A
MARGINAL
JEW

VOLUME TWO

THE ANCHOR BIBLE REFERENCE LIBRARY is designed to be a third major component of the Anchor Bible group, which includes the Anchor Bible commentaries on the books of the Old Testament, the New Testament, and the Apocrypha, and the Anchor Bible Dictionary. While the Anchor Bible commentaries and the Anchor Bible Dictionary are structurally defined by their subject matter, the Anchor Bible Reference Library will serve as a supplement on the cutting edge of the most recent scholarship. The series is open-ended; its scope and reach are nothing less than the biblical world in its totality, and its methods and techniques the most up-to-date available or devisable. Separate volumes will deal with one or more of the following topics relating to the Bible: anthropology, archaeology, ecology, economy, geography, history, languages and literatures, philosophy, religion(s), theology.

As with the Anchor Bible commentaries and the Anchor Bible Dictionary, the philosophy underlying the Anchor Bible Reference Library finds expression in the following: the approach is scholarly, the perspective is balanced and fair-minded, the methods are scientific, and the goal is to inform and enlighten. Contributors are chosen on the basis of their scholarly skills and achievements, and they come from a variety of religious backgrounds and communities. The books in the Anchor Bible Reference Library are intended for the broadest possible readership, ranging from world-class scholars, whose qualifications match those of the authors, to general readers, who may not have special training or skill in studying the Bible but are as enthusiastic as any dedicated professional in expanding their knowledge of the Bible and its world.

David Noel Freedman
GENERAL EDITOR

THE ANCHOR BIBLE REFERENCE LIBRARY

A MARGINAL JEW

RETHINKING

THE HISTORICAL JESUS

VOLUME TWO
MENTOR, MESSAGE, AND MIRACLES

JOHN P. MEIER

ABRL

Doubleday

NEW YORK LONDON TORONTO SYDNEY AUCKLAND

THE ANCHOR BIBLE REFERENCE LIBRARY

PUBLISHED BY DOUBLEDAY
a division of Bantam Doubleday Dell Publishing Group, Inc.
1540 Broadway, New York, New York 10036

The Anchor Bible Reference Library, Doubleday, and the portrayal of an anchor with the
letters ABRL are trademarks of Doubleday, a division of Bantam Doubleday Dell Publishing
Group, Inc.

Book design by Patrice Fodelo

Library of Congress Cataloging-in-Publication Data

Meier, John P.
  A marginal Jew.
  (The Anchor Bible reference library)
  Includes bibliographical references and
index.
  Contents: v. 1. The roots of the problem
and the person — v. 2. Mentor, message, and
miracles.
  1. Jesus Christ—Historicity. 2. Jesus
Christ—Jewishness. I. Title.
B303.2.M465 1991   232.9   91-10538
ISBN 0-385-46992-6 (v.2)

Imprimatur—New York, December 10, 1993—The Most Rev. Patrick J. Sheridan, V.G.

10 9 8 7 6 5 4 3 2 1

To my friends and colleagues
who have made this volume possible

אוהב אמונה אוהב תוקף ומוצאו מצא הון

BEN SIRA 6:14

CONTENTS

PART TWO
MESSAGE

CHAPTER 14
*The Kingdom of God: God Coming in Power to Rule
Part I: Background   237*

CHAPTER 15
*The Kingdom of God: God Coming in Power to Rule
Part II: Jesus' Proclamation of a Future Kingdom   289*

CHAPTER 16
The Kingdom of God: God Coming in Power to Rule
Part III: The Kingdom Already Present   398

PART THREE
MIRACLES

CHAPTER 17
Miracles and Modern Minds   509

CHAPTER 18
Miracles and Ancient Minds   535

CHAPTER 19
The Historicity of Jesus' Miracles: The Global Question   617

CHAPTER 20
Jesus' Exorcisms   646

CHAPTER 21
Jesus' Healings   678

CHAPTER 22
Raising the Dead   773

ACKNOWLEDGMENTS

Even more than was the case with Volume One, Volume Two of *A Marginal Jew* has enjoyed the support and collaboration of many valued colleagues, only a few of whom can be mentioned here. Professors at the Catholic University of America who read the manuscript and made suggestions include Christopher T. Begg, John P. Galvin, Francis T. Gignac, William P. Loewe, and Frank J. Matera. I regret that the late Professor Carl J. Peter did not live to see Volume Two in print; his wise counsel will be missed. Professors from other institutions who have aided me in my research include Harold W. Attridge of the University of Notre Dame; Myles M. Bourke, formerly of Fordham University and now of Portsmouth Priory; Raymond E. Brown, Professor Emeritus of Union Theological Seminary in New York; John J. Collins of the University of Chicago; Joseph A. Fitzmyer, Professor Emeritus of Catholic University; Daniel J. Harrington and John S. Kselman, both of Weston School of Theology; and John P. Reumann of Lutheran Theological Seminary.

I am especially grateful for the assistance of a number of distinguished Jewish scholars, including Professor Shaye J. D. Cohen of Brown University, Louis H. Feldmann of Yeshiva University of New York, Jacob Neusner of the University of South Florida and Burton L. Visotzky of Jewish Theological Seminary of New York. My thanks to these scholars should not be taken to mean that any of them agrees with all that I have written here. I must take sole responsibility for the positions adopted in this volume.

I wish to give separate and special recognition to the general editor of the Anchor Bible Reference Library, Professor David Noel Freedman, whose tireless editorial eye has prevented me from committing any number of embarrassing errors. A word of gratitude is due Professor John Smolko, whose knowledge of computers contributed in no small way to the production of the manuscript.

I also wish to thank the staff members of the libraries at the Catholic University of America; the Woodstock Theological Library at Georgetown University; the Berkeley Theological Union; the Dominican House of Studies, Washington, D.C.; Union Theological Seminary of New York; St. Joseph's Seminary, Yonkers, N.Y.; Weston School of Theology and Episcopal Divinity

School; and the Harvard Divinity School. Finally, I owe a word of gratitude to Thomas Cahill, Michael Iannazzi and Jane Donahue, my editors at Doubleday, for their skill in shepherding this volume through to publication.

The substance of the excursus on John the Baptist in Josephus appeared in a different format as "John the Baptist in Josephus: Philology and Exegesis," *JBL* 111 (1992) 225–37. I am grateful to the journal for its permission to use the material in this volume.

A
MARGINAL
JEW

VOLUME TWO

INTRODUCTION TO VOLUME TWO

I. WHY THE ROAD LIES LONG AND DUSTY

The best laid schemes of mice and exegetes. . . . In the beginning, *A Marginal Jew* was to have been a one-volume work on the historical Jesus. Then two volumes became necessary; now there will be three. Apart from the verbosity of the author (the modern, not the ancient one), why the apparent overkill? Four reasons have persuaded me to broaden the original scope of this work.

First, *A Marginal Jew* is not an autonomous project. It belongs to a larger one, the Anchor Bible *Reference Library*. Hence, *A Marginal Jew* is not free simply to parade its own positions, while ignoring contentious and contrary voices. A reasonably broad and representative sampling of authors and views is required for any "reference library." Inclusiveness and fairness have thus come to demand more floor space in this library than I had originally envisioned.

The second reason for expanded coverage is closely connected to the first. *A Marginal Jew* is being written in and seeks to contribute to a lively period of Jesus research, one that some critics have dubbed the "third quest for the historical Jesus."[1] The first quest, which produced a string of "liberal lives" of Jesus in 19th-century Germany, reached its climax and conclusion in Albert Schweitzer's *The Quest of the Historical Jesus* (1906). These liberal lives often reflected the overactive imagination of their authors rather than the data in the Gospels. The second quest, pursued especially by "post-Bultmannian" scholars like Ernst Käsemann and Günther Bornkamm in the 1950s, tried to be more careful in enunciating criteria for historical judgments. But, at least in Germany, the second quest carried the heavy freight of 20th-century existentialist philosophy. The more intensely existentialist a book on the historical Jesus was, the more it was hailed in the '50s and '60s, and the more dated it seems today. Nothing ages faster than relevance.

In the 1990s, the third quest has tried to be more sophisticated in its methodology, more self-aware and self-critical in dealing with a given author's preconceptions and biases, and more determined to write history rather than covert theology or christology. The third quest benefits from recent

1

archaeological discoveries, a better knowledge of the Aramaic language and the cultural context in 1st-century Palestine, a more differentiated view of the Judaism(s) developing around the turn of the era, and new insights from sociological analysis and modern literary theory. Obviously none of these advances exempts present-day questers—myself included—from being influenced by personal or institutional biases. The best these advances can do is to act as hedges on unbridled imagination and ideological agendas.

All the more reason, then, for me to plunge into the flood of contemporary literature and join other authors in today's lively debate on the historical Jesus. In Jesus research, debate is not simply a matter of being a gregarious intellectual who loves a good fight; debate is essential if Jesus research is to remain an honest academic endeavor. In addition to the criteria of historicity and other methodological guidelines, debate among and mutual criticism by scholars are pivotal to preventing authors from veering off into fantasy worlds of their own making, a not unknown result of searching for the historical Jesus.

This need to dialogue with the vast literature generated by the third quest—as well as representative works of the first two quests—is thus another reason why, in Volume Two, the bibliographical material is so extensive and the end notes so numerous. In order to keep the basic line of argument clear to the educated layperson, I have adhered to the format I adopted in Volume One: the main text pursues major topics as directly and simply as possible, given the complexity of the issues at stake. The end notes, directed mainly at scholars, furnish bibliographical references, further detailed information, and arguments on secondary questions. In this way I hope to deal fairly with the explosion of books and articles occasioned by the third quest without overwhelming the general reader.

A third reason for the length of Volume Two—as well as the need for a Volume Three—is the growing realization on my part that too often in the past vital decisions on the historicity of individual words or deeds of Jesus were made with surprisingly little argumentation. Writing Volume Two has provided me the opportunity to reread such classics as Rudolf Bultmann's *History of the Synoptic Tradition* and Günther Bornkamm's *Jesus of Nazareth*—but this time "in slow motion" as I analyzed individual Gospel texts in great detail.[2] What has struck me repeatedly is the disconcerting way in which these and other great authors would decide the weighty question of the historicity of the material in a few sentences or at times simply with an airy wave of the hand. Often, when I tested the authors' terse pronouncements for their cogency, the arguments did not hold. And yet these arguments have been repeated from book to book and from generation to generation, mainly because of the authority of the exegetical giants being quoted. This experience convinced me that the case for or against the historicity of particular words or deeds of Jesus must be argued at length; hence the length of Volume Two. In the end, readers may not agree with my decisions on individual texts, but at least they will know on what grounds I have made my decisions and on what grounds they disagree.

My fourth and final reason for writing such a large volume derives from the subject matter of the volume's third part: Jesus' miracles as recounted in the Four Gospels. In the past, all too many quests for the historical Jesus either ignored the miracle stories or gave them the polite nod of a single chapter. But such short shrift does justice neither to the broad attestation of Jesus' miracle-working activity in practically all the layers of the Gospel tradition nor to the great impact this activity had on at least some Jews of 1st-century Palestine.

This is not just latter-day Christian surmise or apologetics; Josephus is our guarantor on this point. Josephus, a 1st-century Jewish historian hailing from Palestine, spends only a few words on Jesus' public ministry, but prominent in his thumbnail sketch is the claim that Jesus was "a doer of startling deeds [*paradoxōn ergōn poiētēs*, i.e., a miracle worker like the prophet Elisha]."[3] Along with Jesus' being a wise man and a teacher who attracted a large following, miracle-working is all that Josephus mentions about the public ministry before he abruptly tells us that Jesus was accused by Jewish leaders to Pilate, who condemned him to be crucified. Thus Josephus, as well as the Gospels, leaves us with the impression that Jesus' *reputation* for working miracles played no little part in his ability to attract both the favor of the crowds and the not-so-favorable attention of the authorities, Jewish as well as Roman. I stress the word *reputation*, since it is not my intention here or elsewhere in this book to make the theological claim that Jesus actually worked miracles. It is sufficient for the historian to know that Jesus performed deeds that many people, both friends and foes, considered miracles. That is the key to so much.

I remember well how the late Professor Morton Smith would often emphasize in the NT seminars at Columbia University that, without his miracles, Jesus would never have attracted both the enthusiasm and the opposition that marked and finally ended his public life.[4] There were many prophets and teachers in Palestine in the first centuries B.C. and A.D. None of them had the combination of such success, such a disastrous fate, and such a lasting impact as the Nazarene. A key reason for the difference lies in the atypical configuration of Jesus' characteristics, a configuration in which miracles played an important part.

Because of his claim to work miracles, a claim accepted by many, Jesus was not just another prophet or teacher. At one and the same time he acted as (1) the prophet of the last days, which were soon to come and yet were somehow already present in his ministry; (2) the gatherer of the Israel of the last days, the twelve tribes of Israel being symbolized by the circle of the twelve disciples Jesus formed around himself; (3) the teacher of both general moral truths and detailed directives concerning the observance of the Mosaic Law (e.g., divorce); and last but not least (4) the exorcist and healer of illnesses who was even reputed, like Elijah and Elisha, to have raised the dead.

It is the explosive convergence and mutual reinforcement of all these usually distinct figures in the one Jesus of Nazareth that made him stand out, for better or for worse, in his own time and succeeding ages. More to the point, of all the elements in this "mix," miracle working probably contributed the most to his prominence and popularity on the public scene—as well as to the enmity he stirred up in high places.[5] To be blunt, without miracles, one wonders how much popularity this particular Jewish preacher and teacher would have enjoyed. Without miracles, many Palestinian Jews might have seen Jesus merely as a more "upbeat" version of John the Baptist, an echo of his former master but lacking the master's striking asceticism and stark venue. Without miracles, the figure, fame, and fate of Jesus would have been quite different and probably quite diminished. Without miracles, one is left with the paper cutout manufactured by Thomas Jefferson and all subsequent questers for a reasonable Jesus.

In short, it is to redress the usual absence of any serious consideration of the miracle tradition in most treatments of the historical Jesus that I spend so much time on this feature of his ministry. Consequently, the third part of Volume Two supplies not only a global overview of the many-layered miracle tradition but also a detailed inventory and evaluation of all the stories of Jesus' miracles found in the Four Gospels. This is why the road lies long and dusty.

II. THE RULES OF THE ROAD

The methodology governing *A Marginal Jew* was laid out in Part One of Volume One (pp. 1–201). But even the valiant souls who journeyed down those two hundred pages would probably welcome a quick refresher course on the rules of the road.

In brief, the "historical Jesus" is not to be naively identified with the total reality of Jesus of Nazareth, i.e., all that Jesus thought, said, did, and experienced during his lifetime, or even just during his public ministry. The totality of Jesus' life, or even simply a reasonably complete account of his life, is impossible to reconstruct today, given the vast gap in time and the sparse sources available.

In contrast to the "real Jesus," the "historical Jesus" is that Jesus whom we can recover or reconstruct by using the scientific tools of modern historical research. The "historical Jesus" is thus a scientific construct, a theoretical abstraction of modern scholars that coincides only partially with the real Jesus of Nazareth, the Jew who actually lived and worked in Palestine in the 1st century A.D.

If the historical Jesus is not the real Jesus, neither is he the "theological Jesus" investigated by theologians according to their own proper methods and criteria. To illustrate what a *historical*, as distinct from a *theological*, investigation of Jesus must involve, I propose the fantasy of the "unpapal conclave": a Catholic, a Protestant, a Jew, and an agnostic—all honest historians cognizant of 1st-century religious movements—are locked up in the bowels of the Harvard

Divinity School library, put on a spartan diet, and not allowed to emerge until they have hammered out a consensus document on Jesus of Nazareth.

An essential requirement of this document would be that it be based on purely historical sources and arguments. Its conclusions would have to be open to verification by any and all sincere persons using the means of modern historical research. No doubt, such a consensus document would suffer from a narrow focus, a fragmentary vision, perhaps even some distortions. It certainly would not claim to present a complete, let alone ultimate and definitive, interpretation of Jesus, his work, and his intentions.[6] Nevertheless, at least it would provide an academically respectable common ground and starting point for dialogue among people of various faiths or no faith.

As Volume One showed, there are very few sources for knowledge of the historical Jesus beyond the four canonical Gospels. Paul and Josephus offer little more than tidbits. Claims that later apocryphal Gospels and the Nag Hammadi material supply independent and reliable historical information about Jesus are largely fantasy. In the end, the historian is left with the difficult task of sifting through the Four Gospels for historical tradition. The task is difficult indeed, for these documents are all products of Christian churches in the second half of the 1st century A.D. Written some forty to seventy years after Jesus' death, they are shot through with Christian faith in Jesus as the risen Lord of the church. Hence, only a careful examination of the Gospel material in the light of the criteria of historicity can hope to yield reliable results.

In the quest for the historical Jesus, five criteria have proved especially useful:

(1) The criterion of embarrassment pinpoints Gospel material that would hardly have been invented by the early church, since such material created embarrassment or theological difficulties for the church even during the NT period (e.g., the baptism of Jesus by John).

(2) The criterion of discontinuity focuses on words or deeds of Jesus that cannot be derived either from the Judaism(s) of Jesus' time or from the early church (e.g., Jesus' rejection of voluntary fasting).

(3) The criterion of multiple attestation focuses on sayings or deeds of Jesus witnessed in more than one independent literary source (e.g., Mark, Q, Paul, or John) and/or more than one literary form or genre (e.g., a saying of Jesus about a certain type of miracle plus a story about the same type of miracle). For example, that Jesus forbade divorce is supported by the independent witness of Mark, Q, and Paul. That Jesus was reputed in his own lifetime to have given sight to the blind is supported by a saying in Q and by narratives in both Mark and John.

(4) The criterion of coherence is brought into play only after a certain amount of historical material has been isolated by other criteria. The criterion of coherence holds that other sayings and deeds of Jesus that fit in well with the preliminary "data base" established by the other criteria have a good chance of being historical.

(5) Instead of judging individual sayings or deeds of Jesus, the criterion of Jesus' rejection and execution looks at the larger pattern of Jesus' ministry and asks what words and deeds fit in with and explain his trial and crucifixion. A Jesus whose words and deeds did not threaten or alienate people, especially powerful people, is not the historical Jesus.

Various secondary criteria may also be invoked, but usually only as "backup" or confirmation for the primary criteria. These secondary (some would say dubious) criteria include traces of the Aramaic language in the sayings of Jesus and echoes of the early 1st-century Palestinian environment in which Jesus lived. Still weaker as criteria (some would say useless) are the vivid and concrete nature of a narrative and the supposed general tendencies of the Synoptic tradition as it develops.

As will be seen in Part Three, I think that, by way of exception, there is one clear tendency of the Gospel tradition that may be useful in our quest. In all Four Gospels, the miracle tradition has a remarkable tendency to be anonymous. Usually neither the petitioner, nor the beneficiary of the miracle, nor the exact place of the miracle, nor the time of its occurrence is mentioned. At the very least, a miracle story that "names names" runs counter to the fairly uniform tendency of the miracle tradition to remain anonymous.

Given the difficulty involved in articulating and applying these criteria, it is not surprising that some scholars brush aside the whole question of method and criteria. They prefer to "muddle through."[7] Yet every scholar engaged in the quest for the historical Jesus is de facto operating with some method and criteria, however inchoate and unexamined. The danger in "muddling through" is that one easily begins to draw from the data the conclusions one wants rather than the conclusions the data warrant. The importance of criteria applied methodically to the data is that they can force the quester to draw conclusions he or she has not foreseen and perhaps does not desire.

I experienced the truth of this observation firsthand when I was writing Chapter 15, which deals with the question of whether Jesus proclaimed the kingdom of God as a future event. I had originally expected that certain Gospel texts in which Jesus prophesies the coming of the kingdom within the life span of his own generation would provide the clearest proof that Jesus thought of the kingdom as future-yet-imminent. However, when I examined these key sayings of Jesus (Matt 10:23; Mark 9:1; Mark 13:30) in the light of the criteria, I was forced to a different conclusion. Most likely, these sayings were produced by early Christians who sought to reassure themselves of Christ's coming in glory as the years passed by with no parousia in sight.

Time and time again while writing this volume, I have been constrained to reverse my views because of the weight of the data and the force of the criteria. My own experience has convinced me that, while methodology and criteria may be tiresome topics, they are vital in keeping the critic from seeing in the data whatever he or she already has decided to see. The rules of the road are never exciting, but they keep us moving in the right direction.

III. A ROAD MAP FOR TRAVELING THROUGH VOLUME TWO

Those who have read Volume One of *A Marginal Jew* know that it is largely programmatic, a prolegomenon to the work as a whole, an extended method-plus-introduction. It lays out the problem of the historical Jesus, the method to be used to meet the problem, information about Jesus' origins and background, and finally a rough chronological grid of his life. With this setting of the stage Volume One ends.

It is only the present volume, Volume Two, that begins to grapple directly with the words and deeds of Jesus during his public ministry. Since this volume is much larger than the first, the reader may find it useful to have a guide or road map through the parts and chapters that make up this book.[8]

Volume Two is divided into three main parts: mentor, message, and miracles. "Mentor" deals with John the Baptist, "message" deals with Jesus' proclamation of the kingdom of God, and "miracles" deals with the Gospel narratives of exorcisms, healings, raising the dead, and the so-called nature miracles.

(1) The first part, "mentor," focuses on the one person who had the greatest single influence on Jesus' ministry, namely, John the Baptist. All too often in books on the historical Jesus, the Baptist, like the miracle stories, gets a perfunctory nod and short shrift. Yet one of the most certain things we know about Jesus is that he voluntarily submitted himself to John's baptism for the remission of sins, an embarrassing event each evangelist tries to neutralize in his own way. But the Baptist is not so easily neutralized. For all the differences between John and Jesus, some key elements of John's preaching and praxis flowed into Jesus' ministry like so much baptismal water. Hence, not to understand the Baptist is not to understand Jesus—a dictum borne out in the work of some recent scholars.

To counteract the tendency to play down John's influence, I have devoted the first two chapters of Volume Two to the Baptist. The first chapter, Chapter 12 in the total work, is called "John Without Jesus: the Baptist in His Own Rite." Here, with the help of Josephus as well as the Gospels, I try to understand the ministry, preaching, baptism, and death of John apart from any relationship he may have had to Jesus. Especially when writing for Christians accustomed to the Gospel presentations, any scholar must struggle to inculcate the picture of the Baptist as an independent Jewish prophet possessing his own importance and meaning, prior to any connection with Jesus.

The picture of the Baptist that emerges is that of a 1st-century Jewish prophet proclaiming an eschatological message with some apocalyptic traits. John announced an imminent, fiery judgment that was about to break in upon Israel, a judgment against which sinful Israel could protect itself only by inner repentance, by the concrete reform of one's exterior life, and by the acceptance of a once-and-for-all baptism administered by John himself. In his penitential practice, in his use of a water ritual, and in his implicit critique of the temple and its institutions as *the* way of pleasing God and obtaining forgiveness, John has some characteristics in common with other Jewish penitential figures of the time in the region of the Jordan valley, notably the Jewish sectarians at Qumran.

But the Qumran connection, especially the romantic picture of John being raised in a prep school in the Judean desert, can be overdone. Certain traits mark John off from Qumran, and indeed from most other forms of Judaism in 1st-century Palestine. These traits include a once-and-for-all baptism tied to his own person (so tied to him that it gave him his second name), his outreach to all Israel without differentiation and without concern for detailed questions of legal observance or the creation of a new sectarian community within Judaism, and his apparent lack of concern about the future of the Jerusalem temple, however purified and restored.

What specifically John awaited in the near future by way of judgment and salvation is hard to say. He speaks of the coming of some figure superior to himself, a "stronger one," who will baptize with the holy spirit as opposed to John's mere water ritual. But whether the stronger one is an angelic or human figure, a heavenly "Son of Man" or an earthly Messiah, or simply God himself is unclear. Perhaps the vague language indicates that John's prophecy remained unclear to John himself.

Whatever the details of John's message, he had—as Josephus indicates—a broad and deep impact on the Jews of his day, so much so that Herod Antipas, the tetrarch of Galilee, thought it best to remove him by a "preemptive strike," lest his influence on the people be used for seditious purposes. As Josephus makes clear, any idea of revolt lay in Herod's ever-suspicious brain, not in John's message and deeds.

It was to this eschatological prophet with his unique baptism that Jesus of Nazareth pledged adherence in the Jordan River sometime around A.D. 28. I take up the relationship of John and Jesus in Chapter 13, entitled "Jesus With and Without John." That Jesus accepted John's baptism and thus presumably his message made him at least in some broad sense a disciple of John. Further hints in the Gospels, especially the Fourth Gospel, suggest that Jesus may have stayed for a while in the inner circle of John's disciples. At some point, however, Jesus left the circle of John, perhaps with some of John's erstwhile disciples, to pursue a ministry of his own.

The precise relationship between Jesus' former attachment to the Baptist and his new independent ministry has been much debated recently, with scholars adopting extreme positions at both ends of the spectrum. Hendrikus Boers, for instance, stresses the perduring links between John and Jesus. According to Boers, Jesus continued to see John, and not himself, as the decisive, pivotal figure, the final eschatological figure before the coming of God's kingdom. John did not point to Jesus; Jesus pointed to John as the central human figure at the climax of salvation history. At the other end of the spectrum, Paul Hollenbach speaks of Jesus' "apostasy" from John. Supposedly Jesus at first continued John's practice of baptizing as well as John's message of an imminent fiery judgment. But at a certain point Jesus shifted to a message of God's mercy present now, and correspondingly the practice of baptism gave way to the practice of exorcism and healing.

Actually, in order to create their simplistic scenarios, both of these extremes ignore part of the complex data of the Gospels. Sayings that contradict a particular theory are abruptly declared to be inauthentic, and different time periods in Jesus' ministry are posited with no firm foundation in the Gospel text. If, instead, we carefully sift the traditions found in the Four Gospels, the following picture emerges:

The Fourth Gospel is probably correct when it indicates that Jesus imitated John's practice of baptizing. This is a valuable point of contact between John and Jesus, a point either forgotten or suppressed by the Synoptics. More importantly still, contrary to what Hollenbach supposes, there is no reason to think that Jesus ever gave up the practice of baptizing once he started it. It is likely that the practice of baptizing flowed like water from John through Jesus into the early church, with the ritual taking on different meanings at each stage of the process.

Since Jesus did move the emphasis of his preaching from God's imminent fiery judgment to the offer of God's mercy, baptism as a graphic symbol for extinguishing the fire to come naturally receded into the background of Jesus' own ministry. Still, for all the emphasis on God's mercy and forgiveness, experienced now in Jesus' healings and table fellowship, Jesus never gave up John's proclamation of a future coming of God in judgment, a coming close at hand. Indeed, a Baptist with a message of future eschatology on one side of Jesus and a church with a message of future eschatology on the other side of Jesus makes a Jesus totally bereft of future eschatology a suspicious figure from the start. This poses a major problem for the whole approach of Marcus J. Borg and John Dominic Crossan, both of whom want to do away with the future eschatology in Jesus' preaching. No matter how much Jesus moved beyond John, he always carried a great deal of his former master with him. In a sense, Jesus never was without John.

(2) All this talk about eschatology naturally brings us to the second part of Volume Two, namely, "message." It is so taken for granted that at the heart of Jesus' message lay the key symbol "kingdom of God" that, when writing Volume Two, I purposely tried at first to see whether I could challenge that assumption. In an initial probe of the material I attempted to show that "kingdom of God" was either mostly a linguistic relic preserved from Judaism before Jesus or a key element of early Christian preaching read back into Jesus' message. Interestingly, no matter how much I tried to pursue this revisionist argument in Chapter 14, which investigates the term "kingdom of God," I could not make such a subversive theory work, and so I abandoned it. The facts of the case and the criteria of historicity point too much in the opposite direction. While the dynamic symbol of God assuming his powerful rule over a rebellious creation is found in various parts of the OT, in the pseudepigrapha,

and at Qumran, the precise phrase "kingdom of God" is extremely rare prior to Jesus, especially when used in a context of imminent future eschatology.

Yet we see an explosion of the use of this set phrase as a central symbol in the sayings of Jesus in the Synoptic Gospels. Such a way of speaking does not seem to be retrojected from early Christian usage, since the phrase "kingdom of God" is relatively rare in Paul, all but disappears in John, and is simply absent from certain NT books. The only logical conclusion is that the historical Jesus quite consciously chose an unusual phrase to be the enigmatic vessel, the "tensive symbol," of his complex message about God's rule and kingdom.

Two basic tendencies, again at the two ends of the spectrum, can be detected in recent research on the kingdom of God in the teaching of Jesus. Some scholars, notably Crossan and Borg, claim that Jesus spoke only of the kingdom as present in his ministry or, alternately, as universally present in human experience for those who have the eyes to see. All references to a future eschatological kingdom are judged to come from the early church. On the contrary, in his highly praised book *Jesus and Judaism*, E. P. Sanders maintains that Jesus spoke clearly only of an imminent-future coming of the kingdom. Sanders denies that any of the authentic sayings clearly proclaims the kingdom as already present in Jesus' ministry.

Once again, I think the truth lies somewhere in between the two extremes. The massive number of Jesus' sayings that speak of a future kingdom, sayings found in various sources, makes it very difficult to eliminate all future references in the teaching of the historical Jesus. Even if one completely omits the sayings connected with the mysterious Son of Man, evidence for future eschatology in Jesus' teaching is abundant. In Chapter 15, I argue at length the case for future eschatology on the basis of four key sayings that I claim to be authentic: (a) the petition "Thy kingdom come" in the Lord's Prayer (Matt 6:10 par.); (b) the Last Supper tradition in which Jesus announces that he will no longer drink wine until the arrival of the kingdom (Mark 14:25 parr.); (c) the promise that many will come from the east and the west and sit down at table with the patriarchs in the kingdom (Matt 8:11–12 par.); and (d) the various future promises in the Q beatitudes (e.g., "they shall be satisfied," "for they shall be comforted" in Matt 5:3–12 par.).

I think it clear, then, that Jesus did speak of an eschatological future coming of the kingdom. At the same time, Jesus does seem both to proclaim in his words and to dramatize by his deeds that in some sense "the kingdom of God is in your midst" (Luke 17:21). Especially significant is the key saying in Q by which Jesus interprets his practice of exorcism: "If by the finger of God I cast out demons, then the kingdom of God has come upon you" (Luke 11:20 par.). Sanders strives to avoid the obvious consequence of this authentic saying. But, as I try to show in Chapter 16, along with a number of other sayings, it clearly speaks of God's kingdom as already present, however proleptically and imperfectly, in the ministry of Jesus, especially in his exorcisms and healings.

Recently some critics have objected that a kingdom both future and present is an intolerable contradiction in terms. One might reply that the Semitic minds behind a good part of our biblical literature were not overly troubled by our Western philosophical principle of noncontradiction. But more to the point, the kingdom of God is a tensive symbol that encapsulates a dynamic event, a whole mythic drama of God coming in power to conquer his enemies and establish his definitive rule in Israel. A static kingdom of God understood as a set place or a set state of affairs could not be both present and yet coming. But the kingdom of God as a dynamic mythic drama does allow for a coming in stages, with strategic battles already won, yet the final victory still to come.

(3) One of the striking manifestations of God's kingly rule already present in Jesus' ministry was Jesus' practice of exorcisms, healings, and other miracles. The topic of Jesus' message of the kingdom naturally leads us to Jesus' praxis of the kingdom in miracle-working. The thorny and complicated question of miracles takes up the third and last part of Volume Two.

In Chapter 17 I deal briefly with the theoretical problems that the very idea of miracles creates for many educated people in the Western world today. While I review in passing the modern objections against miracles from philosophy and science, writing an apologetic in defense of a belief in miracles is not my concern. My major point is that a decision such as "God has worked a miracle in this particular healing" is actually a theological, not a historical, judgment. A historian may examine claims about miracles, reject those for which there are obvious natural explanations, and record instances where the historian can find no natural explanation. Beyond that, a purely historical judgment cannot go.[9]

Just as a historian must reject credulity, so a historian must reject an a priori affirmation that miracles do not or cannot happen. That is, strictly speaking, a philosophical or theological proposition, not a historical one. Even more so must the historian reject the unsubstantiated—indeed, the disproved—claim made by Bultmann and his disciples that "modern man cannot believe in miracles." Simply as an empirical fact of the social sciences, a Gallup survey in 1989 showed that about 82 percent of present-day Americans, presumably modern men and women (including educated and sophisticated people), do accept the proposition that *even today* God works miracles. Bultmann and company cannot tell me what modern man *cannot* do when I have empirical sociological data proving that modern man *does* it.

Chapter 18 moves to the ancient problem of miracles. With regard to the ancients' understanding of miracles and magic, authors like Morton Smith, David Aune, and John Dominic Crossan have raised a sharp challenge to traditional Christian views on the nature of miracles. According to these scholars, who use both ancient Greco-Roman texts and the modern social sciences to bolster their positions, there is no real, objective difference between miracles and magic. "Magic" is simply the pejorative label polemicists stick on the miracles of their religious adversaries. In other words, *my* religious heroes perform miracles, while *your* religious heroes perform magic.

While this approach has at first glance the appeal of scientific objectivity and evenhandedness, things are not so simple. After comparing the characteristics of the Greek magical papyri with the characteristics of the Gospel miracle stories, I come to a conclusion similar to that held by some anthropologists: miracle and magic as two ideal types at the two ends of a spectrum of religious experience. At one end of the spectrum, the ideal type of magic involves the elements of (1) automatic power possessed by a magician (2) in virtue of secret formulas and rituals, with (3) the resultant coercion of the divine powers by humans (4) in search of quick solutions to practical problems. Also, magic is usually marked by (5) a spirit of individualism or entrepreneurship as opposed to a perduring community of faith.

At the other end of the spectrum, miracle belongs in general to a context of (1) faith in a personal God to whose will one submits one's own will in prayer, (2) a perduring community of belief, and (3) a public manifestation of God's power (4) that is not dependent on a set ritual or formula. I stress that "magic" and "miracle" are ideal types at the two ends of the spectrum; concrete cases will often float somewhere in between. For instance, the Greek magical papyri regularly reflect the ideal type of magic, though at times elements of prayer and humble supplication appear. Similarly, most of the Gospel healings of Jesus tend toward the miracle end of the spectrum, though some, like the healing of the woman with the hemorrhage, have elements of the magical.

In short, I do not think that the collapse of miracle and magic into one undifferentiated phenomenon is helpful or does justice to the complexity of the data. Hence I do not agree with Smith's and Crossan's characterization of Jesus as a Jewish magician. Miracle-worker is a more helpful category that reflects the Gospel material more accurately. If Crossan and Aune wish to put Apollonius of Tyana into that same category, I have no objection. It provides a less polemical and emotionally charged starting point for examining and evaluating the data.

In Chapter 19 I come to the miracles of Jesus as recounted in the Four Gospels. This chapter supplies an initial overview of the miracles attributed to Jesus. I use the criteria of historicity to establish the global assertion that, during his public ministry, Jesus claimed to work miracles, that Jesus was thought to work miracles by his contemporaries, friends and foes alike, and that Jesus did indeed do some extraordinary deeds that his adversaries explained by claiming that he was in league with demonic powers. In other words, the attempt to see the miracle tradition of the Gospels purely as the creation of early Christian missionary propaganda is a fallacy of certain tendencies in form criticism. This fallacy suffers shipwreck on the shoals of the criteria of historicity, especially the criterion of the multiple attestation of sources and forms. A completely non-miraculous Jesus, an idea propagated by Enlightenment thinkers like Thomas Jefferson, is a prime example of recasting a 1st-century Jewish prophet to fit the sensibilities of a modern intellectual elite.

That much, I think, is clear. Things become more murky as I move from this global assertion to a complete inventory of the miracle stories in all Four Gospels. In Chapters 20, 21, 22, and 23 I take up, in turn, Jesus' miracles of exorcism, healing bodily afflictions, raising the dead, and finally the grab-bag category of the so-called nature miracles (a category I in fact reject). In these chapters judgments of historicity are extremely hazardous. The best one can do, I think, is to distinguish those stories that are most likely creations of the early church pure and simple from those stories that have a claim to go back in some form to the historical Jesus, however much they may have been reworked by later Christian preaching.

The results of applying the criteria of historicity to make this distinction are sometimes surprising and not always what I would have expected or even wanted. For instance, in my opinion, behind the bizarre story of the Gerasene demoniac named Legion in Mark 5 does lie an exorcism that Jesus performed in the Decapolis district of Gerasa. Yet the beautiful story of the Syrophoenician woman begging Jesus for the exorcism of her daughter seems most likely to be an early Christian creation intent on symbolizing the relation of Jews and Gentiles in the Christian mission. Most of the so-called nature miracles seem to stem from the early church, but the story of Jesus feeding the multitude may reflect a special meal Jesus held during his public ministry.

All these judgments, I admit, are highly debatable. What they underline is a basic point hammered home throughout Volume Two: the only way to reach even probable judgments is lengthy analysis of the data and painstaking application of the criteria of historicity. We return to the reason why the road lies long and dusty. But now at least we have a road map as we begin the journey.

NOTES TO THE INTRODUCTION

[1] On the tendencies of this new stage of the quest, see Craig A. Evans, "Life-of-Jesus Research and the Eclipse of Mythology," *TS* 54 (1993) 3–36.

[2] So as not to multiply notes unduly, I do not repeat in these introductory comments all the bibliographical references to major works found in the body of Volume Two.

[3] *Ant.* 18.3.3 §63–64; on the authenticity and meaning of the core text of Josephus' *Testimonium Flavianum* (Josephus' "testimony" about Jesus), see *A Marginal Jew*, 1. 56–88.

[4] As will be made clear, I agree neither with Smith's equation of miracle and magic nor with his portrait of Jesus as a secretly antinomian magician. But along with scholars like David E. Aune, E. P. Sanders, and John Dominic Crossan, Smith helped to correct the nearsightedness of critics who conveniently could not see the massive presence of miracle stories in all layers of the Jesus tradition, even the earliest.

[5] See Evans, "Life-of-Jesus Research," 29.

[6] Not unlike the formatting of hard disks in computers, which allows of various levels of formatting, the writing of history and biography, while always interpretive to some degree, allows of various levels of interpretation. The very gathering of data and the passing of judgment as to their historicity involve a certain "low level" of interpretation. Beyond that unavoidable low level, *A Marginal Jew* attempts as much as possible to let any overarching interpretation of Jesus and his work emerge gradually and naturally out of the convergence of the data judged historical. In particular, *A Marginal Jew* does not intend to impose on the data any predetermined interpretive grid, be it political, economic, or sociological. Such grids can be useful at a later stage of interpretation, but in the quest for the historical Jesus they neither generate data concerning Jesus nor solve the problem of the data's historicity. To be sure, *A Marginal Jew* works with presuppositions, but they are the general presuppositions of historiography.

[7] Geza Vermes proclaims his disdain for "methodology" and his preference for "muddling through" in *The Religion of Jesus the Jew* (Minneapolis: Fortress, 1993) 7. The problem is, though, that any scholarly investigation that is not totally erratic operates by certain rules, whether or not they are acknowledged, labeled, and thought through. The danger of not thinking through one's method and criteria becomes evident almost immediately in Vermes's work. (1) He implicitly works with the criterion of multiple attestation of sources, but does not use the criterion properly. For example, to show that Jesus was observant of the cultic law, Vermes (p. 18) states that "all three Synoptic Gospels report that after curing a leper, he [Jesus] enjoined him to appear before a priest for examination"; Mark 1:44 is cited as evidence. Yet, in the judgment of most commentators, the Matthean and Lucan versions of the story are simply their theological adaptations of the Marcan story. There is, then, only one independent source attesting to the historical event. The Matthean and Lucan parallels certainly attest to what Matthew and Luke thought about Jesus, but they supply no independent evidence as to the historicity of the event. (Even if one preferred the view that Mark depended on Matthew, there would still be only one independent source.) (2) Vermes also uses something like a combination of the criteria of embarrassment and discontinuity (p. 17). However,

when using such a criterion, one must be very careful in appealing to rabbinic material. Unfortunately, Vermes is disconcertingly free and easy in using not only the Mishna (redacted ca. A.D. 200) but also the Tosefta, the various midrashim and targums, and even the Jerusalem Talmud (redacted in the first half of the 5th century) and the Babylonian Talmud (redacted in the first half of the 6th century, achieving its final form in the 8th century). The problem of using rabbinic material to understand Judaism(s) in the early 1st century A.D., a problem highlighted by the works of Jacob Neusner in particular, is not taken seriously (pp. 7–10). In contrast, see the careful weighing of the question—though hardly with agreement on all sides—in E. P. Sanders, *Jewish Law from Jesus to the Mishna. Five Studies* (London: SCM; Philadelphia: Trinity, 1990); idem, *Judaism. Practice & Belief 63 BCE–66 CE* (London: SCM; Philadelphia: Trinity, 1992); Craig A. Evans, "Mishna and Messiah 'In Context': Some Comments on Jacob Neusner's Proposals," *JBL* 112 (1993) 267–89; and, in reply to Sanders and Evans, Jacob Neusner, "Mr. Sanders' Pharisees and Mine," *SJT* 44 (1991) 73–95; idem, "The Mishna in Philosophical Context and Out of Canonical Bounds," *JBL* 112 (1993) 291–304. For Neusner's evaluation of my work, see Jacob Neusner, "Who Needs 'The Historical Jesus'?" *Bulletin for Biblical Research* 4 (1994) 1–14.

[8] In view of the expansion of the project to three volumes, I have decided to divide each volume into separate parts, each volume beginning with its own "Part One." This alters my original plan to number all the parts consecutively throughout the entire work (see Volume One, p. 13).

[9] Cf. Evans, "Life-of-Jesus Research," 17.

PART ONE

MENTOR

John, who was surnamed the Baptist . . .
bade the Jews join in baptism
JOSEPHUS, *ANT.* 18.5.2 §116–17

CHAPTER 12

JOHN WITHOUT JESUS:

The Baptist in His Own Rite

I. THE HISTORICAL EXISTENCE OF JOHN THE BAPTIST [1]

Our study of the chronology of Jesus' life at the end of Volume One had a somber result. It placed two historical figures, both connected with two striking symbols of judgment and death, at two dates that bracket the ministry of Jesus: John the Baptist with his baptism at the beginning of A.D. 28 and Pontius Pilate with the cross on April 7, A.D. 30. The fearful symmetry was not lost on the evangelists or later Christian writers.

Yet, however much history has been elaborated by later theology, the historical Baptist and the historical Pilate remain, framing the ministry of Jesus like the two massive pillars in front of the Jerusalem temple.[2] Their symmetry extends beyond the symbolic and theological. Both the Baptist and Pilate have their existence confirmed not only by all Four Gospels and Acts but also by Josephus.

Unlike the *Testimonium Flavianum* (*Ant.* 18.3.3 §63–64) explored in Chapter 3, Josephus' account of John the Baptist in *Ant.* 18.5.2 §116–119[3] does not require a lengthy defense of its anthenticity. The basic text is witnessed in all relevant manuscripts of the *Jewish Antiquities*,[4] and the vocabulary and style are plainly those of Josephus, especially as evidenced in books 17–19 of the *Antiquities*.[5] Unlike the *Testimonium*, Josephus' treatment of the Baptist is clearly referred to by Origen in his *Contra Celsum* (1.47) as he seeks to prove the existence of the Baptist: "For in book 18 of the *Jewish Antiquities*, Josephus bears witness to John as the one who became 'the Baptist' and who promised cleansing for those who were baptized."[6] The whole text of Josephus' passage on the Baptist is given, with slight variations, by Eusebius in his *Ecclesiastical History* (1.11.4–6).[7]

The content of the Baptist passage also argues for its authenticity. The account Josephus gives of the Baptist is literarily and theologically unconnected with the account of Jesus, which occurs earlier in Book 18 and correspondingly lacks any reference to the Baptist. The passage about the Baptist, which is more than twice as long as the passage about Jesus,[8] is also more laudatory. It also differs from (but does not formally contradict) the Four Gospels in its presentation both of John's ministry and of his death. Hence it is hard to imagine a Christian scribe inserting into Book 18 of the *Antiquities* two passages about Jesus and the Baptist in which the Baptist appears on the scene after Jesus dies, has no connection with Jesus, receives more extensive treatment than Jesus, and is praised more highly than Jesus. It is not surprising, therefore, that few contemporary critics question the authenticity of the Baptist passage.[9]

The Baptist passage in Josephus is also unlike the *Testimonium* in that its Greek is more difficult to translate accurately. Readers who are interested in the problems involved in rendering Josephus' thought with all its nuances will find the material laid out in an excursus at the end of this chapter. Here I simply give the translation that has resulted from my own grappling with the Greek text. This passage is actually a parenthesis inserted by Josephus after he has narrated the defeat of the army of Herod Antipas by the Nabatean King Aretas IV:

§116. But to some of the Jews it seemed that the army of Herod was destroyed by God—indeed, God quite justly punishing [Herod] to avenge what he had done to John, who was surnamed the Baptist.[10]

§117. For Herod killed him, although he was a good man and [simply] bade the Jews to join in baptism, provided that they were cultivating virtue and practicing justice toward one another and piety toward God. For [only] thus, in John's opinion, would the baptism [he administered] indeed be acceptable [to God], namely, if they used it to obtain not pardon for some sins but rather the cleansing of their bodies, inasmuch as [it was taken for granted that] their souls had already been purified by justice.

§118. And when the others [namely, ordinary Jews] gathered together [around John]—for their excitement reached fever pitch as they listened to [his] words— Herod began to fear that John's powerful ability to persuade people might lead to some sort of revolt, for they seemed likely to do whatever he counseled. So [Herod] decided to do away with John by a preemptive strike, before he sparked a revolt. Herod considered this a better [course of action] than to wait until the situation changed and [then] to regret [his delay] when he was engulfed by a crisis.

§119. And so, because of Herod's suspicion, John was sent in chains to Machaerus, the mountain fortress previously mentioned; there he was killed. But the Jews were of the opinion that the army was destroyed to avenge John, God wishing to inflict harm on Herod.

Josephus' agreements with and differences from the Gospel narratives will be noted as we go along. Suffice it to say here that Josephus either suppresses or is ignorant of John's eschatological expectations.[11] For Josephus' largely pagan audience, the Baptist is transformed into a popular moral philosopher of Stoic hue, with a somewhat neo-Pythagorean rite of lustration. Yet, as we shall see, Josephus is probably more reliable than Mark when it comes to the story of John's execution. For now, however, we are interested in Josephus' account simply for its affirmation of the Baptist's existence and the broad outline of his ministry and death.

Even apart from Josephus, the Gospels themselves would give good grounds for affirming the historicity of the Baptist. The criterion of multiple attestation is satisfied by the independent witness of Mark, Q, possibly a stray saying in M (Matt 21:32), and John.[12] Just as important is the criterion of embarrassment, for the Baptist is a "wild card" in the Gospel tradition. As we shall see, he was an independent Jewish prophet, active ca A.D. 28, who might have had face-to-face contact with Jesus of Nazareth only once. His independent worth in the eyes of 1st-century Jews is mirrored both in Josephus' longer and more laudatory treatment (as compared with the *Testimonium Flavianum*) and in groups of "Baptist disciples" who continued to venerate him after his death, who refused to become Christians, and who therefore became a rival movement to early Christianity.

Accordingly, all Four Gospels have to struggle to "make John safe" for Christianity. For instance, the very first verses of Mark's paradoxical Gospel present a major paradox: the OT prophesied the Baptist as the one who would prepare the way for Jesus; yet John never penetrated the mystery of Jesus' identity, even when he baptized him (Mark 1:2–3,4–8,9–11). Thus the messianic secret is kept even from the Messiah's forerunner. In contrast, Matthew has John recognize Jesus' dignity and publicly confess his own inferiority to Jesus just before he baptizes him (3:13–15). Luke makes the Baptist a relative of Jesus so that the fetus of the Baptist may greet and bear witness to the fetus of Jesus at the visitation of Mary to Elizabeth (Luke 1:41–44). This somewhat precocious testimony is necessitated by the fact that this is the only time Jesus and John directly meet in Luke's narrative. Thanks to Luke's curious ordering of events, John's imprisonment is narrated before the baptism of Jesus, and we are never explicitly told who baptizes Jesus (Luke 3:19–21).

In the Fourth Gospel, John the Baptist is not the Baptist; the title is never used of him. He himself denies that he is Elijah (2:21), even though Jesus in the Synoptics intimates (Mark 9:13) or flatly says (Matt 11:14; 17:12–13) that he is. John's baptism, which is clearly called a baptism of repentance for the forgiveness of sins in the Synoptics (Mark 1:4 parr.), is never connected with repentance and sin in the Fourth Gospel; it rather becomes a tool of christological revelation (1:31). The main function of the un-Baptist is not to baptize; indeed, his baptism of Jesus is neither narrated nor mentioned in passing. Instead, John's raison d'être is to *witness* to Jesus; he is the first person in the Gospel to be presented as witnessing (1:7–8,19). Not only does he witness to Jesus as the light (1:7), the Lord (1:23), the Lamb of God who takes away the sin of the world (1:29), the Chosen One (or Son) of God (1:34), the bridegroom who must increase while John decreases (3:29–30); he also witnesses to

Jesus as the Preexistent Word who has entered human history. In 1:15, right after the ringing climax of the Prologue ("the Word became flesh and dwelt among us"), John is suddenly reintroduced into the Prologue to witness that "he who comes after me ranks before me, because he existed [ēn, the verb used for divine existence throughout the Prologue] before me." The un-Baptist becomes the first witness in the Gospel to the undergirding christological claim that Jesus is the Preexistent Word/Son who has become human.

This incredible diversity, not to say conflict, of interpretations in the Four Gospels is due to a simple fact. Right at the beginning of the ministry of Jesus stands the independent ministry of the independent Baptist, a Jewish prophet who started his ministry before and apart from Jesus, who won great popularity and reverence apart from Jesus, who also won the reverence and submission of Jesus to his baptism of repentance for the forgiveness of sins, and who left behind a religious group that continued to exist apart from Christianity. The Baptist constituted a stone of stumbling right at the beginning of Christianity's story of Jesus, a stone too well known to be ignored or denied, a stone that each evangelist had to come to terms with as best he could. The embarrassment of the evangelists as well as the diverse, not to say contradictory, ways in which they try to bend the independent Baptist to a dependent position within the story of Jesus argues well for his historical existence. The evangelists (and their sources before them) did not go out of their way to create a monumental problem for their own theologies by creating John the Baptist.

In short, both the Gospels and Josephus may be taken as witnesses to the historical existence and ministry of the Baptist. Despite all their differences, these diverse sources establish a few bare facts that can frame our further discussion. Around the year A.D. 28, there appeared on the religious scene of Palestine a Jewish prophet, holy man, and ascetic. He was named John and surnamed the Baptist because of the striking and unusual rite he practiced: he, on his own authority, baptized other Jews (apparently only once) as a sign of their turning away from past iniquities, of being cleansed of their sins, and of resolving to live a new, morally pure life. He attracted great crowds, but his wide influence and/or disturbing teaching caused Herod Antipas, tetrarch of Galilee and Perea, to take preventive measures by arresting and then executing him. The execution took place in or before A.D. 30 or 33 (according to the Gospels, who have John die before Jesus) or, at the very latest, before A.D. 36 (when King Aretas IV of Arabia defeated Herod's troops, the event that triggers Josephus' mention of Herod's execution of the Baptist). A feeling of veneration for John did not cease with his death. On the one hand, Josephus recalls that "some Jews," apparently years after the execution, spontaneously interpreted Herod's defeat by Aretas as divine retribution for killing John. On the other hand, the Gospels and Acts reflect an ongoing rivalry with Baptist disciples. In death as in life, John remained an independent figure whom the evangelists had difficulty domesticating for Christianity.

Since Jesus did associate himself with John and John's baptism soon before he began his own ministry, it is important to discern what John, his message, and his baptism were all about, since they can give us an indication of Jesus' own spiritual stance at the start of his ministry.

II. JOHN'S "INFANCY NARRATIVE" IN LUKE 1

Unfortunately, it is not so easy as some authors think to fill out the bare bones of our knowledge of John, as sketched above, and to give a detailed account of what John's ministry, message, and baptism meant to himself and his followers. Along with Walter Wink, I cannot help wondering at the naive confidence certain writers have in their detailed historical reconstructions of the Baptist's life. As Wink remarks, "ironically, while the quest for the historical Jesus had its messengers of defeat, the quest for the historical John had none."[13] A sober realization that we have to contend with not only the theological interpretation of the Baptist by Christian sources but also reverence for or faith in the Baptist by his own followers (who may be the source for at least some of the Baptist material in our Gospels) should make us modest in our claims.

I think this holds true especially of the account of John's birth that we read in Luke 1. It is by no means certain that we can know anything about John's origins or background before he appears on the stage of history as a prophet. In this he differs from Jesus, about whose parents, family, place and date of birth, age, and tribal lineage we can know at least a little. In the case of John, we may have to reconcile ourselves to a complete blank.

In saying this, I realize that I am at odds with those scholars who think that some, if not all, of John's "Infancy Narrative" in Luke 1 can be used to sketch in the origins and background of the Baptist.[14] One need not be a fundamentalist to take this more confident route. Scholars as skeptical as Dibelius and Bultmann thought that some of the Baptist material in Luke 1 might have been derived ultimately from John's followers.[15] Hence, some (though not Dibelius or Bultmann) would hold that, once we strip the narrative of its OT motifs and legendary accretions, we can use it as a quarry for historical information about the Baptist's birth and youth.[16]

I must confess that I remain skeptical about such attempts. If they are difficult in the case of the Infancy Narratives of Jesus in Matthew 1–2 and Luke 1–2, they are nigh impossible when all we have to rely upon are parts of Luke 1 and the supposed Baptist traditions that lie behind them. A number of considerations urge caution:

(1) At least in the case of Jesus we have two distinct Infancy Narratives, which allow us to compare the similarities amid all the differences and arrive at some sober conclusions about common early tradition behind both narratives. With no such check on the Baptist narrative in Luke 1, we are left with largely unverifiable speculation as to what was contained in the pre-Lucan tradition.[17]

(2) From Dibelius onwards, it has often been remarked that the Infancy

Narratives of the Baptist and Jesus basically parallel each other, with some trait of superiority being assigned to Jesus at each stage of the symmetrical narrative.[18] But it is by no means clear how this symmetry was achieved. We could suppose that a fairly full narrative of John's birth existed first and then a story of Jesus' birth was fashioned on the model John supplied; but the reverse process is also conceivable, with John being assimilated to Jesus.[19] Actually, it is highly likely that, whatever the starting point of Luke's Infancy Narrative, each cycle of birth traditions influenced the other as the two were woven together.[20] An artificial connection of the two cycles is visible in Luke's account of the visitation of Mary to Elizabeth; one wonders how many other artificial connections and parallels were created as the traditions grew together. All this makes declaring individual points of the Baptist's Infancy Narrative sober history risky at best.

(3) Distinguishing between history and theological interpretation is made all the more difficult by the fact that Luke 1–2 belong to the huge literary and theological masterpiece that is Luke-Acts.[21] Many themes in the first two chapters are carefully placed there to provide a starting point or foreshadowing for later events in the saga of Jesus and the early church.[22] Beginning the whole story with the priest Zechariah praying in the temple in chap. 1 creates connections not only with the presence of the infant and boy Jesus in the temple in chap. 2 but also with the apostles returning to pray in the temple after the risen Jesus blesses them in priestly fashion[23] as he is taken up into heaven (Luke 24:50–53)—to say nothing of the various scenes in the temple in Acts. Of course, none of this disproves the existence of a priest called Zechariah who was the Baptist's father, but such literary and theological symmetry, so typical of Luke's strategy for knitting together his two-volume work,[24] should make us wary of presuming historicity without further ado.

We may therefore have to reconcile ourselves to leaving aside Luke 1 in our quest for the historical Baptist. To be fair, though, I should point out one element of the Baptist infancy tradition that may have some claim to historicity. Applying the criterion of coherence (i.e., how the portrait of the Baptist in Luke 1 coheres with statements about the adult Baptist in Mark and Q), I think that, if anything of value can be salvaged from Luke's narrative, it is the idea that John was the only son of a priest who functioned in the Jerusalem temple.[25] This would be a most significant nugget of information, for the only son of a Jerusalem priest would have a solemn duty to follow his father in his function and to make sure that the priestly line was continued by marriage and children. If this was in fact the historical situation, John at some point must have consciously turned his back on and—in Jewish eyes—scandalously rejected his obligation to be a priest in his father's footsteps and to supply priestly descendants after him. Forsaking family duty as well as his priestly duty to the Jerusalem temple—therefore, forsaking all that was most sacred to Judaism— he went into the wilderness of Judea to announce imminent judgment and the dire need for moral cleansing on the part of all Jews.

Such radical, "charismatic" action that wipes out traditional lines of authority and continuity certainly coheres well with the action and message of John as presented in the Marcan and Q traditions. The Baptist of the Q document views his fellow Jews as a "brood of vipers" who foolishly trust in descent from Abraham as protection from the coming judgment when in fact neither descent from Abraham nor the usual cultic mechanism but only individual repentance and good deeds, coupled with John's baptism, can save one from destruction (Luke 3:7–9 par.; cf. Mark 1:4–5,12). Such a radical vision, acted out in John's radical rejection of an ordinary lifestyle in favor of nomadic life in the wilderness (Mark 1:3,6), coheres strikingly well with the idea only implied in Luke's narrative: the only son of a priest turned his back on the vocation decreed for him by his birth, effectively rejected both his priestly family and the temple, and struck out into the desert to embrace the role of an Israelite prophet of judgment. The coherence is all the more impressive because Luke never draws these lines of convergence himself. Naturally, this does not prove that the nugget of information in Luke 1 about John's priestly lineage is historical. But this argument from coherence does at least give one pause. Perhaps alone among the Baptist traditions in Luke 1, this element does enjoy a certain plausibility, though personally I think the whole question must remain unresolved.[26]

Since the discovery of the Dead Sea Scrolls, one more item in Luke 1 has received a positive historical assessment from many writers, namely the cryptic statement that ends the Baptist's Infancy Narrative: "Now the child grew and gained strength in the spirit, and he was in the desert places until the day of his manifestation to Israel" (Luke 1:80). We have already seen that Josephus depicts Essenes adopting children and training them in their customs while they are still docile (*J.W.* 2.8.2 §12). John could have been such a child trained at Qumran since boyhood.[27] The theory is not impossible, and John and the Qumranites shared many common traits. Both of them rejected ordinary lifestyles (urban or rural), stood in tension to the contemporary form of temple priesthood and worship, were active in or around the wilderness of Judea, had a sense that the definitive intervention of God in history was imminent, looked to Isa 40:3[28] as a prophecy of their work in the desert preparing for that intervention, called true Israelites to repentance in view of the approaching end of present history, predicted salvation or doom for Israelites depending on their response to the warning proclaimed to them, and practiced some water ritual or rituals as a sign of interior cleansing.

All this makes for a plausible argument, and yet one must at the same time recognize significant differences between the Qumranites and John. When we first come upon the adult John, he is a solitary figure whose only "community" consists of his own disciples; there is no indication that he or they once belonged to a larger group or sedentary community. Most of John's disciples—if we may use that word in the broadest sense, to encompass all those who accepted his teaching and submitted to his baptism—returned to their ordinary lives and occupations. True, some of those John baptized seem to have stayed around him as an "inner circle" of disciples, as chaps. 1 and 3 of John's Gospel suggest. But there is no sign of any organization or, indeed, any permanent membership in the group. A stronger group consciousness and perhaps some minimal organization would have crystallized after John's death, especially when the Baptist disciples found themselves in competition with the early Christians.

As for other differences between John and Qumran: John practices not the frequent lustrations of Qumran but a once-and-for-all baptism administered to others by himself. So closely is his own person identified with this unique kind of ritual washing that he alone, among the many Jews of his day who practiced rites of cleansing, is called "the Baptist."[29] Indeed, everything seems to depend upon his own person; there is no place for the hierarchical structures that guarantee order and succession at Qumran. While Qumran is obsessed with the false priests, calendar, and ritual practiced in the defiled Jerusalem temple and with the pressing need for the temple's purification and restoration, John—especially if he be of priestly stock—is remarkably silent on the temple question. Moreover, and even more telling, while Qumran is noted for its super-stringent interpretation and observance of the Mosaic Law, so much so that they look upon even the Pharisees as laxists, the sayings and actions of John preserved in the Gospels and Josephus show a total lack of concern with detailed legal questions. We could, of course, posit a wrenching break between the adult John and the Qumran community, which nurtured him physically and spiritually.[30] But before we descend further and further into novel writing, we should first consider two points.

(1) Luke 1:80, which has set off so much of this speculation about a prep school in the desert, should first be read in the light of Luke's mode of composition. It is typical of Luke that he will carefully conclude a scene by "getting rid of" characters not needed for the immediately following scene. A prime example is the end of the visitation scene (1:39–56), where we are told that "Mary remained with her [Elizabeth] about three months and returned to her home" (v 56). At first glance, it seems as though Luke is saying that Mary returned home before the birth of the Baptist, which is related in the next pericope (1:57–66). That seems strange, though, since presumably Mary had undertaken her journey at least in part to aid her aged relative as the birth of John approached. Actually, there is no need to think that in v 56 Luke intends to affirm Mary's departure before John's birth. He is simply bringing a particular scene to its graceful conclusion and removing the character not needed for the next scene.[31]

Something similar happens in 1:80: John, who has been the major focus of chap. 1, will not be needed in chap. 2, and so Luke "gets him out of the way" in v 80. More to the point, he faces with the infant John the same sort of problem both Matthew and Luke face with the infant Jesus: how to get him from the geographical location of his infancy to the place where the common Synoptic tradition places him in his adulthood. We have seen how Matthew and Luke create different narrative bridges to connect the tradition of Jesus' birth at Bethlehem with his adult "origin" from Nazareth, the only origin known in the common Synoptic tradition. A similar ploy was needed to bring the plot of John's Infancy Narrative to a graceful conclusion. This special tradition places the infant John in a priestly family in the hill country of Judea, surrounded by neighbors and relatives (1:58); the Marcan tradition introduces the adult John as a solitary traversing the wilderness of Judea by the Jordan. Some narrative link between the two traditions had to be forged. Luke 1:80 may be nothing more than a literary bridge, created to connect the special infancy tradition with the Marcan tradition Luke takes over in 3:2–4.[32]

(2) Thus, Qumran may simply be beside the point,[33] especially when we recall that Qumran did not have a monopoly on ascetic holy men practicing ritual purification in the Judean wilderness around the Jordan. Josephus tells us about Bannus, "who lived in the wilderness, wearing clothing from trees, obtaining his food from uncultivated plants, frequently washing day and night with cold water for purity's sake" (*Life* 2 §11). In the light of the work of Joseph Thomas, it is wise to view Qumran, Bannus, and John as particular manifestations of a much larger Jewish penitential and baptizing movement around the region of the Jordan in the 1st centuries B.C. and A.D.[34] Hence, while it is not impossible that John was "educated" at Qumran, that hypothesis may be taking too narrow a view of a much wider religious phenomenon, of which John, Bannus, and Qumran were individual examples.

Looking at the meager results of our attempt to find some historical information in John's Infancy Narrative, we are left with two wan candidates, two tantalizing possibilities: (1) that the only son of a priest turned his back on his filial duty of continuing the priestly line and ministering in the Jerusalem temple because he felt called to function as an anti-establishment prophet; and (2) that this priestly scion may have had his anti-establishment views nourished by being reared at Qumran or some other Essene settlement. Both hypotheses are possible, neither provable. Because the first, unlike the second, is supported by the heart of the narrative in Luke 1, I am more disposed to give it credence, especially since it coheres well with what we know of the adult John.[35]

III. THE WORDS AND DEEDS OF THE ADULT JOHN IN THE GOSPEL TRADITIONS

Our concern here is not to survey the various redactional portraits of John in the Four Gospels,[36] but to glean from the Gospels reliable historical tradition about John. From the start one must make a methodological distinction between (1) what Q and Mark say that the Baptist said and did and (2) what Q and Mark say that Jesus said about the Baptist. The first category will be treated in this chapter, the second in the next.

A. The Q Tradition of John's Words and Deeds: The First Baptist-Block[37]

John the Baptist plays a remarkably large role in Q, notably in the two great "Baptist-blocks" of material: Matt 3:7–12 ‖ Luke 3:7–9,15–18 and Matt

11:2–19 ‖ Luke 7:18–35.[38] In this chapter we shall examine the first Baptist-block, in which the Baptist speaks for himself. In the next chapter, after Jesus comes on the scene and is baptized, we shall study the second Baptist-block, in which Jesus speaks to and of the Baptist. Both of these Q passages on the Baptist are striking in that they demonstrate some of the closest word-for-word correspondence between Matthew and Luke that we find in the Q material (see especially Matt 3:7–10 ‖ Luke 3:7–9). Hence it is likely that this Baptist material was fixed early on; much of it either shows no explicit relation to Jesus or Christians (so Matt 3:7–10 par.)[39] or expresses John's relation to Jesus in a way untypical of the early church (so much of Matt 11:2–19 par.). The criterion of discontinuity, as well as confirmation at times from Mark, John, or Josephus, makes the core of the Q tradition on the Baptist fairly reliable.[40] It also coheres well with the overall picture of the Baptist we were able to reconstruct in section I.

(1) *Matt 3:7–10 par.* presents John as a grim prophet of fiery imminent judgment. Even the Jews who come out to the Jordan to be baptized by him are greeted with the harsh epithet "brood of vipers."[41] They are no better than a bunch of snakes who are desperately fleeing from danger (perhaps fire in the underbrush, if we may anticipate the image at the end of Matt 3:10). That danger, shorn of metaphor, is the wrath of God which will soon inflict punishment on all who rebel against his will. God's fiery, destructive wrath is a frequent theme of both the narrators of Israel's history and the classical prophets.[42] The wrath of God is the holiness of God automatically reacting against all that is not holy in Israel's conduct, especially the apostasy and idolatry that break that basic covenant relationship between God and his people. God's wrath is often described with metaphors of fire, heat, and blasting wind; and its seething temperature only rises in the angry apocalyptic literature of the 1st centuries B.C. and A.D.[43] John certainly stands in this prophetic and apocalyptic tradition as he warns the whole people of Israel that, despite all the external mechanisms of religion, they are subject to fierce judgment.

In the Greek of Matt 3:7, the wrath John predicts is qualified as *mellousēs*, which carries the idea of a future event that is imminent and/or certain.[44] It is a description meant to inspire fear, but John warns the candidates for baptism that mere fear as a motive for being baptized is not a sufficient shield from the coming judgment. Along with baptism John demands both interior and exterior change. Within, one must change one's mind and heart about what is important in life and then change one's outward life accordingly. This is *metanoia*, that change of mind which is heart-felt repentance.[45] It is the Greek equivalent of the rabbinic Hebrew *tĕšûbâ* (Aramaic *tĕtûbā'*), the inner attitude that replied to the prophets' cry of *šûb* (Aramaic *tûb*),[46] "return," that is, turn back from your sins, apostasy, and idolatry to the one true God. That turning must first take place in the depths of one's being; and no flurry of external religious busy-ness, including baptism, can take its place.[47] On the other hand, the turn within must become enfleshed in a change in one's day-to-day actions without, a change to good deeds that are the "fruit(s)[48] worthy of [i.e., corresponding to and manifesting prior] repentance."

But John knows he faces a difficult task in convincing this "brood of vipers" that mere physical descent from Abraham, like mere physical baptism, will not be sufficient protection on the day of judgment.[49] "*We* have Abraham for our father" bespeaks a collective consciousness as the chosen people that was meant to instill trust in God's covenant-promises but which instead could breed smug complacency.[50] It is to shatter that complacency that the Baptist shatters the significance of a biological link with Abraham. The omnipotent Creator can make children of Abraham out of the stones lying at the audience's feet[51] just as easily as he can give that status to people—and that status is as meaningless for persons as for stones in view of the imminent judgment (v 8bc).[52]

A point should be made here that must be understood in all the threatening speeches of John and Jesus that we shall examine throughout this book. Both John and Jesus proclaim their threats and woes to Israel precisely as Israelite prophets working within and for Israel. Like Amos or Jeremiah, they fiercely condemn Israel and breathe fiery threats of judgment because they are so passionately concerned about Israel's salvation. Although the words may remain the same, this prophetic critique of Israel *within Israel* will take on an entirely different meaning when the early church uses it in its debates with Israel and as a justification for separation from Israel. Once and for all, let it be made clear that, in the quest for the historical Jesus, such prophetic indictments must be heard as coming from a committed Israelite seeking to wake up his own people to what he discerns as imminent danger threatening the covenant community. It is within this context that John uses a powerful image of discontinuity, of the abrogation of claims based on salvation history, claims that his audience takes for granted as protection against the final judgment, to "shake up" his listeners and arouse them from their spiritual lethargy. Yet, while John is employing rhetoric, it is not "empty rhetoric"; he does mean this abrogation to be taken seriously. As with Jesus, so with John, we have here a notable element of discontinuity with much of the Judaism of John's own time.

In John's view, the danger is indeed imminent.[53] "*Already* the ax is laid to the root of the tree" (v 10a). There is no time to lose because—resuming the fruit image for the good deeds manifesting the genuine conversion of sinners—"every tree not bearing good fruit is being cut down and is being thrown into the fire" (v 10b). Presumably the tree bearing good fruit is spared, but it is telling that John formulates his prediction in dire negative terms. John's preaching, while holding open the hope of salvation, stresses the fearful punishment to come. So too, the saying in Matt 3:12 par. ends on the negative theme of inextinguishable fire.

The image of the ax cutting down the tree has forebears in the OT depiction of judgment (cf. Isa 10:33–34; 32:19). What stands out here by comparison is the great emphasis on the imminence of judgment: the woodsman has already laid bare the roots of the tree and is carefully adjusting the angle of the ax to the tree just before the first stroke.[54] A woodsman who has already done all this does not then stop to consider whether the tree should be given more time to grow. Some would see in the tree a metaphor for the collectivity of Israel (cf. Jer 11:16);[55] but the emphasis on *"every* tree" seems to envision the individual Israelite, an interpretation which makes sense in a sermon calling individuals to decision and prophesying a clear division between good and bad on the last day (v 12).[56]

To whom is this sermon addressed? Matthew speaks of "many of the Pharisees and Sadducees coming to be baptized by him." The combination "Pharisees and Sadducees," used to indicate the joint subjects of some action or doctrine, is found only in Matthew's Gospel (3:7; 16:1,6,11–12), and comparisons with Marcan and Q material (Mark 8:11–21; Luke 3:7) show that it is Matthew's own creation.[57] Whether or not Luke's precise designation ("the crowds coming out to be baptized by him") stood in Q, his more generic description of the audience fits the material that follows. Being children of Abraham was something all Israelites, not just Jerusalem priests or Pharisees, would claim; and the basic division between good and bad that runs through this mini-sermon is cast in the most general terms possible. Moreover, the Lucan depiction of the generic "crowds" receives support from Josephus' mention of the large, undifferentiated group of "the others" *(tōn allōn)*. Hence the potential addressees of John's sermon are any and all Israelites.[58]

What is striking, therefore, is that the threat of the sermon contained in Matt 3:7–10 ‖ Luke 3:7–9 is directed at the ordinary Jews who have taken the time and trouble to come out to John to be baptized. It is to them, to the ostensibly well disposed, that John utters this withering denunciation.[59] Thus, in this little shocking gem from Q, we already have a cameo of John's message: in the face of an imminent fiery judgment, in the face of God's holy wrath blazing forth and threatening to consume his apparently holy but actually unholy people, even the ostensibly devout are in danger.[60] There must be confession of sin, not only of one's own individual sins, but also of the corporate sins of the people of God who have gone astray and have therefore lost their assurance of salvation on the day of judgment. Hence not all members of the empirical society called Israel will be part of the eschatological Israel saved by God. Only the swift decision to accept John's baptism and to combine it with a profound change of both inner attitude and external conduct can rescue the individual Jew from the fire soon to come.[61]

Things gone terribly awry among God's people, fearful judgment about to blaze forth, the wicked destroyed by fire, the lone prophetic figure who harks back to the beginnings of Israel's history and exhorts the people in the most dire tones to repent for the end is near, the dissolution of those ties of salvation history and biological peoplehood that gave Israel confidence, salvation possible only for those within Israel who heed and swiftly act on the final revelation mediated through the sad and solitary prophet—all these elements prompt many authors to speak of John as an "apocalyptic" figure.[62] The problem is that "apocalyptic" is a tricky category that present-day scholars debate at

length.[63] John certainly displays some characteristics of the thought and literature of apocalyptic, yet other common elements (mystical visions interpreted
by angels, journeys through the various levels of the cosmos up to heaven and
God's throne, astrological and calendric speculation, timetables of salvation
history, phantasmagoric symbols and esoteric allegories, the question of the
fate of the Gentile nations, and a doctrine of the survival of the individual after
death) are lacking in the material that has come down to us. Perhaps most
telling is the difference that, unlike the apocalyptic movement, John and his
immediate followers produced no literature, especially the pseudepigraphic literature typical of apocalyptic; in a sense he resumed the purely oral preaching
of Elijah and other OT prophets. He feels no need to clothe himself in pseudepigraphic writings and the language of mystery to gain legitimacy. In clear,
simple speech he preaches on the basis of his own personal authority, which
apparently he feels comes directly from God.[64]

It may therefore be more accurate to describe John as an eschatological
prophet tinged with some apocalyptic motifs.[65] "Eschatological" as a category
is perhaps no less problematic than apocalyptic, especially since some forms of
eschatology *are* apocalyptic.[66] But in general it may be used to refer to the
definitive end of the history of God's people as they have experienced it from
the time of their election. It is an end—but also a new beginning—brought
about by God's wrathful judgment and extermination of sinners within his
holy people and by the salvation of those who have proved faithful or who
sincerely repent in the last hour—in some cases, by accepting the just rule of
a new, ideal king, in other cases by obeying the preaching of a final prophet
sent to them. All these themes, in various combinations, can be encompassed
under the rubric of the "prophetic eschatology" found in the OT and in some
works of the intertestamental literature. The extent to which the state of Israel
after the end-and-new-beginning is in continuity with ordinary, earthly realities and the extent to which Israel is transferred into an idealized, magical, or
heavenly world vary from author to author. The greater the transformation of
the whole cosmos, the closer one approaches to apocalyptic. In any case, the
motif of imminent judgment, the threat of annihilation by fire (a fire that does
not seem to be purely a metaphor),[67] the denunciation of even the apparently
sincere as really evil, and the rupture of salvation history (being "children of
Abraham" no longer means anything at the judgment), as well as the generally
dark and dire view of the future (much is said about punishment, little about
salvation), help push John's eschatology in the direction of apocalyptic, without fully arriving there.[68]

We will see how this eschatological outlook is confirmed and developed in
other material on John. But even this preliminary glance at his eschatology
should cause misgivings about recent interpretations of Jesus that wish to play
down or exclude the element of future eschatology from his message.[69] If Jesus
accepted John's message and baptism, presumably he affirmed John's basic
eschatological outlook. To be sure, Jesus may have developed or even moved
away from John's eschatology later on. But a totally un-eschatological Jesus

trips over the very stumbling-stone early Christianity found so difficult: John the Baptist, the independent Jewish prophet of fiery imminent eschatology, to whom Jesus himself adhered.[70]

Finally, what is perhaps most striking about the basic proclamation of John in Matt 3:7–10 par. is that, while eschatological and even slightly apocalyptic, it lacks all specifically Christian character and makes not even a glancing reference to Jesus or to any human mediator of God's final judgment.[71] Taken by itself, Matt 3:7–10 seems to say that it is God himself who lays the ax to the root of the tree and presumably throws the bad tree into the fire. The only human involved is John, who does not wield the ax but simply reveals its ominous presence and offers a way to avoid it. Read in isolation, Matt 3:7–10 provides a good argument for those who claim that John saw himself as the forerunner of God alone, just as in the pre-Christian period Judaism generally thought of Elijah as the forerunner of God alone, and not of some human messiah.[72] Whether or not John presented himself as the returning Elijah, the eschatology of 3:7–10, without Christianity or its Christ, fits in perfectly with the independent Baptist, who felt no need to define himself by his relation to Jesus of Nazareth. Hence there is no serious reason to doubt the substantial authenticity of these verses.

(2) The same basic tone of fiery eschatology touched with apocalyptic remains in the next Q pericope, *Matt 3:11–12 ‖ Luke 3:16–18* (cf. Mark 1:7–8; Acts 13:25; John 1:26–27,33d). However, the Baptist begins to describe two topics heretofore either not touched upon or only mentioned in passing: (1) his baptism and its proper place in the end-time drama; and (2) the relation of his baptism to the coming salvation. It is as his message takes this more positive turn that the possibility of some further mediator of salvation beyond John makes its appearance.

We might, at first glance, suspect a Christian creation, but a number of considerations make the authenticity of Matt 3:11–12 par. fairly secure.[73] Beyond the observations made above about the early nature of the Baptist material in Q, we have here one of the rare cases of a "Mark-Q-Acts-John overlap." That is to say, the part of the Q material that speaks of a mysterious figure still to come (i.e., Matt 3:11bc) is also witnessed, with largely (but not entirely) the same vocabulary, in Mark 1:7–8, in Acts 13:25, and to a surprising degree in John 1:26–27,33d.[74]

Interestingly, though, the order of the components in this common logion is different in Mark and Q, with John vaguely similar to Q. Mark first presents the promise of the stronger one who comes after John and whose sandal strap John is not worthy to untie (v 7); then comes the contrast between John's baptism with water and the stronger one's baptism with the holy spirit (v 8). Mark thus gives us two sayings with two parts each.

The Q logion is more artistically formulated in an A–B–A' structure. First comes the statement that John baptizes with water (Matt 3:11a par.). Then there immediately follows the promise of the stronger one (Matt 3:11bc par.). The saying concludes with the other half of the contrast between the two baptisms: the stronger one will baptize with the holy spirit and fire (Matt 3:11d par.). The Fourth Gospel contains the vague outline of the Q pattern, though other material intervenes, and the A' element is not spoken until the following day in the Johannine narrative! The variety in structure and in the description of the future baptism (Mark and John's "holy spirit" versus Q's "holy spirit and fire") argues well for a very early tradition that developed into the separate forms reflected in Mark, Q, and John. Moreover, it may well be that the core saying proclaiming John's unworthiness may be represented by an independent tradition in Acts as well. Granted, Acts 13:25 could be just a consciously abbreviated citation by Luke of what he has presented more fully in his Gospel. Yet the agreement between John and Acts (as opposed to Luke's Gospel) in (1) the omission of *ho ischyroteros mou* ("the one stronger than I"), (2) the use of *hypodēmatos* ("sandal") in the singular (the Synoptics all read the plural), and (3) the use of *axios* instead of the Synoptic *hikanos* for "worthy" does at least create the possibility that Acts represents not a Lucan redactional variation but another tradition, similar to the one known by John. Finally, aside from the question of multiple attestation in the sources, there is a general consideration that tells in favor of authenticity. The additional Q saying in Matt 3:12 par. continues the fiery eschatology that we have already seen in 3:7–10; and, even with the promise of a stronger one to come, the isolated sayings have no specifically Christian content. Hence we have good reason to accept this as substantially the Baptist's own teaching.

Although there is no way to be certain, I tend to think that the natural, straightforward order of Mark (introduction of the stronger one, then comparison of his baptism with John's in strict parallelism)[75] is more original, while the more artistically intricate structure of Q may be a secondary development, with the Fourth Gospel expanding even further a structure similar to Q's and blurring the A–B–A' pattern in the process. At any rate, for the sake of clarity of presentation, it is easier to follow Mark's order by considering first the mysterious "stronger one" and then his baptism. The basic agreement and the minor differences among Matthew, Mark, Luke, Acts, and John make a hypothetical earliest form possible to reconstruct, though some individual points naturally remain debatable: "There comes [after me] the one stronger than I, the strap of whose sandal I am not worthy to loose. I baptize(d) you with water, but he will baptize you with the holy spirit."[76] Let us take a closer look at this dense statement.

The Baptist abruptly introduces "the one stronger than I," who is to appear after him on the stage of salvation history. This oblique way of referring to a central figure in the eschatological drama is strange,[77] and the lack of any elucidation has led some exegetes to interpret the image by invoking the immediately preceding context: the stronger one can be no other than God himself. God, after all, has already been described in Q with the image of the peasant farmer who cuts down the bad tree and hurls it into the fire. This image for God's judging activity in the end time is continued with the idea of his baptizing people with fire (if one accepts the Q wording), with his cleansing of *his* threshing floor (*whose* threshing floor if not God's?), and his burning of the chaff in inextinguishable fire (the return to the fire motif that was connected with God's judging action in Matt 3:10 par.). Hence there is good reason to take the "stronger one" as referring to God himself. The message of Matt 3:7–10 par. would thus remain unmodified: John is the eschatological prophet preceding God himself, with no other figure intervening.

As appealing as this interpretation is, it suffers from some severe problems.[78] To be sure, in the OT and intertestamental literature, God is *the* strong one, indeed, the Almighty. But it makes no sense whatsoever for John to stress that God is "the one stronger than I," especially with regard to the final judgment. Who would have thought otherwise? Liturgy and preaching can certainly employ veiled references or solemn circumlocutions for God. But for John to use "the one stronger than I" as a veiled name for the God he has directly and plainly referred to just a few verses ago (at least in the Q material in Matt 3:9 par.) seems downright silly. Ernst seeks to avoid this difficulty by rewriting the verse. He omits "than I" as a secondary addition (though it is present in all three Synoptics) and then interprets the comparative adjective as a superlative. All this is quite arbitrary, especially since the immediate context, which compares the baptism of John with that of the stronger one, makes the strictly comparative sense of "the stronger one" the natural sense as well.[79]

The interpretation of the stronger one as God threatens to border on the nonsensical when the sentence continues with the affirmation that John is not worthy to untie the strap on the sandals of the stronger one. Granted, the OT does at times use the metaphor of God's shoe (Pss 60:10; 108:10), though the metaphor is rare and occurs in an entirely different context (the subjugation of enemy territory). A metaphor presenting John untying God's shoelaces seems to go beyond the bounds of any OT example. More to the point, it is an incredibly contorted way of proclaiming the mind-boggling truism that God is superior to John.[80] Finally, to place in parallelism two acts of baptizing, John's and the stronger one's, is extremely strange if the stronger one is God. Why would there be any need to stress that whatever God does, including baptism (an odd action on God's part), would be superior to John's action in the same vein? Hence it is likely that "the stronger one" does contain a veiled reference to some figure in the eschatological drama other than God.

But who? Naturally, the Gospels take for granted that Jesus is meant, and their narratives proceed accordingly. But the logion on "the one stronger than I," if taken in isolation from the overarching framework of the evangelists, need not carry such a clear christological reference. Various modern interpreters have suggested that John was referring to the returning Elijah, the apocalyptic Son of Man, or some other transcendent "messianic" figure. One could certainly add other heavenly figures known from Jewish literature at the time, e.g., the mysterious figure of the heavenly priest Melchizedek, probably identified with the angel Michael in the Qumran fragment 11QMelch.[81] Furthermore, one need not think that John himself was a Qumranite to suppose that he was familiar with other eschatological ideas alive at Qumran, ideas that conceived of eschatological leaders of Israel in more human or earthly terms, e.g., a priestly Messiah, a Davidic Messiah, or some sort of eschatological prophet. Since John himself already seemed to fulfill the last named function, he could possibly have been thinking of a messiah of priestly or royal lineage. Yet the image of the judge of the last day using inextinguishable fire to punish the wicked does not seem to jibe with these purely human, earthly figures. All these suggestions—and others that could be made as well—simply remind us how multifaceted, mutually influencing, and at times jumbled Jewish eschatological expectations were in the 1st centuries B.C. and A.D.

This last observation may give us the real solution to John's mysterious "one stronger than I." The vagueness may have been intentional on John's part. In other words, John did expect some further agent of God who would bring the eschatological drama to its proper denouement, but he had no clear idea who that would be.[82] Perhaps, with a humble and sober realization that he existed, both geographically and spiritually, only on the fringes of Judaism, only as a very "marginal" figure, John did not look upon himself as the most apt or effective final agent of God for the last days. God would rather bring his plan of judgment and salvation to completion through some mysterious figure still to come, someone "stronger" than John when it came to actually executing that plan.[83] It would be up to this agent of salvation to effect the final separation of good and bad among God's people, a separation represented by the image of the peasant separating wheat from chaff on his threshing floor. Strictly speaking, while Matt 3:10 par. presents God destroying the wicked with fire, it does not attribute to God the precise action of distinguishing and separating the good and the evil on the last day. That judicial function is apparently handed over to "the stronger one."[84]

Yet John never says who the one stronger than he is. Perhaps the reason is that John never moved much beyond the general idea that he himself was not powerful enough to complete the eschatological task God had begun with him. Therefore God would send some other, greater agent after John to bring the eschatological drama to completion.[85] It is this very vagueness on a point that Christians would consider all important that argues well for the logion's coming from John himself instead of being invented later by Christians. To be sure, the vagueness allowed the Christians to preserve the saying and apply it to Jesus; but the saying, left to itself, remains open-ended, as John intended.

A major point of contention among exegetes is the original wording of the contrast between the baptisms of John and of the stronger one. All the sources agree that John's baptism is (merely) with water and hence inferior to a more spiritual type of baptism still to be conferred. The coming baptism, however, is described in two different ways in various branches of the Gospel tradition. Q (Matt 3:11 ‖ Luke 3:16) says that "he [the stronger one] will baptize you with [literally, in] holy spirit and fire." Mark 1:8 has the same wording, except that he lacks the final two words "and fire." With slightly different wording the Fourth Gospel supports Mark: ". . . he is the one who baptizes with holy spirit" (John 1:33d).

There may be another source supporting Mark and John over against Q. Although Luke in his Gospel clearly uses the Q form, twice in the Acts of the Apostles Luke has first Jesus and then Peter echo the statement of the Baptist about the two baptisms in what is basically Mark's form.[86] In Acts 1:5 Jesus reminds the eleven apostles: "John indeed baptized with water, but you will be baptized with holy spirit not many days hence." Here Luke is obviously applying the prophecy of future baptism to the Pentecost event. All the stranger, then, is his use of a form closer to Mark than to Q. The Q form, after all, contains the relevant "and with fire," corresponding perfectly to the tongues of fire at Pentecost (Acts 2:3)—which is what Acts 1:5 is predicting.[87]

Again, in 11:16, Peter recounts to the Jerusalem church the conversion and baptism of Cornelius, occasioned by the descent of the holy spirit on him and his household: "I remembered the word of the Lord when he said [practically citing Acts 1:5]: 'John indeed baptized with water, but you shall be baptized with holy spirit.' " It is possible that in both passages in Acts Luke has simply chosen to cite the Marcan form rather than the Q form, which he used in his Gospel. Why he should have done that, especially when the reference to fire would have been so apt just before the Pentecost event, is not clear. When we remember that the Baptist's statement in Acts 13:25 shows surprising similarity to its parallel in the Fourth Gospel, and when we consider that Acts 1:5 and 11:16 likewise side with John (and Mark) over against Q in omitting "and fire," it may well be that the Baptist statements in Acts are neither mere Lucan redaction nor a sudden strange preference for Mark over Q. Rather, they may represent a distinct stream of tradition in the sources of Acts closer to John than to Q. If that be the case, we have three distinct sources, Mark, John, and Acts, in favor of baptism with (only) holy spirit, as opposed to baptism with holy spirit and fire, which is supported by only one source, Q.

Other considerations support the shorter Marcan reading of baptism by holy spirit. First of all, I have argued above that the strict parallelism and balance of Mark 1:8, unbroken by the separate statement about the stronger one (1:7), is the more original form of the saying about the two baptisms. If that is correct, then the balance between water and the holy spirit fits in perfectly with the overall balanced structure and strict parallelism of the saying, while baptism with holy spirit and fire unbalances the logion. Moreover, "and fire" looks especially suspicious because it comes at the very end of the whole logion, the natural place for an addition to be made.

Secondly, if we champion the shorter Marcan form as more original, we should be able to offer a reasonable—though necessarily speculative—explanation of how the addition "and fire" entered into the Q tradition early on, perhaps in the oral stage. One explanation lies right at hand. If Matt 3:7–10 and 11–12 represent more or less the order of the sayings in Q, it is noteworthy that the phrase "and is thrown into fire" (v 10c) immediately precedes "I indeed baptize you with water" (v 11a), while "he will baptize you with holy spirit and fire" (v 11d) is immediately followed by the metaphor of the winnowing fan (v 12), which ends with "but the chaff he will burn with inextinguishable fire." In other words, in the Q tradition, the logion about the two baptisms was framed by two sayings, each of which ended with a reference to fire. If this was the traditional order when this little Q collection on the Baptist was still circulating in oral form, it is quite understandable that the "framing" references to fire might creep into the saying comparing the two baptisms. With the first image in the comparison being "water," the natural tendency would be to supply a sharper contrasting image than "holy spirit"; and fire, the opposite of "water," lay right at hand on either side of the logion.

Many exegetes, however, have defended the Q form as more original.[88] It is telling, though, that they are remarkably divided among themselves as to what baptism with holy spirit and fire means. Some claim that the whole phrase should be taken together as hendiadys: a fiery wind. Most would keep the two images distinct, but they do not agree on what each image represents. Obviously, holy spirit is a positive image, whether one stresses the spirit's purifying or life-giving function. The real difficulty—perhaps not without reason—is the image of fire. Some take it to be purely punitive or destructive. Certainly the immediate context both before and after (Matt 3:10,12 par.) uses it that way, and it seems forced to introduce a contrary meaning in v 11.[89] Yet some exegetes try to read the fire positively, after the manner of Mal 3:2: "He is like the fire of a refiner. . . . he shall sit refining and purifying silver, and he shall purify the sons of Levi." Similarly, the stronger one to come will purify penitent Israelites definitively, completing the purification John has begun with his water baptism. While that is possible, the order seems somewhat strange. Why does the purifying fire follow upon rather than precede the gift of the holy spirit?

All in all, the punitive or destructive function of the fire seems at first glance to make more sense. Yet this approach has its own difficulties. When John says in Matt 3:11a, "I indeed baptize you with water," he is referring to one type of baptism administered to one group of people ("you"), the people who have accepted John's proclamation and submitted to his demands. The punitive sense of fire demands that the stronger one administer in effect two baptisms, one salvific and one destructive. We must take "with holy spirit and fire" to mean really "with holy spirit *or* fire," the "and" *(kai)* being actually disjunctive in meaning. After all, it would make no sense to say that at the final judgment the same group of people would receive both a salvific and a destructive "baptism."[90]

This brings us to a further difficulty. Not only must the stronger one administer in effect two different baptisms. He obviously must do so to two different groups: those who are to be saved and those who are to be punished or destroyed.[91] Yet the recipients of these two very different recompenses on the last day are the very same group ("you") who, alone among the Jews of John's day, have heeded his voice and submitted to his baptism ("I baptize *you* with water"). To import a distinction between the "you" who are ready to repent and the "you" who are not is gratuitous and does violence to the text.[92] Does John mean instead that even some of those who accept his message and bap-

tism will still be destroyed on the last day? The candidates for his baptism
might indeed ask: Why bother? And why are some of the baptized saved and
some lost? We might supply some moral criterion by suggesting that some of
the baptized produced the "fruit of repentance" (Matt 3:8) while others did
not, but once again that is a totally gratuitous distinction not made in the Q
text.[93] If we follow the Q saying to its logical conclusion, we are left with John
affirming, with no explanation, that some of the Jews he baptizes will be saved
on the last day, while others he baptizes will suffer the same fate as those who
were never baptized. This is a strange way for John to promote his baptism.

I suggest that the reason why these explanations of the words "and fire" in
Matt 3:11 par. are both numerous and unsatisfactory is that the phrase is an
addition to a saying that made perfect sense without it.[94] Not only does the
Marcan form enjoy multiple attestation; it also provides a clear, simple, balanced contrast as opposed to an unbalanced one that provides only grist for
various contorted explanations.

Surprisingly, some who agree in rejecting Q's "holy spirit and fire" as original have attempted another, more radical solution: namely, none of the present
forms of the saying on two baptisms—neither Mark, Q, Acts, nor John—
preserves the original wording. By a strange process of subtraction, the original
wording is seen to be "but he shall baptize you with fire."[95] One argument for
this form is that it contains an even more balanced contrast, the one word
"water" contrasted with one word that is its natural opposite, "fire." This
hypothetical form suffers, however, from grave difficulties. First of all and
most obviously, it claims that the phrase "holy spirit," present in all the many
forms of the logion, is not original, while the word "fire," present only in Q
alongside "holy spirit," is. This is to turn source criticism on its head. Secondly, the problem of what the fire means remains. If the fire is punitive or
destructive, the saying becomes even more bizarre: *all* the people submitting
to John's baptism ("you") will also undergo the punitive fire on the last day.
The question Why bother? becomes all the more pressing. In addition, the
saying lacks even a hint that some will be saved on the last day, a promise
clearly made in 3:12. If instead the fire is seen as purifying and so ultimately
salvific, the old difficulty arises of its having a meaning diametrically opposed
to the fire in Matt 3:10 and 12. Moreover, one wonders what is the point of
John's baptism and the inner and outer moral transformation of the baptized
now if basic purification is still needed on the last day.

In short, on the basis of multiple attestation, a balanced structure, and a
pellucid meaning, the basic Marcan form (Mark 1:7–8) shows all the signs of
being more original. I am well aware that many exegetes favor the full or truncated form of the Q saying as more primitive, but I think that this is a glaring
example of a well-known academic prejudice: namely, in the case of a conflict
between Mark and Q, Q is to be preferred. Even if one were to admit such a
stance as a theory, here is a clear case where theory must yield to evidence and
argument. It is telling that, in his painstaking study of this Mark-Q overlap,
Rudolf Laufen takes a somewhat different line of argumentation from what I

have offered above and yet arrives at the same basic conclusion: in the overlap, Mark offers the more original form of the tradition.[96] I conclude therefore that the earliest available wording of the Baptist's promise concerning the future baptism is the Marcan form: "He will baptize you with the holy spirit."

Granted this, the flow of the primitive form of the entire "sermon" preserved in Matt 3:7–12 par. becomes fairly clear. After issuing dire threats to those endangered by a fiery doom (Matt 3:7–10)—thus encouraging his audience to an inner and outer change sealed by his baptism—the Baptist turns to the positive side of his message, the promise to those who wholeheartedly accept his message and baptism. The promise is cast in the form of a double comparison, of persons and of baptisms. First, John himself is not the ultimate figure in the eschatological drama he proclaims and to some extent initiates. After John (the original sense can only be temporal)[97] there comes (with the weighty, prophetic sense of that verb) someone stronger than John, someone so superior to John that the Baptist, by comparison, would not even be worthy to perform the humiliating service reserved to a non-Jewish slave in rabbinic literature: to loosen the strap of the sandals of this stronger one.[98]

Yet his audience might well ask John: In what way is this other person "stronger" than you? John answers with the second comparison: the superiority of the stronger one is grounded in his superior baptism. He is stronger because with his baptism he can fully effect what John's water baptism only signifies and foreshadows. John's pouring out of water on the repentant of Israel only prefigures the pouring out of God's spirit upon the true Israel, a pouring out promised in the prophets, the intertestamental literature, and notably at Qumran.[99] While the water of John's baptism naturally symbolized the washing away of sin, that symbolism looked to a past that would soon disappear. The more important aspect of his baptism looked to the imminent future, when those who had accepted John's message and his pouring out of water (which gives life to the parched land of Palestine on the natural level) would experience the pouring out of the holy spirit, which brings eternal life instead of destruction on the last day.[100]

The "sermon" then ends fittingly with the carefully balanced prophecy of Matt 3:12 par. Matt 3:12 a + b recapitulates the dire message of 3:7–10, especially the agricultural image of v 10. "Already the ax is laid to the root of the tree" is transformed into "his winnowing fan is in his hand and he shall cleanse his threshing floor."[101] The act of harvesting is over and the threshing of the harvested grain is all but done, as people react positively or negatively to John—so imminent is the judgment, so profoundly eschatological is John's preaching and baptism. All that remains is the final, definitive separation, expressed in the metaphors of 3:12 c + d: "And he shall cleanse his threshing floor (i.e., by separating the edible grain from the light and inedible chaff) and shall gather his wheat into the barn, but the chaff he shall burn with inextinguishable fire." For the first and only time in the sermon, salvation and damnation are juxtaposed and given equal weight. In a sense, 3:12c resumes and reinforces the positive hope of 3:11, while 3:12d resumes and sharpens the dire warnings of 3:7–10. The whole of Matt 3:7–12 par. is thus seen to be a coherent unit with a tight, logical flow of thought, often expressed in carefully balanced, two-part statements—all the more so, interestingly, if we replace Matt 3:11 par. with Mark 1:7–8 as the original statement prophesying the stronger one and his baptism.

To summarize the picture of the Baptist that we receive from this sermon contained in Q (plus an overlap with Mark, Acts, and John): John appears as a prophet proclaiming an imminent judgment on an unrepentant Israel, an Israel that as a people has strayed from the right path. There is a dark, threatening tone to most of his message, which speaks sharply even to those who approach him for baptism. Though not fitting a fully rounded definition of an apocalyptic seer, John does stress the imminence of fiery punishment that looms for every Israelite. Being the offspring of Abraham, being a member in good standing of God's people provides no automatic shield; only inner change of heart, outward change of life, and acceptance of a once-and-for-all baptism administered by John can give protection from the consuming fire soon to come. There is no arguing with John, because he presents no arguments to establish his position. There is no explicit argument from Scripture, no invocation of a previous rabbinic teacher, not even the prophetic legitimation, "The word of the Lord came to me, saying. . . ." John knows the end is near, he knows the conditions for escaping destruction, and that is the end of the matter. To the extent that, in a situation of perceived crisis, a forceful and striking personality claims direct, intuitive knowledge of God's will and plans—knowledge unmediated by the traditional channels of law, temple, priesthood, or scribal scholarship—and is able to draw notable crowds of people to himself and his message, the label "charismatic" may be added to "eschatological" as part of this prophet's description. Most of John's message would leave one with the impression that he sees himself, Elijah-like, as the direct forerunner of God. Yet John goes on to describe a shadowy "stronger one" who is still to come, whose sandal strap John is not worthy to loose, who is stronger because his baptism with the holy spirit shows John's baptism to be only a symbolic foreshadowing of what the stronger one will accomplish: the great outpouring of God's spirit on the true Israel, as the prophets had promised for the last days. Whether this stronger one is God, Michael, Melchizedek, "one like a son of man," Elijah, Moses, a prophet like either of them, a royal messiah, a priestly messiah, or a final prophet is unclear to us perhaps because it was unclear to John. Yet even in this one glimmer of hope and promise a warning is implied. The spirit will be poured out in the future only on those repentant Israelites on whom John pours out his water now; for all others there waits only the fire.

B. The L Tradition of John's Moral Directives

Before we turn to the Marcan tradition, we should look briefly at Luke 3:10–14, which the evangelist inserts between the two blocks of Q material we have just investigated, Luke 3:7–9 and 15–18. The tone, subject matter, and vocabulary of this insert are notably different from what immediately precedes and follows. Crowds, soldiers, and toll collectors come to John, asking what concrete actions they should perform, no doubt as "fruits of repentance" (Luke 3:8). John tells the crowds to share their clothing and food with the less fortunate, the toll collectors not to exact more than established tolls fixed on goods shipped across borders, and the soldiers not to practice extortion by threatening to bring false accusations against people, but instead to be satisfied with their pay. Scholars often describe this triplet of questions and answers as a sermon on the duties of one's state in life *(Standespredigt)*, a moral catechism, or baptismal parenesis. Whether any of this material comes from the historical Baptist is hotly disputed.[102]

From the start, one should distinguish two questions: (1) Did the historical John engage in moral exhortation and directions? (2) Does this particular "cat-echism" come from him? As for the first question, there is no reason to doubt a priori that John would have given moral directions to those who came for baptism. Some critics might object that John was an eschatological prophet proclaiming imminent judgment on all Israel, something that would make homely admonitions about daily living in this present world trivial and super-fluous. Yet the OT prophets of judgment from Amos onward, the Qumran community preparing for the final battle between the sons of light and the sons of darkness, the apocalyptic literature like *1 Enoch* and the *Testament of the Twelve Patriarchs*, Jesus the eschatological prophet, and early Christians in-tensely waiting for their Lord's return all engaged in detailed moral admoni-tions ranging from avoidance of prostitution and divorce to getting along with one's neighbor in the eschatological community.[103] John would have been a most unusual spiritual guide within Judaism at the turn of the era if he had not delivered some teaching on morality and daily conduct.

This a priori consideration is bolstered by various scattered hints in our sources. Mark, Q, Luke, Acts, and John all report that the Baptist had disciples (cf. Mark 2:18; 6:29; Matt 11:2 par.; Luke 11:1; John 1:35; 3:25; Acts 19:1–7), people who apparently maintained a closer relationship with him than most people who came to him for baptism. The sources indicate that he taught them special ways to fast and pray; those two points are not likely to have exhausted his instruction. Moreover, both Luke 3:12 and John 3:26 depict people ad-dressing John as "rabbi" or "teacher," the very titles the same Gospels use elsewhere of Jesus. The natural impression is created that John too was some-thing of a teacher of concrete morality. While Josephus, with an eye to his audience, obviously recasts John the eschatological prophet as a Greco-Roman moral philosopher, the very fact that Josephus felt he could take this tack sug-gests that there was some basis for this transformation in the tradition about John that Josephus knew.[104] All in all, there is no reason to think that John the teacher of morality is purely a product of that notorious bourgeois Christian and peddler of early Catholicism, Luke.[105]

None of these considerations, though, proves that the precise teaching in

Luke 3:10–14 goes back to the Baptist.[106] Every opinion imaginable has been put forward concerning the source of these verses. Bultmann declared that the passage was a relatively late Hellenistic creation, spun out of the traditional saying about a person with two tunics giving one away in v 11; Luke himself may have done the spinning.[107] Others suggest that the material comes from Q, with which it shares similar vocabulary and themes.[108] Still others speak of L, Luke's special source.[109]

Each theory has its difficulties. Verses 10–14 have a number of stylistic and linguistic traits not typical of Luke's redaction.[110] As for Q, that hypothetical document is by definition the material Matthew and Luke have in common that is not found in Mark; and there is no convincing reason why Matthew, an evangelist intent on moral catechesis, should have omitted this moral sermon from his Gospel. Moreover, if 3:10–14 is from the Baptist material in Q, why does it break in such a jarring way the natural connection between the two Q units contained in Luke 3:7–9 and 15–18? One might prefer the theory of L tradition, yet the material does contain signs of Lucan redaction.[111] If truth be told, no one position really has a decisive argument that can exclude the counter-positions. After struggling with the various theories, Ernst concludes the material comes not from the Baptist himself but from later Baptist disciples, who interpreted and expanded the master's call to repentance, applying it to concrete states of life. This likewise is possible, but no more so than the other theories.

When I treated the criteria of historicity in Chapter 6, I noted that at times no amount of criteria will make a murky situation clear. Sometimes we must resign ourselves to a verdict of *non liquet:* the evidence available allows for no firm decision one way or the other. Here is a case in point. There is sufficient reason for thinking that, like many other Jewish prophets, John joined concrete moral exhortation to his eschatological message. Whether Luke 3:10–14 gives us an accurate historical presentation of such exhortation must remain undecided, at least for the time being. It may be that when we examine Josephus' account of the Baptist in the excursus to this chapter and later study the stray traditions in Matt 21:31–32 and Luke 7:29–30 (in Chapter 13), we will be able to modify our judgment.

C. MARK 1:1–8 ON THE APPEARANCE OF THE BAPTIST

Moving from the Q and L traditions on the Baptist, made up of sayings material, to the introductory prophecy and narrative of John's ministry in Mark 1:1–8 means entering a different world. The sayings in Matt 3:7–12 par. and Luke 3:10–14 could just as easily stand in some Jewish report on the Baptist, so lacking are they in specifically Christian content. In contrast, Mark 1:1–8, taken as a whole, is a clearly Christian composition from the very first words: "The beginning of the good news of Jesus Christ, the Son of God." This is one reason why we started with the Q material, to give ourselves a better basic orientation. Now that we have some initial grasp of the historical Baptist, we can search for elements in the Marcan narrative that cohere with or supplement our preliminary sketch.

Christian reinterpretation of the Baptist is not the only obstacle making the use of Mark 1:1–8 for historical reconstruction difficult. From the initial words of v 1 onward, the entire pericope is plagued with minor problems of grammar and syntax, medium problems of text criticism, and major problems of overall meaning.[112] I will ignore many of these intriguing puzzles in order to keep the focus solely on what is said about the Baptist, and more particularly on what might have a claim to being historical tradition. Hence Mark's own redactional theology, both fascinating and elusive, is not my concern here.

Thus, the first subsection of 1:1–8, the introductory sentence and prophecy (vv 1–3), will be put aside as Christian interpretation, though an eye must be kept on how it may have influenced or even created the narrative that follows. The third subsection, a summary of John's prophecy of the stronger one and his baptism with the spirit (vv 7–8), has already been examined along with the parallel Q material in Matt 3:11–12 par. That leaves for our consideration the second subsection (vv 4–6), the narrative describing the external circumstances of John's ministry (place of activity, nature of his baptism, reaction of the populace, his clothing and food). From this middle subsection we will examine three major historical concerns: (1) the actual place(s) of John's activity, (2) his clothing and food and their possible symbolic meaning, and (3) the nature of the baptism he conferred.[113]

(1) A number of independent traditions witness to John's activity in the "wilderness" or "desert," i.e., a place devoid of permanent human habitation and farming, though at times used for grazing. It is regularly designated in our Greek Gospels as *hē erēmos* (the plural form is found in Luke 1:80).[114] That John exercised his ministry in a "desert" is affirmed in Mark 1:3–4 parrs.; Q (Matt 11:7 ‖ Luke 7:24, all the more impressive because the reference is "in passing"); and implicitly in the Baptist's modified quotations of Isa 40:3 in John 1:23: "I am a voice of one crying out in the desert, 'Prepare the way of the Lord.' "[115] Qumran's use of Isa 40:3 to justify its own existence in the desert of Judea (1QS 8:13–14; 9:19–20) and Josephus' description of Bannus, "who stayed in the wilderness [*tēn erēmian*]" (*Life* 2 §11), remind us that such a desert-existence was actually lived by certain Jews during the years of John's and Jesus' public ministries.

What particular "desert" area is intended is indicated at least by Matthew in a specification he adds to Mark 1:4 in Matt 3:1: "in the desert *of Judea*." In the OT, Judges 1:16 and Ps 63:1 use the phrase "the desert of Judah" (in Hebrew: *midbar yĕhûdâ*) to designate the barren land that slopes down from the ridges of the Judean hills eastward toward the western/northwestern side of the Dead Sea, precisely the area in which Qumran was located. Since the region directly north of the Dead Sea (i.e., the southern-most part of the Jordan valley) has basically the same sparse rainfall, nearly infertile soil, and barren appearance, the designation "desert of Judea" might well be extended to the southern part of the Jordan valley.[116] Matthew is probably using the phrase in this larger sense, as the reference to baptism in the Jordan in 3:5 makes likely.[117]

It may strike the modern reader as strange that a river valley should be called a desert or wilderness.[118] Yet, as Robert W. Funk rightly emphasizes, the lower Jordan valley was considered "desert" in both the OT and NT periods.[119] In the LXX the Greek word *erēmos* translates a number of Hebrew words for desert or wilderness, especially *midbār* and in a few cases *ʿărābâ*, the two words used in poetic parallelism in the Hebrew text of Isa 40:3. Even more striking is the case of Isa 35:1. There the two Hebrew words *midbār* and *ʿărābâ* occur in poetic parallelism, and the LXX translates both by the same word *erēmos*.[120] It is especially significant for the question of the Baptist's venue that the Hebrew word *ʿărābâ*, which simply means a depression in the earth, was often used in the OT to designate the deep cleft in which the Jordan valley was situated, the "rift valley" or Ghôr. Yet, at least in a few passages, the region around the lower Jordan could also be called *midbār*. In the story of King David's flight from his rebellious son Absalom, the area around the southern end of the Jordan with its fords is described a number of times as *midbār*, which the LXX translates in each case as *erēmos* (2 Sam 15:23,28; 17:16; cf. 16:14 [LXX]; 17:22).

Hence for the NT accounts of the Baptist, there is nothing strange in the fact that this denizen of the "desert" suddenly appears by the Jordan. For the Bible, the land around the Jordan *was* desert. Josephus shares this view when he speaks of the Jordan River wandering through a great deal of desert (*pollēn . . . erēmian*, the word Josephus uses of Bannus' habitat) on its way from the lake of Gennesaret to the Dead Sea (*J.W.* 3.10.7 §515). Josephus' statement is all the more valuable because he obviously knew the region firsthand and because his comment comes in a context of dry geographical information, not in a piece of "desert theology." That the "desert" area around the lower Jordan is indeed the region Mark had in mind in 1:4 when he writes *en tȩ erēmȩ* is confirmed by his (obviously hyperbolic) statement in 1:5 that "all of the Judean countryside and all the people of Jerusalem" went out to John and were baptized "in the Jordan River."

If this is the correct understanding of the geographical references, then attempts by scholars to see two competing traditions, one more original that placed John by the Jordan for the purpose of baptizing, and a later one that, for the sake of the theological symbolism present in Isa 40:3, placed him in the desert, are beside the point.[121] This critical dissection is neatly refuted by the simple, uncontrived way in which Jesus in the Q tradition (Matt 11:7 ‖ Luke 7:24) affirms that the crowds went out to the "desert" to see John, and not just a "reed shaken by the wind"—precisely what they would find on the banks of the Jordan. Thus, in the minds of the authors of Mark, Q, and John, "desert" and "Jordan" go together instead of being opposites. The conjunction is not some grand theological artifice, but simply reflects the geography of the lower Jordan valley and the northern end of the Dead Sea.

Granted the sprawling nature of the desert of Judea and the southern Jordan valley, we should not imagine that John was fixed at one spot along Jordan's banks as though he had a "baptistery." Indeed, Luke 3:3 speaks of John "coming into all the region around the Jordan."[122] This makes perfect sense. Since, for all his ascetic practices, John wished to encounter, sermonize, and baptize people, he would naturally have gravitated to the various fords of the Jordan, especially those south of Jericho, to find an audience among the people traveling the main trade routes. The roads leading from Jerusalem, Bethel, and Bethlehem met in that area before continuing into Perea on the eastern shore. One remembers the toll collectors and soldiers mentioned by Luke 3:12–14; they would naturally be active on the border between Judea, ruled by the Roman prefect Pontius Pilate, and Perea, part of the tetrarchy ruled by Herod Antipas.

John apparently plied his ministry on the Perean as well as the Judean side of the Jordan, since he was arrested by Antipas, the tetrarch of Galilee and Perea, and incarcerated by him in Machaerus, a mountain fortress in southern Perea east of the Dead Sea. His activity on the eastern bank is confirmed by the Fourth Gospel's reference to his preaching and baptizing in Bethany (or possibly Bethabara) "beyond the Jordan."[123] Yet the Baptist seems to have roamed the western shore of the Jordan as well, if one may trust a geographical reference in the Fourth Gospel that, like many others, appears out of nowhere, has no discernible theological agenda, and disappears just as quickly again. After stating that Jesus and his disciples had come into the Judean countryside,[124] where Jesus proceeded to baptize (3:22), the Fourth Evangelist adds: "Now John too was baptizing in Aenon near Salim, for there was an abundant water supply there, and people were coming and being baptized" (3:23). This juxtaposing of John and Jesus, both baptizing, right after the Evangelist has noted that Jesus had just come into the Judean countryside, would suggest that John was probably at this moment on the western side of the Jordan, as was Jesus.

To be more precise about the location of Aenon near Salim is almost impossible, but it may well have been in either Samaria or the Decapolis.[125] All this reminds us that, while John's activity may have been centered in the lower Jordan valley near the Dead Sea, his desire to reach as many Jews as possible probably caused him to roam the length of the Jordan, seeking out travelers at various crossings and springs. The desire of the Synoptics to dwell on the two theologically charged words "desert" and "Jordan" may have led them to ignore the wider range of John's ministry. However, John certainly did not stay permanently in either the Decapolis or Samaria, since Antipas' rule did not reach that far. The arrest of John by Antipas and his imprisonment in a fortress in Perea point to sustained activity by John in that district.

This little excursus into geography is not meant to perpetuate but rather to overcome the facile opposition still met in Gospel studies between geographical facts and theological symbolism. It is unfortunate that some of the early redaction critics were so absorbed in the theology of Mark or John that they came close to ignoring the geographical realities of Palestine that are reflected at times in the Gospels. For example, Willi Marxsen, echoing Karl Ludwig Schmidt, was so carried away by the theology of the "desert" and by the obvious literary transference of *en tę erēmǭ* from the Isaian prophecy in Mark 1:3 to the narrative about the Baptist in 1:4 that he proclaimed: "The desert is not a geographical place."[126] This misses the whole point—which is certainly *not* that the place names and the Gospel stories are bereft of powerful theological symbolism. Quite to the contrary! But we must realize that the geographical realities called the Judean desert and the Jordan River were suffused with religious meaning for the real inhabitants of Palestine centuries before the Baptist, the evangelists, or redaction critics were attracted by the OT's heritage of "salvation geography."

The desert naturally conjured up for Jews of any stripe the founding events of the exodus from Egypt, the covenant at Sinai, and the forty years of wandering in the wilderness.[127] It was a time of special closeness to and revelation by the God of Israel through the mediation of Moses; yet it was also a time of apostasy and punishment. Closely connected with the wandering in the desert was the Jordan, for it was by crossing the Jordan that Joshua put an end to the desert-wandering and led Israel into the promised land. The Jordan was also connected with some of the legends about the prophets Elijah and Elisha (2 Kgs 2:1–18; 5:1–15). The obvious natural qualities of both desert heat and river water only reinforced the OT traditions of testing and judgment in the wilderness and the gift of new life at the Jordan. The fierce radicalism of the Baptist, as well as his threat of judgment by fire for the nation's apostasy, found its perfect backdrop in the Judean wilderness and the Dead Sea, at the southern end of which lay the traditional sites of the sinful Sodom and Gomorrah. No doubt the appropriateness of the stark scenery had not been lost on the founders of Qumran before John. Likewise, the waters of the Jordan were an apt symbol not only for the washing away of sin but also for the entrance of Israel into a new and better life after its wandering in the desert of rebellion against its God. Thus, the geographical setting in Mark 1:4–6 parr. is indeed steeped in religious symbolism. But it was the traditional symbolism of the real Judean desert and the real Jordan River, exerting a powerful attraction on the imagination of John and his fellow Jews, that helped create the Gospel narratives, not vice versa.[128]

(2) The strange clothing and food of the Baptist are perhaps the things that linger the longest in everyone's memory of John, long after the days of childhood instruction in the Bible are past: "And John was clothed in camel's hair, with a leather belt around his waist, and he used to eat locusts and wild honey" (Mark 1:6 ‖ Matt 3:4). Yet these curious details are the aspect of the Baptist's life that is least attested in the sources, being found only in a single verse in Mark, on which the single verse in Matthew obviously depends. Do we have here simply OT typology and NT theology read into the figure of the Baptist? Or do these odd habits have a basis in history?

To take John's clothing first: Critics sometimes claim that the mantle or cloak made of camel's hair and the leather belt are meant to allude to either the prophet Elijah in particular (cf. 2 Kgs 1:8) or the traditional garb of the prophet in general (cf. Zech 13:4).[129] Often, however, the relevant OT texts are not examined in detail. Actually, the Hebrew text of 2 Kgs 1:8 is by no means clear in its meaning. In the context, Ahaziah, the king of Israel, asks his servants for the identity of a strange man who has told them to deliver a message of doom to the king. Translated very literally the Hebrew text of the servants' reply reads: "They said to him, 'A man [who was] an owner [or: lord] of hair and girded with a girdle [or: a belt] of leather on his loins.' And he said, 'It is Elijah the Tishbite.' "

The chief point of debate is the exact meaning of "an owner [or: lord] of hair" *(ba'al śē'ār)*. Dictionaries and commentaries recognize two possible meanings: a hairy, shaggy man or a man wearing a hairy mantle.[130] Translations vary, with the *NAB* and the *RSV* favoring a hairy mantle, while the new *RSV* favors a hairy man.[131] While both translations are defensible, one must beware of reading into this passage various references to cloaks which occur elsewhere in the Bible, e.g., that of Elijah (1 Kgs 19:13,19; 2 Kgs 2:8,13–14) or of a prophet in general (Zech 13:4). One should note that the word for cloak *(adderet)* that is found in 2 Kgs 2:8,13–14 and Zech 13:4 *(adderet śē'ār, a hairy mantle)* does not appear in 2 Kgs 1:8. Moreover, we should remember that while the phrase "clothed with hairs of a camel" in Mark 1:6 no doubt intends to describe a cloak, mantle, or coat of camel's hair, the word for cloak or mantle does not occur in the Greek text of Mark 1:6, though English translations will sometimes supply some such word.[132] Finally, none of the OT texts listed above speaks of *camel's* hair; that is specific to Mark 1:6 par. All in all, then, John's being clothed in camel's hair may have little or nothing to do with the description of Elijah in 2 Kgs 1:8. There is a possible reference to the traditional cloak of an OT prophet; but it is odd that, if that is what Mark or his tradition had wanted to stress, the word for cloak or mantle is omitted.

As for the leather "girdle" or belt, again the meaning is disputed. While the new *RSV* translates the Hebrew word 'ēzôr as "belt," which has the support of the LXX *(zōnēn dermatinēn,* "leather belt"), the Koehler-Baumgartner dictionary accepts only the meaning of "innermost garment," "loincloth," and that seems to be the meaning accepted by the *NAB, NEB,* and *RSV* ("girdle" or "apron").[133] The best we can say is that Mark or his tradition may be consciously echoing the wording of the LXX of 2 Kgs 1:8 when John is described as having a leather belt.[134] The certainty of such a reference is somewhat weakened if we consider that wearing a leather belt (as opposed to a leather loincloth) was probably not all that unusual in the ancient world. We are thus left with something of a split picture: John's being clothed in camel's hair has no typological reference to Elijah; his leather belt may bear such a reference, but need not.

Since the camel's hair clothing lacks a firm OT type, it may be that John's cloak is simply one expression of the sort of loose cloak that desert nomads (e.g., bedouins) use to protect themselves from the heat during the day and the cold at night. For desert nomads, camel's hair would naturally be the most

readily available material—especially since one could obtain it without necessarily killing a valuable animal. It is therefore possible to understand at least
the camel's hair in Mark 1:6 not as a sign of Elijah-typology or even as the
typical garb of a prophet, but simply as a reflection of the ordinary garments
of desert nomads.[135] The leather belt might be an example of Elijah-typology,
but the parallel is so tenuous (and only to the LXX) that a decision cannot be
clear-cut. If John's clothing points to anything beyond the life of a desert no-
mad, it may underscore the ascetic[136] life John had chosen, a motif that is also
echoed in Q (Matt 11:8 par.).

John's food of locusts and wild honey has occasioned speculation even more
wide-ranging than has his clothing. Otto Böcher compares John to various
religious and philosophical ascetics in the ancient world, including Neo-
Pythagoreans, Neo-Platonists (who would not arise until centuries later), vegetarians, magicians, mystics, and those seeking oracles.[137] All of these, says
Böcher, in one way or another used abstinence from meat and wine as well as
from sexual activity to protect themselves from defilement by demonic powers.
Böcher tries to sustain this view in the case of the Baptist by suggesting that
when Q depicts John "eating no bread and drinking no wine" (Luke 7:33; cf.
Matt 11:18), the Greek word for bread (*arton*) is really a mistranslation of the
Hebrew *leḥem*, which can also mean "meat."

This theory suffers from a number of difficulties, however. First, one should
always be wary of a solution that claims that the Greek text misrepresents the
Aramaic original when the Greek makes perfect sense. Second, the argument
rests on the word "bread," which occurs only in Luke's form of the Q saying;
whether "bread" is original in the logion is debated, as Böcher himself admits.
Third, a comparison of John with strict vegetarians of the ancient world is
really not apt, since locusts belong to the realm of animals, not vegetables.
Finally, there is no indication in the NT text that John is concerned about
avoiding demons. Unlike Jesus, he is never said to speak of them or to perform exorcisms.

Equally questionable is an interpretation of John's food that associates him
with the "nazirites," those men of the OT who were especially consecrated to
God (see Num 6:1–21). The one possible point of contact between John and
nazirites is the avoidance of wine. This might be used as an argument for
John's nazirite status if one could take as historical the words of the angel
Gabriel appearing to Zechariah in Luke 1:15: "Wine and strong drink he
[John] shall not drink." Apart from the problem of taking the words of an angel
as a historical datum, Raymond E. Brown judges that Luke is quite consciously
depicting John in the guise of Samson and Samuel, two OT figures favored
with annunciation-of-birth stories that strike the theme of abstinence from
alcoholic drinks.[138] In any case, nazirites were not forbidden bread or meat,
and nothing is said in the description of John about abstaining from cutting
one's hair, perhaps the single most striking sign of a nazirite (cf. the rules for
nazirites in Num 6:5,9,19).[139] Moreover, nothing in the Gospels indicates that
John saw his special state as a temporary one occasioned by a vow that would

be terminated by an offering in the Jerusalem temple. Yet this is the form of the nazirite state (originally less institutionalized and probably lasting for life) that finds legal expression in Numbers 6. This legal institutionalization of the nazirite state seems foreign to the charismatic and eschatological character of John's prophetic vocation.

The mention of the use of honey by the Essenes and of locusts by the Qumranites naturally entices exegetes to build theoretical bridges between John and Qumran.[140] One might even invoke a story of Josephus in the *Jewish War* (2.8.8 §143), according to which those expelled from the Essenes still felt bound by the rules of the community, refrained from eating the ordinary food of ordinary people, ate only grass, and so starved to death. This last parallel is obviously no parallel, since John's diet was not grass or herbs; and, whatever one thinks of John's eating habits, he did not starve on account of them.

The similarity to the diet of the Essenes or Qumran, while not proving an institutional bond with John, may nevertheless hold the key to John's curious eating habits. His food is actually not so unusual for people who regularly inhabit "desert" regions. As Theodor Zahn observed, not only Palestinians, especially those east of the Jordan, but also inhabitants of Arabia and Ethiopia have been known to eat locusts. The poor, especially in time of famine, use them as a true source of nourishment.[141] Likewise, the honey, pointedly classified as "wild" or "uncultivated," could be either the sweet secretion from certain types of trees or the honey from wild bees.[142]

Clearly, then, both the clothing and the diet of John point first of all simply to his habitation in the desert. Whatever further meaning they may have must be derived from his own stated understanding of his ministry. As we have seen from our examination of the Q material, John was a charismatic, eschatological prophet who called Israel to repentance in light of imminent judgment. In the shadow of that judgment, all the ordinary forms of life are called into question; John's concrete manner of living embodies that question in a graphic way. His turning away from ordinary living acts out the turning away from a sinful past to which he calls every Israelite. Like the prophets of old (cf. Isaiah and Jeremiah),[143] John incorporates his message into his life even as he stakes his life on his message.

(3) Finally we come to what was most unique and striking about John's ministry, his baptism. I have purposely kept this central aspect of his activity to last because it can be properly interpreted only within the larger context of his message and life-style. As a symbol, John's baptism is open to many different meanings; only remote and proximate contexts can narrow down the possibilities.

Water rituals are known throughout the gamut of world religions, and they were especially common in the ancient Near East, notably Iran and Babylonia, as symbols of ritual or spiritual purification and the gift of new life.[144] The OT reflects this milieu with its many prescriptions for ritual washing (e.g., Lev 14:5–6,50–52; Num 19:13,20–21), which the prophets and psalmists in turn used as symbols of interior cleansing (e.g., Isa 1:16; Ps 51:7).[145] The more the present seemed plunged into sin and death, the more Israel's prophets hoped for cleansing and renewal in the future, when God would pour out his spirit like water on his people (e.g., Joel 3:1–5; cf. Ezek 36:25–27). Around the turn of the era, ritual washings of a voluntary sort were on the increase in various sections of Judaism, for various reasons. The Pharisees, disgusted at what they considered the corruption of the aristocratic priests in Jerusalem, sought to live out aspects of priestly purity in their daily lives. Joseph Thomas has documented how Syria and Palestine, especially the trans-Jordan area, were a hotbed for baptizing groups in the 1st centuries B.C. and A.D.[146] Qumranites, with their frequent lustrations, and Josephus' guru Bannus, who frequently washed with cold water day and night, are two examples of a strange phenomenon: Jewish desert washers. Significantly, both examples are contemporaneous with the Baptist and located in the same general area of the "wilderness of Judea" and of the lower Jordan valley.

While Bannus is mute, the documents from Qumran give some explanation of their water rituals, as we saw when we explored the wording of Matt 3:11 ‖ Mark 1:8.[147] God's holy spirit brings about atonement and purification for sinful human beings; this cleansing is somehow connected with being sprinkled with the water of purification and cleanliness, which symbolizes being sprinkled with the spirit (1QS 3:6–9; 4:20–22; 1QH 7:6–7; 17:26). But what is the connection? The water imagery in Qumran was not simply verbal; it was concretized in physical washing (1QS 3:4–12; 5:13–14). But the physical act of washing was not magic. Like Josephus in his sketch of the Baptist, and in keeping with the view of the OT prophets, the Qumran material affirmed that water rituals were of no avail if they were not preceded by inner repentance and obedient lives. This in effect meant entering the new covenant with true repentance, i.e., entering the Qumran community and obeying its interpretation of the torah. Hence the baths of Qumran were not thought to confer forgiveness of sins. Rather, they were the ritual sign affirming that God's spirit had cleansed those who repented, entered the community, and obeyed its statutes.[148] Despite clear differences, the washings of Qumran do provide one context for interpreting John's baptism, since John and Qumran share certain features: in an intense eschatological context, tinged with apocalyptic, water rituals are performed in the wilderness by or near the Jordan by Jews who (1) see all Israel as having gone astray, (2) seek inner purification by repentance and reformed lives, and (3) hope for salvation for themselves when the fearsome day of reckoning comes for others.

At the same time, a great gulf separates Qumran's washings from John's baptism. Qumran's water rituals were part of the highly structured life of a closed community, bound by solemn oaths, while John was the solitary prophet who did not use his baptism as an initiatory rite to create around himself an organized sect or church. There was no "novitiate," no time of testing, and no solemn oath prior to John's baptism. After being baptized by John, most people apparently returned to their homes and occupations.[149] A few devoted disciples seem to have stayed with John in the wilderness at least for a while, but there is no indication of any organized structure before John's death (and really not much afterwards). Admission or exclusion from Qumran's lustrations depended on one's careful observance of all the statutes of the Mosaic Law as interpreted by Qumran, with special concern for ritual purity. In contrast, the few moral directives that are ascribed to John in Josephus and Luke 3:10–14 are of a general social nature and do not bear on specific Mosaic prescriptions, especially of a ritual kind. More to the point are the striking differences in the water rituals themselves. At Qumran, as in Judaism generally, the persons to be cleansed washed themselves. John instead claimed for himself the central and unusual role of immersing the candidates. This was the remarkable difference that gave John his surname *baptistēs*, "the immerser," "the dipper," "the plunger."

Likewise uncommon was the fact that, unlike the repeated washings of Qumran in particular and Judaism in general, John's baptism was apparently administered only once, reflecting no doubt its more explicitly eschatological character. I purposely include the word "apparently" in the previous sentence to signal a point often missed by commentators, who universally affirm that John's baptism was conferred only once. Actually, neither the NT nor Josephus explicitly states this. I think the once-and-for-all character of John's baptism is a legitimate inference from the data, but it is only an inference. We should be clear as to why we infer the unrepeatable nature of John's baptism from aspects of his ministry and message: (1) Since John's baptism included as part of its very essence John's role as administrator of the rite, the baptized who then returned home could not have it repeated unless they hunted down John again along the Jordan River. Unlike self-administered ritual washings among Pharisees or Qumranites, it could not be repeated at will. (2) The core of John's message was imminent, final judgment; his once-and-for-all baptism corresponded to the final, definitive pouring out of the spirit on the repentant, along with the destruction of the wicked, that lay just around the corner. In this context of imminent eschatology, John, like the author of the Epistle to the Hebrews (Heb 6:4–8; 10:26–31), did not apparently allow for the possibility that a candidate might repent and be baptized, then apostatize from that fundamental option, and finally return to that option and wish to be baptized again. Apart from questions of the candidate's sincerity and stability, in John's mind there probably was not enough time left for such a scenario to be taken seriously.[150]

Since the once-and-for-all character of John's baptism disqualifies most Jewish water rituals, including those of Qumran, as strict parallels, some authors champion as a better parallel proselyte baptism, i.e., the ritual bath that a Gentile convert to Judaism took as part of the process of conversion.[151] Certainly John's baptism and proselyte baptism shared some common traits: e.g., unlike many other water rituals, both involved a once-and-for-all immersion, not just a washing or sprinkling that could be repeated.[152] The parallel, if valid, would have intriguing consequences for interpreting John's baptism. All Israelites would be seen as unclean as the Gentiles, needing as much as the Gentiles a ritual of conversion and initiation to bring them into the true people of God at the end time.

The great difficulty with this interpretation is that we have no clear and indisputable proof that proselyte baptism existed as an established, well-known conversion ritual in Judaism in the pre-Christian period. No mention of it is made in Philo, Josephus, the NT, or the text known as *Joseph and Aseneth*, a prime example of Jewish conversion literature from the period.[153] This may be an argument from silence, but in this case the silence stands in sharp contrast to the abundant references to circumcision as the definitive rite of entrance. For example, while Josephus goes on at length about the place of circumcision in the conversion of King Izates of Adiabene to Judaism (1st century A.D.), there is not a word in the account about a ritual bath connected with the process (*Ant.* 20.2.3–4 §34–48). Considering that Christians of the first generation felt impelled to define their entrance rite of baptism over against both John's baptism and Jewish circumcision, we should at least wonder why those same Christians felt no need to distinguish their once-and-for-all ritual bath of initiation from a similar Jewish one—if it existed at the time. If instead the origins of the proselyte baptism lie in the middle-to-late 1st or early 2d century, the silence of the earlier Jewish and Christian sources is perfectly understandable, and proselyte baptism simply disappears as a possible source of John's baptism.

Even apart from the question of dating, many of the features that distinguish John's baptism from the lustrations of Qumran hold true for proselyte baptism as well. Proselyte baptism was part of a process of initiation that transferred a person from one visible socio-religious group (Gentile) to another (Jew); John's baptism did not, and so strictly speaking it was not a rite of initiation. John was not interested in founding a "new Israel" in any visible, sociological sense. Transfer from the Gentile to the Jewish world, not forgiveness of sins, was at the heart of proselyte baptism; the reverse was true of John's baptism. The former had no essential connection with intense eschatological expectation; the latter did. If we may draw a conclusion from the Baptist's focus on the Jordan River and Aenon-near-Salim, the Baptist regularly performed his baptism in the running water of rivers or streams; proselyte baptism did not demand this setting. Proselyte baptism was basically self-administered, though legal witnesses (later, instructors)[154] might participate; John's indispensable and active role in administering his baptism seems to have been unique among the Jewish water rituals of the time.[155]

The conclusion seems to be that, while Qumran and proselyte baptism furnish some points of comparison, the precise nature of John's baptism stems from John's own eschatological vision and message.[156] Certain great religious figures stand out in history precisely because they take the raw material of traditional religious vocabulary and symbol and forge something new out of the old; such is the case with the man whose water ritual was so strikingly singular that he was called the Baptist.[157] Its meaning must be divined first of all not from dubious parallels but from John's own words and actions as known from the various Gospel sources. We have examined most of those words already, and they have revealed a context of fierce imminent eschatology, tinged with apocalyptic: repentant Israelites confess their sins,[158] pledge to live better lives, and receive a once-and-for-all baptism at John's hands in hope of being spared the fiery judgment soon to come and of sharing instead in the great pouring out of God's cleansing and life-giving spirit on the true Israel.

But one explanation of the meaning of John's baptism still remains to be studied. I have purposely put off consideration of it since it is not found in John's own mouth but rather in the narrative of Mark 1:4: along with baptizing in the desert, John was proclaiming a baptism of repentance for [or: unto, or: with a view to] the remission of sins (*kēryssōn baptisma metanoias eis aphesin hamartiōn*). A primary problem with such a description is that it never occurs in the words of John or Jesus; it is clearly a designation that comes from Mark or his narrative source. Moreover, the entire phrase, "a baptism of repentance for the forgiveness of sins" occurs in the NT only in this one verse of Mark and in the Lucan parallel (Luke 3:3), which is clearly dependent on Mark. However, both repentance and forgiveness of sins are great concerns of the Christian mission in Acts, and therefore we must ask whether Christian missionary language is being retrojected into a description of John's baptism. The presence of a key verb for Christian proclamation (*kēryssō*, "to herald," "to proclaim," "to preach") makes one especially suspicious.[159]

A purely Christian creation in Mark 1:4 is certainly possible, and therefore we must be cautious about using the phrase as our chief key for unlocking the meaning of John's baptism.[160] Yet there are serious reasons for thinking that this description derived from the Baptist himself and entered early Christianity through disciples of John who became disciples of Jesus and/or members of the early church. First of all, it is noteworthy that the NT never applies the entire phrase to Christian baptism. Second, it is remarkable that Christians would attribute such power to John's baptism. It is symptomatic that, in the second generation of the gospel tradition, Matthew found the phrase "unto the remission of sins" offensive as a description of John's baptism and transferred it to the blood of Christ symbolized by the wine at the Last Supper (Matt 3:1–2,11; cf. 26:28). Notice: when Matthew (or the liturgical tradition of his church before him) decided to transfer the phrase, he attached it not to Christian baptism but to the eucharist. Third, while it is true that speeches in Acts connect repentance and forgiveness of sins with conversion and baptism, even Acts never describes Christian baptism with the exact phrase of Mark 1:4, though Acts 2:38 comes close.[161] In addition, whole sectors of NT thought, such as the Pauline and Johannine literature, do not connect the vocabulary of repentance and the forgiveness of sins with the rite of baptism.[162] Finally, to all this may be added the criterion of embarrassment. The story of Jesus' baptism by John was important for early Christians because for them it was the event in which Jesus was designated or revealed as the Son of God. It hardly seems likely that Christians went out of their way to invent a phrase that would define the baptism Jesus the Son of God received from John as a baptism of repentance for the forgiveness of sins. Thus, it is by no means certain that "a baptism of repentance for the forgiveness of sins" is a Christian retrojection. The fact that this precise description is never applied to Christian baptism, that the full phrase never occurs anywhere else in the NT, that the various key words are rare or absent in whole sections of NT literature, and that the description creates theological problems when Jesus receives this baptism makes derivation from the Baptist a real possibility.

Still, how much we gain by considering "a baptism of repentance for the remission of sins" an authentic description stemming from the Baptist is another question. That John's baptism required repentance and expressed that repentance in a ritual symbol is something we have already seen. By humbly submitting to a baptism conferred by the preacher of repentance and coming judgment, the candidate acknowledged the truth of what John said, confessed and repented of his past sins, sought a spiritual cleansing, pledged a new and better life, and expressed his hope to be spared the imminent fiery judgment and to receive instead the outpouring of God's purifying and vivifying spirit on the last day. All this is fittingly summed up in the phrase "a baptism of repentance."[163] The real problem is the exact meaning of the final qualification, "for [or: unto, or: with a view to] the remission of sins" *(eis aphesin hamartiōn)*. The Greek preposition *eis* expresses first of all "motion to or toward" and then metaphorically purpose, intention, goal, or result. What is the sense here? When and how are the sins of the baptized remitted or forgiven: when they are baptized or only on the last day? Does the baptism somehow cause or mediate the remission of sins (now or on the last day), or is it simply an expression of a human hope or a divine pledge that they will be forgiven? Does the cleansing water effect spiritually what it signifies visibly? Should John's baptism be considered a "sacrament," a "quasi-sacrament," or an "eschatological sacrament"?[164] Is John the purveyor of a saving gnosis, and should his baptism be compared to "mysteries" celebrated elsewhere in the Greco-Roman world or to rituals practiced among gnostics?

Faced with all these questions and suggestions, one begins to feel that a great deal is being built on a very small basis. Taken in isolation, *eis aphesin hamartiōn* is open to any of the above interpretations, though none can prove itself necessary. Two observations are in order. First, to talk about a "sacrament" or "quasi-sacrament" or to pose questions of sacramental causality is to impose later theological categories on matters that were probably not so clear-cut or thought out by either the Baptist or the baptized. In many of these discussions the ghost of Catholic-Protestant debates over sacraments seems to stalk the academic hallways. It should be remembered that even within Catholicism, theories about the mode of causality and the effects of the sacraments have varied greatly over the centuries—to say nothing of the difference in views between the Eastern and Western churches. To burden the Baptist or even an evangelist with such a *quaestio disputata* is hopelessly anachronistic.

This leads to my second observation: the most likely understanding of *eis aphesin hamartiōn* can be gained only by putting the phrase within the context of everything we have already seen about the Baptist's person and message. John never made himself the chief object of his proclamation. His focus was on the imminent fiery judgment, from which sinful Israelites could escape only by repentance and a baptism which pointed forward to the outpouring of the holy spirit by "the stronger one." The whole point of the image of this future "baptism" with the holy spirit is that, in keeping with the imagery of the OT prophets, the spirit was likened to water that would cleanse and give life. If the water baptism of John conferred forgiveness of sins here and now, one wonders what exactly was left for the stronger one to do with his baptism of the spirit. It would be strange for John to emphasize his vast inferiority to the stronger one, and the inferiority of water baptism to spirit baptism, if the former already accomplished a key saving event, the forgiveness of sins. The slave would seem to be stealing the stronger one's thunder.

Hence I think it more likely that John saw his baptism as (1) acting out the candidate's repentance and pledge of new life as well as (2) symbolically proclaiming, anticipating, and assuring the cleansing from sin that the holy spirit would effect on the last day when it was poured out like water on the repentant sinner by the stronger one. If one wants to call this an "eschatological sacrament" in the sense of a visible ritual symbolizing invisible spiritual change and a sure pledge of salvation in the near future, that is fine—provided the later Christian understanding of sacrament is not read into the phrase. Although Ernst rejects the phrase "eschatological sacrament," his interpretation is similar to mine: ". . . *eis*, with its idea of purpose, probably has a future-eschatological sense. . . . Repentance and the forgiveness of sins can be neither objectivized with the handy formula 'eschatological sacrament' nor reduced to the mere confession of sins and therefore to the subjective act of inner renewal. The baptism of John mediates to the repentant person the firm promise of the remission of sins—at the coming judgment."[165]

We are left, then, with something of a paradox when we try to grasp how John saw himself and understood his role in the eschatological drama. On the one hand, he proclaims his own insignificance and the insignificance of his baptism in the light of the stronger one, who will come soon to baptize with the spirit. Yet he does not offer his baptism as a voluntary pious act of supererogation. Future salvation, including the forgiveness of sins on the last day, is inextricably tied to the reception of John's baptism now, and John's baptism is inextricably tied to the person of John, who alone confers it. Hence, this humble insignificant slave implicitly makes himself a pivotal, indispensable figure in the eschatological drama.[166] Whether or not one can make sense of this paradox, it is important to note it; for we shall see the pattern returning in the case of Jesus.

With this we complete our sketch of "John without Jesus," an attempt to understand this charismatic eschatological Jewish prophet on his own terms, as he was understood by himself and by his fellow Jews apart from the question of his relation to Jesus. What that relation to Jesus was, how

Jesus understood the Baptist and vice versa, and finally how the Baptist met his tragic end will be treated in the next chapter, "Jesus With and Without John."

EXCURSUS ON JOHN THE BAPTIST IN JOSEPHUS

At the beginning of Chapter 12, under the question of the historicity of the Baptist, I noted that the authenticity of Josephus' report of the Baptist's ministry and death (*Ant.* 18.5.2 §116–119) is not a subject of fierce debate among scholars today. The vast majority recognize it as genuine. Still, the nuance of certain phrases and therefore the precise flow of thought do create difficulties for a detailed exegesis of the Greek text. The purpose of this excursus is to suggest a solution to some key problems of syntax and consequently of interpretation. The basic critical text, as edited by Louis H. Feldman, is as follows:[167]

§116. *Tisi de tōn Ioudaiōn edokei olōlenai ton Hērōdou straton hypo tou theou kai mala dikaiōs tinnymenou kata poinēn Iōannou tou epikaloumenou baptistou.*

§117. *kteinei gar dē touton Hērōdēs agathon andra kai tois Ioudaiois keleuonta aretēn epaskousin tai ta[168] pros allēlous dikaiosynē kai pros ton theon eusebeią chrōmenois baptismą synienai. houtō gar dē kai tēn baptisin apodektēn autą phaneisthai mē epi tinōn hamartadōn paraitēsei chrōmenōn, all' eph' hagneią tou sōmatos, hate dē kai tēs psychēs dikaiosynē proekkekatharmenēs.*

§118. *kai tōn allōn systrephomenōn, kai gar ērthēsan[169] epi pleiston tē akroasei tōn logōn, deisas Hērōdēs to epi tosonde pithanon autou tois anthrōpois mē epi stasei tini pheroi, panta gar eōkesan symboulē tē ekeinou praxontes, poly kreitton hēgeitai prin ti neōteron ex autou genesthai prolabōn anelein tou metabolēs genomenēs [mē][170] eis pragmata empesōn metanoein.*

§119. *kai ho men hypopsią tē Hērōdou desmios eis ton Machairounta pemphtheis to proeirēmenon phrourion tautē ktinnytai. tois de Ioudaiois doxa epi timōrią tē ekeinou ton olethron epi tą strateumati genesthai tou theou kakōsai Hērōdēn thelontos.[171]*

As with the study of NT texts, the first step in any analysis, after basic text criticism, is the delimitation of the literary unit. Josephus seems to have been at pains to make clear the beginning and the end of the Baptist passage, perhaps because it was for him a minor parenthesis in the much larger story of Herod Antipas, Agrippa I, and other Herodians. Hence Josephus clearly "packages" his aside about the Baptist with an *inclusio*: certain key words and key themes occur in a cluster at the very beginning (§116 and the first words of §117) and the very end (§119) of the passage.

§116	§119
tisi de tōn Ioudaiōn	*tois de Ioudaiosis*
edokei	*doxa*
olōlenai	*olethron*
ton Hērōdou straton	*tǭ strateumati . . . Hērōdēn*
tou theou +	*tou theou* +
tinnymenou	*kakōsai . . . thelontos*
kata poinēn Iōannou	*epi timōrią tę̄ ekeinou*
kteinei	*ktinnytai*

Thus, with the same or similar words, grouped in roughly the same order, Josephus reiterates the theme that (some) Jews thought that the destruction of Herod's army by the Nabatean King Aretas IV was God's just punishment inflicted on Herod Antipas to avenge his killing of John the Baptist. Since this is Josephus' own conscious framework for the pericope, it is advisable to view as the significant literary unit the whole Baptist passage from §116 to §119, and not simply from §117 to the beginning of §119, as Josef Ernst and some other commentators do.[172]

§116 is fairly straightforward, with the only problematic phrase being *tinnymenou kata poinēn*. In the middle form and with an obviously negative connotation, the verb must mean "avenge" or "punish" and must modify *theou*, the closest noun in the genitive, with Herod as the understood object. The sense is therefore: "God indeed punishing [Herod] quite justly." The laconic *kata poinēn Iōannou* must accordingly mean something like "to avenge what Herod had done to John." This likewise seems to be the sense of the equally compressed *epi timōrią tę̄ ekeinou* in §119.

In §117 things become more complicated, as Josephus begins to explain how John's successful but apparently harmless ministry of promoting virtue led to his execution by Antipas. The basic structure of the first sentence is simple enough: Herod killed[173] him, although[174] he was a good man, a man who bade the Jews join in baptism.[175] More troublesome are the two participles modifying *tois Ioudaiois*, *epaskousin* and *chrōmenois*. They are placed outside the article-noun combination and hence should be judged circumstantial rather than attributive in sense. To translate them merely as relative clauses ("the Jews who cultivated virtue and practiced justice and piety")[176] misses the precise syntactical point. Distinguished scholars like Klausner, Feldman, and Ernst[177] resolve the difficulty of rendering this convoluted sentence by using English parataxis in place of Greek hypotaxis: John commanded the Jews to cultivate virtue, practice justice and piety, and join in baptism. While this is a common technique in dealing with periodic sentences in Latin and Greek, it may be missing a fine point here. What exactly is Josephus expressing by these circumstantial participles?

One way to answer this question is to look ahead to the next sentence, which offers an explanation or reason (*gar dē kai*) for what John did in terms of John's own thought (*autǭ phaneisthai*). The explanation states that, in John's view, his baptism of these Jews was acceptable to God (*apodektēn*)[178] *if and only if* they used this rite not as a means to obtain pardon of certain sins but as a means of purifying their bodies. This was all that his baptism need or could do, since in fact (*hate dē*) their souls had already been cleansed by justice. Once again, as in the previous sentence, we find the verb *chraomai* used as a participle in the circumstantial position describing some activity of those baptized; hence it is quite reasonable to suppose that the same noun, *Ioudaiois*, is understood, though now in the genitive, as the genitive absolute construction demands. Given the context, which is discussing the condition under which John's baptism is acceptable to God, the translation "if" for the genitive absolute seems most likely and is used by both Feldman and Ernst.

Now, if *chraomai*, used as a circumstantial participle describing the Jews, is employed to express a condition for baptism in the second sentence of §117, it may well be that in the immediately previous sentence the same verb (along with *epaskousin*), used likewise as a circumstantial participle describing "the Jews" and specifying some circumstance of receiving baptism, carries the same conditional sense—especially since the second sentence claims to give the explanation or reason for the previous sentence. The first sentence in §117 would therefore read: "For Herod in fact killed him, although he was a good man and bade the Jews—if [or: provided that] they were cultivating virtue and practicing justice toward one another and piety toward God—to join in baptism." If this translation is correct, the practice of virtue is not one of the direct objects of John's command but rather the necessary precondition for obeying the one central command of the *Baptist*, namely, to be *baptized*, the only concept that is made the direct object of *keleuonta*. Only by construing the Greek in this way is the special function of the circumstantial participles in serving Josephus' purpose fully recognized. Josephus is at pains to stress that John's baptism is not a magical substitute for or producer of virtue, just as in the following sentence he stresses that John's baptism washes away pollution from bodies, not sins from souls.[179] Accordingly, John addresses his offer of baptism to Jews on the condition that they are already practicing virtue. A proper appreciation of the circumstantial participles, employed in a conditional sense in both sentences, is therefore of great importance for grasping the thrust of the whole passage.

This understanding of *tois Ioudaiois* in §117 as conditioned by the two circumstantial participles helps in turn to explain the curious *kai tōn allōn* at the beginning of §118.[180] At first glance, the previous concentration of the passage on "the Jews" as the audience of John's preaching might conjure up the idea that the unspecified "others" are Gentiles. There is no support for such an idea in the Four Gospels, but such a double audience would parallel what Josephus (quite mistakenly) says about Jesus' audience in *Ant.* 18.3.3 §63 (*kai pollous men Ioudaious, pollous de kai tou Hellēnikou epēgageto*). However, if we are correct that *epaskousin* and *chrōmenois* in §117 express conditions qualifying *tois Ioudaiois*, there is no need to go outside the immediate context to understand who "the others" at the beginning of §118 are. In §117 John calls to baptism only those Jews who fulfill a particular condition: they are already cultivating a life of virtue. Notice that Josephus gives no indication that this gathering of notably virtuous people around John gave Herod cause for alarm. Indeed, why should Herod have been alarmed? Josephus makes no mention at this point of great agitation on the part of the baptized or of their being ready to do whatever John counseled. Moreover, exceptionally virtuous persons do not usually form the vast majority of people in any given society, and the peaceful gathering of such virtuous persons merely to receive a religious rite is not usually the cause of grave concern among politicians. But if that is the type of Jew being specified in §117, "the others" in §118 would seem to refer to the rest of the Jewish population, the larger group of ordinary people who, as in most other societies, neither rejected their religious heritage nor engaged in the heroic feats of virtue and religious observance that marked sectarians. It is not by accident that when "the others," the larger general population, are introduced into the narrative, we hear about excitement (*ērthēsan*), John's persuasive power over people in general (note the generic *tois anthrōpois*), and Herod's fear that all this could lead to revolt.[181] Josephus, however, is emphatic in attributing any idea of revolt to the mind of Herod, not to the Baptist or the people. He goes on to stress that Herod quite consciously undertook a preemptive strike (*prolabōn*) in doing away (*anelein*) with John. The preacher of virtue and bodily purification might be quite harmless when addressing a religious elite; and even when the common people flocked to him, he did not—at least for the present—urge revolt. But things might change (*metabolēs genomenēs*); so better safe than sorry (*kreitton . . . anelein tou . . . metanoein*).[182] This emphasis on the fact that John's death stemmed from the subjective suspicion of Herod rather than from any objective act of John is repeated at the beginning of §119 by the phrase *hypopsią tę̄ Hērōdou*. §119 then goes on to serve two functions: (1) it rounds out the pericope with the *inclusio* that brings us back to the opening affirmation of §116, and (2) it connects the whole parenthetical Baptist passage with the ongoing Herodian saga, which continues in §120 with the preparations for the expedition of Vitellius, the Roman governor of Syria, to punish Aretas IV.

These philological and exegetical considerations produce the following translation, in which the elements of the *inclusio* are set in bold face, the key elements in the progression of thought are capitalized, and explanatory comments supplied by the translator are put in brackets:

§116. **But to some of the Jews it seemed that the army of Herod was destroyed by God—indeed, God quite justly punishing [Herod] to avenge what he had done to John,** who was surnamed the Baptist.

§117. For Herod **killed** him, although he was a good man and [simply] bade the Jews to join in baptism, PROVIDED THAT they were cultivating virtue and practicing justice toward one another and piety toward God. FOR [ONLY]

THUS, in John's opinion, would the baptism [he administered] indeed be acceptable [to God], namely, IF they used it to obtain not pardon for some sins but rather the cleansing of their bodies, INASMUCH AS [it was taken for granted that] their souls had already been purified by justice.

§118. And when THE OTHERS [namely, ordinary Jews] gathered together [around John]—for their excitement reached fever pitch as they listened to [his] words—Herod began to FEAR[183] that John's powerful ability to persuade PEOPLE might lead to some sort of revolt, for they seemed likely to do whatever he counseled. So [Herod] decided to do away with John by a PREEMPTIVE STRIKE, before he sparked a revolt. Herod considered this a much better [course of action] than to wait until the situation changed and [then] to regret [his delay] when he was engulfed by a crisis.

§119. And so, because of Herod's suspicion, John was sent in chains to Machaerus, the mountain fortress previously mentioned; there **he was killed. But the Jews were of the opinion that the army was destroyed to avenge John, God wishing to inflict harm on Herod.**

The movement of thought is thus clear. §116 introduces the theme of the destruction of Herod's army by God to avenge Herod's killing of John. §117 begins the "flashback" in which John is presented as a harmless dispenser of a water ritual, given to Jews on the condition that they are practicing justice and piety. In §118 "the plot thickens" as larger groups of ordinary Jews, as opposed to the original, select audience of the virtuous, swarm around John and are so stirred up by his sermons that they seem—at least to the mind of the fearful Herod—ready to follow John wherever he might lead, even to insurrection. This is the new development that determines the anxious Herod to make a preemptive strike before it is too late. Hence in §119 the suspicions of Herod lead to John's imprisonment and death, a crime God punishes by the destruction of Herod's army (*inclusio* and transition to Vitellius' intervention).

It is axiomatic that the portraits of John the Baptist in Josephus and in each of the Four Gospels must be studied separately and only then brought together for comparison, contrast, and possible correlation (not harmonization). Having looked at Josephus' presentation of the Baptist on its own terms, I would make three tentative suggestions as to how this "close reading" of the vocabulary, syntax, and structure of the Baptist passage in the *Antiquities* might contribute to the study of the Gospels:

(1) From the initial stark juxtaposition of *kteinei* and *agathon* onwards, Josephus' intention in describing the Baptist is obviously apologetic. Any idea of John's fiery eschatological proclamation of a day of judgment that will make irrelevant all ethnic ties, a judgment to be administered by a mysterious figure to come, a judgment that can be avoided only by submitting to John's baptism of repentance—in short, all these strange, disruptive, or disturbing ideas can have no place in Josephus' presentation, if indeed he ever had any knowledge of them. If Josephus did know these aspects of the Baptist's message, he natu-

rally suppressed them, since he regularly plays down or removes eschatological and messianic expectations present in his sources.[184] One need only think of his presentation of the Essenes compared to the various eschatological and messianic hopes expressed in the literature of Qumran.[185]

Accordingly, in Josephus John is reduced to a popular moral philosopher in the Greco-Roman mode, with a slight hint of a neo-Pythagorean performing ritual lustrations. His message is summed up in those twin virtues seen in Philo and other Jewish Diaspora authors: justice toward one another and piety toward God.[186] The whole point of a special, once-and-for-all baptism, to be administered to Jews only by John (hence his surname), becomes unintelligible. If the Synoptic portrait of the Baptist did not exist, something like it would have to be invented to supply the material that Josephus either suppresses or simply does not know. In a sense, Josephus' portrait of the Baptist is self-transcending; it points beyond itself to some further explanation Josephus does not offer.

(2) Still, even when we grant Josephus' apologetic purpose that leads to a very slanted depiction of the Baptist, there is no reason for thinking that one major aspect of his presentation is wrong—namely, that John's program was a religious one without an activist political agenda and that it was only Herod's fear and overactive instinct for survival that led him to see political danger in a preacher of morality who baptized people.[187] This is not to deny that, unlike our experience of separation of church and state in a secularized Western democracy, religion permeated human life in the ancient Mediterranean world in general and in Palestine in particular. Yet Josephus, like some other ancient writers, is perfectly capable of distinguishing a religious leader with no activist political agenda from other religious leaders with just such an agenda. As a matter of fact, both in the *Jewish War* and in the *Jewish Antiquities*, Josephus does present Jewish religious figures whose actions threaten the political establishment and who accordingly meet speedy opposition at the establishment's hands.[188] Since Josephus has no personal stake in the reputation of the Baptist, his care to distinguish John from such types probably has a basis in fact. The pattern of the purely religious figure, whose growing success leads the rulers of Palestine to fear his possible political influence and whose execution is therefore considered a wise preventive measure, must therefore be taken seriously when the historical question of the trial and death of Jesus is considered.[189]

(3) While Josephus' depiction of the Baptist as a moral preacher concerned with virtue owes a great deal to the author's accommodation to his Greco-Roman milieu, it must be granted that Josephus agrees to a certain extent with Luke's special material on the Baptist (Luke 3:10–14). There, too, the Baptist is presented as inculcating practical deeds of social justice. This correlation might simply be chalked up to two Greco-Roman writers (Josephus and Luke) who, independently of each other, seek to adapt a strange Jewish prophet to cultural models familiar in the wider Greco-Roman world.[190] Yet Luke's material, if traditional,[191] may supply further "missing links" in Josephus' narrative.

Luke divides the various questioners seeking moral catechesis into three groups: the crowds, tax collectors, and soldiers. The intriguing point here is that tax collectors and soldiers might have been counted among "the others," the ordinary, not-especially-religious Jews who, according to Josephus, formed the "second wave" flocking to John.[192] The fact that such important props of his financial and military power as tax collectors and soldiers had come under the influence of John and fervently hung on his every word may have been the *realpolitik* consideration that especially alarmed Antipas and moved him to his preemptive strike. He did not care if some virtuous elite listened to John; he did care if his tax collectors and soldiers were taking orders from a different commander. While Luke is obviously pursuing his own theological purpose with his special material, he may have inadvertently thrown some light on the mysterious *tōn allōn* of *Ant.* 18.5.2 §118 and specifically on the reason why, in the mind of the fearful Herod, the adherence of "the others" to John was a danger that could not be tolerated.

NOTES TO CHAPTER 12

[1] The bibliography on John the Baptist is immense, though much tends toward the devotional or the uncritical. Orientation to major bibliographical resources can be found in the following works, arranged chronologically: Martin Dibelius, *Die urchristliche Überlieferung von Johannes dem Täufer* (FRLANT 15; Göttingen: Vandenhoeck & Ruprecht, 1911); Maurice Goguel, *Au seuil de l'évangile. Jean-Baptiste* (Paris: Payot, 1928); Ernst Lohmeyer, *Das Urchristentum. 1 Buch. Johannes der Täufer* (Göttingen: Vandenhoeck & Ruprecht, 1932); Joseph Thomas, *Le mouvement baptiste en Palestine et Syrie (150 av. J.-C.–300 ap. J.-C.)* (Universitas Catholica Lovaniensis 2d series, 28; Gembloux: Duculot, 1935); Carl H. Kraeling, *John the Baptist* (New York: Scribner's, 1951); J. Leonard Farmer, *John and Jesus in Their Days and Ours. Social Studies in the Gospels* (New York: Psycho-Medical Library, 1956); A. S. Geyser, "The Youth of John the Baptist," *NovT* 1 (1956) 70–75; Paul Winter, "The Proto-Source of Luke I," *NovT* 1 (1956) 184–99; Jean Steinmann, *St. Jean-Baptiste et la spiritualité du désert* (Paris: Seuil, 1957); W. H. Brownlee, "John the Baptist in the New Light of Ancient Scrolls," *The Scrolls and the New Testament* (ed. Krister Stendahl; Westport, CT: Greenwood, 1975, originally 1957) 33–53; Wolfgang Trilling, "Die Täufertradition bei Matthäus," *BZ* 3 (1959) 271–89; Günther Bornkamm, *Jesus of Nazareth* (New York: Harper & Row, 1960) 44–52; William R. Farmer, "John the Baptist," *IDB*, 2. 955–62; J. A. T. Robinson, "The Baptism of John and the Qumran Community," and "Elijah, John, and Jesus," *Twelve New Testament Studies* (London: SCM, 1962) 11–27 and 28–52; Albrecht Oepke, "*baptō*, etc." *TDNT* 1 (1964) 529–46, esp. 536–38, 545–46; Charles H. H. Scobie, *John the Baptist* (London: SCM, 1964); Jean Daniélou, *Jean-Baptiste. Témoin de l'agneau* (Paris: Seuil, 1964); Hartwig Thyen, "*Baptisma metanoias eis aphesin hamartiōn,*" *The Future of Our Religious Past* (Rudolf Bultmann Festschrift; New York: Harper & Row, 1971, originally 1964) 131–68; Raymond E. Brown, "John the Baptist in the Gospel of John," *New Testament Studies* (Garden City, NY: Image, Doubleday, 1968, originally 1965) 174–84; Roland Schütz, *Johannes der Täufer* (ATANT 50; Zurich: Zwingli, 1967); Walter Wink, *John the Baptist in the Gospel Tradition* (SNTSMS 7; Cambridge: Cambridge University, 1968); Otto Böcher, "Ass Johannes der Täufer kein Brot (Luk, vii.33)?" *NTS* 18 (1971–72) 90–92; Ernst Bammel, "The Baptist in Early Christian Tradition," *NTS* 18 (1971–72) 95–128; John H. Hughes, "John the Baptist: the Forerunner of God Himself," *NovT* 14 (1972) 191–218; J. Becker, *Johannes der Täufer und Jesus von Nazareth* (Neukirchen-Vluyn: Neukirchener Verlag, 1972); John Reumann, "The Quest for the Historical Baptist," *Understanding the Sacred Text* (Morton S. Enslin Festschrift; ed. John Reumann; Valley Forge, PA: Judson, 1972) 183–200; Morton S. Enslin, "John and Jesus," *ZNW* 66 (1975) 1–18; Raymond E. Brown, *The Birth of the Messiah* (Garden City, NY: Doubleday, 1977) 256–85, 330–92; John P. Meier, "John the Baptist in Matthew's Gospel," *JBL* 99 (1980) 383–405; Helmut Merklein, "Die Umkehrpredigt bei Johannes dem Täufer und Jesus von Nazareth," *BZ* 25 (1981) 29–46; Paul W. Hollenbach, "Social Aspects of John the Baptizer's Preaching Mission in the Context of Palestinian Judaism," *ANRW* II/19.1 (1979) 850–75; idem, "The Conversion of Jesus: From Jesus the Baptizer to Jesus the Healer," *ANRW* II/25.1 (1982) 196–219; idem, "John the Baptist," *The Anchor Bible Dictionary* (6 vols.; New York: Doubleday, 1992) 3. 887–99; Etienne Nodet, "Jésus et Jean-Baptiste selon Josèphe," *RB* 92 (1985) 320–48, 497–524; Wendy J. Cotter, "The Parable of the Children in the Marketplace," *NovT* 29 (1987) 289–304; idem, "Children Sitting in the Agora. Q (Luke) 7:31–35," *Forum* 5 (1989) 63–82; Carl R.

Kazmierski, "The Stones of Abraham: John the Baptist and the End of Torah (Matt 3,7–10 par. Luke 3,7–9)," *Bib* 68 (1987) 22–39; R. P. Merendino, "Testi anticotestamentari in *Mc* 1, 2–8," *RivB* 35 (1987) 3–25; Edmondo Lupieri, *Giovanni Battista nelle tradizioni sinottiche* (Studi biblici 82; Brescia: Paideia, 1988); idem, *Giovanni Battista fra storia e leggenda* (Biblioteca di cultura religiosa 53; Brescia: Paideia, 1988); M. Cleary, "The Baptist of History and Kerygma," *ITQ* 54 (1988) 211–27; Roger Aus, *Water into Wine and the Beheading of John the Baptist* (Brown Judaic Studies 150; Atlanta: Scholars, 1988); D. A. Black, "The Text of Mark 6.20," *NTS* 34 (1988) 141–45; W. E. Moore, "Violence to the Kingdom: Josephus and the Syrian Churches," *ExpTim* 100 (1989) 174–77; Walter Wink, "Jesus' Reply to John. Matt 11:2–6/Luke 7:18–23," *Forum* 5 (1989) 121–28; Josef Ernst, *Johannes der Täufer. Interpretation—Geschichte—Wirkungsgeschichte* (BZNW 53; Berlin/New York: de Gruyter, 1989); Knut Backhaus, *Die "Jüngerkreise" des Täufers Johannes. Eine Studie zu den religionsgeschichtlichen Ursprüngen des Christentums* (Paderborner Theologische Studien 19; Paderborn: Schöningh, 1991); Robert L. Webb, *John the Baptizer and Prophet. A Socio-Historical Study* (JSNTSup 62; Sheffield: JSOT, 1991); Otto Betz, "Was John the Baptist an Essene?" *Understanding the Dead Sea Scrolls* (ed. Hershel Shanks; New York: Random House, 1992) 205–14. For the special question of the Baptist in Josephus, see Louis H. Feldman, *Josephus and Modern Scholarship 1937–1980* (Berlin/New York: de Gruyter, 1984) 673–79, 957; idem, *Josephus. A Supplementary Bibliography* (New York/London: Garland, 1986) 620, 675.

[2] See the remarks by E. P. Sanders, *Jesus and Judaism* (Philadelphia: Fortress, 1985) 91.

[3] Since almost all contemporary critics discount the two passages dealing with John in the so-called "Old Slavonic" (actually, Old Russian) version of the *Jewish War* as later interpolations, they will not be treated here. Among many other curiosities of the texts, one should note how John is never mentioned by name but always by some description. For a survey of the whole question, see, e.g., Dibelius, *Die urchristliche Überlieferung*, 127–29; Kraeling, *John the Baptist*, 5; Scobie, *John the Baptist*, 19–22; Ernst, *Johannes der Täufer*, 258–63; Webb, *John the Baptizer*, 43–44.
Simply for the sake of completeness, I include the English translation of the two passages as provided by F. J. Foakes Jackson and Kirsopp Lake in their *The Beginnings of Christianity. Part I. The Acts of the Apostles* (5 vols.; Grand Rapids: Baker, 1979; originally 1920–33) 1. 433–35:

> (1) In those days, however, a man wandered among the Jews clad in unusual garments, because he had put on furs about his body, on all parts of it which were not covered by his hair. Moreover, judging from his face, he looked just like a wild man.
>
> This man came to the Jews and summoned them to freedom, saying "God has sent me, that I may show you the way to the law, by which you may free yourselves from the great struggle of sustaining yourselves. And there will be no mortal ruling over you, only the Highest, who has sent me." And as the people heard this, they were happy; and all Judea, which lies in the neighborhood of Jerusalem, followed him.
>
> And he did no other thing to them than to plunge them into the flood-tide of the Jordan and let them go, pointing out to them that they should leave off evil deeds, and promising that there would be given them a king, who would free them and conquer for them all peoples not yet subject to them, but that nobody among those of whom we are speaking would be vanquished. Some reviled him, but others were won over to belief.
>
> And then he was led to Archelaus where the men versed in law had assembled; they asked him who he was and where he had been up to this time. And he answered this question, and spoke thus: "Pure am I, for God's spirit has entered into me, and I nourish

my body on reeds and roots and wood-shavings." But when they threw themselves upon him, in order to rack him, unless he revoked his former words and actions, he then spoke again: "It befits you to leave off your atrocious works and to join yourselves to the Lord, your God."

And in a rage there rose up Simon, by descent an Essene, a scribe, and this one spoke: "We read each day the godly books. But you, who have just come out of the woods like a wild beast, how do you dare, indeed, to teach us and seduce the people with your profligate sermons!" And he rushed forward in order to harm him. But he, rebuking them, spoke: "I shall not reveal to you that secret dwelling within your hearts, for you have not wished it. Thereby an unspeakable misfortune has come upon you and by your own design."

And after he had thus spoken, he went forth to the other side of the Jordan, and since no one dare blame him, each did exactly what he had done formerly.

(2) When Philip was in possession of his power, he saw in a dream how an eagle tore out both his eyes. And he summoned all his wise men. But as each explained the dream differently, that man, of whom we have written before, telling how he went about in the furs of wild beasts and how he purified the people in the waters of the Jordan, came to him suddenly unbidden. And he spoke: "Hear the word of the Lord on the dream which you have had. The eagle—that is your corruptibility, because that bird is violent and rapacious. And that sin will take from you your eyes, which are your power and your wife." And as he had thus spoken, before evening Philip died and his power was given to Agrippa.

And his wife took to husband Herod, his brother. On her account, however, all the men versed in law abhorred him, but dared not accuse him to his face.

Only that man, however, whom people called a wild man, came to him with wrath and spoke: "Why have you taken your brother's wife? As your brother died a remorseless death, so will you too be mowed down by the heavenly sickle. God's heavenly decree will not be silenced, but will cause your death through evil affliction in foreign lands. For you are not producing children for your brother, but are giving rein to your carnal desires, and are carrying on adultery, since four children of his exist."

But when Herod heard this he grew angry and ordered that the man be beaten and driven forth. But he accused Herod so incessantly, wherever he found him, and for so long a time, that finally he offered violence to him and ordered him to be killed.

But his character was unusual and his method of life was not mortal; as, for instance, a fleshless spirit would, so did this man also persist. His lips knew no bread, not once at the Passover did he partake of unleavened bread, saying that in remembrance of God, who had freed the people from servitude, this sort of bread was given for food, as a consolation, for the way was woeful. But he did not allow himself near wine and intoxicating drinks. And he shunned every animal for food, and he punished every wrong, and woodshavings answered his needs.

A somewhat different translation, complete with critical notes and short comments, can be found in John Martin Creed, "The Slavonic Version of Josephus' History of the Jewish War," *HTR* 25 (1932) 277–319, esp. 305–16. Creed remarks (pp. 316–17): "It is tempting to conjecture that the figure of some contemporary eremite has influenced the portrait [of John], but attempts to discover any definite source have not been successful. . . . It [the problem of these Old Slavonic insertions into the *Jewish War*] does not concern Josephus, but a mediaeval version of Josephus."

[4] For alternate and conjectural readings, see the notes of Louis H. Feldman on this passage in *Josephus. Jewish Antiquities. Books XVIII–XIX* (LCL; Cambridge, MA: Harvard University; London: Heinemann, 1981 [No. 433, vol. IX of Josephus]) 80–84; and the more detailed information in the *editio maior* of Benedict Niese, *Flavii Josephi Opera* (7 vols.; 2d ed.; Berlin: Weidmann, 1955; originally 1885–95)

4. 161–62. The critically established texts of Niese and Feldman are substantially the same; some minor differences will be noted later in this chapter. For a recent treatment of the many text-critical problems of the *Antiquities*, with books 1–3 used as a test case, see Etienne Nodet, *Flavius Josèphe. Les antiquités juives. Volume I: Livres I à III. A. Introduction et texte* (Paris: Cerf, 1990) xii–xxii. I use the phrase "all relevant manuscripts" because, as Nodet points out (p. xiii), the manuscripts available for text-critical work are very different for books 11–20 of the *Antiquities* than for books 1–10; for an extensive treatment of these manuscripts, see Niese, *Flavii Josephi Opera*, 3. III–LVII. It should be noted that Nodet's own critical text is intended only as an *editio minor*. I am grateful to my colleague, Professor Christopher T. Begg, for the reference to Nodet's work.

⁵For these and other arguments for authenticity, see Scobie, *John the Baptist*, 18–19; Webb, *John the Baptizer*, 39–41. Scobie emphasizes the lack of any eschatological and/or messianic proclamation by Josephus' John, as well as the very different presentation of John's death. Nevertheless, some authors have argued for knowledge of the Synoptic tradition on Josephus' part; e.g., Schütz (*Johannes der Täufer*, 17) argues that Josephus knew the tradition found in Mark's Gospel. The idea that Josephus knew and used Luke has a venerable parentage; for examples of the debate in the 19th century, see H. J. Holtzmann, "Lucas und Josephus," *ZWT* 16 (1873) 85–93; M. Krenkel, "Ein Nachtrag zu dem Aufsatze: Josephus und Lucas," *ZWT* 16 (1873) 441–44; E. Schürer, "Lucas und Josephus," *ZWT* 19 (1876) 574–82; H. J. Holtzmann, "Noch einmal Lucas und Josephus," *ZWT* 20 (1877) 535–49. In my view, the arguments of Scobie in favor of Josephus' independence of the Four Gospels are convincing; for a similar line of argument, see Graham H. Twelftree, "Jesus in Jewish Tradition," *Gospel Perspectives. The Jesus Tradition Outside the Gospels. Volume 5* (ed. David Wenham; Sheffield: JSOT, 1985) 289–341, esp. 294–95. For the vocabulary and style of the passage as Josephan, see H. St. J. Thackeray, "Josephus and Christianity," *Josephus. The Man and the Historian* (The Hilda Stich Stroock Lectures; New York: Jewish Institute of Religion, 1929) 132, 136.

⁶The Greek text reads: *en gar tǭ oktōkaidekatǭ tēs ioudaikēs archaiologias ho Iōsēpos martyrei tǭ Iōannǭ hōs baptistǭ gegenēmenǭ kai katharsion tois baptisamenois epaggellomenǭ.* For a critical edition, see Marcel Borret (ed.), *Origène. Contre Celse. Tome I (Livres I et II)* (SC 132; Paris: Cerf, 1967) 198. All translations are my own. It may be that Origen does not cite Josephus verbatim because Josephus' insistence that John's baptism confers only bodily purification and not forgiveness of sins contradicts the statement of Mark 1:4: *baptisma metanoias eis aphesin hamartiōn.*

⁷For a critical text, see Gustave Bardy, *Eusèbe de Césarée. Histoire Ecclésiastique. Livres I–IV* (SC 31; Paris: Cerf, 1952) 36–38. §116 and part of §117 are also found (with slight variations) in Eusebius' citation of Josephus in his *De Demonstratione Evangelica Libri Decem* 9.5.15; for a critical text, see Ivar A. Heikel (ed.), *Eusebius Werke. Sechster Band. Die Demonstratio Evangelica* (GCS 23; Leipzig: Hinrichs, 1913) 416.

⁸The "core text" of the *Testimonium Flavianum* contains sixty Greek words (including particles); the passage on the Baptist, one hundred sixty-two words. Naturally, different judgments on text-critical questions might lead to slightly different computations; but the overall result would remain the same.

⁹For an example of a critic who does declare the Baptist passage to be an interpolation, see Léon Herrmann, *Chrestos. Témoignages paiens et juifs sur le christianisme du premier siècle* (Collection Latomus 109; Brussels: Latomus, 1970) 99–104. Not surpris-

ingly, Herrmann judges the *Testimonium Flavianum* and even the passage on James, the brother of Jesus (*Ant.* 20.9.1 [§200]), to be interpolations as well. In contrast, Per Bilde (*Flavius Josephus between Jerusalem and Rome. His Life, His Works, and Their Importance* [Journal for the Study of the Pseudepigrapha, Supplement Series 2; Sheffield: JSOT, 1988] 223) readily accepts the authenticity of the Baptist passage, although he dismisses the *Testimonium Flavianum* as totally "a secondary Christian fabrication."

[10] It is indeed remarkable that Josephus uses the surname *baptistēs*, which otherwise occurs in 1st-century Greek only in the Synoptic Gospels (Matt 3:1; 11:11–12; 14:2,8; 16:14; 17:13; Mark 6:25; 8:28; Luke 7:20,33; 9:19). It does not occur in Acts. The noun is presumably a special Jewish-Greek formation, apparently coined solely for the purpose of describing the strange figure of John. The use of the participle in the attributive position to describe John (*ho baptizōn*) seems to be favored by Mark (Mark 6:14,24; possibly 1:4). Oepke ("*baptō,*" 546) thinks that Luke generally avoids the addition of "the Baptist" in his account; it is totally absent in John's Gospel. Hollenbach ("The Conversion of Jesus," 97 n. 2) thinks that the participial form is "less formal" and "originated first." While both Greek forms may actually have arisen around the same time as alternate translations of an Aramaic original, it may be true that the Greek participle represents more accurately an Aramaic participle (perhaps the hafel participle *maṭbēl*, from *ṭĕbal*, "to dip"). All the more intriguing, then, is the fact that the unheard-of form *baptistēs* became so fixed in Jewish and Christian Greek that both the Gospels and Josephus witness to it. The only noun-formation similar to *baptistēs* known from the period is Epictetus' use of *parabaptistai* in his *Discourses* (2.9.21), if indeed the passage is authentic. Even if the passage comes from Epictetus, it is quite obscure, has been the subject of many different interpretations (are the *parabaptistai* Jews? Christians? converts to Judaism undergoing proselyte baptism?), and has been emended in the Loeb Library edition. On this last point, see W. A. Oldfather (ed.), *Epictetus* (LCL; 2 vols.; Cambridge, MA: Harvard University; London: Heinemann, 1925, 1928) 1. 272–73; cf. the comments by Shaye J. D. Cohen, "The Rabbinic Conversion Ceremony," *JJS* 41 (1990) 177–203, esp. 194–95 and n. 49, which also treats of the obscure text in the fourth of the *Sibylline Oracles*, 4. 165. Cohen does not think that the latter text ("wash your whole bodies in perennial rivers") refers to a conversion ritual. For the contrary view (that the verse does refer to conversion and baptism à la John the Baptist), see John J. Collins, "Sibylline Oracles," *The Old Testament Pseudepigrapha* (ed. James H. Charlesworth; 2 vols.; Garden City, NY: Doubleday, 1983, 1985) 1. 388 n. e2.

[11] It is surprising that so careful a critic as Sanders states (*Jesus and Judaism*, 92): "That John himself was an eschatological prophet of repentance is clearly implied in Josephus's account." In fact, there is nothing that clearly implies eschatology in Josephus' account. Sanders backtracks somewhat in the accompanying footnote (p. 371 n. 4): "That John was an eschatological prophet is less clear in Josephus, who here as elsewhere probably downplays eschatological features." Sanders then proceeds to draw eschatological implications from the fact that Herod executed John because he feared trouble from John's ministry. But a petty tyrant's irrational fear of revolt breaking out because of the Baptist's ministry does not in itself imply any kind of eschatology in the Baptist's preaching.

[12] As a general rule, Luke's references to the Baptist in Acts must be considered dependent on his Gospel. Yet that rule is not absolute; as we shall see, Acts 13:25 may represent a tradition in some respects closer to John 1:27 than to Luke 3:16.

The argument from multiple attestation would be weakened slightly if one granted the hypothesis of J. Lambrecht that Mark knew and used the final redacted form of Q in his treatment of the Baptist; see his "John the Baptist and Jesus in Mark 1.1–15:

Markan Redaction of Q?" *NTS* 38 (1992) 357–84. Actually, throughout his article Lambrecht simply presupposes Mark's knowledge of Q as a working hypothesis rather than ever establishing such knowledge by systematic arguments that take into account large sections of Mark and Q. One can only remark that if one is determined to find traces of Q in Mark 1:1–15, one will do so, as any Rorschach test will confirm. A further question may be raised: does the idea that Mark knew Q ultimately undermine the very arguments that created the two-source theory in the first place? As a practical matter, although the hypothesis of Mark's knowledge of Q has been launched at various times in the 20th century, it has never received general acceptance. At a certain point, hypotheses become too hypothetical.

[13] Wink, *John the Baptist*, x. See also the wise caution urged by Reumann, "The Quest for the Historical Baptist," 187, 194.

[14] For attempts to use Luke 1 in a judicious and critical way to fill in the "blank" of John's birth and early years, see, e.g., Kraeling, *John the Baptist*, 16–32; Scobie, *John the Baptist*, 49–59. Kraeling, though, is given to psychologizing the Baptist in the mode of the 19th-century "liberal lives of Jesus." For example, the roots of John's wilderness ministry lie in a "bitter experience" the young priest-to-be had in his 20s when he left the Judean countryside, went to Jerusalem for ordination, and realized that he could not cope with the magnificence of the secularized priesthood as lived in Jerusalem (pp. 26–27). What is refreshing is Kraeling's honest admission at the end of his psychologizing: "All this is hypothesis, a twentieth-century 'legend' that endeavors to account for an important historical fact from the materials available. Yet whatever be true about this particular suggestion, it is clear that without a catastrophic experience of some sort, John would scarcely have become a dweller in the wilderness" (p. 27). The problem of psychologizing becomes clear in the last sentence: "a catastrophic experience of some sort" describes nothing in particular because it could describe almost anything.

[15] See Dibelius, *Die urchristliche Überlieferung*, 75; Rudolf Bultmann, *Die Geschichte der synoptischen Tradition* (FRLANT 29; 8th ed.; Göttingen: Vandenhoeck & Ruprecht, 1970) 320–21; Scobie, *John the Baptist*, 50–51 (who holds that at an early stage the narrative of John's infancy stood by itself, written in Hebrew or Aramaic); Wink, *John the Baptist*, 59–60 (who prefers to speak only of some "Baptist traditions," not a full Infancy Narrative, brought over to the church by former followers of John); Bammel, "The Baptist," 95–128. For neither Dibelius nor Bultmann, however, does the possibility of a tradition's stemming from a Baptist circle guarantee the historicity of the material involved. This is a point missed by a number of other critics: to show that a tradition about the Baptist originated in a Baptist group does not prove *ipso facto* that it gives us any historically reliable knowledge about the Baptist.

[16] Basically confident about the Baptist Infancy Narrative is J. A. Sint, "Die Eschatologie des Täufers, die Täufergruppen und die Polemik der Evangelien," *Vom Messias zum Christus* (ed. Kurt Schubert; Vienna/Feiburg/Basel: Herder, 1964) 55–163, esp. 55–56.

[17] On various theories of sources for Luke 1–2 and the languages in which they were supposedly composed, see Brown, *Birth of the Messiah*, 244–50; Ernst, *Johannes der Täufer*, 116–20. Ernst does think that some coherent Baptist-legend lies behind Luke 1, while Brown is skeptical of such a claim. Ernst thinks that such a legend portrayed John not as the Messiah but as an eschatological prophet (pp. 122–27). Many of the different theories concerning which verses of Luke 1 belonged to the original Baptist-legend are listed by Ernst on pp. 116–17 n. 10. The bewildering variety of opinions

about what is tradition and what is redaction makes one doubtful about isolating the supposed original legend with any certainty or even high probability. Ernst himself likens the Baptist-legend to Jewish haggada and opines that it is extremely difficult to decide what might belong to a historical core (p. 139).

[18] See Dibelius (*Die urchristliche Überlieferung*, 67), whose position, with adaptations, is presented by Wink, *John the Baptist*, 59; a somewhat different approach to structure is found in René Laurentin, *Structure et théologie de Luc I–II* (Paris: Gabalda, 1957) 32–33. For an overview of theories of structure, see Brown, *Birth of the Messiah*, 248–53; Ernst, *Johannes der Täufer*, 113–15.

[19] Proponents of both positions are listed by Ernst, *Johannes der Täufer*, 115 nn. 4 and 5. Ernst (p. 116) holds that both John's and Jesus' Infancy Narratives had their own history of development; it is difficult to determine how the two independent units were brought together.

[20] Wink (*John the Baptist*, 71–72) holds that we should not think of either the Infancy Narrative of Jesus imitating a prior Baptist Infancy Narrative or vice versa. Rather, "the stories of Jesus and John developed *together*, from the very beginning, as an indissoluble unity. . . ."

[21] On this point, see Brown, *Birth of the Messiah*, 239–43.

[22] This becomes quite understandable if one holds that the Infancy Narrative was added only after the Evangelist had finished writing the body of the Gospel and possibly even Acts; on this, see Brown, *Birth of the Messiah*, 239–43; Ernst, *Johannes der Täufer*, 116.

[23] On the priestly nature of the blessing, see Joseph A. Fitzmyer, *The Gospel According to Luke* (AB 28 and 28A; Garden City, NY: Doubleday, 1981, 1985) 2. 1590; also Walter Grundmann (*Das Evangelium nach Lukas* [THKNT 3; 7th ed.; Berlin: Evangelische Verlagsanstalt, 1974] 453–54), who points out the correlation between Zechariah in the temple at the beginning of the Gospel and the disciples in the temple at its end. Charles H. Talbert goes even further (*Reading Luke. A Literary and Theological Commentary on the Third Gospel* [New York: Crossroad, 1982] 233): "Just as the gospel began with the ministry of the priest Zechariah, so it ends with Jesus acting as priest for his flock. . . ."

[24] For the use of literary patterns, especially parallels, in Luke-Acts, see Charles H. Talbert, *Literary Patterns, Theological Themes, and the Genre of Luke-Acts* (SBLMS 20; Missoula, MT: Scholars, 1974).

[25] This may be the valid point at the center of all of Kraeling's psychologizing approach. Brown (*Birth of the Messiah*, 265–66) considers the names of John's parents and his priestly lineage to be elements of tradition that came to Luke, though he notes that this position does not necessarily indicate that the elements are historical. Ernst (*Johannes der Täufer*, 269–72) favors the historicity of John's origins in a priestly family; he argues from the true-to-life depiction of the Jewish cultic and family milieu in the Baptist-legend. Ernst admits that trying to decide what type of priestly tradition John's family stood in is more difficult. John's family may have belonged to that branch of Zadokite priests from the countryside who opposed the worldliness of the Hasmonean priestly aristocracy but who did not go so far as to break totally with the Hasmoneans in Jerusalem in the way the Qumranites did. Ernst is himself cautious in specifying the milieu of John's family; he notes that some commentators have declared the milieu to reflect spiritualizing or pacifist tendencies (Kraeling), while others see connections with the Zealots (Josephine Massyngbaerde Ford, Paul Hollenbach). In my view, the data are too sparse and tenuous to make any such decisions.

[26] Ernst (*Johannes der Täufer*, 272–74) rightly rejects detailed chronological computations on the basis of the Baptist-legend. Why he thinks that we can say that John was older than Jesus (p. 274)—when, by his own admission, the John and Jesus cycles were originally independent units and were brought together only secondarily—is unclear to me.

[27] See Geyser, "The Youth of John the Baptist," 70–75; Winter, "The Proto-Source," 196; Steinmann, *Saint Jean-Baptiste*, 58–61; J. A. T. Robinson, "The Baptism of John and the Qumran Community," *Twelve New Testament Studies*, 11–27. Scobie (*John the Baptist*, 58–59) prefers to speak in general terms of adoption by some baptist sect, which he simply calls an "attractive" idea; Farmer ("John the Baptist," 960) likewise speaks globally of "some" Essene community. On the general question of the Baptist and Qumran, see Brownlee, "John the Baptist," 33–53.

[28] That this text was important for Qumran is clear from 1QS 8:13–15; 9:19–20. We cannot be so certain about the Baptist, but the multiple attestation of sources would seem to argue that it was deeply rooted in the earliest traditions about the Baptist; it is found connected with him in Mark (1:3), Q (Matt 11:10 ‖ Luke 7:27), L (Luke 1:76), and John (1:23).

[29] Josephus is one with the Christian sources in preserving this title (*Ant.* 18.5.2 §116: *baptistou*); that fact alone underlines how striking and unusual John's practice must have been to the Jews of his day.

[30] This is the suggestion of Steinmann (*Saint Jean-Baptiste*, 60), who hypothesizes that John had been an Essene novice but then became "a dissident of Essenism." According to Steinmann, John heard the prophetic call of the Spirit and left the Essene community, with perhaps some others following him. Again, we seem on the verge of writing a novel. Robinson ("The Baptism of John," 13, 18) prefers to attenuate the extent of John's break with his Qumran past.

[31] Brown (*Birth of the Messiah*, 346–46) observes: ". . . it was Luke's intention to have Mary off the stage before he narrated JBap's birth. . . . the two birth narratives of JBap and of Jesus have their own balanced scenario. In each the two parents and the newborn child are featured, and it would destroy this careful balance to have Mary the parent of Jesus at the birth of JBap. This literary structure is far more important in the Lucan infancy narrative than the psychology of the characters involved, for we are not dealing with memories from family history but with a carefully planned dramatization of the theology of salvation history." The only point on which I would disagree with Brown is his reading of Luke 1:56 to mean that Luke actually affirms Mary's departure for home before the birth of John (p. 338). In my view, Luke is concerned solely with getting Mary off the dramatic stage; he is simply not interested in whether she left before or after the birth of John.

[32] So Brown, *Birth of the Messiah*, 376. Brown goes on to comment in n. 2 on p. 376: "It is pure fiction to draw upon our knowledge of the priestly Essene community of the Dead Sea Scrolls in order to fashion the theory that JBap was brought to Qumran as the child of a priest and raised there in a desert monastery." Fitzmyer (*The Gospel According to Luke*, 1. 389) is more open to the possibility, but he cautions that he views the suggestion simply as a "plausible hypothesis—which cannot be proved or disproved. . . ."

[33] Ernst (*Johannes der Täufer*, 276–77) is likewise skeptical about a stay at Qumran.

[34] See Thomas, *Le mouvement baptiste*; a summary of his views can be found on pp. 435–36. For the particular question of Bannus, see pp. 33–34. Thomas rejects the

suggestion of C. Bugge that Bannus represents a second class of Essenes, those who for a while left the community and went into the desert to live a more austere life. In a similar vein, notes Thomas, M. Friedländer makes Bannus, as well as John the Baptist, an "Essene tertiary," living on the margin of Essene communities and less tied to their rules. But, as Thomas rightly observes, Josephus does not seem to suspect any relation between Bannus, the Baptist, and the Essenes (and he discusses all three). In fact, Josephus does not suggest even the existence of a class of Essene hermits in the Bannus mold. Yet Thomas does hold open the possibility that Bannus belonged to some organized group of "baptizing Jews" that had gone beyond the practices of the Essenes. Personally, I think it best to leave Bannus as Josephus presents him: a solitary. Nevertheless, the very existence of this solitary, practicing lustrations in the desert of Judea, is a good reminder that "marginal Jews," including those with baptismal practices, may have been more numerous than our present sources indicate.

[35] As a matter of fact, many commentators who consider most of the Baptist's Infancy Narrative in Luke 1 to be legend nevertheless accept the claim that he was the son of a priest; so, e.g., Scobie, *John the Baptist*, 56; Farmer, "John the Baptist," 96; Hollenbach, "Social Aspects," 852. Goguel, however, remains doubtful (*Au seuil*, 284).

[36] This is done for all Four Gospels and the traditions lying behind them by Wink, *John the Baptist*, and Ernst, *Johannes der Täufer*, 4–216; for Matthew in particular by Trilling, "Die Täufertradition," and Meier, "John the Baptist."

[37] See Ernst, *Johannes der Täufer*, 39–80, 300–19.

[38] Ivan Havener (*Q. The Sayings of Jesus* [Good News Studies 19; Wilmington, DE: Glazier, 1987] 62) remarks: "[In Q] . . . he [the Baptist] is second only to Jesus in importance, and about a tenth of Q is devoted to materials concerning him."

[39] See the remark of John S. Kloppenborg, *The Formation of Q* (Philadelphia: Fortress, 1987) 102–3 n. 2: "Although Bultmann . . . and Lührmann . . . note the congeniality of Q 3:7b–9 with Christian interests, there is nothing specifically Christian here and the oracle is congruent with what is known of John's preaching."

[40] Becker (*Johannes der Täufer*, 16) considers Q to be "clearly the most reliable and characteristic material" we have on the Baptist. According to Becker, the specific nature of the Baptist could not be satisfactorily sketched from Josephus and Mark alone. I will be monitoring this reliability as we examine each verse—for Q is not to be blindly and automatically preferred to Mark every time we meet a Mark-Q overlap—but here I simply note in general that most commentators accept the basic reliability of the Q tradition on the Baptist, especially such non-Christian material as Matt 3:7–10 par. A notable exception is Bultmann (*Geschichte*, 123), who thinks it likely that this material circulated in the early Christian tradition and was then put into the mouth of the Baptist because Christians wanted to be able to report something of John's preaching of repentance. This supposition might seem to hold true especially of Matt 3:7, since a similar saying appears on the lips of Jesus in Matt 23:33: "Snakes, brood of vipers, how will you flee from the judgment of Gehenna?" Actually, in the case of this logion, as in the case of 3:10 (cf. 7:19), it is more probable that Matthew, in his great desire to make John and Jesus parallel figures, has taken Baptist material and placed it on the lips of Jesus. See the argumentation in Meier, "John the Baptist," 390: "Since 'brood of vipers' was apparently already in the Q sermon of the Baptist (Matt 3:7 = Luke 3:7), and since the other two places in Matthew which have 'brood of vipers' have no synoptic parallel, it is likely that, in this case, Matthew has borrowed a phrase from the Baptist and placed it on the lips of Jesus." Hence there is no need to hypothesize, as Kraeling (*John the*

Baptist, 47) does, that the "brood of vipers" saying circulated separately, in isolation from the other Baptist sayings. Likewise, I do not find the objections to the authenticity of Matt 3:7–10 par. raised by Kazmierski ("The Stones of Abraham," 22–39) convincing, as will appear below. In a manner typical of his whole approach, Thyen (*"Baptisma metanoias,"* 137 n. 26) simply affirms without any proof that Matt 3:7–10 par. has been "very thoroughly retouched by Christian hands, if not . . . completely formulated by them." Thyen's article is a strange collection of highly dubious judgments from the Bultmannian and post-Bultmannian schools.

From all that has been said, it should be clear that I completely disagree with Siegfried Schulz's interpretation of the Baptist material in his *Q. Die Spruchquelle der Evangelisten* (Zurich: Theologischer Verlag, 1972); see, e.g., his treatment of Matt 3:7–12 par. on pp. 366–78. For Schulz, all the references to John the Baptist in the Q tradition come from the later stage of Q as formulated by Hellenistic Jewish-Christians in Syria. I shall try to show in all that follows in Chapters 12 and 13 that this reconstruction does not jibe well with the data.

[41] There may be an implied opposition here to being the offspring of Abraham (Matt 3:9). To see a reference to the snake in the Garden of Eden (Gen 3:1), "the ancient serpent who is called the devil and Satan" (Rev 12:9; 20:2), may be reading too much into the text, especially since *echidnōn* is in the plural. On this point I disagree with Ernst (*Johannes der Täufer,* 301), who does see a reference to the devil.

The epithet "vipers" is puzzling insofar as it is "otherwise unknown in the OT, Josephus, or rabbinical writings" (Fitzmyer, *The Gospel According to Luke,* 1. 467); but similar harsh descriptions of the sinful enemies of God's people are found in the documents of Qumran. Especially striking is the parallel vocabulary of judgment in CD 8:7–13: "And each did what was right in his eyes and each chose the stubbornness of his heart. They did not separate themselves from the [sinful] people; they acted without restraint and with arrogance, walking in the way of the wicked. It was of these that God said, 'Their wine is the venom of dragons and the cruel poison [the Hebrew word can also mean 'head'] of cobras' [Deut 32:33]. The dragons are the kings of the peoples and their wine is their ways. And the head of the cobras is the head of the kings of Greece who came to take vengeance on them . . . ; against all of their assembly the anger of God blazed." This parallel in the *Damascus Document* suggests that the Greek word *echidna* does indeed carry its usual meaning of "poisonous snake," "viper." It is remarkable that John would use similar language not of the open enemies of God's people in high places, but rather of apparently pious Jews who come out to him for baptism. John is obviously intent on ripping away from all Jews every assurance of salvation based on traditional claims.

[42] For a survey of the idea in the Bible, see B. T. Dahlberg, "Wrath of God," *IDB,* 4. 903–8; Hermann Kleinknecht, Oskar Grether, Otto Procksch, Johannes Fichtner, Erik Sjöberg, and Gustav Stählin, *"orgē,"* TDNT 5 (1967) 382–447. The prophets' use of the "vocabulary of wrath" to speak of a future day of judgment led naturally into its use in apocalyptic. For examples in the prophets, see, e.g., Isa 13:9; Zeph 1:14–16; 2:2; Ezek 7:19.

[43] Among the OT prophets see Amos 7:4; Ezek 38:22; Mal 3:2; 4:1; Isa 31:9; among the apocalyptic books both in and outside the OT, see Dan 8:19; 9:16; 11:36; *1 Enoch* 89:33; 90:15–27; 102:1–11; *Apocalypse of Abraham* 29:1–21; *2 Apoc. Bar.* 48:1–50; 64:4; *Jub.* 15:33–34; cf. also *Pss. Sol.* 15:4–5; 1QS 2:4–9; CD 1:5; 2:21.

[44] As often with the words of John or Jesus, the exact wording of the "Aramaic original" can be disputed. For example, *mellousēs* might represent a simple *dî 'ātē',*

"which is coming." But the idea might also be expressed by a periphrastic construction for the future tense employing the adjective *'ătîd*, "ready"; see e.g., Dan 3:15: "You shall be ready to fall down," i.e., "you shall be poised to fall down and shall do so as soon as you hear. . . ." (*'îtêkôn 'ătîdîn . . . tippĕlûn*). In later rabbinic Aramaic, the adjective takes on the sense of "destined," "future."

Since there is no clear way of adjudicating such disputes, I will regularly comment on the Greek text, the only sure datum we have. When there is a possible mistranslation of or special nuance in the hypothetical Aramaic, it will be noted. Since, however, we are usually dealing with words of John or Jesus that were probably repeated often during their ministries, the search for *the* Aramaic original may be misplaced from the start. As I have stressed in Part One, we must in general be satisfied with the substance of what John or Jesus said, the *ipsissima vox*, not the exact words spoken on one precise occasion, the *ipsissima verba*. For an overview of the differences in Matthew's and Luke's wording in Matt 3:7–12 par. and an attempt to discern what originally stood in Q, see Schulz, *Q. Die Spruchquelle der Evangelisten*, 366–69.

[45] For basic NT data on *metanoia* and *metanoeō*, see Merklein, "Die Umkehrpredigt," 29–30, and more extensively see J. Behm, "*noeō*, etc.," *TDNT* 4 (1967) 948–1022, esp. the section on *metanoeō, metanoia*, pp. 976–1008. As Merklein points out, only a few of the occurrences of the word in the Gospels are likely to go back to the historical Jesus ("Die Umkehrpredigt," 41). The striking pattern that results, simply on a linguistic level, is that the *word* repentance (not necessarily the reality) has only a marginal place in the preaching of the historical Jesus, while it seems central to the preaching of John. Five (Matt 3:8,11; Mark 1:4; Luke 3:3,8) out of the eight *metanoia* passages in the Synoptics are connected with the Baptist. Of the other three, Luke 24:47 refers to the preaching of the apostles commanded by the risen Jesus, one refers to the joy in heaven over one sinner who repents as opposed to ninety-nine just who need no repentance (Luke 15:7; there is no reference to repentance in the Q parallel, Matt 18:13–14), and only one refers directly to Jesus' ministry ("I did not come to call the just but sinners to repentance"—an obvious Lucan redactional addition; cf. Mark 2:17).

[46] See, e.g., Jer 3:12,14,22. The use of *metanoeō* and *metanoia* to render the Hebrew concept makes its appearance relatively late in the LXX (Sirach, Wisdom of Solomon), but then becomes common in the pseudepigrapha (especially the *Testament of the Twelve Patriarchs*). Kraeling (*John the Baptist*, 70–71) wisely remarks that nowhere in the NT is repentance defined in detail. The reason for this is that the basic OT idea of repentance was presupposed by the Jewish audience of both John and Jesus. What is different in John's proclamation of repentance is its urgency and the way John ties it to his baptism.

[47] Hence, while receiving John's baptism may indeed be included in the "fruit" demanded, I do not think it exhausts the concept, *contra* Merklein, "Die Umkehrpredigt," 37.

[48] Matthew reads the singular "fruit" (*karpon*), while Luke reads the plural "fruits" (*karpous*). Exegetes argue over which is the original reading of Q. For example, Kraeling (*John the Baptist*, 200 n. 7) argues that Matthew's singular form is to be preferred, partly because Luke is clearly trying to improve the logic and partly because the word itself is usually collective in Aramaic. Kazmierski ("The Stones of Abraham," 27) adds the point that Luke may have written the plural to help introduce the concrete examples of such fruits in Luke 3:10–14. Merklein ("Die Umkehrpredigt," 31 n. 17) thinks that in all three differences in Matt 3:7–10 par. (Matt: *karpon axion*, Luke *karpous axious*; Matt *doxēte*, Luke *arxēsthe*; *kai* with no Matthean equivalent in Luke 3:9), Matthew has the more original form.

All this may well be true, and at the very least such considerations warn us against presuming that Luke always represents the more original form of Q. Yet I must admit that I remain uncertain when it comes to such minor points of wording in the Q tradition. In my view, debates about minor differences between Matthew and Luke in Q sayings are often conducted without sufficient data and to no good purpose. I find it difficult enough to affirm the existence of a Q document, though I do think it the more likely hypothesis. To proceed to highly speculative theories about a coherent Q theology (which I do not think existed), about a Q community (which I likewise do not think existed), about distinct layers of Q material that are earlier or later in the development of the document (which I think is trying to know the unknowable), and about which minor variation in a Q saying is more original is, in my opinion, to build a house on sand. As a general rule throughout this book, I will ignore such minor differences between Matthew and Luke when the differences do not affect the basic meaning of the saying(s) involved.

[49] As Kloppenborg notes (*Formation*, 103), it is possible to distinguish in Luke 3:7–9 par. two different criticisms of false confidence: that baptism by itself will save (7b, 8a) and that national privilege will exempt one from judgment (8b,c). As Kloppenborg rightly judges, there is no need to invent a change of audience for the presence of both themes—and, I might add, there is no reason to posit a different author or stratum of tradition every time a new theme appears in a saying or group of sayings.

[50] Ernst (*Johannes der Täufer*, 303–4) sees here an echo of the idea of "the merits of the fathers," a treasury from which all members of the Israelite people could draw. Abraham was blessed by God (Gen 12:1–3), and already in the later books of the OT Abraham became a source of consolation and security for the faithful (Isa 51:2–3). Later rabbinical literature developed the importance of the merits of Abraham or "the merits of the fathers" as a reason for God granting his blessings to Israel; on this see Str-B, 1. 116–21. In fairness, one should note that not all scholars interpret the rabbinic passages in the same way. E. P. Sanders (*Paul and Palestinian Judaism* [Philadelphia: Fortress, 1977] 183–98) decries the uncritical citation of early and late rabbinic sources to create a theology of a "treasury of merits," according to which the merits of the patriarchs could be transferred to sinful Israelites at the last judgment. Sanders stresses that in the early rabbinic literature there is no idea of transfer of merits in a context of the final judgment. While his treatment is a salutary corrective to inaccurate Christian scholarship, his own presentation does not appear entirely free of a certain apologetic slant.

As for Matt 3:9, some might suspect Christian influence on this saying. After all, Paul and other NT authors also fight against trust in physical descent from Abraham as the sure basis of salvation (cf. Galatians 3; Romans 4; John 8:33–39). But the argument of John the Baptist is notably different from that of the NT authors in that it stays within the orbit of Jewish thought. In Matt 3:7–10, salvation based on descent from Abraham is not opposed to salvation through faith, salvation through Jesus Christ, or even salvation through an unspecified messiah. Smug assurance based on physical descent from Abraham is rather opposed to heart-felt repentance that expresses itself in good deeds. Moreover, despite what authors like Jeremias claim (*New Testament Theology*, 48), there is no implication in John's threat that God would give Israel's place to the Gentiles. At most, 3:9 implicitly places Israel on the same level as the Gentiles with regard to the judgment (so Becker, *Johannes der Täufer*, 32). This is radicalism enough—a radicalism Kraeling tries to blunt in his interpretation (*John the Baptist*, 73).

Farmer ("John the Baptist," 959–61) ties in John's teaching about the children of Abraham with the fact that the children had been disinherited by the Roman legions which "occupied" the promised land. Farmer's whole political interpretation of John's message is open to serious question. Here I simply note: (1) In the whole Q sermon (Matt 3:7–10 par.) there is not one clear allusion to any political question. (2) It is not accurate to refer to the whole of Palestine or "the promised land" as occupied by the Roman legions at the time of the Baptist. Galilee and Perea, where he was especially active, were under the rule of Herod Antipas, who—except in times of crisis—used his own soldiers and did not appeal for help to the Roman legions in Syria. For the sake of keeping his Jewish subjects happy, Antipas cultivated the appearance of a true Jewish monarch, even to the point of not putting his image on his coins. In Judea, the ministries of John and Jesus were conducted during a relatively peaceful period when the presence of Roman legions was not needed (see Emil Schürer, *The History of the Jewish People in the Age of Jesus Christ* [4 vols.; ed. Geza Vermes and Fergus Millar; Edinburgh: Clark, 1973–1987] 1. 362). Auxiliary troops were deemed sufficient to maintain order, keep the trade routes open, enforce payment of taxes and tolls, and defend the imperial borders—all that Rome really wanted out of Palestine. A good deal of day-to-day Jewish life in Judea was controlled by the Jerusalem aristocracy.

[51] The demonstrative *toutōn* ("*these* stones") seems to point dramatically to the stones scattered around the ground of the wilderness (unless we are to think of an overliteral translation of the Aramaic demonstrative adjective used to signify the definite article). That John is engaging in an Aramaic wordplay involving the similar sounding words *'abnayyā'* ("stones") and *bĕnayyā'* ("sons") is possible, but as so often such suggestions about Aramaic rhyme and rhythm depend upon choosing one possible retroversion among several candidates. The word *'eben* is not the only Aramaic word for "stone" or "rock," and (if I may push a point) at least later Aramaic at times uses the plural form *bĕrîn* for "sons"—a form that would not create the supposed rhyme.

[52] The proviso "meaningless . . . in view of the imminent judgment" must be properly understood. John is not saying that being a child of Abraham—or for that matter the whole of Israel's salvation history—is meaningless *simpliciter*. He is simply emphasizing in the most rhetorically effective way possible that being a child of Abraham will not serve as automatic protection at the last judgment, if repentance and good works are not shown. This teaching in itself might be unexceptional for many pious Jews. What makes it exceptional is that John ties the necessity of repentance and good works inextricably to the necessity of accepting his message and his baptism. In doing this he implicitly calls the traditional cultic means of atonement and sanctification in Israel, notably the temple sacrifices, into question. But all this remains implicit.

[53] Gnilka (*Jesus von Nazaret*, 79) thinks that John's expectation of an imminent end is so intense that it makes even the eschatological thrust of apocalyptic and the Essenes pale by comparison. As Gnilka phrases it in German, *Naherwartung* ("imminent expectation") becomes with John *Nächsterwartung* ("expecting the end in the very next moment").

[54] Becker (*Johannes der Täufer*, 20) claims that the expectation of an imminent end is even more intense in the Baptist's message than in most Jewish apocalyptic. In the latter, time is often allowed for the "woes of the Messiah" or woes of the end time, the suffering of God's elect that must precede final judgment and salvation. In John's thought there seems to be no time or space for such interim suffering on the part of the elect.

[55] See Ernst, *Johannes der Täufer*, 302–3.

[56] Yet while John's emphasis may be on the decision of the individual Jew, obviously the individual decisions of many Jews add up to a corporate decision by Israel about its

fate on the last day. As so often in the OT prophets, the responsibility of the social unit and the decision of the individual member of the unit are interwoven.

[57] Matthew's redactional tendency is not taken seriously enough by Ben Witherington, III (*The Christology of Jesus* [Minneapolis: Fortress, 1990] 39–40), who tries to take the Matthean audience as historical. The one time Luke does bring the Pharisees and Sadducees together (Acts 23:6–8) serves merely to highlight their differences and to portray them opposing each other in argument. On "Pharisees and Sadducees" as Matthean redaction, see Becker, *Johannes der Täufer*, 64; Schulz, *Q. Die Spruchquelle der Evangelisten*, 366–67. Hence Kraeling's attempt to restrict the historical audience to the priestly aristocracy (*John the Baptist*, 48–49) confuses redactional theology with historical fact. Kazmierski ("The Stones of Abraham," 27–28) hesitates over the point, in my view to no good purpose. Given the clear redactional hand of Matthew, it is amazing that Hollenbach would say with insouciance: "That MT and LK differ with regard to John's audience is of little consequence in determining who that audience was, since an examination of the speech itself shows the audience clearly enough" ("Social Aspects," 860). Actually, the content of the speech confirms the view that the original audience was not limited to the Pharisees and Sadducees. Hollenbach engages in the same sort of psychologizing that marks his mentor Kraeling (see, e.g., the "Pascalian wager" on p. 861); decisions about which verses are addressed to which audiences are quite arbitrary.

[58] On this, see Ernst, *Johannes der Täufer*, 301.

[59] Strange to say, it is this very fact that moves Kazmierski ("The Stones of Abraham," 29) to suggest that the material in Matt 3:7–10 par. may not come from the historical Baptist after all. I think this is to miss the shocking point of what John was all about.

[60] As Merklein notes ("Die Umkehrpredigt," 33), the Baptist does not say: "Unless you repent, the judgment will come." Instead, he says: "The judgment is coming, therefore repent." The call to repentance flows from the certainty that the judgment will come, no matter what anyone does.

[61] The emphasis in John's preaching is definitely on Israel and on individual Israelites. No concern with the whole world, a universal conflagration, or any theory about the two ages (this age and the age to come) is apparent. In this lack of a cosmic perspective John differentiates himself from a good deal of Jewish apocalyptic (so Becker, *Johannes der Täufer*, 29–30). John's preaching is anthropological rather than cosmological, and it aims not at humanity in general but at Israelites in particular.

[62] For example, Hollenbach ("Social Aspects," 857) speaks of him as "an alienated rural priest who was compelled to take up the role of an apocalyptic prophet. . . ."

[63] For a sample of the various attempts to pin down the elusive category of apocalyptic (a noun which some critics insist should be used only as an adjective!), see D. S. Russell, *The Method and Message of Jewish Apocalyptic* (London: SCM, 1964); Becker, *Johannes der Täufer*, 42–43; John J. Collins, "Apocalyptic Eschatology as the Transcendence of Death," *CBQ* 36 (1974) 21–43; idem (ed.), *Apocalypse: The Morphology of a Genre* (Semeia 14; Missoula, MT: Scholars, 1979)—see in particular John J. Collins's "Introduction: Towards the Morphology of a Genre," 1–20; Paul D. Hanson, *The Dawn of Apocalyptic* (rev. ed.; Philadelphia: Fortress, 1979)—especially the appendix, "An Overview of Early Jewish and Christian Apocalypticism," 427–44; the same basic presentation can be found in Hanson's article on "apocalypticism" in *IDBSup*, 28–34. Hanson's distinctions—"apocalypse" as a literary genre, "apocalyptic eschatology" as

a religious perspective for viewing divine plans in relation to mundane realities, and "apocalypticism" as a symbolic universe that an alienated group uses to establish its identity over against the dominant society—are helpful, but many unrepentant authors continue to use "apocalyptic" as a noun to cover all three realities.

[64] Becker (*Johannes der Täufer*, 59–60) observes that John, like the Teacher of Righteousness at Qumran, speaks in a simple, direct, yet authoritative "I-form." Unlike the common locution often met in the OT prophets, the "I" means not Yahweh, who speaks his message through the prophet he has sent, but rather the individual human person doing the proclaiming. Becker notes (p. 62) that, while the Teacher of Righteousness grounds his authority in a special revelation given to him, John does not seem to feel the need for any such legitimation when he says "I."

Two observations may be made on Becker's claim: (1) It is true that the authentic sayings of the Baptist preserved for us in the Gospels do not ground John's authority in any precise way. But then we must remember how few those sayings are. (2) John's use of an authoritative, prophetic "I" without explicit appeal to legitimation is not without some analogy in the OT. David Noel Freedman has pointed out to me (letter of Dec. 4, 1990) that "practically everything Moses says in the Book of Deuteronomy is also in the first person, meaning Moses rather than Yahweh. Most of it is reminiscence about what happened forty years before, but still in his exhortations, he keeps repeating that Israel must listen to what 'I am telling you today.' "

[65] Becker (*Johannes der Täufer*, 43–62) gives a typology of four prophetic figures: a prophet like the OT prophets, a political-national prophet, an eschatological prophet, and a prophetic charismatic like the Teacher of Righteousness at Qumran. Becker identifies John with this last type; I would include characteristics of a type of eschatological prophet. Ernst likewise offers a typology (*Johannes der Täufer*, 290–300): apocalyptic prophet, visionary prophet, messianic prophet, Elijah the prophetic messenger of judgment, the prophet like Moses, and a prophetic charismatic. Ernst prefers to stress that John fit no one category, although he possessed some elements of almost every category. One cannot help feeling that the neat categories probably exist more in the minds of modern critics than in the consciousness of the ancient Jews.

[66] For brief discussions of the concept of eschatology and its relation to apocalyptic, see Richard H. Hiers, "Eschatology," *Harper's Bible Dictionary* (ed. Paul J. Achtemeier; San Francisco: Harper & Row, 1985) 275–77; Elizabeth Schüssler Fiorenza, "Eschatology of the NT," *IDBSup*, 271–77; Adela Yarbro Collins, "Eschatology and Apocalypticism," *NJBC*, 1359–64.

[67] Becker (*Johannes der Täufer*, 27) comments that the punitive fire is as real for John as the water of baptism.

[68] Becker (*Johannes der Täufer*, 20) rightly warns against calling an eschatological scenario "apocalyptic" simply because it contains some apocalyptic motifs. Against Ernst Käsemann (see, e.g., Käsemann's "On the Subject of Primitive Christian Apocalyptic," *New Testament Questions Today* [New Testament Library; London: SCM, 1969] 111–13), he thinks that the Baptist stands at a considerable distance from apocalyptic, though not in direct contradiction to it (p. 68). Kazmierski's definition of Matt 3:7–10 par. as "the rebellion of a radical Apocalypticism" (a judgment which supports his suspicion that the material in Matt 3:7–10 par. does not go back to the historical Baptist but rather to early Christian charismatic preachers in Palestine) is, in my opinion, too unnuanced a statement; see his "The Stones of Abraham," 33.

[69] For one example, see Marcus J. Borg, *Jesus. A New Vision* (San Francisco: Harper

& Row, 1987), esp. pp. 1–21. It is perhaps not by accident that there is no extensive treatment of John the Baptist and his eschatological outlook in the book.

[70] Adela Yarbro Collins ("Eschatology," 1362) remarks: "The clear eschatological character of JBap's activity and teaching suggests that Jesus ought to be interpreted in the same context." Becker (*Johannes der Täufer*, 71–73) stresses that the Baptist and Jesus shared a basic orientation to a future that was controlled by God alone, though Jesus had his particular stance, which relegated the Baptist to past history (pp. 75–76). Indeed, when Becker summarizes his book in fourteen theses (pp. 105–6), he lays down his third thesis in these words (p. 105): "Jesus shares the exclusive orientation to the future with the Baptist." In my view, that statement shows the same sort of extremism on the part of the "future eschatology" school that Hollenbach shows on the side of the "realized eschatology" school when he claims that, after Jesus broke with the Baptist, "Jesus focuses now (at least for the moment) wholly on the present and all interest in the future is beside the point" ("The Conversion of Jesus," 217). Such a claim cannot be substantiated from any critical reading of the data. Hollenbach often decides that various logia are authentic or inauthentic without detailed argumentation, and he just as uncritically distributes logia over various periods of time or to different audiences without sufficient justification.

[71] Merklein, "Die Umkehrpredigt," 32, echoing Becker.

[72] Morris M. Faierstein ("Why Do the Scribes Say That Elijah Must Come First?" *JBL* 100 [1981] 75–86) maintains that there is no firm proof that the idea of Elijah preparing the way for the Messiah was known in pre-Christian Judaism. Dale C. Allison (" 'Elijah Must Come First,' " *JBL* 103 [1984] 256–58) tries to salvage some pre-Christian tradition; but Joseph A. Fitzmyer ("More About Elijah Coming First," *JBL* 104 [1985] 295–96) holds that Allison does not succeed in undermining Faierstein's basic argument. Also denying that there was a fixed pre-Christian idea of Elijah as the forerunner of the Messiah is J. A. T. Robinson, "Elijah, John and Jesus," *Twelve New Testament Studies*, 28–52.

[73] Hendrikus Boers (*Who Was Jesus? The Historical Jesus and the Synoptic Gospels* [San Francisco: Harper & Row, 1989] 35) states apodictically: "The saying concerning the greater one who is to follow is clearly of Christian origin and again places John in a position secondary to Jesus." As usual in Boers's volume, there is no extended argumentation to establish this point; it is simply affirmed. This exemplifies the larger problem of a slim work that attempts in one hundred thirty-one pages to introduce beginners to a study of the Synoptic Gospels through source and redaction criticism and at the same time to write a sketch of the historical Jesus. It is symptomatic that there are no footnotes and the opinions of other scholars are not seriously debated. Instead, Boers simply announces from the start his thesis that Jesus considered John the final, decisive, eschatological figure who marked the turning of the ages; "the kingdom of God had been initiated by the return of Elijah in the person of John" (p. xiii). Gospel texts are then declared authentic or inauthentic, are rejected or rewritten, according to this thesis. Faced with this lack of a disciplined method, one is not surprised to read: "That his [Jesus'] followers were armed when he was arrested in Gethsemane makes it difficult to deny with certainty that he himself had become involved in armed resistance against the Romans" (p. xv). The book is a tour de force, but also a primary example of arbitrary exegesis engineered to sustain a thesis.

[74] The varied agreements and disagreements of the Johannine form of the logion with Mark, Q, and Acts argues well for John 1:27 representing an independent strand of the oral tradition; see C. H. Dodd, *Historical Tradition in the Fourth Gospel* (Cambridge:

Cambridge University, 1963) 253–56; Raymond E. Brown, *The Gospel According to John* (AB 29 and 29A; Garden City, NY: Doubleday, 1966, 1970) 1. 52. As will be noted below, Acts 13:25 has three readings that agree with John rather than with Luke 3:16; hence Acts may in this case represent not just Luke's rewriting of what he has already presented in his Gospel, but an independent tradition.

[75] For the strict parallelism being more original, see Dibelius, *Die urchristliche Über-lieferung*, 54; Ernst Lohmeyer, *Das Evangelium des Markus* (MeyerK 1/2; 17th ed.; Göttingen: Vandenhoeck & Ruprecht, 1967) 17.

[76] To deal with the major variants: (1) The verb *erchetai* ("there comes") is probably more original than the attributive participle *ho erchomenos* ("the coming one"). It is not by accident that the two Gospels with the two most consistently high christologies, Matthew and John, have transformed the main verb *erchetai* into a "title" of Jesus, a title which, for Matthew, neatly connects with the Baptist's question in Matt 11:3 par.: "Are you the coming one *(ho erchomenos)*?" The title also foreshadows the salutation of Ps 118:26 that the crowd cries out at the triumphal entry in all Four Gospels (Matt 21:9 parr.): "Blessed is the coming one *(ho erchomenos)*." The participial form is there-fore more likely an assimilation to Christian belief (so Ernst, *Johannes der Täufer*, 50); but for some doubts on this point, see Kloppenborg, *Formation*, 104. (2) The phrase "to carry his sandals" instead of "to loose the strap of his sandals" is unique to Matthew and is simply a variation of the basic metaphor; both forms of the metaphor depict the lowly service of a slave. (3) The choice between baptism with the holy spirit (Mark, John) and baptism with the holy spirit and fire (Matthew, Luke) will be discussed at greater length below, but at the very least multiple attestation (Mark, John, and possibly Acts versus Q) argues in favor of the simple "holy spirit," as does rhetorical balance.

It is difficult to make a decision about *opisō mou* ("after me"). Eduardo Arens (*The ēlthon-Sayings in the Synoptic Tradition* [OBO 10; Fribourg: Editions Universitaires; Göttingen: Vandenhoeck & Ruprecht, 1976] 289) thinks that, of the three Synoptic forms, Luke has preserved the oldest; hence the absence of *opisō mou* is original. I remain doubtful because (1) Mark, Matthew, and John (and indirectly Acts 13:25, which has the variant formulation *met' eme*) agree on including *opisō mou*, and (2) in my view Luke's version is not in all respects original, since the Q order A–B–A' in Luke 3:16 seems to me secondary. To indicate my uncertainty, I put the phrase in brackets.

Minor variations like (1) Mark's aorist *ebaptisa* and his graphic *kypsas* (1:7), (2) Mat-thew's addition of *eis metanoian* in v 11, and (3) Acts' omission of *ton himanta* and addition of *tōn podōn* (13:25, which seems to shift the image to taking the sandals off the feet) are most likely secondary. Some, like Gnilka (*Jesus von Nazaret*, 82), think that the logion expressing John's great humility ("There comes after me one stronger than I; the strap of his sandals I am not worthy to loose") arose only later in the tra-dition.

[77] Becker (*Johannes der Täufer*, 34) lists five major streams of interpretation: the stronger one is the Messiah, the Son of Man, God, the eschatological prophet, or some unknown figure. Like Lohmeyer (*Das Urchristentum*, 159) before him, Becker (p. 35) prefers to see here a reference to the Son of Man. Similarly, Kraeling (*John the Baptist*, 57) speaks of the messianic judge who is not human, but rather the "angelic manlike one" of Daniel 7. Scobie (*John the Baptist*, 62–73) claims that John spoke of a Messiah who would baptize with a punitive fire and a saving spirit. Similarly, in his article "Die essenischen Tauchbäder und die Johannestaufe," *RevQ* 3 [1961] 185–207, Joachim Gnilka seemed to lean in the direction of thinking that John was referring to the Mes-siah; however, in his book (*Jesus von Nazaret*, 82) he states that the one who baptizes with the holy spirit is either God or the apocalyptic Son of Man. While issuing no final

decision, he appears to favor the latter. Hughes ("John the Baptist," 195) holds that the stronger one is Yahweh himself; so too Thyen, *"baptisma metanoias,"* 136 n. 15; Ernst, *Johannes der Täufer*, 50, 305, 309. Robinson ("Elijah, John and Jesus," 28–31) suggests that John meant an Elijah-like prophet of the end time.

[78] Hughes ("John the Baptist," 195–96) tries to answer the objections to taking God as the stronger one, but he never really overcomes the difficulties I list.

[79] *Contra* Ernst, *Johannes der Täufer*, 50. Ernst's choice has the strange result of deciding in effect that only Acts 13:25 and John 1:27 come close to the original form at this point: "After me there comes one, the strap of whose sandal. . . ." Arens (*The elthon-Sayings*, 289) claims that *ho ischyroteros* was likewise lacking in the earliest form of the saying, simply because John and Acts omit it. In my opinion, John might well have omitted the phrase "one stronger than I" because his high christology would reject the very idea of making the Word made flesh just comparatively stronger than John. Brown (*John*, 1. 53) thinks that the Fourth Evangelist substitutes the phrase "the one among you whom you do not recognize" for "the one stronger than I" to suggest the idea of the hidden Messiah. It is also possible, though, that the adaptation of the saying to Johannine theology had already occurred in the Johannine tradition before the Evangelist took up the material.

[80] It is symptomatic of the embarrassment that this metaphor causes those who want to interpret the stronger one as God that Ernst (*Johannes der Täufer*, 52) suggests that the motif of untying the strap of the sandals was added secondarily by Luke to a primitive Q logion that lacked the metaphor. The need to rewrite so much of the text to safeguard the interpretation of the stronger one as God should move one to rethink the interpretation. A similar approach is found in Kloppenborg, *Formation*, 104. Kloppenborg argues that the clause referring to the untying of the strap is secondary, but must immediately admit that the addition had to have occurred very early on, since it is found in Mark, Q, and John (some might want to add Acts). Indeed, the multiple attestation amid differences in wording in the whole saying is so strong that the secondary nature of the clause must be considered unlikely. Kloppenborg's only argument for the secondary nature of the clause, namely, that it emphasizes John's inferiority, misinterprets the profession of inferiority. John does declare himself inferior to the coming judge, who may be, in his view, God, an angel, or some other super-human being. It is hardly a sure sign of Christian redaction that John should declare his inferiority vis-à-vis that kind of judge.

[81] Kloppenborg (*Formation*, 104) thinks that the reference is either to God or to some "supra-human (angelic) figure. . . ."

[82] To suggest that the Baptist meant "*the* apocalyptic Son of Man" who will act as judge on the last day is to presuppose that there was a clear, uniform concept of such a figure in Palestinian Judaism in the early 1st century A.D. The fact that the dating of the *Parables of Enoch* (1 *Enoch* 37–71) is still debated, with the *Parables* being possibly later than the 1st century, makes such a presupposition precarious. Likewise, it is questionable whether Judaism at this time looked forward to a Davidic Messiah who would be the judge on the last day and punish the wicked with inextinguishable fire. The picture of the ideal Davidic king in *Pss. Sol.* 17 is much more political and of this world, though he is singularly empowered by God to see justice triumph in Jerusalem.

[83] To appeal for elucidation to the *ischyros* terminology of the Beelzebul controversy (Mark 3:27; Matt 12:29; Luke 11:21–22) may be legitimate on the level of redactional theology, but cannot be done when one is trying to reconstruct the historical proclamation of the Baptist.

[84] The one point of coincidence between Matt 3:10 and 3:12 is the act of burning with fire. The same action in both verses could argue for the identification of the stronger one as God. However, in v 12 the burning is merely the logical conclusion of the central metaphor of separating. One must also accept the fact that apocalyptic is not always consistent in its use of metaphors, indeed, even in its basic line of thought. Another possibility remains: originally, Matt 3:12 belonged with sayings like Matt 3:10; a christological reference was created when Christians who collected the Q material placed 3:12 after 3:11, with which it formerly had nothing to do.

[85] In a letter to me dated Dec. 4, 1990, David Noel Freedman remarks: "The prophet is primarily the messenger, the one who brings the word of God, and not the executor, who in the OT is the royal figure. The prophet may remain as adviser, but usually there is at least one other person to come, who is to carry out the task. Who or what kind of person that should be is left obscure. . . . Given John's obvious prophetic self-assurance . . . , and his insistence that anyone who repented must be baptized personally by him, it is not likely that he was looking for someone who would do much the same thing, but rather for a different kind of person, who would be empowered by the spirit to take over and restore and renew Israel. That could be someone like Moses, who was the prophet par excellence, but better known as Law-giver and Founder of the State, or someone like David who established the kingdom of Israel. Even a priestly type, like Melchizedek, would not be excluded, but John does not seem to have been thinking along those lines."

[86] Although the risen Jesus does not introduce the words of the Baptist with some phrase like "as the Baptist prophesied . . ." (something that would sound ridiculous and demeaning in the mouth of the risen Lord), Luke obviously intends his readers to catch the reference back to Luke 3:16. Putting the matter a little differently, Hans Conzelmann remarks: "The saying cited in our passage seems in the course of the tradition to have changed from a word of the Baptist . . . into a word of Jesus" (*Die Apostelgeschichte* [MeyerK 3; 6th ed.; Göttingen: Vandenhoeck & Ruprecht, 1968] 111).

[87] It is strange that many of the major commentaries on Acts (e.g., those of Jackson and Lake, Haenchen, Bruce, Conzelmann, and Schneider) do not examine the source question in detail, especially the question why Luke should use a form similar to Mark's when the Q form he has already used in his Gospel fits the Pentecost event much better. The same is true of Ernst's treatment of Acts 1:5; 11:16; and 13:25 in his study of the Baptist in Acts (*Johannes der Täufer*, 140–43, 145–47, though see n. 21 on p. 146). Gerhard Lofink (*Die Himmelfahrt Jesu* [SANT 26; Munich: Kösel, 1971] 153, 256–57) thinks that Acts 1:5 has as its source Mark 1:8 and that Luke himself has placed it in Acts 1, where from a tradition-history point of view it is entirely secondary. Why Luke should have chosen the Marcan over the Lucan form when it is the latter that fits the immediate context in Acts 1 is never explained.

One possible solution would be to claim that Luke intends the shorter version of the saying in Acts 1:5 to imply the longer version already known to the reader from Luke 3:16. This presupposes a reader with a long, computer-like memory. More to the point, if Luke intended to write simply a "shorthand" version of Luke 3:16 in Acts 1:5, why did he not abbreviate the prediction in a way that would preserve the one symbol (fire) that was so specific to the Pentecost event?

[88] See, e.g., Scobie, *John the Baptist*, 70–73; Ernst (*Johannes der Täufer*, 16), who thinks that Mark suppressed the words "and fire," which were present in the tradition Mark knew (this brings us close to the self-subverting position that Mark knew Q). With some hesitation, Ernst attributes the idea of baptism with salvific spirit and puni-

tive fire to the Baptist himself, though he allows that Christian reinterpretation may have highlighted the aspect of the salvific spirit (pp. 305–9). Kloppenborg (*Formation*, 106–7) remains uncertain whether Q originally read "spirit and fire" or just "fire."

[89] Rightly Scobie, *John the Baptist*, 67.

[90] The difficulty is not removed by claiming that the fire is either salvific or destructive, depending on the person on whom it is poured. Presumably the spirit is meant in the positive, salvific, cleansing and life-giving sense. What, then, is the sense of the whole statement if it must be understood to say: "He will baptize you with the salvific holy spirit and with the salvific-or-destructive fire"? One can see why some people who ponder this interpretation are finally drawn to the radical expedient of deleting "holy spirit" and retaining only "fire." For my objections to this radical solution, see below.

[91] This is the approach, e.g., of Scobie, *John the Baptist*, 73: "Upon the wicked, the Coming One will pour out a river of fire to punish and destroy them; but on God's people the Coming One will pour out God's spirit. . . ." Similarly, Gnilka, *Jesus von Nazaret*, 81.

[92] It is telling that Ernst (*Johannes der Täufer*, 54) must take this arbitrary approach to make sense of the text.

[93] It is natural for Christian readers to import into the text the message of the parable of the wheat and the weeds or the parable of the wise and foolish virgins. But this is indeed to *import* a Christian (and a strongly Matthean) Gospel theme into a text that is notably lacking in specifically Christian modes of thought.

[94] In favor of the longer Q tradition of the logion one might invoke a principle of text criticism: *lectio difficilior potior* (the more difficult reading is the better reading, since scribes would tend to rewrite a difficult text to make it more intelligible). Yet like any rule-of-thumb in text criticism, this one has its limits. The more difficult reading must still be shown to render some intelligible meaning in the given context. My contention is that this is not the case with the Q version of the saying on the two baptisms.

[95] Perhaps the most famous sustainer of this view is Dibelius, *Die urchristliche Überlieferung*, 50, 56. His arguments, though, are weak. He appeals to the story of the disciples of the Baptist in Acts 19:1–7, with no critical sense that we have here a product of Luke's redactional theology, which wants to promote the irenic idea that disciples of the Baptist are already semi-Christians who only need further instruction. To take their declaration that they had never heard that there was a holy spirit too literally would mean that they had never heard about the "spirit of holiness" spoken of in the OT and reflected upon further in the intertestamental literature and the documents of Qumran; that is hardly likely. What Luke means in his composition is that these sincere followers of John had not realized that the holy spirit was now present and being conferred in the Christian church. Once they find out the truth, they naturally join the church. To deduce from this piece of Lucan propaganda that the historical Baptist, unlike the OT prophets or his neighbors at Qumran, never spoke of the spirit is completely illegitimate. Dibelius seems intent on making the Baptist a preacher almost exclusively of judgment and damnation. See the criticism of Dibelius in Ernst, *Johannes der Täufer*, 306–7.

One might take another tack and argue that the simple "he will baptize you with fire" meets two criteria of text criticism for choosing the original reading: (1) the more difficult reading is the better reading (*lectio difficilior potior*), since scribes would tend to change difficult statements to ones more readily understandable (hence the addition or substitution of "holy spirit"); and (2) all things being equal, the shorter reading is to be preferred, since scribes tended to add rather than subtract. Actually, even in text criticism, these two rules-of-thumb are not absolute, and they really do not apply here. (1) On the surface, the neat balance between water and fire hardly seems the more difficult reading. Paradoxically, though, when one considers what the symbols must mean in the context of John's sermon, one might argue instead that "fire" by itself is not just difficult but unintelligible. (2) NT text criticism knows many cases where later scribes apparently abbreviated longer readings, and so the second axiom is far from axiomatic. More to the point, these rules are meant to be applied when judging among a number of extant readings in various manuscripts. What is forgotten is that "he will baptize you with fire" is witnessed by none of the ancient manuscripts; it is not properly a *lectio* at all. It is a purely conjectural reconstruction, to which appeal should be made only as a last resort, when all the extant readings are judged impossible. That is not the case here.

Another approach which is also open to the objection of preferring purely hypothetical reconstructions to the empirical data of the texts is found in Schulz, *Q. Die Spruchquelle der Evangelisten*, 368–71. The two-source theory is revised so that the final redactor of Mark (as opposed to other redactors of Mark?) knows Q material, although Schulz remains coy about whether this final redactor knows the Q document. This sleight of hand allows almost any reworking of the hypothetical Q text and hypothetical Marcan traditions one desires. Schulz does not seem to have noticed that to posit Mark's knowledge of Q is to destroy the basic argument for the existence of a written Q document—which by definition is the material common to Matthew and Luke but not known to Mark.

[96] Rudolf Laufen, *Die Doppelüberlieferungen der Logienquelle und des Markusevangeliums* (BBB 54; Königstein/Ts.-Bonn: Hanstein, 1980) 93–125. In general, of the nine passages Laufen subjects to detailed analysis in his monograph, Q represents the more original form in four cases, Mark in two cases, while in three cases both Mark and Q contain elements that are more original (p. 385).

[97] It is quite common to see explanations of *erchetai . . . opisō mou* that claim that the saying originally referred to some person who "followed after" John in the sense of following him in his entourage as a disciple. Such explanations then go on to claim that the logion originally described Jesus as a disciple of John. See, e.g., Ulrich Wilckens, *Die Missionsreden der Apostelgeschichte* (WMANT 5; 3d ed.; Neukirchen-Vluyn: Neukirchener Verlag, 1974) 103, including n. 3; he in turn appeals to Lohmeyer, *Das Evangelium des Markus*, 18. While that *might* have been the meaning when the saying was eventually applied to Jesus, such a meaning makes no sense if the historical Baptist actually spoke this prophecy about some future figure, be that figure God or some unspecified greater human or angelic being. In such a context, the *opisō* must carry a temporal sense. Moreover, once Christians did apply this saying to Jesus, it is not clear why they would have wanted to change the temporal reference to a statement about Jesus' being a disciple of the Baptist. Whether or not Jesus was historically John's disciple, it is unlikely that Christians would have gone out of their way to reinterpret sayings to emphasize Jesus' dependence on John when no such thought existed in the original logion.

[98] For citations from the rabbinic literature, see Str-B, 1. 121.

[99] Perhaps the most famous OT prophecy concerning the pouring out of God's spirit in the last days is Joel 3:1–5, cited by Peter in his Pentecost sermon in Acts 2:17–21. But the image of God's spirit being poured out or sprinkled on Israel was widespread in postexilic Judaism, both in the OT and in intertestamental literature. See, e.g., Ezek 39:29 ("I have poured out my spirit on the house of Israel"); Isa 32:15 ("the spirit . . .

is poured out upon us"); 44:3 ("I will pour out water . . . ; I will pour out my spirit"). Important also are passages where the images of water and spirit are used in tandem, even when the spirit is not explicitly said to be poured out or sprinkled: e.g., Ps 51:4,9–14 (water cleanses, spirit renews); Ezek 36:25–27 ("I will sprinkle clean water on you. . . . I will put a new spirit in you"). Remarkable images are found in the Dead Sea scrolls; see 1QS 3:6–9 ("by the spirit . . . are the ways of a man atoned for . . . ; by the spirit of holiness . . . is he cleansed from all his iniquities . . . ; his flesh is cleansed by sprinkling the water of purification and by being sanctified with the water of cleanliness . . ."); 4:20–22 ("God . . . [will] cleanse him with the spirit of holiness from all evil deeds and will sprinkle upon him the spirit of faithfulness like the water of purification . . ."); 1QH 7:6–7 ("you have sprinkled your holy spirit upon me"); 17:26 ("you have sprinkled your holy spirit upon your servant").

As is clear from some of these quotations, there would be nothing unusual in the Baptist speaking of "the holy spirit" or "God's holy spirit." The phrase, especially in the Semitic form "spirit of holiness," is found both in the OT and in the apocryphal/ pseudepigraphic literature, including that of Qumran; see, e.g., Isa 63:10,11 [the Hebrew reads *rûaḥ qodšô*, "the spirit of his holiness," which the LXX translates as *to pneuma to hagion (autou)*, "(his) holy spirit"]; Dan 5:11 [Aramaic: *rûaḥ ʾĕlāhîn qaddîšîn*, "spirit of the holy God," translated by the LXX Dan 5:12 simply as *pneuma hagion*]; Wis 9:17; LXX Sir 48:12 (in the codex Alexandrinus); 4 Ezra 14:22; *Martyrdom of Isaiah* 5:14; *Pss. Sol.* 17:37; 1QS 4:21; 8:16; CD 2:12.

[100] Kraeling (*John the Baptist*, 62–63) has the curious theory that, though "holy spirit," not "fire," was original to the saying, "spirit" referred originally to the purging and destructive breath of the Messiah. (One might recall the spirit-filled scion of David in Isa 11:1–9, who dispenses justice and execution with the breath [= spirit] of his mouth.) Hence later Christians simply added the epexegetical "fire" to explain that John was speaking of the "fiery" holy spirit; this is how the Q form arose. Kraeling's theory of an original form that spoke only of a destructive spirit is basically subject to the objections aimed at the theory that "fire" alone stood in the original saying.

[101] The winnowing fan was a fork-like shovel. The harvested grain was first threshed, i.e., the kernels were beaten or ground free of stalks and straw. Then on the threshing floor (a level space of rock or packed earth exposed to the sky), the farmer would toss the threshed material into the air with the winnowing fan. The heavier edible grain would fall back onto the threshing floor and be gathered into barns. The inedible chaff, being lighter, was blown on the sides of the threshing floor by the wind; it was gathered up and used as fuel.

[102] For a balanced overview of the question, see Ernst, *Johannes der Täufer*, 93–98, 312–13.

[103] See the comments in Kraeling, *John the Baptist*, 65–66.

[104] The question of a possible correlation between what Josephus says about the Baptist's ministry and Luke 3:10–14 is taken up in the conclusion of the excursus on the Baptist in Josephus, placed at the end of this chapter.

[105] I trust the reader appreciates that this description of Luke is a wry caricature of an all-too-common interpretation of Luke, an interpretation I do not share.

[106] It is strange that Scobie (*John the Baptist*, 85–86, 89, 115, 210) seems to presume that the material goes back to the Baptist, but he never argues the point.

[107] Bultmann, *Geschichte*, 155. It is interesting to watch how Bultmann reasons to this conclusion. The material cannot come from the early church, since the profession of

soldier is taken for granted; and it does not seem Jewish. What Bultmann means by either of these affirmations is not clear. More telling is the fact that the possibility that the teaching might really come from the Baptist is never considered. Bammel ("The Baptist," 105) has the curious theory that Luke most likely created 3:10–14 to provide a substitute for something more revolutionary that was in Q; this idea stems from Bammel's misreading of what Josephus says about John. However, the suggestion that Luke may have composed these verses is restricted to no one school; for instance, it is also entertained seriously by Gnilka, *Jesus von Nazaret*, 81. Hence Gnilka rules out these verses as a source of the Baptist's intentions.

[108] See Heinz Schürmann, *Das Lukasevangelium* (HTKNT 3; Freiburg/Basel/Vienna: Herder, 1969) 1. 169. It is strange that he argues that the passage is from Q on the grounds that it is similar to Luke 7:29–30, which contrasts the unrepentant leaders of the people with the people and the tax collectors, who accepted John's baptism. The linchpin of his argument is the presumption that 7:29–30 is also from Q, a point which is by no means certain, since it has only a vague parallel in Matt 21:31–32. Schürmann's further suggestion that Matthew omitted Luke 3:10–14 because he wanted to reserve ethical instruction to Jesus does not jibe well with Matthew's tendency to make John and Jesus parallel figures and to place the basic kerygma and call to repentance of Jesus (Matt 4:17) in the mouth of John (3:2). On such parallelism, see Meier, "John the Baptist in Matthew's Gospel," 383–405. In a manner similar to Schürmann's, Harald Sahlin ("Die Früchte der Umkehr," *ST* 1 [1947] 54–68) attempts to argue that it would have been unnecessary and unfitting for Matthew to include in his Gospel the Q material contained in Luke 3:10–14 when just a chapter or so later Matthew would present a more radical ethic at greater length in the Sermon on the Mount.

[109] Fitzmyer (*The Gospel According to Luke*, 1. 464) leans in this direction, though he does not exclude composition by Luke.

[110] These are listed by Schürmann, *Das Lukasevangelium*, 1. 169 n. 53: *elegen* and *eipen* with the dative, *metadidonai*, *homoiōs*, the absolute *ho echōn*, and *didaskale*.

[111] Schürmann (*Das Lukasevangelium*, 1. 169 n. 54) lists as Lucan redactional traits: *eperōtan*, *eipa*, *de kai*, *diatassō*, *prassō* in the sense of demand or exact, *pleon*, *strateuomai*, *opsōnion*, and *sykophanteō*.

[112] E.g., minor problems of syntax involve the precise relationship of the first four verses of the Gospel. I incline to the view that, since Mark elsewhere in his Gospel never begins a sentence with *kathōs*, the sense of vv 1–2 is: "The beginning of the proclaiming of the good news of Jesus Christ the Son of God [took place] in accordance with what stands written in the book of Isaiah the prophet: 'Behold, I send my messenger before your face. . . .'" Another, though less likely, solution is that *archē* in v 1 is the subject, *egeneto* in v 4 the verb, and *Iōannēs* the predicate nominative of one long sentence, with vv 2–3 a very lengthy parenthesis. Medium problems of text criticism include the presence (so Vaticanus, Bezae) or absence (so Sinaiticus) of "Son of God" in v 1. On grounds of the strong textual attestation, the internal structure of the whole Gospel, and its development of the "Son secret," revealed to humans only in 15:39 (the centurion at the cross), I think it likely that the author lets the audience in on the secret in the first verse.

As for the major problems of overall Marcan theology, a representative sampling of opinions and methods can be found in the following books: William Wrede, *Das Messiasgeheimnis in den Evangelien* (4th ed.; Göttingen: Vandenhoeck & Ruprecht, 1969, originally 1901); James N. Robinson, *The Problem of History in Mark* (SBT 21; Naperville, IL: Allenson, 1957); Willi Marxsen, *Der Evangelist Markus* (FRLANT 67; Göttingen: Vandenhoeck & Ruprecht, 1959); Ulrich W. Mauser, *Christ in the Wilderness* (SBT 39; Naperville, IL; Allenson, 1963); Ernest Best, *The Temptation and the Passion: The Markan Soteriology* (SNTSMS 2; Cambridge: Cambridge University, 1965); Rudolf Pesch, *Naherwartungen. Tradition und Redaktion in Markus 13* (Düsseldorf: Patmos, 1968); Quentin Quesnell, *The Mind of Mark* (AnBib 38; Rome: Biblical Institute, 1969); Karl-Georg Reploh, *Markus—Lehrer der Gemeinde* (SBM 9; Stuttgart: KBW, 1969); Theodore J. Weeden, *Mark. Traditions in Conflict* (Philadelphia: Fortress, 1971); Aloysius M. Ambrozic, *The Hidden Kingdom* (CBQMS 2; Washington, DC: CBA, 1972); Madeleine Boucher, *The Mysterious Parable. A Literary Study* (CBQMS 6; Washington, DC: CBA, 1977); Howard Clark Kee, *Community of the New Age* (Macon, GA: Mercer University, 1977); David Rhoads and Donald Michie, *Mark as Story. An Introduction to the Narrative of a Gospel* (Philadelphia: Fortress, 1982); Ernest Best, *Mark. The Gospel as Story* (Edinburgh: Clark, 1983); idem, *Disciples and Discipleship* (Edinburgh: Clark, 1986); Jack Dean Kingsbury, *The Christology of Mark's Gospel* (Philadelphia: Fortress, 1983); Christopher Tuckett (ed.), *The Messianic Secret* (Issues in Religion and Theology 1; Philadelphia: Fortress; London: SPCK, 1983); Vernon K. Robbins, *Jesus the Teacher* (Philadelphia: Fortress, 1984); Martin Hengel, *Studies in the Gospel of Mark* (Philadelphia: Fortress, 1985); Elizabeth Struthers Malbon, *Narrative Space and Mythic Meaning in Mark* (San Francisco: Harper & Row, 1986); Frank J. Matera, *What Are They Saying About Mark?* (New York/Mahwah, NJ: Paulist, 1987); Burton L. Mack, *A Myth of Innocence* (Philadelphia: Fortress, 1988); Scaria Kuthirakkattel, *The Beginning of Jesus' Ministry According to Mark's Gospel (1,14–3,6)* (AnBib 123; Rome: Biblical Institute, 1990); John Paul Heil, *The Gospel of Mark as a Model for Action* (New York/Mahwah, NJ: Paulist, 1992); Janice Capel Anderson and Stephen D. Moore, *Mark & Method* (Minneapolis: Fortress, 1992); Adela Yarbro Collins, *The Beginning of the Gospel* (Minneapolis: Fortress, 1992); Robert H. Gundry, *Mark* (Grand Rapids: Eerdmans, 1993).

Articles and essays of interest, especially on the opening of Mark's Gospel, Mark's christology, and various aspects of his theology and historical setting include: R. H. Lightfoot, "The First Chapter of St. Mark's Gospel," *The Gospel Message of St. Mark* (Oxford: Oxford University, 1950) 15–30; Leander E. Keck, "The Introduction to Mark's Gospel," *NTS* 12 (1965–66) 352–70; J. M. Gibbs, "Mark 1,1–15, Matthew 1,1–4,16, Luke 1,1–4,30, John 1,1–51. The Gospel Prologues and Their Function," *Studia Evangelica. Vol. VI* (TU 112; ed. E. Livingstone; Berlin: Akademie, 1973) 154–88; Gerhard Arnold, "Mk 1:1 und Eröffnungswendungen in griechischen und lateinischen Schriften," *ZNW* 68 (1977) 123–27; G. Dautzenberg, "Die Zeit des Evangeliums. Mk 1,1–15 und die Konzeption des Markusevangeliums," *BZ* 21 (1977) 219–34 and 22 (1978) 76–91; Rudolf Pesch, "Anfang des Evangeliums Jesu Christi. Eine Studie zum Prolog des Markusevangeliums (Mk 1, 1–15)," *Das Markus-Evangelium* (Wege der Forschung CDXI; Darmstadt: Wissenschaftliche Buchgesellschaft, 1979) 311–55; Eugene Boring, "The Christology of Mark: Hermeneutical Issues for Systematic Theology," *Christology and Exegesis: New Approaches* (Semeia 30; ed. R. Jewett; Decatur, GA: Scholars, 1985) 125–53; Daniel J. Harrington, "A Map of Books on Mark (1975–1984)," *BTB* 15 (1985) 12–16; P. Pokorny, "Das Marcus-Evangelium. Literarische und theologische Einleitung mit Forschungsbericht," *ANRW* II/25.3, 1969–2035; D. Dormeyer, "Die Kompositionsmetapher 'Evangelium Jesu Christi, des Sohnes Gottes' Mk 1.1. Ihre theologische und literarische Aufgabe in der Jesus-Biographie des Markus," *NTS* 33 (1987) 452–68; E. S. Johnson, "Is Mark 15.39 the Key to Mark's Christology?" *JSNT* 31 (1987) 3–22; Andrew T. Lincoln, "The Promise and the Failure: Mark 16:7,8," *JBL* 108 (1989) 283–300; Joel Marcus, "The Jewish War and the *Sitz im Leben* of Mark," *JBL* 111 (1992) 441–62; J. Lambrecht, "John the Baptist and Jesus in Mark 1.1–15," *NTS* 38 (1992) 357–84.

[113] For the points that follow, I am especially dependent on Ernst, *Johannes der Täufer*, 278–89.

[114] For basic treatments of the desert theme in the Gospel material, see C. C. Mc-Cown, "The Scene of John's Ministry and Its Relation to the Purpose and Outcome of His Mission," *JBL* 59 (1940) 113–31, as supplemented and corrected by Robert W. Funk, "The Wilderness," *JBL* 78 (1959) 205–14. Though there seems to be no real distinction in meaning between the adjective-used-as-substantive *erēmos* and the noun *erēmia*, the latter is not used for John the Baptist. In my view, Funk at times presses supposed distinctions in vocabulary too hard. I should note that, while some authors attempt to distinguish between "desert" and "wilderness" in treating the Gospel material, I use the English terms interchangeably.

[115] As commentators regularly observe, there is a notable shift in interpretation from the original sense of Isa 40:3 to the NT use of the text, as exemplified in John 1:23. The Masoretic Text of the Hebrew (followed by Jerome's Vulgate) contains a clear parallelism and a chiasm that indicate that the text should be understood to say:

> "A voice [is] crying:
> '*In the desert* PREPARE the way of Yahweh;
> MAKE STRAIGHT *in the wilderness* a highway for our God.' "

For Deutero-Isaiah, therefore, it is not the voice crying out but the act of preparation that is to be found in the desert. This fits the whole message of Deutero-Isaiah, which speaks often of Israel's path leading from exile, through the desert, back to Israel's homeland. Claus Westermann (*Isaiah 40–46* [OTL; Philadelphia: Westminster, 1969] 37) argues further that even the accents and rhythm of the passage favor this interpretation. The first indication that "in the desert" may be beginning to be interpreted as referring to where the voice is crying is found in the LXX (followed by the Vetus Latina), which probably should be taken to mean: "The voice of one crying in the wilderness: 'Prepare the way of the Lord, make straight the paths of our God.' " (Not surprisingly, the later Jewish translations of Aquila and Symmachus restore the parallelism reflected in the MT.) The lack of the parallel phrase "in the wilderness" in the second half of the cry may indicate that the translator took "in the desert" as going not with the following verb "prepare" but with the preceding participle "crying." This, at any rate, is how the NT understood the passage; one wonders whether this interpretation was already used by the Baptist to authenticate and explain his ministry. Such an interpretation would certainly jibe with his own program: he, the prophetic figure, preached in the desert, while most of the people he baptized went back home to prepare the way of the Lord in their daily lives and world, not in the desert. On the other hand, the *Manual of Discipline* at Qumran follows the sense found in the MT; in 1QS 8:13–14 we read: ". . . to go into the desert to prepare there the way of 'Him' [apparently a circumlocution for 'Yahweh,' though the text may be corrupt here; one might also read: 'the way of faithfulness']. As it is written: 'In the desert prepare the way of Yahweh [the sacred name being represented by four dots]; make straight in the wilderness a highway for our God.' " Any possible confusion is avoided by the omission of the introductory phrase "a voice crying." Qumran saw itself as literally fulfilling Isaiah's prophecy by its life of study and torah-observance situated precisely in the desert of Judea (though historically this was not the desert Deutero-Isaiah had in mind). Hence for Qumran it was the act of preparing, not the voice crying out, that was in the desert. In this, Qumran represents the original sense of Deutero-Isaiah, while the NT (and perhaps the historical John?) represents a reinterpretation: John preached ("cried out") in the desert, but Jesus prepared the way for and at least partially brought in the kingdom of

God in the inhabited areas of Galilee and Judea. If the historical Baptist used Isa 40:3 in the way reflected in John 1:23, then on this one point he stands with the NT tradition over against both the MT and the self-understanding of Qumran. Against the likelihood of John's appealing to Isa 40:3 is Gnilka, *Jesus von Nazaret*, 83.

[116] See Denis Baly, *The Geography of the Bible* (London: Lutterworth, 1957); Yohanan Aharoni, *The Land of the Bible. A Historical Geography* (rev. ed.; Philadelphia: Westminster, 1979) 34; and Funk, "The Wilderness," 208–10.

[117] Whether Matthew enjoyed any special knowledge or source that led him to make the precision "the desert of Judea" or whether he simply drew the inference from the context of the story is not clear; I suspect the latter, as does McCown, "The Scene," 114. Merendino ("Testi anticotestamentari," 14) suggests that Matthew is emphasizing here "the importance of Judea as the place of origin of the Christian event," as he does in 2:1,5 with regard to Bethlehem.

[118] As McCown ("The Scene," 115) points out, one indication of the historicity of the basic traditions about the desert-and-Jordan venue of the Baptist is that the strange geographical situation is simply presupposed, with no sense that one has to explain how John could be in a desert and by a river at the same time.

[119] Funk ("The Wilderness," 208) makes a point of insisting that "C. C. McCown was surely incorrect, then, in stating that no part of the Jordan valley was ever included in *the* wilderness."

[120] Still more striking is the LXX form, which in v 2 creates a new subject for the verbs "will blossom and rejoice": "the desert places of the Jordan" *(ta erēma tou Iordanou)*.

[121] See, e.g., Karl Ludwig Schmidt, *Der Rahmen der Geschichte Jesu* (Darmstadt: Wissenschaftliche Buchgesellschaft, 1969) 22–23; and, adopting his view, Bultmann, *Geschichte*, 261.

[122] In LXX Gen 13:10–11, the same phrase *(pasan tēn perichōron tou Iordanou)* seems to envision a goodly part of the Jordan valley. The equivalent Hebrew phrase, *kikkar hayyardēn* (literally, "the circle of the Jordan," i.e., the territory around the Jordan) occurs in 1 Kgs 7:46 and 2 Chr 4:17 with the implication that the "circle" extended as far north as Solomon's bronze factory at Zarethan/Zaphon (possibly Tell es-Saʿidiyeh, to the east of the Jordan almost halfway up the valley; cf. Aharoni, *The Land of the Bible*, 126). In the LXX version of 2 Chr 4:17, *kikkar hayyardēn* is translated with almost the same words found in Luke 3:3: *en tǭ perichōrǭ tou Iordanou*. It is not clear how far south the "circle" was thought to extend. The Abraham-Lot story in Genesis 13 implies that it included "the territory north of the Dead Sea in the neighborhood of Jericho" (McCown, "The Scene," 117).

[123] The early manuscript evidence is strongly in favor of Bethany; so p[66], p[75], Alexandrinus, Vaticanus, and Ephraemi Rescriptus. There is a perfect reason why later scribes would change Bethany, which usually refers to a town close to Jerusalem, to a place known to be beyond the Jordan; a change in the opposite direction is very difficult to explain. The popularity of Bethabara (a town mentioned in the Talmud) is due especially to Origen; his view was followed by Eusebius, Epiphanius, and Chrysostom. Yet Origen admits that Bethany is the reading in nearly all of the manuscripts he knows; he relies largely on a fanciful etymology of the name Bethabara to establish his case. On this, see Bruce M. Metzger, *A Textual Commentary on the Greek New Testament* (3d ed.; United Bible Societies, 1971) 199–200; Brown, *John*, 1. 44–45. All in all, it is more likely that the Fourth Gospel referred to a trans-Jordanian town named Bethany, no

trace of which remains. For various possible locations (near the wadi el-ḥarrar off the Jordan, or farther north, where the wadi nimrin joins the Jordan), see Rudolf Schnackenburg, *The Gospel According to St John* (New York: Herder and Herder; London: Burns & Oates, 1968) 1. 296; Ernst (*Johannes der Täufer*, 282) follows Dalman in speaking for the ḥadshla-ford of the Jordan.

[124] That at least is the meaning of *eis tēn Ioudaian gēn* (John 3:22) in its present context, where Jesus has just been in Jerusalem, the chief city of Judea. It would therefore make no sense to translate the phrase with what would be its more normal meaning, "the Judean territory" or "the Judean region." However, Brown (*John*, 1. 150–51) thinks that in the original story, before it was placed in its present context, *gēn* would have had its usual meaning.

[125] See Brown, *John*, 1. 151; Schnackenburg, *The Gospel According to St John*, 1. 412–13. The two major candidates, in my view, are (1) in the northern Jordan valley, on the west bank, some eight miles south of Scythopolis (Bethshan); and (2) in Samaria: four miles east-southeast of Shechem, there is a town called Sâlim, eight miles north of which lies ʿAinûn; in the general area there are many springs. A third candidate, in Perea, just northeast of the Dead Sea, seems unlikely to me, granted the way that John 3:22–23 profiles Jesus and John in their baptizing activity; implicitly they seem to be placed near each other on the same side of the Jordan.

[126] Marxsen, *Der Evangelist Markus*, 22. It may be, though, as McCown ("The Scene," 114) and Wink (*John the Baptist*, 4) suggest, that Luke does not understand the geographical references in his sources and so presents John leaving the wilderness when he goes to the Jordan region after his call in 3:2–3. Strictly speaking, however, the interpretation of McCown and Wink is not the necessary logical conclusion arising out of Luke's wording in vv 2–3: *egeneto rhēma theou epi Iōannēn . . . en tē erēmō kai ēlthen eis pasan [tēn] perichōron tou Iordanou.* Luke never says that John *leaves* the desert when he comes to the region around the Jordan.

[127] Funk ("The Wilderness," 207–8) traces how the wilderness terminology, which in the Pentateuch nearly always refers to the wilderness of the forty-year journey of the post-exodus period under Moses, becomes in time "applied to areas adjacent to or in Palestine proper."

[128] See Wink, *John the Baptist*, 5: "It would be more accurate to say, then, that Mark *preserved* the wilderness tradition which he found in his sources because it suited his theological purpose, or better, that this theological purpose was itself *created* by this element in the tradition. Because John *was* 'in the wilderness' the Isaiah citation becomes relevant."

[129] For example, Becker (*Johannes der Täufer*, 26) rejects an allusion to Elijah, but accepts the idea that the camel's hair clothing refers to the typical garb of a prophet; similarly, though somewhat stronger on the Elijah-overtones, is Scobie, *John the Baptist*, 128–29.

[130] See, e.g., Ludwig Koehler and Walter Baumgartner, *Lexicon in Veteris Testamenti Libros* (Leiden: Brill, 1958) 927 s.v.; John Gray, *I & II Kings* (OTL; Philadelphia: Westminster, 1963) 414.

[131] Strongly in favor of "hairy man," to the exclusion of the other possibility, is Philipp Vielhauer, "Tracht und Speise Johannes des Täufers," *Aufsätze zum Neuen Testament* (Theologische Bücherei 31; Munich: Kaiser, 1965) 47–54, esp. 49–50. Vielhauer stresses that the LXX translates *baʿal śēʿār* as *anēr dasys;* when the LXX applies the adjective *dasys* to a man, claims Vielhauer, it means only "having a heavy growth of hair

on one's body." Yet the case of the birth of Esau in LXX Gen 25:25 shows the ambiguity of the word. Esau comes forth from the womb *holos hōsei dora dasys* ("completely hairy like an animal hide").

[132] E.g., the *NEB* (1970) reads: "John was dressed in a rough coat of camel's hair." Many translations, however, are sensitive to what the text does *not* say and translate fairly literally with wording like "John was clothed in camel's hair" (so *NAB;* cf. *RSV,* and the new *RSV*).

[133] Marcus Jastrow (*A Dictionary of the Targumim, the Talmud Babli and Yerushalmi, and the Midrashic Literature* [New York, Pardes, 1950, originally 1903] 37 s.v.) accepts both "belt" and "girdle" as meanings of the word in rabbinic Hebrew.

[134] There is certainly a close correspondence between the LXX's *zōnēn dermatinēn periezōsmenos tēn osphyn autou* and Mark's *zōnēn dermatinēn peri tēn osphyn autou.*

[135] So Kraeling, *John the Baptist,* 14–15; similarly, Gnilka, *Jesus von Nazaret,* 83.

[136] The use of the word "ascetic" often calls forth passionate denials, but only because commentators load down the word "ascetic" with ideological baggage it does not necessarily carry. All "ascetic" need mean is "practicing strict self-denial" or "austere in manner." In that sense John was certainly an ascetic. That asceticism necessarily stems from a gnostic view of the physical world or the body as evil is simply not true. Becker (*Johannes der Täufer,* 26) suggests that John's asceticism was a type of "eschatological demonstration." It was an exodus, a going out, from the status-quo of human life and religion in view of the imminent judgment. This explanation has the advantage of cohering with the desert setting of John's ministry. Becker is quite right in refusing to see priestly concern for ritual purity in John's asceticism; for a different view, see Farmer, "John the Baptist," 960–61.

[137] Böcher, "Ass Johannes der Täufer kein Brot?" 91.

[138] Brown, *Birth of the Messiah,* 273–74 (referring to Judg 13:4–5 and 1 Sam 1:9–15). Brown observes: "Using this stereotyped language, Luke is portraying JBap, traditionally an ascetic, as a Nazirite from his infancy. . . ." Whether the OT considered Samuel a nazirite is not entirely clear. In the MT of 1 Sam 1:11 + 22, Samuel's mother promises *only* that her future child, whom she dedicates to Yahweh for perpetual service in his sanctuary, will never use a razor on his hair. However, both the LXX[B] and a text of Samuel from Qumran (4QSam[a]) have additional words in these two verses that make Samuel a nazirite, and some would argue that the LXX and 4QSam represent the original reading here. For detailed argumentation see P. Kyle McCarter, Jr., *I Samuel* (AB 8; Garden City, NY: Doubleday, 1980) 53–54, 56. Indicative of how difficult and delicate such text-critical decisions are is the fact that McCarter himself opts for the view the *nāzîr* ("nazirite") is secondary in v 11 but original in v 22. Putting all this together with the prophetic figures Elijah and Elisha and with the pairing of "prophets" and "nazirites" in Amos 2:11–12, Francis I. Andersen and David Noel Freedman suggest that in ancient Israel there was a close connection between nazirites like Samuel and Samson and prophets like Elijah and Elisha; see their *Amos* (AB 24A; New York: Doubleday, 1989) 331–32. In my view, it is indeed possible that various popular religious heroes like Samuel, Samson, Elijah, and Elisha influenced both the practice of the Baptist and the way his fellow Jews viewed him. However, I do not see enough historical evidence to support the claim that John was actually a nazirite or that he saw himself as playing the role of Elijah in the end time.

[139] Tony W. Cartledge ("Were Nazirite Vows Unconditional?" *CBQ* 51 [1989] 409–22) states: "The most obvious outward mark [of a nazirite] is the proscription against

cutting the hair, though the prohibition against drinking wine also came to be included as a standard requirement" (pp. 412–13).

[140] An indirect reference to honey can be found in a fragment of Philo's *Hypothetica*, preserved in Eusebius' *Praeparatio Evangelica* 8.11.8: "Some of them till the earth, since they are skilled in sowing and planting, others are herdsmen . . . , and some are bee-keepers." The text goes on to speak of other occupations in which the Essenes engage. Obviously, beekeeping is not the sole agricultural endeavor of Philo's Essenes, nor is honey their only nourishment. For a critical text, see Karl Mras, *Eusebius Werke. Achter Band. Die Praeparatio Evangelica. Erster Teil* (GCS 43/1; Berlin: Akademie, 1954) 455–56. On locusts, see CD 12:14; but the context shows that the locusts are listed among the many different animals that the Qumranites must take care to eat in the proper, pure way. There is not here the slightest idea that locusts form the only or main food of the Qumranites. Their mention simply reminds us that both John and the Qumranites lived in the desert and therefore had their diets restricted accordingly.

[141] Theodor Zahn, *Das Evangelium des Matthäus* (Kommentar zum Neuen Testament 1; 4th ed.; Leipzig: Deichert, 1922, originally 1903) 132–33. Similarly, Vielhauer, "Tracht und Speise," 53; W. D. Davies and Dale C. Allison, *The Gospel According to Saint Matthew* (ICC; 3 vols.; Edinburgh: Clark, 1988) 1. 296.

[142] As Ernst notes (*Johannes der Täufer*, 288 n. 76), some commentators are never satisfied with the text as is; both the locusts and the wild honey have been rewritten in Greek to make the text say what the commentators think it should say. Examples include (1) for the locusts, the tips of various plants, crabs, wild pears, fritters cooked in oil and honey (*egkris*, see Epiphanius, *Panarion* 30.13.4–5), milk, and "St. John's bread-fruit" (the carob tree); (2) for the honey, an edible root. Davies and Allison (*The Gospel According to Saint Matthew*, 296) insist on the strict meaning of honey from wild bees as opposed to the honey marketed by beekeepers; they reject even the alternative of a secretion from certain trees. Various scriptural types have been found for both foods: e.g., the locusts show that John is observing the law of paradise that forbade meat, while the honey recalls the honey from the rock mentioned in Deut 32:13; cf. Ps 81:17. All this is fanciful, and it is by no means clear that locusts would qualify under the apparently vegetarian regimen envisioned in Genesis 2.

[143] While one might think merely of individual symbolic actions of the prophets (e.g., Jeremiah's use of a broken vase or a rotted loincloth), more to the point are the ways in which the very lives of the prophets are significantly altered: e.g., Jeremiah's celibacy (Jer 16:1–4) or Isaiah's three-year nakedness (Isa 20:1–4). In this regard we should also mention the Rechabites in Jeremiah 35, who foreswore city life—or even sedentary agricultural life—in favor of a nomadic "wilderness" way of living in tents (in the wilderness of Judea?); they also foreswore the drinking of wine. Without adopting their way of life for himself, Jeremiah extols them as an example of obedience to their ancestor's commands in the midst of a people that has disobeyed its God. The Rechabites, who may have had some influence on the development of the institution of the nazirite, may also have been among John's religio-cultural folk-heroes. But just as John's ascetic habits do not make him a nazirite, so they do not make him a Rechabite. If one instead adopted the revisionist view of Frank S. Frick ("The Rechabites Recon-sidered," *JBL* 90 [1971] 279–87; cf. the summary of his position in his article "Rechab-ites," *IDBSup*, 726–28), the possible relevance of this group to the Baptist would be notably weakened, since in Frick's view the Rechabites were not nomads but rather metallurgists or smiths whose peculiar habits were derived from their occupations.

[144] For the question of the origins of John's baptism and the many suggestions made

by students of comparative religions, see, e.g., Lohmeyer, *Das Urchristentum*, 1. 145–56. From the time of Richard Reitzenstein onwards, the baptismal practices of the Mandean sect (still extant in present-day Iraq) have been called upon to prove the Iranian origins of John's baptism. While it once enjoyed wide popularity, the Mandean hypothesis is largely discounted today, mainly because of the late date of the Mandean sources that mention John the Baptist. Apparently references to the Baptist were introduced into the Mandean literature after the Arab conquest. The Arabs granted toleration only to those religious groups that could produce sacred books and a prophet; the Mandeans called upon the Baptist to fill the role of prophet for them. On this, see Goguel, *Au seuil*, 113–35; Kraeling, *John the Baptist*, 106–9; Dodd, *The Interpretation of the Fourth Gospel*, 115–30; Scobie, *John the Baptist*, 30–31—all of whom reject any direct relationship between John and the Mandeans. Thomas (*Le mouvement baptiste*, 185–266) is more sympathetic to seeing early roots of Mandeanism in Palestine and allowing that some references to John in Mandean literature might predate the Islamic conquest, but he likewise denies any real historical relation between John and the Mandeans.

[145] For a brief survey of OT views, see G. R. Beasley-Murray, *Baptism in the New Testament* (Grand Rapids: Eerdmans, 1990, originally 1962) 1–10.

[146] This is the basic thesis of his *Le mouvement baptiste*; for succinct statements of his views, see pp. 374, 429–30, 435–36. It is unfortunate that Thomas wrote before the discoveries at Qumran; for a more recent summary of baptist movements before and after John, see Sint, "Die Eschatologie," 83–102.

[147] For water rituals among the Essenes and at Qumran, see Beasley-Murray, *Baptism*, 11–18.

[148] This point is emphasized by Gnilka, "Die essenischen Tauchbäder," 194–95.

[149] One must be careful when talking about "the disciples of John" at the time of the public ministry of Jesus. (1) At least one reference to them (in the question about fasting) seems to place them in Galilee along with the Pharisees and the disciples of Jesus (Mark 2:18 parr.; Matthew's redactional form [Matt 9:14] even makes the disciples of John address the question to Jesus in Galilee). In other words, in this pericope the phrase "the disciples of John" refers not to a special group that remained on a more or less permanent basis around John himself, but rather to those who had received his baptism, returned to their ordinary lives, but tried to live out John's call to repentance in certain observances, such as voluntary fasting (imitating John's perpetual fast in the wilderness?). Thus, to speak of "the disciples of John" is not necessarily to speak of an organized group remaining around John in the wilderness. (2) Whatever the significance of the phrase "the disciples of John" in a given passage, one must remember that statements about them may reflect their situation after the deaths of both John and Jesus, when the Baptist and Christian groups were locked in rivalry as each group tried to define itself over against the other. It is perhaps at this point that some organizational development may have occurred among the Baptist disciples—who remain, however, an ill-defined entity throughout the 1st century A.D. (3) Many authors who speak freely of a group of disciples remaining around the Baptist fail to notice that the only clear depiction of such a state of affairs comes from the much-abused Fourth Gospel (John 1:35–42; 3:25–30), and the passages are clearly marked by the later rivalry between the Baptist and Christian movements. The only other possible (but by no means certain) indicator of disciples remaining around John is the laconic statement at the end of Mark's account of the Baptist's beheading (Mark 6:29 par.), and there the language may be intended to point forward to Jesus' burial (15:45–46). In short, I do not deny that some disciples of John may have stayed with him for some time, forming some-

thing of an inner circle around him. But we must recognize not only that the evidence is quite meager but also that, during the Baptist's lifetime, there is no indication of any organization among his disciples—unlike the case of "the Twelve" within Jesus' group of disciples.

[150] On the once-and-for-all nature of John's baptism, see Gnilka, "Die essenischen Tauchbäder," 199. Gnilka thinks that for the Baptist the final judgment was even closer than it seemed to the Qumranites; hence John's eschatological call to repentance was even more urgent (p. 200). But whether such a comparison is possible may be questioned; we are being forced to compare a few sayings of John with a number of documents from Qumran reflecting various eschatological views and written at different stages of the community's existence.

[151] For a list of scholars who favor the view that John's baptism can be seen as an adaptation of proselyte baptism, see Gnilka, "Die essenischen Tauchbäder," 185; cf. Beasley-Murray, *Baptism*, 18–31. For a treatment of the question within the wider context of the history of conversion to Judaism in the pre-talmudic, talmudic, and post-talmudic periods, see Shaye J. D. Cohen, "The Rabbinic Conversion Ceremony," *JJS* 41 (1990) 177–203.

[152] That John's baptism involved immersion of the candidate's body is implied by the statement that, after Jesus' baptism, he "came up out of the water" (Mark 1:10 ‖ Matt 3:16). This supposition is bolstered (1) by the Baptist's focus on the Jordan River and on Aenon-near-Salim, in which he baptized "because there was an abundance of water there" (John 3:23); and (2) by Josephus' statement in the *Antiquities* that John baptized not to cleanse souls but to purify bodies.

[153] The date of *Joseph and Aseneth* is disputed; suggested dates range between 100 B.C. and Hadrian's edict against circumcision, which is connected with the Second Jewish War (A.D. 132–135); see Christoph Burchard, "Joseph and Aseneth," *The Old Testament Pseudepigrapha*, 2. 187–88. Burchard comments on attempts to find a set ritual of conversion in the work: "It is significant that neither circumcision nor proselyte baptism (supposing that it existed already in the author's day) is mentioned" (p. 193). The washing of Aseneth's hands and face in 14:15 is occasioned simply by her shaking off the ashes from her head; it is hardly a ritual bath.

The earliest reference to proselyte baptism in rabbinic literature is usually said to be the dispute between the school of Shammai and the school of Hillel on whether a person who becomes a proselyte on the day before Passover may immerse himself and consume his Passover-offering in the evening (*Pesaḥ.* 8:8). Yet the larger context deals with various impurities that might keep a Jew from eating the Passover-offering (or other "hallowed things") in the evening and with the question whether an immersion bath can free the Jew from the impurity in time to eat his Passover-offering. Hence one wonders whether we have here a clear case of proselyte baptism as an essential part of the conversion process or simply another *quaestio disputata* about what impurity keeps one (in this case, a Jew recently become so) from eating the Passover-offering and whether washing can remove that impurity in time for the meal. On the passage, see Karl Georg Kuhn, "*prosēlytos*," *TDNT* 6 (1968) 738–39; and the revised Schürer, *The History of the Jewish People*, 3/1. 173–74; both favor taking the passage as referring to proselyte baptism. Also holding that proselyte baptism was already practiced at the time of John is Kraeling, *John the Baptist*, 99–100. More dubious is Thomas (*Le mouvement baptiste*, 357–74), who observes that *Pesaḥ.* 8:8 could refer to an ordinary bath of ritual purity to which the recently converted proselyte was held before eating the Passover. Gnilka ("Die essenischen Tauchbäder," 206) thinks that the *Pesaḥ.* 8:8 passage shows how Jewish proselyte baptism arose out of ordinary immersion baths, originally connected with the levitical purity required for cultic actions. In my opinion, Cohen ("The Rabbinic Conversion Ceremony," 194 n. 46) is right in emphasizing that "neither the House of Hillel nor the House of Shammai is aware that a convert must undergo a separate immersion for the sake of conversion. This Mishna has often been cited as evidence for Jewish proselyte immersion in the first century, but the argument is false." Cohen suggests that a full initiation ritual of conversion to Judaism, including both circumcision and proselyte immersion, was a rabbinic product of the mid-2d century A.D.

[154] See Cohen, "The Rabbinic Conversion Ceremony," 195–96.

[155] For a consideration of the similarities and dissimilarities between John's baptism and proselyte baptism, see Lohmeyer, *Das Urchristentum*, 1. 151–52; similarly, Kraeling (*John the Baptist*, 99–103), who in the end rejects proselyte baptism as the source of John's rite. Wishing to draw a comparison with proselyte baptism, Jeremias (*Theology of the New Testament*, 51) claims that Jesus did immerse himself while John functioned as a witness. To arrive at this position, Jeremias must take two questionable steps:

(1) He claims that the Greek passive *baptisthēnai* represents the intransitive active form *ṭĕbal*, which means "undergo immersion, immerse oneself." There are a number of difficulties involved in this claim. (a) How we are to know that this is the Aramaic wording underlying the Greek wording is never explained. (b) More to the point, the Greek texts of Mark and Matthew say just the opposite, namely, that Jesus was baptized *by* John (true passive voice): *kai ebaptisthē . . . hypo Iōannou* (Mark 1:9); *. . . paraginetai ho Iēsous . . . pros ton Iōannēn tou baptisthēnai hyp' autou. . . . [John objects:] egō chreian echō hypo sou baptisthēnai* (Matt 3:13–14). Here we have a perfect example of Jeremias's tendency to change the clear meaning of the Greek text because of some hypothetical Aramaic substratum that cannot be verified. (c) Further, we must suppose that, if Jeremias is right about the meaning of the Aramaic substratum, then all three Synoptists (or their Greek sources) were clumsy in their translations, since Greek does possess an aorist middle form of *baptizō*, which would have rendered the sense of Jeremias's hypothetical Aramaic text perfectly; cf. Meier, "John the Baptist," 385 n. 7. (d) One might also observe that, at least for the Hebrew form of the verb (*ṭābal*), passive forms are used: so the nifal in Josh 3:15 (with passive, not reflexive sense), and the hofal in *m. Miqw.* 5:6.

(2) Jeremias points to the fact that in Luke 3:7 Codex Bezae and the Vetus Latina read *baptisthēnai enōpion autou* [i.e., *before John*] instead of *baptisthēnai hyp' autou*. The latter is supported by all other Greek texts and almost all of the versions; it is clearly the original reading. Even Jeremias does not claim otherwise. Schürmann (*Lukasevangelium*, 1. 163 n. 7) thinks that the *enōpion autou* of Codex Bezae intended to demolish the characteristic element of John's baptism—which is more or less what Jeremias attempts.

[156] Beasley-Murray (*Baptism*, 31–44) is especially negative toward any influence from proselyte baptism; he is more open to parallels from Qumran (pp. 40–41).

[157] So Kraeling, *John the Baptist*, 109–10.

[158] What exactly this confession of sins involved is not clear. It could have been a general confession of sins similar to the one made at the annual covenant feast at Qumran (see 1QS 1:24–2:1; cf. CD 20:27–30). Such general confessions of sin can be found already in the OT: e.g., 1 Sam 7:6; Isa 64:4–6; Neh 9:16–37; Dan 9:4–19. The confession could instead have consisted in the individual's confession of his or her personal sins, as various rabbis demanded for the celebration of Yom Kippur (see the examples

from the tractate *Yoma* in the Mishna and both Talmuds in Str-B, 1. 113–14). On all this, see Gnilka, "Die essenischen Tauchbäder," 198.

[159] Among those who see *eis aphesin hamartiōn* as a Christian addition to the Baptist's proclamation are Dibelius, *Die urchristliche Überlieferung*, 58; and Goguel, *Au seuil*, 290. Dibelius, however, does not give detailed arguments for his position. Admittedly, the vocabulary of the disputed phrase is found in early Christian preaching. The noun *metanoia* occurs 6 times in Acts, the verb *metanoeō* 5 times; significantly, Luke's Gospel uses the two terms more often (5 and 9 times respectively) than the other three Gospels combined. The results are similar for *aphesis*: Acts uses it 5 times, as does Luke's Gospel. In contrast, Matthew uses it only once, and Mark twice. While *kēryssō* is well represented in the Synoptics (Mark alone uses it 14 times), its important use in early Christian missionary preaching is clear not only from the 8 occurrences in Acts but also from the 19 occurrences in the Pauline corpus. Ernst (*Johannes der Täufer*, 333) is willing to grant that *kēryssōn* reflects Christian usage. At the same time, he is right in doubting Thyen's claim (*Baptisma metanoias*, 132 n. 3) that the original reading of Mark's text was *egeneto Iōannēs baptizōn en tę erēmǭ baptisma metanoias* ("John came baptizing in the wilderness [with] a baptism of repentance"); Thyen rests his claim on the thin basis of Acts 19:4 and a passage in the Gospel of the Ebionites.

[160] A basic mistake of Thyen (*"Baptisma metanoias,"* 131–68) is to take this phrase as the starting point for his treatment of John and the meaning of his baptism.

[161] At the conclusion of his Pentecost sermon, Peter exhorts the crowd: "Repent and be baptized, each one of you, in the name of Jesus Christ for the remission of your sins" (*metanoēsate kai baptisthētō hekastos hymōn epi tǭ onomati Iēsou Christou eis aphesin tōn hamartiōn hymōn*).

[162] Indeed, the vocabulary of repentance and the forgiveness of sins is almost entirely lacking in the literature traditionally attributed to Paul and John (apart from the Revelation of John).

[163] Lohmeyer (*Das Urchristentum*, 1. 68–69) reflects later Christian theological debates when he interprets "baptism of repentance" to mean not the repentance of the human being receiving baptism but rather the act of God in baptism which turns the human being around.

[164] Rudolf Bultmann described John's baptism as an "eschatological sacrament" in his *Jesus and the Word* (London: Collins [Fontana], 1934 [German original 1929]) 26.

[165] Ernst, *Johannes der Täufer*, 334–35. This is much closer to the truth than the claim of Thyen, *"Baptisma metanoias,"* 132: ". . . *baptisma metanoias eis aphesin hamartiōn*. . . . characterizes John's baptism as an eschatological sacrament which effects both repentance and forgiveness." Although Lohmeyer also took a "strong" view of the efficacy of John's baptism, even allowing that it was thought to work *ex opere operato*, he rejected the label "sacrament" because, in the end, John's baptism was sui generis (*Das Urchristentum*, 75, 156, 180). For a review and critique of the use of the category "sacrament" for John's baptism, see Sint, "Die Eschatologie," 79–83; he attempts to express the uniqueness of John's baptism by using the label "quasi-sacrament."

[166] Despite Lohmeyer's questionable understanding of John's "baptism of repentance," he is right that John effectively stood in the middle between God and the candidate for baptism (*Das Urchristentum*, 1. 75); similarly, Becker, *Johannes der Täufer*, 38, 40. In this loose sense, and not in the later specifically Christian sense, John implicitly made himself a mediator of eschatological salvation.

[167] Feldman's text is cited as the one most readily available in the United States; it is dependent on the *editio maior* of Niese, *Flavii Josephi Opera.* The only differences in our passage are Niese's choice of *tinymenou* instead of *tinnymenou* in §116; *hēsthēsan* instead of *ērthēsan* and *apostasei* instead of *stasei* in §118; and *doxan* instead of *doxa* in §119. The only difference that would affect the meaning of the passage (and that only slightly) would be the choice of *hēsthēsan*, which is discussed below.

[168] The *ta* before *pros allēlous* is curious. If it is meant to be the accusative of reference (i.e., justice with regard to those things pertaining to one another), it is strange that a balancing *ta* does not occur before *pros ton theon.* One might appeal to the alternate reading in Eusebius' citation of Josephus in his *De Demonstratione Evangelica* 9.5.15: *tē* instead of *ta;* but that could be simply a scribal correction. It is noteworthy that the Epistle to the Hebrews uses the phrase *ta pros ton theon* in Heb 2:17; *hina genētai . . . pistos archiereus ta pros ton theon;* and 5:1, *pas gar archiereus . . . kathistatai ta pros ton theon.*

[169] Feldman rightly rejects the alternate reading favored by Niese (from Eusebius) of *hēsthēsan*, "they enjoyed," "they took pleasure in," "they delighted in." That people were extremely stirred up, excited, agitated, or carried away *(ērthēsan)* by John's words makes much better sense as the cause of Herod's fear. Moreover, *hēsthēsan* is not witnessed universally in the manuscripts of Eusebius, and the manuscripts of Josephus favor *ērthēsan*.

[170] The *mē* is omitted by Eusebius and is placed in brackets by both Niese and Feldman. It may come from the lingering idea of the object of Herod's fear *(deisas)*. In any case, it does not affect the sense of the passage or its translation.

[171] I have presented my own translation of the text at the beginning of this chapter; see p. 20 above.

[172] See Ernst, *Johannes der Täufer,* 253; the translation Ernst supplies in n. 1 unfortunately omits some words and introduces concepts not present in the Greek text. For example, *ktinnytai* is translated "enthauptet," which introduces into Josephus the idea of beheading, found only in the Synoptic Gospels.

[173] For the sake of vivid narration, Josephus puts both references to Antipas' killing of John into the historical present tense *(kteinei* in §117 and *ktinnytai* in §119). In my translation, I put all the verbs into the past tense.

[174] The adjective *agathon* is pointedly separated from *touton* by *Hērōdēs* and is clearly in the predicate rather than attributive position; likewise, the participle *keleuonta* is circumstantial rather than attributive. The context, with its sharp bipolar contrast between the idea of killing and the idea of a good man, makes the adversative sense of *agathon* and *keleuonta* obvious.

[175] Whether *baptismō synienai* means "join in baptism," "be united in baptism," or "come together for baptism" need not concern us here. In general, commentators tend to read more into these various phrases than the words themselves demand; the decision as to whether John was a leader of a nationalist or perhaps even a revolutionary movement hardly turns on this one phrase (cf. Lohmeyer's interpretation [*Das Urchristentum,* 31–32] that John was leading a national reform movement of Jews who "were uniting themselves" as God's people by means of John's baptism). Ernst (*Johannes der Täufer,* 255) is probably correct when he summarizes the sense of the phrase this way: "Die Juden strömten zusammen zur Taufe, um sich dann wieder recht bald zu zerstreuen. Die Bildung esoterischer Zirkel hat dem Täufer genauso ferngelegen wie die Sammlung zu einem Volksaufstand." In n. 7 he observes that *baptismō synienai* may be compared to *machē synienai,* "to go to war," "to engage in battle." A similar view is held

by Backhaus (*Jüngerkreise*, 268–72), who strongly opposes any idea of the Baptist's founding of a permanent circle or sect by using baptism as an initiation rite. In this he differs from Hermann Lichtenberger ("Täufergemeinden und frühchristliche Täuferpolemik im letzten Drittel des 1. Jahrhunderts," *ZTK* 84 [1987] 36–57), who presents a fanciful reading of Josephus' description of the Baptist as an implicit polemic against disciples of the Baptist resident in Rome toward the end of the 1st century A.D.

[176] This is the translation used by Scobie, *John the Baptist*, 17; he takes it over from H. St. John Thackeray.

[177] See Joseph Klausner, *Jesus of Nazareth. His Life, Times, and Teaching* (New York: Macmillan, 1925; Hebrew original 1922) 239; Feldman, *Josephus*, 81; Ernst, *Johannes der Täufer*, 253.

[178] The phrase "to God" is of course not present in the Greek, and the word *apodektos* need not carry this sense, even in a religious context (cf. the *Epistle to Diognetus* 8:3: "And yet if any of these arguments is acceptable [*apodektos*] . . ."). I think, however, that Feldman and Ernst are correct in supplying it in the Baptist passage. It is the natural sense of the word in its context (what sense would it make to say that John thought that the baptism would be acceptable to John?), and it is supported by the two uses of *apodektos* in the NT (1 Tim 2:3; 5:4). Yet one must remain modest in one's claims, since this is the only time that the word appears in the whole corpus of Josephus' works; it never occurs in the LXX. For the dispute over whether the more accurate translation is "acceptable to" or "pleasing to," see Walter Bauer, *Griechisch-deutsches Wörterbuch zu den Schriften des Neuen Testaments und der frühchristlichen Literatur* (6th ed.; ed. Kurt and Barbara Aland; Berlin/New York: de Gruyter, 1988) 179.

[179] Josephus seems to be consciously combatting the type of understanding of John's baptism that we find in Mark 1:4 ‖ Luke 3:3, *baptisma metanoias eis aphesin hamartiōn* (noticeably lacking in the Matthean parallel, Matt 3:1–6). Since, in my opinion, there is no probative evidence that Josephus knew any of the Four Gospels, it is possible that he is reacting here to claims put forward by followers of John the Baptist, some of whom continued to be active throughout the 1st century A.D. Perhaps Josephus felt that such claims made John's baptism a magical rite that would not appeal to the cultivated Greco-Roman milieu for whom Josephus was writing. The Baptist is accordingly transformed from a preacher of eschatological judgment and the administrator of an eschatological "sacrament" into a Greco-Roman popular philosopher exhorting his fellow citizens to virtue. The combination of exhortation to virtue and concern about a lustration to purify the body gives us a fittingly syncretistic image of a Stoic moralist with a neo-Pythagorean ritual. The attempt by Schütz (*Johannes der Täufer*, 26) to read Josephus as saying that the cleansing of both soul and body took place in John's baptism goes against the obvious sense of the text.

[180] *allōn* obviously created difficulty for both ancient and modern readers: the correction *laōn* is found in codex A and *perplurima multitudo* in the Latin version, while Niese offers the conjectural emendation *anthrōpōn* and Robert Eisler *pollōn* (see Feldman, *Josephus*, 82). All these attempts arise from a failure to understand Josephus' own movement of thought.

[181] This interpretation of *tōn allōn* is found in F. J. Foakes Jackson and Kirsopp Lake, *The Beginnings of Christianity. Part I. The Acts of the Apostles* (5 vols.; Grand Rapids: Baker Book House, 1979, originally 1920–33) 1. 102–3; but there it is not based upon an explanation of the two circumstantial participles as equivalent to conditional clauses.

[182] There is a poignant and—on Josephus' part—unintended irony in the use of

metanoeō for the deliberations of Herod that led to John's execution. Unlike the Synoptics, Josephus says nothing explicit about John as a preacher of *metanoia*.

[183] Since this sentence is so lengthy and convoluted, I have decided to turn the participle *deisas* into a main verb; the causal nexus remains clear from the context. I use the phrase "began to fear" since it is only the gathering of this second group, not the initial preaching to the more virtuous sort, that triggers Herod's anxiety.

[184] This observation is a commonplace among students of Josephus and the NT; see, e.g., Dibelius, *Die urchristliche Überlieferung*, 124; Klausner, *Jesus of Nazareth*, 241; Lohmeyer, *Das Urchristentum*, 31; Goguel, *Au seuil*, 17–18; Kraeling, *John the Baptist*, 52; Scobie, *John the Baptist*, 18–19; Ernst, *Johannes der Täufer*, 254; Backhaus, *Jüngerkreise*, 267–68. Becker (*Johannes der Täufer*, 19) observes that Josephus likewise plays down the eschatological component in the messages of the prophets he mentions.

[185] On this see E. P. Sanders, *Judaism: Practice and Belief. 63 BCE–66 CE* (London: SCM; Philadelphia: Trinity Press International, 1992) 368.

[186] On this see ibid., 193–94.

[187] On the "exclusively religious preoccupations of John," see Goguel, *Au seuil*, 287. This is not to deny that in 1st-century Palestine, the religious activity of a prophetic figure might be viewed by a nervous ruler as possibly having negative political consequences. But to refuse to distinguish what John intended in his preaching and ministry and what Herod feared, as Hollenbach does ("Social Aspects," 863–64), is just as naive as to fail to grasp that religious activity in 1st-century Palestine could, apart from the intention of the agent, be feared by others to hold political consequences. To claim, as Hollenbach does (p. 874), that John was "a social revolutionary" is to confuse our contemporary desire for instant relevance with sober exegesis and historical reconstruction. Interestingly, recasting the Baptist as a revolutionary brings us back to Hermann Samuel Reimarus; cf. the remarks of Reumann, "The Quest for the Historical Baptist," 184–86. Such an approach has had many proponents, some more hesitant than others; see, e.g., McCown, "The Scene," 128–31.

[188] See, e.g., Josephus' description of Theudas in *Ant.* 20.5.1 §97–99 (cf. the garbled reference in Acts 5:36) and "the Egyptian false prophet" in *J.W.* 2.13.5 §261–263 (cf. *Ant.* 20.8.6 §169–172; Acts 21:38). Sanders (*Judaism: Practice and Belief*, 286) suggests that, with the exception of the mob led by the Egyptian, none of the groups that followed prophetic figures in the last decades before the First Jewish Revolt "intended to fight, at least not much." For the Romans, the "at least not much" was more than sufficient reason to act.

For an attempt to sort out such various figures by using the categories of bandits, messiahs, prophets, the fourth philosophy, sicarii, and zealots, see Richard A. Horsley and John S. Hanson, *Bandits, Prophets, and Messiahs. Popular Movements in the Time of Jesus* (Minneapolis/Chicago/New York: Winston, 1985). Quite different from organizers of large bands of people ready to act against the establishment is the solitary Jesus son of Hananiah, an oracular prophet of judgment active in Jerusalem for the last seven years of its existence; see *J.W.* 6.5.3 §300–309. Horsley and Hanson put John the Baptist into the same category as Jesus son of Hananiah and remark: "Nothing in our texts indicates that John intended to found a sect or lead a mass movement in a decisive eschatological event of deliverance. In preaching the baptism of repentance he was attempting to prepare the people, apparently even across class and sectarian lines, for the impending judgment" (*Bandits*, 178).

Against Horsley and Hanson, Webb (*John the Baptizer*, 349–78), who adopts a typology of prophets somewhat different from theirs, places the Baptist in the same basic category as the Egyptian and Theudas, i.e., "leadership popular prophets." I think this is questionable, since there are significant differences between the Baptist and leaders like the Egyptian and Theudas—as Webb himself admits. (1) Most of those baptized by John soon returned to their homes, presumably scattered throughout Palestine. There is no indication that those previously baptized by John ever returned at one time and as one group either to live with the Baptist or to follow him on some march. Hence there never was at any one time the kind of huge massing of people around the Baptist that there was around, e.g., the Egyptian. (2) The "leadership popular prophets" not only gathered a large number of followers around themselves at one time; they also proceeded to lead them on a march to some venerable spot of Israelite history in what could only appear to the ruling authorities as an intentionally provocative act (e.g., the Egyptian led his large group to the Mount of Olives, facing Jerusalem). (3) In the case of the "leadership popular prophets," the authorities deemed it necessary to kill or capture many of the prophets' followers. They, as well as their leaders, were seen to be a real and present danger. As far as we know, nothing similar happened even to those disciples of John who lived in his entourage, to say nothing of the larger group of followers baptized by him. Although he grants most of these points, Webb tries to play down their importance. Cumulatively, however, they argue strongly that the Baptist's "movement" was significantly and perhaps essentially different from the movements of Webb's "leadership popular prophets."

[189] It is curious that Josephus, while so detailed in his explanation of why John was executed, is totally silent on the precise reason why the Jewish leaders accused Jesus before Pilate and why Pilate decided to crucify him (*Ant.* 18.3.3 §64).

[190] Ernst (*Johannes der Täufer*, 257) notes the similarity between the presentation of Josephus and that of Luke.

[191] Fitzmyer (*The Gospel According to Luke*, 1. 464) rightly refers to these verses as "problematic" when it comes to the question of sources; various commentators have championed Q (A. Plummer, H. Schürmann), L, or Lucan redaction (a possibility Fitzmyer leaves open). I. Howard Marshall argues that, since the L source contains no other tradition about the Baptist, Q is the more likely source; Marshall defends the sayings as "the Baptist's teaching, shaped by catechetical use" (*The Gospel of Luke* [New International Greek Testament Commentary; Grand Rapids: Eerdmans, 1978] 142).

[192] Along with the problem of the source of Luke 3:10–14 there is the further problem of the ethnic makeup of the *strateuomenoi* ("those on military duty") who came to John. Various commentators declare them Gentiles (Walter Grundmann, *Das Evangelium nach Lukas* [THKNT 3; 7th ed.; Berlin: Evangelische Verlagsanstalt, 1974] 104), either Gentiles or Jews (Josef Ernst, *Das Evangelium nach Lukas* [RNT; Regensburg: Pustet, 1977] 144), or Jews enlisted in the service of Herod Antipas (Fitzmyer, *The Gospel According to Luke*, 1. 470). While the matter is by no means clear, it seems likely that the army of Antipas included at least some Jewish soldiers. A few commentators (e.g., Jeremias, *New Testament Theology*, 48 n. 3) prefer to think of "police who accompanied the tax-collectors. They would therefore have been Jews." M.-J. Lagrange (*Evangile selon Saint Luc* [EBib; 4th ed.; Paris: Gabalda, 1927] 109–10) thinks these people came from Judea rather than from the forces of Antipas in Perea.

CHAPTER 13

JESUS WITH AND WITHOUT JOHN

We come at long last to the moment when Jesus of Nazareth makes his first appearance on the stage of history as an adult: his baptism by John.[1] It was a simple, at the time unnoticed event that nevertheless poses a string of pivotal questions for any quester. Four questions in particular will engage us in this chapter. First, did this event, i.e., Jesus' baptism by John, actually take place? Second, if it did, what does it tell us about Jesus' religious views or intentions? Third, what was Jesus' relation to John after his baptism—in other words, did Jesus for a time become a disciple of John or perhaps engage in a baptizing ministry? Fourth, what was Jesus' long-term relation to John after Jesus undertook an independent ministry of his own?

I. THE HISTORICITY OF JESUS' BAPTISM BY JOHN

It may strike many readers as strange that anyone should have to mount a defense of the historicity of Jesus' baptism by John. Not only is this dramatic event deeply ingrained in the religious memory of almost every Christian; usually without debate it also serves as the starting point of most scholarly reconstructions of the life of the historical Jesus. With the Infancy Narratives often declared unreliable sources, writers naturally gravitate to what they almost automatically consider firm historical ground.

Yet the matter is not so clear-cut as some would think. The narrative of Jesus' baptism is directly available to us in only one independent source, Mark's Gospel (followed by Matthew and Luke). At first glance, therefore, the criterion of multiple attestation does not apply—though certainly a lack of more than one witness does not prove that a narrated event did not take place. This lack of multiple independent witnesses from the 1st century holds true outside of as well as within the NT. Josephus gives us separate accounts of the ministries of Jesus and John in book 18 of the *Antiquities* without mentioning any connection or meeting between the two, to say nothing of the Baptist baptizing Jesus. Does Josephus' total separation of these two Jewish prophets from the first half of the 1st century reflect historical reality, namely, that Jesus and John never actually met?

100

There is another reason for doubting the historicity of Jesus' baptism: the narrative in Mark is obviously laden with Christian theological interpretation. In fact, the great theophany that follows the baptism (the opening of the heavens, the dove descending, God's voice declaring Jesus his Son) takes up most of the Gospel narrative of the baptismal event and is the main point of the pericope, with the event of the baptism itself being reported in one word. With this weighty freight of Christian theology overshadowing the supposed event of the baptism proper, one must wonder whether the Christian believer's experience of his or her own baptism, the beginning of Christian life, has not been read back into the beginning of Christ's public life. Jesus would thus become a paradigmatic figure for all those Christians who had listened to some earnest preacher proclaiming repentance and salvation and who accordingly allowed themselves to be plunged into water by said preacher to obtain forgiveness of their sins.

If this Christian experience of a new beginning were to be retrojected into the life of Jesus, it would naturally be placed at the beginning of his public life. And who would be more likely to confer a baptism (Christian or otherwise) than the man already known in Jewish and Christian tradition as the Baptist? In fact, who else besides John was even available as a candidate for the office? It is thus at least conceivable that the retrojection of the Christian experience of baptism into the beginning of Jesus' public ministry created a literary and theological—but not a historical—link between John and Jesus. In short, scholars are not totally bereft of arguments in favor of the unhistorical nature of the tradition of Jesus' baptism by John. As a matter of fact, certain exegetes have seriously proposed this position; prominent among them have been the German Ernst Haenchen[2] and the American Morton S. Enslin.[3]

Nevertheless, a number of the criteria argue in favor of the historicity of Jesus' baptism. As we saw in Chapter 6, foremost among the criteria in this case is the criterion of embarrassment. There is no credible reason why the early church of the first generation should have gone out of its way to invent a story that would only create enormous difficulties for its inventor. After all, the story of the baptism presents the church's Lord being put in a position of inferiority to John by accepting from him a baptism of repentance for the forgiveness of sins. The narrative runs counter to the desire of all Four Gospels to make the historically independent John merely the forerunner, proclaimer, prophet, or witness of Jesus. More to the point, the idea that Jesus, whom early Christianity considered sinless and the source of forgiveness of sins for humanity,[4] should be associated with sinners by undergoing a "baptism of repentance for the forgiveness of sins" is hardly a fiction created by the church, unless the church enjoyed multiplying difficulties for itself. Significantly, in this case we are not simply projecting the embarrassment *we* may feel back onto the early church, which in theory might have had different sensitivities on the subject. As a matter of plain fact, the Gospels do evince embarrassment at the story of Jesus' baptism and try to "control the damage" as best they can.

The earliest kind of damage control seems already present in the pre-

Marcan tradition: the overshadowing of the actual event of baptism—which is quickly passed over and barely "narrated" in any real sense—with the theophany that immediately follows. Whether the original point of the theophany was to balance a baptism of repentance for the remission of sins with a heavenly proclamation of Jesus as the Son of God or to counter the claims of a rival Baptist community (which saw the baptism as proof of John's superiority to Jesus) with God's affirmation of Jesus' superiority,[5] the theophany obviously mitigates the theological difficulty that a bare, unadorned account of Jesus' baptism by John would create.

For the later evangelists, though, the baptism was such an embarrassment that even the theophany had to be supplemented by other "safety devices." In Matthew, the theophany after the baptism is balanced by a disclaimer before the baptism (Matt 3:14–15). As soon as Jesus appears, the Baptist recognizes him as the giver of the greater baptism John had foretold. John exclaims that *he* needs to be baptized by Jesus. Why should Jesus come to him to be baptized instead? Replying with perfect Matthean vocabulary, Jesus insists that John permit (*aphes*) this strange inversion of roles for the time being (*arti*) because in this way John and Jesus will join in the eschatological fulfillment of God's plan of salvation, foretold through the prophets (*houtōs gar prepon estin hēmin plērōsai pasan dikaiosynēn*).[6] Only at Jesus' bidding does John permit the baptism to proceed.

Luke takes a more radical approach by proleptically narrating John's imprisonment by Herod Antipas before Jesus comes on the scene to be baptized (Luke 3:19–20). Luke then simply mentions in passing, in an almost offhanded way, that Jesus was baptized; but he conveniently omits the name of the baptizer: "And it came to pass that, when all the people had been baptized, and after Jesus had been baptized and was praying, heaven was opened. . . ." This is not a one-time accidental slip or clumsy literary construction on Luke's part. He readily mentions John's activity of baptizing elsewhere. Indeed, in Acts he emphasizes that it is the beginning of the story about Jesus. But he never states that the reason why it is the beginning of the story about Jesus is that John himself baptized Jesus.[7] On the whole, Luke uses a clever ploy that dodges rather than denies the embarrassing datum.

As is to be expected, the radical Fourth Gospel supplies the most radical solution of all: the event of the baptism is simply suppressed. How, indeed, could the eternal Word made flesh receive baptism from John? Any account of Jesus' being baptized, with or without John, is accordingly absent, though the theophany with the spirit descending as a dove on Jesus is retained (John 1:32), without its traditional mooring in a narrative of Jesus' baptism. In the Fourth Gospel we are never told *when* this theophany takes place, and pointedly the theophany is not addressed to Jesus, as in the Synoptics. For how could the eternal Son of God need to be informed about his sonship? Instead, the theophany is directed to John the Baptist (the exact opposite of Mark's depiction!) to help him identify the one who would baptize with the holy spirit (John 1:33–34). Granted, then, that all Four Gospels, and apparently the tradition before them, felt acute embarrassment over Jesus' being baptized by John, the invention of the incident by the early church seems nigh impossible.

While the criterion of embarrassment is the major argument for the historicity of the baptism of Jesus, there is a slight possibility of constructing an argument from multiple attestation as well—though such an argument must remain indirect, not to say convoluted. While Matthew and Luke are patently dependent on Mark for the substance of their narratives of the baptism-plus-theophany (Mark 1:9–11 = Matt 3:13,16–17 ‖ Luke 3:21–22), there are some curious "minor agreements" of Matthew and Luke against Mark that might come from their use of a Q version of the baptism. These include the use of the aorist passive participle for the actual event of Jesus' baptism (Matthew: *baptistheis*, Luke: *baptisthentos*) as opposed to Mark's main verb *ebaptisthē*; the statement that the heavens were "opened" (Matthew: *ēneōchthēsan*, Luke: *aneōchthēnai*) instead of Mark's statement that they were "rent asunder" or "split" (*schizomenous*); a modifier that is added to Mark's simple "spirit" (Matthew: the spirit of God, Luke: the holy spirit); the statement that the spirit descended "upon him [Jesus]" (*ep' auton*) instead of Mark's "into him" (*eis auton*).

By themselves, these small agreements hardly prove a Q version of Jesus' baptism.[8] There is, though, a second consideration. The Q document clearly begins with the preaching and baptizing activity of John, culminating in his prophecy of the coming of the stronger one who will baptize with the holy spirit (Matt 3:11–12 ‖ Luke 3:16–17). The next Q pericope that we can be sure of is the Q version of the temptation of Jesus, in which Jesus is led by the *spirit* into the *desert* to be tempted by the devil (Matt 4:1–11 ‖ Luke 4:1–13). Was there nothing in between these two pericopes in Q? Do the motifs of the spirit acting on Jesus, the desert, and the title "Son of God" (used by the devil in his temptations) suddenly materialize without any explanation or preparation? That some story intervened in Q between John's preaching and the temptation of Jesus is especially suggested by the way the devil introduces his first two temptations: "If you are God's Son . . ." (Matt 4:3,6 par.).[9] In the Gospels of Matthew and Luke, this clearly picks up the voice of God at the end of the baptismal narrative: "You are [Matthew: This is] my son. . . ." That may have been true of the Q document as well. That the Q version of the temptation both presents the *spirit* as acting on Jesus and describes the testing of Jesus *as Son of God* argues for a connection of the Q temptation narrative with a Q version of the baptismal story such as we find in Mark (i.e., with the motifs of the spirit descending on Jesus and Jesus as Son of God). Granted, such arguments are not strictly probative and leave much room for doubt.[10] Still, if forced to choose between probabilities, I think it more likely that some form of a baptismal story stood in Q between the Baptist's promise of the stronger one (Matt 3:11–12 par.) and Jesus' temptation in the desert (Matt 4:1–11 par.).

Besides Q, the Johannine tradition may also supply an indirect argument for the use of the criterion of multiple attestation. As we have seen, although John the "un-Baptist" (the title is never used in the Fourth Gospel) is prominent in the Gospel, especially in chap. 1, although his activity of baptizing is mentioned a number of times (1:25,28,31,33; 3:23), and although his baptism is positively evaluated as an instrument for revealing Christ to Israel (John 1:31), Jesus' baptism by John is never mentioned, let alone narrated. Yet there is good reason to think that the Fourth Evangelist has purposely suppressed an action that existed in his Gospel tradition, an action that might play into the hands of a rival group, the Baptist sectarians of his day.[11] To avoid anything that would smack of the Son of God's subordination to John, the Evangelist simply omits the story of the baptism.[12]

Telltale traces remain, however, especially in John's statement that he was able to recognize Jesus because he saw the spirit descend like a dove from heaven and remain upon him (*ep' auton* in John 1:32, using the phrase that was probably used by Q as well; cf. Matt 3:16 || Luke 3:22). In effect, the Evangelist has detached the divine attestation of Jesus from the scene of his baptism and situated it instead in some otherwise unspecified vision granted to the Baptist. The tradition of theophany is probably continued in the immediate context when the Baptist says that this theophany has given him the knowledge that "this [Jesus] is the Son of God" (John 1:33–34; cf. Matt 3:17: "This is my son").[13]

A further hint that Jesus' baptism by John was known in the Johannine tradition is given in the First Epistle of John, which was probably written by a Johannine Christian other than the Fourth Evangelist, at a date somewhat later than the composition of the Fourth Gospel.[14] Throughout the Epistle, the author is arguing against a gnosticizing group that has separated from the Johannine community. In opposition to the group's emphasis on the divinity of Christ to the detriment of Jesus' full humanity (or at least the significance of his humanity for salvation), the author of the First Epistle stresses the true and full humanity of Jesus, along with the saving significance of his sacrificial death on the cross. The author sees the opponents' position as in effect splitting Christ into two realities: an earthly Jesus and a heavenly Son of God.

At one point (1 John 5:6), after affirming the identity of the earthly, human Jesus with the Son of God sent from the Father, the author continues: "This is the one who came through water and blood, Jesus Christ—not in the water only, but in the water and in the blood." This cryptic remark has generated many different interpretations in the course of Christian history.[15] Most likely the remark does not refer to the blood and water flowing from Christ's side after his death on the cross (John 19:34). The order of words is different (Gospel: blood and water; Epistle: water and blood).[16] Moreover, the point of the symbols in John 19:34 (by the death of Jesus [blood] the life-giving Spirit [water] is poured out on the believing community [the beloved disciple and Jesus' mother] at the foot of the cross) does not quite fit the Epistle's polemic against those who deny or devalue Jesus' full humanity in favor of the Son's divinity.

In my view, 1 John 5:6 is underlining the fully human dimension of Jesus throughout his earthly ministry by stressing (in true Semitic style) the two extreme points of that ministry, which are also the two extreme examples of how fully human Jesus was: his baptism by John in solidarity with sinful human beings and his bloody death on the cross. 1 John 1:5–6 is stressing that no greater proof of the identity of the heavenly Son of God with the earthly Jesus can be found than the fact that *Jesus Christ* (note the double name) came to save us by means of his humble baptism by John and his brutal yet saving death on the cross.[17] All this presupposes what the Fourth Gospel suppresses and what even the First Epistle alludes to only gingerly: that Jesus was baptized.[18]

Hence I think there are some grounds for claiming that the historicity of Jesus' baptism is also supported by the criterion of multiple attestation, with the Q and Johannine traditions independently alluding to what the Marcan tradition directly narrates. Some might even want to include the Acts of the Apostles, but at that point I think that the indirect argument becomes hopelessly tenuous.[19]

As for the criterion of discontinuity, I do not think that it necessarily casts doubt on the historicity of Jesus' baptism. The surprising thing about all of the NT statements concerning Christian baptism is that no NT author ever directly and explicitly links Christian baptism with Jesus' baptism, and the latter is never explicitly presented as the cause, archetype, or model of the former.[20] This is in marked contrast to the treatment of Christian baptism in the Church Fathers. In the NT, Christian baptism is regularly connected with or seen as a share in Christ's death and resurrection (e.g., Rom 6:3–11). Starting with Ignatius of Antioch, John's baptism of Jesus begins to be seen as the model, even the source of the efficacy, of Christian baptism: ". . . he [Jesus] was baptized in order that he might cleanse the water [of baptism] by his passion" (*Ephesians* 18:2).[21] This idea quickly becomes a common and widespread theme in the Fathers (e.g., Tertullian, Clement of Alexandria, Methodius, Ephraem, Gregory of Nazianzus, Maximus of Turin, Peter Chrysologus, and Proclus). By comparison, the absence of any such explicit link in the NT is remarkable. The idea that Christian baptism generated the account of Jesus' baptism as its prototype, that this link then totally disappeared in all NT documents, and that it then immediately reappeared in Ignatius and spread throughout the patristic period presents us with a splendid pattern of life-death-and-resurrection—but also with a very contorted tradition history. The simpler tradition history, namely, that Jesus' baptism by John historically preceded Christian baptism and only in due time came to be seen as the latter's prototype, is the much more natural reading of the data. Hence, in this limited sense, one might even add the criterion of discontinuity to the principal argument from embarrassment and, in my view, to the criterion of multiple attestation to construct the complete argument in favor of the historicity of Jesus' baptism. There are really no weighty arguments to the contrary. We may thus take the baptism of Jesus by John as the firm historical starting point for any treatment of Jesus' public ministry.[22]

II. THE MEANING OF JESUS' BAPTISM

If Jesus was actually baptized by John in the Jordan River somewhere around the beginning of A.D. 28, what does that mean for our understanding of Jesus? Can we know what his baptism meant to Jesus himself? Some would think the answers to these questions simple. For example, we need only go to the account of the theophany following the baptism (Mark 1:10–11) to find out how Jesus understood his baptism. But this approach is hopelessly naive, even if we adopt the ostensibly "critical" position that the theophany is a mythological representation of some psychological experience Jesus had at the time of his baptism. Such a psychological interpretation was beloved of the "liberal lives" of Jesus and still is found today.[23] The problem is that this approach completely ignores the fact that we have in the narrative of the theophany, as it now stands, a Christian "midrash," a learned use of various OT texts to present the reader of the Gospel with an initial interpretation of who Jesus is. The various echoes of OT texts, interpreted in the light of the developing christology of the early church, are easily listed in summary form:

(1) First of all, even before we come to OT prophecies, there is the question of the fulfillment of NT prophecy, namely of what the Baptist has just said. The descent of the spirit shows that Jesus is the one promised by John,[24] the one who will baptize with the spirit (Mark 1:8), hence the one on whom the spirit rests (with possible royal and prophetic allusions from Isa 11:2; 61:1). Jesus, being the fulfillment of everything John promised, is obviously superior to John. The OT texts then serve to explain in detail why Jesus is superior to John.

(2) As for fulfillment of OT prophecies: the heavenly voice proclaims Jesus to be God's Son in the words of Ps 2:7, the words Yahweh addresses to the Davidic king on the day of his enthronement in Jerusalem. The context of Psalm 2 (one of the royal psalms) and the symbolic "anointing" with the spirit imply that this Son of God is also the promised royal Davidic Messiah. One should not miss the emphasis in "*you* are my Son," i.e., *you*, not John.[25]

(3) The further designation of the Son as "the beloved" (*ho agapētos*) may be meant to conjure up the figure of Isaac, the "only beloved son" of Abraham.[26] From this possible allusion various exegetes draw further conclusions about a reference to the sacrifice of Isaac in Genesis 22 (the rabbinic *ʿăqēdat yiṣḥāq*), meant to foreshadow the sacrifice of Christ on the cross. But such an allusion is by no means certain.[27] Whether or not there is such a reference to Isaac, one point is clear: Jesus, not John, is *the* beloved of the Father.

(4) The final words of the heavenly voice, "in you I am well pleased," come from Isa 42:1: "Here is my servant . . . with whom I am pleased, upon whom I have put my spirit." The Son of God-Messiah is thus also the servant of Yahweh. In (Deutero-) Isaiah, this mysterious servant is empowered by God's

spirit to reestablish the covenant-community of Israel by his justice, his meek-
ness, his teaching, his prophetic ministry, and (if one may look as far ahead as
Isa 52:13–53:12) his sacrificial death for sinners. The regathering of a scattered
Israel, a task some might have seen fulfilled in John, is rather the work of the
servant in whom Yahweh is truly pleased, Jesus.

(5) The setting of the bank of a river, the splitting open of the heavens, and
a symbolic vision calling an individual to a prophetic ministry addressed to a
sinful Israel all recall the inaugural vision of Ezekiel by the river Chebar in
Babylon (Ezek 1:1). No such detailed inaugural vision and call to prophecy are
recounted in the Gospels' description of the adult John.

(6) The splitting open of the heavens that God might descend in an eschatological theophany may also carry overtones of Isa 63:19: "Oh that you would
rend the heavens and come down!" The wider context of Isaiah 63 ties in well
with themes suggested by the story of Jesus' baptism: redemption by passing
through water, exodus from Egypt, Moses the servant, God granting his holy
spirit to the people Israel. Especially relevant are verses like 63:11: "And he
[Israel] remembered the days of old, Moses [and] his people. Where is he
[namely, God] who brought up from the sea the shepherd [namely, Moses] of
his flock? Where is he who placed in their midst his holy spirit?"[28]

The overall impression given by these numerous OT texts, all converging
on the initial event of Jesus' public life, is that the fulfillment of all prophecy
is at hand. To sum up, then, the message of the theophany: the Son of God,
the royal Davidic Messiah, is anointed with God's spirit to be the final prophet
and servant of the Lord sent to a sinful people. On those Israelites who heed
him he will pour out this spirit of the end time, just as it has been poured out
on him. Every point in this rich synthesis of OT prophecy and fulfillment
reinforces a not-so-subliminal message: the person of whom all these things
are true is obviously superior to John the Baptist, even though John confers
the baptism that provides the setting of and prelude to the theophany. Not
accidentally, this early Christian composition stresses that it is the theophany,
and not John's baptism by itself, that reveals the truth about Jesus.

In other words, as Anton Vögtle has argued at length, in the theophany of
Mark 1:10–11 we have a Christian composition interpreting the significance
of Jesus' person and mission vis-à-vis his potential rival John. It is not surprising that one exegete goes so far as to define the literary genre of the account
of Jesus' baptism as "a vision that interprets" (*Deute-Vision*).[29] The theophany
does not mirror some inner experience Jesus had at the time;[30] it mirrors the
desire of the first-generation Christian church to define Jesus as soon as the
primitive Gospel story begins—all the more so because this definition was
needed to counter the impression of Jesus' subordination to John, implicit
in the tradition of the former being baptized by the latter. Indeed, Christian
embarrassment over the *fact* of Jesus' baptism was probably a major factor in
the creation of the *story* of Jesus' baptism, complete with interpretative theophany. A possible *Sitz im Leben* would be the rivalry between Christians and
followers of the Baptist as they competed for candidates for each group's bap-

tism. Be that as it may, I think the basic point is clear: a psychological interpretation of the baptismal story as a path to Jesus' inner experience ignores the basic insights of close to a century of tradition, form, and redaction criticism.

I readily admit that not all would agree with this assessment. Apart from fundamentalists and conservatives who would object on a priori grounds, some exegetes would disagree for more sophisticated reasons. For instance, James D. G. Dunn suggests tentatively that the theophany does give us some entrée into Jesus' personal experience at his baptism. Dunn points out that two key concepts that governed Jesus' preaching and praxis throughout his ministry were the loving care of God as Father and the startling power of the spirit manifest in Jesus' work. These twin realities, which Jesus apparently experienced deeply himself, correlate perfectly with the descent of the spirit and the heavenly voice ("You are my son") after Jesus' baptism. Hence Dunn cautiously raises the question: "Why should the traditions fasten on this episode in Jesus' life [i.e., his baptism] if they had no reason for making the link [between his baptism and these two themes of his ministry] and many reasons against it?" Dunn goes on to answer his own question: "The most probable reason . . . is that Jesus underwent a significant experience—significant in terms of his consciousness of sonship and Spirit—on the occasion of his baptism by John."[31]

Though Dunn's proposal seems reasonable enough, one may ask whether it fully comes to grips with the fact that the narrative of the theophany after the baptism is a Christian composition. To be sure, the narrative encapsulates nicely two main themes of Jesus' preaching and praxis.[32] But what else would we expect from a Christian narrative that sought to supply an initial definition of who Jesus is? Dunn is surely correct on one matter: we must suppose that at some point Jesus crystallized these two key themes of his ministry. But whether this happened before, during, or after his baptism is a difficult, perhaps impossible question to answer. Suffice it to say that during the whole process of leaving his home and occupation, hearing John's message and accepting his baptism, possibly spending some time with John as his disciple, and finally striking out on his own, Jesus no doubt developed intellectually and experienced existentially these key insights into his relationship with God as Father and the powerful activity of the spirit manifest in his own life. Indeed, it is possible that the crystallization of these key themes may have had something to do with Jesus' parting company with John. But to be any more specific about exactly when and how this happened (e.g., at the moment of his baptism) risks going beyond reasonable inference from the data and falling into the psychologizing of Jesus practiced by the old "liberal lives."

If the theophany cannot be used to ascertain the original meaning of Jesus' baptism (i.e., what Jesus intended by it, or how he understood it once it happened, or how he saw it fitting into the course of his life), can anything at all be said about the significance of this event for Jesus?

I think a bare minimum is clear. At the very least, Jesus' baptism meant a fundamental break in his life: baptism as watershed. As far as our meager sources allow us to know, before his baptism by John, Jesus was a respectable, unexceptional, and unnoticed woodworker in Nazareth. Both family and neighbors were shocked and offended by Jesus once he undertook his ministry, and not without reason. Apparently there was nothing in his previous life that foreshadowed or ostensibly prepared for his decision to dedicate himself totally to a religious mission to all Israel, a mission lacking any official sanction. His baptism by John is so important because it is the only external, historically verifiable marker of this pivotal "turning around" in Jesus' life—his "conversion" in the root sense of that word.[33]

Still, saying that Jesus' baptism was the external marker of his conversion does not take us very far. Was it also the cause of the conversion, or the symbolic celebration of a decision already made, or one step on a path leading to a decision still in the future? Any of these options is possible. He could have already decided to "go public" with a religious mission before he approached John for baptism. He could have reached the decision during his reception of baptism. And his decision could have waxed to maturity only some time after the baptism, perhaps after Jesus had spent a period of time in the inner circle of John's disciples. Once the theophany is removed as evidence, we must confess that we do not know. To make the baptism itself the precise moment of Jesus' conversion is to mistake the account of the theophany, composed by later Christian theology, for a clinical report on Jesus' psychological state in A.D. 28.

Nevertheless, no matter the exact time when or circumstances in which Jesus made his basic decision to break with his past and to dedicate his life to a religious mission, the baptism by John tells us something about the nature of his decision and his religious views, at least at the very beginning of his public ministry. To be sure, his plans and ideas may have changed later, but at the beginning of A.D. 28 his coming to John for baptism did say something particular about his religious state at that time.

First of all, the baptism indicates that Jesus knew, presumably by hearing it firsthand, the basic eschatological message of John and agreed with it. In other words—if I may quickly recapitulate what we saw in Chapter 12—Jesus agreed with John on the following points: (1) The end of Israel's history as Israel had experienced it up until now was fast approaching. (2) Israel as a people had gone astray, had in effect apostatized; and so all Israel was in danger of being consumed by the fire of God's wrathful judgment, soon to come. (3) The only way to pass from the present sinful state in which Abraham's children were caught to the state of those Israelites who would be saved on the last day was to undergo a basic change of mind and heart. This interior change had to be reflected in a basic change in the way one lived one's life, and it had to be sealed by submission to the special, once-and-for-all, ritual immersion administered by John. Jesus' radical change, embodied in beginning a full-scale religious ministry, may have had its seedbed in the radical change of life that John demanded of every Israelite receiving his baptism. The public ministry may thus have been Jesus' special way of concretizing John's general call to all Israel for a transformation of one's mind, heart, and conduct. (4) Implicit in all this is Jesus' recognition of John as a prophet sent by God to all Israel in the short, critical time left before the judgment. In other words, Jesus acknowledged John to be *a* or *the* eschatological prophet.[34] As I pointed out in Chapter 12, this basic acceptance of Jesus' message and baptism tells us that Jesus shared John's outlook of imminent eschatology tinged with apocalyptic. At least at this opening stage of Jesus' public life, the picture of an un-eschatological Jesus, Jesus the wisdom teacher concerned with people's lives only here and now—a picture championed recently by some American exegetes—simply does not square with historical reality. It is not surprising that John the Baptist does not play a large role in 20th-century sketches of the un-eschatological Jesus.

These four points are basically unexceptionable and give us a basis to build on. But can we go further in probing what Jesus' baptism might imply? Certainly Jesus' acceptance of John's baptism means that Jesus saw himself very much as a part of the people of Israel—which in John's vision of things means part of a sinful people threatened with divine destruction. Jesus accepted John's baptism of repentance as the divinely appointed means of passage from this sinful Israel to a group of Israelites promised salvation on the day of judgment. This implies two interesting corollaries worth investigating.

(1) First, Jesus was in effect accepting an unofficial, "charismatic" ritual, a once-and-for-all baptism administered only by John, as necessary for salvation.[35] This coheres with something we shall see later on: no matter what reforms of outlook or practice Jesus urged, there is no indication that he simply rejected ritual as a part of religious life, be that ritual connected with the synagogue, the Jerusalem temple, or John's baptism.[36] Indeed, Jesus would have been a very strange 1st-century Jew if he had rejected all religious ritual. Very different types of Jews—from Philo, the Therapeutae, and the Essenes to the Pharisees and the Sadducees—might disagree on what rituals to observe and how to observe them. But they all took for granted that external ritual, accompanied by the proper inner dispositions, was an integral part of religious life. Religion within the limits of pure reason, shorn of public, corporate ritual, was not the spiritual program of 1st-century Jews, not even an allegorizing Philo or an ascetic contemplative from among the Therapeutae, to say nothing of the Baptist or the Nazarene. Indeed, both John and Jesus, at least in early A.D. 28, were centering their religious lives on a new type of rite that lacked the sanction of tradition and the temple authorities. Their eschatological outlook did not mean a cessation of interest in ritual activity. But it did mean the introduction of a new type of ritual that implicitly called into question the sufficiency of temple and synagogue worship as then practiced.

At this point, it may be helpful to stop for a moment and reflect on an important insight stressed by Albert Schweitzer and often ignored since, especially by American scholars eager to "sell" the historical Jesus for public consumption. We first meet Jesus as a 1st-century Palestinian Jew who thought that Israel's world, at least as presently known, was swiftly coming to an end, that all Israel was threatened by God with destruction by an imminent fiery judgment, and that being plunged into the Jordan River by a certain John could—along with repentance and a reformed life—help one escape this judgment. In other words, on the threshold of his public ministry, Jesus strikes us moderns as very strange. Apart from certain extreme religious groups, few people in the United States today could readily identify with such views or even sympathize with them. In the bowels of the Harvard Divinity School library, the unpapal conclave assembled to write a consensus paper on the historical Jesus would have to scratch its collective head.

Actually, this insight into the strangeness of Jesus is all to the good. It keeps us aware of the yawning religious and cultural gap that separates the historical Jesus from modern Americans, be they Christians, Jews, or atheists. The chasm between the historical Jesus and a late 20th-century American Catholic or Protestant is obvious. The triumphant banner of "Jesus the Jew"—to be sure, a valid insight of 20th-century scholarship—may obscure the fact that the gap between Jesus and any American Jew—observant or not—who has come to grips with modernity is almost as great. My point is that a sober estimation of the strange nature of the figure we label the historical Jesus quickly dispels the facile relevance some claim for him. If this historical Jesus holds any relevance for present-day Americans, such relevance can be grasped only after a lengthy hermeneutical reflection that takes seriously the chasm between him and us. While this appreciation of the strangeness of Jesus might be disappointing to some who had already decided what uses they would put him to,[37] it is a gain for scholars who need to be reminded constantly not to project their pet theological agendas onto the legitimating figure of Jesus.

(2) The stress on the fact that Jesus accepts John's baptism as the means of escaping the condemnation threatening the sinful people of Israel and of joining the group of the saved raises a second corollary that is also a thorny question. The Gospel of Mark describes John as proclaiming "a baptism of repentance for the forgiveness of sins" (1:4) and those who receive his baptism as "confessing their sins" (1:6). Needless to say, none of the Four Gospels depicts Jesus confessing his sins as he is baptized, and the conversation between John and Jesus that Matthew inserts before Jesus' baptism is meant to preclude any such idea (Matt 3:14–15). But what of the historical reality? Did Jesus come to John to be baptized because, as an individual, he was driven by a deep personal consciousness of being a sinner? After all, the very definition of John's baptism, according to Mark (and Luke), was a ritual expressing repentance with a view to having one's sins forgiven and so being saved on the day of God's wrathful judgment. If this was the very essence of John's baptism, and if apologetic verses like Matt 3:14–15 are later creations to obviate the theological difficulty Christians felt, are we faced with the unavoidable historical conclusion that Jesus saw himself a sinner in need of repentance and forgiveness? Is it only a theological bias that refuses to see this necessary conclusion from the fact that Jesus sought baptism at John's hands?

Such is the view of Paul Hollenbach, who thinks that theological considerations have kept exegetes from admitting the obvious: Jesus sought baptism from John because, like all the other candidates, he thought himself a sinner.[38] To be sure, Christian faith, armed with NT texts and later church teaching on Jesus' sinlessness, finds such a position unacceptable, even blasphemous. But, in the quest for the historical Jesus, the "rules of the game" allow no appeal to what is known or held by faith; to this extent, Hollenbach is correct. The data and inferences drawn from the data must be equally open to and testable by all observers. This is not to deny the faith stance of orthodox Christians; it is simply to say that such faith cannot function as evidence or argument in the narrowly restricted confines of Jesus-of-history research.[39]

What then of Hollenbach's claim? A number of distinctions need to be made. (1) As we saw in Chapter 12, some exegetes consider "a baptism of repentance for the forgiveness of sins" a Christian formulation,[40] a formulation clearly contradicted by Josephus' description of the Baptist in Book 18 of the *Antiquities.* For those who accept that opinion, the problem may not be felt with all its sharpness. However, I have argued in Chapter 12 that the phrase does correctly express the view both John and his followers held of his baptism. My championing of what might have seemed a "conservative" view in Chapter 12 was probably welcomed by people anxious to guard the historicity of the Gospel narratives in every instance. But championing the historicity of this text, however reassuring it might seem at first glance, only creates a larger theological problem. It is that problem I must grapple with here.

(2) Hollenbach exhorts us to leave behind theological positions and treat the question on purely historical instead of theological grounds. Yet even here distinctions are necessary, as Hollenbach himself realizes.[41] On purely historical grounds, the bald question of whether Jesus had committed sins or was a sinner evaporates. For "sin" is a preeminently *theo*-logical, not historical, category. Sin refers to an offense against God, a radical falling away from fidelity to God, an action that ruptures a person's relationship with God.[42] Strictly speaking, therefore, one cannot render a non-theological, purely historical judgment as to whether Jesus was a sinner. One can speak historically about whether Jesus committed crimes or transgressed certain laws, since "crime," "wrongdoing," and "illegal acts" are all categories that are verifiable empirically and historically. Pilate adjudged Jesus guilty of a crime worthy of death, and so we can say that in the public forum of Roman law Jesus was a criminal. We could go on to discuss from a historical vantage point whether *de facto* Jesus performed certain acts or transgressed certain laws, whether his actions resulted in his rightly being judged a criminal and executed, according to the laws in force at the time. It is theoretically possible that we could reach the historical conclusion: yes, Jesus was a criminal or a wrongdoer in the sense of being clearly a transgressor of a particular law or system of laws (be that law system Roman or Jewish) and of being adjudged such by duly constituted legal authorities.

It is a judgment of an entirely different order to say: yes, *de facto*, Jesus was a sinner. That is tantamount to saying: yes, Jesus had ruptured his relationship with God; or yes, Jesus had proven unfaithful to God; or yes, Jesus had turned decisively away from the all-good Creator and toward some limited, created good. What historian would be in a position to make such a judgment, and on what grounds or by what criteria could he make it? To speak objectively, empirically, with strictly scientific historical methods of Jesus' sins or of Jesus as a sinner is a contradiction in terms. To deal properly with the question is to enter into the realm of faith and theology; those who claim to be "only" historians must wait outside the confessional door.

(3) But what if we change the question? What if we ask not whether Jesus was a sinner or had committed sins, but whether Jesus *considered* himself a sinner and was therefore seeking forgiveness of his personal sins by receiving John's baptism? This is the position of Hollenbach. In theory, a historian might inquire as to whether Jesus considered himself a sinner, just as a historian might ask whether Jesus' adversaries considered him a sinner (according to the Gospels, some did).[43] In fact, though, by posing the question of whether Jesus viewed himself as a sinner, we are once again in danger of reverting to the psychologizing of the "liberal lives." What data allow us to enter into the depths of the individual conscience of the historical Jesus to find out whether he thought himself a sinner or which of his acts he considered sinful? In my opinion, the mere fact of Jesus' acceptance of John's message and baptism does not yield sufficient data to form a judgment in the matter.[44]

Here again we face a cultural and religious gap between the 1st and the 20th centuries. Modern Christians, especially Catholics, think of repentance and confession of sins very much in terms of the personal sins of the individual penitent with an uneasy conscience. For example, despite all the exhortations of the post-Vatican II church, some Catholics who frequent the confessional still tend to see confession as a time for excessive introspection and the dredging up of every past peccadillo that can be recalled. The spotlight is focused on the private conscience of the individual, judging in isolation his or her actions. In this, such Catholics remain heirs of what Krister Stendahl years ago branded "the introspective conscience of the West."[45] At the time, Stendahl was warning against interpreting Paul, who was actually focusing on the fate of whole peoples within the sweep of salvation history, in terms of the later perspective of an Augustine or a Luther, the perspective of the tortured conscience of an introspective individual trying to find a gracious God.

The same warning holds true, a fortiori, of our interpretation of Jesus— especially since we have had our introspective tendencies both deepened by Freud and cheapened by Californian psycho-babble. Confession of sin in ancient Israel did not mean unraveling a lengthy laundry-list of personal peccadilloes, with the result that worship of God was turned into a narcissistic reflection on self. Confession of sin in ancient Israel was a God-centered act of worship that included praise and thanksgiving.[46] Confession of sin often meant recalling God's gracious deeds for an ungrateful Israel, a humble admission that one was a member of this sinful people, a recounting of the infidelities and apostasies of Israel from early on down to one's own day, and a final resolve to change and be different from one's ancestors.[47] Even apart from the question of one's particular personal sins, one was part of this history of sin simply because one was part of this sinful people.

In some cases, the great prayers confessing apostasy in the OT are uttered by religious individuals who actually have taken no personal part in the nation's apostasy, though they deeply feel their involvement in the deeds and fate of the people Israel, from whom they draw their identity. This is the case, for example, with the deeply moving confessional prayers of Ezra (Ezra 9:6–15; Neh 9:6–37):

> My God, I am ashamed and brought too low to raise my face to you, my God. Our iniquities are so many they tower above our heads, and our guilt is as high as heaven. From the days of our fathers our guilt has been great even unto today, and because of our iniquities we have been delivered—we, our kings, and our priests—to the power of the kings of the [foreign] lands, to the sword, to captivity, to pillage, and to shame, as is the case this very day. (Ezra 9:6–7)

> [After mention of God's mercy and Israel's restoration after the exile:] And now, our God, what can we say after this? For we have forsaken your commandments, which you commanded through your servants the prophets. . . . Here we are in your presence with our guilty deeds; but we cannot stand in your presence because of [all] this. (Ezra 9:10–11,15)

> [After a lengthy recital of God's saving deeds for Israel down through the centuries, and Israel's constant backsliding into sin, which led to the exile, Ezra prays:] Behold, we are slaves upon it [the promised land]; and its great produce [is given] to the kings whom you placed over us because of our sins. They rule over our bodies and over our cattle as they will, and we are in great distress. (Neh 9:36–37)

Ezra was certainly not, as an individual, a participant in Israel's national apostasy, which he identified in particular with intermarriage. Indeed, he fought fiercely against it. Yet he was part of this sinful people and its history; and his positive religious function demanded his identification with, not his separation from, the sinful group he sought to lead and form.

It is noteworthy that this same people-centered and history-centered concept of the confession of sins is seen at Qumran, in the ritual by which candidates entered into the covenant community at the annual ceremony for the renewal of the covenant (1QS 1:18–2:2):

> On the occasion of their [i.e., the candidates'] passing over into the covenant, the priests and the levites will bless the God of saving deeds and of all his faithful works. And all those passing over into the covenant will say after them: "Amen, amen." And the priests shall recount the just deeds of God manifested in his[48] powerful works and they shall proclaim all [his] merciful acts of love toward Israel. And the levites shall recount the iniquities of the sons of Israel

and all their guilty transgressions and their sin(s) during the reign of Belial. And all those passing over into the covenant shall confess after them saying: "We have committed iniquity, we have transgressed, we have sinned, we have committed evil, we and our fathers before us, for we walked contrary to the statutes of faithfulness and justice. . . . But he has bestowed upon us his merciful deeds of love from eternity to eternity." And the priests shall bless all the men of the lot of God, who walk perfectly in all his ways. . . .

As in the OT confessions of Ezra and other great leaders, so at Qumran there is an overriding sense of solidarity between those actually making the confession of sins and their sinful ancestors, as well as their sinful compatriots of the present moment. Moreover, there may be in these confessions a sense of complicity insofar as those confessing the sins of the people feel that they personally had not done enough to prevent others from transgressing but instead were somehow accomplices by their silence or inaction. This might especially be true of leaders like Ezra—and possibly the Teacher of Righteousness. Clearly, those who recite these formal confessions at Qumran's renewal of the covenant are not primarily concerned with unearthing and listing their personal failings but in confessing that they are part of a sinful and ungrateful people, part of the history of guilt as well as of salvation—perhaps simply by inaction—even as they ask God to renew his mercy in allowing them to pass from a sinful past and a sinful community into a renewed community marked by the doing of God's will in the end time. To interpret these confessions from the vantage point of "the introspective conscience of the West" is to miss the point.[49]

Am I therefore claiming that these considerations show that Jesus was *not* confessing his personal sins or seeking forgiveness for them as he accepted John's baptism? Certainly not; such a judgment would go beyond the data just as much as a judgment that Jesus was driven to baptism by a consciousness of personal sin. When I treated the criteria of historicity in Chapter 6, I pointed out that at times we must reconcile ourselves to a decision of *non liquet*. As galling as it may seem, some great questions like "the sinfulness of Jesus" do not allow of a clear answer on purely historical grounds. Granted the lack of hard evidence, personal views, including one's faith commitment or anti-faith commitment, will weigh heavily in each scholar's assessment of the situation.

If I may conjure up my mythical conclave in the bowels of the Harvard Divinity School library: the Christians, Jews, and atheists trying to write a consensus paper on Jesus would probably all interpret the particular event of Jesus' baptism according to their different overall perceptions of Jesus. Atheists would probably waive the strictly *theo*-logical category of sin as having no meaning for them, though they would grant that a religious Jew of the 1st century might well have considered himself a sinner. While having great respect for Jesus as a religious figure, the Jews would see no reason to deny that he could commit sin just as much as any other human being. In this they might be joined by some liberal Protestants. Orthodox Protestants and Catholics would hold to their faith in the sinlessness of Jesus and interpret his baptism accordingly. The point is, the mere fact of Jesus' baptism in itself does not decide the question of whether Jesus considered himself a sinner in the sense of having a consciousness of personal sins. In this matter his baptism is open to a number of interpretations, and the data available do not allow us to probe the depths of Jesus' individual psyche for a definitive answer.

Nevertheless, our quest for the historical baptism has not been totally fruitless. We have seen that, around the beginning of A.D. 28, Jesus of Nazareth, no doubt in the company of other Jews, journeyed from Nazareth to the Jordan River to receive John's baptism. By doing this Jesus acknowledged John's charismatic authority as an eschatological prophet, accepted his message of imminent fiery judgment on a sinful Israel, submitted to his baptism as a seal of his resolve to change his life and as a pledge of salvation as part of a purified Israel, on whom God (through some agent?) would pour out the holy spirit on the last day. All this tells us something about Jesus' view of John. But did John have any particular knowledge or opinion of Jesus at the time of the latter's baptism? Mark's Gospel gives no indication here or elsewhere that the Baptist ever recognized Jesus as "the coming one"; the theophany (1:10–11) is directed solely to Jesus, as befits Mark's secretive Gospel. The Q document suggests that John had questions about Jesus' person and ministry at a later date (Matt 11:2–3 || Luke 7:18–19). The Baptist's testimony to Jesus in the Gospels of Matthew and John is clearly later Christian theology, taking the sting out of the embarrassing datum of Jesus' submission to baptism (Matt 3:14–15; John 1:19–36). We therefore have no grounds for thinking that, at the moment of Jesus' baptism, the Baptist saw in this thirty-something Jew from Nazareth anything more than another eager follower presenting himself for John's ritual purification. But was this the end of their relationship?

III. JESUS A DISCIPLE OF JOHN?

The question whether Jesus was a disciple of the Baptist immediately generates a further question: What do you mean by disciple?[50] By definition, the very fact that Jesus left Nazareth, came to the region of the Jordan to hear John, and accepted his message to the point of receiving his baptism means that, in the broad sense of the word, Jesus became John's disciple. Besides being an eschatological prophet, and indeed because of that, John was also a spiritual master and guide who taught a particular ritual observance as a sign of beginning a new way of life. To that extent, by submitting to his message and baptism, Jesus became the disciple, the pupil, the student of this rabbi called John.[51]

This point is usually granted without further ado. What is in dispute is the use of "disciple" in the narrower sense. After his baptism, did Jesus stay with John for some period of time, joining an inner circle of the baptized who followed John on his baptizing tours up and down the Jordan valley (cf. John 1:28,35–37; 3:23), assisted John in his preaching and baptizing (3:25),[52] received more detailed teaching from him about his message (3:26–30), and shared his ascetic spirituality of fasting (Mark 2:18), prayer (Luke 11:1), and perhaps (at least temporarily) celibacy?[53] Immediately, we must put ourselves on guard, since the information about John's disciples in the Gospels and Acts is slight and indirect and might reflect the practice of Baptist sectarians in the early days of the church rather than during John's lifetime. Nevertheless, that there were such disciples during the time of John's ministry is made likely by multiple attestation, as the citations just given from John, Mark, and Luke's special tradition show.

There is no indication, however, of any structured community during John's lifetime, or indeed after his death. Disciples of John continued through the 1st century, as Acts 19:1–7 shows and John's Gospel intimates by its mild polemic. Yet, despite claims about connections with the later religious group known as the Mandeans, an identifiable group of disciples in continuity with the historical Baptist does not seem to have survived into subsequent centuries, though other baptizing sects certainly did. Part of the difficulty of speaking about the disciples of the Baptist arises from their amorphous nature, especially during John's ministry. Jesus, Andrew, and Philip (John 1:35–37,40,43–44) were probably not the only Jews around the Baptist who moved in and out of his ambit. As far as we know, no one who received John's baptism was obliged ipso facto to remain with John, and no one who did remain with him was obliged ipso facto to do so permanently. Hence talk of "defection" or "apostasy" from John's inner circle is questionable, since the group of people around John may well have been largely unstructured and impermanent.[54]

With all these provisos and caveats, we can now pose our question with greater understanding of what we are asking: After his baptism, did Jesus stay for a while in the inner circle of John's disciples? Did Jesus become a disciple of John in the narrower sense of the word? Scholars line up on both sides of the issue. Becker and Hollenbach strongly support the position that Jesus was a disciple of John in the narrower sense.[55] On the other side, Ernst exhibits great reserve in the matter, while Gnilka rejects the idea.[56] Obviously, things are not as clear as some might claim. Two initial points need to be made.

First of all, one should observe the irony that the only evidence, however indirect, that Jesus was a disciple of John comes from the much-maligned Fourth Gospel. The Q material in Matt 11:2–19 par. is sometimes invoked as proof, but the statements there need mean only that John and Jesus were both popular preachers, similar yet different in their ministries, and that therefore Jesus saw a need to define his position vis-à-vis John.[57] A fortiori, the dispute story over Jesus' authority and John's baptism in Mark 11:27–33 parrs. does not prove that Jesus had been John's disciple in the narrower sense. Without Chapters 1 and 3 of the Fourth Gospel, I doubt that the idea would have struck anyone that these Q and Marcan traditions indicate that Jesus had been a disciple of John. The narrative framework of the Synoptic Gospels enforces the impression of a swift succession of events: Jesus is baptized by John, Jesus then immediately spends forty days in the wilderness (the temptation story), John is then arrested, and Jesus then goes into Galilee to begin his ministry.[58] If anything, the Marcan story line is constructed precisely to exclude any time when Jesus might have stayed in John's circle of disciples. Ironically, we owe the breakthrough-insight into the possibility of Jesus' apprenticeship in the "school" of the Baptist to the Gospel that is usually shunted aside as unreliable for reconstructing the historical Jesus. In this one case, many critics are willing to say, at least *sotto voce*, that the Fourth Gospel is right and the Synoptics are wrong.

Second, despite my refusal to rule the Fourth Gospel out of court a priori as unhistorical, I recognize that special caution is called for when treating the Baptist in the Fourth Gospel. To begin with, being dependent on this Gospel alone, we are deprived of multiple attestation. Then, too, while the Fourth Gospel is not to be rejected out of hand as a possible source for the historical Jesus, even its ardent admirers usually admit that the Evangelist's theology has massively reshaped the tradition reflected in his Gospel, especially the sayings tradition. Finally, even if we do accept the narrative in chaps. 1 and 3 of the Fourth Gospel as basically historical, we must be honest: nowhere in these chapters does the Gospel state explicitly that Jesus was John's disciple. Jesus' discipleship is rather inferred from his appearing in the Baptist's ambit, from Jesus' first followers' being drawn from the group of the Baptist's disciples, and from Jesus' apparent imitation of John's practice of baptizing disciples, an imitation that creates a certain rivalry. These are intriguing clues, but only clues; a great deal of argumentation lies between them and any conclusion. Hence one can appreciate Ernst's call for reserve about what must remain speculation.[59] With that caution, let us take a look at each of the clues.

(1) John shares one clue with the Synoptics and Acts: the Baptist's prophecy in John 1:27 about "the one coming after me" (*ho opisō mou erchomenos*; cf. *erchetai ho ischyroteros mou opisō mou* in Mark 1:7 parr.).[60] Those who support the idea of Jesus' being a disciple of John claim that elsewhere in the Gospels *erchomai opisō* always carries the sense of following after a master as a disciple; it never has a temporal sense.[61] Yet, even if we were to grant this claim as far as the later stages of the Christian tradition and redaction of the Gospels go, the idea of discipleship does not in all probability represent the original sense of the saying in Mark 1:7 and a fortiori in John 1:27.[62]

As we saw in Chapter 12, if we accept this logion as coming from the historical Baptist, it must be understood in the context of his own independent ministry, without any reference to Jesus. Consequently, scholars' attempts to identify "the one who comes" usually range from God through a heavenly Son of Man to an earthly Messiah or an Elijah-like prophet. Whatever the correct solution, none of these figures would have ever been designated by the Baptist as one of his disciples.[63] In the mouth of the Baptist, the original saying must have had a temporal sense: "the one who will appear soon after me." It is possible that later Christian tradition understood *erchetai . . . opisō* as referring to discipleship instead. But, granted the tendency of NT authors to make John increasingly subordinate to Jesus rather than vice-versa, I think it more likely that even in our Gospels the sense is temporal: the adult Jesus appears on the stage of history later than the Baptist, and yet he is the Baptist's superior, not merely a follower or successor. Hence the situation is not comparable to Moses and Joshua or Elijah and Elisha. In short, John 1:27 parr. drops out of consideration as proof that Jesus was a disciple of John in the narrow sense of the word.[64]

(2) Thus, we are left with the clues that appear only in John's Gospel. These clues are especially suggestive because the Fourth Evangelist seems to have as one of his opponents—though not the fiercest of them—the "Baptist sectarians," i.e., those who have continued down through the 1st century A.D. to revere the Baptist rather than Jesus as *the* significant religious figure (perhaps the Messiah).[65] Hence the Fourth Gospel does all it can to remove any vestiges of an independent role for John. He is no longer called "the Baptist," the title that expressed his unique position and praxis. His only function in the Fourth Gospel is to be a witness to Jesus. Having rejected all sorts of OT titles in the opening narrative of the Gospel (1:19–22), he will accept only one OT designation: the "voice" of Isa 40:3, the perfect foil yet vehicle of the eternal "Word" made flesh (1:23; cf. 1:14). John's whole role in the Fourth Gospel is summed up by his last directly quoted words (3:30): "He [Jesus] must increase, I must decrease." Yet none of this is a polemic against John himself, who is extolled as the first great human witness to Jesus in the Gospel; rather, it is a polemic against an overly exalted estimation of John by the followers of the Baptist who later refused to become Christians.

Once we understand this basic thrust of the treatment of John and Jesus in the Fourth Gospel, a few statements about their relationship stand out like proverbial sore thumbs, since they run so counter to the redactional intention of the author. Apparently these statements were so firmly rooted in the special Johannine tradition that they could not be effaced, no matter how embarrassing they were (one is reminded of the baptism of Jesus in the Synoptic tradition). The reason for their deep-rootedness may be the fact that some early Christians in the Johannine community did actually stem from the circle of John the Baptist and carried these traditions with them when they gave their allegiance to Jesus (or to the early church).[66] Another reason may be that the Baptist sectarians also knew about the origins of Jesus and his first disciples in the circle of John the Baptist, and in their polemics they did not let the Johannine Christians forget the uncomfortable fact. Let us look at the three passages in the Fourth Gospel that may reflect this situation.[67]

(a) The first group of relevant statements is found in John 1:29–45. We have seen how the Fourth Gospel has consciously suppressed the event of Jesus' baptism by John; as far as this Gospel is concerned, the event never happened. All the stranger then is the fact that Jesus first appears in the Gospel's narrative in a sudden, unprepared-for way, in the ambit of the people surrounding the Baptist—people who are either adversaries (1:19–28) or disciples

(1:35–37). Without explanation, therefore, Jesus *from Nazareth* (his geographical origin is stressed later on in chap. 1, in vv 45–46) makes his debut in the Gospel narrative neither in Bethlehem nor in Nazareth nor in Jerusalem, but in the environs of Bethany across the Jordan, where John is baptizing (1:28). Since Jesus is hardly one of the Baptist's adversaries and is not presenting himself to be baptized, the natural thrust of the narrative suggests he is among the Baptist's disciples—a suggestion that, not surprisingly, is never made explicit.

In the story that follows, a number of John's disciples (at least Andrew and Philip;[68] probably Peter and Nathanael are to be considered his disciples as well) transfer their allegiance to Jesus. Granted the theological program of the Fourth Evangelist, it is difficult to imagine him making up the story that some of the most important disciples of Jesus had first chosen the Baptist as their master and that they then gravitated to Jesus without Jesus taking any initiative. Needless to say, the Baptist's recognition of Jesus as the preexistent Lamb of God who takes away the sin of the world is Christian theology of the Johannine brand, as is also the presentation of John urging his disciples to follow Jesus. Yet when all the Johannine theology is stripped away, an embarrassing and surprising fact remains—a fact one would have never guessed from the Synoptic presentation: some of the most important disciples of Jesus first gave their allegiance to the Baptist, and only after a while transferred it to Jesus, whom they first met in the Baptist's circle.

It is at this point that the Synoptics supply the vital missing link in John's narrative.[69] The reason why Andrew and the others first encountered Jesus in the ambit of the Baptist is that Jesus, like themselves and other disciples of John, had been baptized by their common master. Before Jesus came to John to be baptized, he was unknown to the world at large. If some disciples of the Baptist came to transfer their allegiance to him while they were still in the company of the Baptist, that presumes that Jesus had stayed in the Baptist's orbit long enough for some of the latter's disciples to come to know him and be impressed by him. The particulars of how this happened are lost to us, and the narrative of John 1 is obviously trying to put the best Christian face possible on the train of events. Whatever the details, however, the early traditions lying behind John 1:28–45 do suggest that Jesus remained for a while in the circle of the Baptist's disciples after his own baptism. We cannot be more precise than this.[70]

(b) The second—and more intriguing—group of statements is found in John 3:22–30.[71] After the famous encounter between Jesus and Nicodemus (3:1–21), "*Jesus and his disciples* came into the countryside of Judea, and there *he* spent some time *with them* and *he was baptizing*" (v 22). I emphasize certain words to highlight the careful distinction in subjects: both Jesus and his disciples come into the Judean countryside, but only Jesus is the subject of "spent some time," the disciples being relegated to a phrase in an oblique case, "with them." Thus the way is cleared for the straightforward affirmation that Jesus (and, by inference, Jesus alone) was baptizing, the disciples having been dropped as acting subjects. This will be important when we come to 4:2.

That Jesus alone is in mind as the agent of baptism is confirmed by the next verse (v 23), which suddenly reintroduces John (the Baptist), who is said to be baptizing at Aenon-near-Salim. This juxtaposing of Jesus and John as the two conferrers of baptism apparently sets the stage for an argument about ritual purification between some disciples of John and an unnamed Jew (v 25).[72] The flow of the narrative suggests that the dispute involved the relative merits of John's and Jesus' baptisms, for John's disciples come to their "rabbi" and complain about Jesus. John had given Jesus "his big start," as it were; but, in an act of damnable ingratitude, the upstart has stolen John's thunder by practicing his own baptism, "and all are coming to him" (v 26). The note of annoyance at and rivalry with this Jesus-come-lately is obvious. Echoing the mind-set of the Fourth Evangelist, the Baptist replies that he has made it clear to his disciples from the beginning that he was not the Messiah (cf. 1:20), that he was only sent before the Messiah to prepare his way (cf. 1:23,27,30), that the Messiah is the bridegroom claiming his bride Israel, while John is simply the joyful best man at the wedding, who must fade into the background while the bridegroom claims center stage (3:28–30). In the Fourth Gospel, the Baptist is the perfectly Johannine John.

(c) After a meditation on Jesus the Son of Man as the one who comes "from above" and yet is not accepted by unbelievers here below (3:31–36, which is an *inclusio* harking back to and rounding off some themes from the Nicodemus incident), the Evangelist resumes the narrative of 3:22–30 in 4:1: "Now when Jesus knew that the Pharisees had heard that Jesus was making and baptizing more disciples than John. . . ." Once again the position of Jesus as the sole conferrer of his baptism is affirmed and indeed confirmed by the parallel phrase "was making disciples." In the Fourth Gospel, during the public ministry only Jesus makes disciples. Unlike the Synoptic Gospels, in which Jesus' inner circle of disciples is sent out on mission during his own earthly ministry, in the Fourth Gospel Jesus' disciples are never sent out on mission before the resurrection, and hence they never make any disciples before Easter. It is with perfect consistency, therefore, that in 4:1 both making disciples and baptizing are predicated of Jesus alone.

It is only after we have examined the flow of the narrative from 3:22 down to 4:1 that we can fully appreciate the disruptive nature of the statement that immediately follows in 4:2: "and yet Jesus himself was not baptizing, but rather his disciples [were doing the baptizing]." This verse flatly contradicts the entire picture of contrast and conflict, jealousy and humility, that the Evangelist has so carefully constructed by placing the baptizing Jesus and the baptizing John side by side—a contrast repeated for the inattentive in 4:1. When we notice that not only does 4:2 contradict the main point the Evangelist has been laboring to make from 3:22 onward but that 4:2 also contains in its small compass a stylistic trait never encountered elsewhere in the Greek of the Fourth Evangelist,[73] we are forced to conclude, along with C. H. Dodd, that here if anywhere in the Fourth Gospel we have the hand of the ever-watchful "final redactor."[74] He apparently found the idea of Jesus baptizing objectionable, and in his usual wooden, mechanical way he issues a "clarification" correcting any false impression the narrative might give. Thus, the final redactor supplies us with perhaps the best NT example of how the criterion of embarrassment works.

For it is precisely the criterion of embarrassment that once again comes into play here. If the historical Jesus did baptize, the entire Synoptic tradition was so embarrassed by the fact that it simply suppressed this aspect of Jesus' public life (not unlike the way the Fourth Gospel suppressed the fact that Jesus was baptized!). If such a scenario be correct, the final redactor of the Fourth Gospel would have shared—independently—the negative reaction of the Synoptic tradition. One can see why. To have Jesus emerge from the orbit of John the Baptist—either in the sense of circulating among John's disciples (so the Fourth Gospel) or of being baptized by him (so the Synoptics)—and then to have Jesus begin his own ministry with a baptism that was so much like John's that it produced invidious comparisons and jealousy puts Jesus too much in the permanent shadow of the Baptist. Jesus begins to look like the Baptist's disciple, imitator, and (ungrateful?) rival.[75]

In a sense, the final redactor is being true to a major concern of the Evangelist: he is negating a tradition that could play into the hands of the Baptist sectarians. That the Evangelist himself should have preserved such a tradition, which makes Jesus an imitator or understudy of the Baptist, strikes one as strange. True, the Evangelist makes the best use of it he can, by having it provide the last occasion for the Baptist to affirm his inferior and passing role vis-à-vis Jesus. Still, as with some of the material in chap. 1 of the Gospel, and as with other cases to which the criterion of embarrassment applies, the main reason why the picture of Jesus baptizing is included in the Gospel may be that it was too deeply rooted in the Johannine tradition and too widely known to friend and foe alike simply to be omitted.[76] At a later stage of the Gospel's composition, the heavy-handed redactor considered the datum too dangerous to stand unchallenged, and so he "explains it away" in a not very credible fashion. Interestingly, though, not even he dares to expunge the embarrassing tradition from the Gospel.[77]

This, then, is the argument that can be made for the historicity of Jesus' being for a while a member of the inner circle of the Baptist's disciples, of gathering some of his first disciples from that circle, and of using the rite of baptism in his own ministry. It is an argument that rests almost entirely on the criterion of embarrassment, though a certain argument from coherence might be called upon for secondary support. That is to say, if one grants that deciding to accept John's message and submit to his baptism was a pivotal event in Jesus' religious life, then it makes perfect sense that Jesus might spend some time with John after his baptism and, when leaving to start his own mission, might take with him not only some like-minded disciples of John but also the practice of the ritual that had been so meaningful to himself.

Nevertheless, when all is said and done, these arguments from both the Fourth Gospel and the Synoptics generate only a certain degree of probability—and scholars understandably differ on the degree of probability involved. I myself incline to the view that Jesus' remaining with John for a while as his disciple, his drawing some of his first disciples from John's circle, and his continuation of the rite of baptism in his own ministry is the more probable hypothesis—more probable, that is, than the suggestion that all this was made up (for what reason?) by the Fourth Evangelist or the tradition before him.

Yet I readily grant that the arguments I have used are indirect and complicated. I agree with Ernst's caution that the question must be treated with great reserve, and I can understand how Gnilka reaches the opposite judgment, namely, that Jesus did not become a disciple of the Baptist in the narrower sense. The complicated nature of the evidence is shown by the fact that even Gnilka, while doubting that Jesus himself had been John's disciple, thinks that some of Jesus' disciples (e.g., Andrew, and possibly Peter) had previously belonged to John's circle. Moreover, Gnilka remains open to the possibility that Jesus himself baptized people during his ministry. Hence, while I prefer the view that Jesus was a disciple of the Baptist in the narrower sense and that this fact helps explain why the former continued the latter's practice of baptism in his own ministry, I would not claim for this position the same high degree of probability (or moral certitude) that I assign to the event of Jesus' being baptized by John.

Indeed, even my own position allows of differentiation. I feel more secure about affirming Jesus' practice of baptizing during his ministry than about his staying for a while in the circle of John's disciples. For the latter affirmation we have only inference, since no one verse in the entire NT ever directly makes that claim. In contrast, John 3:22,26 and 4:1 all state explicitly that Jesus did baptize; the final redactor intervenes so forcefully in 4:2 precisely because the affirmations of the Evangelist are so plain. Thus, like Gnilka, I feel more secure about the historicity of Jesus' practice of baptizing and the origin of some of Jesus' early disciples in John's circle. Unlike Gnilka, I am willing to accept Jesus' short stay in the circle of John's disciples as the more likely hypothesis.

If one accepts this hypothesis—or even just the most probable part of it, namely, Jesus' practice of baptizing during his own ministry—what conclusions follow? In my opinion, two insights in particular flow from the position I adopt.

(1) John the Baptist, his message, his life, and his baptism are all to be seen as a vital and indispensable matrix of Jesus' own message and praxis. However debatable other views held by Jürgen Becker in his book on John the Baptist and Jesus may be, this major point of his treatment is well taken. When Jesus begins his public ministry, he proclaims an eschatological message concerning the imminent end of history as Israel has known it up until now, he demands from his fellow Jews a basic change of heart and life in view of the approaching end, he stresses the urgency of the choice he presses on his audience by depict-

ing the dire consequences of not accepting his message, he gathers around himself disciples, including an inner circle who stay with him and share his life, he symbolizes acceptance of his message by conferring on his disciples a ritual washing or baptism, he addresses his ministry to all Israel but undertakes no overt mission aimed directly at Gentiles, he spreads his message by an itinerant style of ministry, and his itinerant life includes celibacy. All these elements—most of which will be examined in greater detail in subsequent chapters—reflect the life, preaching, and practice of the Baptist. It is hardly surprising that a Jew who had just recently gone out of his way to journey to the Jordan to hear John and to accept his baptism should pattern his own religious life, at least to some degree, on that of his religious mentor. It would be the opposite line of action that would need a great deal of explanation.

None of this is meant to deny that Jesus, either immediately or after some time in his ministry, introduces notable shifts of emphasis in both his preaching and his practice. Instead of calling people to come out to the wilderness to meet him, Jesus seizes the initiative by touring Galilee and Judea and by spending time both in towns like Capernaum and in the religious capital of his people, Jerusalem. His message becomes much more a joyful announcement of the offer and experience of salvation now, though the future fulfillment—along with possible future disaster—is by no means forgotten. Healings, exorcisms, and reports of other miracles abound. His conscious outreach to "sinners" causes upset, and his views on aspects of the written Mosaic Law, oral traditions, and the Jerusalem temple embroil him in controversy and conflict with various influential groups within Palestinian Judaism. Jesus was therefore not a carbon copy of John. Yet a firm substratum of the Baptist's message and life remained; and as far as we know, it remained throughout Jesus' ministry.[78] To posit early loyalty to John's views on Jesus' part and then a later "defection" or "apostasy" is to introduce into the Gospel traditions chronological indicators and massive theological turnabouts that are simply not present. To be sure, there was a definite shift away from some of John's views and practices, a certain spiritual "leave-taking." But the idea of a hostile and total break conjured up by words like defection and apostasy lacks solid evidence.

For these reasons, I cannot agree with Hollenbach's ingenious attempt to reconstruct the various stages of the relationship between John and Jesus. Hollenbach traces a trajectory that moves from (1) Jesus the penitent, repenting of his sins of social oppression and going to John for baptism, to (2) Jesus the disciple of John, learning more of John's apocalyptic vision and disciplinary practices, to (3) Jesus the baptizer, plying a ministry similar and simultaneous to John's, and finally to (4) Jesus the healer, breaking with John's approach and practice of baptism because of a drastic "conversion" experience.[79] According to Hollenbach, at some point, to Jesus' own surprise, the Nazarene suddenly found himself able to perform exorcisms and healings. Jesus then turned from preaching repentance and social justice to the powerful of society to a ministry of healing directed to even the least significant members of society.

Hollenbach's reconstruction rests on many unlikely and convoluted interpretations of individual texts, but only some major weaknesses of his overall approach need be mentioned here. First of all, as we saw at the very end of Chapter 11, once we leave the initial events surrounding the baptism of Jesus, and until we reach the final clash in Jerusalem around A.D. 30, we cannot properly speak of a before and after in the public ministry of Jesus, except in a few rare cases. As Karl Ludwig Schmidt showed so well, the order of events in each Gospel is the creation of the respective evangelist. The four different presentations cannot and should not be harmonized. Moreover, once we apply form and redaction criticism and so dissolve the chronological grids invented by the evangelists, we have nothing to take their place. To fill the vacuum, Hollenbach invokes the use of "disciplined historical imagination."[80] As usual in such exercises, his reconstruction displays great imagination, less discipline, and little history. Texts and events are moved around to create his four-stage schema, with no basis in the data.

To take but one example: Hollenbach speaks confidently of some critical point in Jesus' ministry when the Nazarene stopped baptizing and started exorcising.[81] This amazing claim is a glaring instance of uncritical harmonization of the Synoptics and John. As a matter of fact, the Synoptics present Jesus exorcising from the very beginning of his ministry (Mark 1:21–28; Matt 4:24; Luke 4:31–36) and never present him baptizing. The Fourth Evangelist does just the opposite: relatively early on in the ministry (chap. 3) the Evangelist presents Jesus baptizing, never says that Jesus stopped baptizing, and never presents Jesus performing a single exorcism. Moreover, in the Fourth Gospel Jesus does perform various "signs" (including possibly healings) in Jerusalem as well as in Cana before any mention of his baptizing is made (2:1–11,23; 3:2). Thus, Hollenbach arrives at his four-step pattern of Jesus' development only by mixing and rearranging the material of the Synoptics and John without any warrant in either tradition.

Second, Hollenbach commits a basic mistake in methodology by leaping from the general observation that Jesus no doubt experienced development in his thought and strategy to the presumption that we today can know what that development was and how and why it took place. As we saw at the beginning of Chapter 9, there is a great difference between enunciating the truism that Jesus the child and adolescent went through the usual stages of physical and psychological development and claiming that we know the exact course Jesus' development took and what impact it had on him. Similarly, it stands to reason that Jesus the adult developed in his religious thought and practice. But again, what exact course that development took cannot be known a priori, and the Gospels give us almost no data by which we might plot its course. With a few possible exceptions (e.g., Jesus' having to face the possibility of a violent death), the Gospel material cannot be assigned to early or late stages in his career, and appeals to the general principle that Jesus must have developed do not change our state of ignorance about particulars. This is all the more true in the case of the public ministry, since, as we saw in Chapter 11, the duration of the ministry was probably a little more than two years. That there was some development during this relatively short time, I do not doubt. What and how much it was, I do not know, nor does anyone else. General principles do not of themselves generate specific data.

A third problem in Hollenbach's reconstruction is one that frequently appears in the presentations of those who hold that Jesus began his public ministry practicing some form of baptism. Almost automatically an author will raise the question of when Jesus stopped this practice, and then the author will proceed to offer some theory, usually suggesting that Jesus ceased baptizing early on in his ministry, around the time he "broke" with John.[82] There is, of course, an unspoken presupposition here, namely, that Jesus did stop baptizing at some point during his ministry. But how do we know that? If pressed, an author might respond that the Fourth Gospel does not mention Jesus' act of baptizing after 4:1. But the Gospel does not mention Jesus' baptizing before 3:22, either. Using the same sort of reasoning, are we to suppose that therefore Jesus did not practice baptism at the very beginning of his ministry but only after a visit to Jerusalem? Or, to take this line of reasoning a step further: Are we to suppose that, in the mind of the Fourth Evangelist, Jesus never performed any miracle of healing after he healed the man born blind (chap. 9), simply because the Gospel does not mention another incident? Are we to suppose that, because Jesus is never depicted operating in Galilee after 7:9, the Evangelist thought Jesus never went to Galilee or conducted his ministry there after that point? Are we, in short, to forget the Evangelist's own caution in 20:30 about the fragmentary nature of his account? The whole presupposition that Jesus must have stopped baptizing because the Fourth Gospel never mentions it after 4:1 is a curious argument from silence—whether we are considering the mind of the Evangelist or the historical flow of events. Especially in the case of Jesus' baptizing, silence may not betoken much, since the whole Synoptic tradition succeeded in remaining silent about this surprising aspect of Jesus' ministry and our one source, the Fourth Gospel, has preserved only a few passing references. Since, in the case of Jesus' baptizing, the Gospels' silence or reserve probably arises out of theological embarrassment, this silence is hardly a reliable indicator of when or whether Jesus stopped baptizing.

Is there any other reason for supposing that, once Jesus began baptizing at the start of his ministry, he later stopped? One might try to mount a general argument based on the fact that John received the title "the Baptist" because he stood out so strikingly as a unique figure who insisted on baptizing other people. Josephus as well as the Synoptics preserve this title for John; neither applies it to Jesus. One might therefore conclude that baptizing was not characteristic of Jesus as it was of John. Yet all this observation need indicate is (1) that John was the inventor of what was a new ritual practice at his time, a practice Jesus imitated, and (2) that baptizing was not the central and defining characteristic of Jesus' ministry as it was of John's. As we shall see in the subsequent chapters, the new elements of Jesus' ministry vis-à-vis the Baptist included the joyful announcement of the coming-yet-somehow-already-present kingdom of God, the actualization of that presence in healings, exorcisms, and table fellowship with sinners, an authoritative new teaching on how the Mosaic Law and tradition were to be interpreted and practiced, and a critical stance toward the Jerusalem temple. It was this exuberant and perhaps shocking newness that was at the center of Jesus' message, action, and attractiveness (or repulsiveness). Presumably, Jesus' conferral of baptism was the symbol of a disciple's acceptance of the new message Jesus proclaimed and of his or her entrance into the new reality Jesus brought—or more concretely, into the group of disciples Jesus was forming. What else the baptism Jesus conferred might have meant either to the conferrer or to the recipient we cannot say. It was part of, but not the center of, Jesus' message and praxis. It was inherited from the Baptist and hence not one of the startlingly new elements Jesus introduced when he launched his own ministry. Hence we need not be surprised that John, not Jesus, was known as *the* Baptist, even if Jesus continued baptizing throughout his ministry.

Needless to say, I cannot prove that Jesus continued baptizing for the whole of his ministry, any more than Hollenbach can prove the opposite. I do think, however, that baptism as one aspect of Jesus' ministry fits in well with other pieces of data, notably in the Synoptic Gospels, where Jesus' baptizing activity never appears. I have refused to use the later Q or Marcan material that treats of the relation between John and Jesus (Matt 11:2–19 || Luke 7:18–35; 16:16; cf. Mark 11:27–33) as proof for Jesus' being a disciple of the Baptist and of continuing his baptism. But once these points have been made probable on other grounds, it is legitimate to note that they cohere well with what the Q and Marcan material shows us. We shall be looking at this material in greater detail shortly. For the moment I call upon it simply to show that traditions from other sources (Q and Mark) cohere well with what the Fourth Gospel explicitly affirms.

According to Q, during his ministry, Jesus had to face the question of what precisely his relationship to John was (Matt 11:2–3 par.). Jesus seems to have been at pains to strike a careful balance. On the one hand, his own ministry displayed an outburst of miraculous healing power and a proclamation of good news to the poor that differentiated it from John's (11:4–6 par.). On the other hand, Jesus praises John as a courageous prophet, indeed, more than a prophet: he is the greatest human being ever born (11:7–11a par.). Pointedly Matt 11:11b–13 || Luke 7:28b; 16:16 balance this high praise by noting the limitations of John's role in salvation history, but it is unclear whether these verses are partially or totally Christian additions. Difference yet similarity in ministry is underscored in Matt 11:16–19 || Luke 7:31–35. John's ascetic lifestyle and severe message contrast sharply with Jesus' wining and dining as a symbol of the joyous banquet to which all were invited in the kingdom of God. Yet both John and Jesus, the eschatological "odd couple," have met with rejection from their finicky audience, though for opposite reasons. Despite this rejection, Lady Wisdom, who has sent both John and Jesus (her children), will see her divine message vindicated by the denouement of the eschatological drama. No matter what our judgment about the meaning or authenticity of individual words in this "Baptist-block" of Q material, some intriguing points are immediately clear from the general thrust of the passage. There must have been some reason why Jesus had to address at length the question of his relationship to John, despite the fact that Jesus' area of activity, message, and style of ministry were so different. As already noted, the mere existence of two popular "eschatological prophets" active in Palestine around the same time might be sufficient reason for raising the question—a fortiori, if the second was known to have been baptized by the first. But the question would have been all the more pressing, and Jesus and his disciples might feel a detailed answer was all the more necessary, if it was also known that Jesus had remained for a while in the circle of John's disciples, that he had drawn some of his own disciples from that pool, and that he had continued baptizing adherents to his message in imitation of John. It may be telling that when the various implicit and explicit contrasts between John's and Jesus' ministries are listed in these Q sayings (Matt 11:4–6,7,12–13,18–19 par.), baptism or the lack thereof is not mentioned, perhaps because it was not a difference.

To turn to the Marcan tradition: At the very least, the dispute over Jesus' authority (Mark 11:27–33 parr.) once again—but in a different Synoptic source—confirms the view that throughout his ministry Jesus maintained that John's message and baptism were divinely inspired. To the question of the Jerusalem high priests and elders about his authority, Jesus—in good rabbinic style, and apparently without any sense of inconsistency—counters with another question: Was John's baptism of divine or merely human origin? When confronted by the Jerusalem officials about his own "charismatic" authority, which lacks any official sanction, Jesus automatically ranges himself alongside John. Not only does Jesus' counterquestion implicitly argue against any defection or apostasy from John on his part. More to the point, the tacit demand that the Jerusalem officials acknowledge the divine origin of John's baptism is especially relevant to Jesus' argument about his own authority *if* the officials' acknowledgment of John's baptism also entails tacit approval of Jesus' continuation of John's practice of baptizing. To admit that John's baptism did come from heaven (was divinely inspired and authorized) would make it very difficult to evaluate the baptism conferred by John's erstwhile disciple Jesus any differently.

Thus, on the one hand, I would not claim that Jesus' being John's disciple in the narrower sense and of practicing baptism during his own ministry can be supported by the criterion of multiple attestation (these points are *attested* only in the Fourth Gospel). On the other hand, I do think that the criterion of coherence does support the argument made by the criterion of embarrassment. The picture the Fourth Gospel presents does fit well with what the Synoptic traditions tell us about John and Jesus. This does not mean that we are engaging in uncritical harmonization. Once the historicity of Jesus' period of discipleship and his baptizing activity are shown to be probable by applying the criterion of embarrassment to the Fourth Gospel, we may legitimately indicate that these two points (Jesus' being a disciple of John and continuing to baptize) shed further light on the data in the Synoptics.

As an aside, I would also suggest that Jesus' baptizing activity, especially if it did extend throughout the whole of his ministry, cuts through a great deal of speculation about the origins of Christian baptism. If the Baptist did baptize while Jesus emphatically broke at some point with the practice of baptism, then we must construct hypotheses about why and when the early church reinstituted the practice of John's baptism, with a notably different meaning given to it. Such a procedure is not impossible, as the case of voluntary fasting shows: practiced by the Baptist, relinquished by Jesus, resumed by the church. But, all things being equal, the simplest hypothesis that explains all the data is to be preferred. In this case, if Jesus did continue throughout his ministry John's practice of baptism, then the problem of when and why the church practiced baptism disappears. The "problem" was false to begin with and arose only because the Fourth Gospel's statements were ignored or rejected and the silence of the Synoptics was taken to mean Jesus did not baptize (a glaring *non sequitur* in itself).

To sum up what we have seen so far: In my opinion, Jesus' being baptized by John is one of the most historically certain events ascertainable by any reconstruction of the historical Jesus. The criterion of embarrassment strongly argues in favor of it; though less sturdy, the criterion of multiple attestation probably does as well. To a certain degree, even the criterion of discontinuity adds its voice. While it is more difficult to discern exactly what his being baptized meant to Jesus, it (along with the events surrounding it) certainly involved a basic break with his past life, his confession that he was a member of a sinful Israel that had turned away from its God, his turning or "conversion" to a life fully dedicated to Israel's religious heritage and destiny, his acknowledgment of John as an eschatological prophet, his embrace of John's message of imminent eschatology, and his submission to the special ritual washing John alone administered and considered part of the way to salvation. So strong was the impact of John on Jesus that, for a short period, Jesus stayed with John as his disciple and, when he struck out on his own, he continued the practice of baptizing disciples. While these two last points are not as certain as the fact of Jesus' being baptized, I think the criterion of embarrassment, applied to the Fourth Gospel, makes them fairly probable, especially since they are supported by the criterion of coherence as well. That some of Jesus' early disciples also came from John's may be less certain, but the criterion of embarrassment also seems to apply here. At the very least, if we grant the historicity of Jesus' being baptized, his spending time with John, and his continuing the practice of baptism in his own ministry, then the further point of his drawing disciples from among the Baptist's followers coheres well with these three points. If we admit the first three, there seems no reason to deny this last point.

Having explored at length Jesus' relation with John around the time of Jesus' reception of baptism, we will now turn to examine in greater detail what the Gospels have to say about the ongoing relationship between the Baptist and Jesus during the latter's ministry. There are only a few scattered references remaining in the Fourth Gospel; most of the material to be studied comes from Q and Mark.

IV. JESUS ON JOHN

Having examined the words and deeds of the Baptist before Jesus comes on the scene (Chapter 12), and having examined in this chapter the events surrounding Jesus' appearance for baptism, his possible stay with John as a disciple, and his striking out on his own in a ministry that included but did not focus on baptism, we are now in a position to listen critically to the sayings of Jesus, preserved in Q and Mark, that deal with the Baptist. We have seen "John without Jesus" and "Jesus with John." It is only in a qualified sense that our study of the public ministry will treat "Jesus without John." For, as the material in this section reminds us, dead or alive the Baptist was never completely absent from the thought and action of Jesus. John's presence might be felt by either comparison or contrast; but like genetic imprint and parental influence, it remained amid many changes.

A. THE SECOND BAPTIST-BLOCK IN Q

The most important corpus of sayings of Jesus concerning the Baptist is contained in the second "Baptist-block" in Q, the first being the preaching of the Baptist we saw in Chapter 12. This group of related sayings is preserved as a unit in Matt 11:2–19 and in two different places in Luke: 7:18–23 and 16:16. The separate location of Luke 16:16 (= Matt 11:12–13) is a hint that this large block of Q sayings is made up of discrete units that probably circulated separately in an early stage of the oral tradition.[83] We need not think that Jesus spoke all of Matt 11:2–19 at one time or in one situation. Indeed, granted the fame of the Baptist, in or out of prison, Jesus probably faced questions about his relation to the Baptist more than once.

Confirming the secondary nature of the precise narrative setting in the Gospels is the fact that, while Matthew and Luke agree very closely in most of the core sayings in Matt 11:2–19 par., they diverge notably in the wording, though not the basic content, of the sentences that provide the narrative framework of the scene. The remarkable word-for-word correspondence between Matthew and Luke in the key sayings reminds us of the similar situation in Matt 3:7–10 par. and may be one indicator of material that was fixed very early on, either orally or in writing. The great exception to this agreement in the sayings material is the extremely difficult logion that puts John the Baptist into relationship with the kingdom of God that Jesus proclaimed (Matt 11:12–13 ‖ Luke 16:16). Its placement in different contexts in Matthew and Luke supports the impression that it underwent a more complicated and convoluted tradition history than the main Baptist-block of Matt 11:2–19 par.[84] Hence it will be treated separately from the main block, which seems to have reached a fairly "stable state" early on.

Another possible indicator of authentic material in this Baptist-block is that the question of the relationship between John and Jesus is not answered in terms of an explicit "high christology" decked out with titles. In stark contrast to this, many streams of Gospel tradition (e.g., the theophany after the baptism in both Mark and probably Q, the use of the virginal conception in Luke's Infancy Narrative, the Fourth Gospel's use of preexistence and incarnation of the Word) do solve the problem of the Baptist simply by "trumping" John with the christological card. There may be some signs of that tendency beginning to take hold in the "Baptist-block," but the core of the material is surprisingly free of the various christologies of the post-Easter church. Instead, these sayings deal with John in connection with themes that, by the common consent of scholars, are at home in the authentic words of Jesus: the kingdom of God, claims about miracles, and parables. Kingdom, miracles, and parables are all complicated topics that will have to be examined at much greater length in subsequent chapters. In treating the sayings in the Baptist-block, I will simply presume certain points about them that are generally accepted by mainstream scholarship on the historical Jesus.

The Baptist-block of Matt 11:2–19 par. easily divides into three main units,[85] which probably circulated independently before they were brought together in Q: Jesus' reply to the disciples of the Baptist (Matt 11:2–6 ‖ Luke 7:18–23); Jesus' praise of the Baptist spoken to the crowds (Matt 11:7–11 ‖ Luke 7:24–28); and the parable of the children in the market place, spoken against "this generation" (Matt 11:16–19 ‖ Luke 7:31–35).[86] Whether these in turn are made up of still smaller units and whether they are likely to come from Jesus himself must now be examined.

(1) The first unit (Matt 11:2–6) is the only one that supplies a narrative framework. This places the material in the literary category of a "pronouncement story" or "apophthegm," i.e., a short narrative in which people pose a question or problem to Jesus, whose "pronouncement" on the issue serves as the climax of the anecdote. The element of narrative also makes this the only unit that has a time frame: John has been imprisoned by Herod Antipas (hence the need to use disciples as emissaries), but he has not yet been put to death. The second and third units could likewise belong historically to this delicate in-between period, but conceivably they could have been spoken either while John and Jesus were both plying a baptismal ministry or after John had been executed. The second and third units are thus good reminders that, for most of the tradition about Jesus' ministry, there is no before or after. Therefore an interpretation that depends heavily on the temporal sequence of individual events in Jesus' ministry is on shaky ground.

The opening narrative recounting John's sending of his disciples to Jesus is much longer in Luke than in Matthew. Scholars argue whether the former has expanded or the latter abbreviated the Q tradition.[87] As I noted in Chapter 12,

I will ignore such questions of the tradition and redaction of Q material when they do not touch on the substance of Jesus' words—all the more so because we often lack clear grounds for making a choice between Matthew and Luke on minor points.[88] Strictly speaking, Luke 7:18, unlike Matt 11:2, does not state that John was already in prison when he sent his disciples to Jesus. However, Luke, unlike Matthew, has already gone into the details of John's arrest (Luke 3:19–20) and therefore presumes a prison setting for the story.[89] It seems to me more likely that Luke deleted what seemed to him a superfluous reference to prison in his tradition.

The exact formulation of John's question, "Are you *the coming one [ho ercho-menos,* i.e., the one who has been prophesied to come, the one who is to come]?" harks back to John's own prophecy that "there *comes* after me one stronger than I," who will accomplish the eschatological baptism of Israel with the spirit (Mark 1:7; Matt 3:11; Luke 3:16). On the redactional level of the NT documents, "the coming one" is applied at times to Jesus in his first or second coming (e.g., Matt 3:11; Mark 11:9 parr.; Heb 10:37), often with the use of OT citations. But there is no indication that either in Judaism at the time of Jesus or on the level of the Q document "the coming one" was a set title for the Messiah or some other eschatological figure.[90] Rather, both in John's preaching and in his question here the reference to someone who is coming seems chosen not only for its eschatological suggestiveness but also for its vagueness and open-endedness. In Chapter 12 we saw that John may have expressed his own expectations in this unclear way because, while certain that he himself was not powerful enough to complete the eschatological task of bringing repentant Israel to salvation, he was unsure about who exactly would bring the work to fulfillment.

Yet, whether it would be God, an angel like Michael, a heavenly Melchizedek, or a more earthly Messiah, Elijah figure, or generic prophet of the end time, John did seem to be sure about one thing. While the coming one would give repentant Israelites who had accepted John's baptism final purification, this happy event seemed fated to transpire within a larger context of fiery judgment and punishment. Moreover, John's stress on the imminent nature of the disaster enveloping all Israel gives the impression that John himself would be "on the scene" as the final drama unfolded. In the beginning of his ministry, John may have thought so. It is intriguing to note that, in comparable fashion, the Apostle Paul, at least in his earlier epistles, thought that he would still be alive on earth at the time of the parousia. As time went on, as matters developed differently, and especially as Paul had to face the prospect of his own imminent death, he revised the scenario.[91]

In similar fashion, John in Matt 11:2–3 par. seems to be reviewing the situation. The scene of fiery judgment along with the "coming" of the stronger one has not arrived. Instead, one of the very disciples John had baptized has started his own somewhat different ministry. Although Jesus' mission retained from John's the practice of baptism and the threat of destruction soon to come, its emphasis lay elsewhere: the good news of God's kingly rule, already powerfully at work in Jesus' healings and exorcisms, as well as in his welcome and table fellowship extended to sinners and toll collectors. In contrast, neither Josephus, the various Synoptic sources, nor the Fourth Gospel record any tradition about John working miracles.[92] Jesus' reputation as a miracle-worker alone would have been enough to attract larger crowds. Reinforcing this, Jesus' practice of seizing the initiative by touring Galilee and Judea and creating "beachheads" in places like Capernaum and Jerusalem naturally gave him more palpable and widespread success than John. Though Jesus' "star" was already "on the rise" while John was still active, the overturning of John's expectations must have had a greater, not to say crueler, impact on the Baptist once he was imprisoned and his personal activity of preaching and baptizing terminated. As Jesus' success grew, John had to face the prospect of death, with no sign of rescue or vindication from the God he thought had commissioned him. To borrow the words of the Fourth Gospel: it was literally true that Jesus was "increasing" while John was "decreasing" (John 3:30).

It is no wonder, then, that in Matt 11:2–3 par. John is reviewing the situation and posing a heretofore unthinkable question. When John asks, "Are you the coming one?" he is neither feigning ignorance as a means of instructing his disciples nor wavering in the faith he had previously put in Jesus. Previously the historical Baptist had had no faith in Jesus as the fulfiller of his own prophecy. But now he must either rethink his own prophecy or see it proven totally false. John's question is therefore a genuine, tentative probe, allowing that he might have to revise his hopes in order to avoid giving them up entirely.[93] But John is by no means sure, since equating Jesus with "the coming one" would mean more than simply changing one particular identification in John's cast of characters for the eschatological drama. It would mean reshaping John's whole proclamation, centered as it was on fiery threats and imminent doom. Hence the alternative, ". . . or shall we wait for someone else?" is by no means purely theoretical. For John and his disciples ("we") it is very much a live option, since Jesus seems to diverge so sharply from John's own expectations. Even at this early point in our investigation, we sense that this does not sound like what we would expect in a story invented by the early church to exalt Jesus as the definitive eschatological figure or to convert Baptist sectarians by persuading them that "this is what John would have wanted."

This impression is reinforced when we look at Jesus' reply to John's question. There is no attempt to have Jesus proclaim his unique status with explicit titles (e.g., "I am the Messiah," "God has anointed his Son with the spirit," "the Son of Man has come in power") or with explicit claims (e.g., "I fulfill all Scripture"). Jesus instead simply appeals to what is commonly said about him on all sides and what John's disciples can see and hear for themselves: he performs miracles and proclaims the good news of salvation to the poor. This remarkably indirect yet suggestive reply of Jesus needs to be "unpacked."[94]

(a) Jesus' response focuses upon the precise points at which his own ministry strikingly diverges from and goes beyond John's. Jesus asks John to consider the joyful, healing newness that he has introduced into the Baptist's program. At least in the Q text as we can reconstruct it, Jesus summarizes the newness his miracles and preaching represent in language redolent of OT prophecy, especially the promises of eschatological redemption in the Book of Isaiah (29:18–19; 35:5–6; 26:19; 25:8; 61:1–2). Significantly, some of the passages alluded to come from what present-day scholars would call the "Apocalypse of Isaiah" (Isa 24:1–27:13), which speaks of Yahweh's redemption of his people Israel on the great "day of the Lord," as well as from Trito-Isaiah (Isaiah 56–66), which speaks of the glory of a restored Jerusalem after the return of the exiles from the Babylonian captivity.[95] Obviously, neither Jesus nor Q worked with these modern designations and concepts, but it is therefore all the more remarkable that Jesus "zeroes in" on this section of the prophetic Scriptures of Israel to describe his own ministry. Jesus sees in his healing and proclamation of good news to the lowly the fulfillment of all "Isaiah" had promised: on the last day, Yahweh would definitively redeem and heal his people.

(b) One senses immediately how the spiritual center of gravity has shifted from John to Jesus. Jesus has not given up John's hope of a consummation yet to come, including punishment for those who harden themselves against the final offer of salvation.[96] But the accent is now on what a loving, merciful God is already doing to save Israel through the ministry of Jesus. Significantly, in a number of the OT passages Jesus alludes to in his reply (Isa 35:4; 29:20; 61:2), the idea of the vengeance or punishment to be meted out by God is clearly present.[97] Yet that component of the prophet's vision, which would be so congenial to the message of John, is passed over by Jesus in silence. What Jesus underlines is the joy of salvation, not the expectation of punishment. For Jesus, the day of the Lord is already here, though not fully so. And the great good news is that for all who accept Jesus' message, the day of the Lord turns out to be a day of light, not of darkness, the prophet Amos (5:18–20) not withstanding.[98] Yet, while his miracles are indeed wonderful, they all point to and culminate in what Jesus pointedly keeps till last in the list of his deeds: proclaiming good news to the poor, what the prophet anointed by Yahweh's spirit does in Isa 61:1.

(c) There is thus a studied shift yet balance in Jesus' answer. John had asked: Who are you? With allusions to OT prophecy, Jesus replies in effect: The end time prophesied by Isaiah is already here.[99] In Jesus' answer, the shift of focus from his own person to what God is doing through him in these last days is telling. The shift is not the result of some words of Jesus being secondarily adapted to answer a question put in the mouth of the Baptist.[100] Rather, as we shall see in subsequent chapters, this shift of focus is typical of a Jesus who places the powerful rule of God instead of his own person at the center of his proclamation. That does not mean that the person of Jesus is totally lost from view; even here something is implied about the agent and messenger of God's definitive action in Israel's history. But it is only implied. Like many other people, John does not get a direct answer from Jesus as to who he is. He gets instead a list of the deeds wrought by God through Jesus, deeds that proclaim that the end—a joyful rather than fiery end—is at hand.

(d) But Jesus does not end with a list of his saving deeds for Israel. He has given an inventory of his activity not for self-aggrandizement but to launch an appeal. He therefore crowns his reply to John with a beatitude that is at the same time a poignant plea to his former master: "And happy is he who is not scandalized because of me."[101] Jesus the purveyor of beatitudes concludes his answer to John with a beatitude that proclaims the happiness of the person wise enough not to be "put off" because things have turned out so differently than expected, not to be "put off" because Jesus' joyful ministry of healing and comfort has proven to be the surprising and successful denouement of the eschatological drama John was prophesying as imminent.[102] It was indeed imminent, and John has lived to see it—but it is not what John envisioned. Hence it is not people in general but John in particular who is addressed in this beatitude. The blind, the lame, and the poor, indeed, Israelites in general were hardly in danger of being prevented from accepting Jesus because of the healing and comfort he was offering them. Rather, it is specifically John who is in danger of being blocked from believing[103] (i.e., in danger of "being scandalized") because of his shock over how God is fulfilling the prophecies about the end time through the ministry of Jesus.

Thus, behind the discreet formulation of a sweeping beatitude, "happy is he who . . . ," stands a delicate appeal to one particular person.[104] Jesus is tacitly entreating his own rabbi to recognize in his former pupil the unexpected—and for John, disconcerting—consummation of God's plan for Israel. Unlike Jesus' debates with the Pharisees and religious leaders, his rebukes to "this generation," his woes on the unbelieving towns of Galilee, or even his upbraiding of his own obtuse disciples, there are no explicit threats, no harsh language here. The student remains respectful of his teacher even as he gently breaks the news that the latter should put his faith in the former.

(e) And what is John's reply to Jesus' appeal? This is perhaps the most astounding point of this pericope, and perhaps one of the best arguments for its basic historicity. If early Christians invented this pericope as propaganda against the Baptist sectarians of their day, then these Christians had a strange idea of propaganda.[105] The pericope simply ends with Jesus' poignant, delicate entreaty; there is no reply from John. The Q material here and elsewhere never claims that John ever responded favorably to this appeal from Jesus. Likewise, the Marcan story of John's execution, however imaginative and unhistorical it may be, does not dare to assert that the Baptist went to his death professing faith in Jesus or offering his life for the cause of Jesus. Silence there, and nothing more.

Some years ago, James Breech wrote a book entitled *The Silence of Jesus.* What is so striking at the end of Matt 11:2–6 par. is the silence of John. The indirect plea of Jesus to believe is left hanging in the air, as is the initial question of John: "Are you the one to come?" While neither Q nor any other NT tradition makes a definitive statement on the subject, the Q narrative of Matt

11:2–6 leaves us with the impression that John went to his death still questioning, still unsure about Jesus and how he did or did not fit into John's hopes.[106] This may be the stuff of a great 20th-century drama; it is not the stuff of 1st-century Christian propaganda. Everywhere else in the NT traditions about the Baptist, he points directly or indirectly, knowingly or unknowingly, to Jesus. Nowhere else is the Baptist challenged by Jesus to believe in him, only to fail to comply. The silent John of this Q pericope stands out starkly against the background of the Lucan babe leaping in Elizabeth's womb, the Matthean "I should be baptized by you," and the Fourth Gospel's "Behold the lamb of God." Whatever the silence of John is, it is not Christian apologetics. The criteria of embarrassment and discontinuity apply well to the disconcerting conclusion of this Q tradition.

As Martin Dibelius, hardly a *naif* in NT criticism, puts it: "Such a question and such an answer—both may make a claim to historical credibility, for legend would not have let the Baptist, depicted by it as the herald of Jesus, ask the question in such a half-believing [?] way and would not have let the Savior, already clothed by it in the crib with the glory of the Messiah, answer in such an unclear way. In light of such credibility, the historical yield of the narrative is significant, both for our knowledge of Jesus' stance vis-à-vis the title of Messiah [?] and for our understanding of the Baptist's view of Jesus."[107] Dibelius should not have spoken in this context of the precise title of "Messiah," which is simply not present. Still, the basic thrust of his argument is correct and can be supported by other observations as well. For instance, it is intriguing to note how, in this apophthegm, the great scandal that could keep one from believing in Jesus is not his rejection by Israel and its leaders, and certainly not his crucifixion, but rather his success. The church's kerygma of cross and resurrection has left no mark on this text.[108]

Yet perhaps the most disconcerting aspect of the tradition in Matt 11:2–6 par. is the combination of the warning veiled in Jesus' beatitude with the lack of any recorded response from the Baptist. Implicit in Jesus' beatitude is the warning that anyone who allows himself to be blocked from faith in Jesus by the unexpected nature of Jesus' ministry will not share the eschatological happiness Jesus brings. It is shocking to see this implicit threat aimed at the Baptist, all the more so when the Q tradition supplies no "happy ending" by way of a positive response from John. The thrust of this apophthegm goes very much against the type of Christian apologetic common throughout the Gospels: the Baptist is always praised and coopted for Christian faith, while only an overestimation of him by his disciples is censured. Once again, the tradition in Matt 11:2–6 par. puts us in a very different world from early Christian preaching. Its most probable origin (i.e., its originating *Sitz im Leben*) is the life of Jesus.[109] While one cannot speak of Jesus' defection or apostasy from the Baptist, this Q tradition shows that Jesus consciously undertook a different style of ministry and proclaimed a message that contained a notable shift in emphasis from John's preaching. So sure is Jesus of his authority that he dares to intimate that his new way of preaching and acting makes a claim not only on Israel in general, not only on John's disciples in particular, but even on John himself. If Jesus is not an apostate from John's faith, neither is he simply some disciple or successor of John, faithfully carrying through the master's program. Both Hollenbach and Boers err by excess at either end of the spectrum.[110]

(2) The second unit in this Baptist block of Q is Matt 11:7–11 ‖ Luke 7:24–28. It is tied to what precedes in both Matthew and Luke by a genitive absolute indicating that Jesus addresses the crowds as the messengers of John leave. This tie-in to the preceding apophthegm is worded differently in Matt 11:7a and Luke 7:24a. Yet the fact that both evangelists have a genitive absolute with the same thought-content introducing the second unit seems to indicate that there was some such link already in Q. Matthew's and Luke's wording becomes very close starting in Matt 11:7b ‖ Luke 7:24b, as Q announces the theme of the following sayings it has collected: Jesus "began to speak to the crowds *concerning John*." If we count this introductory title as part of the mini-discourse, the second unit shows a remarkable structure of five logia, each logion having three parts. The five logia can in turn be grouped into three main rhetorical questions and three correct explanations of John's identity[111] (for convenience' sake, the verses are labeled according to Matt 11:7–11):[112]

I

7b	*Introductory title*	[Jesus] began to speak to the crowds about John:
7c	*Main rhetorical question (first time)*	What did you go out to the desert to see?
7d	*First answer in form of rhetorical question*	A reed shaken by the wind?

II

8a	*Main rhetorical question (second time)*	But what did you go out to see?
8b	*Second answer in form of rhetorical question*	A man clothed in luxurious [garments]?
8c	*Mocking rejection of the second answer*	Behold, those who wear luxurious [garments] are in the houses of kings!

III

9a	*Main rhetorical question (third time)*	But what did you go out to see?
9b	*Third answer in form of rhetorical question*	A prophet?
9c	*Emphatic acceptance of third answer and first identification*	Yes, I tell you, and more than a prophet!

IV

10a *Second identification by scriptural prophecy:*	This is he concerning whom it is written:
10b *messenger (Exod 23:20)*	Behold I am sending my messenger before your face
10c *forerunner (Mal 3:1 MT)*	who shall prepare your way before you.

V

11a *Third identification with solemn formula*	[Amen,] I say to you:
11b *greatness of John*	There has not arisen among those born of women one greater than John [the Baptist]
11c *limitation of John*	But the least in the kingdom of God is greater than he.

Obviously, we are dealing here with a carefully crafted composition that has probably gone through a number of stages of tradition and redaction. In light of the hypothetical nature of the Q document and the very hypothetical nature of its tradition history, it is not surprising that scholars differ on how many stages of tradition and redaction we can find here and which sayings belong to the earliest stage of the tradition. For example, Josef Ernst reviews the opinions of major exegetes only to discover that they posit between two to four levels of tradition, with the same verse being declared ancient tradition or a later addition by different scholars.[113] All this simply reminds us how speculative and fragile are theories about levels of tradition and redaction in the Q document. More to the point, we should remember that the question of whether Jesus ever spoke a given saying is not the same as the question of when and how this saying entered the Q document and was attached to other sayings. A saying that was actually spoken by Jesus could have circulated independently for some time and so have been added to the Q tradition only at a relatively late stage of Q's development. The late date of its addition to Q would prove nothing about whether it came from Jesus. Hence the precise questions posed in this book (Did Jesus say this or something like this? What did he mean by it?) must be carefully distinguished from the questions posed by researchers of the Q document (Does this saying belong to Q? If so, at what stage was it taken into Q? How does it fit into the overall theology of Q?).

Addressing ourselves to the question of origin from Jesus, we readily see that the five sayings can be divided by form-critical category, structure, and rhetorical tone into three basic traditions: vv 7b–9c, v 10, and v 11. We shall examine each one of these three subunits in detail for indications of their origin and meaning.

(a) Verses 7b–9c form a highly rhetorical piece of thrust-and-parry questions and answers. With an ironic, not to say mocking, tone, Jesus underscores the reason for John's great success in attracting people to his baptism in the wilderness: far from being a vacillating person or soft-living courtier, John was an uncompromising prophet. One can easily imagine Jesus the prophet and wisdom teacher engaging his audience in this lively repartee. The pericope reaches its climax with a final answer that is (typical of Jesus) a riddle-like answer: John is a prophet and more than a prophet (v 9b–c). This open-ended answer to the question of John's identity begs for a further explanation: If he is more than a prophet, what is he? This is the reason why Matt 11:7–9 par. would naturally attract to itself other sayings explaining the nature or function of the Baptist. In itself, that fact does not tell us whether the other sayings came from Jesus or not. It simply reminds us that all the sayings in 11:7–19 par., even if they were spoken by Jesus, may not have been spoken by him at the same time or to the same audience.

As for 11:7–9 itself, there are a number of arguments in favor of its representing a teaching of the historical Jesus. The absence of any christological concern, the total focus on and praise of John without limitations,[114] the classification of John as prophet and super-prophet without any use of categories like forerunner of and witness to Jesus, indeed, the lack of any reference or allusion to Jesus at all, and the lively rhetorical tone that would fit well the context of Jesus' preaching to the crowds, all recommend Matt 11:7–9 as authentic tradition coming from Jesus.

Moreover, Matt 11:7–9 par. may contain a number of passing allusions to the concrete situation of John, Jesus, and possibly Herod Antipas, allusions that would have been taken for granted by Jesus and his audience ca. A.D. 28. Without any preparation or explanation, Jesus challenges the crowd: "What did you go out to the desert to see? A reed shaken by the wind?" The idea of a reed, and therefore of water, in a desert might strike some people as strange. But as we saw in Chapter 12, this saying of the Q tradition simply presupposes what the Marcan tradition likewise takes for granted and never bothers to explain: the lower part of the Jordan River was close to the wilderness of Judea and itself qualified as "desert" or "wilderness" not only in the NT but also in Josephus. Jesus presupposes that the crowds know the special setting of John's ministry, and so he chooses his imagery accordingly.

At the very least, Jesus' first rhetorical question with matching rhetorical answer-in-the-form-of-a-question emphasizes a central trait of John's impressive character. As a stern desert prophet preaching amid the reeds beside the Jordan River, John did not bend to every wind of expediency but spoke the threat of judgment with uncompromising rigor. Gerd Theissen tries to take this basic point a step further. He makes the intriguing suggestion that Jesus is already implicitly contrasting the unwavering integrity of the Baptist with the weaving and bobbing, the unprincipled accommodation and *Realpolitik* of Herod Antipas, the "fox" (Luke 13:32) who had put John in prison (cf. Matt 11:2; Luke 3:19–20). To bolster his case, Theissen produces numismatic evidence that Antipas used the symbol of the reed on coins he issued early in his reign. Theissen claims that not only the tetrarch's policies but even his coins

might have connected him in his subjects' minds with the swaying reed Jesus
contrasts with John.

Such an implicit contrast would have been reinforced by Jesus' repetition
of his rhetorical question, now joined to a new ironic answer: "A man clothed
in luxurious garments?" If in fact Antipas had been alluded to in the first answer, the allusion would become stronger and more biting here, all the more
so when Jesus adds a mocking explanation dismissing his rhetorical answer:
"Behold those who wear luxurious garments are in the houses of kings." The
allusion to Antipas would be all too clear to the Galilean crowds if Jesus spoke
these words after their Galilean ruler had imprisoned or already executed the
Baptist. Indeed, Jesus' statements may intimate that he is already thinking of
John as a figure of the past.

Further resonances would follow upon Jesus' affirmation: "Yes, I tell you,
and more than a prophet."[115] In the concrete context of Antipas' Galilee, Jesus'
insistence that John was a prophet could be understood by the crowds to mean
that John stood in the hallowed line of the OT prophets who were persecuted
by the evil rulers of Israel. Echoes of Elijah, the prophet who had struggled
with and been persecuted by the evil monarchs of the northern kingdom of
Israel, Ahab and his wife Jezebel, might ring loudly in the ears of a Jewish
audience that knew well Antipas and his wife Herodias. At the same time,
Antipas' ruthless manner of dealing with one popular prophet and preacher
might explain why Jesus the prophet considers it prudent to talk to his knowing
audience about recent events with rhetorical questions and allusions rather
than with outright denunciation.[116]

In Jesus' eyes, then, John is a prophet. And yet the title prophet, however
revered, is not sufficient to encompass John's greatness. Jesus prefers to place
his former master and baptizer on a pedestal above that of the prophets, indeed, above any regular category that the Jewish religion supplied. Jesus the
spinner of parables makes John himself into something of a parable, a riddle,
a mind-teaser. Having praised John to the skies, Jesus the Socratic pedagogue
refuses to define him, leaving the crowds to puzzle over the Baptist's identity
and role. Like the story of John's delegation to Jesus (Matt 11:2–6 par.), this
tradition of Jesus' praise of John ends with an implicit question. Like everything else we have seen about this pericope, its parable-like ending points to
its origin in the life of Jesus; nothing demands that it be attributed to the early
church instead.[117] Whether the early church decided to answer Jesus' implicit
question by appending further material must be probed now.

(b) The form and tone of the Q material change suddenly in v 10. From a
string of lively rhetorical questions we go to an explicit citation of Scripture,
introduced in a formal way. Actually, in Matt 11:10 par. we have a mixed citation of Exod 23:20 (corresponding to the LXX text) and Mal 3:1 (reflecting at
least partly the Masoretic Text). Since most of the verse is simply a quotation
of well-known OT material, what judgment if any can be made about its origin
from Jesus? On the one hand, I do not share the view of some form critics that
almost any scriptural citation in the mouth of Jesus is by definition a later

insertion by the early church. Jesus would have been a very strange Jewish teacher in 1st-century Palestine if he had never quoted, commented on, or argued about the meaning of the Jewish Scriptures. On the other hand, a number of points give one pause in this case.

First, we are dealing with a careful weaving together of two similar statements in the OT: Yahweh's promise to send his angel (or messenger) before Israel journeying through the desert after the exodus (Exod 23:20, with the Greek text of Q matching the LXX) and Malachi's prophecy of the coming of the mysterious messenger of Yahweh (Mal 3:1, reflecting the Masoretic Text as well as the LXX). In itself, though, this cleverly crafted scribal creation would not be impossible for Jesus. The discoveries at Qumran have revealed that Hebrew texts of the OT that are closer to the LXX than to the Masoretic Text circulated in 1st-century Palestine alongside proto-Masoretic texts. When one adds to this the existence of written targums at Qumran plus a living oral targumic tradition, one cannot say a priori what types of texts Jesus may or may not have used and woven together to make his point.

But second, the formal scribal tone is reinforced by the elegant formula of introduction: "This is he concerning whom it is written." This is not the simpler and commoner "As it is written"[118] or the special Matthean "in order that what was spoken through the prophet might be fulfilled."[119] This introduction, which is more grammatically intricate than the usual "As it is written," is somewhat similar to an introduction created by Matthew (when redacting Mark 1:2–3) to introduce an OT text applied to John the Baptist: "For this is the one spoken of through Isaiah the prophet, saying . . ." (Matt 3:3). Indeed, no other introduction to an OT citation in the Four Gospels resembles Matt 11:10a par. besides Matt 3:3. The rarity of the formula plus its similarity to what is obviously a redactional scribal creation of an evangelist suggests that it might be the product of Christian scribal activity.

Third, the only other passage where this conflated text appears in the Four Gospels is the opening of Mark's Gospel (1:2), where it likewise defines the role of the Baptist, where it is followed immediately by Isa 40:3 (1:3), and where it is not part of the words of Jesus but of the initial commentary given by the Evangelist. Obviously, Mark 1:2–3 is a creation either of the Evangelist or of some Christian scribal tradition he inherits. This strengthens the case for the same being true of Matt 11:10 par.

Finally, this Q citation may contain a hint of christological reflection by the early church. Matt 11:10c probably echoes the masoretic form of Mal 3:1, which reads: "Behold, I am sending my messenger [or angel] to prepare the way before me." In Malachi's text, "before me" refers to Yahweh; the Q text has changed this to "before you," to have the prophecy refer to Jesus. This easy transfer of OT references from Yahweh to Jesus is seen elsewhere in the early church; for example, "the day of the Lord [Yahweh]" becomes "the day of the Lord [Jesus]." We may have another example of such a transfer here.[120] Granted, none of these arguments is conclusive. But, taken together, they make it advisable that we put aside Matt 11:10 par. as probably a Christian reflection added to an authentic logion of Jesus concerning the Baptist (Matt 11:7–9 par.).[121]

(c) Form, tone, and content change again in Matt 11:11 par., which is a carefully balanced two-part statement on greatness, contrasting John and the least in the kingdom of God ("kingdom of God" being a theme that is absent in the rest of Matt 11:7–11 par.). At first glance, Matt 11:11a par. has the criterion of embarrassment or discontinuity in its favor. It does not seem likely that early Christians would have gone out of their way to infringe on the unique status of Jesus by inventing an affirmation that "there has not arisen among those born of women one greater than John." Where does that leave Jesus? Hence it seems quite reasonable to suppose that v 11b, which declares the least in the kingdom superior to John, is a Christian creation added to restrict the sweeping scope of v 11a.[122] Verse 11a was simply too favorable to John and unfavorable to Jesus to remain alone; it was safely neutralized by being restricted to the time before Jesus began proclaiming and realizing the kingdom of God.

However, things are not that simple. As we saw when we reviewed the criterion of embarrassment in Chapter 6, this criterion is not so automatic and infallible as some might think. Like every other criterion it must be weighed against countervailing considerations—a number of which can be found in 11:11 par. To begin with, it is not so clear that 11:11b can be dismissed as a Christian addition to a supposedly original 11:11a. As a number of critics point out, the two parts of the 11:11 create a terse and taut logion, containing an almost perfect rhetorical as well as theological parallel-with-contrast. The fit seems too neat and snug to have resulted from a secondary doctrinal "clarification" added years after Jesus spoke the original saying.[123] Omitting the introductory "Amen I say to you," we have:

v 11a	*v 11b*
There has not arisen	But the least
among [or: in][124] those born of women	in the kingdom of heaven
one greater	is greater
than John	than he

A number of observations may be made about the two halves of this verse. First, exegetes usually observe that the Matthean form of 11a reflects more strongly a Semitic substratum with its "there has not arisen among those born of women one greater. . . ." As is his wont, Luke has rewritten the Semitic phraseology in more normal Greek: "Among those born of women, no one is greater. . . ."[125] Interestingly, it is the more Semitic-sounding Matthean form that also displays the greater parallelism between the two halves of the saying. At the very least, then, 11b reflects the earlier, more Semitic form of the saying. Along with Semitic form the saying may also reflect a Semitic way of thinking called "dialectical negation." While the Western mind tries to draw distinctions by a careful setting of degrees of difference, the Semitic mind will often oppose two extremes, neither of which is to be taken absolutely, but only in tandem with the other extreme. An example of this dialectical negation can be found in the complaint of Jesus the Revealer in John 3:32–33: "No one accepts his [Jesus'] testimony; he who does accept his testimony has certified that God is truthful." Strictly speaking, the two halves of the statement contradict each other. They are meant to be taken together as two sides of one truth.[126] The two halves of Matt 11:11 par. should perhaps be understood in the same way as a typically Semitic dialectical negation.[127]

Second, without any prompting from the previous verses, v 11b uses the phrase so distinctive of Jesus' own proclamation, "the kingdom of God." The proclamation of the coming of the kingdom of God was one of the distinguishing marks of Jesus' message as compared with John's; for, as far as we can tell, John did not use this key phrase in his own preaching.[128]

Third—and perhaps what is most intriguing—despite the frequent description of this verse's content by scholars, v 11b does not limit John's importance vis-à-vis *Jesus*. Rather, the relationship defined is between John and anyone (starting with the least) who is in the kingdom of God. Whether we take this "being in the kingdom" to refer more to stages in history or to realms of existence, the contrast is between John's supreme dignity among human beings in the ordinary/old world and anyone—the "least" being the most striking member for the sake of the comparison—who is in a new, eschatological type of existence, in other words, in the kingdom of God.

We see, then, that the precise point of 11:11 is not an explicitly christological one at all. As with the tradition in Matt 11:2–6 par., the contrast Jesus draws is not directly between John and himself but rather between John and the new state of affairs that Jesus brings by his preaching and healing. Indeed, in comparison with Matt 11:2–6 par., Jesus is even more "out of the picture." At least in 11:2–6 the miraculous deeds and the good news of Jesus were the points of contrast with John's ministry, with the status of Jesus himself more implied than directly considered. Here in 11:11 neither Jesus nor his deeds are center stage, but rather the person of least importance (and therefore, anybody) within the kingdom of God. Thus, what is striking about 11:11, compared even with 11:2–6, is the total lack of christological content. In this, it is closer to the praise of John in 11:7–9 par.—which may be why it was placed after it. Granted all this, I think it probable that the two halves of 11:11 belong together and that they come from Jesus himself.[129] In 11:11b par. Jesus is not jealously protecting his christological dignity against encroachment by John's special status. He is rather affirming that anyone who has entered into the new "field of force" that is the kingdom of God ranks higher than even the greatest person in the old state of affairs.[130] In sum, considerations of both form (the two halves of the verse belong together) and content (lack of christological concern) argue well for the authenticity of Matt 11:11 par.

To be fair, I should mention one other view that is put forward at times, although I do not think it very convincing. Some authors, impressed by the tight fit of 11:11a + 11:11b, agree that the whole logion was formed at one time. However, they suggest that the entire saying was a product of the early church.[131] There are two difficulties with this position: (i) The often unspoken presupposition of this view is that the saying *must* have been created by the early church, since its whole point is the restriction of John's status in favor of Jesus. But, as we have just seen, that is not an exact description of the content of the saying. The focus is on the kingdom of God, not Jesus—which is precisely the state of affairs mirrored in most reconstructions of the message of the historical Jesus. (ii) The difficulty remains of imagining that the early church, in the midst of proclaiming Jesus to be Messiah, Lord, or Son went out of its way to invent a saying that declared in its first half that John was the greatest human being ever born.[132]

In sum, with the exception of the OT citation in Matt 11:10 par., our second unit (Matt 11:7–11 par.) in this Baptist-block seems to preserve authentic sayings of Jesus. Jesus himself is even more absent in the direct subject matter of 11:7–9,11 than he was in the story of the delegation from John (11:2–6). Jesus praises John as the uncompromising prophet of the wilderness who would not bend (implicitly, to the will of a corrupt Herod Antipas). Indeed, with his baptism and his announcement of definitive, imminent judgment on all Israel, John was more than a prophet—though Jesus leaves open exactly what that eschatological plus sign is. Still, while Jesus here as elsewhere basically affirms and seconds the eschatological message of the Baptist, he likewise indicates the important difference between John and himself. For Jesus, the end time John awaited as just-around-the-corner has arrived, at least to some extent. And it is a time of joyful salvation more than of fiery punishment. Hence even the most insignificant Israelite who has entered into the eschatological kingdom of God that Jesus announces enjoys a privilege and standing greater than John's. We are faced here with a paradox that we shall be seeing often in the words and deeds of Jesus. On the one hand, Jesus makes the kingdom of God, not himself, the direct object of his preaching. Yet what he says about the kingdom and what he promises those who enter it by accepting his message make a monumental though implicit claim: with the start of Jesus' ministry, a definitive shift has taken place in the eschatological timetable. Even here, though, Jesus is in a way imitating his master. The Baptist did not make himself the explicit object of his own proclamation; repentance, baptism, and reformed lives in view of the coming judgment held center stage. Nevertheless, declaring the baptism he alone administered the necessary means of escaping final destruction did make John implicitly a central part of his own message. In this as in many other things, the Nazarene follows in the Baptist's footsteps, even as he shifts the path.

(3) This dialectic of following in the footsteps yet shifting the path, this similarity in the core message yoked with a striking change of emphasis and ministerial strategy, continues in the third unit of the second Baptist-block of Q: the parable of the children playing in the marketplace (Matt 11:16–19 || Luke 7:31–35). Matthew and Luke differ in wording somewhat more here than

in Matt 11:7–9 par., but the basic tradition is clear enough.[133] It contains three subunits: (a) the introductory questions (Matt 11:16a par.), (b) the parable of the children (Matt 11:16b–17), and (c) the application of the parable to John and Jesus (Matt 11:18–19 par.).

(a) The introductory rhetorical questions indicate that the parable deals with "this generation," a pejorative term Jesus uses for his contemporaries who refuse to believe in him.[134] This use of "generation" with a negative tone has sturdy OT roots. For example, Deut 32:5,20 uses it of the archetypal "perverse and crooked generation" that was condemned to die in the wilderness after coming out of Egypt with such high hopes (see also Ps 78:8; cf. Jer 7:29; Ps 12:8). As Friedrich Büchsel remarks, Jesus' use of "generation" (Aramaic: *dār*, Greek: *genea*) reveals both his "comprehensive purpose—he is aiming at the whole people and not at individuals—and his view of solidarity in sin."[135] Again, we hear an echo of the program of the Baptist. It is fitting, then, that these rhetorical questions introduce material that places John and Jesus side by side.

Before we look at the parable and its application, we should note that not all scholars agree that these two subunits formed an original whole in the teaching of Jesus. They could have existed separately and then been welded together in Q.[136] While that is possible, I find it difficult to conceive of the laconic parable of 11:16b–17 circulating by itself for very long in the oral tradition. In such an isolated form, the question of *Sitz im Leben* arises: What would it mean, what would be its function, and why would it especially be preserved? Hence I agree with Norman Perrin that most likely parable and application formed a unit from the beginning,[137] and I shall treat them according to this presupposition. As we proceed through the analysis of the two subunits, we shall see that some arguments against their original unity are not very telling. Moreover, the position that the parable and its application were originally discrete units does not in itself settle the question of whether either stems from Jesus. For instance, while Bultmann thinks that the application is secondary, he is willing to allow that the form of the parable itself may be ancient tradition stemming from Jesus.[138]

(b) The parable of the children playing in the marketplace demands that I say a few preliminary words about Jesus' parables, anticipating the full treatment to come in a later chapter. That parables were a privileged form of Jesus' teaching is a fact accepted by almost all questers for the historical Jesus, however much they may differ among themselves when it comes to interpreting the parables. The abundance of parables in the Synoptic tradition, distributed among all the sources, plus the absence of equally deft, artistic parables elsewhere in the NT, argues well for the origin of many—though not all—of the Gospel parables in Jesus' teaching. The "parable" as a way of teaching reaches back to a flexible, many-faceted form of OT wisdom speech known as a *māšāl*, often translated in the LXX as "parable" (*parabolē*) and in the English OT as "proverb." At the heart of a *māšāl* lies some sort of comparison, used as a tool for teaching and capable of being dressed in many different literary forms. An

OT *māšāl* could be anything from a one-line proverb or aphorism, through a longer taunt-song, riddle, or oracle, up to a lengthy historical recital, a revelatory discourse, or a short story containing a complicated allegory. The word *parabolē* in the Synoptic Gospels likewise carries a wide range of meanings (e.g., proverb, similitude, example, allegory), though scholars tend to restrict the English word "parable" to Jesus' narrative parables.

Taken in this narrower sense, Jesus' parables are an extended similitude or metaphor, a comparison stretched out into a brief story. Against the exaggerated tendency of patristic exegesis to turn Jesus' parables into detailed allegories, the great German scholar Adolf Jülicher emphasized that a given parable usually has only one point of comparison.[139] While Jülicher's emphasis was a healthy corrective against extravagant fantasy, it contained the danger of seeing the great verbal art pieces we call parables as merely clear and convenient tools for teaching eternal truths—tools that can be dispensed with once the truths are grasped. More recent scholarship has stressed the poetic and often puzzling art at the heart of a parable. Though usually drawn from vivid, realistic events in ordinary life, the parable often functions as a type of riddle, intended to startle or tease the mind of the audience, forcing it to ponder both the parable and their own lives as challenged by the parable. Far from being just another pretty story, the parable can embody a fierce polemic thrust. Full of surprises, paradoxes, and sudden reversals, it can be an "attack" on the very way the audience views God, religion, the world, and themselves. The parable is thus often a challenge to change one's vision and one's action; in short, it is one of Jesus' favorite ways of calling people to repentance, a basic change of heart, mind, and life.

Because of the dynamic communication the parable unleashes, the "kingdom of God" proclaimed by the parables is usually not to be equated with any one character in a given parable but rather with the whole situation, the whole action or interaction that takes place in the parable—an interaction that should also take place in the lives of the listeners. The parable is thus a "word event," charged with the power of the kingdom it talks about. Granted this dynamic view of parables that recognizes its poetic power and dialogical nature, there is no reason to insist on a strict dichotomy between Jesus' "simple" parables (with supposedly only one point of comparison) and allegorical interpretations, which, it is claimed, must all be assigned to the evangelists or the later church.[140] Since both the OT prophets before him (especially Ezekiel) and the rabbis after him readily used allegory in their *mĕšālîm* (the plural of *māšāl*), it would be strange if not incredible if Jesus had never used allegorical elements in his parables. Allegorical traits need not militate against a parable's having a main focus, thrust, or challenge.[141]

Armed with this thumbnail sketch of the nature of parables, we are now in a position to take a look at the parable of the children playing:

[This generation] is like children sitting in the marketplace who call out to the other children [or: to one another]:

"We played the pipe for you but you did not dance; we sang laments but you did not mourn."

In light of our quick review of the nature of a parable, we realize that the opening words, "[this generation] is like children sitting in a marketplace," does not necessarily mean that we should immediately identify the generation that refuses to believe in Jesus with the children of the story who call out. It may be that the situation, the attitude, or the action of this generation is compared with some other group in the story or simply with the general situation, attitude, or interaction portrayed in the parable.

At the core of the parable, the basic structure of the children's complaint is clear enough: it is the structure of antithetical parallelism (piping and dancing versus singing a lament and mourning), which Joachim Jeremias identifies as typical of the teaching of Jesus. Unfortunately, the precise game being played by the children is not entirely clear. One could understand the text to mean that the first group of children "plays wedding" by piping a merry tune, while the second group refuses to dance. Then, when the first group tries to suit the mood of the second group by switching to threnodies in a game of "funerals," the finicky second group refuses to join in and beat their breasts in mourning.[142] However, one could interpret the puerile conflict differently. Conceivably, the first group insists on playing wedding and the second group insists on playing funerals. Neither group will give in to the other's moody stubbornness, the only result being frustration, a waste of time, and no action.[143]

Either of these two interpretations can be legitimately drawn from the terse parable. To cut the Gordian knot, Joachim Jeremias emphasizes the detail that the children are "sitting" (*kathēmenois*) in the marketplace. To him, this means that it is the first group, lounging at the side of the street, that is trying to "call the tune" and give directions to the second group, first to dance and then to mourn. When the second group refuses to comply with either set of orders, the first group complains that they are spoilsports. Personally, I am not sure whether the detail of "sitting" solves the whole problem so easily.[144] In either interpretation, though, the general thrust of the parable is the same. "This generation's" flightiness, moodiness, and desire to have its own way (however much that desire may change from moment to moment) are the objects of Jesus' rebuke.[145]

We might hope that this general thrust would be clarified and specified by the application that follows, but once again a number of possibilities arise—as one should expect from this riddle-speech, which is naturally open to multiple interpretations. We should start with what is certain. First, the application falls into a neat antithetic parallelism of both form and content:

Matt 11:18 par.	*Matt 11:19 par.*
For John [the Baptist][146] came neither eating nor drinking,[147]	For the Son of Man came eating and drinking,

and you say:	and you say:
"He has a demon."	"Behold an eater and drinker, a friend of toll collectors and sinners."

What strikes one immediately is that not only the parable but also its application are structured according to antithetic parallelism.

Second, we should notice that not only are the two verses (11:18–19 par.) related to each other and to the parable by this antithetic parallelism; they are also organically united to the parable by a chiastic ("crisscross") structure of A-B-A'-B'. Chiasm is a well-known rhetorical tool in both the Old and the New Testaments and is well exemplified here. The parable moved from joyful dancing typical of weddings to the beating of breasts that occurs at funerals. The parable's order of joy-sorrow is then reversed in the application, where (as befits the chronological order of events) the stern, ascetic prophet of judgment (John) is mentioned first, and then the joyful preacher of good news (Jesus). The chiasm is thus joy-sorrow-sorrow-joy. It is strange that critics from Dibelius onward have judged the union of parable and application to be secondary because supposedly the connection between them is strained or contrived.[148] These scholars seem to have missed the obvious interplay of antithetic parallelism in both parable and application with the chiastic structure tying the two together. This tight, neat fit hardly seems the result of some fortuitous, secondary joining of two disparate traditions that have floated separately in the sea of oral tradition for some time. Thus, my initial supposition about the original unity of the parable and its application seems confirmed.

Still, this does not resolve the basic ambiguity of both the parable and its application. Indeed, one might almost argue that parable and application belonged together originally because the saying about John and Jesus fits in "perfectly" (if that is the right word) with the ambiguity of the parable. Even if Joachim Jeremias is right about the interpretation of the parable (i.e., the group sitting down does all the piping and lamenting, and the second group does all the refusing), the exact way in which parable and application intersect is ambiguous. With Jeremias, one could understand the sitting youngsters to represent "this generation." It has tried to give orders to both John and Jesus by demanding that they trim their message and praxis to fit this generation's mood-of-the-moment. Both John and Jesus—each in his own way—have proven themselves true prophets of God by refusing to adapt their message and manner to meet human whims. This generation has tried to call the tune, but neither prophet would sing from the musical score set in front of him.

This interpretation fits the general drift of the parable-plus-application, but the intricate intersection created by the chiasm might lead one to expect a tighter fit in interpretation as well as in structure. Hence I incline to the view that it is rather John and Jesus who are the children (indeed, Luke 7:35 may intimate, the children of divine Wisdom) who call out in their preaching to this generation, summoning it to decision and action. The ascetic John issued a fierce call to repentance, stiffened with dire warnings of fiery judgment soon to come. This generation refused to join in John's *Dies irae* intoned over the present world. They dismissed the dismal prophet from the desert who ate only locusts and wild honey with contempt:[149] the poor man must be mad (= in religious terms, he has a demon). Jesus the bon vivant issued a very different call to repentance. By extending table fellowship to the religious outcasts of Jewish society, the toll collectors and sinners, Jesus offered an easy, joyous way into the kingdom of God that he proclaimed. With a sudden burst of puritanism, this generation felt that no hallowed prophet sent from God would adopt such a freewheeling, pleasure-seeking lifestyle, hobnobbing with religious low-life and offering assurances of God's forgiveness without demanding the proper process for reintegration into Jewish religious society. How could this Jesus be a true prophet and reformer when he was a glutton and a drunkard,[150] a close companion at meals with people who robbed their fellow Jews (the toll collectors)[151] or who sinned willfully and heinously, yet refused to repent (sinners).[152] Thus, for opposite but equally convenient reasons, this generation, like the recalcitrant second group of children, rejects the call to repentance of both the excessively ascetic John and the excessively jolly Jesus. The result is spiritual paralysis and an apparent frustration of God's saving plan to rescue his chosen people in this last hour of their history.

To understand the seriousness of the charge against Jesus in Matt 11:19 par., we must recall a key insight stressed by E. P. Sanders: despite the presentations of Joachim Jeremias and many others, "sinners" in the Jesus-tradition of the Synoptics are not to be equated with the so-called "people of the land" (the *ʿammê hāʾ āreṣ*).[153] The "people of the land" were the simple and uneducated Jewish masses who did not have the time, learning, or means to follow the punctilious observances of those Jews who banded together voluntarily to keep themselves in a high state of ritual purity (the *ḥăbērîm*). While not maintaining this quasi-sacerdotal purity, ordinary Palestinian Jews were not irreligious and certainly were not looked upon by the zealously observant as "the wicked" or "sinners." Sinners were those who intentionally rejected the commandments of the God of Israel, as these commandments were understood by Jews in general, not just by an elite group of puritans. Jesus' table fellowship was therefore seriously offensive to many Jews, not just to *ḥăbērîm* or Pharisees. He insisted on entering into intimate relationship not only with dishonest Jews who robbed their fellows (the tax collectors) but also with those Jews who, for all practical purposes, had thumbed their noses at the covenant and commandments of God. It was to these wicked that Jesus dared to offer forgiveness and a place in the kingdom of God, without apparently making it a prior condition that they go through the usual process of reintegration into Jewish religious society: prayers of repentance, restitution of ill-gotten goods or recompense for harm committed, temple sacrifice, and commitment to follow the Mosaic Law.[154] His bon vivant existence with robbers and sinners was therefore something much more scandalous and ominous than a mere matter of breaking purity rules dear to the *ḥăbērîm* or the Pharisees.[155]

The serious implications of all this will have to be pursued in subsequent chapters. For now, all that we have seen adds further weight to the arguments in favor of the authenticity of 11:18–19 par. as well as the entire unit of 11:16–19. To begin with, while John and Jesus are contrasted in their style of ministry in vv 18–19, they are nevertheless put on the same basic level as two prophetic—and in many ways parallel—figures who appear on the stage of history. For all their differences, vv 18–19 place them back to back as two emissaries of God who meet with the exact same rejection from "this generation," despite their contrasting styles. That the early church would have created a saying that makes of their crucified and risen Messiah and coming Son of Man nothing more than an equal-though-alternative prophetic figure to John the Baptist seems highly improbable. The improbability becomes a near impossibility when we notice that v 19 preserves, uniquely within the NT, the memory that Jesus was branded as a glutton and a drunkard in his unseemly pursuit of disciples among thieving toll collectors and thoroughly wicked people with whom no decent Jew, Pharisee or non-Pharisee, would associate. It strains credulity to think that the early church would create such a pungent, hostile saying about Jesus when none existed.

E. P. Sanders is extremely strong on this point, showing at length how the criteria of authenticity "really work" in this case.[156] He argues for the historicity of Jesus' promise of salvation to sinners on three grounds. (1) There is multiple attestation in content; the Gospel material is large in extent. (2) There is multiple attestation in form: parables, other sayings, flat declarations of purpose, reports of Jesus' activity, and reported accusations against him. (3) There is the criterion of discontinuity: "A high tolerance for sinners was not a characteristic of the early church, as far as we can know it." It is intriguing to see how Paul Hoffmann has to strain to maintain both his claim that 11:18–19 was a creation of the early church and yet that it reflects true historical knowledge of Jesus.[157] Moreover, one is left wondering why, if 11:18–19 is purely a secondary commentary on 11:16–17, the early church made such a special effort (1) to introduce the Baptist as commentary on a logion that did not suggest his presence, (2) make him a parallel figure with Jesus the Lord, (3) make this Lord the object of scurrilous mockery, and (4) associate the Baptist with a charge of diabolical possession, for which there is no evidence anywhere else in the NT or Josephus. The theory of creation by the early church thus turns out to demand a great number of unverifiable hypotheses and contorted explanations. That 11:18–19 formed an original unity with 11:16–17 and was spoken by Jesus is the much simpler solution.[158]

Moreover, after Easter, the question of the table fellowship practiced by the Nazarene during his earthly life was no longer where the war over Jesus was being waged. The earliest fights about the person of Jesus that raged between ordinary Jews and Christian Jews after Easter centered on the Christian claims that a crucified criminal was the Messiah, that God had raised him from the dead, and that this exalted Jesus was coming soon to judge Israel. It was these stupendous claims that the Christian Jews urged on their compatriots, only to find them rejected by most. That in the midst of all this preaching the early church should bother to invent and circulate a saying about Jesus being a glutton and a drunkard makes no sense, since the battle after Easter was being fought on other ground, and dredging up such memories could hardly in any case help the cause.

A similar argument might be made about John the Baptist in v 18. There is no indication of a long-lived tradition of vituperation of the Baptist after his death. Indeed, apparently years after John's execution by Antipas, some Jews, according to Josephus, saw Herod's defeat at the hand of King Aretas as punishment for the martyrdom of the Baptist (*Ant.* 18.5.2 §116–19). Josephus' account may intend to protect John from misinterpretation as a political agitator who met with a political execution. But the presentation in the *Antiquities* does not give one the impression that Josephus is defending John from unpopularity in general or from a charge of diabolical possession in particular. As with certain other historical figures, martyrdom may have given the Baptist the widespread popularity and even reverence that he did not enjoy in his own lifetime. At any rate, the slander that he was diabolically possessed makes the most sense in the mouths of those dismissing or resisting him while he was on the scene. To create the charge only after he was martyred by Antipas and grew to be revered by many Jews would indeed be strange.

Two minor objections still stand in the way of accepting 11:18–19 par. as coming from Jesus. The first is the solemn use of the verb "came" (*ēlthen*) in a saying in which Jesus speaks of himself—if, as many critics do, we take the aorist form *ēlthen* of Matt 11:19 to be more original than the perfect form *elēlythen* ("he has come") in Luke 7:34.[159] Actually, the very fact that the verb "came" is used equally of the Baptist and Jesus indicates that it need not and certainly does not here convey overtones of preexistence or of the unique mission of the Messiah. In context, the verb connotes the appearance on the public stage of Israel's religious history of two men who claimed to be prophets commissioned by God to speak to his people. As a matter of fact, the idea of some sort of prophetic commission or consciousness is found in Josephus' mouth in a passage in his *Jewish War* (3.8.9 §400), with the verb *hēkō* ("I have come") being used by Josephus as he proclaims a prophetic oracle to Vespasian. All this calls into question the position of Bultmann, who holds that the statement "I have come" (*ēlthon*) in the mouth of Jesus indicates a saying that looks back on the whole earthly ministry of Jesus as a thing of the past and that therefore must be a later church creation. Bultmann's claim is further weakened by the fact that we cannot be sure which Aramaic verb form the Greek aorist *ēlthon* is translating (pĕ'al perfect? pĕ'al participle active?). If it is the pĕ'al perfect form, one should remember that this form of the Aramaic verb 'ătā' ("come") can have at times a present or perfect sense. Moreover, the sense of *ēlthen* (Matt 11:19 par.) in its present narrative context in the Gospel of Matthew—Jesus speaking during his public ministry—demands the meaning "I have come," not "I came" (in the sense of a retrospective glance at a life now finished). If *ēlthen* can have that meaning in the Gospel of Matthew, it is difficult to see why it could not have that same meaning in Q or in the earliest Greek form of the saying. The argument against authenticity from the mere presence of *ēlthen* therefore does not hold.[160]

A second objection against authenticity stems from the presence of "the Son of Man" (*ho huios tou anthrōpou*) as a designation for Jesus in 11:29 par. "The Son of Man" is probably the most problematic and controverted title or designation for Jesus in the whole of the Gospel tradition. We shall examine it at length in a later chapter. Here I would simply point out that its presence in 11:19 par. need not call the authenticity of the whole saying into doubt.[161] The presence of "the Son of Man" can be explained in various ways: (1) It is possible that "the Son of Man" was substituted secondarily for an original "I" (*egō*). This would provide a neat balance if the simple "John" of Matt 11:18 (and not the "John the Baptist" of Luke 7:33) is the original reading of Q.[162] (2) Those who claim that the Aramaic original of "the Son of Man" (*bar* [*ĕ*]*nāšāʾ*) could be used simply as a substitute for "I" in early 1st-century Palestinian Aramaic would have no difficulty with its appearance here. However, there is no firm proof for such a usage in the early 1st century;[163] and other "generic" meanings, such as "a man like myself" or "any man in my condition," do not fit the specific reference here (i.e., the parallel to John the Baptist and the precise accusations). (3) In my own view, it is quite possible that Jesus the parable-maker consciously used the vague *bar* ʾ(ʿĕ)*nāšāʾ* as a parable-like, riddle-like, mind-teasing self-designation—most fittingly in a case like this, where it occurs in the application of a parable. Whichever explanation one prefers, "the Son of Man" does not pose a difficulty sufficiently grave to outweigh the many reasons we have seen for accepting the authenticity of Matt 11:18–19 par. and indeed the unity of the larger unit, Matt 11:16–19 par.[164]

A final difficulty for almost all exegetes, no matter what their stance on authenticity, is the meaning of the curious statement that ends the present form of the pericope: "And wisdom is vindicated by all her children [so Luke 7:35; Matt 11:29 has 'by her works']."[165] The verse suffers from many problems of both translation and interpretation.[166] The verb *edikaiōthē* (literally, "was vindicated," "was justified") should probably be translated as a present tense ("is vindicated"), whether we explain the present sense as an overliteral translation of a Semitic perfect tense, a prophetic aorist (affirming the certainty of what will come to pass by putting the verb in a past tense), or a gnomic aorist ("wisdom is always vindicated").[167] The affirmation that wisdom is or will be vindicated, coming as it does right after two glaring examples of how God's prophets are rejected by God's people, suggests that the introductory *kai* ("and") has an adversative sense and should be translated as "and yet."

The concatenation of a parable, a saying about two eschatological prophets being rejected as they offer Israel salvation in the last hour of its history, and the promise of wisdom's vindication reminds us that Jewish apocalyptic resulted at least in part from the amalgam of prophetic and sapiential influences. In this context, then, "wisdom" (*sophia*) probably refers to God's wise, well-ordered plan of salvation, which is now reaching its climax. God's final prophets are rejected by large numbers of Israelites, and at first glance it might appear that God's wise plan of salvation will be frustrated by Israel's obstinacy. Yet there are those who do accept the prophets' message, and they (the prophets, their audience, or both?) will be the means by which God's wisdom is finally vindicated.[168]

This line of interpretation presupposes that the more original reading of the saying is "and yet wisdom is vindicated by all her children" rather than "by her works." Many Matthean scholars see the reference to the *works of wisdom* in 11:19 as a conscious *inclusio* created by Matthew, who also redacted the very beginning of this Baptist-block in Q to make it read: "Now John, hearing in prison of *the works of the Messiah.* . . ."[169] In contrast, "children" at the end of this Q subunit fits in neatly with its beginning, the parable of the "children" in the marketplace; this *inclusio* over a shorter distance has a better chance of being original—at least in Q, if not in the teaching of Jesus.[170]

Still, what exactly "all her [wisdom's] children" refers to is not clear. The immediate context would make it attractive to see John and Jesus as the two children of wisdom who, by their fidelity to their mission to Israel in the teeth of opposition, see to it that God's wise plan of salvation is vindicated, i.e., that it finally achieves its goal. Such an interpretation would once again put John and Jesus on the same level and so would fit in well with the rest of the unit. The major obstacle to this interpretation is the word "all" in front of "children"; it naturally refers to a larger group than the two solitary figures, John and Jesus. On the other hand, Joseph Fitzmyer points out that "all" is lacking in the Matthean parallel, and so "all" may be Luke's addition—an addition, by the way, that he often makes to his sources.[171] If that be the case, the original Q form of the saying would have spoken simply of wisdom's being vindicated "by her children," and the reference to John and Jesus would fit perfectly. Granted, all this is highly speculative. If, however, "all" is part of the original form of the saying, a reference to only two people would be contrived. Instead, all of wisdom's children would probably refer to all the children of Israel who prove themselves true children of wisdom by accepting her emissaries. Here again, but only implicitly, John and Jesus are yoked together as the two prophets of wisdom, but the focus of the saying is rather on all who heed them.[172]

With so many possible interpretations and no clear means of deciding among them, one must admit that Luke 7:35 par. remains a puzzle. Perhaps it is wiser not to make our treatment of the Baptist-block depend upon the authenticity of Luke 7:35 par. and its original connection with the rest of Luke 7:31–34 par. Fitzmyer may well be correct that Luke 7:35 par. was not yet a part of this unit (7:31–34 par.) at the earliest stage of the tradition. More than one commentator has remarked on the sudden appearance of the word "wisdom" in Luke 7:35, without any preparation for it in the immediate context of the parable of the children or its application. The very difficulty exegetes have in making any sense of 7:35 may reflect the fact that it was joined to the parable and its application only secondarily. The joining may have taken place during the formation of Q, when 7:35 was attracted to the rest of the unit by the catchword "children."[173] Indeed, there may be a rhetorical signpost that the tradition originally ended with the comparison-yet-contrast between John and Jesus in Luke 7:33–34 (= Matt 11:18–19). While the sayings about John and Jesus are carefully constructed according to antithetical parallelism, the accusation against Jesus (introduced by "you say") is twice as long as the one against the Baptist. The longer negative description of Jesus, breaking the parallelism with an extra line ("a friend of toll collectors and sinners"), may be a signal that the pericope has reached its conclusion.[174]

We have come to the end of our study of the three main units (Matt 11:2–6,7–11,16–19 parr.) that make up the second Baptist-block of the Q tradition, the sayings of Jesus dealing with John. While recognizing secondary and tertiary additions on the levels of both Q and the evangelists, we have seen that the substance of these three pieces of tradition fulfills various criteria of authenticity, and so the substance has a good claim to come from the historical Jesus. Not coincidentally, these sayings have already introduced us to a number of themes that belong to a "short list" of major areas of Jesus-research: (1) the kingdom of God; (2) the miracles of Jesus; (3) his table fellowship with toll collectors and sinners; (4) the eschatology that all this implies; (5) Jesus' use of rhetorical techniques like antithetical parallelism and wisdom genres like beatitudes and parables; (6) the category of prophet, the transcending of the category of prophet, and the violent fate of prophets like the Baptist; and (7) the personal claims that seem implicit in all Jesus says and does (the question of "implicit christology"). In subsequent chapters we will have to investigate all these topics in detail.

For the moment, though, what should strike us as we read Matt 11:2–19 par. is that most of these key themes are touched on only in passing. They form only the taken-for-granted backdrop for what is the main focus: John the Baptist and his place in the scheme of things. Many exegetes simply summarize the thrust of this second Baptist-block as "John's relation to Jesus." While that is true in a sense, it is not an exact formulation. As we have seen, Jesus stands strangely to the side, if he is present at all (strictly speaking, he is not even mentioned in the logia of Matt 11:7c–9,11 par.). The theme that binds the substance of Matt 11:2–19 par. together is rather John's relation to the new eschatological situation Jesus has introduced.[175] Jesus' miracles, his proclamation of good news to the poor, his expansive fellowship with the not-so-poor yet religiously marginalized toll collectors and sinners all testify to and to some degree actualize God's definitive coming in power to save his people Israel—in other words, the kingdom of God. It is this new state of affairs that Jesus asks John to accept in the beatitude of Matt 11:6 par. The beatitude, however, is a two-edged sword. Failure to accept the joyful news Jesus brings can lead to eschatological woe instead of happiness. This first unit (11:2–6 par.) thus harbors a dark side, especially since there is no indication of a positive response from John.

Balancing this dark tone is the high praise Jesus lavishes on John in the second unit (Matt 11:7–9,11 par.). Verses 7–9 are totally laudatory, extolling the Baptist as an uncompromising, courageous prophet and more than a prophet (as opposed to the conniving tetrarch who finally killed him). Indeed, says v 11a (probably originally a separate tradition), there has arisen among those born of women no one greater than John. Just at this pinnacle of praise, however, a sharp restriction is voiced. Despite scholarly voices to the contrary, the restriction most likely does not come from the early church but from Jesus. For it does not restrict John's greatness vis-à-vis Jesus but rather vis-à-vis anyone who accepts and enters into the new state of affairs, the kingdom of God that Jesus proclaims. By a different route, v 11a + b strikes the same tense balance seen in 11:2–6 par. There John was treated with the greatest deference and diplomacy, and yet a lack on his part is delicately broached. He is invited to embrace a kingdom that has come in keeping with the deepest thrust of his message and yet contrary to his detailed conceptions, a kingdom that has come not only after him but apart from him. In 11:11, respect for John is raised to profuse praise even as the delicate hint of John's limitations is raised to a blunt statement of his inferiority. Whether the blunter mode of expressing the relationship is due to John's refusal to accept Jesus' invitation or merely to the fact that John had already been executed and so quite literally belonged to the past, we cannot say. But both form and content argue that the two sides of the dialectic in 11:11 come from Jesus.

This *basso continuo* of respect for John coupled with emphasis on the new situation Jesus brings is heard even in Matt 11:16–19 par., which gives the clearest expression to the idea of John and Jesus as parallel figures. The parallel and therefore the high dignity of John are obvious: Both he and Jesus are prophets who have come on a mission from God to call a recalcitrant Israel ("this generation") to repentance. Significantly, though, the parallelism is an antithetical parallelism. John the desert ascetic issued a fierce warning of imminent destruction and a stringent call to inner reform, while Jesus the bon vivant celebrated the joy of salvation by holding banquets with religious lowlife. Significant also is the fact that the parallelism is not only antithetical but also weighted in one direction. John comes first, Jesus after; John is stern, Jesus joyful; and even when it comes to accusations hurled against this eschatological odd couple, Jesus gets an extra line of notice. Not by accident, it is only in this last unit of the two Baptist-blocks that Jesus himself emerges as the direct object of reflection.[176] If Matthew and Luke do reflect the basic order of the Q material on the Baptist, and if in turn Q itself reflects the configuration of sayings of and about the Baptist in the oral tradition, then very early on the sayings of John and of Jesus about John were ordered to produce a little theological tract culminating in Jesus the Son of Man bringing in the joy of the kingdom in the teeth of opposition. Be that as it may, the point remains that, for all the parallelism between John and Jesus in Matt 11:16–19 par., the eschatological plus sign definitely lies on the side of Jesus. If I am correct in my analysis, the plus sign, however delicate and indirect, comes from Jesus himself and makes explicit the implied eschatological plus sign that is present from 11:2 onward.

In this second Baptist-block seen as a whole and then examined in its parts, there is a special kind of multiple attestation. In the earliest stage of the oral tradition, Jesus' various statements about the Baptist most probably circulated in small, unconnected units clothed in various literary forms. Yet, despite the variegated nature of the Baptist tradition in both form and content, the basic message remains remarkably the same. Whether we look at the apophthegm, the chain of rhetorical questions, the parable, or the straightforward statements about the Baptist cast in antithetical parallelism—sayings which Jesus probably spoke at various times in varying conditions—a clear and tense balance is struck: John the Baptist is respected, praised, even exalted to the pinnacle of the human world. And yet that world is passing away as the healing, joy, and feasting of the kingdom come in the mission of Jesus. From all we have seen, this delicate and tense balance, though elaborated by the early church, goes back to Jesus himself as he negotiated a perilous passage from being a disciple of John to becoming a parallel and perhaps rival prophet alongside John, to finding himself the sole prophet after John's imprisonment and martyrdom, to facing the prospect of becoming a martyred prophet himself. Where exactly along this line of development each individual saying about the Baptist belongs we cannot always say. What remains striking, however, is how Jesus maintains his careful stance of balance-in-tension throughout. Along with all the other criteria already invoked, one can point to a basic coherence.

(4) When I surveyed the three major units of Matt 11:2–19 par., I purposely passed over some of the material contained in Matthew's version of the second Baptist-block, namely, 11:12–15. It is to these verses, which properly do not belong in the second Baptist-block, that I now turn.

Verses 14–15 may be quickly dismissed as Matthean redaction. The direct affirmation that John *is* Elijah (v 14) occurs neither in the parallel passage of Luke, nor elsewhere in Q, nor anywhere else in the whole of the Gospel tradition with the exception of Matthew's reworking of Mark 9:11–13. In Mark 9:11–13, the descent of Jesus and his disciples from the mount of the transfiguration, Jesus answers in a contorted way a question of the disciples about the supposed return of Elijah to restore all things. Jesus assures them that Elijah will come first (before the full establishment of the Messiah's reign?). But then Jesus makes the dialectical affirmation that Elijah has already come, "and they did to him what they wished, as it is written about him" (v 13). While the exact sense of the verse is obscure, there seems to be a veiled reference by the secret Messiah to John the Baptist as Elijah incognito. As is his wont, Matthew does away with this secrecy and with the puzzlement of Jesus' disciples by ending his version of the pericope with the clarification: "Then the disciples understood that he had spoken to them about John the Baptist" (Matt 17:13). This is the same sort of direct equation of the Baptist and Elijah that we find in Matt 11:17 and nowhere else in the Gospels. The concluding v 15, "let him who has ears hear," is taken over from Mark 4:9,23 and is used by Matthew here and in Matt 13:9,43. In 11:15 it is meant to call attention to the revelation—completely new within the Gospel tradition—that the Baptist is to be directly identified with "Elijah who is to come."

The famous logion in Matt 11:12–13 (= Luke 16:16) is not so easily dismissed—but then, it is not so easily understood. As the Lucan parallel shows, it probably belongs to Q, though the notable difference in wording and order of the clauses makes such a judgment more difficult in this case than for most of the material in the two Baptist-blocks. Scholars cannot even agree on where Matt 11:12–13 par. might have stood in the Q document. The present position in Matthew, the present position in Luke, and total agnosticism on the question have all been espoused.[177] As we shall see below, heavy Matthean redaction, which makes the logion more of a statement about John the Baptist than it was in Q, may also be the reason why it stands in the second Baptist-block in Matthew's Gospel. In my opinion, that Matt 11:12–13 par. did not originally belong to the second Baptist-block of Q is indicated by its position in Luke's Gospel within the Lucan context of 16:14–18, a string of heterogeneous sayings joined only by a loose association of ideas. There is no conceivable reason why Luke should have moved the logion from its place within the second Baptist-block to a context with which it has practically no connection except the weak link of the word "law." Rather, as is often the case, Luke the psychologist seems to have preserved the "stream of consciousness" order (if that is the word) of the Q document, while Matthew the great verbal architect has built his equivalent of Luke 16:16 into a large structure with homogeneous content, namely, the second Baptist-block. Therefore, since Matt 11:12–13 par. was originally a free-floating logion, one may not use its present context in Matt 11:2–19 to settle the questions of its original wording, order, or meaning.[178]

This is one reason why critics are so divided on these questions. Another is that, while some redactional tendencies are clear (especially those of Matthew), exegetes cannot agree in every instance as to what is a redactional trait of an evangelist and what is primitive wording or order. The great difficulty of reaching the earliest form of this saying and the vast diversity of opinion among commentators are two reasons why I have set aside this saying for separate treatment. It is important that our basic findings on Jesus and the Baptist not depend upon this one especially troublesome logion. If it can shed further light on what we have already seen from the second Baptist-block, well and good. If it instead proves intractable or inscrutable, the results of our survey of the three major units in Matt 11:2–19 par. still stand.

The problems involved in reconstructing even the original Q form of the saying, not to mention a hypothetical saying of the historical Jesus, become clear as soon as we look at the two versions of the logion (with verbal similarities emphasized):[179]

Matt 11:12–13	*Luke 16:16*
12 *From the days* of John the Baptist until now, *the kingdom of heaven suffers violence,* and the violent plunder it.	16 a *The law and the prophets until John;*

13 For all the *prophets and the law*   16 b *From then the kingdom of God* is
prophesied *until John*   being proclaimed, and every one
                                                     is pressed into it.

Some of the differences between Matthew and Luke strike the eye immediately. One obvious difference is in the basic order of the two halves of the
saying: the first half of the saying in Luke (Luke 16:16a) corresponds to the
second half of the saying in Matthew (Matt 11:13), while the second half of
the saying in Luke (Luke 16:16b) corresponds to the first half of the saying in
Matthew (Matt 11:12). Then there is a notable difference in length. The first
half of the Lucan saying is extremely terse, without even a verb; the slightly
longer Matthean form (11:13) supplies one. To complicate matters further, a
few of the Greek words (*biazetai, biastai, harpazousin*) are difficult to translate
in this context. As can be seen above, I have sided with those exegetes who
favor a negative sense for all three words in the Matthean version of the logion;
the Lucan version may have a more positive meaning. Certainly detailed studies of the three words, as well as their close configuration in a small compass,
favor the negative sense of violence and rapine in the Matthean form.[180]

Granted the many uncertainties, it is best to start with the clearly redactional hands of Matthew and Luke. The most glaring Matthean trait is his
massive reworking of the statement about the "law and the prophets." We can
confidently speak of "the law and the prophets" as the original reading, since
that is the order witnessed in the LXX and the NT, as well as at Qumran;[181]
neither the LXX, the NT (outside of Matt 11:13), nor Qumran has a single
instance of "all the prophets and the law."[182] Matthew in effect is standing the
OT "canon" on its head, with the torah being understood prophetically and
in the light of the OT prophets. For Matthew, the OT prophets are "the canon
within the canon" (note the "all the" before "prophets"), pointing forward to
the great turning point of salvation history, the Christ-event, especially the
death and resurrection of Jesus. Even the law is taken up into this grand prophetic function of the OT. Hence, when Matthew supplies a verb for this
logion, he chooses a verb that never serves as the predicate of "law" (*tôrâ*,
nomos) anywhere else in the Hebrew OT, the LXX, or the NT: "prophesied"
(*eprophēteusan*). For Matthew, what is true of the prophets is true of the torah:
its major function was to point ahead to its eschatological fulfillment in Jesus.[183] Matthew no doubt would have felt especially free to insert his own
theologically charged verb into the saying if it was simply bereft of a verb.

I tend to think, therefore, that Luke's stark, puzzling, *māšāl*-like logion is
what stood in Q: "The law and the prophets until John." In my view, this
terse, lapidary statement, which immediately raises questions as to its meaning,
would naturally stand at the beginning of a unit, with some further explanation
or comment to follow. Moreover, as Jacques Schlosser points out, the two
parts of the Lucan saying follow the natural order of salvation history (first the

law and prophets, then the kingdom). In contrast, the exact logical flow of Matt 11:12 + 13 is difficult to grasp. How does the statement "for all the prophets and the law, etc." ground or explain the previous statement about the violence the kingdom suffers?[184] Thus, it may well be that Luke has preserved the original order as well as the original wording of 16:16a. This would fit in with the general observation critics make: Luke seems to have preserved the original order and wording of Q more often than Matthew. While such a sweeping "rule" does not hold true in all cases and must always be tested in the individual instance, it seems to be valid here.

The second half of the statement (Luke 16:16b = Matt 11:12) is more troublesome because redactional clues are not as clear and the meaning of key words remains in doubt. To begin with, Luke's verb "is proclaimed [with the implication of good news]" (*euaggelizetai*) is a favorite of Luke's, while the corresponding verb in Matthew ("suffers violence," *biazetai*) never occurs again in Matthew, or indeed anywhere else in the NT outside of this Q passage. Moreover, while *biazetai* does not occur at this point in the Lucan form of the saying, it does "pop up" in the next clause, where Matthew uses another verb denoting violence ("plunder," "snatch away" wrongfully) along with the subject *biastai* ("those who use violence"). All the indicators point to the vocabulary of violence (*biazomai, biastēs*) being original to the saying, while proclaiming good news is a happy thought that the joyful Luke has inserted into a somber setting.[185] Matthew's emphasis on violence and struggle from start to finish appears more original in the second half of the saying.[186]

A few other minor insights into the original wording of Q are possible. As all admit, "kingdom of *heaven*," a phrase unique to Matthew in the NT, comes from his hand, while the otherwise universally attested "kingdom of *God*" (which even Matthew uses in a few cases)[187] stood in Q. Luke-Acts does not use *apo tote* ("from then") elsewhere, while the phrase occurs in Matthew at 4:17; 16:21; and 26:16, all three cases being probably redactional[188] contributions of the Evangelist. Hence there would be no reason for Matthew to delete the phrase here, and no special reason for Luke to insert it; it most likely stood in Q. Another observation supports this judgment. If "the law and the prophets until John" was the original opening of the Q saying, then "from the days of John the Baptist until now" is an unnecessarily long and specific time designation to begin the second half of the logion. Moreover, Matthew may have introduced "from the days of John the Baptist until now" in the beginning of 11:12 and appended "until John" toward the end of 11:13 to supply redactional links with the Q saying in 11:11 and his own equation of John with Elijah in 11:14.[189] In contrast, Luke's simple "from then" makes perfect sense as the beginning of the second half of the isolated saying and fits the laconic style of the first half.

While realizing how tentative much of this is, I think the best hypothetical reconstruction of the Q saying is roughly Luke's order and laconic tone, as emended by some of the vocabulary of Matthew's version:

16a The law and the prophets [lasted?] until John;
16b From then on,
    the kingdom of God suffers violence,
    and the violent plunder it.[190]

While not necessarily coming from the same time or situation as Matt 11:16–19 par. (the parable of the children in the marketplace), the saying probably does reflect the same atmosphere of growing opposition, an opposition that Jesus experienced just as John did. The point, though, does not lie with the parallelism-yet-difference between John and Jesus, as seen in 11:16–19 par. Rather, opposition is seen in a more nuanced time frame and from a different perspective. Already during the classical period of Israel's prophets, Israel's history was divided by the seers into various stages or periods. This periodization of Israel's history (and cosmic history as well) underwent expansion, refinement, and numerical exactitude in apocalyptic literature. Jesus the eschatological prophet with apocalyptic traits may reflect something of this tendency to periodize Israel's history in this saying, though his periodization is quite simple, unlike the baroque constructions of apocalyptic.[191] All of Israel's history up until the time of John the Baptist is placed under the rubric of Israel's sacred literature, summarized as the law and the prophets. God's instruction about both the founding events of Israel's existence and the proper response of Israel in worship and daily life (law) and the further inculcation of duties under the covenant plus promises of punishment yet final restoration in the future (the prophets) had molded and guided Israel's existence for centuries. But in some sense that holds true only "up until John." From the time of John onwards, a new state of affairs has broken in on the scene.[192] This new state of affairs, the kingdom of God, has met with violent opposition and the people using violence are plundering (or trying to plunder) the kingdom.

What all this means is by no means clear. Whether the violent opposition is thought to come from spiritual powers that stand behind earthly rulers, or Antipas, who killed John, or the Jerusalem high priests, or the Roman authorities, or the Pharisees, or the scribes, or antinomians, or legalists, or the rabble, or from armed nationalist freedom fighters has been debated at length by scholars with no clear results,[193] since we are dealing with a single logion whose translation is difficult and whose original context is lost. If the saying in some form comes from Jesus, the best method is to try to interpret it in the light of the results we have achieved from studying the more accessible material in the second Baptist-block of Q.

To begin with, the saying places us in a theological environment not unlike the one presupposed by the story of the delegation to Jesus (Matt 11:2–6 par.) or by the saying on the greatness yet limitations of John (11:11 par.). In all these cases, John's place is being fixed not so much in direct relation to Jesus as in direct relation to the new state of affairs or existence brought about by the coming of the kingdom of God. In none of these cases is John said to proclaim or bring in the kingdom. Indeed, there is no reliable indication inside or outside the Gospels that the historical John ever actually spoke of "the kingdom of God," present or future. Hence we must be careful about what Luke 16:16 par. says or does not say about John.

John is present in the two halves of this logion as a time- or period-marker; he is not the main point of the saying. In both halves he is the object (explicitly or implicitly) of prepositions indicating the flow and limits of time: "up until John" (*mechri* or *heōs Iōannou* in 16a) and "from then [i.e., from the time of John]" (*apo tote* in 16b). It is most important to realize that, just as John is not said to proclaim or teach the law and the prophets in the first half of the saying, so he is not said to be the one who proclaims the kingdom of God in the second half of the saying.[194] In other words, "from then," "from the time of John," should not be misread to mean that John was the one who started the proclamation of the kingdom. As far as we know, he wasn't. As we have already seen, the kingdom of God, proclaimed to the poor, actualized in healings and other miracles, and celebrated by table fellowship with religious outcasts, was the hallmark that differentiated Jesus from John.

Hence, as so often in the sayings in the second Baptist-block, Jesus lies hidden beneath talk about the kingdom of God or its manifestations. It is the kingdom that is the central focus of the logion. "The kingdom of God," as shall be shown in Chapter 14, allows of no easy definition, since it is a many-faceted symbol having a whole range of meanings. Central to this symbol is the idea of God coming in power to judge and save his sinful people Israel at the end of their history. Yet that image unavoidably generates others. If God's powerful rule is actually being exercised and having an effect on people through the ministry of Jesus, then what is in itself transcendent (God's judging and saving power) has become immanent and palpable in the lives of individuals as well as in the corporate existence of Israel as a people. By its coming into the present world through the ministry of Jesus, the kingdom sets up a certain field of force or realm of human existence in which the power of the kingdom is concretely experienced. Hence people are said to "enter into" the kingdom, to "be in" the kingdom, or to "see" the kingdom. It is in this sense—the kingdom as a palpable reality in human lives and history—that the kingdom can be said to "suffer violence" or to be "plundered" by the violent. At this point *hē basileia tou theou* (the kingdom of God) begins to take on the imagery of a spatial kingdom as well as dynamic rule.[195]

We are roughly in the situation envisioned by Matt 11:19 par.: in his proclamation and realization of God's kingdom, Jesus has met with fierce opposition. If anything, the sky seems to be growing darker in Luke 16:16 par. While Matt 11:19 par. speaks of insult and mockery (with just a hint that the precise accusation, echoing Deut 21:20, might lead to lethal punishment), the opposition in Luke 16:16 is described in terms of violence. One might thus be tempted to assign 16:16 to a later stage of Jesus' ministry, when the Baptist has become just a temporal marker and it is now Jesus' turn to face the possibility of a violent death because of his preaching. While that is a plausible reading of the logion, one must remember the danger of trying to place Jesus' sayings on a precise time-line of our own making. Strictly speaking, it is the kingdom, not Jesus himself, that is said to suffer the violence; and one must always allow for hyperbole in a context of oral religious polemic.

At any rate, the fact that John is now over on the sidelines as a temporal divider, while the kingdom of God is the real subject of the saying, may indicate why this saying was not brought into the second Baptist-block of Q. It is Matthew, who doubles the explicit reference to John (12a + 13b), increases the emphasis on prophecy and prophetic fulfillment, and adds a direct identification of John with Elijah, who makes the logion suitable for Q's miniature treatise on the Baptist. Indeed, if it were not for Matthew's influence on our memory of Gospel sayings, we might not even think of Luke 16:16 as a saying about John the Baptist. Actually, it isn't; it is a saying about the kingdom of God.[196]

Still, the precise place of John the Baptist in Jesus' view of God's plan is a question raised, however peripherally, by the logion. Hans Conzelmann both established the basis of his interpretation of Luke-Acts and unleashed a fierce debate by deciding that this saying, at least in its Lucan form, placed the Baptist in the period of the law and the prophets and separated him from the time of Jesus, who proclaims the coming of the kingdom.[197] Yet, while Conzelmann seemed to think that his interpretation of Luke 16:16 was obvious and so needed no detailed defense, many exegetes have questioned his approach. As Paul S. Minear remarks: "It must be said that rarely has a scholar placed so much weight on so dubious an interpretation of so difficult a logion."[198] As Walter Wink notes, Luke 16:16 could easily be interpreted in the exact opposite direction, namely, that in Luke's view John does belong to the "midpoint of time," the central time of Jesus.[199] At the very least, Conzelmann's failure to integrate Luke's infancy narrative into his overarching interpretation of Luke-Acts hurts the credibility of his position.

This difficulty of interpreting John's position as portrayed in Luke 16:16 even within its Lucan redactional context should make us very wary of deciding what the original logion intended to say—if anything—about John's place in the larger scheme of things. Perhaps the best starting point is John's place in the rhetorical structure of the saying. It may not be a total accident that he is placed at the extreme end of the first half, dealing with the law and the prophets, and at the very beginning of the second half, describing the fate of the kingdom of God. This linchpin position in the logion may reflect the view that John's position in Israel's history was pivotal in the literal sense of the word. He was the pivot on which the ages turned, the hinge or link between the time of the law and the prophets and the time of the kingdom proclaimed by Jesus.[200] What Fitzmyer says about Luke 16:16 in its redactional form may be true to some extent even of the original logion: "Verse 16 now makes not only John the Baptist but also the time of his appearance a transition; it at once ends the Period of Israel and begins or inaugurates the Period of Jesus."[201] In John's case, then, "pivotal" is not the same thing as "central." Luke 16:16 suggests that John was *pivotal* to the process by which the time of the law and the prophets came to an end and the time of the kingdom commenced.[202] Yet the very same saying focuses not on John but on the kingdom, as proclaimed by Jesus, as its *central* concern.

Needless to say, there is no way of providing strict proof that this was the intent of the original Q saying, to say nothing of the intention of Jesus. Walter Wink thinks that an argument can be mounted from the criterion of discontinuity: "It is unlikely that the church, engaged as it was in asserting Jesus' superiority over John, would have created a passage which credits John with the decisive act in the shift of the aeons. . . ."[203] For those who do not find such an argument cogent, another approach is possible. In the hypothetical form and content distilled above, this saying does at least meet the criterion of coherence. Consider some of the themes conjured up by this logion: John's relationship not directly to Jesus but to the kingdom, the recognition of John's unique, pivotal role, yet the still greater importance of the kingdom of God proclaimed by Jesus, who meets opposition in realizing the kingdom. We have seen all of these in the three major units of the second Baptist-block (Matt 11:2–6, 7–9,11, and 16–19 parr.). That an isolated Q logion that did not belong to the Baptist-block should, when restored to what seems its earliest form, reflect the same basic constellation of ideas that we have attributed to Jesus' thought on the Baptist, does constitute a reasonable argument, though not a decisive one, in favor of accepting Luke 16:16 par. as Jesus' own viewpoint. Since, however, the line of argument must remain highly speculative, it is wise not to make our major conclusions depend on Luke 16:16 par.[204] For those who wish to accept the primitive form of Luke 16:16 par. as coming from Jesus, it provides further confirmation of what we have already seen about Jesus' view of the Baptist.

B. The Origin of John's Baptism (Mark 11:27–33)

We have concluded our survey of the most important sayings of Jesus dealing with the Baptist; for the most part, they are also the traditions with the best claim of actually coming from Jesus. Among the remaining traditions, the only Marcan pericope that is concerned directly with John and Jesus is the question about Jesus' authority in Mark 11:27–33 parr.[205] Since Matthew and Luke are dependent on Mark and show no sign of using any independent tradition,[206] I shall restrict my observations to Mark's version.

In his redaction, Mark (or his source)[207] has placed this pericope in a pivotal position in his "Passion Week." On the one hand, looking backward, it connects with Jesus' second day in Jerusalem, which was taken up with the "cleansing" of the temple (11:15–19). It is specifically to the cleansing that the high priests, scribes, and elders (i.e., the whole Sanhedrin that will try him) refer when they ask: "By what authority [or, right] do you do these things? Or who gave you the authority to do these things?" (v 28).[208] On the other hand, this initial dispute story (*Streitgespräch*) introduces all that is to follow on this third day in Jerusalem: Jesus' parable of the evil tenants of the vineyard (12:1–12), which the authorities know Jesus has aimed at them; and the four disputes or scholarly dialogues about paying taxes to Caesar, the resurrection, the first commandment, and the descent of the Messiah from David (12:13–37). In the question about authority we therefore hear the opening cannon blast of a day of polemics, a day that will conclude with Jesus' turning the tables on the supposed authorities by showing himself the superior teacher and finally by denouncing the scribes (explicitly in 12:38–40, implicitly in 12:41–44). The eschatological discourse, prophesying God's judgment on the Jerusalem temple and on the whole world, simply broadens the scene of conflict and condemnation to apocalyptic proportions (chap. 13). In the end, the Jerusalem authorities who refused to believe in John will refuse to believe in Jesus and will put him to death (chaps. 14–15).

If one looks solely at the core of the initial dispute about Jesus' authority (11:28–30), one realizes that the material is not necessarily tied to the setting we find in Mark's Gospel.[209] This is not to say that one can prove that Mark's setting is not historical; it is just to observe that the basic story is quite general in nature. Indeed, it is difficult to give the story its proper form-critical category. Especially if we think that the original story ended with the pregnant counterquestion of Jesus in v 30,[210] one might classify it in general terms as an apophthegm. If we include the whole of vv 27–33, with the hostile authorities confessing their ignorance and Jesus speaking a final word of triumphant refusal in v 33, the unit approaches closer to the subdivision of the apophthegm called a dispute story, though one of a very general nature.[211]

In any case, at the core of the story lies a typical rabbinic pattern of challenge by way of question and parry by way of clever counterquestion.[212] Some group (not necessarily the high priests, scribes, and elders of the present form of the story)[213] addresses a basic question and challenge to Jesus: What is the nature and source of your authority? Whether the authority they question refers more to Jesus' teaching, his general mode of action, or some particular practice may not have been specified in the earliest form of the tradition. However, the emphasis on "doing these things" (vv 28–29,33), which serves as a leitmotif throughout the pericope, seems to favor the idea that some action or practice of Jesus is the occasion of the challenge—be it the temple cleansing, as in Mark, or some other well-known action of Jesus.[214]

In the sort of game of wits that is beloved of peasants and is often found in folklore, Jesus suggests a type of contest or wager. If his questioners can first answer a question Jesus proposes—and thus establish that they have the wisdom one would expect of religious interrogators—then he will answer their question.[215] By this initial response, Jesus has already turned the tables. He has put himself "in the driver's seat" by setting the rules of the game, and his offer is based on an unspoken presupposition: of course he can answer his opponents! The only question is on what conditions he will choose to do so.

Silence apparently betokens consent, so Jesus poses his question, which turns out to be more of a trap than his opponents' relatively straightforward query. As Ernst Lohmeyer rightly stressed,[216] all too many commentators (including Bultmann) miss the point of Jesus' question when they paraphrase it as: What was the source of John's authority—God or a mere human? While that paraphrase creates the neat parallel between John's authority and Jesus' authority that commentators want, that is not exactly how Jesus poses the dilemma. Rather, without explanation, he shifts from the general question of authority to the very concrete case of John's baptism: Was that divine or human in its origin? This formulation of the question—especially if we allow that the fuller form of the story down to v 33 is not simply Marcan redaction—implies three important points:

(1) That such a question should create a difficulty or dilemma for Jesus' interrogators presumes that they would feel some embarrassment in admitting the divine origin of John's baptism, and yet would feel constrained to avoid claiming it was merely human. This "job description" of the interrogators seems to preclude ordinary Jews in general or disciples of the Baptist in particular. Neither group, especially the latter, would feel embarrassed declaring the divine origin of John's baptism. The interrogators apparently would—which points in the direction of some ruling group that opposed John or at least declined to receive his baptism (so explicitly in v 31, which may be Marcan redaction). The "Herodians" would be one candidate; the priests and other Jerusalem authorities would be another. Why, however, the Herodians would necessarily fear adopting the other option, namely, that John's baptism had a merely human origin, is not clear. On the other hand, the Jerusalem priests, dependent to a certain degree on the good will or at least tolerance of pious Jews as they acted as tools of the Roman prefect, would not care to alienate the devout by in effect declaring John a fraud, when so many considered him a prophet.[217] Hence it may well be that, even in the early form of the story, the interrogators were in fact certain Jerusalem priests, perhaps guided by some of their scribes. Even though the precise location of this pericope as the opening struggle on the great day of the Jerusalem *Streitgespräche* may be due to Mark's redaction, the general atmosphere of a debate between Jesus and some Jerusalem authorities may be original to the story. As we shall see, the parallel structure in John 2:13–22 seems to support this view.

(2) Especially if we allow that this story was originally situated in Jerusalem toward the end of Jesus' ministry (as Rudolf Pesch claims),[218] then Jesus' counterquestion, whatever else it means, implies that, throughout his ministry, Jesus continued to look upon John's baptism—and therefore John's whole mission—as divinely inspired. This coheres well with what we have seen in both Q and Johannine traditions. Even apart from the criterion of coherence, the fact that a tradition claiming to depict Jesus during the last week of his life would at the same time present Jesus as ranging himself alongside the Baptist and thus implicitly defending himself on the grounds that he was just "another example of the same kind of thing" argues against a pure creation by the early church. The more one thinks about it, the more startling it is that Jesus, in justifying himself before Jerusalem authorities, thinks it a sufficient defense to claim—by implication rather than directly—the same sort of sanction the Bap-

tist enjoyed. This is hardly the christology of Mark's Gospel.[219] Indeed, as Pesch points out, it is striking that the story lacks any attempt to orient John to Jesus as the precursor or preparer of the latter's work.[220] The perspective is one of simple parallelism, with no hint of superiority. This is not the view of John from the vantage point of any NT writer or tradition. The criterion of discontinuity or embarrassment seems to apply, and it gives us further insight into what Jesus implicitly claimed he was. He is not here casting himself in the role of a traditional Jewish sage, scribe, or (to use a term anachronistically) rabbi. By comparing himself with John, he places himself more or less in the category of an eschatological prophet who does not derive his authority not from institutional channels like the law or the temple.

(3) Once we appreciate the remarkable strategy of Jesus' counterquestion, the more pressing becomes a further question: Why does Jesus counter a question about his "authority to do these things" by asking about the divine or human origin of John's *baptism* in particular rather than John's *authority* in general? Granted that the general thrust of Jesus' reply is to range himself alongside the Baptist as some sort of similar case, the most natural explanation is that Jesus focuses on John's baptism because it is very relevant to Jesus' own kind of ministry and the authority it seems to claim. As we saw in section III above, it is probable that Jesus took over from John and continued throughout his ministry the practice of baptizing. Hence the nexus between the divine origin of one's baptism and the divine origin of one's authority holds true both for John and for Jesus. It becomes extremely difficult for the Jerusalem authorities to recognize John's baptism as divinely authorized and yet deny the same status to the very same kind of baptism, which John's former disciple now continues to administer in imitation of his revered and martyred master. Indeed, if originally the authorities' question about Jesus' authority "to do these things" referred not specifically to the cleansing of the temple but to the various startling "charismatic" actions of his ministry, Jesus may have deftly replied by focusing on the one concrete practice in his ministry that most clearly derived from and imitated the ministry of John: baptism.[221] It was the one practice of Jesus that the authorities would find inexpedient to label merely human, since it was simply the continuation of the practice of a martyred prophet revered by the people. Yet to acknowledge John's baptismal practice as divine in origin would in effect imply the same sanction for Jesus' continuation of that practice—and by extension, for Jesus' ministry in general. The authorities are indeed impaled on the horns of a dilemma and choose a humiliating profession of ignorance as the only way out.

If this interpretation of what "lies behind" Jesus' strategic counterquestion is correct, we have a further indication of a tradition that predates Mark and in fact runs counter to the whole Synoptic tradition. As we have seen, the idea that Jesus himself baptized was either suppressed or forgotten very early on in the Synoptic tradition. Yet in this pericope the real force of Jesus' counterquestion is felt only on the supposition that Jesus had continued John's baptism and that it was very much acknowledged by both Jesus and his opponents to be *John's* baptism, and not some other new baptism Jesus had invented *ex nihilo*. The roots of this dispute story therefore go back very early and cohere surprisingly well not with other material in the Synoptic Gospels but with the statements about Jesus baptizing in John 3:23,26 and 4:1.

One might also argue for the basic authenticity of Mark 11:27–33 by appealing to the criterion of multiple attestation—if, as Raymond Brown holds, the narrative of the temple cleansing in John 2:13–22 is independent of the Synoptics.[222] For in John 2 we have the same basic configuration of temple cleansing leading to a challenging question from the Jerusalem authorities about Jesus' right "to do these things" (*tauta poieis*, the same words as in Mark 11:28). In John, however, the tradition is developed according to the Fourth Evangelist's usual "christological concentration," with a prediction of the destruction and raising up of the temple—which temple turns out to be the risen body of Jesus. Nevertheless, behind all this Johannine reworking of the tradition, we do find the skeletal outline of a story not unlike Mark 11:27–33. Granted, all these arguments are indirect and rest on a chain of hypotheses. Yet the criteria of coherence and discontinuity (and perhaps multiple attestation) do give some pointers in the direction of authentic Jesus tradition, while nothing argues strongly that the core of the tradition was a creation of the early church.[223]

C. Stray Traditions in Matt 21:31–32 and Luke 7:29–30

In both Matthew and Luke we have a passing reference to reactions to the Baptist by tax collectors on the one hand and certain Jewish leaders on the other. The debate as to whether these traditions are simply two redactional expressions of one Q saying or whether they should be assigned to the special traditions of Matthew and Luke respectively (or even to the creativity of each evangelist) rages on.[224] A glance at the two passages shows the reasons for this disagreement:

Matt 21:31–32	*Luke 7:29–30*
Jesus says to them: Amen I say to you that *the tax collectors* and the prostitutes are entering the kingdom of God ahead of you. For *John* came to you in the way of justice, and you did not believe him. But the tax collectors and the prostitutes did believe him.	And all the people, hearing [this], —and *the tax collectors*—declared God just, having been baptized with the baptism of *John*.
But when you saw this, not even later on did you change your mind so as to believe him.	But the Pharisees and the lawyers spurned God's plan for them, not having been baptized by him [John].

The similarities between the two texts are clear but few: (1) Both texts are short additions to other traditions (M and Q respectively) with which they originally had no connection.[225] (2) Both texts set up a contrast between two groups that did accept John's message and a group of Jewish leaders that did not. (3) Each tradition has a description of what each group did or did not do, along with a theological evaluation of how this affected their stance vis-à-vis God. (4) The exact verbal parallels are limited to "the tax collectors" (*hoi telōnai*) and "John" (*Iōannēs*). A partial parallel can be found between Matthew's "way of justice" (*hodǭ dikaiosynēs*) and Luke's "declared just" or "justified" (*edikaiōsan*).

The differences are much more massive and significant: (1) With the exception of "the tax collectors" and "John"—the absolute minimum needed for the two texts to contain a similar idea—the vocabulary and content of the two texts are notably different. (2) In particular, Matthew focuses on two examples of religious and social outcasts, tax collectors and prostitutes. Luke, with an all-encompassing vision, and with a contorted order in the clause, speaks of "all the people," and then almost as an afterthought adds "and the tax collectors."[226] The possibility that the mention of the tax collectors is secondary in the Lucan tradition has serious consequences, since it touches one of the two solitary words on which derivation from Q is based. (3) The Jewish leaders who act as a foil are different in the two texts. Matthew, locating the tradition after the first of his three parables of judgment on Israel during Jesus' last days in Jerusalem, implicitly makes the "you" rebuked by Jesus the high priests and elders of the people, who asked Jesus about his authority in Matt 21:23. Luke, appending his comment to part of the second Baptist-block of Q (immediately after the saying about the least in the kingdom being greater than John), places the tradition within the context of Jesus' Galilean ministry and accordingly presents not Jerusalem officials but rather Pharisees and lawyers as the foil. (4) Luke's tradition is in the form of a narrative comment by the Evangelist, recounting the joyful reaction of the people and the tax collectors to Jesus' approbation of John.[227] Matthew's tradition claims to transmit words of Jesus that supply an application to the parable of the two brothers, one of whom says yes to his father and the other no (21:28–31). (5) Both the reaction of each group to John and the theological effect of the reaction are described in different terms. In Matthew it is a question of believing or not believing John, which boils down to a matter of repentance.[228] This reaction is interpreted theologically as entering or not entering the kingdom of God.[229] In Luke, one group had itself baptized by John, the other did not. The refusal by the latter group is evaluated theologically as nullifying God's saving plan for them, while those baptized readily recognize God's just claim on them.[230] (6) This involves a final difference, remarkable in that John the Baptist is the touchstone by which all these groups are judged. Luke mentions John's baptism and makes acceptance or refusal of it decisive for right relationship with God. Matthew does not mention baptism in this text, and in keeping with his general presentation describes John as a preacher calling people to repent (*metemelēthēte*, "repented") and to do God's will ("justice" or "righteousness").[231] Considering the numerous and weighty differences between the two texts, I agree with Fitzmyer: ". . . the formulation is so different that it is difficult to think that we are dealing with a 'Q' parallel."[232]

Thus, we are dealing with two stray traditions, one from M and the other from L,[233] which mention the important detail that John's message and baptism were well received by at least some religiously and socially marginal groups like tax collectors and prostitutes, while they were largely rejected by Jewish leaders.[234] That this tidbit of information may indeed have a historical basis[235] is made likely by its echo both in Luke 3:10–14 (the crowds, the tax collectors, and the soldiers all seek moral guidance from John) and in the *Jewish Antiquities*, where Josephus seems to distinguish a first wave of adherents to John, made up of morally zealous Jews, and a second wave, made up of ordinary Jews (*Ant.* 18.5.2. §116–19).[236]

This is not to harmonize all four statements; they are not all saying the same thing. Yet there is an interesting convergence here that suggests that at least some religiously or socially disreputable Jews, such as tax collectors and prostitutes, sought out John to respond to his call to repentance. Even if an exegete were still to doubt that John engaged in detailed moral directives, the very fact that these outcasts accepted his message of repentance and his purifying baptism certainly implies that they would have modified or even totally changed their concrete lifestyles. All of this is significant for our appreciation of the pattern of similarity-yet-difference that, throughout the historically reliable material, marks the relationship between John and Jesus. It is not correct to portray John as a super-puritan who would have shrunk from contact with tax collectors, prostitutes, or other marginal figures of Jewish society if they had come to him with repentance. He apparently received the well-disposed and baptized them, no doubt with at least a minimal exhortation about how they should live their lives in the time left to them before the day of judgment. Yet there is no indication that John went out of his way to pursue such marginal Jews. Indeed, his tie to the "desert" (however widely that designation be interpreted), his need to have abundant water at hand for numerous baptisms, his own ascetic diet of locusts and wild honey, and perhaps his jaundiced view of what was going on in the Jerusalem temple, all kept him within a restricted area and thus kept him from a wide-ranging, all-inclusive mission. On the whole, sinful and therefore marginal Jews came to the ascetic and therefore marginal John, not vice versa.

In contrast, Jesus undertook an itinerant mission throughout Galilee, parts of Judea, parts of Perea, parts of the Decapolis, and perhaps areas north of Galilee reaching as far as Tyre and Sidon—as well as engaging in numerous journeys to Jerusalem. All this cannot be put down to small-town wanderlust. Jesus was consciously reaching out to all Israel in its last hour, especially to marginal groups like tax collectors, prostitutes, and sinners in general, as well as to the not-especially-sinful but not-especially-well-shepherded poor. Thus, we see again the familiar pattern of nexus-yet-shift. Jesus picked up on John's contact with the morally marginal, but shifted to a more expansive approach, an aggressive program of outreach through a peripatetic mission throughout Israel and its environs. Corresponding to this geographical and psychological shift was a shift in the basic message. Moving from the Baptist's fierce stress on repentance in the face of imminent doom, Jesus, while not entirely abandoning John's call and eschatology, shifted the emphasis to the joy of salvation that the repentant could experience even now as they accepted Jesus' proclamation of the kingdom of God, somehow present and yet to come.[237]

D. STRAY TRADITIONS IN THE GOSPEL OF JOHN

In section III of this chapter we examined the key data that critical analysis can extricate from the highly Christianized picture of the Baptist in the Fourth Gospel: namely, that for a short period Jesus was probably a close disciple of the Baptist, that he may have drawn some of his own close disciples from the Baptist's circle, and that he continued John's practice of baptism. Almost everything else in the Fourth Evangelist's portrait of the Baptist must be assigned to the author's desire to make the Baptist a key witness to the Word made flesh (John 1:15,30), the Lamb of God who takes away the sin of the world (1:29). However, there may be a few stray nuggets in the rest of the Fourth Gospel that reflect historical tradition.

The passing mention of John as a witness to Jesus in the great discourse on the authority of the Son in John 5:19–47 only reminds us how diminished a figure John is in the Fourth Gospel's larger scheme of things. In 5:33–36, while speaking of the convincing witness Jesus enjoys both from himself, his works, and his Father, Jesus raises the question of the Baptist merely as an *ad hominem* argument against the Jewish leaders. They sent a delegation to John, therefore implicitly acknowledging the importance of what he said. John clearly bore true witness to Jesus. Jesus has no need of such human witness, but he allows it into court simply for the sake of his opponents' salvation. With categories typical of the Fourth Gospel, the Baptist is depicted as a "burning and shining *lamp*" (*lychnos*), in tacit comparison to Jesus the light of the world. The light John sheds is positively evaluated as a witness to Jesus, but is obviously limited, derivative, and ineffectual. The tone is clearly apologetic and polemic, aimed at Jewish groups in general and Baptist sectarians in particular.[238]

The apologetic and polemic tone is equally clear in the passing reference to the Baptist toward the end of Jesus' ministry (10:40–42). The Baptist is mentioned to emphasize that Jews who had listened to him (symbolizing the Baptist sectarians?) and had heard him speak about Jesus now know firsthand that everything John said about Jesus is true. In other words, Jesus, not John, is the true Messiah. Hence "many" stream to Jesus—as the Baptist sectarians should. For the Fourth Evangelist, a strong argument for Jesus' superiority is that he worked "signs" (i.e., symbolic miracles), while John did not. This statement, however polemical in context, may be based on historical tradition. Not only all the various Gospel sources but also Josephus indicate that Jesus was known as a miracle-worker among his contemporaries, while John apparently was not. In book 18 of the *Jewish Antiquities*, where Josephus gives a short sketch of Jesus' ministry and later on a somewhat longer sketch of John's, one of the first things Josephus says about Jesus is that he was a "doer of marvelous deeds" (*paradoxōn ergōn poiētēs* [18.3.3 §63], with a possible reference to the wonder-working prophet Elisha).[239] In contrast, Josephus says not a word about miracles supposedly performed by John.[240] It may well be that the Fourth Evangelist, in emphasizing this difference between John and Jesus, was consciously rebutting a claim from Baptist sectarians that the Baptist had worked miracles.[241] But, from the combined witness of all the Gospel sources plus Josephus, it would seem that the sectarians had created such a claim secondarily during the course of the 1st century to compete more effectively with Christian missionary propaganda. To restrict matters to the claims people made: as far as the sources allow us to know, Jesus claimed to perform miracles or "deeds of power" or "signs" (including healings and exorcisms), while John did not. This absence or presence of the claim of miracles may correlate to some degree with John's emphasis on imminent judgment and Jesus' stress on the joy of the kingdom already present in his ministry.

V. THE DEATH OF THE BAPTIST

Finally,[242] we come to the tradition about the Baptist's execution by Herod Antipas, recounted in Mark 6:17–29 and repeated in an abbreviated form by Matthew in 14:3–12.[243] I shall not spend much time on the Marcan story, for two reasons: (1) Even if it is basically historical, it has little or nothing to do with the historical Jesus. (2) The strongly legendary tone of the Marcan story as well as its differences with Josephus' account incline me to the view that the Marcan account contains little of historical worth, even with reference to the historical John.

The first reason is self-evident to anyone who reads Mark's narrative. Jesus is never mentioned in the account of the events leading up to John's execution (6:17–29). Indeed, the story in Mark 6:17–29 is much more a story about Herod Antipas and his family than it is about the Baptist—to say nothing of Jesus. In fact, exegetes are hard pressed to find a reason why this story was inserted by Mark into his Gospel. A few tenuous connections of a literary or theological nature can be suggested.[244] To begin with, the story of John's death provides an interlude while Jesus' twelve disciples go out on mission and then return to Jesus (6:6–13 + 30–31). More importantly, the theme of the rejection and execution of the prophet-martyr John ties in with the rejection of Jesus the prophet at Nazareth (6:1–6) and ultimately with Jesus' own martyrdom in Jerusalem. Various Greek words and phrases in Mark 6:17–29, along with certain governing ideas, are probably intended by the Evangelist to point forward to the Passion Narrative.[245] But that vague nexus is the best explanation one can offer for the presence in Mark of a relatively lengthy story that has nothing directly to do with Jesus. Thus, even if every word of 6:17–29 reflected historical events exactly, it would add nothing to our knowledge of the historical Jesus.

There are, however, indications that not every word in Mark's narrative can be taken as historically accurate. I do not mean to deny that the story has a historical core, since the core is confirmed by Mark's basic agreement with the very different description of John's death by Josephus. The core, though, is small: John was arrested and then executed by Antipas.[246] In addition, Antipas' rejection of his first wife and his marriage to Herodias, who was previously married to one of Antipas' half-brothers, act as background or motivation for the execution in both accounts, though in very different ways. Beyond this meager core, the two presentations by Mark and Josephus are quite dissimilar, although they do not formally contradict each other on each and every count.

In considering the elements that are probably not historical in Mark's story, pride of place must be given to his inaccurate statement that Antipas' second wife, Herodias, had previously been the wife of Antipas' half-brother Philip. This is simply incorrect, as we know from Josephus' *Jewish Antiquities* (18.5.4 §136).[247] In fact, Herodias, the sister of Herod Agrippa I and the granddaughter of Herod the Great, first married a half-brother of Antipas known simply as Herod (a son of Herod the Great by his wife Mariamme II; Antipas was Herod the Great's son by the Samaritan woman Malthace). Herod (i.e., Antipas' half-brother) and Herodias had a daughter named Salome; it was this Salome who married another half-brother of Antipas named Philip (a son of Herod the Great by his wife Cleopatra of Jerusalem). To try to save Mark from a glaring historical error, Christian commentators have traditionally spoken of "Herod Philip" (salvation by conflation), but such a Herodian poltergeist never existed outside the minds of conservative exegetes.[248]

Similarly, to maintain that Josephus is somehow wrong or confused would be a gratuitous assumption made to rescue Mark's accuracy at any cost.[249] Josephus shows a much greater knowledge of Herodian genealogy than does Mark. When one looks at the bewildering chart of the descendants of Herod the Great and his ten wives, one can sympathize with Mark's confusion; but sympathy should never lead to a coverup. Indeed, Mark may have made more than one genealogical mistake in this story. There is a good chance that the text of Mark 6:22a should read: "And when *his* [Antipas'] daughter Herodias had come in and danced. . . ." If that is the correct reading, then Mark is operating under the erroneous impression that Antipas and his wife Herodias had a daughter named Herodias.[250] Be that as it may, the main point is clear simply from his mistake about "Philip": if Mark can be so wrong about the basic familial relationships that are the driving engine of the plot of his story about John's execution, why should we credit the rest of his story as historical?

Other aspects of Mark's story do not reassure one. Josephus gives us the precise place of John's execution: the fortress Machaerus to the east of the Dead Sea. While Mark does not specify the place of the great birthday party for Antipas that serves as the setting for John's execution, the natural inference from the Galilean setting of almost the whole of Jesus' public ministry is that the fateful scene is set in Galilee, perhaps at Antipas' new palace in Tiberias. This general impression is reinforced by a concrete detail as Mark paints the scene: the guests of Antipas include "his courtiers, military officers, and *the leading men of Galilee*." Notice: the leading men of Galilee, not of Perea, the other part of Antipas' tetrarchy, where Machaerus was located.[251] Hence it seems probable that Mark intends to place the imprisonment and execution of John in Galilee (therefore geographically as well as theologically close to Jesus). There is no reason to think that Josephus, who is well-informed about Machaerus,[252] is mistaken in his information; and so once again Mark is wrong in his presentation.

It will not do to attempt an escape-hatch solution, such as the suggestion that the party took place in Galilee, whence Antipas issued the order that the Baptist be executed in the fortress at Machaerus. Mark's own narrative demands that the Baptist be imprisoned where the party is taking place: after the dancing daughter makes her request for John's head, she waits until the executioner carries out Antipas' command. Then, having received the head from the executioner, the daughter gives it to her mother (6:27–28). If instead we seek to salvage something in Mark's narrative by massively rewriting or amending it, the question arises: why should we bother trying to salvage it at all? The simpler solution is to distinguish between the reliability of the Synoptics in recounting John's eschatological ministry, message, and baptism on the one hand and their reliability in narrating his death on the other. In the former case they are superior to Josephus, in the latter not so. For the historian, it is merely a matter of letting the chips fall where they may instead of playing favorites.

These observations are supported by a literary analysis of Mark's story. As all admit, the narrative resonates with echoes of various OT traditions: the prophet Elijah's struggle with King Ahab and his evil wife Jezebel (e.g., 1 Kgs 19:1–2; 21:17–26), the persecuted and martyred prophets in general, and the folkloric motifs in the Book of Esther.[253] These folkloric motifs find parallels in Greco-Roman stories of love, revenge, rash oaths, and women asking for what kings would rather not give, all in the context of royal banquets.[254] We seem to be dealing with folklore tinged with strong anti-Herodian feeling (perhaps aimed especially at the "liberated" female members of the Herodian dynasty),[255] folklore that was then reformulated (by Baptist sectarians or Christians?) as a legend of the martyr's death, and then redacted by Mark to make John a forerunner of Jesus in death as well as in life. With such a complicated tradition history, it is no wonder that exegetes debate the exact form-critical category to which Mark 6:17–29 belongs. A report of martyrdom, a legend, and an anecdote have all been suggested. After considering these various suggestions, Gerd Theissen opts for "court anecdote" or "court legend" as the best label.[256] In my view, this describes well the original form of the story, but does not do full justice to the story in its final setting in Mark's Gospel, where the death of the martyr-prophet mutely prophesies the death of the Son of Man (cf. Mark 9:11–13).

One question that remains is whether the reason for the Baptist's imprisonment and death did in fact have anything to do with his rebuking Antipas about his irregular marriage to Herodias.[257] In Josephus' account, there is no such rebuke. Herodias is involved in the overall story in a different way, one that does not connect her directly with John. Antipas, having fallen in love with Herodias, plans to divorce his first wife, the daughter of the Nabatean King Aretas IV. When his first wife gets wind of the plans, she finds an excuse to go to Machaerus, which is situated close to the border between Antipas' and Aretas' territories. She then flees to her father. This is only the beginning of a quarrel that is further aggravated by a dispute between Antipas and Aretas over territorial boundaries. In the end, a battle is fought in which Antipas' whole army is destroyed. It is at this point that Josephus pauses to give us the "flashback" about the ministry and death of the Baptist, since some Jews saw the destruction of Herod's army as punishment from God for the execution of John.[258] Thus, in Josephus, the connection between Antipas' marriage to Herodias and his execution of the Baptist exists only indirectly and only in the minds of certain devout Jews who see retribution from God in a particular human event. There is no chain of causality on the merely human, empirical level. Not so in Mark, where John rebukes Antipas for his second marriage: "It is not licit for you to have your brother's wife [as your wife]."[259] This angers Herodias more than Antipas, and it is her animus that leads to John's death.[260]

As Josef Ernst, Gerd Theissen, and other scholars point out, there is no strict contradiction between Mark and Josephus on the reason for John's imprisonment and execution. Mark emphasizes John's ethical rebuke aimed at Antipas' second marriage, while Josephus focuses on Antipas' political fears that John's influence on the Jewish masses could lead to an uprising. Historically, there could have been a fatal interaction between John's moral concerns and Antipas' political suspicions. If Antipas was experiencing a threat to his borders by Aretas because of his desire to marry Herodias, and if in addition the religious sensibilities of ordinary Jews in Antipas' realm were offended by a "liberated" Hellenistically educated Herodian princess taking the initiative in divorcing her first husband to marry his half-brother, the purely moral concerns of the Baptist (who at times operated near the Nabatean border) would inevitably and inextricably become entwined with *realpolitik* considerations of the tetrarch.[261] Faced with the possibility of war on the border and unrest at home, all because of his irregular marital situation, Antipas would naturally read the ethical rebuke of John the ascetic prophet as a challenge to the legitimacy of his rule. He accordingly took preemptive action to cut off the internal critique by cutting off John's head.

This harmonization of the accounts of Mark and Josephus is certainly possible,[262] but I personally remain skeptical. As we have seen, the story in Mark 6:17–29 is erroneous in key historical matters (i.e., the marital problem that set off the conflict with John, the place of John's imprisonment and execution, and perhaps the identity of the daughter) and is suffused with legendary and folkloric traits. Moreover, the links between the accounts of Mark and Josephus exist largely in the mind of the modern exegete. Mark knows nothing of political considerations leading to John's death; Josephus—although he, unlike Mark, presents John as a preacher of morality—knows nothing of a moral rebuke to Antipas. The absence of the motif of ethical rebuke in Josephus' account is all the stranger since Josephus seems to have had the apologetic intent of stressing John's purely moral and religious mission, to protect him from any charge of having revolutionary intentions.[263] Furthermore, in Josephus the initiative to arrest and execute John comes from Antipas alone, while Herodias is the driving force in Mark's story.

All in all, I consider attempts at harmonization, while not impossible, ill-advised. When it comes to the imprisonment and death of John, Josephus, not Mark, must serve as our main source. Receiving a folkloric legend already remodeled as a pious account of a martyr's unjust execution, Mark used the story for his own purposes. The tradition he inherited preserved the most basic facts: sometime after Jesus' baptism, John was imprisoned and executed by Antipas. Mark's story also had a vague recollection that Antipas' irregular marriage to Herodias was somehow connected with the Baptist's death, but lively imagination and OT allusions had long since developed the nexus in a different direction from what we read in the *Antiquities*. Coming as it does from a diverse matrix and being developed in a very disparate fashion, Mark's account supplies valuable independent confirmation of the most basic points of Josephus' report. Beyond those, Josephus is to be preferred for history; Mark is to be mined for tradition history and theological intent.[264]

In any case, what is important for our study of the historical Jesus remains firm no matter how we judge the exact relation between the accounts of Mark and Josephus on John's death. The ascetic prophet who was the determinative influence setting Jesus on the course of his public ministry, the eschatological prophet whose announcement of the imminent end of Israel's history Jesus had accepted, the charismatic prophet who administered a once-and-for-all baptism that Jesus had received at his hands, the preacher of repentance whose call Jesus recycled and extended to all Israel, this prophet called John met a violent death at the hands of the (ostensibly) Jewish ruler of Galilee, the very place where Jesus the prophet was plying a good deal of his eschatological ministry. Seen simply in itself, this grim execution of a holy man whom many revered after his death as a martyr could not help but turn the mind of Jesus the prophet to the dangers involved in continuing John's recycled and reinterpreted ministry.

Moreover, in 1st-century Palestine John's violent death did not occur in a theological vacuum. The people of Israel had known a long line of prophets sent by God to his sinful people, prophets who were often rejected and sometimes martyred. The Books of Samuel and Kings, especially as redacted by the so-called "deuteronomistic historian," as well as 1-2 Chronicles, inculcated this pattern,[265] and the lives of prophets like Jeremiah made it much more than a literary pattern. The tradition of and the veneration for martyred prophets grew apace in some Israelite circles in the 1st centuries B.C. and A.D. In due time, the dignity of martyrdom was extended to other prophets (e.g., Isaiah), and the adornment and veneration of the tombs of the martyred prophets became popular.[266] Granted this wider religious context, the martyrdom of the eschatological prophet John necessarily possessed deep resonance for the eschatological prophet Jesus, John's former disciple. When, in a later chapter, we study the question of how Jesus might have faced the possibility of a violent death, we will have to remember that the possibility had become a very real one for the Nazarene, thanks to the fate of his former master. When and if Jesus pondered the prophetic literature on the persecution and death of God's messengers, he needed no special hermeneutical aid to apply it. John had become its midrash incarnate.[267]

VI. CONCLUSION: FINISHING AND NOT FINISHING WITH JOHN

Our survey of all of Jesus' sayings and actions that connect him with his religious matrix, the Baptist, has led us far and wide over all Four Gospels and Acts. That in itself is significant. Even after the Baptist's arrest and execution, Jesus was never entirely "without John." If my view is correct, he carried John's eschatology, concern for a sinful Israel facing God's imminent judgment, call to repentance, and baptism with him throughout his own ministry, however much he recycled and reinterpreted this inheritance. It is also significant that Jesus' sayings about John the Baptist come to us in material that speaks of a wide range of topics: the kingdom of God proclaimed to the poor, Jesus' miracles, his nonascetic lifestyle, his table fellowship with tax collectors and sinners, his more "realized" eschatology, his relation to the law and the prophets, disciples in the kingdom, his teaching in parables and beatitudes, his standing in parallel position to John the prophet, his rejection by people in general, his confrontation with Jerusalem authorities in the temple, and opposition from rulers that could lead to martyrdom.

When one stops to look back on all the themes we have covered simply because they were connected with Jesus' views on John, we realize that almost every topic that remains to be treated in this work on the historical Jesus is somehow touched on in Jesus' sayings about the Baptist. This stands to reason since, having emerged from John's circle with some of John's disciples, Jesus would find it necessary to explain to interested Israelites and potential enemies alike how he continued yet differed from the Baptist's preaching and praxis. Hence almost every major aspect of the historical Jesus' ministry—especially those matters in which he differed from John—finds some echo in the sayings on the Baptist examined in this chapter. One can now appreciate that it was not merely concern for chronological nicety that placed John first in our treatment of Jesus' ministry. By treating the John-material in detail, we have already been brought into the center of Jesus' own concerns.[268] As we "unpack" and study these varied concerns in subsequent chapters, it is good for us to remember that, we, like Jesus, never completely leave John behind.

Among the many themes that have surfaced in Jesus' sayings about the Baptist, the key phrase "the kingdom of God" appears three times (Matt 11:11 par.; 11:12 par.; Matt 21:31), more than any other important theological image specific to Jesus' preaching. This correlates perfectly with the position of many exegetes that the kingdom of God was *the* central and governing image in Jesus' proclamation. It is therefore to the kingdom of God that we now turn to begin our study of the proclamation and praxis of the historical Jesus.

EXCURSUS ON THE Q DOCUMENT

Our study of the traditions from and about John the Baptist led us into a detailed examination of key pericopes of the Q document, especially the two "Baptist-blocks" of Matt 3:7–12 par. and 11:2–19 par. This initial delving into Q material offers an occasion to expand upon my sketchy remarks about the Q source, given in Chapter 2.

Unlike many writers on Q today, I feel obliged to begin my treatment by stressing that the existence of the Q document during the first two Christian generations is a hypothesis, and only a hypothesis. Those authors who, like myself, espouse this hypothesis must recognize that a number of respected exegetes throughout the 20th century have felt quite capable of doing their work while "dispensing with Q."[269] This group naturally includes those scholars who first of all reject the priority of Mark, the *sine qua non* of any argument in favor of the existence of Q.[270] Yet even some exegetes who accept that Mark was the first Gospel to be written have felt no need to posit a single written document that would be the chief source of sayings found in both Matthew and Luke but not in Mark.[271] Various collections of oral traditions or a number of written documents of different size and provenance are called upon to explain the "double tradition" of Matthew and Luke.

While I appreciate the objections these scholars raise against the Q hypothesis, it still seems to me that the existence of the Q document is the theory that best explains the data found in Matthew and Luke. These data raise a basic question: if we grant that Mark was the first Gospel to be written, that Matthew and Luke both used Mark, and that Matthew and Luke did not know each other's Gospels, how do we explain the fact that Matthew and Luke contain blocks of common material not derived from Mark? The simplest answer remains the Q document. Arguments in its favor include:[272] (1) a high degree of verbal agreement between Matthew and Luke in at least some of the Q sayings—notably in most of the two Baptist-blocks we have examined in Chapters 12 and 13; (2) "doublets," i.e., pericopes that occur in different forms and with different wording in Mark on the one hand and in material common to Matthew and Luke on the other (e.g., the prohibition of divorce, found in both a Marcan *Streitgespräch* [Mark 10:2–12 ‖ Matt 19:3–12] and in an isolated logion [Matt 5:32 ‖ Luke 16:17]); (3) unusual phrases that are rare in the LXX, the rest of the NT, and in other early Christian literature and yet appear in this material common to Matthew and Luke; (4) a significant amount of agreement in the order of the pericopes common to Matthew and Luke, an agreement that is difficult to explain on the basis of various blocks of oral or written tradition. While not excluding all doubt,[273] these arguments do tip the balance in favor of a single written source (arbitrarily labeled Q by scholars)—though additional contributions from stray oral traditions or written sources known to both Matthew and Luke cannot be entirely ruled out.

I must admit, though, that the affirmation of Q's existence comes close to exhausting my ability to believe in hypothetical entities. I find myself increasingly skeptical as more refined and detailed theories about Q's extent, wording, community, geographical setting, stages of tradition and redaction, and coherent theology are proposed.[274] I cannot help thinking that biblical scholarship would be greatly advanced if every morning all exegetes would repeat as a mantra: "Q is a hypothetical document whose exact extension, wording, originating community, strata, and stages of redaction cannot be known." This daily devotion might save us flights of fancy that are destined, in my view, to end in skepticism.

I do think that something can be known about the extent of the Q document and the order of pericopes within it. John Kloppenborg's conservative approach to the extent of Q is common today.[275] Kloppenborg has likewise shown how a rough consensus on order has been reached by scholars like B. H. Streeter, Bruno de Solages, and Vincent Taylor.[276] The order of most of the large blocks of material is fairly clear. For instance, Q begins with John the Baptist prophesying imminent judgment, moves through various sapiential and prophetic sayings of Jesus, and culminates in Jesus prophesying imminent judgment in somewhat different terms. The order of individual sayings, however, is not always certain, though Luke seems to have preserved the order of Q more often than Matthew, who has reordered Q material and meshed it with Mark and M to create his five great discourses. While most scholars would follow Kloppenborg's conservative approach to the extent of Q, delineating exactly how large it was remains problematic. We have no way of knowing whether both Matthew and Luke omitted some large block of material, whether a pericope we label M or L actually stood in Q, or whether a Q pericope quite similar to Marcan material was replaced by said material (e.g., the baptism of Jesus). More troublesome still is the question of the exact wording of any Q pericope or saying. In a sense, we were spoiled by treating the two Baptist-blocks first, for they supply some of the clearest verbal agreements available in Q material. Yet even in the Baptist material, the decision between Matthean and Lucan order and wording was not always easy, Luke 16:16

(= Matt 11:12–13) being a notorious example. Other Q pericopes prove more difficult still. Nevertheless, some educated guesses can be made on the order, extent, and even wording of Q—though they must all remain in the realm of the hypothetical.

It is at this point that my ability to believe is exhausted—which just happens to be the point at which most speculation about Q begins to "rev up." Contemporary scholars have sought to pinpoint the community that produced the Q document, the geographical area from which it originated, the stages of tradition and redaction it went through (some scholars assigning almost every verse of Q to a particular stratum of tradition or redaction), and its different theological stances. It is here that I fear that exegetes are trying to know the unknowable. To adapt a famous dictum of Ludwig Wittgenstein: whereof one does not know thereof one must be silent.[277] I doubt that we have the data and the methods sufficient to answer questions about the community, locality, tradition process, and coherent theological vision that supposedly produced Q.

To begin with, I am not sure that we are justified in speaking of *a* or *the* "Q community." I do not see any historical proof that one and only one community either created, gathered, or carried the Q tradition through early Christianity until it wound up in the Gospels of Matthew and Luke.[278] On the contrary, the very fact that Q apparently existed and functioned for some time in each of these evangelists' churches before it was absorbed into their Gospels tells against this idea of one Q community.[279]

Allied with my doubts on a single Q community are my doubts about one coherent theological vision in Q, or even a number of different theological visions at different stages of Q. The Q collection certainly reflects a number of dominant theological concerns, including prophecy, eschatology, apocalyptic, and wisdom, as well as a number of "key players," including Jesus, the Baptist, Jesus' disciples, "this generation," and the Pharisees. But this does not add up to a coherent theological vision. At times sayings of very different—not to say contradictory—viewpoints stand side by side. For example, as we saw in our study of Matt 11:12–13 (= Luke 16:16), most likely Luke 16:16 originally belonged not to the Baptist-context in which Matthew has placed it (Matt 11:2–19), but rather to the small cluster of logia in Luke 16:16–18.[280] Luke 16:16, in its primitive form, seems to distinguish the past age of the law and the prophets which lasted until John; after that pivotal point, the kingdom of God is being exposed to violence. Luke 16:17, in its primitive form (probably something close to Matt 5:18bc),[281] proclaimed the eternal validity and immutability of the Mosaic Law, down to its smallest points. Luke 16:18 immediately proceeds to announce the blanket abrogation of an important institution of the Mosaic Law, divorce.[282] What has brought these sayings together into their small Q cluster is the common theme of law, but hardly a coherent theology of law. It might be possible to create some theological synthesis that would embrace all three sayings. Indeed, this is what Matthew and Luke, in their different ways, struggle to do. But this is precisely what Q does *not* do. At times, Q simply juxtaposes sharply divergent logia, with no overarching theological vision to mediate the differences. Often what seems to draw the logia into clusters is rather a catchword, a common theme, or a common literary form. Taken as a whole, Q is something of a theological as well as form-critical grab bag. When it comes to theological coherence in Q, the wish is father of the thought, and both wish and thought seem to exist only in the mind of the modern commentator.

It is the disconcerting diversity of Q that leads some critics to distinguish strata of tradition and redaction in Q. In my view, behind this attempt lies the drive of the modern Western mind to systematize, and not any clear indicator of tradition and redaction in Q. The presupposition of contemporary attempts at the redaction criticism of Q is that there *must* have been coherence in form, interests, and theology in the various strata of Q; diversity in these matters thus becomes the key to separating the different strata. One senses more than a hint of a circular argument here. Indeed, one might argue more reasonably in the opposite direction. Considering the rudimentary form any initial stage of Q would have had in the first Christian generation, we are justified in asking: Why *must* there have been any theological or form-critical coherence? I think it much more likely that Q "grew like Topsy." That it grew I have no doubt. That it grew in neat stages of tradition and redaction, with a dominant theological view in each stage, lacks not only solid proof but even verisimilitude. In contrast, Migaku Sato suggests as a model for the development of Q a "ring book," loose-leaf binder, or notebook, as exemplified from parchment remains of the 2d century A.D.[283] The gradual growth that such a "ring book" would have expedited may make talk of precise stages of redaction in Q beside the point. With such a fluid medium, one must reckon with the possibility of different versions of Q circulating in the first two Christian generations. Indeed, a number of scholars have suggested that Matthew and Luke worked with versions of Q that had already assimilated the special traditions of the evangelists' respective churches: hence the sigla Q^{Mt} and Q^{Lk}.[284]

In light of all this, I find the attempt of, e.g., Siegfried Schulz to distinguish two levels of redaction, the first done by a Jewish-Christian community somewhere on the border of Palestine and Syria, and a second by a Hellenistic Jewish-Christian community in Syria, with a final redaction by Gentile Christians—with almost every verse of Q assigned to one of these stages—an exercise in trying to know the unknowable.[285] Like many other critics of Q, Schulz tries to distinguish strata by distinguishing theological interests. For example, in Schulz's view, the earlier stratum of Q concentrated on the imminent coming of the apocalyptic Son of Man, while the more recent stratum shifted its focus to the earthly Jesus. We need not be surprised that other scholars, using various theological and linguistic criteria, have offered different theories of Q's redaction that range from one to four stages.[286] The problem with Schulz's reconstruction is the problem found equally in the reconstructions of the other scholars: we lack the adequate data and criteria to discern what is primary and what is secondary in Q. It comes as no surprise that, while Kloppenborg posits an initial sapiential stage of Q, with prophetic material being added secondarily, Sato posits just the opposite process. Accordingly, when it comes to designating the literary genre of Q, Kloppenborg sees it as a type of wisdom-sayings collection with prophetic additions, while Sato sees it in analogy to the OT prophetic books, with sapiential additions.[287] Both of these scholars are highly intelligent experts possessing deep knowledge of the Q material. The fault lies not in their expertise but in the supposition that we can know the unknowable. Indeed, the distinct stages of the redaction of Q, with distinct theological emphases and *Gattungen*, are all the more unknowable if—as I suspect—they never existed in this Topsy-like grab bag.

In any case, a final consideration makes a good deal of this speculation about the Q document's development irrelevant to the quest for the historical Jesus. Even if one could establish with fair certitude that a particular logion entered into the Q document at a secondary stage of its composition, that in itself would tell us nothing about whether the logion originally came from Jesus or was created by the early church. As I emphasized when dealing with the second Baptist-block of Q, to suggest a reason why the early church found a particular saying useful is not to prove that the early church created the saying instead of preserving or adapting it from the teaching of the historical Jesus. The authenticity of a saying does not depend on the time of its entrance into the Q document, even if that could be established with reasonable certitude.

In short, my procedure throughout this book is to accept the hypothesis that the Q document represents a distinct and valuable source for the sayings (and, in a few cases, the deeds) of Jesus and John. Realizing, however, the hypothetical nature of Q—and, indeed, the hypothetical nature of my entire project—I think it unwise to make my conclusions depend on detailed hypotheses about Q that are tenuous at best.

NOTES TO CHAPTER 13

[1] I must apologize to the reader beforehand for some lengthy, cumbersome phrases that will have to be used in this chapter. The problem arises from two ambiguities that I try to avoid. (1) The phrase "Jesus' baptism" can have two meanings, and both occur in this chapter: (a) the event of Jesus' being baptized by John (according to the Synoptic tradition), the subject matter of section I; and (b) the baptism that Jesus supposedly administered during his public ministry (according to John 3:22 and 4:1), the subject matter of section III. Sometimes the meaning of the phrase "Jesus' baptism" is clear from the context, but to make sure that all ambiguity is avoided I sometimes have recourse to more lengthy phraseology. (2) Phrases like "the Fourth Gospel" and "the Fourth Evangelist" are used very frequently, especially in section III. The reason for the repetition is that I try to reduce the number of times I refer to the Fourth Evangelist or his Gospel as "John," since that name occurs frequently in this chapter for the Baptist. For the same reason, I retain the title "the Baptist" even when speaking of him in the Fourth Gospel—where the title is never used—since this helps clarify the meaning of the ambiguous name "John."

[2] See Ernst Haenchen, *Der Weg Jesu* (2d ed.; Berlin: de Gruyter, 1968) 60–63. Haenchen meshes together too quickly the separate questions of (1) the historical origin of the narrative of the theophany after the baptism and (2) the historicity of the baptism itself. His appeal to Christian baptism as the origin of the idea that Jesus was baptized is proposed without sufficient proof of its likelihood; actually, probability points to a tradition history running in the opposite direction, as we shall see below. Another of Haenchen's objections is that there was too much of a difference between John and Jesus ever to suppose that Jesus would have accepted baptism from John. One must carefully distinguish here. That there was a difference between the preaching and praxis of John on the one hand and Jesus on the other is readily granted by most commentators; that the difference was the vast chasm Haenchen suggests is questionable.

[3] Morton S. Enslin, "John and Jesus," *ZNW* 66 (1975) 1–18. In a strange way, this article mixes the psychologizing of the "liberal lives" of Jesus (e.g., the Baptist's execution led Jesus "to an emotional upheaval," p. 18) with Schweitzer's picture of Jesus as an apocalyptic prophet who in the end despaired on the cross (p. 16). Among the article's many flaws, there is a notable lack of understanding of Matthew's redactional theology; see his remarks on Matt 28:16–20 vis-à-vis Matt 10:5–6 (pp. 7–8) and cf. John P. Meier, "Salvation-History in Matthew: In Search of a Starting-Point," *CBQ* 37 (1975) 203–15. Enslin's failure to deal adequately with questions of tradition and redaction reaches its low point when he assigns the denial that Jesus himself baptized (John 4:2) to "primitive tradition" (p. 8), when almost all critics would agree that here, if anywhere, we have the hand of the final redactor contradicting what the Evangelist has said from 3:22 onward. For example, Dodd (*The Interpretation of the Fourth Gospel,* 311 n. 3) states that John 4:2 "has a better claim to be regarded as an 'editorial note' by a 'redactor' than anything else in the gospel except the colophon xxi. 24–5." On this point, see section III below.

Actually, Enslin does have some perceptive things to say about the increasing tendency of the Four Gospels to demote the Baptist and to downplay the event of Jesus' baptism. Where Enslin crosses the line into improbable hypotheses is his claim that John and Jesus never met and that the early church invented the story of Jesus' being baptized by John. He claims that the universal practice of baptism in the Christian church helped create the story; yet, as we shall see, it is the patristic period, not the NT, that forges such a connection. More to the point, Enslin claims that the church invented the story to counter a rival movement made up of John's disciples by co-opting their hero (pp. 10–11). He never explains why the church was not content with a strategy of co-option that made John the forerunner, prophet, and witness to Christ and why it created the only story in the NT that clearly subordinates Jesus to John by having the former voluntarily undergo a baptism of repentance for the forgiveness of sins at the hands of the latter. This is the Achilles' heel of Enslin's whole approach.

There is one final weakness in his reconstruction. Enslin is at pains throughout the article to stress that the paths of John and Jesus never crossed and that Jesus, unlike many other Jews, did not flock to John to accept his baptism. Yet Enslin suggests that it was the shock of the execution of John that propelled Jesus to begin his own ministry. One is left wondering why a Jew who apparently was not interested enough in John even to go to hear him preach, let alone receive his baptism, should have reacted so emotionally to his death when none of John's close followers was galvanized by the Baptist's death to start his own ministry. It is an odd ending to an odd article. It is no wonder that this theory about John's death being the catalyst of Jesus' ministry was relegated to a footnote in Enslin's earlier book, *The Prophet from Nazareth* (New York: Schocken, 1968, originally 1961) 84 n. 9. It should have been left there.

[4]Jesus as sinless: 2 Cor 5:21; Heb 4:15; John 8:46; 1 Pet 1:19; 2:22; Jesus as the source of the forgiveness of sins: 1 Cor 15:3; Rom 3:23–26; 4:25; 5:8–21; Col 1:14; Eph 1:7; 1 Tim 1:15; Mark 2:1–12; Matt 1:21; 26:28; Luke 7:36–49; 24:46–47; Acts 5:31; Heb 1:3; 1 Pet 2:24–25; 3:18; John 1:29; 1 John 1:7–2:2.

[5]The latter view is taken by Anton Vögtle, "Die sogenannte Taufperikope Mk 1,9–11. Zur Problematik der Herkunft und des ursprünglichen Sinns," *Evangelisch-Katholischer Kommentar zum Neuen Testament. Vorarbeiten Heft 4* (Zurich/Einsiedeln/Cologne: Benziger; Neukirchen: Neukirchener Verlag, 1972) 105–39. Vögtle gives a good survey of different opinions on the subject.

[6]For a consideration of the Matthean vocabulary and theology in Matt 3:14–15, see John P. Meier, *Law and History in Matthew's Gospel* (AnBib 71; Rome: Biblical Institute, 1976) 73–80, with the literature cited there.

[7]It is remarkable how in the kerygmatic summaries of the Gospel story in Acts, Luke makes clear that John's ministry of proclaiming a baptism of repentance was the prelude or even the beginning of Jesus' ministry, yet any direct reference to Jesus' being baptized—with or without John—is avoided; see Acts 1:22; 10:37; 13:24–25; 19:3–4. In 10:37–38 there is an allusion back to Luke 3:22; 4:1,14,18; but the absence of any direct reference to Jesus' being baptized is all the more striking.

[8]The force of the argument stems from the fact that these four stylistic changes, introduced by Matthew and Luke independently of each other into the Marcan text, all occur in one-and-a-half verses of Mark's text. The reason why this observation is not strictly probative of a Q source is that it is not inconceivable that both Matthew and Luke, as cultured writers whose Greek style was definitely superior to Mark's, might have—independently of each other—been led by their literary sensitivities to make the same sort of changes in the Marcan text. On this, see John S. Kloppenborg, *The Formation of Q. Trajectories in Ancient Wisdom Collec-*

tions (Philadelphia: Fortress, 1987) 85 n. 157. Alternatively, one might argue that Matthew and Luke both knew forms of Mark's Gospel slightly different from the one we know. But this solution (sometimes in the form of an *ur-Markus* hypothesis) always has the air of an escape hatch or a *deus ex machina*.

[9] Kloppenborg tries to dismiss this argument in *Formation*, 85: "Finally, that a Son of God Christology is presupposed by 4:1–13 is obvious; but that in itself is no reason to posit a special narrative justifying that Christology. . . ." He points to the lack of any narrative justification for the "Son" titles that appear elsewhere in Q. But this is to ignore the special way in which the title is introduced into the story of the temptation: "*If* you are the Son of God. . . ." There is almost necessarily a reference backwards here, and the baptismal narrative is the only viable candidate.—While the question of the original order of the three temptations in Q is still disputed, I think it more likely that Matthew represents the original order: stones turned to bread, pinnacle of the temple in Jerusalem, and the offer of all the kingdoms of the earth. Luke's use of the temptation that occurs on the pinnacle of the temple as the climax of his story is due to his well-known redactional interest in Jerusalem and the temple. This is the position adopted by Fitzmyer, *The Gospel According to Luke*, 1. 165, 507–8; for the opposing view, see (besides the authors listed by Fitzmyer) Walter Grundmann, *Das Evangelium nach Matthäus* (THKNT 1; Berlin: Evangelische Verlagsanstalt, 1972) 100 (though tentatively). Others who favor Matthew's order as the original one include Ulrich Luz, *Matthew 1–7* (Minneapolis: Augsburg, 1989) 183; and Wilhelm Wilkens ("Die Versuchung Jesu nach Matthäus," *NTS* 28 [1982] 479–89), who thinks however Luke is directly dependent on Matthew for the story. In any case, Matthew's third temptation, involving direct worship of the devil and thus direct contravention of the first commandment of the Decalogue, naturally comes last in the series. After the devil makes such a blatant demand for worship of his person, no further dispute is possible, for the ultimate choice lying behind all other temptations has been revealed: God or Satan.

[10] Vögtle ("Die sogenannte Taufperikope," 107–11) is doubtful about a baptismal pericope in Q, though he does not absolutely exclude the possibility. In his view, if Q did contain such a pericope, it would not have differed essentially from Mark's narrative. This seems a reasonable conclusion, given the fact that both Matthew and Luke follow Mark, with only "minor agreements" against him. On the other hand, Schürmann (*Das Lukasevangelium*, 1. 197, 218) inclines toward the presence of a baptismal pericope in Q; likewise W. D. Davies and Dale C. Allison, *The Gospel According to Saint Matthew* (ICC; 3 vols.; Edinburgh: Clark, 1988) 1. 329. Alfred Suhl (*Die Funktion der alttestamentlichen Zitate und Anspielungen im Markusevangelium* [Gütersloh: Mohn, 1965] 99) is also willing to entertain it as a hypothesis; even stronger in his affirmation of such a Q pericope is Grundmann, *Das Evangelium nach Lukas*, 106–7. In his study *Die Christologie der Logienquelle* (WMANT 45; Neukirchen-Vluyn: Neukirchener Verlag, 1977) 2, Athanasius Polag counts the narrative of Jesus' baptism-plus-theophany among those pericopes that were "vermutlich" ("presumably" or "by conjecture") present in Q. For Polag, "vermutlich" ranks above "möglich" ("possibly") and below "wahrscheinlich" ("probably"). Unfortunately, Polag does not provide a detailed argument for the presence of a baptismal narrative in Q. In contrast, Migaku Sato (*Q und Prophetie. Studien zur Gattungs- und Traditionsgeschichte der Quelle Q* [WUNT 2/29; Tübingen: Mohr (Siebeck), 1988] 18, 25–26) considers the presence of a narrative of Jesus' baptism in Q "wahrscheinlich" and gives arguments much like my own. For a list of major

critics pro and con, see John S. Kloppenborg, *Q Parallels. Synopsis, Critical Notes, &* *Concordance* (Sonoma, CA: Polebridge, 1988) 16.

[11] See Wink (*John the Baptist,* 98–105), who takes a balanced view (p. 104): "Polemic and apologetic directed at contemporary 'disciples of John' clearly seems to be present, yet Baptists are not the chief opponents of the Evangelist's church. The prime target is Pharisaical Judaism. . . ." Although Ernst (*Johannes der Täufer,* 215–16) quotes Wink approvingly, he is less disposed to see a polemic aimed at Baptist sectarians.

[12] See the remarks of Goguel, *Au seuil,* 157–61: The Fourth Evangelist, who knows the story of Jesus' baptism, neither narrates nor presupposes it in his Gospel. Rather, he eliminates it and replaces it with a simple manifestation to the Baptist. According to Goguel, the Fourth Evangelist does this because he cannot accept the more or less adoptionistic meaning that the baptismal account originally had. The radical nature of the Fourth Evangelist's solution to the problem of Jesus' baptism by John is missed by Wink (*John the Baptist,* 90, 104) when he says: "Apparently Jesus has already been baptized before [John] 1:19ff. begins (note the past tenses in 1:30–4). . . . Jesus is baptized *before* the narrative begins, and his baptism is for *John's* sake, so that John might recognize the Lamb of God." When, therefore, Wink speaks of the Evangelist omitting the scene of Jesus' baptism (p. 91), he fails to grasp the full impact of this "omission": in the Fourth Gospel, Jesus' baptism is not presupposed, for it never took place. Hence the evaluation of Ernst (*Johannes der Täufer,* 204) likewise misses the point: "The Johannine 'report' [*Bericht*] of Jesus' baptism—a narrative [*Erzählung*] as in the Synoptics is simply not offered—emphasizes only the experience of the Baptist." What Ernst fails to realize is that in the Fourth Gospel there is no report of Jesus' baptism, only a report of a vision the Baptist receives, with no indication of *when* or *where* he receives it. John 1:32–34 is one of the most glaring cases of even critical scholars engaging in uncritical harmonizing of John with the Synoptics.

[13] The similarity of the two declarations is striking in the Greek:

Matt 3:17   *houtos estin ho huios mou*
John 1:34   *houtos estin ho huios tou theou*

There is, however, a problem with the text of John 1:34. A few texts read "the chosen one of God" instead of "the Son of God" (i.e., *eklektos* instead of *huios*): apparently p[5] (3d century), the first hand of Sinaiticus (4th century), some manuscripts of the Vetus Latina, and the Curetonian and Sinaitic Syriac. Almost all other Greek manuscripts (including p[66], p[75], Alexandrinus, Vaticanus), versions, and patristic citations favor *huios*. Metzger (*Textual Commentary,* 200) concludes: "On the basis of age and diversity of witnesses a majority of the Committee preferred the reading *ho huios,* which is also in harmony with the theological terminology of the Fourth Evangelist." That last point, though, inadvertently brings up the strongest argument in favor of *ho eklektos*: the more difficult reading is the better reading. Granted the reading "Son of God," there is no reason why Christian scribes would have changed this thoroughly Johannine phrase to "chosen one of God," which never occurs again in John's Gospel or indeed—in this precise form— anywhere else in the NT (though Luke does use the absolute *ho eklektos* during the mockery of the crucified Jesus in 23:35). Given the totally unparalleled "chosen one of God," Christian scribes accustomed to the terminology of the Fourth Gospel and to the Synoptic versions of Jesus' baptism would naturally change *eklektos* to *huios*. Actually, even if *eklektos* is original in the Johannine text, the connection with a primitive tradition about Jesus' being baptized by John is still likely, since the *eklektos* would probably hark back to the prophecy about the servant of the Lord in LXX Isa 42:1: *ho eklektos mou*: "Jacob is my servant, I shall uphold him; Israel is my chosen one, my soul has received him [in the MT: (in him) my soul is well pleased]; I have given my spirit upon him." It is this verse that is echoed (more in its MT form) in the heavenly voice at Jesus' baptism, as found in Mark 1:11 parr.: ". . . in you [or: in whom] I am well pleased."

[14] For these and other introductory questions concerning the context and theology of the Johannine Epistles, see Raymond E. Brown, *The Epistles of John* (AB 30; Garden City, NY: Doubleday, 1982) 3–115. For somewhat different approaches, see I. Howard Marshall, *The Epistles of John* (NICNT; Grand Rapids: Eerdmans, 1978) 9–48; Stephen S. Smalley, *1,2,3 John* (Word Biblical Commentary 51; Dallas: Word, 1984) xxiii–xxxii.

[15] For the problems both of text criticism and interpretation, see Brown, *The Epistles of John*, 572–78.

[16] The order "water and blood" in John 19:34 is witnessed by some ancient versions and patristic citations, but by only one Greek manuscript; it is obviously an assimilation to 1 John 5:6 or to a sacramental interpretation of the Gospel passage (water and blood symbolizing baptism and the eucharist). On this see Brown, *The Gospel According to John*, 2. 936. For the interpretation of the blood and water in the Gospel, see pp. 949–50; similarly, Rudolf Schnackenburg, *Das Johannesevangelium* (HTKNT 4; 3 vols.; Freiburg/Basel/Vienna: Herder, 1975) 3. 344–45. Most commentators rightly see the key to the blood and water of 19:34 in 7:37–39: "Jesus stood and cried out saying: 'If anyone thirsts, let him come to me, and let him who believes in me drink. As Scripture says, "Rivers of living water shall flow from his innermost being [literally: stomach]."' He said this concerning the spirit which those who believed in him would receive. For as yet there was no spirit [i.e., the spirit had not yet been given to believers], since Jesus had not yet been glorified [i.e., crucified and risen]." With the shedding of his blood on the cross, the glorification of Jesus has reached its climax, and so at least symbolically the living water of the spirit can be given to believers (cf. the equally symbolic "giving over" of the spirit in 19:30).

[17] Brown (*The Epistles of John*, 576) calls this "the most common theory." Brown himself prefers to see the imagery as referring only to the death of Jesus, with John 19:34 the key to proper interpretation. If the author of the First Epistle were so clearly picking up on the phrase in 19:34 and inculcating basically the same meaning, I find it difficult to understand why he would change the order of the words. My own approach is closer to that of Marshall (*The Epistles of John*, 231–33), though I would not base my position on speculation about the heresy of Cerinthus.

[18] Even if one were to hold with Brown (*The Epistles of John*, 578) that it is the secessionists who stress the coming of the Son of God at Jesus' baptism and that the author of 1 John is combating this view by emphasizing Jesus' saving death, the point I wish to make remains: there is independent attestation of Jesus' baptism in the Johannine tradition, though the authors of the canonical Johannine writings suppress it or allude to it only indirectly.

[19] To find independent attestation of Jesus' baptism by John in Acts, one would have

to grant three postulates: (1) While the kerygmatic speeches of Acts are in their present form the products of Lucan redaction, behind them are discernible the main lines of pre-Lucan summaries of the kerygma. (2) The stress on John's preaching and baptism of repentance, standing at or as the beginning of Jesus' ministry (Acts 1:22; 10:37; 13:24–25) makes sense only if the pre-Lucan kerygma mentioned or at least presupposed Jesus' baptism by John. This is especially true of 10:37–38 (which is plagued by rough syntax): "You know the events that happened throughout all of the land of the Jews, beginning from Galilee after the baptism which John proclaimed, how God anointed Jesus from Nazareth with the holy spirit and power. . . ." The anointing with the holy spirit obviously refers to the theophany after the baptism, which in turn was preceded by John's preaching. The missing link in this recital of events is the explicit mention of Jesus' baptism by John, the lacuna being due perhaps to Luke's redactional tendencies in Acts. (3) Hence it seems that, while Luke's Gospel suppresses the precise role of John in Jesus' baptism, in Acts Luke goes even further. He suppresses, à la the Fourth Evangelist, the whole event of the baptism, which was known in the tradition he used in Acts.—It may be that all these postulates are true, but I see no way of proving all of them.

[20] See Vögtle, "Die sogenannte Taufperikope," 127–28.

[21] The Greek words I translate as "by his passion" are *tǭ pathei*; in my opinion, they refer to Christ's suffering and death on the cross. Ignatius thus links the beginning and end of Jesus' public life in a way reminiscent of 1 John 5:6. Some might prefer to follow the translation of Kirsopp Lake: ". . . by himself submitting [to baptism] . . ."; cf. his edition of *The Apostolic Fathers* (LCL; Cambridge, MA: Harvard University; London: Heinemann, 1912) 193 n. 1. Against this view is William R. Schoedel (*Ignatius of Antioch* [Hermeneia; Philadelphia: Fortress, 1985] 85), who notes that *pathos* always means "passion" in Ignatius.

[22] This position is sustained, with various emphases, even by Bultmann and many post-Bultmannians, not known for their excessive credulity in accepting events in the Gospels as historical. In *Jesus and the Word* (pp. 26, 110–11), Bultmann leans toward accepting the historicity of Jesus' baptism although his statements remain very guarded; he is more open in his acceptance in his *Geschichte*, 263 n. 1, where he states that he cannot share the skepticism of Eduard Meyer in the matter. Needless to say, while Bultmann does not dispute the historicity of Jesus' baptism by John, he classifies the narrative in the Gospels as a "legend of faith" because of the essential role of miraculous and edifying elements, depicting Jesus' consecration as Messiah (pp. 263–64). For the post-Bultmannians, see, e.g., Ernst Käsemann, "On the Subject of Primitive Christian Apocalyptic," *New Testament Questions Today* (New Testament Library; London: SCM, 1969) 108–37, esp. 112: ". . . the baptism of Jesus by John belongs to the indubitable happenings of the life of the historical Jesus." Günther Bornkamm agrees: "His [Jesus'] own baptism by John is one of the most certainly verified occurrences of his life" (*Jesus of Nazareth* [New York: Harper & Row, 1960] 54). Even Herbert Braun, skeptical in so many matters, pronounces: "To be sure, Jesus was baptized by John the Baptist . . . that is very likely historical" (*Jesus of Nazareth. The Man and His Time* [Philadelphia: Fortress, 1979] 55). Hans Conzelmann uses a more cautious formulation, yet the implication of his remarks is acceptance of Jesus' baptism as historical: "All four Gospels [sic] report that Jesus was baptized by John the Baptist. The account is, of course, in its present form, legend. It remains as a historical fact, however, that Jesus emerged out of the Baptist's movement; John's proclamation of the kingdom of God and call to repentance he acknowledged" (*Jesus* [Philadelphia: Fortress, 1973] 31). It is perhaps symptomatic of this school of exegesis that often the historicity of the baptism

is simply affirmed; rarely are detailed arguments given. At least some basic reasons for affirming historicity are given by Goguel, *Au seuil*, 139–40; Kraeling, *John the Baptist*, 131; Jeremias, *Theology of the New Testament*, 45; Ernst, *Johannes der Täufer*, 337; Gnilka, *Jesus von Nazaret*, 83–84.

[23] See, e.g., Scobie, *John the Baptist*, 146: "In this original account of the baptism [i.e., Mark 1:10–11] we have, very probably, an account by Jesus himself of an experience which was of tremendous importance to him personally. As only Jesus experienced the vision, it must be to him that we owe the description of the heavens opening, the Spirit descending, and of the heavenly voice. . . ." In a cautious formulation, Ernst (*Johannes der Täufer*, 337) leaves open the possibility that at his baptism Jesus experienced the call to undertake his special vocation.

[24] The debate over the precise meaning of the dove as the symbol of the spirit continues unresolved: allusion to the spirit of God over the waters in Gen 1:2 (new creation theme); allusion to the dove bringing the olive leaf to Noah after the flood in Gen 8:11 (the restoration of humanity after God's judgment); allusion to Deut 32:11, where Yahweh stirs up his people to the exodus as an eagle stirs its nestlings; the dove as a symbol of the holy spirit, as seen in the later targum to the Canticle of Canticles 2:12 ("the song of the dove is heard in the land"); the dove as a symbol of a goddess in the ancient Near East or as a messenger of the gods; the whole phrase signifying originally not the way the spirit looked but the manner in which it descended ("descended like a bird in flight"). For supposed mythological parallels, see Bultmann, *Geschichte*, 264–69; a negative response to this approach is given by Leander E. Keck, "The Spirit and the Dove," *NTS* 17 (1970–71) 41–67. For a critique of most of the suggestions offered, see Fitzmyer, *The Gospel According to Luke*, 1. 484. Fortunately, the question does not affect our quest for the historical event.

[25] The emphatic *you* (*sy*) is the earliest available form of the heavenly voice, as represented in Mark 1:11 and followed by Luke 3:22. In view of his story of the virginal conception (Matt 1:18–25) and of God's announcement (in Matt 2:15, through the prophet Hosea) that Jesus is God's Son, Matthew, ever concerned with consistency in his christology—at least more concerned than is the eclectic Luke—changes the *you* (addressing Jesus) to the demonstrative *this* (*houtos* in Matt 3:17), pointing out Jesus to the Baptist (and perhaps others). Apparently Matthew saw no point to having Jesus informed of his divine sonship in chap. 3 of the Gospel after the matter was dealt with at length in the Infancy Narrative of chaps. 1–2. Moreover, it is typical of Matthew's Gospel that revelation tends to go public, as opposed to Mark's secrecy about Jesus' messiahship and sonship.

[26] Behind *agapētos* in this text may lie the Hebrew *yāḥîd*. The Hebrew word strictly means "only," "only one." But in a context of family relationships, when applied, e.g., to a son, it may mean "only beloved" or "uniquely beloved." This seems to be the sense when it is applied to Isaac (Gen 22:2,12,16), since Abraham (at least according to the canonical form of Genesis) did have other children by other women, notably Ishmael by Hagar. The sense of love contained in *yāḥîd* is underlined in the first verse that uses it of Isaac: "Take your son, your only one, whom you love, Isaac" (Gen 22:2). It may also be the Hebrew word behind *monogenēs* ("only"), a common description of Jesus the Son in John's Gospel. Interestingly, in the LXX, in every instance where *yāḥîd* in the Hebrew text is translated by *agapētos*, it is used of an "only" or "only beloved" son or daughter who has died or who is destined for death: Isaac in Gen 22:2,12,16; Jephthah's daughter in Judg 11:34; mourning as for an only son in Amos 8:10 and Jer 6:26; and the mysterious "pierced one," who is mourned as an only son in Zech 12:10.

[27] The debate continues to rage on this point. For examples of the two positions (the first in favor of such a reference, the latter opposed), see Robert J. Daly, "The Soteriological Significance of the Sacrifice of Isaac," *CBQ* 39 (1977) 45–75, esp. 68–71; and P. R. Davies and B. D. Chilton, "The Aqedah: A Revised Tradition History," *CBQ* 40 (1978) 514–46. See also W. R. Stegner, "The Baptism of Jesus. A Story Modeled on the Binding of Isaac," *Bible Review* 1 (1985) 36–46; James Swetnam, *Jesus and Isaac. A Study of the Epistle to the Hebrews in the Light of the Aqedah* (AnBib 94; Rome: Biblical Institute, 1981).

[28] The basic sense of 63:11 is clear, though some phrases are disputed: e.g., "Moses [and] his people" might possibly be read instead as "Moses his servant" (the LXX omits the whole phrase); the MT reads "brought them up from the sea," but 1QIs[a] and the versions favor omitting "them"; the MT also reads "shepherds" instead of "shepherd," found in the LXX; some commentators would emend "he remembered" to "they remembered," making the subject of the verb clearly the people Israel. My point here is not the exact grammar and syntax of the verse but the cluster of evocative themes, especially in the wider context of the whole of Isaiah 63. Claus Westermann (*Isaiah 40–66* [OTL; Philadelphia: Westminster, 1969] 389) notes that some exegetes hold that the "sea" (*yām*) referred to in v 11 is not the Reed Sea but the Nile River. Although this would give a closer correlation with the baptismal scene, this meaning of *yām* would be most unusual in biblical Hebrew. Still, Helmer Ringgren considers it a possibility in his article on "*yām*," *TDOT* 6 (1990) 95.

[29] Fritzleo Lentzen-Deis, *Die Taufe Jesu nach den Synoptikern* (Frankfurter Theologische Studien 4; Frankfurt: Knecht, 1970), esp. 195–289.

[30] So rightly Martin Dibelius, *Die Formgeschichte des Evangeliums* (6th ed.; Tübingen: Mohr [Siebeck], 1971) 273; cf. Bultmann, *Geschichte*, 263.

[31] James D. G. Dunn, *Jesus and the Spirit* (Philadelphia: Westminster, 1975) 63. Although not following the exact reasoning of Dunn, Jeremias (*Theology of the New Testament*, 55–56) comes to a similar conclusion.

[32] That the two motifs of God as Father and the spirit powerfully active in Jesus' work were actually important themes of the public ministry must be shown later. For now the point is simply granted for the sake of argument with Dunn.

[33] Having just rejected attempts to psychologize the baptism of Jesus, I trust it is clear that I use the word "conversion" without filling it with all the tired religious rhetoric and emotionalism that often plague the word in popular religion today.—I find it strange that Hollenbach ("The Conversion of Jesus," 196–219) uses the word "conversion" not of the break connected with Jesus' coming to baptism but of a later, hypothetical shift in Jesus' life when Jesus received a prophetic revelation just as John had (p. 199). According to Hollenbach, this shift involved his "defection" or "apostasy" from John's movement and vision (pp. 215–16). Supposedly, while baptizing, Jesus discovered that he could exorcise. Giving up his earlier ministry of baptizing the powerful for repentance, Jesus instead began healing the sick and outcast members of society. He thus substituted new "secular, personal, and social actions and insights" (p. 216) for his former ritual activity. This whole reconstruction rests on uncontrolled conflation and rearrangement of Johannine and Synoptic passages, with a large injection of forced relevance by way of liberation theology. In my opinion, if the word "conversion" is to be used at all, it belongs rather with the events connected with Jesus' baptism, i.e., at the verifiable basic turn that Jesus makes from a good but ordinary Jewish life off the stage of history to a total commitment to a new kind of religious life on the stage of history.

[34] We shall have to return to this concept later, but here I simply admit the unavoidable vagueness of the concept, covering everything from the "prophet like Moses" promised in Deut 18:15,18–19 (and alluded to in Qumran's 4QTestim 5–8), through a returning Elijah (or an Elijah-like prophet), to the prophet mentioned alongside the two messiahs in the *Manual of Discipline* of Qumran (1QS 9:11). We need not suppose that the concept was known to or accepted by all Israelites. Indeed, Richard A. Horsley (" 'Like One of the Prophets of Old': Two Types of Popular Prophets at the Time of Jesus," *CBQ* 47 [1985] 435–63, esp. 437–43; cf. the summary statement in Horsley and Hanson, *Bandits, Prophets, and Messiahs*, 148–49) argues that the idea was quite restricted in early 1st-century Israel. In my opinion, he pushes a good case too far. In any case, at the very least, certain groups (Qumran, the disciples of the Baptist, the early Palestinian disciples of Jesus during his earthly ministry) did operate with the reality indicated by "eschatological prophet," if not with the formal concept or title itself.

[35] "As necessary for salvation" may seem too strong a formulation to some, but in my opinion it does reflect the astounding claim implicit in John's "sermon of wrath and repentance" (Matt 3:7–10 par.) and in his promise of the coming one (Matt 3:11–12 parr.), as interpreted in Chapter 12. It seems to me that the presumption must be that the reason why Jesus submitted to John's baptism is that he accepted John's claim about his baptism.

[36] See the contrary view in Hollenbach, "The Conversion of Jesus," 217: "[After leaving John's group] Jesus no longer seeks God in and through either performing religious ritual or calling upon the mighty to perform deeds of justice. . . ." Only by arbitrarily assigning Gospel material to hypothetical stages of Jesus' public life can Hollenbach arrive at this conclusion.

[37] The article of Hollenbach ("The Conversion of Jesus") especially comes to mind here.

[38] "The Conversion of Jesus," 199–201. Hollenbach opines that Jesus repented and was baptized when he "discovered that he had participated directly or indirectly in the oppression of the weak members of society." In Hollenbach's view, Jesus was a member of a small middle class which enjoyed "considerable standing in society"; indeed, Jesus himself was "a substantial member of society." We are back to the "liberal lives" mixed with a goodly dose of liberation theology. One practical problem of reconstituting Jesus according to the academic movement of the moment is that the resulting portrait may look very dated a decade from now.

[39] Various attempts by Christian theologians to explain Jesus' submission to John's baptism are listed by Scobie, *John the Baptist*, 148: "Jesus has been thought of as undergoing baptism in order to consecrate the sacrament and provide the example for Christians to follow; or his repentance has been thought of as not being on his own behalf, but on behalf of others; or his submission has been thought of as part of his complete self-identification with sinners." Scobie's own approach seems to be summed up thus: "Repentance was certainly demanded by John, but we will remember how repentance signified a positive turning towards righteousness, just as much as a turning from sin." Somewhat similar is the approach of Kraeling, *John the Baptist*, 136: we need only "replace the negative virtue of sinlessness in this context with the positive virtue of holiness for which there is ample justification in the record. History shows that the holiest of men have also been the ones most ready to humiliate themselves before God. To this rule Jesus was undoubtedly no exception."

[40] So, e.g., Dibelius, *Die urchristliche Überlieferung*, 58.

[41] It is curious that, while Hollenbach seeks to eschew the role of the theologian in favor of the historian, he inevitably becomes involved in theological reasoning—and unfortunately his theological reasoning is not always clear or sound. For example, he states ("The Conversion of Jesus," 201): "Now it may be in some sense abstracted from history that Jesus never sinned, but historically speaking that issue cannot be determined one way or another." I am at a loss to understand precisely what this means. An even more difficult exercise in theological reasoning is found on p. 202: "For if he [Jesus] came to be baptized for some theologically appropriate reason, then he was in fact a deceiver, which was again reason enough indeed for him to need John's baptism of repentance even if Jesus himself was unaware of it."

[42] This firmly and radically *theo*-logical conception of sin fits in with the preaching of both John and Jesus, neither of whom was primarily concerned with sin as a trespass against a particular ritual or purity command of the Law or tradition. When it comes to a question of sin, what is at stake for both John and Jesus is basic fidelity or infidelity to the God of the covenant.

[43] See, e.g., John 9:24; Mark 2:7; 14:63–64; and implicitly Matt 11:19 ‖ Luke 7:34. One must make allowances, however, for the polemical nature of these passages.

[44] Here is the clearest point of opposition between my view and that of Hollenbach, who claims ("The Conversion of Jesus," 201): "Historically, the fact that Jesus came to John for baptism shows demonstrably that Jesus thought he was a sinner who needed repentance." As I indicate below, further nuance is needed in the very concept of the confession of sins before the question can be adequately considered.

[45] See the revised version of this seminal article in Krister Stendahl, "The Apostle Paul and the Introspective Conscience of the West," *Paul Among Jews and Gentiles and Other Essays* (Philadelphia: Fortress, 1976) 78–96. The main essay in the book, "Paul Among Jews and Gentiles" (pp. 1–77), restates the key insights in more developed form.

[46] The joining of these (to us) disparate concepts of praise/thanksgiving and confession of sins is found even in the double meaning of the Hebrew verb *ydh*: in hifil it usually means "praise (and thank)"; in hitpael it usually means "confess one's sins." On this see G. Mayer, J. Bergman, and W. von Soden, "*ydh, tôdâ*," *TDOT* 5 (1986) 427–43.

[47] See the description W. A. Quanbeck gives in his article on "Confession," *IDB*, 1. 667.

[48] The reading "his" involves a slight emendation of the Hebrew text, which is confused but seems to read "their." The confusion probably arose because a *mem* from a later word was accidentally written at the end of the word for "power" (represented in my translation as "powerful").

[49] Gnilka (*Jesus von Nazaret*, 80) thinks that it may well have been that any candidate for John's baptism made a general kind of confession of sins, "comparable to the confession of sins on the Jewish Day of Atonement or at the feast of the renewal at Qumran. . . ."

[50] The need to distinguish between disciples in the wider and in the narrower sense (when applying the term to both John's and Jesus' disciples) is pointed out by Kraeling, *John the Baptist*, 162.

[51] As noted previously, "rabbi" was used in a fluid sense in the early 1st century A.D. and had not yet been restricted to its later, more institutional sense.

[52] By "assisted" I do not mean that John's disciples themselves conferred baptism. We have no indication from either the NT or Josephus that anyone besides John *the Baptist* actually administered John's baptism. A number of NT texts state or imply that John personally baptized all the people who came to him: see Mark 1:5 par.; Mark 1:8 (= Q tradition in Matt 3:11 || Luke 3:16); Mark 1:9; Matt 3:13; Luke 3:7. Interestingly, the Fourth Evangelist seems to say the same thing about Jesus baptizing: note the distinction between Jesus and his disciples in John 3:22 and the juxtaposing of Jesus alone and John alone in the verses that follow. As we shall see below, it is only the final redactor of the Fourth Gospel who introduces the idea of Jesus' disciples conferring baptism in 4:2. Hence one must beware of reading later Christian liturgical practice (where others besides the chief figure or official present might baptize) back into the practice of John or Jesus.

[53] I should stress that the references to the Fourth Gospel at this point are concerned only with the existence of the Baptist's disciples and their basic activities and not with the precise content of the Baptist's supposed instruction, which is, for the most part, nothing but the theology of the Fourth Evangelist put into the mouth of the Baptist.

[54] This point is missed by Hollenbach ("The Conversion of Jesus," 215–16) when he speaks of Jesus' "defection" and "apostasy" from John.

[55] Becker, *Johannes der Täufer*, 12–15, 105; Hollenbach, "The Conversion of John," 203–4. The seeds of this position go back a long way and include (with differences of emphasis) such notable scholars as Bultmann (*Jesus and the Word*, 26), Dibelius (*Die urchristliche Überlieferung*, 65–66), Goguel (*Au seuil*, 292), and Scobie (*John the Baptist*, 153–56).

[56] Ernst, *Johannes der Täufer*, 338–39; cf. his separate essay, Josef Ernst, "War Jesus ein Schüler Johannes' des Täufers?" *Vom Urchristentum zu Jesus* (Joachim Gnilka Festschrift; ed. Hubert Frankenmölle and Karl Kertelge; Freiburg/Basel/Vienna: Herder, 1989) 13–33; Gnilka, *Jesus von Nazaret*, 84–85. Jeremias also seems negative to the idea; see his *New Testament Theology*, 48–49.

[57] If the Q tradition did presuppose or actually narrate Jesus' baptism by John, Jesus' subsequent need to clarify his relationship to John would be all the more understandable, without our having to suppose that Q hints at Jesus' being John's disciple for some period of time. Hence, contrary to Hollenbach ("The Conversion of Jesus," 205–6), I do not think that the Q material helps prove the claim that Jesus had become a disciple of John in the narrower sense or that Jesus had undertaken a baptizing ministry. As we shall see, though, the Q material may have a confirmatory function if we can first establish these claims on other grounds.

[58] Luke goes even further: he prevents the idea of Jesus' becoming a disciple of John after his baptism from even entering the reader's mind by narrating John's arrest before he narrates Jesus' baptism (3:20–21).

[59] Ernst, *Johannes der Täufer*, 338–39.

[60] As we saw in Chapter 12, the parallel texts are Matt 3:11 and Acts 13:25 (with *erchetai met' eme* instead); Luke 3:16 lacks *opisō mou*.

[61] Those in favor of taking *erchetai opisō mou* in the sense of discipleship include Lohmeyer, *Das Evangelium des Markus*, 18: "Now the phrase 'come after someone' in the NT always has a precise sense; it indicates subordination or less power." Lohmeyer then continues in n. 3: "A temporal meaning of *opisō* is attested nowhere [presumably, in the NT], only a spatial [meaning is attested]." See also Wilckens, *Die Missionsreden*

der Apostelgeschichte, 103, including n. 3; it should be noted, however, that Wilckens is speaking specifically of the sense of the phrase in Mark's Gospel. The contrary view of *erchetai opisō mou* in the mouth of the Baptist is held by Heinrich Seesemann, *"opisō, opisthen," TDNT* 5 (1967) 289–92, esp. 290: "Again, when Jesus is called *opisō mou erchomenos* by the Baptist (Jn. 1:15,27,30; cf. Mk. 1:7 and Mt. 3:11), the *opisō* is not theologically significant [?], but simply indicates the time." In n. 5 Seesemann observes that the temporal sense of *opisō* is witnessed in the LXX: e.g., 1 Kgdms 24:22; 3 Kgdms 1:24.

[62] To begin with a general observation: it should be noted that *opisō* in itself does not contain the idea of discipleship. For example, in the Gospels, *opisō* appears with other verbs of motion to create a hostile meaning that is just the opposite of "following after as a disciple." For instance, in Mark 8:33 par., *hypage opisō mou satana* probably carries the primary sense of "Out of my sight, Satan!" In Luke 19:14 (the parable of the minas), the citizens hate the candidate for kingship and *send* a delegation *after him* (*apesteilan presbeian opisō autou*) to try to prevent him from obtaining the kingship. In John 6:66, those disciples who find Jesus' saying "hard" turn away (*apēlthon eis ta opisō*) and leave the company of his disciples.

More relevant to our question are two cases in the NT where the spatial sense of *opisō* may yield to a temporal sense. (1) In Phil 3:13, Paul forgets the things that lie behind (*ta men opisō*); the sense here is actually temporal, the things lying behind being a metaphor for his past life. (2) In John 1:15 and its almost word-for-word repetition in 1:30, Johannine theology as seen in the Prologue makes a temporal sense likely. In light of the opposition between the divine *ēn* and the created *egeneto* throughout the Prologue (1:1–18), *ho opisō mou erchomenos emprosthen mou gegonen, hoti prōtos mou ēn* probably means "he who comes after me [in the flow of events] ranks ahead of me [in dignity in salvation history], for he existed before me [in his divine preexistence]." For this translation, see Brown, *John*, 1. 56; Schnackenburg, *The Gospel According to St. John*, 1. 273–74; Haenchen, *John 1*, 120. This then is also the sense of the verse when it is repeated with slightly different wording in 1:30. Therefore, when we come to the Synoptic-like form of the saying in 1:27, poised as it is between 1:15 and 1:30, the phrase *ho opisō mou erchomenos* in 1:27 (the exact same wording as in 1:15) most likely also carries the temporal sense. Hence it is not true to say that *every* case of *erchomai opisō* in the Four Gospels clearly or most likely has the spatial sense and is used as a metaphor for discipleship. At least in John 1, the theological context makes the temporal sense more probable. It is not surprising that the Bauer-Aland *Wörterbuch* (col. 1166) includes not only John 1:15,27,30 but also Matt 3:11 and Mark 1:7 under the rubric of the temporal sense of "after."

[63] So rightly Scobie, *John the Baptist*, 64. Speaking of the "discipleship interpretation," he remarks: "This is an ingenious explanation, though rather far-fetched. It contradicts the clear evidence that John pictured this figure as being still in the future. John had no thought of identifying the coming Judge with Jesus."

[64] If one were to adopt the view of Arens (*The ēlthon-Sayings*, 289) that the absence of *opisō mou* in Luke 3:16 represents the original form of the saying, the same final conclusion would be reached by a different route: without *opisō mou*, the saying would not even have the possibility of referring to discipleship. The opinion of Arens is shared by Ernst, *Johannes der Täufer*, 49–51.

[65] For a balanced evaluation of the Fourth Gospel's treatment of these Baptist sectarians, see Raymond E. Brown, *The Community of the Beloved Disciple* (New York/Ramsey, NJ: Paulist, 1979) 69–71. Brown rejects the exaggerated emphasis on supposed anti-

Baptist polemic in the Gospel, an emphasis that stems from the work of W. Balden-sperger (*Der Prolog des vierten Evangeliums. Sein polemisch-apologetischer Zweck* [Tü-bingen: Mohr (Siebeck) 1898]). "The fact that they [the non-Christian followers of John the Baptist] are refuted in the Gospel, not by direct attack upon them as non-believers, but through careful correction of wrong aggrandizements of JBap may mean that the Johannine Christians still held hope for their conversion . . ." (pp. 70–71).

[66] So Brown, *Community of the Beloved Disciple*, 29–30.

[67] It is important to consider all three passages; Ben Witherington, III (*The Christology of Jesus* [Minneapolis: Fortress, 1990] 54) is too brief in his consideration of the question when he states: ". . . 3:22–23 does not indicate that Jesus was in the Baptist's circle, or that he baptized with or under his tutelage." This is true of 3:22–23 considered in isolation, but not of John 1:19–4:1 read as a whole. To be fair, one must remember that at this point in his argument, Witherington is reacting to the detailed reconstruction of Eta Linnemann, "Jesus und der Täufer," *Festschrift für Ernst Fuchs* (ed. G. Ebeling et al.; Tübingen: Mohr [Siebeck] 1973) 219–36. Witherington gives a summary of Linnemann's thesis on p. 53.

[68] Traditional exegesis was accustomed to see in the "two of his disciples" standing with John the Baptist in John 1:35 Andrew (so v 40) and John the beloved disciple. But there is no basis in the text for the latter identification. If we look at the structure of chap. 1 instead, the parallels between vv 40–41 and vv 44–45 suggest that Philip is understood by the Evangelist to be the other disciple:

v 40	*ēn Andreas*	v 44	*ēn de ho Philippos*
v 41	*heuriskei* + accusative indicating another disciple *kai legei autō* *heurēkamen* + accusative indicating status of Jesus	v 45	*heuriskei* + accusative indicating another disciple *kai legei autō* *heurēkamen* + accusative indicating status of Jesus

The idea that Philip is the companion of Andrew in 1:35 fits perfectly with the fact that (1) elsewhere in the Fourth Gospel Andrew and Philip are singled out in the same pericope (6:5,8; 12:22), and (2) in 1:44 the Evangelist goes out of his way to explain that Philip was from the same city as Andrew and Peter, Bethsaida.

[69] I am well aware of the danger of uncritically harmonizing John and the Synoptics, but I do not think that this is the case here. On the one hand, the historicity of the baptism of Jesus by John was established on critical grounds in the first section of this chapter. The second section explored how this event manifested Jesus' basic embrace of the Baptist's message and vision. We are now probing indications in the Fourth Gospel of a further relationship between the Baptist and Jesus. To attempt a critical correlation of these insights is not the same as to engage in an artificial kind of harmonization.

[70] Since the stay of Jesus with John after the former's baptism is itself a conclusion reached only by reading between the lines of the Fourth Gospel, it is useless to debate how long this stay lasted. We simply have no way of knowing. My own surmise—and it is no more than that—is that the stay was not lengthy. If I am correct in thinking that the whole ministry of Jesus lasted just a little over two years, there simply is not a great deal of time for Jesus' period of discipleship with John, when one considers all the events that must be fit into the time frame between Jesus' baptism and his death.

[71] See Ernst, *Johannes der Täufer*, 206–10. In "Jesus und der Täufer," Linnemann

discerns two different traditions contained in John 3:22–4:3 that attest to Jesus' baptizing: 3:23,25–27 and 3:22; 4:1–3. Linnemann thinks that these two mutually independent reports reflect historical facts about the ministry of Jesus, including the fact that Jesus gave up his baptizing activity when he heard that his own success had come to the notice of the Pharisees. The Baptist was supposedly involved in a conflict with the Pharisees, and Jesus did not want to cause his former master embarrassment before his enemies. Linnemann's detailed reconstruction of events is highly speculative and at times does violence to the natural sense of various texts. However, she is right in her basic point: that Jesus did actually baptize is most likely a historical fact, and not an invention of the Fourth Evangelist.

[72] The exact wording of the text is not certain in 3:25. p[75], Alexandrinus, Vaticanus, and other codices read "with a Jew"; p[66], the original hand of Sinaiticus, and other codices read "with Jews." On the question, see Brown, *John*, 1. 152; Metzger, *Textual Commentary*, 205. Fortunately, this question does not affect the overall flow of the text and the point I am making. However, Brown (ibid.) remarks that some commentators (e.g., Loisy, Bauer, Goguel) have suggested that the text originally read "Jesus," but that piety caused Christian scribes to change "Jesus" to "Jew" or "Jews" to avoid the "scandal" of a dispute between Jesus and the disciples of John. Ernst (*Johannes der Täufer*, 208) seems to take the suggestion of "Jesus" as the original reading seriously; Scobie (*John the Baptist*, 154) considers it "a very probable emendation." While such a hypothetical reading would fit in nicely with my interpretation of the flow of thought, it lacks all basis in the papyri, Greek codices, versions, and commentaries of the Fathers. With Brown and Metzger, I incline to accepting "a Jew" as the original reading.

[73] 4:2 uses *kaitoi ge* for "and yet"; *kaitoi ge* never occurs elsewhere in the Fourth Gospel, or indeed in the rest of the NT, except for the *textus receptus* of Acts 14:17. At Acts 14:17 the *UBSGNT*[3] reads simply *kaitoi*, which is also found in Heb 4:3. *kaitoi ge* is, however, used by some other authors of the period, including Josephus (*J.W.* 1.1. §7).

[74] In a work that stresses the unity of the Fourth Gospel as the work of one author, C. H. Dodd admits (*The Interpretation of the Fourth Gospel* [Cambridge: Cambridge University, 1965] 311): "The statement [that Jesus baptized] is repeated in iv. 1, but immediately corrected in iv. 2, in a parenthesis which ruins the sentence, and perhaps has a better claim to be regarded as an 'editorial note' by a 'redactor' than anything else in the gospel except the colophon xxi. 24–5." His view of 4:2 is standard among commentators; see, e.g., J. H. Bernard, *The Gospel According to St. John* (ICC; 2 vols.; Edinburgh: Clark, 1985, originally 1928) 1. 133–34; Rudolf Bultmann, *Das Evangelium des Johannes* (MeyerK 2; 19th ed.; Göttingen: Vandenhoeck & Ruprecht, 1968) 128 n. 4; Schnackenburg, *The Gospel According to St John*, 1. 422 n. 6; Brown, *John*, 1. 164. Attempts to avoid Dodd's conclusion are usually contorted and contrived. It is telling that critics who question the theory of a final redactor of the Fourth Gospel usually do not give great attention to 4:2; see, e.g., Paul S. Minear, "The Original Functions of John 21," *JBL* 102 (1983) 85–98; Peter F. Ellis, *The Genius of John* (Collegeville, MN: Liturgical Press, 1984).

An approach to the problem of 4:2 that eschews historical questions and focuses rather on literary criticism and rhetorical techniques is found in Jeffrey Lloyd Staley's *The Print's First Kiss: A Rhetorical Investigation of the Implied Reader in the Fourth Gospel* (SBLDS 82; Atlanta: Scholars, 1988) 96–98. In Staley's analysis, the abstract "implied reader" is purposely tripped up by the equally abstract "narrator" in order to force the implied reader to reevaluate his relationship to the narrator and the story. In the face of the flat contradictions between 3:22–4:1 and 4:2, Staley claims: "Yet the implied reader cannot accuse the narrator of being unreliable, for he set accounts straight with 4:2. . . ." Does he? How is the implied reader to know that the narrator is now telling the truth in 4:2 when he apparently lied on purpose in 3:22–4:1? This flat contradiction is not on the same level as the various ambiguous and ironic statements of the Fourth Gospel that play with double meaning. There is no double meaning here, only flat contradiction and (in Staley's reading) intentional lying. Even on the presuppositions of modern rhetorical criticism, Staley's explanation is strained.

[75] No doubt the desire to avoid Jesus' appearing as a mere subordinate who imitates the master's baptism is one reason the final redactor inserts 4:2; in this he is probably at one with the thrust of the Synoptic tradition, which simply lacks any depiction of Jesus baptizing. There may, however, be another reason for the redactor's intervention, one more "internal" to the theology of the Fourth Gospel. The final redactor apparently had a luxury the Evangelist did not have, namely, the leisure to read the whole Gospel again and again over a period of time and perhaps to experience its use in a local Johannine community. The redactor perhaps noticed that a major theme of the Gospel is the gradual giving of the spirit. The spirit descends and *remains* on Jesus in 1:32. But no one else receives the spirit during the public ministry, as 7:37–39 indicates. After Jesus promises "streams of living water" to the believer, the Evangelist comments: "He said this concerning the spirit, which those who believed in him would receive; for as yet there was no spirit, because Jesus had not yet been glorified" (7:39). It is only by Jesus' full glorification in his death-resurrection that the spirit is conferred on believers. In 19:30, the dying Jesus "gives over the spirit" (*paredōken to pneuma*) to the believing community at the foot of the cross; in 19:34, blood [= Jesus' saving death] and water [= the spirit] flow from the side of the dead Jesus; in 20:22, the risen Jesus breathes out the spirit on the assembled disciples on Easter Sunday. The final redactor apparently appreciated this overarching schema; he also appreciated the fact that having Jesus baptize during his public ministry threw the whole theological process into confusion. If Jesus was baptizing during his public ministry, the reader of the Fourth Gospel was caught in a dilemma. *Either* Jesus' baptism conferred the spirit—and how could a baptism conferred by Jesus himself not do that, if baptism conferred by Christian ministers does it?—but then the whole overarching process of the promise of the spirit during the public ministry and its bestowal in the death-resurrection is destroyed. *Or* the process is saved by claiming that Jesus did not confer the spirit when he conferred his baptism during the public ministry—which seems an impious thought, granted the high christology of the Fourth Gospel. The redactor resolves the tension (at the expense of the tension of 4:2) by issuing a "clarification" that denies that Jesus himself baptized. An intriguing point here is that, unlike the ecclesiastical redactor posited by Bultmann, the final redactor who emerges from this analysis is passionately committed to the basic theology of the Fourth Gospel and wants to neutralize any detail in the Gospel that could threaten the overall vision of the Fourth Evangelist. He corrects the Gospel by way of "friendly amendment." His amendment, however, unleashed a stream of controversy in the patristic, medieval, and modern periods. For a short review of patristic and medieval opinions, along with an attempt to deal with the problem of John 3:22 in a precritical, dogmatic mode, see Simon Weber, *Jesus taufte. Eine Untersuchung zu Ev. Joh. 3,22* (Offenburg: Huggle, 1895).

[76] For similar reasoning that defends the historicity of overlapping ministries of John and Jesus, see W. Schenk, "Gefangenschaft und Tod des Täufers. Erwägungen zur Chronologie und ihren Konsequenzen," *NTS* 29 (1983) 453–83, esp. 458–59.

[77] Dibelius (*Die urchristliche Überlieferung*, 111–13) seems to miss the whole point of the embarrassing nature of the tradition in 3:22–30; 4:1 when he states that the dispute

that arises over Jesus' baptizing was created by the Evangelist to stress the *independence* of Jesus and his baptism from John's baptism. Any natural reading of the material would suggest just the opposite. Bultmann also thinks that 3:22–26 is the creation of the Evangelist, though he allows for the possibility of v 25 representing some tradition (*Das Evangelium des Johannes*, 122–23). Linnemann argues against the positions of both Dibelius and Bultmann in "Jesus und der Täufer," 219–36.

[78] Needless to say, this is not to endorse the extreme view of Boers (*Who Was Jesus?*, xiii, 31–53), who claims that Jesus considered John "the final . . . decisive eschatological figure," the one who caused Jesus to realize that he was "living in a time when the kingdom of God had already arrived" (p. xiii). For Boers, Jesus remains dependent on John to a degree that does violence to the messages of both John and Jesus. In a sense, Boers stands at the opposite extreme from Hollenbach's theory of Jesus' defection and apostasy from John's movement. As so often happens, truth and sanity are to be found somewhere in the middle. Becker (*Johannes der Täufer*, 68) comes closer to the truth in a balanced formulation that holds the two poles of the paradox in tension: Jesus' message cannot simply be explained by derivation from the Baptist, but one cannot understand Jesus without the Baptist.

[79] As with so many imaginative reconstructions, all this verges on writing a novel— and any number can play the game. For example, with the same data Linnemann ("Jesus und der Täufer," 229–31) constructs a scenario according to which (1) the Baptist refused to baptize toll collectors and prostitutes; (2) this led to a split in the Baptist movement, when Jesus decided to accept these outcasts for baptism; (3) then at a later date Jesus, who was more successful in his baptizing ministry, gave up baptizing entirely to avoid embarrassing the Baptist before his enemies, the Pharisees.

[80] Hollenbach, "The Conversion of Jesus," 206 n. 27.

[81] "The Conversion of Jesus," 206–7.

[82] Besides Hollenbach, see for this theory Goguel, *Au seuil*, 235–74, and 292. Although Witherington would disagree with Hollenbach's reconstruction on many points, he too speaks of Jesus' getting "the idea for a *brief* baptizing ministry from John . . ." (*The Christology of Jesus*, 54; emphasis mine). Witherington goes on to suggest "that Jesus, out of respect for John, ceased his own parallel ministry so as not to compromise John's work." According to this reconstruction, the imprisonment of John may have led Jesus to think that God was "urging him to go a step further than the Baptist, perhaps with a somewhat different emphasis or modus operandi" (ibid.).

[83] See Ernst, *Johannes der Täufer*, 55–56.

[84] For the different theories of the original position of Matt 11:12–13 in Q, see Ernst, *Johannes der Täufer*, 56 n. 72.

[85] So emphatically Dieter Lührmann, *Die Redaktion der Logienquelle* (WMANT 33; Neukirchen-Vluyn: Neukirchener Verlag, 1969) 25. He rightly opposes the view of Dibelius (*Die urchristliche Überlieferung*, 6), who sees Matt 11:7–19 par. as one unit, treated in one subsection of chapter one of his book, while Matt 11:2–6 par. is treated later on in a different subsection. To be fair to Dibelius, however, one should note that he does distinguish two groups of sayings in Matt 11:7–19, the second group beginning with the parable of the children.

[86] See Bultmann, *Geschichte*, 22. As Lührmann points out (*Die Redaktion der Logienquelle*, 23), the divisions are fairly obvious from the change of addressees: disciples of John in Matt 11:2; crowds in 11:7; and indirectly, the evil generation that rejects both

John and Jesus in 11:16. Form-critical *Gattungen* change accordingly: an apophthegm (vv 2–6), a string of two- and three-part logia built around rhetorical questions (vv 7–11), and a parable with application (vv 16–19). What ties the three units together is not form but content: the question of the relation between John and Jesus.

[87] For example, W. G. Kümmel (*Promise and Fulfilment. The Eschatological Message of Jesus* [SBT 1/23; 3d ed.; London: SCM, 1957] 109 n. 15) holds that "in Luke the framework has been dramatized secondarily by a description of Jesus' healing activity taking place just at the time of this inquiry"; cf. the remarks of Dibelius about Luke's tendency, as seen here, to provide a lively narrative (*Die urchristliche Überlieferung*, 33 n. 1). Ernst (*Johannes der Täufer*, 57) weighs the arguments on both sides of the issue but does not take a position himself.

[88] For an attempt to detect the redactional tendencies of Matthew and Luke in this pericope, see, e.g., Schulz, *Q. Die Spruchquelle der Evangelisten*, 190–92; Ernst, *Johannes der Täufer*, 56–57.

[89] So Dibelius, *Die urchristliche Überlieferung*, 38 n. 2. Compare the relatively detailed statement of Luke 3:19–20 with the laconic notice in Matt 4:12, a reworking of Mark 1:14. Matthew would be more likely to keep a reference to prison if it occurred at this point in Q, since his vague *paredothē* ("was handed over") in 4:12 could use further specification, which is not needed by Luke. Note also that both the Marcan and Johannine traditions know independently of the Baptist's imprisonment (Mark 1:14 and John 3:24, either before the beginning of or early on in Jesus' ministry); therefore the presence of such knowledge in the Q tradition would hardly be surprising. In his *Q Parallels. Synopsis, Critical Notes, & Concordance* (Sonoma, CA: Polebridge, 1988) 52, John S. Kloppenborg prints *en tō desmōtēriō* ("in prison") as part of the "generally accepted extent of Q" (see p. xxiii). However, Polag, in his reconstruction of Q printed in Havener's *Q. The Sayings of Jesus* (p. 128), considers the presence of the words "in prison" merely "possible." Ernst (*Johannes der Täufer*, 57) lists scholars on both sides of the issue and leaves the question open. If the mention of prison is a Matthean addition (as Lührmann [*Die Redaktion der Logienquelle*, 26 n. 4] thinks), the historical setting of Jesus' reply could be the period when John and Jesus were still active simultaneously. Obviously, a setting after John's execution is excluded, unless we delete the entire narrative framework and leave the beatitude without a precise addressee.

While the question cannot be solved simply by investigating the use of *desmōterion* ("prison"), Matthew's preference for *phylakē* for "prison" should give pause to those who insist that "in prison" is Matthean redaction in 11:2. Matthew willingly takes over *phylakē* in the sense of "prison" from both Q (Matt 5:25) and Mark (Matt 14:3,10). More significantly, *phylakē* is Matthew's word-of-choice in material that is either special M tradition or Matthean redaction: 18:30; 25:36,39,43,44. The examples in chap. 25 are especially striking, since the idea is the same as that found in Matt 11:2 (visiting someone in prison), and the whole passage depicting the last judgment is either a Matthean creation or heavily redacted by Matthew. In contrast, *desmōterion* occurs only at 11:2 in Matthew's Gospel. While these facts do not decide the case, I think they do help tip the balance in favor of *desmōterion* being in Q's story about John's question to Jesus. Much more likely candidates for being Matthean redactional formulations are "the works of the Messiah" in 11:2 and "by her works" in 11:19—the sort of *inclusio* Matthew often uses.

As an aside, one may note that objections to historicity that arise from the access John has to his disciples while he is in prison (so Ernst, *Johannes der Täufer*, 318) ignore the situation of many prisoners in the ancient Mediterranean world, so different from prison conditions in the United States today. Often prisoners were dependent on family and friends for food and other supplies, which the imprisoning officials sometimes did not provide. While strict confinement without any visitors was known, the presumption of almost all the NT texts that deal with the topic is that access to the imprisoned is possible (e.g., Heb 13:3; Acts 23:16). Hence, both in his epistles and in the Acts of the Apostles we see Paul in frequent contact with his friends while he is imprisoned. If Paul could write a whole epistle from prison, the Baptist could probably send at least a verbal message from prison. The same sort of situation is taken for granted in Matt 25:36 ("... in prison and you came to me").

[90] See Kümmel, *Promise and Fulfilment*, 110; Bultmann (*Geschichte*, 22) does not sufficiently take this point into account. Fitzmyer (*The Gospel According to Luke*, 1. 663–66) and Witherington (*The Christology of Jesus*, 43) point out that certain key "messianic" texts in the OT and Qumran speak of the Davidic king or anointed one as "coming": so Zech 9:9 ("Behold, your king comes to you"); 1QS 9:1 ("... until there come the Anointed Ones of Aaron and Israel"); 4QPBless 3 ("... until there comes the Anointed One of justice, the sprout of David"). Fitzmyer, however, prefers to understand "the coming one" in reference to the "messenger of Yahweh" who "suddenly comes to his temple," an Elijah redivivus, as prophesied in Mal 3:1; 3:23–24. The element of the miraculous in Jesus' answer does conjure up the idea of the miracle cycles of Elijah and Elisha (certainly not a royal Davidic Messiah); others might want to add to the mix the idea of the prophet like Moses, since Moses performed wonders in the context of the first exodus.

One could add to these texts many other eschatological passages both in and outside the OT (e.g., the coming of one like a son of man in Dan 7:13, the coming of God in Zech 14:5). However, all that these texts necessarily show is that the verb "come" (Hebrew *bōʾ*, Aramaic *ʾătāʾ*, Greek *erchomai*) can take on a solemn eschatological resonance in a given eschatological context. The verb in itself is not attached to any one eschatological figure. Indeed, in an eschatological context, almost everything and anything is said to "come," including the days. As Ferdinand Hahn (*The Titles of Jesus in Christology* [London: Lutterworth, 1969] 380) remarks, "*ho erchomenos* can hardly be associated in a fixed terminological sense with a definitive stratum of tradition. 'Coming' means all that stands in association with the time of salvation, the new aeon, the dominion of God, the world judge, Elias, the Messiah, etc." On the vagueness of "the coming one," see also Hughes, "John the Baptist," 204–5.

It should be noted that only Matthew, with his bookkeeper's mind that likes neat cross-references, changes the prophecy of the Baptist in 3:11 so that instead of saying "there comes one stronger," the Baptist says "the coming one ... is stronger." Matthew thus creates a closer fit between John's prophecy in 3:11 and John's question in 11:3 (and the acclamation of the crowd in 21:9). It is therefore on the level of Matthew's redaction rather than on the level of Q that "the coming one" begins to sound like a title.

[91] Compare the confident "we" (apparently including Paul) in the expectations of the parousia in 1 Thess 4:15 ("*we* who are living, who survive until the parousia of the Lord, will certainly not precede those who have fallen asleep [in death]") and 1 Cor 15:51–52 ("the dead shall be raised incorruptible, and *we* [i.e., the living who will not be raised from the dead] will be changed") with Paul's taking into account the possibility of his dying and leaving his audience behind in this life in Phil 1:20–26 and 2 Cor 4:16–5:10.

[92] The absence of any mention of miracles in Josephus' account of the Baptist (*Ant.* 18.5.2 §116–19) is striking because, in the same book of the *Antiquities* (18.3.3 §63), one of the first descriptions Josephus applies to Jesus is *paradoxōn ergōn poiētēs* ("a doer

of startling deeds"). The use of *paradoxa . . . erga* of Elisha (*Ant.* 9.7.6 §182) confirms the sense of miracles worked by a prophet. The contrast implicit in the presentations of Josephus and the Synoptics is made explicit by the observation of the "many" who are attracted to Jesus in John 10:41: "On the one hand, John worked no sign; on the other, everything that John said about this man [Jesus] is true." This follows a debate between Jesus and the Jerusalem authorities in which Jesus appeals to the "many good works" that he has performed. In the larger context of chap. 10, this alludes in particular to the healing of the man born blind (chap. 9), recalled in 10:21.

The multiple attestation of sources that suggests that John was not thought by his contemporaries to have worked miracles during his ministry is overlooked by John M. Hull, *Hellenistic Magic and the Synoptic Tradition* (SBT 2/28; London: SCM, 1974) 105. It is astounding that Hull rests his claim that John was thought to have worked miracles largely on the prophecy of the angel Gabriel during his appearance to Zechariah in the temple in Luke 1:17 ("And he shall go before him in the spirit and power of Elijah . . ."). Needless to say, prophecies spoken by angels in apparitions in Infancy Narratives do not provide the most solid historical sources for the activity of the historical Baptist. Moreover, whatever the sources of Luke's Infancy Narrative, Gabriel's speech in its present form has probably been shaped by Luke's redactional activity; see Brown, *Birth of the Messiah*, 279. In any event, the reference to the spirit and power of Elijah is explained in 1:17 in terms of preparing God's people Israel for the Messiah by way of conversion and reconciliation; nothing hints of the idea of miracles. On the whole question see Ernst Bammel, " 'John Did No Miracle,' " C. F. D. Moule (ed.), *Miracles. Cambridge Studies in Their Philosophy and History* (London: Mowbray; New York: Morehouse-Barlow, 1965) 181–202. On p. 187, Bammel grants that certainty in the matter is not to be had, but then concludes: "Probably, the statement of John 10.41 is in agreement with the facts. . . ."

[93] Some critics declare it unthinkable that the Baptist would address a question like "Are you the coming one?" to Jesus. But their objection rests upon too narrow and fixed an understanding of John's preaching and prophecy in Matt 3:7–12 par. This is the problem, e.g., with the objection of Kraeling (*John the Baptist*, 129): "There is for John no possible meeting-ground between the wonder-working preacher of the Kingdom and the transcendent 'man-like one' who destroys the wicked in unquenchable fire, save on the assumption of a break with his fundamental convictions, for which there is no adequate justification." This presumes that the Baptist had had a clear conception of the one to come as a transcendent Son of Man. As we saw in Chapter 12, the prophecy of John seems much more open-ended and perhaps purposefully vague. Kraeling also dismisses in too cavalier a fashion the possibility that John's altered circumstances could have led him to rethink his position. It is surprising to see how often Kraeling's view and even his very words are repeated by later critics with no probing of the validity of his assertions; see, e.g., Sato, *Q und Prophetie*, 141. I am puzzled by Kloppenborg's objection to authenticity (*Formation*, 107): "The story deliberately invokes Baptist expectations in its use of the title 'the Coming One,' but infuses the title with specifically Christian content. There is no indication that John expected a miracle worker." That is just the point: John's expectations have been challenged by Jesus, and John is now probing the new situation he had not foreseen. In all this, I do not see "specifically Christian content."

[94] On all this, see Kümmel, *Promise and Fulfilment*, 110–11. For a brief argument in favor of the historicity of Matt 11:2–6 par., see Scobie, *John the Baptist*, 144. For a thorough application of the various criteria of historicity to the passage, see Wink, "Jesus' Reply to John," 121–27. While I agree with most of Wink's conclusions on

historicity, I do not accept the larger theological conclusions he draws from his exegetical work.

[95] The reference to lepers may reflect the story of the cleansing of Naaman the Syrian by Elisha in 2 Kings 5. This would fit in with the Elijah-Elisha atmosphere that pervades a great deal of the Baptist-Jesus material. If this be true, then other echoes of the Elijah-Elisha cycle might be found in Jesus' reply: e.g., the raising of the dead could allude to 1 Kgs 17:17–24; 2 Kgs 4:18–37; 13:20–21. Yet the very fact that we must go searching outside the books of the classical writing prophets for an allusion to the cleansing of lepers (found in a narrative in what the Jewish canon calls the "former prophets") reminds us that Jesus is first of all speaking of what he has done and only secondarily clothing it in scriptural language. In my view, references to the miracles of Elijah and Elisha in Matt 11:5 par. remain mere possibilities; I prefer not to build any grand theories on them.—Two other minor points concerning this list of miracles should be noted: (1) No mention is made of Jesus' exorcisms. The absence is puzzling, since they are referred to in both Mark and Q, as well as in special M and L material. Perhaps one of the purposes of the list—presenting Jesus' miracles as signs of the end time foretold and prefigured by the OT prophets—leads to their omission, since there is no prophecy of or story about an exorcism in the OT prophetic books. (2) While the allusions are to what we call the canonical OT, we should remember that healings as part of the salvation offered at the end time was a living idea in Jewish apocalyptic literature around the turn of the era; see, e.g., *Jub.* 1:29; 23:30; *1 Enoch* 96:3; *2 Apoc. Bar.* 29:7; 73:2. As Schulz points out quite bluntly (*Q. Die Spruchquelle der Evangelisten,* 198), there is no justification in the Q text for interpreting the miracles in some spiritualized sense or as some generic description of the end time. Jesus introduces his list of miracles by telling John's emissaries: "Go, tell John what you see and hear. . . ."

[96] While the emphasis in Jesus' answer lies on the "already," on what God is already doing to save Israel in these last days, the "not yet" is implied in the very fact that Jesus' message and ministry are nevertheless ambiguous even to so sincere a person as the Baptist and that Jesus must end his recital of his saving deeds with a plea that John believe, a plea that seems to go unanswered, a plea that contains a veiled eschatological warning.

[97] See Joachim Jeremias, *Jesus' Promise to the Nations* (SBT 1/24; rev. ed.; London: SCM, 1967) 46.

[98] On the day of the Lord in Amos, see Francis I. Andersen and David Noel Freedman, *Amos* (AB 24A; New York: Doubleday, 1989) 521–22. One cannot avoid the impression that the Baptist would have felt quite at home with Amos' message; Jesus is more at home with Isaiah's.

[99] This point is emphasized by Dibelius, *Die urchristliche Überlieferung,* 37; and, in a different way, by Jacques Dupont, "L'ambassade de Jean-Baptiste (Matthieu 11,2–6; Luc 7,18–23)," *NRT* 83 (1961) 805–21, 943–59, esp. 956. Dupont, however, uses the terms "messianic" and "Messiah" in his explanation; what is striking here is the total absence of such terminology.

[100] This is a suggestion made by Bultmann (*Geschichte,* 22), who thus misses the whole point of the shift in Jesus' answer.

[101] As Dupont points out ("L'ambassade de Jean-Baptiste," 952 n. 52), of the sixty-five beatitudes in the Greek Bible, only Matt 11:5 par. and Luke 14:14 are introduced by *kai* ("and"). There is a reason why such a grammatical connection is unusual. The distinct type of wisdom saying called a beatitude has the form of an exclamation; hence

it usually enjoys a certain grammatical independence. Here, though, the appeal to John that it launches is closely tied to the signs of the end time that should move him to believe in Jesus. One might almost translate this *kai* as "and so" or "and therefore."

[102] Even this small unit of Q (Matt 11:2–6) thus implies a complex picture of Jesus: he is a miracle-worker, a preacher of good news to the poor, an eschatological figure rivaling in some way John the Baptist, and a wisdom teacher (note the use of beatitudes here and elsewhere in Q).

[103] Witherington (*The Christology of Jesus*, 44) speaks of John "perhaps even losing confidence in him [Jesus]. To this Jesus replies in effect: blessed is the one who does not give up faith in me." This is perfectly true on the level of Matthew's redaction, but questionable on the level of the historical Jesus. On the latter level, there is no proof that John before his imprisonment ever had any "faith" in Jesus; and so there was no danger of giving it up. Rather, the question is whether the Baptist will, for the first time, come to faith in his former pupil or whether his shock and disappointment will prevent him from believing. That this is a possible meaning of the verb *skandalizō* is recognized by Gustav Stählin, "*skandalon, skandalizō,*" *TDNT* 7 (1971) 339–58, esp. 345: "The *skandalon* is an obstacle in coming to faith and a cause of going astray in it." Stählin goes on to observe: "When in the Gospels an *en tini* added to *skandalizomai* gives the reason for going astray or falling, the reference in each case is to Jesus, Mt. 26:31,33; 11:6 par. Lk. 7:23; Mt. 13:57 par. Mk. 6:3 . . ." (p. 349). Although Jesus' appeal to John is gentle and respectful, the use of *skandalizō* carries an ominous undertone: "Every beatitude and every woe . . . on the lips of Jesus is an eschatological judgment. . . . it is of decisive significance in the Last Judgment whether a man loses confidence in Him or not. . . . The present age [while an age of salvation] is also the age of decision. It offers two possibilities, that of faith and that of unbelief, and both in Jesus; for the presence and work of Jesus have the power to awaken faith but they can also result in the missing of faith" (p. 350). Thus, in an almost bizarre, ironic way, the use of *skandalizō* in this beatitude of Jesus conjures up two themes he inherited and retained from John: future eschatology and judgment. In Jesus' proclamation, future judgment and condemnation may take second place to the joy of salvation already present and soon to be fully realized, but they are still there.

[104] Here I would agree with Dupont ("L'ambassade de Jean-Baptiste," 952–53) over against Fitzmyer (*The Gospel According to Luke*, 1. 668), who thinks that the beatitude is "intended to be generic, as is made clear by the conj. *hos ean.* . . ." I would distinguish: grammatically, the construction is generic; but in the rhetorical situation the generic cast of the beatitude is a discreet veil thrown over a very pointed address. The poignancy of this beatitude is heightened when one remembers that elsewhere in the Q material Jesus congratulates those who do believe in him with a beatitude: "Happy the eyes that see what you see. For amen I say to you that many prophets and kings desired to see what you see, but they did not see it, and to hear what you hear, but they did not hear it" (Matt 13:16–17 ‖ Luke 10:23–24).

[105] This is a major weakness of the approach of Schulz (*Q. Die Spruchquelle der Evangelisten*, 192–203), who not only assigns the creation of this apophthegm to Q but also holds that it belongs to a later stratum of Q, when salvation was being attributed to the time of the earthly Jesus. Apart from the difficulty of seeing how a pericope that ends with an apparently unbelieving Baptist would help the church in its apologetic-polemic dialogue with Baptist sectarians, Schulz's reconstruction suffers from the larger problem encompassing his whole project. In my view, to posit two distinct "Q communities" whose preaching and teaching are summed up in the Q document, to presume

further that one can distinguish stages of tradition and redaction in Q, each with its own coherent christology and eschatology, and finally to claim enough knowledge to assign a tradition to the earlier Q community on the border of Palestine and Syria or to the later Q community of Syria is to go beyond what we can know of Q and to indulge in highly speculative hypotheses. Schulz's treatment of Matt 11:2–6 par. points up another difficulty in his mode of argumentation. It is one thing to show how a piece of tradition might have been used or adapted (as best that tradition allowed) to fit into some theological interest of Q; it is another thing to show that the most plausible hypothesis is that the author(s) of Q had precise reasons to create a given tradition.

[106] For the different ways in which John's question to Jesus has been interpreted—often with a view to softening its disturbing implications—see Dupont, "L'ambassade de Jean-Baptiste," 806–13. For an interpretation of John's question similar to my own, see Hughes, "John the Baptist," 203–9.

[107] Dibelius, *Die urchristliche Überlieferung*, 37. My only reservation about Dibelius's view is his freewheeling use of the word "Messiah," a term that needs careful explanation. As Witherington (*The Christology of Jesus*, 44) observes: "The evidence that in early Judaism the Messiah was expected to be a healer is slender."

Jeremias (*New Testament Theology*, 20–25) claims that the reply of Jesus in Matt 11:5–6 par. reflects a common speech pattern of Jesus in Aramaic: a line with a two-beat rhythm (in this case, six of them in v 5), followed by one three-beat line in v 6. According to Jeremias, the two-beat rhythm urgently impresses upon the hearer the central ideas of Jesus' message, while the three-beat line reflects a wisdom background. As I explained when I treated criteria of authenticity in Chapter 6, this sort of "Aramaic argument" can at best serve only as a secondary criterion. It can be useful only if—as in our present case—the authenticity of the material is probable on other grounds. After all, Jesus was not the only gifted, Aramaic-speaking teacher among Jews and Christians in 1st-century Palestine. Presumably the permanent disciples of Jesus, traveling with and learning from him for about two years, would have picked up some of his speaking and teaching techniques. Since we have already accepted the authenticity of the core of Matt 11:2–6 par. on other grounds, I am happy to acknowledge the corroborating evidence that Jeremias supplies. However, the ambiguity of such evidence can be seen from the fact that Sato (*Q und Prophetie*, 143) uses the poetic structure of Matt 11:5 par. as an argument against its coming from Jesus! The tendency of Sato to use apodictic statements instead of engaging his opponents in debate is obvious from the fact that Jeremias's position is simply never considered.

[108] On this see Lührmann, *Die Redaktion der Logienquelle*, 26.

[109] The very fact that this tradition was later preserved in Q and then in Matthew and Luke shows that the early church found a use for it in its preaching, apologetics, and polemics (e.g., dialogue and debate with Baptist sectarians). But Matt 11:2–6 par. is a striking reminder that to suggest or discern the *Sitz im Leben* of a pericope in the life of the early church is not to prove that such a *Sitz im Leben* was the original *Sitz im Leben* of the material. Hence the question that concerns us throughout this book is not whether a pericope had a *Sitz im Leben* in the early church; by definition, its inclusion in a Gospel makes it very likely that it did. The question is whether there are indications that the tradition had an earlier *Sitz im Leben* in the life of Jesus. At least in the case of Matt 11:2–6, such indications are clearly present. Hence I must disagree with the judgment of Ernst (*Johannes der Täufer*, 315–19), who, though hesitant, prefers the view that Matt 11:2–6 par. is a creation of the early church. A similar view—presented with only sketchy arguments—can be found in A. George, "Paroles de Jésus sur ses miracles

(Mt 11,5.21; 12,27.28 et par.)," *Jésus aux origines de la christologie* (BETL 40; 2d ed.; ed. J. Dupont; Leuven: Leuven University/Peeters, 1989) 283–301, esp. 290–92. This view seems all the stranger when one remembers that even the skeptical Bultmann (*Geschichte*, 163) allowed that at least the beatitude in Matt 11:6 par., reflecting Jesus' prophetic consciousness and containing no specifically Christian tone, came from Jesus himself. Although Sato (*Q und Prophetie*, 141) opposes a number of Bultmann's judgments about this pericope, he does follow him to the extent of judging the beatitude older than the rest of the apophthegm. However, he does not justify this literary amputation with any detailed argument.

[110] In a letter to me (dated April 29, 1992), David Noel Freedman tries to hammer out his own "middle position" between these two extremes. Freedman suggests that the point at issue in Matt 11:2–6 par. is the question of who will be the replacement or successor for John in the Baptist movement once John is imprisoned (and later executed). As this question arises among the Baptist's followers, Jesus "discovers something about himself . . . , namely that he can do something that John couldn't, perform miracles." According to Freedman, Jesus' initial intention was not to create a new movement, but to lead the Baptist movement—with a notable difference. The new element was the performing of miracles, which cast Jesus in a Moses-Elijah-Elisha light. More importantly, it indicated that Jesus, unlike John, was not merely proclaiming an imminent end but was actually initiating the kingdom of God during his ministry. This in turn naturally led to a greater emphasis on the joyful aspect of Jesus' message and deeds. In effect, the startling new element of miracles and the emphasis on the joy of salvation already present meant that Jesus could not be just another John. As things turned out, Jesus succeeded in getting only some of John's followers to come with him, while others went a different way, keeping the framework of John's message.

While there is much that is attractive in Freedman's reconstruction, there are also a number of difficulties. (1) As Freedman himself admits, there is a certain element of "psychologizing" that belongs back with the 19th-century "liberal lives" of Jesus: e.g., at a certain point after the Baptist's arrest Jesus discovered he could perform miracles and this led him to a view of the kingdom as partially present. The basic problem is that such psychologizing—as well as the exact time frame within which a chain of events supposedly takes place—is simply not open to any sort of verification. All sorts of psychologizing scenarios enjoy a certain verisimilitude, and there is no way to adjudicate competing claims. (2) Freedman's scenario suggests that Jesus did not undertake any distinctive ministry of his own until after John was arrested. I have argued above that the "embarrassing" and "discontinuous" material in the Fourth Gospel makes it more likely that Jesus struck out on his own while the Baptist was still active and that for a while each pursued his own distinctive—and perhaps rival—ministry. (3) Freedman must place the material in Matt 11:2–6 par. at a particular critical juncture, i.e., soon after the Baptist has been arrested and before Jesus has fully contoured his special type of ministry. Yet the original context for the core material in Matt 11:2–6 par. is disputed. While some reject the reference to John's being imprisoned as a secondary element, I am willing, along with many exegetes, to accept it as the historical *Sitz im Leben* for the questions that the disciples of John put to Jesus. However, I think that by this time Jesus had long since been active in his own characteristic ministry, a ministry that had shown him to be something more than just a replacement or successor for John.

[111] The reason why the five logia can be analyzed into three questions and three explanations is that the answer to the third question is also the first correct explanation.

[112] Convenience is not the only reason for using the verse enumeration from Mat-

thew's Gospel: (1) As a number of writers on Q note, Matthew appears in this unit to be more faithful, on the whole, to the original wording of Q; so, e.g., Hoffmann, *Studien*, 194; Ernst, *Johannes der Täufer*, 61. (2) This leads me to a second observation. As most critics of Q emphasize, Luke more often than Matthew seems to retain the order and wording of Q. Hence a number of commentators on Q simply take over the chapter-and-verse enumeration of Luke to identify Q sayings (so, e.g., Kloppenborg in his *Q Parallels*; see p. xv). While the simplicity of this system has much to say for it, I am concerned that we can all too easily fall into a presumption that Luke always represents the more original wording of Q. The present unit reminds us that this is not always the case, as Kloppenborg carefully notes. Hence, simply to fight against critical inertia, I purposely designate Q material by such notations as Matt 11:7-11 ‖ Luke 7:24-28 or Matt 11:7-11 par. Needless to say, this should not be taken to mean that I think that Matthew usually preserves the more original wording of Q. He does not. Since practically no one thinks that he does, my system of notation will be less likely to lull us into an unexamined presumption as we study various Q sayings.

[113] Ernst, *Johannes der Täufer*, 61 n. 94; see also the tradition history suggested by Kloppenborg, *Formation*, 108-10.

[114] This point is pressed by Kraeling, *John the Baptist*, 138.

[115] Not only does Sato (*Q und Prophetie*, 240) argue from the content of 11:7b-9 par. to the authenticity of the material in the mouth of Jesus; he also points out that this authentic material is prime evidence for the authoritative "I say to you" (here organically embedded in 11:9c as the climax of the rhetorical ascent of the series of questions) as a usage of the historical Jesus. Sato goes on to observe that, since this "I say to you" usage is witnessed abundantly not only in Q but also in Mark, M, and L, the spread of frequent occurrences over the four major Synoptic sources would be unintelligible if Jesus himself had not used the formula frequently.

[116] For the concrete historical allusions that may stand behind the Q tradition in Matt 11:7-9 par. see Gerd Theissen, "Das 'schwankende Rohr' in Mt 11,7 und die Grundungsmünzen von Tiberias," *Lokalkolorit und Zeitgeschichte in den Evangelien. Ein Beitrag zur Geschichte der synoptischen Tradition* (Novum Testamentum et Orbis Antiquus 8; Freiburg: Universitätsverlag; Göttingen: Vandenhoeck & Ruprecht, 1989) 26-44. Theissen's argument about Antipas' coins may strike some as highly speculative, and I would not want to insist on the details of his thesis. However, it does seem likely to me that, given the Baptist's arrest by the tetrarch and the probability that Jesus' words would have been spoken during John's imprisonment or after his execution (note how John already sounds like a figure of the past), the reference to a man clothed in luxurious garments in the houses of kings—mentioned precisely as a counterimage to John—would naturally conjure up in the minds of a Galilean audience the figure of Antipas. (The use of the plural, "the houses of kings," might be a case of studied and prudent vagueness on Jesus' part.) And once we grant that Antipas is alluded to in the second rhetorical answer, it becomes possible to see an allusion to him in the first as well, whatever one may think of the evidence from Antipas' coins.—As an aside, it may be noted that there is no problem in seeing an allusion to Antipas in the phrase "the houses of kings," even though Antipas technically was only a tetrarch, never a king like his father Herod the Great. Harold W. Hoehner (*Herod Antipas* [SNTSMS 17; Cambridge: Cambridge University, 1972] 149-51) makes a good case for "king" being a title used of Antipas in popular speech or out of courtesy.

[117] So, e.g., Lührmann, *Redaktion*, 27; Hoffmann, *Studien*, 216-18. Those who hold the opposite view include Ernst (*Johannes der Täufer*, 60-63), who does not even in-

clude a consideration of these verses in the section of his book dealing with a reconstruction of the historical John the Baptist. As further support for the authenticity of
11:7–9 par. some might want to appeal to the supposedly independent attestation in
the Coptic *Gospel of Thomas* (saying #78, in the translation of Bentley Layton, *The
Gnostic Scriptures* [Garden City, NY: Doubleday, 1987] 394): "Jesus said, 'Why have
you [plural] come out into the countryside? To see a reed shaken by the wind? And to
see a person dressed in fine apparel [like your] governors [or: kings, emperors] and
members of court, who wear fine apparel and cannot recognize the truth?' " In my
view, this saying is a prime example of why the sayings tradition in the *Gospel of Thomas*
often, if not always, seem secondary vis-à-vis the canonical Gospels. The direct historical reference to John the Baptist preaching in the desert is given up in favor of a vague
polemic against the rich and powerful of this world, who lack the true knowledge enjoyed by the gnostic. Likewise lost is the neat, taut three-step rhetorical structure of
question and counterquestion. The fact that a concrete saying about John the Baptist
has been recycled to inculcate gnostic teaching is obvious from the last words: ". . . and
cannot recognize the truth?"

[118] The various Greek forms of this phrase (with the verb *graphō*) are listed in Joseph
A. Fitzmyer, "The Use of Explicit Old Testament Quotations in Qumran Literature
and in the New Testament," *Essays on the Semitic Background of the New Testament*
(SBLSBS 5; Missoula, MT: Scholars, 1974, originally 1971) 3–58, esp. 9. He does not
list the intricate form we treat here, probably because no exact parallel exists in the
Qumran literature.

[119] For standard treatments of the Matthean "Reflexionszitate" or formula quotations, see Krister Stendahl, *The School of St. Matthew* (Acta Seminarii Neotestamentici
Upsaliensis 20; 2d ed.; Lund: Gleerup, 1968); Robert Gundry, *The Use of the Old Testament in St. Matthew's Gospel* (NovTSup 18; Leiden: Brill, 1967); R. S. McConnell, *Law
and Prophecy in Matthew's Gospel* (Theologische Dissertationen 2; Basel: F. Reinhardt
Kommissionsverlag, 1969); W. Rothfuch, *Die Erfüllungszitate des Matthäus-Evangeliums*
(BWANT 88; Stuttgart: Kohlhammer, 1969); George M. Soares Prabhu, *The Formula
Quotations in the Infancy Narrative of Matthew* (AnBib 63; Rome: Biblical Institute,
1976).

[120] The case is not totally clear, since Matt 11:10c could also be influenced by Exod
23:20: "Behold, I am sending my angel before you to guard you along the way." For
the many problems connected with Matt 11:10 par. and the various theories concerning
them, see Stendahl, *The School of St. Matthew*, 49–54. Some scholars claim that the
conflation seen here is of pre-Christian Jewish origin. That is certainly possible, but
the texts in which we find such a conflation are post-Christian. Even if the conflation
is pre-Christian, that fact does not tell us whether it was first used by Jesus or by a
Christian scribe.

[121] As a matter of fact, this is the judgment of most exegetes; see Ernst, *Johannes der
Täufer*, 61 n. 94. However, Hughes ("John the Baptist," 211) defends the use of Mal
3:1 as coming from Jesus. Focusing more on the tradition history of Q, Kloppenborg
(*Formation*, 108 n. 29) states that "the intrusive character of Q 7:27 [= Matt 11:10 par.]
is widely recognized. While 7:24–26 [=Matt 11:7–9] declares that John is greater than
a prophet, 7:27 places him in the role of Elijah. . . .' "

[122] See, e.g., the view of the origin and development of 11:11 in Dibelius, *Die urchristliche Überlieferung*, 12–15, 121 n.1. Dibelius operates under a number of questionable assumptions: e.g., that Jesus viewed the kingdom as purely future and therefore
would not have spoken of it as present. Others who think v 11b is an addition by

the early church to an authentic saying of Jesus include Bultmann, *Geschichte*, 177–78; Kraeling, *John the Baptist*, 138; Hoffmann, *Studien*, 219–20.

[123] This point is well made by Schulz (*Q. Die Spruchquelle der Evangelisten*, 233), who also notes the parallel with rabbinic discussions on being small and great in this age and the age to come (see n. 378). As usual, Schulz, while defending the unity of the logion, proceeds to ascribe its origin not to Jesus but to the "Q community" at a second stage of its existence. His observation in n. 378 is revealing: the supposition that this verse is to be ascribed to the preaching of Jesus himself is unlikely; but this supposition is "for our context indeed also without significance. . . ." Here Schulz unwittingly touches on one of the unspoken problems of a work that focuses so minutely on Q and its hypothetical communities and stages of tradition. Given the fierce desire for exactitude in assigning material to this or that stage of Q, there is a subtle built-in bias against ascribing material to the historical Jesus.

[124] The usual translation masks the fact that the two prepositions are parallel: *en gennētois gynaikōn meizōn* and *en tȩ basileia tōn ouranōn meizōn*.

[125] So Hoffmann, *Studien*, 194; similarly Schulz, *Q. Die Spruchquelle der Evangelisten*, 229–30; Jacques Schlosser, *Le règne de Dieu dans les dits de Jésus* (EBib; 2 vols.; Paris: Gabalda, 1980) 1. 158–59. Hoffmann suggests that the three Matthean redactional traits in this verse are the initial "Amen," the addition of "the Baptist," and the use of "heaven" instead of "God." On the whole, though, he thinks that Matthew may have preserved the more original form of the Q saying.

[126] Brown (*The Gospel According to John*, 1. 161) comments: "The 'no one' is not categorical, as the next verse (33) shows." For similar examples of this dialectical way of developing an idea, see John 1:11–12; 8:15–16; 12:37 + 42. To appeal to a different source or stage of redaction for every instance is contrived.

[127] Using different terminology, Jeremias sees Matt 11:11 par. as an example of antithetic parallelism, which he specifies in the case of 11:11 as "the combination of an opposition with a negation" (*New Testament Theology*, 14–16); similarly, Schlosser, *Le règne*, 1. 160. On p. 17 Jeremias points out that "all four strata of the synoptic tradition [Mark, Q, M, and L] are unanimous in attesting that Jesus frequently used antithetic parallelism. It is still more important that this parallelism is distributed approximately equally among the sayings of Jesus in the four strata."

[128] Its appearance in the mouth of the Baptist in Matt 3:2 is obviously due to Matthew's redaction of Mark 1:4 (John's proclamation) and Mark 1:14–15 (Jesus' proclamation). The transfer of Jesus' proclamation to the Baptist fits perfectly Matthew's redactional tendency to make John and Jesus parallel figures. Hence they proclaim the same message in Matt 3:2 and 4:17 respectively (see Meier, "John the Baptist," 388). For basic statistics on the phrase "kingdom of God [or heaven]" on the lips of Jesus in the Gospels, see Jeremias, *Theology of the New Testament*, 31–35. For the argument over whether the kingdom is seen in this verse as future or present, see Schlosser, *Le règne*, 1. 162–64.

[129] This is the position of Becker, *Johannes der Täufer*, 75; Schlosser, *Le règne*, 1. 160–61. Becker interprets Matt 11:11 par. to mean that the past had no one greater to offer than John, but in relation to the new he is clearly part of the past. Kloppenborg (*Formation*, 109) defends the unity of 11:11 and leaves open the possibility of its origin from Jesus. However, as part of his argument Kloppenborg calls upon *Gos. Thom.* saying #46. As I indicated in Chapter 5, I do not view the *Gospel of Thomas* as an independent source for Jesus' sayings. A glance at saying #46 confirms this stance: "Jesus said:

From Adam unto John the Baptist there has been none among the offspring of women who has been more exalted than John the Baptist, so that such a person's eyes might be broken [? possibly: should be averted]. But I have said that whoever among you [plural] becomes a little one [or: a child] will know the kingdom, and will become more exalted than John." We have here an expansive paraphrase, inserting the gnostic leitmotif of saving knowledge (the kingdom becoming its object), mention of Adam (perhaps reworking Matthew's "from the days of John the Baptist until now" in Matt 11:12), a repetition of the introductory "I say" from Matt 11:9 + 11, and a reduplication of the title "the Baptist," which is probably a Matthean addition to begin with. More to the point, a terse and carefully balanced two-part logion has been stretched out of shape and made nigh unintelligible.

[130] Some critics (e.g., Schlosser, Le règne, 1. 162) suggest that the word "in" in the phrase "in the kingdom of God" reflects the Hebrew/Aramaic bĕ in its causal sense: "As for the most insignificant person, because of the kingdom of God he is greater than John." While this is possible, I see no reason not to take "in the kingdom of God" in its usual sense, which is perfectly intelligible in this verse.

[131] See, e.g., Lührmann, Redaktion, 27; Ernst, Johannes der Täufer, 62–63. Ernst gives mikroteroi the narrow sense of the new prophets active in the Q community, who are declared superior not only to the OT prophets but also to the Baptist.

[132] I have omitted a consideration of an alternate understanding of mikroteros (translated as "least" in my text) because in itself the alternate understanding does not decide the question of authenticity and because it could conceivably fit any of the theories I have surveyed. From the time of the Church Fathers onwards, some have suggested that mikroteros, which is strictly speaking a comparative form of the adjective, should be understood as a true comparative ("the lesser of two"), rather than as a superlative ("the least"). The question then arises as to whom "the lesser" refers. Following one line of patristic interpretation, some modern critics have championed the view that mikroteros refers to Jesus as the person "lesser" in the sense of "younger" than John or a disciple of John. On this see Franz Dibelius, "Zwei Worte Jesu," ZNW 11 (1910) 188–92, esp. 190–92; Oscar Cullmann, "ho opisō mou erchomenos," The Early Church (Philadelphia: Westminster, 1956) 177–82; idem, The Christology of the New Testament (Philadelphia: Westminster, 1959) 32; Schlosser, Le règne, 1. 164–66. Hoffmann (Studien, 220–24) adopts this approach, although he thinks 11:11b is a later addition to the authentic 11:11a.

While this interpretation is theoretically possible, there are a number of difficulties, especially if we are asking about the sense of the logion in the mouth of the historical Jesus. (1) The idea that Jesus is "younger" than the Baptist is contained nowhere in the NT except for the Lucan Infancy Narrative, chap. 1. Since the idea of Jesus' being a younger relative of John is of doubtful historicity, and since there is no indication that such a Lucan concept ever existed in the Q material (indeed, it has no further impact on Luke's own presentation of John and Jesus), to appeal to such an idea to explain Matt 11:11 par. is highly questionable. To employ mikroteros to describe Jesus as a disciple of John would also be a strange usage in the NT. (2) Even if we accepted such an interpretation of mikroteros, it is extremely difficult to explain how such an idea functions in Matt 11:11 and a fortiori within the flow of the larger context of the second Baptist-block of Q. (3) To support his interpretation, Cullmann (Christology, 24, 32) wants to read "in the kingdom of heaven" with "is greater" rather than with "the least." While that is possible, the word order favors taking "in the kingdom of heaven" with the immediately preceding "least"; this is in fact the interpretation of most modern English translations. On this point, see Kloppenborg, Formation, 109 n. 32. (4) The comparative interpretation of *mikroteros* is by no means demanded by the grammar of Hellenistic Greek in general or NT Greek in particular. In koine Greek the superlative form of adjectives tended to disappear, its function being taken over by the comparative form; see BDF §60; C. F. D. Moule, *An Idiom-Book of New Testament Greek* (Cambridge: Cambridge University, 1960) 97–98. As a matter of fact, the Bauer-Aland *Wörterbuch* (col. 1055) gives Matt 11:11 as an example of this usage (see Luke 9:48 for another example). Not surprisingly, the translations of Luther, the *KJV*, Goodspeed, the *NEB*, the revised *JB*, the revised *NAB* NT, and the new *RSV* all adopt the understanding of *mikroteros* as a superlative.

[133] For the weighing of differences, see Ernst, *Johannes der Täufer*, 72–73; the fact that Ernst locates the more original reading at one moment in Matthew and the next in Luke reminds us that we should not presume that either evangelist is the guaranteed conduit of the original Q tradition.

[134] Jesus' use of "this generation" (without as well as with further descriptive adjectives) as a pejorative way of speaking of his unbelieving contemporaries is witnessed in a number of texts of both the Marcan and Q tradition, with possible examples in M and L as well. By comparison, the simple "this generation" with a pejorative sense is practically absent from the rest of the NT, the only other example (Heb 3:10) being part of a lengthy formal quotation of LXX Ps 94:7–11. This points in the direction of an authentic usage of the historical Jesus. Bultmann (*Geschichte*, 186) thinks that the double rhetorical question in Luke is original; so too Hoffmann, *Studien*, 196; Ernst (*Johannes der Täufer*, 72), who considers it a sign of Semitic influence. Similarly, Dibelius considers the doubling of the question to be a trait of Q and therefore considers Matthew's single question to be secondary (*Die urchristliche Überlieferung*, 15); however, he thinks that Matthew may have preserved the more original form of the parable. One is reminded how difficult it is to reach any certainty on these minor variants in Q and how dangerous it is to hang a whole position on any such decision.

[135] Friedrich Büchsel, "*genea*, etc.," *TDNT* 1 (1964) 662–65, esp. 663.

[136] This is the position, e.g., of Arens, *The ēlthon-Sayings*, 222–23, 242–43. His arguments on pp. 222–23 are surprisingly brief and not very cogent. The facile and questionable distinction between "Hellenistic" and "Palestinian" elements surfaces frequently in his treatment. Further, he does not seem to conceive of the possibility that sayings of Jesus might at times have been translated into Greek by persons with a good command of Greek, who would naturally use ordinary Greek words and phrases. The verdict of authenticity is made to depend too much on having wooden translations that exactly reflect a hypothetical Aramaic substratum. Schulz (*Q. Die Spruchquelle der Evangelisten*, 381) typifies a regrettable habit among exegetes. In telegraphic style he lists in about four lines the five reasons of Bultmann and other critics for rejecting the original unity of Matt 11:16–19 par. and thinks that is sufficient argumentation. Schulz is willing to consider the possibility that the original parable comes from Jesus, but the application comes (according to him) from the later Hellenistic Jewish-Christian stage of Q.

[137] Norman Perrin, hardly an uncritical quester, is quite strong in his judgment (*Rediscovering the Teaching of Jesus* [New Testament Library; London: SCM, 1967] 121): ". . . there is no doubt but that the parable and its application have belonged together in the tradition from the very beginning. . . . both are certainly from Jesus, and the comparison between them is so apt and striking that it is impossible to imagine that they ever belonged, separately, to other bits of tradition now lost, or that they were originally independent units which were brought together only in the tradition." For

arguments for the original unity of parable and application, see also Franz Mussner, "Der nicht erkannte Kairos (Mt 11,16–19 = Lk 7,31–35)," *Bib* 40 (1959) 599–612. Kloppenborg (*Formation*, 110) argues against the original unity of parable and application. He points out that the application involves allegorization and that the order of John first and then the Son of Man in the application "does not accord" with the order of the verbs in the parable. As we shall see, neither objection is probative.

[138] Bultmann, *Geschichte*, 186.

[139] Adolf Jülicher, *Die Gleichnisreden Jesu* (2 vols.; Tübingen: Mohr [Siebeck], 1888, 1899).

[140] On this point see Raymond E. Brown, "Parable and Allegory Reconsidered," *New Testament Essays* (Garden City, NY: Doubleday [Image Books], 1968, originally 1965) 321–33; Hans-Josef Klauck, *Allegorie und Allegorese in synoptischen Gleichnistexten* (NTAbh 13; Münster: Aschendorff, 1978); Charles E. Carlston, "Parable and Allegory Revisited: An Interpretive Review," *CBQ* 43 (1981) 228–42; John Drury, *The Parables in the Gospels. History and Allegory* (New York: Crossroad, 1985); John R. Donahue, *The Gospel in Parable* (Philadelphia: Fortress, 1988) 11–13.

[141] Failing to come to grips with this fact weakens the presentation of Arens, *The ēlthon-Sayings*, 221–48.

[142] This sense is suggested by Matthew's use of *heterois* ("to the others") in 11:16. Joachim Jeremias (*The Parables of Jesus* [New Testament Library; rev. ed.; London: SCM, 1963] 161) adds to the colorful concreteness of the scene by observing that, according to Jewish custom, the boys (= men) would be involved in the wedding dance, while the girls (= women) would be involved in the funeral dirge. Whether the statements of later rabbinic literature about weddings and funerals can really tell us what children in early 1st-century Galilee would do or not do in their games remains unclear; more to the point, the male-female question does not affect the interpretation of the parable and seems to be just an attempt by Jeremias to throw in a little local color. Jeremias also suggests (p. 160 n. 37) that there is an underlying wordplay and rhyme in the original Aramaic, though here he must rely on the later Syriac versions: *raqqēdtûn* ("you danced") and *'arqedtûn* ("you lamented"). Jeremias thinks that *'arqedtûn* may be the source of both Matthew's "you did not beat your breasts" and Luke's "you did not weep."

[143] This understanding is suggested by Luke's use of *allēlois* ("to one another") in 7:32.

[144] For example, Hoffmann (*Studien*, 226) uses the same detail of sitting to support his thesis that it is the sitting children who do not play and so waste time.

[145] For a slightly different way of listing the alternatives in interpretation, see Dieter Zeller, "Die Bildlogik des Gleichnisses Mt 11:16f./Lk 7:31f.," *ZNW* 68 (1977) 252–57. He notes that, in the history of interpretation, the generation that Jesus rebukes has been identified with the children who call to the others, the others who refuse to play, and both groups of children. In any case, the strongly negative meaning of "this generation" in the sayings of Jesus makes it very improbable, in my view, that the parable originally referred to the followers of John and the followers of Jesus, who had been exchanging recriminations (this interpretation is mentioned, but not adopted, by Fitzmyer, *The Gospel According to Luke*, 1. 678). "This generation" regularly denotes those who reject Jesus or who are hostile to him.

[146] The presence or absence of "the Baptist" in the original form of the Q sayings is

difficult to decide. Arguing that Luke tends to omit *ho baptistēs* when he finds it in his sources, Arens (*The ēlthon-Sayings*, 226) favors its presence in Q. I agree with him; Matthew probably omits the title here because he has used it recently in both 11:11 and 11:12. Schulz, however, thinks Luke has added "the Baptist" here (*Q. Die Spruchquelle der Evangelisten*, 379–80).

[147] With Ernst (*Johannes der Täufer*, 73), I consider Luke's "neither eating bread nor drinking wine" to be a secondary expansion; so too Arens, *The ēlthon-Sayings*, 226. As I have already indicated, the attempt by Böcher to preserve the longer reading as original ("Ass Johannes der Täufer kein Brot?" 90–92) is contrived and rests on the uncontrolled use of many later sources.

[148] See, e.g., Dibelius (*Die urchristliche Überlieferung*, 18), who is followed by Hoffmann, *Studien*, 224–25. See also the list of objections in Ernst, *Johannes der Täufer*, 73–74, who in turn is dependent on Schulz, *Q. Die Spruchquelle der Evangelisten*, 381. Many of the objections to the original unity of parable and application rest on questionable presuppositions: (1) The correspondence between the two could be only by way of direct parallelism and not chiastic structure; (2) Jesus' parables can have only one simple point and cannot have allegorical traits (the heritage of Jülicher!); (3) Jesus would never give an explanation or application of a parable (unlike, say, the prophet Nathan?); (4) the use of "Son of Man" shows that the application must be secondary (as though all agreed on what Son of Man means and what its origin is); (5) the final remark about divine Wisdom is surely secondary (whether it is or not, that does not decide the question for the main part of the application). When Kloppenborg (*Formation*, 111) objects that the application "fits so artificially with the parable. . . ," one can only observe that artificiality is often in the eye of the beholder. It is interesting, by the way, to note how those exegetes who separate parable and application cannot agree which is primary in the tradition (Kloppenborg, ibid.).

[149] Like the "eater and wine-drinker" that describes the Son of Man, "neither eating nor drinking" must be understood as a compressed, laconic phrase. Obviously John had to eat and drink something; the sweeping negation simply emphasizes the extreme asceticism of his diet. As opposed to Jesus, he enjoyed neither the food of a banquet nor the wine that went with it.

[150] Viewed simply from the viewpoint of etymology, all the words *phagos kai oinopotēs* need mean are "eater and wine-drinker." It is the sharp antithetic parallelism to the exaggerated "neither eating nor drinking" that confirms, in this mocking polemical context, the hostile sense of "glutton and drunkard." Even apart from these verses, Palestinian people of poor or moderate means would tend to identify regular drinking of wine—so regular that the person in question became known for it in public—with both affluence and indulgence.

[151] On the identity of toll collectors and the reasons why they were disliked by fellow Jews, see John R. Donahue, "Tax Collectors and Sinners. An Attempt at Identification," *CBQ* 33 (1971) 39–61. According to Donahue, the toll collectors of the Gospels are not Jews "who made themselves like Gentiles" and hence traitors. They are rather Jews who are disliked by their fellow Jews because they are held to be dishonest. Jesus is therefore scorned because he regularly associates with dishonest people, at least in Galilee (where this tradition is laid). However, in Judea and Jerusalem, under direct Roman rule, toll collectors might have been viewed as traitors.

[152] This is the definition proposed by E. P. Sanders, *Jesus and Judaism* (Philadelphia: Fortress, 1985) 177. I am indebted to Sanders for the remarks that follow in the text

about sinners. Nevertheless, in view of Donahue's work ("Tax Collectors and Sinners"), Sanders may put the two categories of sinners and toll collectors together too quickly under the rubric of "they were all traitors" (p. 178).

[153] See Sanders's chapter on "The Sinners" in *Jesus and Judaism*, 174–211. James D. G. Dunn has criticized Sanders's views on the categories of "Pharisees" and "sinners" in his "Pharisees, Sinners and Jesus," *The Social World of Formative Christianity and Judaism* (Howard Clark Kee Festschrift; ed. Jacob Neusner et al.; Philadelphia: Fortress, 1988) 264–89. While Dunn's point about the relative reliability of Mark's portrayal of the Pharisees deserves consideration, I think that his critique of Sanders's views on "sinners" is weak.

[154] On this, see Sanders, *Jesus and Judaism*, 206–8. I would not be as sure as Sanders is that the vocabulary of repentance was notably absent from Jesus' proclamation. It may well be that Jesus reformulated repentance in terms of accepting his message and himself. In this connection, one would like to know whether Jesus baptized those who accepted his message, baptism thus being for him as for John a sign of repentance. Unfortunately, the Synoptic tradition, which is the source of our knowledge about these "tax collectors and sinners" around Jesus, has suppressed any idea of Jesus' baptizing ministry, and so there is no way of knowing. At the very least, though, if one speaks (as Sanders does) of Jesus not demanding that the sinners who accepted him go through the usual process of repentance, one should reckon with the possibility that Jesus, in effect, had redefined repentance in terms of following him and his teaching, which may have included accepting baptism from him.

[155] According to Jeremias (*Parables*, 160), the accusation "an eater and a wine-drinker" echoes Deut 21:20: *zôlēl wĕsōbēʾ*. If it does, the seriousness of the accusation becomes clearer. Deut 21:18–21 treats of a stubborn and unruly son. He is so disobedient to his father and mother that they accuse him before the town elders: "He is a glutton [or, more generally, a wanton person] and a drunkard." The penalty prescribed is death by stoning at the hands of the townspeople. Against the background of John's imprisonment (and possible execution), such an accusation against Jesus could have very ominous overtones. However, the allusion is not certain. Fitzmyer (*The Gospel According to Luke*, 1. 681) points out that the LXX translates Deut 21:20 differently: *symbolokopōn oinophlygei* ("given to feasting, he is drunk"). Yet, while the translation of the LXX has a bearing on whether there is an intentional allusion in Q or Luke, it really does not affect the question of whether there was an allusion in the accusation when it was first raised and repeated by Jesus in Aramaic.

[156] For the remarks that follow, see Sanders, *Jesus and Judaism*, 174.

[157] Hoffmann, *Studien*, 227–28.

[158] It is telling that even Arens (*The ēlthon-Sayings*, 242–43), who is so strong on separating Matt 11:16–17 par. from 11:18–19 par., on pruning away the second half of v 19 as secondary, and on insisting that vv 18–19b do not preserve the original words of Jesus, admits in the end that vv 18–19b were probably spoken by Jesus, though not in the present "Hellenistic" wording (?).

[159] Ernst (*Johannes der Täufer*, 72–73) follows von Harnack in judging Luke's perfect form to be a stylistic improvement. While that is likely, the Greek perfect tense might instead represent a translation variant of an Aramaic pĕʿal perfect verb form.

[160] For older literature on the problem of the *ēlthon* words, see Adolf von Harnack, " 'Ich bin gekommen.' Die ausdrücklichen Selbstzeugnisse Jesu über den Zweck seiner Sendung und seines Kommens," *ZTK* 22 (1912) 1–30. Von Harnack correctly notes

that "to come" need not have a messianic sense even in the NT. Against the view of Bultmann, Johannes Schneider ("*erchomai*, etc.," *TDNT* 2 [1964] 668) cautions against taking for granted that *ēlthon* words are all necessarily creations of the early church. For his part, it is true that Bultmann (*Geschichte*, 164–67) argues that in general the "Ich Worte" ("I words") that speak of Jesus' coming are products of the community. But he does allow that some may go back to Aramaic logia and that in Aramaic the word for *ēlthon* may mean "I come," "I am here." In effect, though, this admission undermines one of his basic objections to the authenticity of the *ēlthon* words in general. Granted their possible "present" sense in Aramaic, the objection that these words look back on Jesus' historical ministry as something of the past falls to the ground. Bultmann makes the general reply that the secondary character of some of the *ēlthon* words makes him skeptical about all of them (p. 168). O. Michel (" 'Ich komme' (Jos. Bell. III, 400)," *TZ* 24 [1968] 123–24) points out that Josephus (in *J.W.* 3.8.9. §400) announces his prophetic oracle with *hēkō: egō d' aggelos hēkō soi meizonōn* ("I have come to you as a messenger of greater things"). Michel suggests that the idea here is that, in the encounter between the prophet and his audience, the prophetic oracle has already begun to be realized. Gerd Theissen and Philipp Vielhauer, in the fourth edition of the *Ergänzungsheft* to Bultmann's *Geschichte* (Göttingen: Vandenhoeck & Ruprecht, 1971, p. 62), take up this suggestion and state: "Possibly all the *ēlthon* sayings stood in the present." Jeremias stresses the present meaning of the supposedly original Aramaic verbs ("I come," "I am here") to defend his view that Jesus did speak some of the *ēlthon* sayings (e.g., Matt 5:17); see his *New Testament Theology*, 83. According to Jeremias, the underlying *'ātayit* can mean "I am there," "I will," "it is my task." On all this, see also Arens, *The ēlthon-Sayings*, 240.

[161] For reasons for thinking "Son of Man" was not original in this saying, see Arens, *The ēlthon-Sayings*, 233–34. While this is not the place to debate the question at length, I do not find Arens's arguments cogent.

[162] This argument, of course, presupposes that the simple "John" of Matt 11:18 is original; so Ernst, *Johannes der Täufer*, 73; Fitzmyer, *The Gospel According to Luke*, 1. 678. The contrary opinion is held by Schürmann, *Lukasevangelium*, 1. 426 n. 133. He points to passages where Luke lacks the title in Q material when Matthew has it: Matt 11:11–12; Luke also lacks it in 3:2 (cf. Mark 1:4, if *ho baptizōn* is the correct reading). If "John the Baptist" is the original reading in Q, that would argue by way of parallelism for the title "the Son of Man" being original as well.

[163] See Joseph A. Fitzmyer, "The Study of the Aramaic Background of the New Testament," *A Wandering Aramean* (SBLMS 25; Missoula, MT: Scholars, 1979) 1–27, esp. 14 and 25 n. 71.

[164] One scholar who does question the authenticity of the entire unit is Wendy J. Cotter, "Children Sitting in the Agora. Q (Luke 7:31–35)," *Forum* 5,2 (1989) 63–82. Her reasons, however, are not all that cogent. For example, she considers the parable inauthentic because it does not cohere with what Jesus says elsewhere about children. That is to say, it would be the only saying of Jesus which uses the child as a vehicle of humiliation and an accusation of foolishness. There are a number of difficulties with this approach. (1) Irrespective of whether John and Jesus are identified with the first or second group of children, children are used in this parable as symbols of both the prophets sent from God and the generation that rejects them. In other words, the world of children and their games symbolizes the world of adults and their more serious games. Children *qua* children are not held up to ridicule in this parable. (2) The precise application of the parable aside, a person who loves children deeply will hardly think of

himself as going contrary to that love if he rebukes finicky and inconstant adults for being "childish." Moreover, loving children does not mean overlooking the limitations of children. One could go on in this vein, but the point is clear: the mode of reasoning in this article is not very rigorous. Likewise, many of the positions taken are highly imaginative and lack any substantive proof (e.g., the insults leveled against the Baptist are artificial, but the insults against Jesus are real).

[165] On the text-critical problems, see Schürmann, *Lukasevangelium*, 1. 427–28 nn. 144, 148, and 150.

[166] One minor problem of translation that is often ignored is the fact that, taken literally, the saying reads: "And wisdom is vindicated *from* [*apo*] all her children." Most commentators take for granted that we have here a case of *apo* ("from") = *hypo* ("by"); on the grammatical phenomenon, see Max Zerwick, *Graecitas Biblica* (5th ed.; Rome: Biblical Institute, 1966) 30 (#90). This is certainly the most likely solution, but not the only one. For instance, Dibelius (*Die urchristliche Überlieferung*, 19 n. 3) appeals to the myth of divine wisdom that descends from heaven to take up her dwelling among her children (see, e.g., *1 Enoch* 42:1–2); in some forms of the myth, she finds rejection and must return to heaven. Hence Dibelius thinks that "her children" refers to all the Jews (or human beings in general) who reject divine wisdom in the persons of John and Jesus; *apo* would therefore mean that wisdom is finally vindicated "far from her children." Another suggestion, namely, that *apo* reflects the Aramaic *min qŏdām* (so Jeremias, *Parables*, 162 n. 43) in the sense of "in view of" does not fit the Lucan wording.

[167] See, e.g., Moule, *An Idiom-Book*, 11–13; Zerwick, *Graecitas Biblica*, 85–87 (#256– 60).

[168] As Schürmann observes (*Lukasevangelium*, 1. 427) "to be justified" or "vindi- cated" in this context means to be acknowledged as being in the right and therefore to be obeyed.

[169] See, e.g., Heinz Joachim Held, "Matthäus als Interpret der Wundergeschichten," Günther Bornkamm, Gerhard Barth, and Heinz Joachim Held, *Überlieferung und Aus- legung im Matthäusevangelium* (WMANT 1; 5th ed.; Neukirchen-Vluyn: Neukirchener Verlag, 1968) 155–87, esp. 237–40; Eduard Schweizer, *Das Evangelium nach Matthäus* (NTD 2; Göttingen: Vandenhoeck & Ruprecht, 1973) 165–68. Robert H. Gundry (*Matthew. A Commentary on His Literary and Theological Art* [Grand Rapids: Eerdmans, 1982] 213) suggests that by speaking of "the works of the Messiah" in 11:2 and the "works" of wisdom in 11:19, Matthew intends to equate Christ with wisdom (cf. Matt 23:34 and Luke 11:49). On *teknōn* as the original reading, see also Schulz, *Q. Die Spruchquelle der Evangelisten*, 380; Kloppenborg, *Formation*, 110 n. 36. As Schürmann correctly judges, the remarkably close agreement in the wording of the Q material in this Baptist-block of Matthew and Luke makes redactional alterations rather than mistranslations of an Aramaic source the more likely reason for divergences in wording. Hence there is no need for a convoluted theory that appeals to a supposedly original Aramaic word (e.g., ʿbdyh' or ʿbdy') that was vocalized and then translated differently to produce "her children" or "her works"; on this, see Gottlob Schrenk," "*dikē*, etc.," *TDNT* 2 (1964) 214 n. 13. Even Jeremias calls the transformations postulated by this theory "a conceivable though complicated process" (*Parables*, 162 n. 44). As Arens (*The elthon-Sayings*, 227–28) points out, there is no proof that ʿbd would be translated as *teknon* rather than as *pais* or *doulos*; indeed, the LXX never translates ʿbd as *teknon*.

[170] In our present Greek text, the *inclusio* remains one of sense, not wording, since Luke 7:32 reads *paidiois*, while 7:35 reads *teknōn*. But if all of these sayings stood origi-

nally in Aramaic, the words used (e.g., *běnayă*) might well have been the same in both places.

[171] Fitzmyer, *The Gospel According to Luke*, 1. 681. Just as a matter of statistical fact, Luke uses the adjective *pas* ("all") more often than any other author in the NT; he has a "generic predilection" for the adjective (ibid., 524). The one who comes closest to Luke's predilection is Matthew. Hence, the lack of "all" in the Matthean parallel 11:19 (where it would fit nicely) could be seen to argue for *pantōn* as Lucan redaction of Q in 7:35. The few Lucan manuscripts that omit *pantōn* do not, however, affect the argument; practically all commentators reject this shorter reading as secondary. Kloppenborg (*Formation*, 111) takes *teknōn* to refer to John and Jesus.

[172] This may well be the sense of the verse in its Lucan redaction, since Luke places before this whole subunit a separate tradition stating that, when Jesus praised the Baptist, "*all* the people and the toll collectors, hearing this, acknowledged God's just claim on them [literally, "vindicated God," using *edikaiōsan*, the same verb that occurs in Luke 7:35]." On all this, see Hoffmann, *Studien*, 228–30; Schulz, *Q. Die Spruchquelle der Evangelisten*, 386. Wink (*John the Baptist*, 22) favors the idea of the children being the poor and the sinners, who streamed to both John and Jesus. This interpretation arises not out of the logion or even its immediate context in Q, but rather out of Wink's reconstruction of John's ministry and its relation to Jesus'. One is struck immediately by the automatic—and questionable—yoking of the poor and the sinners, a combination that scholars like E. P. Sanders have criticized. On the level of the theology of Q, Kloppenborg (*Formation*, 112) sees "the fusion of the well-known sapiential motif of Sophia as a preacher of repentance (Prov 1:20–33; 8:1–21) and as indwelling the prophets (Wis 7:27) with the theological schema of the deuteronomistic conception of the history of Israel."

[173] Fitzmyer, *The Gospel According to Luke*, 1. 677–79. Arens (*The ēlthon-Sayings*, 229) thinks that the use of *sophia* to signify God as the author of the plan of salvation is "foreign to the outlook of v.18–19b." Hence Arens suggests that "the *sophia*-clause was originally unrelated to its present context."

[174] Arens (*The ēlthon-Sayings*, 228) misses this point when he decides that the longer negative description of Jesus means that "a friend of tax collectors and sinners" is a later addition to the saying.

[175] Failure to appreciate this point is a major weakness of the whole approach of Boers in his *Who Was Jesus?* The most primitive tradition within Q presents a Jesus who sees himself as bringing in an eschatological situation qualitatively different from that proclaimed or realized by the Baptist.

[176] This would be all the more striking if "the Son of Man" is original and serves as some sort of mysterious or solemn designation of Jesus.

[177] For the list of proponents of each view and a brief digest of arguments, see Kloppenborg, *Q Parallels*, 56; idem, *Formation*, 112–13. To give only a few examples: Wink (*John the Baptist*, 20) thinks that "neither context appears to be original." In favor of Matthew's representing the original position (because one can hardly find a reason why Matthew would have inserted 11:12–13 where it now stands in his Gospel) is Lührmann, *Redaktion*, 27–28. Fitzmyer (*The Gospel According to Luke*, 2. 1114) seems to favor the Lucan order (yet see the opposite opinion expressed in his *Luke*, 1. 662). Schlosser (*Le règne*, 2. 509–10) carefully considers the arguments pro and con and concludes that it is unlikely that Luke would have dismantled a relatively satisfying composition like Matt 11:2–19 to create a less satisfying one at Luke 16:15–18. For extensive arguments

in favor of Luke's having preserved the place of the logion in Q, see Peter Scott Cameron, *Violence and the Kingdom. The Interpretation of Matthew 11:12* (Arbeiten zum Neuen Testament und Judentum 5; Frankfurt: Lang, 1984) 214–26. In my view, Schlosser and Cameron have the better part of the argument; but, obviously, any decision remains fragile.

[178] See the similar assessment in Schulz, *Q. Die Spruchquelle der Evangelisten*, 263.

[179] As might be imagined, practically every opinion conceivable concerning the earliest available form of the logion has been put forward by scholars. For example, Wink (*John the Baptist*, 20) renders the lapidary judgment that "Matthew's form of the saying is the more difficult and is probably older." In itself, that is a questionable criterion of authenticity: sometimes difficulties in interpretation arise because of the tension between tradition and redaction. For a history of interpretation and a detailed study of the problem—only from the Matthean side of the question!—see Cameron's *Violence and the Kingdom*. Obviously, what follows in the text can only be a schematic summary of the arguments for my position.

[180] For a detailed study of the words in Josephus, as well as for further literature, see Ernest Moore, "*biazō, harpazō,* and Cognates in Josephus," *NTS* 21 (1974–75) 519–43. From the usage of Josephus, Moore argues for the negative sense of forcing people or things against their will or nature. More questionable is Moore's suggestion that the logion is denouncing the Pharisees, who "provided the resistance movement with its theology . . ." (p. 541). Frederick W. Danker ("Luke 16:16—An Opposition Logion," *JBL* 77 [1958] 231–43) also thinks the saying is aimed at the Pharisees, but thinks that the context is the Pharisees' complaint that the reign of law and order has come to an end.

Independently Wink (*John the Baptist*, 20–21) reaches this conclusion about the words' negative sense": "The parallelism of *biazetai* and *harpazousin* in Matt. 11:12 surely denotes an act of violence in a negative sense"; similarly Dibelius, *Die urchristliche Überlieferung*, 24–25 (with a critique of the positive sense proposed by von Harnack); Kümmel, *Promise and Fulfilment*, 122; Schlosser, *Le règne*, 2. 517–18; Kloppenborg, *Formation*, 114. After considering all the philological possibilities, Gottlob Schrenk ("*biazomai, biastēs,*" *TDNT* 1 [1964] 609–14) favors the negative passive sense for Matt 11:12: ". . . it [the divine rule] is contested, attacked or hampered by contentious opponents." On the other hand, he interprets the more positive context of Luke (with *euaggelizetai*) to mean that everyone is pressing into the kingdom, a sign of the success of the Gentile mission, a grand theme of Luke-Acts; cf. Philippe H. Menoud, "Le sens du verbe *biazetai* dans Lc 16,16," *Mélanges bibliques en hommage au R. P. Béda Rigaux* (ed. Albert Descamps and André de Halleux; Gembloux: Duculot, 1970) 207–12. On this point, see also Fitzmyer (*The Gospel According to Luke*, 2. 1117–18), who gives a list of authors who favor the positive and the negative meaning in the Lucan logion. Even in the case of Matthew's version, however, one must always allow for the possibility that Jesus is using negative words in an ironic or paradoxical sense: e.g., sinners are doing violence to the kingdom of God by rushing into it, i.e., by massively accepting Jesus' message; this is the interpretation of Schlosser, *Le règne*, 2. 521–22.

Against the ironic or paradoxical interpretations of scholars like Danker, one must ponder the observation of Mussner ("Der nicht erkannte Kairos," 608): in such a case, one would expect some introductory phrase like *hōs legete* ("as you say"). That this is not an unreasonable expectation is seen in the second Baptist-block itself. The mockery hurled at John and Jesus is introduced with "you say" (so Luke 7:33–34) or "they say" (so Matt 11:18–19). This is not the only Gospel passage that makes clear that Jesus is quoting the real or supposed objections of his enemies; see, e.g., Luke 4:23.

181 In the LXX see the *Prologue* of Sirach, though the operative pattern here is actually the three-part one of law, prophets, and the other books (1–2,8–10,23–25). Except for Luke 24:44 (where "the Psalms" holds the third place), the NT knows only the two-part division. In the NT, this two-part division occurs ten times: Matt 5:17; 7:12; 11:13 (but with the reversal of the usual order); 22:40; Luke 16:16; John 1:45 (but not perfectly coordinated); Acts 13:15; 24:14; 28:23; Rom 3:21. Luke also has three times "Moses and the prophets" (16:29; 16:31; 24:27). Similar to this Lucan style of "Moses and the prophets" is the usage found at Qumran, where, moreover, "Moses" and "the prophets" may appear in different clauses; see, e.g., 1QS 1:3 ("as he [God] commanded through Moses and through all his servants the prophets"); 8:15–16 ("This is the study of the law, which he commanded through Moses, that it be done according to all that has been revealed from time to time, and as the prophets have revealed through his holy spirit").

182 The attempts by a few critics (e.g., Alexander Sand, *Das Gesetz und die Propheten* [Biblische Untersuchungen 11; Regensburg: Pustet, 1974] 179 n. 8) to champion Matthew's text as the original wording of Q fail to deal adequately with this sharp difference in usage, which fits so well into Matthean vocabulary and theology. The Matthean text is "the more difficult" reading (as Sand argues in favor of its primitiveness) only if one is looking at regular OT and NT usage; it hardly creates difficulty for the special thought-world of Matthew.

183 This compressed statement summarizes one of the main theses of my book *Law and History in Matthew's Gospel* (AnBib 71; Rome: Biblical Institute, 1976); see esp. 85–89. It is surprising that Ernst misses this point and judges Matthew's formulation to be more primitive than Luke's (*Johannes der Täufer*, 66). He is perhaps unduly influenced by the arguments of Hoffmann (*Studien*, 51–60), which show a poor understanding of the redactional style and theology of Matthew.

184 Schlosser, *Le règne*, 2. 511. Kloppenborg (*Formation*, 114) attempts to defend the Matthean order of the two parts of the logion. He echoes the argument of others that since the order of Matthew is more difficult and seems illogical, it is original. He fails to consider the possibility that the tension and lack of smooth flow in Matthew's version are due to heavy Matthean redaction of the Q material.

185 This is perhaps the best reason for thinking that Luke has also changed the sense of *biazetai* to a positive meaning (the urgent, demanding invitation of the preacher). It coheres well with Luke's wording of the parable of the supper (Luke 14:23: "make them come in"; contrast Matt 22:9–10) as well as with his use of the compound verb *parabiazomai* in the middle voice in Luke 24:29 and Acts 16:15 with the sense of "urge strongly" or "prevail upon" someone in the context of an invitation to a meal or lodging.

186 This is the judgment of Fitzmyer, *The Gospel According to Luke*, 2. 1118; cf. Dibelius, *Die urchristliche Überlieferung*, 23–24; Hoffmann, *Studien*, 51; Kloppenborg, *Formation*, 113–14; Gnilka, *Jesus von Nazaret*, 151 n. 25.

187 Matthew uses *basileia* ("kingdom") fifty-five times, *basileia tōn ouranōn* ("kingdom of heaven") thirty-two times, and *basileia tou theou* ("kingdom of God") four times (12:28; 19:24; 21:31,43).

188 This is made likely by the parallel passages in Mark, which lack the precise phrase Matthew has.

189 See Ernst, *Johannes der Täufer*, 64–65. Hoffmann (*Studien*, 52) affirms rather than argues to the position that "from the days of John up until now" is the more original

text; he does not deal with the reasons we put forth for considering Luke's *apo tote* the primitive reading.

[190] This is the hypothetical Q form favored by Schulz, *Q. Die Spruchquelle der Evangelisten*, 261–62; Schlosser, *Le règne*, 2. 515; Kümmel, *Promise and Fulfilment*, 122.

[191] Hence I do not see the cogency of Schlosser's argument (*Le règne*, 2. 517) that Jesus probably did not say Luke 16:16a because it shows theological reflection on salvation history. Schlosser prefers to restrict the authentic logion to a hypothetical form of Matt 11:12, equivalent to my hypothetical Q form of Luke 16:16b given in the text.

[192] Kümmel (*Promise and Fulfilment*, 124) may be reading too much into this one logion when he summarizes its statement on salvation history thus: ". . . Jesus not only claimed to replace the Old Testament revelation by the perfect revelation, but he also proclaimed that thereby the eschatological consummation is already in the present bringing the old aeon to an end." That may be true of the overall message of Jesus distilled from all available authentic sayings, but it seems to go beyond what this individual logion is affirming.

[193] For various suggestions, see Cameron, *Violence and the Kingdom*, 2. When the violence is taken in a positive sense, the violent have at times been identified with Jesus, the Baptist, believers, ascetics, sinners, or Gentiles. Cameron himself argues at length for Antipas as the violent one who has breached the kingdom of God by killing the Baptist (pp. 226–46). Cameron spends a great deal of time theorizing about the Semitic substratum of the saying. Yet, strange to say, almost all of his conjectures deal with OT Hebrew rather than with the Aramaic Jesus presumably would have spoken.

[194] See Fitzmyer, *The Gospel According to Luke*, 2. 1117.

[195] On the possible spatial metaphor of "kingdom" in the logion under consideration, see Cameron, *Violence and the Kingdom*, 234–35. I do not think that Schlosser's definition (*Le règne*, 2. 526) of kingdom in this logion as simply "the salvific activity of God" quite captures the sense of the passage.

[196] In this it differs from Matt 11:11 par., where the whole first half of the saying is taken up with the Baptist, while the second half limits his importance by introducing the concept of the kingdom of God. On this see Fitzmyer (*The Gospel According to Luke*, 2. 1115): "Only indirectly can the first part of v. 16 [of Luke 16:16] be considered a saying about John the Baptist. . . ."

[197] See, e.g., Hans Conzelmann, *The Theology of St. Luke* (New York: Harper & Row, 1961) 20, 23, 26–27, 161, 185 n. 2. For Conzelmann, in Luke-Acts the kingdom does not come, even partially, in the earthly ministry of Jesus: ". . . the Kingdom of God, far from being made into a historical entity, is removed into the metaphysical realm" (p. 113).

[198] Paul S. Minear, "Luke's Use of the Birth Stories," Leander Keck and J. Louis Martyn, *Studies in Luke-Acts* (Paul Schubert Festschrift; London: SPCK, 1968) 111–30, p. 122.

[199] Wink, *John the Baptist*, 51–57. As Ernst notes (*Johannes der Täufer*, 66 n. 114), when *apo* and *heōs* are used with proper names, the sense can be either inclusive or exclusive; in themselves, the prepositions do not solve the question.

[200] See the cautious formulation in Polag, *Die Christologie der Logienquelle*, 48: "[The saying] deals with a designation of epochs . . . , and John is mentioned to indicate a kind of limit or turning point. . . . So with John it is not a matter of fulfillment and

eschatological re-presentation of prophecy. What exact role belongs to him is not clear from the saying; in any case his person is acknowledged and Jesus himself is nevertheless separated from him."

[201] Fitzmyer, *The Gospel According to Luke*, 2. 1115. A balanced summation of the problem whether (according to this logion) John belonged to the time of the law and the prophets or to the time of the kingdom is presented by Fitzmyer on p. 1116. Commenting on the statement "the law and the prophets up until John," Fitzmyer observes: "I.e. up until John inclusive, in that he was a Jewish reform-preacher; but also exclusive, because he was 'something greater than a prophet'. . . ." This catches well his pivotal, threshold quality. A similar evaluation can be found in G. R. Beasley-Murray, *Jesus and the Kingdom of God* (Grand Rapids: Eerdmans, 1986) 94: "John the Baptist forms the bridgehead between the old order and the new, not in such a fashion as to belong to *neither*, but in such a fashion as to belong to *both*." Schulz (*Q. Die Spruchquelle der Evangelisten*, 264–67) is too one-sided in insisting that Q always sees John as belonging to the old age.

[202] Implicit in this seems to be an astounding claim about the kingdom of God (notice, not Jesus himself) somehow making the function of the law and the prophets otiose. Yet all this remains implied, and nothing like a Pauline theory of "Christ the end of the law" (Rom 10:4) or a Matthean theory of Jesus the fulfiller of the law and the prophets (Matt 5:17) is so much as hinted at; cf. Polag, *Die Christologie der Logienquelle*, 79. Gnilka (*Jesus von Nazaret*, 214) is correct in saying that, in the context of this kingdom-saying, the opposition between the law and the prophets on the one hand and John the Baptist on the other suggests that the law and the prophets have come to a certain end or at least have been moved into a new perspective. The kingdom of God assigns the torah a new position, which is no longer the central position it once possessed. Schulz (*Q. Die Spruchquelle der Evangelisten*, 264–66) tries to solve the problem by asserting that, while the Q document upholds and intensifies the law, the law and the prophets as an epoch of salvation history are brought to a close by the coming of the kingdom. But if the old and now superseded epoch was formed and defined precisely by the law and the prophets, the question of the function of the law and the prophets in the new, different epoch is necessarily raised. We have here but one example of Schulz's attempt to make Q a repository of coherent theological views when it is much closer to a grab bag.

[203] Wink, *John the Baptist*, 21. Wink goes on to claim that this logion also portrays Jesus "as merely John's successor" (pp. 21–22). I think that his very strong formulation of the content is not supported by a critical reading of the hypothetical text I have reconstructed. In general, the post-Bultmannians were not as skeptical about the authenticity of this logion as was Bultmann himself (*Geschichte*, 177–78). Those in favor of authenticity (but with various reconstructions of the primitive logion) include Ernst Käsemann, "The Problem of the Historical Jesus," *Essays on New Testament Themes* (SBT 41; London: SCM, 1964) 42–43 (but note that "Matt. 11.25f." on p. 42 is a misprint for "Matt. 11.12f."); James M. Robinson, *A New Quest of the Historical Jesus* (SBT 25; London: SCM, 1959) 116–17; Bornkamm, *Jesus of Nazareth*, 51; Perrin, *Rediscovering the Teaching of Jesus*, 75–77.

[204] One is made especially wary by the way in which, down through the centuries, theologians and exegetes have used this logion as a vehicle for their own theological agendas; see the summary in Cameron, *Violence and the Kingdom*, 254. On the other hand, one should not let questionable presuppositions prevent one from seriously considering the possibility that something like the primitive form of the logion was spoken

by Jesus. Contrast the approach of Schulz (*Q. Die Spruchquelle der Evangelisten*, 263), who almost automatically assigns sayings tinged with realized eschatology to a second stage of the Q document, coming from a Hellenistic Jewish-Christian community in Syria.

[205] The question about why Jesus and his disciples do not fast (Mark 2:18–22) is raised in reference to (and perhaps by) the *disciples* of John and (the disciples of) the Pharisees. Since the focus in this pericope is on the praxis of Jesus as distinct from other pious movements in Judaism (with the Baptist himself only indirectly involved), I prefer to treat this pericope in Chapter 16.

[206] See the judgment of Virgil P. Howard, *Das Ego Jesu in den synoptischen Evangelien* (Marburger Theologische Studien 14; Marburg: Elwert, 1975) 116. A defense of Marcan priority and of the dependence of Matthew and Luke on Mark alone is given by Gam Seng Shae, "The Question on the Authority of Jesus," *NovT* 16 (1974) 1–29, esp. 3–4.

[207] This brief treatment of one Marcan pericope does not allow detailed consideration of whether Mark was a conservative redactor of large blocks of tradition already formed before he wrote his Gospel (so, e.g., Rudolf Pesch in the two volumes of his *Das Markusevangelium*) or a creative writer who devised his Gospel narrative out of bits and pieces of individual traditions (so many of the authors in Werner H. Kelber [ed.], *The Passion in Mark* [Philadelphia: Fortress, 1976]). Hence, in this discussion, phrases like "Mark's redaction" may be interpreted by the "Pesch school" to mean the pre-Marcan Passion Narrative Mark inherited. Even if one does not accept the large pre-Marcan Passion Narrative Pesch posits, it is common to suggest that this initial dispute story was part of a pre-Marcan collection of Jesus' disputes in Jerusalem that corresponded to a pre-Marcan collection of Jesus' disputes in Galilee (Mark 2:1–3:6). On this, see Martin Albertz, *Die synoptischen Streitgespräche* (Berlin: Trowitzsch & Sohn, 1921) 16–36, 107–8, 110, 113–14; cf. Bultmann, *Geschichte*, 347 n. 2. Nevertheless, Joanna Dewey doubts that such a pre-Marcan collection existed in the case of Mark 12; see her arguments in *Marcan Public Debate* (SBLDS 48; Chico, CA: Scholars, 1980) 55–63; similarly, Howard, *Das Ego Jesu*, 109–10. I do not find Dewey's arguments very cogent, since she presupposes that such a pre-Marcan collection would show some unity of content, form, and purpose. Unlike our present Gospels, it may well be that the pre-Gospel sources were very much "grab bags" of heterogeneous material loosely tied together by association in form or content. In my view, that is precisely what the Q document was.

[208] Howard (*Das Ego Jesu*, 109) emphasizes the plural form *tauta* and holds that the word must refer to more than a single action of Jesus. In Mark's context, one could refer it to everything Jesus has done from his triumphal entry onward. Indeed, Shae ("The Question on the Authority of Jesus," 26) thinks that in the larger context of Mark's Gospel *tauta* points back to all of the activities of Jesus which demonstrate his authority; cf. J. Kremer, "Jesu Antwort auf die Frage nach seiner Vollmacht. Eine Auslegung von Mk 11,27–33," *BibLeb* 9 (1968) 128–36. However, one must be careful not to press the plural form; *tauta* as a substantive often appears in the NT where we in English would use "this" or "that"; cf. such phrases as *meta tauta*. Taking a different tack, Dewey (*Marcan Public Debate*, 58) claims: "The logical narrative antecedent of 'these things' is Jesus' acts and words in the temple cleansing." For a listing of opinions among exegetes, see Vincent Taylor, *The Gospel According to St. Mark* (2d ed.; London: Macmillan, 1966) 469–70.

[209] Strange to say, Bultmann (*Geschichte*, 18) seems to think that this holds true of

the pericope even in its present setting. He claims that *tauta poieis* in v 28 has no reference. In my view, he misses the redactional intention of Mark (see Ernst, *Johannes der Täufer*, 34). Arguing from the Johannine parallel (which we shall examine below), Jürgen Roloff (*Das Kerygma und der irdische Jesus* [Göttingen: Vandenhoeck & Ruprecht, 1970] 91–92) holds that the *tauta poieis* may well have referred to the temple cleansing, which he suggests was originally connected directly with this dispute story. On the other hand, Roloff is willing to assign the identification of the questioners, as well as the division of days, to Mark's redaction.

[210] This is the view of Bultmann (*Geschichte*, 18), who argues from the style of dispute stories in rabbinic literature. Taylor (*The Gospel According to St. Mark*, 469) replies that this is "arbitrary." In my opinion, it is not cogent to argue from the general form rabbinic dispute stories take to a conclusion about how one concrete dispute of Jesus (which does not perfectly fit this rabbinic pattern anyway) was recounted in the oral tradition of the early church—to say nothing of proceeding to a historical conclusion about what really happened in the life of Jesus. Fitzmyer (*The Gospel According to Luke*, 2. 1272) wisely issues a reminder that none of the rabbinic "parallels" usually invoked antedates the 4th century A.D. More specifically, Howard (*Das Ego Jesu*, 111) argues that Bultmann's rabbinic parallels do not really fit our pericope. According to Howard, among the many parallels cited by Bultmann and Strack-Billerbeck, there is not a single one in which the reply to the question posed by the opponents is made dependent on a prior reply to a counterquestion. But that is exactly what Jesus does in Mark 11:29: "I will ask you one question. Answer me, and I will tell you by what authority I do these things." Therefore, Bultmann's whole form-critical argument is beside the point.

Howard also finds lacking a different rabbinic parallel suggested by David Daube, *The New Testament and Rabbinic Judaism* (London: Athlone, 1956). The rabbinic form put forward by Daube contains (1) a question by an opponent, (2) a counterquestion, (3) a reply by the opponent that leaves him exposed to attack, and (4) a rejection of the reply on the basis of the consequence that flows from the answer. As Howard points out, this supposed parallel is not satisfying either. Not only does it demand that vv 31–32 be dropped; more importantly, Daube can produce only one rabbinic example of this form (*b. Sanh.* 65b), which is not an exact parallel in any case. It does not contain a rejection of the question; rather, the counterquestion contains the answer, which is then explained in the third and fourth steps. While rejecting such rabbinic parallels, in the end Howard himself (p. 115) adopts a three-stage theory of the tradition history of the saying: (1) The question and answer contained in vv 28 and 30 regarding Jesus' authority go back to a historical situation in the life of Jesus; (2) the narrative framework in vv 29,31–33 shows the reflection of the first Christians over Jesus' rejection by his opponents; (3) Mark then identifies these opponents in v 27 and the dialogue thus receives a firm setting in time and place. Once again, I would raise the practical question of *Sitz im Leben*. How and why were the two isolated questions in vv 28 and 30 carried along in the oral tradition—and what sense did they make—before Christians decided to give them a narrative framework?

An even more refined tradition history, also in three stages, but differing from Howard's, is spun out by Shae, "The Question on the Authority of Jesus," 14–29. Especially when one compares Shae's results with the many differing opinions of other scholars who have proposed their hypothetical tradition histories, it seems wise not to make one's conclusions depend on some atomistic dissolution of the tradition into pieces of verses, disassembled and reassembled on dubious grounds. When one compares the highly speculative theories of Howard and Shae with the lapidary affirmations of Pesch that Mark has made no redactional change in his source and that the text is a uniform whole with no secondary additions (*Markusevangelium*, 2. 209), one realizes that it is best not to claim to know the unknowable.

[211] This is the classification given the pericope by Bultmann, *Geschichte*, 18. As Taylor (*The Gospel According to St. Mark*, 468) observes, "It is . . . a 'controversy-story,' but in the course of transmission the narrative elements have fallen away almost entirely, and little more is left than the pointed question. . . ." Taylor has an intriguing point here. Most form critics cited in these notes toil to see how much they can trim away from Mark 11:27–33 to arrive at the original tradition. But could the process have moved in the opposite direction: an originally circumstantial narrative was increasingly boiled down to its bare essentials and thus became more dense and obscure?

For the essential features of a dispute story and the extent to which Mark 11:27–33 fits the pattern, see Shae, "The Question on the Authority of Jesus," 10–11. If one does classify this pericope as a *Streitgespräch*, one must acknowledge that it differs in content from most other *Streitgespräche*, which usually concentrate on some particular question (e.g., plucking grain on the Sabbath, divorce, the nature of the resurrection). If, however—as I think is the case—Jesus shifts the question from his authority to John's baptism to spotlight his own practice of baptism, the pericope has a narrower focus than might at first appear.

[212] For the pattern, see Str-B, 1. 861–62. However, as Howard (*Das Ego Jesu*, 111) points out, the typical pattern seen in the rabbinical stories is not perfectly verified in Mark 11:27–31. I am not interested in putting the Marcan pericope on a Procrustean bed to make it fit the full rabbinic pattern by whatever pruning is demanded. I am concerned only with the basic pattern of question and counterquestion. One must be especially wary of changing the Marcan text to force it to conform to a rabbinic pattern because, as C. S. Mann points out (*Mark* [AB 27; Garden City, NY: Doubleday, 1986] 457), "the method of question and counterquestion was a well-known device in Hellenistic culture, and is found as early as the fifth century B.C."

[213] As Bultmann (*Geschichte*, 18) admits, it is difficult to decide how far v 27 (which names the interrogators) stems from Mark, though he inclines to the view that the identification of the questioners is Marcan redaction.

[214] Bultmann (*Geschichte*, 18) thinks that while the temple cleansing may have already been the occasion for the question in an earlier stage of the Marcan tradition, it was not the original catalyst, since (claims Bultmann) Jesus' cleansing of the temple would not be the suitable occasion for a rabbinic debate. Nevertheless, Bultmann goes on to point out (in n. 3) that the (transferred) story of the cleansing of the temple in John 2:13–22 also unleashes a challenge to Jesus from the Jerusalem authorities. Bultmann dismisses this with a vague surmise that John had used the source of Mark. For those who think John's Gospel is independent of the Synoptics, the presence of a similar configuration in John 2 does argue that the connection of temple cleansing and challenging question from the authorities was at least very early in the tradition, if not original.

[215] There may be a hint in Jesus' challenge that these questioners, who are taken for religious teachers by the people, must first demonstrate to Jesus their competence to teach and so their right to interrogate him. If this is the case, scribes might most easily fit the role of the interrogators. But the hint is nothing more than that.

[216] Ernst Lohmeyer, *Das Evangelium des Markus* (MeyerK 1/2; 17th ed.; Göttingen: Vandenhoeck & Ruprecht, 1967; reprint of 10th ed., 1937) 242 n. 3. He is objecting to Bultmann's acceptance of the judgment of A. Merx that the counterquestion of Jesus

implies the answer: "As the Baptist had his authority from God and not from any human being, so also I!" On this, see Bultmann, *Geschichte*, 18. However, when Lohmeyer proceeds to read the counterquestion to mean that Jesus sees John's baptism (and what he experienced in it) as the basis of his own authority, he goes beyond what is either said or implied in this one pericope; so too, Jeremias, *New Testament Theology*, 56. One must also remember that Jesus' answer is a clever, witty riposte meant to defend him against his enemies; it is something of an *ad hominem* argument that forces them to face a dilemma. One should not seek a full statement of Jesus' understanding of his own authority in this pericope.

[217] This explanatory aside in Mark 11:32 ("for all considered John to be a genuine prophet") may be a Marcan redactional insertion into the tradition. Yet it coheres well with a number of other Gospel sources, all of which know that various people viewed John as a prophet. See, e.g., Jesus' accolade in Q (Matt 11:9 = Luke 7:26); the popular estimation reflected in the question of the Jerusalem authorities in John 1:21,25; the Benedictus, a hymn embedded in the Lucan Infancy Narrative (Luke 1:76); and Antipas' opinion (Matt 14:5, probably Matthean redaction).

[218] Pesch, *Markusevangelium*, 2. 212.

[219] Ernst makes this point effectively in *Johannes der Täufer*, 36.

[220] Pesch, *Markusevangelium*, 2. 212.

[221] David Noel Freedman has pushed this suggestion even further by suggesting to me in correspondence that originally the authorities' question ("On what authority do you do these things") referred precisely to Jesus' practice of baptizing. While this suggestion is attractive, I hesitate to accept it because of the agreement of Mark and John on a setting after the cleansing of the temple (see below).

[222] Brown, *The Gospel According to John*, 1. 118–20. As Brown points out, the immediate connection in John between the temple cleansing and the challenging question of the authorities may be original in the earliest tradition. It may have been Mark or his tradition that split up these two elements and assigned them to successive days (perhaps to allow for the story of the cursed fig tree). On all this, see Roloff, *Kerygma*, 90–95. As many commentators note, the question underlying John 2:18 (literally: "What sign do you show us, that you do these things?") is: What is your authority to cleanse the temple and how will you prove you have it? See, e.g., Bernard, *Gospel According to St. John*, 1. 92; Ernst Haenchen, *John* (Hermeneia; 2 vols.; Philadelphia: Fortress, 1984) 1. 184. Schnackenburg (*The Gospel According to St John*, 1. 348) comments: ". . . their demand resembles very much that put forward in the 'question of authority' which is narrated by the Synoptics soon after the cleansing of the temple, . . . though not linked directly to it."

[223] It is perhaps telling that even the skeptical Bultmann (*Geschichte*, 19) is uncertain about the question of historicity. He affirms that the core tradition in vv 28–30 is "an authentic Palestinian apophthegm." But he is uncertain about whether it is a historical account or a creation of the early church, which uses it to argue against those who did accept the authority of the Baptist but not of Jesus (or of Christian missionaries, as Ernst [*Johannes der Täufer*, 36] suggests). However, if the questioners in the original form of the story were hostile Jerusalem authorities (which the Fourth Gospel's independent version seems to confirm), the suggested *Sitz im Leben* of an apologetic aimed at Baptist sectarians will not hold. Simply as a matter of fact, most of the exegetes cited in this section who investigate the pericope at length come to the conclusion that at least the core of the story is authentic. Some, like Lohmeyer (*Das Evangelium des Mar-*

kus, 243), think it is useless to try to trim away a verse here or a verse there and so, while admitting stylistic modifications, declare the unit as a whole to be authentic; cf. Fitzmyer, *The Gospel According to Luke*, 2. 1272–73.

[224] For a list of exegetes pro and con with a summary of reasons, see Kloppenborg, *Q Parallels*, 58.

[225] On Matt 21:32, see Joachim Jeremias (*The Parables of Jesus* [New Testament Library; London: SCM, 1963] 80): 21:32 is an allegorical interpretation that does not really fit the parable in vv 28–30. Jeremias goes on to speculate that the latter part of v 31 originally had nothing to do with v 32. Verse 32 would have been attracted to this Matthean unit because of the verbal association with "the tax collectors and the prostitutes" at the end of v 31. Jeremias thinks the connection was made in the pre-Matthean tradition. As an alternative theory, I would suggest that the original parable in the M tradition ended with Jesus' probing and accusing question in v 31a ("Which of the two sons did the will of the father?") or just possibly with the self-condemning answer of his adversaries in v 31b ("And they say: 'The first.' "). In this case, everything from "and Jesus says to them" in v 31c would be a later addition to the parable, perhaps in two stages (first the rest of v 31, later the application to the Baptist in v 32). Obviously, all of this is hypothetical, but the main point remains: at least v 32, and perhaps the latter part of v 31, did not originally belong to the parable of the two sons. A weighty consideration for Ernst (*Johannes der Täufer*, 180–81) is the strongly Matthean wording of v 32. As for Luke 7:29–30, the intrusion of a short narrative into the midst of a dense collection of Q sayings on the Baptist (the second Baptist-block) is a priori suspicious, especially when both vocabulary and theological interests link up with Lucan style and concerns elsewhere in the Third Gospel; see Fitzmyer, *The Gospel According to Luke*, 1. 675. For a list of Lucan vocabulary in Luke 7:29–30 as compared with the usage of the other Gospels, see Ernst (*Johannes der Täufer*, 103 n. 79), who leans toward a Lucan redactional creation.

[226] In the Greek text, "hearing" [*akousas*] modifies only the preceding noun "people," and not the phrase that follows, "and the tax collectors."

[227] In fairness, I should note that this opinion is not accepted by all commentators; for a list of exegetes pro and con, see Marshall (*Luke*, 297). I agree with Marshall's judgment: "In its Lucan form the passage cannot be anything other than a comment by the narrator"; likewise Fitzmyer, *The Gospel According to Luke*, 1. 670.

[228] This is shown both by the use of *metemelēthēte* ("changed your mind") and the choice of such low-life as the tax collectors and the prostitutes as paradigms of those who did respond properly to John.

[229] As many exegetes suggest, *proagousin* [literally, "they go before you"] may well have an exclusive sense ["they enter and you do not"], especially if a Semitic substratum is involved. On this see Zerwick, *Graecitas Biblica*, 48–49 (#145).

[230] *atheteō*, used of the Pharisees and the lawyers, carries the idea of annulling, setting aside, thwarting, disregarding. *dikaioō*, used of the people and the tax collectors, carries the idea of recognizing God to be in the right and therefore of recognizing God's just claim and demand on sinners to repent and live according to his will.

[231] "John came to you in the way of justice [righteousness]" (Matt 21:32) could refer to John himself as living and therefore exemplifying God's way of righteousness, or to preaching what God's righteous will demanded of people's lives, or (especially on the level of Matthean redaction) to John's obedient execution of his proper role in the flow and fulfillment of salvation history (cf. 3:15). On this see Meier, *Law and History in*

Matthew's Gospel, 77–79; cf. his *Matthew* (New Testament Message 3; Wilmington, DE: Glazier, 1980) 240–42.

[232] Fitzmyer, *The Gospel According to Luke*, 1. 671. Ernst (*Lukas*, 248), remarking that Luke 7:29–30 has no corresponding passage in Matthew, judges that it was inserted into the Q context either by Luke or by an earlier hand (the concept of an expanded form of Q, Q^{Lk}). Marshall (*Luke*, 297) hesitates, but inclines to Q as the source. In favor of Q is Schürmann, *Lukasevangelium*, 1. 422.

[233] The similarities noted above make it likely that we are dealing with two traditions containing some common ideas rather than with two purely redactional creations of Matthew and Luke respectively. In the latter case, the similarities would involve remarkable coincidences. At the same time, both traditions have been heavily reworked by the two evangelists, as the characteristic vocabulary shows.

[234] I purposely use the vague phrase "Jewish leaders" to cover such disparate groups as the aristocratic priesthood in Jerusalem, with coercive legal power over Jews in their jurisdiction, and voluntary groups like the Pharisees, who influenced others by personal example, the esteem they enjoyed, and (perhaps where they were numerous) social pressure.

[235] The stray Matthean and Lucan traditions we are looking at have another claim to historicity as well: discontinuity with Christian theology along with coherence with Gospel material we have already judged historical. Nowhere in Matt 21:31–32 or Luke 7:29–30 is there any indication that John's role was mainly or solely to be the precursor or preparer of the way for Jesus. He is spoken of as a prophet, baptizer, and preacher of repentance in his own right, without the question of his relationship to Jesus even being raised. If anything, there is an implied parallelism. As tax collectors and sinners (e.g., prostitutes) accepted John, so they accepted Jesus. As Jewish leaders rejected John, so they rejected Jesus. One is reminded of the parallelism of rejection in Matt 11:18–19 par.

[236] For Luke 3:10–14, see the treatment in Chapter 12, section III B. For the relation of all of this to Josephus' presentation of the Baptist, see the excursus at the end of Chapter 12, especially observation (3) at the end of the excursus. The observations I make here help push Luke 3:10–14 out of the category of *non liquet* (where I left it in Chapter 12) into the category of probably historical at least with regard to its basic thrust: i.e., John did give moral directives to those who came to him for baptism, some of whom were religious or social outcasts in Palestinian Judaism.

[237] The connection between John and Jesus in this matter would be all the stronger if, as I have argued in section III of this chapter, Jesus did continue John's practice of baptism, while not placing the same emphasis and interpretation on it that John did.

[238] Ernst (*Johannes der Täufer*, 211) stresses that the Baptist sectarians are not the only catalyst for the christology of the Fourth Gospel. Wink (*John the Baptist*, 97) is even stronger: "Here again, the primary polemical thrust is directed against Pharisaical Judaism and not the Baptist community." This may play down the role of the Baptist sectarians a little too much.

[239] Of Elisha the prophet Josephus says: *thaumasta gar kai paradoxa . . . epedeixato erga* ("for he performed astounding and marvelous deeds," *Ant.* 9.7.6 §182). As far as I can see, the only two passages in the whole of Josephus' works where a person is said to perform *paradoxa erga* are the descriptions of Elisha and Jesus.

[240] Granted, both in Josephus and in the Gospels (outside of John 10:41) this is an

argument from silence—but it is an argument within a larger context where silence does betoken something. In Book 18 of the *Jewish Antiquities*, Josephus treats two remarkable prophetic figures, Jesus and John. Although the treatment of Jesus is much shorter than that of John, one of the first things Josephus says about Jesus is that he was a worker of marvelous deeds. That Josephus should not say something similar anywhere in his longer description of John does allow us to draw the legitimate inference that miracles were not something John was noted for among his Jewish contemporaries—especially since the same distinction appears implicitly in most Gospel sources and finally explicitly in John 10:41.

[241] See Ernst, *Johannes der Täufer*, 212. It would be a mistake to support belief in the miracle-working power of the Baptist during the life of Jesus by appealing to the remark of the common people (or possibly of Herod Antipas, if we accept the variant reading in the Greek text) that introduces Mark's account of the Baptist's execution (Mark 6:14): "John the Baptist has been raised from the dead and therefore miraculous powers are at work in him." (1) As we shall see, the whole story of the Baptist's execution in Mark is highly suspect from a historical point of view. (2) A further difficulty is created if we accept the alternate reading in the Greek text in 6:14 (supported by Sinaiticus and Alexandrinus), which assigns the opinion to Antipas rather than to people in general (see Metzger [*Textual Commentary*, 89], who gives *elegon* ["they said"] a "B" rating [the preferred reading, but with some degree of doubt]). Mark's report of how Herod Antipas personally explained the miracles of Jesus can hardly be other than a redactional creation of Mark. How would Mark have entrée to the private thoughts of Antipas on the miracles of Jesus? (3) More to the point, the redactional nature of Mark 6:14–16 is seen from the fact that it brackets the so-called "bread-section" in Mark (from 6:32–44 to 8:14–21), where almost every pericope has some reference to bread. The bread-section culminates in the story of Peter's confession of faith near Caesarea Philippi, in which the enumeration of theories about Jesus' true identity (6:14–16) is repeated in 8:28. (4) Even in the redactional statement of Mark 6:14, the reference to miraculous powers means that *because* the Baptist has been *raised from the dead, therefore* miraculous powers are at work in Jesus. In other words, it is not the Baptist *qua* Baptist who is the source of the miracles, but rather the Baptist *qua* raised from the dead by supernatural power who is the source of supernatural power in the one called Jesus. On all this, see Brown, *The Gospel According to John*, 1. 413; Walter Grundmann, *Das Evangelium nach Markus* (THKNT 2; 6th ed.; Berlin: Evangelische Verlagsanstalt, 1973) 126, 168.

[242] Certain traditions about the Baptist are not considered at length because they have no solid claim to stem from the historical Baptist or the historical Jesus. One of these is the discussion about the return of Elijah and Jesus' cryptic identification of Elijah with the Baptist in Mark 9:9–13. Since there seems to have been no idea in pre-Christian Judaism about Elijah returning to prepare the way for a messiah (as opposed to preparing the way for God himself), the dialogue as it stands is probably a Christian creation. For the debate on this point, see Faierstein, "Why Do the Scribes Say That Elijah Must Come First?" 75–86; Allison, " 'Elijah Must Come First,' " 256–58; and Fitzmyer, "More about Elijah Coming First," 295–96. The Marcan pericope may reflect Christian scribal attempts to reconcile the Jewish tradition about Elijah returning to restore all things and the specifically Christian proclamation of the suffering Son of Man. Mark's own solution is to have a secret Messiah (Jesus) explain to his disciples the mystery of a secret Elijah (John); see Wink, *John the Baptist*, 13–17. All of this may explain why the pericope is so disjointed as to be almost unintelligible. As Ernst remarks (*Johannes der Täufer*, 30), "the argumentation [of Mark 9:9–13] is so incoherent and illogical that it is difficult to recognize a definite leading idea."

[243] For the dependence of Matthew and Luke on Mark, see Joachim Gnilka, "Das Martyrium Johannes' des Täufers (Mk 6,17–29)," *Orientierung an Jesus. Zur Theologie der Synoptiker* (Josef Schmid Festschrift; ed. Paul Hoffmann et al.; Freiburg/Basel/Vienna: Herder, 1973) 78–93, esp. 89–90. For Matthew's redaction of Mark's account according to the former's own theological program, see Meier, "John the Baptist in Matthew's Gospel," 399–400. The mention in passing of John's arrest in Luke 3:19–20 is most probably based solely on Mark 1:14 + 6:17–29. Luke proceeds to omit Mark 6:17–29, preserving only a reference to John's beheading as Antipas puzzles over Jesus in Luke 9:9. As Fitzmyer observes (*The Gospel According to Luke*, 1. 476), "if we had only this Lucan account of John's imprisonment [in 3:19–20], it would be hard to understand what is really behind these verses. They are intelligible only because we know the longer form of the story from Mark or Matthew." There is no reason to suppose that Luke knew anything about John's imprisonment and execution beyond what Mark's Gospel told him. The Fourth Gospel knows of John's imprisonment (3:24, though the authority involved is never specified), but his execution is never directly mentioned. The tone of the remarks in both 5:33–36 (v 35: "John *was* [imperfect tense] a lamp burning bright") and 10:40–42 ("John did [aorist tense] no sign") suggests that John is already dead by the time Jesus speaks these words.

[244] Schenk ("Gefangenschaft," 470–73) rejects the following suggestions in favor of a "legitimation pattern of the vindicated martyr," which he claims to find in the redactional passage Mark 6:14–16. According to Schenk, 6:16 presents the confession of a remorseful Antipas, who has taken advantage of Jesus' offer of repentance (cf. 6:12)! Such contorted exegesis needs no refutation.

[245] Ernst, *Johannes der Täufer*, 28–29. For another attempt to see Mark 6:17–29 within Mark's larger theological context, see Ignace de la Potterie, "Mors Johannis Baptistae (Mc 6,17–29)," *VD* 44 (1966) 142–51, esp. 149–51. The exact extent of Marcan redaction in the story is still debated by exegetes. Not surprisingly, Pesch (*Markusevangelium*, 1. 337) argues that Mark, the conservative redactor, has made no substantive change in the tradition he has received, while Schenk ("Gefangenschaft," 468–70) sees Marcan redactional traits throughout. Schenk thinks that there was no coherent text prior to Mark, who constructed the present text out of various stories about the Baptist's death and out of motifs from fables. Most exegetes favor some mix of tradition and redaction; see de la Potterie, "Mors," 142–45.

[246] This may seem a disconcertingly small core, but I am not alone in my judgment; see the carefully weighed conclusion of Gnilka, "Martyrium," 91.

[247] See Theissen, "Die Legende des Täufers—eine Volksüberlieferung mit Nachbarschaftsperspektive?" *Lokalkolorit*, 85–102, esp. 92. However, I do not share all his theories about the geographical and chronological origin of the Marcan story.

[248] For attempts to save Mark, see Robert A. Guelich, *Mark 1–8:26* (Word Biblical Commentary 34A; Dallas: Word, 1989) 331; Hoehner, *Herod Antipas*, 131–36. It is surprising that Hoehner, who is a reputable scholar, engages in conservative apologetics and special pleading to avoid admitting that Mark has made a mistake. Many of his arguments rest on vague generalizations and gratuitous suppositions (e.g., that the author of Mark's Gospel would have known members of Antipas' court like Joanna and Manaen). The ultimate argument seems to be the dogmatic one: the evangelist could not have made such a mistake. To quote Hoehner: "It seems incredible that the evangelists who had access to reliable sources would have made so many gross historical errors" (p. 134). The honor of conservative scholarship is upheld by Taylor (*The Gospel According to St. Mark*, 312), who inclines to the view that Mark is in error here. There

is no proof that Herod the son of Mariamme II was also known as Philip; arguments that "he could have been" hardly make it probable that he was. The whole exercise cannot hide its true nature as a desperate attempt to harmonize Mark and Josephus.

[249] The great Josephan scholar Louis H. Feldman, who is a model of judicious caution, comes to the conclusion that Mark is mistaken in this matter; see his comment on *Ant.* 18.5.1 §109 in *Josephus. Jewish Antiquities. Books XVIII–XIX* (LCL), 76 n. b.

[250] The text of Mark 6:22 printed in the *UBSGNT*[3] reads: *kai eiselthousēs tēs thygatros autou Hērōdiados kai orchēsamenēs* ("and *his* [Antipas'] daughter *Herodias* having entered and danced"). Metzger (*Textual Commentary*, 89–90) reviews the confusing textual situation and reports that with reluctance the majority of the editorial committee decided to print the text given above, but with a "D" rating (very uncertain). Actually, I would not be so pessimistic. The printed text enjoys the attestation of Sinaiticus, Vaticanus, and Bezae. Unlike some of the attempts at emendation in other manuscripts, the Greek given above makes perfect sense—provided the reader does not know the historical state of affairs from Josephus! It is not the Greek text of Sinaiticus, Vaticanus, and Bezae that creates the problem, but the historical information and dogmatic presuppositions that Christian scribes (both ancient and modern) bring to the text. If the text given above was the original one, it is perfectly clear why later Christian scribes would have altered it to avoid an error on Mark's part. If one of the other readings (making the dancing girl Herodias' daughter) was original, it is difficult to see why Christian scribes would have gone out of their way to change the text to introduce a historical error. Therefore, if one measures the text given above by the basic rules of text criticism (the reading attested in the best and earliest manuscripts is to be preferred, the more difficult reading is the better reading, the reading that would explain the rise of the other readings is to be preferred), it must be judged original—and Mark must be judged to have committed another historical error. On this see Theissen, "Die Legende des Täufers," 94; also Schenk, "Gefangenschaft," 467–68.

[251] This point is made by Theissen, "Die Legende des Täufers," 85–102, esp. 91. On the other hand, one should not argue that Machaerus could not have been the locus of a birthday party for Antipas. Excavations at Machaerus indicate otherwise; see Ernst, *Johannes der Täufer*, 343, esp. nn. 246 and 248; cf. Othmar Keel and Max Küchler, *Orte und Landschaften der Bibel* (2 vols.; Zurich/Einsiedeln/Cologne: Benziger; Göttingen: Vandenhoeck & Ruprecht, 1982) 2. 449–50; Benedikt Schwank, "Neue Funde in Nabatäerstädten und ihre Bedeutung für die neutestamentliche Exegese," *NTS* 29 (1983) 429–35. Rainer Riesner ("Johannes der Täufer auf Machärus," *BK* 39 [1984] 176) points to the discovery of two dining halls in Machaerus, presumably one for the men and the other for the women according to Jewish custom. This agrees with Mark's depiction of the daughter *coming in* to dance for Antipas, then *going out* to speak to her mother, and then *coming in* again to speak to Antipas (Mark 6:22–25). However, all that these observations show is that (1) the Marcan story was created by Jews or Jewish Christians who would have taken for granted the Jewish separation of men and women at banquets, and (2) Antipas, as other sources also indicate, was careful not to offend the Jewish sensibilities of his subjects and so tended to observe Jewish law and custom when he was in his tetrarchy. None of this really establishes anything about the historicity of the particular narrative in Mark 6:17–29.

[252] See his description of Machaerus and his narrative of its siege by the Romans in *J.W.* 7.6.1–4 §164–209; also the scattered references in *Ant.* 14.5.2 §83, 14.5.4 §89, 14.6.1 §94 and 96.

[253] Similar motifs can be found in Esth 1:1–3,9–11; 5:6; 7:2–6. Aus (*Water into Wine,*

39–74) places heavy emphasis on the role of the Book of Esther in the formation of Mark 6:17–29. In his view, the story was first composed in Aramaic (or possibly Hebrew) in either Palestine or Syria. It should be categorized as "etiological haggada." Aus specifically rejects the attempts of Hans Windisch and other scholars to save the historicity of Mark's story: "Finally, the Baptist narrative [in Mark 6:17–29] is not historical . . ." (p. 73). While I think that this last point is correct, Aus's heavy emphasis on midrashic expansion and adaptation of the Esther story seems strained, especially since he has to rely on targums and midrashim on Esther that belong to later centuries (see his apologia on pp. 25–26). Similar to Aus's approach is de la Potterie's emphasis on the midrashic character of Mark 6:17–29, with clear echoes from the Book of Esther ("Mors," 149). Gnilka more wisely rejects a one-sided insistence on Esther and sketches the many different motifs that find parallels in both the OT and Greco-Roman literature ("Martyrium," 87–89).

[254] See the parallels pointed out by Hans Windisch, "Kleine Beiträge zur evangelischen Überlieferung. 1. Zum Gastmahl des Antipas," ZNW 18 (1917–18) 73–81. I find it astounding that Windisch thinks that the highly imaginative anecdotes he culls from Athenaeus and Herodotus support the historicity of Mark 6:17–29. On the contrary, if they illustrate anything, it is the kind of ancient Near Eastern folklore that has helped form the Marcan story.

[255] See Theissen, "Die Legende des Täufers," 96–101.

[256] Theissen, "Die Legende des Täufers," 85–102. He points out that the story lacks the depiction of torture and the defense of the martyr spoken before the judge that one would expect in a report of martyrdom or in the *Acta* of the martyrs. Neither is Mark's story a typical legend of a holy man; it does not seize the opportunity to depict the holy man in his exemplary piety (indeed, the Baptist hardly appears on stage intact). "Anecdote" is too general a term, and "novella" likewise does not catch what is characteristic of this story. Theissen prefers the designation "court anecdote" or "court novella," which focuses on court intrigue and misuse of power (we might add: with some love interest directly or indirectly involved). Theissen thinks that the idea that a holy man falls victim to such court intrigue makes Mark 6:17–29 distinctive. For other views on the literary genre, see Dibelius, *Die urchristliche Überlieferung*, 78–80; Haenchen, *Der Weg Jesu*, 241; de la Potterie, "Mors," 146–48; Gnilka, "Martyrium," 84–86.

[257] Theissen ("Die Legende des Täufers," 87–88) holds that the way the moral rebuke is phrased in Mark 6:18 indicates that the story was not formulated by a learned Jewish or Jewish-Christian scribal group. The statement "It is not licit for you to have the wife of your brother [as your wife]" is not false from a Jewish view, but it needs greater precision. A more accurate statement would be: "It is not licit to marry your brother's wife as long as he is still alive." After all, if the brother died childless, it would be a positive obligation of the surviving brother to marry the widow and raise up offspring for the deceased brother (the law of levirate). Aggravating the fault of Herodias in the eyes of ordinary Palestinian Jews was her flouting of ancestral custom: she took the initiative in divorcing her first husband Herod in order to marry his half-brother Antipas while Herod was still alive (*Ant.* 18.5.4 §136: *Hērōdias epi sygchysei phronēsasa tōn patriōn Hērōdē gameitai tou andros tō homopatriō adelphō diastasa zōntos*). Theissen thinks that behind the Marcan story we have not the offense of scribes at a transgression of the law but popular anger at an autonomous, mobile woman of the ruling class. There are none of the traits we would expect if the story had been first formulated by Baptist disciples or Christians.

[258] As we saw in the treatment of chronology in Chapter 11, Josephus' flashback

technique should not lead us to think that John's execution had taken place only shortly before Antipas' defeat by Aretas. There is no reason to date John's death ca. A.D. 35 or 36; see Ernst, *Johannes der Täufer*, 345–46. One must remember the remarkably loose way in which Josephus strings together various events in Book 18 of the *Jewish Antiquities*: e.g., Jesus dies before John the Baptist appears on the scene! Moreover, Josephus does not tell us the exact amount of time that transpired between the various events recounted in the story of Antipas' marital and territorial difficulties with King Aretas. More importantly, Josephus simply indicates that the military disaster Antipas suffered seemed to some Jews to be a punishment from God for the death of John. These Jews would no doubt include—if not be totally identifiable with—the Baptist sectarians who nurtured the memory of the Baptist and therefore resentment against Antipas. It is hardly surprising that they would have connected any major disaster befalling Antipas with divine vengeance for John's execution, no matter how many years had intervened (in fact, only about seven years had transpired). After all, according to Luke 11:51 "this generation" will have to answer for the unjust slaying of everyone from Abel to Zechariah; and Christians had no difficulty seeing the destruction of Jerusalem as divine punishment for the death of Jesus (e.g., Mark 12:1–11), though crime and punishment were separated by forty years. On this delay between the crime and the punishment there is a valuable analogy in the OT story of Sennacherib's siege of Jerusalem (701 B.C.) and his assassination at the hands of two of his sons (681 B.C.), treated in the Bible as a direct consequence of his attack on Jerusalem (see 2 Kings 18–19). Similarly, the deuteronomistic historian blames the fall of Jerusalem in 587/86 B.C. on the sins of Manasseh, who died in 642. Unfortunately, Schenk ("Gefangenschaft," 463–64) fails to appreciate these points, misinterprets Josephus, and winds up having the Baptist outlive Jesus by some five years. On the overall chronological question, see Theissen, "Die Legende des Täufers," 95–96. He points out that it is not impossible that by the end of the twenties of the 1st century A.D. (when John was put to death), Salome was already married to Philip; see also Schenk, "Gefangenschaft," 465–66. If this were true, the whole Marcan story would be fantasy.

[259] Whether the Baptist is rebuking only Herod's act of adultery (Exod 20:14) or is censuring both adultery and incest (Lev 20:21; cf. 18:16) is not clear. Schenk ("Gefangenschaft," 468–69) thinks that the emphasis lies on the charge of adultery. If, however, Theissen ("Die Legende des Täufers,") is correct in thinking that we have here a story that originally expressed the common people's dislike of a "liberated" woman of the Herodian dynasty who left one husband to marry another, the whole question of transgression against the Mosaic Law may be beside the point.

[260] Matthew, for his own theological purposes, shifts the moral burden to Antipas himself.

[261] See the reconstruction by Theissen, "Die Legende des Täufers," 87.

[262] The approach that stresses that Mark and Josephus are complementary rather than contradictory is taken by Scobie, *John the Baptist*, 178–86; and, more cautiously and with greater nuance, by Ernst, *Johannes der Täufer*, 340–46.

[263] Nevertheless, some authors see political intentions in the Baptist's activity as recorded by Josephus; so Lohmeyer, *Das Urchristentum*, 111–12; McCown, "The Scene of John's Ministry," 128–31.

[264] The many differences in the accounts of Josephus and Mark make it nigh impossible that Josephus had access to the Marcan tradition of John's death; so rightly Gnilka, "Martyrium," 90. Perhaps more important than the individual contradictions is the

overall perception that the Josephan and Marcan accounts breathe different air in different universes. The rare view that Josephus had some knowledge of the Marcan tradition is defended (not very well) by Schütz, *Johannes der Täufer*, 17–18.

[265] For a summary of this whole view of Israel's history up to the exile, see 2 Chr 36:15–16. Jeremiah was not the only prophet to complain bitterly of rejection; see, e.g., Amos 7:16; Micah 2:6–11. For all his complaints, Jeremiah was not actually put to death in Jerusalem by the king, probably because he had powerful protectors at court. Quite different was the fate of another prophet, Uriah, who was put to death by King Jehoiakim (Jer 26:20–24). The difference apparently was that, for all his sufferings, Jeremiah, like Isaiah, was an "insider" in that he had important sympathizers at court. Uriah was an "outsider" because he had none. As David Noel Freedman has pointed out to me, in this sense both the Baptist and Jesus were outsiders; both were marginal Jews.

[266] One well-known example of how prophets who were not martyrs became martyrs in later Jewish piety and literature is the apocryphal work *The Martyrdom of Isaiah*; its basic story, probably written originally in Hebrew, could go back as early as the 2d century B.C. See the observations by M. A. Knibb, "The Martyrdom and Ascension of Isaiah," *The Old Testament Pseudepigrapha*, 2. 143–54. Later on (but probably in Christian circles) even Enoch and Elijah became martyrs; see O. S. Wintermute, "Apocalypse of Elijah," *The Old Testament Pseudepigrapha*, 1. 724–26. See also Joachim Jeremias, *Heiligengräber in Jesu Umwelt (Mt. 23,29; Luk. 11,47). Eine Untersuchung zur Volksreligion der Zeit Jesu* (Göttingen: Vandenhoeck & Ruprecht, 1958); Odil H. Steck, *Israel und das gewaltsame Geschick der Propheten* (WMANT 23; Neukirchen-Vluyn: Neukirchener Verlag, 1967).

[267] See, e.g., Farmer, "John the Baptist," *IDB*, 2. 962.

[268] In a curious way one is reminded of the opening words of Rudolf Bultmann in his *Das Evangelium des Johannes* (MeyerK 2; 10th ed.; Göttingen: Vandenhoeck & Ruprecht, 1968) 1, as he meditates on the strange character of the Prologue of the Fourth Gospel. At first glance it seems hardly an introduction (*Einführung*), since it is complete in itself and nicely rounded off; it needs nothing to follow it. It is more a riddle than a key to understanding the Gospel; it can be fully understood only by the person who knows the whole Gospel. And yet it is an introduction in the sense of an overture that takes us out of everyday life and leads us into a new and strange world. Mutatis mutandis, the same can be said of a study of the historical Baptist as an introduction to the study of the historical Jesus. Indeed, for some 1st-century Jews, John *was*— unbeknownst to himself—the prologue and introduction to Jesus.

[269] The reference is to the famous essay by A. M. Farrer, "On Dispensing with Q," *Studies in the Gospels. Essays in Memory of R. H. Lightfoot* (ed. D. E. Nineham; Oxford: Blackwell, 1967) 55–88. Farrer's suggestion is that the Gospels were written in the order Mark—Matthew—Luke—John, with each evangelist knowing the work of the previous evangelists. If this theory worked, it would have simplicity on its side. Unfortunately—if I may judge from my own labors in writing a commentary on Matthew's Gospel—the theory creates more problems than it solves. For a good summary of the arguments in favor of the two-source theory (and hence in favor of the existence of a Q document), see Davies and Allison, *The Gospel According to Saint Matthew*, 1. 97–127.

[270] In recent years here in the United States, rejection of Marcan priority has often entailed espousing the Griesbach hypothesis; see, e.g., William R. Farmer, *The Synoptic Problem* (New York: Macmillan, 1964); idem, "A Fresh Approach to Q," *Christianity,*

Judaism and Other Greco-Roman Cults. Studies for Morton Smith at Sixty (SJLA 12; 4 vols.; ed. Jacob Neusner; Leiden: Brill, 1975) 1. 39–50; C. S. Mann, *Mark* (AB 27; Garden City, NY: Doubleday, 1986). Various other critiques of Marcan priority include B. C. Butler, *The Originality of St. Matthew. A Critique of the Two-Document Hypothesis* (Cambridge: Cambridge University, 1951); P. Benoit and M.-E. Boismard, *Synopse des quatre évangiles en français* (2 vols.; Paris: Cerf, 1966, 1972); Hans-Herbert Stoldt, *Geschichte und Kritik der Markushypothese* (Göttingen: Vandenhoeck & Ruprecht, 1977); John M. Rist, *On the Independence of Matthew and Mark* (SNTSMS 32; New York: Cambridge University, 1978).

[271] Besides Farrer see, e.g., Joachim Jeremias, "Zur Hypothese einer schriftlichen Logienquelle Q," *Abba* (Göttingen: Vandenhoeck & Ruprecht, 1966) 90–92; Hans-Theo Wrege, *Die Überlieferungsgeschichte der Bergpredigt* (WUNT 9; Tübingen: Mohr [Siebeck], 1968); G. Schille, "Bemerkungen zur Formgeschichte des Evangeliums. II. Das Evangelium des Matthäus als Katechismus," *NTS* 4 (1957–58) 101–14; M. D. Goulder, *Midrash and Lection in Matthew* (London: SPCK, 1974).

[272] For these arguments, see Kloppenborg, *Formation*, 42–51; Frans Neirynck, "Q," *IDBSup*, 715–16.

[273] Not all the verbal agreement is of a high degree, and at times scholars must choose between Matthew and Luke to reestablish what they think is the original order of Q. Especially in the case of parallels with low verbal agreement, one must be ready to entertain the possibility of oral tradition coming to each evangelist in somewhat different form. On the problem of the original order of Q, see Kloppenborg, *Formation*, 64–80.

[274] Major theorists include Dieter Lührmann, *Die Redaktion der Logienquelle* (WMANT 33; Neukirchen-Vluyn: Neukirchener Verlag, 1969); idem, "The Gospel of Mark and the Sayings Collection Q," *JBL* 108 (1989) 51–71; Siegfried Schulz, *Q. Die Spruchquelle der Evangelisten*, (Zurich: Theologischer Verlag, 1972); Paul Hoffmann, *Studien zur Theologie der Logienquelle* (NTAbh 8; 2d ed.; Münster: Aschendorff, 1975); Richard A. Edwards, *A Theology of Q. Eschatology, Prophecy, and Wisdom* (Philadelphia: Fortress, 1976); Athanasius Polag, *Die Christologie der Logienquelle* (WMANT 45; Neukirchen-Vluyn: Neukirchener Verlag, 1977); Petros Vassiliadis, "The Nature and Extent of the Q Document," *NovT* 20 (1978) 49–73; Rudolf Laufen, *Die Doppelüberlieferungen der Logienquelle und des Markusevangeliums* (BBB 54; Königstein: Hanstein, 1980); Ivan Havener, *Q. The Sayings of Jesus* (Good News Studies 19; Wilmington, DE: Glazier, 1987); John S. Kloppenborg, *The Formation of Q. Trajectories in Ancient Wisdom Collections* (Philadelphia: Fortress, 1987); Migaku Sato, *Q und Prophetie. Studien zur Gattungs- und Traditionsgeschichte der Quelle Q* (WUNT 2/29; Tübingen: Mohr [Siebeck], 1988); David Catchpole, *The Quest For Q* (Edinburgh: Clark, 1993). See also the various essays in John S. Kloppenborg with Leif E. Vaage (eds.), *Early Christianity, Q and Jesus* (Semeia 55; Atlanta: Scholars, 1992). An attempt to use the Q document to reconstruct Jesus as a Jewish Socrates who was later mythologized into the Christ of the NT can be found in Burton L. Mack, *The Lost Gospel. The Book of Q and Christian Origins* (San Francisco: Harper, 1993). My opinion on such an attempt can be divined from my comments in the main text on claiming to know too much about Q. For reports on the work of the International Q Project, see the notices by James M. Robinson in *JBL* 109 (1990) 499–501; 110 (1991) 494–98; 111 (1992) 500–508.

[275] *Formation*, 80–87.

[276] *Formation*, 64–80.

[277] Wittgenstein's own dictum, enunciated both in his preface and as the last proposition (#7) in the main text of his famous *Tractatus Logico-Philosophicus*, is "whereof one cannot speak, thereof one must be silent [Wovon man nicht sprechen kann, darüber muss man schweigen]." See Ludwig Wittgenstein, *Tractatus Logico-Philosophicus* (translation by C. K. Ogden; London/New York: Routledge, 1922) 26–27, 188–89. The meaning of this statement in the context of the *Tractatus* is discussed by Ray Monk, *Ludwig Wittgenstein. The Duty of Genius* (New York: The Free Press [Macmillan], 1990) 155–56.

[278] Appeal is often made to the seminal essay of Gerd Theissen, "Legitimation and Subsistence: An Essay on the Sociology of Early Christian Missionaries," *The Social Setting of Pauline Christianity. Essays on Corinth* (Philadelphia: Fortress, 1982) 27–67. One tends to forget how speculative a reconstruction Theissen's own group of itinerant charismatics is.

[279] For a similar reason, I am dubious about the idea that the community or communities that carried and used Q did not also know some form of narrative or proclamation about Jesus' death and resurrection. The high probability that Q itself had no Passion Narrative (to me, the most likely position) in no way demonstrates what other traditions or documents a "Q community" might or might not have known as well. To take the cases we do know: for some years, both the church of Matthew and the church of Luke presumably used Q in their liturgy and catechesis, while at the same time knowing the passion kerygma from Mark's Gospel, also in use in their worship and teaching.

[280] So Kloppenborg, *Formation*, 79.

[281] For the arguments for this position, see Meier, *Law and History*, 57–65.

[282] On the question of the abrogation of the Mosaic Law in Jesus' teaching on divorce, see Meier, *Law and History*, 140–50.

[283] Sato, *Q und Prophetie*, 62–65 (photographs on pp. 66–68).

[284] For one form of this approach, see J. P. Brown, "The Form of 'Q' Known to Matthew," *NTS* 8 (1961–62) 27–42.

[285] For a brief summary of his views, see Schulz, *Q. Die Spruchquelle der Evangelisten*, 481–89.

[286] For a survey of approaches, see John S. Kloppenborg, "Tradition and Redaction in the Synoptic Sayings Source," *CBQ* 46 (1984) 34–62.

[287] For summaries of the two views, compare Kloppenborg (*Formation*, 317–28) with Sato (*Q und Prophetie*, 406–11). Kloppenborg readily admits the influence of James M. Robinson, "LOGOI SOPHON: On the Gattung of Q," *Trajectories Through Early Christianity* (Philadelphia: Fortress, 1971) 71–113; see also Robinson's "Foreword" to Kloppenborg's *Formation*, xi–xiv. For another treatment of Q that emphasizes the prophetic rather than the sapiential, see M. Eugene Boring, *Sayings of the Risen Jesus. Christian Prophecy in the Synoptic Tradition* (SNTSMS 46; Cambridge: Cambridge University, 1982) 137–82, esp. 180–81. Closer in overall approach to Sato, but with a different perspective, is Arland D. Jacobson, "The Literary Unity of Q," *JBL* 101 (1982) 365–89. Jacobson thinks that the deuteronomistic-Wisdom perspective in Q represents a shift away from the earlier apocalyptic view focused on the imminent expectation of the Son of Man (p. 389).

PART TWO

MESSAGE

*Jesus, a wise man, . . . was . . . a teacher of people
who receive the truth with pleasure*
JOSEPHUS, *ANT.* 18.3.3 §63

CHAPTER 14

THE KINGDOM OF GOD:

God Coming in Power to Rule

PART I:
BACKGROUND

I. INTRODUCTORY CONSIDERATIONS

Our study of Jesus' baptism by John and his subsequent relation to John (Chapter 13) has already launched us into Jesus' public ministry. Once so launched, we must constantly remind ourselves of a basic rule: between Jesus' baptism and the last weeks of his life, there is no before or after.[1] The time frame and plot line of each evangelist are his own creation; and once that redactional grid is dissolved by form and redaction criticism, there are very few indicators of time in the individual units of the Jesus tradition.[2] Hence the major sayings and deeds of Jesus during his ministry must be studied topically. The question becomes: which topic first?

(1) *The Kingdom of God as a Major Part of Jesus' Message.* That I should begin such a topical study with Jesus' proclamation of the kingdom of God will startle no one acquainted with the quest for the historical Jesus.[3] Many scholars have voiced in various ways the ringing affirmation of Joachim Jeremias: "Our starting point is the fact that the central theme of the public proclamation of Jesus was the kingly reign of God."[4] Norman Perrin, a former pupil of Jeremias, makes an even more categorical claim and draws a sweeping conclusion from it: "The central aspect of the teaching of Jesus was that concerning the Kingdom of God. On this there can be no doubt and today no scholar does, in fact, doubt it. Jesus appeared as one who proclaimed the Kingdom; all else in his message and ministry serves a function in relation to that proclamation and derives its meaning from it."[5] This last point, in particular, needs to be tested rather than taken for granted. It is one thing to say that the kingdom of God was *a* central or at least *a* major part of Jesus' message. It is quite another to claim that it was *the* central element from which every other part of his message derives its meaning.

That the kingdom of God was at least a significant component of Jesus' message is clear simply from the number and spread of occurrences of the phrase in the sayings of Jesus. The criterion of multiple attestation of sources is more than satisfied: the phrase "kingdom of God" or its equivalents (e.g., "kingdom of heaven," "kingdom of my Father," etc.) occur in 13 sayings in Mark, in some 13 sayings in Q, in some 25 sayings in M, in some 6 sayings in L, and in 2 sayings in John.[6] Moreover, this wide attestation in a variety of sources is matched by wide attestation in a variety of form-critical categories: e.g., parables, prayer, beatitudes, eschatological prophecies, miracle stories, conditional sentences stating the requirements for entrance into the kingdom, a concise two-part statement on John the Baptist, and a concise summary of the proclamation of both Jesus and his disciples. Needless to say, this does not prove that every saying in which "kingdom of God" appears is therefore authentic. Most likely both oral tradition and the evangelists imitated Jesus' vocabulary and message. This is especially true in the case of the special tradition and the redactional activity of Matthew, which represent a disproportionate number of occurrences. But the multiple attestation of both sources and forms does argue well for the position that "kingdom of God" formed a major part of the message of the historical Jesus.

This preliminary observation is bolstered by the criterion of discontinuity. The precise phrase "kingdom of God" does not occur as such in the Hebrew OT, and occurrences in the deuterocanonical/apocryphal books of the OT, the OT pseudepigrapha, Qumran, Philo, Josephus, and most of the targums are either rare or nonexistent.[7] Use of "kingdom of heaven" increases somewhat in the rabbis, but even there usage is restricted largely to certain stereotyped phrases.[8] Corresponding to this sparse representation of the phrase in early Jewish literature is the relative dearth of occurrences of "kingdom of God" in other parts of the NT. In the whole corpus of undisputed Pauline epistles, the phrase occurs in only seven passages (1 Thess 2:12; Gal 5:21; 1 Cor 4:20; 1 Cor 6:9–10 [2 times]; 1 Cor 15:24,50; and Rom 14:17), and many of these seem to represent baptismal or parenetic traditions that Paul is taking over rather than minting himself.[9] It is striking that, although Paul's epistles represent the first complete Christian literary corpus preserved for us after Jesus' historical ministry, "kingdom of God" does not play a large role in Paul's own thought and language. When it does appear, it seems to be an echo of earlier Christian proclamation, itself echoing the usage of the master. The scattered references in the disputed Pauline letters (2 Thess 1:5; Col 1:13; 4:11; Eph 5:5; 2 Tim 4:1,18) are fewer still and, if anything, less central to the message of these letters. The Acts of the Apostles has slightly more examples (Acts 1:3,6; 8:12; 14:22; 19:8; 20:25; 28:23,31), but we must take into account Luke's redactional tendency to link the time of Jesus (the Third Gospel) with the time of the church (Acts) by using Gospel phrases in Acts (e.g., "disciples"). Indeed, an examination of the individual texts in Acts that mention the kingdom of God suggests that most if not all of them stem from Luke's redactional activity.[10]

Outside of the Pauline orbit, references to the eschatological kingdom of

God are understandably present in the Revelation of John, but again the occurrences are surprisingly few (Rev 1:9; 11:15; 12:10).[11] Interestingly, none of the occurrences of "kingdom of God" in the Book of Revelation is placed on the lips of the risen Jesus, to whom a fair number of sayings are attributed in this work. Hence, in the one clear case where a Christian prophet is putting words into the mouth of (the risen) Jesus, those words do not include "kingdom of God." As for the rest of the NT, the yield is extremely meager. The Epistle to the Hebrews uses the phrase only in 1:8 (when Ps 45:7 is addressed to Christ) and 12:28. The Epistle of James has only one reference (2:5); a reference in 2 Pet 1:11 rounds out the not overly impressive attestation outside the Synoptic Gospels.

This brief survey implies that the frequent appearance of "kingdom of God" on the lips of the Synoptic Jesus cannot be traced to its popularity and regular use in either pre-Christian Judaism or 1st-century Christianity. Outside the Synoptic Gospels and the mouth of Jesus, it does not seem to have been widely used by either Jews or Christians in the early 1st century A.D. Significantly, we do not find the NT authors who use it outside the Gospels putting it into the mouth of Jesus; the Revelation of John is especially striking in this regard. In the Synoptic Gospels themselves, "kingdom of God" is found almost always in the mouth of Jesus, rarely in the comments of the evangelist (e.g., Mark 15:43 par.; Luke 19:11) or in the mouths of other persons (e.g., Luke 14:15). Consequently, our initial impression is reinforced: the only adequate explanation for the heavy concentration of "kingdom of God" in the sayings of the Synoptic Jesus, contrasting sharply with the relative dearth of the phrase in early Judaism and the rest of the NT, is that the frequent occurrences faithfully reflect Jesus' own usage and emphasis.[12] At the very least, "kingdom of God" was a major component of Jesus' message.

(2) *"Kingdom of God and Kingdom of Heaven."* With the exception of Matthew's Gospel, the form of the phrase that is regularly used throughout the NT is "the kingdom of God."[13] Matthew alone uses instead the set phrase "the kingdom of heaven," though he does employ "kingdom of God" four times (12:28; 19:24; 21:31,43).[14] Various Matthean critics have sought to discover some distinction in meaning (e.g., present versus future kingdom, or great emphasis on the transcendent origin of the kingdom by the use of "heaven"),[15] but Matthew's own usage tells against such subtleties. Matthew uses the two phrases interchangeably in two succeeding verses of a single pericope (19:23 + 24), thus making any real distinction in meaning nigh impossible. Matthean usage is better explained by the fact that Matthew's tradition and formation stem from a church that had been strongly Jewish-Christian in its early days.[16] The use of "heaven" in place of "God" is simply a pious Jewish periphrasis to avoid constantly naming the Deity in the oblique case of a set formula. Hence the surprising appearance of "kingdom of God" in four Matthean passages should be considered a pointer to what was the earlier and perhaps original form of the phrase.

This hypothesis is strengthened by the fact that every other author in the

NT who uses the set phrase employs "kingdom of God," never "kingdom of heaven." From many other types of Gospel sayings, we can see that Jesus did not as a rule avoid the name God,[17] and there is no reason to think that he would have sought to avoid it when speaking of God's kingdom. Moreover, Jewish intertestamental literature before Jesus does not use "kingdom of heaven," while a few examples of "kingdom of God" do appear.[18] On the other hand, rabbinic use of "kingdom of heaven" can be documented only after Jesus.[19] Thus, while Jesus may have varied his usage, all indicators point to "kingdom of God" (in Aramaic: *malkûtā' dî 'ĕlāhā'*) as his regular if not sole way of referring to the kingdom.[20]

(3) *"Kingdom" or "Reign"?* I have used the word "kingdom" in the title of this chapter and in the discussion up until now because "the kingdom of God" is the traditional English translation of *hē basileia tou theou*, because it is the phrase enshrined in the titles of so many books and articles on the subject, and finally because any newcomer to the discussion would probably be confused if from the start I used one of the alternate—and more accurate—phrases ("reign," "rule," "kingship," "kingly power," etc.). While bowing to English tradition, I readily admit that "kingdom of God" is misleading to anyone who does not know the biblical background of the phrase. "Kingdom of God" is a vague and abstract-sounding locution that, if it conveys anything, conveys the idea of a set territory or realm over which God rules. Both connotations—abstractness and emphasis on territory—create a false impression. As we shall see, "kingdom of God" is meant to conjure up the dynamic notion of God powerfully ruling over his creation, over his people, and over the history of both. The point has been put succinctly by a number of writers: the kingdom of God means God ruling as king. Hence his action upon and his dynamic relationship to those ruled, rather than any delimited territory, is what is primary.

Nevertheless, "kingdom" is not entirely out of place as a translation of *basileia*. If God rules and controls the whole universe and in particular his people Israel, logically there must be some concrete created reality that is ruled, a reality in space and time that in some sense constitutes a realm or kingdom in which God exercises and visibly manifests his power. The sayings of Jesus that use phrases like "enter into the kingdom" or "be in the kingdom" necessarily conjure up a spatial image, however un-spatial the ultimate reality that the image points to may be. Consequently, I am willing to keep "the kingdom of God" as a stock translation of *hē basileia tou theou*, provided the dynamic rule of God that establishes his kingdom is understood to be the primary component of the symbol. At times, though, I will use "kingship," "kingly rule," or "reign" instead to make sure that we are not lulled into accepting the territorial imperative latent in the symbol.[21]

(4) *The Kingdom of God as a Symbol.* Having just referred to the kingdom of God as a symbol, I should note the influential view of Norman Perrin, who in his last book on parables insisted that the kingdom of God was a particular sort of symbol and should not be called an idea or conception. Taking over a

distinction made by Philip Wheelwright,[22] Perrin observed that there are certain symbols that always have a one-to-one relationship to the things they represent (e.g., the mathematical symbol *pi* or a red signal light at an intersection).[23] These are steno-symbols; they are useful precisely because they have a single, clearly defined, and clearly understood meaning. Quite different are those symbols which can conjure up in our minds and hearts a whole range of meanings, experiences, or yearnings. To ask what is the single, clearly defined meaning of Michelangelo's *Pietà* or *The Last Judgment* is to miss the point and brand oneself a Philistine. As a symbol moves from mathematical precision to artistic suggestiveness, as it plays with Jungian archetypes and mythic stories, as it addresses the meaning of the universe and of human life, it increasingly defies any attempt to nail it down with one neat definition. Such a "deep symbol" is what Perrin calls a "tensive symbol." It evokes not one meaning but a whole range of meanings. Since the kingdom of God is such a tensive symbol, says Perrin, it is a mistake to try to reduce it to any one idea or conception. This is why one is always frustrated when one attempts to "define" the kingdom of God. The kingdom of God does not have a definition; it tells a story.

The mythic story evoked by the phrase "the kingdom of God" stretches from the first page of the Bible to its last, and a given context will highlight one aspect of the multifaceted symbol rather than another.[24] If we were to construct an artificial summary of the story of the kingdom, it would include God's creation of his good and ordered universe, creation's corruption by human sin and rebellion, God's gracious choice of the people Israel to be his very own, his liberation of them from slavery in Egypt, the experiences of sin and salvation at the Reed Sea and Mt. Sinai, the desert journey, and entrance into the promised land. The story might include the kingdom of the all-too-human-but-later-idealized King David, God's choice of Jerusalem and Mt. Zion for his dwelling place alongside the king, the disasters caused by David's less than ideal successors, the descent of Israel into ever greater idolatry and sin, Israel's rejection of the prophets' warnings, the destruction of Jerusalem and the Babylonian exile, the promise of future restoration that would include a rebuilt Jerusalem and a new, purified temple, the subjection of the hostile Gentiles, and the establishment among human beings of God's eternal kingdom of peace and justice (with or without a human vicegerent or intermediary). Depending on how apocalyptic a given storyteller might be, the final kingdom might be envisioned as a restoration-but-vast-improvement of David's original kingdom, or a return to paradise on earth, or a heavenly kingdom beyond this world of time and space.

The reader must excuse me for "fast-forwarding" the whole of the OT and intertestamental apocalyptic literature, but only such a breathless literary marathon can encapsulate the vast world of meaning that "the kingdom of God" can evoke. Obviously, no one use of the phrase is meant to conjure up every aspect of the story equally, nor does every use have the same theological intent. A particular OT psalm may extol God's constant and unchallenged rule over heaven and earth without reflecting on human sinfulness, punishment, and eschatological restoration. The story of God's rule may at times focus solely on Israel, without the Gentiles even being mentioned. At other times, the conflict between Israel and the Gentiles may hold center stage. Some retellings may dispense with David, Jerusalem, and the temple; others may make them central. The grand story of the kingdom has many twists and turns, and not a few alternate endings. As in the case of a good piece of music, every literary "performance" actualizes certain potentialities of the tensive symbol, while passing over others. Like any masterpiece of art, the tensive symbol is not exhausted by the performer; rather, it exhausts both performer and audience and then invites everyone back for more. So it is with our attempt to understand the kingdom of God—in the Bible in general and in Jesus' message in particular.

Perrin's emphasis on kingdom as a tensive symbol is a salutary warning against treating a mythic archetype like a mathematical formula. Yet, as other critics have noted, Perrin may have drawn some illegitimate conclusions from his distinction between a steno-symbol and a tensive symbol. First, Perrin insists that we must not talk about the kingdom as an idea or a conception, but only as a symbol.[25] Actually, this does not follow logically, unless there is some unwritten law that an idea or a concept must be a clear, neatly defined mental construct that always has a one-to-one relation to the reality it represents. But that is hardly the case. Even the most logical and precise of systematic theologians works with ideas and concepts that are multifaceted, ambiguous, or downright murky. There is no reason why we must become caricatures of Descartes, restricting the use of "idea" or "concept" to what is clear and distinct. When at times I use "idea" or "concept" of the kingdom of God, I intend the same sort of richly textured, multilayered, never-fully-captured reality I intimate with the designation "tensive symbol."[26]

There is a second problem with Perrin's view that the kingdom of God in Jesus' preaching is a tensive symbol. Perrin moves too quickly from this insight to the position that the symbol carries no particular indication of the time of the kingdom's arrival (already arrived in the present? coming in the near future? both present and future?).[27] Rejecting any of these choices, Perrin insists that Jesus evokes the myth of God's royal activity "to mediate the experience of existential reality."[28] Apart from this sounding more like a 20th-century Bultmannian than a 1st-century Jew, it does not follow that the kingdom of God, simply because it is a multifaceted tensive symbol, does not or cannot, in individual instances, convey a reference to the time of the kingdom's arrival.[29] A time frame, however vague or mythic, was part of the underlying story of the kingdom evoked by the tensive symbol. Thus it seems more reasonable to argue that the tensive symbol of the kingdom would tend to evoke a number of possible time frames rather than none. We should not slip into a basic mistake of the deconstructionists; multiplicity of meaning is not the same thing as no meaning. At any rate, whether in fact Jesus' use of "kingdom of God" points to one or more particular time frames can be decided only by an analysis of the pertinent texts, not by global considerations about tensive symbols.

(5) *The Kingdom and Eschatology.* Even these initial, sketchy observations on the kingdom suggest how closely intertwined the questions of kingdom and eschatology are in any study of Jesus' message, no matter what one's ultimate decision about their precise relationship may be. Actually, the topic of the kingdom only serves to open up the larger question of the eschatological views Jesus held; "kingdom of God" does not exhaust everything Jesus had to say (or do) about eschatology. The question of Jesus' eschatological stance pervades almost every other aspect of Jesus' ministry as well: parables, miracles, table fellowship, his call of disciples (especially the Twelve), and the way he faced his own death. Only at the end of our study of Jesus' message, ministry, and fate can we seek to formulate an adequate evaluation of his eschatology. Yet, granted the pivotal role of the kingdom in Jesus' proclamation, studying the kingdom is perhaps the best way to begin the larger project of understanding Jesus' eschatology. At the same time, we need not be surprised that our attempt to grasp Jesus' message of the kingdom will involve us in other dimensions of his ministry as well (e.g., his miracles). The broad extent of "kingdom language" in Jesus' sayings plus the pervasive nature of his eschatological vision make neat packets of topics, hermetically sealed off from one another, impossible. In the very act of trying to divide up and treat separately the varied components of Jesus' ministry, we begin to feel the centripetal force that ties them together. Kingdom and eschatology are certainly part of that force.

As we turn to the OT background of Jesus' use of the phrase and symbol "kingdom of God," one point should be made clear. In what follows I do not propose a thorough exploration of all the ramifications of the symbol of God as king in the OT. That would take a monograph in itself and would not ultimately serve the goal of this chapter. Since we are interested in the possible linguistic and conceptual background to Jesus' use of one particular phrase, "the kingdom of God," I shall focus the following study precisely on the OT's use of words and phrases connected with God's kingship, kingly rule, and kingdom.[30]

II. GOD'S KINGLY RULE IN THE OT

When we examine the OT (including the deuterocanonical/apocryphal books), we are faced with a paradox: the OT contains only one example of the precise phrase "kingdom of God," and yet the OT is supremely important as background for Jesus' usage.[31] On the one side of the paradox, the only occurrence of "kingdom of God" (*basileian theou*) is found in the deuterocanonical/apocryphal Wisdom of Solomon (10:10). In the books of the Hebrew canon the exact phrase "kingdom of God" never occurs. "Kingdom of Yahweh" occurs once in the relatively late 1 Chronicles (1 Chr 28:5), where David speaks of Solomon sitting on the throne "of the kingdom of Yahweh" (*malkût yahweh*).[32] The word "kingship" or "kingdom" (*malkût*) does occur at times in other contexts that make plain that the kingdom or rule belongs to God, but no set phrase is used: e.g., Pss 103:19 ("his kingdom"); 145:11,12,13 ("your kingdom"); 1 Chr 17:14 ("my kingdom").[33] The related Hebrew word *mĕlûkâ* is employed to state that the "kingship" belongs to Yahweh in Obad 21 and Ps 22:29. Another Hebrew word, *mamlākâ*, is used to attribute "kingship" or "kingly rule" to Yahweh in 1 Chr 29:11 ("to you, Yahweh, belongs kingship"). As for Aramaic equivalents, the Aramaic portions of the Book of Daniel are not abundant in examples either. The Aramaic word *malkûtāʾ* ("kingship," "kingly rule," "kingdom")[34] is used of God in the phrase "his kingdom" in Dan 4:3 [English text, 3:33 in the Aramaic]; 4:34 [English text, 4:31 in the Aramaic]; and 7:27, while Dan 2:44 speaks of the "God of heaven" establishing "a kingdom."

This sums up the hardly overwhelming use in the OT of phrases similar to Jesus' "kingdom of God." Indeed, there are whole parts of the OT that have no explicit reference to God as king or to God's kingship. It is not coincidental that the few examples of an abstract noun plus some possessive noun or pronoun to signify God's kingship or kingdom occur almost entirely among the late books of the Hebrew canon,[35] while the one precise parallel occurs in the Book of Wisdom, composed in Greek probably in the 1st century B.C.—thus the last book to be written in the larger (so-called "Alexandrian") canon of the OT accepted by Catholic and Orthodox Christians.[36] To judge from the sparse and late OT evidence, Jesus apparently took up a relatively recent way of referring to God's kingly rule, and he may well have been the first to forge and employ regularly the fixed phrase "the kingdom of God" to evoke the OT mythic story.

On the other side of the paradox, it is certainly the OT that establishes the basic mythic story line later encapsulated in the set formula of "the kingdom of God." Typically, though, the OT does this through dynamic verbs rather than abstract nouns. Cultic proclamations of *yahweh mālak* ("Yahweh has become king!" or "Yahweh rules as king!")[37] and prophetic promises of *yahweh yimlōk* ("Yahweh will reign as king") set the tone for the OT's view of God's past, present, and future act of ruling as king.[38]

As an aside, I should point out here to the reader that many studies of God's kingly rule in the OT carefully divide up the material according to sources and try to trace a hypothetical tradition history of the symbol of God's kingship. Some proceed to engage in complex speculation about a New Year's feast of Yahweh's enthronement as king, supposedly celebrated each autumn with a ritual enactment of Yahweh's defeat of the powers of chaos.[39] While such approaches can be fascinating, they really are not useful for our purpose, which is to grasp the scriptural background for Jesus' view of the kingdom of God. Jesus obviously did not read the sacred books of Israel from the modern perspective of tradition history; hence a synthetic presentation of the material is more in keeping with the way he would have understood the OT's message.

Particularly from Isaiah and the Psalms Jesus would have learned the basic truth that God as Creator has ruled, is ruling, and always will rule over his creation, be it obedient or rebellious. Whatever precise aspect of God's kingship a text might underline, the presupposition of any biblical writer was that God is "the king of the ages," the eternal king. Hence the psalmist can sing (and no doubt Jesus at worship sang, too): "Your kingdom is a kingdom for all ages, and your kingly rule lasts for all generations" (Ps 145:13). "Yahweh has established his throne in the heavens, and his kingly power rules over all" (Ps 103:19). Indeed, Yahweh is king precisely because he has created and continues to govern all things by his unlimited power (Ps 93:1–4; cf. Ps 96:10; Ps 97:1–6).

Some scholars, following the lead of Sigmund Mowinckel, consider Psalms 47, 93, 96, 97, 98, and 99 to be "royal enthronement psalms" that celebrate Yahweh's kingly rule over creation, Israel, and the history of both.[40] Whatever the precise form-critical category of these psalms, their basic message is clear. In various ways, these psalms proclaim that, while God has always been king, he has exercised his creative kingship in a new and special way by creating the people Israel, by ruling it through particular laws (the Pentateuch) and leaders (e.g., Moses, Aaron, and Samuel), and by choosing the Jerusalem temple, the footstool of his heavenly throne (cf. Ps 99:1–9). Some scholars also see in the psalms' acclamation of Yahweh's kingship an expression of eschatological hope.[41] The central importance of all these references in the psalter to Yahweh as king flows from the function of the Book of Psalms as the "hymn book" of Judaism. Constantly repeated, the psalms were a major way in which the symbol of Yahweh's kingly rule—in all its various aspects—was regularly absorbed into the religious consciousness of Judaism, which longed for a new manifestation of God's kingship.

Yet the theme of God's kingship over Israel is by no means restricted to the Book of Psalms. The basis for Yahweh's claim to kingship is laid out in the narrative books of the OT—though, intriguingly, the meager examples in the Pentateuch are all in poetic contexts. This is a good reminder that, even in the narrative books, God's kingship is a poetic metaphor. Yahweh made himself Israel's king by fighting for it as a divine warrior against the Egyptians and delivering it at the Reed Sea. The great Song of the Sea in Exodus 15 fittingly ends with an acclamation that moves from the original act of redemption to the unlimited future: "Yahweh will reign as king forever and ever" (Exod 15:18). Yahweh's status as king is then legally sealed by the covenant at Mt. Sinai, where Israel becomes for its God "a kingdom of priests" (Exod 19:6: *mamleket kōhănîm*; cf. Deut 33:5).[42] On the whole, though, one is surprised to see how few passages in the Pentateuch—in comparison with the Psalms and the Prophets—explicitly mention the idea of Yahweh as Israel's king, though the symbol does surface in some highly significant contexts (the crossing of the Reed Sea, the covenant at Sinai, Balaam's oracles, and the blessing of Moses). From these passages it is clear that the Pentateuch thinks in terms of Yahweh's kingship over Israel rather than over heaven, earth, or the whole of creation.

Since Yahweh had established his kingship over Israel by the events at the Reed Sea and Mt. Sinai,[43] the attempt to create a human king in the promised land at the time of Saul was looked upon by some as the rejection of the divine king (1 Sam 8:6–22; cf. Gideon's refusal in Judg 8:23). Yet other texts in 1 Samuel take a positive view of human kingship as instituted by God (1 Sam 9:1–10:16; 12:1–2,13).[44] An acceptable modus vivendi was worked out with Saul's successor, David, whom later Scripture exalted as the ideal human king, humbly acting as vicegerent or vassal of the divine king. In return, through the prophet Nathan, Yahweh promised David that his descendants would always sit upon his throne (2 Sam 7:8–17), a prophecy that later became the basis of hopes for a Davidic king in the end time. In fact, the increasing failure of David's successors to live up to the Davidic ideal caused the prophets to look resolutely to the future for a more obedient vassal of the divine king (e.g., Isa 7:10–14; 9:6–7 [MT 9:5–6]). Despite the prophets' warnings, the sinfulness of Judah, including both king and people, multiplied until the divine king (cf. Isa 6:1–13)[45] delivered his kingdom into the hands of the king of Babylon.

It was out of the depths of despair during the Babylonian exile that the prophets spoke of a future restoration of God's kingdom in Judah, with Jerusalem once more as a holy capital. This is the "good news" that Deutero-Isaiah (which Jesus would naturally have read simply as part of the Book of Isaiah) proclaims to the exiles: "How beautiful on the mountains are the feet of him who brings the news, announcing peace, bringing good news, announcing salvation, saying to Zion, 'Your God reigns as king [*mālak 'ĕlōhāyik*]!' " (52:7).[46] Here is a turning point in Israel's vision of God ruling as king (besides 52:7, the title is used in 41:21; 43:15; 44:6). Israel's breaking of the covenant by its innumerable sins should have spelled the end of its existence as the special locus of God's kingly rule. But in his saving mercy, which is also his justice, God the King forgives and redeems his people, bringing them out of their captivity in a new exodus, creating them anew as his kingdom (see Isa 43:1–8,15; 44:6). His royal power is revealed before the nations in his gathering of the scattered remnants of Israel back together in a purified Jerusalem. As we shall see, (Deutero-) Isaiah's rethinking of God's kingly rule in terms of forgiving love, of the regathering of fragmented Israel into a restored unity centered on the holy city, resonates in the message and activity of Jesus. Jesus, who naturally would not have distinguished later "apocalyptic additions" to the Book of Isaiah such as chaps. 24 and 33, would have found in 24:23 ("Yahweh of hosts reigns as king on Mt. Zion and Jerusalem") and 33:22 ("Yahweh is our king, he is the one who saves us") further support for the idea of Yahweh's eschatological kingship, exercised in an apocalyptic context.[47]

The promise of a hope-filled future is not, of course, restricted to the Book of Isaiah. The image of merciful restoration and joyful return to Zion is found in the other great prophets as well. The Book of Jeremiah, which records the prophet's continual struggle with the sinful kings of Judah, knows that Yahweh alone, who dwells on Mt. Zion, is the king of the nations, the king of eternity (Jer 8:19; 10:7,10; cf. 46:18; 48:15; 51:57).[48] Jeremiah 31–33 is replete with promises that God will reunite all twelve tribes of the shattered people (31:1: "I shall be the God of *all* the tribes [or: clans] of Israel"). Closely connected with this prophecy is the promise of a new David to preside over the restored kingdom of Israel (see especially 30:8–9; cf. 33:14–26). Similar hopes are expressed in the Book of Ezekiel, which also knows the image of Yahweh as king of Israel (20:33), in the context of the promise of a new exodus and a new judgment. As the book unfolds, the way in which Yahweh will govern his redeemed people becomes clearer. The divine shepherd will gather and pasture the reunited flock of Israel through a human shepherd, the Davidic prince (Ezekiel 34; 37:15–28). Similar hopes of Yahweh reigning as king in a restored Jerusalem are also found scattered throughout the minor prophets: e.g., Mic 2:12–13; 4:9; Zeph 3:15; and Obad 21.

However, when the exiles of Judah did return to Palestine, the glorious promises hardly seemed fulfilled in the hard times that followed. In the midst of moral chaos (Trito-)Isaiah promises that Yahweh will once again act the role of the divine warrior, establishing a just order in society (59:9–21).[49] The hope is once more voiced that the scattered tribes of Israel will be gathered together in Jerusalem, whither all the Gentile nations will bring tribute (chap. 60). In the Book of Zechariah, the exalted status of Jerusalem vis-à-vis the nations begins to be imagined in apocalyptic terms, with a final world-battle that the warrior God wins for his holy city. Paradisiac conditions will prevail when Yahweh becomes king over all the earth (Zech 14:9: *wĕhāyâ yahweh lĕmelek ʿal-kol-hā ʾāreṣ*). His universal kingship will be acknowledged by the remnants of the Gentiles, who will come on pilgrimage every year to worship Israel's divine king in Jerusalem (14:16–19).

Sad to say, the promise was once again delayed. In the first part of the 2d century B.C., the horrors of persecution under the Seleucid monarch Antiochus IV Epiphanes (reigned 175–164) called forth the first full-blown apocalyptic book of the Bible, Daniel. It is hardly surprising that the vocabulary of kingdom and kingship plays an important part in chaps. 1–7 of the book, since Daniel has as one of its major apocalyptic themes the divine king's control over all history and all kingdoms as he brings them to their cataclysmic consummation, while his own kingdom endures forever (e.g., 4:14,22,31–32,34).[50] In Daniel, the traditional schema of four great kingdoms succeeding one another[51] ends in the definitive defeat of the hostile Gentile nations and the establishment by God of an everlasting kingdom in which his holy ones rule (2:36–45; 7:1–27). The coming of this kingdom seems to be an act of God alone, without human intervention. As Daniel emphasizes in his interpretation of Nebuchadnezzar's dream in chap. 2, the stone that symbolizes the eternal kingdom is cut from the mountain "not by [human] hands" (2:34,45).[52] For the first time in the Bible, these last days are clearly connected with the resurrection of individual faithful Jews who shall live in glory, while the wicked shall rise to be punished (12:1–3,13).[53]

While most of the deuterocanonical/apocryphal books of the OT do not share the full apocalyptic vision of Daniel,[54] they do continue key themes seen in the "prophetic eschatology" of Isaiah, Jeremiah, and Ezekiel. Fittingly, this hope for the future of God's people is often expressed in prayers and hymns. The postexilic hopes for a regathered Israel and a renewed Jerusalem are clearly reflected in the canticle that helps conclude the book of Tobit (chap. 13), a canticle in which the theme of God's kingly rule and lordship over Israel and the world is dominant (vv 2,4,7,9,11,13,15,16,17,18).[55] God, whose kingdom lasts forever, is blessed because, although he has scattered the children of Israel among the nations, he will again gather his repentant children (vv 1–5). Hence Tobit calls on all sinners to repent, that they may receive mercy in a Jerusalem that the king of the ages, the king of heaven, first afflicted for its sins but will now restore (vv 6–10). Indeed, God the great king will rebuild Jerusalem with every kind of precious stone to be his house for all ages. It will become the shining light for the nations who will make pilgrimage to bring gifts to the king of heaven (vv 11–17; the prophecies of the Book of Isaiah [2:2–5; 54:11–12; 60:1–14; 66:10–14] are thus recycled). The same pattern of exile for sin but hope of being regathered by God on Mt. Zion is seen in the Book of Baruch (3:1–8; 4:21–5:9).

Jesus ben Sira, summing up a great deal of the wisdom tradition of the professional Jerusalem scribe, nevertheless shares this same "Jerusalem eschatology of regathering." In a great prayer (Sir 36:1–17)[56] to the "God of the universe [literally: of the all]," Ben Sira prays that God will work new signs and wonders (echoing Moses' miracles at the time of the exodus). Ben Sira hopes that, while fire will consume the hostile nations, God will "gather together all the tribes of Jacob" so that "they may receive their inheritance as in the days of old." God's mercy is especially implored for Jerusalem and its temple, "your holy city . . . the place where you dwell." Ben Sira prays that all the promises of the prophets may be fulfilled, so that the one true God may be known to the ends of the earth.[57]

Needless to say, these shining hopes about Jerusalem were hardly fulfilled in the 1st centuries B.C. and A.D. The turbulence often engulfing Jerusalem is reflected in the folkloric novel (with some apocalyptic touches) that makes up the Book of Judith.[58] The enemy, with traits of all the major foes of Israel in the OT, once more threatens God's sacred house on Mt. Zion, and so Judith turns in prayer to the king of all creation, the divine warrior who alone protects Israel (9:12–14). In her final triumphant hymn,[59] Judith praises the Lord Almighty who will take vengeance on Israel's persecutors "on the day of judgment"; they will be tortured forever. The traditional hope that Jerusalem will be protected by the divine king displays some apocalyptic traits here, although the Book of Judith is by no means a full-blown apocalypse.

Israel exposed to pressure and possible extinction—but in exile rather than in the holy land—is a main theme of the Book of Esther, contained in the Hebrew Bible. Far from being apocalyptic or even eschatological in tone, the book tells basically a secular wisdom tale—so secular that neither God nor major Israelite religious institutions (except fasting) are mentioned.[60] Interestingly, the later apocryphal additions to the book, which seek to infuse an explicitly religious tone into the story,[61] emphasize the role of God as king of all, controlling what seems on the surface to be purely human politics and saving his people from destruction (e.g., 13:9–17; 14:3–19).[62] Even King Artaxerxes is made to profess that God "rules over all things . . . and has directed the kingdom for us" (16:16,18,21).

The Wisdom of Solomon, written in Greek probably in Alexandria in Egypt, breathes a different atmosphere, that of the philosophical movement known as Middle Platonism. A forerunner or contemporary of Philo of Alexandria, the author of the Wisdom of Solomon fuses Platonic views with reinterpretations of Israel's history (as presented in its sacred books), eschatology, and speculation on divine wisdom. One can see in the book the coalescence of sapiential, mystical, and eschatological traditions that would conspire—in other works—to produce apocalyptic literature. While certainly not an apocalypticist, and while steeped in the wisdom traditions of Israel, the author is very much concerned to affirm that the just person wrongly put to death will both enjoy immortality and be vindicated by God at the last judgment (2:10–3:12; 4:20–5:23). Indeed, as a *huios theou* ("son of God"), the just shall share the judging and ruling power of the divine judge, "and the Lord shall rule over them as king forever" (3:8).[63] In contrast, the wicked shall be terrified at the last judgment as they face their punishment.

Precisely because he is not pursuing our inquiry into the symbol "kingdom of God," it is interesting to see how David Winston, a commentator on the Wisdom of Solomon, summarizes the book's presentation of God's action on the last day: ". . . God will now devastate and smash the lawless kingdoms of the earth, thus inaugurating a new, trans-historical era of divine rule."[64] The Book of Wisdom thus meshes (1) the pattern of the persecuted-but-vindicated just person (seen in the psalms, e.g., Psalm 22, and in Isa 52:13–53:12),[65] (2) the Platonic doctrine of the immortality of the soul, and (3) Jewish apocalyptic expectation of a final judgment of the good and the wicked (though without any idea of a resurrection of the body). What is most interesting for our search is that in the context of this eschatology the divine judge is referred to as king, powerfully establishing his eternal rule at the end of the world in an act of judgment that definitively rewards the just and punishes the wicked. Moreover, the very word "kingdom" (*basileia*) is used in this eschatological context. Divine wisdom is said to lead just rulers to inherit an eternal kingdom, which consists in immortality (6:20–21: ". . . the desire for wisdom leads to a kingdom . . . ; honor wisdom, that you may reign as kings forever"). Yet the kingdom that wisdom gives can be experienced in some partial way even in this life. The rulers of this world are supposed to be the servants of God's kingly rule (6:4, *tēs autou basileias*), and for that reason unjust rulers will receive a stricter judgment on the last day. More significantly for our survey, within the history of Israel divine wisdom was already active in showing heaven, the kingdom of God, to the just. It revealed heaven, the locus of the kingdom of God (*basileian theou*), to Jacob in his dream at Bethel and gave him knowledge of the holy ones (i.e., the angels on the staircase),[66] just as it gave the scepter of kingship (*skēptra basileias*) to the wronged but vindicated Joseph (10:10,14).

The Wisdom of Solomon thus presents us with an intriguing and complex picture. While basically sapiential and philosophical in thrust, it has a firm eschatological vision.[67] Living according to divine wisdom assures one of sharing after death in the kingdom of heaven, i.e., in immortality. Indeed, certain just men of old were privileged to share in wisdom's kingdom even while on earth. Moreover, on the last day, the just not only will be ruled by the divine king but also will share in his eternal kingship, as they see the evil oppressors of their earthly life condemned. This is not, of course, the eschatology of Jesus or most of the NT.[68] But, granted the special eschatological outlook of the Wisdom of Solomon, the occurrence of "kingdom of God" in this book—the sole occurrence in the whole of the OT, Hebrew or Greek—should not go unnoticed. Perhaps most relevant to the study of Jesus' proclamation is the fact that a Jewish work roughly contemporaneous to him could use kingdom/ kingship imagery of both God's eternal rule in heaven and of the blessed state of the just on the last day. In this basic but complicated structure of thought, the Wisdom of Solomon reflects the tendency of such protocanonical books as Daniel. When the question is raised whether Jesus' eschatology and in particular his message of the kingdom could contain both a present and a future dimension, we should remember that Jewish works like Daniel and the Wisdom of Solomon had already achieved this paradoxical combination. Jesus may or may not have mirrored this juxtaposition of eschatologies, but to claim a priori that he *could* not have combined present and future elements in his eschatology flies in the face of the evidence of at least some eschatological writings of early Judaism that subsequently entered into the canon of the synagogue or the church.

The situation of both 1 Maccabees and 2 Maccabees is obviously different from the other volumes of the deuterocanonical/apocryphal OT, since the focus is on the earthly, human, political kingdom in the here-and-now that the Maccabees and their descendants in the Hasmonean dynasty erect. Especially in 1 Maccabees, God seems somewhat distant; such words as "king" and "kingdom" are regularly used of earthly rulers, not of God. Indeed, this relatively untheological work never uses the word "God" for the God of Israel, substituting "heaven" instead.[69] There is no talk of a kingdom of heaven, let alone a kingdom of God or any equivalent; *basileia* is an earthly, human, political reality.[70] Still, at least once in 1 Maccabees, a traditional eschatological hope may peek through. Granted the desire of this book to extol the levitical line of the Maccabees, whose descendants would create a non-Davidic monarchy in Israel, it is noteworthy that the dying Mattathias, the father of Judas Maccabeus and the other Maccabean leaders, recalls in his testamentary address that King David "received as his heritage a throne of kingship forever" (1 Macc 2:57).[71] Otherwise, though, the spotlight in 1 Maccabees is on the emerging Hasmonean dynasty, of levitical lineage. Jonathan A. Goldstein goes so far as to say that "we are justified in calling the author of First Maccabees the 'Hasmonaean propagandist.' "[72]

A political focus (though of a different sort) is also present in 2 Maccabees,[73] but there is more of a theological tone to the work. Indeed, granted the book's political concerns,[74] some of its theological and eschatological statements are all the more striking. God is himself the creator of the universe and its only king (1:24: *kyrie ho theos, ho pantōn ktistēs . . . ho monos basileus*), the "king of kings" (13:4), whose almighty power has restored to his people Israel their heritage, kingdom (or kingly rule, *basileion*), priesthood, and the sacred rites (2:17). It is this divine king who guarantees that martyred Jews will rise in their own bodies on the last day (2 Maccabees 7). The story of the martyrdom of the Jewish mother and her seven sons in chap. 7 pointedly contrasts the cruel earthly king, who is denied any resurrection to life (7:14), with God the creator, "the king of the world," who will raise up the martyrs to live again forever (7:9,23,28–29).[75] The theme of the creator God and king who will see justice done on the last day by raising up his martyred subjects to eternal life contributes an apocalyptic note to a book that aims at being Hellenistic history.[76]

Summing up what we have seen in the deuterocanonical/apocryphal books of the OT, we detect a persistent concern on the part of postexilic Israel: the many members of God's people scattered among the Gentile nations (hence the word "Diaspora") or subjected to the Gentile yoke in Palestine, and the apparent inversion of what Israel expected salvation history to mean, namely, the subjugation of the Gentiles to God's people. Hope for the future naturally translates into God's gathering of all the dispersed members of his people (at times emphatically: *all* the tribes or clans) back to a liberated Jerusalem, Mt. Zion, and the temple. The once proud Gentiles will first be defeated in a great final battle; then their remnants will humbly come on pilgrimage to offer gifts to God in the Jerusalem temple. It is intriguing to see how this "Jerusalem eschatology of regathering" can at times emphasize God's status as king (so Tob 13:1–15, echoing Isa 52:7; Zech 14:16–17) and at times prescind from the image of God's kingship (so Sir 36:1–17). At other times God's kingship, in connection with his power over all creation, can be used to ground eschatological hopes of immortality and vindication on the last day (Wisdom of Solomon, chaps. 2–5) or even apocalyptic hopes of resurrection (so 2 Maccabees 7). In short, the image of God's kingly rule over the world, Israel, and the final lot of both is still alive in these late OT books, and even at times it helps ground a particular eschatological hope, be it in this world or the next. But God's kingship or kingdom is by no means either a dominant theme throughout these works or the necessary basis of the eschatological hopes they harbor. That the precise phrase "kingdom of God" should occur only once in the whole corpus of deuterocanonical/apocryphal books, and then in a noneschatological context, stands in stark contrast to the heavy concentration of the phrase, in a specifically eschatological sense, in the teaching of Jesus.

Stepping back and looking at the entire range of OT books, we see some of these insights confirmed for the entire library we call the OT. On the one hand, the imagery of God's kingship/kingdom is not a gigantic clasp that can bind the whole of the OT together, a great underlying theme that can provide the basis for a theology of the OT—à la the word "covenant" in the work of Walther Eichrodt.[77] The imagery connected with God's kingship is absent from whole parts of the OT; and in the books in which it does appear, it is not the one dominant symbol that gives coherence to everything else. Only in smaller units can the claim of a dominant metaphor be made: e.g., in some of the "enthronement psalms" or perhaps in the canticle of Tobit.

On the other hand, the symbolism of God's kingship/kingdom does enjoy a widespread use throughout many strands of OT tradition. Beyond the mere range of usage, the symbolism is impressive in that it appears at pivotal moments in the OT story of God's dealings with his people Israel. For instance, God's kingship and kingdom are not dominant themes in the Pentateuch, yet for that very reason their surfacing at the crossing of the Reed Sea and the making of the covenant at Sinai is striking. The same can be said of the symbol's appearance in the histories of the Deuteronomist and the Chronicler when the question of King David's successors is raised. However, it is especially in the Psalms and the Prophets that the symbol of God's kingship/kingdom comes into its own. An increasingly—but not exclusively—eschatological tone is notable in some of the deuterocanonical/apocryphal literature; in some cases, the eschatological message puts on apocalyptic clothing, the style being set by protocanonical Daniel. The result of all this development is that, by the time of Jesus, the symbol of God's kingship/kingdom has acquired many facets and dimensions. Eternal, present, and future expressions of God's rule can sit side by side within the same work. Reading the various volumes of the Jewish Scriptures, we today—and presumably the Jews of Jesus' time—can put together the overarching story suggested by the variegated usages of *malkût* and *basileia*. No one OT book spelled out the whole story in detail, but the constant reading of at least the most significant books quietly inculcated the basic structure of the myth. Hence, both because the symbol itself was multivalent and because the overall story was conveyed subliminally over a long time rather than by one detailed telling, the meaning of any one use of the symbol has to be understood in the larger context of the messenger and his entire message. The OT supplied Jesus with the language, symbols, and story of God's kingly rule, and hence with a range of meanings. What he fashioned out of that heritage only an investigation of his sayings and actions will show.

A final word on our study of God's kingship in the OT. To some it might seem anachronistic to set apart the canonical literature of the OT for special consideration. In reply, I readily admit that even the Hebrew canon of Scripture was not closed until some time between the end of the 1st and the end of the 2d century A.D.,[78] with the Christian canon used by Catholics and Orthodox not being settled until centuries later.[79] Yet it is one thing to determine when the canon was definitively closed; it is quite another to recognize that, by the time of Jesus, the canon had been developing for some time and that some books, especially the Pentateuch and the major prophets, had achieved an authoritative status within most sectors of Judaism (cf. Sirach 44–49 and his grandson's Prologue).[80] In this sense, the Pentateuch, the Prophets, and the Psalms cannot be studied as "background" to Jesus' teaching in the same way that Qumran or Philo can be studied. There is no proof that Jesus ever read a word of Qumran's *Manual of Discipline* or Philo's *On the Contemplative*

Life. There is every reason to think that Jesus regularly read or heard the Torah and the Prophets and sang the Psalms. Even if Jesus had read Philo, there is no reason to think that the Nazarene would have considered Philo's works authoritative for all Jews. There is every reason to suppose Jesus thought that about the Five Books of Moses, the Prophets, and at least some of the Writings besides (especially the Psalms).[81] In short, there is background and there is background. Some background is authoritative source, other background is not. While the authoritative status of some of the books we examined, especially the deuterocanonical/apocryphal ones, is debated and no doubt was debated in the days of Jesus, the divine authority of the core of the canon was a given for devout Jews by the time of Jesus.

Even some of the books that were at the margins of the evolving canon and that finally were not accepted into the Hebrew (or "Palestinian") canon (e.g., Sirach and Tobit) were nevertheless the object of study by devout Jews, as the fragments of manuscripts from Qumran and Masada now testify.[82] What is noteworthy here is that neither Tobit nor Sirach was produced at Qumran or championed a specifically Essene theology. Presumably, then, if the Qumranites were studying these works of "outsiders," other Jews who took their religion seriously were studying them, too. At the very least, such works show us what was "in the air" that pious Jews breathed in the 1st centuries B.C. and A.D. I readily admit, though, that for many Jews of the early 1st century there probably was not too much—if any—distinction between most of the deuterocanonical/apocryphal books and the intertestamental literature to which we now turn.

III. GOD'S KINGLY RULE IN THE PSEUDEPIGRAPHA

Obviously, space does not allow a full treatment of the vast amount of writings that fall under the vague rubric of the "OT Pseudepigrapha" or "intertestamental literature."[83] Here I will give only a brief survey of the use of the symbol of the kingship/kingdom of God in major Jewish religious works that fall outside the canon and that were written—as far as we can tell—before or during the lifetime of Jesus.[84] To provide some pedagogical order and clarity, and also to respect the integrity of a special theological movement, the literature of Qumran will be treated separately.

(1) *The Sibylline oracles* comprise various Jewish and Christian poems,[85] written in Greek and purporting to be the (often political and minatory) prophecies of various famous prophetesses of the ancient world.[86] The most significant composition for our purposes is the Third Sibylline Oracle, written ca. the middle of the 2d century B.C. in Egypt. Since by nature the oracle is a collection of individual sayings, it is difficult and perhaps misleading to draw up a clear succession of prophesied events. Yet a general scenario seems fairly clear. *Sib Or* 3:97–161 raises the topic of kingship and concludes with a list of

world kingdoms. 3:192–93 tells how God sends a savior king who puts an end
to all war and grants deliverance to the Jews. The reference is to some Hellenistic Egyptian ruler, either Ptolemy VI Philometor or his successor. The concluding section of the oracle prophesies a kingdom that God will raise up
(3:767–795). The hopes of Isaiah are echoed as the Jerusalem temple becomes
the goal of pilgrimage for all the nations, the conditions of paradise return,
and universal peace prevails. This final kingdom apparently comes after the
kingdom of the heroic Ptolemaic king. The final kingdom is still an earthly
one, though it puts an end to the succession of world kingdoms and apparently
to death as well. All this is done by God, who is referred to throughout the
oracle as "the great King" (499, 560, 616, 808). Additions were made to the
Third Oracle in the 1st century B.C. They prophesy the coming of a "holy
prince" who will rule over a universal kingdom, inaugurated by the fiery judgment of "the great king, immortal God." Again, all this takes place on the
earth.

The Third Sibylline Oracle is distinctive in that it is one of the few Jewish
writings of the time that forcefully welds together the themes of a this-worldly
eschatology, a monotheism that is proclaimed to all the nations, and the kingdom of God, open to all who will worship the one true God and king.[87] Noting
that the Sibylline oracles represent a "somewhat atypical strand of Diaspora
Judaism," John J. Collins observes: "The Egyptian Sibylline tradition is remarkable for its lack of the otherworldly dimension so characteristic of the
apocalyptic literature. There is no talk of angels and no expectation of resurrection."[88]

(2) The mixed bag of the Sibylline oracles seems almost simple compared
to the terribly complex library of apocalyptic literature we refer to as *1 Enoch*.[89]
The work is made up of five disparate compositions, plus additions. For those
who have studied the place of God's kingship/kingdom in the OT, what is
most startling about *1 Enoch* is that, in an apocalyptic book of 108 chapters, the
symbol of God's kingly rule plays such a small role. Only in the first "book" of
1 Enoch, "The Book of the Watchers" (chaps. 1–36), does God's kingship receive any significant mention. The Book of the Watchers delights in creating
lengthy series of titles for God. These series are always concluded with the
title of king, and regularly God is specifically said to be "the king of the ages,"
i.e., the eternal king (see 9:4; 12:3; 25:3–5,7; 27:3). God's kingship includes,
but is not restricted to, his power to pass judgment on the last day; at the same
time, the final judgment is not tied essentially to the image of God as king. In
the fourth book, "The Book of Dream Visions" (chaps. 83–90), "king" occurs
in a prayer to God (84:2–6) and once again encapsulates all other divine predicates. In the "Ten-Week Apocalypse" (93:3–10; 91:11–17), which is part of
the fifth book, "The Epistle of Enoch" (chaps. 91–107), we are told that in
the "eighth week," after the just execute judgment on sinners, "the temple of
the kingdom of the great [God] will be built" (91:13, presumably by God
himself).[90] The overall concept seems to be that God will reign as king over
the just on a renewed earth, purified of sin. In the much-debated second book,

"The Parables [or Similitudes] of Enoch" (chaps. 37–71), which mentions a mysterious "Son of Man" or "Chosen One" and probably dates from the end of the 1st century A.D., God is called king only once, in the context of prayer (63:2–4), while his regular title is "Lord of the Spirits." In sum, *1 Enoch* is a sobering reminder that one of the longest and most influential works of Jewish eschatology and apocalyptic around the turn of the era could speak at length about the last days without ever mentioning "the kingdom of God" and with very little use of the image of God as king.[91]

(3) The fact that fragments of some 11 Hebrew manuscripts[92] of the *Book of Jubilees* have been found at Qumran, not to mention fragments from Masada, has reinforced the view that the work bears Essene traits, e.g., the promotion of a solar calendar. Yet it is by no means certain that *Jubilees* was actually written at Qumran. It might well be a work stemming from the early stages of either the "Hasidic" or Essene movements of the 2d century B.C.; at a later date the work would have been brought to Qumran.[93] *Jubilees* is actually a midrashic rewriting of the narrative in Genesis 1 to Exodus 14. Corresponding to its sources, *Jubilees* touches on the theme of God's kingship in only a few passages. God is king on Mt. Zion for all eternity (1:27–28). Rejecting astrology as a kind of idolatry, Abraham prays to the one true God, the creator of all things: "I have chosen you and your kingly rule" (12:19). The Sabbath is a day of God's "holy kingship for all Israel" (50:9). In other words, choosing monotheism and keeping the Sabbath are how faithful Jews concretely subject themselves to God's kingly rule. Reworking Exod 19:6, *Jub.* 16:18 promises that the offspring of Jacob will be "a kingdom and a priesthood and a holy people" (cf. a similar usage in 33:20).[94] In this case the sense may indeed be "kingdom," the concrete place where God exercises his royal rule.[95] All in all, it is striking how small a role the symbol of God's kingship plays in this fifty-chapter retelling of the foundational events of Israel's existence. One conclusion seems to be forming already. Whether one was looking forward to an eschatological future or back to Israel's origins, the symbol of the kingdom of God or its equivalent was neither thought necessary nor used frequently in some Jewish religious works around the turn of the era.

(4) The situation seems more promising in the case of the *Testament of Moses*. However, our relief in finding an apocalyptic work in which the symbol of God's kingship is important must be tempered by the ongoing debate over the date and unity of this apocalyptic work. Estimates of the time of its composition range from the period of the Maccabean revolt (168–165 B.C.), through the first three decades of the 1st century A.D., to the first half of the 2d century A.D. (most likely just before the Second Jewish Revolt of A.D. 132–135).[96] Given these options, the position that the work has its roots in the early 2d century B.C. but reached final form in the early 1st century A.D. appears the most likely. Actually, any theory that admits that the work as a whole would have been known in Palestine in the first part of the 1st century A.D. qualifies it for our consideration—and in fact, its existence in the 1st century A.D. is widely accepted today.

The *Testament of Moses* has two passages that deal with God as king. In 4:2, within a prayer (as so often in the deuterocanonical and pseudepigraphic literature), God is addressed with the words "O Lord of all, king on a high throne, who rule over the world." The theological context is God's choice of Israel as his own people, the covenant he made with their ancestors, their sin, which has caused their exile, and God's compassion in moving an earthly king (Cyrus) to pity them and allow them to return to the promised land.

More important is the grand vision of the revelation of God's kingdom at the end of time, which takes up chap. 10. One should not, however, overlook the incident that immediately precedes this in chap. 9. There a mysterious Levite named Taxo and his seven sons voluntarily undergo martyrdom at the hands of a pagan persecutor (Antiochus Epiphanes) so that their deaths may provoke God to avenge their blood by manifesting his final kingdom—which is precisely what happens in chap. 10. Thus, chap. 10 stands out amid the scarce references to the kingdom of God in the pseudepigraphic literature prior to Jesus. For here we are told that the voluntary deaths of martyrs unleash the end-time appearance of "his [i.e., God's] kingly reign [or kingdom, *regnum* in the Latin version] throughout all of his creation." The devil is definitively defeated, and sadness is banished with him (10:1). God arises from his royal throne (literally, "the throne of his kingdom") and goes forth from his holy dwelling in heaven to avenge "his sons" (10:3). An earthquake, the darkening of sun and moon, and other cosmic catastrophes announce in true apocalyptic style that the end of the old age has come (10:4–6). After punishing the Gentiles, the one true God raises Israel to the heights of heaven, to live there in happiness (10:7–10).

Here at least, we have a clear portrayal of God the king powerfully establishing his rule over the universe at the end of time, as he responds to the death of innocent martyrs by wreaking vengeance on Israel's enemies and exalting his people to heaven. All this is defined as the revelation of God's kingdom in v 1, which acts as something of a superscript and summary of all that follows in chap. 10, itself the climactic vision of the *Testament of Moses*. Hence, while kingship terminology is not widely used throughout the whole work, it is significant by its pivotal location, its eschatological content, and its apocalyptic coloring. How much of the apocalyptic coloring the author(s) took seriously remains a problem in this pseudepigraphon as it does in most of its literary siblings and cousins. At the very least, the *Testament of Moses* expects a sudden, dramatic, and definitive reversal of fortunes, by which Israel is elevated directly by God to a situation of permanent joy, while its enemies lie forever prostrate. Whether this elevation will be literally to the heavenly world and hence an entirely new mode of existence (a thoroughgoing apocalyptic hope, beyond this present world) or is meant to be symbolic of Israel's complete and permanent triumph (the eschatology of the OT prophets in apocalyptic dress) is unclear. Needless to say, this is a constant problem with eschatological and apocalyptic symbolism. Because "kingdom of God" is a tensive symbol, open to many meanings and interpretations, there is no reason why one speaker or author might not take the dramatic visions literally and another only meta-phorically. As always, only the larger context—if it exists—can help clarify the meaning of the symbol intended by any one speaker, saying, vision, or doc-ument.[97]

(5) God's kingly rule is an even more prominent theme in some of the psalm-like poems known collectively as the *Psalms of Solomon*.[98] These 18 psalms stem from a pious group of Jerusalem Jews, identified by some as early Pharisees, who were thrown into a spiritual crisis by the horrors of the capture of Jerusalem and the defilement of the temple by the Roman general Pompey the Great in 63 B.C. Written in Hebrew, probably between 63 and 42 B.C., they reflect in part the OT wisdom psalms that grapple with the problems of the suffering of the innocent. At the same time, they move beyond the canoni-cal psalms especially in their eschatology, which is sometimes clothed in apoca-lyptic imagery. Having despaired of the evil rulers (both Jewish and Gentile) of this present world, their authors look forward to the speedy intervention of God the true king, who will set up his eternal kingdom through the agency of the Son of David, the Lord Messiah. This emphasis on an end-time Davidic Messiah as the vicegerent of God's kingly rule is one element that sets the *Psalms of Solomon* apart from a good deal of the OT Pseudepigrapha of the pre-A.D. 70 period.

The images of God as king and of his kingly rule, as well as the more gen-eral theme of God's sovereign control of the fate of both nations and individu-als, are found in various passages of the *Psalms* (e.g., *Pss. Sol.* 2:30,32; 5:19; 8:24; 17:3). Certain psalms, however, focus especially on God's kingship and kingdom. In *Ps. Sol.* 2:18–37, God is praised as the great judge who shows no favoritism. He has justly judged and punished both the sinful inhabitants of Jerusalem (vv 1–17) and their pagan oppressors, the Romans (vv 19–32). Par-ticularly striking is the contrast between Pompey "the Great," who imagined himself to be lord of earth and sea, and God "the Great," the all-powerful, who is king in heaven and judges kings and powers on earth. Thus, in the mind of the author of *Psalm of Solomon* 2, the basis for hope is that, in the sudden death of the mighty Pompey, God the true king is seen to be active once again in recent historical events, controlling them with his royal power. The recent past thus becomes a pledge of what God the king will soon accomplish in totally destroying sinners and bringing his servants into his presence forever (vv 33–37).

Psalm of Solomon 5 moves from precise historical events to more general considerations about God's care for all his creation, as he nourishes everything from birds and fish to kings and princes and peoples (5:8–11). Unlike the lim-ited generosity of humans, the mercy of the Lord extends to all the earth. This contemplation of God's limitless goodness to his creatures culminates with praise of the special goodness God will show to Israel "in your kingdom" (or, "by your kingly rule," *en tē basileią sou*) (5:18). While this praise could be understood as a statement of fact ("Your goodness *is* upon Israel in your kingdom"), one should probably supply a verb in the optative ("May your goodness be upon Israel in your kingdom").[99] This mention of Israel and God's kingdom may thus have an eschatological thrust. The whole psalm then ends with what is surely a wish in v 19: "Blessed [be] the glory of the Lord, for he is our king." While the faithful members of the psalmist's community hope for Israel's full entrance into God's kingdom when their present sufferings pass away, they nevertheless believe that God is their king even now, even in the midst of persecution.

The most famous of the *Psalms of Solomon* is *Psalm of Solomon* 17, in which God's eschatological rule as king is manifested and realized through the rule of the Son of David, the Lord Messiah. The relationship between the divine king and the human king is carefully enunciated throughout the psalm. Significantly, the psalm begins and ends with an *inclusio* that stresses that God alone is king in the absolute sense: "Lord, you yourself [are] our king forever and always" (v 1a) and "the Lord himself [is] our king forever and always" (v 46).[100] From the beginning, then, it is clear that whatever kingship the human Messiah exercises is subordinate to and at the service of God's kingly rule. Verse 3 contains the precise phrase *hē basileia tou theou*, but the context shows that the sense is not "the kingdom of God" but rather "God's kingly rule." This rule is defined by way of an interesting parallelism: "The might of our God [endures] forever with mercy [on us who hope in him as our savior, as v 3a indicates], and the kingly rule of our God [*hē basileia tou theou hēmōn*] [endures] forever over the Gentiles [or nations, *ethnē*] in judgment." God's kingly rule is placed in parallel with his might, indicating that *basileia* here means not "kingdom" but "the powerful exercise of the king's rule." This is confirmed by God's *basileia* being depicted as enduring over the Gentiles in (his exercise of) judgment; *basileia* here is hardly a place or state of salvation.

Having first affirmed the eternal and all-encompassing kingly rule of God in the "prologue" of vv 1–3, the author now feels free in v 4 to recall how, in the Books of Samuel, the Lord chose David to be king over Israel and how he swore to David that his descendants would always exercise the kingly rule (*basileion*) in his presence (the prophecy of Nathan in 2 Sam 7:11–15). Sadly, the sins of the basically faithful Israelites allowed hardened sinners to displace them from their rightful position of power. The pejorative reference here is to the levitical Hasmoneans, who in due time assumed the title "king," which the author sees as a violation of the rights of the house of David (vv 5–6). God punished and destroyed the Hasmonean rulers by bringing upon them Pompey ("a man foreign to our race," v 7), who ravaged Jerusalem (vv 7-14). Yet the pious likewise suffered, being scattered over the face of the earth, which is then subjected to a drought (vv 15–20). Since all hope of change by human means is lost, the author turns to prayer, beseeching the Lord to raise up for the faithful "their king, the son of David" to rule over Israel at the time God himself has chosen (v 21). God is asked to supply (literally, "undergird") the Messiah with the strength needed to cleanse Jerusalem of the evil Gentiles (vv 22–25). Like the enthroned "son of God" in Ps 2:9, he will smash the proud sinners like a potter's vessel, and he will shatter all they possess with an iron rod. Although he is a human being, this son of David is endowed with God-like powers in that the mere word of his mouth can destroy the lawless Gentiles (v 24; cf. Isa 11:4b). On the positive side, his power will gather together the tribes of Israel (what God himself does in Tobit and other writings from the deuterocanonical/apocryphal OT and the pseudepigrapha), leading them back to a holy land redistributed according to the ancestral tribal allotments. No impure Gentile will have a share, but will instead submit to the yoke of the Messiah (vv 26–30), who will give back to Jerusalem its original purity. The prophecies of Isaiah (e.g., 2:2–4; 55:5; 60) will be fulfilled as the Gentiles come in pilgrimage to Jerusalem to bring back the exiled Israelites and to see the glory of the Lord shining forth in the holy city (v 31). The just messianic king shall be taught by God himself (the proper lines of authority being thus preserved), and under his rule all Israelites will be holy, "and their king will be the Messiah [and] Lord" (v 32).[101] Once again, the author emphasizes that this is true only in a subordinate sense: "The Lord [God] will himself be his [the Messiah's] king" (v 34). Having reaffirmed God's supremacy, the author continues to describe the Messiah in the most exuberant terms: he will be free from sin, he will never suffer weakening of his powers, he will be the faithful shepherd of the Lord's flock, his words will be like the words of angels (vv 35–44). The psalm then ends with an eschatological petition that all this be swiftly brought to pass by the merciful God, who alone is king of Israel in the absolute sense (vv 45–46).

Psalm of Solomon 18 continues to pray to God concerning the days of the Messiah, though now it is God himself who cleanses his people Israel to prepare them for the day he has chosen to begin his Messiah's reign. A final burst of praise connects the God of eschatological salvation with the God who created and still orders the stars in their courses (cf. Judg 5:20). As is usual in apocalyptic, the savior God is identified with the creator God.

In summation, the *Psalms of Solomon* hold strenuously to the monotheistic faith as well as to the eschatological hope of Israel: the one true God is the one true king of his people, whom he shall save from their enemies and their own sins at the end of the present age. Yet in some of the psalms, especially 17, the divine king chooses to bring about the destruction of the Gentiles, the regathering and purification of Israel, and its ongoing governance by a human king, the Son of David, Messiah and Lord. The Messiah is both completely human and yet God-like in his qualities and power: totally sinless, he smashes the sinful Gentiles simply by the power of his word—a power very reminiscent of God's word in the OT. Paradoxically, it is precisely the emphasis throughout the psalm on the one God who is the one true king that allows such God-like attributes to be bestowed on his vicegerent on earth, the Davidic Messiah. We would like to know more about this Messiah, but the psalm is tantalizing rather than detailed in its description. With the emphasis on the Messiah's personal sinlessness, on the supernatural power of his word, and on the fact that he will not "weaken" because of God's power working through him, it is probable that the Messiah is not simply a symbol for a whole line of Davidic rulers, but rather a single human who will presumably live forever, ruling over God's eschatological Israel—though this is an inference from rather than an affirmation of the psalm. This inference is made stronger by the fact that other psalms in the collection speak of the faithful rising to eternal life or living forever (3:12; cf. 13:11; 14:3; 15:13).[102] At the same time, one must admit that apocalyptic literature is not especially noted for its consistency, especially when one is dealing with a collection of psalms, written perhaps by different people at different times. In any case, taken as a whole the *Psalms of Solomon* are unique among the OT pseudepigrapha prior to Jesus for their strong emphasis on the eschatological rule of God the king, realized through a human but God-like Davidic Messiah, the earthly king of a regathered and purified Israel, which apparently includes those risen from the dead.

(6) With the *Psalms of Solomon* we exhaust (apart from the Dead Sea documents) the material from the intertestamental literature that can be safely dated to a period prior to the ministry of Jesus. A number of documents float in a twilight zone, insofar as they may embody traditions anterior to the time of Jesus but have a date of final composition no earlier than the late 1st century A.D.—and in some cases, much later.

Prominent among these works is the collection of twelve compositions purporting to be the last words of the twelve sons of Jacob to their descendants, known as the *Testaments of the Twelve Patriarchs*. Judgments on their dating and provenance vary widely. Howard Clark Kee defends the position that they were composed by a hellenized Jew in the 2d century B.C.; he restricts to an absolute minimum passages deemed Christian interpolations.[103] On the other end of the spectrum, Marinus de Jonge originally upheld the view that the *Testaments* were a Christian composition, though with some Jewish background. He later modified his view to make more allowance for older Jewish traditions at the origin of the *Testaments;* however, he still held strongly to heavy Christian redaction.[104] The discovery of an Aramaic *Testament of Levi* in the Cairo Genizah (published in 1910) and more recently of Aramaic fragments of a *Testament of Levi* at Qumran argues for the origin of at least some of the *Testaments* in Judaism around the turn of the era. Yet the present form of the *Testaments* clearly exhibits Christian interpolations, and in my view Kee is unduly restrictive in his admission of Christian interventions in the text. It is probably fair to say that today most scholars would admit a Jewish substratum to the *Testaments*, with the final product the result of Christian redaction. The problem, though, is that this leaves us uncertain as to whether any given verse can be assigned to a Jewish hand prior to the ministry of Jesus.[105] The problem is only compounded by the different textual traditions of the manuscripts of the *Testaments* and by the fact that the Christian interpolations seem concentrated in the sections dealing with the future, the very sections in which we are especially interested.

Some basic patterns of thought may well stem from the work's Jewish origins: e.g., the pattern of sin-exile-return that runs through the *Testaments*, as well as the passages that speak of messiahs from the tribes of both Levi and

Judah (an idea that finds a parallel at Qumran).[106] The presentation of Levi as an ideal priest, contrasted with his sinful sons, and the emphasis on a king from the tribe of Judah may reflect criticism of the Hasmonean priest-kings in control of the Jerusalem temple and the Israelite state by the end of the 2d century B.C. The eschatology in the *Testaments* is multifaceted, not to say confusing. There is talk of the restoration of Israel with all twelve tribes, some share of the nations in salvation, a final manifestation of God, rule by the messianic high priest and the Davidic king, the resurrection of the dead, and the last judgment. Critics disagree on whether this plethora of eschatological images proves that many hands were at work on the composition of the document over a long period of time or simply that Jewish eschatology was not especially concerned with logical consistency.

With regard to our search for references to God's kingship/kingdom, one cannot claim that the symbol dominates the whole of the *Testaments*. There are a few passages, however, where the imagery does appear and where one can argue for basic Jewish tradition rather than Christian redaction. In the *Testament of Dan* 5:13, there is an example of the concept of God's kingly rule within a larger eschatological context. From 5:10 onwards we hear of the Lord's salvation, which will arise from the tribes of Judah and Levi. Eternal peace is granted to those who call upon the Lord; the saints are rewarded with life in Eden and in the New Jerusalem, where the Lord himself lives. This eschatological vision climaxes in v 13 with the promise: "The Holy One of Israel [will be] ruling as king over them . . . and he who believes in him will rule as king in truth in the heavens."[107] In the *Testament of Benjamin* 9:1–2, there is an obscure passage which in v 1 may identify the kingly rule of the Lord over Israel with the rule of the human king of Israel (in this case, Saul the Benjaminite). Immediately after this mention of the Lord's kingship exercised through a human king, there is a prophecy of a final *(eschatos)* temple of God, more glorious than the first (v 2). The twelve tribes will be gathered around this temple, along with all the Gentile nations, until the Most High sends his salvation through the visitation of the unique prophet. At the very least, the theme of the regathering of the twelve tribes of Israel around the eschatological temple in Jerusalem is quite possibly Jewish material. Even the mention of a unique *(monogenous)* prophet might be a reflection of the theme of the prophet-like-Moses (Deut 18:15,18) or the eschatological prophet mentioned in some of the documents of Qumran. However, the appearance of the very Christian sounding adjective *monogenēs* (used regularly in John's Gospel for "the only Son"), plus a clearly Christian interpolation in v 3, makes one wary of putting too much weight on this passage. In the *Testament of Benjamin* 10:6–10 there is a detailed description of the order of the resurrection of the dead on the last day: first Enoch, Noah, Shem, Abraham, Isaac, and Jacob. Then the twelve patriarchs will be raised, each (ruling) over his tribe; and they shall adore the king of heaven. Then all shall be raised, some for glory, others for dishonor. God will judge first the Israelites and then the Gentiles. The connection of God's kingly rule with the general resurrection at the end of time and the final judgment fits in with what we have seen in other examples of Jewish apocalyptic. However, the presence of Christian interpolations in the Greek version of this prophecy again makes one wary about claiming too much.[108] This is even truer of the *Testament of Joseph* 19:11–12. Verse 12 predicts of the Lord's final rule: "His kingdom is an everlasting kingdom which shall not pass away." The fact that the present form of the Greek text predicates this rule of "the Lamb of God" shows that it is Christian. Various attempts are made to reconstruct what was supposedly the earlier form of the text, but all remain highly speculative.[109]

All in all, not much can be garnered with certainty from the *Testaments of the Twelve Patriarchs*. At best, one can find an echo of a typically Jewish apocalyptic scenario. At the end of time, the dead will rise and be judged. The twelve tribes, along with all the Gentiles, will be gathered back to a paradisiac Jerusalem, where God will rule as king in a glorious eschatological temple, his vicegerents being a messianic high priest from the tribe of Levi and a messianic king from the tribe of Judah. In short, God's kingly rule is mentioned at times in the eschatological passages of the *Testaments;* but even if we admit all the relevant passages as original, one cannot claim that God's kingship/kingdom is a dominant theme.

(7) The problem of dating also bedevils attempts to exploit occurrences of the symbol of God's kingly rule in the Aramaic translations of the Hebrew Bible known as the targums.[110] The targums started out as oral translations of the Hebrew Scriptures read in the synagogue. They were necessitated by the gradual shift of the popular language spoken by Palestinian Jews from Hebrew to Aramaic.[111] Fragments from Qumran (e.g., 4QtgJob, 11QtgJob, 4QtgLev [targum on Leviticus]) show us that written targums existed by the 1st century A.D., although for the most part the Qumran material points to a type of targum that was a fairly literal translation of the Hebrew. The later, so-called "classical" targums, many of which have lengthy expansions of the sacred text, received their final forms only in the centuries subsequent to Jesus. For example, the targums of Onqelos on the Pentateuch and Jonathan on the (Former and Latter) Prophets, while containing early Palestinian material, underwent extensive redaction in Babylon around the 5th century A.D. We are thus left in a quandary not unlike the one we faced in the case of the *Testaments of the Twelve Patriarchs:* some of the traditions that diverge from what the OT says may indeed be older than the 1st century A.D., but it is difficult to judge in individual cases.

A further problem arises from the fact that not all the targums exhibit exactly the same tendencies when it comes to "recycling" the OT language about God's kingly rule. The targums on Chronicles and on the Psalms, which in any case are quite late, contain almost nothing of interest for our purpose. Some passages in the targums on the Pentateuch (Onqelos, Jerusalem targum I [Pseudo-Jonathan], the fragmentary form of Jerusalem targum II, and Neofiti) are more instructive. Onqelos, which on the whole stays fairly close to the Hebrew text, encapsulates a general tendency of the targums when in Exod

15:18 it changes the MT's "Yahweh shall reign as king forever and ever" to "Yahweh, his kingly rule [shall last] forever and for all ages." Instead of the MT's dynamic verbal proclamation *yahweh yimlōk* ("Yahweh shall reign as king"), the targums in general prefer abstract formulations like "the kingly rule *(malkûtāʾ)* of Yahweh." This fits in with the overall tendency of the targums to avoid anthropomorphisms (e.g., the verb "to rule" directly predicated of God) and to guard the transcendence of God by providing "buffer words" between himself and his creatures (hence "the glory of the kingdom of Yahweh" is revealed to humans rather than Yahweh himself). What is both striking and telling is that, in the translation of Exod 15:18, while each targum on the Pentateuch paraphrases the text somewhat differently, the Hebrew verb "to reign as king" *(mālak)* is replaced in each case by the abstract noun "kingdom," i.e., "kingly rule" *(malkûtāʾ)*.[112] The reference in the targums' translations seems to be primarily to God's constant rule over all things, though some translations (e.g., Pseudo-Jonathan, the fragmentary targum) explicitly include in this his rule over "the age to come" as distinct from "this age." The abstract noun *malkûtāʾ* is also added to the text in Neofiti on Gen 49:2 and in the fragmentary targum on Exod 15:3. Like "name," "glory," and "power" that stand in parallel to it, "kingly rule" in these passages refers to a mode of God's being, appearing, and acting in the world, rather than primarily to a spatial kingdom.

It must be stressed that, while these examples are helpful, one must be cautious about drawing general conclusions from the limited number of occurrences. One cannot claim that the symbol of God's kingly rule suddenly becomes dominant in the targums on the Pentateuch or that the symbol takes on a heavily eschatological tone. When it comes to "the kingdom of God" and its equivalents, the thrust of the targums on the Pentateuch, for all their paraphrases, does not diverge all that much from the original Hebrew of the Pentateuch.

Things are somewhat different in the targum Jonathan on the Prophets. To be sure, the targum Jonathan is still willing to use the noun "king" *(melek)* of Yahweh, usually in an eschatological prophecy of judgment (e.g., Isa 33:17, 22). But especially in a context dealing with Israel's eschatological salvation, the books of the classical writing prophets, both major and minor, tend to use "the kingdom of God" as a substitute for "God" or "Yahweh." For example, in the apocalyptic scenario of Isa 24:23, while the MT prophesies that "Yahweh of hosts will reign as king on Mt. Zion and in Jerusalem," the targum rephrases this to read "the kingly rule of Yahweh of hosts will be revealed on Mt. Zion and in Jerusalem." The use of "the kingdom of God will be revealed" as a substitute for God himself acting is especially noteworthy in three key passages of eschatological prophecy: Isa 52:7 (for "your God reigns as king"); Isa 40:9 (for "behold, your God"); and Isa 31:4 (for "the Lord of hosts shall come down"). In all three cases, the eschatological prophecy depicts Yahweh the divine king or warrior bringing salvation to Jerusalem or Mt. Zion. In contrast, in Ezek 7:7,10, "the kingdom is revealed" is introduced into a text to announce the day of final judgment. The idea of both salvation for Zion and judgment on the Gentiles is present in Obad 21, where the targumic phrase "the kingdom of Yahweh will be revealed" replaces the simpler "the kingdom will be Yahweh's." In Zech 14:9, the straightforward statement "Yahweh will be king over all the earth" becomes "the kingdom of Yahweh will be revealed over all those who dwell on the earth."

In sum, the targum Jonathan regularly avoids the verbal statement "Yahweh reigns as king," most notably by using the periphrasis "the kingdom of Yahweh is [or, will be] revealed," especially in eschatological contexts. In fairness, it should be noted that Bruce D. Chilton has attempted to reinterpret the passages from the targum on Isaiah as referring to the ever-present activity and self-disclosure of God as king. "The kingdom of God" is simply a vivid way of saying that God is present and active among us; it is not to be limited by any one time reference, including an eschatological one.[113] This interpretation flies in the face of the obvious meaning of many of the prophetic passages and seems dictated by Chilton's own theological program, which includes removing apocalyptic traits from Jesus' proclamation of the kingdom. Contrary to Chilton's claim, in the targum Jonathan "the kingdom of Yahweh is [or, will be] revealed" often does carry an eschatological tone.

However, whether or not Chilton is right, there remain serious problems in employing Jonathan's striking phrase as "background" to Jesus' use of "the kingdom of God." First, as noted above, there is the problem of dating. Second, while the substitution of "kingdom of Yahweh" or similar phrases for more direct statements about God's ruling is arresting, even in Jonathan one cannot claim that the symbol of God's kingship dominates the theology of any one prophet or the entire corpus. In the whole collection of the prophetic targums, there are only eight passages containing the precise phrase "kingdom of God" or "kingdom of Yahweh."[114] Third, whatever Jesus' reason for using "kingdom of God" so often, it obviously is not that of the targums, namely, to avoid anthropomorphisms and to distance God from direct contact with humans. To anticipate what we shall see later on: Jesus' "God-talk" is full of direct references to God, revels in daring anthropomorphisms, and is a stranger to any distancing of God from humans.

At best, then, the targums join the general witness of the deuterocanonical/apocryphal books of the OT and the pseudepigrapha: the symbol of God ruling as king was alive and well in the "intertestamental" period and was often connected with eschatological hopes (sometimes with apocalyptic elements) concerning the restoration of all Israel gathered around Mt. Zion or Jerusalem. At the same time, we are reminded that, while this symbol was "available" and basically intelligible in the Judaism of Jesus' time, it was by no means the only or dominant symbol of Israel's faith. Israel's hope for the future was expressed with many different, hardly reconcilable images; moreover, the symbol of God's rule was not tied down to any one theological definition or time frame. In other words, this symbol was available and useful to Jesus, being known to his audience and suggesting many facets of Israel's life and faith; but it was restricted to no one aspect of that faith. At the same time, as only one symbol among many, it was not something imposed on Jesus as the necessary way in which he had to present his message. His choice of it as a key theme is just that: a conscious, personal choice, and for that reason the symbol is a privileged way of entering into Jesus' message.

IV. GOD'S KINGLY RULE AT QUMRAN

Although the documents arising from the Qumran community could be placed under the vague rubric of "intertestamental" literature, it is useful to give separate consideration to this body of Jewish writings, stemming as it does from one concrete group existing at one place in Palestine from about the middle of the 2d century B.C. to A.D. 68. Here we shall be focusing on those documents which most probably originated in and so reflect the inner life of the Qumran community.[115] Hence the pseudepigrapha that were probably composed outside Qumran and then found their way into the community (e.g., *Jubilees, 1 Enoch*) have been treated above in section III. Even when we restrict ourselves to the Qumran documents in this narrow sense, we are still faced with a massive amount of material, from full works to tiny fragments, the chief writings often having complicated tradition histories, many lacunae in the text, and numerous difficulties in interpretation. To provide some order to this brief overview, I will divide the significant material into four categories: (1) community rules (e.g., 1QS), (2) liturgical ordinances and songs (e.g., 1QSb, 4QŠirŠabb [*Songs of the Sabbath Sacrifice*], 4Q510–511, 1QH), (3) exegetical literature (e.g., 4QFlor, 11QMelch, 5Q10), (4) and the rules for the eschatological war (1QM).[116]

(1) In the *Manual of Discipline* or *Community Rule* (1QS), there is no emphasis on the kingship/kingdom of God. In 1QS 9:24, there may be a reference to God's entire dominion or realm (*bĕ kôl mimšālô*). However, the immediate context makes it more likely that the phrase refers to the "master" or "instructor" (*maśkîl*), an official in the community who is told to be "a man zealous for the commandment and its [proper] time [of observance] for the day of vengeance, to carry out [God's] pleasure in everything that he [the master] puts his hand to and in all his [probably the master's] domain."[117] This "pedestrian" sense of the word "domain" (*mimšal*) fits the fact that it appears only here in 1QS, while a similar noun for kingdom, dominion, or rule (*memšālâ*) does appear elsewhere. One hears, for instance, of the evil dominion of Belial (1:18,23; 2:19). In the tract on the two spirits (3:13–4:26) we learn that two spirits battle within each individual. One is the prince of light, in whose hand is the dominion of the sons of justice, just as the angel of darkness has dominion over the sons of iniquity (3:20–21). This is a classic example of the cosmological and anthropological dualism of Qumran, expressed in terms of two dominions or fields of force at war with each other in history and in each person. In the light

of all we have seen in the OT and the pseudepigrapha, however, the amazing thing is that this dominion/rule terminology is not applied to God but rather to Belial, to the prince of light, and to the angel of darkness. The author probably intends to preserve God's transcendence vis-à-vis the battle among his creatures by not having his activity described in terms of dominion or rule; such a description could draw him into comparison or competition with other beings who exercise some sort of dominion.

(2) Among liturgical ordinances and songs special notice should be given to a fragmentary text (1QSb), a collection of blessings written on the same scroll as the *Manual of Discipline*. The document contains blessings for all the members of the covenant community, then apparently for the eschatological high priest (the Messiah of Aaron), then for the sons of Zadok (the priests), and finally for the "prince of the congregation" (the Messiah of Judah). Significantly, the blessing for the prince of the congregation prays that God will renew the covenant of the community with him, so that he (apparently the prince) may establish "the kingdom of his people (*malkût ʿammô*) forever" (1QSb 5:21). With the allusions in the context to Isa 11:1–5, it is likely that "his kingdom" refers to the messianic kingdom of a Davidic ruler. The promise of kingly rule seems also to be given to the high priest in 1QSb 3:5 (again *malkût* is used), but the manuscript is so fragmentary at this point that the overall message is difficult to discern. The idea of two messianic figures, with the Messiah of Aaron taking precedence over the Messiah of Israel, is witnessed elsewhere in Qumran (e.g., 1QS 9:11; 1QSa 2:11–14,18–20); it may be reflected here as well.[118] The word for kingly rule (*malkût*) occurs for a third time in the blessing of the priests (4:25–26). The blessing prays that the priest may serve God forever "in the palace of the kingdom," i.e., in the eschatological temple. This reflects the traditional OT idea that God is enthroned as king in his temple. But the image does not dominate 1QSb in particular or the Qumran material in general.

How strikingly lacking in references to God's kingship the hymnic or liturgical documents from Qumran can be is highlighted by the greatest single collection of hymns, the *Thanksgiving Hymns* or *Hôdāyôt Psalms* (1QH), composed perhaps (at least in part) by the founder of the community, the Teacher of Righteousness. In the entire corpus of some 25 hymns, God is addressed as king only once, and even then it is only one title in a string of titles: "Behold, you are the prince of gods and king of the glorious ones and lord of every spirit and ruler of every creature" (1QH 10:8). The *Thanksgiving Hymns* are thus an extreme example of what is true of most of the Qumran material: the image of God's kingship may be present, but it is hardly pervasive or dominant.

One exception to this general observation is the work, unfortunately preserved only in fragments, called *Songs for the Holocaust of the Sabbath* or *Songs of the Sabbath Sacrifice* (4QŠirŠabbᵃ⁻ʰ, MasŠirŠabbⁱ, and 11QŠirŠabbʲ).[119] In the fashion typical of Qumran, the songs link the worship of the Qumran community with the liturgy offered to God by the angels in the heavenly temple-palace. Building on the visions of God's throne-chariot and of the new temple from the Book of Ezekiel, the songs suggest a heavenly sanctuary, complete with the throne-chariot, the *merkābâ*, which would be the source of much mystical speculation in the later "merkabah mysticism" and "hekaloth" (heavenly palaces) literature of ancient and medieval Judaism. The emphasis on the heavenly liturgy in God's temple-palace helps make the songs noticeably different from most of the Qumran literature in one aspect: the images of the divine king and of his kingdom permeate the texts. Indeed, so pervasive are these images that, even when they are not present in a given fragment, we can feel fairly sure that this is due only to the incomplete nature of the fragment. The longer fragments speak repeatedly of the "king of glory" or "majesty" and of his "kingship." We might add to this witness the fragments of two other manuscripts from Cave 4, called *The Songs of the Sage* (4QŠir a-b, made up of 4Q510 and 4Q511). The images of king and kingship do not pervade the whole work, but the title at the beginning of 4Q510 is "[Songs] of praise: bless[ings for the ki]ng of glory." His kingly rule (*memšaltô*) is declared to be over the mighty champions, i.e., the evil spirits who flee from "the dwelling of the glory of his kingdom [*malkûtô*]." In 4Q511 God is also praised as "the king of glory." For the sake of completeness, it should be noted that the vocabulary of king and kingship is found at times in other fragments of liturgical texts from Qumran, but the lack of a context prevents any use of them in drawing larger conclusions. All in all, the liturgical prayers and songs of Qumran are remarkably sparse in their use of the imagery of God's kingship. The one exception is the *Songs of the Sabbath Sacrifice*, and even here God's kingship is conceived of as a mystical, heavenly reality to which the Qumranites have access through the esoteric liturgy of the community, which joins in the worship offered by the angels. This is hardly the imminent-yet-somehow-present eschatological rule of God that Jesus publicly proclaims to all Israel.

(3) Exegesis, the interpretation of the sacred biblical texts in the light of the history and hopes of the Qumran community, played an important part in the sect's life, since such exegesis both authoritatively defined the group's identity vis-à-vis other parties in Judaism and promised that in the end the sect would be vindicated and triumphant. Passages dealing with God's kingship tend not to be found in those exegetical works that are running commentaries on a single biblical book (e.g., the *Pesher on Habakkuk*). Rather, such passages tend to occur in compositions that draw together and rework texts and allusions from a number of books, usually in an eschatological context. A prime example is the *Midrash on the Last Days*, also called the *Eschatological Midrash* or the *Florilegium* (4QFlor or 4Q174). It combines the promise of Nathan in 2 Sam 7:10–14 with Ps 1:1 and other biblical passages to identify the Qumran community as the true temple and to predict the coming of two messianic figures, "the branch of David" and "the interpreter of the law." In 4QFlor 1:3, Exod 15:17–18 is cited: "In the sanctuary, O Lord, which your hands have established; Yahweh will rule as king forever and ever." It is telling that the theme of God's kingship, introduced here simply to stress that the Qumran

community is the authentic temple that God builds and governs, is not taken up in what follows in the text.

Another exegetical piece that has roused great interest is the eschatological *Midrash on Melchizedek* (11QMelch), which in many ways is more like a pesher on the biblical prescriptions regulating the Jubilee years (see Leviticus 25), reinterpreted in eschatological terms. According to the midrash, the stages of history will end with the final judgment of Satan and the deliverance of the faithful, to be performed by a heavenly Melchizedek (probably to be identified with the angel Michael) on the Day of Atonement that will end the tenth Jubilee cycle. The text is a tissue of scriptural allusions, including the key text about God's kingship from Isa 52:7 (11QMelch 2:15–16): "This is the day of salvation [or possibly, peace] of which God spoke through the words [or, the mouth] of Isaiah the prophet, who said: 'How beautiful on the mountains are the feet of him announcing the message of peace, announcing good news of salvation, saying to Zion: "Your God reigns as king." ' " Almost every word in this citation is then picked up and exegeted in what follows—except, apparently, for the central concept of God as king, which seems left by the wayside.[120] The silence speaks volumes about Qumran's relative lack of interest in God's kingship, even in (or especially in?) an eschatological context of final judgment and deliverance from evil.

(4) The final document in our survey, the *War Rule* or *War Scroll* (1QM), is a type of community rule, but a rule for a very specific situation: the eschatological war between the sons of light (i.e., the members of the Qumran community) and the sons of darkness. With such a scenario we might expect that here, if anywhere in the Qumran documents, we might find references to God's kingship, and we are not entirely disappointed. God is called king in 1QM 12:8 and 19:1 (in both cases, "holy," "Lord," and "king of glory" are all predicated of God). In 6:6 we are told that the kingship (*mĕlûkâ*) will belong to the God of Israel. In 12:7 God is addressed: "And you, O God, are awe-inspiring in the glory of your kingship (*malkûtĕkâ*)." The same prayer praises God, who will rule as king (*limlōk*) for all the times and ages (12:3,16). In column 19, after God has been referred to as the king of glory, the defeat of the kings of the hostile nations is predicted (19:6), with the Lord's kingship being shared by Israel (19:7–8, although lacunae in the manuscript make the precise wording uncertain here). A final reference is found in a fragment of a different version of or addition to the *War Rule*, recovered from Cave 4 (4Q491 *fragment 11* [= M^a]), entitled "The Song of Michael and the Just." The speaker (Michael?) states at the end of the fragment that "I am reckoned with the 'gods,' and my glory is with the sons of the king [presumably, the Lord God]."[121] Interestingly, 1QM follows the pattern set by 1QS: when reference is made to the dualistic division of the world into good and evil men and spirits, the vocabulary for the two realms or dominions of created beings at war with each other is regularly taken from the more general verb *māšal* ("to rule," so 1:5,15; 10:12; 13:10–11; 14:9–10; 17:5,7; 18:1,11), not the verb

mālak, which is more closely tied to kingly rule and which belongs properly to God alone.[122]

For our purposes, therefore, the *War Rule* is the most important document from Qumran, since it alone mentions God's kingship a number of times in the context of the eschatological struggle of good with evil, while distinguishing God's transcendent kingship from the dualistic dominions of good and evil creatures. God, of course, is king in heaven forever; but at the end time he will exercise his kingly rule through faithful Israelites (i.e., the Qumranites), who will defeat the forces of evil and share forever in God's dominion.[123] Even here, however, we must admit that the image of God's kingship—to say nothing of the precise phrase "kingdom of God"—does not dominate the entire work. Moreover, the rather bloodthirsty and gleeful description of how, at the end of this present world, one small sect within Judaism will slaughter all evil (i.e., non-Essene) Jews[124] along with the Gentiles does not exactly coincide with Jesus' message about the kingdom of God.

In short, despite all its idiosyncrasies, the documents from Qumran generally coincide with the overall picture that emerges from the protocanonical and deuterocanonical OT as well as the pseudepigrapha. The image of God's kingship/kingdom is absent from some of the literature, mentioned in passing in other works, and significantly present in still others, though hardly anywhere can it be said to dominate or to be a central theme of a whole book. At Qumran, the mystical and liturgical *Songs of the Sabbath Sacrifice* may rank as a lone exception. The precise phrase "the kingdom of God" appears only very late (in the OT, only in the deuterocanonical Wisdom of Solomon) and remains relatively rare in the material written before or around the time of Jesus. Hence what I suggested at the beginning of this chapter seems verified. Not only does the criterion of multiple attestation argue strongly for Jesus' use of the vocabulary and imagery of "the kingdom of God"; the criterion of discontinuity also highlights Jesus' usage as markedly distinct from all the Jewish religious literature that can be safely dated before him—as well as, surprisingly, from most of the NT literature (outside of the Gospels) that follows him. Thus, Jesus seems to have seized upon imagery and language that was present but hardly central to the OT and intertestamental traditions of Judaism and consciously decided to make the symbol of God's kingly rule one of the central themes of his own message.

As we move to Jesus' own use of the symbol, one point deserves special mention. As we have seen, while the symbol of God's rule continued to be used in the "intertestamental" period to refer to God's kingship in Israel's past and present as well as throughout eternity, the symbol was especially prominent in eschatological or apocalyptic contexts, conjuring up hopes of Israel's definitive salvation in the future. If, as some critics have claimed, Jesus did not want his use of the symbol to embody eschatological hopes for the future, it would have been absolutely necessary for him—unless he did not care about being misunderstood—to make clear that he did not intend an eschatological dimension when he employed the symbol. If he did use the symbol with reference to the future or in connection with apocalyptic imagery, and yet had no intention of teaching anything about the eschatological future (when God would reign definitively over Israel), he would have been inexplicably condemning himself to being misunderstood. Put simply: Jesus, like every teacher throughout history, had to work under certain constraints. However new or creative a teacher's insights, unless he or she can find a way to communicate those insights to an audience operating with certain received images, ideas, presuppositions, and worldviews, the new insights will never be effectively taught.[125] Whatever else Jesus was, he was an effective teacher who cared passionately about communicating what he believed and convincing people of its truth. Presumably, then, if he used the symbol of the kingdom of God in a sense directly counter to the eschatological connotations with which it was often connected, he would have made his own usage clear—all the more so if he wanted to negate any and all eschatological expectations.

These observations do not solve a priori the issue of eschatology in Jesus' message, nor do they claim that the usage of the apocrypha, pseudepigrapha, or Qumran was normative for Jesus. They simply remind us that, whatever his own message, Jesus was working within a religious tradition and with set religious symbols that had their own long history. If Jesus wished to reshape those symbols to fit his own message, he still had to do so within the constraints of history. Everything we have seen in this chapter has been aimed at helping us understand these constraints, which Jesus either accepted, rejected, or modified, but which he could hardly have ignored if he had wanted to be understood. How in fact Jesus adapted and recycled the symbol of God's kingship, and what ultimately he meant to convey by it, will be explored in the next two chapters.

NOTES TO CHAPTER 14

[1] Some might wish to posit one event that can be placed between the baptism and the body of the public ministry: the temptation of Jesus. One must grant that the temptation does enjoy multiple attestation, being represented by a puzzling, laconic notice in Mark 1:12–13 (the actual temptation narrative being restricted to v 13!) and a much longer narrative of a triple temptation in Q (Matt 4:1–11 ‖ Luke 4:1–13). Beyond the bare idea of Jesus' being tempted in the wilderness by the devil, the Marcan and Q presentations diverge widely. For Mark, the temptation takes place over forty days, but there is no mention of Jesus' fasting. Indeed, the statement that the angels "were ministering [*diēkonoun*] to him" apparently the whole time suggests that they were serving him food (one of the root meanings of *diakoneō*) during the forty days. The presence of the wild beasts in Mark is difficult to interpret; perhaps they are meant to suggest a return to the peace of paradise (Jesus as the new Adam?). On this, see Eduard Schweizer, *Das Evangelium nach Markus* (NTD 1; 2d ed.; Göttingen: Vandenhoeck & Ruprecht, 1968) 22.

The Q tradition instead has Jesus fasting for forty days; implied is the idea that only at the end of that period does he actually feel hunger. Luke states that the devil was tempting Jesus during the whole forty days, while Matthew seems to say that the actual temptations began only at the end of the forty-day period. The three temptations, with Jesus and the devil battling each other with quotations from Deuteronomy and Psalm 91, revolve around the true understanding of what it means to be the Son of God and the royal Messiah (harking back to the divine voice at the baptism). With these massive differences between the Marcan and Q versions of the temptation, the only thing they have in common is the idea that, immediately after his baptism, Jesus was led by the spirit into the desert, where he was tempted by the devil and emerged victorious (though even this last point is implicit rather than affirmed in Mark's text). On Matthew's redaction of Q, see Grundmann, *Das Evangelium nach Matthäus*, 99–104; for Luke's redaction, see Fitzmyer, *Luke*, 1. 507–20. Kloppenborg (*Formation*, 246–62) notes how many critics of Q find the temptation narrative a puzzling embarrassment; part of Kloppenborg's solution to the problem is to proclaim the narrative a late addition to Q. I think instead that the presence of this narrative in Q supports my thesis that Q must be accepted for what it is, a theological "grab bag."

One should also note that, as is to be expected, the Fourth Gospel lacks any corresponding temptation narrative. Such a struggle would not fit the high christology of a Gospel that begins with the proclamation of the Word made flesh. The motif of Jesus' battle with the devil, which ends triumphantly with the grand exorcism accomplished by Jesus' crucifixion (the event that truly expels Satan from the world [John 12:31–32]), appears at various places throughout the Fourth Gospel, especially from chap. 8 onwards. On this, see Raymond E. Brown, "Incidents That Are Units in the Synoptic Gospels but Dispersed in St. John," *CBQ* 23 (1961) 143–60, esp. 152–55. No other writing in the NT supplies us with a reference to the Marcan or Q temptation narrative.

Granted the paucity of sources and their conflicting presentations of the temptation of Jesus, any judgment about a historical event is extremely difficult. More to the point, though, since the heart of the temptation narrative concerns Jesus' struggle with a preternatural being in the desert, with no eyewitnesses present, the narrative really does not belong to the Gospel material that is in principle open to verification by any and all inquirers, believers and nonbelievers alike. At best, one could argue that the attestation of both Mark and Q indicates that, immediately after his baptism, Jesus retired for a while into the Judean wilderness and there underwent an inner spiritual struggle in preparation for his public ministry. While that is possible, one must also recognize that the entire tradition of Jesus' temptation by Satan in the wilderness may be a symbolic representation of the apocalyptic struggle between God and the devil which was prophesied for the last days and which—according to Christian faith—became a reality in the ministry (especially the exorcisms) of Jesus, culminating in his cross and resurrection. All this is obviously a statement of faith. That does not make it untrue or unreal, but it does withdraw it from the kind of examination and weighing of evidence undertaken in this book. For the suggestion that the narrative is a type of haggadic midrash based on texts from Deuteronomy, see Davies and Allison, *Matthew*, 1. 353; yet the authors hold open the possibility of a historical nucleus (p. 357). For a similar and even more imaginative attempt to preserve some historical nucleus (which admittedly is very small and vague), see Jeremias, *Theology*, 70–74. After considering various solutions (literalistic interpretation, parabolic interpretation, figurative language or dramatization of what Jesus experienced during his ministry), Fitzmyer sagely observes (*Luke*, 1. 510): ". . . in the long run, their import [i.e., of the scenes of temptation] is of greater importance than any salvaging of their historicity." See also Jacques Dupont, *Les tentations de Jésus au désert* (StudNeot 4; Bruges: Desclée de Brouwer, 1968); Ernest Best, *The Temptation and the Passion. The Markan Soteriology* (SNTSMS 2; 2d ed.; Cambridge: Cambridge University, 1990, 1st ed. 1965). For a different view of the sources, see Wilhelm Wilkens, "Die Versuchung Jesu nach Matthäus," *NTS* 28 (1982) 479–89.

[2] For detailed consideration of this point, see section III, "A Final Summary and a Final Caution," in Chapter 11.

[3] The bibliography on the kingdom of God is vast. For basic introduction to the symbol or concept of the kingdom of God, along with suggestions for further reading, see Karl Ludwig Schmidt, *"basileia,"* *TDNT* 1 (1964) 579–90; Rudolf Otto, *The Kingdom of God and the Son of Man* (Lutterworth Library 9; rev. ed.; London: Lutterworth, 1943); Amos N. Wilder, *Eschatology and Ethics in the Teaching of Jesus* (rev. ed.; Westport, CT: Greenwood, 1978, originally 1950); Reginald H. Fuller, *The Mission and Achievement of Jesus* (SBT 12; London: SCM, 1954); O. E. Evans, "Kingdom of God, of Heaven," *IDB*, 3. 17–26; Gösta Lundström, *The Kingdom of God in the Teaching of Jesus. A History of Interpretation from the Last Decades of the Nineteenth Century to the Present Day* (Edinburgh/London: Oliver and Boyd, 1963); Norman Perrin, *The Kingdom of God in the Teaching of Jesus* (Philadelphia: Westminster, 1963); idem, *Rediscovering the Teaching of Jesus*, 54–108; idem, *Jesus and the Language of the Kingdom* (Philadelphia: Fortress, 1976); Oscar Cullmann, *Christ and Time* (rev. ed.; Philadelphia: Westminster, 1964); George Eldon Ladd, *Jesus and the Kingdom. The Eschatology of Biblical Realism* (2d ed.; Waco, TX: Word, 1964); Richard H. Hiers, *Jesus and Ethics. Four Interpretations* (Philadelphia: Westminster, 1968); idem, *The Kingdom of God in the Synoptic Tradition* (University of Florida Humanities Monograph 33; Gainesville, FL: University of Florida, 1970); idem, *The Historical Jesus and the Kingdom of God. Present and Future in the Message and Ministry of Jesus* (Gainesville, FL: University of Florida, 1973); Bruce D. Chilton, *God in Strength. Jesus' Announcement of the Kingdom* (The Biblical Seminar; Sheffield: JSOT, 1987, originally 1979); idem (ed.), *The Kingdom of God in the Teaching of Jesus* (Issues in Religion and Theology 5; Philadelphia: Fortress, 1984); Odo Camponovo, *Königtum, Königsherrschaft und Reich Gottes in den frühjüdischen Schriften* (OBO 58; Freiburg: Universitätsverlag; Göttingen: Vandenhoeck & Ru-

precht, 1984); Dale C. Allison, Jr., *The End of the Ages Has Come* (Philadelphia: Fortress, 1985); George R. Beasley-Murray, *Jesus and the Kingdom of God* (Grand Rapids: Eerdmans, 1986); Wendell Willis (ed.), *The Kingdom of God in 20th-Century Interpretation* (Peabody, MA: Hendrickson, 1987); Benedict T. Viviano, *The Kingdom of God in History* (Good News Studies 27; Wilmington, DE: Glazier, 1988); Bruce J. Malina, "Christ and Time: Swiss or Mediterranean?" *CBQ* 51 (1989) 1–31; Marc Zvi Brettler, *God is King. Understanding an Israelite Metaphor* (JSOTSup 76; Sheffield: JSOT, 1989); Gnilka, *Jesus von Nazaret*, 141–65.

[4] Jeremias, *Theology*, 96. For similar statements, see, among others, Johannes Weiss, *Jesus' Proclamation of the Kingdom of God* (Lives of Jesus Series; ed. Richard Hiers and David Holland; Philadelphia: Fortress, 1971, originally 1892) 57–60; Rudolf Bultmann, *Theology of the New Testament* (2 vols.; London: SCM, 1952) 1. 4; Bornkamm, *Jesus of Nazareth*, 64; Hiers, *The Historical Jesus and the Kingdom of God*, 11–12. This emphasis is naturally taken over by liberation theologians such as Jon Sobrino (*Jesus in Latin America* [Maryknoll, NY: Orbis, 1987] 81–97), since their presentations of the historical Jesus rely heavily on the reconstructions of European scholars like Jeremias and Bornkamm.

[5] Perrin, *Rediscovering the Teaching of Jesus*, 54.

[6] See Evans, "Kingdom of God," 20. The qualifier "some" has to be used in reference to Q, M, and L since these sources must be reconstructed hypothetically. What one critic might attribute to M another might attribute either to Q or to Matthew's redaction; but the overall picture would not be appreciably altered by such individual decisions. For example, the count of Jeremias (*Theology*, 31) yields 13 times in Mark, 9 times in Q, 27 times in Matthew, 12 times in Luke, and 2 times in John.

[7] As we shall see, occurrences do increase in the targum Jonathan on the Prophets, but dating the material is notoriously difficult.

[8] On this see Jeremias, *Theology*, 32.

[9] On this see Karl Paul Donfried, "The Kingdom of God in Paul," in Willis (ed.), *The Kingdom of God in 20th-Century Interpretation*, 175–90.

[10] Acts 1:3 presents the risen Jesus speaking of the kingdom of God to his disciples prior to his ascension. In 8:12, Luke summarizes in his own words the preaching of Philip. In 14:22, "It is through many tribulations that we must enter the kingdom of God" could be a traditional saying put on the lips of Paul and his companions. However, Haenchen (*Die Apostelgeschichte*, 377) claims that 14:22 shows pronounced traits of Lucan style; Schneider (*Die Apostelgeschichte*, 2. 165–66) points out how the verse fits perfectly into Lucan theology. In 19:8, Luke summarizes in his own words Paul's preaching. In 20:25, *kēryssōn tēn basileian* in Paul's address to the elders of Ephesus may be a conscious attempt by Luke to link Paul's missionary preaching with that of Jesus and Jesus' earliest disciples; cf. Luke 8:1; 9:2. Finally, in 28:23,31, Luke twice summarizes Paul's preaching in Rome in terms of proclaiming the kingdom of God. As can be seen, almost all of the occurrences in Acts are either Luke's own summary of what someone said or very likely Luke's formulation of direct discourse that he puts in someone's mouth.

[11] To these instances might be added Rev 1:6 and 5:10, where Jesus is said to make "us" or "them" a "kingdom and priests" for God. The sense appears to be that the slain and risen Christ has made believers into a group of royal priests of-

fering worship to God—an idea that differs from the notion of "kingdom of God" in the Gospels.

[12] Jeremias (*Theology*, 32–34) further bolsters his argument by noting the many Gospel phrases involving the word "kingdom" that "have *no parallels* (not even secular ones) in the language of Jesus' contemporaries" (p. 32). The view that only a few kingdom-sayings are authentic and that "the kingdom of God" was not the central concept for the historical Jesus is maintained by Ernst Bammel, "Erwägungen zur Eschatologie Jesu," *Studia Evangelica. Vol. III* (TU 88; ed. F. L. Cross; Berlin: Akademie, 1964) 3–32, esp. 7–19 and 28–32. Bammel's picture of an uneschatological Jesus depends on his cavalier dismissal, with little or no argumentation, of a number of key kingdom sayings that do point to future eschatology in the message of the historical Jesus. Some of these will be examined at length—and judged authentic—in Chapter 15. But it is sobering to remember that there are exegetes like Bammel who deny future eschatology and the symbol "kingdom of God" a central place in the preaching of the historical Jesus. Hence a careful, detailed examination of the symbol and its function within the eschatological thought of Jesus is necessary.

[13] Though at times alternate phrasing is used, e.g., "his kingdom" (2 Tim 4:18) or "the kingdom of his son" (Col 1:13).

[14] In Matthew, *basileia* ("kingdom") is used 55 times, *basileia tōn ouranōn* ("kingdom of heaven[s]") 32 times, and *basileia tou theou* ("kingdom of God") 4 times. The plural *ouranōn* (literally, "of heavens") reflects the plural form in the corresponding and probably underlying Aramaic phrase *malkûtā' dî šĕmayyā'*. Because Matthew or his tradition tends to multiply references to the kingdom, one must be careful when using specifically Matthean material to establish the historical Jesus' message of the kingdom. For example, Lundström (*The Kingdom of God*, 236) too readily uses texts like Matt 5:20 and 5:48 without asking whether they might be Matthean redactional creations in whole or part.

[15] For one attempt, see Margaret Pamment, "The Kingdom of Heaven According to the First Gospel," *NTS* 27 (1981) 211–32. She tries to show that "kingdom of heaven" in Matthew is an imminent but entirely future reality, while "the kingdom of God" represents a present kingdom. Her theory breaks down especially in 11:11–12 and 19:23–24.

[16] For the justification of this statement, see my reconstruction of the history of the Matthean church in Raymond E. Brown and John P. Meier, *Antioch and Rome* (New York/Ramsey, NJ: Paulist, 1983) 12–72.

[17] Occurrences of the name God in sayings of the Synoptic Jesus: Mark 35 times, Matthew 33 times, Luke 65 times.

[18] The one occurrence in the deuterocanonical/apocryphal books of the OT is Wis 10:10: "She [divine wisdom] showed him [Jacob] the kingdom of God" (*edeixen autō basileian theou*). The reference is to Jacob's dream (at Bethel) of a stairway or "ladder" going up to heaven in Gen 28:10–17. Notice the difference from NT usage; in Wis 10:10 the kingdom of God is that kingdom which is located in heaven and which is revealed to the chosen one through a vision. Scattered occurrences are found in the OT pseudepigrapha; see, e.g., *Ps.Sol.* 17:3: "the kingdom of our God" (*hē basileia tou theou hēmōn*).

[19] On all this, see Jeremias, *Theology*, 97.

[20] His use of the construct form *malkût 'ĕlāhā'* is also a possibility, as well as the elegant *malkûtēh dî 'ĕlāhā'*.

[21] At the same time, one must acknowledge that some of the alternate phrases are not without difficulty as well. For example, because of the constitutional situation of the monarchs still "reigning" in certain countries of Western Europe, to modern Americans "reign" carries the connotation of "reign, not rule." "Rule," while in many ways preferable, suffers from a disability not shared by "kingdom" or "reign": of itself, it in no way denotes or connotes royal or kingly rule. All "rule" means (as a noun) is "the exercise of authority or control; dominion" (*Webster's Ninth New Collegiate Dictionary*, s.v.). Among the possible meanings of the verb is included "to exercise authority or power over, often harshly or arbitrarily." Obviously, no one word is a completely satisfactory translation; hence I choose to stay with the stock translation and explain the range of meanings it can bear in a biblical context.

[22] Philip Wheelwright, *Metaphor and Reality* (Bloomington, IN/London: Indiana University, 1962) 45–69, 92–110. A similar distinction between a transparent "sign" and an opaque "symbol" is made by Paul Ricoeur, *The Symbolism of Evil* (Boston: Beacon, 1967) 10–18.

[23] Perrin, *Jesus and the Language of the Kingdom*, 29–34.

[24] Brettler observes toward the end of his monograph (*God is King*, 165): "Although I have referred in general terms to 'the' metaphor 'God is king', it is not a single, unified metaphor. Individual uses of the metaphor in different contexts and in different time-periods recall different specific entailments of God's kingship."

[25] Perrin, *Jesus and the Language of the Kingdom*, 33.

[26] This seems to be what Dale Patrick ("The Kingdom of God in the Old Testament," in Willis [ed.], *The Kingdom of God in 20th-Century Interpretation*, 67–79) is getting at when he remarks (p. 70) that "Jesus employs the expression *basileia tou theou* . . . to arouse in his listeners a complex of ideas, associations, and metaphors. They already have some idea of what he is talking about. Whatever particular twist he wishes to give to this idea, he relates it to the various conceptions his hearers have in their minds"—which includes conflicts he may intend to ignite with received opinions on the kingdom. A similar point is made by Lundström, *The Kingdom of God*, 232.

[27] For an outline of the various possibilities in interpreting the time-reference of "kingdom of God," see Everett Ferguson, "The Kingdom of God in Early Patristic Literature," in Willis (ed.), *The Kingdom of God in 20th-Century Interpretation*, 191–208, esp. 191–92. The major positions of 20th-century interpreters (Johannes Weiss and Albert Schweitzer defending purely imminent eschatology, C. H. Dodd defending realized eschatology, Rudolf Bultmann defending an eschatological Jesus demythologized into authentic existence in the present moment of the believer, Werner Georg Kümmel and George Eldon Ladd defending a mediating position of already/not yet [similar to Joachim Jeremias's eschatology in the process of realization], and Amos Wilder and Norman Perrin emphasizing kingdom as a literary symbol and metaphor) are reviewed and analyzed in the following essays in the Willis volume: Wendell Willis, "The Discovery of the Eschatological Kingdom: Johannes Weiss and Albert Schweitzer," 1–14; Richard H. Hiers, Jr., "Pivotal Reactions to the Eschatological Interpretations: Rudolf Bultmann and C. H. Dodd," 15–33; Eldon Jay Epp, "Mediating Approaches to the Kingdom: Werner Georg Kümmel and George Eldon Ladd," 35–52; W. Emory Elmore, "Linguistic Approaches to the Kingdom: Amos Wilder and Norman Perrin," 53–65.

[28] Perrin, *Jesus and the Language of the Kingdom*, 45.

[29] M. Eugene Boring, "The Kingdom of God in Mark," in Willis (ed.), *The Kingdom of God in 20th-Century Interpretation*, 131–45, esp. 134–45. Perrin's position is pushed even further by Bernard Brandon Scott, *Jesus, Symbol Maker for the Kingdom* (Philadelphia: Fortress, 1981) 10–11. Any reference to the future is rejected in favor of an elastic symbol that "uses God's past dealings with his people as King to indicate how God deals with them now." Scott's view is strongly criticized by E. P. Sanders, *Jesus and Judaism* (Philadelphia: Fortress, 1985) 7, 125–29. Simply from the nature of the method employed, Scott's ahistorical, synchronic, modern literary approach to the parables, while supplying interesting esthetic insights, cannot put us into touch with a particular 1st-century Jew called Jesus.

[30] Hence I have no quarrel with the contention of Brettler (*God is King*, 161) that a thorough study of all the associations connected with the metaphor of God as king must go beyond an examination of the Hebrew root *mlk*.

[31] I should emphasize from the outset that the focus of our investigation in this chapter is the symbol/concept "kingdom *of God*" in its strict *theo*-logical sense. I am not attempting in this chapter to examine in detail all the various intermediary or messianic figures (e.g., angels, Michael, Melchizedek, Davidic king, eschatological high priest or prophet) that might or might not play an instrumental role in the establishment or rule of God's kingdom. Such considerations belong more properly to an investigation of Jesus' view of himself and his role in the coming of God's kingdom—a subject that will be raised in a later chapter. As we shall see even from the present survey, Jewish presentations of God's kingdom could both employ and dispense with intermediary figures.

[32] The new *RSV* renders the Hebrew literally as "the throne of the kingdom of the Lord," while the *NAB* is freer: "the Lord's royal throne." Similar to 1 Chr 28:5 is the usage within Nathan's promise to David (1 Chr 17:14): "And I will make him [the offspring of David] stand in my house and in my kingdom [*malkûtî*] . . . ." Notice how in these two passages the kingdom of Yahweh is connected with the throne and offspring of David. Some authors think that the Chronicler's view of the Davidic kingdom as a realization of God's rule betokens a messianic conception connected with the idea of Yahweh's eschatological kingship; on this, see Camponovo, *Königtum*, 90–91.

[33] Some might add Ps 45:7 (MT), but the statement that "the scepter of uprightness is the scepter of your kingship" is most likely directed to the enthroned Israelite king, who by court etiquette receives the honorific *ĕlōhîm* ("God").

[34] As Walter Baumgartner notes in his entry on *malkû* in the Aramaic part of the Koehler-Baumgartner *Lexicon in Veteris Testamenti Libros* (p. 1094), it is not always easy to distinguish the cases where *malkû* means "kingdom" or "realm" from the cases where it means "kingship." To take a concrete example, Klaus Koch ("Offenbaren wird sich das Reich Gottes," *NTS* 25 [1978–79] 158–65) holds that in the targum Jonathan on the Prophets, *malkûtā'* usually carries the spatial sense of kingdom, though in fact this sense cannot be totally divorced from the dynamic one of the exercise of royal power. Camponovo (*Königtum*, 430), while allowing a variety of meanings in a variety of contexts, is not so ready to admit a predominantly spatial sense in the case of the eschatological kingship/kingdom of Yahweh. The same ambiguity holds true for the Hebrew equivalents. Camponovo (*Königtum*, 70) notes the difficulty of deciding the exact meaning of any one of the Semitic "royal" words in a given OT passage. To take another concrete example: John J. Collins ("The Kingdom of God in the Apocrypha

and Pseudepigrapha," in Willis [ed.], *The Kingdom of God in 20th-Century Interpretation*, 84) distinguishes in the Book of Daniel three aspects of the Aramaic *malkû*: the sovereignty of God, who disposes of all kingdoms; the earthly dominion of the Jewish people in a kingdom set up by God at the end of time; and the apocalyptic kingdom of the angels, which involves the exaltation of righteous human beings after death. Whether these distinctions hold will be examined below.

[35] So Camponovo (*Königtum*, 70, 73), who suggests that the abstract form in *-ût* may have increased in use under Aramaic influence.

[36] David Winston (*The Wisdom of Solomon* [AB 43; Garden City, NY: Doubleday, 1979] 20–24) points out that a date as early as 220 B.C. has been defended, but he himself argues strongly for the turbulent days of the Roman Emperor Gaius Caligula (reigned A.D. 37–41). This dating is also given serious consideration by George W. E. Nickelsburg, *Jewish Literature Between the Bible and the Mishnah* (Philadelphia: Fortress, 1981) 184. If this late date should be accepted, it would have some intriguing consequences for those Christians who accept the Wisdom of Solomon as canonical. For them, the so-called "intertestamental period" would have lasted, from a literary point of view, about ten years (1 Thessalonians is usually dated ca. A.D. 50).

[37] The question of whether the verb *mālak* should be understood in an ingressive sense ("Yahweh has become king") or a perduring sense ("Yahweh is reigning as king") or both is discussed by Camponovo, *Königtum*, 78. Camponovo wisely observes that the verb in itself is capable of either meaning and that therefore the context must decide the individual case.

[38] See Patrick ("The Kingdom of God in the Old Testament," 72) for a list of OT passages that use verbal forms like *yimlōk* or nominal formations with *melek* ("king") in reference to God. As Patrick remarks on p. 74, the verb *šāpaṭ* ("to judge"), when used with God, is often functionally equivalent to the verb *mālak*. While the verbal forms are perhaps the most important expressions of the royal symbol, one should not overlook the use of the noun *melek* for Yahweh, especially in psalms and prayers.

[39] Especially associated with such a view is Sigmund Mowinckel, *The Psalms in Israel's Worship* (2 vols.; Oxford: Blackwell, 1962) 1. 106–92. For an overview of the problem and doubts about Mowinckel's approach, see Brettler, *God is King*, 139–58, 166–67.

[40] For a summary of opinions on the subject, see Camponovo, *Königtum*, 76–78. On pp. 91–95 he briefly reviews the content of these psalms. On pp. 95–102 he adds a consideration of other psalms that touch on the theme of Yahweh's royal rule: Ps 29:10; 68:25; Psalms 145 and 146; Ps 149:2; 24:7–10; 95:3; 10:16; 103:19; 22:29; 44:5; 74:12; 5:3; 48:3; and 84:4.

[41] See Camponovo, *Königtum*, 77–78 (especially with reference to Claus Westermann, who sees the influence of Deutero-Isaiah in these psalms).

[42] For the difficulty of fixing the exact sense of Exod 19:6, see Camponovo, *Königtum*, 81; similarly, for Deut 33:5, see pp. 83–84.

[43] The establishment of Yahweh's kingship over Israel by his saving deed is also indirectly alluded to in the second oracle of Balaam (Num 23:21). The text is somewhat obscure; the new *RSV* translates: "The LORD their God is with them, acclaimed as a king among them."

[44] On the problem of the two strains of thought in the deuteronomistic history, see Camponovo, *Königtum*, 85–89.

[45] As Camponovo observes (*Königtum*, 103), it is of significance that the oldest OT reference to Yahweh as king that can be dated with certainty (i.e., Isa 6:5) connects the kingship of Yahweh with the Jerusalem temple.

[46] For a commentary on Isa 52:7–10, see Claus Westermann, *Isaiah 40–66* (OTL; Philadelphia: Westminster, 1969) 249–52.

[47] For comments on Isa 24:21–23 and 33:1–24, see Otto Kaiser, *Isaiah 13–39* (OTL; Philadelphia: Westminster, 1974) 192–96, 336–50.

[48] Presumably Jesus would have read the title of king in the last three citations, although some of the occurrences may be later additions to the text; see Camponovo, *Königtum*, 110. In any case, they would have been added before the time of Jesus.

[49] Here it is important to remember that Jesus and his contemporaries would have read the Book of Isaiah as a whole, without making our modern distinctions between Deutero- and Trito-Isaiah. Actually, Trito-Isaiah does not use the image of the divine king as the basis of his hopes and exhortations, but naturally a 1st-century reader would have taken his prophecies as one with those of Deutero-Isaiah, who does exploit the symbol of Yahweh as king.

[50] In the text I give the verse enumeration in the MT, followed by the *NAB;* the new *RSV* has the following enumeration: 4:17,25,32,34–35,37. See also 3:33 in the MT (in the new *RSV* 4:3, in the *NAB* 3:100): "His [God's] kingdom is a kingdom of eternity [= an everlasting kingdom], and his sovereign rule is from generation to generation"; and 6:27: "His [God's] kingdom shall not be destroyed, his sovereign rule shall not end." In the great hymn of the three young men that is found in the LXX and in the Theodotion version of Daniel, God is presented as seated on "the throne of your kingdom" (LXX Dan 3:54). On the secondary nature of the hymn of the three young men, see Carey A. Moore, *Daniel, Esther and Jeremiah: The Additions* (AB 44; Garden City, NY: Doubleday, 1977) 43–44.

[51] On the idea of four successive world-empires, see Louis F. Hartman and Alexander A. Di Lella, *The Book of Daniel* (AB 23; Garden City, NY: Doubleday, 1978) 29–42; Collins, "The Kingdom of God in the Apocrypha and Pseudepigrapha," 81–95, esp. 81–82. The origin of the pattern may lie in Persia.

[52] The original context of these prophecies is the hope for a speedy deliverance from the persecution of Antiochus IV Epiphanes. Naturally, Jesus and his contemporaries would not bother themselves about a historical-critical interpretation of a text like Daniel. Qumran gives us (e.g., in the *pešer* on Habakkuk) clear examples of how old prophecies were reread as addressing the present and prophesying the near future.

[53] At least in the final form of the Book of Daniel, one must somehow bring the resurrection of the dead in chap. 12 into relation to the everlasting kingdom God establishes for his holy ones in chaps. 2 and 7. From this point of view I have difficulty with Collins's description of the everlasting kingdom of 2:44 ("The Kingdom of God in the Apocrypha and Pseudepigrapha," 82): "From the context we should suppose that it is a Jewish kingdom which will rise to replace, and destroy, the previous gentile kingdoms. It differs from other kingdoms insofar as it will not pass away, but it is presumably a political, earthly kingdom like them." Collins's solution to the problem is to distinguish between the everlasting kingdom in chap. 2 and the everlasting kingdom in chap. 7. In chap. 7, but not in chap. 2, the kingdom has two levels, angelic and earthly; it is to the angelic kingdom that the risen Jews will belong. In my view, the distinctions made to produce this synthesis seem somewhat artificial. Among other things, it seems strange that the Book of Daniel should introduce the relatively new idea (to Judaism, anyway)

of the resurrection of the just on the last day, only to assign the Jews raised in their bodies to an angelic heavenly realm rather than to the everlasting kingdom of Jews on earth. The whole construction also rests heavily on the identification of the "one like a son of man" with the angel Michael (pp. 83–84). On the difficulties involved in this identification, see Alexander A. Di Lella, "The One in Human Likeness and the Holy Ones of the Most High in Daniel 7," *CBQ* 39 (1977) 1–19. If instead the human figure is to be identified with the truly human kingdom of faithful Jews (as opposed to the bestial kingdoms that preceded it), it seems to follow that this final human (and Jewish) kingdom has a heavenly or transcendent aspect. That, however, does not solve the precise question of the where and how of this final kingdom of the faithful. The author of Daniel may not have been all that interested in the details implicit in his own grand vision (cf. Camponovo, *Königtum*, 125–26).

[54] The treatment of the deuterocanonical/apocryphal material is encumbered by many disputed questions of the dating of tradition and redaction, text-critical variants, and various recensions. It may well be that some of the material treated here was actually composed before the final redaction of the Book of Daniel. This is certainly the case for Ben Sira; it may also be true of Tobit. At the same time, we must remember that Daniel itself had a lengthy tradition history, with some elements going back to the 3d century B.C. or even earlier. For the sake of an orderly survey, however, all the deuterocanonical material is brought together here.

[55] Once again, we are plagued by different editions and translations using different verse enumerations. The numbers in the text reflect the verse enumeration printed in Rahlfs's two-volume edition of the LXX.

[56] The evidence is all the more impressive in the case of Ben Sira because this prayer is preserved in Hebrew in the fragments from the Cairo Genizah; for the Hebrew, Greek, Latin, and Syriac texts, see Francesco Vattioni, *Ecclesiastico* (Naples: Istituto Orientale di Napoli, 1968) 186–91. For commentary, see Patrick W. Skehan and Alexander A. Di Lella, *The Wisdom of Ben Sira* (AB 39; New York: Doubleday, 1987) 420–23.

[57] God is addressed as king in the Greek and Syriac versions of Sir 51:1; the Hebrew text, however, reads "God of my father." Skehan and Di Lella (*The Wisdom of Ben Sira*, 560) prefer the reading with "king." Praise of God as the king of kings also appears in chapter 51 in a separate hymn (line 14, by Camponovo's enumeration) that occurs only in manuscript B from the Cairo Genizah and does not seem to have been an original part of Ben Sira; see Skehan and Di Lella, *The Wisdom of Ben Sira*, 569.

[58] For the problem of a proper form-critical designation, see Carey A. Moore, *Judith* (AB 40; Garden City, NY: Doubleday, 1985) 71–76.

[59] On the problems raised by "Judith's Song," see Moore, *Judith*, 252–57. Whether this song was originally part of the Book of Judith need not concern us, since it would have been accepted as part of the work by the ancient reader.

[60] On this see Carey A. Moore, *Esther* (AB 7B; Garden City, NY: Doubleday, 1971) xxxii–xxxiv.

[61] See Moore, *Daniel, Esther and Jeremiah: The Additions*, 158–59.

[62] Giving chapter and verse references to the Greek additions to the Book of Esther is always a problem, since different translations use different systems. I adopt here the chapter and verse references employed by the new *RSV*, which preserves the chapter and verse numbers of the *KJV*.

[63] Camponovo (*Königtum*, 365–68) emphasizes that, in his view, the scene in 3:1–9

refers not to an individual judgment immediately after death, but to the general judgment, "the day of Yahweh." Thus, in Camponovo's view, the author is consciously meshing the Greek idea of the immortality of the soul with traditional Jewish views on eschatology. It is at the final judgment that the just will receive the kingly crown (*to basileion*) of glory (5:16), i.e., the share in God's rule that immortality makes possible.

[64] Winston, *Wisdom of Solomon*, 33.

[65] See Nickelsburg, *Jewish Literature*, 175–79; see further George W. E. Nickelsburg, *Resurrection, Immortality, and Eternal Life in Intertestamental Judaism* (HTS 26; Cambridge, MA: Harvard University, 1972).

[66] Heaven is God's kingdom in the sense that it is the place in which and from which he exercises his eternal sovereign power; hence we are told that God's throne is in heaven in Wis 9:4,10; 18:15.

Winston (*Wisdom of Solomon*, 217) notes that some commentators take *hagiōn* (which he, along with the *NAB* and the new *RSV*, translates as "of holy things") in 10:10 to refer to the heavenly temple (this is the sense of *ta hagia* in Heb 9:12) or to the heavenly Jerusalem. Considering, however, the presence of the angels in the Bethel story (*hoi aggeloi tou theou* of LXX Gen 28:12), I think the genitive plural *hagiōn* is best taken as masculine. It is more difficult to decide whether the genitive is subjective (i.e., the knowledge of God and heaven that angels possess [so Camponovo]) or objective (i.e., knowledge about these heavenly beings). For various interpretations of the verse, see Camponovo, *Königtum*, 373–75.

[67] On the problems of the eschatology of the Book of Wisdom, see Addison G. Wright, "Wisdom," *NJBC*, 511. A comparison between Ben Sira and the Wisdom of Solomon on the question of eschatology can be found in Alexander A. Di Lella, "Conservative and Progressive Theology: Sirach and Wisdom," *CBQ* 28 (1966) 139–54.

[68] Because of their common ground in Middle Platonism and Jewish-Alexandrian theology (as seen to fullest extent in Philo), there are some affinities between the Wisdom of Solomon and the Epistle to the Hebrews.

[69] See Jonathan A. Goldstein, *I Maccabees* (AB 41; Garden City, NY: Doubleday, 1976) 13. Goldstein thinks that the absence of *theos* used for the God of Israel is due to reverence for the divine name. Whether total avoidance of "God" out of reverence can be shown to have existed among Jews so early is debatable; one might point instead to the relative lack of strictly theological concerns in 1 Maccabees as opposed to 2 Maccabees. It should also be noted that in 1 Macc 3:18 some manuscripts do read *tou theou* ("God") instead of *tou ouranou* ("heaven").

[70] It is telling that, in his survey of the varying ideas of the kingship, kingly rule, and kingdom of God in the deuterocanonical/apocryphal OT, Camponovo (*Königtum*, 185) gives no separate treatment of 1 Maccabees, but instead passes immediately to 2 Maccabees.

[71] But see Goldstein (*I Maccabees*, 240–41), who interprets the plural *eis aiōnas* to mean "for ages," not "forever." While he offers a good argument for his choice, his attempt at distinguishing between *aiōn* in the singular and in the plural seems strained.

[72] Jonathan A. Goldstein, *II Maccabees* (AB 41A; Garden City, NY: Doubleday, 1983) 4.

[73] Goldstein (*II Maccabees*, 82) goes so far as to claim that Jason of Cyrene (whose

history was abridged to create 2 Maccabees) wrote his work to discredit 1 Maccabees, which contained "the propaganda of the hated Hasmonaeans."

[74] The mixture of political and theological concerns sometimes makes it difficult to judge the exact import of a statement. For example, when the author writes that Jason "fell away from" or "revolted against the holy land and the kingdom" (2 Macc 1:7), is the kingdom that of the Seleucid monarch, of the legitimate high priest, or of God? Camponovo (*Königtum*, 186–88) chooses the last, but the matter is by no means clear (see p. 187 n. 42 for other suggestions).

[75] See Goldstein, *II Maccabees*, 305. It is curious that Camponovo, in his review of divine kingship in 2 Maccabees (*Königtum*, 185–90), gives short shrift to chap. 7 (p. 189).

[76] Since some count 3 Maccabees among the deuterocanonical/apocryphal books of the OT, mention should be made here of references to the divine king in 3 Maccabees. There are two significant passages, both prayers. In 3 Macc 2:1–20, the high priest Simon prays to the divine king to prevent the Egyptian king from entering the holy of holies. God is presented as king of heaven and lord of all creatures, the creator of all, who nevertheless has chosen as his own the city of Jerusalem. His people, justly oppressed for their sins, cry out in their helplessness to the all-powerful God who can save them in their need. In the similar prayer of the elderly priest Eleazar (3 Macc 6:1–15), God is king precisely because he is the all-powerful creator of all things, who has used and will now again use his power to save his people Israel when they are threatened with destruction. In 4 Maccabees, which is more of a philosophical tract, *basileus* is used not of God, but of the pious martyr (7:10) and of reason, which allows the seven Jewish brothers to endure martyrdom (14:2, but there is a variant reading). This comes close to the philosophical commonplace that the wise man is king, a view taken over by Philo (*On the Migration of Abraham* 197; *On Abraham* 261; *On Dreams* 2. 244). In general, the more Jewish thought moved into the Hellenistic culture of the Greco-Roman world, the more spiritualized and rationalized the concept of kingdom became. Reading Philo, one gets the feeling of being worlds away from the proclamation of Jesus.

[77] See especially Volume One of his *Theology of the Old Testament* (2 vols.; Philadelphia: Westminster, 1961, 1967). It is for this reason that I feel some unease with the ingenious book of Beasley-Murray, *Jesus and the Kingdom of God*. In this work, "the kingdom of God" becomes such a broad, overarching concept or symbol that it seems to encompass just about everything and anything Beasley-Murray wishes to include in his grand theological synthesis of the Old and New Testaments. I readily grant that we must not focus narrowly on just the precise words "kingdom of God." As I have stressed already, "kingdom of God" is a tensive symbol that certainly evokes a whole range of meanings. Yet even that range, even that whole mythic story, has a certain coherence and integrity to it. To expand "kingdom of God" to cover the very general affirmation that God controls all things is to rob the symbol of its specificity and power and to miss the special contours of the thought and language of various books (and parts of books) in the OT, the pseudepigrapha, and Qumran. Even if one were to grant a very wide meaning to "kingdom of God," I still do not think it is true to say, as Beasley-Murray does: "It was Yahweh's sovereign action on which the attention of Old Testament writers focused. . . ." Is that true of Qoheleth or Esther or 1 Maccabees? And even when OT authors did "focus" upon God's sovereign control, why did some "focus" on language connected with God's *kingly* rule while others did not? Does the difference in focus mean anything? I think that, as he attempts to write a sweeping

biblical theology, Beasley-Murray misses the special nature of the particular statements that do speak explicitly of God's kingdom or kingly rule. It is on those specific statements that we must focus for the primary background of Jesus' use of the symbol "kingdom of God."

[78] See Raymond E. Brown (with Raymond F. Collins), "Canonicity," *NJBC*, 1040: "The safest statement about the closing of the Jewish canon is one which recognizes that, although in the 1st cent. A.D. there was acceptance of 22 or 24 books as sacred, there was no rigidly fixed exclusive Hebr canon until the end of the 2d century. In this period various Jewish groups continued to read as sacred, books not included in the 22/24 count."

[79] Actual practice among Orthodox and Oriental Christians has varied in the past and continues to vary today; see Raymond F. Collins (with Raymond E. Brown), "Canonicity," *NJBC*, 1043.

[80] I purposely use vague language like "authoritative status" to accommodate the wide range of opinions in early 1st-century Judaism. I intentionally choose a phrase that says less than "divinely inspired," for it is quite possible that, for Jewish scribes in Jerusalem, Sirach may have enjoyed great authority and esteem without having been considered divinely inspired. Indeed, Sirach seems to have continued in use among some Jews until around the 11th century. The attitude of the rabbis toward it was complex. It was considered outside the canon, and yet at times it would be cited in the Talmud with the introductory phrase reserved for canonical Scripture: "it is written." On this, see Skehan and Di Lella, *The Wisdom of Ben Sira*, 20.

In the pluralistic situation of Judaism in the early 1st century A.D., no doubt some books enjoyed more authority or status in some Jewish groups or parties than in others. For instance, as far as we can tell, the Pharisees attributed more authority to the literary prophets than did the Sadducees. But any such statement must be made warily, since we have no theological literature from the Sadducees of the early 1st century A.D. Some would count Ben Sira as a "proto-Sadducee." If that is true, it is significant that he includes Isaiah, Jeremiah, Ezekiel, and the twelve minor prophets in his praise of the ancestors (Chapters 44–50, especially 48:20–49:10). Obviously, whether he is a proto-Sadducee or not, Ben Sira is not defining a canon as he praises the great figures of Israel's history; but implicitly he is indicating what prophetic writings he considered in some sense authoritative. In the opinion of David W. Suter (*Harper's Bible Dictionary*, 238), Ben Sira's praise of the ancestors "makes it clear that by 200 B.C. both the Torah and the Prophets are fixed divisions of Scripture in Palestinian Judaism." At first glance, this may seem a very strong statement. But Skehan and Di Lella (*The Wisdom of Ben Sira*, 544) observe that "Ben Sira lists 'the Twelve Prophets' (49:10a) as a single book and places them after Ezekiel, as in the Hebrew canon." While the canon is not closed, it certainly has taken on some firm contours. For the grandson of Ben Sira (Sirach, Prologue, 24–25), those contours included the threefold division enshrined in the Hebrew Bible: the Law, the Prophets, and the rest of the books (= the Writings).

[81] I purposely express myself cautiously here to avoid the anachronism of presuming a fixed and closed canon of Scripture at the time of Jesus. To be sure, Josephus mentions a collection of twenty-two sacred books of the Jews in *Ag. Ap.* 1.8 §39–41. But *Against Apion* was written at the very end of the 1st century, three decades after the watershed of A.D. 70. Whether Josephus represents a view that almost all Palestinian Jews held in the early decades of the century is not certain. Moreover, Josephus' own list is not without its ambiguities. It may be that Josephus counted among his thirteen prophetical books some works later assigned to the Writings. He also speaks vaguely of four books

of hymns and precepts. By this he probably means Psalms, the Song of Songs, Proverbs, and Qoheleth, though his reference remains unclear. It is telling that the four books receive no collective rubric such as "the Writings." In short, I agree with the estimation of Brown ("Canonicity," *NJBC*, 1039): "At least one may say that the 22 books enumerated by Josephus enjoyed wide acceptance among Jews. It is another question to what extent Josephus meant to exclude other books or reflected universal Jewish thought in so doing."

[82] Archaeology has revealed that a Jewish community at the fortress of Masada, overlooking the Dead Sea, used a Hebrew copy of Sirach some time in the 1st century B.C. More importantly, in this manuscript the verses of Sirach were written stichometrically (each verse on a separate full line, with the two halves of the verse appearing on the right- and on the left-hand sides of the manuscript respectively). Such a practice was also used in the two Hebrew fragments of Sirach from Cave 2 at Qumran. This writing practice was usually reserved for books that were later considered canonical. The fact that Sirach also underwent successive Hebrew and Greek recensions in Palestine highlights at the very least its great importance and esteem in the eyes of some Jewish groups. On all this, see Skehan and Di Lella, *The Wisdom of Ben Sira*, 20. Both Tobit and Sirach are represented by fragments at Qumran that come from several copies of each book.

[83] For a brief treatment of the problems surrounding both the word "pseudepigrapha" and the extent of the material it comprises, see James H. Charlesworth, *The Pseudepigrapha and Modern Research* (SBLSCS 7; Ann Arbor, MI: Scholars, 1981) vii, 15–25.

[84] Hence I do not consider here some important Jewish pseudepigraphic (especially apocalyptic) works that, by scholarly consensus, are dated after the time of Jesus: e.g., 4 Ezra and 2 Baruch *(the Syriac Apocalypse of Baruch)*. Both were written after and reflect the crisis caused by the destruction of the Jerusalem temple in A.D. 70. The original form of 4 Ezra (without the additions made around the 3d century A.D.) dates from ca. A.D., 100; 2 Baruch probably comes from the early 2d century A.D. For a brief consideration, see Beasley-Murray, *Jesus and the Kingdom of God*, 47–48. The schema of a succession of kingdoms, seen in the Book of Daniel, is retained and recycled.

[85] The present-day collection of Sibylline oracles includes oracles ranging from the 2d century B.C. to the 7th century A.D. While the final compositions are either Jewish or Christian, some probably contain material deriving from pagan sources.

[86] For basic orientation see John J. Collins, "Sibylline Oracles," *The Old Testament Pseudepigrapha*, 1. 317–24. For his introduction to the Third Sibylline Oracle, see pp. 354–55; the text of the oracle is found on pp. 364–80. Another brief introduction can be found in Nickelsburg, *Jewish Literature Between the Bible and the Mishnah*, 162–65. For more detailed treatments, see V. Nikiprowetzky, *La troisième Sibylle* (Etudes Juives 9; Paris/La Haye: Mouton, 1970); John J. Collins, *The Sibylline Oracles of Egyptian Judaism* (SBLDS 13; Missoula, MT: Scholars, 1972). For the Sibylline oracles viewed within wider cultural and theological contexts, see John J. Collins, *Between Athens and Jerusalem* (New York: Crossroad, 1983) esp. 61–72; idem, *The Apocalyptic Imagination* (New York: Crossroad, 1987) esp. 93–101, 187–94.

[87] See the summary of Camponovo, *Königtum*, 350–52.

[88] Collins, "The Kingdom of God in the Apocrypha and Pseudepigrapha," 86. In keeping with the limitations of this section, I do not treat the Fourth Oracle (ca. 80 A.D., which has more of an apocalyptic eschatology) or the Fifth Oracle (early 2d century A.D., depicting a savior king who builds up an eschatological Jerusalem as the

center of a universal kingdom). As Camponovo, following Collins, observes, the later additions to this and the other Sibylline oracles tend to be more enmeshed in political events, more nationalistic, and more pessimistic (*Königtum*, 356).

[89] For introduction and text, see E. Isaac, "1 (Ethiopic Apocalypse of) Enoch," in *The Old Testament Pseudepigrapha*, 1. 5-89. Isaac dates the various parts of *1 Enoch* from the 2d century B.C. to the 1st century A.D. (the Parables of Enoch being placed at the end of the 1st century A.D.). See further Nickelsburg, *Jewish Literature*, 46–55, 90–94, 145–51, 214–23; Collins, *The Apocalyptic Imagination*, 33-63, 142–54.

[90] For this passage Aramaic fragments from Qumran are available (4QEn[g]); the text in question reads literally: "The temple of the kingdom of the Great One [*hêkal malkût rabbā*', i.e., the royal temple of the Great God] will be built in greatness for all generations and ages."

[91] As Camponovo observes (*Königtum*, 258), *2 Enoch* (also called *Slavonic Enoch*), which may date in its original form to some time in the 1st century A.D., contributes nothing new or noteworthy to our study of the kingdom of God in the pseudepigrapha. God is called "the eternal king" in *2 Enoch* 64:4, and Enoch sees the Lord on a lofty throne in 20:3. Since *3 Enoch*'s final redaction may be placed somewhere around the 5th or 6th century, it is not treated here. For introductions to and the texts of both works, see F. I. Andersen, "2 (Slavonic Apocalypse of) Enoch," *The Old Testament Pseudepigrapha*, 1. 91–221; and P. Alexander, "3 (Hebrew Apocalypse of) Enoch," ibid., 1. 223–315.

[92] Since we are dealing with fragments, it is not surprising that estimates of how many manuscripts are involved differ; various scholars have suggested 10, 11, or 13 manuscripts.

[93] See O. S. Wintermute, "Jubilees," *The Old Testament Pseudepigrapha*, 2. 44: "It is more accurate to think of Jubilees as a work that was produced within a community of Hasidim or Essenes prior to the withdrawal of some of the members of the sect to Qumran." See also Raymond E. Brown, "Apocrypha," *NJBC*, 1058–59; Camponovo, *Königtum*, 230; Nickelsburg, *Jewish Literature*, 73–80; Collins, *The Apocalyptic Imagination*, 63–67.

[94] If one follows the Latin version, the citation would read: "a priestly kingdom and a holy people." In favor of "a kingdom and a priesthood and a holy people," see Camponovo, *Königtum*, 235 n. 19.

[95] So Camponovo, *Königtum*, 236.

[96] For a discussion of the introductory questions, see J. Priest, "The Testament of Moses," in *The Old Testament Pseudepigrapha*, 1. 919–25, esp. 920–21; cf. Nickelsburg, *Jewish Literature*, 80–83, 313–14; Collins, *The Apocalyptic Imagination*, 102–6; idem, "The Kingdom of God in the Apocrypha and Pseudepigrapha," 89. Camponovo (*Königtum*, 142–62) proposes a detailed hypothesis of a basic document written in a hasidic group before the beginning of the Maccabean revolt, with a revision in the early 1st century A.D. One need not adopt his whole theory to accept the general insight that we are dealing with a document that had a complicated tradition history. Provided we accept the widely held position that the final form of the document comes from early in the 1st century A.D., the usefulness of the *Testament of Moses* for our purposes is established.

[97] Given the context of the *Testament of Moses*, the judgment of Collins ("The Kingdom of God in the Apocrypha and Pseudepigrapha," 90) seems justified: "In the Testa-

ment, as in Daniel and the Similitudes of Enoch, the kingdom of God is brought about by the transcendent power of God and his angels. It is not to be attained by human revolution and does not even involve the earthly career of a messiah."

[98] For introductory questions, see Camponovo, *Königtum*, 200–206; R. B. Wright, "Psalms of Solomon," *The Old Testament Pseudepigrapha*, 2. 639–49. Camponovo defends the view that the "Hasidim" who resisted the Hellenization campaign of Antiochus Epiphanes in the first half of the 2d century B.C. later split into the moderate Pharisees and the more radical Essenes, of whom the Qumranites were the most extreme expression. Camponovo attributes the *Psalms of Solomon* to the Pharisees, perhaps as they were developing from a political party under the Hasmoneans to a religious sect under Herod the Great and his successors. Wright, on the other hand, thinks that we know too little of Pharisaic theology in the 1st century B.C. to be sure about assigning the *Psalms of Solomon* to them; yet the theology of the *Psalms* does not seem to fit the Essenes either. Instead, Wright sees as the *Sitz im Leben* of the *Psalms* a community of devout Jews in Jerusalem who sought to answer with apocalyptic messianism the theological crisis brought on by Pompey's invasion. For other presentations of the problems involved, see Nickelsburg, *Jewish Literature*, 203–12; Collins, *The Apocalyptic Imagination*, 113–14.

[99] This is the position of Camponovo (*Königtum*, 216), who also argues for the conjectural optative reading *euphrantheiēsan* ("may those who fear the Lord rejoice in good things") in v 18a. Yet the MSS read the aorist indicative, which is the reading followed by Wright in his translation ("Psalms of Solomon," 657): "Those who fear the Lord are happy with good things." Apart from the arguments of Camponovo, which rest partly on a hypothetical reconstruction of the Hebrew text, it seems to me that the abstract noun signifying an attribute of God (*chrēstotēs [sou]*) in 18b naturally parallels the abstract noun signifying an attribute of God (*doxa [kyriou]*) in v 19, just as *basileia sou* in 18b naturally parallels *basileus hēmōn* in v 19. If v 18b actually belongs together with v 19, and if the natural sense of v 19 is clearly optative (as even Wright admits in his translation: "May the glory of the Lord be praised"), then the form of the verb "to be" that is to be supplied in v 18b should be optative, too.

[100] In the Greek, the two statements are word-for-word the same, except that the vocative *kyrie* of v 1a becomes the nominative subject of the sentence *kyrios* in v 46 and, correspondingly, the subject pronoun *sy* of v 1a disappears in v 46. In each case the main verb is understood—an eternal present being the most likely choice, though in the context of eschatological prophecy a future tense is also possible.

[101] The Greek MSS read "Messiah Lord" (*christos kyrios*), but many commentators think that this is a Christian emendation of an original "Messiah of the Lord" (*christos kyriou*), reflecting the Hebrew "the anointed of Yahweh." Camponovo (*Königtum*, 225 n. 78) argues for the emendation, pointing out that (1) the immediate context is clarifying the exact relationship of the Messiah to God and (2) elsewhere in the *Psalms of Solomon*, *kyrios* always designates God. These arguments are forceful, yet I prefer the reading "Messiah [and] Lord." (1) As Wright points out ("The Psalms of Solomon," 667 n. z), this is the uniform reading of both the Greek and the Syriac MSS. (2) The context is also one that confers on the Davidic Messiah God-like powers: he destroys the Gentiles with the word of his mouth, he regathers and purifies the tribes of Israel, he is completely free of sin, and his words are like the words of the angels. Since the psalm pointedly and repeatedly confers on the Messiah the title *basileus*, which it insists in the full sense belongs only to God, I do not see why, in a context exalting the Messiah to almost God-like status, the author might not also confer on the Messiah the title

kyrios. Like "king," he is obviously "lord" only in a subordinate sense, as v 34 makes clear.

[102] As Wright ("The Psalms of Solomon," 655 n. o) correctly observes, "It is unclear whether this is the resurrection of the body (rise from the grave) or immortality of the spirit (rise to God), or, indeed, if this author distinguished the two."

[103] See Howard Clark Kee, "Testaments of the Twelve Patriarchs," *The Old Testament Pseudepigrapha*, 1. 775–80, esp. 777–78. See also his "The Ethical Dimensions of the Testaments of the XII [*sic*] as a Clue to Provenance," *NTS* 24 (1978) 259–70, where he suggests instead that "a likely date for the composition of the basic Jewish document [of the *Testaments*] is 100 B.C."

[104] For a review both of the shift in de Jonge's own position and of other critics' theories, see Marinus de Jonge, "The Interpretation of the Testaments of the Twelve Patriarchs in Recent Years," *Studies on the Testaments of the Twelve Patriarchs* (SVTP 3; ed. Marinus de Jonge; Leiden: Brill, 1975) 183–92. In the same volume see his "The New Editio Maior," 174–79; and "Christian Influence in the Testaments of the Twelve Patriarchs," 193–246. In his article "The Main Issues in the Study of the Testaments of the Twelve Patriarchs," *NTS* 26 (1980) 508–24, de Jonge seems to move back in the direction of his earlier view: he stresses that we cannot be sure that a Jew ever composed a collection of twelve testaments; the author could have been a Christian working with various Jewish materials. See also his "The Testaments of the Twelve Patriarchs: Central Problems and Essential Viewpoints," *ANRW* II/20.1, 359–420. For other presentations of the problems involved, see Nickelsburg, *Jewish Literature*, 231–41; Collins, *Between Athens and Jerusalem*, 154–62; idem, *The Apocalyptic Imagination*, 106–13.

[105] Camponovo (*Königtum*, 309) calls the *Testaments* "an irritating work" in that much of the material in the haggadic and parenetic parts is "neutral," i.e., conceivable in Judaism, but also conceivable as Christian appropriation of the OT.

[106] See, e.g., *T. Jud.* 1:6; 24:1–6 for the royal rule of Judah; for both Levi and Judah as leaders, see *T. Jos.* 19:1–11; for Levi as the key agent of salvation, see *T. Levi* 18:1–14.

[107] Camponovo (*Königtum*, 323–24) considers the second half of the quotation to be a Christian interpolation; not so Kee, "Testaments of the Twelve Patriarchs," 810. The wide divergence of views among commentators on what is original and what is secondary in the *Testaments* is a major reason why I do not place much weight on the document's testimony.

[108] For the problems of the Greek and Armenian texts, see Camponovo, *Königtum*, 328 n. 66.

[109] See Camponovo, *Königtum*, 329–30. Notice the overall judgment of Collins ("The Kingdom of God in the Apocrypha and Pseudepigrapha," 91), who believes that the *Testaments* do contain Jewish material from the 2d century B.C.: "Unfortunately, the Testaments do not provide independent evidence of Jewish beliefs but need corroboration from the sources."

[110] For a brief overview, see Camponovo, *Königtum*, 401–8; Kevin G. O'Connell, "Texts and Versions," *NJBC*, 1097–98; Martin J. McNamara, "Targums," *IDBSup*, 856–61.

[111] On this see Volume One, chapter nine, section II.

[112] The different versions are conveniently laid out by Camponovo, *Königtum*, 408–9.

[113] See his running argument throughout his *God in Strength. Jesus' Announcement of the Kingdom* (Sheffield: JSOT, 1987, originally 1979); pp. 277–93 of this monograph are also printed as a separate essay, "God in Strength," in Bruce Chilton (ed.), *The Kingdom of God in the Teaching of Jesus* (Issues in Religion and Theology 5; Philadelphia: Fortress; London: SPCK, 1984) 121–32. Chilton published a summary of his views in "Regnum Dei Deus Est," *SJT* 31 (1978) 261–70; a popularization of his approach can be found in *A Galilean Rabbi and His Bible* (Good News Studies 8; Wilmington, DE: Glazier, 1984). Various essays applying this approach to individual problems and texts can be found in Bruce Chilton, *Targumic Approaches to the Gospels* (Studies in Judaism; Lanham, MD/New York/London: University Press of America, 1986). See also his *The Glory of Israel: The Theology and Provenience of the Isaiah Targum* (JSOTSup 23; Sheffield: JSOT, 1982); and, with J. I. H. McDonald, *Jesus and the Ethics of the Kingdom* (Grand Rapids: Eerdmans, 1987). Camponovo sharply criticizes Chilton's stance in *Königtum*, 428–29. In my view, Camponovo is correct that the contexts of the key prophetic passages are eschatological; it is only by contorted exegesis that one can avoid the eschatological thrust. As Collins astutely observes ("The Kingdom of God in the Apocrypha and Pseudepigrapha," 94): "The phrase ['the kingdom of God' in the targum on Isaiah] is used in contexts where the MT is already eschatological. The characteristic Targumic phrase 'the kingdom of the Lord will be revealed' puts the emphasis on the expectation of an eschatological event." The eschatological nature of the kingdom of Yahweh in the targum Jonathan on the latter prophets is also maintained by Koch, "Offenbaren wird sich das Reich Gottes," 158–65.

Nevertheless, it should be said in Chilton's favor that many of his insights are helpful. He is correct in maintaining that "the kingdom of God" basically means "God come in strength" to save his people. The effects of the kingdom's coming cannot be separated from the person of the God who comes as king. Thus, "the kingdom of God" is not a political movement or a program for social improvement. Chilton is intent on preserving the God-centeredness of the kingdom of God from any dissolution into ideology or a theological abstraction. All that is to the good, but there are two major problems in his project. (1) Given the problems about dating, it is questionable whether the targum on Isaiah can be elevated to the great hermeneutical key to Jesus' message that Chilton makes of it; see Collins, "The Kingdom of God in the Apocrypha and Pseudepigrapha," 93–94. Interestingly, Chilton himself admits the problem of dating, but he thinks that his method is able to deal with the difficulty (see, e.g., "Regnum Dei Deus Est," 263). Yet the type of argument he uses on p. 265 to support 1st-century dating of targumic statements about the kingdom of Yahweh (Zech 14:9; Obad 21) is surprisingly weak. (2) It is true that in both the targum Jonathan and the Gospels time references involving the kingdom are flexible; we are dealing with "a tensive symbol." Yet in specific passages in both literatures the references to a future, indeed, an eschatological future, are quite clear. One must therefore go on to ask whether the future dimension of the kingdom in Jesus' proclamation is just one aspect of his thought among many or whether it gives a definite thrust to the whole of his message. This is a problem we shall have to explore in subsequent chapters.

[114] The count is Chilton's ("Regnum Dei Deus Est," 264); the passages are Isa 24:23; 31:4; 40:9; 52:7; Ezek 7:7,10; Obad 21; Mic 4:7,8; Zech 14:9.

[115] In saying this I do not deny the possibility of an initial stage of some of the Qumran documents prior to the group's settlement at Qumran. But I think it safe to presume that the documents in their final form were written at Qumran.

[116] For this division, as for much of what follows, I am heavily indebted to Camponovo, *Königtum*, 259–307; see also Benedict T. Viviano, "The Kingdom of God in the

Qumran Literature," in Willis (ed.), *The Kingdom of God in 20th-Century Interpretation*, 97–107. Viviano supplies statistics covering the major documents of Qumran: *malkût* (kingship or kingdom) is used 15 times, though three of these cases are textually uncertain; *mĕlûkâ* (kingship) is used twice; *mamlākâ* (royal dominion, kingdom, sovereignty) is used once; *melek* (king) is applied to God 11 times; and the verb *mālak* (to rule as king) is used of God twice. *memšālâ* (a more general word for dominion or rule) is used 31 times; *miśrâ* ([princely] dominion or rule) is used 3 times.

[117] This seems to be the understanding of Geza Vermes in his translation (*The Dead Sea Scrolls in English* [3d ed.; London: Penguin, 1987] 75): "He shall perform the will of God in all his deeds, and in all his dominion as He has commanded" (note the lack of capitalization in both occurrences of "his").

[118] The idea may also be present in a fragmentary text of an Aramaic *Testament of Levi* from Qumran (1QTLevi ar 1:2): ". . . the kingly rule [*malkût*] of the priesthood is greater than the kingly rule. . . ." Unfortunately the rest of the statement has been lost.

[119] The material consists of fragments from eight manuscripts from Cave 4 of Qumran (4Q400–407), small fragments from Cave 11 (11QŠirŠabb), and a large fragment from Masada (MasŠirŠabb). For reconstructed texts, translations, commentaries, and photographs of the original fragments, see Carol Newsom, *Songs of the Sabbath Sacrifice: A Critical Edition* (HSS 27; Atlanta, GA: Scholars, 1985). An English translation may be found in Vermes, *The Dead Sea Scrolls in English*, 222–30. Newsom (*Songs of the Sabbath Sacrifice*, 1–4) considers the possibility of a pre-Qumran origin of the *Songs*, but decides that the evidence weighs more heavily on the side of composition at Qumran.

[120] One must say "apparently" because there are some lacunae in the text. For a critical edition and detailed discussion of 11QMelch, see Paul J. Kobelski, *Melchizedek and Melchireša*ᶜ (CBQMS 10; Washington, DC: CBA, 1981) esp. 5–23. Note the differences between his translation and that of Vermes, *The Dead Sea Scrolls in English*, 300–301; cf. Camponovo, *Königtum*, 287–89 (translation into German).

[121] This translation is taken from Vermes, *The Dead Sea Scrolls in English*, 126.

[122] Hence I think that the claim of Viviano ("The Kingdom of God in the Qumran Literature," 107) needs further nuance: "We have found kingdom of God terminology in the Qumran literature, particularly in the dualistic theology and eschatology of a section of the Community Rule and in parts of the War Scroll." The documents in question seem intent on distinguishing between the supreme kingly rule of the Lord God of Israel and the various other kinds of dominion or rule exercised by his creatures in conflict. Talk of *God's own* rule or kingdom is noticeably absent from 1QS.

[123] For detailed exegesis of individual passages in 1QM, see Camponovo, *Königtum*, 296–305.

[124] This seems to be the point of adding after the list of the traditional OT enemies of God's people (1QM 1:1-2) a reference to those "with them as allies, the evildoers of the covenant" (1:2).

[125] For a treatment of this basic insight, see A. E. Harvey, *Jesus and the Constraints of History* (Philadelphia: Westminster, 1982) esp. 1–10. See, e.g., p. 6: "No individual, if he wishes to influence others, is totally free to choose his own style of action and persuasion; he is subject to constraints imposed by the culture in which he finds himself."

CHAPTER 15

THE KINGDOM OF GOD:

God Coming in Power to Rule

PART II:
JESUS' PROCLAMATION OF A FUTURE
KINGDOM

I. INTRODUCTION

In the previous chapter, we learned two important things about the symbol or concept "the kingdom of God." (1) The kingdom of God is a central part of Jesus' proclamation. (2) If it is central, then Jesus must have consciously and purposely made it so, since in general the symbol cannot be said to be central to the protocanonical or deuterocanonical/apocryphal OT, to the OT pseudepigrapha, or to the Qumran literature taken as a whole. When the symbol does appear in key passages of exilic or postexilic Jewish literature, it often—though not always—has a future reference, sometimes connected with hopes of the restoration of a glorious Jerusalem, with all twelve tribes of a regathered Israel present in the holy city, receiving gifts and tribute from the defeated Gentiles.

This "tone" of the symbol around the turn of the era plus the matrix of Jesus' ministry in the eschatological message of the Baptist makes the hypothesis of an un-eschatological Jesus proclaiming an un-eschatological kingdom of God initially suspect. It also creates problems for those who claim that the kingdom of God in Jesus' preaching is entirely or predominantly present and realized in the Nazarene's ministry. Still, it is conceivable that Jesus, as a creative thinker and teacher, consciously reworked what was largely an eschatological symbol to signify either God's timeless, ever-present reign or its present, definitive realization in Jesus' words and deeds. However, as I noted at the end of the last chapter, given the background and connotations of the symbol, it would have been necessary for Jesus to make an important shift in the symbol's significance clear to his audience if he did not want to guarantee that he would be misunderstood.

The only way to resolve the question of the extent to which Jesus accepted, reworked, or rejected the ideas and hopes connected with "kingdom of God" is to examine certain key sayings that contain the phrase and have some claim to being authentic in the mouth of Jesus. To sort out the many conflicting interpretations of what Jesus meant by "kingdom of God" in particular and to begin the much larger project of grasping Jesus' eschatological message as a whole (which involves more than just the phrase "kingdom of God"), I will examine in this chapter certain pivotal sayings which seem prima facie to speak of a future kingdom of God, and in the next chapter some sayings that seem prima facie to speak of the kingdom of God present and active in Jesus' ministry.[1]

Some readers may be surprised to see that very few parables are used in the main part of my argument. This may seem strange to those who have been taught to turn immediately to Jesus' parables of the kingdom as the main route into his eschatology. For all their differences, both C. H. Dodd and Joachim Jeremias saw in the parables a privileged way of intuiting the heart of Jesus' eschatological message.[2] Yet recent scholarship, by approaching the parables as autonomous pieces of rhetorical art, has reminded us how open is each parable to multiple interpretations—at least if taken by itself, in isolation from the rest of Jesus' message and praxis. That is why recent parable research has been so rich in its suggestiveness but also so variegated to the point of confusion when it comes to determining what the parables meant or intended as they came from the historical Jesus. In addition, many of the parables are found in only one independent literary source, and so the criterion of multiple attestation cannot be used.[3] Granted the goal and method of *A Marginal Jew*, I think it is advisable first to derive an initial sketch of Jesus' message from his sayings that are not full-blown parables, as well as from certain striking actions typical of his ministry. One will then be better positioned to understand the parables within a particular historical framework. Needless to say, I do not claim that such an approach exhausts the potential of the parables. Nor do I desire to restrict their meaning to what was intended by the historical Jesus. Nor do I forget that this riddle-speech might well have multiple meanings in the mouth of Jesus himself. Nevertheless, since in this book I am concerned with the meaning of the parables *as intended by the historical Jesus*, my specific goal justifies the methodological strategy of putting off a treatment of the individual works of verbal art called parables until I have suitable historical frames in which to place them.

As I begin to study in detail certain sayings of Jesus concerning a future yet imminent kingdom of God, I should note that a decade or two ago there would have been no need to belabor Jesus' teaching on a future eschatological kingdom. That Jesus spoke of an eschatological future was one of the "assured results" of critical scholarship from the time of Johannes Weiss and Albert Schweitzer at the end of the 19th century. But assured results have a way of becoming unsure again. In recent years some scholars have called into question the view that Jesus taught about an eschatological kingdom that was soon to come. Emphasis has shifted to Jesus the Cynic philosopher or Jesus the charismatic man of the Spirit who urged people to find God and/or ultimate meaning in the present moment. It is against the exaggerations of this new type of "realized eschatology," which at times is strangely reminiscent of the 19th-century liberal lives of Jesus, that I aim this present chapter.[4] To show that a future yet imminent kingdom of God was an essential part of Jesus' message, we shall examine five highly significant blocks of Jesus' sayings: (1) the Lord's Prayer, in particular the petition "your kingdom come" (Matt 6:10 ‖ Luke 11:2); (2) the Last Supper tradition that Jesus would no longer drink wine until the arrival of the kingdom (Mark 14:25 parr.); (3) the place of the Gentiles at the banquet in the kingdom (Matt 8:11–12 ‖ Luke 13:28–29); (4) the beatitudes of the Sermon on the Mount/Plain (Matt 5:3–12 ‖ Luke 6:20–23); and (5) various sayings which set a time limit for the arrival of the kingdom (Matt 10:23; Mark 9:1; Mark 13:30). The advantage of selecting these particular sayings is that not only do they contain theologically important material; they also involve, directly or indirectly, all the major strands of Gospel tradition (Mark, Q, M, L, and tangentially John). Moreover, in addition to this multiple attestation of sources, the passages also display multiple attestation of forms (prayer, eschatological prophecy in the form of an Amen-word with temporal terminus set within a narrative, eschatological prophecy in the antithetical form of weal and woe, and beatitudes).[5]

II. JESUS' SAYINGS CONCERNING A FUTURE KINGDOM

A. "YOUR KINGDOM COME" (MATT 6:10 ‖ LUKE 11:2)

1. Introductory Considerations

Probably the single best-known phrase of Jesus that contains the word "kingdom" is the second petition in the prayer Christians have named "the Lord's Prayer" or "the Our Father":[6] "Your kingdom come." To attempt a thorough exegesis of the whole of the Lord's Prayer at this point would take us too far afield from the main point of this chapter. I shall return to the Lord's Prayer later on; right now I will simply make some introductory remarks to provide a context for my observations on "Your kingdom come" and what this petition tells us about Jesus' message of the kingdom.[7]

The predominant opinion today is that the two versions of the Lord's Prayer (the longer one in Matt 6:9–13, the shorter in Luke 11:2–4)[8] reflect the expansions (mostly Matthean) or modifications in wording (mostly Lucan) of two Christian liturgical traditions, though the influence of the final redactors cannot be excluded.[9] In general, Luke has kept the basic size and structure of the prayer, while Matthew has preserved at some points the more original wording. In the two versions below, capital letters show the additions of the

Matthean tradition, while italics show the modifications in wording of the Lucan tradition:

Matthew		*Luke*
OUR Father, WHO [ARE] IN HEAVEN,	(Address)	Father,

I. "You Petitions"

hallowed be your name.	(1. petition)	hallowed be your name.
Your kingdom come.	(2. petition)	Your kingdom come.[10]
YOUR WILL BE DONE, AS IN HEAVEN, SO ON EARTH.	(3. petition)	

II. "We Petitions"

Our daily bread
  give us
  today.
	(1. petition)	Our daily bread
		  keep giving us
		  everyday

And forgive us
  our debts
as we also forgive
  our debtors.
	(2. petition)	And forgive us
		  our *sins,*
		for we also forgive
		  everyone indebted to us.

And do not lead us
  to the test
	(3. petition)	And do not lead us
		  to the test.

BUT DELIVER US FROM THE EVIL ONE.[11]	(4. petition)	

If we omit what Matthew or his liturgical tradition has added but keep to his more laconic and Semitic wording in the petitions common to both versions, we wind up with:

(Address)   Father,

I. "You Petitions"

(1. petition)   hallowed be your name.
(2. petition)   Your Kingdom come.

II. "We Petitions"

(1. petition)   Our daily bread give us today.
(2. petition)   And forgive us our debts
                 as we forgive our debtors.[12]
(3. petition)   And do not lead us to the test.

Various experts have attempted a retroversion of this primitive form into Aramaic.[13] Since we are poorly informed of the exact type of Aramaic Jesus spoke, scholars naturally differ in details. Joseph A. Fitzmyer offers the following as a hypothetical original form:[14]

(Address)   ʾabbāʾ

I. "You Petitions"

(1. petition)   yitqaddaš šĕmāk,
(2. petition)   tēʾtêh malkûtāk,

II. "We Petitions"

(1. petition)   laḥmānāʾ dî mistĕyāʾ hab
                    lanāh yômāʾ dĕnāh,
(2. petition)   ûšĕbuq lanāh ḥôbaynāʾ
                    kĕdî[15] šĕbaqnāʾ lĕḥayyābaynāʾ,
(3. petition)   wĕʾal taʿēlinnanāʾ lĕnisyôn.

The structure is tight and laconic, eminently suitable for memorization. Jeremias discerns in the Aramaic a pattern of a two-and-four-beat rhythm, along with a number of rhymes.[16] The address to God, made up of a single word, is followed by two short, carefully paralleled petitions focusing directly on "the matters of God" (*your* name, *your* kingdom).[17] These in turn are followed by three somewhat longer petitions focusing on the needs of the petitioners (*our* bread, *our* debts, do not lead *us*). One gets the impression of a short prayer that is so direct and to the point that it almost offends the sensibilities of those who are accustomed to the longer rhythmic phrases of the Matthean version. The hypothetical form, while not the prayer of an isolated individual (as the "we" petitions show), has not undergone either the rhetorical expansions fostered by liturgical use within a community (the Matthean form, with phrases parallel to those in Jewish synagogal prayers) or a shift away from a thoroughgoing future-eschatological vision toward the ongoing daily needs of life in the present world (the first and second "we petitions" in Luke). This fits well with the idea that the hypothetical form had its original *Sitz im Leben* not in the early church but among the disciples of the historical Jesus when they were still a loose band gathered around him. Certainly, the very fact that this Aramaic form existed earlier than either of the two forms of the prayer that were already traditional in the churches of Matthew and Luke prior to the composition of their Gospels—indeed probably before the Q tradition was collected[18]—argues for a very early date for the prayer. In addition, a pointer to a Palestinian-Aramaic milieu can be found in the use of "debt" and "debtor" for "sin" and "sinners." In both classical and Hellenistic Greek, the words for "debt" and "debtor" retained their secular reference and were not used metaphorically in a religious context for sin. On the contrary, the equivalent Aramaic word was so used;[19] at the very least, then, we are dealing either with a very early creation of the Aramaic-speaking Palestinian Christians or with a teaching of Jesus himself.

A number of considerations argue that the earliest form of the prayer comes from Jesus himself. Despite the doubts of some recent scholars, Jeremias was probably correct in maintaining that the laconic, almost disconcerting "Father" (Luke's *pater*) probably reflects Jesus' striking use of the address *'abbā'* ("my own dear father") for God.[20] The surprisingly direct and short petitions are meant to reproduce the trusting and unaffected attitude of a child dependent on an all-powerful and loving father. Besides the use of *'abbā'*, the prayer contains another remarkably unique usage that argues for the origin of the prayer in Jesus' own instruction. The linking of God's kingdom and the verb "to come" in a prayer-petition (or even in a direct affirmation) is unknown in the OT, in ancient Judaism before Jesus, and in the rest of the NT outside of the Gospel sayings of Jesus.[21] On the other hand, such a unique occurrence fits in perfectly with a Jesus who consciously and purposely chose the symbol of God's kingship to be central to his message when it was not central to the OT or ancient Jewish literature (and would not be central to the NT outside the Synoptic Gospels). Similarly, while the "hallowing" or sanctification of God's name has roots in the OT (as we shall see), it is hardly a key concept in the NT and does not point in the direction of a creation by the early church.

To my own mind, one of the most weighty arguments for the origin of the prayer in the mouth of Jesus is the simple fact that both the Matthean and Lucan traditions, for all their differences, agree on attributing the prayer to Jesus and having him specifically command his disciples to use it.[22] At first glance, this may not seem strange or unusual, but within the NT it is. The NT swarms with prayers, hymns, and confessional statements, some of them apparently going back to the earliest days of the church. Yet nowhere else in the NT—inside or outside the Gospels—is it claimed that the words of a particular prayer or hymn were directly taught to the disciples by Jesus during his public ministry.[23] We have a curious instance of the criterion of discontinuity here. It was not the custom of the early church to attribute to Jesus of Nazareth the exact words of its prayers or hymns; the Our Father stands out as a sole exception. If we join this point to the other considerations of philology and thought-content already listed, I think that we have more than sufficient reason to judge the substance of the hypothetical Aramaic form to be authentic.[24]

2. The Two "You Petitions"

After this initial survey of the structure and content of the Lord's Prayer, as well as the reasons for thinking that the substance of the "primitive" form comes from Jesus, it would be natural to turn immediately to the direct object of our investigation, the petition for the coming of the kingdom. However, things are not so simple; the second petition cannot be treated adequately apart from the first. The structure of the first main part of the prayer ties together the two "you petitions" ("Hallowed be your name, your kingdom come") by means of parallel structure, parallel rhythm, and even rhyme (certainly in the Greek, most probably in the Aramaic). Since these links are often lost in modern-language translations, it is important to look at the parallelism in the Greek and hypothetical Aramaic versions:

Greek	Aramaic
hagiasthētō to onoma sou (hallowed be your name)	*yitqaddaš šĕmāk*
elthetō hē basileia sou (your kingdom come)	*tēʾtêh malkûtāk*

In each petition the order of the Greek words is: finite verb in the aorist imperative (in the Aramaic this was no doubt the imperfect with a jussive sense), then the noun that is the grammatical subject, and finally the 2d singular possessive pronoun (in the Aramaic, attached to the noun as a suffix). In both Greek and Aramaic each line has two beats, one on the verb and one on the noun. Thanks to the possessive pronouns, both lines end in the same sound and therefore rhyme in both Greek and Aramaic. Unlike the "we petitions" in the second half of the prayer, the two "you petitions" are not tied together by "and" (Greek *kai*, Aramaic *wĕ* or *û*). The absence of "and" (known technically as asyndeton) actually has the rhetorical effect of binding the two petitions more closely together. All these linguistic phenomena, plus the fact that the two lines make up the whole of the first main part of the prayer, suggest that these two parallel lines, if not completely synonymous, certainly go together and help explain each other. Hence, to understand the second petition, we must start with the first.

a. *"Hallowed be your name."* The idea of hallowing (sanctifying, making holy) the name of God is totally absent from the rest of the Synoptic sayings of Jesus, and indeed from almost all of the NT apart from a partial echo in a prayer of Jesus addressed to the Father (!) in John 12:28: "Father, glorify your name."[25] To understand the motif of the sanctification of God's name, we must look back to its roots in the OT and to how it found expression in Jewish literature and liturgy.

In the OT, the sanctification of God or God's name occurs in two basic contexts, both using the Hebrew verb *qiddaš* ("make holy"). In the first context, Israel does or should sanctify God's name, as opposed to profaning it.[26] This sanctification includes believing God's word, trusting his promises, standing in awe of his majesty, praising him in worship, and observing his precepts in cult and everyday life. More frequent is the second context, in which God sanctifies himself or his name. He does this by manifesting his power, glory, and holiness (= his transcendence, his "otherness," his "God-ness") in the blazing light of a theophany that can bring either salvation or condemnation.[27] The Book of Ezekiel is conspicuous for its use of the concept of God's sanctifying *himself* or his *name* in the context of Israel's sin and restoration. Indeed, in the very same verse (Ezek 36:23) both ways of expressing the thought are used: "And I will sanctify my *name* [piel form of the verb: *wĕqiddaštî 'et-šĕmî*] . . . when I sanctify *myself* by means of you [nifal form of the verb: *bĕhiqqādĕšî bākem*]." This text is a parade example of the equivalence of a person and the name of the person in biblical usage.[28] The name of God is God as revealed, present, and active among his people. The idea that God sanctifies his name precisely by manifesting himself in order to make himself known to both Israel and the hostile Gentiles in a powerful act of salvation and judgment is also contained in Ezek 36:23: "And I will sanctify my great name, profaned among the Gentiles, which you [the Israelites] have profaned in their midst, *in order that the Gentiles may know* that I am Yahweh—oracle of the Lord Yahweh— when I sanctify myself by means of you in their eyes."[29] Indeed, among the prophets, Ezekiel in particular stresses the theme of God sanctifying himself by a powerful intervention that will bring the scattered people Israel out from among the Gentile nations and back home to their own land—through no merit of their own.[30] This manifestation of God's power in saving and judging will make him known to friend and foe alike. While God had manifested his holiness in various events of Israel's history, Ezekiel seems to envision a complete and definitive (in this sense, eschatological) manifestation of God's holiness in this regathering of Israel (see especially Ezek 36:16–38 and 38:18–23). In manifesting his holiness, God will give the regathered Israel a thorough cleansing with water as well as a new heart and a new spirit (36:25–26). After defeating a final fierce foe (with the mysterious name of Gog) amid cosmic cataclysms (38:18–23),[31] God will place Israel in a Palestine that, though formerly desolate, will now be transformed into a garden of Eden (36:35).[32]

Ezekiel's emphasis on the manifestation of God's holiness in some great eschatological intervention resounded down the centuries of subsequent Jewish thought. In his great prayer to "the God of the universe" for Israel's deliverance, Jesus ben Sira prays that God will strike the Gentiles with fear as they see his mighty deeds (Sir 36:1–3). Then, echoing the language of Ezekiel, he prays that, "just as you sanctified yourself in their eyes by means of us, so in our eyes reveal your glory by means of them" (36:4). As in Ezekiel, the ultimate purpose of this manifestation is that the Gentiles may share Israel's knowledge of the one true God (36:5).[33] The constellation of these key themes from Ezekiel surfaces again in the depiction of the eschatological battle between the sons of light and the sons of darkness at Qumran. In the *War Scroll*, God is said to deliver the enemies of his people into the hands of the poor and lowly, to humble the warriors of the Gentiles. This act of judgment on the wicked will earn God an eternal name, showing him to be great and holy in the eyes of the remnant of the Gentiles when he executes judgment on Gog (1QM 11:13–15, with obvious allusions to Ezekiel 38–39).[34]

The two ideas of God's sanctifying his name and establishing his kingdom in an eschatological context are strikingly joined together in the ancient Jewish prayer known as the *Qaddish*: "Magnified and hallowed be his great name in the world [or: age] that he has created according to his good pleasure; may he cause his kingdom to reign [i.e., may he establish his kingdom] . . . in your lives [i.e., in your lifetime] and in your days and in the lives of the whole house of Israel, very soon and in a near time [i.e., in the near future]."[35] Like the passages in Ezekiel to which the prayer alludes, the sanctification of God's name is understood in the *Qaddish* to be the work of God, not of human beings, who are rather saved or judged by God's action. The parallel petition that God quickly cause his kingdom to rule obviously sees this event as God's act alone; presumably the parallel act of sanctifying the name belongs to God as well. Hence "hallowed be his great name" is not, at least primarily, a pious exhortation to praise God or a pledge to live according to his precepts. The passive voice is a true "theological passive," reverently referring indirectly to the divine agent, who is asked to manifest himself in all his world-creating and royal power in the near future.

Whether or not this early form of the *Qaddish* can be dated to the time of Jesus,[36] it demonstrates the continuing trajectory of a theme launched by Ezekiel and perduring in Judaism in the 1st centuries B.C. and A.D., especially in the context of prayer: God is besought to bring about a definitive manifestation of his power, glory, and holiness by defeating the Gentiles, gathering the scattered tribes of Israel back to the holy land, and establishing his divine rule fully and forever. It is within this trajectory that Jesus' prayer that God will sanctify his name and bring in his kingly rule is to be understood.

Hence "hallowed be your name" in the Lord's Prayer is probably neither a prayer that people will honor and praise God's name nor, as it were, an exhortation to oneself to do the same. Granted the trajectory we have seen from Ezekiel through Ben Sira and Qumran to the *Qaddish*, Jesus' petition most probably carries the same theological concentration: God alone can rightly and fully manifest himself in all his power and glory, that is to say, God alone can sanctify his name, which, it is hoped, he will do soon. This interpretation is supported by the close connection between the first and second "you petitions." Certainly only God can make his kingdom come; the tight parallelism between the two petitions would seem to argue that the same is true of sanctifying the name. That such an idea is not unheard of in NT literature is shown by the Johannine equivalent of the prayer in John 12:28a: "Father, glorify your name" (*pater, doxason sou to onoma*).[37] All this does not exclude, but rather presupposes, the idea that humans will respond to God's sanctification of his name with praise and obedience; but that is not the primary object of the first "you petition." Instead, the God whom the disciples are taught to address with the name "my own dear Father" (*'abbā'*) is besought to reveal himself as Father once and for all at the end time. The eschatological thrust of the petition is clear from its roots and parallels in Ezekiel, Ben Sira, Qumran, and Jewish liturgical prayers like the *Qaddish*.[38] Thus, the petition is both God-centered and eschatological; this already gives us an orientation toward understanding the second petition, our major concern.

b. "Your kingdom come." The God-centered and eschatological orientation made plausible by the first petition is fully confirmed by the second petition. In the previous chapter we saw that "the kingdom of God" is simply an abstract way of speaking of God ruling powerfully as king. The focus on God himself is inherent in the symbol, which is merely one particular way of speaking about him and his actions. Just as the name of God in the first petition means God as revealed, so the kingdom of God in the second petition means God as ruling. We also saw in the previous chapter that, especially in exilic and postexilic Jewish literature (protocanonical OT, deuterocanonical/apocryphal OT, pseudepigrapha, and Qumran), the symbol of God's kingly rule often took on eschatological overtones, notably with regard to the regathering of the scattered tribes of Israel. We concluded that, if Jesus wanted to make "the kingdom of God" central to his message and yet desired to avoid or negate future eschatology, he would have to make the differences in his use of the symbol crystal-clear.

Instead, in this key prayer taught to his disciples, Jesus makes the kingdom of God the subject of the petitionary verb "come"—which is all the more striking because of its novelty. In OT prophecies, all sorts of eschatological realities (God, the hoped-for king, days, etc.) were said to come—but, pointedly, not the kingdom of God or some equivalent phrase.[39] Actually, this absence of talk about the kingdom of God "coming" is not so puzzling in itself. The problem is, we are so accustomed to hearing the words "thy kingdom come" from the Our Father that we do not notice that it is a curious phrase and concept. Whether we translate *malkûtā* / *basileia* as kingdom, kingly rule, or kingship, in what sense do we pray that a kingdom or kingly rule or kingship "come"?[40] When one pauses to consider it, the idea is strange and awkward; and, apart from the traditional prayer, we probably would not think of expressing ourselves in that way. Certainly, most of the authors of the OT, the pseudepigrapha, and the Qumran literature did not.

Why, then, does Jesus choose this unusual phrase, almost unheard of in the OT and strange to untutored ears?[41] To begin with, Jesus' innovative locution indicates that he takes with utter seriousness the observation made above: the kingdom of God is simply a more abstract way of speaking of God as king. It does indeed sound strange to speak of a kingdom or kingly rule coming. It makes perfect sense—given OT prophecies and eschatological expectations of 1st-century Judaism—to speak of God coming or, as is the case here, to pray that he come. That God comes to save is a common affirmation in the OT, and from the time of Deutero-Isaiah onward it carries special weight in eschatological prophecy. For example, Isa 35:4 proclaims: "Say to the faint-hearted, 'Be strong, fear not; behold, your God will *come* with vengeance and his own recompense; he will *come* and save you.' "[42] Similarly, Isa 40:9–10 states: "Behold your God, behold the Lord Yahweh will *come* in strength, and his arm will rule for him." This God who comes in power is the very one of whom the herald proclaims the good news in Isa 52:7: "Your God reigns as king!" Prophecies of God's definitive coming to save Israel can also be found in Isa 59:19–20; 66:15,18; Mal 3:1–2; cf. Pss 96:13; 98:9. Zech 14:5–9 is of special interest, since there the promise that Yahweh will *come* is closely connected with the eschatological battle against all the hostile nations gathered against Jerusalem. In the end, after winning the battle, "Yahweh will become *king* over all the earth. On that day Yahweh will be one and his *name* [will be] one" (v 9). The hope for the eschatological coming of God to save his people continued in the Jewish pseudepigrapha, as can be seen in *1 Enoch* 1:3–9 (v 9 alludes to Zech 14:5 and in turn is quoted in Jude 14); 25:3; *Jub.* 1:22–28, where God's coming to restore his people is connected with his being both king on Mt. Zion and a father to his sons; and the *Testament of Moses* 10:1–12, in which God's coming is connected with the appearance of "his kingdom."

In short, when Jesus prays that God's kingdom come, he is simply express-ing in a more abstract phrase the eschatological hope of the latter part of the OT and the pseudepigrapha that God would come on the last day to save and restore his people Israel.[43] Once we realize this, we can see that the dispute whether the noun *malkûtā' / basileia* in the second "you petition" is more properly translated as kingdom or kingly rule is probably misplaced. Neither of those entities can, in the strict sense of the word, be said to come. Rather, according to the OT, it is God as king who is the one who comes, and that is the meaning of Jesus' petition. The sense of the second petition is thus: "Come, O Father, to rule as king." Accordingly, the sense of the whole first half of the Lord's Prayer is: "Father, reveal yourself in all your power and glory [= hallowed be your name] by coming to rule as king [= your king-dom come]."

This interpretation underlines the eschatological as well as the God-cen-tered nature of the petition and, indeed, of the whole first half of the Our Father. Nourished as he was on the Scriptures of Israel, Jesus was quite aware that God as creator had always been king, that he had exercised his kingship in choosing, liberating, punishing, and restoring his people Israel, and that he continued to hold kingly sway over all things. If, then, Jesus makes a major object of his prayer the petition that God come to rule as king, this naturally means that in some sense, according to Jesus, God is not yet fully ruling as king. Jesus' petition thus refers to that future, definitive coming of God as king which Jewish literature had connected with the symbol of God's kingship from the time of the exile onward. Both the immediate context of the first petition and the larger context of the use of the symbol of God's kingship in Jewish literature and liturgy confirm this conclusion. As a matter of fact, the theme of God's eschatological kingship is sounded not only in the *Qaddish*, but also in other Jewish prayers, notably the *Eighteen Benedictions* (the *Shemoneh Esreh*, also called the *Amidah* or *Ha-Tefilla*). Once again, the tradition history of the prayer is complicated and it is difficult to say exactly what form, if any, would have been known to Jesus.[44] But Benediction 11 (in the Palestinian recension) seems to be fairly ancient: "Restore our judges as at the beginning and our counselors as at the start, and reign over us, you alone. Blessed are you, O Lord, who love [just] judgment." If Jesus and his contemporaries knew and prayed this eschatological prayer, it is difficult to see how Jesus' own prayer, "Your kingdom come," would be understood differently (i.e., non-eschatologically) by his disciples.[45]

Thus, our first probe of "kingdom sayings" supports the position that Jesus' message was focused on a future coming of God to rule as king, a time when he would manifest himself in all his transcendent glory and power to regather and save his sinful but repentant people Israel. Only contorted exegesis can remove the element of future eschatology from Jesus' proclamation, as mirrored in the only prayer he ever taught to his disciples.

This is the major point I wish to draw from the Our Father at the present moment; I will return to other aspects of the prayer in other contexts. Still, it may be useful to take a quick overview of the whole prayer from the eschatological perspective that has just been vindicated.

One of the first things that should strike us about the Our Father is the apparently jarring yet purposeful juxtaposition of the initial cry of "Father" with the dominant theme (in the first half) of the glorious manifestation of God's power in the end time, when God comes to rule fully as king. God as father and God as king might seem to be a curious concatenation in eschatology, but such a yoking of diverse images of God lies at the heart of Jesus' message. Actually, the contrast would not have been as great in a 1st-century Mediterranean society as it is in modern America today. While a 1st-century father might be a symbol of love for his children, he was most certainly a symbol of sovereign power over their lives and fates, since within the homes of most 1st-century Mediterranean societies the father was the supreme arbiter of life and death, to say nothing of careers, marriages, and inheritance. The father was a symbol of supreme power in matters domestic; and so he was the object of obedience and reverence, even fear, as well as love. Conversely, at various times ancient kings, however ghastly and bloody their political record, boasted of being the fathers of their people insofar as they protected and cared for them, especially the poor and the weak (or so said the state propaganda). Father and king were therefore not contradictory symbols in religious discourse. Nevertheless, the stark juxtaposition of the single, intimate word 'abbā' (properly used of one's own human father and never used in Jewish liturgical prayer of the time for God)[46] with the powerful symbol of God as king coming to rule in the end time does create the type of rhetorical and theological clash that Jesus often used in his parables, a clash that brings together apparent opposites in a higher truth. Jesus teaches his disciples to pray for the longed-for coming of God as king, the king who would manifest his power and glory by regathering Israel in the end time. Yet this transcendent, almighty king of creation and history is addressed by the disciples as their own dear father. Measureless divine might, about to explode in the final act of human history, is accessible even now in prayer by those who enjoy intimacy with the divine king, who is also their loving father. This union of opposites in a few tight words encapsulates in miniature a good deal of Jesus' message. Among other things, it already hints at the connection between future eschatology, emphasized in the two "you petitions," and realized eschatology, implied by the very fact that the disciples even now are empowered to address the coming king as their own father.

3. The Three "We Petitions"

It is from this strong eschatological perspective, explicitly future and implicitly realized, that the three "we petitions" should probably be understood.[47] The bread-petition might well be read in the context of the eschatological banquet depicted in some of Jesus' parables and acted out in his table fellowship with tax collectors and sinners.[48] But even if we do not press for so precise a reference, the bread-petition shows us that Jesus shares with a good deal of OT, pseudepigraphic, and Qumranite writings an eschatological hope that involves concrete bodily existence, and not just disembodied souls in heaven. Hence bread in the present moment and bread in the final kingdom need not have been as discontinuous in Jesus' thought and prayer as they might be in ours.

The petition for forgiveness has in view the fearful final judgment that God the king will hold on the last day. It is most significant that Jesus makes the disciples' forgiveness of others in the present the condition of God's definitive forgiveness of them on the last day; again, an element of realized eschatology peeks through the predominantly future perspective. Making God's final forgiveness of individual believers depend on their forgiveness of others in the present moment may create problems for Christian theology. But, since Jesus was not a Christian theologian, he seems sublimely unconcerned about the problem.

The final petition of the prayer ("and lead us not into temptation") is probably eschatological in its thrust, too. In the more elaborate depictions of the end time in the OT, the pseudepigrapha, and Qumran,[49] a monumental struggle between good and evil, a cosmic battle with fearful casualties, or a bloody persecution of the righteous remnant of God's people is usually part of the eschatological scenario prior to God's ultimate triumph. In the crucible of suffering God's faithful people would be exposed to one last fearsome testing, and some would fall into apostasy under the pressure of the final crisis. The last petition seems to be a request that the Father spare his children the horror of that final clash between good and evil, lest they succumb (cf. Mark 13:20). Hence the *peirasmos* of the Greek text refers not to everyday "temptations" but rather to the final "test" that God in his sovereign control of history will bring upon the world in its last hour.[50]

Many commentators who take this approach go on to explain the difficult "and lead us not" by supposing that the Aramaic verb is in the hafel (causative) form, which at times can have a permissive sense: "And do not allow us to come to the test." Moreover, when a negative particle is used with such hafel causative forms, the negation can at times belong not to the causative action performed by the subject of the verb but rather to the result of the action. In the case of the Our Father, this would mean that a proper translation would run "cause us not to come to the test" instead of "do not cause us to come to the test." While all this may be true, one should remember that many writers in the OT and the NT were not bothered by problems of primary and secondary causality. In keeping with their strong monotheism, usually expressed by mythic stories rather than by philosophical theology, they frequently attributed all events directly to God, with no great concern about whether these events were good or bad. The important point was to exclude any second power, good or evil, that might seem equal to God.[51] This simple and direct faith in the one God who controls all things corresponds perfectly to the simple and direct petitions that make up the Our Father. Worrying about whether God directly causes or merely permits evil may lie beyond the horizon of this utterly simple prayer.[52]

In the end, though, whether the "we petitions" do express future eschatology is a matter of secondary importance for us in this chapter. What is of primary importance is that, in the only prayer that Jesus ever taught his disciples (as far as we know), the first concern voiced in the petitions is not a need or problem of this present world but rather a strictly eschatological desire that God reveal himself in all his power and glory ("hallowed be your name") by coming to Israel to reign fully and definitively as king ("your kingdom come"). The claim that at the center of Jesus' message and hopes was the coming of the eschatological kingdom of God—something God alone could achieve and something the disciples could only pray for—thus receives a firm, if preliminary, basis. We must now see whether other sayings of Jesus support this view.

B. DRINKING WINE IN THE KINGDOM OF GOD (MARK 14:25)

Just as I tried to keep my treatment of "thy kingdom come" from turning into a full-scale exegesis of the Our Father, so I will restrict my focus in this section to the saying of Jesus at the Last Supper recorded in Mark 14:25 parr.: "Amen I say to you that I shall no longer drink of the fruit of the vine until that day when I drink it new in the kingdom of God." Since I am focusing on this saying, I will not present here a full treatment of either the Last Supper or of the eucharistic words of Jesus, which immediately precede Mark 14:25.[53] Suffice it to say that the historicity of a final farewell meal held by Jesus with his disciples is generally accepted by scholars across the spectrum, since its existence is supported both by the criterion of multiple attestation and the criterion of coherence.[54]

As for multiple attestation, the event of the Last Supper is affirmed by Mark 14, John 13–17 (some would add a special tradition in Luke 22), and 1 Cor 11:23. The independent attestation by Paul is especially significant. Writing to the Corinthians ca. A.D. 55, some 25 years after the original event, Paul stresses that he transmitted the tradition about the Supper to the Corinthians when he instructed them in the faith (ca. A.D. 50–51), just as he received the tradition when he was instructed in the faith (ca. A.D. 33–34): "For I received from the Lord what I also handed on to you . . . " (1 Cor 11:23). Paul goes on to specify the time when Jesus spoke the eucharistic words he quotes ". . . on the night in which he was handed over . . ."; this agrees with the chronology of all Four Gospels. The use of the bread and the cup of wine obviously conjures up the idea of a meal, something Paul confirms with the words that introduce the cup in v 25: "Likewise also the cup, after he had finished supper. . . ." What is more, the use of wine, which was not common among poor Jews for everyday meals, betokens a meal of some importance and solemnity.

This witness of multiple attestation is supported by the criterion of coherence. A solemn festive meal which Jesus used to communicate a share in eschatological salvation would not have been something utterly unheard of in his ministry. We have already seen in Chapter 13 how Jesus was mocked by his adversaries because, in contrast to the ascetic John, he was seen as an "eater and drinker, a friend of tax collectors and sinners" (Matt 11:19 par.). In the eyes of the stringently pious, Jesus' table fellowship with the ritually or morally unclean communicated uncleanness to Jesus himself. Jesus, of course, saw it the other way round: he was communicating salvation to religious outcasts. His meals with sinners and the disreputable were celebrations of the lost being found, of God's eschatological mercy reaching out and embracing the prodigal son returning home (see, e.g., Mark 2:13–17; Luke 15:1–32). His banquets with sinful Israelites were a preparation and foretaste of the coming banquet in the kingdom of God—a metaphor that appears in various sayings and parables (see, e.g., Mark 2:19; Luke 13:28–29 par; 14:15–24 par.). Thus, the Last Supper does not stand in splendid isolation. It is instead quite literally the "last" of a whole series of meals symbolizing the final feast in the kingdom of God. There is therefore nothing strange about Jesus' holding a special, symbolic meal with his disciples (especially if he sensed his approaching arrest or death) or about his connecting the meal with the coming kingdom of God.

The saying under consideration, Mark 14:25, certainly belongs from its inception to the narrative of the Last Supper. We can be sure that it was not brought into the Last Supper context secondarily by Mark or his tradition, since what it states would make sense nowhere else in Jesus' ministry. For Jesus to affirm that he would never again drink wine (the sign of a special festive meal) until he does so in the kingdom of God is to affirm *ipso facto* that this is the last festive meal of his life in this present world. Hence, whether or not this saying is authentic, it was always connected with the story of the Last Supper.

Is in fact the saying authentic in the mouth of Jesus? As many writers point out, the vast majority of commentators agree that it is, though the precise reason for this agreement is not always spelled out.[55] Some, like Jacques Schlosser, appeal to the criterion of multiple attestation, since Mark 14:25 is paralleled in Luke 22:18. This Lucan verse forms the conclusion of a special Lucan unit of the Last Supper: "And he said to them: 'I have greatly desired to eat this Passover meal with you before I suffer. For I say to you that I will not eat it until it is fulfilled in the kingdom of God.' And receiving a cup

[and] giving thanks, he said: 'Take this and share it among yourselves' " (Luke 22:15–17). It is at this point that the parallel to Mark occurs:

Mark 14:25	Luke 22:18
Amen I say to you,	For I say to you,
I shall no longer drink	I shall not drink from now on
of the fruit of the vine	of the fruit of the vine
until that[56] day when	until
I drink it new[57]	
in the kingdom of God.	the kingdom of God comes.

As I indicated when treating chronological questions about the Last Supper in Chapter 11, I am doubtful of claims made by Heinz Schürmann and those following him that Luke 22:15–16 represents an early, independent tradition about what Jesus said at the Last Supper. I prefer the view that Luke 22:15–16 is a redactional creation of Luke,[58] who transposes Mark 14:25 to a position before the eucharistic words and expands upon it to create a neat pattern of food-word/drink-word, in order to balance the food-word/drink-word pattern in the institution of the eucharist. Thus Mark's awkward, dangling conclusion (i.e., Mark 14:25) of the pericope on the eucharist is deleted, allowing the unit to end instead with Jesus' solemn affirmation about "my blood poured out for you" (Luke 22:20). The transposition and expansion of Mark 14:25 in Luke 22:15–18 also provide Luke an opportunity to label this meal a Passover meal, a designation that is notably lacking in every other narrative of the Last Supper proper. As I noted in Chapter 11, both the many Lucan redactional traits in the wording of Luke 22:15–16 and the historically improbable presentation of the Last Supper as a Passover meal make it likely that most if not all of the Lucan unit 22:15–16 (as well as the connecting v 17) is a creation of Luke himself.[59]

But what of the precise parallel of Mark 14:25, Luke 22:18, taken by itself? Unlike 22:15–16 it says nothing about the meal being the Passover feast; and, being at times word-for-word the same as Mark 14:25, it is certainly not a purely Lucan creation. Either it is Luke's partial rewriting of Mark 14:25 or it is an alternate version of Mark 14:25 preserved in Luke's special tradition. While I incline to the former view, Schlosser does present some weighty arguments in favor of the latter. True, even Schlosser readily admits that some aspects of Luke 22:18 could be seen as Luke's redaction of Mark 14:25: e.g., the omission of Jesus' introductory "Amen," the formula "for I say to you" (probably redactional in Luke 22:37 as well), and the addition of "from now on" (apo tou nyn, a typically Lucan phrase).

Yet Schlosser can also point to traits that are not readily explainable as Lucan redaction of Mark. For example, in the phrase "to drink of the fruit" Mark uses the preposition ek while Luke uses apo. Both constructions are unusual in normal Greek but frequent in the LXX, reflecting the Hebrew preposition *min.* There is no discernible reason why Luke should have substituted *apo* for Mark's *ek*; the difference could therefore be a translation variant in two independent translations of the same Aramaic logion. Also, while Luke's "until" (*heōs hou*) is typical of his style, there is again no clear reason why he would avoid Mark's more specific "until that day when." More importantly, there is no reason why Luke should have avoided the clear imagery of the heavenly banquet (which he gladly uses elsewhere) or the phrase "in the kingdom of God" found at the end of Mark's logion: "when I drink it new in the kingdom of God."[60] At the same time, Schlosser points out that the image of an eschatological banquet is not unique to Jesus in ancient Judaism or early Christianity, and that the number of sayings containing the precise phrase "in the kingdom of God" that can be attributed to the historical Jesus with fair certitude is not great.[61]

Hence Schlosser maintains that possibly Mark's formulation is secondary. In contrast, as we have seen in the second petition of the Our Father, neither the OT, nor intertestamental Judaism, nor NT Christianity apart from the sayings of Jesus made the kingdom (of God) the subject of the verb "to come" (*erchesthai*). Schlosser thus concludes that at least the final part of Luke 22:18 may represent a more primitive form of Jesus' saying than does Mark 14:25. In any case, according to Schlosser the basic saying would enjoy multiple attestation of sources: Luke 22:18 would be an independent form of an eschatological saying of Jesus at the Last Supper recorded also in Mark 14:25. While I am not convinced by Schlosser's arguments, in fairness I should note that he does represent a good number of exegetes who defend the independent status of Luke 22:18 and thus the applicability of the criterion of multiple attestation in judging the historicity of the saying.

In my own view, the more telling criterion is that of discontinuity. Mark 14:25 reflects christological, soteriological, and eschatological ideas—or the startling lack thereof—that are at variance with almost any stream of early Christian tradition but are perfectly understandable in the mouth of the historical Jesus. To establish this point I must undertake an exegesis of Mark 14:25, all the while keeping an eye on the Lucan form as well, since Schlosser may be right that the ending of the saying is more reliably preserved in Luke. This is a prime example of being fairly certain about the general content and structure of a logion, while not being completely sure about the exact wording.

The initial "Amen" is, as Jeremias so often stressed, a typical introductory affirmation that Jesus used in some of his solemn sayings.[62] Here the affirmation strengthens the certainty of the prophecy Jesus is about to make. This rhetorical strengthening is carried forward by another locution typical of Jesus, "I say to you." What follows is obviously of great import in the eyes of Jesus. The total beginning that the "Amen I say to you" creates provides no bridge backward to the eucharistic words that immediately precede in Mark. Indeed, Jesus' speaking in a generic fashion of his drinking of the fruit of the vine sounds a bit strange after the solemn identification of the wine with his blood. All this may indicate that Mark 14:25 was an isolated logion, necessarily connected by its content with the Last Supper, but not originally connected with the eucharistic words. For those who see Luke 22:18 as an independent tradition, its position before the eucharistic words confirms this view, which is likely in any case.[63]

Jesus' basic affirmation that he will no longer drink wine (the sign of a special, festive meal) is expressed in an emphatic form in the Greek: the double negative *ou mē* + the subjunctive *piō* ("drink"), all preceded by the further negative *ouketi* ("no more," "no longer"). The whole clause is awkward, even "barbaric," in the Greek and may be a not totally happy rendering of an Aramaic tradition.[64] Luke's alternate formulation ("I shall not drink from now on") is, in Schlosser's view, not a Lucan redaction of the Marcan text, but Luke's attempt to render the same underlying Aramaic tradition, where the nuance of "no longer" would be understood rather than expressed.[65]

In any event, what is the main thrust of the logion? In the second German edition of his classic *The Eucharistic Words of Jesus*, Jeremias claimed that Jesus was uttering a vow of abstinence. Acting out his role as the suffering servant, Jesus was supposedly abstaining from the Passover lamb and wine in front of him at the Last Supper as a part of his intercessory prayer for a sinful Israel. This interpretation lacked any real basis in the text, since what Jesus utters is not a set formula used for a vow. In the third German edition of his book, Jeremias tried to step back slightly from his original position by saying that Jesus uttered not a strict vow of abstinence but rather "an avowal of abstinence" or "a declaration of forgoing [the food at the Last Supper]" (*Verzichter-klärung*).[66] However, this seems to be a distinction without a difference, since in his explanation of the text Jeremias all but returns to his original view that what Jesus utters is a vow.

If instead we simply look at the grammatical structure of Mark 14:25, we see a solemn, emphatic introduction ("Amen I say to you") to a promise/prediction/prophecy of what Jesus will not do in the immediate future (drink wine at a festive meal) until some further future event occurs (the day on which he drinks it new in the kingdom of God). The initial "Amen" not only gives solemnity to what follows but more importantly indicates that Jesus is authoritatively uttering a prophecy about the end time.[67] This end-time prophecy involves a veiled reference to his death, and for such a reference the particular grammatical structure and literary form of Mark 14:25 are well suited. A number of Jesus' sayings in various Gospel traditions have the same basic form, though not all have a clear eschatological reference. They include Mark 9:1; 13:30; Matt 10:23; Matt 5:26 || Luke 12:59; Matt 23:39 || Luke 13:35; and John 13:38. We shall be examining the first three at greater length in section E of this chapter. For now, let us look at Mark 9:1 as an especially apt parallel to Mark 14:25:[68]

Mark 14:25	*Mark 9:1*
Amen I say to you that	*Amen I say to you*
	there are some of those
	standing here

I shall no longer *drink*	who shall not *taste*
of the fruit of the vine	death
until that day when	*until*
I drink it new	they see
in *the kingdom of God*	*the kingdom of God*
	come in power.

The parallels in structure and content are clear. An initial "amen" introduces a prophecy that some event will not happen in this world (in both cases expressed by the emphatic *ou mē* + the subjunctive) before the final kingdom of God comes and is experienced by the person(s) who will not perform the action (drinking, tasting) mentioned in the main part of the prophecy. More specifically, in these two Marcan sayings the non-drinking and non-tasting both function as metaphors connected with death. The difference lies in the fact that Jesus in Mark 14:25 uses the pattern to prophesy his death before the full coming of God's kingdom, while in Mark 9:1 Jesus uses the same pattern to deny that some of the bystanders will die before the full kingdom of God comes. This precise pattern of prophecy (amen + negated future action + time-span until future experience of kingdom of God occurs) is a specific case of a more general biblical pattern in which it is prophesied that a person's death will not take place until some saving event occurs (see, e.g., Luke 2:26; John 21:23; outside the Bible *Jub.* 16:16; and, in a more diffuse way, the *Testament of Isaac* 3:3,12). It is this pattern, rather than any vow or oath formula, that Mark 14:25 fits.[69]

Clearly, then, given both the literary form of his statement and the general context of the Last Supper, what Jesus is prophesying is his approaching death, though one should be careful about speaking of his "imminent death." All Mark 14:25 implies is that Jesus will die before he has occasion to join in another festive banquet—a somewhat open-ended timetable (as is the timetable in Mark 9:1).[70] Jesus' state of non-drinking has in turn its own set limit, expressed in the temporal clause: he will resume drinking wine "in the kingdom of God." As most commentators note, "in the kingdom of God" is probably to be taken in a temporal rather than spatial sense and hence is roughly equivalent to the temporal clause in Luke 22:18: "until the kingdom of God comes." Thus, whichever version is more original, the basic sense is the same. As in the Our Father, so in Mark 14:25, the kingdom of God, at least in its full reality, is still to come. For all the powers of the kingdom already unleashed by the preaching and healings of Jesus, Jesus himself still looks forward to and urges his disciples to pray for the coming of the kingdom.

We are now in a better position to appreciate (1) what the historical Jesus would have meant when he spoke Mark 14:25 ‖ Luke 18:22 at the Last Supper and (2) the argument from discontinuity that supports the authenticity of this saying. As Jesus comes to the Last Supper, he is faced with the fact that his ministry, from a human point of view, has been largely a failure. All Israel has not heeded his message and accepted him as the eschatological prophet sent from God. Worse still, the bankruptcy of his life-project may be comple-mented by the bankruptcy of his life, as the possibility of a violent death looms. Jesus senses that his death is near; that is the thrust of his prophecy that he will not drink wine at a festive meal again. But his prophecy does not end on this gloomy note. Jesus is convinced that his cause is God's cause and that therefore, despite Jesus' personal failure and death, God will in the end vindi-cate his cause and his prophet by bringing in his kingdom and seating Jesus at the final banquet, to drink the festive wine once again. The prophecy in Mark 14:25 is thus a final cry of hope from Jesus, expressing his trust in the God who will make his kingdom come, despite Jesus' death. To the end, what is central to Jesus' faith and thought is not Jesus himself but the final triumph of God as he comes to rule his rebellious creation and people—in short, what is central is the kingdom of God.

With this understanding of the logion, we can appreciate the full force of the argument from discontinuity, supporting the authenticity of Mark 14:25 ‖ Luke 22:18. The basic affirmation of hope in this verse is utterly discontinuous with the christological, soteriological, and eschatological ideas of the early church, no matter what stream of the Christian tradition we look at. As far as christology and soteriology are concerned, not only is no title mentioned in this saying, no messianic role or function is assigned to Jesus in the final tri-umph of the kingdom.[71] Instead of saving anyone from death Jesus needs to be saved out of death himself, and only God can do that. The death itself is spo-ken of indirectly (Jesus will never enjoy another festive meal in this world). Its nearness, while intimated, remains indistinct; no timetable is given.[72] Neither is any cause-and-effect relation created between Jesus' death and the coming of the kingdom; indeed, the only relation between the two events is that the kingdom's arrival will somehow bring Jesus out of death. There is no hint of Jesus' death as atoning sacrifice, to say nothing of an explicit affirmation of his resurrection, exaltation, or parousia.[73] In all this, there is something discon-certing to Christian expectations. Not only does Jesus not mediate access to the eschatological banquet for others; there is no indication in the saying that he will enjoy any special place in the banquet, even as host. He is simply placed at the banquet table drinking wine; he is one of the saved, no more, no less. Not surprisingly, Matthew alters this non-christological saying by changing "in the kingdom of God" to "in the kingdom of my Father," thus insinuating the Evangelist's Son-christology into a logion notably devoid of it.

Even a communitarian or ecclesiological dimension is lacking in the ver-sions of the saying found in Mark and Luke. The logion says nothing about Jesus being reunited with his disciples at the final banquet, nothing about the broken fellowship being restored.[74] Significantly, once again it is Matthew, the evangelist intent on ecclesiology, who adds the phrase "with you" to the prom-ise that Jesus will drink wine in the kingdom (Matt 26:29). Granted, a commu-nitarian element is already implied in the imagery of a banquet. Still, it is telling that (1) no specific reference is made in the Marcan and Lucan versions to the disciples and their relationship to Jesus in the kingdom and that (2)

Matthew felt it necessary to insert this neglected dimension. If Mark 14:25 may be called a word of comfort, it is a word of comfort that Jesus speaks more to himself than to his disciples. In the face of failure and approaching death, Jesus consoles himself with the promise of ultimately being seated by God at the final banquet, despite the collapse of his mission in this present world. Thus, the focus of the saying is on Jesus' death as a sign of failure rather than of salvation, and on the coming of God's kingdom as the salvation of Jesus rather than the parousia of Jesus. This is simply not the christology, soteriology, and eschatology of the first generation of Christians, no matter what branch or stream of tradition we examine. Hence it is especially the criterion of discontinuity that argues for the authenticity of Mark 14:25 ‖ Luke 22:18. As Anton Vögtle says, we have in Mark 14:25 part of the bedrock of the Last Supper tradition.[75] For us, the important point here is that Mark 14:25 confirms from the Marcan tradition and from the form-critical category of prophecy what we already knew from Q and from the form-critical category of prayer: Jesus looked forward to a future coming of God's kingdom—and continued to do so even at the end of his life.

C. RECLINING AT TABLE WITH ABRAHAM IN THE KINGDOM (MATT 8:11–12 ‖ LUKE 13:28–29)

The next kingdom saying to be examined (Matt 8:11–12 ‖ Luke 13:28–29) most likely comes from the Q document, though one cannot be absolutely sure.[76] Both the different order of the two-part saying in the Matthean and Lucan versions and variations in the wording leave open the possibility that either or both evangelists drew the saying from independent special tradition. However, most commentators explain the differences in terms of the redactional activity of Matthew and Luke and hence assign the logion to Q.[77] The two versions read as follows:

Matt 8:11–12	*Luke 13:28–29*
I say to you that many from east and west shall come and shall recline at table with Abraham and Isaac and Jacob in the kingdom of heaven. But the sons of the kingdom shall be thrown out into the outer darkness. In that place there shall be weeping and grinding of teeth.	In that place there shall be weeping and grinding of teeth when you see Abraham and Isaac and Jacob and all the prophets in the kingdom of God, but you thrown out. And they shall come from east and west, from north and south, and shall recline at table in the kingdom of God.

For the most part, commentators agree that the larger contexts in which the tradition stands in both Matthew and Luke are secondary.[78] This is relatively clear in the case of Matthew, who has inserted the saying bodily into the markedly different literary genre of a miracle story, namely, the healing of the centurion's servant (Matt 8:5–13 ‖ Luke 7:1–10; cf. John 4:46–54). Matthew's insertion of the saying, plus some of his redactional changes (e.g., "the sons of the kingdom" designating Israel seen as a whole), adds to this story of a centurion's faith (the real point) a polemical thrust against an unbelieving and consequently rejected Israel. Such a fierce polemic is foreign to the original story, which simply compares the centurion's faith favorably with the faith Jesus has found in Israel.[79] In contrast, the Matthean insertion depicts an Israel that, taken as a whole, is rejected from the kingdom. Both the Lucan version of the healing of the centurion's servant and the more distant parallel in John (the healing of the royal official's son)[80] know of the theme of faith and unbelief related to miracles, but neither parallel reflects the idea of Israel's wholesale rejection on the last day. Indeed, it seems that Matthew himself noticed that his polemical insertion disrupted the miracle story's major theme of faith. He attempted to bring back the major theme at the end of the story by having Jesus' praise of the centurion's faith in 8:10 echoed in Jesus' final words of dismissal and promise (not present in Luke): "Go. As *you have believed*, let it be done unto you" (8:13).[81]

The context of Luke is more difficult to judge, for it is a typical collection of disparate Q and L traditions linked by similar themes and by the grand overarching theme of the journey to Jerusalem. The theme that is common to Luke 13:22–27 (the Lord locking the door in the face of those who claim to know him well) and 13:28–29 (the heavenly banquet with the patriarchs) is the separation of the good and the evil on the last day; this similarity may have invited Luke to link the two traditions. At the same time, there are certainly strong dissimilarities in the two traditions that argue against the theory that the link was original. (1) The theme of the ingathering of people (probably Gentiles) from the ends of the earth to eat with the patriarchs while at least some Israelites ("you") are thrust out of the kingdom is missing in vv 22–27; the separation runs along different lines and by different criteria. (2) The motif of the sorrow and pain of those expelled from the kingdom in 13:28 is lacking in vv 22–27. (3) The presence of the "Lord" (clearly Jesus) as the final judge in 13:25–27 is quite different from the completely "non-christological" judgment scene in vv 28–29.

In short, it appears that neither Matt 8:11–12 nor Luke 13:28–29 had anything to do originally with its present context. This isolation of Matt 8:11–12 par. has important consequences for interpreting this tradition. Neither the Matthean nor the Lucan context should be read into the tradition—something that critics often do unconsciously.[82] We must rather strip away the contexts of the two Gospels as well as any redactional changes in wording and then interpret the logion on its own terms.

Fortunately, for all the differences and disagreements between Matthew and Luke and despite the logion's original isolation, the basic message of the two-part saying is clear. In one half of the saying, it is prophesied that people will come from the east and the west and recline at table with Abraham, Isaac, and Jacob in the kingdom of God. The other half of the saying warns that another group will be thrown out (of the kingdom); there (i.e., outside) they will weep and grind their teeth in sorrow and pain. The two forms this logion takes in Matthew and Luke are difficult to compare, since the parts of the saying occur in different order. If we number the individual phrases of Matthew in the order in which they occur, we can then see where the equivalent phrases occur in the Lucan form. In the following outline, phrases that have no corresponding form in the version of the other evangelist are emphasized.

	Matt 8:11–12		*Luke 13:28–29*
	(verse 11)		(verse 28)
1	*I say to you that*	9	In that place
2	many from east and west		there shall be
	will come	10	weeping and grinding
3	and will recline		of teeth
	[at table]		*when you see*
4	with Abraham and Isaac	4	Abraham, Isaac,
	and Jacob		and Jacob
			and all the prophets
5	in the kingdom of heaven.	5	in the kingdom of God,
	(verse 12)		
6	But the sons of the kingdom	6	but you
7	will be thrown out	7	thrown out.
8	*into the outer darkness.*		
			(verse 29)
9	In that place	2	And they will come
	there shall be		from east and west,
10	weeping and grinding of teeth.		*from north and south,*
		3	and shall recline
			[at table]
		5	*in the kingdom of God.*

A glance at the outline shows us that the themes in the middle part of the saying (elements # 4, 5, 6, 7) are basically the same in both versions: a contrast with the patriarchs in the kingdom and some group ("the sons" or "you") who are thrown out. We are dealing with a prophecy of weal and woe on the last day. The great inversion takes place at the two ends of the prophecy. Matthew begins the prophecy with the positive note of the people who come from east and west to recline at table (#2, 3) and ends it with the negative note of weeping and grinding of teeth (#9, 10). Luke reverses the order, beginning negatively with the weeping and ending positively with reclining in the kingdom. In addition, each evangelist has two phrases proper to his version. Matthew prefaces the whole saying with the authoritative prophetic introduction, "I say to you that . . . ," and he specifies that when the sons are thrown outside, they are thrown "into the outer darkness." Luke joins "all the prophets" to the mention of the patriarchs and rounds out "east and west" with the other two points of the compass. Finally, Matthew has "sons of the kingdom" where Luke has simply "you," and Luke states that the group called "you" *see* the patriarchs in the kingdom, although the group itself is thrown out.

Which evangelist represents the more original order and/or the more original wording? The reader will not be surprised to learn that scholars are divided on the issue. As for the order of the phrases in the logion, Schlosser maintains that Luke preserves the original order, while Dupont and Schulz uphold the order of Matthew as more primitive.[83] Both sides present good arguments, but there is a fatal flaw in the position of Schlosser. Since he supports the Lucan order, he must maintain that the independent tradition began in Greek with the adverb *ekei* ("there," "in that place"). Schlosser tries to escape this difficulty by urging that the word could instead mean "then";[84] but, while there are some rare examples of this usage outside the NT, there is no clear case of this meaning in NT Greek. Unless one ignores the natural sense of the word for the sake of special pleading, one must translate the beginning of Luke 13:28 as "in that place *(ekei)* there will be weeping," etc. To begin an independent logion in that way is quite harsh since, in contrast to the present Lucan context, there would be nothing for the adverb to refer back to. It seems more likely, therefore, that the Matthean order is more original.[85] Luke has reversed the order of the saying to latch onto the end of the Q saying in 13:25–27, which concludes with the rejection of the wicked.[86] It is this inversion and partition of various elements in the original logion that occasions Luke's repetition of the phrase "in the kingdom of God."

Beyond the question of the original order, we must face the question of whether Matthew or Luke has preserved the more original wording of the tradition. As so often, the answer is that neither evangelist can be called "more original" *simpliciter*. Both have made their own additions and modifications. While one must be wary of an automatic "method of subtraction" (i.e., the presumption that deleting words or phrases found in only one evangelist will give us the more original form), the subtraction method does seem to work in this case. In other words, the phrases unique to either Matthew or Luke are probably secondary, as an examination of individual cases will show.

To take Matthew first: while "I say to you" does seem to have been characteristic of Jesus' speech, Matthew has the habit of imitating and multiplying phrases that he finds in his sources and likes. As with locutions such as "Father" applied to God, the introductory "I say to you" is an example of a usage that may have originated with Jesus but then tended to be multiplied in Matthew's redaction of Jesus' words. The absence of it in the Lucan parallel makes it likely, though not certain, that it is secondary here.[87] For Matthew, it is a useful way both to insert alien material into the story of the centurion's servant and to stress the prophetic authority of Jesus. As for other Matthean redactional traits: needless to say, "kingdom of heaven" is Matthew's reformulation of "kingdom of God." The phrase "into the outer darkness," found only in Matthew's Gospel within the NT, also occurs in Matthew's redactional and allegorical addition to the parable of the great supper (Matt 22:13, with no equivalent passage in the simpler Lucan form of the parable, Luke 14:15–24). The phrase is probably also redactional when it appears in Matthew's version of the parable of the talents in 25:30; again, it is absent in the Lucan version of the parable. The redactional nature of the phrase in both Matt 22:13 and 25:30, plus its absence in Luke 13:28, points to its redactional nature in Matt 8:12 as well.

One word in Matthew's version is not so easily adjudicated. Matt 8:11 says that "*many* will come," while Luke 13:29 simply says that "they [even the pronoun is merely understood in the verb] will come." Since all of the other additions and expansions in this logion appear secondary, one is inclined to view "many" as secondary, too. But here the decision is not so clear. If element 2 of the logion originally began the whole saying, "many" would certainly be a better and clearer opening than a vague "they" contained in the verb. Moreover, Kloppenborg judges that the word "many" *(polloi)* in Jesus' sayings in Matthew's Gospel usually represents tradition that Matthew has received rather than Matthean redaction.[88] Hence I am inclined to retain "many," while I admit that the matter is far from certain.

On the Lucan side: once Luke made what was originally the concluding words of the logion ("in that place there shall be weeping and grinding of teeth") the introductory statement instead, he needed some way of attaching these words to the main part of the prophecy in 13:28, which focuses on the patriarchs at the banquet in the kingdom of God. The clause "when you see" in v 28 seems to be the redactional link created by Luke to forge this bond. The two other special phrases in Luke are literary and theological expansions. Luke complements "Abraham and Isaac and Jacob" with "and all the prophets," stressing as usual that all that was best in the history of Israel is in continuity with and finds its fulfillment in Jesus and the church. If "and all the prophets" had been original, there would have been no reason why Matthew, who is very much taken with the OT prophets, should have omitted the phrase.[89] "From north and south" in Luke 13:29 is also probably a Lucan addition to "from east and west"; it simply underlines the message of universalism, a theme dear to Luke.[90]

One point of difference between Matthew and Luke is not a matter of addition but of variation in wording. Matthew calls the people thrown out of the kingdom "the sons of the kingdom," while Luke has a simple and unspecified "you." Elsewhere in the NT "sons of the kingdom" is found only in Matthew's redactional and allegorical interpretation of the parable of the wheat and the weeds (13:38: ". . . the good seed: these are the sons of the kingdom").[91] Hence, the vague "you," no doubt specified by the presence of the original audience, is more original. The direct address is especially fitting in a prophetic oracle of threat and announcement of judgment. The sudden change from a promise in the third person to a threat in the second person is part of the saying's antithetical parallelism.

The upshot of all this analysis is that the primitive tradition would have been close to Matthew's version, minus Matthew's redactional additions.[92] It would have run something like this:

8:11 (2)   Many [or: they] from east and west shall come
     (3)   and shall recline [at table]
     (4)   with Abraham and Isaac and Jacob
     (5)   in the kingdom of God.
8:12 (6 and 7) But you shall be thrown out.[93]
     (9)   In that place there shall be
     (10)   weeping and grinding of teeth.

Although we may not feel sure about every single word in this reconstruction, the basic structure and content are clear. We have a prophetic oracle in two parts, promising eschatological salvation in the kingdom of God and threatening definitive exclusion from the kingdom. As Sato observes, the logion seems to have been stamped from the beginning by this structure of antithetical parallelism. Or as Dupont puts it, the point of the logion lies precisely in its contrast.[94]

Admittedly, certain details of the oracle are not so clear, especially now that we have stepped back from the redactional contexts and additions of the evangelists. To begin with, who are the "many" (or possibly, the vague "they") who will come from east and west? Many commentators immediately think of the Gentiles, and one can certainly appeal to the numerous prophecies in the OT and pseudepigrapha that present Gentiles as involved in the drama of the end time: e.g., either by their worshiping the one true God or by their coming to Israel, specifically Jerusalem, when the end time arrives (see, e.g., Isa 2:1–4; 25:6–8; 51:4–6; 59:19; Mic 4:1–4; Zech 14:16; Mal 1:11; Tob 13:11; 14:6).[95] Needless to say, the way in which the Gentiles are involved in the events of the end time varies from writer to writer. For example, their coming to Jerusalem is sometimes imagined in a positive way (the Gentiles as devout pilgrims, joining Israel in its worship of Yahweh), sometimes in a negative way (the defeated Gentiles are made to bow down before a triumphant Israel).[96] Since such ideas about the Gentiles were often connected with the hope that all Israel would be regathered to the Promised Land and Zion, and since Jesus seems to have shared this hope for a regathered or reconstituted Israel, there is nothing impossible or anachronistic about the historical Jesus speaking of the coming of the Gentiles in the context of the kingdom of God.

At the same time, we must be cautious in our claims. The saying neither alludes to any one OT text nor explicitly mentions Jerusalem or Zion. The "many" are said to come to a banquet with the patriarchs, not to Mt. Zion. Moreover, we must not imagine that, at the time of Jesus, there was some homogenized doctrine about the coming of the Gentiles to Mt. Zion. As with

so much of his use of the OT, Jesus employs the tradition creatively to communicate his own message.[97]

Indeed, if the "many" are the Gentiles, this depiction of their coming to
salvation *only* at the final banquet in the kingdom does not fit the situation of
the early church, which conducted a lively mission to the Gentiles in the decades after Jesus' crucifixion. On the other hand, a prophecy that the Gentiles
would come to salvation *only* at the final banquet (and hence not within ordinary human history) would fit the situation of the historical Jesus, who did not
view either himself or his disciples as charged with the task of undertaking a
mission to the Gentiles while this present world ran its course. Jesus understood his own mission as directed solely to his own people Israel, and his immediate disciples—notably the *Twelve!*—were likewise sent by him only to
Israel.[98] This was one reason why a programmatic mission to the Gentiles
during the course of this present world was such a wrenching departure for the
early church and caused so much controversy in the first Christian generation.
Neither the actions nor the words of the historical Jesus had given precise and
detailed instructions for such an initiative. Rather, Jesus' words in Matt
8:11–12 par. presuppose just the opposite: the Gentiles will come to join those
who are saved (= obedient Israel) *only* at the final banquet in the kingdom.[99]
They have no key role in the drama before then. They (or, at least "many" of
them) are to be saved on the last day, but how or on what basis is not said.
Notably, nothing is said about their being saved by accepting or believing in
Jesus.

To be fair, I should note as an aside that, theoretically, the "many" might
be taken as referring not to the Gentiles but to Diaspora Jews as opposed to
Palestinian Jews (this is what the "you" of the contrast would then seem to
mean).[100] While that is not impossible, it results in a curious contrast. For no
clear reason, the Diaspora Jews are contrasted most favorably with the Palestinian Jews. The latter group will be cast out of the kingdom—with the contrast apparently making no distinction between those Palestinian Jews who did
not accept Jesus and those who did. All this makes for a strange opposition. In
addition, nowhere else in the authentic words of Jesus is there any indication
that Jesus ever reflected upon the special situation and fate of Diaspora Jews
as distinct from Palestinian Jews. He seems rather to have hoped for the ingathering of all Jews to reconstitute the twelve tribes of Israel in the end time.

More likely, then, the "many" are the Gentiles, who are mentioned as traditional participants in the end-time events to underscore the punishment of
"you." Who then are the "you"? The people of Israel, seen as a whole and as
a group that has rejected Jesus and so will be rejected at the final judgment? It
is surprising to see that some critics claim that this might be the sense of the
original logion.[101] Yet that is to read the highly polemical Christian theology
of Matthew's Gospel and Matthew's redactional form of the logion back into
its primitive form and message. Abstracted from its redactional context, the
saying does not specify who the threatened "you" are. They are certainly not
"all Israel," since the patriarchs, no doubt representing all the righteous of the

OT, are at the banquet, and presumably Jesus would include at the table his own disciples (especially the Twelve, representing the reconstituted twelve tribes) as well as the tax collectors, sinners, and other assorted Israelites who heeded his message. The "you" must be those among his contemporaries in Israel who made a point of rejecting his mission. Whether in this particular instance they were the priestly aristocracy in Jerusalem, some scribes who opposed his teaching, or certain Pharisees who felt that Jesus' "reform movement" was much too freewheeling when it came to the Law cannot be decided on the basis of this isolated logion.

What can be decided is that there is no reason to deny this saying to the historical Jesus and a number of reasons for attributing it to him. (1) Negatively, the idea of Gentiles coming to the final banquet in the kingdom need not be seen as a retrojection of the Gentile mission of the early church. Indeed, one can formulate this point more positively from the viewpoint of the criterion of discontinuity. The lack of any idea in the logion of a mission to the Gentiles during this present age, the presumption that the Gentiles will "come into play" only at the final banquet in the kingdom, runs counter to what was in fact beginning to happen only a few years after the crucifixion. The saying makes more sense in the mouth of Jesus than in the mouth of the early church. (2) Also negatively, once the logion is stripped of its redactional context (especially in Matthew), there are no grounds for speaking of "the rejection of all Israel." Nothing in the saying indicates that *all* Israel is involved, only some unspecified group of Israelites who oppose or reject Jesus' message.[102] (3) More positively, and also from the viewpoint of discontinuity, neither the OT nor the Judaism of the time of Jesus brought together in such brief compass the three motifs of the eschatological pilgrimage of the Gentiles, the eschatological banquet, and the symbol of "the kingdom of God."[103] Moreover, the joining of the eschatological banquet to the kingdom of God coheres with other sayings of Jesus, including Mark 14:25, which we examined above. (4) The criteria of discontinuity and coherence have further bearing on Matt 8:11–12 par. This logion portrays Gentiles and patriarchs participating in the final banquet, yet nothing is said or intimated about Jesus' role as mediator or host—or in this case, even as guest—at the meal. Granted, one might suggest that there is an implied christological claim in this logion insofar as acceptance or rejection of Jesus seems to be the basis for one's own acceptance or rejection on the last day. But even this implicit claim must be read into the logion from other sayings and actions of Jesus; no such claim is made in Matt 8:11–12 par., taken by itself. Indeed, no mention is made of any mission by either Jesus or his disciples.[104] The lack of any christological role for Jesus as mediator or host of the banquet is discontinuous with early Christian preaching and coheres remarkably with Jesus' words at the Last Supper in Mark 14:25.[105] Hence probability lies on the side of a primitive form of Matt 8:11–12 par. coming from the historical Jesus.[106]

The main point here, within the overarching purpose of this chapter, is that we have another clear example of Jesus' belief in a future, definitive coming of

God's kingly rule, represented under the metaphor of a banquet. With the affirmation that the Gentiles will join the long-dead patriarchs of Israel at the banquet, Jesus indicates that this fully realized kingdom of God is not only future but also in some way discontinuous with this present world. Whether Jesus is thinking in this logion more of the resurrection of the dead or of the souls of the saved in heaven is not clear.[107] How "transcendent" or "earthly" the kingdom exactly is in Jesus' mind is not illuminated by this prophecy, which obviously operates in the realm of religious symbols. But the idea of the Gentiles streaming into the kingdom of God to be joined by the long-dead but now obviously living patriarchs of Israel surely brings us beyond any political kingdom of this present world, including a mere reconstitution of the kingdom of David on a grander scale.[108] While one cannot call Jesus' prophecy in this logion full-scale apocalyptic,[109] the hope of eternal life beyond this present world (including the resurrection of the dead?), enriched as it is by a note of universalism, does reflect some apocalyptic motifs. In particular, the depiction of the three great patriarchs as alive and participating in a heavenly banquet implies both the transcendence of death and the regathering of the people of Israel not only from all places but also from all times.[110] Such prophecy must be considered apocalyptic to some degree, even if all the required characteristics of full-blown apocalyptic are not present. This fits in with what we saw of both John the Baptist and Jesus in Chapters 12 and 13: both were eschatological prophets with some apocalyptic traits,[111] yet without all the characteristics of what scholars today classify as an apocalyptic message or an apocalyptic worldview.

In sum, according to Matt 8:11–12 par., the historical Jesus did expect a future coming of God's kingdom, and that kingdom was in some way a transcendent one, surmounting this world's barriers of time, space, hostility between Jews and Gentiles, and finally death itself. A completely un-eschatological Jesus, a Jesus totally shorn of all apocalyptic traits, is simply not the historical Jesus, however compatible he might be to modern tastes, at least in middle-class American academia.

D. The Beatitudes as Confirmation[112]

It may strike the reader as strange that so important a text as the beatitudes of the Sermon on the Mount/Plain (Matt 5:3–12 ‖ Luke 6:20–23) are treated only toward the end of a chapter on Jesus' proclamation of the imminent coming of the kingdom.[113] The reason is a strategic one, and is not unlike the reason why the treatment of the parables is reserved to a later chapter. If isolated from any larger context, the beatitudes are open to a number of different interpretations. Hence I have purposely kept them until now, so that all that we have seen so far in this chapter may provide an interpretive framework. As in the case of the Lord's Prayer, the Last Supper tradition, and the question of the salvation of the Gentiles, my goal in this section is not to provide a full treatment of the material, but only to see what it has to contribute to our knowledge of Jesus' proclamation of a future kingdom.

1. *An Initial Inspection of the Beatitudes*

To clear a path through the thicket of exegetical questions surrounding the beatitudes, we need at least an initial survey of the two forms of the beatitudes in the Sermon.[114] It will help us make some basic decisions about sources and the earliest available form of the tradition. Once that is done, we can deepen our appreciation of what the beatitudes mean and prepare for the question of authenticity by looking back at the development of the beatitude form in the OT and the pseudepigrapha.

The two forms of the beatitudes line up as follows:[115]

Matt 5:3–12	*Luke 6:20–23*
1. Happy the poor in spirit for theirs is the kingdom of heaven. (v 3)	1. Happy the poor for yours is the kingdom of God. (v 20)
2. Happy the mourners for they shall be comforted. (v 4)	[3. Happy those weeping now for you shall laugh. (v 21b)][116]
3. Happy the meek for they shall inherit the earth. (v 5)	
4. Happy those hungering and thirsting for justice for they shall be satisfied. (v 6)	2. Happy those hungering now for you shall be satisfied. (v 21a)
[See Matt 5:4]	3. Happy those weeping now for you shall laugh. (v 21b)
5. Happy the merciful for they shall be shown mercy. (v 7)	
6. Happy the pure of heart for they shall see God. (v 8)	
7. Happy the peacemakers for they shall be called sons of God. (v 9)	

8. Happy those persecuted
   for the sake of justice
   for theirs is the kingdom
   of heaven. (v 10)

9. Happy are you   4. Happy are you
   when they revile you   when men hate you
   and persecute [you]   and when they separate you
   and say every kind   and cast out your name
   of evil against you   as evil
   [falsely]
   for my sake.   for the sake of the Son of Man.
   Rejoice[117] and be glad   Rejoice on that day and leap
                                           [for joy]
   for your reward is great   for behold your reward is great
   in heaven.   in heaven.
   For so   For in the same way
   they persecuted   their fathers acted
   the prophets [who were]   toward the prophets. (vv 22–23)
   before you. (vv 11–12)

Some points are immediately clear. Matthew has nine beatitudes (eight short, one long), while Luke has four beatitudes (matched by four woes;[118] the beatitudes are three short and one long). Following the two-source theory and using Matthew's order of the beatitudes, we can say that beatitudes 1 (poor), 2 (mourners), 4 (hungry), and 9 (long one on persecution) come from Q, while beatitudes 3 (meek), 5 (merciful), 6 (pure of heart), 7 (peacemakers), and 8 (short one on persecution) come from either Matthew's special source (M), Matthew's creative redaction, or a mixture of both.

Since most scholars judge the original form of the Q beatitudes to be very early tradition and among the best candidates for authentic sayings of Jesus, we shall focus our attention on the Q beatitudes, with the M beatitudes kept for consideration at the end of our survey.

The Q Beatitudes

Matthew

Luke

1. Happy the poor in spirit   1. Happy the poor
   for theirs is the   for yours is the
   kingdom of heaven.   kingdom of God.

2. Happy the mourners   [3. Happy those weeping
                                          now
   for they shall be comforted.   for you shall laugh.]

3. Happy those hungering and   2. Happy those hungering

thirsting for justice   now
for they shall be satisfied.   for you shall be satisfied.

                                    3. Happy those weeping
                                         now
                                         for you shall laugh.

4. Happy are you   4. Happy are you
   when they revile you   when men hate you
   and persecute [you]   and when they separate you
   and say every kind   and cast out your name
   of evil against you   as evil
   [falsely]
   for my sake.   for the sake of the Son of
                                         Man.
   Rejoice and   Rejoice on that day and
   be glad   leap [for joy]
   for your reward is   for behold your reward is
   great in heaven.   great in heaven.
   For so   For in the same way
   they persecuted   their fathers acted toward
   the prophets [who were] before you.   the prophets.

Scholars argue over which evangelist reflects the original (or more original) form of Q. As we have learned to suspect by now, neither evangelist can be said to represent the original form in its pristine purity. The wording of each beatitude must be judged on its own merits. As for the difference between the 3d person plural in Matthew and the 2d person plural in Luke, the 3d person is much more common and traditional both in the OT and in the intertestamental literature. More to the point, the 2d person plural is totally lacking in the first part of the first three beatitudes of Luke—an absence that is most unusual in beatitudes directly addressing an audience. In such beatitudes one expects a pronoun or a verb in the 2d person plural. Instead, "yours" or "you" occurs only in the *hoti* ("for") clause of Luke. The suspicion arises that Luke has secondarily introduced the 2d person plural form into beatitudes that originally stood in the 3d person. Moreover, throughout his work Luke betrays a certain stylistic penchant for the 2d person. Hence, despite the claim that Luke represents the more lively, fiery proclamation of Jesus the prophet preaching to the poor of Galilee, many authors view Matthew's 3d person as more original, except for the final beatitude, which (as we shall see) seems to have had a different origin.[119]

Matthew's "poor in spirit" is usually judged secondary to Luke's simple "poor." Since throughout the list Matthew shows a tendency to spiritualize, moralize, and generalize the beatitudes, turning them into spiritual attitudes applicable to all believers, it seems likely that the addition of "in spirit" serves the same purpose here. Moreover, the bare phrase "the poor" matches better the equally bare "mourners" and "hungry" in the second and third Q beatitudes.[120] However, it must be noted that "poor in spirit" or a close equivalent is found more than once at Qumran.[121] "In spirit" could represent an early development of the wording of the Q beatitudes in the Matthean community prior to Matthew's own composition (the siglum Q^Mt is sometimes used to symbolize this possible evolution of Q within Matthew's church).[122] Luke's "kingdom of *God*" is obviously more primitive than Matthew's redactional "kingdom of *heaven*."

In the second beatitude,[123] on mourners, the exact wording of the primitive Q form is not clear. Various authors argue for the priority of Matthew's or Luke's wording; yet the whole question is moot if the differences go back to translation variants in different Greek recensions of Q. Fortunately, for our purposes a decision on such minor points is not vital. On the whole, I am impressed by the arguments of Schlosser, Fitzmyer, Davies, and Allison that Luke's wording has a better chance of being redactional than Matthew's.[124]

In the beatitude on the hungry, "justice" *(dikaiosynē)* looks suspiciously like Matthew's redaction or at least the contribution of Matthew's tradition. "Justice" is a favorite Matthean word—it occurs seven times in Matthew, once in Luke, and never in Mark or John—and it supplies the theme for the first part of his Sermon on the Mount (while love and mercy are more central to Luke's Sermon on the Plain).[125] The neat balancing of "justice" in the fourth beatitude and "justice" in the eighth beatitude is a fine example of Matthew's love of symmetry and patterns. The phrase "hunger and thirst" is traditional in the OT, and so the joint verbs could be original. However, the first three primitive Q beatitudes, which seem to have been strikingly terse, probably named all these groups with a single stark word. Matthew and his tradition loved long, rolling, rhythmic phrases redolent of the OT, as is clear from his version of the Lord's Prayer. Most likely, therefore, the original form of the third beatitude was the laconic "Happy are the hungry, for they shall be satisfied [i.e., fed to the full]."[126]

The final long beatitude on persecution is much more complicated in form and in the problem of deciphering its original wording. Luke's "when they separate you . . . and throw out your name as evil" may refer to the exclusion of Jewish Christians from synagogues toward the end of the 1st century.[127] Matthew's vaguer wording may be more original. On the other hand, there is no clear case where Luke substitutes "Son of Man" for a personal pronoun, while there are cases of Matthew's substituting a personal pronoun for "Son of Man" (see, e.g., Matt 16:21; cf. Mark 8:31).[128] Moreover, "Son of Man" was a key—some would say the only—christological title in Q. Hence Luke's "for the sake of the Son of Man" is probably original. The use of the clarifying "on that day" and of the verb "leap" *(skirtaō* only in Luke's Gospel in the whole of the NT) may well betray Luke's redactional hand.[129] Since in beatitudes *hoti* ("for") is the usual word for describing a reward, Luke's "for behold" *(idou gar)* may also be redactional.[130] The reference to the persecution of the OT prophets occurs with variations in both Matthew and Luke and hence was already in Q. However, since such further explanations fall outside of the beatitude form proper, the reference to the persecution of the prophets may be a secondary development within the Q tradition, which was very interested in prophets and prophecy, both Jewish and Christian.[131]

A likely hypothetical form of the four beatitudes of Q would therefore run something like this:

1. Happy are the poor   for theirs is the kingdom of heaven.
2. Happy the mourners for they shall be comforted.
3. Happy the hungry   for they shall be satisfied.
4. Happy are you   when [people] revile you and persecute [you] and say every kind of evil against you on account of the Son of Man. Rejoice and be glad, for your reward is great in heaven.

Critics usually separate the fourth Q beatitude from the other three since it is so notably different in length, form, and content. The first three are terse, the fourth is longer than the first three combined. The first three speak of particular groups of people in a state of socioeconomic distress that they have not chosen, that has nothing to do with commitment to Jesus, and about which they can do nothing. The first three beatitudes proceed to promise these people a direct reversal of their particular state of distress on the last day (i.e., the mourners will be comforted, the hungry will be fed to the full). The fourth beatitude speaks of those who have voluntarily undergone persecution because of their freely chosen commitment to the Son of Man (= Jesus). Instead of a direct reversal of a concrete state, the persecuted receive a general promise of reward. Moreover, the fourth beatitude differs form-critically. Instead of a terse, tight pattern of (1) *makarios* ("happy") + (2) the definite article with an adjective or participle + (3) a brief *hoti* ("for") clause describing the reversal of one's suffering, the fourth beatitude is formulated in the 2d person ("happy are you"),[132] without the definite article with adjective or participle, and with *hotan* ("when") instead of *hoti*. Functionally, the lengthy *hotan* clause takes the place of the stark adjective or participle in describing the plight of those declared happy. Only after this description and two imperative verbs enjoining jubilation is the reason (*hoti*) for happiness given in a vague promise of future reward in heaven.

It is advisable, therefore, to put aside the fourth beatitude.[133] Length, form, and content all suggest that it did not originally belong with the collection of the first three. Moreover, in its redactional form it may well reflect the persecution experienced by the early church.[134] In contrast, the three "core" beatitudes of Q[135] may have been uttered together and passed down together from the beginning. As we shall see from our examination of the OT, apocrypha, pseudepigrapha, and Qumran, such stringing together of three or more beatitudes, while unknown in the Hebrew OT, began to appear in the intertestamental period. In addition, the first beatitude of the Q series seems to act as a general, sweeping statement, the two categories of the "poor" (*'ănāwîm*) and the "kingdom of God" being extremely broad. In contrast, the two subsequent beatitudes concretize the general beatitude by employing more specific groups and promises (the mourners and their consolation, the hungry and their being fed to the full). In short, the earliest form of the Q beatitudes available to us reads as follows:

	Felicitation of state	*Reversal of state*
1.	Happy are the poor *makarioi hoi ptōchoi*	for theirs is the kingdom of heaven. *hoti autōn estin hē basileia tōn ouranōn*
2.	Happy are the mourners *makarioi hoi penthountes*	for they shall be comforted. *hoti autoi paraklēthēsontai*
3.	Happy are the hungry *makarioi hoi peinōntes*	for they shall be satisfied. *hoti autoi chortasthēsontai*

Having isolated what seems to be the earliest attainable Q tradition of a series of beatitudes, let us step back for a moment to gain a deeper appreciation of the meaning and function of this series from its background in the OT and intertestamental literature.

2. Beatitudes in the OT and Intertestamental Literature

As a specific form of wisdom-teaching, beatitudes (or "macarisms," from *makarios*, "happy," "fortunate") were known in ancient Egypt, Greece, and Israel. In the OT, beatitudes appear especially in the Psalms (26 times) and wisdom literature (12 times), notably the Book of Proverbs. The biblical beatitude is easily recognized from its opening: it is introduced in Hebrew by the noun *'ašrê* ("happiness") and in Greek by the corresponding adjective *makarios* ("happy"). On the face of it, a beatitude is a cry of admiration, congratulation, and felicitation: "O the happiness of the one who [does such and such]!" The wisdom teacher shows by such descriptions of the happy person what actions or attitudes make for true and lasting happiness in this life.[136] Implicitly the teacher exhorts his students to follow the course of action or kind of life he describes in his beatitude. Hence, while formally descriptive, the beatitude is functionally parenetic: the happiness explicitly described is implicitly held up as a goal to be pursued.

The basic OT beatitude is made up of two major parts: the initial exclamation ("O the happiness of . . . !")[137] and a description of the person who is happy in terms of his actions or attitudes. For instance, the very first verse of Psalm 1 exclaims: "O the happiness of the one who walks not in the counsel of the wicked . . . !" Sometimes the reward or fortunate consequence of such wise action is mentioned in the context, as in v 3 of Psalm 1: "He shall be like a tree planted near streams of water, which produces its fruit in due season and whose leaves do not fade; and all he does prospers." Interestingly, however, the causal link between right action and reward is not regularly made an explicit part of the form of the beatitude (e.g., with a "because" or "for" introducing the reward right after the description of the action). A few cases of such a causal link can be found in the Book of Proverbs, e.g., Prov 3:13: "Happy the person who finds wisdom, and the person who obtains insight, for *(kî)* its gain is better than the gain of silver."[138] An important form-critical point to note is that the Hebrew canon of the OT does not use long series of beatitudes strung together; but the joining of just two beatitudes in a row does occur in Pss 32:1–2; 84:5–6; 119:1–2; 137:8–9; and 144:15.

The beatitude was very much ensconced in the thought-world of OT wisdom, which saw a correlation between human behavior and reward or punishment, all to be experienced in this present life. (For most of the OT, the idea of reward or punishment beyond the grave was simply not on the theological horizon.) This simple, not to say simplistic, view of human life came under increasing challenge after the Babylonian exile, first from the darker, questioning type of wisdom literature found in Job and Qoheleth, and then in the first half of the 2d century B.C. from the fearful persecution during the reign of the Seleucid monarch Antiochus Epiphanes, when faithful Jews were horribly tortured and martyred. It became painfully obvious that the good did not always enjoy happiness in this life; and so wisdom, flowing together with prophecy to form apocalyptic, developed a second type of beatitude. This apocalyptic beatitude kept the nexus between right living and happiness, but projected that happiness into a future beyond this present world.

One example of such an apocalyptic beatitude is found at the end of the Hebrew version of the Book of Daniel.[139] After prophecies concerning persecution, the resurrection of the dead, and the vindication of the faithful, the book closes with a beatitude and a promise: "Happy the one who endures and attains to the one thousand three hundred and thirty-five days [when salvation comes after disaster]. And you [Daniel], go your way and take your rest [i.e., die]. You shall stand [i.e., rise from the dead] to receive your lot [i.e., reward] at the end of the days [i.e., on the last day, the time of final reward and punishment]" (Dan 12:12–13). The wisdom beatitude, congratulating the good person who leads a good life and thus enjoys happiness on this earth, is thus transformed by apocalyptic into both a call to endure the present suffering of this evil world and a promise that consolation awaits the faithful in the next life. The apocalyptic beatitude thus involves a certain contrast, paradox, or reversal: those who suffer in this present world are nevertheless happy even now because they are assured of happiness, vindication, and a reversal of their lot in the next world. The underlying thought-structure is: Happy are the unhappy, for God will make them happy (on the last day). Indeed, this is the formal as well as the theological structure of the Q beatitudes of the Sermon.

The apocalyptic beatitude spread throughout the Jewish apocalyptic writings of the intertestamental period, notably in various parts of the Enoch literature.[140] Even in an eschatology (or a proto-apocalyptic vision) tied more to this world, i.e., even in Jewish eschatological hope centered on a restored Jerusalem and a regathered Israel, the future beatitude of consolation appears. For example, in the great canticle of praise and prophecy toward the end of the Book of Tobit, three beatitudes appear in a row: "O happy are those who love you [the rebuilt Jerusalem], and happy are those who shall rejoice over your peace; and happy are all those who will grieve over all your blows, for they shall rejoice in you and see all your glory forever. My spirit, bless the Lord the great king" (Tob 13:15–16).[141] What is striking here is the development and conjunction of a number of traits present only rarely or not at all in the beatitudes of the Hebrew OT: the joining together of three or more eschatological beatitudes in a series, the paradoxical idea of the happiness of those who grieve, the express mention of the reason for the happiness in a *hoti* ("for") clause indicating a reversal of fortune, and a reference to God as king. All these elements return in the beatitudes that begin Jesus' Sermon on the Mount/Plain.

This stringing together of three or more beatitudes, a phenomenon foreign to the Hebrew canon of the OT, becomes more common in the intertestamental period. We find this concatenation not only in Tobit but also in Ben Sira, Qumran, and the Enoch literature; the phenomenon thus appears both in the more traditional wisdom beatitude and in the more recent apocalyptic beatitude. In the case of Ben Sira, not only does he present us with the occasional two beatitudes joined together (14:1–2); he actually strings together a carefully compiled list of ten beatitudes (25:7–10), although *'ašrê* is not repeated at the beginning of each one (cf. 14:20–27 for a series of eight). At Qumran, the fragment called 4Q525 presents us with four affirmations, each beginning with *'ašrê*. They are preceded by the end of another affirmation whose beginning has not been preserved.[142] It seems probable, however, that this fragmentary affirmation also began with *'ašrê*; it in turn may have been preceded by other beatitudes. Thus we probably have a series of at least five beatitudes, each beginning with the exclamation *'ašrê*. The first four are short, falling into two halves (one positive, one negative), while the last goes on for nine clauses. One is reminded of the eight short beatitudes in Matt 5:3–10 followed by the notably longer one in 5:11–12. The upshot of all this is that in Palestinian Judaism of the 1st century A.D. it would not have been at all strange if Jesus had not only used beatitudes for both eschatological promise and moral parenesis but also strung them together in an artful series. But can we move beyond this general statement? Are there positive reasons for thinking that the core beatitudes we have isolated from the Q tradition actually come from the historical Jesus?

3. The Question of the Authenticity of the Core Beatitudes in Q

That Jesus, as wisdom teacher and eschatological prophet, would have used beatitudes at times in his preaching enjoys antecedent probability. Indeed, since the protocanonical and deuterocanonical OT, the OT pseudepigrapha,

Qumran, NT writers, and later rabbis all used beatitudes, it would be exceedingly strange if Jesus the Jewish teacher proved a solitary exception. As a matter of fact, multiple attestation makes the probability that Jesus uttered beatitudes quite strong. Granted, beatitudes are lacking in Mark's Gospel; but this is not very surprising, since Mark has fewer sayings and less discourse material than any other Gospel and does not emphasize the portrait of Jesus as wisdom teacher. Matthew, Luke, and John all represent Jesus as speaking beatitudes of various sorts. The bulk of such cases stems from Q (e.g., in the Sermon on the Mount/Plain), but they are also found in M (Matt 16:17), L (11:28; 14:14; 23:29), and Johannine tradition (John 13:17). The question is thus not whether Jesus ever spoke beatitudes but whether any particular beatitude in the Gospels can be attributed with fair probability to the historical Jesus.

The question of attribution is especially difficult in the case of beatitudes, since they belong in part to the wisdom tradition, the most "ecumenical" and "international" of the biblical traditions. Beatitudes were used inside and outside Israel for centuries before and after Jesus. How are we to tell whether an individual beatitude was actually spoken by him instead of merely being attributed to him by later Christians? Fortunately, the likelihood of intrusion from without into the Jesus tradition is narrowed somewhat in the case of the beatitudes in the Sermon on the Mount/Plain, since they reflect not general wisdom traditions rife throughout the ancient Near East but rather particular eschatological/apocalyptic hopes that jibe with the eschatological message of Jesus we have already seen. Still, it remains possible that early Jewish-Christian prophets first spoke these beatitudes in the name of the risen Jesus and that secondarily they were put into the mouth of the earthly Jesus. Just how strong is the possibility of such transferred authorship in the case of the beatitudes, especially the three core beatitudes, of the Sermon on the Mount/Plain?

As a matter of fact, the likelihood of such transferred authorship from Christians to Jesus is much slighter than might at first appear. Outside of the Gospels and—significantly—the Book of Revelation, beatitudes are used relatively rarely by NT authors. In the first Christian generation, Paul almost never uses them. In all of the undisputed Pauline Epistles, *makarios* is employed only four times, and only three cases involve beatitudes. Two of these cases are citations from the OT, i.e., LXX Ps 31:1–2 in Rom 4:7–8. While Paul pointedly speaks about and argues from the "happiness" (*makarismos*, vv 6 + 9) extolled in the psalm, his exegesis of the text does not lead him to formulate any beatitude of his own. Indeed, in all of the Pauline Epistles (disputed as well as undisputed), the only time Paul or a Pauline author[143] ever speaks a beatitude is in Rom 14:22, toward the end of a lengthy argument over eating or abstaining from certain foods: "Happy is the one who does not judge [i.e., condemn] himself by what he approves [i.e., by the food he decides to eat]." In both content and form, this is a far cry from the beatitudes of the Sermon.

Turning to the great wisdom document of the NT, the Epistle of James, we rightly expect to find beatitudes there; and we are not wholly disappointed.

The Epistle of James contains two beatitudes.[144] The first is perhaps the closest we come in general form, though not in exact wording and length, to the beatitudes of the Sermon. It is found in Jas 1:12: "Happy the man who endures temptation, for, having become approved, he shall receive the crown of life that he [God] promised to those who love him." We have here the basic idea of endurance of suffering in this life being a source of happiness because *(hoti)* it leads to eternal life. There are, however, many differences. Unlike the beatitudes of the Sermon, the beatitude in Jas 1:12 is much longer and diffuse, with subordinate clauses; after the initial *makarios* it uses the common LXX form "a man who" *(anēr hos* + relative clause)[145] rather than the laconic article + participle or adjective of the core beatitudes of the Sermon; the reception of the reward is expressed by an active verb ("he shall receive")[146] instead of the divine passive verb ("for they shall be satisfied," i.e., by God); and the strong note of the reversal of the precise concrete condition one presently suffers is absent. In a manner unusual in the NT, the *hoti* ("for") clause expressing the reward is followed by a further relative clause ("that he promised to those who love him").

The other beatitude in James (1:25) is likewise diffuse in form and, in its placement of *makarios* toward the end of the sentence, quite unlike most NT beatitudes: "But the one who bends over [to look closely] at the perfect law of freedom and who continues [to do so], becoming not a forgetful hearer but an active doer—this one shall be happy in what he does." In addition to the different and diffuse form, the content is basically sapiential rather than eschatological.[147]

In a curious way, the First Epistle of Peter is a better quarry than James in that it contains two "beatitude-like" statements that echo beatitudes of the Sermon. In 1 Pet 3:14, "but even if you should suffer for the sake of justice, happy [would you be]" is reminiscent of Matt 5:10: "Happy are those who have been persecuted for the sake of justice, for theirs is the kingdom of heaven." As far as the form is concerned, however, 1 Pet 3:14 is not strictly a beatitude in the usual biblical mold: the use of a conditional clause with the optative (lifting the whole condition onto a hypothetical plane), followed by a bare *makarios*, does not fit either the OT or the NT models. The same holds true of 1 Pet 4:14: "If they revile [*oneidizesthe*] you on account of the name of Christ, happy [are you], for [*hoti*] the spirit of glory and of God rests upon you." Here the statement has a *hoti* clause, which however does not speak of a future reward in heaven reversing one's present state. More to the point, the form is again shaped by a conditional clause and a bare *makarios*, contrary to the regular biblical form of a beatitude. Nevertheless, there is a weak echo (in both form and content) of Matt 5:11 || Luke 6:22: "Happy are you when [*hotan*, which is close to a conditional particle] people revile [*oneidisōsin*] you and persecute [you] and say every kind of evil against you for my sake [Luke: for the sake of the Son of Man]." In addition, in the previous verse (4:13), 1 Peter urges those Christians sharing the sufferings of Christ to rejoice (*chairete*) that they may rejoice and be glad on the last day (*charēte agalliōmenoi*). It seems just too much of a coincidence that the Matthean form of the long beatitude on persecution contains the double imperative *chairete kai agalliasthe*. But in which direction does the line of dependence run? All things considered, instead of the two cases in 1 Peter being examples of Christian prophets composing new beatitudes that are then put into the mouth of Jesus, 1 Pet 3:14 and 4:14 seem more like examples of a Christian parenesis that is reworking Jesus' beatitudes from the Sermon for the specific theological purposes of the Epistle.[148] It is telling that in place of "for my sake" or "for the sake of the Son of Man," 1 Pet 4:14 uses "for the name of Christ," which practically means "because you bear the name of Christian" (cf. v 16: "But if [any of you suffers] as a Christian . . .").[149]

So far, the rest of the NT does not support the theory that Jesus' beatitudes in the Sermon were most likely early Christian products. The candidates from the Epistles are few in number and different in form and sometimes in content. But we have not yet examined the largest repository of NT beatitudes outside the Gospels, the Book of Revelation. Just as Revelation speaks of seven churches, seven letters, seven spirits, seven lamp stands, seven stars, seven seals, seven horns, seven eyes, seven trumpets, seven thunders, seven heads, seven diadems, seven angels, seven plagues, seven bowls, seven hills, and seven kings, so—hardly by accident—the book contains exactly seven beatitudes. Not surprisingly, the beatitudes of Revelation are eschatological rather than sapiential in content. One definite surprise is that the majority of them are not placed on the lips of Jesus. In 1:3, the author of the book speaks in his own person an opening beatitude on all who read his work; he addresses another beatitude to his audience in 20:6 (with *hagios* ["holy"] added to *makarios*). As we shall see, the author thinks nothing of suddenly stopping the flow of the narrative or discourse to address a beatitude to his audience, only to return immediately to the flow of his text. At times this tendency creates problems in discerning the precise speaker of some of the beatitudes in Revelation.

Two other beatitudes are spoken by an anonymous heavenly or angelic voice (14:13; 19:9). In three cases the risen Jesus may be the speaker, but not every case is clear. Rev 16:15b is a beatitude immediately preceded by a sudden and unprepared-for "I statement" in 16:15a: "Behold I come as a thief." Although no speaker is identified, these words must be those of Jesus. Yet the larger context immediately before and after "Behold I come as a thief" is third-person narrative by the author. It is thus not entirely clear whether the third-person beatitude in 16:15b is meant to be a statement by Jesus or by the author responding to Jesus: "Happy is the one keeping watch and guarding his garments, in order that he may not walk naked and see his shame."

Rev 22:6–7 is also unclear. Robert H. Mounce remarks: "This section [22:6–21] consists of a number of rather loosely related utterances which are difficult to assign with any certainty to specific speakers."[150] The passage begins with a vague "and he said to me," which is used elsewhere in Revelation of an anonymous heavenly voice or angel.[151] The content of v 6 also seems to point in that direction. But v 7a states: "And behold I come quickly," words apparently spoken by the risen Jesus, although J. P. M. Sweet thinks it more likely that the words are spoken by the interpreting angel in Jesus' name.[152] In v 7b there follows a beatitude: "Happy the one who keeps the words of the prophecy of this book," which echoes by way of inclusion the initial beatitude written by the author at the beginning of the book (1:3). Compounding the confusion, the author continues in 22:8–9: "And I, John, am the one who hears and sees these things. And when I heard and saw, I fell down to adore before the feet of the angel who showed me these things. And he [the angel] says to me. . . ." Hence whether the beatitude in 22:7a is to be understood as spoken by Jesus, the author, or the angel remains uncertain.

The confusion continues in 22:9–16. In vv 9–11 the angel is speaking. Then, without any indication of a change of speaker, the text states: "Behold I come quickly. . . . I am the Alpha and the Omega . . . ," where obviously Jesus is the speaker. Verses 14–15 switch to a beatitude and a curse-like statement in the third-person, and v 16 resumes with the first-person speech of Jesus: "I, Jesus, sent my angel. . . ." Hence, of all the examples, 22:14, surrounded as it is by the first-person utterances of Jesus, is the most likely candidate for a beatitude put into the mouth of Jesus by the author of Revelation. Indeed, within the whole of the NT, it is perhaps the only clear case of Jesus' being represented as speaking a beatitude outside the Gospels. At the very least, then, we can say that the Book of Revelation did not engage in massive attribution of the author's beatitudes to the risen Jesus. That is a fortiori true of the rest of the NT outside the Gospels.

If we now turn to the *literary form* of the beatitudes in the Book of Revelation, we notice another significant point. Nowhere in Revelation do we have the tight series of three or more beatitudes, each a laconic affirmation that the miserable are happy because God will reverse their lot on the last day; yet this is precisely what we find in the core beatitudes of the Q Sermon. Moreover, in no case in Revelation is a reward explicitly and immediately attached to the beatitude by a *hoti* clause. Indeed—most extraordinarily for the NT— sometimes a purpose clause introduced by *hina* is added instead (so Rev 16:15; 22:14).

To sum up: despite the great continuity of the use of beatitudes in the Hebrew OT, the apocrypha, the pseudepigrapha, Qumran, and the NT, there is a certain amount of discontinuity between most Jewish and NT beatitudes composed up until the end of the 1st century A.D. on the one hand and the core of the beatitudes from the Q Sermon on the other. A glance at the form and content of the three core beatitudes in their primitive Q form makes this clear:

1. Initial felicitation: *makarios* is always put first.
2. The designation of the sufferers: only the definite article + an adjective or a participle.
3. The eschatological reason for happiness: the *hoti* clause introduces the promise of future salvation by God, described in the second and third beati-

tudes by a future passive indicative that is a divine passive (i.e., God is the unmentioned agent).

All too often the rarity of this precise form of NT beatitude is not noted. In no other case in the whole of the NT do we have (1) a chain of at least three beatitudes, (2) all expressed in a remarkably terse manner, (3) using the precise form of (a) an initial *makarios*, (b) a suffering group designated simply by the definite article + adjective or participle, and (c) the reason for their happiness expressed with a *hoti* clause promising the reversal of their present misery by some eschatological gift or action of God. One should ponder well the fact that (1) most of the NT outside of the Gospels is remarkably bare of beatitudes; (2) such beatitudes as do exist outside the Gospels in the NT do not adhere to the form and concatenation of the core beatitudes of the Q Sermon; (3) only once in the rest of the NT (Rev 22:14) do we find a clear example of a beatitude being put on the lips of (the risen) Jesus; (4) and in this one case the form (long purpose clause with *hina* instead of a terse causal clause with *hoti*) and the content (virtuous action of the faithful with a view to what the faithful will be able to do on the last day) are strikingly different from the core beatitudes. In light of all this, I think that one can forge a good argument from discontinuity for ascribing the core beatitudes of the Q Sermon to Jesus himself rather than to early Christians.

One can also appeal to the criterion of coherence. As we have already seen in this chapter, Jesus sums up all eschatological good, all that is to come and to be hoped for, in terms of the kingdom of God. It is not for nothing that "thy kingdom come" is the key petition of the Lord's Prayer (Matt 6:10 ‖ Luke 11:2). The coming of the kingdom brings the comfort that will reverse the present sorrow of mourners and the heavenly banquet that will feed the famished to the full. This idea of reversal at the eschatological banquet, the reversal of the lot of the sorrowing with eschatological joy and comfort, is reflected in Jesus' own self-comfort in Mark 14:25, when he consoles himself, as he faces death, with the prospect of the reversal of his fate and his vindication at the heavenly banquet in the kingdom. The idea of reversal, of the outsiders becoming the insiders and vice versa, is also voiced in the promise that many Gentiles would be included at the final banquet, while Jesus' opponents in Israel would be excluded (Matt 8:11–12 ‖ Luke 13:28–29). Thus the core beatitudes of the Q Sermon fit perfectly with other sayings on the kingdom of God already judged authentic in this chapter. If the unhappy are paradoxically happy, it is precisely because of the imminence of the kingdom of God, because God is about to seize his rightful rule over his rebellious creation and people and set things right. The beatitudes make no sense without, indeed demand as their proper context, Jesus' proclamation of the imminent coming of the kingdom of God.[153] Furthermore, as in so much of Jesus' proclamation of the kingdom, there is no explicit christology. However much his importance may be implied by his function, the messenger effaces himself in favor of his message.[154]

In addition, if we may anticipate what we shall see in later chapters and note how it coheres with the core beatitudes: Jesus proclaimed the loving forgiveness of God the Father, a prodigal father who freely bestows his forgiveness on sinners who have no strict claim on God's mercy (see, e.g., the parables of the prodigal son, the lost coin, the lost sheep, the unmerciful servant, the great supper, the two debtors, the rich man and Lazarus, and the Pharisee and the publican).[155] It is God alone who acts in the end time to establish his kingdom of justice and love; humans can only wait for it (see, e.g., the parable of the seed growing by itself and probably the original sense of the parable of the sower). This emphasis on the gratuitous nature of God's eschatological saving action, this emphasis on the fact that God himself is the sole sufficient reason for his saving action, which humans need and can receive but cannot deserve, demand, or force, jibes well with the core beatitudes. Unlike the M beatitudes, which focus on good people doing good things and receiving corresponding good from God, the core beatitudes of the Q Sermon focus on people who are not explicitly said to be good or virtuous, but simply in need: the poor, the mourners, and the hungry in Israel. God helps them not because they deserve his help but because they desperately need it and no one else can or will supply it.

In the background of these beatitudes stands the whole OT picture of God as the truly just king of the covenant community of Israel, the king who does what Israel's human kings often failed to do: defend widows and orphans, secure the rights of the oppressed, and in general see justice done (so, e.g., Ps 146:5–10).[156] It is not by accident that the first of the core beatitudes has as its promise the kingdom of God. What human kings have not done and apparently will never do in Israel, God the king will do on the last day. (This, by the way, is why one should not play off a "purely" socioeconomic sense of "the poor" in the beatitudes against a "purely" religious sense; given the OT background in the Prophets and Psalms, the first sense implies the second.)[157] The core beatitudes indeed declare a revolution, but it is a revolution wrought by God alone as this present world comes to an end.

We begin to see why Jesus was not interested in and did not issue pronouncements about concrete social and political reforms, either for the world in general or for Israel in particular. He was not proclaiming the reform of the world; he was proclaiming the end of the world. Hence there is an important difference in emphasis between Jesus and some of the great OT prophets (e.g., Amos, Hosea, Isaiah, and Jeremiah). The latter, while prophesying judgment and salvation in the future, were also passionately concerned about particular social and political evils of their day. To take but a few examples: Amos denounces the cruel treatment of prisoners of war (Amos 1:3–2:3) and selling the poor into slavery to pay a paltry debt (2:6–7).[158] Hosea pronounces judgment on the dynasty of the Israelite King Jehu for Jehu's massacre of the previous royal house of Omri (Hos 1:4).[159] The Books of Isaiah and Jeremiah are replete with concrete commands and warnings that the prophets give to the kings and officials of Judah, even on particular matters of statecraft and international diplomacy (see, e.g., Isa 7:1–16; chaps. 36–39; Jer 21:1–10; chaps. 27–29; 34–

44). One searches in vain for correspondingly explicit pronouncements of Jesus on the burning social ills and political policies of his day: e.g., slavery, Roman rule in Judea, or unjust economic practices oppressing the poor in the face of inflation. Direct excoriation of economic exploitation, so prominent in certain OT prophets, is largely absent from Jesus' words and can be read into them only by contorted exegesis. The reason for this disconcerting silence is simple: Jesus was an eschatological prophet tinged with apocalyptic in a sense that at least some of the OT prophets were not. The definitive arrival of God's kingly rule was imminent; calls for social and political reform, launched—and often botched—by human beings, were thus beside the point.

Besides the criteria of discontinuity and coherence, one might construct a limited sort of argument from multiple attestation—but only with regard to the *content* of some of the beatitudes of the Sermon, not their *form*. As we have seen, 1 Pet 3:14 and 4:14 seem to echo the short and long beatitudes on persecution respectively. M. Eugene Boring, who has explored the application of the criteria of authenticity to the beatitudes at great length, judges that the two texts from 1 Peter may indeed be independent reflections of pre-Gospel tradition.[160] Granted, the two examples in 1 Peter are not attributed to Jesus, but such weaving of Jesus-tradition into the seamless garment of Christian parenesis—without explicit attribution—seems to be the usual style of NT Epistles, and indeed of later Christian literature like the *Didache* and the *Shepherd of Hermas*.[161] The few references that Paul makes to Jesus as the source of certain sayings are the exceptions that prove the rule.

In my view, the two texts from 1 Peter are unfortunately the only solid case of multiple (and independent) attestation we have for the beatitudes. Boring is most likely correct that the echo of the beatitudes in Polycarp's Letter to the Philippians (*Phil.* 2:3) is not independent of Matthew and Luke.[162] After citing a number of examples of "what the Lord said when he taught"—various short logia from the Gospels of Matthew and Luke—Polycarp concludes by quoting: "Happy are the poor, and they who are persecuted for the sake of justice, for theirs is the kingdom of God." One can readily see here the conflation of the canonical Gospels that was already under way in the 2d century. "Happy are the poor, for theirs is the kingdom of God" is the Lucan form of the first beatitude, except that Matthew's use of the third person has been imported into the Lucan text. This Matthean bent is quite understandable since right in the middle of the first Lucan beatitude Polycarp implants the eighth Matthean beatitude, the short one on persecution, which ends with the Matthean "for *theirs* is the kingdom of heaven."[163] Polycarp must therefore drop out of consideration as an independent witness to Jesus' beatitudes.

When he comes to the Coptic *Gospel of Thomas*, specifically the beatitudes in sayings 54, 68, 69a, and 69b, Boring leaves open the question of the dependence of the *Gospel of Thomas* on the Synoptics.[164] I think something more definite can be said on the issue. As I have argued at length in Chapter 5 of *A Marginal Jew*, the Synoptic-like sayings in the *Gospel of Thomas* are most likely dependent, directly or indirectly, on the canonical Gospels. I think my position is borne out by the four sayings in question: "Jesus said, 'Happy[165] are the poor, for yours [plural] is the kingdom of heaven [plural]' " (saying 54); "Jesus said, 'Happy are you [plural] whenever they hate you and persecute you. And wherever they have persecuted you, they will find no place' " (saying 68); "Jesus said, 'Happy are those who have been persecuted in their hearts. It is they who have truly come to be acquainted with the Father' " (saying 69a); and "Happy are they who hunger for the belly of the needy to be satisfied" (saying 69b).

I will point out only the most obvious examples of dependence on Matthew and Luke in these four sayings. Saying 54 follows Luke's beatitude on the poor, which is hardly surprising since the *Gospel of Thomas* often bends in a Lucan direction. Yet the growing influence of Matthew's Gospel in the 2d century is clear from the telltale "kingdom of heaven" instead of Luke's "kingdom of God." Within the beatitudes "kingdom of heaven" is clearly Matthean redaction; as Christopher Tuckett has pointed out, this sort of "redactional test" repeatedly confirms the dependence of the *Gospel of Thomas* on the canonical Gospels.[166]

It is also only in Matthew's Gospel—and precisely as a result of Matthew's redactional conflation of Q and M beatitudes—that two beatitudes on persecution are put back-to-back. His redactional pattern is reduplicated in sayings 68 and 69a. This example is all the more remarkable because the *Gospel of Thomas* tends elsewhere to tear apart and scatter blocks of material created by the Synoptics. In addition, saying 68 seems to be a conflation of Matthew and Luke. It reflects the final long beatitude on persecution by starting out: "Happy are you [plural] *whenever* [*hotan*]. . . ." Significantly, the Greek word *hotan*, used by Matthew and Luke only for the last beatitude in their series, is taken over into the Coptic text of *Thomas'* saying 68. The wording of the beatitude seems to be a conflation of Matthew and Luke. Matthew alone in his version of the beatitude uses the Greek word *diōkō* ("persecute"), and this Greek word is taken over into the Coptic text of *Thomas*. On the other hand, Luke alone uses the verb "hate" in this beatitude, and that too appears in *Thomas'* version. Once again, rather than representing an independent stream of Jesus' sayings, the *Gospel of Thomas* fits perfectly into the 2d-century phenomenon of Gospel conflation and harmonization.[167]

One might go on to examine how the future eschatology of Jesus' beatitudes has been typically collapsed by *Thomas* into the present moment and the interior life of the gnostic, especially in saying 69a.[168] But the basic point that the *Gospel of Thomas* cannot be used as an independent source for Jesus' beatitudes is abundantly clear. The two texts from 1 Peter must remain the only sources for a meager argument from multiple attestation. Affirmation of the authenticity of the core beatitudes of the Q Sermon must rest mainly on the criteria of discontinuity and coherence; in my view, the criteria indicate that their authenticity is the more probable opinion.[169]

4. *The Question of the M Beatitudes*

We have finished the most important part of our probe of the beatitudes of the Sermon on the Mount/Plain. The core beatitudes of the Q Sermon confirm what we have seen repeatedly in this chapter: at the heart of Jesus' message is the promise of the definitive coming of God as king, who will bring to an end the present state of things by revealing himself in all his power and glory. In the kingdom that he will establish, he will vindicate those who unjustly suffer in this world: the sorrowing will be comforted, the hungry will be fed to the full at the eschatological banquet (cf. the bread petition in the Lord's Prayer), the debt of sin will be remitted by God just as the saved will forgive one another's debt, and even the unclean Gentiles will be admitted to table fellowship with the patriarchs of Israel—as will Jesus himself, who will be saved out of death and brought into the kingdom he once proclaimed. In short, the core beatitudes cohere with and solidify the case for future eschatology (with some apocalyptic coloration) as an essential part of Jesus' preaching.

But what of the special Matthean beatitudes in Matt 5:3–12, i.e., the beatitudes on the meek, the merciful, the pure of heart, the peacemakers, and those persecuted for justice' sake? Often these special Matthean beatitudes are shunted aside because it is taken for granted that they do not come from Jesus but from early Christian tradition or even Matthew's creative redaction.[170] In addition, at times they are positively denigrated for being moralizing "entrance requirements" for admission into the kingdom.[171] In contrast to the Q beatitudes that promise salvation to the helpless simply because they are helpless, the "call to action" in the special Matthean beatitudes, along with the rewards in the second half of each beatitude that correspond to the virtuous human actions in the first half, seem to some critics suspiciously Pelagian.

Yet the neglect or even disparagement of the special Matthean beatitudes is hardly justified. First of all, it is by no means clear that they are simply the redactional creations of a supposedly moralistic Matthew. In fact, two of the special Matthean beatitudes (no. 4 on the meek and no. 8 on the persecuted) seem strangely redundant if they are viewed as solely Matthew's creations, formed on the model of the Q beatitudes.

(1) The beatitude on the meek seems somewhat redundant because both *ptōchoi* ("poor" in Matt 5:3) and *praeis* ("meek" in 5:5) are ways the LXX translates the key Hebrew adjectives *'ănāwîm* (which carries more of the idea of humble and meek) and *'ăniyyîm* (which carries more of the idea of afflicted and oppressed).[172] These two beatitudes in Matt 5:3 + 5 might almost be considered functional equivalents. Not only are *ptōchoi* and *praeis* translation variants for the same Hebrew terms, but also the idea of inheriting "the earth" (i.e., *hā'āreṣ*, the promised land) is a "theological variant" for possessing the kingdom of God.[173] Both conjure up central OT images of the final saving good for which Israel yearns and toward which it tends.

(2) Similarly, the short Matthean beatitude on persecution for justice' sake (5:10) collides awkwardly with the longer Q beatitude on persecution that fol-

lows immediately and ends the whole series (5:11–12). Indeed, so gauche is the succession of the two beatitudes on persecution that it is difficult to imagine the literarily skillful Matthew going out of his way to manufacture a second beatitude on persecution to stand ungainly alongside another that was already disproportionately long. The juxtaposition of the two beatitudes on persecution is much more likely the result of the conflation of two different traditions of beatitudes than of an inept *creatio ex nihilo* by Matthew.

That the intervening special Matthean beatitudes on the merciful, the pure of heart, and the peacemakers may also be M tradition rather than Matthean redaction is suggested by the fact that none of the words in these beatitudes can be labeled uniquely or even specifically Matthean. Indeed, "merciful" (*eleēmōn*) occurs only here in Matthew's Gospel; "peacemaker" (*eirēnopoios*) occurs only here in the whole of the NT and never in the LXX. Some critics point to Matthew's hand in the use of "meek" (*prays*). But of the two other occurrences in Matthew, *prays* in 21:5 is simply part of a citation of Zech 9:9; and Jesus' self-description in 11:29 ("I am meek and humble of heart") is part of a passage that, in view of its un-Matthean vocabulary, is more likely M tradition than Matthean redaction.[174] In brief, there are no strong reasons for attributing the special Matthean beatitudes to Matthew's redaction, while there are some indications of M tradition.[175]

If the M beatitudes do indeed come from a pre-Matthean tradition, a remarkable parallel comes into view. Namely, both the Q beatitudes and the M beatitudes began with a beatitude about the *'ănāwîm* ("poor" or "meek"), listed a number of other beatitudes, and then concluded with a beatitude on persecution. It may be that these Q and M lists represent but two surviving examples of various lists of beatitudes that circulated in the early church and were attributed to Jesus.

Be that as it may, what basically does the existence of a separate M list of beatitudes tell us? At the very least we have multiple attestation not only for Jesus' use of beatitudes but also of his use of chains of beatitudes, à la Ben Sira and Qumran. Interestingly, the M beatitudes reflect the same structure as the short Q beatitudes, as opposed to the long Q beatitude on persecution. In both the Q and the M lists, the beatitude begins with *makarios*, continues with the definite article + an adjective or participle, and concludes with a short *hoti* ("for") clause promising salvation on the last day. Some of the M beatitudes agree with the second and third Q beatitudes in describing this future salvation with a future passive verb expressing obliquely God's action (e.g., "they shall have mercy shown them" = "God will show them mercy"; "they shall be called sons of God" = "God will call them his sons").

Yet other *hoti* clauses, reflecting the M beatitudes' emphasis on human action, describe the final reward in terms of what the disciples will do on the last day ("will inherit the earth," "will see God"). While this is a real difference in the tone of the two sets of beatitudes, the call to human action now and the corresponding reward on the last day cannot be ruled out of court a priori as impossible in the mouth of Jesus. Jesus certainly did enjoin on his followers the energetic and zealous doing of deeds of love and mercy (e.g., the parable of the good Samaritan, the command of love of one's enemies, the various exhortations to be merciful, giving, and forgiving).

Moreover, like the whole of the OT and intertestamental Jewish tradition, he did not shrink from speaking about a reward from God.[176] As a matter of fact, the Greek word for reward (*misthos*) occurs in the sayings of Jesus in all Four Gospels, including Marcan, M, and Johannine traditions. Even apart from a particular word, the reality of God's reward is often held up to the disciples as a motivating force (see, e.g., Matt 6:19–21 par.; 24:45–51 par.; 25:14–30; Mark 10:21,29–30). Indeed, the special tradition of Luke, without using *misthos*, presents Jesus at a meal exhorting his host to invite to his meals only those who cannot pay him back (Luke 14:12–13). Significantly, this teaching is concluded by a beatitude that parallels well the tone of some of the M beatitudes: "Happy (*makarios*) will you be, for (*hoti*) they have no means to repay you; for repayment will be given you [by God, divine passive in the *hoti* clause of a beatitude] at the resurrection of the just" (14:14).[177] Thus, a call to action coupled with the promise of a reward, while characteristic of the M beatitudes of the Sermon on the Mount, appears also with different vocabulary but the same basic form in a beatitude specific to the L tradition. This should warn us against dismissing beatitudes that exhort to virtuous action by using the promise of a final reward as aberrations of Matthew or his church. That this parenetic use of beatitudes, as old as the OT, might cause problems for some strands of Christian theology did not enter the mind of the Jew called Jesus—nor for that matter the minds of the Christians called Matthew and Luke.[178] Hence, neither the call to merciful action nor the promise of a reward from God can automatically brand the M beatitudes as inauthentic. There is no reason to think that Jesus used beatitudes only when he wished to convey the eschatological promise characteristic of the Q beatitudes.

Needless to say, none of these considerations nor all of them together prove that the historical Jesus did speak some or all of the M beatitudes. But if one judges at least some of the M beatitudes to be authentic—and one could certainly mount an argument from their coherence with Jesus' basic exhortations to mercy, love, and forgiveness as well as from the parallel of form and function found in Luke 14:14—they reinforce the basic point seen in the Q beatitudes: Jesus did look forward to definitive future salvation from God. The M beatitudes see this salvation more in terms of God's faithful reward of the faithful members of his covenant people, but the final M beatitude on persecution maintains at least implicitly the tone of eschatological vindication of the unjustly oppressed—and so of eschatological reversal.[179]

E. Did Jesus Give a Deadline for the Kingdom?

So far we have examined four key sayings or blocks of sayings uttered by Jesus: the petition "your kingdom come" in the Lord's Prayer; Jesus' prophecy at the Last Supper that, his approaching death notwithstanding, he would share in the eschatological banquet; Jesus' prophecy that Gentiles would come from the ends of the earth to share the heavenly banquet with the great patriarchs of Israel; and the beatitudes that promise to the poor, the mourners, and the hungry the reversal of their present suffering when the kingdom comes.

Each of these pivotal sayings has been tested by various criteria and judged authentic. Furthermore, taken together they clearly indicate (1) that Jesus expected a future, definitive coming of God to rule as king; (2) that this hope was so central to his message that he bade his disciples make it a central petition of their own prayer; (3) that the coming kingdom would bring about the reversal of present unjust conditions of poverty, sorrow, and hunger; (4) that this final kingdom would bring about an even more astounding reversal: it would include at least some Gentiles, not as conquered slaves but as honored guests who would share the eschatological banquet with the Israelite patriarchs (risen from the dead?); and (5) that, despite the possibility of his impending death, Jesus himself would experience a saving reversal: he would share in the final banquet, symbolized by the prophetic event of the Last Supper. The last two points make it clear that the final kingdom is in some sense transcendent or discontinuous with this present world. Quite apart, therefore, from the tangled and hotly debated problem of the Son of Man sayings, future eschatology, tied to the symbol of a transcendent kingdom of God, is a central part of Jesus' message.

But how close or distant is this future kingdom that is coming? Exegetes commonly and almost blithely use phrases like "imminent, "very soon," or "just around the corner" to describe the kingdom's coming. Yet in the sayings we have examined, as well as in certain other future sayings with a good claim to authenticity, there is a notable absence of phrases that state explicitly that the coming of the kingdom is very imminent. Among the authentic sayings of the historical Jesus, it is difficult to find the equivalent of the express promise of the risen Jesus in the Revelation of John: "Yes, I am coming soon" (Rev 22:20).

Does this mean that the note of imminence has been read into Jesus' message by early Christians and/or by modern exegetes? While that suspicion is not without some basis,[180] there are reasons for holding that Jesus himself thought of the kingdom's coming as imminent. First of all, there is the global observation, urged by such scholars as Ben F. Meyer, that the OT prophets in general prophesied events not in the far-distant future but in the immediate future.[181] Indeed, using insights from the social sciences, Bruce Malina claims that the mentality of the Mediterranean peasant did not easily lend itself to thought about the distant future.[182] More to the point, though, it hardly made sense for Jesus to give up entirely his normal mode of living, to ask some of his disciples to do likewise, to dedicate himself full-time to the proclamation of the kingdom's coming, to call people to a radical reform of their attitudes and lives in light of the kingdom's future arrival, to issue dire warnings about what will happen to those who reject his message, to make the kingdom's coming the object of the terse, concentrated prayer he teaches his disciples, and to find in the kingdom's coming his sole consolation in view of his own impending death, if he did not think that the kingdom would soon arrive. More specifically, his creation of a special inner group of twelve disciples, apparently representing the reconstituted twelve tribes of Israel in the end time, and his demand that this group leave their regular employment and families to follow him constantly in his itinerant ministry also point in the same direction.[183] Surveying the authentic sayings of Jesus, we hear a note of urgency and intense anticipation, a fierce concentration on the theme of the kingdom's coming, which is out of all proportion if Jesus did not imagine the kingdom's coming to be close at hand. Then, too, there is the general argument from historical continuity. John the Baptist proclaimed an imminent-future eschatology tinged with apocalyptic, and the first-generation church did the same, at times moving over into full-blown apocalyptic. That the Jewish Jesus who proceeded from the Baptist movement and from whom the earliest leaders of the first-generation church in turn proceeded did not share the imminent-future eschatology of his Jewish predecessor or Jewish successors is possible, but not on the face of it likely.[184]

To these general considerations further ones may be added, if I may be allowed for a moment to anticipate what we shall see in later chapters. Many of Jesus' parables are parables of growth and/or contrast, presenting a striking comparison between small or unpromising beginnings and huge, overwhelming, and startling outcomes in the future (e.g., the parable of the sower, the parable of the mustard seed, and the parable of the yeast in the lump of dough). While the metaphors of these parables cannot be pressed into allegories, the symbolizing of the final coming of the kingdom as the full growth and/or harvest coming from the initial seed (or as the spread of the yeast throughout the dough) naturally conjures up a relatively near consummation, organically tied to the present, rather than a distant event in a vague future. Allied with these parables are various "parables of crisis" (e.g., the unjust steward, the two men on the way to court), which, as Jeremias stresses, serve as warnings that one must decide in favor of Jesus' message immediately, for any moment may be too late: one may be overtaken by the final cataclysm at any time. Certain of Jesus' prophetic actions may mirror the urgency of these parables and his sense of an imminent denouement of the eschatological drama. If Jesus' triumphal entry into Jerusalem a few days before his death and then, compounding the provocation, his "cleansing of the temple" were both, at least in essence, historical actions, they hardly made sense if Jesus did not feel that the kingdom whose coming he was announcing—and perhaps even setting in motion by his prophetic actions—was not imminent.

Yet how imminent is imminent? Looking at the authentic sayings of Jesus, it is difficult to say. Along with the sense of urgency in view of the proximity of the kingdom, there is a strange vagueness about exactly *when* the kingdom is coming. In this Jesus again resembles John the Baptist. There is a good deal of the eschatology of the OT prophets in both, along with some motifs from Jewish apocalyptic. But unlike a number of apocalyptic works, neither John nor Jesus engages in timetables or speculation about successive periods or ages. Part of the tension involved in Jesus' warnings to be ever watching and waiting arises from the fact that the kingdom could come at any time soon, but no particular time is designated.

Some scholars might object at this point that there are a few sayings of Jesus, sayings with a good claim to authenticity, that do set at least a general time limit to the kingdom's coming. Matt 10:23, Mark 13:30, and Mark 9:1 are the texts most often brought forward to support this view.[185] While at first glance the evidence looks strong, I think that further investigation makes it likely that all three sayings derive not from Jesus but from the early church and reflect the latter's preoccupations.

(1) Matt 10:23, which occurs only in Matthew's Gospel, is part of the large and multifaceted "missionary discourse" that makes up chap. 10 of the Gospel. Although the discourse purports to be Jesus' instructions to the twelve apostles as he sends them on a short, limited mission to Israelites in the holy land (10:1–2, 5–6; 11:1), the sermon—like all the large sermons in Matthew—is actually a composite of various sources and sayings (Mark, Q, and M), some sayings wandering far from the supposed setting and purpose of the missionary discourse.[186] The directions proper to the missionary discourse are found mostly in 10:5–16. With 10:17–25 we pass to more general warnings to disciples about persecution to come from both Jews and Gentiles. The disciples will be delivered over to local Jewish sanhedrins and scourged in the synagogues (v 17); they will be brought before governors and kings for the sake of Jesus (v 18). Indeed, families will be rent asunder by betrayal as brother hands over brother to death (v 21). The disciples will be hated by all because of the name of Jesus, but the one who endures to the end will be saved (v 22). Needless to say, such a detailed scenario about the disciples' being involved in legal procedures before Jewish courts and before the tribunals of pagan governors and kings, to say nothing of suffering the death penalty for acknowledging one's allegiance to Jesus, reflects the time of the early church, not the time of the historical Jesus. To be sure, I do not reject in principle the idea that Jesus the eschatological prophet may have spoken prophecies about the fate of his disciples. But the detailed scenario of a far-flung mission that is given here, reflecting as it does the type of events seen in the Epistles of Paul and the Acts of the Apostles (e.g., 2 Cor 11:23–27; Acts 16:20–24; 18:12–17), makes it likely that we are hearing not the words of the historical Jesus but the words of Christian prophets of the early church, speaking consolation, direction, and warning to Christians in the name of Jesus. Significantly, a good deal of this material in Matt 10:17–25 is borrowed by Matthew not from Mark's short missionary discourse (Mark 6:7–11) but rather from Mark's longer eschatological discourse (Mark 13:5–37), Matthew wishing to depict the mission of the post-Easter church as part of the eschatological drama.

It is right after these apocalyptically colored predictions about the persecution experienced by the first-generation Christian church that Matt 10:23 occurs: "When they persecute you in one city, flee to the next. For amen I say to you, you shall not have finished [going through] the cities of Israel until [or: before] the Son of Man comes."[187] Both the immediately preceding context and the content of the logion itself argue in favor of its being a product of some Christian prophet in the first Christian generation.[188] The setting presupposed by the saying is not the very brief, programmatic mission of the twelve during the ministry of the historical Jesus, but a thoroughgoing mission to each and every town (*poleis*, "cities" in the Greek, actually signifying "towns" of any size) in Israel—presumably all of the Jewish-inhabited towns of both Galilee and Judea. The Christian missionaries were to meet fierce persecution in some of these towns, and the question would naturally arise whether one's duty was to stay and risk martyrdom or to flee to another, perhaps more hospitable town, where one might be able to succeed in one's task.[189] In reply, some Christian prophet, speaking in the name of Jesus, assured the missionaries that they would not even have time to exhaust all the towns to be evangelized in Israel before the Son of Man would come in glory to bring the present age to its end. Hence the advice of the prophet was to flee the hostile town, since there would always be more than a sufficient number of Israelite towns in which to do one's work up until the (obviously imminent) coming of Jesus the Son of Man. As Martin Künzi shows in his survey of the history of the interpretation of Matt 10:23, "until the Son of Man comes" can refer only to the parousia (which is thus placed within the life span of the missionaries addressed). To suggest any other interpretation for "until the Son of Man comes" is to go against the united witness of the whole Synoptic tradition.[190]

The natural conclusion from all this is that the setting presupposed by the saying is the first Christian generation. There was no thoroughgoing mission by Jesus' disciples to all the towns of Israel during his public ministry, and there certainly was no fierce, widespread, and possibly lethal persecution of Jesus' disciples by their fellow Israelites prior to Jesus' death.[191] On the other hand, the disruption in Palestine caused by the First Jewish War (A.D. 66–70), the destruction of Jerusalem, and the reorganization of social and political life after the war seem to have spelled an end to any organized, wide-ranging mission of Jewish Christians to their fellow Jews in the holy land. Hence the original and originating setting of the prophetic logion in Matt 10:23 was most likely the first Christian generation in Palestine, as the Jewish-Christian missionaries pondered strategy in the light of the persecution they had experienced from their Jewish brethren. The logion does set a time limit for the final coming of the *kingdom* (translated, quite naturally for Christians, into the coming of the *Son of Man*). But it is a time limit set by Christian prophets as consolation and instruction for weary, persecuted Christian missionaries longing for the coming of the kingdom that would signal their deliverance. It has nothing to do with the historical Jesus.[192]

One cannot help but pause at this juncture to ponder parenthetically the fragile nature of our quest for the historical Jesus, especially as mirrored in the interpretation of Matt 10:23. As is well known, Albert Schweitzer uncritically took Matthew 10 to be a reliable report of what the historical Jesus said to his disciples as he sent them out on a short-term Galilean mission, a mission intended to precipitate "the messianic woes," the sufferings preceding the end of this age.[193] Accordingly, Schweitzer interpreted 10:23 to mean that Jesus thought he would not see his disciples again in this present age, since the Son of Man would come before they had completed their Galilean mission. When the disciples instead returned to Jesus without the occurrence of the Son of Man's parousia, Jesus decided that he himself must precipitate the end of the age by going to Jerusalem, confronting the authorities, and taking the messianic woes upon himself, even to the point of death.

As G. R. Beasley-Murray remarks, "It is extraordinary that a man of Schweitzer's intellectual brilliance could not bring himself to accept the simple fact that the discourses of Matthew were constructed by the evangelist from sources available to him."[194] The lack of serious source criticism in Schweitzer's work, to say nothing of form and redaction criticism (which still lay in the future), renders his reconstruction of the eschatological Jesus as uncritical and imaginary as the many theories that lie beneath his own on the scrap heap of history. One may indeed be grateful for the more refined methodologies at our disposal today. At the same time, the monumental blunder of such a great genius as Schweitzer stands as a warning to all who are tempted to be overly confident about the certainty of their own positions on the historical Jesus. Still, having heeded this caution, one must render one's own verdict. Looking at all the evidence and arguments, I think that the most probable conclusion is that Matt 10:23 comes not from Jesus but from the early church.

(2) More problematic and more disputed is the prophecy of Jesus in Mark 9:1: ' And he said to them: 'Amen I say to you that there are some of those standing here who shall not taste death until they see the kingdom of God (having) come in power.' "[195] As in the case of Matt 10:23, the immediately preceding context seems to be an artificial and composite one.[196] After Peter makes something of a "half-way" breakthrough to the truth of the messianic secret by proclaiming Jesus to be the Messiah (Mark 8:29), Jesus orders silence about his messiahship and speaks the first of the three great predictions of the passion of the Son of Man (8:31). Peter rebels against the necessity of the cross, and Jesus in return sternly rebukes him by calling him "Satan" (8:32–33). In 8:34, Jesus summons both the crowd and his disciples and inculcates the necessity of any would-be disciple accepting the cross in his or her own life. Here begins a string of originally discrete sayings that stress that the disciple must take up his or her cross and follow Jesus (8:34), must lose his or her life to find it (8:35), must realize that there is no profit in gaining the whole world and losing one's real life (8:36–37), and must be warned that the person who disowns Jesus the Son of Man before an earthly tribunal will be disowned by him before the heavenly tribunal on the last day, "when he [the Son of Man] *comes* in the glory of his Father with the holy angels" (8:38).[197]

It is perhaps the general theme of the judgment on the last day plus the specific motif of its glorious and powerful coming that occasions the addition of Mark 9:1 as the last in the series of sayings on present suffering and future vindication (or punishment). As 8:38 connects the powerful coming with the negative theme of damnation, so 9:1 antithetically connects it with the positive hope of seeing (i.e., experiencing or enjoying) the full reality of God's kingdom. Still, even in Mark's final composition of his Gospel, 9:1 stands somewhat isolated.[198] Unlike the preceding sayings in 8:35–38 it receives its own separate introduction: "And he said to them. . . ."[199] Immediately following 9:1 is a formal and precise temporal introduction to the distinct narrative of the transfiguration: "And after six days Jesus takes Peter and James and John. . . ." All this suggests that originally 9:1 circulated as an isolated logion without a larger interpretive context. Either Mark or a pre-Marcan collector of sayings gave 9:1 its present location at the end of a string of logia on the general theme of present suffering leading to future vindication.

Most probably it was Mark himself who, writing about A.D. 70, devised a way of reinterpreting and thus preserving the promise of 9:1 at a time when the remnant of the first Christian generation was passing away without the prophecy being fulfilled.[200] Mark most likely intended his readers to see the prophecy fulfilled, at least partially, in the transfiguration story. Peter, James, and John fit perfectly the designation of "some of those standing here" (i.e., the crowd plus "his disciples" in 8:34). Obviously they do not *die* ("taste death") before they *see* ("there appeared to them," 9:4) the powerful coming of the kingdom in the transfiguration of Jesus as the *Son* of Man ("this is my son," 9:7). With the transformation of Jesus into a being of light and the appearance of Elijah with Moses, the whole scene is suffused with heavenly mystery and eschatological glory. Thus Mark can solve the problem of the non-fulfillment of 9:1 by placing it just before the transfiguration, which is made into its (at least partial) fulfillment.

All this is, of course, highly artificial.[201] It hardly makes sense to characterize Peter, James, and John with the solemn designation of those "who will not taste death" when the transfiguration occurs only six days after the prophecy. The natural impression given by a prophecy concerning "some of those standing here who will not taste death until they see the kingdom" is that some of the bystanders will survive until the denouement of the eschatological drama, while others will not. An interval of some years, not days, is suggested.[202] Moreover, given all we have seen about Jesus' hope of a future, definitive coming of the kingdom of God that would include the Gentiles at the heavenly banquet, the fleeting vision of heavenly glory granted to only three disciples who do not understand its significance can scarcely qualify as that "kingdom of God come in power" which was a central theme of Jesus' proclamation.

From all that we have seen already, especially in reference to Matt 10:23, the difficulty of assigning Mark 9:1 to the historical Jesus—the embarrassment of an unfulfilled prophecy notwithstanding[203]—is considerable. Jesus proclaimed the imminent coming of the kingdom of God as the motivating force for radical conversion in the present moment, for any moment might be too late. To proceed to assure his disciples that "some of those standing here" would not die until they saw the kingdom come would have the effect of cutting the ground out from under the urgency and imminent nature of his own proclamation.[204] The natural implication of speaking about the "some" who will survive is to admit that some others, perhaps a good number, of the present generation will die before the kingdom comes.[205] In effect, then, Mark 9:1 moves the arrival of the kingdom somewhere into the second half, if not the end, of the present generation that Jesus addresses. To urge his audience to be prepared at every moment for the kingdom's proximate coming and then to hint that decades might well intervene before its arrival, with some or many of his listeners dying before that date, seems a strange way of motivating prospective disciples. A setting that does make sense of Mark 9:1 would rather be a church of the first generation, probably in Palestine,[206] that has experienced the death of some, perhaps many, of its members and so has come to wonder about Jesus' promise of an imminent coming of the kingdom. In response to this crisis of faith, a Christian prophet within the community utters assurance in the person of Jesus that "some of those standing here" (i.e., at least some Christians of this first-generation community)[207] will not die before they experience the fulfillment of Jesus' promise of the coming kingdom.

To be sure, it is not quite accurate to say that Mark 9:1 is addressing the same problem as Paul in 1 Thess 4:13–18 (what will happen to those Christians who have already died when Jesus comes in glory to take the still-living Christians into the air with him? will the dead be at a disadvantage?)[208] or 1 Cor 15:51–53 (how will those surviving until the parousia attain to the "spiritual body" that the resurrected Christians will have?).[209] Yet behind all three texts there are certain common presuppositions and problems. The time between Jesus' death-resurrection and his longed-for parousia is lengthening into decades, some of those who expected to live to see his coming have died, and those still surviving raise various questions about the fate both of their departed friends and of themselves at the time of the parousia. In each of the three texts, the speaker presupposes that at least some of those whom he addresses will still be living at the parousia: compare Mark's "some of those standing here" with Paul's confident "we the living, the ones left until the parousia of the Lord" (1 Thess 4:15) as well as his "we shall not all sleep" (i.e., "die" in 1 Cor 15:51). In each case the lot of these survivors is compared in some way with the future fate and state of their fellow Christians who have already died.

Moreover, in each case instruction, assurance, and consolation are given in a *prophetic* revelation of the eschatological future. Mark 9:1 clearly speaks in a prophetic style typical of the words of Jesus: the initial prophetic assurance ("Amen I say to you") is followed by an affirmation that a future event will not occur (emphatic double negative *ou mē* with the aorist subjunctive: "shall not taste death") until (*heōs an*) the kingdom of God (or alternately, the glorified Jesus/Son of Man) comes. We have already encountered this prophetic style in our study of Mark 14:25. Both Pauline passages also carry traits of Christian prophetic revelation. Paul introduces his instruction in 1 Thess 4:15 with a solemn affirmation: "For this we say to you in a word of the Lord." This "word of the Lord" that explains in detail the order of precedence when believers dead and alive are caught up into the air to meet the Lord Jesus at the parousia does not resemble any authentic saying of Jesus concerning the last day. "We say to you in the word of the Lord" probably identifies a revelation that the risen Lord is thought to have conveyed through the saying of some Christian prophet, possibly though not necessarily Paul himself.[210] Similarly, in 1 Cor 15:51 Paul introduces his instruction on the resurrection in prophetic tones as he conveys a new Christian revelation: "Behold, I tell you a mystery."[211] Accordingly, many exegetes today suggest that Mark 9:1 is likewise the utterance of a first-generation Christian prophet.[212] Not unlike Matt 10:23, it reflects the concerns of first-generation Christians, not those of the historical Jesus.

(3) For some exegetes, the least problematic of Jesus' sayings that set a time limit for the coming of the kingdom is Mark 13:30: "Amen I say to you that this generation shall not pass away until all these things come to pass."[213] Scholars like Helmut Merklein feel that they can quickly dismiss this saying since, in their view, it is obviously a redactional creation of Mark, fashioned on the model of Mark 9:1.[214] Actually, whether or not it is created by Mark himself, if Mark 13:30 is secondary to and patterned on Mark 9:1, it is necessarily inauthentic. However, not all admit that the dependence runs in this direction. Some critics have tried instead to show that Mark 9:1 is a secondary formulation patterned on 13:30.[215] In my view, it is not necessary to reach a firm judgment as to which logion is dependent on which to decide that Mark 13:30 most probably does not go back to the historical Jesus. There are a number of reasons for judging 13:30 inauthentic.

To understand these reasons, one must first appreciate the place and function of 13:30 within the remarkable composition that takes up the whole of chap. 13 of Mark's Gospel, namely, the eschatological (or apocalyptic) discourse. The exact stages of the composition of this discourse—a lengthy discourse, given the proportions of Mark's Gospel—are disputed among exegetes.[216] It is not surprising that over his many years of study of Mark 13, the renowned Marcan scholar Rudolf Pesch felt constrained to change his opinion of how Mark 13 was formed.[217] However, whatever one's particular theory, it is hardly debatable that the present form of Mark 13 is composite, made up of various sayings and blocks of sayings whose common eschatological theme helped draw them together over time, with Mark supplying the final form and framework.[218]

The major literary building blocks leading up to 13:30 are clear. After one of Jesus' disciples marvels at the wonderful stones and structures that make up the temple complex, Jesus replies that not one stone of the buildings will be left standing (13:1–2). Then, in a secret revelation on the Mount of Olives, the inner circle of Peter, James, John, and Andrew (harking back by way of inclusion to the call of the first four disciples in 1:16–20) asks Jesus for (1) the *time* when this will take place and (2) the *sign* indicating when all these things are about to be accomplished (13:3–4). Responding to the two questions in reverse (chiastic) order, Jesus begins to describe the various signs—stock apocalyptic motifs such as false teachers, wars, revolts, earthquakes, and famines—that will precede the end. Mark emphasizes that these events are not themselves the end but only "the start of the birthpangs" or messianic woes (13:5–8). The signs that will more directly affect the disciples will be persecution and judicial trials at the hands of both Jewish and Gentile authorities, as well as betrayal by one's own family (this is the section of Mark's eschatological discourse that Matthew inserted into his missionary discourse as the context for Matt 10:23). Indeed, before the end can come, the gospel must first be preached to all the nations (13:9–13).

The more specific signs of tribulation that are then mentioned probably echo conflicts between Jews and the occupying Roman power in Palestine: perhaps first the Emperor Caligula's attempt in A.D. 40 to set up in the Jerusalem temple a statue of himself in the guise of Jupiter (the "abomination of desolation" of v 14?)[219] and then the beginning of the First Jewish War (A.D. 66–70). The tribulation external to the church in this chaotic period will be matched by chaos within as false messiahs and prophets appear (13:14–23). At last the end arrives, accompanied by chaos in the cosmos, as the Son of Man comes on the clouds to gather his elect from the four corners of the earth (13:24–27).

It is at this point that the disciples' first question in 13:4 ("*when* will this happen?") begins to be answered. Just as summer follows quickly after the fig tree produces leaves (13:28),[220] so too, when these signs occur, the Son of Man is near, even at the gates.[221] The question about the time of the end is thus answered by way of the description of the signs of the end: when all the signs Jesus describes ("these things") occur, then the time of the end is at hand.

Verse 30 proceeds to make this time limit more precise. Taking up the phrase "these things" from v 29 (where it clearly refers to all the signs described in 13:5–25), v 30 declares: "Amen I say to you, this generation will not pass away until *all these things* [presumably, both the signs leading up to the coming of the Son of Man, vv 5–25, and the coming itself, vv 26–27)[222] come to pass." Curiously, this fairly precise calendar is then balanced or perhaps canceled out by 13:32–33: "But about that day or hour no one knows, neither the angels in heaven nor the Son, but [only] the Father. Watch out, keep awake; for you do not know when the time is." This ignorance of the time of the end then acts as the basis for a final exhortation to vigilance (including the parable of the master who returns at a time unknown to his servants) in 13:34–37.

This brief overview of chap. 13 highlights a number of relevant points. First, one can appreciate the heterogeneous nature of the various components that make up this multilayered discourse. Indeed, not all the parts of Mark's eschatological discourse can be said to cohere perfectly. The discourse is introduced by Jesus' prediction of the destruction of the Jerusalem temple. That event is obviously the most specific object of the disciples' two questions: when and after what signs? Yet curiously, the destruction of neither the temple nor Jerusalem is explicitly referred to in the body of the discourse that follows. We hear instead of a desolating sacrilege in v 14. The language of "the abomination of desolation" is borrowed from Dan 11:31; 12:11, where it refers to the erecting of an altar and/or image of the pagan god Zeus in the Jerusalem temple in Maccabean times.[223] The more immediate allusion in the Marcan discourse may be to Caligula's attempt to install a statue of himself in the same temple.[224] Be that as it may, the initial prophecy of Jesus in 13:1–2 does not jibe with the prophecy in the body of the discourse. Tension can also be seen in the list of apocalyptic signs leading up to the end, an end which is then set within the lifetime of Jesus' own generation (13:30). This fairly specific time limit is immediately contradicted by affirmations of the unknowability of the time of the Son of Man's coming and hence the need to watch at every moment (13:32–36). There are other tensions within the composition as well: the necessity that the gospel be preached to all the nations before the end can come coheres poorly with the assurance that the end will come before the present generation passes away. Clearly, no more than in Matthew's Sermon on the Mount do we have in Mark's eschatological discourse a single address given by Jesus or even by an early Christian prophet at one time and place. The tree trunk of the eschatological discourse displays the many rings of long, organic growth.

The relevance of all this for the authenticity of Mark 13:30 is clear. First of all, 13:30 is carefully positioned at the conclusion of the list of apocalyptic signs. More specifically, it picks up and expands on "when you see these things occurring" in v 29. When, therefore, 13:30 assures its audience that "this generation will not pass away until *all these things occur*," it is referring back to the whole list of apocalyptic signs,[225] plus the actual coming of the Son of Man. In other words, the meaning and function of 13:30 depend on its position in its present context at the end of the catalog of signs. Hence 13:30 presupposes the composition of the catalog of signs—itself a composite piece that no doubt developed over some time in the early church, reflecting as it does various events of the first Christian decades. In short, 13:30, as the summation and conclusion to the catalog of signs, arose at a later stage in the history of the composition of Mark 13. It was most probably composed precisely for this place in the eschatological discourse, since it makes little sense as a stray, isolated logion. Of its very nature, the saying sets a time limit that in turn demands a larger context. To say that this generation (i.e., the Jewish contemporaries of Jesus)[226] will not pass away "until *all these things* occur" is to prophesy nothing unless there is an immediately preceding context that states what "all these things" are—which is what Mark 13:5–25 does. To suggest that Mark 13:30 once had some other context, now lost, is to engage in speculation about the unknowable in order to avoid the natural conclusion: v 30 was composed to act as the climax of the list of apocalyptic signs, summing up and specifying further the time limit they constitute. Granted the lengthy and complicated composition of Mark 13:5–25, the verse that was composed to summarize and specify this list of signs can hardly be assigned to the historical Jesus.

A second consideration from Mark 13 also argues against the authenticity of v 30. Almost immediately after this verse there occurs a concluding pericope, made up of individual sayings and a short parable, all of which stand in tension to the list of signs in general and v 30 in particular by stressing the unknowability of the time of the end. While this final pericope is itself composite, we have already seen in Chapter 6 (on the criteria of authenticity) that the criterion of embarrassment makes it likely that Mark 13:32 in particular is authentic: "But about that day or hour no one knows, neither the angels in heaven nor the Son, but only the Father." If this verse is authentic, the natural conclusion would be that the contradictory verse, 13:30, is not. It will not do to try to harmonize 13:32 with v 30[227] and the preceding list of signs by claiming that 13:32 simply means that the *exact* date and time of the end (alternately, of the coming of the Son of Man) are not known except to the Father. Verse 32 is actually quite general in its sweep: "But no one knows about [or concerning: *peri*] that day or hour." The ignorance is about the final day in general, not simply about its exact time. When one considers the wide range of Gospel sayings in Mark, Q, M, and L that are attributed to Jesus and that prophesy the events preceding the end, one appreciates how embarrassing Mark 13:32 really is. To deny its authenticity, one would have to suppose that some early Christian prophet went out of his way both to attribute ignorance of the Son of Man's coming to the exalted Son of Man himself[228] and to contradict various prophecies about the end already attributed to the Son of Man. The authenticity of 13:32 seems a much more likely hypothesis, but that in turn connotes the inauthenticity of 13:30.[229]

In sum, the three sayings that are the most promising candidates for logia in which Jesus sets a time limit for the kingdom's arrival (Matt 10:23; Mark 9:1 parr.; Mark 13:30 parr.) all appear, on closer examination, to be creations of the early church.[230] I realize that the skeptical reader might be tempted to remark: "How convenient! This way Jesus was not mistaken about the time of the kingdom's arrival, and one avoids all sorts of uncomfortable theological questions." In reply I would offer the following four points for consideration. First, it is hardly just the hidebound orthodox who paradoxically champion a judgment of inauthenticity in these three cases. As Martin Künzi has shown in his two monographs on the subject,[231] the decision for or against the authenticity of these three sayings cuts across confessional lines as well as the more war-torn boundary between liberals and conservatives. For example, Rudolf Bultmann, who is not usually accused of bending historical criticism to satisfy Christian piety, judges that all three of our texts come from the early church, not from Jesus.[232] Second, the truth of the matter is that I approached the examination of these three sayings with a presumption in favor of the authenticity of Mark 9:1 and/or 13:30. It was only after weighing all the arguments pro and con that I changed my mind. Third, and most importantly, what count in any decision are not the parties and ideologies involved but simply the data and the arguments. These latter have been examined here at length, indeed at much greater length than is often found in books on the historical Jesus that nevertheless serenely pass judgment on the authenticity of the three logia. Finally, if I had decided that the evidence favored a judgment of authenticity, I would have adopted that position. Such a conclusion would not, in my view, create insuperable theological difficulties.

As it is, though, I think that all the data and arguments point toward the conclusion that the three sayings do not come from the historical Jesus. Most likely, they were formulated by Christian prophets as words of consolation, encouragement, and direction to first-generation Christians who were facing both increasing hostility and an unexpectedly lengthy interval between resurrection and parousia. The upshot of our excursus into eschatological deadlines is that, while Jesus proclaimed an imminent, definitive coming of God's kingdom, he did not specify any timetable or time limit for this coming. In his reticence on the subject he is closer to traditional OT prophecy (and to John the Baptist) than to full-blown apocalyptic.

I would suggest that this conclusion carries with it an interesting corollary. In this section we have examined three sayings referring to the eschatological future that have turned out to be creations of first-generation Christianity. They give us a partial view of what early Christians were doing and what they were concerned about when they fashioned such logia. What we see in the case of these three sayings is not Christians inventing future eschatology out of whole cloth and imposing it upon an uneschatological Jesus. Rather, faced with the given of Jesus' proclamation of an eschatological kingdom coming in the near future, the first-generation Christians are rather producing sayings that seek to adjust Jesus' imminent eschatology to their own lived experience and resulting problems. What we saw in our first three sections is thus confirmed: it is the historical Jesus who is the origin of the imminent-future eschatology in the Synoptics. The early church soon found itself pressed to come to terms with the problems occasioned by that eschatology as the years (and deaths of Christians) multiplied. Imminent-future eschatology has its origins in Jesus; attempts to set time limits for that eschatology have their origin in the early church.

III. CONCLUSION

In Chapter 14 we determined that the symbol "kingdom of God" formed a central part of Jesus' preaching. We then explored the significance of this tensive symbol of God's powerful rule over his creation and his people throughout the protocanonical and deuterocanonical OT, the pseudepigrapha, and Qumran. We noted that, especially in the postexilic period and most especially in eschatological and apocalyptic material, the symbol of God's kingly rule increasingly came to be connected with the hope that God would bring to an end the present state of the world and would embark upon his full and definitive rule over his rebellious creation and people. We were therefore faced with the question whether Jesus incorporated into his preaching of God's kingdom this idea of a definitive future act of God establishing his kingly rule, or whether Jesus purposely changed "kingdom of God" into a very different symbol, one that expressed God's timeless or ever-present rule in daily life. This is the question that has been probed at length in Chapter 15.

To make the initial probe as representative as possible, I purposely selected sayings of Jesus on the kingdom of God that came from different sources (Mark, Q, M, and indirectly L and John) and represented different literary forms: prayer, an Amen-word promising Jesus' ultimate vindication beyond death, an eschatological prophecy about the Gentiles' participation in the heavenly banquet, and various kinds of beatitudes. In each case the material chosen contained pivotal statements of Jesus that were of major theological import: the Lord's Prayer, a prophecy of Jesus at the Last Supper, Jesus' prediction that some Gentiles would share in the final banquet while some Israelites would be excluded, and Jesus' use of the hallowed form of the beatitude to convey his promise of eschatological comfort to his suffering followers. Across all these strands and forms of the Jesus tradition one point was constantly confirmed: Jesus did understand the central symbol of the kingdom of God in terms of the definitive coming of God in the near future to bring the present state of things to an end and to establish his full and unimpeded rule over the world in general and Israel in particular. Although the urgent tone of Jesus' message emphasized the imminence of the kingdom's arrival, Jesus, unlike much apocalyptic literature and like his master John the Baptist, did not set any timetable for the kingdom's appearance. The three major examples of sayings that vaguely approach a timetable (Matt 10:23; Mark 9:1 parr.; Mark 13:30 parr.) have been judged products of a first-generation Christianity that grew increasingly concerned about the delay of the parousia, the fate of those Christians who had already died, and the hope of those Christians who were still alive.

The four examples of kingdom-sayings we have examined in this chapter can hardly yield a complete sketch of how Jesus pictured this future kingdom, but at least some points are clear. The eschatological kingdom Jesus proclaimed, which was to be the object of intense expectation and prayer on the part of Jesus' disciples (Matt 6:10 par.), would mean the reversal of all unjust oppression and suffering, the bestowal of the reward promised to faithful Israelites (the beatitudes), and the joyful participation of believers (and even of some Gentiles!) in the heavenly banquet with Israel's patriarchs (Matt 8:11–12 par. and the bread-petition of the Lord's Prayer). That the banquet would be shared with Abraham, Isaac, and Jacob implies the transcendence of death itself, a transcendence that becomes personal in Mark 14:25 parr., when Jesus prophesies that God will save him out of death and seat him at the final banquet. The symbol of the banquet is "unpacked" with various images of consolation, the satisfaction of hunger, the inheritance of the land, the vision of

God, the bestowal of mercy—as well as with other metaphors meant to suggest and evoke what cannot properly be put into words: the fullness of salvation wrought by God beyond this present world. From all that we have seen, it is clear that this future, transcendent salvation was an essential part of Jesus' proclamation of the kingdom. Any reconstruction of the historical Jesus that does not do full justice to this eschatological future must be dismissed as hopelessly inadequate.

A number of corollaries flow from the basic insight we have gained in this chapter. First, by the criterion of coherence, those Synoptic sayings of Jesus which do not show traces of early Christian concerns or the redactional theology of the evangelists but which do speak of a future salvation beyond this present world have a good chance of being authentic, at least in their substance—all the more so if they use the key symbol of "kingdom of God."

Second, the global question of whether Jesus spoke of an eschatological future—especially with the symbol "kingdom of God"—must be carefully distinguished from the more specific question of whether he spoke of himself or anyone else as a future-eschatological figure called the Son of Man. We have affirmed the global point while avoiding for the time being and for strategic reasons the second more particular and terribly complicated question. Even if one were to judge all the Son of Man sayings inauthentic, this decision would in no way negate the fundamental insight we have gained in this chapter. Jesus' message of future eschatology and a future kingdom does not rise or fall with Jesus' statements about the Son of Man—a point some critics fail to grasp.[233]

Third, the importance of the eschatological future in Jesus' message of the kingdom cannot help but have an impact on our understanding of his parables of the kingdom. We will turn to them only in a later chapter, but already an approach such as C. H. Dodd's, which tries to collapse the message of the parables of the historical Jesus into a completely realized eschatology, must be viewed with suspicion.[234] If the future-eschatological kingdom of God was central to Jesus' message, one would expect a priori to see this reflected in Jesus' parables of the kingdom, those extended metaphors that suggest what the kingdom is like.

Fourth, even as we examined the key sayings in this chapter for all they could tell us about Jesus' expectations of a future-yet-imminent kingdom, we almost necessarily sensed that not everything in Jesus' message and praxis could be explained simply in terms of the future. The disciples are enjoined even now to address God as their Father, to pray for the coming of his kingdom, and to forgive those indebted to them, that they may likewise be forgiven. Even now they share Jesus' table fellowship—especially his table fellowship and his cup at the Last Supper—as a sign and pledge of sharing the final banquet in the kingdom. Even now the poor, the mourners, and the hungry are paradoxically happy, since they have Jesus' sure promise of the reversal of their lot by God when his imminent kingdom arrives.[235] Thus, even the few kingdom-sayings we have examined in a chapter that is focused on future eschatology already intimate that the present situation of Jesus and his disciples is radically altered, both in the way it is perceived and in the way it is to be lived, by the imminent eschatological future Jesus proclaims, a future impinging on and shaping the present moment. It is therefore natural for us to move from our study of the future kingdom in Jesus' message to the kingdom insofar as it is in some sense already present in his words and deeds. This will be the subject of Chapter 16.

NOTES TO CHAPTER 15

[1] For the general question of the present and yet future kingdom of God in the teaching of both Jesus and the Four Gospels, see the various essays in *Gegenwart und kommendes Reich* (Anton Vögtle Festschrift; SBB; ed. Peter Fiedler and Dieter Zeller; Stuttgart: KBW, 1975).

[2] Their positions are found in their two classic works: C. H. Dodd, *The Parables of the Kingdom* (rev. ed.; London: Collins [Fontana], 1961); and Joachim Jeremias, *The Parables of Jesus* (rev. ed.; London: SCM, 1963). Typical are the opening remarks of each author: "The parables are perhaps the most characteristic element in the teaching of Jesus Christ. . . . Certainly there is no part of the Gospel record which has for the reader a clearer ring of authenticity" (Dodd, *Parables*, 13). "The student of the parables of Jesus . . . may be confident that he stands upon a particularly firm historical foundation" (Jeremias, *Parables*, 11). However, Dodd, with bracing honesty, immediately proceeds to affirm: "But the interpretation of the parables is another matter. Here there is no general agreement." For that reason, I think it wiser to put off a full-scale treatment of the parables until a general framework of Jesus' message and praxis can be established so as to provide a historical context for the interpretation of the parables.

[3] Some sobering remarks about the limitations of using the parables to reconstruct the historical Jesus can be found in Georg Strecker's "The Historical and Theological Problem of the Jesus Question," *Toronto Journal of Theology* 6 (1990) 201–23. On p. 207 Strecker remarks: "Analysis of the parable tradition for the reconstruction of Jesus' preaching has as its premise a Jesus picture which would first have to be established. For that reason, the parables in the Gospels cannot provide the sole basis for investigating Jesus' (historical) preaching."

[4] The rejection of future eschatology in the message of the historical Jesus has been prominent among many participants in the "Jesus Seminar," which has its headquarters in Sonoma, California. See, e.g., Robert W. Funk, Roy W. Hoover, et al., *The Five Gospels. The Search for the Authentic Words of Jesus* (New York: Macmillan, 1993) 3–4. It is intriguing that a scholar like Helmut Koester, who has emphasized so much the importance of the gnostic material from Nag Hammadi, nevertheless thinks this removal of future eschatology from the historical Jesus is unwarranted; see his "Jesus the Victim," *JBL* 111 (1992) 3–15, esp. 14–15. Koester argues that Paul became a Christian only a few years after Jesus' death and that the Christianity to which Paul gave adherence was already proclaiming a future-eschatological message. Indeed, Paul was persecuting this eschatological group before he joined them. As Koester remarks, "That leaves precious little time in which the followers of a noneschatological Jesus could have developed an entirely new eschatological perspective without a precedent in the preaching and actions of Jesus" (p. 14). While Koester's point is well-taken, his own approach employs a freewheeling and undifferentiated use of various terms like "utopian," "apocalyptic," and "eschatological," with such different phenomena as the slave revolt of Spartacus, the imperial propaganda of Caesar Augustus diffused by the poets Horace and Vergil, and the proclamation of Jesus all fitting under a very wide utopian/apocalyptic/eschatological tent.

[5] Needless to say, a number of other sayings concerning the future kingdom might be added to the list. I have tried to restrict the candidates to the logia that have (1) the best claim to authenticity, (2) the clearest reference to the "final fu-

ture" coming of the kingdom on the last day, and (3) a certain theological richness or suggestiveness, to aid us as we try to grasp some implications of Jesus' proclamation of a future kingdom.

No doubt some critics would want to include in our initial list of sayings about the future kingdom some or all of the sayings of Jesus that refer to entering the kingdom of God. Such "entrance-into-the-kingdom sayings" include Mark 9:47 (cf. vv 43 + 45); 10:15 parr. (including perhaps Matt 18:3); Mark 10:23,24,25; Matt 5:10; 7:21; 21:31; 23:13; John 3:5 (cf. v 3). Such a block of material enjoying multiple attestation might seem to be a promising starting point, but there are two difficulties in using these entrance sayings in an initial probe of logia referring to the future kingdom:

(1) Some of the sayings are patently redactional. A prime example is Matt 5:20: "For I say to you that unless your justice exceeds that of the scribes and Pharisees, you shall not enter the kingdom of heaven." As I argue in my *Law and History in Matthew's Gospel* (pp. 116–19), there are many signs that 5:20 is completely redactional: redactional links backwards and forwards with the rest of chap. 5; typically Matthean vocabulary; and position and content that enable 5:20 to function perfectly as both résumé of 5:17–19 and introduction to 5:21–48. There are other cases of entrance sayings that are either redactional or at least secondary in the tradition. For example, according to Schlosser (*Le règne de Dieu*, 2. 549–52), the entrance sayings in Mark 10:23–24 are secondary to the one saying that may go back to Jesus, 10:25: "It is easier for a camel to pass through the eye of a needle than for a rich man to enter the kingdom of God." Schlosser (pp. 451–64) likewise thinks that Matt 21:31b ("Amen I say to you that the toll collectors and the prostitutes are going before you into the kingdom of God") has a good chance of coming from Jesus.

(2) But even if we can locate some entrance sayings that most likely go back to Jesus, there is the further problem of determining whether the kingdom of God referred to is understood to be future, present, or possibly both. The problem is especially pressing when the primitive forms of these sayings are isolated from the larger contexts that give them a more definite meaning. It is significant that Beasley-Murray, while treating the entrance sayings within his chapter on the kingdom as future (*Jesus and the Kingdom of God*, 174–80), nevertheless allows for the possibility of a reference to the present in some of the sayings. That an entrance saying could stand in and be interpreted according to a context of realized eschatology is clear from John 3:5.

The upshot of all this is that, since I am seeking as my starting point sayings of Jesus that have both solid arguments in favor of their authenticity and an unambiguous reference to the final coming of the kingdom on the last day, I think it wiser not to call upon the entrance sayings—though some of them may indeed be authentic. For further treatment of the entrance sayings, see the classic essay by Hans Windisch, "Die Sprüche vom Eingehen in das Reich Gottes," *ZNW* 27 (1928) 163–92.

⁶For convenience' sake, I will use the phrase "the Our Father" for both forms of the prayer, even though strictly it applies only to Matthew's version.

⁷The bibliography on the Our Father is vast, though much is of a devotional or popular nature and so does not interest us here. However, even the scholarly material is daunting; a good beginning can be made with the special bibliographies on the subject: *Vater-unser Bibliographie. Jubiläumsgabe der Stiftung Oratio Dominica* (ed. Monica Dorneich; Freiburg: Herder, 1982); and the supplementary volume, *Vater-*

unser Bibliographie. Neue Folge. Jubiläumsgabe der Stiftung Oratio Dominica (ed. Monica Dorneich; Freiburg: Herder, 1988). For orientation on the major introductory questions, see Paul Fiebig, *Das Vaterunser* (Gütersloh: Bertelsmann, 1927); Ernst Lohmeyer, *Das Vater-Unser* (Göttingen: Vandenhoeck & Ruprecht, 1946) (= *The Lord's Prayer* [London: Collins, 1965]); Karl Georg Kuhn, *Achtzehngebet und Vater-unser und der Reim* (WUNT 1; Tübingen: Mohr [Siebeck], 1950); Henri van den Bussche, *Le "Notre Père"* (Etudes religieuses 747; Brussels/Paris: La pensée catholique/office général du livre, 1960) (= *Understanding the Lord's Prayer* [London: Sheed and Ward, 1963]); Heinz Schürmann, *Das Gebet des Herrn* (3d ed.; Freiburg: Herder, 1965) (= *Praying with Christ* [New York: Herder and Herder, 1964]); idem, *Das Gebet des Herrn als Schlüssel zum Verstehen Jesu* (4th ed.; Freiburg: Herder, 1981); P. Bonnard, J. Dupont, and F. Refoulé, *Notre Père qui es aux cieux* (Cahiers de la traduction oecuménique de la Bible 3; Paris: Cerf/Les bergers et les mages, 1968); Jean Carmignac, *Recherches sur le 'Notre Père'* (Paris: Letouzey & Ané, 1969), with extensive bibliography on pp. 469–553; Joachim Jeremias, "Das Vater-Unser im Lichte der neueren Forschung," *Abba. Studien zur Neutestamentlichen Theologie und Zietgeschichte* (Göttingen: Vandenhoeck & Ruprecht, 1966) 152–71 (= "The Lord's Prayer in the Light of Recent Research," *The Prayers of Jesus* [SBT 2/6; Naperville, IL: Allenson, 1967] 82–107); Raymond E. Brown, "The Pater Noster as an Eschatological Prayer," *New Testament Essays* (Garden City, NY: Doubleday [Image], 1968, originally 1965) 275–320; W. Marchel, *Abba, Père! La prière du Christ et des chrétiens* (AnBib 19A; Rome: Biblical Institute, 1971) esp. 179–97; Anton Vögtle, "Der eschatologische Bezug der Wir-Bitten des Vater-unsers," *Jesus und Paulus* (Werner Georg Kümmel Festschrift; Göttingen: Vandenhoeck & Ruprecht, 1975) 344–62; Jakob J. Petuchowski and Michael Brocke (eds.), *The Lord's Prayer and Jewish Liturgy* (New York: Seabury, 1978); James H. Charlesworth et al. (eds.), *The Lord's Prayer and Other Prayer Texts From the Greco-Roman Era* (Valley Forge, PA: Trinity, 1994).

[8] I do not list the version in *Didache* 8:2 since it is either "almost certainly dependent on the Matthean [version]" (so Fitzmyer, *Luke*, 2. 897) or at least derived from the M tradition that lies behind the text in Matthew's Gospel. Either way, it does not represent a separate tradition; cf. Anton Vögtle, "The Lord's Prayer: A Prayer for Jews and Christians?" in Petuchowski and Brocke (eds.), *The Lord's Prayer and Jewish Liturgy*, 112 n. 1.

[9] For authors who hold other opinions about the origins of the divergent forms of the Lord's Prayer (e.g., both are equally echoes of the teaching of Jesus, or Matthew preserves the primitive form), see Schlosser, *Le règne de Dieu*, 1. 247–48. Lohmeyer (*The Lord's Prayer*, 294) waives any attempt to establish a "primitive" form, suggesting instead that "the version of the Lord's Prayer in the First Gospel was in Galilaean dialect, that in the Third in the common West-Aramaic language." This difference is in turn explained by the hypothesis that Matthew's Gospel represents the Galilean tradition of Jesus' ministry, while Luke's Gospel is rooted in the tradition of Jerusalem. These distinctions, as well as Lohmeyer's overall explanation of early Christianity in terms of the poles of Galilee and Jerusalem, have not had a great following recently. The relatively rare view that Matthew preserves the original form of the Our Father is championed by Marchel, *Abba, Père!*, 179–89; his arguments often depend more on his theological presuppositions than on historical-critical reasoning. Even more unusual is the view of Carmignac (*Recherches*, 18–52), who holds that Jesus taught the Matthean form of the Lord's Prayer in Hebrew and that Matthew then enshrined it in his Hebrew

gospel, which was later translated into Greek (cf. Jean Starcky, "La quatrième demande du Pater," *HTR* 64 [1971] 401–9). Such a position flies in the face of most recent theories about the composition of the Synoptic Gospels; it is not surprising that Carmignac's view has not been followed by most scholars (cf. Anton Vögtle, "The Lord's Prayer: A Prayer for Jews and Christians?" 93–117, esp. 93–94. For good brief treatments of tradition and redaction that represent the mainstream of research, see Jeremias, *Theology of the New Testament*, 193–203; and Fitzmyer, *The Gospel According to Luke*, 2. 896–907. As both note, the expansions in Matthew clearly betray the special style of Matthean tradition and/or redaction. "Our" and "who [are] in heaven" are often appended to "Father" by Matthew or his tradition; see 5:16,45; 6:1; 7:11,21; 10:32–33; 12:50; 16:17; 18:10,14,19. The phrase is never used by Luke. Elsewhere in the Gospels "thy will be done" occurs only in the Matthean version of Jesus' prayer in Gethsemane before his arrest (Matt 26:42) and obviously comes from Matthew's redactional hand rewriting the Marcan narrative he has inherited. "But deliver us from the evil one" helps round off and give balance to the prayer's ending. The abrupt, almost harsh "and lead us not into temptation" is the only negative petition in the Our Father; its dark tone called forth, by way of compensation, not only the Matthean addition but also later on the famous doxology ("for thine is the power and the glory forever"), first seen in the *Didache*'s text (8:2). Not by accident, the three additional Matthean clauses occur at the end of the address, the end of the "you petitions," and the end of the "we petitions"—exactly at the locations where additions could be most easily inserted into a tightly constructed oral unit. While it is clear why Matthew or his tradition would desire to insert these phrases, there is no reason why Luke would have deleted them if they had already stood in the venerable prayer he had inherited.

Luke's modification of the wording is both theological and stylistic. The substitution of the present imperative in the first "we petition" (*didou*, "keep giving," as opposed to Matthew's aorist *dos*) blatantly breaks with the string of punctiliar aorist imperatives that make up the body of the prayer, even in his own version. The durative or iterative present imperative fits the pastoral concerns of Luke, the theologian of salvation history, who knows that the church must settle down for the long haul of life in this present world. This sense of ongoing Christian life in the present age is reinforced by his replacement of "today" with "every day"; similarly, he inserts "every day" into the Synoptic command to take up one's cross (9:23; contrast Mark 8:34 ∥ Matt 16:24). Luke apparently felt that the "debts/debtors" metaphor (Matthew's *opheilēmata* and *opheiletais*) for sins and sinners would not be immediately intelligible to his Greek-speaking audience, which would not ordinarily use "debt" in Greek as a metaphor for sin. Here Luke compromises with his tradition. He substitutes "sins" (*hamartias*) for "debts" in the first half of his petition, while allowing "debtor" (*opheilonti*, a participial form) to remain in the second half. Presumably Luke thought that the straightforward theological word "sin" in the first half would make the metaphor in the second half intelligible. Luke, the theologian of universal salvation and personal forgiveness, both universalizes and personalizes the second half of the petition by specifying "everyone who is indebted to us." The present-tense form of the verb "forgive" in the second half (*aphiomen*) may be Luke's clarification of the difficult aorist tense (*aphēkamen*) seen in Matthew's version, although it might instead be an independent attempt to render an Aramaic perfect tense having a present meaning. In any event, the present tense certainly fits Luke's focus on Christian existence continuing to be lived out in this present world.

[10] A few manuscripts of Luke have alternate readings at this point, but the scattered evidence is hardly sufficient to overturn the vast majority of Lucan manuscripts. The evidence is summarized and evaluated by Bruce M. Metzger, *A Textual Commentary on the Greek New Testament* (New York: United Bible Societies, 1971) 154–56. The reading "Your Holy Spirit come upon us and cleanse us" is found in place of the Lucan petition for the kingdom (with slight variation in the wording) in the 11th-century MS 700 and the 12th-century MS 162. The same basic reading is referred to in quotations by Gregory of Nyssa (4th century) and Maximus of Turin (5th century, perhaps in dependence on Gregory). Earlier, Tertullian seems to know of a petition for the Holy Spirit right after the invocation "Father"; it is followed by the petition for the kingdom. Whether Tertullian is referring to the Lucan form of the Lord's Prayer known to him or to the 2nd-century heretic Marcion is not clear. At any rate, it is possible that at some time in the 2d or 3d century some manuscript(s) had the petition for the Spirit in place of the petition for the hallowing of the name (not the petition for the coming of the kingdom!). Codex Bezae (D) may have a weak echo of this when it has "Hallowed be your name" followed by "Upon us may your kingdom come"; but, as Metzger points out, Bezae's reading is not necessarily a remnant of the petition for the Spirit. Moreover, the reference from Tertullian comes from a work he wrote during his Montanist period, "when he had a special fondness for texts pertaining to the Holy Spirit; in his earlier exposition of the Lord's Prayer he betrays no knowledge of the existence of such a petition" (p. 155). Most likely, the petition for the Spirit comes from the use of the Lord's Prayer in the liturgy, especially at baptism or the laying on of hands. Beyond the very weak attestation in the manuscripts, there is another reason for rejecting the petition for the Spirit as original in Luke. There would be no reason for Christians to replace such a perfectly Christian idea with what would have struck them as a vaguer one about the kingdom. Hence the attempt by Robert Leaney to rehabilitate the petition for the Holy Spirit as original in the text of Luke and perhaps even original in the prayer Jesus taught has not found general acceptance; see his "The Lucan Text of the Lord's Prayer (LK xi 2–4)" *NovT* 1 (1956) 103–11. Erich Grässer (*Das Problem der Parusieverzögerung in den synoptischen Evangelien und in der Apostelgeschichte* [BZNW 22; 2d ed.; Berlin: Töpelmann, 1960] 109–12) leans toward the originality of the petition for the Spirit, but only in Luke's text—and he does not commit himself fully to that position.

[11] The Greek phrase *apo tou ponērou* could be taken as either masculine ("from the evil one" [= Satan]) or neuter ("from evil"). Zerwick notes that the use of the prepositions *apo* and *ek* in the LXX and the NT favors the masculine interpretation; see his *Graecitas Biblica*, 29 (§ 89). This would certainly fit in with the Gospels' presentation of Jesus' ministry and passion as the eschatological struggle with the devil. For further arguments for taking *ponērou* as masculine, see Brown, "The Pater Noster," 317–19. Considerations favoring the neuter are given by Vögtle, "The Lord's Prayer: A Prayer for Jews and Christians?" 101. All this remains academic for us, since we are concerned with the form coming from Jesus, not the additions made by Matthew's tradition or Matthew himself.

[12] Within this hypothetical primitive form, critics point to the "proviso" clause "as we forgive our debtors" as the most likely candidate for being a later addition. To be sure, it alone among the petitions is a subordinate clause conditioning the basic petition and in the process creating a petition noticeably longer than most of the others in this strikingly laconic prayer. Moreover, this proviso clause alone

among the clauses in the Our Father focuses on our action rather than God's. Yet the idea of the necessity of our granting forgiveness to others as a condition for receiving God's (definitive) forgiveness on the last day is not alien to other streams of tradition of Jesus' words; cf. Mark 11:25 and Matt 18:35 (indeed, the whole preceding parable of the unforgiving servant); also Matt 5:23–25 and Luke 6:37 ‖ 7:1–2. The basic teaching is thus attested in Mark, Q, and M, and so cannot easily be dismissed. A fortiori, it cannot be dismissed because it goes against a particular understanding of Christian theology by introducing a proviso or condition into the teaching of God's limitless forgiveness or by making God's action dependent on human actions. It may indeed pose a problem for those studying Christian theology in general or Pauline theology in particular; but Jesus of Nazareth was not formulating Christian theology, and no one told him that he had to conform to it. For an attempt to get around the embarrassment Christian theologians often feel over this proviso, see Jeremias (*New Testament Theology*, 201), who suggests that the sense is "as *herewith* we forgive our debtors." Whether this really solves the theological problem Jeremias sees is questionable. In my opinion, the whole problem is a red herring.

[13] For a list, see Schulz, *Q. Die Spruchquelle der Evangelisten*, 86 n. 208 (continued on p. 87).

[14] Fitzmyer, *The Gospel According to Luke*, 2. 901. A slightly different version is offered by Jeremias, *New Testament Theology*, 196. Some of the differences between the two versions are merely orthographic, while some others result from doubt about the underlying Aramaic word represented in the Greek. This is especially true in the case of the problematic adjective *epiousion*, for which I retain the stock translation "daily." For detailed consideration of the many different ways *epiousion* might be translated, see Fitzmyer, ibid., 2. 900, 904–6.

[15] The vagueness of the Aramaic conjunction *kĕdî* may explain why Matthew's version reads "as we also forgive" while Luke's version reads "for we ourselves also forgive."

[16] Jeremias, *New Testament Theology*, 196. Such an observation is properly made at the end of the process of reconstructing a primitive text, not at its beginning. The strange results produced by making considerations of rhythm, rhyme, and parallelism major criteria for what is the original version of the Lord's Prayer can be seen in Günther Schwarz, "Matthäus VI. 9–13/Lukas XI. 2–4. Emendation und Rückübersetzung," *NTS* 15 (1968–69) 233–47. Schwarz deletes words that are common to Matthew and Luke, keeps a clause present only in Matthew, and inserts a word present in neither to arrive at the perfect pattern of rhythm, rhyme, and parallelism that he has decided the original form of the Lord's Prayer must have exhibited. His article is a remarkable example of the tyranny of arbitrary presuppositions.

[17] Joseph Heinemann ("The Background of Jesus' Prayer in the Jewish Liturgical Tradition," in Petuchowski and Brocke [eds.], *The Lord's Prayer and Jewish Liturgy*, 85) espouses the curious position that the words "Hallowed be thy name, may thy kingdom come" constitute an "expression of praise" preliminary to the petitions proper. This contorted reading should serve as a caution against conforming the Our Father to patterns of rabbinic prayer at any and all costs.

[18] One could question in what sense the Lord's Prayer should be said to belong to the Q material. If Q is defined broadly as whatever Matthew and Luke have in common that is not derived from Mark, obviously the Lord's Prayer is Q material. If, however,

one is thinking more specifically of one written document, one must allow for a number of possibilities. (1) The Lord's Prayer was in the copies of Q known to both Matthew and Luke, and each evangelist faithfully copied the form contained in his copy of the Q document, with at most a few redactional changes. Polag (*Die Christologie der Logienquelle*, 3) considers the presence of the Our Father in Q as "sure" or "very probable." Hoffmann (*Studien zur Theologie der Logienquelle*, 39–40) interprets the prayer within the context of what he discerns to be Q's theology. Schulz, who is one of the few recent Q-critics to devote a good deal of attention to the prayer within the context of Q (*Q. Die Spruchquelle der Evangelisten*, 84–93), thinks that "in the Our Father we have before us the 'prayer-formula' of the oldest Jewish-Christian Q community of Palestine" (p. 87). Perhaps some Q-critics pass over the Our Father in relative silence because they feel unsure about its presence in Q. All this leads us to a consideration of two other possibilities. (2) Some form of the Lord's Prayer was contained in each evangelist's copy of Q; but each evangelist, when he came to write down the Lord's Prayer in his own Gospel, naturally wrote the form of the prayer he regularly recited, however much it may have diverged from the form written in Q. (3) The Lord's Prayer was not contained at all in the Q document; rather, it was known to both Matthew and Luke through independent oral traditions, communicated especially by the liturgical praxis of their local churches. Naturally, some of these possibilities could be combined or nuanced further: e.g., a written version in Q, modified at points by the evangelist because of the liturgical praxis of his church, Q material already conflated with the special M or L material, etc.

[19] On this, see Fitzmyer, *The Gospel According to Luke*, 2. 906. It was long known that *ḥôbāʾ* was used in this way in rabbinic writings. We now have attestation from Qumran. In 4QMess ar 2:17 "sin and debt [= guilt]" are found together: *ḥṭʾh wḥwbtʾ*. For text and commentary, see Joseph A. Fitzmyer, "The Aramaic 'Elect of God' Text from Qumran Cave 4," *Essays on the Semitic Background of the New Testament* (SBLSBS 5; Missoula MT: Scholars, 1974) 127–60. Brown ("The Pater Noster," 309) adds the observation that the Greek verb used for forgiveness is *aphiēmi*, which, with the metaphor of debt, carries the meaning of "remit." This idea of remitting debts "is also more Semitic than Greek, for 'remission' has a religious sense only in the Greek of the LXX, which is under Hebrew influence."

[20] This point will have to be examined more closely later on when the question of Jesus' implicit or explicit claims about himself is taken up. I readily admit that Joachim Jeremias and scholars dependent on him have overplayed the "Abba card" in their treatment of Jesus. However, I think that some recent scholars have unfortunately gone to the opposite extreme in claiming that it cannot be shown—at least as the more probable hypothesis—that Jesus ever used father-language in general or *ʾabbāʾ* in particular. For the moment, I simply note that Fitzmyer (*The Gospel According to Luke*, 2. 898) is one with Jeremias in holding that Jesus' use of *ʾabbāʾ* in his prayer to God was "exclusive to himself and otherwise unknown in pre-Christian Palestinian Jewish tradition." Few scholars' knowledge of Jewish Aramaic at the turn of the era can equal Fitzmyer's. For Jeremias's treatment, see his lengthy essay "Abba" in his collected essays, *Abba*, 15–67 [= "Abba," *The Prayers of Jesus*, 11–65]; more succinctly in his *New Testament Theology*, 61–68.

Critical of the whole "Abba approach" to the historical Jesus is Mary Rose D'Angelo, "*Abba* and 'Father': Imperial Theology and the Jesus Traditions," *JBL* 111 (1992) 611–30. She justly criticizes exaggerated claims about Jesus' use of *ʾabbāʾ* and father-language and about the supposed absence of father-language for God in Judaism around the turn of the era. But in reaction to inflated claims she indulges in some inflated or unfounded claims of her own. To state flatly that "*abba* cannot be shown . . . even to have been used by Jesus" (p. 616) or that "father" as an address to God "may also, but need not, have gone back to the practice of Jesus and his companions" (p. 618) is to go beyond what sober exegesis can establish as probable and to engage in advocacy exegesis instead. If it cannot be established as the more probable hypothesis that Jesus did use father-language of God, I suggest that the criteria of historicity be abandoned along with the quest as a whole. The problem here is that late 20th-century agendas are obscuring sober historical research and exegesis. When one reads (p. 630) that "neither Jesus nor the NT can be shown to have used the word 'father' in a way that constitutes a transhistorical revelation that is unique and will be irreparably lost if twentieth-century theology and practice choose other imagery for God," one realizes that something other than a desire for accurate reconstruction of the historical Jesus has been the driving force of the investigation. If it was wrong for Joachim Jeremias to bend the data for his own theological or philosophical purposes, then it is wrong for more recent exegetes to bend the data for their own purposes, however right and just they may be.

[21] See Schlosser, *Le règne de Dieu*, 1. 261–62 (including his treatment of the apparent exception in Micah 4:8). As Schlosser points out (p. 301 n. 101), the presence of the phrase in the mouth of a Pharisee in Luke 17:20a is only an apparent exception to the rule. Most likely the half-verse is a secondary elaboration created by the redactor. That is to say, the "lead-in" question of the Pharisee, "When does the kingdom of God come?" is most probably a "back-formation" from the originally independent saying of Jesus, "The kingdom of God does not come with observation [i.e., with signs that can be observed]."

[22] The agreement is all the more striking in that otherwise the contexts of Matthew and Luke are so different. Matthew places the Our Father within the Sermon on the Mount, the first great discourse of his Gospel. More specifically, he places it within the triple teaching on the correct way for disciples to give alms, pray, and fast (Matt 6:1–18). Still more specifically, the Our Father forms the middle section of a triple instruction on the proper way to pray: avoidance of lengthy prayers (vv 7–8), the Our Father itself (vv 9–13), and the separate injunction repeating and inculcating the need for forgiving one's fellow human beings if one is to receive the Father's forgiveness (vv 14–15). On the question of pre-Matthean collections behind 6:1–18, see Hans Dieter Betz, "A Jewish-Christian Cultic *Didache* in Matt. 6:1–18: Reflections and Questions on the Problem of the Historical Jesus," *Essays on the Sermon on the Mount* (Philadelphia: Fortress, 1985); Stephenson H. Brooks, *Matthew's Community. The Evidence of His Special Sayings Material* (JSNTSup 16; Sheffield: JSOT, 1987) 78–80. By an interesting coincidence, Luke likewise situates the Lord's Prayer in a larger tripartite pattern: the Lord's Prayer (with biographical introduction, 11:1–4), the parable of the persistent friend (11:5–8), and various sayings on the efficacy of persistent prayer (11:9–13); see Fitzmyer, *Luke*, 2. 896 (though a five-part pattern instead is discerned by Marshall, *The Gospel of Luke*, 454). Granted the great difference in contexts, what stands out amid all the disagreement is that Matthew and Luke agree on presenting the Lord's Prayer as a prayer taught by Jesus to his disciples.

It is sometimes claimed that Luke intends his version of the Lord's Prayer to serve as a set formula, while Matthew (6:9: "pray thus") thinks more of an example or model that disciples can follow as they form their own prayers. This may both overinterpret Matthew's adverb *houtōs* ("thus," which in an ancient Greek manuscript could simply serve as opening quotation marks; so Matt 2:5) and set up a false dichotomy. By consigning their versions to writing, both Matthew and Luke obviously intended to confer a certain fixity on the precise form of the prayer they knew, yet they may well have thought that the Lord's Prayer could also serve as a pattern for other prayers of the disciples' own devising.

[23] The closest example of such a phenomenon would be the "words of institution" at the Last Supper. But these are neither a prayer nor a hymn. Moreover, as a form-critical analysis would indicate, the injunction to the disciples to repeat the words is a later addition to the tradition. Words of the risen Jesus naturally fall outside the scope of our investigation.

[24] Relatively few exegetes deny outright the origin of the Our Father, in some primitive form, from Jesus himself. One author who comes close to that position is Grässer, *Problem*, 95–113. Grässer does leave open the possibility of some form going back to Jesus. But for Grässer even the "you petitions," while future-eschatological, represent a later stage of eschatology that fits the early church better than Jesus. Grässer holds that this is a fortiori true of the "we petitions," which he interprets in terms of everyday needs in the ongoing world. Significantly, Grässer does not attempt a step-by-step reconstruction of a hypothetical Aramaic form; he tends to focus on the Matthean and Lucan versions as they stand in the Gospels. A larger problem is that his treatment of the Our Father seems very much determined by his overarching thesis about the imminent eschatological expectation of Jesus and its rapid transformation in the early church. For an approach to the Our Father that sees it arising from a Jewish-Christian community, see S. van Tilborg, "A Form-Criticism of the Lord's Prayer," *NovT* 14 (1972) 94–105.

[25] As Schlosser (*Le règne de Dieu*, 1. 247–84) emphasizes throughout his treatment, God's glory and God's holiness are often associated in OT and ancient Jewish texts dealing with theophany. The linking of the themes of glory, sanctification, and God's name in a prayer of Jesus is seen in "the high-priestly prayer" of John 17, which has some intriguing verbal and thematic links with the Our Father, especially in its Matthean form. On this, see William O. Walker, Jr., "The Lord's Prayer in Matthew and in John," *NTS* 28 (1982) 237–56—though some of the similarities listed are at best tenuous.

[26] See Lev 22:32; Num 20:12; 27:14; Deut 32:51; Isa 8:13 (text not certain); 29:23.

[27] For the context of salvation, see Num 20:13; Ezek 20:41; 28:25; 36:23; 39:27; for the context of condemnation, see Lev 10:3; Isa 5:16; Ezek 28:22; 38:16, 23. It is significant that in many of these passages the themes of salvation and condemnation are closely intertwined. Note the large representation of passages from Ezekiel and the connection of God's sanctification with the theme of the regathering of a scattered Israel.

[28] The interchangeability of sanctifying God and sanctifying his name is seen also in Isa 29:23.

[29] I take the perfect form of the verb with *waw consecutivum* to have a final sense. In other texts in Ezekiel, the purpose of God's sanctifying of himself is likewise the making of himself known; see Ezek 28:22; 38:16, 23. On this idea, see John W. Wevers, *Ezekiel* (NCB; Grand Rapids: Eerdmans, 1969) 191–92: "The recognition formula ['that they may know that I am Yahweh'] is here the key of the passage. His identity will be recognized by the nations in the act of restoration since he is the actor, the Israelites those acted upon, and the nations the viewers of the action. . . . Yahweh will be recognized throughout the world as the God who acts for his people."

[30] Walther Eichrodt puts it very well in *Ezekiel* (OTL; Philadelphia: Westminster,

1970) 496–97: "If Israel can still possess any sort of hope, it must have as its sole basis the certainty that God's fidelity to his own intrinsic nature (and that is precisely what is ultimately meant by the hallowing of his name) must necessarily lead to his sanctifying and renewing the people whom he has rejected. . . . What is at stake is not an impressive position for Israel, but the justification of God's claim to reveal himself to the world as its God. . . . God's turning to his people is a pure act of grace. . . ."

[31] Eichrodt (*Ezekiel*, 519) says of the whole of chaps. 38–39, which deal with the final battle with Gog: "The overriding objective that determines the whole prophecy is the hallowing of the name of Yahweh before the nations, which is emphasized again and again as a result of the divine judgment now to be executed. This is a theme well known to the prophet Ezekiel, and one about which he has much to say in his oracles to the nations."

[32] These passages may well be additions made when the apocalyptic impulse already present in an earlier form of the Book of Ezekiel had borne fruit in full-blown apocalyptic. Needless to say, Jesus and his contemporaries would have read the Book of Ezekiel without such literary-critical distinctions. For theories of stages of composition, see, e.g., Wevers, *Ezekiel*, 190–91, 198–200; Walther Zimmerli, *Ezekiel 2. A Commentary on the Book of the Prophet Ezekiel. Chapters 25–48* (Hermeneia; Philadelphia: Fortress, 1983) 245–46, 296–302.

For commentary on Ezekiel 36–39, see Wevers, *Ezekiel*, 188–206; Zimmerli, *Ezekiel 2*, 236–324; G. A. Cooke, *The Book of Ezekiel* (ICC; Edinburgh: Clark, 1936) 385–424; Georg Fohrer, *Ezechiel* (HAT 13; Tübingen: Mohr [Siebeck], 1955) 200–218; H. F. Fuhs, *Ezechiel II 25–48* (Die Neue Echter Bibel; Würzburg: Echter, 1988) 200–224; Ronald M. Hals, *Ezekiel* (The Forms of the Old Testament Literature 19; Grand Rapids: Eerdmans, 1989) 254–85.

[33] For textual questions and commentary, see Skehan and Di Lella, *The Wisdom of Ben Sira*, 415, 420–21.

[34] The text is unfortunately fragmentary at this point, but the general sense as well as the allusion to Ezekiel is clear.

[35] For the Aramaic text, see Gustaf Dalman, *Die Worte Jesu* (Leipzig: Hinrichs, 1898) 305. Note the variant reading of the key phrase "may he cause his kingdom to reign" (so MS B): "may his kingdom reign" (so Yemen MSS I and II).

[36] The *Qaddish* is often introduced into the discussion of the Our Father with simply a vague statement that the core of the *Qaddish* is very ancient and probably predates the Lord's Prayer. So, e.g., Jeremias, "The Lord's Prayer in the Light of Recent Research," *The Prayers of Jesus*, 98: "[The two 'you petitions'] recall the *Kaddish*, . . . with which Jesus was no doubt familiar from childhood." Indeed, some authors would make Jesus consciously dependent on the *Qaddish* in his wording of the Our Father. For instance, Perrin claims (without arguing his case or producing detailed evidence) that the *Qaddish* was "in regular use in the Jewish synagogues immediately before the time of Jesus. . . . the prayer of Jesus [i.e., the Our Father] is a deliberate modification of the Kaddish prayer . . . (*Jesus and the Language of the Kingdom*, 28–29). Schlosser considers this kind of claim excessive. His own way of phrasing the matter is more cautious (*Le règne de Dieu*, 1. 254), but he does think that the hypothetical primitive form of the *Qaddish* (which I quote in the text) dates from before A.D. 70, since there is no mention of the destruction of the Jerusalem temple. One should ponder, however, the cautious presentation in the *Encyclopaedia Judaica*, which includes the statement ("Kaddish," *EncJud*, 10. 661): "The *Kaddish* is mentioned as part of the prescribed synagogue daily

prayers for the first time in tractate *Soferim* (c. 6th century C.E.)." Strictly speaking, the *Qaddish* does not seem to have originated as one of the "statutory prayers" in the communal worship of the synagogue but rather as a prayer concluding the public sermon in the "house of study" or "beth midrash" (see Petuchowski and Brocke [eds.], *The Lord's Prayer and Jewish Liturgy*, 59–60). This use of the prayer is attested by at least the 4th century A.D. In his *Prayer in the Talmud* (SJ 9; Berlin/New York: de Gruyter, 1977) 256, Joseph Heinemann judges: "Although our present versions may have later additions, the nucleus: 'Let His great name be blessed . . . ,' and almost certainly also the beginning: 'Magnified and sanctified be His great name . . . may He establish His kingdom,' date from the Tannaitic period." But the tannaitic period does not end until ca. A.D. 200. With great honesty, Heinemann says bluntly in his essay, "The Background of Jesus' Prayer in the Jewish Liturgical Tradition" (Petuchowski and Brocke [eds.], *The Lord's Prayer and Jewish Liturgy*, 81): ". . . the *Kaddish*, in spite of the prominent place which it occupies in the prayers of the synagogue today, did not do so until the end of the Talmudic period in the fifth century C.E.; hence it can hardly be considered an example of 'Jewish norms of prayers' in the first century." In the light of all this, it is not surprising that Fitzmyer (*The Gospel According to Luke*, 2. 901) urges caution when using the *Qaddish* as a parallel to the Our Father. Accordingly, in exegeting the Our Father I do not put as much weight on the *Qaddish* as some other critics do.

[37] It is intriguing to note that in Ezek 38:23, the statement in the Hebrew text is expanded in the LXX by the addition of the verb "glorify" (*endoxazō*): "And I will be magnified and sanctified [MT: *hitqaddištî*; LXX: *hagiasthēsomai*] and glorified [added by the LXX] and known before many nations, and they shall know that I am the Lord." Interestingly, John's Gospel also has an example of God as the subject of the verb "to sanctify" in a prayer of Jesus addressed to the Father, namely, John 17:17 (cf. 10:36): "Sanctify them in the truth."

[38] Since we are dealing with the hypothetical Aramaic form, we cannot appeal to the aorist tense of the two imperative verbs in the Greek text of our Gospels and then proceed to claim that the aorist as opposed to the present tense indicates an eschatological meaning (arising from the punctiliar, "once-and-for-all" nature of the aorist). No such argument can be based on a Semitic imperfect used in a jussive sense. Moreover, even in the Greek version, such an argument from the aorist is shaky at best. Greek prayers regularly used the aorist (the "complexive" aorist) for petitions, though it is true that the present would be used to ask for a lasting favor or for a favor that had to be repeated. For an appeal to the aorist to support an eschatological meaning here, see Brown, "The Our Father," 275–320, esp. 289–93. For the complexive aorist in liturgical prayers, see Zerwick, *Graecitas Biblica*, 85 (§ 255); for the occasional use of the present, see Blass-Debrunner-Rehkopf, *Grammatik des neutestamentlichen Griechisch*, 276 (§ 337, 4).

[39] The one apparent exception is Micah 4:8, where the rule and kingship (*memšālâ* and *mamleket*) of "daughter Jerusalem" are said to "come." In context this seems to refer to the regathering of the scattered remnant and Judah's regaining of its political sovereignty through a future Davidic king. The sense of the nouns here is not "the kingdom of God" or some equivalent thereof. On this see Schlosser, *Le règne de Dieu*, 1. 262.

[40] Schlosser (*Le règne de Dieu*, 1. 256) thinks that "kingdom" does not fit "come" in this context, but that "reign" does. I find neither locution natural.

[41] Schlosser (*Le règne de Dieu*, 1. 261) observes that joining the noun "kingdom" to

the verb "come" appears elsewhere in words of Jesus that have a claim to authenticity: e.g., Mark 9:1; Luke 17:20–21; Luke 22:18.

[42] The subject of the first "will come" is not absolutely clear in the Hebrew; some would translate instead "vengeance comes, the recompense of God" (so Otto Kaiser, *Isaiah 13–39* [OTL; Philadelphia: Westminster, 1974] 360). But Kaiser joins other translations in rendering the last line: "He [God] will come and save you." The attempt to read the verbs "to come" in the hifil (causative) form (e.g., "He will cause vengeance to come") is unnecessary.

[43] Thus, it is in the OT's prophecies of God's coming to save rather than in the rabbis' talk about "this age" and "the age to come" that the source of Jesus' phraseology should be sought. Although the "rabbinic" distinction can already be seen in the great apocalyptic works of 4 Ezra (end of the 1st century A.D.) and *2 Baruch* (early 2d century A.D.), clear attestation of the precise distinction between this age and the age to come is very rare—some would say nonexistent—in Jewish literature that can be dated indisputably before A.D. 70. (One might also point out the authoritative nature of books like Isaiah and Zechariah as compared to rabbinic sayings or later Jewish pseudepigrapha.) Interestingly, some of the earliest datable occurrences of the two-part distinction appear in the NT (Mark 10:30 par.; Matt 12:32; Luke 20:34–35; Eph 1:21). In each case, the occurrence of the distinction in the words of Jesus is most likely due to the redactional work of the evangelist. In fact, it is doubtful whether the distinction was much used in the first Christian generation. With the exception of Mark, all the cases are clearly from the post-A.D. 70 period.

[44] See the careful evaluation in "Amidah," *EncJud*, 2. 839–40: "It is almost certain that by the end of the [Second] Temple period the 18 benedictions of the weekday *Amidah* had become the general custom. However, their exact sequence and the content of the individual benedictions probably still varied. . . . The absence of anything resembling the *Amidah* in the liturgical fragments of the Dead Sea Scrolls found so far may be significant. . . . Soon after the destruction of the Temple, the *Amidah* was 'edited' finally in Jabneh. . . . Even then only the order, general content, and benediction formula were standardized; the actual wording was left to be formulated by the individual worshiper or reader. Attempts to reconstruct the 'original' text of the *Amidah* or to ascertain the date when each section was 'composed' are pointless. . . . It was probably in the early geonic [i.e., post-talmudic] period only that definite versions of the *Amidah* were established and committed to writing. . . ." A curious attempt to establish parallels between the Eighteen Benedictions and the Lord's Prayer (an attempt which includes the claim that the Lord's Prayer had "no fixed text" in the patristic church of the first few Christian centuries) is made by Gordon J. Bahr, "The Use of the Lord's Prayer in the Primitive Church," *JBL* 84 (1965) 153–59. For a detailed study of the development of the Eighteen Benedictions and other Jewish prayers of the talmudic period, see Heinemann, *Prayer in the Talmud*, esp. 1–76, 218–50; cf. Kaufmann Kohler, "The Origin and Composition of the Eighteen Benedictions," *Contributions to the Scientific Study of Jewish Liturgy* (ed. Jakob J. Petuchowski; New York: Ktav, 1970) 52–90; Louis Finkelstein, "The Development of the Amidah," ibid., 91–177. The problematic nature of the dating of the *Amidah* is the reason why I do not put as much emphasis on the Eighteen Benedictions as some critics do in their treatment of the Our Father.

[45] Similar prayers for the appearance of God's definitive kingly rule over Israel and over the whole earth can be found in such synagogal prayers as the *Musaf* for New Year's Day and the *'Aleinu*. However, the problem of dating these prayers prior to or contemporary with Jesus is as great if not greater than the case of the primitive forms

of the *Qaddish* and the Eighteen Benedictions. On the *Abinu Malkenu* prayer for the High Holidays, see Simon Lauer, "*Abhinu Malkenu:* Our Father, Our King!" in Petuchowski and Brocke (eds.), *The Lord's Prayer and Jewish Liturgy,* 73–80.

[46] This point will have to be explored at greater length later on; for the moment, see Jeremias, "The Lord's Prayer in the Light of Recent Research," *The Prayers of Jesus,* 95–98; also the whole essay "Abba," ibid., 11–65.

[47] I qualify my statement with "probably" because an impressive number of exegetes interpret at least some, if not all, of the "we petitions" as referring to the present situation of the person praying (see Brown, "The Pater Noster," 301 n. 82). One of the most forceful, though concise, expositions of this view is presented by Vögtle, "Der 'eschatologische' Bezug," 346–62; much less cogent is the thoroughgoing rejection of eschatology in the Our Father by Carmignac (*Recherches,* 337–47), whose arguments betray a heavy apologetic tone. Vögtle stresses that the bread-petition is the key to understanding all three of the "we petitions." He goes on to criticize the future-eschatology approach of Jeremias and Brown by pointing out that they must read a great deal into "give us today our bread" to arrive at a reference to the future heavenly banquet of salvation. However, even Vögtle admits that his own solution ("give us today the food we need so that we may be free to be concerned wholly and solely with doing your will") also demands a certain amount of reading between the lines and interpreting Jesus' words here by his teaching elsewhere. On the whole I find the approach of Jeremias and Brown more satisfying because it gives this very terse and taut prayer a simple and unified sense. A similar eschatological approach is championed by Jacques Dupont and Pierre Bonnard in *Notre Père qui es aux cieux,* 77–115. Schulz (*Q. Die Spruchquelle der Evangelisten,* 84–93) likewise champions a thoroughly future interpretation of the eschatology in the Our Father; however, Schulz interprets the prayer as coming from the early Palestinian Christian community rather than from Jesus.

[48] Since we cannot be sure what Aramaic word lay behind the Greek adjective *epiousios* (traditionally translated "daily"), it is unwise to construct a whole argument on what the Aramaic *may* have said and meant. Nevertheless, Jeremias ("The Lord's Prayer in the Light of Recent Research," *The Prayers of Jesus,* 100–101) weaves an intriguing web of argumentation as he stresses the eschatological nature of this as well as every other petition in the Our Father. The linchpin of Jeremias's approach is the claim by Jerome that in the lost Aramaic *Gospel of the Nazarenes* the word *māḥār* (literally, "tomorrow") appears at this point in the first "we petition" of the Our Father. Now Jeremias readily admits that the *Gospel of the Nazarenes* depends on the canonical Greek text of Matthew; hence he does not argue naively that the Aramaic text of the *Gospel of the Nazarenes* must naturally preserve the more original form of the Our Father. Rather, his argument is more subtle and is based on what we might well expect an Aramaic-speaking Christian to do as he translated Greek Matthew into Aramaic. Ordinarily he would follow the Greek text fairly literally. However, when he came to the Our Father, he would naturally write down the oral version of the prayer prayed by Aramaic-speaking Christians in unbroken usage from the 1st century onward. Hence *māḥār* represents the original wording of the prayer not because the *Gospel of the Nazarenes* is on the whole more primitive than canonical Matthew but because the tenacity of the oral tradition preserved the primitive wording in this special case of the Lord's Prayer. Jeremias then goes on to observe that Jerome remarks that *māḥār* can mean "future"; moreover, in ancient Judaism the word did at times refer to the final consummation.

All this is impressive, but two points should make us cautious: (1) Jerome is not always reliable in reporting about readings in various documents. (2) We know nothing about the individual who composed the *Gospel of the Nazarenes*. It is likely that the individual, when translating the Our Father, would have operated in the way Jeremias suggests; but there is no way of verifying the hypothesis. At any rate, if Jeremias is correct, he simply solidifies what is probable on other grounds, namely, that the bread-petition has an eschatological reference: "Give us today the bread of tomorrow"—i.e., bring us even today to the eschatological banquet.

[49] Also witnessed at Qumran is the concatenation of a petition for forgiveness of sins and a petition for escape from temptation or evil. See, e.g., the incomplete Psalms Scroll from Cave 11 (11QPs^a): col. 24, lines 11–12, and col. 19, lines 13–16. For an English translation, see Vermes, *The Dead Sea Scrolls in English*, 210–12.

[50] Brown ("The Pater Noster," 316) points to a parallel in Rev 3:10, where the risen Christ promises the church at Philadelphia: "I will keep you from the hour of the test (*peirasmou*), which hour is about to come upon the whole inhabited world, to test those who dwell upon the earth." An objection to this approach might be the absence of the definite article before *peirasmon* in the Our Father (so Vögtle, "Der 'eschatologische' Bezug," 355, who argues at length against the eschatological understanding of *peirasmon* in the Lord's Prayer). But the presence or absence of definite articles before nouns in prepositional phrases is erratic in NT Greek to begin with, and the fact that we are dealing with translation Greek muddies the waters even more. Therefore I do not think that the mere absence of the definite article is all that probative. For example, in Mark 14:38, Jesus' command to the sleepy disciples in Gethsemane is "Pray that you may not enter *eis peirasmon*," where *peirasmon* lacks the definite article, yet in the context probably carries the sense of the great eschatological test (though perhaps with more of a tone of "realized eschatology": so Taylor, *The Gospel According to St. Mark*, 554–55; Mann, *Mark*, 591–92; for the opposite view, see Haenchen, *Der Weg Jesu*, 491–92). In sum: it may indeed be true that *peirasmos* is an unusual term for the eschatological crisis, but then the Lord's Prayer has a number of unusual phrases (e.g., *'abbā'* as divine address in prayer, the joining of "kingdom" and "come").

[51] Increasing sensitivity on this point is found in some of the later parts of the OT. Notice, e.g., the change in the story of David's census from 2 Sam 24:1 (Yahweh incites David to take the census and then punishes him for doing so) to 1 Chron 21:1 (Satan, not Yahweh, incites David to take the census). Not surprisingly, it is especially the wisdom stream of OT and NT traditions that begins to see a problem with God's being the direct cause of tempting or testing. That God is not the source of temptation or sin is affirmed in Sir 15:11–13 and Jas 1:13. Nevertheless, large sections of both the OT and NT seem unconcerned with the problem.

[52] Another point that may also lie beyond the horizon of this terse prayer is whether God is asked (1) not to bring us to the final great test or (2) not to allow us to succumb in the midst of the test. Relying on the wording of a Jewish evening prayer recorded in *b. Ber.* 60b and on an extracanonical saying cited by Tertullian, Jeremias ("The Lord's Prayer in the Light of Recent Research," *The Prayers of Jesus*, 104–5) favors the latter interpretation. I think the former is the more natural way of understanding the wording of the petition. The idea of God's elect being brought to salvation without being subjected to the great final testing is certainly possible in apocalyptic; see, e.g., Rev 3:10 (cf. the prayer of the Synoptic Jesus in Mark 14:35–36). On this see Schulz (*Q. Die Spruchquelle der Evangelisten*, 92 n. 241), who rejects the objection of Peter Stuhlmacher (*Gerechtigkeit Gottes bei Paulus* [FRLANT 87; 2d ed.; Göttingen: Vandenhoeck & Ruprecht, 1966] 254 n. 1) that such an interpretation would mean that the petitioner would be asking for a delay of the parousia (so similarly Grässer, *Das Problem*, 103–4).

Stuhlmacher's objection lacks cogency. For believers to pray that they be spared or not succumb to the terrible suffering accompanying the end of this present world and engulfing at least the wicked and perhaps humanity in general does not necessarily mean that they do not want the end to come or that they want it delayed. The idea of being spared the fearful eschatological test is already contained seminally in the archetypal events of the plagues in Egypt prior to the exodus, when Israel was spared the tribulations visited upon the Egyptians. The eschatological recycling of these plagues is prominent in the Book of Revelation (e.g., 15:1–16:21).

[53] A full treatment of the Last Supper and the eucharistic words must wait for a later chapter. For general treatments of the Last Supper and the eucharistic words—including consideration of Mark 14:25 ‖ Luke 22:18—see Joachim Jeremias, *The Eucharistic Words of Jesus* (New Testament Library; London: SCM, 1966); Eduard Schweizer, *The Lord's Supper According to the New Testament* (FBBS 18; Philadelphia: Fortress, 1967); Hermann Patsch, "Abendmahlsterminologie ausserhalb der Einsetzungsberichte. Erwägungen zur Traditionsgeschichte der Abendmahlsworte," *ZNW* 62 (1971) 210–31; idem, *Abendmahl und historischer Jesus* (Stuttgart: Calwer, 1972); Ferdinand Hahn, "Zum Stand der Erforschung des urchristlichen Herrenmahls," *EvT* 35 (1975) 553–63; Helmut Feld, *Das Verständnis des Abendmahls* (Erträge der Forschung 50; Darmstadt: Wissenschaftliche Buchgesellschaft, 1976); Helmut Merklein, "Erwägungen zur Überlieferungsgeschichte der neutestamentlichen Abendmahlstraditionen," *BZ* 21 (1977) 88–101, 235–44; Rudolf Pesch, *Das Abendmahl und Jesu Todesverständnis* (QD 80; Freiburg/Basel/Vienna: Herder, 1978); Eugen Ruckstuhl, "Neue und alte Überlegungen zu den Abendmahlsworten Jesu," *Studien zum Neuen Testament und seiner Umwelt* 5 (1980) 79–106; Karl Kertelge, "Das Abendmahl Jesu im Markusevangelium," *Begegnung mit dem Wort* (BBB 53; Heinrich Zimmermann Festschrift; ed. Josef Zmijewski and Ernst Nellessen; Bonn: Hanstein, 1980) 67–80; I. H. Marshall, *Last Supper and Lord's Supper* (Grand Rapids: Eerdmans, 1980); John Reumann, *The Supper of the Lord* (Philadelphia: Fortress, 1985) 1–52.

[54] In addition, it also coheres well with the chronology of the last days of Jesus that I reconstructed in Chapter 11.

[55] Like so many other authors, Merklein simply notes the general acceptance of Mark 14:25 as authentic without arguing the case at length ("Erwägungen," 236). As a matter of fact, agreement on the saying's authenticity extends from the rather skeptical Grässer (*Das Problem*, 53–56) and the post-Bultmannian Bornkamm (*Jesus of Nazareth* [New York: Harper & Row, 1960] 160–61) through the moderately critical Hahn ("Zum Stand," 557) and Xavier Léon-Dufour (*Sharing the Eucharistic Bread. The Witness of the New Testament* [New York/Mahwah, NJ: Paulist, 1987] 85–90, 165–68) to the very accepting Pesch (*Markusevangelium*, 2. 354–63). Bultmann thinks that Mark 14:25 represents an early stage of the Last Supper tradition, but does not commit himself to its authenticity (*Geschichte*, 286–87).

[56] The demonstrative "that," if taken with full force, could refer to the *yôm yahweh*, that "day of Yahweh" proclaimed in prophetic and apocalyptic literature, the final day of judgment and salvation for God's people. However, it is also possible that the Greek *ekeinēs* ("that") is an overliteral translation of a pleonastic Aramaic demonstrative that is better ignored in English translation (so Jeremias, *The Eucharistic Words*, 183–84). If that be the case, the sense of the Marcan text ("until the day when") hardly differs from that of the Lucan text ("until").

[57] No word corresponding to "new" is found in the Lucan version of the logion. Jeremias (*The Eucharistic Words*, 184) notes that this predicate accusative construction

of the adjective "new" would be unusual in both Hebrew and Aramaic. Hence Schlosser (*Le règne de Dieu*, 1. 386) thinks that the adjective was added at the Greek stage of the tradition. That may well be, but it remains possible that "new" (*kainon*) is a free rendering of some Aramaic adverb modifying the verb "drink."

[58] This is basically the position of Merklein ("Erwägungen," 235 nn. 52, 53, and 54), who lists scholars on both sides of the issue.

[59] For a review of the many Lucan redactional traits in vv 15–17, see Schlosser, *Le règne de Dieu*, 1. 376–80. While stressing the fragile nature of any hypothesis in such a small compass of material, Schlosser inclines to the view of Lucan redaction for these verses.

[60] At best one might argue that, since Luke had already used the phrase "in the kingdom of God" in his redactional creation in v 16, he sought an alternative way of saying the same thing in v 18. In this case, "until the kingdom of God comes" might be a conscious echo of the Lord's Prayer.

[61] Schlosser, *Le règne de Dieu*, 1. 387–89. The image of the eschatological banquet (sometimes of a gruesome rather than a joyful nature) has its roots in OT prophecy: e.g., Isa 34:6–8; Jer 46:10; Zeph 1:7; and esp. Isa 25:6–10. The image is found in the words of Jesus in the Gospels, less often elsewhere in the NT (see notably Rev 3:20; 19:9). It continues in both Jewish rabbinic and Christian patristic literature. Often cited in this context is *1 Enoch* 62:14: "The Lord of the Spirits will abide over them [the righteous]; they shall eat and rest and rise with that Son of Man forever and ever." Unfortunately, this passage occurs within the *Parables [or Similitudes] of Enoch* (*1 Enoch* 37–71), whose dating is still disputed. If *1 Enoch* 62:14 is brought into the discussion, what is striking by way of comparison is the lack of any christological title in Mark 14:25 ‖ Luke 22:18. On all this, see Johannes Behm, "*deipnon, deipneō*," *TDNT* 2 (1964) 34–35.

[62] In the OT, *'āmēn* was used by the individual and the community to affirm acceptance of an allotted task, to confirm the personal application of a divine threat or curse, or to attest the praise of God in response to a doxology; its basic function was thus "responsorial." The LXX usually translates it by the optative *genoito*, but occasionally transcribes it with *amēn* in Greek letters. Especially interesting is the use in Jer 28:6 (MT): *'āmēn* stands at the beginning of a wish of Jeremiah, but it is probably to be understood as an answer to Hananiah in v 4 and hence still responsorial. The corresponding verse in the LXX, Jer 35:6, has *alēthōs*. In its widespread use in Judaism (notably in the synagogue), *'āmēn* keeps its character of response, though it is sometimes used as a response to one's own prayer. In the NT and the Christian world, *amēn* is used as a liturgical acclamation and as a conclusion to Christian prayers and doxologies. It could also be placed at the beginning of a prayer, especially when it formed the link between two doxologies. For continuation of Jewish usage in the NT outside the Gospels, see 1 Cor 14:16, 2 Cor 1:20; Rev 5:14; 7:12; 19:4; 22:20.

In the NT and the early 1st century A.D., the usage of Jesus as presented in the Gospels stands out as strikingly characteristic, if not unique. Jesus alone places *amēn* before his own sayings in the Synoptic Gospels in a fashion that is clearly not responsorial. It occurs 31 times in Matthew, 13 times in Mark, and only 6 times in Luke, since Luke often either drops the word entirely or substitutes *alēthōs* or *ep' alētheias*. If we look only at Matthew and Luke, *amēn* occurs 9 times in Q material (always the Matthean, never the Lucan version), 9 times in Matthew only, and 3 times in Luke only. In John it is used 25 times in a doubled form, therefore 50 times in all (perhaps reflecting Jewish liturgical usage). The criterion of multiple attestation and the criterion of discontinuity therefore argue strongly that the striking usage of *amēn* in the Gospels derives from Jesus himself. That does not mean that every instance in the Four Gospels comes from the historical Jesus. For instance, as with the use of "Father" for God, so also with the use of *amēn*, Matthew may well have imitated and multiplied the impressive usage of Jesus that he found in his sources.

As for the meaning of "amen" in the mouth of Jesus, Dalman (*Die Worte Jesu*, 186–87) suggests that Jesus' use of *amēn* reflects his avoidance of oaths, but Heinrich Schlier ("*amēn*," *TDNT* 1 [1964] 337–38) denies this. Schlier for his part seems to be writing biblical theology when he says: "The point of the Amen before Jesus' own sayings is rather to show that as such they are reliable and true, and that they are so as and because Jesus Himself in His Amen acknowledges them to be His own sayings and thus makes them valid. . . . Thus in the *amēn* . . . of Jesus we have the whole of Christology *in nuce*" (p. 338). Jeremias (*New Testament Theology*, 36) instead compares Jesus' "Amen I say to you" formula to the messenger-formula used by the OT prophets ("thus says the Lord") to show that their words were not their own wisdom but a divine message. In a similar way "Amen I say to you" expresses the authority of Jesus.

Jeremias is perhaps the most forceful proponent of the position that the "non-responsorial" amen was unique to Jesus. He claims that it "is without any parallel in the whole of Jewish literature and the rest of the New Testament. . . . in this unprecedented [i.e., non-responsorial] usage it is strictly confined to the words of Jesus" (*New Testament Theology*, 35; cf. "Kennzeichen der ipsissima vox Jesu," in *Abba*, 145–52, esp. 148–51).

Not all have accepted Jeremias's view of the originality of Jesus' usage. Klaus Berger (*Die Amen-Worte Jesu* [BZNW 39; Berlin: de Gruyter, 1970] 4) points to two examples of *amēn* at the beginning of a sentence (thus corresponding to the supposedly unique usage of Jesus) in Jewish-Greek apocalyptic literature, i.e., in the *Testament of Abraham* (recension A, 8:7 ["Amen I say to you"] and 20:2 ["Amen, amen I say to you"]). His thesis suffers from a number of difficulties: (1) The date of the composition of the *Testament of Abraham* remains disputed; E. P. Sanders ("Testament of Abraham," *Old Testament Pseudepigrapha*, 1. 874–75) suggests a date ca. A.D. 100. (2) More to the point, the longer recension A is commonly judged to be later than recension B and to show Christian influence in some of its phraseology. Berger (*Die Amen-Worte*, 5 n. 7) admits this point, but denies its relevance to the texts he uses for the proof of his thesis, even though the critical "amen" does not appear in the B recension.

A different approach is taken by V. Hasler, *Amen. Redaktionsgeschichtliche Untersuchung zur Einführungsformel der Herrenworte "Wahrlich ich sage euch"* (Zurich/Stuttgart: Gotthelf, 1969). Hasler, like Berger, denies that the NT usage of "amen" goes back to Jesus. But Hasler disagrees with Berger on the true origin of the amen-sayings in the NT. While Berger points to apocalyptic currents in Hellenistic-Jewish Christianity, Hasler refers to the charismatic prophets speaking in the name of the exalted Lord. When one considers the clear evidence of the Gospels as weighed by the criteria of multiple attestation and discontinuity as well as the highly disputed nature and function of Christian prophets in the NT period, especially with regard to the creation of sayings of the Lord, Hasler seems to be rejecting the obvious explanation of a phenomenon in favor of a very dubious one.

A still more unlikely hypothesis is put forward by J. Stiassny in "Jésus accomplit la promesse," *BVC* 59 (1964) 30–37, esp. 33. Stiassny suggests that Jesus used not *ʾāmēn* but *ʾākēn* (the second word, like the first, being an affirmation of certainty). The letter *kaf* in *ʾākēn* was supposedly confused later on with the letter *mem*, thus producing *ʾāmēn*. Apart from the overall complexity and improbability of such a hypothesis, it attributes too much importance to the literary transmission of Jesus' words in the first

Christian generation. The oral transmission (in which such a confusion would be highly unlikely) existed prior to any written tradition and continued to exert influence through preaching, catechesis, and liturgy even after the Jesus tradition began to be written down.

One could go on with other theories (see, e.g., Bruce Chilton, " 'Amen'—an Approach through Syriac Gospels." *ZNW* 69 [1978] 203–11; and a cogent refutation in W. D. Davies and Dale C. Allison, Jr.; *The Gospel According to Matthew* [ICC; 3 vols., Edinburgh: Clark, 1988] 1. 490 n. 23), but the main point is clear. In reviewing all these solutions one cannot avoid the feeling that various esoteric and convoluted explanations are being preferred to the obvious one. Jeremias treats a number of these alternate explanations and indicates their weaknesses in "Zum nicht-responsorischen Amen," *ZNW* 64 (1973) 122–23; cf. *New Testament Theology*, 36 n. 2; and Fitzmyer, *Luke*, 1. 536–37.

As for Mark 14:25, the mere presence of *amēn* does not prove the authenticity of the logion, but secondarily it does reinforce the major argument from discontinuity that I make in the text. While the *amēn* could be a later addition to an authentic saying of Jesus, it is interesting to note that the redactional tendencies we can observe in this case go in the opposite direction: both Matthew and Luke independently omit the *amēn* of Mark's version.

[63] As Kertelge observes ("Das Abendmahl," 71), "The saying of Jesus in v 25, in both form and content, falls outside the framework of the words of interpretation [of the bread and wine] in vv 22c.24." Matthew apparently noticed the lack of any connection between the eucharistic cup-word and Mark 14:25 and so tried to create one by adding "this" (*toutou*) to the phrase "fruit of the vine" in Matt 26:29. While the connection between Mark 14:25 and 14:22–24 (the eucharistic words) was probably not original, the link may have been created very early in the oral tradition. Paul reflects a similar concatenation of ideas when he concludes his tradition of the eucharistic words with "you proclaim the death of the Lord *until he comes*" (cf. "until the kingdom of God comes" in Luke 22:18, immediately preceding the eucharistic words).

[64] So Jeremias, *The Eucharistic Words of Jesus*, 182.

[65] Schlosser, *Le règne de Dieu*, 1. 382.

[66] See Joachim Jeremias, *The Eucharistic Words of Jesus* (London: SCM, 1966) 207–18, esp. n. 6 on pp. 207–8. The 1966 English translation is based on the revised 3d edition of the German text, in which Jeremias's original term *Entsagungsgelübde* ("vow of abstinence") is replaced with *Verzichterklärung*, which carries the idea of a declaration of forgoing (food or drink) or, as the English translator renders it, an "avowal of abstinence." For the older translation ("vow of abstinence"), see Joachim Jeremias, *The Eucharistic Words of Jesus* (New York: Macmillan, 1955) 165–72. The more recent translation "avowal" captures well how close Jeremias actually remains to the idea of a vow even in the revised form of his thesis. See, e.g., p. 209: the words of Jesus "are in the *form of a careful declaration of intent, almost an oath*" (the emphasis is Jeremias's). As Jeremias must admit, however, Jesus does not use the technical formula of a vow. Jeremias continues to maintain in his revised presentation that Jesus abstained from the Passover lamb and wine—and probably all food—during the Last Supper (p. 212). One can therefore understand why Jeremias must maintain the priority of the wording and placement of Luke 22:18 over Mark 14:25. In Mark 14:25 the meal has been underway for some time (the pericope is introduced with "and while they were eating" in 14:22), and Mark's wording includes *ouketi* ("I will *no longer* drink of the fruit of the vine").

[67] Relying on the work of Berger in *Die Amen-Worte Jesu*, Pesch (*Markusevangelium*, 2. 355; cf. 1. 216) describes the function of the amen-saying thus: with the amen-saying "the speaker of the prophecy claims insight conferred by revelation." Often the revelation transmitted through the prophet or apocalyptic seer concerns the criteria for God's judgment on the last day. This fits Mark 14:25 insofar as Jesus prophesies that the unjust judgment of humans will be reversed by God, who will seat Jesus at the final banquet in the kingdom.

[68] The parallel between these two logia is highlighted here simply to clarify the meaning of Mark 14:25 as indicated by its structure and basic content. This should not be taken to mean that Mark 9:1 is authentic in the mouth of Jesus. As section E will show, the opposite seems to be true. For a study of the literary form of these sayings, see Barry S. Crawford, "Near Expectation in the Sayings of Jesus," *JBL* 101 (1982) 225–44. Crawford's presentation is weakened by (1) his presumption that, if some of the Gospel logia having this form can be shown to be the creation of early Christian prophets, one may quickly move to the inference that the rest are too; there is no reason why Christian prophets might not have imitated the prophetic style of Jesus; (2) his inadequate treatment of Matt 5:18 ‖ Luke 16:17, a saying which really does not belong in this form-critical category, since its primitive form did not have the final *heōs an* clause (see Meier, *Law and History*, 57–65); (3) his highly speculative attempt to explain Mark 14:25 as a creation of an early Christian prophet presiding at the eucharist; what the saying would have meant in such a context is never explained adequately (see pp. 239–40). Nevertheless, as will become clear in section E below, I think that he is correct in holding that Matt 10:23; Mark 9:1; and Mark 13:30 are creations of the early church.

[69] As Pesch observes (*Markusevangelium*, 2. 356), some vows of abstinence may have structures that are similar to this pattern, but they lack a clear promise of salvation. In their place often stands the time-limit set by the person making the vow for the carrying out of the action he or she has promised to perform; see, e.g., 1 Sam 14:24; Acts 23:12,14, 21. This is one reason why Jeremias's attempt to see either a vow or an avowal of abstinence misses the point with regard to both literary form and content.

[70] Feld comments (*Das Verständnis*, 56): "The eschatological prospect (Mk 14, 25) shows quite clearly that Jesus must have supposed that a certain amount of time would elapse prior to the banquet in the kingdom of God. While he did not give chronological specification to his future-expectation, still he certainly awaited the inbreaking of the kingdom of God in the *very near* future. . . . Whether a basis for a dogmatic ecclesiology is thus provided, as Patsch seeks to establish, is however very questionable . . ." (the emphasis is Feld's).

[71] Grässer (*Das Problem*, 54) stresses the absence of any messianic function or any intimation of a parousia. This is true on the level of the historical Jesus. Yet no doubt Mark and his church would have seen in the phrase "in the kingdom of God" a reference to the parousia (so Kertelge, "Das Abendmahl," 77).

[72] Contrast, e.g., Jesus' prediction of his death to his disciples in Matt 26:2: "You know that after two days the Passover is celebrated and the Son of Man is handed over to be crucified." The vagueness of reference makes it futile to ask whether Mark 14:25 expects the kingdom to come immediately after Jesus' death or whether some interim period is envisioned.

[73] Pesch (*Das Abendmahl*, 101–2) overinterprets Mark 14:25 when he sees intimated in it the destiny of Jesus as the Son of Man, his atoning death, and his resurrection.

[74] Strangely, Grässer (*Das Problem*, 53–54), in the midst of his basically correct defense of the historicity of Mark 14:25, reads the theme of Jesus' reunion with his disciples into the text. Hence he sees the logion as a word of comfort to the disciples who are left behind. He then proceeds, rather lamely, to note that Matthew emphasizes this point by his addition of "with you." Without any basis he claims: "*Expressis verbis* this idea is lacking in Mark, but the expectation of the kingdom [in Mark 14:25] makes it self-evident" (p. 55). Grässer reaffirms his interpretation of Mark 14:25 as indicating a reunion of Jesus and his disciples in *Die Naherwartung Jesu* (SBS 61; Stuttgart: KBW, 1973) 114. Anton Vögtle is more cautious in claiming that Jesus makes an "indirect promise" to his disciples that their table fellowship with him will find its fulfillment in the kingdom; see his *Das Neue Testament und die Zukunft des Kosmos* (Kommentare und Beiträge zum Alten und Neuen Testament; Düsseldorf: Patmos, 1970) 148–49. But would we think even of an indirect promise if we did not know the Matthean version of the logion?

[75] Anton Vögtle, "Der verkündende und verkündigte Jesus 'Christus,' " *Wer ist Jesus Christus?* (ed. Joseph Sauer; Freiburg/Basel/Vienna: Herder, 1977) 27–91, esp. 68.

[76] Kloppenborg (*Q Parallels*, 154) notes that most critics do assign the tradition to Q, the major point of dispute being whether Matthew or Luke represents the original order found in Q. Petros Vassiliadis ("The Nature and Extent of the Q-Document," *NovT* 20 [1978] 49–73, esp. 68) puts himself in a small minority by claiming that at least part of this tradition (Luke 13:28a = Matt 8:12b) was not in Q; he leaves open the possibility of a proverbial saying possibly stemming from oral tradition.

[77] Actually, the question of the precise source of the saying is not of the greatest importance for our treatment of this logion. It would have some bearing if it could be established that one or both versions of the logion came not from Q but from some special source of the evangelist. In that case, the criterion of multiple attestation of sources would come into play. However, as we shall see, the differences in Matthew and Luke are best explained as redactional changes each evangelist made in a Q logion.

[78] So, e.g., Jacques Dupont, " 'Beaucoup viendront du levant et du couchant . . .' (Matthieu 8, 11–12; Luc 13, 28–29)," *ScEccl* 19 (1967) 153–67, esp. 153; Dieter Zeller, "Das Logion Mt 8, 11f/ Lk 13, 28f und das Motiv der 'Völkerwallfahrt,' " *BZ* 15 (1971) 222–37; 16 (1972) 84–93, esp. 223 (in first article) and 91 (in second article).

[79] One should note the precise tenor of the statement Jesus makes in praising the centurion's faith: "I have not found such great faith in any person in Israel" (Matt 8:10), or "not even in Israel have I found such great faith" (Luke 7:9). The presupposition of the praise is that Jesus has found *some* faith in Israel, but it does not measure up to the centurion's faith. There is nothing here that speaks of a total rejection of Jesus by Israel or of a total rejection of Israel by Jesus.

[80] The distant Johannine parallel is best explained as representing a distinct stream of the oral tradition rather than a reworking of a story that John copied from the Gospel of Matthew or Luke; so Dodd, *Historical Tradition in the Fourth Gospel*, 194; and Brown, *The Gospel According to John*, 1. 192–93. Notice that in John's version there is no indication that the royal official is a Gentile. See Chapter 21, Section V below.

[81] Notice the similar redactional insertion of the theme of faith at the end of Matthew's version of the healing of the daughter of the Syrophoenician/Canaanite woman: "O woman, great is your faith! Be it done unto you as you wish" (Matt 15:28, not present in the equivalent Marcan verse, 7:29). On Matt 8:13 as a redactional creation meant to bridge the disruption caused by the insertion of 8:11–12, see Schlosser, *Le*

règne de Dieu, 2. 603. For a consideration of the few exegetes who argue that Matt 8:11–12 originally belonged to the miracle story and for a refutation of their arguments, see Uwe Wegner, *Der Hauptmann von Kafarnaum* (WUNT 2/14; Tübingen: Mohr [Siebeck], 1985) 3–5. Significantly, after weighing the arguments pro and con on pp. 3–5, Wegner simply omits Matt 8:11–12 par. from further consideration in the treatment of the miracle story.

[82] In my view, the treatment of Schulz (*Q. Die Spruchquelle der Evangelisten*, 323–30) suffers from unconsciously reading the fiercely negative Matthean redactional tone into the primitive logion. This is even more the case with the interpretation of Joachim Jeremias, *Jesus' Promise to the Nations* (SBT 24; London: SCM, 1967) 51: "[Matt 8:11–12 par.] is equally severe and equally devoid of hope for Israel. . . . The full horror of the threat that in the final judgment Gentiles will take the place of the sons of the Kingdom can best be measured by the fact that no Jewish scholar and no Jewish apocalyptist had ever dared to utter such a thing. . . ." Notice how the redactional form of Matthew (with "sons of the kingdom") is treated as the authentic saying of the historical Jesus.

[83] Schlosser, *Le règne de Dieu*, 2. 608–14; Dupont, " 'Beaucoup,' " 156; Schulz, *Q. Die Spruchquelle der Evangelisten*, 323.

[84] Schlosser, *Le règne de Dieu*, 2. 613, 650 n. 71. As noted in H. Liddell-R. Scott, *A Greek-English Lexicon* (Oxford: Clarendon, 1940) 505 *s.v.*, the temporal meaning is rare even in classical authors. As for NT Greek, Bauer does not even list a temporal meaning in the entry on *ekei* in his *Wörterbuch*, cols. 481–82.

[85] Schulz (*Q. Die Spruchquelle der Evangelisten*, 323) adds other arguments to support this conclusion. For him, the structure of the Matthean form is far more compact and logical: the acceptance of the Gentiles into the kingdom is then followed by the rejection of Israel (*sic*!). Some of Schulz's arguments (e.g., Luke's use of a second person verb, which is judged secondary to Matthew's use of the third person) are unconvincing, especially when Schulz himself accepts "you" in Luke 13:28 as original rather than "sons of the kingdom" in Matt 8:12. For a list of authors championing Matthew's or Luke's order as original, see nn. 1 and 2 on p. 323.

[86] So Kloppenborg, *The Formation of Q*, 226.

[87] One clear example of Matthew's insertion of "I say to you" into an already existing text is found in Matt 19:9; cf. Mark 10:11. It should be noted, however, that most of the other examples put forth by Schlosser (*Le règne de Dieu*, 2. 645 n. 21) are not probative. For the opposite view, that "I say to you" is original in the saying, see Schulz, *Q. Die Spruchquelle der Evangelisten*, 323–24.

[88] Kloppenborg, *The Formation of Q*, 227 n. 227; cf. 224 n. 217. Kloppenborg also suggests that Luke had good reason to omit "many" in 13:29, since it might appear to contradict what he had just written in 13:24: "*Many* shall seek to enter [by the narrow gate], but will not be able." Schlosser (*Le règne de Dieu*, 2. 606–7) argues in the opposite direction: (1) The indefinite "they" may reflect an Aramaic original. (2) Matthew has simply made more explicit a theme commonly met in the biblical texts on the eschatological pilgrimage of the nations. It is more likely that Matthew added the explicit reference than that Luke went out of his way to do away with it. (3) Matthew strongly contrasts the "many" with "the sons of the kingdom," and the latter phrase is commonly viewed as Matthean redaction. The contrast makes it probable that the former phrase is likewise redactional. Also in favor of Matthean redaction is Dupont, " 'Beaucoup,' " 157.

As so often, the arguments on these matters of detail are finely balanced. For example, while Schlosser sees the impersonal "they" contained in the verb as a trace of Aramaic background, Jeremias (*Jesus' Promise*, 73 n. 1) claims that *polloi* reflects a Semitic locution with the inclusive sense of "a great multitude, a countless number." While I think that critics like Kloppenborg have the better part of the argument, I readily admit that certainty is not to be had. Fortunately, my basic position does not depend upon such minor questions.

[89] See, e.g., Alexander Sand, *Das Gesetz und die Propheten* (Biblische Untersuchungen 11; Regensburg: Pustet, 1974), esp. 125–77. Kloppenborg (*The Formation of Q*, 226 n. 226) points out that the phrase "all the prophets" is found in the NT, apart from Matt 11:13 (with the word "Law"), only in Luke-Acts: Luke 11:50; 13:28; 24:27; Acts 3:18, 24; 10:43. Schlosser (*Le règne de Dieu*, 2. 605) likewise judges "all the prophets" to be an insertion by Luke.

[90] Schlosser (*Le règne de Dieu*, 2. 606) suggests that Luke may be influenced in his formulation by some texts of the LXX dealing with the great ingathering of dispersed Israelites; see, e.g., LXX Ps 106:3; Isa 43:5–6. Both texts use the pattern "from the east and from the west, from the north and from the south."

[91] See Armin Kretzer, *Die Herrschaft der Himmel und die Söhne des Reiches* (SBM 10; Stuttgart: KBW; Würzburg: Echter, 1971); also Wolfgang Trilling, *Das wahre Israel* (SANT 10; 3d ed.; Munich: Kösel, 1964) 88. In n. 85 Trilling points out that, besides 13:38, Matthew uses similar phrases in material unique to him: 23:15 ("a son of Gehenna") and 17:25–26 ("their sons," i.e., the sons of kings). Indeed, Schlosser (*Le règne de Dieu*, 2. 607) suggests that, especially in redactional passages, Matthew readily uses "son(s)" in metaphorical phrases having a Semitic flavor, while Luke does not show the same interest in such redactional creations, though he will keep "son" phrases when he finds them in the tradition. The absolute use of *basileia* ("kingdom") is also characteristic of Matthew. In favor of "sons of the kingdom" being more original are (with hesitation) Dupont, " 'Beaucoup,' " 157–59; and Kloppenborg, *Formation of Q*, 227 n. 227. Curiously, Kloppenborg argues that "sons of the kingdom" was original in Q by noting that in 13:38 the phrase refers to Christians while in 8:12 it refers to Jews. But that is part of Matthew's redactional theology: the older group of "sons of the kingdom" (i.e., Israel) has been replaced by the newer group of "sons of the kingdom" (i.e., the church). The use of the same phrase may also serve as a warning to the new "sons" that they are not automatically exempt from the judgment that befell the old "sons"; see Peter Fiedler, "Der Sohn Gottes über unserem Weg in die Gottesherrschaft," *Gegenwart und kommendes Reich* (Anton Vögtle Festschrift; SBB; ed. Peter Fiedler and Dieter Zeller; Stuttgart: KBW, 1975) 91–100, esp. 96–97; also Günther Bornkamm, "Enderwartung und Kirche im Matthäusevangelium," in Günther Bornkamm, Gerhard Barth, and Heinz Joachim Held, *Überlieferung und Auslegung im Matthäusevangelium* (WMANT 1; Neukirchen-Vluyn: Neukirchener Verlag, 1968) 13–47. For a different understanding of "sons of the kingdom"—one that perhaps owes too much to present-day concerns—see Amy-Jill Levine, *The Social and Ethnic Dimensions of Matthean Salvation History. "Go nowhere among the Gentiles . . ." (Matt. 10:5b)* (Studies in the Bible and Early Christianity 14; Lewiston/Queenston/Lampeter: Mellen, 1988) 107–30.

[92] For the opposite view, see Schlosser, *Le règne de Dieu*, 2. 614.

[93] Sato (*Q und Prophetie*, 137) suggests that Luke's participial form *ekballomenous* may be a direct translation of a participle in Galilean Aramaic, carrying the sense of imminent future action. That is indeed possible, but one must also take into account the fact

that the grammatical construction of Luke's *hymas de ekballomenous* ("but you cast out") results from his redactional insertion of *hotan opsēsthe* ("when you see").

[94] Sato, *Q und Prophetie*, 137; Dupont " 'Beaucoup,' " 158. Hence I agree with Sato that the hypothesis that two distinct sayings came together secondarily is highly unlikely.

[95] Zeller ("Das Logion," 232–36) traces the further development of the theme in Jewish apocalyptic and rabbinic literature.

[96] On all this, see Schlosser, *Le règne de Dieu*, 2. 618–20; Jeremias, *Jesus' Promise*, 57–62. Sanders (*Jesus and Judaism*, 213–14) distinguishes in the biblical prophets at least six different types of predictions about the fate of the Gentiles in the end time, ranging from the Gentiles' salvation with Israel to their destruction. Sanders criticizes Jeremias for claiming that Judaism at the time of Jesus "almost universally took a negative view towards the Gentiles" (*Jesus and Judaism*, 212); Sanders argues that most Jews at the time would have expected "many Gentiles to turn to the Lord when his glory was revealed" (p. 218). Sanders's criticisms of what he considers Jeremias's misrepresentations of Judaism have sparked a fierce debate. Critical of Sanders is Ben F. Meyer, "A Caricature of Joachim Jeremias and His Scholarly Work," *JBL* 110 (1991) 451–62; Sanders's reply, "Defending the Indefensible," is found in the same issue of the *JBL*, pp. 463–77.

[97] On all this, see Zeller, "Das Logion," 236–37. Zeller stresses that the Jewish literature does not employ the imagery of the pilgrimage of the nations to Mt. Zion to solve the explicit theological question of how the Gentiles will attain to salvation in the end time. The Gentiles do not appear as an independent theme; they are oriented to the glory of God and/or Israel.

[98] The classical texts in this regard are Matt 15:24 ("I was sent only to the lost sheep of the house of Israel") and 10:5–6 ("Do not go to the Gentiles and do not enter a city of the Samaritans; rather, go to the lost sheep of the house of Israel"). Many different sources have been suggested as the origin of these two sayings (Matthean redaction, special M material, a Q saying not taken over by Luke, and—whatever the immediate source—ultimately the historical Jesus himself). On both sayings, see the various opinions surveyed in Levine, *The Social and Ethnic Dimensions*, 1–57, 131–64. With no precise parallels in the Synoptic tradition, it is difficult to adjudicate claims. In any case, the two sayings do reflect accurately the entire picture of Jesus' mission that arises from a reading of all the sources of all Four Gospels: nowhere does Jesus undertake a programmatic mission to the Gentiles. This impression is indirectly supported by the distinction that Paul (who is actually treating another question) makes in Rom 15:8: "Christ has become a servant of the circumcision [i.e., he ministered to the Jews] for the sake of God's faithfulness, to confirm the promises made to the patriarchs, but [also] in order that [in due time, through the ministry of Paul and other missionaries like him] the Gentiles might glorify God for his mercy." Notice that Paul does not claim that Christ ever ministered directly to Gentiles, however much such a claim might have aided his cause. He—and no doubt many other Christians of the first generation—were well aware that Jesus had directed his mission in principle only to his own people. The Synoptic Gospels, as is well known, present a few exceptions in some individual cases of healing (the centurion with the sick servant, the Syrophoenician woman with the possessed daughter); John's Gospel knows of no such exceptions. On the philological and theological problems connected with Rom 15:8, see C. E. B. Cranfield, *The Epistle to the Romans* (ICC; 2 vols.; Edinburgh: Clark, 1975, 1979) 2. 740–44; James D. G. Dunn, *Romans* (Word Biblical Commentary 38A and B; Dallas: Word,

1988) 2. 846–49. On the general question of Jesus' desire to restore the whole of Israel in the end time and the symbolic significance of the twelve disciples (= the twelve tribes), see Sanders, *Jesus and Judaism*, 61–119, esp. 95–106.

[99] Zeller ("Das Logion," 93) thinks instead that the logion neither develops a program for a mission to the Gentiles in this world nor excludes it. Granted, the question is simply not raised explicitly in this short logion. Yet the fact that the "you" are apparently thought to be in the kingdom before the end time and therefore must be "thrown out" of it while, in contrast, the Gentiles are said only then to "come" implies, to my mind, that it is only then that the Gentiles are in any sense of the word "called." Paul and presumably other early Christian missionaries did see their mission as the eschatological gathering of the Gentiles, who are "called" even in this present age (e.g., Rom 1:6–7,13; 15:7–29).

[100] Hence the formulation of Sato (*Q und Prophetie*, 137) may be too strong: ". . . the traditional expression 'coming from east and west' must mean first of all the Gentiles." Likewise too hasty is Dupont, " 'Beaucoup,' " 159. An attempt to interpret the prophecy in terms of Diaspora Jews is made by George Wesley Buchanan, *Jesus. The King and His Kingdom* (Macon, GA: Mercer University, 1984) 34–35, 114. His interpretation is part of his larger program of seeing the kingdom proclaimed by Jesus as a political kingdom of this world, with Jesus as king. Needless to say, the element of prophetic eschatology tinged with apocalyptic that is present in this logion (reclining at the eschatological banquet with Abraham, Isaac, and Jacob) is ignored. Buchanan's whole book suffers from an uncritical use of sources and curious arguments to arrive at a still more curious position.

[101] Most emphatic on this point is Zeller, "Das Logion," 87: "In fact, the many—as a kind of 'substitute'—take the places at the meal of the patriarchs that were reserved for the Jews." He speaks in general terms of the logion's "opposition between the many and the Jews" (p. 87). It is a saying about "the rejection of Israel" (p. 88). "The saying is directed against the Jews as such" (p. 90). It is this extreme (and, in my view, erroneous) interpretation of the opposition in the saying that leads Zeller to attribute the saying to early Christians rather than to Jesus. Sato (*Q und Prophetie*, 138) considers this a possible meaning of the prophecy. However, Sato thinks that, if one adopts this harsh interpretation, the saying must be attributed to a prophet in the Q tradition, and not to the historical Jesus, who would not have said such a thing. Sato himself seems to incline toward the interpretation I suggest, and he then allows for the possibility of origin from the historical Jesus. Schulz (*Q. Die Spruchquelle der Evangelisten*, 327) speaks in a sweeping manner of the generation of Jesus' contemporaries as the ones excluded from the banquet.

[102] So, rightly, Schlosser, *Le règne de Dieu*, 2. 615.

[103] The attempt by Schlosser (*Le règne de Dieu*, 2. 622–24) to find a few examples prior to Jesus is not convincing.—The reader will note that I speak here simply of the eschatological pilgrimage of the Gentiles. Whether this pilgrimage is still thought to be to Mt. Zion in particular cannot be answered on the basis of this logion alone. Dupont (" 'Beaucoup,' " 160) thinks that the kingdom of God has replaced Jerusalem or Mt. Zion as the goal of the pilgrimage, but that may be reading too much into the silence of the logion on this point, just as Jeremias (*Jesus' Promise*, 62) may be reading too much into it by declaring Matt 8:11 par. to be "a succinct summary of the Old Testament utterances concerning the eschatological pilgrimage of the Gentiles to the Mount of God. . . ." Zeller ("Das Logion," 86) leaves open the possibility that the eschatological meal of the patriarchs is connected with Jerusalem. Zeller goes on to

stress that what is truly surprising in this logion is the connection made between the eschatological pilgrimage of the Gentiles, the meal with the patriarchs, and the kingdom of God.

[104] Dupont ("'Beaucoup,'" 161) points out the remarkable reticence of Matt 8:11–12 par. on this score, especially when compared with the parable of the great supper in Luke 14:15–24 (highly allegorized in Matt 22:1–10), which is accepted by many as a parable of the historical Jesus. Dupont sees here an a fortiori argument in favor of the authenticity of Matt 8:11–12 par.

[105] Schulz (Q. Die Spruchquelle der Evangelisten, 324–25) goes beyond what Matt 8:11–12 par. says when he summarizes the message of the logion thus: "At the parousia of the Son of Man, the Gentile nations will stream [to Zion] from all four corners of the earth in a great pilgrimage of the nations according to the OT pattern." Here is a prime example of Schulz reading his own idea of Q christology into a particular Q saying in which such a christology is notably absent.

[106] Sato (Q und Prophetie, 137) lists stylistic traits of the logion that he thinks point at least to early oral tradition of a prophetic sort, if not to Jesus himself: intense imminent eschatological expectation, a participle used for the future tense (reflecting Galilean Aramaic), and the divine passive. As I indicated in Chapter 6, these are at best secondary and post factum criteria, confirming an origin from Jesus after other criteria have already made such an origin likely. That seems to be the case here. Zeller ("Das Logion," 89) notes that Rudolf Bultmann hesitated on the question of authenticity, while Ferdinand Hahn opted for authenticity; Zeller himself, following Ernst Käsemann, inclines against it (p. 91). While hesitant about our ability to know with certainty what sayings containing future eschatology come from the historical Jesus, Koester ("Jesus the Victim," 15) includes Luke 13:28–29 par. in a short list of likely candidates.

[107] In dealing with such questions, one must remember that (1) many different ideas about eschatology and the final state of human beings circulated in Judaism at the time of Jesus; and (2) the different conceptions were not necessarily viewed as mutually exclusive. The latter point is especially true of apocalyptic thought and literature, never known for their perfect consistency. For some reflections on what Jesus may have understood about the final state of humanity in the kingdom, see Schlosser, Le règne de Dieu, 2. 624–41.

[108] Hence such sayings as Matt 8:11–12 par. create major difficulties for the everpopular, Reimarus-like view of Jesus as a this-wordly, political revolutionary attempting to seize power and make himself "King of the Jews." For one example of this approach, see Buchanan's Jesus. The King and His Kingdom.

[109] Schulz (Q. Die Spruchquelle der Evangelisten, 325) may go too far when he asserts: ". . . in distinction from these prophetic promises of the Old Testament [concerning the pilgrimage of the nations to Zion] [Matt 8:11–12 par.] treats of a strictly apocalyptic event. . . ." Anton Vögtle may be too intent on excluding apocalyptic views (understood in terms of a transformed or recreated earth) from this logion, though he is correct that we must not look for a detailed eschatological scenario in the symbols of a single saying; see his Das Neue Testament und die Zukunft des Kosmos (Kommentare und Beiträge zum Alten und Neuen Testament; Düsseldorf: Patmos, 1970) 148–49.

[110] On the transcendence of death as crucial to apocalyptic eschatology, see John J. Collins, "Apocalyptic Eschatology as the Transcendence of Death," CBQ 36 (1974) 21–43. Collins's attempt to work out a typology of Jewish apocalyptic can be found in his "Introduction: Towards the Morphology of a Genre" and his "The Jewish Apoca-

lypses," *Apocalypse. The Morphology of a Genre* (Semeia 14; ed. John J. Collins; Chico, CA: Scholars, 1979) 1–20 and 21–59 respectively.

[111] As most scholars today admit, the dividing line between the prophetic eschatology of the late OT and (proto-)apocalyptic is often very fine and difficult to define. The great rush to declare apocalyptic "the mother of all Christian theology" à la Ernst Käsemann (see his "The Beginnings of Christian Theology," *New Testament Questions of Today* [London: SCM, 1969] 82–107, esp. 102) has tended to obscure the continuity of prophetic eschatology in the OT, in Jesus' ministry, and in early Christianity. For some suggestions on the close similarities, see Walter Harrelson, "Prophetic Eschatological Visions and the Kingdom of God," *The Quest for the Kingdom of God* (George E. Mendenhall Festschrift; ed. H. B. Huffmon, F. A. Spina, and A. R. W. Green; Winona Lake, IN: Eisenbrauns, 1983) 117–26.

Ben F. Meyer ("Jesus's Scenario of the Future," *DRev* 109 [1991] 1–15) stresses the importance of the temporal succession of John the Baptist (who proclaimed imminent eschatology), Jesus, and the first generation of Christians (who proclaimed imminent eschatology). A priori it would be surprising, granted the links backward and forward, if Jesus' proclamation had no element of imminent eschatology. Echoing the research of scholars like August Strobel (*Untersuchungen zum eschatologischen Verzögerungsproblem auf Grund der spätjüdisch-urchristlichen Geschichte von Habakuk 2,2ff.* [NovTSup 2; Leiden: Brill, 1961] 299–305) and Jon D. Levenson (*Theology of the Program of Restoration of Ezekiel* [HSM 10; Missoula, MT: Scholars, 1976] 53 n. 33), Meyer observes (p. 6) that "the tradition of prophecy in Israel *always* strikes the note of imminence. There is no prophecy of the distant future. . . . his [Jesus'] prophecy—if, as a history-of-religion phenomenon, it was in any sense significantly aligned with that of the prophets of Israel—bore on the immediate future." Meyer's statement may be somewhat exaggerated. Ezek 12:26–28, for instance, seems to presuppose the category of prophecies meant for the distant future. Still, taken as a generalization (and therefore omitting the emphatic "always"), Meyer's dictum is a fair description of the overall nature of Israelite prophecies concerning the future.

[112] The literature on the beatitudes is immense. An initial orientation to problems and bibliography can be found in the magisterial work of Jacques Dupont, *Les béatitudes* (3 vols; 2d ed.; Paris: Gabalda, 1969 [vols. 1 and 2], 1973 [vol.3]). Basic philological data can be found in F. Hauck and G. Bertram, *"makarios,"* TDNT 4 (1967) 362–70; and Henri Cazelles, " *'ashrê,"* TDOT 1 (1974) 445–48. For further exegetical discussion and bibliographies, see Klaus Koch, *Was ist Formgeschichte?* (2d ed.; Neukirchen-Vluyn: Neukirchener Verlag, 1967) 6–9, 21–23, 36–37, 50–55, 74–48; N. Walter, "Die Bearbeitung der Seligpreisungen durch Matthäus," *Studia Evangelica. Vol. IV* (TU 102; ed. F. L. Cross; Berlin: Akademie, 1968) 246–58; Raymond E. Brown, "The Beatitudes According to Luke," *New Testament Essays*, 334–41; Hubert Frankemölle, "Die Makarismen (Mt 5,1–12; Lk 6,20–23)," *BZ* 15 (1971) 52–75; Schulz, *Q. Die Spruchquelle der Evangelisten*, 76–84; Eduard Schweizer, "Formgeschichtliches zu den Seligpreisungen," *Mattäus und seine Gemeinde* (SBS 71; Stuttgart: KBW, 1974) 69–77; Schlosser, *Le règne de Dieu*, 2. 423–50; Neil J. McEleney, "The Beatitudes of the Sermon on the Mount/Plain," *CBQ* 43 (1981) 1–13; Fitzmyer, *Luke*, 1. 625–46; Robert A. Guelich, *The Sermon on the Mount* (Waco, TX: Word Books, 1982) 62–118; Hans Dieter Betz, "The Beatitudes of the Sermon on the Mount (Matt. 5:3–12): Observations on Their Literary Form and Theological Significance," *Essays on the Sermon on the Mount* (Philadelphia: Fortress, 1985) 17–36; Ingo Broer, *Die Seligpreisungen der Bergpredigt* (BBB 61; Bonn: Hanstein, 1986); Kloppenborg, *The Formation of Q*, 172–73, 187–90; Georg Strecker, *The Sermon on the Mount* (Nashville: Abingdon, 1988) 27–47;

M. Eugene Boring, "The Historical-Critical Method's 'Criteria of Authenticity': The Beatitudes in Q and Thomas as a Test Case," *The Historiccal Jesus and the Rejected Gospels* (Semeia 44; ed. Charles W. Hedrick; Atlanta: Scholars, 1988) 9–44; idem, *The Continuing Voice of Jesus*, 192–206; Davies and Allison, *The Gospel According to Saint Matthew*, 1. 429–69; Ulrich Luz, *Matthew 1–7. A Commentary* (Minneapolis: Augsburg, 1989) 224–46; Alexander A. Di Lella, "The Structure and Composition of the Matthean Beatitudes," (Joseph A. Fitzmyer Festschrift; ed. Maurya P. Horgan and Paul J. Kobelski; New York: Crossroad, 1989) 237–42; Emile Puech, "4Q525 et les péricopes des béatitudes en Ben Sira et Matthieu," *RB* 98 (1991) 80–106; Benedict T. Viviano, "Eight Beatitudes at Qumran and in Matthew?" *Svensk Exegetisk Årsbok* 58 (1993) 71–84.

[113] Compare, e.g., the treatment of the beatitudes in Merklein, *Jesu Botschaft von der Gottesherrschaft*, 45–51. The beatitudes are the first significant piece of Jesus tradition Merklein examines in detail when he takes up the topic of future salvation in the kingdom of God.

[114] In what follows, when I use the phrase "the Sermon" without further qualification, it always means the Sermon on the Mount/Plain or the basic Q Sermon that lies behind both the Matthean and the Lucan versions.

[115] To avoid confusing the educated lay person, I have stayed as close as possible to a traditional translation of the beatitudes. However, the educated lay person should be warned that a number of traditional phrases may not adequately render the sense of the Greek text, its OT background, and the theology of the evangelists. For example "the meek" (*hoi praeis*) are not "soft" people who are easily "pushed around," but rather people who are humble in their relationship with God (readily admitting their total dependence on him) and gentle in their relationships with other people (not egotistically pursuing their own desires to the detriment of others). The Matthean phrase "hunger and thirst for justice" denotes a fierce desire for God's salvation (that is the Matthean sense of "justice," *dikaiosynē*, in this text); for the opposite view (that "justice" refers here to human moral action), see Davies and Allison, *The Gospel According to Saint Matthew*, 1. 451–54. Such hungry people "will be satisfied," i.e., they will be fed to the full (the Greek verb, *chortazō*, originally referred to feeding animals); the imagery is that of the joyful banquet in the kingdom. The "pure (or clean) of heart" are those who stand before God with complete honesty and integrity; they are perfectly sincere, obedient, and loyal toward God. In Matthean terminology, those persecuted "for the sake of justice" are persecuted because they do the will of God according to the teaching of Jesus (the other sense of *dikaiosynē* in Matthew). The Lucan reference to "when they separate you and cast out your name as evil" may refer to social ostracism (e.g., a family rejecting a member who has accepted the teaching of Jesus) or the exclusion of Jewish Christians from synagogues toward the end of the 1st century A.D.

[116] In order to facilitate the comparison of the wording of Matthew and Luke, I anticipate Luke's third beatitude and place it in brackets alongside Matthew's second beatitude. Then, to show its proper position in Luke, I repeat his third beatitude in its regular place, without the brackets.

[117] Because my goal is the authentic teaching of the historical Jesus, I do not dwell upon fine points of difference between the Greek texts of Matthew and Luke that would make no difference in our hypothetical reconstruction of Jesus' statements. Hence, e.g., I do not try to represent in the translation the difference between Matthew's present imperative *chairete* (perhaps: "keep on rejoicing") and Luke's 2d aorist deponent imperative *charēte* (the "punctiliar" aorist being chosen perhaps because of Luke's pinpointing of the rejoicing "on that day").

[118] I agree with the majority opinion that the woes in Luke's text are not an original part of the beatitude tradition of the Q Sermon. The arguments for this position are laid out by Dupont (Les béatitudes, 1. 299–342), who is followed by many others. Whether the woes existed in a different place in Q, came from a special L tradition, or are simply the redactional creation of Luke need not concern us here. Broer (Die Seligpreisungen, 19–38) thinks that Luke did not create the woes but rather had access to a more developed form of the Sermon tradition, in which the beatitudes and the woes were already both present; a similar position can be found in Walter, "Seligprei-sungen," 249–50. In contrast, Fitzmyer (The Gospel According to Luke, 1. 627) thinks that "the heavy incidence of Lucan vocabulary in these verses" indicates that "they should be ascribed to Lucan composition. . . ." For the minority view that the woes were a part of the Q Sermon but were omitted by Matthew because (1) he had already planned a list of woes in chap. 23 and (2) the woes in the Q Sermon would not fit the theme and tone of the great initial discourse in chaps. 5–7, see Frankemölle, "Makaris-men," 64–65.

[119] For authors on both sides of the issue, see Fitzmyer, The Gospel According to Luke, 1. 631–32. Fitzmyer argues for the originality of the 3d person form on the grounds that (1) the 3d person plural form "has better OT antecedents"; (2) it is more likely that Luke changed the 3d person to the 2d person to match the 2d person form natural to the woes (ouai hymin) that Luke added and made parallel to the beatitudes; (3) Luke's style shows a certain preference for the 2d person plural. Also in favor of the originality of the 3d person plural is Bultmann, Geschichte, 114 along with n. 3.

But is this line of argumentation entirely probative? Dupont (Les béatitudes, 1. 274–82) goes into the question in some detail and holds that a mere appeal to what is the more usual form of the beatitude in the OT and later literature is not sufficient, since the 2d person plural, while rarer, is not impossible. Dupont proceeds rather from the point that the first part of Luke's first three beatitudes gives no indication of the 2d person plural ("happy the poor," etc.). It is only the hoti clause that in each case indi-cates the 2d person ("for yours is the kingdom of God"). This, says Dupont, is most unusual. If a beatitude were originally cast in the 2d person, it would naturally indicate the direct address in the first part of the beatitude, as is the case in the final long beatitude in both Matthew and Luke (makarioi este: "happy are you"). The lack of either a 2d person pronoun or a 2d person verb in the first part of Luke's first three beatitudes makes it much more likely that Luke has introduced the 2d person into the hoti clause of three beatitudes that originally were entirely in the 3d person. Dupont reinforces this argument by an appeal to the hypothetical Aramaic original. The Ara-maic construct plural form tûbê (from tûbā', "goodness," "happiness"), which is the functional equivalent of the Hebrew 'ašrê in beatitudes, calls for a pronominal suffix. So in the original Aramaic form of the beatitudes there probably stood either tûbêhôn ("O the happiness of those who") or tûbêkôn ("O the happiness of you who"). If the 3d person plural stood in the original, it would be quite normal for the Greek translator to translate the Aramaic with makarioi hoi [+ adjective or participle], with no need to put in an autoi after makarioi to represent the 3d person plural pronominal suffix. If, however, the Aramaic original was in the 2d person plural, it is strange that the Greek translator would not have represented the pronominal suffix by using hymeis (or alter-nately este). I find Dupont's argumentation especially convincing. For a representative of the opposite view, see Walter, "Seligpreisungen," 253.

[120] Davies and Allison (Matthew, 1. 442) offer two further reasons for considering "in spirit" redactional: (1) in another Q passage, Matt 11:5 ∥ Luke 7:22, "poor" occurs without any modifier or qualification; (2) Luke 6:24, the first woe, "has 'the rich' with-

out qualification, which probably implies an unqualified 'the poor' in at least Q^{Lk}." See also Broer, *Die Seligpreisungen*, 69–71.

[121] See 1QM 14:7, with the possible reading *bĕʿanwê rûaḥ* ("and by the poor [or humble] of spirit . . ."), though this translation has been disputed. In a fragmentary text in 1QH 14:3 *wĕʿanwê rûaḥ* appears. The difficulty of deciding the proper reading of the 1QM 14:7 text can be seen in the change of opinion by Jacques Dupont. He at first accepted the reading given above; see his "Les pauvres en esprit," *A la rencontre de Dieu. Mémorial Albert Gelin* (Le Puy: Mappus, 1961) 265–72, esp. 269–72. Later on he preferred the reading *ʿanwî rûaḥ*; see his "le *ptōchoi tǭ pneumati* de Matthieu 5,3 et les *ʿnwy rwḥ* de Qumrân," *Neutestamentliche Aufsätze* (Josef Schmid Festschrift; ed. Josef Blinzer, Otto Kuss, and Franz Mussner; Regensburg: Pustet, 1963) 53–64. In any case, the possible occurrence of the phrase at Qumran raises the question whether it might refer to voluntary poverty; Matthew certainly knows of such poverty as one response to Jesus' call to discipleship (e.g., Matt 19:16–30).

[122] On this see J. P. Brown, "The Form of 'Q' Known to Matthew," *NTS* 8 (1961–62) 27–42.

[123] The original order of the second and third beatitudes in the Q document cannot be known with certainty; see Schlosser, *Le règne de Dieu*, 2. 424. The matter is of no great importance for our purposes. For the sake of convenience, I follow the order of Matthew.

[124] Schlosser, *Le règne de Dieu*, 2. 425–29; Fitzmyer, *The Gospel According to Luke*, 1. 634. Fitzmyer notes that the verb *gelan* ("to laugh") "appears only here and in the corresponding woe in the gospel tradition; this seems to indicate that it is Luke who has modified his source." Fitzmyer also suggests that Matthew's *hoi penthountes* ("those who mourn") may reflect the theme of those who mourn for Zion (Isa 61:2) and so may echo the words of Jesus, who in turn was echoing the Book of Isaiah. However, as Guelich points out, the reference to Isa 61:2 could be due to Matthew's redaction (*The Sermon on the Mount*, 80). Actually, the widespread appeal to Isa 61:1–3 as a source of the thought and structure of the beatitudes is highly questionable—certainly so on the level of the primitive Q beatitudes, and perhaps even on the level of Matthean redaction. The clear influence of Isaiah 61 is probably limited to Matt 5:4's *hoi penthountes*. For this healthy skepticism about the influence of Isaiah 61, see Broer, *Die Seligpreisungen*, 64–67. More probative is the observation of Davies and Allison (*Matthew*, 1. 447), who note that *pentheō* ("mourn") is probably original because it resurfaces in telltale fashion in Luke's woe on those who laugh now (probably created as a mirror-image of the primitive beatitude): "Woe, those who laugh now, for you shall mourn (*penthēsete*) and weep."

One might dismiss the whole argument by holding that "mourn" and "weep" are simply Greek translation variants. While that is possible, it may not be the most likely solution in this particular case. In the LXX, *klaiō* ("weep") regularly translates the Hebrew verb *bākâ*—and never *ʾābal*—while *pentheō* ("mourn") regularly translates *ʾābal* ("mourn") and only once *bākâ*.

[125] On *dikaiosynē* in Matthew, see Dupont, *Les béatitudes*, 3. 211–384; also still useful is the older study of Albert Descamps, *Les justes et la justice dans les évangiles et le christianisme primitif hormis la doctrine proprement paulinienne* (Gembloux: Duculot, 1950); and the more recent work of Benno Przybylski, *Righteousness in Matthew and His World of Thought* (SNTSMS 41; Cambridge: Cambridge University, 1980).

[126] Again, one must stress that certitude in such a minor matter is not to be had. For

instance, Fitzmyer (*The Gospel According to Luke*, 1. 634) thinks that since the verbs "hunger and thirst" are found as a pair in OT passages (e.g., Isa 49:10; 65:13), Matthew may be preserving the original form of Q. Guelich (*The Sermon on the Mount*, 83) takes the opposite view: Luke represents the original wording referring to those who were literally "hungry," a stark single word standing in parallel to the stark single word "poor." Davies and Allison (*Matthew*, 1. 451) advance two arguments in favor of the single verb "hunger" being original: (1) The Greek is awkward (the accusative after "hunger and thirst"), and the first half of the beatitude is lopsided compared with the simple *autoi chortasthēsontai* of the second half. (2) The *kai dipsōntes* breaks the "p" alliteration in the first four beatitudes: *ptōchoi, penthountes, praeis,* and *peinōntes.*

[127] So Fitzmyer, *The Gospel According to Luke*, 1. 635. This should not be taken to mean that Jesus might not have warned his disciples about possible harassment and persecution (the verb *diōkō* can mean both).

[128] So Schürmann, *Lukasevangelium*, 1. 334 n. 62; Guelich, *The Sermon on the Mount*, 95; less confidently, H. E. Tödt, *The Son of Man in the Synoptic Tradition* (New Testament Library; London: SCM, 1965) 123. For the opposite view, see Fitzmyer, *The Gospel According to Luke*, 1. 635. The fragility of any decision on this question is shown by the fact that, while Matthew substitutes the personal pronoun for the title Son of Man in his Marcan source in Matt 16:21 ∥ Mark 8:31, he does just the opposite in Matt 16:13 ∥ Mark 8:27.

[129] Fitzmyer, (*The Gospel According to Luke*, 1. 635) thinks that Luke has added "on that day" as a parallel-contrast to the "now" that he has likewise added to the first half of his second and third beatitudes. As Fitzmyer also notes, Luke has substituted *skirtaō* for *agalliaō*, which Matthew preserves from Q and which he uses only here in his Gospel. In contrast, Luke uses *agalliaō* elsewhere (1:47; 10:21).

[130] On a minor point: Matthew's plural form *en tois ouranois* (literally, "in the heavens") may reflect a Semitic substratum (in both Hebrew and Aramaic "heaven" is always a plural noun), while Luke's singular *en tǭ ouranǭ* may be an adaptation to common Greek usage.

[131] Kloppenborg (*The Formation of Q*, 173), following Odil H. Steck (*Israel und das gewaltsame Geschick der Propheten* [WMANT 23; Neukirchen-Vluyn: Neukirchener Verlag, 1967] 258–59), suggests that 6:23c does not fit the flow of logic in vv 22–23b. Verse 6:23c ("for so they persecuted the prophets") does not provide a further reason supporting v 23b ("for your reward is great in heaven"), which is the real—and sufficient—grounding of the imperatives in 23a ("rejoice and be glad"). See also Schulz, *Q. Die Spruchquelle der Evangelisten*, 456 n. 404.

[132] I am presuming here the position for which I argued above, namely, that Matthew's 3d person plural formulation is more original in the first three beatitudes of the Q Sermon.

[133] The fact that the fourth beatitude lacks the initial alliteration of the "p" sound found in the other three beatitudes (*ptōchoi, penthountes,* and *peinōntes*) may be another indication that it did not belong to the original series of beatitudes when the series first appeared in Greek dress.

[134] On this see Boring, *The Continuing Voice of Jesus*, 203–6. Guelich (*The Sermon on the Mount*, 112–13) recognizes that the long beatitude on persecution probably existed in the earliest tradition as an independent logion, but he stresses that the theme of suffering was part of Jesus' teaching to his disciples. Indeed, Dupont (*Les béatitudes*, 2. 317–18) argues from the reserved nature of the original Q beatitude, which says noth-

ing about the disciples dying for their faith in Jesus, that the beatitude ultimately comes from Jesus and not from early Christian catechesis. To maintain this point, however, he must concede that the precision "for the sake of the Son of Man" is probably a secondary addition by the church (pp. 377–78).

[135] Whenever in what follows I use the phrase "the core beatitudes," I mean these first three beatitudes in Q.

[136] While the beatitude ultimately arose out of the congratulations or felicitations of daily life, scholars argue over the technical, literary *Sitz im Leben* of the beatitude. The two main candidates are the liturgy of the Jerusalem temple and the wisdom school. In favor of the latter is the originally "secular" and international nature of the beatitude, as well as the beatitude's focus on human action and happiness. Indeed, in the OT *ʾašrê* is never predicated directly of God. In this it stands in sharp contrast to the liturgical cry *bārûk* ("blessed"), the prayer of blessing and thanksgiving (the *běrākâ*) which is regularly directed to God in the Psalms and in other prayers, public and private. It is to maintain this distinction of vocabulary and form that I regularly translate *ʾašrê* (Greek: *makarios*) as "happy" and *bārûk* (Greek: *eulogētos* and *eulogēmenos*) as "blessed." This is not to deny that as beatitudes became theologically grounded and both literary forms developed in the biblical tradition a certain commingling occurred (cf. Luke 1:42,45; 1 Tim 1:11; 6:15). On the dispute concerning form and *Sitz im Leben*, see Guelich, *The Sermon on the Mount*, 63–66.

[137] By way of exception, the forms *ʾašrāyw* and *ʾašrēhû* are found in the postpositive position in Prov 14:21; 16:20; and 29:18.

[138] Another example is Prov 8:33–34. Job 5:17–18 might qualify except for the fact that a negative jussive intervenes between the beatitude and the *kî* ("for") clause. Examples from the Book of Psalms are not so clear. One case may be Ps 128:1–2: "Happy is everyone who fears Yahweh, who walks in his ways; for (*kî*) you shall eat of the labor of your hands." However, the *kî* is not represented in the LXX, and its position in the Hebrew text may indicate that it is rather an emphatic particle meaning "indeed, to be sure, certainly." Still another uncertain example may be Ps 94:12–14; the problem here is that the *kî* ("for") clause beginning v 14 is distant from and only loosely connected with the initial *ʾašrê haggeber* ("happy the man") beginning v 12. Some might want to add Gen 30:13, but two considerations prevent it from being a true example of the form *ʾašrê* + noun (or other description of the person) + *kî* expressing a reward: (1) Instead of the usual *ʾašrê* at the beginning, we have the *hapax legomenon* phrase *běošrî*, "by my luck!" If (as some critics suggest) one substitutes instead *bāʾ ošrî* ("my luck has come"), the difference in form is even greater. (2) The *kî* clause in 30:13 seems to be more an exegesis of the initial exclamation than a statement of a reward. Hence the *NAB* translates: "And Leah said, 'What good fortune!'—meaning, 'Women call me fortunate.'" A similar translation is adopted by E. A. Speiser, *Genesis* (AB 1; Garden City, NY: Doubleday, 1964) 229: "Said Leah, 'How fortunate! It means that the women will consider me fortunate.'" That the *kî* clause simply spells out what is contained in the initial exclamation seems to be the understanding of the LXX as well: *makaria egō hoti makarizousin me hai gynaikes.*

[139] Isa 30:18 and 32:20 might also count as eschatological beatitudes when their larger contexts are taken into account; but they are less clearly eschatological in content than Dan 12:12.

[140] See, e.g., the series of eight woes in *1 Enoch* 98:9–99:2 (cf. 99:11–16); the joining of woe and beatitude in *1 Enoch* 103:5 and *2 Apoc. Bar.*10:6–7; the nine beatitudes in *2 Enoch* 42:6–14; and the seven intercalated beatitudes and curses in *2 Enoch* 52:1–14.

[141] This is the translation of Sinaiticus; Vaticanus and Alexandrinus differ slightly in wording, but the basic point remains the same.

[142] See Puech, "4Q525," 82–90. From the fragmentary evidence Puech draws sweeping conclusions that seem to go beyond the fragile data.

[143] 1 Tim 1:11 and 6:15 use *makarios* of God. This shows the influence of pagan Greek thought and linguistic usage, in which the gods are considered the supremely happy ones. Such usage runs counter to the Hebrew OT, where *'ašrê* is never predicated directly of God. In the same Greek manner, Tit 2:13 calls Christians' hope for the parousia *makarios*.

[144] For a list of all the possible allusions to the Synoptic tradition in the Epistle of James, see Peter H. Davids, "James and Jesus," *Gospel Perspectives. Volume 5. The Jesus Tradition Outside the Gospels* (ed. David Wenham; Sheffield: JSOT, 1984) 63–84, esp. 66–67. Material from the Sermon on the Mount is especially prominent in the survey. However, Davids's analysis is not very penetrating. For example, Matt 10:22 is listed as a possible parallel to Jas 1:12, with no mention of the beatitude-form or of a possible parallel to the beatitudes of the Sermon, which Davids does discern elsewhere in James. The same holds true of Jas 1:25.

[145] See Martin Dibelius, *Der Brief des Jakobus* (MeyerK 15; 11th ed.; ed. Heinrich Greeven; Göttingen: Vandenhoeck & Ruprecht, 1964) 118.

[146] To be more precise: a future middle verb (*lēmpsetai*) with active meaning.

[147] As Dibelius (*Der Brief des Jakobus*, 153) notes, the verb *estai* is a logical, not an eschatological, future and might well be translated by the present tense. On this whole difficult passage in James, see Luke Timothy Johnson, "The Mirror of Remembrance (James 1:22–25)," *CBQ* 50 (1988) 622–31.

[148] See, e.g., Edward Gordon Selwyn, *The First Epistle of St. Peter* (2d ed.; Grand Rapids: Baker, 1981; originally 1946) 191–92, 222. For a debate on the extent and use of Gospel tradition in 1 Peter, see Robert H. Gundry, " 'Verba Christi' in I Peter: Their Implications Concerning the Authorship of I Peter and the Authenticity of the Gospel Tradition," *NTS* 13 (1966–67) 336–50; the reply by Ernest Best, "I Peter and the Gospel Tradition," *NTS* 16 (1969–70) 95–113; and the reply to Best by Gundry in his "Further *Verba* on *Verba Christi* in First Peter," *Bib* 55 (1974) 211–32. Gundry's presentation of the Gospel tradition in 1 Peter is influenced by his desire to affirm authorship of the Epistle by the Apostle Peter, a position that Best convincingly refutes. Gerhard Maier ("Jesustradition im 1. Petrusbrief?" *Gospel Perspectives. Volume 5. The Jesus Tradition Outside the Gospels* [ed. David Wenham; Sheffield: JSOT, 1984] 85–128) calls 1 Pet 4:14 a case of the "verifiable dependence of 1 Peter on words of the Lord, precisely as they are preserved in Matthew" (p. 102). It is strange that Maier, unlike Gundry and Best, does not give serious consideration to 1 Pet 3:14. Concerning 1 Pet 3:14 Best ("1 Peter," 109) states: "We thus assume that in our present instance Matthew received it [Matt 5:10] in the tradition and that the author of 1 Peter knew this tradition, whence he derived it." Gundry for his part considers the relationship between 1 Pet 3:14 and the beatitude on those who suffer for justice' sake "indubitable" ("Further *Verba*," 228). In his conclusion, Best suggests that, if 1 Peter was written in Rome toward the end of the 1st century A.D., it may well reflect the same sort of dependence on an oral form of the Gospel tradition found also in *1 Clement*.

[149] See Edouard des Places, *La Première Epitre de saint Pierre* (Rome: Biblical Institute, n.d.) 56–57. He holds that *en onomati Christou* of v 14 and *Christianos* of v 16 go together; "from the beginning the persecutions suffered by Christians . . . were 'for the

name.' . . ." Davids ("James and Jesus," 68–69) points out that not only NT authors like James and Paul (and we might add the author of 1 Peter) but also postcanonical writings like the *Didache* and the *Shepherd of Hermas* do not always explicitly mention Jesus as the source when they cite his words, even though by the early 2d century the authors are no doubt aware of the ultimate (reputed) source of the sayings.

[150] Robert H. Mounce, *The Book of Revelation* (NICNT; Grand Rapids: Eerdmans, 1977) 389.

[151] So Mounce, *Revelation*, 390.

[152] J. P. M. Sweet, *Revelation* (Westminster Pelican Commentaries; Philadelphia: Westminster, 1979] 314): ". . . [the interpreting angel] like the OT prophets both reports the words of his principal and speaks in his person." A similar possibility is left open by Mounce, *Revelation*, 391 n. 7. E.-B. Allo allows for the possibility that "behold I am coming soon" is understood as spoken by either the author or the angel, who is recalling the words already spoken by Jesus earlier in the Book of Revelation; see his *Saint Jean. Apocalypse* (EBib; 2d ed.; Paris: Gabalda, 1921) 329.

[153] As Dupont says (*Les béatitudes*, 2. 140), "They [the core beatitudes of Q] appear at the same time a variant and a concrete illustration of the proclamation that the kingdom of God is imminent. The poor are happy precisely because God is about to inaugurate his reign. . . ."

[154] See Dupont, *Les béatitudes*, 2. 141.

[155] For now I simply accept the fact that at least the substance of many of these parables is acknowledged by most critics as reflecting the authentic message of the historical Jesus. The material will have to be probed at greater length later on. But even now we can see that the core message of God's gratuitous mercy extended to those who have no claim on it is attested in the parables in multiple sources, as it likewise is elsewhere in multiple forms.

[156] Speaking in general of the ideas about the poor and of the function of the king toward them in the ancient Near East, Dupont (*Les béatitudes*, 2. 88) says: "If the king is obliged to be concerned about them [the poor], it is not because they are perhaps better citizens than anyone else, but because one of the essential attributes of the royal function consists in assuring justice to all subjects, which means in practice assuring their proper rights to the weak, those incapable of defending themselves against the powerful and the oppressors. The foundation of what one can call the privilege of the poor is not found therefore in an idealized conception of their poverty, but in an ideal of the royal function." Dupont then points out that this same conception held for the gods in general and for the God of Israel in particular (p. 89): "As the just king, God cannot help but be the protector of the disinherited."

[157] For an extensive treatment of "the poor" in the Bible in general and in the beatitudes in particular, see Dupont, *Les béatitudes*, 2. 19–278. For shorter discussions of the topic, see Friedrich Hauck and Ernst Bammel, "*ptōchos*, etc.," *TDNT* 6 (1968) 885–915; Guelich, *The Sermon on the Mount*, 67–72; and Broer, *Seligpreisungen*, 68–75. To summarize: while *ptōchos* in ancient pagan Greek had solely a socioeconomic sense, the Hebrew adjective ʿānî (along with its more recent linguistic "cousin," ʿānāw) carried a double sense: both socioeconomic status and religious attitude. ʿānî connoted more of the former, ʿānāw more of the latter; but a certain interchangeability can be seen, especially in some of the later psalms of the Psalter (see Bammel, "*ptōchos*," 892). The socioeconomic status designated by ʿānî involved not simply lack of money or possessions, but first of all powerlessness and vulnerability vis-à-vis the powerful (and often

arrogant) members of society. The word thus denoted first of all a certain negative relationship within society rather than simply an absolute state of not having money or goods. There is an implication of "being unjustly deprived of one's rights and goods" in ʿānî; accordingly, the regular adversaries of the "poor" in the OT are not the rich but the wicked, the arrogant, and the oppressors. This status often evoked—at least according to many religious affirmations in the OT—an attitude of humility toward and reliance upon God, before whom one had to stand empty-handed, without pretensions but with hope. The poor's trust in God was based on God's being the guarantor as well as chief partner in the covenant, with all its stipulations of social justice. According to the united witness of Law, Prophets, and Psalms, Yahweh took the side of the poor and oppressed and vindicated their rights against their rich and powerful oppressors. The Babylonian exile brought a further development, for in a sense the whole of the people became "poor" and helpless. Increasingly the vindication of Israel—or at least the faithful and pious remnant thereof—was promised in eschatological and then apocalyptic terms. The sectarian documents from Qumran often refer to the members of the community as the "poor," i.e., the pious Qumranites who scrupulously obey the will of God in the torah, interpreted correctly by the Teacher of Righteousness. Still, the socioeconomic dimension has not evaporated into pure spirituality at Qumran, since the Qumranites practiced a community of goods and saw as their chief adversaries the rich and powerful priestly aristocracy in Jerusalem.

All this provides a fitting background for the beatitudes of Jesus, the eschatological prophet sent to Israel in its last hour. He addresses the core beatitudes to those who are really poor, mournful, and hungry—no doubt a good percentage of Galilean peasants, people who do not have the means to lift themselves permanently out of their impoverished, sorrowful, and famished state. But in the light of the OT and intertestamental thought, these literally poor were also thought to be those who had seen through the lying promises of the power and wealth of this world and therefore had put their ultimate trust in God alone. It is to these Israelites who are socioeconomically *and* religiously "poor" that Jesus speaks the eschatological hope of the kingdom with its reversal of the present unjust state of things. One must beware of letting this dual sense of poverty be obscured by the Lucan tradition of the beatitudes, where the "poor" are simply opposed to the "rich" in the corresponding woe (Luke 6:24). It is not very surprising that Jesus the marginal Jew showed special concern for those Jews who, in varied ways, were marginalized within the larger society. That Jesus did give his attention especially to the "poor" in this broad sense is borne out by the various Gospel sources and literary forms that present him being sought after or reaching out to the physically and mentally ill (e.g., lepers, the epileptic boy in Mark 9:14–27), those thought to be possessed by demons, public sinners, tax collectors (many of whom were not as rich as Zacchaeus), women, and children (on this, see Gnilka, *Jesus von Nazaret*, 180–82; for the similarity between the poor on the one hand and little children and sinners on the other in the proclamation of Jesus, see Dupont, *Les béatitudes*, 2. 143–278). That Jesus saw an important part of his ministry to be proclaiming the "good news" of the coming kingdom of God to the poor—the very thing he is doing in the Q beatitudes—is confirmed by the reply to the disciples of John the Baptist (Matt 11:2–6 ‖ Luke 7:18–23). The reply, after reciting various miracles, reaches the climax of its narration of Jesus' ministry with an allusion to Isa 61:1: "And the poor have the good news preached to them." As we saw in Chapter 13 there is good reason for taking the substance of this pericope as historical.

All that is said above should not be taken to mean that *every* follower of Jesus was literally poor or that Jesus never addressed anyone but the poor. From Jairus, the centurion with the sick servant (or the royal official with a sick son?), and the ministering women mentioned in Luke 8:2–3 (some of whom may have had connections in high places) to Zacchaeus, the woman at Bethany with her expensive ointment, and the anonymous Jerusalemite who was able to give Jesus hospitality for the Last Supper, there are signs that—not unlike Paul's urban churches—the many poor disciples (along with Jesus or Paul himself) could look to a few more affluent or influential disciples for some practical help and support. In this sense, at least, those who were economically well-off could count themselves among Jesus' "poor" provided that they accepted Jesus' message and formed their lives accordingly. In one sense, then, the phrase "poor in spirit," be it from Matthew's redaction or from Q^{Mt}, does capture one aspect of those who followed Jesus.

[158] On the problem of interpreting Amos 2:6, see Francis I. Andersen and David Noel Freedman, *Amos* (AB 24A; New York: Doubleday, 1989) 310–13.

[159] On the passage see Hans Walter Wolff, *Hosea* (Hermeneia; Philadelphia: Fortress, 1974) 17–19. This political denunciation by Hosea is all the more intriguing because it seems that historically the revolt of Jehu was either inspired by or at least approved by "the prophetic circles gathered around Elijah and Elisha (2 Kgs 10:30)" (p. 18).

[160] Boring, *The Continuing Voice of Jesus*, 195; see also the remarks by Best ("I Peter," 105–6, 109, 111–13), who suggests that the author of 1 Peter, like *1 Clement*, knew blocks of oral Gospel tradition. On 1 Pet 3:14, Best thinks that the difference between the use of *diōkō* in Matt 5:10 and *paschō* in 1 Pet 3:14 is not important "since the meaning is not greatly affected and the latter word is a particular favorite in 1 Peter" (p. 109 n. 2).

[161] On the existence of a parenetic tradition of Jesus' words in the NT Epistles, distinct from the Synoptic Gospel tradition of his words—both traditions going back to Jesus himself but developing in different *Sitze im Leben* in the early church—see John Piper, *'Love Your Enemies'* (SNTSMS 38; Cambridge: Cambridge University, 1979).

[162] Boring, *The Continuing Voice of Jesus*, 195.

[163] In place of Matthew's relatively rare perfect passive participle *dediōgmenoi* ("having been persecuted") Polycarp uses the simple present *diōkomenoi*, perhaps with a view to the church's experience of persecution in his own day.

[164] Boring (*The Continuing Voice of Jesus*, 195) states: "It is not clear whether or not this [i.e., the group of Synoptic-like beatitudes in the *Gospel of Thomas*] is an independent witness. . . ." In more recent conversations, Boring has indicated to me that he now inclines to the view of dependence on the Synoptics for at least some of the material in the *Gospel of Thomas*. For a convenient listing of the ten beatitudes in the *Gospel of Thomas*, see Davies and Allison, *Matthew*, 441.

[165] In each of the sayings, the Coptic text takes over the Greek word *makarios*.

[166] Christopher Tuckett, "Thomas and the Synoptics," *NovT* 30 (1988) 132–57. That saying 54 is a mixed citation from Matthew and Luke is affirmed, after an analysis of the Coptic text, by Michael Fieger, *Das Thomasevangelium. Einleitung, Kommentar und Systematik* (NTAbh 22; Münster: Aschendorff, 1991) 164. Fieger thinks that in saying 54 the kingdom has become a present reality for the poor gnostic who turns away from matter.

[167] See Fieger, *Das Thomasevangelium*, 198. Fieger sees saying 69a related to Matt 5:10, with "heart" coming from Matt 5:8; saying 69b is seen as "a free combination" of Matt 5:6 and Luke 6:21. On all this, see pp. 199–200.

[168] See the systematic summary of the gnostic theology of the *Gospel of Thomas* in Fieger, *Das Thomasevangelium*, 281–89.

[169] Hence I find it astounding that in his full-dress treatment of the teaching of the historical Jesus (*Rediscovering the Teaching of Jesus*), Perrin never takes up a consideration of the beatitudes; apparently he did not feel that they qualify as authentic Jesus tradition. In this there was a silent but significant shift away from Perrin's earlier stance in his *The Kingdom of God in the Teaching of Jesus*, 181–82: "In their present form these [beatitudes] are undoubtedly editorial in arrangement, but that Jesus did teach something very like this there can be no doubt." Serious consideration of the beatitudes is likewise lacking in Perrin's last major work, *Jesus and the Language of the Kingdom*. Perhaps he had become influenced by the opinion of Ernst Käsemann, who asserts rather than proves his view that the beatitudes in the Sermon on the Mount/Plain are wholly products of early Christian prophecy; see his "The Beginnings of Christian Theology," *New Testament Questions of Today* (New Testament Library; London: SCM, 1969) 82–107, esp. 100–101.

[170] For the position that they arose (with the exception of 5:10 and possibly a few slight redactional touches) in an early, pre-Matthean stage of the Christian tradition, see, e.g., Guelich, *The Sermon on the Mount*, 114–15; for the position that they are Matthew's creations, see, e.g., Walter, "Seligpreisungen," 247–49; cf. Frankemölle, "Makarismen," 74; for the position that they are partly traditional and partly redactional, see, e.g., Broer, *Seligpreisungen*, 53–63 (see his list of opinions and representative authors on pp. 53–54).

[171] See the treatment of the question in Robert A. Guelich, "The Matthean Beatitudes: 'Entrance-Requirements' or Eschatological Blessings," *JBL* 95 (1976) 415–34. One senses that Christian theological problems that lie far from the main interests of the historical Jew named Jesus are intruding here.

[172] With similar spellings and similar meanings, it is not surprising that these two Hebrew adjectives/nouns often alternate with each other in the Qere and Ketib of the Hebrew manuscripts.

[173] See Guelich, *The Sermon on the Mount*, 82–83: "This promise [of inheriting the earth] also stands as a parallel to *the Kingdom of Heaven* in 5:3. The inheritance of the land was part of Israel's prerogative as the People of God (Deut 4:1; 16:20). It came to be an expression of God's intervention on their behalf in the future as seen, for example, in Isa 61:7. . . ."

[174] Many critics opt for some sort of underlying tradition rather than pure Matthean redaction for Matt 11:28–30; however, they differ on what source is being used. Georg Strecker (*Der Weg der Gerechtigkeit* [FRLANT 82; 3d ed.; Göttingen: Vandenhoeck & Ruprecht, 1971] 172–73) rejects the idea of Q as the source and champions instead a special M tradition; a creation by Matthew is unlikely because of the un-Matthean vocabulary, including six *hapax legomena*. In contrast, Bultmann (*Geschichte*, 172) speaks vaguely of 11:28–30 being a citation from a Jewish wisdom book, put into the mouth of Jesus. Dibelius (*Formgeschichte*, 281) takes the surprising view that the whole of 11:25–30 stood together as a three-strophe unit in Q. Sato (*Q und Prophetie*, 51) rejects the idea of a Matthean creation, but hesitates between M tradition and Q. Gerhard Barth, however, follows E. Hirsch and B. W. Bacon in seeing 11:28–30 as a creation of Matthew; see his "Das Gesetzesverständnis des Evangelisten Matthäus," in Günther Bornkamm, Gerhard Barth, and Heinz Joachim Held, *Überlieferung und Auslegung im Matthäusevangelium* (WMANT 1; 5th ed.; Neukirchen-Vluyn: Neukirchener Verlag,

1968) 96 n. 1. On the whole, I think that Strecker's choice of a special M tradition is the best grounded in solid philological arguments.

[175] Guelich (*The Sermon on the Mount*, 114–15) also offers an argument based on verbal links between Matt 5:7–9 and the primitive Sermon as discerned from Luke: "Each [of the beatitudes in 5:7–9] correlates with one of the following three major sections of the Sermon tradition, in particular with the tradition as it now stands in Luke" (p. 114). Such an argument is by its nature more subtle and speculative, and not everyone will see the links as clearly as Guelich.

[176] See the comment by Fitzmyer, *The Gospel According to Luke*, 1. 635.

[177] For commentary, see Fitzmyer, *The Gospel According to Luke*, 2. 1045. It is symptomatic that Marshall (*Luke*, 583) is worried about the saying being misunderstood. Nevertheless, he sums up the basic message well: ". . . it can surely not be Jesus' meaning that one is to do good deeds simply because they bring a better and more durable reward. The point is rather that one should seek to do good to those who are so needy that they cannot do anything in return, and leave the whole question of recompense to God. . . ."

[178] For a standard (perhaps all-too-standard) treatment of the vocabulary and the concept of reward in the Bible, see H. Preisker and E. Würthwein, "*misthos*, etc.," *TDNT* 4 (1967) 695–728. Abundant material is supplied from both Greek pagan, OT, Jewish, and Christian sources; but a particular theological viewpoint governs all. Preisker openly acknowledges that both Jesus and NT writers "spoke quite freely of reward" (p. 728). The way Preisker deals with this potentially embarrassing fact is clear from his very next sentence: "But for all the formal dependence, the Jewish idea of reward is completely transcended." The whole *TDNT* article is dedicated to this thesis and consequently revels in a caricature of Judaism that the NT is declared to overcome. Set over against the NT is the dogma of human achievement and merit in "Late Judaism" (!). On p. 714 we read: "Judaism . . . does not dare to rest man wholly on God's grace. It insists on man and his achievement. It seeks to merit a just reward and hence does not escape impotence and anxiety." There is a passing admission that some rabbinic texts reject an obedience that is simply looking for a reward (e.g., *m. 'Abot* 1:3), but we are assured that such voices "do not prevail" (p. 713).

It was against such biased presentations of what is more rightly called "early Judaism" that E. P. Sanders wrote his *Paul and Palestinian Judaism* (Philadelphia: Fortress, 1977); see esp. pp. 107–82. Sanders's treatment is not without its own difficulties, but it is a refreshing corrective to older, one-sided presentations of Judaism at the time of Jesus and in the immediately subsequent centuries. Sanders stresses that one should not try to turn the *ad hoc* statements of various rabbis into a systematic theology of merit. What the rabbis intended above all when they spoke of reward and punishment was to affirm that God is just and to motivate Israelites to obey his commandments. Statements that tend in the direction of commercial metaphors must be balanced against the great emphasis on God's mercy and on the means he has supplied for atonement when one sins.

As one might expect, Preisker contrasts his slanted picture of Judaism with the genuine teaching of Jesus in the Synoptic Gospels. Not surprisingly, to obtain this genuine teaching Preisker must discount a fair amount of Synoptic tradition that is judged to be suspiciously Jewish and therefore doubtful as authentic tradition coming from Jesus (pp. 715–16). This is the criterion of discontinuity run amok. A certain number of "reward" sayings are accepted as coming from Jesus, but a great deal of windy homiletics proceeds to inculcate how much Jesus "transcended" (the word is a favorite solution in this article) his Jewish milieu. Needless to say, it is quite correct to stress that Jesus rejected any idea that one could calculate the reward due one's good deeds and thus have a claim on God; his emphasis was completely on God's loving mercy and forgiveness of sinners. It is regrettable, however, that some scholars think that this point can be made adequately only by contrasting Jesus with a hopelessly inadequate presentation of early Judaism.

[179] I do not press the point that the *hoti* clause of 5:10 again mentions the kingdom, since this could well be due to Matthean redaction, creating an *inclusio* between the first and eighth beatitudes.

[180] For one expression of this suspicion, see the programmatic essay by Eta Linnemann, "Hat Jesus Naherwartung gehabt?" in J. Dupont (ed.), *Jésus aux origines de la christologie* (BETL 40; 2d ed.; Leuven: Leuven University/Peeters, 1989) 103–10. I think that Linnemann is correct in holding that imminent expectation is often predicated of the historical Jesus and of various sayings within the Gospels without testing the authenticity of the sayings or asking whether they must be understood as speaking of an imminent-future coming of the kingdom. I also think that she is correct in holding that Matt 10:23; Mark 13:30; and Mark 9:1 are most likely inauthentic and that sayings like Matt 12:28 ∥ Luke 11:20 should not be twisted into referring to imminent expectation when the natural sense of the logia points to the presence of the kingdom during the ministry of Jesus. However, apart from its brevity and sketchiness, Linnemann's essay suffers from a number of weaknesses: (1) She never seriously considers the converging lines of evidence that I point to in the main text, evidence that argues that for Jesus the coming of the kingdom was indeed imminent. This failure is even more evident in one of Linnemann's "predecessors" in the "anti-imminent" position, Ernst Bammel; see his "Erwägungen zur Eschatologie Jesu," 3–32. (2) Her claim that the imminent-future eschatology of both the Baptist immediately before Jesus and the Christian church immediately after him does not point to imminent expectation in Jesus' own teaching is not sufficiently substantiated. On this pivotal matter Linnemann claims total discontinuity between the Baptist and Jesus on the one hand and Jesus and the church on the other. That is a possible but nevertheless curious scenario. It would need to be argued at much greater length to be accepted as the most probable solution. Sanders argues convincingly instead for basic continuity in this matter of imminent eschatology; see his *Jesus and Judaism*, 91–95. (3) Once she eliminates imminent expectation in Jesus' teaching, Linnemann does not entirely escape the danger of falling into the opposite extreme. Although Linnemann holds that Jesus did expect a future coming of the kingdom, the lack of imminence means for her that Jesus' eschatology must be interpreted from the starting point of the presence of the kingdom in his ministry. This is to make the opposite mistake of authors like Sanders (*Jesus and Judaism*, 129–56), who are so focused on the imminent future kingdom that they cannot bring themselves to admit that Jesus also spoke of the kingdom as already present in his ministry. For the problems inherent in Sanders's position, see the next chapter, especially the treatment of Matt 12:28 ∥ Luke 11:20.

[181] Meyer, "Jesus's Scenario," 6.

[182] Bruce J. Malina, "Christ and Time: Swiss or Mediterranean?" *CBQ* 51 (1989) 1–31. There are, however, problems in Malina's presentation. Some of the NT texts are given unlikely interpretations; and other countervailing texts are ignored. One gets the impression of a good point being pressed too far.

[183] I will pursue this point in a later chapter; for now, see the presentation in Sanders, *Jesus and Judaism*, 95–106.

[184] For this argument, see Sanders, *Jesus and Judaism*, 91–95.

[185] These are the three usually singled out for detailed discussion by critics; see, e.g., Lorenz Oberlinner, "Die Stellung der 'Terminworte' in der eschatologischen Verkündigung des Neuen Testaments," *Gegenwart und kommendes Reich* (Anton Vögtle Festschrift; SBB; ed. Peter Fiedler and Dieter Zeller; Stuttgart: KBW, 1975) 51–66. For the views of exegetes (e.g., W. G. Kümmel, O. Cullmann, and H. Patsch) who defend some or all of these texts as coming from the historical Jesus, see pp. 53–59.

[186] This is a commonplace among commentators on Matthew; see, e.g., Walter Grundmann, *Das Evangelium nach Matthäus* (THKNT 1; 3d ed.; Berlin: Evangelische Verlagsanstalt, 1972) 284–85. That it is especially true of v 23 is affirmed by Martin Künzi, *Das Naherwartungslogion Matthäus 10, 23. Geschichte seiner Auslegung* (BGBE 9; Tübingen: Mohr [Siebeck], 1970) 177. A survey of the disparate material in the discourse is given from a modern literary-critical point of view by Dorothy Jean Weaver, *Matthew's Missionary Discourse. A Literary Critical Analysis* (JSNTSup 38; Sheffield: JSOT, 1990) 13–16.

[187] For a survey of the history of the interpretation of this puzzling saying, see Künzi, *Das Naherwartungslogion Matthäus 10, 23*. For a reading of the text from a modern literary-critical point of view, see Weaver, *Matthew's Missionary Discourse*, 99–101. A reading of the text on the level of Matthew's redaction that also seeks to work out a modern hermeneutic by way of typology can be found in Charles H. Giblin, "Theological Perspective and Matthew 10:23b," *TS* 29 (1968) 637–61.

As Künzi notes, "you shall not have finished [*ou mē telesēte*]" could refer to either fleeing through the cities of Israel or proclaiming the kingdom; Künzi favors the former (p. 178). As with many other secondary riddles in this logion, the choice does not greatly affect the overall decision about authenticity and so will not be given separate treatment. I agree with Künzi that "the cities of Israel" refers to the cities of Palestine (and not to some wider, metaphorical meaning).

[188] Along with Künzi (*Das Naherwartungslogion Matthäus 10, 23*, 178) and Helmut Merklein (*Jesu Botschaft von der Gottesherrschaft. Eine Skizze* [SBS 111; 2d ed.; Stuttgart: KBW, 1984] 55), I judge that Matt 10:23 is not made up of two separate sayings that were brought together only secondarily (contra Kümmel, *Promise and Fulfilment*, 61–62). The chiastic pattern of the whole verse (temporal clause with a verb in the subjunctive + main clause with a verb in the 2d person plural indicating an action that relates to a city [of Israel] + solemn Amen-formula in the center of the logion + main clause with a verb in the 2d person plural indicating an action that relates to the cities of Israel + a temporal clause with a verb in the subjunctive) seems too neat to be a happy coincidence resulting from the secondary welding together of two independent sayings.

[189] Boring (*The Continuing Voice of Jesus*, 250–51) suggests that Matt 10:23 supplied "a word of the risen Lord to settle an ambiguous situation for which there was no clear or satisfactory dominical saying in the tradition." The problem was that some sayings of Jesus in the early tradition called for steadfastness in the face of opposition and would therefore seem to forbid flight to another town as a sign of defeat and/or cowardice. But at times staying in a hostile town and accepting martyrdom might endanger the very mission given the missionaries by the risen Lord. In such cases Matt 10:23 legitimized flight. Boring sees this as an example of the early Christians' belief in the Spirit, speaking through the community's prophets, justifying a break with tradition.

[190] Künzi, *Das Naherwartungslogion Matthäus 10, 23*, 179.

[191] So Merklein, *Jesu Botschaft*, 55; see also Oberlinner ("Die Stellung," 64–65), who observes that in Matt 10:23 the missionary activity of the disciples takes on a certain independent existence. If there actually was a mission of the disciples during Jesus' public ministry, it would rather have been a brief, intense period of activity meant to support and extend Jesus' own mission to Israel. Instead, in Matt 10:23 the mission of the disciples has become an object of reflection and a theological problem in its own right.

[192] It is significant to note that Perrin, who formerly had defended the authenticity of Matt 10:23 on the basis of its being an unfulfilled prophecy (*The Kingdom of God in the Teaching of Jesus*, 83), finally decided against its authenticity, largely on the grounds presented above (*Rediscovering the Teaching of Jesus*, 201–2). An important methodological point is brought to light here. An unfulfilled prophecy among the words of Jesus is certainly a sign of an earlier rather than a later stratum of tradition. But whether the unfulfilled prophecy comes from the time of Jesus or from the early days of the church must be investigated in each case. Here again we see the limits of the criterion of embarrassment. Matt 10:23 may indeed have become something of an embarrassment for the church of the second or third generation. It certainly seems to have become an embarrassment for the early patristic church; v 23b is not cited before Origen and not often after him (see Künzi, *Das Naherwartungslogion Matthäus 10, 23*, 165; yet Künzi himself [p. 181] denies that the reason for the silence in the early church was embarrassment). To be sure, the embarrassment of the later NT or patristic church does not of itself prove that the saying comes from Jesus. A further question is how Matthew understood the logion in the final redaction of his Gospel. My opinion is that he may have reinterpreted it to refer to the coming of the risen Jesus as the exalted Son of Man to his church in the final scene of his Gospel, a sort of "proleptic parousia" (see Meier, *Matthew* [New Testament Message Series], 110–11); similarly, Levine, *The Social and Ethnic Dimensions*, 51. Other suggestions (e.g., a rendezvous between Jesus and the Twelve during the latter's brief mission, the event of Pentecost, the spread of the Gospel and the growth of the church, the crisis of the First Jewish War) have been made; see Beasley-Murray, *Jesus and the Kingdom of God*, 283–91, esp. 285–86; Boring, *The Continuing Voice*, 251; and the whole monograph of Künzi.

Others who argue that Matt 10:23 is a creation of the early church include Grässer, *Problem*, 138; Boring, *The Continuing Voice*, 250–52 (see p. 250: "The saying in 10:23 is particularly noteworthy as an example of a saying of a Christian prophet added to the tradition"); Gnilka, *Jesus von Nazaret*, 154: ". . . today this logion is almost unanimously assigned to the post-Easter situation." Künzi, *Das Naherwartungslogion Matthäus 10, 23*, 180) and Beasley-Murray (*Jesus and the Kingdom*, 289–91) are among those contemporary critics who maintain the logion's origin from the historical Jesus; neither's argument is all that rigorous. In particular, Beasley-Murray's argument, which claims to base itself on taking seriously the fact that Jesus was a Jew, is not a model of clarity or cogency.

[193] The great summary of his thesis is found in chapter 21, "The Solution of Consequent Eschatology," in his *Geschichte der Leben-Jesu-Forschung* (Siebenstern-Taschenbuch 79/80; 2 vols.; Munich/Hamburg: Siebenstern Taschenbuch, 1966 [originally 1906]) 2. 402–50.

[194] Beasley-Murray, *Jesus and the Kingdom of God*, 286.

[195] For the history of the interpretation of Mark 9:1 parr. (with an appendix on Mark 13:30 parr.), see Martin Künzi, *Das Naherwartungslogion Markus 9,1 par. Geschichte seiner Auslegung* (BGBE 21; Tübingen: Mohr [Siebeck], 1977).

[196] It is telling that even Rudolf Pesch, who champions the idea of a primitive, coherent pre-Marcan Passion Narrative reaching from 8:27 to 16:8 (*Das Markusevangelium*, 2. 1–2), considers 8:34–38 to be a separate chain of sayings that did not belong to the primitive Passion Narrative but was added to it by Mark. According to Pesch, it was Mark who added 9:1 to this chain of sayings (p. 57). While the conservative critic Vincent Taylor favors the authenticity of all the sayings in 8:34–9:1, he admits that the pericope "consists of excerpts from a collection of sayings and is inserted at this point for topical reasons" (*The Gospel According to St. Mark*, 380).

[197] Whatever be the case with the historical Jesus, certainly on the level of Marcan redaction and also the pre-Marcan tradition, Jesus and the Son of Man were identified in this saying. This is granted even by H. E. Tödt, who claims that the historical Jesus did not identify himself as the Son of Man; see Tödt's *The Son of Man in the Synoptic Tradition* (New Testament Library; London: SCM, 1965) 42.

[198] See Oberlinner, "Die Stellung," 63.

[199] Like many other critics, Schlosser (*Le règne de Dieu*, 1. 323) considers the introductory formula *kai elegen autois* to be typical of Marcan redaction. Schlosser (pp. 323–24) also echoes the majority of scholars in viewing the parallel verses in Matt 16:28 and Luke 9:27 to be simply Matthean and Lucan redactions of Mark 9:1. These parallel verses will therefore be ignored in what follows.

[200] So Pesch, *Das Markusevangelium*, 2. 67; see also Grundmann, *Das Evangelium nach Markus*, 177.

[201] The artificial nature of the connection makes it unlikely, in my view, that Mark himself created 9:1, as Perrin argues in *Rediscovering the Teaching of Jesus*, 199–201. But even if Perrin were correct, the basic position I am defending would remain the same: the logion does not come from the historical Jesus.

[202] On all this see Beasley-Murray, *Jesus and the Kingdom of God*, 187–88. On pp. 188–89, he likewise shows that the saying does not fit the resurrection of Jesus, the growth of the church, or the destruction of Jerusalem in A.D. 70. A similar exclusion of unlikely candidates (often championed throughout the history of the exegesis of this verse) is undertaken by Künzi, *Das Naherwartungslogion Markus 9,1 par*, 199–203.

[203] On this see Merklein, *Jesu Botschaft*, 54. As Merklein points out, Mark 9:1 would be an embarrassment for a Christian community late in the 1st century A.D., but not for the earliest community that had not yet sensed the so-called "delay of the parousia" as a problem. Hence, as in the case of Matt 10:23, an origin early in the first Christian generation seems likely. For an uncritical attempt to assign the saying to the historical Jesus and to have it refer to his resurrection, see Heinz Giesen, "Mk 9,1—ein Wort Jesu über die nahe Parusie?" *TTZ* 92 (1983) 134–48.

[204] Indeed, this point is an argument against taking any of the three sayings that set a time limit as authentic; see Oberlinner, "Die Stellung," 53–59.

[205] On the uselessness of trying to avoid the natural sense of Mark 9:1, see Anton Vögtle, "Exegetische Erwägungen über das Wissen und Selbstbewusstsein Jesu," *Gott in Welt* (Karl Rahner Festschrift; Freiburg/Basel/Vienna: Herder, 1964) 1. 608–67, esp. 611–12. It is telling that, in order to save the authenticity of Mark 9:1, Schlosser (*Le règne de Dieu*, 1. 349) allows that the distinction between the living and the dead expressed by "some" (*tines*) was introduced secondarily. But that is a solution of desperation; nothing indicates that "some" is not original to the logion.

[206] Schlosser (*Le règne de Dieu*, 1. 327–42) underscores the many Semitisms present in the logion.

[207] Thus, one cannot appeal to the concrete reference of "some of those standing here" to argue that the saying makes sense only in the mouth of the historical Jesus addressing his disciples. It makes equal sense in the mouth of a Christian prophet addressing his particular community (contra Schlosser, *Le règne de Dieu*, 1. 344). On p. 349, Schlosser presses the perfect form of the participle *hestēkotōn* to maintain that it refers to the narrow group of disciples right around Jesus. As with a number of other cases, though—one thinks of the *ēggiken* in Mark 1:15 and the perfect participle *elēlythuian* in Mark 9:1—we cannot be sure what verb form in the Aramaic is represented by the Greek perfect. Nor is it always easy to say what exact force the perfect has when it is not a finite verb in the indicative.

[208] As Béda Rigaux points out (*Saint Paul. Les épitres aux Thessaloniciens* [EBib; Paris: Gabalda; Gembloux: Duculot, 1956] 524–51), the burning question for the Thessalonians is not the basic Christian teaching on the parousia or the resurrection of the dead (which is presupposed) but rather the precise problem of the lot of those Christians who have already died prior to the parousia. Will they somehow be left behind or "taken care of" only later on when Jesus comes in glory to take "us survivors" into the air with him? The possibility of such a scenario is what causes the Thessalonians to grieve. Paul's answer to their anxious question is a firm no. Instead, the order will be the reverse of what the Thessalonians fear: *first* the dead will rise (1 Thess 4:16); only *then* will "we survivors" be caught up with them on the clouds to meet the Lord in the air (4:17). On all this, see John Gillman, "Signals of Transformation in 1 Thessalonians 4:13–18," *CBQ* 47 (1985) 263–81, esp. 268–71. Gillman argues convincingly for the basic compatibility of Paul's doctrine of the resurrection in both 1 Thess 4:13–18 and 1 Cor 15:51–53. There is more emphasis on continuity in 1 Thessalonians 4 and more emphasis on the transformation of the living in 1 Corinthians 15, but intimations of transformation are already found in the former text.

[209] As Gordon D. Fee (*The First Epistle to the Corinthians* [NICNT; Grand Rapids: Eerdmans, 1987] 799) points out, in 1 Cor 15:51 Paul is concerned "with the nature of the body that believers will assume *at the resurrection.* . . . They, too [i.e., the living], must be changed before they are fitted for immortality."
The differences among the three texts are correctly noted by Schlosser, *Le règne de Dieu*, 1. 343–44. Yet, while he is right in underlining the differences in the problems that the three passages are addressing, he fails to appreciate the underlying similarities that point to the first Christian generation as the matrix of all three texts.

[210] See Boring, *The Continuing Voice of Jesus*, 161, 164. Raymond F. Collins ("The First Letter to the Thessalonians," *NJBC*, 778 [#33]) remarks on 1 Thess 4:15: "Although some commentators continue to think of sayings of the historical Jesus, either one akin to Matt 24:30 or an agraphon, and others suggest a personal revelation to Paul, it is preferable to think that Paul is making use of a dictum of early Christian prophecy." This position is argued convincingly and at length by David E. Aune, *Prophecy in Early Christianity and the Ancient Mediterranean World* (Grand Rapids: Eerdmans, 1983) 253–56. For a consideration of other views, see Rigaux, *Les épitres aux Thessaloniciens*, 538–39. Like Rigaux, David Hill (*New Testament Prophecy* [Atlanta: John Knox, 1979] 130) leans toward the view that "in a word of the Lord" of 1 Thess 4:15 refers to the apocalyptic teaching of Jesus taken as a whole.

[211] See Boring, *The Continuing Voice of Jesus*, 161, 164, 236. Fee (*The First Epistle to the Corinthians*, 800 n. 17) comments: "Although one cannot be certain, the usage here

probably reflects that of 13:2, where as a prophet Paul has been given special revelation, a kind of charismatic knowledge (cf. 12:8)." Aune (*Prophecy in Early Christianity*, 250) begins his treatment of 1 Cor 15:51–52 by observing: "Modern scholarship widely regards 1 Cor. 15:51–52 as a prophetic revelation received by Paul." Aune then goes on to establish this point by an examination of the oracle's form, content, and function. Immediately after considering 1 Thess 4:15, Hill (*New Testament Prophecy*, 131) affirms: "It is with much greater assurance that we may point to Romans 11.25f. and 1 Corinthians 15.51 as examples of Paul's prophetic unveiling of *mysteria.*"

[212] So, e.g., Boring, *The Continuing Voice of Jesus*, 236. Others, like Beasley-Murray (*Jesus and the Kingdom of God*, 192), prefer to see it as a conscious adaptation of the earlier logion Mark 13:30. In either case, it does not come from the historical Jesus. For a slightly different line of reasoning, which nevertheless ends at the same conclusion of inauthenticity, see Gnilka, *Jesus von Nazaret*, 154–55. A long list of 20th-century critics who favor or reject the logion's authenticity can be found in Künzi, *Das Naherwartungslogion Markus 9,1 par*, 193–95. After Künzi spends a whole monograph studying the history of the saying's interpretation, it is disappointing to see how quickly and uncritically he decides on the saying's authenticity, without any serious application of the criteria of historicity (pp. 204–7). With equal swiftness he then resolves the theological question of an apparent error on Jesus' part with some murky remarks on the development and extension of salvation history, in obvious dependence on the views of Oscar Cullmann (pp. 207–12).

[213] The history of the exegesis of Mark 13:30 parr. is dealt with in an appendix of Künzi, *Das Naherwartungslogion Markus 9,1 par*, 213–24. After Künzi's uncritical treatment of the question of the authenticity of Mark 9:1, one is not surprised to find the question of the authenticity of 13:30 resolved summarily in a single sentence on p. 224: "As in Matt 10:23 and Mark 9:1 parr., nothing speaks against the acceptance of the authenticity of our saying."

[214] Merklein, *Jesu Botschaft*, 54. Since Merklein judges Mark 9:1 to be a Christian creation, a fortiori Mark 13:30 is. But even Schlosser (*Le règne de Dieu*, 1. 325–27), who tries to defend the authenticity of Mark 9:1 in an altered form, admits that Mark 13:30 is secondary.

[215] So, e.g., Anton Vögtle in his article "Exegetische Erwägungen," 647. The tenuous nature of all these theories of which verse was formulated on the basis of which verse is seen in the fact that Vögtle, on further reflection spurred by the work of Pesch, changed his opinion and opted for the view that Mark 13:30 was actually created on the basis of 9:1; see Vögtle, *Das Neue Testament und die Zukunft des Kosmos*, 100, including n. 52. For authors on both sides of the question, see the references given in the notes of Schlosser, *Le règne de Dieu*, 1. 352–53; and Beasley-Murray, *Jesus and the Kingdom of God*, 190–93 and 381–82.

[216] See, e.g., Jan Lambrecht, *Die Redaktion der Markus-Apokalypse. Literarische Analyse und Strukturuntersuchung* (AnBib 28; Rome: Biblical Institute, 1967); he gives a brief overview of various theories on pp. 8–12.

[217] Compare Rudolf Pesch's approach to Mark 13 in his earlier *Naherwartungen. Tradition und Redaktion in Mk 13* (Kommentare und Beiträge zum Alten und Neuen Testament; Düsseldorf: Patmos, 1968) with that presented in his later commentary, *Das Markusevangelium*, 2. 264–318. In *Naherwartungen*, Pesch carefully distinguishes between pre-Marcan clusters of tradition (logia on persecution in 13:9,11,13a; two logia in 13:31–32; and an "apocalyptic pamphlet" in 13:6,22,7b,8,12,13b,14–17,18[?],19–

20a, 24–27) and the considerable amount of Marcan redaction (including the whole of vv 1–5,7,10, 21, 29–30,35–37) which allowed the pamphlet to be taken into his Gospel along with other sayings from the Jesus tradition. In contrast, in his two-volume commentary on Mark, Pesch shifted to the view of Mark as a conservative redactor. Hence most of chap. 13 is now seen by Pesch as one traditional apocalyptic discourse, to which Mark contributed only vv 1–2, 23,32,33–37. In *Naherwartungen*, Pesch clearly assigned v 30 to Marcan redaction (pp. 181–87); in his commentary it is rather part of the traditional discourse, though perhaps not an authentic saying of Jesus (*Markusevangelium*, 2. 305–11).

Similarly, as I have already noted, over time Anton Vögtle changed his opinion on the origin of Mark 13:30. Granted these turnabouts in judgments by major scholars, I seek to have my argument about 13:30 operate on a general plane, using not any one detailed theory of tradition and redaction but rather general observations that would not be widely disputed. In this way my position on 13:30 avoids depending on any one particular (and often intricate) theory about the development of Mark 13 in general or 13:30 in particular.

[218] So, along with many other commentators, Grundmann, *Das Evangelium nach Markus*, 260. Even conservative exegetes like C. E. B. Cranfield (*The Gospel According to Saint Mark* [Cambridge Greek Testament Commentary; Cambridge: Cambridge University, 1959] 390) grant the composite nature of the chapter. Grundmann observes that scholars oscillate between two possibilities: (1) the basic source of Mark 13 is a Jewish apocalypse, to which have been added Christian sayings; or (2) a string of Jesus' sayings has been expanded by the addition of material from Jewish apocalyptic. In either case, the sayings of Jesus must in turn be divided into those of the historical Jesus and those spoken by Christian prophets in the name of Jesus. For a description of the details of the theories of various authors, see Taylor, *The Gospel According to St. Mark*, 498–99.

[219] For various theories on the succession of historical events involved in Caligula's plans regarding the temple in Jerusalem, see Anthony A. Barrett, *Caligula. The Corruption of Power* (New Haven/London: Yale University, 1989) 188–91.

[220] Taylor (*The Gospel According to St. Mark*, 520) comments on the parable of the fig tree: "The fig tree is mentioned because in Palestine, where most trees are evergreens, the rising of the sap in its branches and the appearance of leaves is a sure sign that winter is past." Mann (*Mark*, 534) emphasizes the importance of the "predictability" and reliability of the fig tree: "The gradual emergence of the fig tree into leaf in spring is always the first *definite* sign of the season: the almond tree, by contrast, may often flower prematurely and then have the flowers cut by a late frost."

[221] The subject of the Greek *eggys estin* ("is near") is not expressed. The description of the coming of the Son of Man is the immediately preceding context (13:24–27), and so he is the most likely subject. However, a vaguer subject such as "the end" (*to telos* in v 7) is also possible. The question is hardly a vital one since, on the level of Marcan redaction, the end, the definitive coming of the kingdom of God, and the coming of the Son of Man on the clouds of heaven are all essentially the same event.

[222] So, rightly, Künzi, *Das Naherwartungslogion Markus 9,1 par*, 224.

[223] To be more precise, the altar and/or image was that of the Semitic god "Baal of the Heavens" (*baʿal šāmēn*), the equivalent of *Zeus Olympios* in Greek; on this see Hartman and Di Lella, *The Book of Daniel*, 299.

[224] On this see the explanation and the literature cited by Beasley-Murray, *Jesus and the Kingdom of God*, 328–29.

[225] On this see Oberlinner, "Die Stellung," 62.

[226] After considering all other possible interpretations (e.g., the Jewish people down to the end of the world, all believers), Künzi, *Das Naherwartungslogion Markus 9,1, par,* 224) rightly judges that this is the only possible meaning of "this generation" in the immediate and larger Gospel context.

[227] So, rightly, Oberlinner, "Die Stellung," 52.

[228] If Mark 13:32 were first spoken by some Christian prophet, the saying would originally have been understood as an utterance of the risen Jesus, speaking through his prophet. Only secondarily, when inserted into its present context, would the saying become an utterance of Jesus during his public ministry.

[229] For a list of 20th-century critics who favor or oppose authenticity, see Künzi, *Das Naherwartungslogion Markus 9,1 par,* 221–24.

[230] This is the conclusion of Oberlinner, "Die Stellung," 65–66.

[231] *Das Naherwartungslogion Matthäus 10, 23* and *Das Naherwartungslogion Markus 9,1 par.*

[232] See his *Geschichte,* 128–30. For Bultmann, Mark 9:1 is "indeed a formulation of the community," Matt 10:23 is "clearly a Christian prophecy from the time of the [church's] mission," and Mark 13:30 never existed independently in its present form; it could be "a variant of 9:1, which was reformulated for the present context." However, Bultmann thinks that it is also possible that 9:1 originally belonged to the conclusion of the Jewish apocalypse that stands behind Mark 13.

[233] See, e.g., Marcus J. Borg, *Jesus. A New Vision* (San Francisco: Harper & Row, 1987) 14, 20 nn. 25 and 26, 168 n. 28, and the literature cited there.

[234] Dodd, *The Parables of the Kingdom;* see pp. 61, 82, 103, and 113–14 for typical enunciations of his view. A good summation of his analysis of various parables can be found on pp. 129–30: "It seems possible, therefore, to give to all these 'eschatological' parables an application within the context of the ministry of Jesus. They were intended to enforce His appeal to men to recognise that the Kingdom of God was present in all its momentous consequences [in his earthly ministry]. . . ." It was the early church, according to Dodd, that adapted Jesus' parables to make them refer to a still future world-crisis, the second coming of Christ.

[235] It is interesting to note that in some books on Jesus' eschatological preaching of the kingdom, the beatitudes are treated under the rubric of "the kingdom as a present gift"; so, e.g., Ladd, *Jesus and the Kingdom* 202–3. This would seem to have a certain basis in the text, insofar as the first beatitude concludes with the statement "for theirs *is* [Greek present tense: *estin*] the kingdom of God." However, the present tense of the Greek verb *estin* is hardly probative for the sense of the beatitudes in the mouth of the historical Jesus. Quite often in Hebrew and Aramaic, the verb "to be" is simply omitted from these types of clauses (nominal or stative clauses). This is the approach Franz Delitzsch took to Matt 5:3 in his translation of the New Testament into biblical Hebrew. In Matt 5:3, the concluding *hoti* clause reads in his Hebrew: *kî lāhem malkût haššāmāyim* (literally, "for to them [is] the kingdom of the heavens"). At other times in biblical Hebrew or Aramaic, the place of the verb "to be" is taken either by a pronoun (*hû'* or *hî'*) or by a substantive that can take a pronominal suffix (*yēš* in Hebrew, *'îtai* in Aramaic); in either case the tense is not indicated by the word itself and must be divined from the context. Hence, in the hypothetical Aramaic of the three core beatitudes of

Q, the unspoken copulative verb might easily have been understood as future, since the corresponding clauses in the second and third beatitudes were explicitly future.

As a matter of fact, even in the present Greek text, commentators often note that the present tense of *estin* can easily be understood as a "proleptic present," anticipating in the present (on the strength of Jesus' word) the future good of the kingdom, already partially experienced in Jesus' ministry. Interpreting on the level of Matthew's Gospel, Luz (*Matthew*, 1. 235) remarks: "Matthew 4:17 and the future tenses of vv. 4–9 make clear that it [the kingdom] is still in the future." Indeed, Davies and Allison (*The Gospel According to Saint Matthew*, 1. 445) stress the future sense: ". . . the meaning is neither that the poor now possess the kingdom (it is God's possession) nor that the kingdom consists of the poor; rather are we to think, 'To the poor will be given the kingdom of heaven.' " However, Guelich (*The Sermon on the Mount*, 76) emphasizes the present aspect of the kingdom and so takes the present tense of *estin* at full value.

THE KINGDOM OF GOD:

God Coming in Power to Rule

PART III:
THE KINGDOM ALREADY PRESENT

I. INTRODUCTION

In the last chapter we saw that any attempt to strip the historical Jesus of his eschatological message concerning the kingdom runs counter to the evidence. In particular, we concluded that the future, definitive, and imminent arrival of God's kingly rule was central to Jesus' proclamation.

The question we must now ask is whether Jesus viewed this final arrival of God's kingdom as purely future or whether he also claimed that in some way the kingdom of God had already arrived—however partially and symbolically— in his own words and actions. The question is especially pressing because of the sharp divergence of opinion among critics. As we have seen, some scholars have excluded future eschatology from the preaching of the historical Jesus (e.g., Marcus J. Borg, C. H. Dodd for the parables of the kingdom).[1] Yet others strongly oppose this collapse of Jesus' eschatology into the present—even to the point of excluding or minimizing any teaching by Jesus that would depict the kingdom as already present in his ministry.

Significant in this regard is the discomfort E. P. Sanders feels about speaking of the kingdom as not only future but also present. While acknowledging that Jesus thought God was working through him during his ministry, Sanders stresses that Jesus' emphasis lay on the kingdom as immediately future. When speaking of God's present action in Jesus, Sanders prefers formulations like "he [Jesus] was God's spokesman, God's agent. . . . Many of the sayings which some have seen as pointing to the presence of the kingdom actually point to Jesus' view of his own importance. . . ."[2] When it comes to the kingdom, "the future event is what primarily defines Jesus' view of 'the kingdom.' "[3] Indeed, Sanders thinks it better, when dealing with Jesus' sayings about present and future, "to distinguish the referents of the word 'kingdom.' "[4] This may explain why Sanders himself does not readily use "kingdom" when he speaks of Jesus' sense of God at work in his ministry.

Obviously the question must be resolved not by what strikes us moderns as a priori likely but by what Jesus himself said and did. Do his words and deeds indicate that the kingdom that he promised for the near future was paradoxically, in some strange way, already present in his work? To some modern minds such a paradox may seem an intolerable contradiction. Yet, to take an analogous case, throughout both the OT and the NT we find individual authors making apparently contradictory statements about divine control of events and human responsibility, statements that have driven theologians of Western Christianity to distraction, if not to the stake.[5] The ancient Semitic mind, not unlike the outlook of many third-world peoples today, was not overly concerned with the principle of noncontradiction, however revered the principle may be by Western logic. Accordingly, in this chapter our primary duty is simply to find out whether the historical Jesus did speak of the kingdom as already present in his ministry. How or indeed whether such a teaching contradicted, reversed, or revised Jesus' proclamation of a future but imminent kingdom is a question that can be answered only later—and therefore a question that must not be allowed to interfere with our initial weighing of the evidence.

We will begin the weighing of the evidence by reviewing various sayings of Jesus about John the Baptist that may imply a presence of the kingdom in Jesus' ministry (the second Baptist-block in Matt 11:2–19 par.). Then we will move to the "star witness" for the presence of the kingdom in Jesus' ministry, Luke 11:20 par.: "If by the finger of God I cast out the demons, then the kingdom of God has come upon you." Also to be examined is the cryptic—and variously translated—claim of Luke 17:21: "The kingdom of God is in your midst." While these two sayings will be seen to provide good grounds for the idea of a present kingdom, we shall discover that another famous saying of Jesus, "The kingdom of God has drawn near" (Mark 1:15), is much more problematic and is best left aside. Our quest will conclude with two allied sayings that do not explicitly mention the kingdom yet imply its presence in Jesus' ministry: the beatitude congratulating those who see what the disciples see (Luke 10:23–24 par.) and Jesus' rejection of voluntary fasting (Mark 2:18–20 parr.).

II. SAYINGS ALREADY EXAMINED: THE SECOND BAPTIST-BLOCK (MATT 11:2–19 PARR.)

One relatively "painless" way of entering into this thorny and complicated question is to look back over various sayings of Jesus that we have already examined in other contexts and have judged authentic. At the end of the last chapter I noted how (1) Jesus' invitation to his disciples to address God as '*ābbā*' when they prayed for the coming of the kingdom and (2) his paradoxical declaration in the beatitudes that the unhappy are happy both intimate that the future kingdom already exerts a transformative power over the present of the believer. In some sense, the believer is already under the sway of God's eschatological kingdom. But that is not the same thing as saying that the kingdom is already present. Do some of the sayings we have tested go further than the Lord's Prayer or the beatitudes in indicating that the eschatological kingdom is already present during Jesus' lifetime and through his activity?[6]

One promising area of investigation is the "second Baptist-block" from Q (Matt 11:2–19 ‖ Luke 7:18–23; 16:16), which we examined in Chapter 13. As we saw there,[7] with the exception of Matt 11:12–13 ‖ Luke 16:16, the two versions of this second Baptist-block show a surprising degree of word-for-word correspondence, especially in the core sayings. Apparently these core sayings reached a fairly fixed state in the Q tradition early on. Likewise noteworthy is that the problem of how Jesus relates to the Baptist is not answered by christological titles or conceptual frameworks typical of the "high christologies" found in the Gospels. Beyond these general considerations, indications of authentic Jesus tradition are also found in the individual units that make up the block.

In the first unit (Matt 11:2–6 par.), John, through his envoys, does not pose the question of Jesus' identity with any of the major christological categories of the early church. Rather, he raises a vague, open-ended question that suggests but does not define some eschatological figure: "Are you the one who is to come [literally, the coming one]?" Neither pre-Christian Judaism nor the Q document used "the coming one" as a set title for the Messiah or any other particular eschatological personage. Nothing in the question or the context suggests that John's puzzlement is feigned in order to bring his disciples to Jesus. Nor is his question the anguished cry of one whose faith in Jesus is wavering, for nothing in the immediate context or in Q as a whole suggests that John had ever come to faith in Jesus. John is groping toward the possibility that he must rethink his view of the imminent denouement of Israel's history. He is groping toward the possibility that, contrary to his earlier expectations, Jesus, the healer and preacher of good news, and not some fiery judge, may be the instrument of that denouement.[8] However, the opposite possibility, that Jesus is not the expected one, is still quite real for John and his disciples ("or should we wait for someone else?"). If the pericope was originally invented by Christians to persuade followers of the Baptist to become Christians, the form of propaganda chosen can only be described as curious.

Like the Baptist's question, Jesus' reply is bereft of the kind of clear-cut christological claims made by the early church. Jesus answers John indirectly and suggestively by pointing to the public record of what the former has been doing and saying, and then letting the Baptist draw the conclusion for himself: the blind see, the lame walk, lepers are cleansed, the deaf hear, the dead rise, and the poor have the good news proclaimed to them (Matt 11:5 par.). If the Q text reflects Jesus' reply with any accuracy, Jesus may well have been alluding to various passages in the Book of Isaiah where such miraculous healings are symbols of God's redemption of Israel from the Babylonian exile and the return of the people to a renewed Jerusalem.[9]

If this is so, Jesus' reply signals a shift in emphasis from John's ministry. While Jesus does hold on to John's warning of an imminent end, the threat of judgment awaiting those who refuse the call to repentance, and probably even the rite of baptism, he emphasizes instead the God who comes in power and mercy to heal and redeem his people, gathering the scattered fragments of Israel into an eschatological whole. Indeed, the climactic action of Jesus in bringing in the end time, the action Jesus keeps to last in his list, is not any healing but rather the proclamation of good news to the poor—the good news spoken of in Isa 61:1, the good news Jesus quite literally proclaims to the "poor" in his first beatitude in the great Q sermon (Matt 5:3 ‖ Luke 6:20).

Jesus then ends the description of his gentle ministry with a gentle appeal to his erstwhile master, an appeal fittingly clothed in a beatitude: "And happy is he who is not scandalized [= kept from believing] because of me." As we saw in Chapter 13, what is so surprising, almost shocking, is that the anecdote ends at this juncture, hanging in midair, with no indication here or elsewhere in Q (or in any early tradition in the Synoptics) that the Baptist ever responded positively to Jesus' appeal for faith in himself. We are even left wondering: if John did not proffer the faith that was connected with the happiness promised in the beatitude, was he actually thought of as excluded from eschatological happiness? Even the slightest intimation of such an idea would be counterproductive for any attempt to attract former disciples of John to Christianity. In short, the criteria of both embarrassment and discontinuity speak strongly here, as elsewhere in the pericope, for authentic tradition coming from Jesus.

As is obvious to any reader, this tradition in Matt 11:2–6 par. does not use the phrase "kingdom of God." Yet it supplies us with important background for understanding the phrase when it does appear in the next Baptist section from Q (Matt 11:7–11,12–13 ‖ Luke 7:24–28; 16:16).[10] Vis-à-vis the Baptist, Jesus stands out as one who performs miracles of healing and proclaims good news to the poor as he travels throughout Israel in fulfillment of Isaiah's prophecies. Implicitly we are prepared for the insight that this is how God's kingly rule of Israel in the end time operates concretely and is experienced right now, through the ministry of Jesus. Something new and different is occurring in the prophetic work of Jesus. Everyone, including the Baptist, is challenged to accept the truth that God is the ultimate agent at work in Jesus' words and actions, however much the events contradict one's preconceived ideas of what the end time would be like for Israel.

All this is of great importance as we move on to the second unit in the Baptist-block. As we saw in Chapter 13, Matt 11:7–11 ‖ Luke 7:24–28 is a carefully constructed unit made up of a number of independent sayings, not necessarily spoken in the same historical situation as that depicted in Matt 11:2–6 par. Yet the subject matter, namely, the Baptist, is the same; and presumably Jesus did not radically change his views on the Baptist from month to month. The total focus of Matt 11:7–9 is on the greatness of John, who is seen as a prophet and (mysteriously) more than a prophet. The absence of any of the categories that would orient him toward Jesus (witness, forerunner), indeed, the absence of any reference to Jesus at all, recommends this highly rhetorical give-and-take passage as authentic Jesus tradition.[11] Other elements in the passage likewise speak for its authenticity. For instance, the allusive, indirect nature of Jesus' reference to Herod Antipas makes perfect sense if Jesus the prophet, the former disciple of John, is speaking in Galilee about the prophet whom Herod has recently imprisoned.

If we put aside the OT quotation in Matt 11:10 as probably an early Christian creation, we continue with the two-part evaluation of John in Matt 11:11 ‖ Luke 7:28. This saying not only concludes the Q unit but also gives us the first occurrence of "kingdom of God" in this second Baptist-block: "There has not arisen among those born of women one greater than John [the Baptist] (11:11a); but the least in the kingdom of God is greater than he" (11:11b).[12] As we saw in Chapter 13, some would claim that v 11b is a Christian correction of the embarrassing and sweeping statement in v 11a. Yet the terse and taut structure of the whole of v 11, the neat rhetorical parallel-with-contrast, especially clear in the more Semitic form of the saying, and the typically Semitic way of expressing comparison and contrast by radically opposite and apparently mutually exclusive statements (dialectical negation) all argue for the authenticity of the whole of v 11 as a unit. Moreover, cohering perfectly with all that we have seen about "the kingdom of God" (a phrase noticeably absent from the preaching of the historical Baptist), the phrase is absent from this passage when the focus is solely on John (Matt 11:7–11a) and suddenly appears when John is compared with those who accept Jesus' message, i.e., the message of the kingdom. A vital point here is that v 11b does not compare John directly with Jesus but rather with anyone (typified by "the least") who is already in the new, eschatological state of affairs, the new type of existence made possible by the kingdom of God. Indeed, Jesus himself is not explicitly referred to in v 11; there is no specifically christological content to this logion. The contrast is between John's supreme greatness in the old human world and the superior state enjoyed by anyone who has entered into and so lives in the new "field of force" that is the kingdom of God. The focus of the saying is thus not on Jesus but on the kingdom—which jibes perfectly with what is seen in a good deal of the authentic Jesus tradition.

What is important for us is that the statement about the kingdom of God in v 11b demands that it in some sense be already present. The whole point of the comparison and contrast in v 11 is that while, in the old world, the Baptist is the greatest of human beings, anyone who accepts Jesus' joyful message and healing ministry enjoys a higher status because he is already in the kingdom of God, already experiencing God's powerful, redeeming, healing, gladdening rule in his life. The whole point of this contrast between two people, each in his particular, concrete existence, is that the "least" in v 11b is not simply promised a kingdom that will arrive at some future date. He exists in the kingdom now as he experiences the power of God transforming his life. Hence he is not promised that he will be greater than the Baptist when the kingdom comes; he is greater than the Baptist now precisely because he is in the kingdom now.[13] The end time John awaited and proclaimed has in some sense arrived. The corner has been turned. The kingdom of God is here, ready to be experienced in the ministry of Jesus.

The second saying in this block of Baptist material that seems to refer to the kingdom as already present is a much more difficult text to interpret. It is the highly disputed Q logion on the Baptist, the kingdom, and violence that appears in two divergent forms in Matt 11:12–13 ‖ Luke 16:16. Some critics would reject it as authentic Jesus material, while others would despair of ever reconstructing the original form of the saying. As I indicated in Chapter 13, I think credible arguments can be mounted both for an original form of the logion and for the authenticity of such a form. The lengthy and delicate source criticism undertaken in Chapter 13 suggested that the original Q saying ran something like this (with the verse enumeration of Luke 16:16):

16a The law and the prophets [lasted?] until John.
16b From then on,
    the kingdom of God suffers violence,
    and the violent plunder it.

While the saying suffers from both obscurity and ambiguity, it does seem to indicate that John the Baptist was, in Jesus' eyes, a pivotal figure (in the sense of a key transitional figure, not the central figure) in a major shift in Israel's history. Before him the law and the prophets stood securely in place as *the* summation and guide of Israel's religious life. After him the new, all-determining reality is the kingdom of God, subjected to violence on the part of those who oppose it. As usual, it is the kingdom, not Jesus himself, that is the primary focus of the saying.

Amid all the problems of interpretation that plague this saying, one point is fairly clear. The kingdom of God, understood in this saying as the palpable, immanent manifestation of God's kingly rule in Israel's history, and more particularly in the ministry of Jesus, is suffering violent opposition. While the source and nature of this opposition is not apparent in the logion, one presupposition of v 16b is. The kingdom of God could not be suffering violent opposition as Jesus speaks if it had not taken on concrete, visible form in the words and deeds of Jesus. The very idea of the kingdom of God suffering from such violence is an astounding notion, foreign to the OT, the intertestamental literature, and the rest of the NT.[14] The idea implies that what is in essence transcendent, eternal, invisible, and almighty—God's kingly rule—has somehow become immanent, temporal, visible, and vulnerable in Jesus' ministry. While the present kingdom appeared in a basically positive context in Matt 11:11b ‖ Luke 7:28b, its context in Matt 11:12–13 ‖ Luke 16:16 is darker and more troubling.[15]

Granted, little has been gained by this review of the Baptist material beyond the basic but vital fact that Jesus did at times speak of the eschatological kingdom of God as already present in his ministry. Still, one specific point emerges. As opposed to the kingdom's future coming in glory, which (according to Jesus) will surely occur soon, the present kingdom is ambiguous. It is a powerful source of joy and greatness for those who experience it now, but also a sign of contradiction, subject to violent opposition on the part of those who reject it now. There is no reason to think that this present kingdom is some separate reality, essentially different from the future kingdom soon to arrive. It is that same eschatological kingdom present now—but only partially so, with healing power mixed curiously with vulnerability and violence. The two kingdom passages from the Baptist-block are thus as much questions as answers and invite us to explore other sayings of Jesus that may throw further light on how the kingdom is already present.

III. OTHER SAYINGS ABOUT A PRESENT KINGDOM

A. "IF BY THE FINGER OF GOD I CAST OUT THE DEMONS, THEN THE KINGDOM OF GOD HAS COME UPON YOU": MATT 12:28 ‖ LUKE 11:20 AND RELATED SAYINGS ON JESUS' EXORCISMS (MARK 3:24–27 PAR.)

Up until relatively recently, there was one saying of Jesus that was almost unanimously accepted by scholars as authentic and that was moreover seen by many as referring to a present kingdom, namely, Matt 12:28 ‖ Luke 11:20: "But if by the finger [Matthew: spirit] of God I cast out the demons, then the kingdom of God has come upon you." Beasley-Murray may be exaggerating slightly when he claims: "This statement is one of the few logia in the gospel traditions relating to the kingdom of God that is universally acknowledged to be authentic."[16] Still, the basic truth of his assertion is admitted even by E. P. Sanders, who is skeptical about the legitimacy of such a scholarly consensus.[17] It is not that Sanders feels that he can prove with certainty that the saying is not authentic; he simply questions whether the arguments for authenticity and for an interpretation in terms of a present kingdom are all that probative. Given this disagreement and the pivotal nature of the saying, it is necessary to examine the logion in great detail, exploring the various problems it involves one at a time.

1. The Initial Problem of Modern Sensibilities and Ancient Beliefs

We shall be examining the problem of miracles in the Jesus tradition in Part Three of this volume, but the special problem posed to modern minds by talk about exorcism and demons requires a few preliminary observations here. As soon as modern Americans hear the word "exorcism," images from Hollywood horror movies naturally flood their memories. The cultural chasm between the

1st and 20th centuries yawns especially wide when we touch on the question of exorcism. The idea that evil spirits could not only inflict suffering on people from without (demonic obsession) but could even invade and take over their bodies (demonic possession) was widespread in ancient cultures.[18] Indeed, it can be found in a good number of third-world cultures today—to say nothing about popular belief in demonic possession in Europe and North America.[19] In the ancient Near East, ideas about demonic obsession and possession were already present in Sumerian and Akkadian religions, which were equipped with rites of exorcism that often employed incantations as well as sympathetic or imitative magic. Similar ideas and practices can be found in ancient Babylonian, Assyrian, and Egyptian religions. In contrast, such beliefs and rituals are largely absent in the Hebrew canon of the OT; the evil spirit that tormented King Saul stands out by way of exception (1 Sam 16:14–23; 18:10–11; 19:9–10).[20] On the other hand, what ordinary Israelite people, much given to syncretistic practices before the exile, might have been doing by way of exorcisms is difficult to judge.

In postexilic literature, demonic activity becomes a more prominent topic, with the apocryphal/deuterocanonical Book of Tobit providing what is more properly called a case of demonic obsession (attack from without) than possession (Tob 6:7–8,16–18; 8:3). But demonic possession as well as obsession became a frequent theme in the Jewish literature of the intertestamental period. King Solomon in particular enjoyed a growing reputation in Jewish legends as an expert in exorcisms, as Josephus relates in his *Jewish Antiquities* (8.2.5 §45). In the same chapter, Josephus proceeds to recount how he himself witnessed a Jew named Eleazar perform exorcisms in the presence of Vespasian by using a ring with special roots under its seal and by invoking the name and incantations of Solomon.[21]

Fragments from the Dead Sea Scrolls make it clear that Qumran likewise knew of exorcism, though it is by no means certain that exorcism was actually practiced at Qumran. In the *Genesis Apocryphon*, Abraham is besought by Pharaoh to pray and lay hands on him so that the plague and the evil spirit that afflict Pharaoh and his people may depart (1QapGen 20:16–29).[22] In the *Prayer of Nabonidus* (4QprNab), the Babylonian king Nabonidus recounts how a Jewish exorcist from among the exiles of Judah cured his ulcer and forgave his sins.[23] A strange form of Psalm 91, known among later rabbis as an exorcistic psalm, has been found at Qumran; in it Solomon's name appears just before the term for "demons."[24] The image of Solomon as exorcist finds fullblown literary expression in the pseudepigraphic *Testament of Solomon*, probably written sometime between the 1st and 3d centuries A.D.[25] In later Jewish lore, the founding father of rabbinic Judaism, Johanan ben Zakkai, is presented (in an *ad hominem* argument with a pagan) as comparing the OT ritual of the red heifer (Num 19:2) to the pagan ritual of burning roots and sprinkling water to exorcise an evil spirit (*Pesiq. Rab Kah.*, pisqa 4:7).[26] Also from a later period we have Jewish incantation bowls, written in Aramaic; a number of them mention "King Solomon, Son of David" and his seal ring.[27]

Judaism was hardly alone in its belief in demonic possession and the efficacy of exorcism in the 1st centuries B.C. and A.D. Similar ideas existed in both pagan religions and Christianity and tended to increase in tandem with syncretism and magic in the late Roman empire.[28] The earliest Christians viewed themselves as empowered by Jesus himself to perform exorcisms; all three Synoptic Gospels include exorcism in Jesus' commission to his disciples when he sends them out on mission (Mark 6:7; Matt 10:1,7; Luke 9:1; cf. Mark 9:38–40). The Acts of the Apostles presents Paul as an exorcist (Acts 16:16–18; 19:12) whom his Jewish rivals attempt to imitate without success (19:13–20).[29] The striking power of Christians to exorcise was an argument used by patristic writers against paganism. So important did this power become in the church that by the 3d century there was in Rome a special office of exorcist, which perdured in the Roman church as a "minor order" down until the latter part of the 20th century.

Granted the long history of exorcism in paganism,[30] its existence in Judaism around the turn of the era, and its presence in Christianity from its earliest days, it would be surprising not to find any trace of exorcism in the thought or practice of the 1st-century Jewish prophet, teacher, and miracle-worker named Jesus. As a matter of fact, both the Marcan and Q traditions, along with M and L, attest abundantly that Jesus practiced exorcism (Mark 1:23–28 par.; 3:22–27 parr.; 5:1–20 parr.; 7:24–30 par.; 9:14–29 parr.; Matt 12:22–23 ‖ Luke 11:14–23; see also Matt 9:32–34 and Luke 13:10–17,31–33).[31] They are also mentioned in various summaries of Jesus' activity. Exorcisms enjoy not only multiple attestation of sources but also multiple attestation of forms: they occur both in narratives (miracle stories, narrative summaries) and in various types of sayings (dispute stories, missionary charges). Indeed, exorcisms make up the largest single category of healings in the Synoptics.[32] One might also appeal to the criterion of embarrassment insofar as the exorcisms led Jewish leaders to charge Jesus with collusion with the prince of devils (Mark 3:22 parr.). In due time such charges developed into the accusation of practicing magic, an accusation found in later Jewish and pagan writings.[33] To a certain degree, one might even appeal to the criterion of discontinuity in that Jesus' mode of exorcism was different from many "techniques" of the time. In the strict cases of demonic possession in the Synoptics (as opposed to healing miracles with overtones of exorcism),[34] Jesus—contrary to common practice in the ancient world—does not actually pray to God, lay on hands, or use elaborate incantations, spells, or religious objects. He does not even cast out demons "in the name" of someone, as opposed to the early Christians, who expelled demons in the name of Jesus (Acts 16:18; 19:13).[35] All Jesus does is "rebuke" (*epitimaō*), "command" (*epitassō*), and "cast out" (*ekballō*) the demon.[36]

Hence, however disconcerting it may be to modern sensibilities, it is fairly certain that Jesus was, among other things, a 1st-century Jewish exorcist and probably won not a little of his fame and following by practicing exorcisms (along with the claim of performing other types of miracles).[37] Perhaps in no other aspect of Jesus' ministry does his distance from modern Western culture

and scientific technology loom so large and the facile program of making the
historical Jesus instantly relevant to present-day men and women seem so ill-
conceived. One can approach his exorcisms with greater sympathy if one remembers that Jesus no doubt saw them as part of his overall ministry of healing
and liberating the people of Israel from the illnesses and other physical and
spiritual evils that beset them. Granted the primitive state of medical knowledge in the 1st-century Mediterranean world, mental illness, psychosomatic
diseases, and such afflictions as epilepsy were often attributed to demonic possession. If Jesus saw himself called to battle against these evils, which diminished the lives of his fellow Israelites, it was quite natural for him, as a 1st-
century Jew, to understand this specific dimension of his ministry in terms of
exorcism. All of this simply underscores the obvious: Jesus was a man and a
Jew of his times.[38]

As far as we can tell, by practicing exorcism Jesus stood out from John the
Baptist and certain other Jewish religious figures of his day. Yet exorcism alone
did not make him unique; both the Marcan and Q traditions, as well as Acts,
make clear that there were Jewish exorcists alongside of or in competition with
Jesus—and later on with his followers (Matt 12:27 ‖ Luke 11:19; Acts 19:11–
17; cf. Mark 9:38–40). Actually, what made Jesus unusual, if not unique, was
not simply his role as exorcist but rather his integration of the roles of exorcist,
moral teacher, gatherer of disciples, and eschatological prophet all into one
person. As we have already seen, it may well be no one aspect of Jesus' life and
ministry but rather the special configuration of its various parts, forming a
whole, that should be labeled "unique."

2. Source and Tradition Criticism of Matt 12:28 ‖ Luke 11:20

The saying that explicitly links Jesus' exorcisms with the coming of the kingdom of God (Matt 12:28 ‖ Luke 11:20) occurs within a complicated, multilayered section of Gospel tradition. A dispute between Jesus and certain Jewish
leaders over the true meaning of his exorcisms (triumph of God over evil? or
the prince of the demons empowering Jesus?) was apparently recorded in both
Mark and Q. Hence Mark 3:22–27 and Matt 12:22–30 ‖ Luke 11:14–23 qualify as one of the "Mark-Q overlaps" in the Synoptics.[39] The pericopes as they
stand in Matthew and Luke are clearly composite, reflecting both Marcan tradition and Q material (i.e., material found in both Matthew and Luke but not
in the Marcan parallel). Complicating matters further, even the Q material
contained in Matthew and Luke seems to result from the stitching together of
various sayings of Jesus. Different exegetes detect different hypothetical layers
of the Q material. But most agree that the saying that links Jesus' exorcism
with the kingdom of God (Matt 12:28 ‖ Luke 11:20) was originally an independent logion; it was joined only secondarily to the rest of the Q material to
form the present pericope on the dispute concerning Jesus' exorcisms (Matt
12:22–30 ‖ Luke 11:14–23).[40]

To be more precise: it seems that Matt 12:28 ‖ Luke 11:20 had nothing

Matt 12:25–30	Mark 3:23–27	Luke 11:17–23
[25]Knowing their thoughts, he said to them,	[23]And summoning them, he said to them in parables, "How can Satan cast out Satan? [24]If a kingdom is divided against itself, that kingdom cannot stand.	[17]But he, knowing their thoughts, said to them,
"Every kingdom divided against itself is made desolate, and no city or house divided against itself will stand; [26]and if Satan casts out Satan, he is divided against himself; how then will his kingdom stand?	[25]And if a house is divided against itself, that house will not be able to stand. [26]And if Satan has revolted against himself and is divided, he cannot stand; rather, he is finished.	"Every kingdom divided against itself is made desolate, and house falls upon house. [18]And if Satan also is divided against himself, how will his kingdom stand? For you say that I cast out demons by Beelzebul. [19]But if I cast out demons by Beelzebul, by whom do your sons cast them out? Therefore they shall be your judges. [20]But if by the finger of God I cast out demons, then the kingdom of God has come upon you.
[27]And if I cast out demons by Beelzebul, by whom do your sons cast them out? Therefore they shall be your judges. [28]But if by the Spirit of God I cast out demons, then the kingdom of God has come upon you. [29]Or how can one enter the house of the strong man and plunder his goods,	[27]But no one can enter the house of the strong man and plunder his goods,	
		[21]When the strong man, fully armed, guards his own palace, his goods are in peace; [22]but when one stronger than he comes against and conquers him, he takes away his armor in which he trusted, and divides his spoil. [23]He who is not with me is against me, and he who does not gather with me scatters."
unless he first binds the strong man?	unless he first binds the strong man;	
Then indeed he shall plunder his house. [30]He who is not with me is against me, and he who does not gather with me scatters."	then indeed he shall plunder his house."	

originally to do with the verses that immediately precede and follow it in the present form of Matthew and Luke. As for the material that immediately follows it (the parable of the binding of the strong man in Matt 12:29 ‖ Luke 11:21–22), the matter is fairly clear. The same parable of the strong man occurs at roughly the same point in the Marcan form of the dispute story (Mark 3:27), but without any parallel to the Q saying that links exorcism and kingdom.[41] The same lack of an original connection seems to hold for the verse immediately preceding Luke 11:20 par., namely, Matt 12:27 ‖ Luke 11:19: "And if I cast out demons by [the power of] Beelzebul, by whose power do your sons [i.e., your followers, your disciples, or the members of your group] cast them out?" Apparently this verse was originally independent of the preceding argument about kingdoms and houses being divided against themselves (Matt 12:25–26 ‖ Luke 11:17–18), since that argument is paralleled in Mark 3:23–26, while Matt 12:27 ‖ Luke 11:19 has no equivalent in the Marcan tradition.

Whether or not the question about the sons casting out demons (Matt 12:27 ‖ Luke 11:19) was originally connected with the saying on exorcisms and the kingdom (Matt 12:28 ‖ Luke 11:20) is more difficult to decide, but probably they were not united from the beginning.[42] For one thing, the thrust of the two sayings is notably different. Matt 12:27 par. is a rhetorical question that mounts an *ad hominem* argument. For the sake of argument Jesus grants that the followers or members of some unnamed Jewish group ("your sons") actually perform exorcisms.[43] The mere fact that they do so hardly proves that they hold their power from Beelzebul, the prince of demons—a conclusion the Jewish leaders would reject in any case with respect to their followers. By what right, then, do these leaders conclude from the mere fact of successful exorcisms that Jesus receives his exorcistic power from the prince of demons? Thus, the followers of the leaders are themselves the living refutation of the leaders' accusation against Jesus ("therefore they themselves shall be your judges").

The tone and thrust of Matt 12:28 ‖ Luke 11:20 differ notably from the preceding verse.[44] Instead of a rhetorical question and an *ad hominem* argument, Jesus makes a flat claim in a declarative conditional sentence that contains nothing that he considers really hypothetical: "But if by the finger [Matthew: spirit] of God I cast out the demons, then the kingdom of God has come upon you." More to the point, the adjective "your" or the pronoun "you" does not seem to refer to the same people in Matt 12:27 par. as in 12:28 par. In v 27, when "*your* sons" are called upon ironically to be "*your* judges," the "you" who are addressed seem to be certain Jewish leaders who are making a most serious accusation against Jesus: he is in league with the prince of demons. The word "your" in v 27 would make no sense ("your sons" are to be "your judges") if it referred to Israelites in general, Jesus' audience in general, Jesus' disciples in particular, or the people Jesus has exorcised. "Your" must refer to the Jewish leaders who oppose (or at least question) Jesus' exorcising activity.

The pronoun "you" seems to demand a different referent in v 28. For it is by no means clear why, if Jesus is exorcising by the finger of God, the kingdom has therefore (*ara*) come precisely to the Jewish leaders who are nevertheless rejecting his exorcisms as the work of the chief demon. These Jewish leaders who oppose and stigmatize Jesus' exorcisms would seem to be the one group to which the kingdom is not coming *via* Jesus' exorcisms. "You" in v 28 seems to demand some other referent, such as Jesus' audience in general, or the disciples whom he is instructing about the true meaning of his exorcisms, or possibly even the recipients of his exorcisms. That without any indication of a shift of audience "your" and "you" should refer to two such different groups in two successive sentences would be hopelessly confusing in an actual conversation of Jesus or even in an original composition created from the start by Q. The natural conclusion is that v 27 and v 28 did not belong together from the beginning of the tradition.[45]

Furthermore, some commentators point out that if v 27 and v 28 were joined together from the beginning, a curious conclusion might be inferred from the link between the two sayings.[46] If Jesus appealed to the legitimacy of the exorcisms of the followers of his adversaries as an argument in favor of the legitimacy of his own exorcisms (v 27), and if he then immediately proceeded to identify his exorcisms as concrete vehicles by which the kingdom of God comes right now (v 28), would not Jesus logically be allowing that the exorcisms of the disciples of his adversaries were likewise and equally vehicles of the coming of God's kingdom right now? Would Jesus really grant such a conclusion about the religious activity of his adversaries?[47] Even apart from the present ending of the Q pericope (Matt 12:30 par.: "The one who is not with me is against me, and the one who does not gather with me scatters"), Jesus' own special claims as herald of the kingdom and his scathing attacks on his various adversaries make such a conclusion highly unlikely. All things considered, therefore, the more probable view is that the key saying linking Jesus' exorcisms and the kingdom originally circulated apart from its present context in Q.

The upshot of all this is that Matt 12:28 ‖ Luke 11:20 must be interpreted by itself, apart from the larger literary context in Q, though of course not apart from the general context of Jesus' exorcising ministry. One question of source and tradition criticism remains, namely, whether Matthew's "by the spirit of God" or Luke's "by the finger of God" is more original in the saying.[48] Many commentators favor Luke, and with good reason. The spirit is a favorite theological theme of both Luke's Gospel and the Acts of the Apostles. It is unlikely that, without some pressing reason, Luke would replace one of his favorite theological words and symbols with the unusual phrase "finger of God." The word "finger" (daktylos) occurs only twice elsewhere in the whole of Luke-Acts (Luke 11:46; 16:24). In neither case is "finger of God" used, in neither case does the word serve as a weighty theological symbol, and apparently in neither case is "finger" due to Luke's redaction.[49] In contrast, "spirit" (pneuma) occurs 36 times in Luke's Gospel and 70 times in Acts—106 times in all, while the entire NT uses "spirit" 379 times. To be more precise, when pneuma is used to designate the divine spirit, it is used three times as often in Luke's Gospel as in Mark. As for the Acts of the Apostles, chaps. 1–12 have comparatively the greatest number of occurrences of this meaning of pneuma in the whole of the NT: 37 instances.[50] Luke's propensity for "spirit" in the sense of God's spirit is clear. That he would purposely replace a favorite theological word (and concept) with "finger of God," a phrase otherwise unattested in the NT, is, to say the least, improbable.

Matthew, on the other hand, while not as expansive in his use of "spirit," certainly has nothing against the word, using it 19 times in his Gospel in all the strands of his tradition. More to the point, he may well have introduced the word into Matt 12:28 to supply redactional links backward and forward in his composition. Just prior to the Beelzebul dispute in Matthew's Gospel, Matthew has inserted a formula quotation from Isa 42:1–4, which contains the phrase "I shall place my spirit [*to pneuma mou*] upon him [i.e., upon the servant of the Lord]." Right at the end of the Beelzebul dispute in Matthew—but not in Luke!—we find the statement about blasphemy against the spirit (*tou pneumatos*, Matt 12:31). The equivalent verse does not occur in Luke until 12:10. Hence Matthew, but not Luke, had good redactional motives for replacing the unusual "finger of God" with the usual and perfectly intelligible "spirit of God." Therefore, Luke's version of the verse is probably the original Q form: "But if by the finger of God I cast out demons, then the kingdom of God has come upon you."[51]

3. The Meaning of the Earliest Q Form of the Saying

If we are to understand how the Q saying in Luke 11:20 par. interprets the exorcisms of Jesus,[52] two key phrases need to be examined: "by the finger of God" (*en daktylǭ theou*) and "has come" (*ephthasen*).

(a) As the former phrase occurs nowhere else in the NT and is not common in the OT or the pseudepigrapha as a symbol of God's power working a miracle through a human agent,[53] "the finger of God" seems to be a direct reference to the one clearly parallel text, Exod 8:15.[54] In Exod 8:12–15 we have the story of the third plague that Yahweh sends upon Egypt and its recalcitrant Pharaoh, namely, the plague of gnats. Aaron extends his rod and strikes the dust of the earth, which turns into a vast number of gnats. Pharaoh's magicians, who had been able to ape the two previous wonders wrought by Moses and Aaron (Exod 7:22; 8:3), cannot reproduce this one. They confess their failure by saying: "This is the finger of God."[55] At the very least, Jesus is indicating by the phrase that he places himself alongside Moses and Aaron, genuine messengers from God who were empowered by him to perform symbolic miracles connected with Israel's liberation from slavery. By implication, Jesus is now doing the same; his authorization and power to perform miracles, specifically, liberating exorcisms, come from the God of Israel, not from demons. As Heinrich Schlier puts it, "'finger of God' denotes God's direct and concrete intervention" in Jesus' exorcisms.[56]

There is a possibility that something more precise is in Jesus' mind. T. W. Manson, followed by Norman Perrin, appeals to a text in the rabbinic midrash on the Book of Exodus, *Exodus Rabbah*, to explain Jesus' allusion.[57] In *Exod. Rab.* 10:7, when the magicians see that they cannot reproduce the plague of gnats, they recognize that the plagues are "the work of God and not the work of demons." The implication is that, in their successful imitation of the first two plagues, the magicians were themselves using power supplied to them by demons. The demons, however, are not able to reproduce the third plague, and hence even the magicians are constrained to admit that this third plague could be wrought only by the superior power of God. Jesus is using a similar line of argumentation, reflected also in the Marcan-Q parables on the divided kingdom and the divided house.[58] It would be absurd for demons to supply the power necessary to cast out demons; they would only be destroying themselves. But if the demons are ruled out as the source of Jesus' supernatural power, the only other possible source is God. Moreover, if the God of Israel, who once used his miraculous power to liberate his people from Egypt, is now exerting that same power to liberate Israelites enslaved by demonic power, and if he is doing so precisely through a Jesus who is proclaiming the imminent coming of God's eschatological kingdom, then God's eschatological royal power has already reached out, touched, and transformed the lives of certain Israelites (i.e., the possessed) even now.[59]

While the tradition in *Exodus Rabbah* seems at first glance to be helpful in illuminating the implications of Jesus' claim, one must remain very wary. Some scholars date the final form of *Exodus Rabbah* between the 10th and 12th centuries A.D.,[60] though various haggadic traditions contained in the work are much earlier. Whether the interpretation of Exod 8:15 found in *Exodus Rabbah* was actually known in the early 1st century A.D. cannot be determined with certainty. All one can say is that the midrashic tradition does fit in perfectly with Jesus' allusion to Exod 8:15 in the context of his claim to miraculous power coming from God.

(b) The major focus of debate in Luke 11:20 par. is the verb *ephthasen*, translated above as "come." The verb *phthanō* had a wide range of meanings in classical Greek: anticipate, precede, overtake, outstrip, come first, act first, arrive at, attain to. In the NT, however, 1 Thess 4:15 seems to be the only case where the classical meaning of "precede" or "come first" survives: "We who are [still] living, who survive until the parousia of the Lord, will by no means *precede* [into heavenly glory] those who have fallen asleep [= Christians who have died]." The other six passages, including Luke 11:20 par., mean simply "come," "arrive," "attain to," or "reach."[61]

What, then, is the plain meaning of Luke 11:20 par.? Here one must distinguish carefully between the Greek text that lies before one's eyes and a hypothetical Aramaic reconstruction of what the historical Jesus said. For the moment, I am dealing only with the former. Given the philological data we have just seen, the only possible translation of the Greek text is that given above: "But if by the finger of God I cast out the demons, then the kingdom of God has come upon [or: to] you." The aorist tense of *ephthasen* can hardly be made to mean something else in this verse than "has come," "has arrived," "has reached." To decide, without any special basis in the text, that *ephthasen* is a "prophetic" or "proleptic" aorist ignores the precise argument about and explanation of Jesus' exorcisms that this verse purports to give. Such an appeal to a prophetic or proleptic aorist cannot help but look like special pleading, geared to avoiding an unwelcome theological conclusion about the presence of the kingdom of God in Jesus' ministry—at least according to plain sense of this Greek verb in this Greek text.[62]

Likewise unconvincing is E. P. Sanders's observation that the aorist of *phthanō* "frequently means 'came' in the sense of 'the coming was determined,' not 'the coming was accomplished.'" He points to the *Testament of Abraham*, where we are told that the cup of death "came" (*ephthasen*) to Abraham (*T. Abr.* 1:3 in Recension A), and yet Abraham lives on for nineteen more chapters.[63] But this supposed parallel is not apposite. The "cup of death" is a very particular symbol; it does not in itself mean the actual death of a person. The dying of a person is rather expressed by the further symbol of the person's "drinking [or: tasting] the cup" of death—so, most notably, Jesus in his prayer in Gethsemane.[64] The cup of death has already been "decreed" for Jesus, to use Sanders's phrase; but Jesus can still pray—in his first "prayer session"—that the cup pass him by, i.e., that he not actually die (Matt 26:39). In the second "prayer session," when things look bleaker, Jesus prays instead: "If this cup cannot pass me by *unless I drink it*, your will be done." In this symbol-system, the act of dying is not the coming of the cup but the drinking of it. Hence there is nothing strange in the cup of death coming to Abraham at the beginning of the *Testament of Abraham* and Abraham's actual death nineteen chapters later. In contrast, nowhere in Jesus' sayings about the kingdom, future or otherwise, does the coming of the kingdom refer to a potential arrival or a potential coming that must then be ratified by human action or experience before the kingdom's coming is real. The parallel Sanders offers is really no parallel at all. This is a good example of the danger of claiming to find parallels when one simply finds the same word in another context. It is the context, not the single word, that determines meaning and produces a real parallel of sense. In short, the natural sense of the aorist verb *ephthasen* within Matthew's and Luke's Greek narratives, which tell of a past event of Jesus' exorcism and explain the meaning of that exorcism, is "has come."[65]

4. The Question of the Authenticity of Luke 11:20 Par.

Once the questions concerning the sources of the saying, its original meaning in the earliest Q form, and the natural meaning of the Greek text have been resolved, we must face the further question of whether Jesus ever uttered this saying. As with almost all of Jesus' sayings, one must wrestle with various criteria and arguments that can at best produce only a high degree of probability.

What is actually surprising in this particular case is how united the vast majority of critics are in accepting the authenticity of Luke 11:20 par., sometimes with very little argumentation. The skeptical Bultmann makes the surprising declaration that Luke 11:20 par. can claim "the highest degree of authenticity that we are in a position to accept for a word of Jesus; it is filled with the feeling of eschatological power that the appearance of Jesus must have conveyed."[66] This is a strangely subjective, not to say romantic, judgment on the part of the master skeptic of form criticism. Stranger still is the fact that many exegetes after him have been content to quote Bultmann, advert to the fact of almost universal agreement on the saying's authenticity, and then move on to another question. One is left asking: Is the logion's much-vaunted authenticity a house built on the sand of received and unexamined opinion? Or are there serious arguments in favor of authenticity?

While the matter is not so crystal-clear as some commentators suppose, I think that there are reasons for holding Luke 11:20 par. to be authentic. One major point touched on earlier bears repeating. As we saw in Chapter 14,[67] the phrase "kingdom of God" does not occur in the Hebrew OT, and occurrences in the deuterocanonical/apocryphal books of the OT, the OT pseudepigrapha that can be dated prior to Jesus, Qumran, Philo, Josephus, and most of the targums are either rare or nonexistent. The phrase is likewise relatively scarce in the NT outside the Synoptic Gospels; within the Synoptic Gospels it is almost completely restricted to the words of Jesus.

Moreover, as we saw in Chapter 15 in the interpretation of the Lord's Prayer, the linking of "the kingdom of God" with a verb meaning "to come" in a direct affirmation is unknown in the OT, in ancient Judaism before Jesus, and in the rest of the NT outside of the Gospel sayings of Jesus.[68] Indeed, in OT prophecies, all sorts of eschatological realities (God, the hoped-for king, days, etc.) were said to come—but pointedly, not the kingdom of God or some equivalent phrase. I suggested in Chapter 15 that the absence of talk about God's kingdom coming is really not so strange. Instead, it is talk about God's kingdom coming that is strange—though we moderns generally do not notice that because the sayings of Jesus in the NT (especially the petition in the Lord's Prayer) have made us accustomed to the unusual phraseology. Whether we translate *hē basileia tou theou* as God's kingdom or kingship or kingly rule, it is really not the most natural thing to speak of a kingdom or kingship or kingly rule as "coming." Hence, most of the people who wrote the OT, the pseudepigrapha, and the Qumran literature did not spontaneously speak that way.

Yet Jesus did, because "the kingdom of God" was simply his special and somewhat abstract way of speaking of God himself coming in power to manifest and exercise his definitive rule in the end time—a concept (though not phraseology) that was indeed common in OT prophecy, especially in Deutero-Isaiah, as well as in some works of the pseudepigrapha. God coming in power to rule in the end time: that is the point of Jesus' phraseology, phraseology almost unique to him in early 1st-century Judaism, phraseology not cultivated by NT writers outside the Synoptic Gospels, and phraseology that fits perfectly the striking scenario of Jesus expelling a demonic power from some troubled Israelite.

To understand this point, it is important to realize that, in the view of Jesus, as in the view of Qumran before him and of Paul and John after him, human beings were not basically neutral territories that might be influenced by divine or demonic forces now and then. In the eschatological and apocalyptic views of Jews and Christians around the turn of the era, human existence was seen as a battlefield dominated by one or the other supernatural force, God or Satan (alias Belial or the devil).[69] A human being might have a part in choosing which "field of force" would dominate his or her life, i.e., which force he or she would choose to side with. But no human being was free to choose simply to be free of these supernatural forces. One was dominated by either one or the other, and to pass *from* one was necessarily to pass *into* the control of the other. At least over the long term, one could not maintain a neutral stance vis-à-vis God and Satan. To refuse to submit oneself wholeheartedly to the former after an exorcism would necessarily involve lapsing back into the control of the latter—a lesson inculcated by the Q parable about the seven demons (Matt 12:43–45 ‖ Luke 11:24–26).

Hence, in this either-or universe, for a tortured demoniac to be freed from the power of demons by the power of God working in Jesus was ipso facto to be delivered from the control of demons into the sovereign control of God. God, powerfully exerting his kingly rule in the end time through Jesus, had transformed the demoniac's life by "invading it," expelling the rival power, and claiming it as his own.[70] In this sense, at least, the kingdom of God, God's sovereign rule, had already come to a formerly enslaved Israelite, as well as to those who witnessed this epiphany of God's eschatological power and believed in what had happened. Thus, not only does talk about the coming of God's kingdom belong to Jesus' authentic words by the criterion of *discontinuity*; such talk also *coheres* perfectly with the special event of Jesus' exorcisms.

A further argument from discontinuity may be mounted for the striking phrase "by the finger of God." As we have seen, the phrase occurs nowhere else in the NT, though the NT certainly contains other stories of exorcisms both in and outside the Gospels, as well as many other graphic depictions of God's struggle with and defeat of Satan. Yet for all the colorful metaphorical language used to describe this cosmic battle, especially in the Book of Revelation, the striking anthropomorphism "finger of God" never recurs. Significantly, the phrase is never used in the description of exorcisms performed by disciples of Jesus or by early Christians. Hence it is very difficult to assign this saying to Christian writers or prophets instead of Jesus himself. As far as we can tell from our limited evidence outside the Gospels, Christians of the 1st century, when they did perform exorcisms, did not do so with the simple, direct, authoritative command that Jesus used and that is reflected in the stark "I-word" of Luke 11:20 par. Rather they sought to expel demons by invoking the name of Jesus in their commands to the demons (see Acts 16:18; 19:13).[71] Such was the case even with a certain Jewish exorcist mentioned in Mark 9:38–41 ‖ Luke 9:49–50—whether we understand the situation to reflect the time of the historical Jesus or the early days of the church.[72] Either way, the disciple John informs Jesus that the unnamed man has expelled demons "in your name," i.e., by invoking Jesus' name or by adjuring the demons in Jesus' name—and notably not by "the finger of God" or by a simple direct command that did not mention any higher power. This invoking of the name of Jesus is thus a different style of exorcism from Jesus' direct, authoritative command to the demons, which is fittingly reflected in Jesus' simple "I-word" of Luke 11:20 par. In short, nowhere else in the NT is Exod 8:15 cited or alluded to in any context, exorcistic or otherwise. Hence, within the NT, both in and outside the Gospels, the usage in Luke 11:20 par. is unique.

Interestingly, a similar claim of uniqueness can be made for the text that supplies the image, Exod 8:15. Nowhere else in the OT is "finger of God" used in the precise context and with the precise sense found in Exod 8:15, i.e., as a metaphor for God's power performing a specific miracle through human agency to liberate his people and/or punish his foes. Instead, in Ps 8:4 the heavens are the works of God's fingers, while in Exod 31:18 and Deut 9:10 the tablets of the Mosaic Law are said to be written by the finger of God. A miraculous context can be found in the Aramaic text of Dan 5:5, where a message of judgment is written on the wall in King Belshazzar's palace. But in Dan 5:5 the fingers (in the plural) are described as "fingers of a hand of a man," not "the finger of God"; and no human agent is acting to bring about this miraculous event, unlike Moses unleashing the plagues in Egypt. Moreover, in Exod 8:15 "finger of God" is simply a metaphor for God's power manifest in a miracle, while in Dan 5:5 fingers actually appear and are seen by the king. Thus, the usage of Exod 8:15 is unique within the OT, whether one looks at ʾeṣbaʿ ("finger") in the Hebrew of the MT or the equivalent daktylos in the Greek of the LXX.

The same basic lack of interest in developing the imagery of Exod 8:15 seems to hold true for the intertestamental literature in Palestine around the time of Jesus. Exod 8:15 is not an object of special interest or speculation in the Qumran literature.[73] Significantly, in the Book of Jubilees (2d century B.C.), the precise phrase "the finger of God" is not even mentioned in the recounting of the plagues inflicted on the Egyptians in Jub. 48:5–12. In fact, the tradition about Pharaoh's magicians imitating the first two plagues is glossed over in Jub. 48:9–11. Pseudo-Philo's Biblical Antiquities (1st century A.D.) likewise omits any reference to "the finger of God" when it gives a brief digest of the plagues (Bib. Ant. 10:1).[74] Josephus, in contrast, narrates the third plague in detail in his Jewish Antiquities; all the more surprising, then, is the disappearance of Moses, Aaron, Aaron's rod, and the phrase "finger of God" from the narrative (Ant. 2.14.3 §300–302). As for Jewish tradition after the time of Jesus, the phrase "finger of God" is avoided by many of the Aramaic targums when they translate Exod 8:15; apparently they sought to circumvent the anthropomorphism.[75] The image of the finger of God is used in some of the rabbinic midrashim, such as the Mekhilta and Genesis Rabbah, but we must remember both that these works received their final redaction centuries after Jesus and that they use the image in ways quite different from that of Jesus.[76]

At the very least, then, set over against the OT, the NT, and Jewish-Palestinian writings datable to or earlier than the 1st century A.D., Jesus' way of describing the divine power at work in his exorcisms, with a conscious allusion to Exod 8:15, appears unique.[77] When we put together "finger of God," the eschatological symbol of the kingdom of God coming, and the connection of both with exorcisms, the strikingly "discontinuous" language and thought of

Luke 11:20 par. argue for the saying's origin from the historical Jesus, and not from either the early church or contemporary Judaism.[78] Indeed, Gerd Theissen goes so far as to claim that "Jesus is unique in religious history" because of the particular way in which he combines apocalyptic eschatology with the actual performance of exorcisms.[79] Qumran mentioned exorcisms in a few of its documents, but it made no intrinsic connection between the future end of the world and such miracles in the present.

5. The Coherence of Luke 11:20 Par. with Other Sayings on Exorcism

Like the argument from discontinuity, the argument from coherence may also be set in a larger context.[80] Jesus' claim in Luke 11:20 par. coheres well with other sayings of Jesus that describe how he understood his exorcisms. Among these is the double parable of the divided kingdom and the divided house, found in both Mark and Q (Mark 3:24–25; Matt 12:25–26 || Luke 11:17–18).[81] In the Marcan form it reads: "If a kingdom is divided against itself, that kingdom cannot stand. And if a house is divided against itself, that house cannot stand." Without using the phrase "kingdom of God," the double parable nevertheless illuminates the point made in Luke 11:20 par. The implication of the double parable is that the exorcism of demons means that the kingdom or royal house of the prince of demons is being destroyed—certainly not by the prince himself, which would be absurd—but by the opposite royal power seizing control of human beings through a striking miracle.[82] This jibes perfectly with the terse, explicit claim of Luke 11:20 par., made with the combined images of "finger of God" and "kingdom of God."

Luke 11:20 par. is also coherent with the short parable of the despoiling of the "strong man" that immediately follows it in both Matt 12:29 and Luke 11:21–22. The parable also occurs within the Marcan material on the Beelzebul controversy, at Mark 3:27. It seems that we have here another example of a Mark-Q overlap. For the parable of the strong man occurs at exactly the same point in both Matthew and Luke—precisely after their common Q saying on the kingdom of God (Matt 11:28 || Luke 11:20). Thus, both evangelists independently agree in putting the parable at a different place in the Beelzebul complex than does Mark, who situates it immediately after his double parable about the kingdom and the house divided against themselves. All this argues strongly for the parable's being in the Q document as well as in Mark. The greater length, the dissimilar structure, and the variant wording of the parable of the strong man in Luke (but not in Matthew, who basically follows Mark's wording) likewise suggest that Luke possessed a version of the parable different from that of Mark. Hence it is reasonable to conclude that, while Matthew reflects Mark's form of the parable,[83] Luke—as so often proves to be the case—stays close to the Q wording. The un-Lucan character of much of the vocabulary in Luke's form of the parable makes this especially likely.[84] The Marcan and Lucan forms of the parable are as follows:

Mark 3:27	**Luke 11:21–22**
No one, entering the house of the strong man,[85]	As long as the strong man, fully armed, guards his palace,[86]
can plunder his goods,[87]	his possessions are safe. But when a man stronger than he,
unless he first bind	entering, conquers him, he takes away his armor
the strong man, and then he will plunder his house.	on which he had relied and divides the armor [that he stripped] off him.

Which form is more primitive, Mark's or Q's? In my view, we have another case where, despite a common prejudice in favor of the originality of Q when compared to Mark, Mark 3:27 represents the more primitive form of the parable. One notices immediately the short, compact form in Mark as compared to the longer and more detailed form in Luke. Mere length, however, does not prove that Luke's version is secondary. More to the point, in Mark we have a simple and rather vague story about "no one" being able to enter the house of a strong man to plunder his goods. Nothing is demanded beyond some bandit breaking into a wealthy man's house, tying him up, and robbing his possessions. Probably this was a not uncommon event in 1st-century Palestine.

Luke's version has "blown up" the story: the strong man now seems to be a warlord, prince, or king who guards his palace and possessions while being fully clothed in armor.[88] The adversary, now designated as "the stronger man," does not simply tie up the strong man. Rather, he "conquers" him in battle and then strips him of his full complement of armor, which now becomes the object of division (apparently as spoils among the stronger man's soldiers). Still more significant is the transformation of a colorless figure without concrete identification (Mark's "*no one* can enter the house" and Matthew's "how can *anyone* enter the house") into Luke's *ho ischyroteros*, "the stronger man." Luke's change may aim at introducing an implicit christological reference into the wording of the parable. It may not be pure coincidence that Jesus is referred to as "the one stronger than I" (*ho ischyroteros mou*) by the Baptist in Luke 3:16 parr.[89] All things considered, therefore, Mark's version of the parable seems more original.[90]

What is the meaning of the parable? As we have seen, the Beelzebul controversy in both Mark and Q is a composite piece, made up of various sayings touching on Jesus' practice of exorcism. Since, however, the material already occurs as a composite in both Mark and Q, the basic traditions are no doubt quite early. There is no reason to think that the parable of the strong man in particular ever had a setting apart from the general question of the source and meaning of Jesus' exorcisms, and—as we shall see—the image of "binding" argues positively for such a *Sitz im Leben*. Simply as a matter of fact, no other setting in the life of Jesus seems a viable alternative.

The parable therefore refers to Jesus' victory over Satan (or Beelzebul or demons) as demonstrated in his exorcisms. As the parable stands in the Gospels, the strong one is obviously Satan. As we have seen, Mark's "no one" (Matthew's "anyone"), and not Luke's "a stronger one," is most likely the original reading of the parable. If so, then probably Mark's "no one" is Jesus, who typically refers to himself, when he does so at all, in an indirect or veiled way. This vague, colorless way of speaking of the person who binds Satan is one reason for thinking that the person intended is Jesus, and not God. True, exegetes often point to Isa 49:24–25 as background for the parable: "Shall spoils be taken from a strong man [or: warrior], and captives from a powerful man [or: tyrant]? Thus says the Lord: Yes, captives shall be taken from a strong man, and spoils shall be rescued from a powerful man." While it is possible that the parable alludes to this text, one must note that the Isaian verses have more of a connection with the Q version of the parable and may even have been a catalyst in transforming the earlier Marcan form into the Q form.[91] In my opinion, a more probable candidate for an OT allusion is the image of "binding" the strong man. Indeed, the choice of the verb "binds" especially fits the context of exorcisms, reflecting as it does both OT images and intertestamental Jewish traditions about binding a demon or a leader of demons.

An OT basis for this image of binding can be found in the late "Apocalypse of Isaiah" section of Isaiah, Isa 24:21–22: "And it shall be on that day that Yahweh will punish the host of the heavens in the heavens and the kings of the earth on the earth. And they shall be gathered together [here the Hebrew text is somewhat doubtful] like prisoners [literally: like one bound, *'assîr*] in the pit, and they shall be shut up in a prison." The images of binding demons/Satan and locking them/him in a pit or dungeon become key themes in Jewish and Christian apocalyptic literature, as well as in other religious works not strictly apocalyptic. For example, in Tobit 8:3 the angel Raphael pursues the demon that has afflicted Sarah into Upper Egypt and there binds him hand and foot. In *1 Enoch* 10:4 Raphael likewise receives a command from the Lord to bind Azazel, a leader of the fallen angels, hand and foot and cast him into the darkness. The theme of binding, which is applied to other figures as well (e.g., the disobedient stars of heaven, the disobedient shepherds) is found in various strata of *1 Enoch*: e.g., 13:1; 18:16; 21:6; 69:28; 90:23. In *Jub.* 10:3–8, Noah prays that God will bind and shut up the demons (alias the evil spirits, the sons of the Watchers). But Mastema, their chief, obtains permission to have some of them remain free to lead astray evil men. In the *Testament of Levi*, Levi promises the coming of a new priest who will bind Beliar and give his offspring power to trample on evil spirits (*T. Levi* 18:12; but the text may be Christian). The imagery is gladly taken over into Christian literature, as the binding of Satan (alias the dragon, the ancient serpent, and the devil) in Rev 20:1–3 shows; cf. Jude 6 and 2 Pet 2:4. In short, the metaphor of binding in the parable of the strong man definitely points to a context of exorcism and to the strong man as Satan.

One issue that remains unclear is whether one should press the parable to

the point where the goods or possessions of the strong man should be understood as the demoniacs whom Jesus frees from Satan's possession by his exorcisms. Some might object that this smacks too much of allegory. Yet we already
have three equations: strong man = Satan, the one who plunders = Jesus,
binding = exorcism. Not only are these three equations not forced, they are
actually necessary if the parable is to make sense or have any application in the
context of Jesus' exorcisms. Granted this, the identification of the strong man's
possessions with possessed individuals seems to flow naturally from these three
equations, instead of being an artificial identification thought up and imposed
on the parable after the fact.

In our decision on this point we should not be intimidated by the dogma
that Jesus as teacher and prophet never used allegory. He would have been a
most unusual Jewish teacher and prophet if he had abided by that strange rule.
The OT is no stranger to allegory, notably in prophetic literature connected
with Ezekiel, Zechariah, and Daniel.[92] Allegory continues in the pseudepigraphic writings around the time of Jesus (e.g., the Enoch literature), flows
into Jewish apocalyptic at the end of the 1st century A.D. (e.g., 4 Ezra and the
Syriac Apocalypse of Baruch), and is cultivated by the later rabbinic literature. To
be sure, we must be careful to distinguish the original parables of the historical
Jesus from the Christian allegory that the early church sometimes added to
them. But this does not mean that we should deny any and all allegory to Jesus
himself. Hence I think it not unlikely that, in the parable of the strong man,
the plundered goods are meant to signify the possessed persons whom Jesus
frees from the power of "the strong man," Satan. That such a metaphor was
not impossible in early Jewish or Christian thought is seen from the *Testament
of Naphtali*, where the devil is said to dwell in an evil man as his own vessel or
instrument (*T. Naphtali* 8:6: *skeuos*, the word used in Mark 3:27).[93]

As for the authenticity of Mark 3:27 par., there is no particular reason to
deny its authenticity, and a number of considerations that argue for it. The
very fact of the Mark-Q overlap shows that, at the very least, we are dealing
with material that existed very early on in more than one stream of Christian
tradition (multiple attestation of sources). As for the criterion of coherence, it
is satisfied in a number of ways. The saying certainly coheres with both the
basic fact of Jesus' exorcistic activity and the other disparate sayings in the
Beelzebul block of material. It also coheres well with Jesus' tendency to speak
of himself only in veiled or indirect ways, even when he is talking about his
own miracles (cf. Matt 11:2–5 par.). The lack of any explicit christological
claim in the Marcan version is highlighted by the beginning of such a tendency
in Luke's reference to "the stronger one." In contrast, the Marcan Jesus implicitly identifies himself with the robber of the parable, not the most exalted
form of christology.

Moreover, the whole underlying imagery of a struggle with Satan for the
control of humanity in the end time fits in perfectly with the eschatology-
colored-by-apocalyptic that we have seen in both the Baptist and his most
famous follower. Likewise, we have seen that, while Jesus inherited this kind

of eschatology from the Baptist, he differentiated himself from his master by acting out or actualizing his more optimistic view of the eschatological crisis, struggle, and victory by performing miracles, notably exorcisms.

Besides the criteria of multiple attestation and coherence, one might even appeal, to a limited degree, to the criterion of discontinuity. Interestingly, the use of *ischyros* ("strong") as a substantive in the masculine singular and in the positive degree never occurs anywhere else in the NT.[94] More specifically, *ischyros*, which is used twenty-nine times in the NT, never occurs again in the NT for Satan, the devil, or a demon. "The strong one" was simply not a Christian way of speaking of Satan or his minions in the NT writings. Along with the vocabulary of binding, we may have here another case of Jesus' tendency to rework creatively OT themes and vocabulary to describe a fulfillment of eschatological hopes in his own actions. Moreover, the parable of the strong one is discontinuous with early Christian thought as well as language. In the rest of the NT, the triumph of Jesus over the demonic or cosmic "powers" is usually connected with the themes of his cross, resurrection, and exaltation in heaven (e.g., Col 2:6–23; Eph 1:15–23), not with his earthly ministry in general or his exorcisms in particular.

In short, all the relevant criteria point in the direction of the authenticity of Mark 3:27 par.; nothing argues against it. In turn, Mark 3:27 coheres well with and therefore supports the authenticity of Luke 11:20 par. Without using the key phrase "kingdom of God," Mark 3:27 proclaims the same basic reality: through Jesus' exorcisms the God of Israel is even now exercising his rule in the end time by breaking the power of Satan and/or demons and thus liberating his people.

One facet of the argument from coherence that I have just used in favor of the authenticity of Mark 3:27 par. may be applied a fortiori to Luke 11:20 par., a saying in which the key phrase "kingdom of God" does appear. As we have seen from Chapter 12 onwards, and as I have just reiterated with regard to Mark 3:27 par., Jesus, like his former master John, engaged in an intriguing but puzzling dialectic when it came to any assertion about his person. While implicitly claiming to be *a* or *the* central figure in the eschatological drama (acceptance or rejection of him and his message would mean eternal salvation or damnation), Jesus did not usually put himself explicitly at the center of his preaching. Rather, the kingdom of God, not Jesus the proclaimer of the kingdom, was the main object of Jesus' preaching. The kingdom was the reality he sought to communicate, however partially or proleptically, by activities such as exorcism and table fellowship with sinners. As Theodor Lorenzmeier notes, we have the same basic pattern here in Luke 11:20 par.[95] Jesus does imply that, in some unspecified way, the kingdom of God is connected with his person insofar as the kingdom becomes present, becomes an event now, through his exorcisms. Yet in Luke 11:20 par. Jesus places not his own person but his message proclaiming and his action communicating the kingdom in the spotlight. Characteristically, Jesus leaves the precise relationship between his person and the kingdom he proclaims unclear.

All in all, then, both the criterion of discontinuity and the criterion of coherence argue for the authenticity of Luke 11:20 par., while nothing points in
the direction of an early Christian creation. Along the way, we have seen that
a similar claim can be made for Mark 3:27 par.[96]

6. The Question of the Original Aramaic Form of Luke 11:20

Having proceeded carefully step by step, we have arrived at two major conclusions: (1) The Greek saying enshrined in Luke 11:20 and earlier in the Q
document states that Jesus' practice of exorcism demonstrates that the kingdom of God has already come upon (or to) the recipients and/or witnesses of
his exorcisms. (2) All available indicators point to the authenticity of Luke
11:20—as well as of Mark 3:27, which says much the same thing without using
the phrase "kingdom of God." But at this point we run up against the most
difficult part of any quest of the historical Jesus through his sayings in general
and Luke 11:20 in particular. As I have often stressed, we cannot usually expect
to be certain about the exact wording of what the historical Jesus said, especially as we try to reach back to the hypothetical Aramaic form of a given
saying. The problems we face are manifold: (1) The Greek words of the sayings in our Gospels may at times have more than one possible Aramaic equivalent. (2) Jesus may have spoken the same basic teaching more than once, with
slightly different wording. (3) One translator may possibly have translated
more freely than another, preferring good Greek style to a literal, wooden
translation. Hence, getting back to the exact words Jesus used often proves
elusive; we must be satisfied with knowing the substance of what he said with
varying degrees of probability.

It must be emphasized, however, that this limitation affects not simply Luke
11:20 but all the sayings of Jesus. In explaining his doubt that Luke 11:20 par.
proves that Jesus spoke of the kingdom as a present as well as a future reality,
E. P. Sanders complains that the "principal sayings that support" this view
"are not absolutely firm, either with regard to their original context or their
precise wording. . . ." The problem is that the same objection could be leveled
against almost any saying of Jesus used to establish any aspect of his teaching.
It certainly could be leveled against the predictions of the destruction of the
temple or Jerusalem on which Sanders places so much weight for his pivotal
interpretation of Jesus' "cleansing" of the temple in his *Jesus and Judaism*.[97]
We cannot ask that our views be "absolutely firm"; all we can hope is that
they are solidly probable in representing the substance of what Jesus said on a
particular issue.

Granted all this, there is no weighty reason to doubt that Luke 11:20 par.
represents the substance of what Jesus said at some time in his ministry concerning his exorcisms, whether or not we can know the exact Aramaic wording
of the logion. If we do want to attempt an Aramaic retroversion, we have at
least some indicators. The pivotal question in any such retroversion is the
Aramaic equivalent of the Greek verb *ephthasen*, "has come" or "has arrived."

In the Greek OT, *phthanō* represents a number of Semitic verbs, notably the Hebrew *nāgaʿ* and the Aramaic *mĕṭāʾ*, both of which mean "arrive," "reach," or "come." Since *ephthasen* is the aorist indicative active, the natural equivalent in Aramaic would be the verbal form known as the pĕʿal perfect, which indicates a completed action, corresponding to the English present perfect, simple past, and past perfect.[98] Hence *ephthasen* very likely represents the Aramaic *mĕṭāʾ*,[99] with a past meaning that can be rendered in English by the present perfect: "the kingdom of God has come" or "has arrived." One possible retroversion into Aramaic would therefore be:

English:	but if	by the finger of God	I cast out the demons
Greek:	*ei de*	*en daktylǭ theou*	*egō ekballō ta daimonia*
Aramaic:	wĕhēn	bĕʾeṣbĕʿāʾ dî ʾĕlāhāʾ	ʾănâ mĕṭārēk šēdayyāʾ

English:	then	upon you has come	the kingdom of God
Greek:	*ara*	*ephthasen eph' hymas*	*hē basileia tou theou*
Aramaic:	miṭʾat	ʿalêkôn	malkûtāʾ dî ʾĕlāhāʾ[100]

Admittedly, one must always leave open the possibility that there has been a mistranslation of an Aramaic imperfect tense, which could have a future meaning. In addition, the Aramaic pĕʿal or the Greek aorist could be understood as a "proleptic" or "prophetic" past, actually pointing with assurance to the future. While all these explanations are possible, they are in no way restricted to or especially applicable to Luke 11:20 par. alone. Mistaken translations or misunderstood tenses remain a constant possibility when moving from the hypothetical Aramaic forms of Jesus' sayings to the Greek text we possess. They remain just as much a possibility for various sayings on which Sanders relies as for Luke 11:20 par.[101] There is no special reason to invoke such a possibility here, where the most natural retroversion makes perfect sense—unless, on theological grounds, one is already committed to denying that any saying about a present kingdom could come from the historical Jesus.

Such an agenda seems operative in some exegetes' rejection or forced reinterpretation of Luke 11:20.[102] The simplest, most natural interpretation of both the Greek text of Luke 11:20 and its most likely Aramaic retroversion is the translation I have proposed. Jesus does present his exorcisms as proof that the kingdom of God that he proclaims for the future is in some sense already present. How this coheres—or whether it coheres—with what Jesus says about the kingdom soon to come remains an open question.[103] But that further problem should not lead us to suppress or twist some of the evidence that creates the problem, all for the sake of a neat systematization that was not a major concern of Jesus.

B. "THE KINGDOM OF GOD IS IN YOUR MIDST": LUKE 17:20–21

Another possible reference to the kingdom of God as present in Jesus' ministry is found in Luke 17:20–21.[104] At least at first glance, the saying depicts Jesus rejecting apocalyptic calculations about the time and place of the coming of the kingdom and asserting instead that "the kingdom of God is in your midst." This affirmation seems so clear and straightforward that some critics, such as John Dominic Crossan,[105] give it a prominent place in their argument that Jesus viewed the kingdom as already present. I have purposely placed this saying instead after the consideration of a number of other sayings because the apparently simple statement of Luke 17:20–21 actually bristles with complicated problems of translation and interpretation. The meaning of individual words is unclear, the source of the logion is debated, and the saying lacks multiple attestation.[106] Hence it is vital to proceed step by step.

1. The Meaning of the Saying in the Context of Luke's Gospel

Unlike Mark and Matthew, Luke creates two distinct "eschatological discourses," the first in 17:20–37, on the road to Jerusalem, and the second in 21:5–36, delivered in the Jerusalem temple.[107] The first is made up largely of Q and L sayings about the coming of the Son of Man and the end of the world. The second, basically following the eschatological discourse in Mark 13 (= Matthew 24), focuses more on the destruction of Jerusalem, which is carefully distinguished from the coming of the Son of Man, though the latter is also described. All this reflects a general pattern in the Synoptic Gospels: Luke tends to keep his Marcan material separate from Q and L, while Matthew tends to mesh Mark, Q, and M in the same discourse (so, e.g., Matthew 24–25).

In chap. 17, Luke's first eschatological discourse is easily divided into two parts: (1) a short introductory section made up of a question by the Pharisees and a reply by Jesus on the time and place of the kingdom's arrival (17:20–21); and (2) a main section addressed by Jesus to his disciples and dealing with the coming of the Son of Man, accompanied by the final cataclysm (17:22–37). One possible translation of the introductory section (vv 20–21) is as follows:

20a Asked by the Pharisees when the kingdom of God is coming, he [Jesus] answered them and said:
   b "The kingdom of God is not coming with [close] observation [*meta paratēr-ēseōs*].

21a Nor will they say, 'Behold, here or there.'
   For behold, the kingdom of God is [*estin*] in your midst [*entos hymōn*]."

I call this "one possible translation" because the English version hides a number of difficulties in the Greek text. Jesus' answer in v 20b says that the kingdom of God is not coming *meta paratēreseōs*, which I translate "with [close] observation." The most likely reference of this puzzling phrase is to the close scrutinizing of signs in nature, the heavens, and historical events. Apocalyptic circles looked for such signs in order to calculate and predict the end of this present age (see, e.g., the Apocalypse of Weeks in *1 Enoch* 91 and 93; and the vision of the cloud and the black and white waters in *2 Apoc. Bar.* 53–74). In rejecting the Pharisees' request that he prophesy the exact time when the kingdom is to come, Jesus likewise rejects all traditional apocalyptic techniques and speculation employed to predict that time. This flat dismissal of such calculations as unsuited to the true nature of the kingdom fits in perfectly with Luke's redactional tendency. He regularly dismisses fiery apocalyptic expectations and urges his church instead to settle down for the long haul of history and the practice of perseverance amid suffering (see Luke 21:7–24; 19:11; Acts 1:6–7). This pastoral message to his church, rather than concern about correcting erroneous views held by Pharisees in A.D. 30, is the most natural sense of the phrase in Luke's Gospel.

There are, however, two other possible interpretations of *meta paratērēseōs*. Since the Pharisees are the ones asking the question, the phrase could mean "with stringent observance of the Law." Later rabbinic literature at times reflects the view that pious Jews could hasten the coming of the Messiah or the time of redemption by keeping the Torah.[108] Jesus would supposedly be rejecting this view of human works forcing God's hand. The problem with this interpretation is threefold: (1) nothing in the immediate context of chap. 17 suggests such a theological backdrop to the exchange; (2) the rabbinic texts espousing such an idea are chronologically later; and (3) such a theological problem does not appear to be a major issue in Luke's church or his theology. We must beware of reading Paul's agenda into a text that is innocent of it.[109]

An even more involved theory, and one that is even more enmeshed in rabbinic (and patristic) texts is the interpretation proposed by August Strobel.[110] Luke supposedly composed most of vv 20–21 to combat a belief that some Jewish Christians had taken over from Judaism: the kingdom of God and/or the Messiah would come on Passover night (i.e., the night that concludes the 14th of Nisan and begins the 15th of Nisan). Such a night was referred to in Jewish literature as "the night of observation [or watching]," *lêl šimmûrîm* in Hebrew, *nyx paratērēseōs* in Greek. Strobel seeks to trace such an idea in early Christianity as well. This effort is a dazzling tour de force, but so many of the writings are later than Luke's Gospel and the supposed connections among them are so hypothetical that one must conclude that there is no solid evidence that Luke ever knew of or faced such a problem in his church. Certainly, neither the immediate context nor the overall theology of Luke-Acts points to such a background. On balance, therefore, a rejection of apocalyptic calculations predicting the precise time of the end of this age is the most natural reading of v 20b.[111]

In light of this, v 21a ("nor will they say, 'Behold, here or there' ") most likely contains a rejection of apocalyptic predictions of the exact *place* of the kingdom's appearance, corresponding to v 20b's rejection of any calculation of the exact *time*.[112] The future tense "nor *will* they say" may be understood as a "modal" future,[113] equivalent to "nor *can* they" specify any particular spot

("here or there," e.g., the desert or Jerusalem, as did some of the "false prophets" mentioned by Josephus).

The reason why apocalyptic speculation about the future date of the kingdom's arrival is futile is given in the very difficult v 21b. The introductory
phrase "for behold" signals Jesus' correct statement of the matter, as opposed
to the false positions just rejected. In content and formulation, v 21b parallels
yet contrasts with v 20b: (1) "The kingdom of God" is the subject of both
sentences. (2) In v 20b, the kingdom "is coming" (*erchetai*) in an imminent-
future sense; in contrast, in v 21b it "is" now. (3) Each statement qualifies its
affirmation about the kingdom with a prepositional phrase: *meta paratērēseōs*,
which Jesus rejects, and *entos hymōn*, which he now affirms.

While in theory it would be possible to take the verb "is" (*estin*) as a prophetic way of speaking of the imminent future, one is left wondering how the
banal statement that "the kingdom of God will be in your midst" is supposed
to act as the climax of this unit. A future expectation of the kingdom is presupposed by both parties in the dialogue and is a commonplace throughout the
Gospel. To save v 21b from being a mere truism, an adverb like "suddenly" or
"unexpectedly" is sometimes interpolated by critics.[114] But the problem inherent in such a solution is clear. To make sense of "is" as a future prophecy, a
key word that Luke could easily have supplied but pointedly did not is read
into a text that lacks it. The plain present sense of "is" seems by far the more
natural reading.

This brings us to the most difficult phrase of all, *entos hymōn*, translated
above as "in your midst" (or "among you")—a rendering common in modern
translations today. Some exegetes protest against this rendering and claim that
entos never meant "in the midst of" in ancient Greek. However, the evidence
of Greek texts—notably, Greek texts *translated* from a Semitic language—is
against them. That the preposition *entos* certainly had the meaning "in the
midst of" in ancient Greek is proven by two passages in Aquila's translation of
the OT (done probably a few decades after the completion of Luke-Acts) and
is supported as well by the translation of the OT done by Symmachus toward
the end of the 2d century A.D.[115]

Still, the most common meaning of *entos* is "within," and in the past—from
the patristic period through the Middle Ages into the early modern period—
most interpreters preferred this "interiorization" and "spiritualization" of Jesus' saying. In effect, Jesus would be saying: Do not look for a visible, spectacular, cosmic coming of the kingdom, for the kingdom is already present in your
hearts. But the context of the saying in Luke's Gospel makes this translation
doubtful. That Jesus should affirm that the kingdom would not come in the
future because it was already present in the hearts of his adversaries the Pharisees—and not especially in the hearts of his disciples (an equivalent statement
is never applied by the Lucan Jesus to his followers)—would be passing
strange.[116] More to the point, no matter what stage of the NT tradition is
being considered, the idea of the kingdom of God as a purely interior, invisible, present spiritual state of individual hearts is a foreign intrusion. It is at

home in 2d-century Christian Gnosticism (so the *Gospel of Thomas*, sayings 3, 51, and 113), 19th-century German liberal Protestantism, and some 20th-century American quests for the historical Jesus, but not in the canonical Gospels in general or Luke in particular.[117]

Another possible way of interpreting *entos hymōn* was suggested by Colin H. Roberts and championed by such scholars as Alexander Rüstow: the kingdom of God lies within your reach, in your possession, at your disposal, i.e., in your power to receive it.[118] That is to say, by choosing to accept Jesus' challenge to repent and believe, a person is capable of entering the kingdom. Jesus thus rejects idle apocalyptic speculation in favor of serious moral commitment and action in the light of the kingdom's coming. This interpretation does fit some of Luke's moral exhortations elsewhere in the Gospel (e.g., 13:22–30). But how widespread such a sense of *entos* was in 1st-century Greek is not all that clear. Some supposed examples of the usage have been disputed.[119] Moreover, one may ask whether a stress on human effort in v 21b catches correctly the contrast between v 20b and v 21b and, indeed, the whole rhetorical thrust of the saying. Since the first part of the logion rejects the idea that the kingdom of God is coming "with close observation," the natural thrust of the saying as a whole would seem to include the rejection of all human control over or calculation of what is God's action alone: his coming in power as king in the end time. An emphasis on the idea that the kingdom of God "lies in your power (or: possession)" or "is at your disposal" hardly seems to fit the contrast that the two parts of the statement set up.[120]

In my view, the translation "the kingdom of God is among you" remains the preferable one.[121] It is not surprising that it is favored by many modern translations.[122] For one thing, it coheres admirably with statements the Lucan Jesus makes elsewhere in the Gospel. Prior to this passage in Luke's Gospel, the presence of salvation has been stressed in Jesus' answer to the Baptist, which lists his eschatological miracles (7:18–23). Indeed, the least in the kingdom *is* greater than the Baptist (7:28). As we have already seen, the exorcism of demons specifically demonstrates that the kingdom has in some sense already arrived (11:20). It may not be totally by accident that Jesus' proclamation that "the kingdom is among you" follows directly upon the story of the healing of the ten lepers, one of whom hears from Jesus the joyful news: "Your faith *has saved* you [perfect tense]."

All things considered, then, the translation I proposed above is the most likely in the context of Luke's Gospel and his overall theology. Pressed by the Pharisees for a prophecy of the precise date of the kingdom's arrival, Jesus rejects all apocalyptic speculation about and calculation of the time and place of the coming of the kingdom. He instead seeks to turn his adversaries' eyes from the speculative future to the concrete present. If the Pharisees would only open their eyes, they would see the kingdom already present in Jesus' healing and teaching ministry. Because they refuse to see it now, they will not share in its future coming either.[123] Thus, at least on the level of Luke's redaction, the unit does proclaim the presence of the kingdom in the words and deeds of the earthly Jesus, while the following verses in the discourse predict his future coming as the Son of Man on the last day.

2. Luke's Redaction and Possible Sources

Only 17:21a ("Nor will they say, 'Behold, here or there' ") has a parallel in another Gospel, namely, in Mark 13:21 (= Matt 24:23): "And then if anyone says to you: 'Behold, here is the Messiah [or] behold there [he is],' do not believe [him]." It may well be, then, that 17:21a is due to Luke's transferral of a reworked form of Mark 13:21 to this place in Luke's Gospel, especially since Luke omits this verse in chap. 21, which largely runs parallel to the eschatological discourse of Mark 13.[124]

Apart from 17:21a, we are left in the dark about possible sources, since the rest of 17:20–21 has no exact parallel in any Gospel. Some educated guesses, however, are possible. Luke has the tendency to introduce sayings of Jesus with a redactional question from some bystander(s).[125] He also tends to put questions (as well as statements) into indirect discourse.[126] Both stylistic tendencies are seen in v 20a: "When asked by the Pharisees when the kingdom of God is coming, he answered them and said. . . ." As Bultmann and Dibelius observe, by this introduction Luke assimilates a saying or sayings of Jesus to the common Greek literary form known as the apophthegm or chreia: a short narrative framework or initial question introduces a pithy and memorable saying of a philosopher or some other great person.[127] Moreover, when vv 20–21 are read together with vv 22–37, they reflect a redactional pattern found elsewhere in Luke's great journey narrative (chaps. 9–19): allied theological themes are treated in two consecutive scenes, one involving teaching directed to the Pharisees, the other involving teaching directed to the disciples.[128] Hence it is likely that the two introductory verses that name the two audiences (v 20a: Pharisees and v 22a: disciples) are products of Lucan redaction.

If this be the case, we are left with 17:20b and 21b as the only candidates for special pre-Lucan tradition:

20b The kingdom of God is not coming with [close] observation.

21b (For) behold,[129] the kingdom of God is in your midst.

The intriguing point here is that, once we remove what probably comes from Luke's editorial activity, the remaining sayings turn out to form a carefully balanced two-part statement (a negative statement about the future followed by an opposite positive statement about the present),[130] a statement that displays both parallelism and chiasm. Both sentences have the same subject (the kingdom of God) plus a verb in the present tense plus a qualifying prepositional phrase. In the first statement the verb stands at the beginning of the Greek sentence (*erchetai*, "is coming"), in the second statement at the end (*estin*, "is").[131]

All this is relevant to the question of sources since it would be a curious procedure on Luke's part first to compose a carefully balanced two-part statement on the kingdom, only to turn around and obscure its crisp parallelism with his editorial additions. That the two-part statement is not Luke's own creation is confirmed by the fact that these two short sentences contain two key words that never occur elsewhere in Luke-Acts: *paratērēsis* ("observation") and *entos* ("in the midst of").[132] Indeed, *paratērēsis* and *entos* (used as a preposition) never occur elsewhere in the whole of the NT.[133] Moreover, one should also remember that talk about the kingdom of God "coming" is characteristic of the speech of the historical Jesus.[134] On balance, then, it is more likely that vv 20b and 21b are pre-Lucan tradition rather than Luke's own creation.[135]

A few authors, such as Schürmann and Schnackenburg, suggest that the traditional saying may have existed in the Q document, but their reasoning is highly speculative.[136] Q is by definition the tradition Matthew and Luke share but Mark lacks; but Luke 17:20b + 21b has no parallel in either Mark or Matthew. The mere fact that this special tradition occurs just before a block of Q material and has thematic and verbal similarities to the Q tradition hardly proves that it comes from Q.[137] The same could be said for a good amount of the L traditions that Luke weaves together with Q material during his great "journey narrative" that runs from 9:51 to 19:27.

Hence, if we exclude both Lucan creation and the Q document as the source of vv 20b + 21b, the obvious conclusion is that this two-part saying comes from Luke's special tradition (L). Admittedly, this does not tell us all that much, since L is simply a convenient umbrella term for any and every stray tradition in Luke not derived from Mark or Q.[138]

3. An Authentic Saying of Jesus?

The stray nature of the isolated logion behind vv 20b + 21b makes it difficult to reach any firm conclusion about its authenticity. That is one reason why it has been kept to this late place in Chapter 16. Yet I think that total skepticism on the subject is not warranted.[139] Even such a noted skeptic as Bultmann judges the traditional logion to be authentic, though he does not spell out in convincing detail the reasons for this judgment.[140] In my view, a number of considerations tip the balance in favor of authenticity. There is, first of all, the presence of the key phrase "the kingdom of God" joined to the verb "come," a way of speaking characteristic of the historical Jesus and notably absent from the NT outside of the Synoptic Gospels. This typical locution appears as the central concern in a concise, carefully balanced two-part saying with the pattern of negative-then-positive. All these characteristics are found elsewhere in sayings of Jesus considered authentic on other grounds.[141]

Then, too, there is the criterion of coherence of content. The surprising message that the kingdom Jesus promises for the imminent future is somehow already present in his ministry[142] coheres well with the other sayings and deeds of Jesus that we have studied in this chapter. In answer to the probing question of the Baptist, Jesus points to his miraculous activity as an indication that the prophesied time of salvation has come (Matt 11:2–6 par.). Hence, among Jesus' followers, the least in the kingdom is greater than the Baptist (Matt 11:11 par.). But all is not sweetness and light in this kingdom already present. Insofar as it is now here, the kingdom Jesus announces and actualizes is exposed to violent opposition (Matt 11:12–13 ‖ Luke 16:16). Perhaps to encourage followers who are shaken by such opposition, Jesus points to the kingly power of God clearly displayed in the exorcisms he performs (Luke 11:20 par.). They plainly show that the kingdom has arrived—at least for those who have personally experienced this gripping manifestation of God conquering evil. Such obvious indicators of the kingdom already present and exercising its power should turn people's eyes and minds *away from* futile apocalyptic calculations of the time of the kingdom's arrival (Luke 17:20b) and *toward* the kingdom which "is in your midst" (v 21b). Yet, as in many of the other sayings on the kingdom that we have examined, any christological reference in vv 20b + 21b is at best indirect or implicit.[143]

I readily admit that none of these considerations is probative by itself; L is, after all, a minor source. Still, I think that the convergence of the signs of pre-Lucan tradition, the vocabulary foreign to most NT writers and yet typical of Jesus, and the coherence of the saying with the general style and content of the sayings of Jesus already judged authentic makes the view that Luke 17:20b + 21b is authentic more probable than the opposite opinion. However, the tenuous nature of the evidence has led me to take up this saying only after the more weighty logia have been considered.[144]

C. "THE KINGDOM OF GOD HAS DRAWN NEAR": MARK 1:15

As Mark concludes the introduction to his Gospel (1:1–15) and opens the narrative of the public ministry,[145] he presents Jesus proclaiming: "The kingdom of God has drawn near" (1:15). Those scholars who follow the theory of realized eschatology propounded so forcefully by C. H. Dodd[146] would no doubt make the proclamation by Jesus in Mark 1:15 a major part of their argument: the kingdom of God is a present reality even as Jesus speaks. Other scholars would just as forcefully argue that the kingdom proclaimed in v 15 belongs to the imminent future rather than to the present moment.[147] The debate on Mark 1:15 is complicated by the fact that there is no consensus on which parts of the saying attributed to Jesus in v 15 come from Mark the redactor, from pre-Marcan tradition, or from Jesus himself.

The saying in v 15 is introduced by a short Marcan narrative in v 14, whose wording, by definition, does not go back to Jesus himself:

v 14 After John [the Baptist] was handed over [i.e., put into prison by Herod Antipas], Jesus came into Galilee proclaiming the gospel of God

v 15 and saying: "The time is fulfilled and the kingdom of God has drawn near. Repent and believe in the gospel."

One can find exegetes who consider the whole of the saying in v 15 a creation of Mark, who wishes to have a dense summary statement of Jesus' proclamation standing at the beginning of his public ministry.[148] Other critics, while waiving questions of precise wording, claim that at least the basic content of v 15 goes back to Jesus.[149] Still others would differentiate between parts of the saying that reflect the vocabulary of the mission of the early church after Easter and other parts that might well come from Jesus.[150]

Matters are still more complicated for us, since we are posing not just the usual question of historicity but also the precise question of whether Mark 1:15 provides further evidence that the historical Jesus proclaimed a kingdom already present during his ministry. To the first question I think a fairly clear-cut answer can be given. To the second question I think the reply must be an exasperating "not clear." Even if parts of v 15 go back to the historical Jesus, we cannot tell from the text before us whether he was speaking in this particular logion of the kingdom as present or future. Three major difficulties conspire to create this uncertainty about the meaning of 1:15.

The first major difficulty stems from the fact that—as I have just indicated—scholars disagree on exactly how much of the saying goes back to Jesus himself. Jacques Schlosser,[151] who is certainly sympathetic to the project of locating kingdom-sayings that can be attributed to the historical Jesus, admits that most of v 15 must remain under a question mark. With the exception of "the kingdom of God has drawn near," the logion in v 15 lacks multiple attestation. Moreover, the vocabulary and phrasing of both "the time is fulfilled" and "believe in the gospel" point in the direction of the missionary preaching of the early church, though derivation from Jesus cannot be completely excluded. The basic imperative "Repent!" is hardly impossible in the mouth of Jesus, but as Schlosser admits and E. P. Sanders emphasizes, sayings that mention repentance and that can be seriously attributed to Jesus are relatively few, if any.[152]

There is one exception to our general uncertainty on the question of origin from Jesus. The one part of v 15 that has a good chance of coming from Jesus is the core proclamation "the kingdom of God has drawn near (*ēggiken hē basileia tou theou*)." As we have seen in the last two chapters, sentences with the kingdom of God as the subject and a verb of motion (come, arrive, draw near) as the predicate are characteristic of the historical Jesus, while they are practically absent from Jewish writings before him as well as from the rest of the NT outside of the Synoptic Gospels.

This argument from discontinuity and coherence is not, however, the only factor to be considered. The core proclamation of the kingdom in v 15 also enjoys multiple attestation of sources since it has a parallel in Q, specifically in Jesus' missionary discourse to his disciples. In this case, though, the argument from multiple attestation of sources is a complicated one. On the one hand, Mark's version of the missionary discourse (6:7–13) makes no reference to the disciples proclaiming, "The kingdom of God has drawn near." On the other hand, both Matthew and Luke have this saying in their accounts of the missionary discourse, and so the possibility of the core proclamation existing in the Q version of the discourse arises.

Unfortunately, the way in which Matthew and Luke present their respective missionary discourses makes the whole matter even more complex. Like Mark, Matthew has only one missionary discourse (Matt 10:1–42); but, as is Matthew's wont, his missionary discourse is a mixture of Mark, Q, and M traditions. Within this mélange of traditions, Jesus says in Matt 10:7: "Go forth and proclaim, saying 'The kingdom of heaven has drawn near.'" At first glance, one might suspect that Matthew has decided to put on the lips of Jesus' disciples the proclamation made by Jesus himself in Matt 4:17. The reason for thinking this is that Matthew also puts Jesus' proclamation of the kingdom on the lips of John the Baptist in 3:2. According to this theory, Matthew's intent would be to create a neat parallel and satisfying sense of continuity reaching from the Baptist through Jesus to Jesus' disciples.

While such a theory seems at first attractive, it does not fit what we find in Luke's Gospel. Luke, as is his wont, has kept his Marcan and Q traditions separate. As a result, Luke creates two missionary discourses, one addressed to the Twelve in 9:1–6 (basically following Mark 6:7–13) and one addressed to seventy-two other disciples[153] (apparently drawn from Q, as can be seen from the Matthean parallels in Matt 10:1–42 that have nothing corresponding in the Marcan text).[154] What is striking here is that, in the Q version of his missionary discourse, Luke, like Matthew, has the core proclamation: "The kingdom of God has drawn near" (Luke 10:9). What is even more striking is that Matthew and Luke, for all the differences in their respective discourses, place the core proclamation either directly before (Matt 10:7–8) or directly after (Luke 10:9) a command to heal the sick (Matthew: *asthenountas therapeuete*; Luke: *therapeuete tous . . . astheneis*). On the whole, therefore, it is likely that the core proclamation "the kingdom of God has drawn near" existed in Q as well as in Mark. We thus have another example of a Mark-Q overlap,[155] a phenomenon we have already seen in the Baptist's prophecy of the coming one (Mark 1:7–8 parr.) and the Beelzebul controversy over Jesus' exorcisms (Mark 3:22–27). Hence, granted the multiple attestation it enjoys and the vocabulary typical of Jesus, "the kingdom of God has drawn near" is the one part of Mark 1:15 that has a good chance of coming from the historical Jesus.[156]

Nevertheless, even if this core-proclamation of the kingdom is authentic, a second major difficulty arises for anyone who wishes to use it to show that Jesus spoke of the kingdom as already present. The precise meaning of the Greek verb *ēggiken* ("has drawn near") has been a battleground for exegetes for a good part of the 20th century. We have already touched on the problem when dealing with the logion in Luke 11:20 par. ("If by the finger of God I cast out the demons, then the kingdom of God has come [*ephthasen*] to you"). However, in Mark 1:15 ‖ Luke 10:9 par., the key verb is not *phthanō* ("to arrive," "to come") but the verb *eggizō*. In the present tense the verb *eggizō* means "to draw near," "to come near," "to approach."[157] That is clear enough, but our problem stems from the fact that the form of the verb in the core-proclamation of Mark 1:15 is not the present but the perfect tense in the Greek (*ēggiken*). Now the Greek perfect is a very subtle and precise tense. It denotes an action (1) that was completed in the past but (2) whose effect perdures into the present.[158] For example, when Paul in Rom 4:25 uses the aorist (simple past) tense to proclaim the belief that Christ "was raised" from the dead (*ēger-thē*), the aorist tense emphasizes the once-and-for-all unrepeatable nature of the past event.[159] In contrast, when in 1 Cor 15:4 Paul uses the perfect tense to affirm that Christ "has been raised" from the dead (*egēgertai*), the emphasis is on the idea that the past act of resurrection has resulted in a permanent risen state for Christ. Just prior to this affirmation, Paul uses the aorist tense to say that Christ "died . . . and . . . was buried (*apethanen . . . kai . . . etaphē*)" since he views these events as over and done with—and pointedly not creating a permanent state for Christ.[160]

Therefore, since the form of the verb in the core kingdom-proclamation of Mark 1:15 ‖ Luke 10:9 par. is in the perfect tense (*ēggiken*), the literal translation of the verse must read "the kingdom of God *has drawn near*" in the sense that the act of drawing near is now over and done with and the kingdom is now in a state of having drawn near. But does this unwieldy paraphrase mean that the kingdom *is* now here or simply that it has drawn so close and become so imminent that it is "at the door"—or, to use another image, that it is like a train just about to pull into the station (a favorite, if curious, metaphor among modern commentators). Obviously, it is difficult to draw a fine line here because of the very nature of this spatial or temporal metaphor. A reality imminent in time or space can approach so close that it is practically, if not literally and technically, present. A train pulling into a station might be described by one waiting passenger as arriving and by another as just about to arrive. It is not surprising, therefore, that proponents of both realized and future eschatology can find texts in Hebrew, Aramaic, and Greek that support their interpretation of *ēggiken* in Mark 1:15 parr. as "has drawn very near" or "is here." One has more than sufficient reason to remain skeptical about a clear resolution of the debate even on the level of the Greek text in Mark 1:15 parr.[161]

All this leads to the third major difficulty, one geared to make total skeptics out of those who ask not simply about the meaning Mark 1:15 parr. in the Greek text but also about the meaning of this kingdom-proclamation (future or realized eschatology?) in the mouth of the historical Jesus. To cut the Gordian knot: all the arguments about the exact meaning of the Greek perfect tense are beside the point when one is questing for the historical Jesus. Jesus presumably spoke this kingdom-proclamation in Aramaic. But there is no precise equivalent to the Greek perfect tense in Aramaic. We are left asking: What meaning did this verb in the Greek perfect represent and how should it be retroverted into Aramaic? Which Aramaic verb (e.g., *qĕrēb* ["draw near"] or *mĕṭāʾ* ["reach," "come"]) does the Greek verb translate? What form would the Aramaic verb take? Would it be a finite verb in the pĕʿal perfect (simple past)? Or possibly a participle—or even an adjective—with a finite verb understood? There is no way to be sure about the answers to these questions, as can be shown from the various tenses of *eggizō* used in the LXX to translate the same basic Hebrew forms in (to take but one example) the Book of Isaiah.[162] Hence I think it unwise to use Mark 1:15 parr. as one of the key texts to document either the future or the realized dimension of Jesus' proclamation of the kingdom.[163]

This is not to say that the kingdom-proclamation in Mark 1:15 parr. has no bearing on the quest for the historical Jesus or the eschatology he proclaimed. The saying certainly has a claim to authenticity on the grounds of both characteristic vocabulary and multiple attestation. At the very least it does show that Jesus spoke about the kingdom of God drawing near, whether he thought that it had already arrived by the time he was speaking or whether he thought that it would soon do so. In any event, the kingdom-proclamation of Mark 1:15 parr. does give us another example of Jesus' proclamation of the kingdom as an eschatological reality coming to human beings at some given time, and not just a general experience of God that is ever-present and ever-available in all human existence.[164] Nevertheless, the kingdom-proclamation in Mark 1:15 cannot be used as evidence for realized as opposed to future eschatology (or vice versa) in the preaching of the historical Jesus. When faced with that alternative, our logion turns into a sphinx.

D. ALLIED SAYINGS ABOUT PRESENT SALVATION: THE BEATITUDE ON EYEWITNESSES AND THE REJECTION OF FASTING

We have now reviewed the major authentic sayings and actions of Jesus that indicate that, at least at some times and in some circumstances, Jesus considered the kingdom of God to be already present. Significantly, authentic sayings of this type are not as numerous and prominent in the Synoptic tradition as sayings of Jesus referring to a future coming of the kingdom. That may be a matter of chance. But, given the growing tendency in the Four Gospels to exalt the present salvation Jesus brings and to play down the promise of an imminent end to the present age (or the promise of an imminent parousia of the Son of Man),[165] the relatively small number of authentic sayings that clearly affirm the presence of the kingdom during Jesus' ministry may echo the relative weight Jesus himself gave to the future and present dimensions of his kingdom-preaching.

It would be a mistake, however, to limit indications of a kingdom already present in Jesus' ministry to those sayings that use the phrase "the kingdom of God." Be it in its future or its present aspect, Jesus' teaching on eschatology was not restricted to that one phrase. Before we conclude this chapter, it would be helpful to note a few other traditions that intimate or presuppose some sort of presence of the kingdom during Jesus' ministry, even though the phrase "kingdom of God" does not appear.

1. The Beatitude on Eyewitnesses (Matt 13:16–17 ‖ Luke 10:23–24)

In a stray Q tradition, which both Matthew and Luke secondarily joined to other blocks of material in their Gospels, Jesus uses a beatitude to felicitate those who are privileged to experience his ministry firsthand. The wording differs somewhat in Matthew and Luke, but fortunately the differences do not affect the substance of the beatitude. A likely reconstruction of the original Q form of the beatitude (using the verse enumeration of Luke 10:23–24) would run as follows:

v 23   Happy (are) the eyes that see what you see
        [and the ears that hear what you hear].

v 24   For [amen] I say to you that
        many prophets and kings longed
            to see what you see and did not see [it],
            and to hear what you hear and did not hear [it].[166]

One is immediately struck by the coherence of this beatitude with two other Q traditions we have already judged authentic: the Q beatitudes at the beginning of the Sermon on the Mount/Plain (Luke 6:20–23 par.) and Jesus' reply to the emissaries of John the Baptist (Matt 11:2–6 par.). As in Luke 6:20–23, we see Jesus using the literary genre called "beatitude" to congratulate actual or potential disciples. Moreover, the overall structure of the beatitude in Luke 10:23–24 corresponds roughly to that of the three beatitudes of the Sermon: (1) initial cry of "happy" (*makarios*), followed by (2) a terse description of the people who are happy (definite article plus adjective or participle in the plural), followed in turn by (3) a causal or explanatory clause (*hoti*, "for," in the beatitudes of the Sermon, *gar*, "for," in Luke 10:24) that gives a reason for the eschatological happiness Jesus ascribes to his audience, a reason involving a reversal of expectations in the end time. Unlike many beatitudes in the OT, Jesus' beatitude in Luke 10:23–24 is addressed to a given audience and so is phrased in the 2d person plural.[167]

Luke 10:23–24 displays a number of telling "mutations" in the basic pattern of Jesus' beatitudes. The beatitude as a whole is noticeably longer than the Q beatitudes of the Sermon, mostly because the explanatory (*gar*) sentence is much more complex. The entire sprawling beatitude is built in an intricate fashion on the principle of parallelism: parallelism in both its large and small units, parallelism that is both synonymous and antithetical, parallelism that rests upon the two primordial images of seeing and hearing. The parallelism in the smallest units of the beatitude results from the simple repetition of these two images. In the first half of the beatitude (v 23), this parallelism is simply synonymous: ". . . the eyes that *see* what you *see* . . . the ears that *hear* what you *hear*." In the second half (v 24, the explanatory *gar* clause), this pattern is repeated but also expanded by adding antithetical to synonymous parallelism: ". . . to *see* what you *see* and [= but] did *not see* [it], and to *hear* what you *hear* and [= but] did *not hear* [it]." On a larger scale, the two verses that make up the beatitude may be seen as standing in a rough sort of antithetical parallelism that contrasts two groups.[168] Verse 23 felicitates the eyes that see and the ears that hear (i.e., the happy audience of Jesus), while v 24 contrasts these happy eyes and ears with the prophets and kings of Israel's past who did not see or hear.

What is intriguing here is that, despite all the differences between Luke 10:23–24 and the core beatitudes in the Q Sermon on the Mount/Plain, a basic pattern perdures. The first half of the beatitude declares happy a certain group of people who are described in terms of some state or action of theirs (poor, hungering, mourning, seeing) that is true now, even as Jesus speaks. Why this state or action constitutes happiness even now (perhaps contrary to the judgment of outsiders) is then explained in the *hoti* or *gar* clause, which involves an eschatological reversal. Here we touch upon the most significant difference between the Q beatitudes of the Sermon and the beatitude in Luke 10:23–24. In the Q beatitudes of the Sermon, the *hoti* ("for") clause prophesies the reversal of the present sad lot of Jesus' audience when the last day comes: those mourning will be comforted by God, and those hungering will be fed to the full by God at the eschatological banquet.

Now, Luke 10:24 also expresses a kind of eschatological reversal, but one of a notably different type.[169] The antithesis now lies not between present suffering and future joy but between past frustration of desire and its present fulfillment. The great prophets and kings of Israel longed to see and hear the fulfillment of God's promise of final salvation, but they did not. Instead, contrary to any sane expectation, a bunch of ragtag Galilean peasants is said by Jesus to be experiencing now the hoped-for salvation denied to the heroes of Israel's sacred past. This is indeed eschatological reversal, but now the reversal lies in the present moment, because the definitive object of Israel's centuries-long hopes and prophecies is present in what Jesus' audience is seeing and hearing.

The repeated emphasis on "seeing" and "hearing" reminds us of Jesus' reply to the emissaries sent by the Baptist. As an indirect, cryptic answer to their direct question about his identity and role, Jesus orders the emissaries to tell John what they "see" and "hear" (Matt 11:4 ‖ Luke 7:22). What follows is *both* a list of various miraculous healings performed by Jesus *and* the climactic point that the poor have the good news proclaimed to them (Matt 11:5 ‖ Luke 7:22). This, then, is what the emissaries "see" and "hear": the deeds of Jesus (especially the miracles) and his message of good news to the poor. Most likely, this is also what is intended by the reference to what Jesus' audience sees and hears in Luke 10:23–24: the astounding deeds and joyful message of Jesus.[170] As we have already seen in this chapter, Jesus saw his exorcisms as proof that the kingdom of God had already come to those who experienced them, and in his preaching he dared to claim that the kingdom of God was already "in the midst" of his hearers. This is why Jesus' audience can be described as possessing an eschatological happiness that leaves Israel's prophets and kings behind in the dust. In seeing and hearing what Jesus does and says, his audience experiences to some degree, however partially, what the great figures of Israel's past could only hope for and what many pious Jews of Jesus' day still looked for at some future date: the kingdom of God, God come in power to reign definitively over his people Israel. That hoped-for future event happens now, in the ministry of Jesus.

How remarkable this claim of eschatological salvation in the present moment must have seemed to many pious Jews of Jesus' day can be grasped from two beatitudes that we read in the pseudepigraphical *Psalms of Solomon*, written by devout Jews in Jerusalem during the 1st century B.C.[171] These two beatitudes occur, significantly, in two psalms that pray for the coming of the "Son of David," "the Lord Messiah," in "the last days," within the larger theological context of God's kingship, fully realized in the end time. *Ps. Sol.* 17:44 presents us with this eschatological beatitude: "Happy [shall be] those born in those days, to see the good things of Israel, when God brings about the gathering of the [twelve] tribes." Similarly, *Ps. Sol.* 18:6 proclaims: "Happy [shall be] those born in those days, to see the good things of the Lord, which he shall accomplish for the coming generation under the rod of discipline of the Lord Messiah." The eschatological happiness that is extolled, the people who will know this happiness, and the experience of God's salvation all lie in the future.

In sum, from the comparison of the beatitude in Luke 10:23–24 with the Q beatitudes of the Sermon and the reply to the emissaries of John, and from the contrast with the *Psalms of Solomon*, we can draw four conclusions: (1) Jesus felicitates his audience for experiencing what was hoped for but never experienced by the great ones of Israel's past.[172] (2) Jesus' audience therefore lives in the time of the fulfillment of Israel's hopes and prophecies, a time that many pious Jews of Jesus' day still expected at some future date. (3) This fulfillment, which the audience is seeing and hearing right now, is contained in the miraculous deeds Jesus performs and the good news he preaches. (4) Finally, if we may draw upon what Jesus says explicitly elsewhere (Luke 11:20 par.; 17:21), what the audience is now experiencing through his deeds and words is nothing less than the coming of God's kingdom—even though the key phrase is not directly mentioned in the beatitude.[173] Reginald Fuller's attempt to water down the implication of this beatitude by claiming that the disciples "see and hear [only] the signs of the coming Kingdom, . . . not its arrival, but its dawning" hardly does justice to the amazing antithesis in the saying between the longing of all the great figures of Israel's past and the actual experience of the disciples of Jesus.[174] Was the object of the prophets' longing merely the signs of the kingdom, and not the kingdom itself—merely its dawning, and not its arrival? That does not seem to be the implication of Luke 10:23–24.

The claim of this beatitude is so amazing that we might well wonder whether it can be ascribed to the historical Jesus. To be sure, the lack of multiple attestation of sources makes any conclusion difficult. Yet even a skeptic like Bultmann thinks that Luke 10:23–24 comes from the historical Jesus.[175] In my view, the argument from coherence is in this instance fairly strong, especially since we find more than one kind of coherence. There is first of all coherence in literary form and structure, since Luke 10:23–24 evinces more or less the same striking beatitude-form seen in Jesus' beatitudes of the Sermon on the

Mount/Plain. As we noted in Chapter 15, the rest of the NT does not reflect a great interest in or production of new beatitudes, especially ones that imitate the form and message exhibited in the beatitudes of Jesus.

Then, too, there is a coherence in the implied message of the presence of the kingdom in and through the ministry of Jesus. The new, happy state of things proclaimed in Luke 10:23–24, a state that sharply demarcates the time of Jesus and his disciples from Israel's sacred past, jibes perfectly with many of the sayings and actions of Jesus we have examined in this chapter: Jesus' reply to the emissaries of the Baptist (Matt 11:2–6 par.); Jesus' assertion that the least in the kingdom of God is greater than John (Matt 11:11 par.; cf. the prophets and kings who long to see what the disciples see); Jesus' claim that from the time of John onward a new situation with regard to the kingdom exists (Matt 11:12–13 ǀǀ Luke 16:16); Jesus' appeal to his audience to recognize that through the exorcisms he performs the kingdom of God has come to them (Luke 11:20 par.); and Jesus' dismissal of apocalyptic calculations of a future coming of the kingdom with the assertion that the kingdom is already in their midst (Luke 17:21b).

There is a further aspect of coherence in Luke 10:23–24 that argues in favor of the saying's authenticity as opposed to a creation by first-generation Christians. When we examined many of the sayings just mentioned—as well as sayings that refer to a future coming of the kingdom—we observed an intriguing pattern. Implicitly Jesus made himself and his ministry the pivotal means by which the kingdom would or had come, and yet we usually found no direct reference to him in the sayings in which he announces the kingdom.[176] What personal references there may be tend to be allusive or oblique. In Matt 11:2–5, miracles are mentioned, but not the one who performs them. In Mark 3:27, Jesus the exorcist is alluded to under the hardly flattering metaphor of a robber. So too, in Luke 10:23–24, what the happy disciples see and hear is ultimately the presence of the kingdom. But it stands to reason that what they are immediately seeing and hearing are the deeds and words of Jesus—though this is not openly affirmed in the logion. As in other sayings, Jesus is implicitly made the sole and necessary mediator of this present experience of the kingdom. Yet here as elsewhere he does not appear in the saying; his role is implied rather than expressed. The various christologies of the post-Easter church are simply absent.

There is a final observation that points in the direction of authenticity rather than a creation by the early church. The whole rhetorical argument of Luke 10:23–24 draws its force from the unique experience of being eyewitnesses of Jesus' ministry. Those witnessing Jesus' activity are uniquely happy because, unlike all the great religious figures of Israel's past, they are directly, personally, on a firsthand basis experiencing the deeds and words of Jesus and thus the kingdom's presence: "Happy are the eyes that see what you are seeing." The happiness extolled in the beatitude is thus implicitly restricted to those who are actually seeing and hearing what Jesus says and does as he goes about healing and preaching. Such a beatitude is strikingly dissimilar to—

indeed, the very opposite of—the beatitude with which the Fourth Evangelist ends his Gospel (John 20:29). After the risen Jesus comments ironically on the belief of Thomas, who demanded firsthand experience of the risen Lord before he would believe, a final beatitude praises the members of the later church who did not have or need the experience of being eyewitnesses in order to believe: "Have you [i.e., Thomas] come to believe because you have seen me? Happy [*makarios*] are those who have not seen and [yet] believe."

Actually, John 20:29 reflects the very reason why sayings of Jesus were created or adapted by the early church: to make the past event and teachings of Jesus of Nazareth speak to and be relevant to the very different present of the church. In a sense, Luke 10:23–24 does just the opposite by emphasizing the unique experience and happy privilege of the eyewitnesses of Jesus' public ministry—a privilege members of the later church could not have, a privilege that might even be seen to devalue the status of members of the church vis-à-vis Jesus' original audience. When one takes this point together with the converging lines of coherence and the lack of any explicit christological claim, it seems on the whole more likely that Luke 10:23–24 is a saying of the historical Jesus rather than a creation of the church. Hence, according to this logion, Jesus saw his ministry as the unique time that fulfilled Israel's hopes and prophecies, the time when the kingdom of God that was to come was in some way already present.[177]

2. The Question About Fasting (Mark 2:18–20 parr.)

When dealing above with the exorcisms of Jesus (Luke 11:20 par.), I remarked how in practice it is often impossible to separate the actions of Jesus from the sayings that are called forth by his actions and in turn interpret them. A prime example of this inextricable union of deeds and words is the brief question-and-answer pericope about the lack of fasting on the part of Jesus' disciples. The earliest form of the unit is found in Mark's Gospel (2:18–20),[178] where it already shows signs of development and expansion in the Christian tradition:[179]

v 18a And the disciples of John and the Pharisees were fasting,
    b and they come and say to him [i.e., Jesus]:
    c "Why do the disciples of John and the disciples of the
        Pharisees fast,
    d but your disciples do not fast?"

v 19a And Jesus said to them:
        "Can the wedding guests[180] fast
            when the bridegroom is with them?[181]
    b As long as they have the bridegroom with them
        they cannot fast.

v 20a But days will come
        when the bridegroom will be taken away from them,
    b and then they will fast on that day."[182]

a. *The Marcan form of the pericope.* Although Mark's version of the question on fasting may be too repetitious for our tastes (indeed, it was too repetitious for Matthew and Luke!), it is a fine example of the "duality" (saying things twice in parallel form), the use of key words, and the reversal of word order that we often find in Mark's Gospel. The key word "to fast" (*nēsteuō*) occurs three times in the introductory material of v 18 (setting the scene and asking the question) and three times in Jesus' reply in vv 19–20 (twice of the present impossibility of fasting in v 19, once of future fasting in v 20). In the introductory material of v 18, the Greek verb "to fast" always occurs at the end of a clause—and at the end of the whole verse—for emphasis. Another key word that dominates v 18 is "disciples" (*mathētai*), which occurs four times in a pattern of three units: "the disciples of John" (v 18a) / "the disciples of John and the disciples of the Pharisees" (v 18c) / "your disciples" (v 18d)—each unit being connected with one occurrence of the verb "to fast." In the first two units, the phrase "the disciples *of*" (either John or the Pharisees) is used, a pattern which helps to emphasize the final mention of "disciples," accompanied as it is by a different sort of modifier: "*your* disciples." All these verbal patterns highlight the contrast between other Jewish disciples (be they of John or of the Pharisees) and Jesus' disciples on the question of fasting.

Verses 19–20 (the reply of Jesus) show a similar use of the repetition of key words and the reversal of order. The key word "disciples" disappears, and the new key word that accompanies the verb "to fast" is "bridegroom" (*nymphios*). In fact, vv 19a, 19b, and 20 all contain one occurrence of "to fast" and one occurrence of "bridegroom." The figure of the bridegroom remains secondary in the sense that he always appears in a subordinate clause. It is the verb "to fast" that dominates the main clauses. As in v 18, the two occurrences of "to fast" in v 19 (where the action of fasting is negated each time) appear last in their clauses, while the emphatic "they cannot" appears each time first in the clause. All the more striking, then, is the reversal of word order and expectations when "to fast" appears in the last line of the pericope. For the only time in the story, "to fast" occurs toward the beginning of its clause as, contrary to expectations, it is now asserted that the wedding guests *will* fast when the ominous time-period designated "on that day" arrives. This reversal motif is strengthened by the chiastic relation of the subordinate temporal clause to the main clause in v 19a and v 19b: "The wedding guests cannot . . . *when* . . . (v 19a) / "*as long as* . . . they cannot . . . (v 19b)."

All these stylistic observations help us to appreciate the carefully balanced artistic whole created either by Mark or by some pre-Marcan collector of dispute stories whose work Mark has appropriated.[183] Mark employs the pericope's meticulous balance-with-contrast to bring into relief two major theological affirmations about the fasting practiced by Jesus' disciples, each affirmation having its own justifying reason:

(1) Verses 18–19 tell us that, during Jesus' public ministry, his disciples

stood out from other pious Jewish groups in that they did not fast. The reason for this—on the level of Mark's redaction—was that Jesus the bridegroom had introduced the joyful time of salvation, the time of his espousals with his bride, the people of Israel. In this theological justification we hear the Christian use of "bridegroom" as a symbol for the Messiah—a symbol, interestingly, that was not used for the Messiah or any human eschatological figure in the OT or early Judaism.[184] According to Mark, Jesus has made present the joyful marriage feast of the Messiah with Israel; hence it would be unthinkable, impossible ("they *cannot* fast") for his disciples, his closest friends at the wedding, to fast during his ministry.[185] Such a gesture of sorrow or mourning would be totally out of place in the presence of the Messiah-bridegroom.

(2) But the end of v 19b ("*as long as* they have the bridegroom with them") already hints at the possibility of a time when the disciples will be bereft of the bridegroom. The hint is then spelled out in the eschatological prophecy of v 20, which justifies the disciples' change of practice with regard to fasting. With the solemn introduction often used by the prophets ("days will come," with the corresponding "on that day" forming an inclusion),[186] Jesus prophesies that he, the bridegroom, will be "taken away" from his friends (namely, by violent death on the cross, as the Gospel will increasingly make clear). His death will introduce a time of bereavement as opposed to wedding joy, a time when his friends will mourn over his (physical) absence.[187] Fittingly, then, they will practice fasting "on that day."[188] In short, while vv 18–19 justify the disciples' past practice of not fasting during Jesus' ministry, despite the fasts practiced by disciples of John and the Pharisees, v 20—and thus the ultimate thrust of the whole pericope—justifies to the present-day church of Mark its own quite different practice of fasting.[189]

The veiled reference to Jesus' death in 2:20 also fits neatly into the larger cycle of dispute stories in Mark 2:1–3:6. In the first dispute story, the healing of the paralytic (2:1–12), adversaries ("the scribes" in v 6) make an accusation against Jesus for the first time in the Gospel: "He *blasphemes*" (v 7). This forms an ominous inclusion with the last time this accusation is made against Jesus in the Gospel. Just before Jesus is condemned to death by the Sanhedrin, the high priest says: "You have heard the *blasphemy*. What do you think?" (14:64). The reference to Jesus' death in 2:20 also points forward to the end of the cycle of dispute stories (3:6), where for the first time we hear of a plot to put Jesus to death: "And going out the Pharisees immediately took counsel with the Herodians against him as to how they might destroy him." Standing as it does at the midpoint in the cycle of dispute stories,[190] the question on fasting connects with the references to Jesus' death at the beginning and end of the dispute cycle, while also pointing forward to the Passion Narrative.[191]

From all that we have seen it is clear that Mark 2:18–20 as it now stands is a Christian composition, aiming ultimately at explaining to Christians why their practice of fasting is the opposite of what Jesus' disciples practiced during his public ministry. The answer takes for granted the special nature of "the time of the church," poised as it is between the initial joy of the appearance of the Messiah during his earthly life and his final appearance in glory at the parousia.[192] While one might label this pericope a pronouncement story, an apophthegm, or a chreia (it is not strictly speaking a dispute story),[193] it functions in effect as a piece of church order, commanding ("then they *will* fast"), justifying, and interpreting the Christian practice of fasting in terms of the death of Jesus and the in-between time of the church.[194]

b. *The earliest attainable pre-Marcan form.* The characteristics of the redaction of Mark or of the collection he took over already point us in the direction of what may lie behind the present form of the text. When we join these formal considerations to observations about content and meaning, we begin to sense which parts of the pericope might be secondary additions to the tradition. As we saw above, v 18a and v 18c reflect Marcan "duality" inasmuch as they say basically the same thing. Since the question in v 18c + d is the immediate occasion of Jesus' counterquestion in v 19a (a typically rabbinic way of arguing), which in turn lies at the heart of the whole tradition, it is more likely that the unnecessary opening statement in v 18a is a product of Marcan duality. Significantly, 18a compresses the diffuse and somewhat puzzling "the disciples of John and the disciples of the Pharisees" into the briefer and more intelligible "the disciples of John and the Pharisees." The greater focus on the Pharisees as a group in v 18a ties 2:18–20 more closely to the surrounding dispute stories in Mark 2:1–3:6, where the Pharisees themselves are on the scene (2:16, 24; 3:6) and show hostility to Jesus or his disciples—which is pointedly not the case in 2:18–20. Thus, an earlier version of the story probably began with v 18b, the indefinite and impersonal third-person plural of the verb in Aramaic being equivalent to "some people came and said to Jesus. . . ."[195] There is no hint of hostility as the traditional story opens; the disciples of John or the Pharisees are not presented as being on the scene.

As just noted, within the question voiced in v 18c, "the disciples of the Pharisees" is a curious phrase. It occurs in this precise form nowhere else in the NT. Since historically the Pharisees were for the most part a pious group of stringently observant Jewish laymen,[196] most of whom were not learned teachers, one would not expect them *as a group* to have "disciples." The type of phrase one would expect is the one found in Mark 2:16: "the scribes of the Pharisees," i.e., those men within the Pharisaic movement who had formally studied the Torah, became teachers, and could thus act as guides for the other members of the movement.[197] In v 18c, "the disciples of the Pharisees" must be taken in a somewhat looser sense to mean people who were attracted to and adopted the teachings and practices of the Pharisaic movement. This may be the meaning of the phrase when it occurs in Matt 22:15–16: "The Pharisees . . . sent their disciples to him [i.e., Jesus]."

Such usage is not necessarily anachronistic or indicative of a poor knowledge of Judaism. Writing in the *Jewish Antiquities* (13.10.5 §288–89), Josephus refers to the Hasmonean ethnarch and high priest John Hyrcanus I (reigned 134–104 B.C.) as a disciple (*mathētēs*) of the Pharisees before he switched his allegiance to the Sadducees. This probably does not mean that Hyrcanus, a worldly ruler involved in wars and international politics, carefully observed every detail of the Pharisaic way of life. Rather, the context suggests that he courted the support of the Pharisees, sought their advice, and flattered them with protestations of how much he was influenced by them.

Another point should be kept in mind as well: both Matthew and Josephus use the designation "disciple(s) of the Pharisees" toward the end of the 1st century A.D., when the Pharisees (or the early rabbis in their wake) had gained the ascendancy as the leading group in post-A.D. 70 Judaism.[198] Thus, while the phrase may not be dismissed simply as an anachronism, its use by Mark, Matthew, and Josephus may have been fostered by developments after the First Jewish Revolt.

All this may give us a hint about the tradition history of the question in Mark 2:18c. On the one hand, Mark, Matthew, and Josephus give reason to think that the phrase "disciple(s) of the Pharisees" would be at home especially in a post-A.D. 70 situation. On the other hand, within Mark's Gospel, Pharisees are a significant Jewish group in opposition to Jesus. In contrast, with the exception of a passing reference at the burial of the Baptist (6:29), the disciples of John the Baptist never appear again in the Gospel. As we know from John's Gospel, some of Jesus' disciples—and in some sense, Jesus himself—emerged from the circle of disciples around John the Baptist. Accordingly, people naturally raised questions about Jesus' relation to John, questions reflected in various forms in both the Q and the Johannine traditions (Matt 11:2–6 par.; John 3:22–26). With the exception of 2:18–20, Mark seems innocent of such questions or tensions regarding the disciples of John—while questions from and tensions with the Pharisees abound. Then, too, we notice that, while the phrase "the disciples of the Pharisees" is not necessarily incorrect, it does seem out of place in the present context. Two other groups of disciples are present in the brief story: the disciples of John and "*your* disciples," i.e., the disciples of Jesus. In both cases, the phrases "the disciples of John" and "your disciples" describe a religious group in terms of a single revered teacher around whom people gather and by whom they are taught. Whatever its precise sense, "the disciples of the Pharisees" does not fit this pattern of meaning—and this in a terribly concise, three-verse story where, as we have seen, the repetition of the same key words and phrases structures the whole narrative.

Three significant points arise from these considerations: (1) the Pharisees are quite important to Mark both for the plot of the Gospel as a whole and in particular for the cycle of dispute stories in 2:1–3:6 (appearing as they do in 2:16,24; 3:6). (2) With the exception of Mark 6:29, the disciples of John never appear again and play no role either in the larger plot of the Gospel or in the cycle of dispute stories in 2:1–3:6. (3) The phrase "the disciples of the Pharisees" in the question of v 18c does not fit the other uses of "disciples" in v 18. All this justifies us in supposing, along with Knut Backhaus and other exegetes, that the pre-Marcan tradition has added "the disciples of the Pharisees" to a primitive story that originally concerned only the relationship of the disciples of John to the disciples of Jesus on the question of fasting.[199] Since the disciples of John are of no interest to the pre-Marcan cycle of dispute stories, which are held together and reach their climax in the ever-increasing hostility of the Pharisees, it seems likely that "the disciples of the Pharisees" was added to the original story about fasting to provide a link to the larger literary unit. Hence, the earliest form of the story probably mentioned only the disciples of John in the question voiced in v 18c. In the later Marcan tradition the focus is shifted from the question of the disciples of John vis-à-vis the disciples of Jesus to the question of Christianity versus Pharisaic (or early rabbinic) Judaism.

Another later development in the tradition may be seen at the other end of the pericope, namely v 20. The majority of scholars declare v 20 to be a prophecy after the fact (*vaticinium ex eventu*), created by the early church to reflect its different, post-Easter situation. One must be clear here on the reason for accepting such a judgment about the authenticity of v 20. I do not accept the a priori position that Jesus could never have considered the possibility of his meeting a violent end and could never have spoken about it to his disciples. If, merely as a matter of historical fact, such different religious leaders as Martin Luther King, Jr., and Archbishop Oscar Romero could foresee and speak of what their likely end would be—and that soon before their actual deaths—a historian cannot a priori exclude such a possibility in the case of a Jewish teacher of 1st-century Palestine who understood himself in prophetic terms. This would be especially true after John the Baptist, the eschatological prophet who was Jesus' own mentor, met a bloody end at the hands of Herod Antipas, the ruler of Jesus' native Galilee. The whole question of the sayings of Jesus concerning his death will be taken up in a later chapter. Here I simply make the point that it is illegitimate to reject Mark 2:20 simply on the grounds that it would be impossible for Jesus to have foreseen or talked about his violent end.

But the mention of Jesus' approaching death is not the sole or even the main reason for thinking that v 20 comes from the early church. The death of Jesus does not stand, either grammatically or theologically, at the center of v 20. Rather, as we have already seen, the main point of v 20 is the enunciation and the validation of a "change of policy"—one is almost tempted to say a change in canon law. The policy of not undertaking voluntary fasts—the very policy whose validation is the point of vv 18–19—is abrogated in favor of the opposite policy in v 20. In fact, *that* is the major point of v 20, the death of Jesus serving in the subordinate clause as the justifying reason. This prophecy of a change in the practice of fasting by Jesus' disciples, justified in turn by an oblique prophecy of his death, becomes all the more startling when we remember that the people to whom Jesus is speaking are neither his own disciples nor the disciples of John, but rather some anonymous inquirers. Is it at all historically likely that Jesus would have addressed a prophecy of a change in fasting regulations affecting his disciples not to those disciples but to some outsiders, and would he have gone on to justify the future change to the outsiders by alluding to his future death? How could outsiders, who were inquiring about the fasting practice of Jesus' disciples vis-à-vis John's disciples, have understood the prophecy in v 20 about a future change of practice based on the death of Jesus? More to the point, how could the historical Jesus have expected outsiders to understand his prophecy? At this juncture the whole scenario becomes wildly improbable. Both the content of v 20 and the way it functions within the whole narrative argue conclusively for its being a later addition to the tradition.[200]

A further observation that supports this conclusion is the movement from a simple, intelligible metaphor in v 19 to the beginning of a forced allegory in v 20. The basic thrust of the metaphor in v 19 is that fasting by Jesus' disciples as they experience the time of salvation their master brings is just as incompatible or unthinkable as fasting would be on the part of wedding guests as they celebrate the wedding with their host, the bridegroom. The metaphor is direct and uncomplicated, with at best an oblique reference to the person of Jesus. That is not the case in v 20, where the metaphor begins to be developed into an allegory: at some future date Jesus the bridegroom will be taken away by death,[201] and his friends (i.e., his disciples) will respond to the new situation by reversing their practice and taking up fasting as a sign of mourning. Not only has the imagery become more complicated—which would not be impossible in the mouth of Jesus—but it has also become forced and contrived as it turns into allegory. The friends of any bridegroom would naturally avoid fasting during his wedding. But there is no natural reason why, when the wedding is over and the bridegroom has departed—or even for some reason been taken away—the wedding guests should begin to fast. Indeed, one might ask whether it would not be more natural at the end of a wedding feast for the guests to depart and for the bridegroom to remain where he is. In any case, the subsequent history of Jesus and the early church is obviously peeking through and forming the artificial allegory of v 20, as opposed to the natural metaphor of v 19. The allegorical nature of v 20 thus reinforces our conclusion that it is secondary.[202]

Should we draw the same conclusion about the second half of Jesus' answer in v 19 ("as long as they have the bridegroom with them they cannot fast")? Here scholars become more doubtful and opinions divide.[203] While the case is not as clear as v 20, I incline to the view of such exegetes as Rudolf Pesch and Knut Backhaus that v 19b is likewise a Christian expansion on the original tradition. First of all, there is the phenomenon of Marcan duality. The question about fasting in v 18cd is answered in true rabbinic fashion by Jesus in 19a with a counterquestion employing a concrete metaphor. All that need be said by way of an answer is contained in Jesus' counterquestion. The affirmative form of Jesus' answer in v 19b is little more than a mirror image of the counterquestion, and so may easily be an example of Marcan duality. Yet v 19b does provide one slight development over its rhetorical "twin brother" in v 19a. Instead of referring simply to the time "when" (*en hǭ*, literally "in which") the bridegroom is with the wedding guests, v 19b uses a more specific phrase: *hoson chronon*, "as long as" the wedding guests have the bridegroom with them. "As long as" discreetly raises the idea of a time limit and termination of the bridegroom's presence among his friends and so quietly opens up the way for the prophecy of the bridegroom's being taken away in v 20. Verse 19b thus acts as the literary and theological bridge to the new theme of v 20. If, as seems necessary, we judge v 20 to be a later Christian addition, the same judgment appears to follow logically for v 19b, the sentence that links it to the earlier tradition.[204]

c. *The authenticity of the core tradition.* Having removed apparent additions to the story, additions made during the first Christian generation, we have arrived at the earliest available form of the tradition enshrined in Mark 2:18–20:

> v 18b (And) they come and say to Jesus:[205]
>   c "Why do the disciples of John fast,
>   d but your disciples do not fast?"
>
> v 19a And Jesus said to them:
>   "Can the wedding guests fast
>   when the bridegroom is with them?"

This primitive tradition is less elegantly balanced and knit together than the final form of the pericope in Mark's Gospel. Still, this extremely concise unit possesses a basic symmetry. At the heart of the unit lies the irreducible core of question and counterquestion: the question about fasting posed to Jesus by some anonymous inquirers and the answer by way of rhetorical counter-question spoken by Jesus. Both question and answer divide into two halves of roughly equal length.[206] The two two-part questions are then framed by two introductory clauses (v 18b and v 19a), each clause having exactly five words in the Greek.[207] The triple use of the key word "fast" cuts across these two-part structures and binds the unit together with the word that sums up the point at issue.

This primitive tradition, made up of v 18bcd and v 19a, is the smallest unit that could have been transmitted in the oral tradition and still have made sense. Obviously, the question in v 18, apart from some answer, could not have stood on its own in the oral tradition. Similarly—despite some exegetes who suggest otherwise—Jesus' counterquestion in v 19a would have been unintelligible if transmitted in isolation.[208] Its very nature as a rhetorical counterquestion that presumes a previous attitude, comment, or question to which it is reacting demands something like v 18.

All of this brings us to the climactic question toward which our consider-ations have been tending: Can the substance, if not the exact wording, of the tradition in v 18bcd and v 19a be traced back to an actual exchange in the life of the historical Jesus and correspondingly to a particular practice of his disci-ples with regard to fasting?[209] Despite the lack of multiple attestation of sources for this dialogue, a number of criteria argue strongly for the tradi-tion's authenticity.

First, the criterion of discontinuity points out that voluntary fasting[210] was an honored practice among the devout, both in 1st-century Judaism and in the early church. Possibly at least some Pharisees, as Luke mentions in the parable of the Pharisee and the Toll Collector (Luke 18:9–14), fasted twice a week (Mondays and Thursdays seem suggested by *Did.* 8:1 and the later *b. Taʿan.* 12a; cf. *m. Taʿan.* 1:6; 2:9; and the Tosefta to *Taʿan.* 2:4).[211] We are not informed as to the exact practice and schedule of fasting among the disciples of the Baptist during the time of Jesus. Presumably they did not follow the radically restricted diet of their master (locusts and wild honey), but from the austerity and severity of the Baptist we may reasonably infer a strict practice of fasting among his devoted followers. Not for nothing was the original form of the question probably posed in terms of the disciples of John alone; perhaps they overshadowed even the Pharisees in their zeal for fasting. In line with John's preaching, fasting for his disciples no doubt signified sorrow for sin and repentance, along with fierce supplication to God to be spared the fearful judgment on the last day.[212]

Various streams of 1st-century Christianity knew the practice of fasting as well. It is reflected not only in the willingness of Matthew and Luke to take over Mark 2:18–20, but also in the special M material of Matthew (Matt 6:16–18), in Luke's depiction of the early church leaders, including Paul (Acts 13:2–3; 14:23),[213] and in the detailed instructions of the *Didache* (7:4; 8:1). Even when we do not hear individual NT writers affirming the practice of fasting, what is notable is that no NT writer polemicizes against it or categorically forbids it as a pious practice. This is all the more remarkable when one considers the battles in the Pauline churches over the question of whether one should avoid certain foods altogether—which, of course, is not the same thing as fasting.[214] Granted the widespread practice of fasting in the 1st-century church, it is hardly credible that the early church both invented a prohibition of voluntary fasting (Mark 2:18–19a) and then in somewhat awkward fashion turned around and invented an explanation as to why the prohibition no longer held (Mark 2:19b–20). Simply as a matter of fact, we have no clear evidence anywhere in the NT for some group of Christians in the early church that in principle refused to fast.[215] Thus, the rejection of voluntary fasting by the disciples of Jesus during his ministry—presumably because of the practice and teaching of Jesus himself[216]—stands out in contrast to the practice of devout Jews in the 1st centuries B.C. and A.D. and also to the practice of the 1st-century church.

Alongside the criterion of discontinuity comes the criterion of coherence with other sayings and deeds of Jesus' ministry. As we have seen, Jesus himself commented ironically on the sharp difference in practice between the ascetic Baptist and Jesus the eater and drinker, noting how critics found something to object to in both types of conduct (Matt 11:16–19 par.). Perhaps to some observers, his table fellowship with tax collectors and sinners (Mark 2:13–17; Matt 11:19; Luke 19:7; cf. Luke 15:1) was all the more objectionable because it was in no way balanced by voluntary fasting at other times. All these aspects of Jesus' conduct cohere with that dimension of his message which we have been studying in this chapter: not only was the kingdom of God very near, in some sense it was already present in Jesus' ministry, bringing healing and joy to those who accepted it. The eschatological banquet of salvation, promised in the near future to many coming from east and west (Matt 8:11 par.), was in some way already available to those who shared Jesus' joy at mealtime.[217]

This refusal to fast, which Jesus inculcates and his disciples practice, takes on special resonance in a 1st-century Jewish Palestinian milieu. We have from Palestine of the 1st century A.D. an Aramaic text called the *mĕgillat taʿanît*, the Scroll of Fasting. As a kind of liturgical calendar it lists the days of the year when fasting and mourning were prohibited because the stated days were days of joy, commemorating happy events in Israel's history such as victories and recognition of Jewish prerogatives.[218] The intriguing point here is that we see witnessed in a 1st-century Palestinian text the idea that a special day of joy in Israel's history excludes the possibility of fasting. In effect, then, Jesus is implying by his general prohibition of voluntary fasting that every day is a special day of joy for his disciples, a day in which they rejoice at the wedding banquet of salvation Jesus brings. While the saying in Mark 2:19a does not explicitly mention the kingdom of God, that is in all likelihood the reality referred to by the imagery of the wedding. What other sayings examined in this chapter explicitly proclaim Mark 2:18–19a intimates: in some way the kingdom is already present, bringing Jesus' disciples a constant joy that excludes the very thought of fasting.

To these two major criteria other secondary observations may be added. The sharp antithetical metaphors of fasting and a wedding, compressed into a single rhetorical question, are typical of the forceful rhetoric and parabolic speech of Jesus. As for the metaphor of the bridegroom, we see once again an aspect of Jesus' teaching that we have already noted frequently. When Jesus does refer to his own role in the eschatological drama, he tends to do so indirectly, often in surprising or even disconcerting metaphors and parables (e.g., Mark 3:27, the robber in the parable of the strong man). Since there was no tradition in the OT or early Judaism that depicted the Messiah or any other human eschatological figure as a bridegroom, the image could remain on the level of a passing metaphor, one way of making the basic point of comparison: guests do not fast at a wedding. Yet the very fact that Jesus chooses to speak of the time when the guests do not fast with the words "when the bridegroom is with them" rather than simply with a phrase like "during the wedding" may indicate that he intends an oblique or teasing reference to himself as the prophetic proclaimer—and in some sense realizer—of the kingdom. Without him his disciples would not know the joy of a constant wedding feast or feel authorized to reject all voluntary fasting because of it.

Besides implications for Jesus' understanding of himself, the pericope on fasting also holds implications for Jesus' disciples. Backhaus says of Mark 2:18–20 that it offers "the first sure evidence of a sociologically circumscribed group of disciples around John the Baptist."[219] Looking at all that the Gospels tell us about the Baptist's disciples, we are given what amounts to a description of a clearly defined sociological group—some would say a "sect"[220]—within 1st-century Palestinian Judaism, which had more than its share of such movements. Certainly, the Baptist's disciples possessed distinctiveness and coherence as a group within the greater Jewish community of Palestine. They had a single famous leader, a preacher and teacher who gathered around himself followers to whom he administered a once-and-for-all baptism closely associated with his person (hence, John *the Baptist*). This group created a certain sociological identity within the larger religious community of 1st-century Palestinian Judaism by reciting special prayers taught them by the Baptist (Luke 11:1) and by observing special voluntary fasts (Mark 2:18), as they eagerly awaited a final judgment that would soon put an end to the present state of things.

But if all this constituted the Baptist's disciples as a distinct sociological group within Palestinian Judaism, the same must be said about the disciples of Jesus. To anticipate what we shall see in later chapters: while many people may have been attracted to Jesus and agreed with his message, Jesus went out of his way to call certain individuals to a more stable kind of companionship with himself (Mark 1:16–20; 2:14; Luke 5:1–11; John 1:35–51). Some of these relatively permanent followers formed an inner circle around Jesus called "the Twelve."[221] At least with regard to his more permanent followers, what was true of the disciples of John was also true of the disciples of Jesus. As I have argued in Chapter 13, Jesus most likely continued the unusual practice of baptizing others that he had learned from the Baptist. He also taught his disciples at least one memorable prayer (the so-called Lord's Prayer). Perhaps even more importantly from the viewpoint of sociological boundaries, Jesus pointedly demarcated his group of disciples not only from the Baptist's disciples or the Pharisees but from any and all pious Jews of the time by forbidding in principle the practice of voluntary fasting on the grounds that the joyful time of salvation had arrived. The intriguing point here is that a practice setting up a sociological boundary was grounded by Jesus in his intensely eschatological message. As we have seen throughout the present chapter, Jesus asserted that the kingdom he was proclaiming for the future had in some sense arrived. As a result, far from conveying a mere inner belief about the state of one's soul or a fiery hope about the imminent future, Jesus' proclamation of the kingdom of God had a concrete impact on the socio-religious lives of those who closely followed him—noticeably in the question of fasting.

In this regard it is important to emphasize that Jesus *as a matter of principle* proclaims that it is *impossible* for his disciples to undertake voluntary fasts because of the joyful time of salvation he announces and brings (Mark 2:18–19a). Now, devout Jews might decide to fast or not to fast voluntarily as they saw fit.[222] Apart from stated days of joyful celebration on the calendar, no one was in a position to tell pious Jews that they could not fast at a particular time or in a particular way. It was a matter of free choice. Different groups of Jews who had banded together for religious purposes might decide to fast on different days, e.g., the Pharisees on one day and the Baptist's disciples on another.

But what is unheard of is for some individual Jewish teacher to tell outsiders that what marks off his disciples from every other pious Jewish group is that in principle his disciples cannot fast at all because of his particular message and ministry. In effect, then, at least on this one issue of voluntary fasting, Jesus is distinguishing his disciples from all other Jews. Here is at least one way in which the disciples of Jesus during his public ministry constituted a distinct sociological group (again, some would go so far as to use the term "sect") within Palestinian Judaism—as were the Baptist's disciples, the Pharisees, the Essenes, and the Sadducees.

Obviously the distinctiveness of any one subgroup within a larger society allows of varying degrees of strength or weakness. I do not think that the distinctiveness of Jesus' disciples during his ministry reached that point of separateness which Shaye J. D. Cohen considers necessary for the designation "sect." Cohen defines a sect thus: "A small, organized group that separates itself from a larger religious body and asserts that it alone embodies the ideals of the larger group because it alone understands God's will."[223] Significantly, Cohen is willing to apply the term to early Christianity after Jesus' death, but he does not use it (rightly, I think) in reference to the disciples gathered around Jesus during his ministry.[224]

In sum, the brevity of the tradition in Mark 2:18–19a belies its great significance. Not only does it provide one more indication of the idea that the kingdom of God is present in Jesus' ministry, it also shows that this presence was for Jesus not simply an idea but a reality and power that would naturally mold and indeed change his disciples' religious practice. In Jesus' view, the kingdom as present was to have concrete consequences for community living within Palestinian Judaism.[225]

IV. CONCLUSION: THE KINGDOM AS PRESENT

The upshot of all we have seen in this chapter is clear. A number of sayings and actions of Jesus argue strongly for the view that Jesus at times spoke of the kingdom as already present in some way or to some degree in his ministry. Some of the sayings refer only in a vague, global way to Jesus' ministry as the sign or vehicle of the kingdom's presence: "The kingdom of God is in your midst" (Luke 17:21). . . . "Happy the eyes that see what you see" (Luke 10:23). Other sayings focus more specifically on particular actions of Jesus as manifestations or instruments of the kingdom's presence. The most important witness, and hence the one on which we have spent the most time, is found in Luke 11:20: "If by the finger of God I cast out the demons, the kingdom of God has come upon you." Effectively, Jesus declares his exorcisms to be both manifestations and at least partial realizations of God's coming in power to rule his people in the end time. The same basic message is intimated by the parable about binding the strong man (Mark 3:27 parr.).

Cohering with all this is Jesus' reply to the Baptist's disciples, a reply that points to Jesus' miracles and proclamation of the kingdom to the poor as indicators that the prophesied time of salvation is now present (Matt 11:2–6 par.). Jesus' rejection of voluntary fasting for himself and his disciples (Mark 2:18–20 parr.) implies the same vision.

As we survey this material, one point should strike us immediately. The most significant *sayings* of Jesus about the kingdom's presence contain references to significant *actions* of Jesus that communicate or symbolize this presence. As we have seen any number of times, one cannot separate the words and deeds of Jesus into two neat packets of information; they are inextricably bound together in the Gospel traditions. To this extent, scholars like Morton Smith and E. P. Sanders are correct in rejecting an approach to Jesus that focuses on Jesus' sayings with detriment to his deeds. Yet against Smith's presentation of "Jesus the Magician" we have observed in this chapter how Jesus' striking deeds are connected with and grounded in his proclamation of the kingdom coming yet somehow present. Moreover, as we shall see in subsequent chapters, Jesus' core message of the kingdom was not without its moral or ethical dimension, impacting on Jesus' interpretation of the Mosaic Law. An amoral or antinomian magician, unconnected with the eschatological fate and ethical concerns of Israel, is not the historical Jesus that emerges from the most reliable traditions of his words and deeds.

While we have gained some clarity on the presence of the kingdom in Jesus' ministry, our findings raise a number of further questions:

(1) The precise relationship between the coming and the present kingdom remains unspecified. Merely to establish that Jesus did speak of the kingdom as both future and present does not ipso facto provide an explanation of how this paradox holds true. Exegetes and theologians usually adopt various slogans and set phrases to try to elucidate the relation between the future and the present kingdom: e.g., it is an example of the "already/not-yet" tension in Jesus' message; the exorcisms are "signs" of the coming kingdom; the future kingdom is "dawning" in Jesus' ministry; or the future kingdom is so imminent that it overshadows, impinges upon, and shapes the present moment.

From the start I am leery of doing theology by slogans, though such an approach is not unknown in the United States today. More to the point, phrases like "the kingdom is dawning" or "the kingdom is impinging" hardly do justice to the clear and blatant claims of Jesus like "the kingdom of God *has come* upon you" or "the kingdom of God is in your midst." These sayings proclaim more than a rosy-fingered dawn impinging on one's consciousness.[226]

To speak of an "already/not-yet" tension provides a better label for what we have seen in the past two chapters, but in itself it provides nothing more than a vague description, not an explanation. Theologians may proceed to develop a whole theology of the NT or salvation history from the phrase, but obviously they are going beyond what the historical Jesus himself ever claimed.[227] Needless to say, Jesus never used any such phrase to describe or explain the strange juxtaposition of a future and a present kingdom in his message. In fact, we have no way of being sure that he ever noticed the juxtaposition or considered it a problem. History knows of other great religious leaders and thinkers who were noted more for their charismatic personalities and powerful preaching than for their logical consistency. If a historian may question whether great philosophers like Epictetus or Benedict de Spinoza were always consistent in their statements about God, a historian may ask the same question concerning Jesus' statements about the kingdom of God. Moreover, as I stressed at the beginning of this chapter, the problem of logical consistency that the modern Western mind may raise with regard to the systematic writings of a Spinoza may be beside the point when dealing with an itinerant Jewish preacher and miracle-worker of 1st-century Palestine. Our concern about the principle of noncontradiction might have been greeted with a curious smile by the Nazarene and his audience.

Nevertheless, I am inclined to think that the juxtaposition of future and present in Jesus' proclamation of the kingdom is not due solely to a fit of absentmindedness on his part or to a lack of concern with consistency. After all, Jesus had purposely seized upon the phrase "kingdom of God"—a phrase not widely used in previous Jewish writings or traditions—and pointedly made it a central part of his words and deeds. Judging by the large proportion of sayings on the future kingdom in the authentic Jesus material, we can surmise that his message of the kingdom focused predominantly on the imminent future, as Chapter 15 suggested. "Kingdom of God" was the privileged phrase Jesus chose to speak of that future. Yet he did not simply speak; he also acted—indeed, acted out. In his exorcisms, in his other striking deeds judged miraculous by his contemporaries, in his formation of an inner circle of disciples, in his table fellowship with toll collectors and sinners, in his "cleansing" of the Jerusalem temple—in all these deeds he was "acting out" his message. Hence it is significant and hardly accidental that at least on some occasions Jesus chose to explain such striking actions in terms of the kingdom of God having already come to his audience.

I would suggest that the reason why Jesus would not feel a need to explain what strikes us as a paradox may not be simply his lack of concern with the principle of noncontradiction. The real answer to the paradox may lie in the very nature of the kingdom of God. Indeed, it is telling that not any and every symbol Jesus used but precisely the set phrase "kingdom of God" embodies the "already/not-yet" tension we find in the Gospels. As we have seen repeatedly from Chapter 14 onwards, the kingdom of God is not primarily a state or place but rather the entire dynamic event of God coming in power to rule his people Israel in the end time. It is a tensive symbol, a multifaceted reality, a whole mythic story in miniature that cannot be adequately grasped in a single formula or definition. This is why Jesus can speak of kingdom as both imminent and yet present. When Jesus says in Luke 11:20 that experiencing his exorcisms is experiencing the kingdom already come, he is in effect making a startling identification: one of his powerful deeds is equated with the powerful action of God assuming his rightful control of Israel in the end time, an action that has already begun and will soon be completed.[228] Thus, in Jesus' eyes his exorcisms are not individual acts of kindness, or even individual acts of power. They are part of the eschatological drama that is already underway and that God is about to bring to its conclusion. In sayings like Luke 11:20 and 17:21, the emphasis lies on the claim that the drama has already begun: God's liberating power in favor of his people Israel is already being experienced by those Israelites who have encountered it in Jesus.

Whether or not we use terms like "pledge," "foretaste," or "proleptic realization"—terms Jesus never used—the important point, in my view, is that Jesus consciously chose to indicate that the display of miraculous power in his own ministry constituted a partial and preliminary realization of God's kingly rule, which would soon be displayed in full force.[229] It was to underline this organic link between his own ministry in the present and the full coming of God's eschatological rule in the near future that Jesus chose to employ "the kingdom of God" for both. That much, I think, can be inferred from the strange double usage of Jesus.[230] Perhaps like the parables this paradoxical usage was meant to be something of a riddle, aimed at teasing the mind into active thought (to borrow the famous words of C. H. Dodd).[231] In my view, this is all that we can say. To go beyond this minimal explanation of the kingdom present yet future is to leave exegesis and engage in systematic theology.

(2) At the end of our survey of the kingdom future yet present, the question of Jesus' understanding of himself, of his place and function in the eschatological drama he proclaimed, becomes all the more pressing. As far back as our treatment of John the Baptist in Chapters 12 and 13, we noticed the pattern of an eschatological prophet who in one sense avoids making himself the explicit object of his preaching and yet implicitly places himself squarely within the eschatological drama as a key figure. In the case of the Baptist, acceptance not only of his message but also of his unique kind of baptism at his own hands was apparently deemed a necessary condition for salvation. His explicit modesty is thus balanced by an implicit but astounding claim to play a pivotal role in the events of the end time.

The same pattern continues in his disciple Jesus, who, likewise in the role of eschatological prophet, claims to know that the kingdom is imminent, and who presumes to teach his disciples the proper way to address God (as ʾābbāʾ) and to petition him for the coming of his kingdom. Moreover, unlike the Baptist, Jesus declares that certain of his actions (e.g., his exorcisms) mediate a partial experience of the future kingdom even now. Even more than in his proclamation of the future kingdom, Jesus' proclamation-plus-realization of the kingdom as present inevitably moves the spotlight onto himself.

And yet Jesus persists in veiling himself in indirect references and metaphors. He alludes to himself in Mark 3:27 under the curious image of a bandit. He speaks of the miracles of the end time to John's disciples without ever saying "I" (Matt 11:2–6 par.). Even when he does speak in the first person, he often does so indirectly, as in the famous subordinate clause "If by the finger of God I cast out the demons. . . ." It is almost as though Jesus were intent on making a riddle of himself. Whether or to what extent he ever unraveled the riddle must be explored in subsequent chapters. But already we have the outline of a fairly large riddle: a 1st-century Jewish eschatological prophet who proclaims an imminent-future coming of God's kingdom, practices baptism as a ritual of preparation for that kingdom, teaches his disciples to pray to God as *'ābbā'* for the kingdom's arrival, prophesies the regathering of all Israel (symbolized by the inner circle of his twelve disciples) and the inclusion of the Gentiles when the kingdom comes—but who at the same time makes the kingdom already present for at least some Israelites by his exorcisms and miracles of healing. Hence in some sense he already mediates an experience of the joyful time of salvation, expressed also in his freewheeling table fellowship with toll collectors and sinners and his rejection of voluntary fasting for himself and his disciples. To all this must be added his—at times startling—interpretation of the Mosaic Law.

Whoever or whatever Jesus was, he was a complex figure, not easily subsumed under one theological rubric or sociological model. In this sense as well, he was a marginal Jew. In short, up to this point in our investigation the data suggest some sort of fusion of eschatological prophet, baptizer, exorcist, miracle-worker and healer, and rabbinic teacher of the law. But this vague configuration must be clarified and filled in by what we uncover in subsequent chapters.[232]

(3) Finally, the question of the kingdom as present has already confronted us with perhaps the most intractable problem in any historical-critical sifting of the Jesus traditions, namely, the traditions about his miracles. Up until now, they have been tangential to the main point we have been treating: Jesus' claim that, through his supposedly miraculous deeds (exorcisms, healings), the kingdom of God had already become present. It is time to shift our focus from this message of the kingdom as present to the supposed channels of its presence, the actions of Jesus that the Gospels depict as miracles.

NOTES TO CHAPTER 16

[1] This is also the position of John Dominic Crossan in his *The Historical Jesus. The Life of a Mediterranean Jewish Peasant* (San Francisco: Harper, 1991); see, e.g., pp. 238–59. A more popular version of his position can be found in his *Jesus. A Revolutionary Biography* (San Francisco: Harper, 1994) 54–74. For some reactions to Crossan's project, see Jeffrey Carlson and Robert A. Ludwig (eds.), *Jesus and Faith* (Maryknoll, NY: Orbis, 1994). Not unlike Borg (*Jesus. A New Vision*, 1–21), Crossan tends to jump from an absence of an apocalyptic Son of Man in Jesus' message to an absence of future eschatology in Jesus' message. The first absence does not necessarily prove the second. For the connection of Jewish wisdom with Jewish apocalypticism around the turn of the era, a connection reflected in the sayings of Jesus, see Richard J. Dillon, "Ravens, Lilies, and the Kingdom of God (Matthew 6:25–33/Luke 12:22–31)," *CBQ* 53 (1991) 605–27, esp. 615.

[2] Sanders, *Jesus and Judaism*, 153.

[3] Sanders, *Jesus and Judaism*, 154.

[4] Sanders, *Jesus and Judaism*, 155.

[5] Sanders himself notes how at least some Jews combined God's providence and human free will while not working out the relation between them philosophically (*Judaism: Belief and Practice*, 251): "They [i.e., such Jews] did not see the need to solve the problem of the incompatibility between God's providence and human free will, and they simply asserted both." Sanders suggests that these Jews tended to stress God's total control of all things when they considered the whole sweep of history; they spoke of free will when they considered individual human behavior. He makes similar observations about the Pharisees (pp. 418–19). Even more to the point, Sanders likewise acknowledges that, while the Dead Sea Scrolls witness to a fierce future hope, they also reflect "to some degree" a realized eschatology: ". . . some of the benefits of the new age had already been realized in the community" (p. 370).

[6] Hence there is a point to our asking whether certain sayings of Jesus go beyond the general idea of the future impinging on the present. Do some sayings strongly and explicitly affirm the presence of the kingdom in Jesus' ministry? If such sayings do exist, then the distinction between future and realized eschatology in Jesus' sayings is not simply a creation of modern scholarship that should be dismissed as an anachronism. For the opposite view, see Dillon, "Ravens," 615.

[7] See Chapter 13, section IV. A. For the convenience of the reader, I repeat here in digested form the major conclusions about the authenticity and interpretation of texts arrived at in section IV. A. What is new over and above the treatment in Chapter 13 is the focus here on what the logia tell us about Jesus' view of the kingdom of God as already present in his ministry.

[8] David Noel Freedman has suggested to me that, beside the theological content of the question put to Jesus, something very practical may also be intended. John is in prison, facing possible execution. Naturally there arises the question of who might be John's replacement or successor. Jesus indicates that he is willing to be that successor, but he also indicates something more. He has performed miracles, something John never did. With the figures of Moses, Elijah, and Elisha as the great miracle-workers of the OT looming in the background, Jesus intimates that he is something more than just a replacement or successor of John. With his min-

istry of proclamation-plus-miracles, a new stage in the eschatological drama has begun.

[9] Jeremias (*New Testament Theology*, 103–5) concludes from the symbolic language in the Book of Isaiah that Jesus' reply is likewise symbolic and does not refer to any miracles that he has supposedly performed (which is rather the meaning Matthew and Luke give to his words). The real sense of the passage, according to Jeremias, is: ". . . now help is extended to those in the depths of despair, now those who were as good as dead are raised to life." Jeremias apparently senses an obvious objection to this interpretation, and so he adds somewhat lamely (p. 105): "It should be noted that the lepers and the dead are not mentioned in the three lists in Isaiah. That Jesus mentions them means that the fulfilment goes far beyond all promises, hopes and expectations." Rather, the natural conclusion should be that Jesus, while alluding to Isaiah, is nevertheless recounting various miracles he is reputed to have performed; his "track record" does not neatly correspond to any of the lists in Isaiah.

[10] Beasley-Murray (*Jesus and the Kingdom of God*, 83) summarizes the point of Matt 11:2–6 par. in this fashion: "God in his gracious, sovereign power as Redeemer is encountered in the word and work of Jesus, and through him that sovereignty is experienced in the present, even as it is to be inherited through him in the future." Admittedly, talk of God's "sovereign power" may introduce kingdom language into a pericope that does not explicitly use it. In Beasley-Murray's defense, it should be noted that he writes this summary after treating the question of the arrival of God's kingdom in Jesus' exorcisms (Matt 12:28 || Luke 11:20) and perhaps with this related saying in mind.

[11] At the same time, in the larger context of the whole Baptist-block, an unspoken contrast may be detected between the stern, ascetic, uncompromising desert prophet and the joyful Jesus, the bon vivant, the eater and drinker, the friend of tax collectors and sinners, who brings healing to the sick and good news to the poor (Matt 11:2–6 and 11:18–19 par.).

[12] This hypothetical reconstruction of the original wording of the Q saying rests on the arguments presented in Chapter 13, section IV. A. The same holds true for other reconstructions of Q sayings discussed in the main text.

[13] Needless to say, it would be perilous to make the "present" interpretation of v 11b hang on the Greek verb *estin* ("is"), when we are not sure what it might represent in the underlying Aramaic logion (*bû*? *'îtai*? some form of the verb *hāwâ*? or a nominal sentence with no pronoun, substantive, or verb representing "is"?). But as Schlosser remarks (*Le règne de Dieu*, 1. 163), to make "in the kingdom of God" in v 11b refer solely to the future kingdom makes no sense, since the upshot of the whole logion would then be to exclude the Baptist totally from the future kingdom (i.e., even the person "on the lowest rung of the ladder" in the future kingdom would be greater than the Baptist—effectively excluding the Baptist from that kingdom). This is hardly the point of the logion or the thrust of a passage that is on the whole highly laudatory of John; John's status in the future, definitive form of the kingdom is simply not treated here. The point of contrast is rather the status of John now vis-à-vis the status of the lowliest follower of Jesus now. All this argues for understanding the kingdom as present. In my view, Sanders misses the whole point when he objects (*Jesus and Judaism*, 148): "The saying about John the Baptist [in Matt 11:11 par.] does not seem to imply that the kingdom is present, but rather that it is future. When the kingdom comes, the least in

it will be greater than the greatest figure in this age. Those who urge that the say-ing implies that the kingdom is present do not explain just where that leaves the Baptist. Does Jesus claim that the least of his followers is greater than John?" Yes, he does—at least for now, as a critical corner is turned. Indeed, this is precisely the startling point of the logion: the least follower of Jesus is greater than John *now* precisely because he is in the kingdom *now*.

As an aside, I should note that it is in this kind of saying that *basileia* begins to take on more of a stative or spatial sense: the state of being, the field of force, brought about by God's kingly rule at work in the world to heal and save be-lievers.

[14] See Beasley-Murray, *Jesus and the Kingdom of God*, 95.

[15] Admittedly, one might prefer less likely alternate translations and interpreta-tions of the key phrases *hē basileia . . . biazetai kai biastai harpazousin autēn* (e.g., "the kingdom . . . presses forward mightily, and people press mightily to enter into it"). The saying's darker tone might thus be eliminated. But the basic point I have emphasized—the present nature of the kingdom—would remain.

[16] Beasley-Murray, *Jesus and the Kingdom of God*, 75.

[17] Sanders states (*Jesus and Judaism*, 136): "There probably is no other verse in the Gospels about which there is so much unanimity." On p. 134 he admits that the com-mon scholarly view is that the verse is authentic. As a matter of fact, authenticity is accepted by a number of scholars whose focus is not on the historical Jesus but on the redaction of Q; see, e.g., Hoffmann, *Studien*, 299; Sato, *Q und Prophetie*, 133. In con-trast, Schulz, as is his wont, sees a creation of the Q community, indeed, one from the more recent stage of the tradition (*Q. Die Spruchquelle der Evangelisten*, 210).

[18] Care should be taken in distinguishing various phenomena described both inside and outside the Bible; e.g., one should not mix together indiscriminately demonic pos-session, obsession, punishment inflicted by God, an angel, or a holy man, and simple illness not attributed to supernatural causes. Such care is not always taken by John M. Hull in his *Hellenistic Magic and the Synoptic Tradition* (SBT 2/28; London: SCM, 1974). Likewise confused is his attempt to define magic and miracle; his exegesis of Synoptic texts is also often muddled. A major problem throughout the whole work is the use of various distinctions ("magical miracle" versus "eschatological" or "religious" miracle, objective reality versus subjective vision, etc.) that are never fully explained and justi-fied. The problem of distinguishing magic from miracle will be taken up in Chapter 18.

[19] For one example of the many serious anthropological studies of exorcisms in third-world countries today, see Bruce Kapferer, *A Celebration of Demons. Exorcism and the Aesthetics of Healing in Sri Lanka* (Bloomington, IN: Indiana University, 1983). Some important methodological points may be garnered from Kapferer's treatment: (1) Al-though exorcism may be understood as a kind of healing rite, its meaning is not ex-hausted in such a category (p. xiii). (2) Any anthropological interpretation must adopt one consistent school of thought and, in that very act, may exclude certain other schools (pp. 2–6). (3) Kapferer sees exorcism as one way in which the disorder caused in a social world by the invasion of the abnormal into the normal is undone and order is restored (p. 1). Obviously this interpretive framework does not fit the eschatological thrust of Jesus' exorcisms, which look forward to and partially realize the breaking-in of a new and different ordering of the cosmos. For the practice of exorcism in Christian Ethiopia today, see the analysis by Gerd Theissen, *The Miracle Stories of the Early Christian Tradi-tion* (Philadelphia: Fortress, 1983) 250 (= *Urchristliche Wundergeschichten* [SNT 8; Güt-ersloh: Mohn, 1974] 248).

Interest in exorcisms performed in the United States in recent years has usually expressed itself in more sensationalistic forms, from novels and movies to a television presentation of what the participants claimed to be a genuine exorcism. For a more sober description of phenomena connected with supposed cases of possession, especially in the 20th century, see Adolf Rodewyk, *Dämonische Besessenheit heute. Tatsachen und Deutungen* (Aschaffenburg: Pattloch, 1966).

[20] The playing of the lyre by David to calm the troubled Saul cannot be considered a ritual of exorcism in the strict sense. I think James D. G. Dunn may be reading too much into the original OT narrative when he claims that ". . . David, upon whom the Spirit of the Lord had come mightily . . . in effect acted as exorcist to deliver Saul from the evil spirit which tormented Saul . . ." ("Matthew 12:28/Luke 11:20—A Word of Jesus?" *Eschatology and the New Testament* [George Raymond Beasley-Murray Festschrift; ed. W. Hulitt Gloer; Peabody, MA: Hendrickson, 1988] 29–49, esp. 40 n. 29). The case is different with the midrashic reworking of the material, with a possible reference to Solomon, the son of David and exorcist, in Pseudo-Philo's *Bib. Ant.* 60:1–3; cf. the expansion of the story in Josephus, *Ant.* 6.8.2 §166–69. As Dennis C. Duling ("The Eleazar Miracle and Solomon's Magical Wisdom in Flavius Josephus's *Antiquitates Judaicae* 8.42–49," *HTR* 78 [1985] 1–25) points out, this is one of only two stories of exorcism in the whole of Josephus' works (the other being *Ant.* 8.2.5 §42–49), and there are few exorcism stories in non-Christian Jewish texts dating from around the turn of the era.

[21] On this account see Duling, "The Eleazar Miracle," 1–25.

[22] For the Aramaic text and an English translation, see Joseph A. Fitzmyer, *The Genesis Apocryphon of Qumran Cave I. A Commentary* (BibOr 18A; 2d ed.; Rome: Biblical Institute, 1971) 64–67. Fitzmyer notes (p. 138) that the verb used of Abraham's commanding the spirit to depart is *g'r*. The basic meaning of the verb is "to rebuke", "scold." It is rendered in the LXX by *epitimaō*, the verb used by Marcan narratives and their parallels for Jesus' exorcisms (see, e.g., Mark 1:25; 9:25; Luke 4:39). The sense of the verb in 1QapGen 20:29 thus seems to be "to exorcise." Also significant is the fact that this is the first time in Jewish literature that the rite of healing takes place by the laying on of hands; it does not appear in the OT or rabbinic literature. The laying on of hands occurs in a number of NT passages; both rebuking and laying on of hands occur in Luke 4:40–41, though not with reference to the exact same person being cured. Rebuking is used of both the healing of Simon Peter's mother-in-law (v 39) and of those possessed by demons (v 41); the laying on of hands is mentioned only in the general reference to Jesus' healing of the sick (v 40). The laying on of hands figures in a case of diabolical obsession in Luke 13:10–17 (Jesus' healing of a crippled woman on the Sabbath). Fitzmyer notes that, while the rite of exorcising with the laying on of hands is unknown in the OT, it is found in older Assyrian and Babylonian texts. It is possible that the Essenes in general or Qumranites in particular borrowed the gesture from Babylonian magic rites and belief in demon-sickness. But one must be wary of using texts like the *Genesis Apocryphon* and the *Prayer of Nabonidus* to reconstruct rituals actually performed at Qumran. We cannot be sure that these documents were composed at Qumran as opposed to being written elsewhere and later brought into the community's library. Moreover, the Qumran ideology of a holy community made up only of the converted and purified of Israel would seem to exclude the need for exorcism within the community. On this see Walter Kirchschläger, "Exorzismus in Qumran?" *Kairos* 18 (1976) 135–53. See also Joseph A. Fitzmyer, "The Contribution of Qumran Aramaic to the Study of the New Testament," *A Wandering Aramean. Collected Aramaic Essays* (SBLMS 25; Missoula, MT: Scholars, 1979) 85–113, esp. 96–97. It

should also be noted that neither of the key Qumran texts speaks of demonic possession, but rather of demon obsession: the demon has not taken over the victim's body and personality, but rather afflicts the person's body with illness.

[23] For the Aramaic text of the *Prayer of Nabonidus* with English translation, see Joseph A. Fitzmyer and Daniel J. Harrington, *A Manual of Palestinian Aramaic Texts* (BibOr 34; Rome: Biblical Institute, 1978) 2–5; for text description and bibliography, see pp. 191–93. For another English translation of the *Prayer of Nabonidus*, see Geza Vermes, *The Dead Sea Scrolls in English* (3d ed.; London: Penguin, 1987) 274. See the comment on both Qumran texts by D. C. Duling, "Testament of Solomon," *The Old Testament Pseudepigrapha*, 1. 945: "Abraham in the Genesis Apocryphon and probably Daniel in the Prayer of Nabonidus are viewed as types of exorcists." An indirect reference to Daniel is found in a partially preserved clause in fragment 4 of 4QPrNab, line 4: ". . . how you resemble Da[niel] . . ." (Fitzmyer and Harrington, *Manual*, 4–5).

[24] See J. M. van der Ploeg, "Le Psaume XCI dans une recension de Qumrân," *RB* 72 (1965) 210–17; idem, "Un petit rouleau de psaumes apocryphes (11QPsAPᵃ)," *Tradition und Glaube. Das frühe Christentum in seiner Umwelt* (Karl Georg Kuhn Festschrift; ed. G. Jeremias et al.; Göttingen: Vandenhoeck & Ruprecht, 1971) 128–39.

[25] The date, authorship, and provenance of the *Testament of Solomon* are still debated. For a survey of views, see Duling, "Testament of Solomon," 935–59. In its final form, the *Testament of Solomon* is either a Christian work or a Jewish work redacted by a Christian; but it obviously derives from Jewish sources and traditions.

[26] The date of the redaction of *Pesiqta de Rab Kahana* (one of the homiletic midrashim) is debated. A 5th-century A.D. date is likely, though no doubt much of the material is older. On this see H. L. Strack and G. Stemberger, *Introduction to the Talmud and Midrash* (Edinburgh: Clark, 1991) 321. For a translation of *Pesiqta de Rab Kahana*, see William G. Braude, *Pĕsiḳta dĕ-Rab Kahăna* (Philadelphia: Jewish Publication Society of America, 1975).

For a general treatment of demonology in early Judaism, see Str-B, 4/1. 501–35; exorcists (including both King Solomon and Jewish rabbis of the talmudic period) are treated on pp. 533–35. However, in using this material one must beware of the tendency of Str-B to create ahistorical syntheses out of many different Jewish writings from different centuries.

[27] On all this see the revised Schürer, *The History of the Jewish People*, 3/1. 342–43 (exorcism), 352–55 (incantation bowls and amulets in Hebrew and Aramaic), and 372–74 (*Testament of Solomon*).

[28] See, e.g., the plates, text, and translation of the Paris Magical Papyrus, lines 3007–3085, in Adolf Deissmann, *Licht vom Osten* (4th ed.; Tübingen: Mohr [Siebeck], 1923) 216–25; the material dates from ca. A.D. 300. More to the point as a parallel to the saying in Luke 11:20 is the photograph, text, and translation of an ostracon from the Egyptian town of Ashmounein in Egypt (pp. 259–60). Addressed to the god Kronos, it contains a magical spell that seeks to shut someone's mouth and prevent him from speaking to another person. The significant phrase is *exorkizō kata tou daktylou tou theou* ("I adjure you by the finger of God"). Deissmann sees here a mixture of pagan and Jewish elements, while B. Couroyer ("Le 'doigt de Dieu' (*Exode*, VIII, 15)," *RB* 63 [1956] 481–95) suggests that the text is the work of a syncretistic Egyptian Jew (p. 482). In any case, the ostracon belongs to the further history of the influence of Exod 8:15 (and possibly Luke 11:20?), since it dates from the late Roman imperial period. The

image of the finger of God then continues in syncretistic texts from Coptic Christianity in Egypt. A more complete and up-to-date edition of Greek magical papyri (but without the original Greek texts) can be found in Hans Dieter Betz (ed.), *The Greek Magical Papyri in Translation, Including the Demotic Spells* (Chicago/London: University of Chicago, 1986).

For a good example of a narrative of exorcism in pagan literature of the early 3d century A.D., see the story of the exorcism of a young man by Apollonius of Tyana in Philostratus' *Vita Apollonii*, 4.20; the Greek text and translation can be found in F. C. Conybeare (ed.), *Philostratus. The Life of Apollonius of Tyana* (LCL; 2 vols.; London: Heinemann; Cambridge, MA: Harvard University, 1912) 1. 390–93. Another exorcism narrative can be found in 3.38. Three other stories (2.4; 4.10; 4.25) are not, strictly speaking, stories of possession and exorcism but rather cases of a hobgoblin, a demon, or a vampire taking visible form to do harm to humans.

[29] On some of the difficulties connected with the story of the seven sons of Sceva in Acts 19:14–16, see Joseph A. Fitzmyer, " 'A certain Sceva, a Jew, a chief priest' (Acts 19:14)," *Der Treue Gottes Trauen. Beiträge zum Werk des Lukas* (Gerhard Schneider Festschrift; ed. Claus Bussmann and Walter Radl; Freiburg/Basel/Vienna: Herder, 1991) 299–305.

[30] One qualification is important here: "Possession of individuals and subsequent exorcism is unknown in ancient and classical Greece, but the seed of the idea is already present in the *Odyssey* (V. 396) . . ." (Hull, *Hellenistic Magic*, 62). Hull also points out (p. 63) that while we have considerable evidence of a history of exorcism in the ancient Near East by the 1st century A.D., actual stories of individual cases are relatively rare.

[31] For an initial survey of relevant Synoptic texts, with an emphasis on the idea of the kingdom or rule of Satan, see Heinz Kruse, "Das Reich Satans," *Bib* 58 (1977) 29–61. See also the articles by Werner Foerster in the *TDNT*: "*Beelzeboul*," 1 (1964) 605–6; "*Beliar*," 1 (1964) 607; "*daimōn*, etc.," 2 (1964) 1–20; (with Gerhard von Rad) "*diaballō, diabolos*," 2 (1964) 71–81; (with Knut Schäferdiek) "*satanas*," 7 (1971) 151–65.

[32] Dunn ("Matthew 12:28/Luke 11:20," 32) tries to launch something of an argument from discontinuity by pointing out the relative lack of mention of exorcisms in the activity of the early church as portrayed in Acts and the total lack of any mention of exorcisms in the various forms of the post-Easter commission (Matt 28:18–20; Luke 24:26–29; John 20:21–23; Acts 1:8). The grand exception is the so-called "longer ending of Mark," specifically Mark 16:17, which however dates from the 2d century. Granted Dunn's basic point, one must still allow for the possibility that the early church saw the narratives of Jesus' exorcisms, coupled with the empowerment of the disciples in the missionary discourse to perform exorcisms (Mark 6:7,13; Matt 10:1,8; Luke 9:1), as sufficient commissioning to continue doing what Jesus had done. The post-Easter commissions tend to focus on what is to be new and different in the disciples' activity after Easter.

[33] For Jewish and pagan texts charging Jesus with the practice of magic, see Morton Smith, *Jesus the Magician* (San Francisco: Harper & Row, 1978) 45–67. Since I am trying to establish particular facts about and sayings from a particular 1st-century Jew, I remain as close as possible to the words and categories of the primary sources. From the viewpoint of the sociology of religions, the charge of casting out demons by Beelzebul (i.e., by invoking Beelzebul's name) may indeed be equivalent to the charge of being a magician; on this see David E. Aune, "Magic in Early Christianity," *ANRW* II/23.2, 1507–57, esp. 1540–41. I am simply pointing out here that the words *magos*, *mageia*, and *mageuō* are not used in Mark 3:22 parr. or anywhere else in the NT of

Jesus, while they are used elsewhere in the NT of other figures (Simon in Acts 8:9,11; Bar-Jesus in Acts 13:6,8)—and later on in pagan sources. The question of magic and miracles will be taken up in Chapter 18.

For an attempt to understand the Synoptic dispute stories surrounding Jesus' exorcisms in terms of the model of witchcraft used by cultural anthropology and in terms of social-scientific theories of labeling and deviance (applied specifically to Matthew's Gospel), see Bruce J. Malina and Jerome H. Neyrey, *Calling Jesus Names. The Social Value of Labels in Matthew* (Sonoma, CA: Polebridge, 1988) 3–67. For a basic theoretical disquisition on how to approach any study of the demonic in the Greco-Roman world, see Jonathan Z. Smith, "Towards Interpreting Demonic Powers in Hellenistic and Roman Antiquity," *ANRW* II/16.1 (published 1978), 425–39.

[34] For example, Jesus uses spittle as a healing agent in Mark 7:33; 8:23; and indirectly in John 9:6 (making clay out of spittle as part of the process of healing a blind man). Clearly beliefs common in Jesus' milieu are reflected in these stories, and no doubt Jesus shared such beliefs. Hence my affirmation in the text should not be understood as some sort of apologetic. What I am pointing out is the striking fact that, even though Jesus at times may have used means like spittle in some of his healings (assimilating them to some degree to exorcisms?), in the stories that professedly deal with possessed persons (the *daimonizomenoi*) such techniques and material aids are noticeably lacking. This point is perhaps not sufficiently appreciated by Theodor Lorenzmeier, "Zum Logion Mt 12,28; Lk 11,20," *Neues Testament und christliche Existenz* (Herbert Braun Festschrift; ed. Hans Dieter Betz and Luise Schottroff; Tübingen: Mohr [Siebeck], 1973) 289–304, esp. 292–93.

[35] On this see Aune, "Magic in Early Christianity," 1545.

[36] Dunn ("Matthew 12:28/Luke 11:20," 40–41) points out how this lack of paraphernalia and incantations fits in perfectly with Luke 11:20: it is by the finger of God, and not by any of the rituals others might use, that Jesus casts out the demons. Luke 11:20 par. "expresses a claim to exercise the eschatological power of God with an immediacy and directness that is borne out by the accounts of Jesus' exorcisms and which effectively distinguish Jesus' exorcistic technique from the practice of his Jewish contemporaries" (p. 41). See also Fitzmyer, *The Gospel According to Luke*, 2. 922. The absence of paraphernalia and formulas is one reason why Ben Witherington III objects to the application of the category "magician" to the historical Jesus by Morton Smith in the latter's *Jesus the Magician*; for Witherington's argument, see his *The Christology of Jesus*, 202. At the same time, one should note that the vocabulary used to describe Jesus' exorcisms and some of the phrases Jesus is reported to use can be paralleled in other exorcism stories in ancient Jewish and Greek literature. This point is well made by Graham H. Twelftree, " '*Ei de . . . egō ekballō ta daimonia . . . ,* '" *Gospel Perspectives. Volume 6. The Miracles of Jesus* (ed. David Wenham and Craig Blomberg; Sheffield: JSOT, 1986) 361–400, esp. 368–87. However, his case is somewhat weakened by (1) his use of "parallels" whose written forms are centuries later than the Gospels (e.g., the Babylonian Talmud, Philostratus' *Life of Apollonius of Tyana*, and some of the magical papyri); and (2) his acceptance of a story like the Gerasene demoniac in Mark 5:1–20 as a reliable record of what Jesus and a demon(iac) said to each other on a particular occasion. When both the skeptical Haenchen (*Der Weg Jesu*, 189–204) and the trusting Pesch (*Das Markusevangelium*, 1. 282–95) think that the underlying exorcism story has undergone a great deal of development in the oral tradition, caution is advised.

[37] Summing up the evidence, Perrin (*Rediscovering the Teaching of Jesus*, 65) states: "The evidence for exorcism as a feature of the ministry of Jesus is very strong indeed:

exorcisms are to be found in every strata of the synoptic tradition, and the ancient Jewish texts regard Jesus as a miracle-worker, i.e. an exorcist." All the evidence for this conclusion is examined by Twelftree, " '*Ei de . . . egō ekballō ta daimonia . . .* ,' " 361–400, esp. 363–68; see also his full-length monograph, *Jesus the Exorcist* (WUNT 2/54; Tübingen: Mohr [Siebeck], 1993). Twelftree notes that the very fact that other Jews during or shortly after the life of Jesus sought to use his name in exorcisms indicates that he had quickly gained fame as a powerful exorcist. Yet, if Matt 11:2–6 par. represents accurately the substance of Jesus' reply to the doubtful Baptist, Jesus could at times summarize his activity during his ministry without referring explicitly to his exorcisms. In other words, while exorcisms were an important part of Jesus' ministry, they hardly summarized everything he did or intended (pp. 387–93). Still, Dunn ("Matthew 12:28/ Luke 11:20," 31) is quite right to point out how little attention Sanders pays in *Jesus and Judaism* to Jesus' reputation as an exorcist, despite Sanders's emphasis on secure facts about Jesus' activity. As Twelftree stresses in his monograph, playing down or omitting the importance of Jesus' exorcisms during the public ministry may make Jesus more understandable or acceptable to moderns, but it results in a distorted picture of the historical Jesus.

[38] On this point see Otto Böcher, *Christus Exorcista* (BWANT 5/16, 96; Stuttgart: Kohlhammer, 1972) 16–19, 166–67. Böcher thinks that the saying about the unclean spirit who is expelled and then returns with seven spirits worse than himself (Matt 12:43–45 ‖ Luke 11:24–26) most probably goes back to the historical Jesus (p. 17). However, Bultmann (*Geschichte*, 176–77), while admitting that the lack of Christian traits makes derivation from the early church unlikely, also thinks that the saying, in form and content, is different from the rest of Jesus' words; he suggests that it is perhaps derived from a Jewish document. Hence, in my own presentation, I thought it best to focus on a saying that Bultmann does deem authentic.

[39] Hence its inclusion in Laufen's *Die Doppelüberlieferungen*, 126–55. In the view of Schlosser (*Le règne de Dieu*, 1. 127), Matthew, as is his wont, meshes Mark and Q, while Luke depends basically on Q. This is the usual approach of both evangelists when the opportunity to combine Mark and Q arises.

[40] For one possible history of the growth of the whole Q tradition on the Beelzebul dispute, see Dunn, "Matthew 12:28/Luke 11:20," 34–37; for another attempt, see Schlosser, *Le règne de Dieu*, 1. 127–32. I consider any attempt to write a complete history of the development of this Q tradition extremely speculative. Since it does not materially affect my use of Luke 11:20 par., I waive any such undertaking.

One result of the stitching together of originally independent sayings is that the distinct terms "Satan," "Beelzebul," "the prince of demons," and "demons" have been drawn together into a demonic synthesis. The most natural interpretation of the redactional level of all three Synoptics is that Satan and Beelzebul (a uniquely NT and early Christian name) are identified as the ruler of the whole demonic kingdom. Theoretically possible, however, in the confusing and variegated world of demonology is the interpretation that Satan is indeed the king of the "kingdom" of demons (notice the *basileia* in Matt 12:26), while Beelzebul is one of his subordinate ruling princes (hence *archōn*). The idea of a "centrally organized" world of demons under the one ruler Satan is foreign to the OT. The beginnings of such an idea surface in some of the OT pseudepigrapha. In 1QS 3:20–25 we meet the angel of darkness (the opposite of the prince of light or angel of truth), who rules over the sons of wickedness and the spirits of darkness (= the spirits of his lot), even though God has created them. In 1QM 18:1–3, we hear of "Belial and the whole army of his rule," "the throng of Belial," against whom God will raise his hand in the final battle. In 11QMelch 2:12–13, God, through his angelic vicegerent Melchizedek, exacts eschatological vengeance on "Belial and the spirits of his lot." Although the text is fragmentary, Paul J. Kobelski (*Melchizedek and Melchireša'* [CBQMS 10; Washington, DC: CBA, 1981] 8) restores line 13 to read: "And Melchizedek will exact the vengeance of El's judgments and he will protect all the sons of light from the power of Belial and from the power of all the spirits of his lot." In lines 15–16, this salvation fulfills the promise of Isa 52:7: "Your God is king." The herald of this good news seems in line 18 to be called an anointed prince. Perhaps the Beelzebul complex in the Synoptics reflects similar ideas about the reign of Satan/Beelzebul over a kingdom of demons, ideas held by Jewish peasants in Palestine around the turn of the era. Naturally, the last thing we should look for in popular beliefs about Satan and demons is the consistency of systematic theology.

[41] The parable of the strong man will be treated below, after Matt 12:28 ‖ Luke 11:20 is examined at length.

[42] Dunn ("Matthew 12:28/Luke 11:20," 40–41) thinks a firm decision on this point cannot be reached, but he does not consider a decision one way or the other to have much impact on the question of the meaning and authenticity of Luke 11:20 par. Those who argue strongly that the two logia were originally separate include Schlosser, *Le règne de Dieu*, 1. 130–32. Indeed, he suggests that v 19 was created secondarily to facilitate the joining of the originally independent v 20 to the Q material in Luke 11:14–15,17–18a. Verse 19 is seen as a creation of "rational" Christian apologetics by Ernst Käsemann, "Lukas 11,14–28," *Exegetische Versuche und Besinnungen* (2 vols.; 4th ed.; Göttingen: Vandenhoeck & Ruprecht, 1965) 1. 242–48, esp. 243–44. Contrasting with it, according to Käsemann, is the kerygmatic proclamation in v 20 (which is authentic) that the kingdom is breaking in through the activity of Jesus.

[43] Kruse ("Das Reich Satans," 29–61, esp. 38 n. 22) suggests that an unspoken presupposition of this argument is that the exorcists among Jesus' adversaries or at least exorcists who did not follow Jesus have successfully cast out demons *in Jesus' name*. Here Kruse illegitimately meshes the Q tradition of Matt 12:27 par. with the Marcan tradition in Mark 9:38–41 par.

[44] Schlosser (*Le règne de Dieu*, 1. 130) stresses a form-critical difference. While Luke 11:19 par. is a three-part logion reflecting the form of a dispute story (*Streitgespräch*) that concludes with a threat (*Drohwort*), v 20 is instead a two-part logion, a prophetic word reflecting the proclamation of salvation (*Heilspredigt*). Schlosser also thinks that the emphatic and antithetical "I" (*egō*) of v 19 differs from the less emphatic "I" in v 20 (which furthermore is only partially attested in the Greek manuscript tradition).

[45] On this point see Sato, *Q und Prophetie*, 133; cf. Gnilka, *Jesus von Nazaret*, 135; A. George, "Paroles de Jésus sur ses miracles (Mt 11,5.21; 12,27.28 et par.)," *Jésus aux origines de la christologie* (BETL 40; 2d ed.; ed. J. Dupont; Leuven: Leuven University/Peeters, 1989) 283–301, esp. 297–300.

[46] See, e.g., Bultmann, *Geschichte*, 12; Kümmel, *Promise and Fulfilment*, 105–6; Schlosser, *Le règne de Dieu*, 1. 130. Not all find this argument persuasive; hence I place it after the arguments that strike me as more weighty.

[47] This line of argument can be found in Bultmann, *Geschichte*, 12. He is followed by many commentators after him; see, e.g., Perrin, *Rediscovering the Teaching of Jesus*, 63–64.

[48] The meaning of the saying is not substantially altered by the choice, for both "finger of God" and "spirit of God" designate the power of God in action; so rightly Schlosser, *Le règne de Dieu*, 1. 132. However, the choice does have some impact on the

argument concerning authenticity, especially on the use of the criterion of discontinuity.

[49] Luke 11:46 is most likely a Q tradition (*daktylos* occurs in Matt 23:4, a parallel in substance if not in wording). As a matter of fact, most critics include Luke 11:46 par. in their reconstructions of Q; see Kloppenborg, *Q Parallels*, 112. Luke 16:24 is found in the parable of the rich man and Lazarus, a parable that probably comes from the L tradition rather than from pure Lucan redaction. Fitzmyer (*The Gospel According to Luke*, 2. 1125) judges: "A few traces of Lucan redaction can be detected in it [the parable]. . . . The amount of non-Lucan formulation in the story is, however, noteworthy . . . , stemming from the pre-Lucan source." Also in favor of pre-Lucan tradition in the parable are Bultmann, *Geschichte*, 193; Marshall, *Luke*, 634; Ernst, *Das Evangelium nach Lukas*, 472–73.

[50] For these statistics, see Eduard Schweizer, "*pneuma*, etc.," *TDNT* 6 (1968) 404.

[51] This conclusion is contested by such scholars as George ("Paroles de Jésus," 299) and C. S. Rodd ("Spirit or Finger," *ExpTim* 72 [1960–61] 157–58), but their arguments are not convincing; see Schlosser, *Le règne de Dieu*, 1. 133. Fitzmyer (*The Gospel According to Luke*, 2. 918) and Gnilka (*Jesus von Nazaret*, 135) likewise hold that "finger of God" was the original reading of Q. The fact that Luke attributes prophecy, apostolic testimony, and the very message of Jesus to the spirit hardly proves that he could not or would not also attribute Jesus' exorcisms to the spirit. Indeed, in one passage Luke joins *dynamis* and *pneuma* as the divine equipment with which Jesus performs healings on those "oppressed by the devil, for God was with him" (Acts 10:38). George also points to exodus-Moses typology in Luke's portrait of Jesus. Actually, such typology is stronger in Acts than in the Gospel of Luke; for its presence in Acts, see Luke T. Johnson, *The Literary Function of Possession in Luke-Acts* (SBLDS 39; Missoula, MT: Scholars, 1977) 70–76. In the Gospel of Luke, other OT typologies, especially those of Elijah and Elisha, seem equally or even more influential. As a matter of fact, Moses typology is stronger in Matthew, yet he has not inserted "finger of God" or any other Mosaic allusion into this verse. One might also observe that, strictly speaking, the third plague in Exodus 8 that occasions the mention of "the finger of God" is brought about by Aaron, not Moses. It is perhaps telling that George does not present a detailed study comparing Luke's linguistic usage with that of Matthew.

It is true, as Dunn points out (*Jesus and the Spirit*, 46) that Luke drops a reference to the spirit in 20:42 and perhaps 21:15. However, neither case is exactly the same as Luke 11:20 par. In the Marcan tradition taken over in Luke 20:42, Luke's "in the Book of Psalms" is hardly the functional equivalent of Mark's "in the holy spirit." Luke has decided to make a totally different point: the place in Scripture in which David's quotation is found instead of the divine power by which David prophesied. This is not the same phenomenon as one metaphor for divine power (e.g., the finger of God) replacing another metaphor for the same reality (e.g., the spirit of God). The case of Luke 21:15 is less clear, since we cannot be sure that Luke is intending to reproduce the tradition in Mark 13:11 ‖ Matt 10:19–20. He could be either reproducing a different tradition or composing freely. In any case, a very similar statement with "holy spirit" does occur in Luke 12:11–12. In short, I do not think that we can find anywhere else in Luke an example of Luke's replacing the divine spirit with an equivalent metaphor, while maintaining the rest of the traditional logion as is. Hence, I do not think an agnostic position on the priority of the Matthean or Lucan version is justified; for such a position, see Lorenzmeier, "Zum Logion Mt 12, 28; Lk 11, 20," 289–304, esp. 290–91.

[52] Once again we are reminded how futile is the debate over whether one should

seek the surest starting point in the quest for the historical Jesus in the actions or the words of Jesus. One cannot hope to interpret the actions without a context of interpreting words, just as the words float in a vacuum without an interpretive context of deeds. Hence I find Sanders's championing of actions over deeds misguided; for his position, see *Jesus and Judaism*, 3–18 (where "deeds" or "actions" are curiously referred to simply as "facts"—as distinguished from "sayings"!). It is telling that in his pivotal chapter on the "cleansing of the temple" (pp. 61–76), his argument in favor of interpreting Jesus' action in the temple as a symbolic prophecy of destruction would be very weak if he could not call upon certain sayings of Jesus that prophesy the temple's destruction. As the reader has no doubt already noted, I have attempted no division between Jesus' actions and his sayings in my work. The opening chapter of this volume, on John the Baptist, had to consider both his words and his actions; the same held true of the next chapter, which took up Jesus' initial actions and the statements in which he described his relationship to the Baptist. The chapters on Jesus' teaching concerning the kingdom of God naturally emphasize what he said about the kingdom, though once again I connected the sayings with his typical actions. Jesus' actions as interpretive of his sayings will be studied in subsequent chapters. In short, I find any dichotomy in the treatment of Jesus' words and deeds questionable in theory and unworkable in practice.

[53] In this, "finger of God" is notably different from the common OT anthropomorphisms "hand of God" and "arm of God."

[54] Exod 8:15 is the chapter-and-verse enumeration of modern editions of the MT and the LXX. However, the Vulgate and some modern translations (e.g., the *RSV*) number this verse Exod 8:19, an enumeration that is also found in some reference works on the Bible. Robert W. Wall (" 'The Finger of God': Deuteronomy 9.10 and Luke 11.20," *NTS* 33 [1987] 144–50) tries to explain the phrase in terms of the finger of God writing the tables of the covenant in Deut 9:10. His farfetched explanation rests in turn on a convoluted theory that the great central section of Luke's Gospel (Luke 9:51–19:10) is arranged in midrashic style to parallel Deuteronomy 1–26. Even Wall admits that this theory has met with strong objections. The reference to Exod 8:15 is much more direct and natural.

[55] In the MT this reads: ʾeṣbaʿ ʾĕlōhîm hîʾ; in the LXX, *daktylos theou estin touto*.

[56] Heinrich Schlier, "*daktylos*," *TDNT* 2 (1964) 20–21. While most exegetes understand Exod 8:15 to mean "this [plague] is [wrought by] the finger [= power] of God" or "[here] is the finger [= power] of God," B. Couroyer takes a different approach in his two articles, "Quelques égyptianismes dans l'Exode" and "Le 'doigt de Dieu' (*Exode*, VIII, 15)," *RB* 63 (1956) 209–19 and 481–95. Appealing to various parallels in ancient Egyptian religion (e.g., in the Egyptian Book of the Dead), where a concrete object that resembles a finger (e.g., a rod or a bar) is likened to the finger of a god, Couroyer suggests that the original sense of Exod 8:15 was: "This [rod of Aaron] is the finger of God [or: a god]." Couroyer admits, however, that later Jewish tradition lost sight of the original reference to the rod of Aaron. Thus Jesus' saying in Luke 11:20 par. does equate the finger of God with the power of God, as do later syncretistic Jewish and Christian-Coptic texts from Egypt. Hence Couroyer's thesis, which in any event may take too literalistic an approach to the striking metaphor in Exod 8:15, does not materially affect our interpretation of Luke 11:20 par.

[57] T. W. Manson, *The Teaching of Jesus. Studies of Its Form and Content* (2d ed.; Cambridge: Cambridge University, 1935) 82–83; Perrin, *Rediscovering the Teaching of Jesus*, 66–67.

[58] As I have argued above, the Marcan-Q parables on the divided kingdom and the

divided house probably did not form an original literary unit with Luke 11:20 par. and might well have been spoken by Jesus on a different occasion. Nevertheless, all these various sayings of Jesus reflect his understanding of the meaning of his exorcisms, especially in the face of misunderstanding or hostile criticism. Hence it is not unreasonable to suppose that Jesus' various utterances explaining and defending his exorcistic practice rested on the same basic mode of argumentation. On the whole Beelzebul *Streitgespräch* in Mark and Q, see Laufen, *Die Doppelüberlieferungen*, 126–55; his consideration of the material in the mouth of the historical Jesus is on pp. 136–38. Laufen's conclusion is that, despite all the stylizing of the material in the oral tradition, the core of the *Streitgespräch* represents an actual debate between Jesus and his opponents on the question of the source and meaning of his exorcisms.

[59] Perrin (*Rediscovering the Teaching of Jesus*, 67) points to two possible theological contexts of Jesus' claim: (1) the new exodus of Israel from slavery, wrought by the eschatological power of God working through Jesus' exorcisms (though Perrin does not insist on this context); and (2) the holy war theology seen in Qumran's *War Scroll*, depicting the eschatological struggle of the sons of light against the sons of darkness. Of this second context Perrin says: "When an exorcism is a manifestation of the Kingdom of God, then that Kingdom is manifested in terms of a conflict between good and evil, between God and Satan, between the Sons of Light and the Sons of Darkness. The Kingdom is not only God acting; it is God acting in a situation of conflict" (p. 67). I do not agree with Perrin's further point, that Jesus is stressing the experience of the individual rather than that of the people as a whole. Sanders rightly stresses throughout his *Jesus and Judaism* that Jesus was intent on addressing and regathering a broken and scattered Israel in the end time. I would draw the natural conclusion from this insight, as applied to Jesus' exorcisms. His exorcisms, while obviously worked on individual Israelites, addressed and symbolically promised eschatological liberation to all of Israel—a liberation that had already become a reality for some individual Israelites.

[60] See Strack and Stemberger, *Introduction to the Talmud and Midrash*, 336–37.

[61] For the basic philological data on *phthanō*, see Gottfried Fitzer, "*phthanō*, etc.," *TDNT* 9 (1974) 88–92; he shows that the LXX anticipates the NT in reflecting mostly the weakened sense of "come," "arrive," "attain to." Fitzer states with regard to Luke 11:20 par. (p. 91): "Here as in the LXX . . . the meaning of *phthanō* is 'to attain to,' 'to come.'" Commenting on Erich Grässer's attempt to soften *ephthasen* to mean that "God's lordship is present already but only in the sense that it is dawning," Fitzer remarks curtly (p. 92 n. 29): "But the verb *phthanō* does not mean 'to be dawning.'" For Grässer's view, following in the tradition of Johannes Weiss, see his *Das Problem*, 6–8. Blass, Debrunner, and Rehkopf (*Grammatik des neutestamentlichen Griechisch*, 79 n. 82) observe that the sense of "come," "arrive" is continued in late ancient Greek and in modern Greek. See also Beasley-Murray, *Jesus and the Kingdom of God*, 77–79; Schlosser, *Le règne de Dieu*, 1. 137; Howard, *Das Ego Jesu*, 161 n. 2 (with a list of other authors who accept the meaning "has come to you" in Luke 11:20 par.). Interestingly, Beasley-Murray checked all the contributors to the Kittel-Friedrich *TDNT* who alluded to the meaning of Luke 11:20 par. and found that, without exception, they "expounded it as demonstrating the presence of the kingdom of God in the ministry of Jesus" (p. 78).

[62] For various attempts by exegetes and theologians to get around the clear past or present-perfect sense of *ephthasen*, see the survey by Beasley-Murray, *Jesus and the Kingdom of God*, 76. For concrete examples, see, e.g., Reginald Fuller, *The Mission and Achievement of Jesus* (SBT 12; London: SCM, 1967) 25–26, 37–38 (Jesus the prophet

speaks of a future event as though it were already present; the exodus typology shows that the real saving event still lies in the future). Rudolf Bultmann seems to be of two minds about the meaning of Luke 11:20 par. and the exorcisms in general. In his *Theology of the New Testament* (2 vols.; London: SCM, 1952) 1. 7, he states that Jesus sees "God's Reign already breaking in in the fact that by the divine power that fills him he is already beginning to drive out the demons." A few lines later, however, Bultmann emphasizes that this "does not mean that God's Reign is already here; but it does mean that it is dawning." The precise relation among "God's Reign has come upon you," "God's Reign already breaking in," God's reign "dawning," and God's reign not "already here" is never explained. In a number of commentators one notices a multiplying of metaphors to escape the clear import of Luke 11:20 par. Hans Conzelmann (*Jesus* [ed. John Reumann; Philadelphia: Fortress, 1973] 70) says that the kingdom "is not yet here. But it already casts its light in that it becomes operative in Jesus." This cryptic utterance is then explained with an existentialistic analysis of human life and understanding (pp. 75–77). How God's kingdom, understood as God's kingly rule, can be operative now, but not here now, never becomes clear.

Rejecting all these modes of circumvention and accepting the obvious sense of the Greek text in the Gospels and in Q before them is Schulz, *Q. Die Spruchquelle der Evangelisten*, 209–11; see also Kümmel, *Promise and Fulfilment*, 105–9; similarly, though with a somewhat different emphasis, Tödt, *The Son of Man in the Synoptic Tradition*, 261–63. The same sense of kingdom as present is vindicated for the Matthean form of the text by Strecker, *Der Weg der Gerechtigkeit*, 168–69.

[63] Sanders, *Jesus and Judaism*, 134.

[64] For similar cases with *geuomai* ("taste"), see Mark 9:1 parr.; John 8:52; Heb 2:9. For a similar case with *pinō* ("drink"), see Mark 10:38–39 par. Dunn ("Matthew 12:28/ Luke 11:20," 47 n. 45) prefers to see *T. Abr.* 1:3 as "a summary statement of the whole story which is about to unfold . . ."; he could well be correct. Dunn holds—rightly, in my view—that such cases as (Theodotion) Dan 4:24 (cf. v 28) and 1 Thess 2:16 use the verb in the sense of something that is already occurring. In the case of Dan 4:24, Dunn is correct in judging that the verb relates to "the decree which Daniel is at that very moment in process of delivering to the king. . . ." As for 1 Thess 2:16, Rigaux (*Les épitres aux Thessaloniciens*, 451–52) correctly rejects attempts to give *ephthasen* a future reference; its sense is rather "est *déjà* arrivé," with perhaps a note of suddenness and unexpectedness. Interestingly, there seems to be a tone of suddenness and unexpectedness in the cup of death coming to Abraham in *T. Abr.* 1:3: "But even to him [Abraham] came the common and inexorable bitter cup of death and the unforeseen end of life" (translation by E. P. Sanders, *The Old Testament Pseudepigrapha*, 1. 882). Note, by the way, that, unlike the coming of the kingdom in Jesus' preaching, the coming of death to Abraham is not some unique, world-changing event, but simply the "way of all flesh" that holds true even for the good and the pious.

[65] To this limited extent Dodd is correct in his interpretation of *ephthasen* (*The Parables of the Kingdom*, 36–37 with n. 15). However, I think he is wrong to mesh the question of *ephthasen* with that of *ēggiken*, the perfect tense of *eggizō*. A similar objection might be raised against the treatment of the two verbs by Kenneth W. Clark, "Realized Eschatology," *JBL* 59 (1940) 367–83; his treatment of *phthanō* is especially unsatisfactory. The root meaning of the two Greek verbs is different, and in the concrete Gospel texts one is in the aorist and the other in the perfect tense. Hence, at least on the level of the Greek, the two verbs must be treated separately. Furthermore, the Semitic verbs that these two Greek verbs translate in the LXX also tend to be different. While both data and arguments from the data are complex, the overall situation can be summed up

fairly simply: the Greek verb *eggizō* represents the Semitic root *qrb* ("approach," "draw near") often, but *ngᶜ* (Hebrew for "touch," "reach to," "arrive") and *mṭˀ* (Aramaic for "reach," "attain to," "come to") only rarely; *phthanō* represents *ngᶜ* or *mṭˀ* almost uniformly and *qrb* not at all. On this point, see Perrin, *The Kingdom of God in the Teaching of Jesus*, 64–65. Debates over the meaning of the various Semitic and Greek verbs have spawned a whole literature of their own; the basic data and arguments, as well as further bibliography, can be found in the following articles. In *ExpTim* 48 (1936–37), three noted critics published short essays on different sides of the issue of the "realized eschatology" espoused by C. H. Dodd. The three essays, all with the title "'The kingdom of God has come,'" were written by J. Y. Campbell (pp. 91–94), C. H. Dodd (pp. 138–42), and J. M. Creed (pp. 184–85). Further comments on the debate were made in the article by Clark mentioned above. A later and fuller review of opinions was supplied by Robert F. Berkey, "*eggizein, phthanein,* and Realized Eschatology," *JBL* 82 (1963) 177–87. Berkey stresses the ambiguity inherent in both the Semitic verbs and the concepts involved, as well as the multistage nature of the coming of the kingdom in the Gospels; the individual context must decide the sense of a given passage.

[66] Bultmann, *Geschichte*, 174.

[67] In Chapter 14, section I ("Introductory Considerations").

[68] This point is stressed in reference to Luke 11:20 par. by Erich Grässer, "Zum Verständnis der Gottesherrschaft," *ZNW* 65 (1974) 3–26, esp. 7–11.

[69] Consequently, Otto Betz sees Jesus' exorcisms (including Matt 12:28 par.) and his other miracles in the context of the OT tradition of the holy war, especially as this tradition was understood in an eschatological context by Qumran; see his "Jesu Heiliger Krieg," *NovT* 2 (1958) 116–37. For a brief summary of Jewish ideas about Satan and his reign around the time of Jesus, see Schlosser, *Le règne de Dieu*, 1. 135–36.

[70] T. W. Manson (*The Sayings of Jesus* [London: SCM, 1949] 86) sums up the point in this way: "[In Luke 11:20 par.] the exit of the evil spirits is the *result* of the Divine presence, not the *preparation* for it." Manson contrasts this idea with that of the neo-Platonist Porphyry: elaborate preparations are necessary to fit men for communion with the deity, "that when they [the evil demons] have departed the Parousia of the god may take place." Manson's valid insight makes the attempt to avoid the obvious sense of the logion by Richard H. Hiers suspect. In his *The Kingdom of God in the Synoptic Tradition*, 33, Hiers tries to fit Luke 11:20 par. into his completely imminent-future view of Jesus' eschatology by claiming: "The connection between exorcism and the Kingdom of God, then, is that the former prepares for the coming of the latter." But that is not what Luke 11:20 par. says; if anything, it says just the opposite. As Schlosser points out (*Le règne de Dieu*, 1. 136–37), *hē basileia tou theou* in Luke 11:20 par. encompasses both the powerful action of God in the end time and the saving good that human beings receive from this action.

[71] Böcher (*Christus Exorcista*, 167) includes here the anointing of the sick with oil by the presbyters of the church "in the name of the Lord [Jesus]." This, of course, is to take exorcism in the widest sense, including the healing of all physical illnesses. Dibelius (*Der Brief des Jakobus*, 299–300) views the whole rite of prayer and anointing in the name of the Lord as an exorcism, which expels the demon causing the illness.

[72] Böcher (*Christus Exorcista*, 167) argues that the tradition goes back to Jesus; Jesus' tolerant attitude toward the successful Jewish exorcist who uses Jesus' name without being one of his disciples would not have been created by the early church and in fact was suppressed by Matthew. Indeed—we might add—by implication Jesus' tolerant

attitude is extolled over against the intolerance of John the son of Zebedee, a noted leader of the early Jerusalem church. Are we to suppose that there was a special anti-John polemic in some section of first-generation Christianity that invented this story? Outdoing Böcher, Pesch (*Das Markusevangelium*, 2. 109) gives six different reasons for holding to the authenticity of *Schulgespräch* in Mark 9:38–39. Not all are of equal weight, but the cumulative effect of the six considerations is cogent. One reason for hesitation, though, is the way John speaks of the strange exorcist as someone who "does not follow *us*." That mode of speaking might possibly reflect the situation of the early church. This consideration, along with the whole idea of performing exorcisms in the name of Jesus, leads Bultmann (*Geschichte*, 23–24) to assign the tradition to the early church. Haenchen (*Der Weg Jesu*, 327) tries to build a more extensive case against the authenticity of the incident, but some of his arguments are as questionable as some of Pesch's (e.g., 1 Cor 2:8 [!] shows that Jesus did not actually perform as many great miracles in his ministry as the Marcan tradition would have us think). It should be noted, by the way, that the text-critical situation is somewhat confused, but the use of "us" is not in doubt; see Metzger, *Textual Commentary*, 101.

[73] While one must be cautious about claims about the Qumran literature, since not all the material is yet available in definitive critical editions for examination, it is significant that, when Joseph A. Fitzmyer lists all the quotations from the OT found in the Qumran literature available to him, Exod 8:15 occurs only in a passage from a copy of the Book of Exodus written in archaic Hebrew script, 4QpaleoExod[m]; see his *The Dead Sea Scrolls. Major Publications and Tools for Study* (SBLSBS 20; Atlanta: Scholars, 1990) 206. 4QpaleoExod[m] contains no variant reading for Exodus 8:15, according to Judith E. Sanderson, *An Exodus Scroll from Qumran. 4QpaleoExod[m] and the Samaritan Tradition* (HSS 30; Atlanta: Scholars, 1986) 328. Interestingly, 'eṣba' ("finger") occurs only twice in Karl Georg Kuhn's *Konkordanz zu den Qumrantexten* (Göttingen: Vandenhoeck & Ruprecht, 1960) 22; the two texts are 1QS 11:2 and 1QM 5:13. Neither has anything to do with Exod 8:15 or "the finger of God." One must remember, however, that Kuhn's *Konkordanz* covers only the nonbiblical Hebrew texts from cave 1, as well as the Damascus Document and material from cave 4. The word is not listed at all in Kuhn's "Nachträgen zur 'Konkordanz zu den Qumrantexten,'" *RevQ* 4 (1963) 163–234, in E. Puech (ed.), "Konkordanz zu XIQMelkîsédeq," *RevQ* 12 (1985–87) 515–18, or in the Aramaic-Greek-Ethiopic Glossary in J. T. Milik's *The Books of Enoch. Aramaic Fragments of Qumrân Cave 4* (Oxford: Clarendon, 1976) 367–407. The word does occur once in the *Genesis Apocryphon* (20:5), but of human fingers (Sarai's). These findings are confirmed by the list of occurrences of 'eṣba' in James H. Charlesworth, *Graphic Concordance to the Dead Sea Scrolls* (Tübingen: Mohr [Siebeck]; Louisville: Westminster/John Knox, 1991) 33 (the concordance does not include biblical texts found at Qumran). The occurrences listed by Charlesworth are the same three already mentioned: 1QS 11:2; 1QM 5:13; and 1QapGen 20:5.

If we broaden our search beyond "finger of God" and the third plague in Qumran literature, we do find the more general theme of the Egyptian magicians Jannes and his brother (= Jambres) opposing Moses and Aaron. Just as the prince of lights raises up the latter pair, Belial is said to raise up the former pair (CD 5:18–19). Hence at least the overall theme of God and Satan struggling through Moses and Aaron on the one hand and the magicians on the other is present in the interpretation of the Egyptian plagues in general.

[74] That the *Biblical Antiquities* was written in Hebrew in Palestine during the 1st century A.D. is the position sustained by Daniel J. Harrington, "Pseudo-Philo," *The Old Testament Pseudepigrapha*, 2. 299–300.

[75] *Targum Onkelos* reads: "It is a plague from before Yahweh." *Targum Pseudo-Jonathan* reads: "It is a plague sent from before Yahweh." *Neofiti 1* does have in its text: "It is the finger of the power from before Yahweh," but the margin reads instead: "It is the power from before Yahweh." The *Samaritan Targum A* uses the phrase "God's potence." Besides *Neofiti 1*, the anthropomorphism is retained in the LXX, the Peshitta, and *Samaritan Targum J*. On the various readings, see Israel Drazin, *Targum Onkelos to Exodus* (Hoboken, NJ: Ktav, 1990) 96 n. 18; Roger Le Déaut, *Targum du Pentateuque. Tome II. Exode et Lévitique* (SC 256; Paris: Cerf, 1979) 60–61; Alejandro Díez Macho, *Neophyti 1. Targum Palestinense MS de la Biblioteca Vaticana. Tomo II. Exodo* (Madrid/ Barcelona: Consejo Superior de Investigaciones Científicas, 1970) 47. While this survey of targumic readings is useful for gaining a sense of the general thrust of Jewish exegesis (e.g., obviously "the finger of God" was not an object of great interest or speculation among Jews in the early centuries A.D.), one must remember that the final forms of most of the targums come from the late ancient or early medieval period. No doubt they contain ancient exegetical traditions, but distinguishing early from late and dating individual traditions are notoriously difficult.

[76] For an example from the *Mekilta*, see Jacob Neusner, *Mekhilta According to Rabbi Ishmael. An Analytical Translation* (Brown Judaic Studies 148, 154; 2 vols.; Atlanta: Scholars, 1988) 1. 170. The text is in *Beshallah*, chap. 7, 21.B.–C. (according to Neusner's system of enumeration): "In connection with the punishment in Egypt, what does Scripture say? 'Then the magicians said to Pharaoh, "This is the finger of God"' (Ex. 8:15), while in connection with the punishment at the sea: 'And Israel saw the great hand which the Lord did against the Egyptians.' How many plagues were inflicted with a finger? Ten plagues. Then in Egypt they were smitten with ten plagues, and at the sea, fifty." One sees immediately that the use made here of Exod 8:15 is completely different from that in Luke 11:20 par. It is the question of scholarly deductions from ancient sacred texts versus the charismatic use of Scripture to interpret charismatic actions in the present.

For an example from *Genesis Rabbah*, see Jacob Neusner, *Genesis Rabbah. The Judaic Commentary to the Book of Genesis. A New American Translation* (Brown Judaic Studies 104, 105, and 106; 3 vols.; Atlanta: Scholars, 1985) 1. 39. In this passage (*Gen. Rab.* 4:4 [1.E.]), Rabbi Meir argues (against a Samaritan's objection) that the upper water of Genesis 1 is suspended merely by God's word. He acts out an analogy by stopping up a syringe with his finger. When the Samaritan objects that what he is doing is not comparable to God's holding back of the upper water merely by a word, Rabbi Meir replies: "Now if I, a mere mortal, am able to stop up the water just by putting my finger [over the aperture], as to the finger of the Holy One . . . how much more so! This proves that the upper water is suspended by a word." Once again, we are in the world of scholarly argumentation over texts, not charismatic actualization.

For the sake of completeness, I should note that Schlier ("*daktylos,*" 20–21) mentions (1) a reference to the finger of Ashirat in a letter to Ashirat-jashur found at Ta'annek and (2) an Egyptian ostracon that uses "the finger of God" in an exorcism formula.

[77] I specify "Jewish-Palestinian writings" because, in the Diaspora, Philo does occasionally develop the image of the finger of God in the story of the third plague. However, as one might expect, Philo's allegorical interpretations in terms of timeless truths about God have nothing to do with Jesus' eschatological interpretation of his exorcisms. Moreover, Philo gives different interpretations of the finger of God in different passages. In his *Life of Moses* (*De Vita Mosis*), God's finger is interpreted as signifying an intervention (i.e., the plague of gnats) in which only a small part of his power is used—

as distinct from God's hand, which not even the entire universe could oppose (*Mos.* 1.19.112). However, in his *On the Migration of Abraham* (*De Migratione Abrahami*), Philo interprets the finger of God as meaning what is written by God, i.e., the divine wisdom enshrined in the tablets written by God's finger, a wisdom that is wiser than human sophistry (*Mig.* 15.85).

[78] One is amazed to see how Hull (*Hellenistic Magic*, 79), without any detailed exegesis of Luke 11:20 or its OT background, blithely interprets "by the finger of God" with the banal idea "that it was Jesus' practice to touch the possessed wherever this was practicable." Hull takes this strange route because he wants some evidence that Jesus touched the possessed he cured, and the NT inconsiderately supplies him no example.

[79] Theissen, *Miracle Stories*, 277–80. See, e.g., his remark on p. 279: "Nowhere else do we find miracles performed by an earthly charismatic which purport to be the end of the old world and the beginning of the new." Theissen sees the starting point for an eschatological interpretation of Jesus' miracles precisely in his exorcisms: "Because Jesus casts out demons he can proclaim that the end has entered into the present. There is a close connection between present eschatology and the eschatological interpretation of the miracles" (p. 279). For a similar view, see Dunn, "Matthew 12:28/Luke 11:20," 42.

[80] For the argument from coherence presented in a slightly different way, see Dunn, "Matthew 12:28/Luke 11:20," 42–46. Like many other questers, Dunn does not put great emphasis on distinguishing those eschatological sayings that explicitly mention the kingdom from roughly equivalent sayings that do not. In both Chapter 15 and Chapter 16 I have tried to keep the focus on sayings that do use the phrase "kingdom of God" in one form or another. Sayings speaking of future or present salvation with other various terms and symbols have also been considered, but I have tried to alert the reader to the fact that, while they may ultimately convey the same message as the kingdom sayings, they do not contain the key locution.

[81] For this double parable within the context of the whole Beelzebul dispute, see Charles E. Carlston, *The Parables of the Triple Tradition* (Philadelphia: Fortress, 1975) 16–21, 66–69, 129–36 (for the redactional theology of Matthew, Luke, and Mark respectively). For the differences between the Marcan and Q versions of the parable, see Kruse, "Das Reich Satans," 29–61, esp. 38. Since I treat Mark 3:23–26 parr. only in passing, I do not bother to engage in a detailed argument about authenticity. Suffice it to say that the appearance of the double parable in a Mark-Q overlap (multiple attestation of sources) and the lack of any discernible christological or Christian concerns point in the direction of authenticity; there seem to be no countervailing objections. If, however, one should doubt the authenticity of this double parable and consider it instead a common secular proverb that entered secondarily into the Jesus tradition, such a decision would make no great difference to the overall argument of this section.

For treatment of the Marcan material in the whole Beelzebul section, see the standard commentaries, including Lagrange, *Saint Marc*, 71–75; Taylor, *The Gospel According to St. Mark*, 240–44; Haenchen, *Der Weg Jesu*, 139–52; Lane, *The Gospel According to Mark*, 140–46; Pesch, *Das Markusevangelium*, 1. 209–20.

[82] One could also interpret the parable as offering the two horns of a dilemma. If in fact Satan is casting out Satan (as the initial rhetorical question suggests in Mark 3:23), then the critics of Jesus should be happy, because such a "palace revolution" or schizophrenic action on Satan's part means that his rule is at an end (so v 26). If instead such an explanation is rejected as absurd, then the only other viable explanation is that Jesus

is expelling Satan by the superior power of God—and Jesus' critics should likewise rejoice. Either way, the critics should stop criticizing.

[83] Since Matthew's form shows only slight variations from Mark, only the Marcan and Lucan versions are given here. Matthew does alter the syntactical structure of the first half of the verse, probably to create a closer connection between the form of the parable he takes over from Mark and the preceding Q version of the saying on Satan being divided against himself (rhetorical question introduced by *pōs* in Matt 12:26 [cf. Luke 11:18] echoed by rhetorical question introduced by *pōs* in Matt 12:29). We thus see displayed Matthew's usual tendency to mesh different sources skillfully to create a new, neatly structured whole. Indeed, all the differences in the Matthean version of the parable of the strong man vis-à-vis Mark's form can be easily understood as Matthean redaction of Mark; on this see Robert H. Gundry, *Matthew. A Commentary on His Literary and Theological Art* (Grand Rapids: Eerdmans, 1982) 235.

[84] A good deal of the vocabulary in the Lucan version that differs from the Marcan version turns out to be atypical of Luke as well. The unusual verb *kathoplizomai* is found only this time in the whole of the NT. The noun *aulē* is not a typically Lucan word; outside of this verse it appears in Luke-Acts only in the story of Peter's denial in the Passion Narrative, where it most probably reflects Marcan tradition. While the verb *nikaō* is used 27 other times in the NT, this is its only occurrence in Luke-Acts. The noun *panoplia* likewise occurs only here in Luke-Acts; *skylon* occurs only here in the NT. When one considers all these *hapax legomena* in Luke-Acts or in the whole of the NT, all occurring in two consecutive verses, it seems highly unlikely that Luke freely composed 11:21–22 as a substitute for the form of the parable that stood in Q. Even the vocabulary that can be found elsewhere in Luke-Acts (*phylassō, eirēnē, airō, peithō, diadidōmi*) is by no means unique to Luke and so could easily have stood in the text of Q. At most, Luke may have lightly rewritten Q with a few words of his own (e.g., *diadidōsin*).—That the parable of the strong man is only loosely connected with the larger context in both the Marcan and the Q traditions and that therefore it was originally an independent, isolated saying is rightly maintained by Kruse, "Das Reich Satans," 42.

[85] Commentators often note that in the phrase *tou ischyrou* ("of the strong man"), the definite article should be understood as generic: "a strong man." But, given the context of exorcism, which seems to be the original setting of the parable, the article should perhaps be given its full force.

[86] *aulē* has a wide range of meanings, from an open space around a house, and hence a courtyard, to a court, a house, a farmhouse, and a palace. The last translation seems to fit the overall imagery best: a full complement of armor, a warrior guarding his possessions with his arms, the "conquering" of the strong man, the stripping off of the full complement of armor, and the dividing of the armor (apparently among the soldiers of the stronger man) as spoils of war. All this has bearing on the question of the more primitive form of the parable.

[87] Mark's *ta skeuē* and Luke's *ta hyparchonta* are given different English translations ("goods," "possessions") to reflect the different Greek substantives they represent.

[88] On the differences in Luke's version, see Dodd, *The Parables of the Kingdom*, 92–93 (Dodd suggests "a border incident on the frontiers of Syria, always exposed to Bedouin raids"); John Drury, *The Parables in the Gospels* (New York: Crossroad, 1985) 117–18.

[89] At the same time, one must recognize the differences in sense. In Luke 3:16 parr. Jesus is stronger than the Baptist; in Luke 11:22 he is stronger than Satan. On the

redactional level of Luke all this might be understood synthetically to mean that Jesus is stronger than the Baptist precisely in his ability to conquer Satan. Indeed, it is just possible that such a theological connection between the two *ischyroteros* sayings already existed in Q.

[90] This is likewise the judgment of Kruse, "Das Reich Satans," 42; and Gnilka (*Jesus von Nazaret*, 137), who correctly observes: "The parallel text of Luke 11, 21f allegorizes the parable."

[91] This holds true a fortiori of Isa 53:12, where it is said of the suffering servant: "He shall divide spoils with the mighty." To be noted is that the LXX of both Isa 49:24–25 and Isa 53:12 uses *skyla* for "spoils"; in the whole of the NT, the word occurs only in the Lucan version of the parable of the strong man. In any case, there is a notable difference between dividing the spoils *of* the mighty (so the Lucan version of the parable) and dividing the spoils *with* the mighty (the Isaian prophecy). In my opinion, Kruse ("Das Reich Satans," 43–44) makes too much depend on a reference to this text, which at best is connected with the secondary Lucan form of the parable.

[92] On this point see Drury, *The Parables in the Gospels*, 7–38; Raymond E. Brown, "Parable and Allegory Reconsidered," *New Testament Essays* (Garden City, NY: Doubleday [Image Books], 1968 [originally 1965]) 321–33; Hans-Josef Klauck, *Allegorie und Allegorese in synoptischen Gleichnistexten* (NTAbh 13; Münster: Aschendorff, 1978); Charles E. Carlston, "Parable and Allegory Revisited: An Interpretive Review," *CBQ* 43 (1981) 228–42.

[93] The relevant text of *T. Naphtali* 8:6 reads: *kai ho diabolos oikeioutai auton hōs idion skeuos* ("and the devil dwells in him as his very own vessel [or: instrument]"). For the critical Greek text, see Marinus de Jonge, *The Testaments of the Twelve Patriarchs* (PVTG 1/2; Leiden: Brill, 1978) 123.

[94] The comparative degree (*ischyroteros*) does occur in two contexts for Jesus: as superior to the Baptist in Mark 1:7 parr., and as superior to Satan in Luke 11:22. The Book of Revelation does use *ischyros* as an adjective for an angel in 5:2; 10:1; and 18:21; and for God in 18:8.

[95] Lorenzmeier, "Zum Logion Mt 12, 28; Lk 11, 20," 302.

[96] Since the kingdom of God as a present reality is the object of inquiry in this chapter, Mark 3:27 par. has been kept in a subordinate and confirmatory position simply because it lacks the key phrase "kingdom of God." Obviously, though, it points to the same basic reality that is referred to by the phrase in Luke 11:20 par., namely, the presence even now in Jesus' ministry of the liberating, saving rule of the God of Israel as he defeats the powers of evil and liberates his people.

[97] See Sanders, *Jesus and Judaism*, 61–76. For a critique of Sanders's interpretation of the cleansing of the temple, see Craig A. Evans, "Jesus' Action in the Temple: Cleansing or Portent of Destruction?" *CBQ* 51 (1989) 237–70. The often unexamined questions of method that are involved in arguing for or against the historicity of the cleansing of the temple are considered by Robert J. Miller, "The (A)Historicity of Jesus' Temple Demonstration: A Test Case in Methodology," *Society of Biblical Literature 1991 Seminar Papers* (ed. Eugene H. Lovering, Jr.; no. 30; Atlanta: Scholars, 1991) 235–52. If nothing else, we are reminded that not everyone considers the historicity and interpretation of the cleansing as secure a starting point for the quest for the historical Jesus as does Sanders.

In my view, two things are surprising about Sanders's treatment of the "cleansing" of the temple (*Jesus and Judaism*, 61–76): (1) Sanders emphasizes that priority is to be

given to the deeds or actions of Jesus, which are a more secure starting point in the
quest for the historical Jesus; the sayings are assigned a relatively secondary role
(pp. 3–18). Yet Sanders's whole case for a particular meaning of the cleansing remains
surprisingly weak until he calls upon the sayings of Jesus concerning the destruction of
the temple to clarify what, according to Sanders, Jesus intended by the cleansing
(pp. 71–76). Here is a prime example of the fact that the deeds of Jesus, deprived of his
interpreting words, remain either mute or ambiguous. Sanders's presentation has
weight only because he meshes the deeds and sayings of Jesus concerning the temple. I
have sought to do much the same here with the deeds of exorcism and Jesus' interpreting words. (2) Sanders's handling of Jesus' sayings about the temple is not as effective
as it might have been. The application of the criteria of authenticity is not entirely
clear (cf. the remarks of Miller, "The (A)Historicity of Jesus' Temple Demonstration,"
236–38). This is partly due to the fact that Sanders has enunciated no clear and coherent position on the Synoptic problem in his introduction to *Jesus and Judaism*. Yet the
criterion of multiple attestation can be used effectively only when one has sound reasons for deciding when a particular saying in a particular Gospel constitutes an independent strand of tradition. For example, the fact that all three Synoptic Gospels contain Jesus' "simple prediction" of the destruction of the temple in Mark 13:1–2 parr.
(p. 71) means nothing for multiple attestation if one holds—as many do—that Matthew
and Luke are literarily dependent on Mark for this saying. On another point: Sanders's
appeal to the testimony of the witnesses during the Jewish trial (Mark 14:57–58 par.)
cannot carry much weight without some extended consideration of the problems of the
whole tradition of the Jewish trial in Mark. Especially troubling is Sanders's lack of
appreciation for the peculiarly Matthean style and theology seen in the Matthean forms
of sayings both here and elsewhere in the triple tradition. Sanders then goes on
(pp. 72–73) to appeal to the parallel saying about the destruction of the temple in John
2:18–22. But, without some idea of how Sanders stands with reference to the overall
problem of John's relationship to the Synoptics, one might conceivably take the position of Frans Neirynck: John is literarily dependent on the Synoptics, and so this saying
in John does not represent independent tradition and therefore cannot be used for the
criterion of multiple attestation.

All of this is not to deny the basic correctness of Sanders's position on the cleansing
of the temple. It does, however, point out problems in Sanders's own approach, especially with regard to the criteria of authenticity, which are treated only briefly in his
introduction. More importantly, all this underscores that Sanders cannot claim that
"the principal sayings which support" his interpretation of the temple cleansing are
"absolutely firm, either with regard to their original context or their precise wording"
(cf. p. 140). Yet he proceeds to put great weight on them. He can hardly object to those
who do likewise with sayings like Luke 11:20 par., especially when the methods of
tradition, source, and redaction criticism—as well as the criteria of authenticity—have
been carefully applied to such sayings. (It was after writing my critique of Sanders's
treatment of Luke 11:20 par. and the underlying methodological problems it involved
that I discovered a similar critique in Dunn, "Matthew 12:28/Luke 11:20," 46–49. I
am encouraged to see that another student of the problem arrived independently at the
same basic position.)

[98] See, e.g., Franz Rosenthal, *A Grammar of Biblical Aramaic* (Porta Linguarum Ori-
entalium; Wiesbaden: Harrassowitz, 1968) 42.

[99] Favoring *mĕṭā'* is Dalman, *Die Worte Jesu*, 88. Much less likely, though not absolutely impossible, would be the general verb for "to come," *'ātā'*.

[100] Obviously, many aspects of this retroversion must remain hypothetical. Both *de*

and *ara* could have been added by the Greek translator. Since *wĕhēn* is a fairly common beginning of a conditional statement, I have taken the *de* to be the equivalent of *wĕ*. *ara* is more difficult; although one could theorize that it represents a *waw* introducing an apodosis of a conditional sentence, my guess (and it can be nothing more) is that the Greek translator added it to strengthen the rhetorical force of the conclusion. Instead of the emphatic form of the noun plus *dî* for "finger of God" and "kingdom of God," a construct chain would be possible. For *egō ekballō* I have chosen the pronoun plus the participle, with the verb "to be" understood; this construction can indicate either immediate present action or habitual action. It is by no means clear what verb *ekballō* represents; the pa"el of *trk* seems an acceptable choice. The 3d person singular feminine of *mĕṭā*' appears in more than one form. The Elephantine papyri from Egypt have *miṭ'at* (also *mityat*), while the MT of Dan 4:19,21 has *mĕṭāt*.

[101] In his objection about the highly speculative nature of any retroversion of the logion into Aramaic, Sanders follows in the footsteps of Hans Conzelmann, "Present and Future in the Synoptic Tradition," *God and Christ. Existence and Province* (Journal for Theology and the Church 5; ed. Robert W. Funk; New York: Harper & Row, 1968) 26–44, esp. 35 n. 40. For a similar objection, see Hiers, *The Historical Jesus and the Kingdom of God*, 62.

[102] A whole monograph could be written on the various ways the obvious sense of Luke 11:20 par. has been dodged. A classic example is given by the father of thoroughgoing (or "consequent") future eschatology, Johannes Weiss; see his *Jesus' Proclamation of the Kingdom of God* (ed. Richard Hyde Hiers and David Larrimore Holland; Philadelphia: Fortress, 1971, originally 1892) 74–79. Weiss's meandering observations boil down to three attempts at "damage control" to defend his thoroughly future-imminent interpretation of Jesus' eschatology: (1) Jesus is talking about an event that now exists only in heaven; it is not yet a historical event on earth; (2) Jesus speaks in Luke 11:20 in a way he rarely does elsewhere; (3) Luke 11:20 exemplifies a rare moment "of sublime prophetic enthusiasm, when an awareness of victory comes over him [Jesus]" (p. 78). One cannot escape the impression that an embarrassing piece of evidence is being swept under the rug.

[103] Beasley-Murray (*Jesus and the Kingdom of God*, 79) summarizes his position with the simple formula: ". . . it is the *arrival* of that kingdom being spoken of here [i.e., in Luke 11:20 par.], not its *consummation*." A more extensive explanation, one that depends on a great deal of complicated thought and terminology, can be found in Polag, *Die Christologie der Logienquelle*, 50–51. Merklein (*Jesu Botschaft*, 65) remarks more intelligibly: "The 'kingdom of God' is for Jesus a dynamic concept that denotes an *event* in which the eschatological future already includes the present." Dunn ("Matthew 12:28/Luke 11:20," 48–49) attempts to resolve the tension between present and future eschatology by appealing to Jesus' own spiritual experience: ". . . it was the experience (as Jesus understood it) of God's final rule already manifesting itself through him which probably convinced or reassured Jesus that the complete manifestation of that rule could not long be delayed." This is an intriguing move: from Jesus' intense experience of the kingdom as present in his ministry, especially his healings and exorcisms, to Jesus' conclusion that the full kingdom must be imminent. One has to ask, however, whether this approach is not in danger of reverting to the "psychologizing" of the 19th-century liberal lives of Jesus. This certainly is not Dunn's intent. For his earlier thoughts on the religious experience of Jesus and Luke 11:20 par., see his *Jesus and the Spirit* (Philadelphia: Westminster, 1975) 44–49; idem, *Unity and Diversity in the New Testament* (Philadelphia: Westminster, 1977) 184–89. Taking a different tack, Lorenzmeier ("Zum Logion Mt 12,28; Lk 11,20," 300–301) remains skeptical about any at-

tempt to harmonize Jesus' two kinds of statements about the kingdom, present and future, although Lorenzmeier thinks that Jesus uttered both types: "The present and future statements about the kingdom stand side by side without harmonization. All attempts to reconcile these statements remain hypotheses. One must be satisfied with the affirmation that the juxtaposition and interlocking of the present and future statements obviously burst the time frame of the doctrine of the [two] ages [i.e., this age followed by the age to come]."

[104] For general discussions of this logion and further bibliography, see P. M. S. Allen, "Luke xvii.21," *ExpTim* 49 (1937–38) 476–77; idem, with same title, *ExpTim* 50 (1938–39) 233–35; Beasley-Murray, *Jesus and the Kingdom of God*, 97–103; Hans Conzelmann, *The Theology of St. Luke* (New York: Harper & Row, 1961) 120–25; André Feuillet, "La double venue du Règne de Dieu et du Fils de l'homme en Luc XVII, 20–XVIII,8," *Revue thomiste* 81 (1981) 5–33; Fitzmyer, *The Gospel According to Luke*, 2. 1157–63; Ruthild Geiger, *Die lukanischen Endzeitreden. Studien zur Eschatologie des Lukas-Evangeliums* (Europäische Hochschulschriften, Series 23, Theology, vol. 16; Bern: Herbert Lang; Frankfurt: Peter Lang, 1973) 29–52; Gnilka, *Jesus von Nazaret*, 155–56; J. Gwyn Griffiths, "*entos hymōn* (Luke xvii.21)," *ExpT* 63 (1951–52) 30–31; Hiers, *The Kingdom of God in the Synoptic Tradition*, 22–29; Jeremias, *New Testament Theology*, 100–101; Kloppenborg, *The Formation of Q*, 155; Kümmel, *Promise and Fulfilment*, 32–36; Franz Mussner, " 'Wann kommt das Reich Gottes?' Die Antwort Jesu nach Lk 17, 20b.21," *BZ* 6 (1962) 107–11; Bent Noack, *Das Gottesreich bei Lukas: Eine Studie zu Luk. 17,20–24* (SymBU 10; Lund: Gleerup, 1948); Perrin, *Rediscovering the Teaching of Jesus*, 68–74; Harald Riesenfeld, "*tēreō*, etc.," *TDNT* 8 (1972) 140–51; idem, "Le règne de Dieu, parmi vous ou en vous?" *RB* 98 (1991) 190–98; Colin H. Roberts, "The Kingdom of Heaven (Lk. xvii.21)," *HTR* 41 (1948) 1–8; James M. Robinson, "The Study of the Historical Jesus after Nag Hammadi," *The Historical Jesus and the Rejected Gospels* (Semeia 44; ed. Charles W. Hedrick; Atlanta: Scholars, 1988) 45–55; Alexander Rüstow, "ΕΝΤΟΣ ΥΜΩΝ ΕΣΤΙΝ. Zur Deutung von Lukas 17:20–21," *ZNW* 51 (1960) 197–224; Schlosser, *Le règne de Dieu*, 1. 179–243; Rudolf Schnackenburg, "Der eschatologische Abschnitt Lk 17,20–36," *Mélanges bibliques en hommage au R. P. Béda Rigaux* (ed. Albert Descamps and André de Halleux; Gembloux: Duculot, 1970) 213–34; Andrew Sledd, "The Interpretation of Luke xvii.21," *ExpTim* 50 (1938–39) 235–37; Richard Sneed, "The Kingdom of God Is Within You (Lk 17, 21)," *CBQ* 24 (1962) 363–82; Josef Zmijewski, *Die Eschatologiereden des Lukas-Evangeliums. Eine traditions- und redaktionsgeschichtliche Untersuchung zu Lk 21,5–36 und Lk 17, 20–37* (BBB 40; Bonn: Hanstein, 1972) 361–97.

[105] See his *The Historical Jesus*, 282–83.

[106] To obtain multiple attestation, Crossan (*The Historical Jesus*, 282–83) appeals to various versions or echoes of the saying in the Coptic *Gospel of Thomas*, specifically sayings 113, 3 (with a slightly different form in POxy 654:9–16), and 51. Perrin (*Rediscovering the Teaching of Jesus*, 70–72) likewise appeals to these sayings, especially 113. As I have indicated in Volume One of *A Marginal Jew*, 124–39, I think the evidence strongly favors the view that the *Gospel of Thomas* is dependent on the Synoptic Gospels. Interestingly, even Crossan (p. 283) admits that sayings 3 and 51 are "derivative." But the same holds true for saying 113, which Crossan wants to treat as an early independent witness to a saying of the historical Jesus. As we have seen elsewhere, some sayings from the *Gospel of Thomas* reflect in particular the Lucan form of the sayings of Jesus, and saying 113 is a case in point. That saying 113 reflects the redactional form of Luke 17:20–21 is shown by the analysis of Schlosser, *Le règne de Dieu*, 1. 197–99; and Michael Fieger, *Das Thomasevangelium*, 276–78.

The text of saying 113 reads: "His disciples said to him, 'When is the kingdom going to come?' [Jesus said,] 'It will not come by being waited for. They are not going to say, "See, here," or "See, there." But the kingdom of the Father is spread out over the earth and people do not see it.' " As we compare this saying with Luke 17:20–21, one point is especially telling. As we shall see in the discussion of Luke 17:20–21 in the main text, form and source criticism make it likely that Luke had before him a two-part saying made up of 17:20b + 21b. Luke expanded the saying into a Hellenistic-type apophthegm or chreia by prefacing an introductory question about when the kingdom would come (v 20a); he also introduced the theme of the *place* of the kingdom's coming to balance the theme of the *time* of the kingdom's coming by taking over and inserting here a version of Mark 13:21. As can be readily seen, saying 113 of the *Gospel of Thomas* contains both of these elements (initial question about time and the reply that includes a reference to place). In other words, saying 113 reflects faithfully the Lucan redactional form of the saying. Indeed, the clause, "they are not going to say: 'See, here,' or 'See, there,' " in saying 113 reproduces perfectly Luke 17:21a (repeated in v 23a) rather than the Synoptic parallels in Mark 13:21 and Matt 24:23.

What is intriguing in all this is the shift in meaning that the *Gospel of Thomas* deftly accomplishes with minor changes. The *Gospel of Thomas* presents esoteric teaching to disciples rather than exoteric teaching to Pharisees. Nongnostics could hardly receive such secret revelation. Jesus' teaching in saying 113 rejects not merely apocalyptic observation of signs and calculation of the precise time of the end but also any and all expectation of a future coming of the kingdom. The *Gospel of Thomas* proclaims the typical gnostic gospel of a radically realized eschatology that has no place whatever for future eschatology. Notice also that the *Gospel of Thomas* characteristically avoids "the kingdom of God" in favor of "the kingdom of the Father."

Others who doubt the independence of *Thomas* in the sayings parallel to Luke 17:20–21 include Robert M. Grant and David Noel Freedman, *The Secret Sayings of Jesus* (Garden City, NY: Doubleday, 1960) 190; Geiger, *Die lukanischen Endzeitreden*, 50–52; Beasley-Murray, *Jesus and the Kingdom of God*, 98–99; Fitzmyer, *The Gospel According to Luke*, 2. 1157–58. It is remarkable that James M. Robinson ("The Study of the Historical Jesus," 50–53) chooses sayings 3 and 113 to illustrate how important the *Gospel of Thomas* is as an independent source for the study of the Synoptic Gospels and the Jesus tradition. Actually, the sayings show just the opposite.

[107] On these two discourses, see Geiger, *Die lukanischen Endzeitreden*; and Zmijewski, *Die Eschatologiereden*. There is also a collection of eschatological sayings in Luke 12:4–13:30, though it is difficult to designate it as one eschatological discourse since sayings that do not deal with the end of the world intervene at times (notably in 12:22–34). With regard to the eschatological discourse in 17:20–37, some may wish to include the parable of the widow and the judge in 18:1–8 as the concluding section of the discourse (so Feuillet, "La double venue," 5, 25–28). Notice how the reference to the Son of Man in 18:8 forms an inclusion with the mention of him at the beginning of the main section of the discourse in 17:22 + 24. However, the separate introduction at 18:1, indicating that Luke understands the parable mainly as an exhortation to persevering prayer, weakens the possible connection of the parable with the preceding discourse.

[108] A wide variety of rabbinic sayings attribute the ability to hasten (literally: "bring near" [*mqrb*]) the day of redemption (*hg'wlh*) to various human acts: repentance, observance of the commandments (e.g., keeping two Sabbaths properly), study of the Torah, or charitable deeds. For examples, see *b. Yoma* 86b; *b. Sanh.* 97b; 99b; *b. B. Bat.* 10a. A different "rabbinic" interpretation of "observance" is given by Dalman, *Die Worte Jesu*,

117: Speculation about the time of redemption must not distract the pious from their study of the Torah.

[109] Zmijewski (*Die Eschatologiereden*, 391–97) takes the unusual position of claiming that *meta paratēreseōs* means both observance of Torah and observing signs. I find it difficult to imagine v 20b meaning two so notably different things at the same time.

[110] See his "Die Passa-Erwartung als urchristliches Problem in Lc 17:20f.," *ZNW* 49 (1958) 157–96; "A. Merx über Lc 17:20f.," *ZNW* 51 (1960) 133–34; "In dieser Nacht (Luk 17,34). Zu einer älteren Form der Erwartung in Luk 17, 20–37," *ZTK* 58 (1961) 16–29; "Zu 17,20f.," *BZ* 7 (1963) 111–13. For a wider treatment of the whole topic, see R. Le Déaut, *La nuit pascale. Essai sur la signification de la Pâque juive à partir du Targum d'Exode XII 42* (AnBib 22; Rome: Biblical Institute, 1963). Le Déaut expresses his agreement with Strobel's view of Luke 17:20–21 on p. 272 n. 21 and on pp. 284–85.

[111] After reviewing a number of possible interpretations, Schlosser (*Le règne de Dieu*, 1. 195) judges the "anti-apocalyptic" approach the most likely.

[112] Some indirect confirmation of this position can be derived from the use of the corresponding verb *paratēreō* in the Gospels and Acts. The five cases in which the verb occurs in the Gospel and Acts (Mark 3:2; Luke 6:7; 14:1; 20:20; Acts 9:24) show (1) that the verb is used more frequently by Luke than by any other NT author (though four occurrences are not overly impressive) and (2) that the sense is always one of people intently watching someone (Jesus in the Gospels) or something (the gates of Damascus in Acts) with hostile purpose to see whether somebody will do something or something will happen. This meaning of the verb corresponds roughly with the "apocalyptic" meaning I attribute to the noun: intently watching to see whether something will happen. The only occurrence of the verb in the sense of legal observance is found, significantly, not in the Gospels or Acts but in Paul (Gal 4:10). Yet even here the precise legal observance that Paul mentions—observance of days, months, seasons, and years—involves calendrical calculations.

[113] See Beasley-Murray (*Jesus and the Kingdom of God*, 100), who suggests the translation "they cannot rightly say"; Zmijewski (*Die Eschatologiereden*, 368–69) suggests the sense of "one cannot say," "one may not say," or even "one need not say." It is not entirely clear whether this modal sense should be kept in the future tense or be put into the present; that depends upon whether one emphasizes v 21a's connection backward to v 20b (*erchetai* having a future sense) or forward to v 21b (*estin* having a true present sense).

[114] So, e.g., Bultmann, *Geschichte*, 128; Jeremias, *New Testament Theology*, 101 (who in addition moves all too easily back and forth between Luke's redactional text and the historical Jesus). See Otto's critique of this attempt to insert some adverb like "suddenly" in his *The Kingdom of God and the Son of Man*, 134–35; see also Schlosser, *Le règne de Dieu*, 1. 211. Conzelmann (*The Theology of St. Luke*, 120–25) and Hiers (*The Kingdom of God in the Synoptic Tradition*, 22–29) both reject the idea of the kingdom as present in 17:20–21, but both do so because of their overall theory of the meaning of the kingdom in Luke or in the Synoptics respectively. Hiers in particular makes the mistake of assimilating 17:20–21 to the main part of the discourse that follows instead of appreciating its contrasting message as an introduction.

[115] A clear example of the meaning of "in the midst of" for *entos* can be seen in Aquila's translation of Exod 17:7: "Is the Lord in the midst of us or not?" The MT has *běqirbēnû* for "in the midst of us." The LXX has the laconic *en hēmin*, which theoreti-

cally could mean "in us" but here obviously means "in the midst of us." Symmachus comes closest to representing the MT with *en mesǭ hēmōn*, while Aquila has *entos hēmōn*, where *entos* clearly means "in the midst of." Aquila uses *entos* in the same way in Exod 34:9, where the MT again has *bĕqirbēnû* and the LXX has *meth' hēmōn*. On all this see Strobel, "In dieser Nacht," 28–29; Perrin, *Rediscovering the Teaching of Jesus*, 73–74; and Beasley-Murray, *Jesus and the Kingdom of God*, 101–2. Symmachus likewise evinces the use of *entos* in the sense of "in the midst of" in his translation of Lam 1:3 (*bên* with a plural noun is rendered *entos tōn thlibontōn autēn*); and Ps 87:5 (where the MT has *bammētîm* the LXX reads *en nekrois*, Symmachus *entos nekrōn*, and the Vulgate *inter mortuos*; the *NAB* translates the Hebrew as "my couch is among the dead"). Ps 140:5 is more problematic, since the meaning of the Hebrew text is unclear, but the sense of the Hebrew phrase in question (*bĕrā'ôtēhem*) might be "in the midst of their wicked deeds." Symmachus accordingly renders the phrase *entos tōn kakiōn autōn*. An intriguing further point arises from this brief review of usage: the use of *entos* to mean "among" is found both in a translation of the OT that is painfully and at times ungrammatically literal (Aquila's) and in a translation that is much closer to idiomatic Greek (Symmachus').

In the light of this OT evidence—to say nothing of pagan texts—it is astounding that Riesenfeld ("Le règne de Dieu," 195) tries to maintain that the meaning "among" or "in the midst of" is not found "in any text of Greek literature, either profane or biblical." It is all too telling that the texts from Aquila are never mentioned. Riesenfeld tries to "defuse" the evidence from Symmachus by paraphrasing *entos* as "sojourning in the house or region of," "in the country of," "in the context, framework, sphere, of," etc. But all these paraphrases (Riesenfeld speaks of supposing a "slight ellipsis" in the texts) are simply ways of avoiding the natural sense of each text when translated literally, i.e., "among." This type of avoidance by paraphrase is nothing new; it was used by Allen ("Luke xvii.21," 476–77) in 1938. Interestingly, Allen too had problems with Aquila and Symmachus! The strategy of Allen and others usually consists in substituting a singular noun for the plural noun that follows the preposition *entos* in the Greek text; not surprisingly, once the singular noun replaces the plural, the preposition "among" no longer fits. All this proves nothing except the ingenuity of the exegete who does not want to translate *entos* as "among." For an approach to *entos* similar to that of Riesenfeld, see Feuillet, "La double venue," 7–11.

[116] Some critics try to read a favorable view of the Pharisees (at least at times) into Luke's Gospel; see, e.g., J. A. Ziesler, "Luke and the Pharisees," *NTS* 25 (1978–79) 146–57. However, as John T. Carroll ("Luke's Portrayal of the Pharisees," *CBQ* 50 [1988] 604–21) shows quite convincingly, this is to miss the plot-line that Luke lays out in his Gospel. "Luke has shaped his sources to depict an evolution of hostility between Jesus and the Pharisees" (p. 607). Indeed, "it is within the travel narrative that conflict between Jesus and the Pharisees reaches its peak" (p. 611). On this point see also Frank J. Matera, "Jesus' Journey to Jerusalem (Luke 9.51–19.46): A Conflict with Israel," *JSNT* 51 (1993) 57–77. According to Carroll, Luke 17:20–21 is a prime example of the conflicts between Jesus and the Pharisees that present two incompatible understandings of the kingdom of God (pp. 611, 613). Halvor Moxnes (*The Economy of the Kingdom. Social Conflict and Economic Relations in Luke's Gospel* [Overtures to Biblical Theology; Philadelphia: Fortress, 1988] 153) misses this point and the whole redactional approach of Luke's Gospel to the Pharisees when he claims that in 17:20–21 Luke presents them in a positive light. A similar tack is taken by Feuillet ("La double venue," 9–11), though he also attempts to solve the problem by generalizing the "you," which, he claims, does not refer especially to the Pharisees. This is certainly strange on the redactional level since (as we shall see below) Luke probably went out of his way to

introduce the Pharisees as Jesus' interlocutors. If the kingdom of God is already present "among you Pharisees," then this kingdom must be some sort of objective reality—however difficult to discern—whose presence does not depend upon the subjective dispositions of the people addressed.

That the phrase "among you" must refer first of all to the hostile Pharisees is likewise a weakness of the interpretation of Riesenfeld ("Le règne de Dieu," 197), who tries in addition to wed future eschatology with *entos*, understood in terms of human interiority. The resulting translation is forced and arbitrary. Riesenfeld is reduced to claiming that in Luke 17:21 *hē basileia tou theou* means "the criteria of the coming of the kingdom of God" (a novel rendering in the history of interpretation!). According to Riesenfeld, at the moment of the kingdom's arrival, these criteria are found "in the interior consciousness of human beings." Not surprisingly, Riesenfeld never raises the question of the possible redactional nature of vv 20a + 21a.

[117] Sneed ("The Kingdom of God Is Within You," 369–74) creates a curious variation on this position by yoking Luke 17:20–21 with Rom 14:17 to produce a reference to the indwelling of the Holy Spirit. He is followed in this by Feuillet, "La double venue," 14–15. Needless to say, this is synthetic biblical theology, not an exegesis of the Lucan text. Strange to say, Sneed never bothers to justify his all-important translation "within you." On the level of Luke's intended meaning, the perfect critique of the whole "interiority" approach is given by Fitzmyer, *The Gospel According to Luke*, 2. 1161: ". . . elsewhere in Lucan writing the kingdom is never presented as an inward reality or an inner condition of human existence. . . . the presence of the kingdom is never equated with the presence of the Spirit." One notices how foreign to the Synoptic Gospels the whole "interiority" interpretation is when Feuillet ("La double venue," 11–12) explains "the kingdom of God" in Luke 17:21b in terms of "the grace now offered to human beings . . . [with] immediate repercussions in the innermost being of [their] souls, . . . hidden in the secret of [their] hearts." Perhaps this sounds more convincing in French.

[118] Roberts, "The Kingdom of Heaven," 6–8; Rüstow, "ΕΝΤΟΣ ΥΜΩΝ," 213–16. It is strange that Beasley-Murray (*Jesus and the Kingdom of God*, 102–3) prefers this meaning and yet maintains that Luke 17:20–21 represents the view that the kingdom is present. To say that the kingdom lies within the audience's reach if they repent and believe in Jesus' proclamation does not necessarily signify that the kingdom is already present.

[119] In some of the Greek texts adduced, *entos* may mean not "in one's power" or "possession" but rather "in one's home" or "at one's home," or possibly "on this side of." On this point, see the caveats of Kümmel, *Promise and Fulfilment*, 35 n. 54; and Fitzmyer (*The Gospel According to Luke*, 2. 1161–62), who relies here on Riesenfeld. However, Schlosser (*Le règne de Dieu*, 1. 202) thinks that, despite some doubts, the existence of the meaning "in one's power" can no longer be denied. How widely it was used in the 1st century A.D. and whether it can be stretched to include the theological sense some exegetes see in 17:21b remain open questions. When Schlosser comes to a final decision himself, he prefers the meaning "in the midst of" (p. 204).

[120] On this point, see Zmijewski, *Die Eschatologiereden*, 377–78.

[121] In this I basically agree with Kümmel, *Promise and Fulfilment*, 35.

[122] For example, the *NAB*, the revised *NAB* NT, the *RSV*, the new *RSV*, the *NEB*, the *Revised English Bible*, the *JB*, and the *New Jerusalem Bible*.

[123] For the threat implied in vv 20–21, see Carroll, "Luke's Portrayal of the Phari-

sees," 613. Needless to say, everything affirmed here about the Pharisees refers only to Luke's polemical theological portrait of the Pharisees, not to the historical Pharisees living during the ministry of the historical Jesus.

[124] This would fit Luke's supposed tendency to avoid doublets of Marcan material. However, Luke's attitude toward doublets is more complicated than some may think; see Fitzmyer, *The Gospel According to Luke*, 1. 81–82.

[125] For this tendency in Luke, see Schnackenburg, "Der eschatologische Abschnitt," 217; Geiger, *Die lukanischen Endzeitreden*, 31. Geiger (p. 32) goes on to point out how frequently the Pharisees appear in material found only in the Third Gospel. Geiger thinks it a mistake to see the Pharisees' question as a hostile test.

[126] On this see Zmijewski, *Die Eschatologiereden*, 361–62. Compare, e.g., Luke 8:9, where Luke reformulates Mark 4:10 to create an indirect question (notice also how Mark's *ērōtōn* becomes *epērōtōn* in Luke). The same use of *eperōtaō* with an indirect question is found in Acts 23:34, where presumably Luke is composing with greater freedom vis-à-vis tradition than in the Gospel narrative of Jesus' public ministry. Other passages where Luke changes the direct discourse of Mark to indirect discourse include Luke 5:14; 8:29,32,41; 18:40; 20:7; 21:5; 22:23.

[127] Bultmann, *Geschichte*, 24; Dibelius (*Die Formgeschichte des Evangeliums*, 162 n. 2) remarks that Luke 17:20a corresponds word-for-word to the pattern of the chreia.

[128] See Zmijewski, *Die Eschatologiereden*, 382. Examples can be found in 11:37–54 (Pharisee) followed by 12:1–12 (disciples); 13:31–14:24 (Pharisee) followed by 14:25–35 (but in this case addressed to the crowds on the requirements for becoming a disciple); 15:1–32 (Pharisees) followed by 16:1–13 (disciples); 16:14–31 (Pharisees) followed by 17:1–10 (disciples); 18:9–14 (those who are self-confident about their righteousness, including no doubt Pharisees, as the Pharisee in the parable suggests) followed by instruction to the disciples (18:15–17). A full listing of the sequence of audiences from 10:1 to 18:34 can be found in Carroll, "Luke's Portrayal of the Pharisees," 609 n. 24.

[129] One or both of these words could be Lucan additions to the traditional logion. Zmijewski (*Die Eschatologiereden*, 371 n. 48), following Schnackenburg ("Der eschatologische Abschnitt," 218), observes that *idou gar* ("for behold") occurs relatively often in Luke (six times in Luke-Acts), while it never occurs in Matthew or Mark. Elsewhere in the NT it is found only once, in 2 Cor 7:11. On this see also Schlosser, *Le règne de Dieu*, 1. 188.

[130] For this pattern of negative-positive in another statement of present eschatology that probably comes from the historical Jesus, see Matthew 11:11 ‖ Luke 7:28. Notice how in Matt 11:11 the negative *ouk* stands at the beginning of the first statement and the verb *estin* stands at the end of the second statement, just as in Luke 17:20b + 21b. That the *erchetai* in Luke 17:20b has a future rather than a present sense is clear from context; a detailed argument is laid out by Schlosser, *Le règne de Dieu*, 1. 189.

[131] See Zmijewski, *Die Eschatologiereden*, 387.

[132] A possible further confirmation might be seen in the initial *ouk* of v 20b. Strictly speaking, it does not qualify the verb *erchetai* that immediately follows but rather the prepositional phrase *meta paratērēseōs* at the other end of the sentence. Such word order may betray a Semitic substratum; see Zmijewski, *Die Eschatologiereden*, 364. Yet one must be cautious with this kind of argument. Luke is capable of imitating Semitisms found in the LXX when he so desires. Hence this point is at best confirmatory of what

is said in the main text. However, the fact that *paratērēsis* occurs only here in Luke-Acts and that 17:20b + 21b as it stands forms a remarkably parallel structure makes it difficult for me to follow Schlosser's minority view that *meta paratērēseōs* is a redactional addition by Luke; see his *Le règne de Dieu*, 1. 196–201.

[133] The only other occurrence of *entos* in the NT is as a noun in Matt 23:36. There it is preceded by the definite article *to* and has the meaning "the inside of." Zmijewski (*Die Eschatologiereden*, 384) adds to the non-Lucan vocabulary and style the use of the preposition *meta* to indicate accompanying circumstance.

[134] The terminology of the coming of the kingdom does occur in the redactional creation of v 20a, but that is a "back-formation" created by Luke, i.e., a clause that takes its vocabulary from the traditional logion that it is meant to introduce.

[135] So with Zmijewski (*Die Eschatologiereden*, 384–90) and against Strobel, who proposes Luke's creation of the logion in his "Die Passa-Erwartung," 182; and "Zu Lk 17,20f.," 111–13. See the critique of Strobel's whole theory in Perrin, *Rediscovering the Teaching of Jesus*, 69–70. Lucan redaction for the whole of 17:20–21 is also maintained by Geiger, *Die lukanischen Endzeitreden*, 49–50. In holding to Luke's creation of the whole logion, Strobel and Geiger are in a definite minority.

[136] See Heinz Schürmann, "Zu lukanischen Sondertraditionen. Das Thomas-evangelium und das lukanische Sondergut," *Traditionsgeschichtliche Untersuchungen zu den synoptischen Evangelien* (Kommentare und Beiträge zum Alten und Neuen Testament; Düsseldorf: Patmos, 1968) 228–47, esp. 237; more hesitatingly, Schnackenburg, "Der eschatologische Abschnitt," 213–34. For a critique of their position, see Kloppenborg, *The Formation of Q*, 155.

[137] There is need for methodological rigor here, lest it turn out that "Q is only what you make it." Q must be defined as the verses Matthew and Luke clearly have in common over against Mark. Mere similarity in wording or themes between Q material and special Lucan material does not prove that the latter belongs to Q. Presumably Luke would join L material to Q material precisely because they shared common phrases or themes. (In any case, even if vv 20b and 21b were from Q, it would not materially affect the basic argument in the main text.)

[138] While I accept "L" as a minor source for the Synoptics and as a possible source of knowledge of the historical Jesus, I do not subscribe to the theory of "proto-Luke," a primitive Lucan Gospel made up of L and Q and later joined to Marcan material to create our present Third Gospel. On the problem of proto-Luke and reasons for doubting its existence, see Fitzmyer, *The Gospel According to Luke*, 1. 89–91.

[139] Simply as a matter of fact, as Schlosser notes (*Le règne de Dieu*, 1. 214), the vast majority of critics do accept some form of 17:20b + 21b as authentic.

[140] Bultmann, *Geschichte*, 24, 55–58.

[141] Indeed, one might raise the question whether we have here a typical Semitic pattern of speech known as "dialectical" or "relative" negation. In dialectical negation, although the opposition between two realities or ideas seems so absolute that one term or idea is simply excluded or rejected, in fact the sense of the affirmation is "not so much A as rather B." An example is the original sense of Hosea 6:6: "I desire covenant-love and not sacrifice." Hosea is not speaking as an 18th-century Enlightenment philosopher, rejecting all sacrificial cult or all external public worship. Rather, he is emphatically proclaiming that covenant-love is much more important to Yahweh than cultic sacrifice; indeed, it is only the former that gives the latter true meaning. On this pattern

of speech and how it might apply to both OT and NT sayings, see Arnulf Kuschke, "Das Idiom der 'relativen Negation' im NT," *ZNW* 43 (1950–51) 263; and Heinz Kruse, "Die 'dialektische Negation' als semitisches Idiom," *VT* 4 (1954) 385–400.

[142] The question of the time-reference of v 21b arises again when we move back from a Greek version of the saying in the L source to a hypothetical Aramaic form of the text. Most likely in Aramaic the verb was simply understood, though either *hî'* or *'îtai* might stand behind the Greek *estin*. Neither Aramaic form would carry a time indication. However, (1) the rhetorical opposition to v 20b and (2) the banality, if not meaninglessness (in the climax of the two-part saying), of having v 21b say simply "the kingdom of God will be in your midst" both argue for the present tense as the original meaning in v 21b. In contrast, *entos hymōn* creates no great difficulty when it moves back into Aramaic. Whether the preposition *bĕ* or *bên* (or possibly some other preposition such as *bĕgô'*) stands behind *entos*, the context makes clear the sense of "in the midst of."

[143] Klaus Berger ("Hellenistisch-heidnische Prodigien und die Vorzeichen in der jüdischen und christlichen Apokalyptik," *ANRW* II/23.2, 1428–69, esp. 1460–62) sees a much stronger christological claim than I do in Luke 17:20. Indeed, according to Berger, the verse makes a claim of exclusivity: in order to prepare for the end time one is dependent on Jesus alone, and not on any apocalyptic signs that might be interpreted as indications of or instructions concerning the end. It is not that apocalyptic is being rejected in Luke 17:20, says Berger; rather, it is a matter of focusing apocalyptic concepts on a christological perspective. Jesus himself is *the* apocalyptic portent, and the only one; he absorbs all apocalyptic signs into himself.

Unfortunately, Berger treats only the sentence "the kingdom of God does not come with observation." He does not supply any overall analysis of Luke 17:20–21, nor does he indicate what if anything in the unit might come from the historical Jesus. In my view, his strong christological interpretation may have validity in the total context of Luke's Gospel. I doubt whether it can be read into what I suggest is the most primitive form of the logion.

[144] Granted the many puzzles connected with the Greek text, it may seem almost foolhardy to attempt an Aramaic retroversion. Still, if positions adopted here on the meaning of debatable Greek words and the earliest attainable Greek form are correct, the following retroversion may not be too far from the truth:

20b *ouk erchetai hē basileia tou theou meta paratērēseōs*
 lā' 'ātĕyāh malkûtā' dî 'ĕlāhā bĕmantĕrāh

21b *[idou?] hē basileia tou theou entos hymōn estin*
 [bā?] malkûtā' dî 'ĕlāhā' bênêkōn hî'

[145] On Mark 1:15 and its place within the prologue of the Gospel, see R. H. Lightfoot, "The First Chapter of St. Mark's Gospel," *The Gospel Message of St. Mark* (Oxford: Oxford University, 1950) 15–30; James M. Robinson, "II. The Marcan Introduction: 1. 1–13," *The Problem of History in Mark* (SBT 21; London: SCM, 1957) 21–32; Leander E. Keck, "The Introduction to Mark's Gospel," *NTS* 12 (1965–66) 352–70; Aloysius M. Ambrozic, *The Hidden Kingdom: A Redaction-Critical Study of the References to the Kingdom of God in Mark's Gospel* (CBQMS 2; Washington, DC: CBA, 1972); J. M. Gibbs, "Mark 1,1–15, Matthew 1,1–4,16, Luke 1,1–4,30, John 1,1–51. The Gospel Prologues and Their Function," *Studia Evangelica. Vol. VI* (TU 112; ed. E. Livingstone; Berlin: Akademie, 1973) 154–88; Gerhard Arnold, "Mk 1:1 und Eröffnungswendungen

in griechischen und lateinischen Schriften," *ZNW* 68 (1977) 123–27; Gerhard Dautzenberg, "Die Zeit des Evangeliums. Mk 1,1–15 und die Konzeption des Markusevangeliums," *BZ* 21 (1977) 219–34; 22 (1978) 76–91; Detlev Dormeyer, "Die Kompositionsmetapher 'Evangelium Jesu Christi, des Sohnes Gottes' Mk 1.1. Ihre
theologische und literarische Aufgabe in der Jesus-Biographie des Markus," *NTS* 33
(1987) 452–68; Frank Matera, "The Prologue as the Interpretative Key to Mark's Gospel," unpublished paper delivered at the Catholic Biblical Association meeting, Task
Force on Literary Criticism in the NT, Aug. 18, 1988. I prefer to call Mark 1:14–15 a
"bridge-summary": it both looks back and completes the introduction (a better designation than "prologue") to the Gospel and at the same time opens up the first main
narrative section of the public ministry.

[146] See his interpretation in *The Parables of the Kingdom*, 36–37. As I noted above
when treating Luke 11:20 par. (in section III. A), a major mistake of Dodd is to assimilate the verb *eggizō* ("draw near") in Mark 1:15 to the verb *phthanō* ("arrive") in Luke
11:20 par. "To draw near" and "to arrive"—the basic meanings of the two verbs, a few
exceptional cases aside—are simply different meanings and should not be confused. A
similar confusion can be found in the treatment of the two verbs by Kenneth W. Clark,
"Realized Eschatology," *JBL* 59 (1940) 367–83. As we saw when examining Luke 11:20
par., the Semitic verbs that *eggizō* and *phthanō* translate in the LXX also tend to be
different. While debatable cases can be found, in general the Greek verb *eggizō* represents the Semitic root *qrb* ("approach," "draw near") often, but *ngʿ* (Hebrew for
"touch," "reach to," "arrive") and *mṭʾ* (Aramaic for "reach," "attain to," "come to")
only rarely; *phthanō* represents *ngʿ* or *mṭʾ* almost uniformly and *qrb* not at all; see Perrin,
The Kingdom of God in the Teaching of Jesus, 64–65. For various views on this subject,
see the three short essays published in *ExpTim* 48 (1936–37): the essays, all with the
title " 'The kingdom of God has come,' " were written by J. Y. Campbell (pp. 91–94),
C. H. Dodd (pp. 138–42), and J. M. Creed (pp. 184–85). A judicious survey of opinions
is supplied by Robert F. Berkey, "*eggizein, phthanein*, and Realized Eschatology," *JBL*
82 (1963) 177–87. Berkey wisely emphasizes the ambiguity in both the Semitic verbs
and the concepts they convey, as well as the multistage nature of the coming of the
kingdom in the Gospels; the concrete context of a given passage must determine its
meaning. For an overview of the basic philological data, see Herbert Preisker, "*eggys*,
etc.," *TDNT* 2 (1964) 330–32.

[147] So, among many others, Fuller, *The Mission and Achievement of Jesus*, 21–25;
Hiers, *The Kingdom of God in the Synoptic Tradition*, 34.

[148] So, e.g., Bultmann, *Geschichte*, 124, 134, 366; Bultmann allows that Mark has used
the terminology of the Christian mission in creating this redactional composition. Yet,
as Schlosser shows (*Le règne de Dieu*, 1. 95–96), a good deal of the vocabulary in Mark
1:15 is non-Marcan in the sense that, although the words may appear a few other times
in Mark, the meaning is often quite different from the meaning in 1:15. This is especially true of *plēroō*, "fulfill" (cf. Mark 14:49; 15:28, both times of Scripture). *kairos*,
"time," returns in different senses in 10:30; 11:13; and 12:2. Only the use in 13:33 can
be called explicitly eschatological, and the eschatological moment it refers to is not the
same as the one designated in 1:15. *eggizō*, "draw near," is found in Mark 11:1 and
14:24; but in these two passages the verb is used in a spatial, not temporal, sense as in
1:15. *metanoeō*, "repent," occurs again only in 6:12, where, as part of the narration of
the mission of the Twelve, it serves as a redactional cross-reference to Jesus' proclamation in 1:15. The absolute use of *euaggelion*, "gospel," could be attributed to Marcan
redaction (cf. 8:35; 10:29; 13:10; 14:9), but *pisteuō en tǭ euaggeliǭ*, "believe in the gospel," can also be found in the terminology of the early Christian mission.

[149] So, e.g., Beasley-Murray, *Jesus and the Kingdom of God*, 71–75. The author supplies a good overview of the various scholarly positions on the question.

[150] So, e.g., Schlosser (*Le règne de Dieu*, 1. 105), who concludes that the first and fourth clauses of 1:15 ("the time is fulfilled . . . believe in the gospel") come from Hellenistic-Jewish Christianity, while the second and third clauses ("the kingdom of God has drawn near; repent") are probably authentic fragments of the preaching of Jesus. On pp. 97–98, Schlosser points out that the key words *kairos*, *eggyteron/ēggiken*, and *pisteuō* all occur in the eschatological parenesis of Rom 13:11–12, with *plēroō* occurring (though in a different sense than in Mark 1:15) in 13:8. The idea of fulfillment with reference to time can be found in Gal 4:4 and Eph 1:10 (with the noun *plērōma*). *metanoeō* is not widely attested in the most primitive Gospel traditions, but it is an important word and concept in the type of Christianity enshrined in Luke-Acts and in the Revelation of John. Various configurations of the ideas "repent," "believe," and "gospel" can be found in the writings of early Christianity; see, e.g., Phil 1:27; Rom 10:8–9,16; 1 Cor 15:1–2,11; Rom 1:16–17; Mark 16:15–16. In short, a good deal of Mark 1:15 echoes the missionary vocabulary of the early church; the one notable exception is the whole clause, "the kingdom of God has drawn near." More hesitant about the authenticity of "the kingdom of God has drawn near" is Gnilka, *Jesus von Nazaret*, 154, esp. n. 29.

[151] For what follows, see Schlosser, *Le règne de Dieu*, 1. 91–109.

[152] See Sanders (*Jesus and Judaism*, 106–13), who, however, may be too skeptical about the matter.

[153] On the much-disputed and hardly resolvable question of whether the original text of Luke 10:1 read "seventy" or "seventy-two," see Metzger, *Textual Commentary*, 150–51. Kurt Aland argues strongly for "seventy-two" as the original reading.

[154] For this argument, see Kloppenborg, *Q Parallels*, 72. Kloppenborg notes that Luke's first missionary discourse (taken mostly from Mark) may betray slight influence from Q as well.

[155] For a much more detailed analysis and argument for the Mark-Q overlap, see Laufen, *Die Doppelüberlieferungen*, 221–24. Laufen thinks that Luke in 10:9 has preserved the original order, position, and wording of Q. For a list of scholars who maintain that opinion with regard to the discourse as a whole, see Kloppenborg, *Q Parallels*, 72; for detailed argumentation in favor of this view, see Schulz, *Q. Die Spruchquelle der Evangelisten*, 404. Both Laufen and Schulz hold that Matthew's rewriting of the Q material is explainable on the grounds of his overall reordering and meshing of traditions throughout his notably longer missionary discourse. As for Luke's "to you (*eph' hymas*)" in 10:9b ("the kingdom of God has drawn near *to you*"), Laufen takes a nuanced view. On the one hand, Laufen (likewise Sato [*Q und Prophetie*, 129 n. 48]) holds that "to you" probably belonged to the Q form of the core proclamation of the kingdom (cf. the similar use of *eph' hymas* in Luke 11:20 par. and Matthew's tendency to make the kingdom-proclamations of John, Jesus, and the disciples parallel). On the other hand, Laufen (p. 524 n. 375) suspects that the *eph' hymas* was added to the kingdom-proclamation by Q (assimilating Luke 10:9 par. to Luke 11:20 par.) and so does not go back to the historical Jesus. Schulz (p. 407) would agree with the last point, but attributes *eph' hymas* to the hand of Luke. Whether we prefer the view of Laufen or Schulz, we see verified once again what we noticed in two other Mark-Q overlaps (i.e., John's prophecy of the coming one and the Beelzebul dispute): at times Mark rather than Q (or the Lucan form of Q) has preserved the earliest attainable form of Jesus' saying.

[156] So, among many others, Sato, *Q und Prophetie*, 131. Merklein (*Jesu Botschaft*, 56–58) wavers on the question of authenticity, but on the whole considers it the more likely hypothesis. Merklein is unduly distracted by his attempt to play down the temporal element that, in my view, is necessarily a key part of the core-proclamation of the kingdom in Mark 1:15.

[157] The transitive sense found in secular Greek ("to bring near") does not occur in the NT. Even in secular Greek the transitive sense is not as frequent as the intransitive, and it is rare in the LXX. The verb does not occur frequently in the papyri.

[158] For the basic concept, see BDF §340, with possible exceptions in §343 (the treatment is almost the same in BDR §340, 343). Similarly, Zerwick, *Graecitas Biblica*, §285–89. I purposely take my examples from Rom 4:25 and 1 Cor 15:4 because of the intriguing fact that both formulations are probably early pre-Pauline creedal formulas that Paul is citing.

[159] This fits in well with the theological context of the first main part of Romans: As Christ died and rose once and for all, so too the Christian at the time of his or her conversion experienced (through faith and baptism) a once-and-for-all death to sin.

[160] The perduring risen state of Christ is important in the context of 1 Corinthians 15 as Paul argues from the resurrection of Christ in the past to the resurrection of Christians in the future.

[161] One small point inclines me to suspect that even in the perfect tense *eggizō* was understood by the evangelists to refer to the imminent future: while all three Synoptics use *eggizō* for eschatological statements, the Gospel of John, the great proponent of realized eschatology among the Gospels, never uses *eggizō*. The verb is totally absent from the Fourth Gospel. For the predominance of the imminent-future sense in the NT when *eggys* and *eggizō* are used temporally, see Kümmel, *Promise and Fulfilment*, 19–25, esp. 20; Schlosser, *Le règne de Dieu*, 1. 106.

[162] The hopelessness of trying to specify the precise Semitic substratum and its meaning in the case of *ēggiken* can be documented by the way different tenses of *eggizō* in the LXX translate the same basic form of the Hebrew adjective (not verb!) *qārôb* ("near," with the verb "to be" understood) in the MT—notably in eschatological prophecies. To argue about the precise time-reference in the original saying when the underlying Semitic text may contain no verb but only an adjective is fruitless. It is no wonder that a Hebrew sentence with an adjective but no expressed verb might be translated by a Greek verb put into different tenses in different passages. For example, in Isa 50:8 ("He who justifies me is near") *qārôb maṣdîqî* is rendered *eggizei ho dikaiōsas me* (present tense). Yet in Isa 56:1 ("my salvation is near to come") *qĕrôbâ yĕšûʿātî lābôʾ* is rendered *ēggise . . . to sōtērion mou paraginesthai* (aorist). The example of Isa 56:1 is especially enlightening in that the LXX manuscripts are divided in their reading. While Alexandrinus, Marchalianus, and minuscules 26, 49, 106, and 410 read the aorist *ēggisen*, Vaticanus and Sinaiticus, in addition to other varied witnesses, read the perfect *ēggiken*. For a full list of witnesses on both sides, see *Isaias* (Septuaginta Vetus Testamentum Graecum Auctoritate Academiae Litterarum Gottingensis editum; vol. 14; 2d ed.; ed. Joseph Ziegler; Göttingen: Vandenhoeck & Ruprecht, 1967) 330. On the uselessness of seeking an Aramaic substratum for Luke 10:9, see the remark of Schulz (*Q. Die Spruchquelle der Evangelisten*, 417), who, however, is speaking of the task of interpreting the text as it stands in the Q document. Hoffmann (*Studien*, 300) thinks that, at least in the Q document, Luke 10:9, as compared with Luke 11:20, shows a shift from present eschatology to imminent-future eschatology.

It is difficult to draw significant conclusions about the precise meaning of the perfect of *eggizō* from the LXX because of its sparse occurrence there. There are some 158 cases of *eggizō* in the LXX, but the vast majority of them are in the present, imperfect, future, or aorist. Even if we count dubious alternate readings, there are only about eight cases of the perfect. In two cases the Greek perfect indicative represents the adjective *qārôb*, in one case the qal perfect of the verb *nāgaʿ*, and in the other cases by the qal perfect of the verb *qārab*. As for the use of *eggizō* in the LXX in general, a large majority of relevant cases seem to favor an imminent-future interpretation. But some cases are unclear, and at least one text (in the Book of Jonah) shows that *eggizō* (but here in the aorist, not the perfect) can, at least by way of exception, bear the sense of "come" or "reach." In Jonah 3:6 we read *kai ēggisen ho logos pros ton basilea tēs Nineuē*: "and the report *came* to [or: reached] the king of Nineveh." As Fuller (*The Mission and Achievement of Jesus*, 21) points out, this usage is unusual in the LXX, and the special meaning is made clear by the context. Moreover, the Hebrew verb in the MT of Jonah 3:6 is not *qārab* ("draw near, approach") but rather *nāgaʿ* ("touch," "reach," "come to"). The sense is spatial rather than temporal, and the terminus of the action is expressed in a prepositional phrase. The last two points obviously do not hold for Mark 1:15. Closer to Mark 1:15 is 1 Macc 9:10: *ei ēggiken ho kairos hēmōn* ("if our time [to die] has come"). But even here one might ask whether the time to die has fully arrived or is simply pressing upon the followers of Judas Maccabeus as extremely imminent. Then, too, notice that it is the *time* to die that has come; *death* itself is still imminent. The parallelism of LXX Ps 118:169–70 argues for the sense of "arrive," "come," or "reach": *eggisatō hē deēsis mou enōpion sou, kyrie. . . . eiselthoi to axiōma mou enōpion sou* ("let my prayer come before you, Lord. . . . may my request enter into your presence"). Another likely candidate for the sense of "arrive" is Lam 4:8: *ēggiken ho kairos hēmōn, eplērōthēsan hai hēmerai hēmōn, parestin ho kairos hēmōn* ("our time has come, our days have been fulfilled, our time is here"). In these two last cases, the Hebrew verb is *qārab*, with the probable (though not absolutely certain) meaning of "arrive," "reach." One must admit, however, that this meaning of *eggizō* in the LXX is the exception rather than the rule.

Interestingly, none of these complexities and difficulties daunts Sato (*Q und Prophetie*, 130), who bravely suggests that *ēggiken* is the translation of the Aramaic *pěʿal* perfect *qrbt* (3d person singular feminine). Sato then goes on to suggest that whoever translated this Aramaic verb by the perfect rather than by the aorist tense in Greek probably desired to emphasize the kingdom that had now become present. In this Schlosser's view (*Le règne de Dieu*, 1. 107–8) is remarkably similar to Sato's: behind *ēggiken* in Mark 1:15 stands *qrb*. Originally in the mouth of Jesus it announced the imminent future, while the early church understood the proclamation in terms of the kingdom's presence. Given all the problems mentioned above, the best one can say is that the suggestion of Schlosser and Sato is neither more nor less probable than a number of other theories.

[163] The reader might ask why I am so diffident about translating *ēggiken* in Mark 1:15 parr. when I was more confident about retroverting *ephthasen* in Luke 11:20 par. There are a number of differences between the two cases: (1) *ēggiken* brings with it the special problem of retroverting a verb in the Greek perfect tense, for which Aramaic has no precise equivalent. (2) Detached from its redactional context, *ēggiken hē basileia tou theou* lacks any context that would help interpret the sense. By the nature of its content, Luke 11:20 enjoys the interpretive context of Jesus' practice of exorcism and the argument about the coming of the kingdom that Jesus draws from this practice. (3) There is a great difference when one comes to the question of what Hebrew or Aramaic verb to choose for retroversion. *phthanō*, in the vast majority of cases, translates

either the Hebrew verb *nāgaʿ* or the Aramaic verb *mĕṭāʾ*, both having roughly the same range of meaning ("reach," "attain to," "touch"). In contrast, *eggizō* translates not only a much wider range of verbs but also at times a prepositional phrase, an adjective, or a noun. In short, *eggizō* is a much more problematic verb to retrovert into Hebrew or Aramaic.

[164] Notice the wording of Crossan (*The Historical Jesus*, 292) when he describes the "sapiential" (as opposed to "apocalyptic") kingdom that Jesus proclaimed: it "imagines how one could live here and now within an already *or always available* divine dominion" (emphasis mine). At this point we are indeed not far from a gnostic Jesus.

[165] The common strategy here was not to deny the coming of the end of the age or the parousia of the Son of Man, but to push back the final event into the indefinite future, while keeping the substance of the promise intact.

[166] Although any judgment based on such a small amount of data remains debatable, it seems probable that, with the exceptions of (1) the second line that I insert into v 23 from Matthew's version and (2) the verb "longed" (Matthew's *epethymēsan*) instead of Luke's "wished" (*ēthelēsan*), Luke represents the original Q form of the logion (similarly Manson, *The Sayings of Jesus*, 80; see also Bultmann, *Geschichte*, 114; Schulz, *Q. Die Spruchquelle der Evangelisten*, 420–21). To take the questions of redaction step-by-step:

1. Redactional contexts. The contexts supplied by the evangelists differ widely. Matthew places the beatitude within the explanation of why Jesus speaks to the crowds in parables but restricts his explanations to his disciples. Luke has Jesus deliver the beatitude in private to his disciples (the seventy-two who have returned from their mission?) right after his intimate prayer of joy and thanksgiving to the Father for having given revelation to "the little ones" (i.e., the disciples) rather than to the "wise and intelligent" (e.g., the lawyers and Pharisees). Shorn of these two redactional settings, the beatitude could have been spoken originally to any audience standing before Jesus (cf. Luke 17:21b). Yet the fact that this audience is felicitated as a type or model of anyone who has the experience of seeing and hearing Jesus ("happy are the eyes [of anyone] that see what you see") may point to the circle of committed disciples. While the form of a beatitude does not demand such an audience, it certainly fits it perfectly.

2. Matthew's *hymōn* in 13:16 ("*your* eyes . . . *your* ears") may be a redactional addition that assimilates the Q saying to his Marcan context (Matt 13:10–17 ‖ Mark 4:10–12). In Matt 13:10–17 the Matthean Jesus sharply distinguishes the crowds (13:2,10) who have refused to see and hear (i.e., believe) from the disciples who do see and hear. The latter group does so because knowledge of the mysteries of the kingdom has been given "to you [i.e., the disciples]" (13:11). Hence it is readily understandable why Matthew in the beatitude would emphasize "*your* eyes" and "*your* ears" as contrasted with the eyes and ears of the crowds that do not see, hear, or understand (13:13).

3. Matthew's redactional context in 13:10–15 may also be responsible for the reading "happy your eyes *because* [*hoti*] they see" instead of Luke's "happy the eyes that see *what* [*ha*] you see." As Beasley-Murray notes (*Jesus and the Kingdom of God*, 358 n. 67, depending on C. F. Burney and Matthew Black), the difference between "because" and "what" could reflect alternate translations of the ambiguous Aramaic word *dĭ* (or *dĕ*), which can be either a causal conjunction or a relative pronoun. While possible, such a theory is not necessary to explain Matthew's editing. Matthew's "because" echoes perfectly the redactional change he has made just a few verses earlier in his Marcan text. While Mark 4:12 introduces the quotation of Isa 6:9–10 with a conjunction indicating purpose (*hina*, "in order that . . . they may not see"), Matthew changes the conjunction (in 13:13) to the same causal conjunction he also uses in the beatitude in 13:16 (*hoti*,

"because . . . they do not see"). The same neat redactional link between the Q beatitude and the immediate context is not apparent in Luke.

4. The second line of the beatitude in Matt 13:16 (referring to the disciples' ears that hear) is difficult to judge, since there are arguments both for and against its inclusion in the Q form. Since we already suspect that Matthew is assimilating 13:16 to the larger context, the reference to ears hearing as well as eyes seeing could easily come from the two citations of Isaiah where seeing and hearing are put in parallel position four times within three verses (Matt 13:13,14,15). Nevertheless, there is a consideration arising from the very structure of the Q beatitude that militates against this argument. As I argue in the main text, the beatitude in Matt 13:16–17 par. has a structure built on synonymous and antithetical parallelism. The presence of "ears" in v 16 would fit both the parallelism within the verse and the parallelism between the two verses. Luke may well have omitted the material in Matt 13:16b for stylistic reasons: he felt that the repetition of so many similar phrases and metaphors in two successive verses was clumsy and tiresome for Greek literary taste. I readily admit that neither side in the argument has a clear edge; hence I put Matt 13:16b in brackets when I add it to the end of Luke 10:23. It is not surprising that on the one hand Beasley-Murray (*Jesus and the Kingdom of God*, 84) includes Matt 13:16b in the Q saying, while on the other Havener (*Q. The Sayings of Jesus*, 131) omits it.

5. Matthew's "amen" at the beginning of Matt 13:17 is also difficult to judge. The Gospels give us examples of Matthew adding and of Luke omitting the word in Jesus' sayings. Hence I leave the word in brackets. In any case, it simply adds further to the solemn emphasis of "I say to you." In favor of "amen" being in the Q document's version of the saying is Fitzmyer, *The Gospel According to Luke*, 2. 875; against (though not without hesitation), Schulz, *Q. Die Spruchquelle der Evangelisten*, 420 (also n. 112).

6. While scholars are divided on the issue, I think it more likely that Matthew substituted "righteous men" (*dikaioi*) for Q's "kings" (*basileis*), which is retained by Luke. The word-field of "just, justice, justify" is important to both Matthew and Luke (while being largely absent in Mark and John), and so a decision between "kings" and "righteous men" is not easy. Still, Matthew's Gospel uses the adjective "just" (*dikaios*) more often (seventeen times) than any other book in the NT; moreover, *dikaios* and *dikaiosynē* represent key concepts in Matthew's overall theological vision of morality, eschatology, and salvation history. It may not be sheer coincidence that twice elsewhere in material that betrays his redactional hand Matthew presents righteous men joined to prophets (10:41; 23:29; see Manson, *The Sayings of Jesus*, 80). In contrast, it is in a Q text that Matthew mentions a prophet alongside a monarch (Matt 12:41–42 ‖ Luke 11:31–32). In addition, "kings" goes well with "prophets" as a group of concrete, specific historical figures in Israel's past history recorded in the Scriptures. The kings appear alongside of the prophets not because the former were so admirable as a group but because, along with prophets, they summarize the salvation history of Israel in its thrust forward to fulfillment; Gnilka (*Jesus von Nazaret*, 152) points in particular to King David, the supposed author of the Book of Psalms. "Righteous men" were present at the time of Jesus just as they were in Israel's past; the word "kings" conjures up much better that sacred past. For a different view, see Beasley-Murray, *Jesus and the Kingdom of God*, 84. I consider farfetched the suggestion by McNeile (*The Gospel According to St. Matthew*, 192) that the difference between Matthew and Luke is due to a confusion between the Aramaic *yšryn* ("the upright," "the righteous") and the Aramaic *šryn* ("princes," "leaders"; the Hebrew equivalent [*śār*] is translated as "king" [*basileus*] in the codex Vaticanus text of 3 Kgdms 22:26); Matthew's redactional interest is a much simpler explanation.

For a highly speculative tradition history that derives the phrase "many prophets and kings" from the fourth song of the servant of Yahweh in Deutero-Isaiah, see Werner Grimm, "Selige Augenzeugen, Luk. 10,23f. Alttestamentlicher Hintergrund und ursprünglicher Sinn," *TZ* 26 (1970) 172–83. Grimm tries to extract "many prophets and kings" from the reference to "many nations . . . [and] kings" in Isa 52:15: "Thus shall he [the servant] startle many nations and because of him *kings* shall shut their mouths [i.e., stand speechless]; for those who have not been told shall *see*, and those who have not *heard* shall understand." Supposedly Jesus spoke of "many nations and kings," but later Christian tradition missed the reference to Isaiah and changed the wording. I find this unlikely, though a somewhat similar position is supported by David Noel Freedman in a letter to me dated April 29, 1992. Freedman suggests that, while the prophets are indeed those of Israel, the kings should be understood as the kings of the nations who play a considerable role in the prophecies and poetry of the OT. Freedman feels much more confident than I that behind the beatitude lies an allusion to the suffering servant in Isa 52:15. However, the lack of prophets alongside of kings in Isa 52:15, the fact that "see" and "heard" are not in truly parallel positions, and the absence of any discernible allusion to the suffering servant in the Q beatitude on eyewitnesses make me dubious of the allusion to Isa 52:15. More generally, I think that a statement like "many Israelite prophets and pagan kings longed to see what you see" involves a strange type of ecumenical gathering. Hence I take the view that both "prophets" and "kings" refer to the great figures of Israel's past.

7. There is not much difference between Matthew's *epethymēsan* ("longed," "desired") and Luke's *ēthelēsan* ("wished, wanted"). The one other time Matthew uses the verb *epithymeō* (5:28), it carries the pejorative sense of lusting for a woman who is not one's wife. At the same time, Matthew uses the verb *thelō* more often than any other book in the NT (42 times to Luke's 28 times in his Gospel). Hence it is unlikely that Matthew would have gone out of his way to alter a verb he employs quite often in favor of a verb he uses only once elsewhere, and there in a pejorative sense. As for Luke, he uses the word *epithymeō* in his Gospel four times in a variety of contexts (twice in a neutral or secular sense, twice in a positive religious sense), as well as once in Acts. In contrast, he uses *thelō* not only 28 times in his Gospel but also 14 times in Acts. Thus, it is not surprising that Luke substituted for the relatively rare *epithymeō* a verb he employed much more often. While none of these considerations is strictly probative, taken together they incline me to conjecture that Matthew's relatively rare and emphatic *epithymeō* is original, and Luke's common and bland *thelō* is secondary (so Schulz, *Q. Die Spruchquelle der Evangelisten*, 420).

The original unity of Luke 10:23–24 is supported by the special pattern of beatitude it exhibits, which is typical of Jesus. Against the idea that v 24 was originally a separate saying is Sato, *Q und Prophetie*, 260 n. 464; similarly, Hoffmann, *Studien*, 210; Schulz, *Q. Die Spruchquelle der Evangelisten*, 421.

[167] Here one must distinguish carefully between form and content. Strictly speaking, the form of the beatitude in Luke 10:23 is in the 3d person plural: "Happy are the eyes that see what you see." But obviously this is simply a poetic way of saying: "Happy are you who see." Hence the beatitude is effectively (in its meaning) if not formally (in its wording) in the 2d person plural. On this see Sato, *Q und Prophetie*, 260.

[168] Jeremias (*New Testament Theology*, 14–20) claims that the authentic sayings of Jesus show a preference for antithetical parallelism, since it is found in all four strata in the Synoptic tradition (Mark, Q, M, and L) and is more or less equally distributed among the four strata. Jeremias (p. 15 n. 2) lists Matt 13:16–17 ‖ Luke 10:23–24 as one of the 34 instances of antithetical parallelism in the Q material.

[169] On this point Sato's comment (*Q und Prophetie*, 261) needs further nuance. He

notes that because the experience of the time of salvation is declared to be already present, "therefore the eschatological *hoti* is lacking." But a different sort of explanatory eschatological clause is to be found in Luke 10:24, introduced by "for I say to you that. . . ." This clause, like the *hoti* clause in the Q beatitudes of the Sermon, supplies an eschatological grounding for the beatitude; but now the grounding refers to realized as opposed to future eschatology.

[170] Granted the general nature of the beatitude in Luke 10:23–24, it would probably be a mistake to restrict what the audience *sees* to miracles alone. Other striking actions of Jesus (e.g., table fellowship with tax collectors and sinners, accepting women as disciples) may also be included.

[171] See my comments on the *Psalms of Solomon* in Chapter 14. Comparison with the *Psalms of Solomon* is a commonplace in the interpretation of Luke 10:23–24 par.; see, e.g., Beasley-Murray, *Jesus and the Kingdom of God*, 84–85; Grimm, "Selige Augenzeugen," 173–74.

[172] See the comment of Manson, *The Sayings of Jesus*, 80: "The point of the saying is that what for all former generations lay still in the future is now a present reality. What was for the best men of the past only an object of faith and hope is now matter of present experience." For a similar interpretation, see Kümmel, *Promise and Fulfilment*, 112–13.

[173] So Gnilka, *Jesus von Nazaret*, 152.

[174] See Fuller, *The Mission and Achievement of Jesus*, 34. Fuller's interpretation serves as a good example of a type of exegesis that avoids any kind of realized eschatology in the sayings of Jesus by regularly importing such words as "signs" and "dawning" into texts that do not contain them.

[175] Bultmann, *Geschichte*, 133, 135; so also Hoffmann, *Studien*, 38, 210; Sato, *Q und Prophetie*, 261; Gnilka, *Jesus von Nazaret*, 152. Merklein (*Jesu Botschaft*, 66) remains doubtful about the saying's authenticity, though he thinks that it correctly reflects the eschatological situation proclaimed by Jesus.

[176] Even in the exceptional case of Luke 11:20, Jesus' self-reference ("If by the finger of God I cast out the demons . . .") is in the conditional clause, the main clause being reserved for the proclamation of the kingdom's arrival.

[177] There are a number of other sayings attributed to Jesus in the Gospels that are brought forward by various scholars as examples of authentic logia that demonstrate that Jesus proclaimed the kingdom of God as already present in his ministry. I do not consider them in the main text because I am doubtful of their authenticity and/or their effectiveness in showing that Jesus viewed the kingdom as somehow already present. Chief among these dubious candidates are:

(1) Mark 4:11 (Jesus tells his disciples why he speaks to the crowds in parables): "To you has been given the mystery of the kingdom of God; but to those outside everything is enigmatic [literally: all things happen in parables]." I agree with Jeremias (*The Parables of Jesus*, 13–18), Beasley-Murray (*Jesus and the Kingdom of God*, 103), and many other exegetes that Mark 4:11 (and indeed the whole pericope 4:10–12) did not originally belong to its present context as part of the explanation of the parable of the sower. That at least 4:11, if not the whole of 4:10–12, is pre-Marcan tradition rather than Marcan redaction seems likely. But none of the arguments put forward by exegetes proves, in my view, that the saying goes back to the historical Jesus. It is telling that Pesch, who has such a positive view of the historical reliability of a good deal of the material in Mark, considers it likely that Mark 4:11–12 originates not in Jesus' ministry

but in the mission of the early church. It was the church, not Jesus, that used the vocabulary of "mystery," saw itself on the "inside" and everyone else "outside," and developed a theory of God's "hardening" of Israel to explain the relative failure of its mission to the Jews; see Pesch, *Das Markusevangelium*, 1. 238–39. More to the point, though, I fail to see why, even if 4:11 were authentic, it would demonstrate that Jesus thought that the kingdom was already present. All the logion need mean is that Jesus gives clear instruction on the kingdom to his disciples in private, while using only riddle-like speech (and perhaps actions) when dealing with his larger audience. I do not see how this necessarily shows that the kingdom is already present.

(2) Luke 4:16–30 (Jesus' inaugural sermon in the synagogue at Nazareth): After reading Isa 61:1–2 + 58:6 on the release God gives captives when the eschatological Jubilee Year arrives, Jesus declares: "Today this scripture passage has been fulfilled even as you listened to it" (4:21). While the phrase "kingdom of God" does not appear, the basic idea of God's royal power at work in the present moment to free the imprisoned and the exiled is certainly affirmed. My problem with this pericope is that I incline to the view that Luke's scene of Jesus' inaugural sermon at Nazareth is the result of Luke's creative redaction of Mark's story of Jesus in Nazareth in Mark 6:1–6. For my reasons for holding this view, see Volume One of *A Marginal Jew*, 269–71, with the accompanying notes. It is perhaps significant that most of Beasley-Murray's treatment of Luke 4:16–30 (*Jesus and the Kingdom of God*, 85–91) deals with the Isaiah text that is cited, its midrashic reworking in the Melchizedek fragment from Qumran (11QMelch), and a running commentary on the Lucan text. Nowhere is there any detailed argumentation that the key verse (4:21: "Today this scripture passage has been fulfilled even as you listened to it") comes from the historical Jesus. Both Bultmann (*Geschichte*, 31) and Fitzmyer (*The Gospel According to Luke*, 1. 526–27) apparently consider it more likely that 4:21 comes from Luke's own pen. I do not claim that I can prove that position, but I do not think that the opposite position can be proven either. We are in the galling category of the *non liquet*.

(3) Luke 10:18 (Jesus' reply to the seventy-two disciples returning from their mission and reporting their successful exorcisms of demons): "I saw [literally: was seeing] Satan like lightning falling from heaven." Although some authors argue for the placement of this saying, and indeed the whole of Luke 10:17–20, in the Q document (so Marshall, *The Gospel of Luke*, 427–28, following Schürmann), the lack of a precise parallel demands that the text be labeled L. Luke 10:18 was most likely a stray logion that Luke or pre-Lucan tradition joined to other sayings to construct this short pericope about the seventy-two disciples returning triumphant to Jesus, who comments on their success; on this see Hoffmann, *Studien*, 248–54. In the present context Jesus, either using a dramatic metaphor or referring cryptically to a vision he has had, interprets the disciples' successful exorcisms by employing the apocalyptic scenario of Satan, the great adversary and accuser of God's people, being cast out of heaven in defeat. Satan's power over Israel has been broken, and by implication God's kingly rule has been established. In the Lucan context, therefore, 10:18 does imply the presence of the kingdom of God in the ministry of Jesus and his disciples. However, what the logion meant as a stray saying is more difficult to determine. Moreover, despite the lengthy presentation of Ulrich B. Müller in favor of authenticity ("Vision und Botschaft. Erwägungen zur prophetischen Struktur der Verkündigung Jesu," *ZTK* 74 [1977] 416–48; cf. Merklein, *Jesu Botschaft*, 60; Kümmel, *Promise and Fulfilment*, 113–14), I do not find the argument for authenticity convincing. Indeed, there is an inner conflict in Müller's reasoning. He first tries to show from the Fourth Gospel and Acts that Luke 10:18 is discontinuous with early Christian thought on the subject of Satan's expulsion. But then Müller calls upon Rev 12:7–12 as a major parallel that illumines the sense of Luke 10:18. This move

exposes a major weakness in his whole argument. Why could not 10:18 originate in the same stream of early apocalyptic Christianity that is also the ultimate source of the tradition used in Rev 12:7–12? Interestingly, Müller argues for the authenticity of 10:18 on the grounds that its perspective is wholly theo-logical, not christo-logical. Yet the same thing could be said of the tradition behind Rev 12:7–12, when taken in isolation (which is what Müller is doing with 10:18). Müller's attempt to situate the saying in the life of Jesus (it reflects the personal experience that caused Jesus to leave the Baptist and start his own independent preaching mission) comes close to the psychologizing of the 19th-century "liberal lives." Even more imaginative on this point is Jeremias (*New Testament Theology*, 73–74), who, however, does not see Luke 10:18 as meaning that the kingdom has already come. As with the other sayings considered here, I do not assert that I can demonstrate that Luke 10:18 does not come from the historical Jesus. I am simply saying that I do not see strong reasons for affirming the opposite. The cautious statement of Fitzmyer (*The Gospel According to Luke*, 2. 859) speaks volumes: "If we admit that the original sense of v. 18 is irretrievably lost, the strangeness of the saying may be the best reason for ascribing it to Jesus himself." Gnilka (*Jesus von Nazaret*, 137 n. 55) also shows himself reserved on the whole question. Hence, like Bultmann (*Geschichte*, 174, 176) I remain unsure whether the apocalyptic saying proclaiming triumph over evil in Luke 10:18 comes from Jesus or from some early Christian.

[178] The so-called minor agreements of Matthew and Luke against Mark in this pericope do not point to either a variant tradition in Q or some other solution to the Synoptic problem. The two significant minor agreements are (1) the omission of the setting of the scene in Mark 2:18a ("and the disciples of John and the Pharisees were fasting") and (2) the omission of the affirmative statement of Jesus (as opposed to his rhetorical question) in v 19b ("as long as they have the bridegroom with them they cannot fast"). Both omissions are readily explainable on the same grounds. Both sentences omitted by Matthew and Luke duplicate statements made in other sentences in the Marcan form of the story. Indeed, the omitted sentences are parade examples of "Marcan duality." It is hardly surprising that Matthew and Luke, as is their wont, keep only one form of a sentence for the sake of a less repetitive style. The other differences found in either Matthew or Luke are easily explained by the redactional tendencies of each evangelist. Hence Matthew and Luke are both dependent on Mark, who is the sole literary source for the story. The failure to realize this hobbles the learned essay of André Feuillet, "La controverse sur le jeûne (Mc 2, 18–20; Mt 9, 14–15; Lc 5, 33–35)," *NRT* 90 (1968) 113–36, 252–77. Relying on the Synoptic theory of L. Vaganay (which champions the priority of a hypothetical Aramaic Matthew), Feuillet reaches such unlikely conclusions as the primitive nature of Matthew's "mourn" (*penthein* in Matt 9:15) over Mark's (and Luke's) *nēsteuein* (Mark 2:19 ‖ Luke 5:34). In contrast, a good defense of Marcan priority is given by Karl T. Schäfer, " '. . . und dann werden sie fasten, an jenem Tage' (Mk 2,20 und Parallelen)," *Synoptische Studien* (Alfred Wikenhauser Festschrift; ed. Josef Schmid and Anton Vögtle; Munich/Freiburg: Zink, 1953) 124–47, esp. 125–27.

There is an intriguing corollary to accepting Marcan priority in the case of the question on fasting (Mark 2:18–20 parr.). Our tradition- and redaction-critical observations in this section will lead us to the conclusion that v 18a and v 19b are probably additions made to the original unit by the pre-Marcan tradition or by Mark himself. Once again, we see in Matthew and Luke's redaction the paradox that we have also noted in the *Gospel of Thomas*: later pruning by redactors who wish to omit material because of their theological or stylistic preferences may result in these redactors inadvertently producing a text that by accident coincides with the primitive form of the tradition. Obviously, this does not prove that the later redactors actually knew the primitive tradition.

[179] For the history of this Marcan pericope within the subsequent tradition of the patristic and medieval church, see Franz Gerhard Cremer, *Die Fastenansage Jesu* (BBB 23; Bonn: Hanstein, 1965); idem, " 'Die Söhne des Brautgemachs' (Mk 2, 19 parr) in der griechischen und lateinischen Schrifterklärung," *BZ* 11 (1967) 246–53; idem, "Lukanisches Sondergut zum Fastenstreitgespräch," *TTZ* 76 (1967) 129–54; idem, *Der Beitrag Augustins zur Auslegung des Fastenstreitgesprächs (Mk 2, 18–22 parr) und der Einfluss seiner Exegese auf die mittelalterliche Theologie* (Paris: Etudes Augustiniennes, 1971).

[180] Literally in Greek "the sons of the bridal chamber" (*hoi huioi tou nymphōnos*), i.e., either wedding guests in general or (in the context of Mark 2:19) more specifically the best friends of the bridegroom, the friends whom he has invited to the wedding to assist him at the ceremony and the festivities. Here we have a clear case of a Semitism; the Hebrew equivalent that the Greek phrase translates literally is *běnê ha-ḥuppâ* (see Str-B, 1. 500; Joachim Jeremias, "*nymphē, nymphios*," *TDNT* 4 [1967] 1099–1106, esp. 1103 n. 40; Fitzmyer, *The Gospel According to Luke*, 1. 598).

[181] In the Greek text this rhetorical question is introduced with the interrogative particle *mē*, which indicates that the expected answer to the question is either certainly or probably no. One could translate: "The best friends of the bridegroom cannot fast when the bridegroom is with them, can they?" But since this results in an awkward sentence in English, I prefer to omit the negative in my translation. I think the rhetorical nature of the question and the expectation of a negative response are clear enough from the content and the context.

[182] Almost all commentators admit that the following double-metaphors of the new patch and the new wine (Mark 2:21–22), whatever their ultimate origin, did not belong originally to the tradition about fasting in 2:18–20. The concrete subject matter of 2:18–20 (i.e., divergent customs of fasting among various groups of Jewish disciples), the implicit role of Jesus as bridegroom, and the metaphor of a wedding all differ notably from the very general message about the incompatibility of new versus old, symbolized by metaphors quite dissimilar from that of a wedding. Neither Jesus, his disciples, nor various Jewish groups that might be contrasted with them figure explicitly in 2:21–22. Indeed, it may well be that vv 21–22 are secular proverbs that were used secondarily either by Jesus or by the early church to illustrate the contrast between old and new. Backhaus (*Jüngerkreise*, 149) remains unsure whether vv 21–22 come from Jesus or first-generation Christianity. In any event, vv 21–22 have nothing to do with whatever authentic Jesus-material lies behind vv 18–20.

[183] As usual, opinions differ among critics as to whether we should attribute the final form of this artistic whole to Mark the creative redactor (so Joanna Dewey, *Markan Public Debate* [SBLDS 48; Chico, CA: Scholars, 1980]) or to Mark the conservative redactor who took over a pre-Marcan collection of dispute stories (so Pesch, *Das Markusevangelium*, 1. 170). Strongly against any idea of a pre-Marcan collection of dispute stories, even of smaller compass than the present 2:1–3:6, is Jarmo Kiilunen, *Die Vollmacht im Widerstreit. Untersuchungen zum Werdegang von Mk 2,1–3,6* (Annales Academiae Scientiarum Fennicae, Dissertationes Humanarum Litterarum 40; Helsinki: Suomalainen Tiedeakatemia, 1985) 249–66.

[184] Jeremias ("*nymphē, nymphios*," 1101–3) claims that the metaphor of bridegroom is used for the Messiah neither in the OT nor in later Judaism. Agreeing with this view, J. B. Muddiman ("Jesus and Fasting. Mark 2. 18–22," *Jésus aux origines de la christologie*

[BETL 40; ed. J. Dupont; Leuven: Leuven University; Gembloux: Duculot, 1975] 271–81, esp. 277–79) goes on to suggest that Jesus is alluding to Joel 2:16 ("Let the bridegroom go forth from his chamber"). To support this view Muddiman must maintain that the original form of Mark 2:20 really spoke in the active voice of the bridegroom going out from the bridal chamber (symbolizing Jesus' departure from Galilee and the journey to Jerusalem); later on the verb was changed to the passive *aparthē* to create an allusion to Isa 53:8. All this is farfetched and arbitrary; like a number of other commentators on this passage, Muddiman wants to rewrite the text to make it fit his theory.

For Jesus as bridegroom (with use of the noun *nymphios*), see, besides this pericope and its Synoptic parallels, Matt 25:1,5,6,10 (the parable of the ten virgins); John 2:1–12 (at Cana Jesus is symbolically the bridegroom of the wedding feast, hence the *nymphios* of the story remains anonymous and never speaks); 3:29 (three times, in the Baptist's explanation of Jesus' superiority). The Book of Revelation implicitly presents the risen Jesus as the eschatological bridegroom of the new Jerusalem (the church of the last days) in Rev 21:2,9; 22:17. We hear of the wedding of the lamb and his wedding feast in Rev 19:7,9. The relationship of Christ and his church is compared to that of a husband and his bride or wife in 2 Cor 11:2; and more extensively in Eph 5:22–33. A similar metaphor is applied to Yahweh and Israel in the OT, especially in the prophets; see, e.g., Hos 2:4–25; 3:1–3; Isa 1:21; 50:1; 54:1–8; 62:4–5; Jer 2:2; 3:1–10; Ezek 16:1–34; 23:1–49. We have here a prime example of how metaphors and titles applied to God in the OT were reapplied to Jesus in the NT. One is left to wonder whether the simple metaphor in Mark 2:19a acted as a catalyst in the early church, fostering the development of the image of bridegroom as applied to Jesus.

Against the consensus that "bridegroom" was not used of the Messiah or some other eschatological human figure in early Judaism is William H. Brownlee, "Messianic Motifs of Qumran and the New Testament," *NTS* 3 (1956–57) 12–30, 195–210, esp. 205. Brownlee tries to show from 1QIsaᵃ 61:10 that at Qumran "bridegroom" was applied to the messianic high priest, "the Messiah of Aaron" expected in the last days. Brownlee thinks that the Qumranites purposely changed the text of Isa 61:10 to read: "He has covered me with the robe of righteousness, as a bridegroom, as a priest, with a garland." Brownlee sees this text as an illuminating parallel to the NT passages where Jesus is presented as a bridegroom or as a priest. Rightly critical of Brownlee's highly speculative thesis is Joachim Gnilka, " 'Bräutigam'—spätjüdisches Messiasprädikat?" *TTZ* 69 (1960) 298–301. Gnilka notes that the MT of Isa 61:10 hardly makes sense as it stands and is often emended. The reading in 1QIsaᵃ 61:10 may be only another example of attempts to clarify this difficult text; the metaphor that is added, "like a priest," is simply part of this process of clarification. Nothing indicates that the priestly Messiah of the end time is intended.

[185] The attempt by Schäfer (" '. . . und dann werden sie fasten,' " 140–41) to interpret "fasting" in Jesus' answer in a metaphorical rather than literal sense must be rejected for a number of reasons: (1) Granted, both "wedding guests" (= "sons of the bridal chamber") and "bridegroom" are metaphors in Jesus' reply. Nevertheless, "fasting," the very point of the pericope, stands in its literal sense at the beginning of the whole story and runs through the whole story as a structuring key word. There is nothing to indicate that at some point the word suddenly changes its meaning from literal to metaphorical. The flow of the pericope makes sense only if "fast" retains throughout the pericope the meaning it had at the beginning of the pericope. (2) Schäfer is influenced too much by patristic exegesis on the one hand and Matthew's redactional *penthein* (Matt 9:15) on the other. (3) His interpretation seems ultimately directed by an apologetic desire to affirm that the entire pericope comes from the

historical Jesus. Schäfer is followed in his metaphorical interpretation by Jürgen Roloff, *Das Kerygma und der irdische Jesus* (Göttingen: Vandenhoeck & Ruprecht, 1970) 233.

[186] Schäfer (" '. . . und dann werden sie fasten,' " 140) is right to see "on that day" as meaning the same thing as "the days" at the beginning of the verse; so too Charles E. Carlston, *The Parables of the Triple Tradition* (Philadelphia: Fortress, 1975) 119–20. Georg Braumann (" 'An jenem Tag,' Mk 2, 20," *NovT* 6 [1963] 264–67) tries to interpret "on that day" as referring to the last judgment and "days shall come" as referring to the messianic woes preceding the last judgment. His exegesis is forced, suffering as it does from a lack of a detailed exegesis of the whole pericope, which might serve as a control on his imaginative interpretation of a few words.

[187] The point is the absence of the visible, physical presence of Jesus from his disciples in the time between his death and his parousia. This in no way contradicts the belief, no doubt held by the evangelists (see, e.g., Matt 28:16–20) that in some spiritual way the risen Jesus remains present to his church. Because he misses this point, J. A. Ziesler ("The Removal of the Bridegroom: A Note on Mark II. 18–22 and Parallels," *NTS* 19 [1972–73] 190–94) develops the contorted theory that it is the Pharisees who are like men who have had the bridegroom taken away from them and who therefore are like mourners who fast. This is a prime example of ignoring the obvious sense of a text in favor of a most unlikely and artificial one.

[188] Various commentators have read a particular reference into "that day," e.g., a weekly fast on Fridays, an annual fast at Passover, or an annual fast on Good Friday or Holy Saturday; see Backhaus (*Jüngerkreise*, 147 n. 205) for various opinions. Guelich (*Mark 1–8:26*, 113) argues forcefully against taking "on that day" to refer to some particular day of liturgical observance, and I agree with his position. Granted the inclusion (and presumably parallel meaning) created by "days shall come" at the beginning of v 20a and "on that day" at the end of v 20b, both phrases may simply carry the general sense of eschatological prophecy—in this case, ominous—found in the OT prophets. Apparently both Matthew and Luke took the two phrases as synonymous, since Matt 9:15 simply drops "on that day" and Luke 5:35 changes it to "in those days" to make the reference back to "days shall come" clearer. If "on that day" had referred to a particular annual or weekly observance, one would have thought that the evangelists who belonged to later and more structured churches would have kept it. One might also note that *Did.* 8:1 does not correspond perfectly to Mark's "on that day" (interpreted as a particular day of observance), for the *Didache* speaks not of one but of two days of fasting each week.

One further point worth noting for Marcan scholarship: both the "taking away" of the bridegroom and the fasting of the disciples are prophesied as taking place in an eschatological future and are thus qualified as eschatological events. Hence, the time when the disciples fast is not "empty time" devoid of meaning for the eschatological drama.

[189] Guelich (*Mark 1–8:26*, 113–14) tries to avoid the sharp contrast between two practices (not fasting and fasting) observed by Jesus' disciples in two different time periods; he focuses instead on the christology of the passage. While a christological theme is present (Jesus as bridegroom present and absent), the christological aspect of the pericope has a subordinate role, functioning as the justification for the practice of Jesus' disciples "then and now," which is the main point of the pericope. As we have seen, all the rhetorical structures of the Marcan composition point in this direction.

[190] The cycle of Galilean dispute stories is made up of five major pericopes: (1) the healing of the paralytic, 2:1–12; (2) the call of Levi and the meal with toll collectors

and sinners, 2:13–17; (3) the question about fasting (plus the two metaphors of the patch and the wineskins), 2:18–22; (4) the plucking of grain on the Sabbath, 2:23–28; and (5) the healing of the man with the withered hand, 3:1–6. Standing as it does as the third of the five pericopes, the question about fasting enjoys the middle position in the cycle.

[191] On this see Guelich, *Mark 1–8:26*, 108.

[192] As Roloff observes (*Das Kerygma*, 233), the interpretative addition of 2:19b–20 shows us that the early church (indeed, probably the pre-Marcan church of the first generation) was capable of looking back at the past earthly life of Jesus and distinguishing it theologically and practically from the situation in which it lived. That the early church could not distinguish or did not desire to distinguish between the earthly Jesus and the risen Lord—and the corresponding situations of his original disciples and the later church—does not stand up to the close scrutiny of such passages as Mark 2:18–20.

[193] It is only when Mark 2:18–20 is placed within the larger complex of dispute stories in Mark 2:1–3:6 that it partakes of the increasingly negative and hostile tone that leads to the first occasion in Mark's Gospel when people plot to put Jesus to death (3:6). Only in this larger context is Pesch's designation of 2:18–20 as a "dispute story" or "controversy dialogue" (*Streitgespräch*) correct (*Das Markusevangelium*, 1. 171). Taken by itself, it is not. Alone among the stories in 2:1–3:6, no real or potential adversaries of Jesus (scribes, Pharisees, or Herodians, as in 2:6,16,24; 3:6) appear in 2:18–20 to object to what he or his disciples do. Rather, unnamed persons, who could be either merely curious bystanders or people sincerely interested in religious questions, notice the difference in practice and ask Jesus for its reason. (Unlike most dispute stories, the questionable or potentially offensive action of Jesus or his disciples is not mentioned at the beginning of the story; here what is mentioned at the beginning is what other pious people do.) If the pericope is taken by itself, no tone of hostility is perceivable. Hence, although Bultmann (*Geschichte*, 17) treats the pericope in his section on dispute stories and scholarly dialogues, he denies that the pericope fits the style of a dispute story. For him, the basic question and counterquestion qualify as an apophthegm. Dibelius (*Formgeschichte*, 40) considers the pericope a fairly pure form of what he calls a paradigm. For Taylor (*The Gospel According to St. Mark*, 208) it is a pronouncement story.
  In light of the relatively neutral tone of the story's beginning, it is to be regretted that a number of commentators allow their exegesis to be skewed by speaking in undifferentiated fashion of "the adversaries" who supposedly demand that Jesus' disciples adhere to the practices of the disciples of John and the Pharisees; so, e.g., Schäfer, " '. . . und dann werden sie fasten,' " 124–47. Such language introduces into the story a polemical tone it does not have.

[194] In a letter to me dated April 29, 1992, David Noel Freedman suggests an objection to seeing Mark 2:20 as a reference to a legitimation of the general practice of fasting in the church, a legitimation that asserted that Christ the bridegroom had been taken away from the church by his death and that therefore the church should fast. As Freedman points out, many texts in the NT see the time of the church as a time of the presence of the risen, triumphant Christ in his church, a time when Christ's Spirit enlivens the church and sends it on mission, a time when the kingdom of God has entered upon a more advanced stage of its realization. Given this joyful, positive vision of the presence of the risen Christ to his church, how could the early church justify a resumption of fasting on such lugubrious grounds as the claim that Christ the bridegroom had been taken away from the church by his death?
  The answer to this problem lies in distinguishing carefully various streams of NT

tradition and the various ways in which they evaluate the "time of the church" between Jesus' death-resurrection and his awaited parousia. To be sure, the Gospels of Matthew, Luke, and John all see the time of the church as a time of Christ's real but hidden presence in the community. Matthew's Gospel ends with the risen Jesus not going away from his church but coming to it, to be with it all days until the end of the world (Matt 28:16–20). Luke indeed has Jesus visibly ascend to the Father, but only so that he may send the church the promised gift of the Holy Spirit to guide it on its world-wide mission (Luke 24:44–53; Acts 1–2). Moreover, the risen Jesus himself appears or speaks to various people (e.g., Paul, Ananias) in the Acts of the Apostles; he is not simply "out of the picture." For John, after the resurrection the Holy Spirit plays the special role of the Paraclete, the presence of Jesus when Jesus is absent (e.g., John 16:5–15), as Raymond E. Brown has pointed out so well (*The Gospel According to John*, 2. 1139). In the Pauline epistles there is likewise a lively sense of the present rule of the risen Christ over the church (his body) and the world, along with an almost mystical vision of Christ dwelling in the individual believer.

Methodologically, it is extremely important not to import these theological interpretations of the time of the church into the Gospel of Mark or pre-Marcan tradition, where they are by no means so prominent. Needless to say, the post-Easter community envisioned in Mark's Gospel is not totally bereft of the presence of Christ. His words of instruction (enshrined in the Gospel; cf. Mark 1:1), the insignificant members of the community (the child in 9:37), the celebration of the Lord's Supper (14:22–25), and the Holy Spirit speaking through the inspired witnesses of the church (13:11) all mediate his presence. But, compared with the intense sense of Christ's presence seen in Matthew, Luke, John, and Paul, Mark does seem less emphatic about the joyful presence of Christ during the period between cross-resurrection and parousia. This may well be due to the early date of the pre-Marcan tradition and even Mark's Gospel, a date when the parousia was still felt to be quite imminent (within the present generation, cf. Mark 9:1; 13:30) and when therefore reflection on the continued presence of Christ in his church before the parousia was less of a pressing concern. A church subjected to trials and persecution as it eagerly awaits the imminent return of its Messiah might be a church that would evaluate the present moment less positively, a church that would therefore see a place for fasting to indicate a time of relative absence in between the two types of Christ's presence: provisional-earthly and definitive-heavenly. Hence, I do not see a great problem in Mark 2:20, which sees the "in-between time" of the church as a time when the friends of the bridegroom are deprived of his visible presence and when they therefore fast in longing and eager expectation of his imminent return. It may not be purely accidental that no later NT tradition provides an exact parallel to this stark Marcan idea.

[195] Backhaus (*Jüngerkreise*, 144) holds that the impersonal plural of the verb (in the historical present) is the sort of beginning one would expect in an isolated story circulating in the oral tradition. The periphrastic imperfect tense of v 18a with its specific subjects comes instead from Marcan redaction, which seeks to set the traditional story in a concrete situation. Such a concrete individual situation does not really fit the general rule Jesus intimates in v 19a, a rule that holds for his public ministry as a whole. Thus, says Backhaus, the redactional attempt to create one concrete situation actually distorts the broader issue raised by the original question in 18cd. As Pesch notes (*Das Markusevangelium*, 1. 171 n. 2), even in the Marcan form of the story, "they come and say" (v 18b) has an impersonal sense. If the disciples of John and/or the Pharisees were the inquirers, the question would naturally read, "Why do *we* fast . . . ?" This is what Matt 9:14 does when Matthew rewrites Mark 2:18 to make the disciples of John the inquirers. Hence I am dubious of Kiilunen's suggestion (*Die Vollmacht*, 167) that in the

Marcan form of the story the inquirers are the scribes of the Pharisees who appear in the previous pericope (2:16).

[196] Here is not the place to launch a full-scale discussion of who the Pharisees were in the early 1st century A.D.; see the careful treatment by Sanders, *Judaism: Practice & Belief*, 380–451.

[197] The phrase "the scribes of the Pharisees" is the most likely of the proposed readings in Mark 2:16, since it is attested by early and reliable manuscripts (including Sinaiticus and Vaticanus), is the *lectio difficilior* (the phrase is unique in the NT, but cf. Acts 23:9), and easily explains the other readings, which arose by way of correction to provide a more readily intelligible text (most corrections supply the common Synoptic phrase "the scribes and the Pharisees"). On the textual question see Metzger, *A Textual Commentary*, 78.

[198] I purposely use vague and generic language here to describe the situation in the decades immediately following A.D. 70. This is not the place to enter into the complicated debates about (1) the extent to which the Pharisees as a group survived the First Jewish War and the destruction of Jerusalem (A.D. 70) to begin the reformulation of Judaism according to their program and (2) the exact nature of the relationship between the Pharisees and the post-A.D.-70 rabbis who ultimately created or shaped the corpus of traditions we call the Mishna and the Talmud. Various scholars use different sets of terms to describe the pre- and post-A.D. 70 period. For example, E. P. Sanders uses "Pharisee" for a member of the Pharisaic party before A.D. 70; "rabbis" is used for those scholars after A.D. 70 "who inherited and developed Pharisaic traditions, finally creating 'rabbinic Judaism.'" Sanders allows for some overlap in the case of certain Pharisees who became leading rabbis after the First Jewish War, notably Johannan ben Zakkai. On all this, see Sanders, *Judaism. Practice & Belief*, 496 n. 10, and more generally 380–451. For an overview of the problem of the identity of the Pharisees from a sociological point of view, see Anthony J. Saldarini, *Pharisees, Scribes, and Sadducees in Palestinian Society. A Sociological Approach* (Wilmington, DE: Glazier, 1988) 277–97.

[199] See Backhaus, *Jüngerkreise*, 139–40, along with the literature cited there; see also T. A. Burkill, "Should Wedding Guests Fast? A Consideration of Mark 2:18–20," *New Light on the Earliest Gospel. Seven Markan Studies* (Ithaca/London: Cornell University, 1972) 39–47, esp. 47; Roloff, *Das Kerygma*, 223–29. Alistair Kee ("The Question about Fasting," *NovT* 76 [1967] 129–54) sees this point well, but then proceeds in arbitrary fashion to rewrite 2:19–20 (which he judges to be a product of the church) in order to recover what he imagines to have been the "substance" of Jesus' reply. The important clue to the tradition history that the question in v 18 supplies is missed by Kiilunen (*Die Vollmacht*, 176), who asserts unconvincingly that the disciples of John may have been added secondarily to the tradition. This unlikely position is taken with a view to Kiilunen's further position that the question in v 18 may be secondary, while vv 19–20 should be judged to have existed as a unit from the beginning.

[200] The secondary nature of v 20, which is accepted today by the vast majority of commentators, gives us another case in which the equivalent saying (the second half of 104) in the Coptic *Gospel of Thomas* cannot be claimed to have preserved a more primitive tradition than the Synoptics. Rather, the second half of saying 104 shows signs both (1) of being secondary and (2) of being dependent on the Synoptics, in particular Luke. (1) The second half of the Coptic saying reads (with a number of Greek words used in the Coptic text, as indicated): "Rather (*alla*), when (*hotan*) the bridegroom (*nymphios*) leaves the bridal chamber (*nymphōn*), then (*tote*) let them fast (*nēsteuein*) and pray." The Greek words in the Coptic saying reflect the vocabulary and even the order of the

words in Mark 2:20 parr.; only *nymphōn* reflects v 19. Even more significant is the fact that the basic structure of Mark 2:20 parr. is mirrored in the second half of saying 104: adversative word (*de* or *alla*) + *hotan* (introducing temporal clause with *nymphios* as subject) + main clause introduced with temporal adverb *tote* + verb *nēsteuein*. But, as we have seen, Mark 2:20 is a secondary addition to the authentic saying of Jesus in v 19a. Therefore, the second half of saying 104 is a prime example of a case where the *Gospel of Thomas* preserves *not* the authentic saying of Jesus (i.e., Mark 2:19a, which, with the exception of the one word *nymphōn*, is not represented at all in saying 104) but only the secondary addition (v 20) created later on in the tradition as an expansion of the authentic saying (v 19a). (2) Moreover, and still more damaging to the claims of the *Gospel of Thomas*, the inauthentic tradition of v 20 about fasting has been given in *Thomas* a connection with the theme of prayer, a connection that Luke and Luke alone created in his redactional reworking of the question addressed to Jesus. The question of Mark 2:18 ("Why do the disciples of John and the disciples of the Pharisees fast?") becomes in the redaction of the prayer-loving Luke an affirmation that contains an implied question or criticism: "The disciples of John fast frequently and pray [a redactional theme of Luke], and likewise the (disciples) of the Pharisees; but your (disciples) eat and drink." Since only Luke adds the theme of praying to the Marcan pericope about fasting, the presence of the theme of prayer in *Thomas'* version of Mark 2:20 strongly suggests that once again *Thomas* reflects the Lucan redactional form of a Marcan logion. On all this, see Fieger, *Das Thomasevangelium*, 260–62.

[201] The attempts to make "will be taken away" (*aparthē*) refer to something else than death (and, as is suggested by the passive voice, death inflicted by someone else) are all contrived. It is no wonder that Muddiman ("Jesus and Fasting," 278–79) simply cuts the Gordian knot by (quite arbitrarily) rewriting the text and creating a reference to Jesus' departure from Galilee and his journey to Jerusalem.

To be sure, the verb *aparthę̄* in Mark 2:20 is a puzzle, for the three Synoptic versions of the question on fasting supply the only occurrences of *apairō* in the NT. A number of commentators see in it an allusion to the death of the suffering servant of Yahweh in Isa 53:8. Unfortunately, that verse, which has its own textual difficulties in the MT, offers no sure solution. In the LXX the uncompounded form *airetai* appears, and its subject is *hē zōē autou*. Earlier in the verse we have the aorist passive form *ērthē*, but the subject in the LXX is *hē krisis*. In contrast, the servant himself is the subject of the MT's *luqqāḥ* (as he is of the subsequent *nigzar*). But—as the LXX makes clear—there is no reason why either Hebrew verb must be translated with the precise verb *apairō*, which is found in Mark 2:20. In short, the allusion is possible, but far from certain.

[202] As I have noted previously, I do not consider it impossible that Jesus used allegory, an honored device in the repertoire of Israelite wisdom both in the OT and among the rabbis. However, the forced and contrived nature of the allegory in v 20, as compared with the simple image of v 19a, as well as the precise salvation-historical function of v 20, argues against its coming from the historical Jesus.

[203] E.g., in favor of keeping v 19b as authentic is Jeremias, "*nymphē, nymphios*," 1103; Pesch (*Das Markusevangelium*, 1. 171, 174–75) considers it secondary.

[204] A representative champion of the conservative view (i.e., that vv 19b–20 are authentic words of Jesus) can be found in Taylor, *The Gospel According to St. Mark*, 208–12. Taylor's argument, while making some good points (e.g., allegory is not to be automatically rejected as impossible in the mouth of the historical Jesus), suffers from a basic weakness seen in the position of most of the conservative defenders of the authenticity of vv 19b–20. To sustain his position Taylor must ignore what is the major thrust of

the final form of the pericope: the justification of the change in the disciples' behavior (from not fasting before Jesus' death to fasting after his death). A more fanciful and less critical defense of the authenticity of the whole of vv 19–20 can be found in Roderic Dunkerley, "The Bridegroom Passage," *ExpTim* 64 (1952–53) 303–4; words in the saying that get in the way of his interpretation are dismissed with an airy wave of the hand. For a concise defense of the secondary nature of vv 19b–20, see Haenchen, *Der Weg Jesu*, 116–17.

[205] Presumably, if there was originally no wider context in which this tradition about fasting was set, Jesus' name would have been mentioned at the beginning of the tradition. An explicit mention of Jesus' name was not needed in 2:18b in the pre-Marcan collection of dispute stories, since Jesus' name is mentioned in the preceding verse (Mark 2:17). Indeed, he is the only individual figuring in the text from v 15b onwards; hence the *autǭ* in 2:18 could hardly refer to anyone else.

[206] In the Greek text (omitting "and the disciples of the Pharisees"), each half of the initial question (v 18cd) contains exactly six words, if one includes all particles in the count. Because of the subordinate temporal clause and the placing of the infinitive *nēsteuein* ("to fast") last in the sentence, Jesus' reply (v 19a) does not divide as neatly. However, if we place the break just before the beginning of the temporal clause in Jesus' reply, the first half again has six words in the Greek, while the second half, which is the concluding line of the whole story, is slightly longer at eight words. This division of Jesus' reply cannot be exactly represented in an English translation, since "fast" must be put with the auxiliary verb "can."

[207] One might wonder whether the initial *kai* would have been present in the earliest form of v 18b in Greek. Judging by the way *kai* regularly introduces a new pericope in Mark's Gospel, even when the new pericope has no real connection with what precedes, I think that the presence of the initial *kai* in the earliest attainable Greek form of v 18 is definitely possible, though not certain. In any event, the point of my remarks in the main text is the basic balance of the primitive unit, both in its two-part structure and in the length of corresponding clauses. This point is not affected by the presence or absence of a particular monosyllable.

[208] *Contra*, e.g., Bultmann (*Geschichte*, 17), who thinks in terms of an isolated logion of Jesus that was expanded by the early Christian community into an apophthegm. For Bultmann, this expansion took place when the question of the relationship of the church to the followers of the Baptist was still lively and relevant. But the history of the Marcan tradition, as opposed to that of Q and John, does not seem to reflect any such pressing concern about the relationship of the church to the Baptist's followers in the post-Easter period.

[209] The mere fact that the questionable behavior (i.e., not fasting) is attributed to Jesus' disciples while the inquirers address their question to Jesus should not be taken as an indication that the whole or major part of the pericope is an invention of the later church, which puts its defense in Jesus' mouth. This incorrect assumption lies at the very beginning of Burkill's essay ("Should Wedding Guests Fast?" 39–40) and skews the results of his analysis. As David Daube points out ("Responsibilities of Master and Disciples in the Gospels," *NTS* 19 [1972–73] 1–15), the responsibility of the master for his disciples' actions is a principle widely acknowledged in various cultures and time periods (including the 19th and 20th centuries), and is attested both in Jewish rabbinic literature after Jesus and among Greek philosophers (e.g., Socrates) before him.

[210] For a brief survey of the practice of fasting in the OT and Judaism, see Moshe

David Herr, "Fasting and Fast Days," *EncJud*, 6. cols. 1189–96; E. P. Sanders, *Jewish Law from Jesus to the Mishnah. Five Studies* (London: SCM; Philadelphia: Trinity Press International, 1990) 81–84. Most commentators agree that the point at issue in Mark 2:18–20 is *voluntary* fasting, practiced for various reasons by diverse "reform," "repristination," or "apocalyptic" groups in 1st-century Judaism, including the Pharisees, the Qumranites, and the disciples of the Baptist. Pious Jews of no particular sectarian group might likewise undertake fasts for personal reasons (Tob 12:8; Jdt 8:6). From the time of the OT onwards, individual Israelites as well as whole communities used fasting to express mourning after a death (2 Sam 1:12; cf. 12:21), penance (1 Kgs 21:27; Ezra 10:6), and intense supplication, especially in the face of a real or possible calamity (2 Sam 12:16–23; Neh 1:4; Dan 9:3). Fasting may also have been connected at times with preparing oneself for an encounter with God or the heavenly world by revelation (a possible meaning behind Exod 34:28; 1 Kgs 19:8; Dan 10:3). We have no indisputable evidence that an annual public fast enjoined on the entire Israelite community existed before the exile. Stated fasts for the community in the fourth, fifth, seventh, and tenth months are apparently mentioned in Zech 8:19; cf. 7:3,5. Zechariah declares that these fasts are to be turned into times of joy, but Sanders (ibid., 82) thinks that some may have continued to observe them; indeed, "fasts in addition to that on the Day of Atonement may have been regarded as obligatory in the later biblical period." The most prominent day of fasting imposed on the whole Israelite community in the postexilic period, and the only one enjoined in the Pentateuch, is Yom Kippur (the Day of Atonement), prescribed in Lev 16:29,31; 23:27,29,32; Num 29:7. The use of the Hebrew phrase "to afflict oneself" to describe the observance of Yom Kippur suggests that Jews, including those in the 1st century A.D., did more than just abstain from food and drink; such practices as rending garments, wearing sackcloth, placing ashes or earth on the head, and weeping might have been added.

There is no indication in Mark 2:18–20 or in any other Gospel text that Jesus and/ or his disciples did not observe the Yom Kippur fast. If they had disregarded such a solemn fast incumbent on all Jews, one would have expected a heated dispute story making the "transgression" on the part of Jesus clear. The texts of the canonical Gospels—whether or not they represent accurate history on this point—depict Jesus repealing various individual laws or institutions of the Torah (food laws, divorce, oaths and vows, retaliation), but the fast of Yom Kippur is not among them. The silence is very strange if Jesus actually rejected fasting on Yom Kippur. One is left wondering about other public fasts (e.g., the 9th of Ab, commemorating the destruction of the temple by Nebuchadnezzar) that, though not mandated by the Pentateuch, would have been commonly observed by Palestinian Jews. The Mishna tractate *Ta'an.* 4:7 states that "in the week wherein falls the 9th of Ab it is forbidden to cut the hair or wash the clothes" (Danby translation). What follows in the Mishna suggests that some reduction in the intake of food was generally observed, though rabbis differed on particulars. Sanders (*Jewish Law*, 83) summarizes the situation thus: ". . . it is certain that in Jesus' day there were occasional fasts (e.g., for rain), and there may have been one or more regular fasts in addition to the one on the Day of Atonement. The likeliest candidate is the 9th of Ab."

The point at issue in Mark 2:18–20, however, is that observers wonder at the marked difference in the practice of voluntary fasting between two religious groups (the disciples of John and the disciples of Jesus) who have so much in common, especially with regard to background.

[211] One should recognize the element of inference in this chain of citations. Only Luke mentions the name "Pharisee," and he speaks generally of "twice a week." More-

over, Luke does not claim that this is a practice observed by all Pharisees. Both the *Didache* and the tractate *Ta'anît* ("Affliction") in the Babylonian Talmud mention Monday and Thursday, but Pharisees are not mentioned in the immediate context of either passage. *Did.* 8:1 speaks polemically of "the hypocrites" (an epithet often used of the Pharisees in Matthew's Gospel, on which the *Didache* may directly or indirectly depend). In Sanders's view (*Jewish Law*, 82), the text in the *Didache* does not mean that both Jews and Christians fasted two days of every week; rather, the point at issue is which two days should be chosen when an individual or the community decides to fast. *Ta'an.* 12a speaks very generally: "If a man undertakes to fast on Mondays and Thursdays throughout the year. . . ." A succession of three days of fasting in the order Monday-Thursday-the following Monday is mentioned in the Mishna tractate *Ta'an.* 1:6 (cf. 2:9), but the context here is not regular fasting undertaken voluntarily by a pious individual but rather a community fast enjoined by an authoritative court on the special occasion of a severe drought.

[212] The attempt by some exegetes to see the fast of John's disciples as an expression of mourning after the Baptist's death is completely gratuitous. Apart from the addition of v 18a at a later stage of the tradition, both question and counterquestion are addressing the general practice of two groups, not a particular fast on a particular occasion.

[213] Whether the historical Paul practiced fasting as a Christian is not clear. His references to fasting in 2 Cor 6:5; 11:27 seem to refer rather to going without food (either voluntarily or involuntarily) because of the circumstances of his apostolic mission (e.g., poverty, long hours spent in work and prayer, etc.); see Furnish, *II Corinthians*, 344, 355, 518. Needless to say, this does not prove that Paul did not practice fasting at times; an argument from silence in this matter would be unwarranted. Acts 9:9 presents Saul of Tarsus as neither eating nor drinking, but the passage suffers from a double difficulty: (1) it is one of the three versions of Luke's account of Paul's coming to faith in Christ, and one must allow for a good amount of Christian reformulation and Lucan redaction of the story; and (2) technically, Saul/Paul is not yet a Christian at this point in the story (his baptism and subsequent eating are recounted in 9:18–19). See also Acts 13:2–3.

[214] Roloff (*Das Kerygma*, 230) introduces confusion into his treatment when he refers to such texts as Rom 14:17 and Col 2:21–23 as treating forms of fasting. In the OT and early Judaism, to fast was to abstain from all (or almost all) food and drink for a certain set time (e.g., twenty-four hours). After the fast, one resumed eating the foods from which one had abstained during the fast. Texts like Rom 14:17 and Col 2:21–23, whatever the precise problems they are treating (e.g., food taboos that allow no meat), are concerned with the practice of avoiding particular foods permanently and as a matter of principle—in other words, permanent dietary regulations or food laws. This is not fasting, just as the avoidance of pork by Jews is not fasting. There is no indication that different groups in the early church ever had Paul-like disputes over the question of fasting.

[215] When Carlston (*The Parables of the Triple Tradition*, 121–25) tries to deny the authenticity of Mark 2:18–19a and attribute the entire pericope to debates among various Christians in the early church, he is forced to compose an ecclesiastical scenario for which there is no real evidence. Contrary to his claims, and provided one does not read vv 19b–20 into 19a, there is no reason why "when the bridegroom is with them" in v 19a must be taken as indicating a time-limit and therefore as constituting "a very indirect passion-prediction" (p. 122). Nor is it clear that "bridegroom" in v 19a "implies a fairly distinct Messianic consciousness" (p. 121). The use of "bridegroom" could

be intelligible to inquirers on a very simple level of the metaphor: "Wedding guests cannot fast at a wedding [or: when the bridegroom is standing right there], can they?" I readily concede that the use of "bridegroom" does implicitly point to Jesus as a or the pivotal figure in the present time of salvation; but we have seen that such a veiled or implicit self-reference exists in a number of Jesus' other authentic words and/or actions. A veiled reference to his own pivotal role is not the same thing as "a fairly distinct Messianic consciousness."

While rejecting a controversy among Christian communities as the origin of Mark 2:18–20, Kiilunen (*Die Vollmacht*, 193–94) suggests that the pericope owes its formulation to a substantially Jewish-Christian community that had always practiced fasting as a matter of course. However, in order to ground firmly its own identity, the community wanted to present Christian fasting as a phenomenon *sui generis*, something different from Jewish fasting. Kiilunen's thesis is built on a number of improbable tradition-history decisions (e.g., the mention of the disciples of John in v 18 is secondary, vv 19–20 formed a unit from the beginning), but perhaps its greatest difficulty is that it never really explains the origin of the idea that Jesus' disciples did not fast during his earthly life. Such an idea would set this hypothetical Jewish-Christian community at variance with the earthly Jesus and inevitably place it in the same camp as the Jews from whom it supposedly wants to differentiate itself. There is an air of contrivance about the whole hypothesis.

[216] Throughout my treatment of Mark 2:18–20, I have spoken about the practice of not fasting on the part of Jesus' disciples, since that is the way the question and counterquestion in Mark 2:18–19 frame the issue. However, as the inquirers in 2:18 and any other Palestinian Jew would take for granted, the teacher of a group of disciples is responsible for their conduct and must answer any questions or objections about it. It is hardly credible that Jesus would have taught his disciples the remarkably different and disconcerting religious practice of not fasting and then not have observed his own teaching. As I show below, that Jesus himself did not fast coheres with other authentic sayings (e.g., Matt 11:16–19 par.).

[217] It is significant that even Jeremias, who does not accept the idea that Jesus spoke of the kingdom as already present during his ministry, is still willing to say: " 'Realized eschatology' is . . . the meaning of Mark 2.19" (*The Parables of Jesus*, 117). Needless to say, Dodd (*The Parables of the Kingdom*, 87) is of the same opinion.

[218] See Fitzmyer, *The Gospel According to Luke*, 1. 598; also Joseph A. Fitzmyer and Daniel J. Harrington, *A Manual of Palestinian Aramaic Texts (Second Century B.C.–Second Century A.D.)* (BibOr 34; Rome: Biblical Institute, 1978) §150 (pp. 185–87). As the commentary on p. 248 notes, the date of composition of the Scroll of Fasting has been variously put at ca. A.D. 7, ca. A.D. 66, and some time toward the end of the 1st century A.D. (the date favored by Fitzmyer and Harrington). In any case, the text has undergone a number of redactions, and some additions have been made to the basic text. For an earlier critical edition with comments, see Gustaf Dalman, *Aramäische Dialektproben* (2d ed.; Leipzig: Hinrichs, 1927) 1–3, 41–45.

[219] Backhaus, *Jüngerkreise*, 151.

[220] For a brief treatment of the problems involved in using the word "sect" in the sociology of religion, especially when it is applied to early Christianity, see Bengt Holmberg, *Sociology and the New Testament. An Appraisal* (Minneapolis: Fortress, 1990) 86–117. Because of all the difficulties Holmberg points out—especially the fact that so many authors give the word "sect" different and even multiple definitions—I avoid using the word of Jesus' disciples in the main text.

[221] A full justification of this statement must wait till later. For a spirited defense of the existence and importance of "the Twelve" during the ministry of the historical Jesus, see Sanders, *Jesus and Judaism*, 95–106.

[222] Sanders (*Jewish Law*, 83) remarks on Mark 2:18–22 that "the accusation [against Jesus and/or his disciples] implies that these two groups [the Pharisees and the disciples of John the Baptist] regarded this particular fast as obligatory." Strictly speaking, there is no "accusation" in the story, and I do not see how one infers a sense of obligation. The contrast in the story seems rather to be between the regular observance of voluntary fasts by two pious groups and the total avoidance of such fasts by Jesus' disciples.

[223] For his definition of "sect," see his fine work *From the Maccabees to the Mishnah* (Library of Early Christianity 7; Philadelphia: Westminster, 1987) 125–27; for his remarks on early Christianity as a Jewish sect, see pp. 166–71. A similar definition of sect is given by Sanders, *Judaism: Practice and Belief*, 352 (cf. 362): "A sect considers itself to be the only true Israel and all other Jews to be apostates. The boundary lines are rigid and impermeable." In practice, the sect would avoid the Jerusalem temple. In contrast, for Sanders a party "has distinctive views and practices, but it does not define itself as being all Israel, and its members constitute a party *within* common Judaism rather than being an alternative to it." In Sanders's view, the Qumranites represented by the Manual of Discipline (1QS) were a sect, while the Essenes represented by the Damascus Document (CD) were "an extremist party." I would take it that, according to Sanders's definitions, the inner circle around Jesus would have been a party, not a sect—at least during Jesus' lifetime.

[224] The problematic nature of applying "sect" even to the Christian movement after Jesus' crucifixion is demonstrated by the widely divergent views on the subject by scholars who have tried to employ the label with reference to parts or all of 1st-century Christianity; see Holmberg, *Sociology and the New Testament*, 86–114. For the questionable usefulness of the traditional distinction between "church" and "sect" as developed by Ernst Troeltsch, see Bryan R. Wilson, *Magic and the Millennium. A Sociological Study of Religious Movements of Protest Among Tribal and Third-World Peoples* (New York: Harper & Row, 1973) 11–16, 31–69. For one possible application of Wilson's sevenfold typology of sects (more precisely, according to Wilson: deviant or minority religious movements) to Palestinian Judaism, see the insightful work of Saldarini, *Pharisees, Scribes and Sadducees in Palestinian Society*, 71–73; cf. Crossan, *The Historical Jesus*, 72–73. Saldarini observes that, granted Wilson's seven types, both the Pharisees and Jesus with his disciples would probably fit into the "reformist" type, which "seeks gradual, divinely revealed alterations in society." Whether this definition fits the imminent eschatology plus realized eschatology of Jesus' message and praxis (including miracles) is at least debatable. For a position that rejects the idea that Jesus founded a sect, see F. W. Dillistone, "St. Mark 2, 18–22," *ExpTim* 45 (1933–34) 253–54; but the thrust of his essay is more homiletic than scholarly.

[225] If one judges that the substance of Mark 2:18–19a is authentic, then it seems likely that Jesus' teaching about the proper way to fast in Matt 6:16–18 is a creation of the early church, reflecting the same general situation as Mark 2:19b–20, namely, the resumption of fasting by Christians.

[226] For examples of the terminology of "dawning," see Fuller, *The Mission and Achievement of Jesus*, 34; Jeremias, *New Testament Theology*, 103–8.

[227] For a classic presentation of the already/not-yet tension in the preaching of Jesus and in the NT as a whole, see Oscar Cullmann, *Salvation in History* (New York: Harper & Row, 1967) 166–85.

[228] Gnilka (*Jesus von Nazaret*, 136) uses two happy formulations for this state of affairs: (1) there is a "dynamic presence" of the future kingdom in the ministry of Jesus; and (2) in Jesus' miracles the kingdom of God can be experienced as definitive salvation, but not yet in all its definitiveness.

[229] Hence one must be careful about saying that Jesus' miracles functioned to prove that he was a legitimate prophet. While Jesus, along with other religious figures of the Greco-Roman world, did combine the functions of prophet and miracle-worker (see the survey by Anitra Bingham Kolenkow, "Relationships between Miracle and Prophecy in the Greco-Roman World and Early Christianity," *ANRW* II/23.2, 1470–1506, esp. 1492–95), his miracles, especially his exorcisms, were intended to do much more than simply prove his legitimacy as a prophet. As a or the eschatological prophet, Jesus performed exorcisms to make partially present the saving rule of God that, according to his proclamation, would soon come in all its fullness.

[230] While in this section of my treatment of the kingdom of God I have concentrated on the dialectic between present and future, the reader must not forget that this dialectic is possible ultimately because, in the biblical view, God's rule, when seen "from above," is eternal and immutable (see, e.g., Pss 145:13; 103:19). Especially in apocalyptic literature, it is maintained that God, for his own good reasons, has allowed the powers of evil to gain the upper hand on earth for a set time. But this is permitted only in order to punish sins, test the faithful, and arrange for a still greater triumphal manifestation of God's power in the denouement of history. For the believing Jew or Christian of the 1st century A.D., a tension between "already" and "not yet" was bearable—perhaps even necessary—because the tension existed beneath the overarching reality of God's supreme, unquestioned, and unchanging rule of his creation, be it obedient or disobedient.

[231] Dodd, *The Parables of the Kingdom*, 16.

[232] Beasley-Murray (*Jesus and the Kingdom of God*, 144–46) considers the roles Jesus implicitly gives himself in the sayings about the kingdom as present under the rubrics of champion of the kingdom, initiator of the kingdom, instrument of the kingdom, representative of the kingdom, mediator of the kingdom, bearer of the kingdom, and revealer of the kingdom. Beasley-Murray readily admits that such descriptions are of later coinage; Jesus claimed none of them for himself. Still, in my opinion, Beasley-Murray (p. 146) then moves too quickly from these latter-day descriptions to the title of Messiah, which was certainly known in 1st-century Palestine and which disciples of Jesus applied to him—at the very latest—soon after his crucifixion. More care and investigation are needed before one can begin to discuss whether, how, and when the title Messiah might be applied to Jesus.

PART THREE

MIRACLES

Jesus . . . was a doer of startling deeds

JOSEPHUS, *ANT.* 18.3.3 §63

CHAPTER 17

MIRACLES AND MODERN MINDS

I. INTRODUCTION: HOW DOES A HISTORIAN TREAT MIRACLE STORIES?

On the first page of Volume One of *A Marginal Jew*, I introduced the reader to the "unpapal conclave," a mythical committee of scholars made up of a Protestant, a Catholic, a Jew, and an agnostic.[1] In my academic fantasy, these worthies were locked up in the bowels of the Harvard Divinity School library and not allowed to emerge until they had produced a consensus statement on what historical research, prescinding from any faith commitment (or anti-faith commitment) could say about Jesus of Nazareth.[2] Anyone who has ever helped compose a consensus statement issued by a committee knows how difficult it can be to find compromise language that is acceptable to all without distorting the truth as seen by each. In the end, no one is completely satisfied, but everyone can "live with" the final document, in spite of its lacunas and ambiguities.

Such has been the approach in these two volumes of *A Marginal Jew*. Needless to say, when I speak of "compromise," such compromise cannot be allowed to affect the basic process of weighing historical evidence and reaching the most probable conclusion. When the data point clearly in one direction, there can be no pulling back from the judgment indicated simply for the sake of compromise. But there are also cases where the data are not so clear, where it would be all too easy to reach a decision more on the basis of one's personal worldview than on the basis of the material at hand. Moreover, beyond individual cases, one's personal philosophical perspective can also begin subtly to order and contour the whole picture (especially in such a complicated question as miracles). Here is where a sense of evenhandedness and compromise is needed in order to find ways of molding and enunciating the results of our research that avoid canonizing any one philosophical perspective to the exclusion of others. Here compromise is not only possible but necessary if one is to craft a consensus document.

Hence in these two volumes, from the question of the virginal conception to the problem of Jesus receiving "a baptism of repentance for the forgiveness of sins,"[3] topics fraught with theological consequences had to be treated in a circumspect fashion in order to obtain some minimal agreement among the different and differing members of our hypothetical committee. At times, no doubt, the compromise language is enough to set the teeth of believers on edge, since treasured affirmations of faith do not appear in the consensus statement when historical evidence is not sufficient to establish the truth of such affirmations. But this does not result in a policy of the least common denominator, which in effect would hand the palm of victory each time to the agnostic. Left to himself or herself, the agnostic would never have written the open-ended treatments of the virginal conception and the baptism of Jesus by John that appear in these two volumes. In the give-and-take of a consensus document, everyone on the committee both wins and loses when it comes to choosing the exact mode of expression. This is acceptable, provided the historical data and the most probable conclusions drawn from them are not skewed in the process. For believers, there should be nothing new or strange in this procedure. There is hardly an ecumenical statement produced by interchurch dialogue that does not reflect the same strategy.

If all this applies to *A Marginal Jew* as a whole, it applies a hundredfold to the treatment of miracles that we now begin.[4] Left to themselves, the Christians in the unpapal conclave would probably want to affirm not only (1) that Jesus performed startling deeds that some of his contemporaries considered miracles but also (2) that such deeds were actually miracles, feats beyond all human capacity, accomplished by the power of God alone and revealing the unique status of Jesus. By the same token, left to himself or herself, the agnostic would state in no uncertain terms that miracles simply do not happen, that modern men and women cannot possibly accept the miracle stories of the Gospels as literally true, and that such stories had their origin either in the creative imagination and propaganda of the early church or in deeds actually performed by Jesus that were later magnified and reinterpreted (or misunderstood) by Christian faith in the light of the OT.

Obviously, if the members of the conclave are ever to forge a consensus statement on miracles, neither side can have its way absolutely. The committee must hammer out some sort of compromise language that will capture at least an essential part of the truth, without however expressing the whole truth as either side sees it. Restricted to the empirical evidence and what can be clearly inferred from it by rational argument, these latter-day Henry Clays will have to be content with modest questions and modest claims. In particular, with so many pitfalls along the way to consensus, the committee will have to take special care to thrash out preliminary but pivotal questions of method. Only then will the conclave be able to treat adequately the real point at issue: the miracles of Jesus narrated in the Gospels and the historical tradition lying behind them.

The chapters of Part Three will follow the path blazed by our mythical committee. They will first grapple with some key questions of method and only then take up directly the miracles of Jesus. The order of our discussion will be as follows: (I) First we will briefly consider the various problems that face modern minds when they take up the Gospel miracles (Chapter 17). For instance, what exactly should be the focus of a historical (as distinct from a philosophical or theological) investigation of the Gospel accounts of Jesus' miracles? What can a historian say or not say about them? On a wider plane: is it true that the *modern worldview* forged by contemporary science and philosophy makes it impossible for any thoughtful, educated individual to hold that miracles can or do occur?

(II) Then we will move to the problems posed by the *ancient worldview* that serves as a backdrop to the Gospels (Chapter 18). In the ancient Mediterranean world, most people readily granted the possibility and reality of miracles. But precisely because of this, sociology and anthropology raise a question many believers may find uncomfortable: is there any justification for seeing a significant distinction between the miracles attributed to Jesus in the Gospels and the magical practices widely reflected in Greco-Roman writings, including magical papyri and popular novels? Are these magical practices anything more than the "bad" miracles of pagans, while the Gospel miracles are simply the "good" magical practices of Jesus? In other words, is there any real difference between magic and miracle? Or is the only difference in the eye of the beholder who happens to be a Christian apologist?

(III) Only after these preliminary questions of method have been pondered can we move on to the Gospel miracles attributed to Jesus, classify them, and ask some modest questions about them (Chapters 19 to 23). The key problem of the historicity of Jesus' miracles will first be treated in a global fashion (Chapter 19): are all the miracle stories of the Gospels pure inventions of the early church, or do at least some reports go back to the time of Jesus himself? Only then will individual types of miracles be examined (exorcisms, healings, reports of raising the dead, and so-called "nature miracles"), to see if any particular stories have a claim to go back to some incident in the life of Jesus. At the conclusion of the survey, the results will need to be incorporated into our evolving sketch of the historical Jesus.

II. MIRACLES AND MODERN MINDS

Can miracles happen? Do miracles happen? The problem of the possibility and actual occurrence of miracles is logically the first question any inquirer would raise in a discussion of the miracles of Jesus. I fear then that I will be disappointing almost all my readers with the answer I give. In my view, these wide-ranging questions are legitimate in the arena of philosophy or theology. But they are illegitimate or at least unanswerable in a historical investigation that stubbornly restricts itself to empirical evidence and rational deductions or inferences from such evidence.

No sooner do I make this claim than I imagine both believers and nonbelievers crying "cop-out!" On the one side, staunch Christian believers—

especially those of a conservative bent—will protest that I am once again giving the victory to agnostics by default: I am in effect saying that miracles are not real events in time and space. On the other side, nonbelievers, non-Christians, and even some Christians will no doubt detect covert Christian apologetics in what seems a refusal to bite the bullet. In their view, I am refusing to pursue a thoroughgoing critical approach to history, an approach that necessarily accepts the conclusions of modern science and philosophy: miracles cannot and therefore do not happen. In their eyes, I am trying to preserve a tiny acre of a bygone mythical world within the otherwise modern universe of historical research.

A. WHAT IS A MIRACLE?

With more than a little chutzpah I reply that both sides are wrong. Before we start an interminable debate, though, I think it essential to be clear on what I mean by a miracle. A quick glance will show that various works of theology, philosophy, and sociology use different definitions.[5] For our purposes in this discussion of the miracles of Jesus within the context of modern philosophy and science, I think a fair general definition would run as follows:[6] A miracle is (1) an unusual, startling, or extraordinary event that is in principle perceivable by any interested and fair-minded observer, (2) an event that finds no reasonable explanation in human abilities or in other known forces that operate in our world of time and space, and (3) an event that is the result of a special act of God, doing what no human power can do. Each of these three components of the definition makes an important point:

(1) Christian rhetoric will at times speak loosely of the miracle of grace, the miracle of Christ's resurrection, or the miracle of Christ's presence in the eucharist. But in the strict acceptation of the term, a miracle involves an event that is in principle perceivable by all interested and fair-minded observers: e.g., a man known to be totally blind from birth, with no hope of a cure, suddenly sees everything with perfect clarity and demonstrates to others that he can do so.[7]

(2) The event is unusual and startling precisely because no reasonable explanation for the event's occurrence can be found in the realm of human abilities or in any other force or power known to exist and operate in our world of time and space.[8] I use this somewhat cumbersome description to avoid the often-heard definition of a miracle as an event that goes beyond, transgresses, violates, or contradicts "the laws of nature" or "natural law." The concept of "nature" or "natural law" is a slippery one, defined differently by different philosophies even within the Greco-Roman period, to say nothing of modern philosophy.[9]

The philosophical idea that the smooth flow of "nature" is regulated by immanent laws finds no direct parallel in the vast majority of the books of the OT written in Hebrew. From the first chapter of Genesis onwards, the created world arises out of and is constantly tending toward chaos. Only the creative power of God, not "natural" laws inherent in the realities of time and space, keeps the world from falling back into disorder. God gives or imposes laws on his creatures; those laws do not arise "naturally" out of the creatures because of their very essence.[10] It is not by accident that we hear of "nature" *(physis)* only when we move to the deuterocanonical/apocryphal Book of the Wisdom of Solomon (7:20; 13:1; 19:20), a work written in Alexandria and reflecting the middle Platonism also seen in Philo.[11] Even here, though, "nature" is understood in the light of the OT tradition, namely as "creation," which is made and governed by God's word and wisdom.[12] Nature is not a self-contained reality that operates according to its own inherent and inviolable laws, not a reality ultimately identifiable with God himself.[13]

Hence, in my own definition of miracles, I purposely avoid the vocabulary of "nature" so as not to inject concepts from ancient Stoicism or Platonism— or later concepts from medieval scholasticism or the 17th- and 18th-century Age of Reason—into texts that for the most part operate with different presuppositions. It is better to speak in general terms of what human beings—as well as other known forces in our world—can and cannot do. For example, no human being—and no other known force in our world of time and space—can suddenly cause a person who is totally blind from birth because of a physical pathology to see with perfect vision, simply by a word of command.

(3) It is of the essence of a miracle that the event is seen to have as its only adequate cause and explanation a special act of God, who alone is able to bring about the miraculous effect.[14] In practice, the question of God's action usually arises because the extraordinary event occurs in a religious context that confers some religious significance or purpose on the event (e.g., a symbol of the salvation God offers his people) and often involves the participation of some human religious figure.

This third component of our definition brings us to the nub of the whole problem. Anyone who claims that a miracle has happened is saying in effect: "God has acted here to accomplish what no human force or any other known power in our world can accomplish. This extraordinary event was caused by God alone."[15] Now it is certainly possible that historians could, in a number of ways, prove that such a claim is false. For instance, they might show that some overlooked human action or power had been at work. Or their investigation might lead to some hitherto unknown force or power operating in our empirical world. Or they might prove fraud, trickery, self-delusion, or psychiatric illness on the part of the person claiming to have worked or received the miracle.[16]

But what if all these explanations are carefully excluded by the historians' investigation? I maintain that even then it is inherently impossible for historians working with empirical evidence within the confines of their own discipline ever to make the positive judgment: "God has directly acted here to accomplish something beyond all human power." The very wording of this statement shows that it is essentially *theo*-logical ("*God* has directly acted . . ."). What evidence and criteria could justify a historian *as a historian* in reaching such a judgment? To be sure, a professional historian who is likewise a believing Christian might proceed from one judgment ("this extraordinary event, occurring in a religious context, has no discernible explanation") to a second judgment ("this event is a miracle worked by God"). But this further judgment is not made in his or her capacity as a professional historian. The judgment that this particular event is a miracle accomplished by God necessarily moves the person making the judgment into the realm of philosophy or theology.

Hence it is my contention that a positive judgment that a miracle has taken place is always a philosophical or theological judgment. Of its nature it goes beyond any judgment that a historian operating precisely as a historian can make. What a historian—or a physicist or a doctor—may say in his or her professional capacity is that, after an exhaustive examination of the evidence, one cannot find a reasonable cause or adequate explanation for a particular extraordinary event. The historian may also duly record the fact that a particular extraordinary event took place in a religious context and is claimed by some participants or observers to be a miracle, i.e., something directly caused by God. But to move beyond such affirmations and to reach the conclusion that God indeed has directly caused this inexplicable event is to cross the line separating the historian from the philosopher or theologian. The same person may make both types of judgments, but he or she does so in a different professional (or amateur) capacity and in a different realm of human knowledge.

All that I have just said holds true of nonbelievers as well. Let us suppose that an atheist has carefully examined a cure that is alleged to be miraculous. Let us also suppose that he has found that, at a certain moment, in a religious setting, a person totally blind from birth because of a physical pathology suddenly saw perfectly. Let us further suppose that the atheist then verifies the fact of the past physical blindness, the suddenness and permanence of the cure, and the truthfulness and sincerity of the blind person as well as of others who witnessed the cure. At this point the atheist can reach the same judgment as a colleague who is a believer: "As far as can be ascertained, this cure cannot be explained by any human ability or action, by any known force in the physical universe, or by fraud or self-delusion." But, just as his believing colleague might proceed to take a further step and judge the event a miracle, the atheist might offer his own further judgment: "Whatever the explanation may be, and even in the absence of an explanation, I am sure that this is not a miracle." The atheist's judgment may be as firm and sincere as the believer's; it is also just as much a philosophical or theological judgment, determined by a particular worldview, and not a judgment that arises simply, solely, and necessarily out of an examination of the evidence of this particular case.[17]

To repeat my main point: the historian can ascertain whether an extraordinary event has taken place in a religious setting, whether someone has claimed it to be a miracle, and—if there is enough evidence—whether a human action, physical forces in the universe, misperception, illusion, or fraud can explain the event. If all these explanations are excluded, the historian may conclude that an event claimed by some people to be miraculous has no reasonable explanation or adequate cause in any human activity or physical force. To go beyond that judgment and to affirm *either* that God has directly acted to bring about this startling event *or* that God has not done so is to go beyond what any historian can affirm in his or her capacity as a historian and to enter the domain of philosophy or theology.[18]

B. A PRACTICAL EXAMPLE

The scenario I have painted, namely, a group of experts divided in their opinions as they try to judge an event that some call miraculous, is not an imaginary one.[19] As a matter of fact, at the shrine of Lourdes in France there is a medical bureau made up (at various times) of doctors of different faiths and no faith.[20] Their task is to examine supposed miraculous cures and ascertain whether there is any explanation in the realm of medical knowledge and the physical sciences in general. When an examination of the records and of the patient causes the doctors to judge that a serious physical pathology did exist, that a cure took place without medical intervention, that the cure was instantaneous or of baffling rapidity, that there has been no reoccurrence of the pathology for a year afterwards, and that there is no indication of fraud or psychological delusion, the medical bureau at Lourdes passes on the case to what is called the International Medical Committee, located in Paris. The committee conducts a further study and draws up a detailed report. If satisfied by all the evidence, the committee may declare that the cure is "medically imexplicable." The doctors involved in this lengthy process distinguish between such cures and those that are considered unusual but not beyond all possible scientific explanation.

Quite rightly, the medical group does not presume to issue any judgment as to whether God has directly acted in a particular case to cure this or that individual. For such a judgment, the records are handed over to church authorities for further examination.[21] At times a particular cure will pass the scrutiny of the medical bureau and the committee only to be disallowed by the ecclesiastical commission set up to investigate it as a possible miracle.[22]

I mention the supposed cures at Lourdes not to claim that they are miracles but to provide a concrete example of the distinction I have been making between a historical and a philosophical (or theological) judgment about inexplicable events. Obviously, the doctors belonging to the medical bureau at Lourdes are free to form their own private judgments on the miraculous character of a given case. A Catholic doctor on the medical team might join in issuing a statement that a particular cure has no discernible explanation and then say privately to himself: "Surely God has cured this patient; it is a miracle." But in forming this further judgment, the Catholic doctor no longer speaks as a doctor but as a believer with a particular worldview.

By the same token, an atheist on the medical team might join in issuing the same statement and then say just as firmly to himself: "God has not acted in this case; whatever the ultimate explanation, there is no miracle here because there is no God to cause it." The atheist would also be speaking not as a doctor but as a person who holds a particular worldview and who judges individual phenomena—even those he cannot rationally explain—by his worldview. Each doctor might well claim that his judgment is a reasonable one, given his worldview. But in neither case does the judgment proceed necessarily from an examination of the data of the individual cure, apart from the philosophical or religious worldview that provides the cure with its final interpretation. The judgment "God has miraculously cured this patient" and the judgment "God has not miraculously cured this patient" both go beyond what is strictly verifiable by medical and historical investigation.[23]

Two insights that arise from this example of the medical team at Lourdes have a relevance for our own question of the miracles attributed to Jesus.

(1) The case histories at Lourdes testify to an indisputable historical fact of our own time. I do *not* mean the fact of miraculous cures; I make no such claim. Rather, the fact I refer to is that certain people, ostensibly seriously ill, *claim* to be suddenly, miraculously cured in a religious setting. As we have seen, at times the medical bureau at Lourdes and the International Medical Committee working with it can find no adequate scientific explanation for these cures. This, then, is a simple fact of our own modern-day experience: certain people, apparently once ill, are now well; they claim that they were suddenly cured by divine power; and no adequate medical explanation of the cure can be found. The principle of historical analogy would suggest that, if this sort of phenomenon has happened in religious circumstances in our own day, it *may be* that something similar has happened in religious circumstances in the past. At least such claims from past history would hardly be surprising, granted our present experience.

To put this in another way: in the face of the Lourdes phenomenon (and others like it), one cannot assert a priori that Jesus never performed inexplicable cures, claimed by some to be miracles. This is simply to argue from historical analogy: if, under a certain set of circumstances, a particular type of event tends to happen in one period of history, similar events *may* (not necessarily *do*) happen in another period of history if a similar set of circumstances is verified.[24] Needless to say, this general observation does not automatically prove that Jesus claimed to perform miracles or that he did so. It simply points out that it is illegitimate to reject such a possibility a priori, granted modern analogies.

(2) As already indicated, the limitations of a doctor's judgment about some recent cure reported at Lourdes are similar to the limitations to which historians are subject when they try to judge the report of a miracle that supposedly occurred at some time in the past. However, in the case of the miracles attributed to Jesus, matters are still more complicated; and the possibility of rendering any sort of judgment—even the limited type I have described above—becomes even more meager.[25] Unlike events at Lourdes, when we examine the events of Jesus' ministry, we have no medical records drawn up by 20th-century physicians; we have no chance to examine the patient after his or her cure to test its reality and permanence; and we cannot interview the recipients of

these supposed miracles to verify their accurate knowledge, truthfulness, sincerity, and mental stability. As with the quest for the historical Jesus in general, so too with the quest for his miracles: the chasm of two millennia makes verification of what a 1st-century marginal Jew did in a marginal province at the eastern end of the Roman Empire extremely difficult.

C. KEEPING OUR QUESTIONS MODEST

Granted the severe limitations of our data, I would suggest that we must be careful to keep both our questions and our conclusions modest. What may we reasonably ask in such a restricted situation? In my opinion, we may reasonably ask and hope to answer the following questions: (1) Are *reports* about Jesus performing miracles totally inventions of the early church as it developed its missionary apologetic and propaganda in a Greco-Roman world that expected miracles from divine figures visiting the earth? Or do at least some of the *reports* of Jesus' miracles go back to the time and activity of the historical Jesus? (2) Do certain kinds of supposed miracles appear to be typical of reports of Jesus' activity, while other kinds are relatively or completely absent, in comparison with other reports of miracles in the ancient world? (3) To move from reports to what Jesus actually did: Did in fact Jesus perform certain startling or extraordinary actions that he and his followers claimed to be miracles? (4) What ultimately did these supposed miracles mean to Jesus, his disciples, and other observers in the total context of his ministry?

The reader will no doubt notice what issues these four questions do not include. In keeping with the position I mapped out above, I do not think that a historian *as a historian* (or an exegete as an exegete) can say yes or no to the further question: Was God directly acting in Jesus' ministry to bring about miracles? I am not saying that such a question is illegitimate; I am simply saying that it lies beyond the specific competence of the historian or exegete. This is all the more true when we move from miracles in general to the miracles of Jesus in particular. As already noted, 1st-century Capernaum is not 20th-century Lourdes. In the case of Jesus, we do not have the detailed medical records, personal interviews, and tracking system that would enable us to say that, in the case of Jesus' miracles, all conceivable explanations from the physical sciences or psychology have been exhaustively tested and excluded. Rather, we can hope to ascertain what Jesus, his followers, and sometimes his adversaries *thought* was the explanation of his startling deeds. In short, modest data dictate modest questions and claims.

To apply all this to our unpapal conclave: by the "rules of the game," the conclave prescinds from what is known either by faith or by theological insight flowing from faith. Hence it cannot and does not try to answer a question such as: "In this particular healing reported in the Gospels did God act directly to effect a startling and immediate cure beyond all human ability?" But, by the same token, the conclave does not admit unverified presuppositions from the agnostic side of the committee table. To judge a priori, before an examination of a particular case, that no matter what the evidence may be, a particular action of Jesus could not possibly have been a miracle is a philosophical judgment, not a historical one. And the agnostic has no more right to impose his or her philosophical worldview on the whole conclave than does a believing Catholic or Protestant. We come back to the point that the "ecumenical" method used in *A Marginal Jew* does not hand the palm of victory to the agnostic by default. If our approach is to be truly open-minded, then the agnostic can no more demand that the committee rule out the possibility of miracles from the start than can a member who is a believer make it the preferred presumption.

I want to emphasize that the careful, evenhanded approach to claims of the miraculous that I have laid out in this chapter has not been invented simply to give Jesus (or Lourdes) special treatment. This evenhanded method is what any serious historian should bring to any serious report of miracles. A prime example of such an approach in a contemporary biography is Daniel Mark Epstein's *Sister Aimee*, a biography of the 20th-century American faith-healer Aimee Semple McPherson.[26] While certainly not an adherent of McPherson's Church of the Foursquare Gospel (a type of evangelical Pentecostalism), Epstein takes great pains to be objective and fair in handling the many reports of miracles, especially miraculous healings, attributed to McPherson. This evenhandedness is all the more remarkable, given the flamboyant and even scandalous aspects of McPherson's career. Ridicule would have been easy; sober evaluation took more effort.

While supplying rational explanations of McPherson's "cures" wherever possible, Epstein does not pretend to be able to explain perfectly all the events McPherson and her followers considered miraculous. After reporting an occasion when McPherson helped another minister receive the "gift of tongues," Epstein observes: "We may compare it [McPherson's conferral of the gift] to the power to induce hypnosis, as long as we respect the distinctions: we must not profane the sacrament we cannot understand."[27] This is typical of Epstein's respect for the religious intention and context of the events reported. He does not seek a reductionist route that would indiscriminately level all the supposedly miraculous experiences to the least common denominator. My point here is a simple one: the respect and evenhandedness that Epstein brings to the study of the miracles attributed to McPherson should likewise be brought to the study of the miracles attributed to Jesus. Far from being a sign of parti pris, such fairness is the sign of an honest historian.

D. Two Concluding Observations

Before I conclude this brief consideration of miracles and the modern mind, two final observations—actually, little more than asides—should be made. They address a position more often silently held than openly stated, namely, that it is silly, embarrassing, and a waste of time to treat the question of miracles at all. Modern science and philosophy have made the whole question passé. No modern educated American can take the question of miracles seriously, let alone believe in them. My two observations do not aim at establishing the possibility or reality of miracles, but rather at replying to this tendency, found especially in some quarters of academia, to brush aside the question as unworthy of serious consideration.[28]

(1) I have emphasized that the decision to restrict my treatment to modest historical questions about Jesus' miracles is a decision that flows from the realization that any theoretical position on the possibility of miracles is a philosophical, not a historical stance. At the same time, this decision involves a convenient practical corollary. Since our limited investigation does not attempt to wrestle with the grand philosophical questions about the possibility and reality of miracles, there is no need to drag the reader down the labyrinthine corridors of modern philosophy from the Age of Reason and the Enlightenment onwards, rehearsing all the arguments for and against miracles. This is not said to disparage such great minds as Benedict (Baruch) de Spinoza (1632–1677),[29] Voltaire (1694–1778),[30] and David Hume (1711–1776),[31] who were among the preeminent philosophical critics of miracles before and during the Enlightenment.[32] Their arguments and the various replies to them are still worth pondering, but they lie outside the narrow focus of our quest.[33]

As an aside, though, I might observe that, while Spinoza's and Hume's positions still command attention, we cannot help noticing that the particular arguments they use may strike an educated person today as somewhat dated.[34] In varying ways, both Spinoza and Hume—as well as many following in their footsteps—reflect the Age of Reason's view of the physical universe as a closed, mechanical system run by precise, eternal, and immutable laws.[35] Indeed, some of the great thinkers of the Enlightenment (e.g., Voltaire) saw God as the supreme craftsman who had set up the physical universe as a smoothly running machine. Having given it unchanging laws to assure its harmony, he had left it to run by these laws. It would betoken lack of knowledge or power on his part ever to intervene and violate the wise order he had established.[36]

While there is a classical simplicity in such a vision of reality, there are also a number of problems with it. Chief among these, in the eyes of some present-day critics, is the conception of the physical universe as what has been dubbed "the Newtonian world-machine," governed by inexorable and immutable laws, with a strict chain of cause and effect. Such an Enlightenment view of the cosmos has given way to a conception molded by such 20th-century breakthroughs as Werner Heisenberg's principle of uncertainty (or indeterminacy).[37] In the light of the "Copenhagen interpretation" of quantum mechanics, of which Heisenberg was an active supporter, the tidy Enlightenment universe of immutable laws and tight chains of cause and effect, knowable in principle to any observer, begins to look outmoded. I say this neither to canonize the Copenhagen interpretation of quantum physics nor to claim that a universe conceived according to Heisenberg's principle of uncertainty is any more hospitable to miracles than is the universe depicted by the Enlightenment. The indeterminacy Heisenberg speaks of belongs to the microcosm of subatomic particles, not to the macrocosm of our everyday world of human action and observation, where we experience as much regularity as did the 18th-century Deists.[38] Rather, my point is that the shifts in 20th-century physics simply serve to remind us that not only theology but also anti-theology, not only the arguments in defense of miracles but also the arguments rejecting them depend in part on the particular view of the physical universe that prevails in a given period of civilization. Once that prevailing vision of the cosmos changes, not only arguments in defense of miracles but also the arguments against them require reformulation.[39]

All this, I stress, is an aside. My main point is the good news that our own approach, with modest historical rather than grand philosophical goals, need not engage in such a reformulation and rehearsing of the classical debate over miracles, whatever direction such a recasting might take in a Heisenbergian universe.

(2) My second observation on miracles and the modern mind concerns what might be called the academic sneer factor. If a full debate on the possibility and reality of miracles were to take place on American university campuses today—a highly unlikely event—such a debate would be tolerated in many quarters only with a strained smile that could hardly mask a sneer. Before any positions were articulated or discussed, the solemn creed of many university professors, especially in religion departments, would be recited *sotto voce:* "No modern educated person can accept the possibility of miracles." Or, to take another authorized version (often not revised to avoid sexist language): "Modern man cannot believe in miracles." Perhaps the most famous formulation of this creed was penned by Rudolf Bultmann: "It is impossible to use electric light and the wireless and to avail ourselves of modern medical and surgical discoveries, and at the same time to believe in the New Testament world of . . . miracles."[40]

In one form or another, this creed has dominated American academic circles for so long that rarely does anyone bother to ask: is it *empirically* true? Please note: the question I raise is not whether modern educated persons *should* believe in miracles, but rather whether they *can* and *do* in fact believe in miracles. Considering Bultmann's exaltation of the scientific wonders available to the modern educated person, and considering the great emphasis today on employing the social sciences in biblical exegesis, one would think that some academics would have consulted the scientific wonder known as the opinion poll—a wonder unavailable to Enlightenment philosophers—to check assertions about what modern persons can and do believe.

As a matter of empirical fact, an opinion survey published by George Gallup in 1989 found that about 82 percent of Americans polled believed that "even today, miracles are performed by the power of God."[41] This 82 percent, as Gallup's detailed table of statistics indicates, embraces more than the poorest and least educated in American society.[42] Presumably it numbers some representatives of the well-educated and affluent, including some scientists and doctors. This can certainly be verified anecdotally by priests and ministers in "upscale" parishes. Indeed, only 6 percent of all Americans polled by Gallup completely disagreed with the proposition that even today God works miracles. If Bultmann and his intellectual disciples are correct in their view on miracles and the modern mind, then it follows that only 6 percent of Americans completely qualify as truly modern persons. A more plausible conclusion is that only 6 percent of Americans share the mind-set of some German university professors.[43]

Bultmann notwithstanding, the fact is that present-day educated Americans are capable of using electric lights and "the wireless" while maintaining at the same time that the Creator's powers go far beyond what human power can achieve or conceive. Whether these educated believers are consistent or reasonable in so thinking is another question. But the *fact* that they do so think is beyond dispute. Hence the academic creed of "no modern person can believe in miracles" should be consigned to the dustbin of empirically falsified hypotheses. After all, that is what is done when other hypotheses are empirically falsified by the social sciences. I fail to see why this particular creed, however passionately held, can apply for a special exemption, simply because so many academics keep reciting it.

To return to my main point: for methodological reasons I will restrict my discussion to the modest questions about Jesus' miracles that I have outlined above. I do not intend to delve into the vast philosophical questions surrounding the possibility and reality of miracles. But I wish to make clear that I take this route not as a covert way of accepting the empirically falsified credo that "no modern person can believe in miracles."

Having briefly surveyed the problems that any treatment of Gospel miracles raises for modern minds, let us now turn to what is in some ways a still more difficult question: how to understand miracles within the mind-set of the ancient world, a world that often believed in magic as well as miracles.

NOTES TO CHAPTER 17

[1] John P. Meier, *A Marginal Jew. Rethinking the Historical Jesus* (Anchor Bible Reference Library; 3 vols.; New York: Doubleday, 1991) 1. 1.

[2] As the attentive reader has no doubt long since realized, this particular approach makes *A Marginal Jew* a noticeably untheological work. This coheres with the aim announced in the subtitle: *Rethinking the Historical Jesus.* There is indeed need for rethinking the whole project, especially the basic question of what it means to "quest" for the historical Jesus. The problem is that, despite loud protestations about a purely historical approach, most authors of books about the historical Jesus mesh their historical agenda with a theological one. This was true of Reimarus; it remains true of post-Bultmannian portraits from Bornkamm and Käsemann—and, I would add, of portraits from supposedly neutral historians like Geza Vermes. One should note, for instance, how Vermes begins his book *Jesus the Jew. A Historian's Reading of the Gospels* (Philadelphia: Fortress, 1973) with a polemic against the Nicene creed and a lament for Jesus as "this man, so distorted by Christian and Jewish myth alike . . ." (p. 17). This does not augur well for a cool, objective reading of the evidence by a historian. Claims to purely historical scholarship notwithstanding, the quest for the historical Jesus is usually part of a theological program that seeks either to replace the Christ of faith with the historical Jesus (Reimarus, Vermes) or to show how the historical Jesus is relevant to present-day concerns (Sobrino, Segundo). I cannot stress sufficiently that I intend to break with this approach; I do not see my own project as a theological one. Rather, in these volumes I intend to prescind from (though not deny) the insights of faith and the developments of theology in order to focus on what all scholars of any persuasion can affirm by using strictly historical evidence and reasoning. To be sure, after the entire work of *A Marginal Jew* is finished, one can raise the further question of how or whether this project can be appropriated by theologians doing christology in a contemporary context. But to press that question now and to insist that from the start the historical investigation conform its method, questions, and answers to the needs or dictates of theology is to nullify the particular historical project I have proposed.

[3] For the virginal conception, see *A Marginal Jew*, 1. 220–22; for Jesus' reception of a baptism of repentance, see Chapter 13 of the present volume, under "The Meaning of Jesus' Baptism."

[4] From the vast literature on the miracles of the Gospels, the following list—chosen to give a sampling of various views—will supply basic orientation and further bibliography: Alan Richardson, *The Miracle-Stories of the Gospels* (London: SCM, 1941); Robert M. Grant, *Miracle and Natural Law in Graeco-Roman and Early Christian Thought* (Amsterdam: North-Holland Publishing Company, 1952); Erich Fascher, *Kritik am Wunder. Eine geschichtliche Skizze* (Arbeiten zur Theologie 2; Stuttgart: Calwer, 1960); Rudolf Bultmann, "New Testament and Mythology," in Rudolf Bultmann et al., *Kerygma and Myth* (ed. Hans Werner Bartsch; New York: Harper & Row, 1961) 1–44 (see also the various responses in the volume, especially Helmut Thielicke, "The Restatement of New Testament Mythology," 138–74); Rudolf Bultmann, "Zur Frage des Wunders," *Glauben und Verstehen. Gesammelte Aufsätze. Erster Band* (2d ed.; Tübingen: Mohr [Siebeck], 1954) 214–28 (= "The Question of Wonder," *Faith and Understanding* [ed. Robert W. Funk; Philadelphia: Fortress, 1969, 1987] 247–61); Reginald H. Fuller, *Interpreting the Miracles* (London: SCM, 1963); H. van der Loos, *The Miracles of Jesus* (NovTSup

9; Leiden: Brill, 1965); C. F. D. Moule, *Miracles. Cambridge Studies in Their Philosophy and History* (London: Mowbray, 1965); Louis Monden, *Signs and Wonders. A Study of the Miraculous Element in Religion* (New York: Desclee, 1966; Flemish original, 1960); Antony Flew, "Miracles," *The Encyclopedia of Philosophy* (8 vols.; New York: Macmillan; London: Collier, 1967) 5. 346–53; Franz Mussner, *Die Wunder Jesu. Eine Hinführung* (Schriften zur Katechetik 10; Munich: Kösel, 1967); Ernst and Marie-Luise Keller, *Miracles in Dispute. A Continuing Debate* (Philadelphia: Fortress, 1969); Richard Swinburne, *The Concept of Miracle* (Studies in the Philosophy of Religion; London: Macmillan, 1970); Rudolf Pesch, *Jesu ureigene Taten? Ein Beitrag zur Wunderfrage* (QD 52; Freiburg/Basel/Vienna: Herder, 1970); Karl Kertelge, *Die Wunder Jesu im Markusevangelium. Eine redaktionsgeschichtliche Untersuchung* (SANT 23; Munich: Kösel, 1970); idem, "Die Überlieferung der Wunder Jesu und die Frage nach dem historischen Jesus," *Rückfrage nach Jesus* (QD 63; ed. Karl Kertelge; Freiburg/Basel/Vienna: Herder, 1974) 174–93; Anton Vögtle, "The Miracles of Jesus against Their Contemporary Background," *Jesus in His Time* (ed. Hans Jürgen Schultz; Philadelphia: Fortress, 1971, originally 1966); Anton Fridrichsen, *The Problem of Miracle in Primitive Christianity* (Minneapolis: Augsburg, 1972, originally 1925); Bryan R. Wilson, *Magic and the Millennium. A Sociological Study of Religious Movements of Protest Among Tribal and Third-World Peoples* (New York: Harper & Row, 1973); Gerd Theissen, *Urchristliche Wundergeschichten. Ein Beitrag zur formgeschichtlichen Erforschung der synoptischen Evangelien* (SNT 8; Gütersloh: Mohn, 1974) (= *The Miracle Stories of the Early Christian Tradition* [Philadelphia: Fortress, 1983]; John M. Hull, *Hellenistic Magic and the Synoptic Tradition* (SBT 2/28; London: SCM, 1974); Dietrich-Alex Koch, *Die Bedeutung der Wundererzählungen für die Christologie des Markusevangeliums* (BZNW 42; Berlin/New York: de Gruyter, 1975); Xavier Léon-Dufour (ed.), *Les miracles de Jésus selon le Nouveau Testament* (Parole de Dieu; Paris: Seuil, 1977); Leopold Sabourin, *The Divine Miracles Discussed and Defended* (Rome: Catholic Book Agency, 1977); Anton Steiner and Volker Weymann (eds.), *Wunder Jesu* (Bibelarbeit in der Gemeinde 2; Basel: Friedrich Reinhardt; Zurich/Cologne: Benziger, 1978); Morton Smith, *Jesus the Magician* (San Francisco: Harper & Row, 1978); Klaus Berger, "Hellenistisch-heidnische Prodigien und die Vorzeichen in der jüdischen und christlichen Apokalyptik," *ANRW* II/23.2 (published in 1980), 1429–69; Anitra Bingham Kolenkow, "Relationships between Miracle and Prophecy in the Greco-Roman World and Early Christianity," ibid., 1471–1506; David E. Aune, "Magic in Early Christianity," ibid., 1507–57; Harold Remus, *Pagan-Christian Conflict over Miracle in the Second Century* (Patristic Monograph Series 10; Cambridge, MA: Philadelphia Patristic Foundation, 1983); Howard Clark Kee, *Miracle in the Early Christian World. A Study in Sociohistorical Method* (New Haven/London: Yale, 1983); idem, *Medicine, Miracle and Magic in New Testament Times* (SNTSMS 55; Cambridge: Cambridge University, 1986); Colin Brown, *Miracles and the Critical Mind* (Grand Rapids: Eerdmans; Exeter: Paternoster, 1984); William R. Schoedel and Bruce J. Malina, "Miracle or Magic?" *RelSRev* 12 (1986) 31–39; William Lane Craig, "The Problem of Miracles: A Historical and Philosophical Perspective," *Gospel Perspectives. The Miracles of Jesus. Volume 6* (ed. David Wenham and Craig Blomberg; Sheffield: JSOT, 1986) 9–48; Gerhard Maier, "Zur neutestamentlichen Wunderexegese im 19. und 20. Jahrhundert," ibid., 49–87; Edwin Yamauchi, "Magic or Miracle? Disease, Demons and Exorcisms," ibid., 89–183; Barry L. Blackburn, " 'Miracle Working ΘΕΙΟΙ ΑΝΔΡΕΣ' in Hellenism (and Hellenistic Judaism)," ibid., 185–218; René Latourelle, *The Miracles of Jesus and the Theology of Miracles* (New York/Mahwah, NJ: Paulist, 1988); Crossan, *The Historical Jesus*, 137–67, 303–32; Yair Zakovitch and Harold E. Remus, "Miracle," *Anchor Bible Dictionary* (6 vols.; New York: Doubleday, 1992) 4. 845–69; Craig A. Evans, "Life-of-Jesus Research and the Eclipse of Mythology," *TS* 54 (1993) 3–36; Werner Kahl, *New Testament Miracle Stories in Their Religious-Historical Setting* (FRLANT 163; Göttingen: Vandenhoeck & Ruprecht, 1994).

[5] It is remarkable that a number of authors who discuss various definitions or conceptions of miracles never make clear which definition they finally adopt for their own extended discussion of miracles. A brief summary of various definitions that have been proposed is given by Swinburne, *The Concept of Miracle*, 1–11; a more detailed history can be found in van der Loos, *The Miracles of Jesus*, 3–47; a detailed treatment of miracle in the ancient Mediterranean world, with an eye to the sociology of knowledge, is given by Remus, *Pagan-Christian Conflict*, 3–94. The general definition Swinburne offers at the beginning of his investigation is as follows: "an event of an extraordinary kind, brought about by a god, and of religious significance" (*The Concept of Miracle*, 1). Aune ("Magic in Early Christianity," 1522) considers Swinburne's formula a "commonly accepted way" of defining miracles. Swinburne later offers what he considers "a more precise definition": "a violation of a law of nature by a god" (*The Concept of Miracle*, 11). *The Oxford Dictionary of the Christian Church* (ed. F. L. Cross; London: Oxford University, 1958) defines a miracle as "a sensible fact . . . produced by the special intervention of God for a religious end, transcending the normal order of things usually termed the Law of Nature." The definition offered by Thomas G. Pater ("Miracles [Theology of]," *NCE*, 9. 890) is similar: "an extraordinary event, perceptible to the senses, produced by God in a religious context as a sign of the supernatural." Wenham and Blomberg, the editors of *Gospel Perspectives. The Miracles of Jesus*, begin the volume with a brief definition of the miracles of Jesus as "those actions of Jesus which . . . appear to have involved the exercise of supernatural power." A much longer theological definition, but one that comes down to the same thing, is given by van der Loos (*The Miracles of Jesus*, 47): "A miracle is a direct act of God in which He reveals to mankind, with an intention, a new observable reality, which can only be fully understood by faith. In this new reality God proclaims, outside and against the known laws of order and regularity in nature, His freedom, power and love." Indeed, van der Loos insists on the quality of being "against nature" as a prerequisite for a miracle (pp. 67–69). A more nuanced expression of this point is given in the definition of miracle by Francis J. Beckwith (*David Hume's Argument against Miracles. A Critical Analysis* [Lanham, MD/New York/London: University Press of America, 1989] 7): "A miracle is a divine intervention which occurs contrary to the regular course of nature within a significant historical-religious context."

For methodological reasons, I think it wise to avoid the language of "natural" and "supernatural" when defining the concept "miracle," since such language may import philosophical and theological distinctions that are foreign to (and in the case of "supernatural," later than) the biblical material we are treating (see Fuller, *Interpreting the Miracles*, 8–11). Hence I likewise have a problem with the approach of Craig ("The Problem of Miracles," 29–30), who seeks to avoid the idea of miracles as "violations of nature" by defining them as "events which lie outside the productive capacity of nature," or as events "which cannot be accounted for wholly by reference to relevant natural forces," or simply as events that are physically or naturally impossible. Some who define miracles in terms of nature (e.g., "an event produced by God Himself in infringement of the laws of nature") then proceed to distinguish among miracles above or surpassing nature (e.g., raising the dead to life), miracles contrary to nature (e.g., the three men in the fiery furnace [Daniel

3] who emerged unscathed), and miracles beyond or beside (*praeter*) nature (e.g., most miraculous healings); see François Leuret and Henri Bon, *Modern Miraculous Cures* (New York: Farrar, Straus and Cudahy, 1957) 9, 21–22.

Kee (*Miracle in the Early Christian World*, 147) specifies that in the Jewish Bible, "miracle appears in two major forms: extraordinary acts said to be performed by the God of Israel, nearly always in behalf of his people or in defeat of their enemies; and acts performed by divinely endowed persons, who function as agents of God." Dealing specifically with healing miracles, Kee (*Medicine, Miracle and Magic*, 3) defines them as healings "accomplished through appeal to, and subsequent action by the gods, either directly or through a chosen intermediary agent."

Meshing German Lutheran piety, a view of science and "the laws of nature" inherited from the Enlightenment, and Heideggerian existentialism, Bultmann ("Zur Frage des Wunders," 214, 217–21) distinguishes between a miracle, which traditionally was understood as an event contrary to nature (a concept that is impossible for a modern person to believe), and a wonder, which properly understood is the revelation to an individual of the grace of God forgiving the godless. On Bultmann's distinction and its debt to an Enlightenment view of the laws of nature, see Latourelle, *The Miracles of Jesus*, 27–29. I will discuss below Bultmann's contention that modern educated persons cannot possibly believe in miracles. What is especially surprising about Bultmann's treatment of miracles in reference to the historical Jesus is his attribution of a later philosophical idea of miracles to Jesus and his contemporaries. In his early *Jesus and the Word* (London/Glasgow: Collins [Fontana], 1958, originally 1926), Bultmann quite rightly stresses that Jesus shared his contemporaries' belief in miracles, a belief that should not be watered down to fit modern sensibilities (p. 123). But then Bultmann goes on to describe this belief of Jesus' contemporaries (p. 124): "But in Jewish thought an event which is contrary to nature, which occurs outside of the known and ordinary chain of cause and effect, is called a miracle and ascribed to a supernatural cause. . . ." This is a strange retrojection of later philosophical terminology and ideas about miracles into the life and times of Jesus. Bultmann's attempt (pp. 125, 128) to clarify his position by adding that Jesus' "concept of causality is not abstract but concrete, referring a specific phenomenon to a specific cause, as daily experience taught him" and that "the concept of miracle, the concept of God in Jesus' sense, does away with the concept of nature" does not help very much. Against this whole approach is Vögtle, "The Miracles of Jesus," 96.

6 Borrowing from many other definitions that have been proposed, I have tried to construct as comprehensive and neutral a definition as possible. By a happy accident, the wording echoes in a number of places the vocabulary of miracles in the Gospels. The Gospels frequently use *dynamis* (power), *ergon* (work), and *sēmeion* (sign), and less frequently *teras* (prodigy, portent, wonder), *thaumasia* (wonderful things), and *paradoxa* (strange or wonderful things). But for the time being, the definition is fashioned mainly with an eye to modern philosophical and scientific discussions. As we shall see in the next chapter, the concept of miracle will have to be rethought when we place the question of miracles in an ancient rather than a modern context.

7 Hence I would not count either Christ's resurrection from the dead or his "real presence" in the eucharist as a miracle, since neither is in principle open to the observation of any and every observer. Granted, in their different critiques of David Hume's rejection of miracles, Michael P. Levine and Francis J. Beckwith regard the real presence and the resurrection respectively as examples of miracles. As

can be seen from my definition of miracles, I think both examples unfortunate, though both are "givens" in the traditional debate over miracles. For the real presence (or more technically, transubstantiation), see Michael P. Levine, *Hume and the Problem of Miracles: A Solution* (Philosophical Studies Series 41; Dordrecht/Boston/London: Kluwer, 1989) 106–22, 133–51. For the resurrection, see Beckwith, *David Hume's Argument against Miracles*, 1, 50, 65–66 (n. 5).

[8]There is a "common sense" formulation of this component in the exasperated cry of the man born blind in John 9:32: "Never has it been heard that anyone [ever] opened the eyes of a person born blind." As many writers on miracles point out, there is a basic problem here: granted the great (miraculous?) strides science has made in the last few centuries, how can anyone know with certainty what will be possible or impossible to human science at some future date? That is a perfectly reasonable objection, which simply points up the historicity of all human knowledge. The observation holds true, as we shall see, not only for arguments in favor of miracles but also for arguments against miracles; they too rest on certain philosophical and scientific presuppositions that may be abandoned at a later date.

However, I think that two general observations may be made in defense of the second component of my definition. (1) While there will always be startling developments in science, most people do not seriously think that at some future date totally blind or actually dead people will be restored to sight or physical life merely by a word of command. (2) More to the point, whether anything like that will be possible in some unimaginable future, no one seriously doubts that it was impossible in the 1st century A.D. This second observation opens up a further interesting speculative question: precisely because of the progress of science, is there such a thing as a historically conditioned miracle? For example, in our present-day world it is by no means impossible for a person to be in Jerusalem early in the morning of a given day and to be in Rome in the evening of the same day. In the 1st century A.D. it would have been miraculous for anyone to have done that.

[9]For different understandings of "nature" and "the natural law," see Remus, *Pagan-Christian Conflict*, 14–24; Grant, *Miracle and Natural Law*, 3–28. Sanders (*Judaism. Practice and Belief*, 268) observes that Diaspora Jews could agree with the Greco-Roman view that life should be lived in accord with "nature" and yet disagree with most Greeks and Romans as to what this entailed in practice.

[10]On this, see, e.g., J. P. Ross, "Some Notes on Miracle in the Old Testament," Moule (ed.), *Miracles. Cambridge Studies in Their Philosophy and History*, 45–60, esp. 46–51; Gerhard von Rad, *Old Testament Theology* (2 vols.; Edinburgh and London: Oliver and Boyd, 1962, 1965) 1. 141, 156–57 (and the whole of pp. 136–60); and the whole of Bernhard W. Anderson's *Creation versus Chaos* (New York: Association, 1967).

[11]Remus (*Pagan-Christian Conflict*, 23) notes that "in Jewish writings in Greek, *physis* appears primarily, and not often, in books composed originally in Greek. . . ."

[12]See, e.g., Wis 19:20, in which God's saving power, delivering his people (especially during the exodus and wandering in the desert) is said to bring it about that water forgets its quenching "nature" (*physeōs* according to Codices Alexandrinus and Sinaiticus, though Codex Vaticanus reads *dynameōs* ["power"] instead). J. P. M. Sweet ("The Theory of Miracles in the Wisdom of Solomon," Moule [ed.], *Miracles. Cambridge Studies in Their Philosophy and History*, 115–26) sees the author of the Book of Wisdom engaged in an intriguing hermeneutic as he rein-

terprets the miracles recorded in Israel's history. He attempts "to hold together the biblical doctrine of Creation—God's constant physical and moral control of the world which he called into being out of nothing—and the assumptions of Greek philosophy, that the world was shaped by God out of pre-existing matter and runs according to the immutable laws then implanted" (p. 116). Sweet sees the value of the author's project in that "it holds together belief both in the uniformity of the world as understood by educated men of the time, and in God's control of the world" (p. 125).

[13] See, e.g., the remarks of Marcus Aurelius in his *Meditations*, 4.21,23; the basic concept of God-equals-nature is represented in modern philosophy especially by Spinoza.

[14] Speaking of the ancient Greco-Roman world, Remus (*Pagan-Christian Conflict*, 27) states: "The premise shared by proponents and opponents of miracle was that explanation of an extraordinary phenomenon by reference to deity was intrinsic to 'miracle.'" Kee (*Medicine, Miracle and Magic*, 3) agrees in making action by the gods central to the ancient conception of a miracle.

Traditional Christian theology raised further questions about distinguishing miracles worked directly by God from miracles worked by angels or the devil; a consideration of pagan polytheism would naturally add questions about miracles worked by gods, "demons" (good and bad), and deified heroes. There were different views on the subject even within the Roman Catholic tradition; see Swinburne, *The Concept of Miracles*, 2. Granted the composition and intent of our "unpapal conclave," which at this point is dealing with the question of "miracles and *modern* minds," we prescind from such questions.

[15] This formulation does not deny that God might use some human being (i.e., a miracle-worker) as an instrument of his power. It rather affirms that no human being could be in himself or herself the adequate cause or explanation of some extraordinary event that surpasses all human power.

[16] Greco-Roman writers, especially philosophers and historians, were not unaware of possible alternate explanations of extraordinary events, and some were not slow to use them to avoid referring such events to the gods; see Remus, *Pagan-Christian Conflict*, 27–47.

[17] As G. F. Woods ("The Evidential Value of the Biblical Miracles," in Moule [ed.], *Miracles. Cambridge Studies in Their Philosophy and History*, 21–32) observes, ". . . the evidential value of the miraculous is closely interwoven with the metaphysical views of those to whom the evidence is offered. . . . the weighing of historical evidence is affected by the metaphysical presuppositions of those who weigh the evidence. There are no metaphysically neutral scales" (p. 30).

[18] Richardson (*Miracle-Stories*, 127) makes the same point in discussing the Gospel miracles in particular: "Thus, the answer to the question, Did the miracles happen? is always a *personal* answer. It is not the judgment of an historian *qua* scientific investigator. . . ." However, Richardson does not seem to accept the possibility that a believer could, for methodological reasons in a historical investigation, bracket his or her faith-judgment and leave the question open for the time being.

[19] Curiously, many treatments of the Gospel miracles make little or no reference to modern claims of miracles occurring in a Christian context in Europe or the United States. This is especially strange when so many recent studies draw upon sociological or anthropological studies of miracles or magic in the ancient Greco-

Roman world or in the present-day Third World. One gets the impression that some authors are comfortable with the topic of miracles only if it is kept "at arm's length." Perhaps scholars are also put off by the bizarre and sensationalistic nature of some modern claims; one need only think of items in the supermarket tabloids. Hence I choose as a modern illustration the supposed miracles at Lourdes, which at least offer some opportunity to check the data.

[20] The fullest documentation of the events surrounding the establishment of the Lourdes shrine can be found in René Laurentin and Bernard Billet, *Lourdes. Dossier des documents authentiques* (7 vols.; Paris: Lethielleux, 1957–66). From the many works written about the cures claimed at Lourdes (and elsewhere), see, e.g., Ruth Cranston, *The Miracle of Lourdes* (New York: McGraw-Hill, 1955); Leuret and Bon, *Modern Miraculous Cures;* Monden, *Signs and Wonders,* 194–250; Alphonse Olivieri (head doctor of the medical bureau at Lourdes) and Bernard Billet, *Y a-t-il encore des miracles à Lourdes? 18 dossiers de guérisons (1950–1969)* (Paris: Lethielleux; Lourdes: Oeuvre de la Grotte, 1970); Sabourin, *The Divine Miracles,* 151–72. Needless to say, not all the studies are positive in their approach. For a critical view, see, e.g., Franz L. Schleyer, *Die Heilungen von Lourdes. Eine kritische Untersuchung* (Bonn: Bouvier, 1949); Schleyer stresses the strong psychological element evident in many of the cures. Likewise critical is D. J. West, *Eleven Lourdes Miracles* (London: Duckworth, 1957); West points out that some cases declared miraculous might have natural explanations, especially psychological ones. In some cases the original diagnosis was uncertain; in others, sufficient documentation was lacking. At the same time, it is only fair to point out that West, unlike the doctors at Lourdes, relied totally on written documents, without any personal interviews with the patients; see the evaluation of his work by Sabourin, *The Divine Miracles,* 156–59. For a sociological approach to the phenomenon of Lourdes, see Alan Neame, *The Happening at Lourdes. The Sociology of the Grotto* (New York: Simon and Schuster, 1967). In recent years the social sciences have been applied to supposed Marian apparitions and cures with some intriguing results. For a study undertaken with a judicious use of the social sciences, see Sandra L. Zimdars-Swartz, *Encountering Mary* (Princeton: NJ: Princeton University, 1991); Lourdes is treated on pp. 43–67; see also Thomas A. Kselman, *Miracles and Prophecies in Nineteenth-Century France* (New Brunswick, NJ: Rutgers University, 1983). A meticulous sociological study of one concrete case of contemporary Marian piety can be found in Robert Anthony Orsi's *The Madonna of 115th Street* (New Haven and London: Yale University, 1985).

[21] This is stressed by Leuret and Bon, *Modern Miraculous Cures,* 102.

[22] The stringency of ecclesiastical procedures can be seen from statistics: between 1948 and 1993 some 1,300 cures have been alleged at Lourdes; of these, only 18 have been judged miracles by church authorities. One perduring problem in the whole process is the difficulty of obtaining complete medical records, especially of the state of the patient before the reputed cure. For criticism of the lack of records in various cases, see Sabourin, *The Divine Miracles,* 156–59.

[23] Monden (*Signs and Wonders,* 343–45) expresses the point of the limitations of scientific inquiry somewhat differently than I, but I think that his distinction is basically the same as mine.

[24] One must be careful about the limitations of an argument from analogy; see the cautions voiced by C. Behan McCullagh, *Justifying Historical Descriptions* (Cambridge: Cambridge University, 1984) 85–90. Hence I stress the provisos of "if the same circumstances are present" and "may."

I am aware that here I am turning the usual objection against miracles drawn from

Ernst Troeltsch's principle of analogy on its head. For Troeltsch's classic articulation of the principle of analogy in historical criticism, see his "Überhistorische und dogmatische Methode in der Theologie," *Gesammelte Schriften* (2d ed.; 4 vols.; Aalen: Scientia, 1962; originally 1913, 1922) 2. 729–53, esp. 731–33. In this I differ from the approach of Craig, "The Problem of Miracles," 41–42. Craig first explains Troeltsch's principle: the past does not differ essentially from the present; the two must be the same *in kind* if historical investigation is to be possible. Craig proceeds to state: "Troeltsch realized that this principle was incompatible with miraculous events . . ." (p. 41). Craig then appeals to scholars like Wolfhart Pannenberg, R. G. Collingwood, and Richard Niebuhr to oppose the wholesale application of Troeltsch's principle to miracles; see in particular Wolfhart Pannenberg, "Heilsgeschehen und Geschichte," *Grundfragen systematischer Theologie. Gesammelte Aufsätze* (2 vols.; Göttingen: Vandenhoeck & Ruprecht, 1967, 1980) 1. 22–78, esp. 44–54 (= "Redemptive Event and History," *Basic Questions in Theology* [2 vols.; Philadelphia: Fortress, 1970, 1971] 1. 15–80, esp. 38–50). Troeltsch, says Craig (following Pannenberg), has illegitimately elevated the postulate of analogy to constrict all past events to purely natural events. But one cannot a priori exclude the possibility of an event bursting all analogies. (I would add a further objection: there is a certain ambiguity from the start in Troeltsch's demand that historical events be "homogeneous" or basically similar in kind [*gleichartig*] while not being identical or the same [*gleich*].)

While a great deal of Craig's and Pannenberg's criticism of Troeltsch's use of historical analogy is valid, I have three reservations: (1) Some of their objections may be understood as lumping together the miracles of Jesus' public ministry and his resurrection. Here an apologist like Colin Brown (*Miracles and the Critical Mind*) is more cautious, and rightly so. For my part, I would not classify the resurrection as a miracle, since it does not fit the definition I have proposed above. That is to say, it is not in principle perceivable by any and all observers (cf. the Apostle Peter's statement in Acts 10:40–41). Indeed, some, while not denying the reality of the resurrection, would question whether it should be labeled a "historical event" at all; see *A Marginal Jew*, 1. 201 n. 2. (2) Rather than surrendering immediately to the claim that there are no modern analogies to the miracle narratives in the Gospels, one should first consider possible analogies from controllable data like the reports of miracles at Lourdes. At the very least we have analogous *claims* of miraculous activity in a religious context connected with faith in Jesus of Nazareth. In my view, neither the historian examining the cures at Lourdes nor the historian examining the supposed miracles of Jesus can ever make the judgment *as a historian* that these events are miracles wrought by God; this, too, is part of the analogy. (3) When one reads Troeltsch's essay on historical method on the one hand and Pannenberg's essay on redemptive event and history on the other, one quickly realizes that the question of historical analogy is being weighed down by excess freight from modern theological debates among German Protestants. This is not to say that such debates are wrong; but the historian or exegete need not be burdened with all the baggage of systematic theology simply because he or she at times argues from historical analogy. Moreover, whether one is well advised to counter Troeltsch's understanding of revelation and history with that of Pannenberg is highly questionable. In my opinion, Pannenberg's overall approach to revelation and faith on the one hand and history and reason on the other creates more difficulties than it solves. At times it comes close to saying that the object of faith can be proven by historical research. On this whole matter, see also Wolfhart Pannenberg, "Dogmatische Thesen zur Lehre von der Offenbarung," *Offenbarung als Geschichte* (*KD*, Beiheft 1; 2d ed.; ed. Wolfhart Pannenberg et al.; Göttingen: Vandenhoeck & Ruprecht, 1963) 91–114.

[25] One is reminded of the observations made in Volume One about the difference between writing ancient and writing modern history; see *A Marginal Jew*, 1. 21–24.

[26] Daniel Mark Epstein, *Sister Aimee. The Life of Aimee Semple McPherson* (New York: Harcourt Brace Jovanovich, 1993).

[27] Epstein, *Sister Aimee*, 77. Epstein discusses the methodological problem that reports of miracles pose to the historian on pp. 57 and 111; see also p. 74. In many ways, in this present chapter on miracles and modern minds, McPherson, a preacher and charismatic miracle-worker like Jesus, would have provided a better case study of the problem of reports of miracles in the modern world than did the shrine at Lourdes. However, since Lourdes has maintained throughout the years a medical bureau charged with examining supposed marvelous cures, it supplies a more serious example of miraculous claims in the 20th century, one that is not so easily dismissed with a wry smile.

[28] On contemporary prejudices, see Monden, *Signs and Wonders*, 184–93.

[29] The most important work of Spinoza with regard to his critique of miracles is his *Tractatus theologico-politicus*. The Latin text can be found in *Benedicti de Spinoza opera quotquot reperta sunt* (ed. J van Vloten and J. P. N. Land; 3d ed.; 4 vols.; The Hague: Nijhoff, 1914) 2. 83–331. An English translation can be found in R. H. M. Elwes (translator and editor), *The Chief Works of Benedict de Spinoza* (2 vols.; New York: Dover, 1951) 1–278. The heart of Spinoza's argument can be found in Chapter 6, "De miraculis" (pp. 156–71 in the Latin edition, pp. 81–97 in the English translation). For evaluations and critiques of Spinoza's arguments, see Leo Strauss, *Spinoza's Critique of Religion* (New York: Schocken, 1965), with a treatment of miracles on pp. 123–36 and a critique on pp. 144–46; Sylvain Zac, *Spinoza et l'interprétation de l'écriture* (Bibliothèque de philosophie contemporaine; Paris: Presses universitaires de France, 1965); André Malet, *Le traité théologico-politique de Spinoza et la pensée biblique* (Publications de l'université de Dijon 35; Paris: Société Les Belles Lettres, 1966), esp. Chapter 5, "Le miracle selon le *Tractatus* et selon la Bible," pp. 171–85, with a critique of Spinoza's views on pp. 183–85.

[30] For a succinct statement of his position, see (François-Marie Arouet) Voltaire, "Miracles," *Dictionnaire philosophique* (Paris: Garnier, 1967) 314–20. An English translation can be found in Voltaire, *Philosophical Dictionary* (ed. Peter Gay; 2 vols.; New York: Basic Books, 1962) 2. 392–98. On p. 314 of the French text (p. 392 of the English) Voltaire gives his definition of a miracle ("the violation of divine and eternal laws") and then states the essence of the Deist (and for the most part the rationalist and Enlightenment) objection to miracles: "It is impossible that the infinitely wise Being has made laws in order to violate them. He has made this immense machine [of the universe] as good as he could." Hence, argues Voltaire, God has no reason to change anything. Voltaire provides an excellent reminder that almost all of the great thinkers of the Enlightenment, despite some fierce attacks on traditional Christianity, were nonetheless theists, not atheists.

[31] The classic expression of Hume's critique of miracles is found in David Hume, *An Inquiry Concerning Human Understanding* (ed. Charles W. Hendel; New York: Liberal Arts, 1955); the relevant chapter is Chapter X, "Of Miracles" (in this edition, pp. 117–41). Besides the critique of Hume's approach given by Craig ("The Problem of Miracles," 37–43), evaluations and critiques of Hume's arguments can be found in Antony Flew, *Hume's Philosophy of Belief. A Study of His First Inquiry* (London: Routledge & Kegan Paul; New York: Humanities, 1961), esp. Chapter 8; R. M. Burns, *The Great Debate on Miracles: From Joseph Glanvill to David Hume* (Lewisburg, PA: Bucknell University; London/Toronto: Associated University, 1981), with a critique of Hume's arguments on pp. 176–246; J. C. A. Gaskin, *Hume's Philosophy of Religion* (2d ed.; Atlantic Highlands, NJ: Humanities, 1988), esp. Chapter 8, "Miracles and Revela-

tion," 135–65; Beckwith, *David Hume's Argument against Miracles*; Levine, *Hume and the Problem of Miracles*; Keith E. Yandell, *Hume's "Inexplicable Mystery." His Views on Religion* (Philadelphia: Temple University, 1990), esp. Chapter 15, "Miracles," 315–38. Gaskin thinks that Hume's famous chapter "Of Miracles" shows too much confidence in one's ability to know what is or is not physically possible. Moreover, Gaskin argues that there is a conflict in Hume's own position between his account of the laws of nature and his definition of a miracle (pp. 159–61, 165). Yandell also thinks that Hume fails to prove his point. Rather, argues Yandell, "logically and philosophically, miracles may occur, and logically and philosophically nothing prevents us from knowingly observing them. What remains is the theological and historical question, 'Have they occurred?' " (p. 338). After a thorough analysis of Hume's arguments against miracles, Levine concludes that Hume's case is "grounded in his peculiarly narrow philosophical empiricism" (*Hume and the Problem of Miracles*, 186); Levine himself concludes "that it is possible for one to justifiably believe that a miracle has occurred, either on the basis of testimony or direct experience" (p. 152). Similarly, Beckwith (*David Hume's Argument against Miracles*, 139) ends his monograph with the judgment that Hume's argument does not overturn "the possibility that one may have enough evidence to make one's belief in a particular miracle-claim epistemologically reasonable." Although Antony Flew is more in the Humean skeptical tradition than these other critics, he too sees weaknesses in Hume's arguments against miracles; see Flew, *Hume's Philosophy of Belief*, Chapter 8, "Miracles and Methodology," pp. 166–213; idem, *David Hume. Philosopher of Moral Science* (Oxford/New York: Blackwell, 1986), esp. Chapter 5, "The Necessity of Causes, and the Impossibility of the Miraculous," 69–89. Flew (*David Hume*, 80) makes an important observation about the precise point of Hume's argument: ". . . Hume was engaged with a question of evidence rather than a question of fact. What he was trying to establish was: not that miracles do not occur, although he does make it very plain that this was his own view as well as that of all other men of sense, but that, whether or not they did or had, this is not something we can any of us ever be in a position positively to know." As Craig ("The Problem of Miracles," 17) puts it, "if Spinoza attacked the possibility of the *occurrence* of a miracle, Hume attacked the possibility of the *identification* of a miracle."

[32] "The Age of Reason," "the Enlightenment," and "Deism" are terms that are sometimes used loosely and almost interchangeably in discussions of Spinoza, Hume, and the philosophical critique of miracles. If one wants to be more precise (and, admittedly, somewhat arbitrary), the Age of Reason may be said to embrace the increasingly rationalistic cast of philosophy in the 17th and 18th centuries, while the Enlightenment is often restricted to the 18th century. Granted these definitions, Spinoza belonged to the Age of Reason as a preeminent example of continental rationalism (along with Descartes and Leibniz), but preceded the Enlightenment. It should be noted that, although Spinoza's view of the universe is sometimes related to Newtonian physics, Spinoza published his pivotal *Tractatus theologico-politicus* in 1670, years before Isaac Newton's *Philosophiae Naturalis Principia Mathematica* (published in 1687). In contrast, the influence of Newton's thought on Voltaire and Hume is obvious. Although Spinoza and Hume are often lumped together because of their contributions to the rationalistic critique of miracles, their philosophies, taken in their entirety, were hardly similar. Spinoza spun out a grand metaphysical system based on a type of pantheism that was essentially materialistic monism. Hume, representing British (especially Scottish) traditions of commonsense, empiricism, and skepticism, disliked grand metaphysical systems.

"Deism" is likewise a tricky category to define; see Burns, *The Great Debate on Miracles*, 13–14. But if one accepts its usual application to thinkers of the 18th-century

English and French Enlightenment like Voltaire, neither Spinoza nor Hume should be called a Deist. On the question of Hume's relation to Deism, see Burns, ibid., 139: unlike the Deists, Hume had no "gospel" of salvific truth, no rational religion to which he zealously sought to convert others. Correspondingly, he did not share the belief of many Deists in the inevitability of human progress. In contrast, Voltaire may with fairness be called an Enlightenment Deist. Even here, though, the terminology is complicated. As Rosemary Z. Lauer points out (*The Mind of Voltaire. A Study in His "Constructive Deism"* [Westminster, MD: Newman, 1961] vii), "the term *deism* . . . is quite justly applied to Voltaire's thought." Yet, while Voltaire used the term earlier on, he came to prefer the term "theist" to "deist"; on this change, see René Pomeau, *La religion de Voltaire* (2d ed.; Paris: Nizet, 1969) 428 with nn. 2 and 3.

[33] For arguments for and against the rejection of miracles by Spinoza and Hume, see Craig, "The Problem of Miracles," 15–43.

[34] For a thumbnail sketch of the history of the relation of scientific thought to the problem of miracles, see van der Loos, *The Miracles of Jesus*, 48–79 (for miracles and the physical sciences, especially physics) and 80–113 (for miracles and medicine).

[35] This is the basis of Spinoza's rejection of the possibility of miracles. In his *Tractatus theologico-politicus*, capite VI, "de miraculis" (Chapter 6, "On miracles"), Spinoza lays down that "nothing happens contrary to nature; rather, nature keeps an eternal, fixed, and immutable order" (translation mine). Since Spinoza identifies this immutable order of nature with God's decrees, which flow from the necessity and perfection of God's nature, it stands to reason that God would not act against his own immutable and perfect nature by performing a miracle. To put the whole matter another way: since Spinoza's view is basically pantheistic (God is identified with nature), it is by definition impossible that God (= nature) would do something contrary to nature, i.e., a miracle. The "miracles" reported in the Bible are either the workings of nature that ancient people could not understand or the results of ancient writers embellishing the events they recounted.

[36] One abiding problem in the whole discussion of miracles is the loaded vocabulary of "violation," "intervention," and "laws." The imagery of God "intervening" in the universe to "violate" the very "laws" he has set up involves a confusing mass of mythological metaphors. In the systematic thought of critical philosophy and theology one would expect instead clearly defined concepts. For one attempt to find an alternative to "intervention" language in a theological framework, see C. F. D. Moule, "Introduction," in Moule (ed.), *Miracles. Cambridge Studies in Their Philosophy and History*, 3–17, esp. 12–17; G. F. Woods, "The Evidential Value of the Biblical Miracles," ibid., 21–32, esp. 29–30.

[37] See David C. Cassidy, *Uncertainty: The Life and Science of Werner Heisenberg* (New York: Freeman, 1992); and the summary of his research in his article, "Heisenberg, Uncertainty and the Quantum Revolution," *Scientific American*, May, 1992, pp. 106–12. For the relation of the indeterminism of quantum physics to the question of miracles, see Mary Hesse, "Miracles and the Laws of Nature," Moule (ed.), *Miracles. Cambridge Studies in Their Philosophy and History*, 35–42, esp. 38–40.

[38] For salutary warnings against seizing upon Heisenberg's principle of indeterminacy as a defense of miracles, see van der Loos, *The Miracles of Jesus*, 62–66; Craig, "The Problem of Miracles," 27–28.

[39] It is intriguing to see how Bultmann ("Zur Frage des Wunders," 215) defends his rejection of miracles on the grounds that they violate the laws of nature: his own con-

ception of the laws of nature, he claims, is not a subjective worldview *(Weltanschauung)*, but a given of human existence in the modern world. One may ask whether such a conception is not rather a given of the Enlightenment view of nature that Bultmann takes for granted. It would be interesting to compare Bultmann's assurance about his view of the physical universe with Heisenberg's dislike of 19th-century atomism, which he saw as a type of mechanistic materialism derived from the atomic theories of Leucippus and Democritus. Heisenberg inclined instead to the view that the contemporary physics of elementary particles "found its meaning in the ancient idealism and transcendent philosophy of Plato" (Cassidy, *Uncertainty*, 544). This is not to say that Bultmann's view of the physical universe is wrong or that Heisenberg's is right; it is simply to remind ourselves that any particular philosophical view of the physical universe may not be so much of a "given" of human existence as its proponent believes.

[40] Bultmann, "New Testament and Mythology," 5. The same sort of worldview is the framework within which Wilson wrote his very useful *Magic and the Millennium;* beyond the sociological analysis proper to the book there looms an entire (though implicit) philosophical position that allows for no reality beyond what can be empirically justified. See in particular the concluding chapter of *Magic and Millennium*, 484–504, notably 484, 500–502. Wilson's version of Bultmann's credo can be found on pp. 502–3. After noting that psychological benefits like reassurance and solace constitute the sole—and feeble—magic that religion dispenses today, he continues (p. 503): "Modern men do not look for a man—or a god—to 'come and save us': they look to impersonal, consciously evolved agencies and organization, and to scientific procedures of enquiry and prescription." A similar view pervades many an exegetical treatment of the miracle stories of the Gospels; see, e.g., Gerd Petzke, "Die historische Frage nach den Wundertaten Jesu, dargestellt am Beispiel des Exorzismus Mark. IX. 14–29 par," *NTS* 22 (1975–76) 180–204 (especially the final pages).

[41] George Gallup, Jr., and Jim Castelli, *The People's Religion. American Faith in the 90's* (New York: Macmillan; London: Collier, 1989) 58; see also pp. 4, 56, 119. The survey is quoted in an article on the prevalence of belief in miracles in contemporary America in *The Washington Post*, Sunday, March 22, 1992, page A14. The author of the *Post* article, Laura Sessions Stepp, observes: "For all the talk about an increasingly secular American culture, the possibility of miracles continues to exert a powerful hold."

One small point about the question Gallup asked concerning belief in miracles should not be overlooked: the proposed statement reads "*even* today, miracles are performed by the power of God" (emphasis mine). The "even" carries the implicit judgment that it would be easier to believe in miracles that took place in the past than in those claimed to occur in the present. If this implicit judgment was shared by those responding to the poll, one might infer that more than 82 percent of the respondents believe that miracles have occurred at some time in the past.

[42] The accompanying table on p. 58 of Gallup's *The People's Religion* indicates that the percentage of agreement remains high for almost all segments of the population, fluctuating, e.g., up to 97 percent for black Evangelical Protestants and down to 77 percent for males in general and for people thirty to thirty-nine years old. For a further breakdown of the figures, see George Gallup, Jr., and Sarah Jones, *100 Questions and Answers: Religion in America* (Princeton, NJ: Princeton Religion Research Center, 1989) 10. Of all the people who reacted to the statement "even today, miracles are performed by the power of God," 51 percent completely agreed, 29 percent mostly agreed, 9 percent mostly disagreed, 6 percent completely disagreed, and 5 percent did not know.

[43] Contrast the results of the Gallup poll with the declaration of Wilson (*Magic and*

the Millennium, 70), speaking of miracles as manifestations of supernatural power: "If, in the orthodox religious traditions of the western world, these elements appear as a survival and perhaps especially so to the religiously sophisticated, they nonetheless persist as an *undercurrent* among the laity. They exist as superstitions . . ." (emphasis mine). Eighty percent may appear to some as more than an undercurrent. Here we have a collision between social fact, as represented by Gallup, and sociological theory, as represented by Wilson. I think it clear which must yield.

CHAPTER 18

MIRACLES AND ANCIENT MINDS

I. SOME BASIC PROBLEMS

As we move from modern to ancient minds, we find that the problem of miracles among the ancients turns out to be almost the exact opposite of the one we have been struggling with up until now. To be sure, skepticism about or denial of miracles can be found among some of the Greek and Roman elite, especially certain philosophers and rhetoricians (e.g., Epicurus, Lucretius, Cicero, Lucian),[1] usually because of more fundamental doubts about popular notions of the gods and their intervention in human affairs. On the whole, however, the ancient Greco-Roman world was one in which miracles were accepted as part of the religious landscape.[2] A major problem that faces the modern historian seeking to enter into the thought world of the 1st century A.D. is not objections to miracles by the elite but the all-too-ready acceptance of them by ordinary people. Naturally, this has ramifications for any attempt to judge the historicity of the miracle stories in the Gospels. For convenience' sake, this problem of miracles in the ancient world can be subdivided into two distinct though allied problems: Greco-Roman parallels to Gospel miracle stories and the relation of miracles to magic. In what follows I will first make a few general observations about pagan and Jewish parallels, while relegating detailed questions on the subject to the excursus at the end of this chapter. Then I will take up the complicated problem of the relation between (or identity of?) miracle and magic.

II. PAGAN AND JEWISH PARALLELS TO GOSPEL MIRACLES

At the beginning of the 20th century, the "history of religion" school (*die religionsgeschichtliche Schule*), especially in Germany, drew attention to the various parallels between the miracles of Jesus recorded in the Four Gospels and the miracles (as well as magic) found in pagan and Jewish sources of the period.[3] The practitioners of form criticism then took up and expanded this approach. In their major works on form criticism, both Bultmann and Dibelius devoted numerous pages to Jewish and pagan parallels to the Gospel miracle stories.[4] In such studies the claim is usually made that reports of Jesus' miracles reflect the literary forms, themes, and motifs found in pagan and Jewish miracle stories circulating in the Mediterranean world around the turn of the era.

There is a great deal of truth to this claim, but at the same time some distinctions are in order. A proper evaluation of pagan, Jewish, and Gospel miracle stories must involve respect for differences as well as similarities. Unfortunately, detailed analyses and comparisons of the different miracle traditions take a great deal of space and time. So as not to burden the reader unduly, I have relegated the technical analysis of the pagan and rabbinic parallels to the excursus at the end of this chapter. Here I will simply make a few general observations based on the results of the excursus, to which the interested reader is referred.

(1) With respect to the dating of the documents containing miracle stories, many of the pagan and Jewish parallels (e.g., Philostratus' *Life of Apollonius of Tyana* or the rabbinic material) come from centuries after the Four Gospels.

(2) Sometimes the "parallel" material fails to parallel the Gospels at a key point: namely, Jesus in the Gospels is presented as a miracle-*worker, performing* miracles by his own power. Both Josephus and the rabbinic material will at times present pious figures whose prayers for special favors (rain, healing) are answered in speedy, spectacular, or superhuman ways, or who receive miraculous protection from God, or who promise miracles at a future date. Stories of this type cannot in the strict sense be called the stories of miracle-*workers*.

(3) Most importantly, there is the question of what exactly the parallels demonstrate. On the one hand, the work of the history-of-religion school and form criticism shows that the miracle stories in the Gospels do in fact parallel *literary forms* found in pagan and Jewish miracle stories. On the other hand, one cannot automatically draw from this fact firm conclusions about the *historicity* of the Gospel stories. That is to say, from the mere fact of form-critical parallels one cannot immediately conclude that most or all of the traditions about Jesus' miracles do not go back to the historical Jesus, but were inserted instead into the Jesus tradition by the early church because it was competing with other religious traditions that extolled miracle-workers.[5]

The reason why such conclusions do not follow necessarily from the mere fact of literary parallelism is clear once we pose a simple question. For the sake of argument, let us grant that Jesus actually performed some extraordinary deeds thought by his audience to be miracles. The natural question then becomes: How would such events have been narrated in the 1st century A.D. if not with the literary forms used in that time-period to recount miracle stories?[6]

Here we run up against a basic limitation in the method of form criticism: the classification, comparison, and history of the literary forms in the Gospels do not of themselves demonstrate whether any particular saying or event ultimately comes from the historical Jesus. For that, the application of the usual

criteria of historicity, discussed in Chapter 6 of Volume One of *A Marginal Jew*, is required. The subsequent chapters will be dedicated to just such an application of these criteria to the Gospel miracle stories.

I should add that what is true of the literary form of miracle stories holds true as well for the basic vocabulary used to describe a miracle. As linguistic studies have shown, there is no radical difference between the vocabulary used for the miracles of Jesus in the Gospels (and later on in the Fathers of the Church) and the vocabulary employed to describe pagan or Jewish miracles.[7] Thus, as is often the case, attempts to establish the uniqueness of Jesus (or more particularly his miracles) solely on the basis of differences in word usage prove to be misguided, especially when the supposed differences evaporate on closer examination.

Actually, the similarity of vocabulary in Christian, pagan, and Jewish miracle stories only stands to reason and should be expected. As we have just seen, in itself similarity in literary form gives no criterion for judging the historicity of a narrative; the same is true of similarity in wording. A terse report of a car accident will use basically the same vocabulary, whether the report appears in a newspaper or a novel. To apply this point to Jesus: let us suppose for a moment that a miracle of healing did take place in the ministry of Jesus. With what other words would the event be narrated than with those already well known and employed in the Hellenistic world to tell miracle stories? We are back to a basic point we have often "bumped up against" in this study: the constraints of history.

In short, studies done by the history-of-religion school and by form critics have greatly helped the investigation of the miracle stories of the Gospels by placing them within the larger culture of the Greco-Roman world. Both similarities to and differences from the non-Christian parallels can help us interpret the Gospel stories according to the presuppositions of the time. But such studies have their limitations when it comes to judging the historicity of the events narrated.

III. MIRACLE AND MAGIC

Pagan and Jewish parallels to the Gospel miracles are not the only problem that confronts us as we take up the question of miracles in the ancient Mediterranean world. Closely allied with, and at times hardly distinguishable from, claims of miracle-working was the widespread practice of magic.[8] To be sure, the surviving papyri texts that contain magical spells and rituals date largely from the later Roman Empire (3d–5th century A.D.).[9] Apparently there was an explosion of interest in magic during the "age of anxiety" that marked the later Roman Empire.[10] Still, some of the magical papyri date from the last centuries B.C. and the first centuries A.D.[11] Other literature, including both novels and histories, supports the view that miracle and magic—or at least belief in them—

were afoot in the 1st century A.D. Moreover, the regular retelling of the stories of such biblical miracle-workers as Moses, Elijah, and Elisha in synagogue celebrations, references to exorcism and horoscopes at Qumran, and some stories and strictures in the Mishna give us united witness that traditions about miracle and/or magic were alive and well among Palestinian Jews around the turn of the era.[12] Thus, both miracle and magic were "in the air" as Jesus began his ministry and performed extraordinary deeds deemed by some to be miraculous. Hence there naturally arises a question that has been pressed insistently in recent decades: whether or to what extent the supposed miracles of Jesus should be understood as Jewish examples of 1st-century Greco-Roman magic.

A. MAGIC AND THE SOCIAL SCIENCES

In the 20th century, the question of the relation of miracle to magic (and of their possible identity) has been enriched and complicated by insights from sociology and cross-cultural anthropology. In a sense, these social-science disciplines have carried forward the investigation of the "setting in life" (*Sitz im Leben*) of the miracle stories begun by form criticism.[13] Still, it is scarcely an exaggeration to claim that the social sciences have added a whole new dimension to the discussion of the Gospel miracles. It was one thing to debate the concept and reality of miracles when scholars were concerned only with modern problems raised by philosophers, theologians, historians, and scientists molded by the mentality of the Western world since the Enlightenment. It is quite another thing to widen our horizons to encompass ideas about miracles and magic from the ancient Mediterranean world as well as from the Third World today.[14] In the rest of this subsection, we will be weighing certain insights of the social sciences regarding miracle and magic.

While many insights from the social sciences have been helpful and readily accepted, some approaches have proved highly controversial. One of the best-known debates revolves around the claim that, from the viewpoint of the social sciences, there is no objective difference between what we commonly label a miracle in the Gospels and what we commonly label magic in various Greco-Roman papyri, novels, and historians.[15] For instance, both John Dominic Crossan and David E. Aune assert that Jesus made use of magical techniques in his exorcisms and healings. Indeed, Crossan, though not Aune, would agree with Morton Smith in labeling Jesus a magician.[16] Despite differences in details, all of them agree that miracle and magic are basically the same thing. Whatever the precise definition, miracle and magic are both a guaranteed way of using divine or (more generally) superhuman power to achieve certain desired ends in the human world, ends not obtainable—or not readily obtainable—by ordinary means.

From these recent scholarly presentations one could easily get the impression that it is only Christian apologetics that calls Jesus' magic miracles and pagan miracles magic. Crossan in particular is quite straightforward in his

charge: "It is endlessly fascinating to watch Christian theologians describe Jesus as miracle worker rather than magician and then attempt to define the substantive difference between those two. There is, it would seem from the tendentiousness of such arguments, an ideological need to protect religion and its miracles from magic and its effect."[17]

The social sciences, it is claimed, cannot make such a tendentious distinction. Viewed simply as phenomena, what Jesus supposedly did and what Hellenistic magicians supposedly did by way of supernatural healings or the control of the forces of nature are the same thing: magic. The designation "magic," it is emphasized, is used as a value-free label, without any pejorative connotation.[18]

One can appreciate this desire of social scientists to find neutral, value-free language to describe religious phenomena; such language is meant to prevent theological judgments from creeping into a nontheological discipline. Nevertheless, in my view, the decision to use the label "magic" as the common designation of both the extraordinary feats ascribed to Jesus in the Gospels and the magical practices described, e.g., in the Greek magical papyri is ill advised, for two reasons.

(1) First, what the social scientists are seeking is a relatively neutral, value-free designation. Yet, as they themselves admit, in the ancient world the word "magic" often—though not always—carried a pejorative connotation,[19] and it continues to do so in popular culture today when the word is applied to religious activity. In the ancient Roman world the African novelist Apuleius (ca. A.D. 125—after 170) stood out as a rare apologist for magic when he argued at his trial that etymologically "magician" was just the Persian word for "priest" and that "magic" was an alternate term for religious observance.[20] Even Apuleius, though, proceeded to acknowledge that there was a more popular conception of magic that was worthy of prosecution.[21] In espousing the higher, "Persian" sense of magic, he could claim to have linguistic truth on his side; but the word "magic" had long since taken on too many negative vibrations in Greco-Roman society for a purely etymological argument to succeed in creating a more benign definition and attitude.

Other examples of a positive sense of magic can be found,[22] but such a view remained in a hopeless minority. What exactly a given writer of the Greco-Roman era would stigmatize as "magic" depended to a great deal on his education, social status, and the specific controversy in which he was engaged. In particular, as recent authors have noted, "social location" influenced the ancients' definition of and approach to magic; the polemical writings of the pagan Celsus (mid-2d century A.D.) and the Christian Origen (A.D. ca. 185—ca. 254) make that abundantly clear.[23] Whatever the exact definition, though, "magic" was viewed by the vast majority as something negative and hence useful as a polemical label.

Things have not changed all that much in our modern world. Social scientists may duly lecture their fellow academics on the neutral meaning of "magic." But let one academic on a religion faculty refer to Catholic sacraments as "magic" or another call a Protestant faith healer a "magician," and supposedly neutral labels quickly turn into fighting words.[24] While I grant the good intentions and intellectual probity of those who propose "magic" as a common, neutral label, I think that we must be realistic. Practically speaking, such usage will never be free of negative connotations, even in academia. It certainly was not free of them in the ancient world we are investigating.

As a matter of fact, if one were determined to find a neutral umbrella term, it would probably be wiser to use "miracle." The word could be applied without bias both to Jesus' extraordinary deeds and to various superhuman feats described in the magical papyri and elsewhere in pagan and Jewish literature. The common term "miracle" could thus have the desired effect of creating a level playing field for the social sciences, and unlike "magic" it would not carry with it a great deal of questionable baggage.

(2) To move from a purely semantic debate about what constitutes the best neutral term to a more substantive point: in my view, the claim that there is no real phenomenological difference between narratives of Jesus' miracles in the Gospels and what we commonly find, for example, in the magical papyri of the Roman period is questionable. Perhaps part of the problem is that the total identification of miracle and magic sometimes championed today may reflect a reaction against the older, acritical assumption that miracle and magic (or religion and magic) are clearly different and even opposite phenomena (with the miracles of one's adversary conveniently labeled "magic").[25] Complete dichotomy may have begotten the opposite view of complete identification.

An even greater problem, though, is finding any modern scientific definition of magic on which all the debate partners—sociologists, anthropologists, historians, theologians—can agree. As Alan F. Segal correctly observes, "although many different definitions of 'magic' have been offered throughout the history of religions and anthropological research, no one definition has reached general use."[26]

Definitions of magic proposed in the scholarly literature are myriad, with different definitions focusing on different characteristics: complicated rituals and elaborate, often unintelligible spells, strings of esoteric names of deities and nonsense syllables, extreme syncretism, an impersonal rather than a personal relation to supernatural powers, coercion of the gods rather than humble supplication, the techniques of an individual professional without a religious community around him, a prescientific "technology" that demands payment for services rendered, secrecy, social disapproval—the list goes on and on. A basic problem with any universal definition is that rarely does any one characteristic hold true of magic in all cultures in all times and places. Hence some scholars prefer to approach magic as the folkloric side of popular religion as opposed to the rationalized religion of the elite. Other scholars stress the subversive, antiestablishment tendencies of magic and claim that illegality is its one universal characteristic. Still others claim that magic should not be considered under the rubric of religion at all. Magic, according to this opinion, is better seen as a worldview, a particular way of understanding things and their mutual connectedness.[27]

Granted this confusion over the proper definition of the sprawling, untidy reality called magic, it is no wonder that scholars disagree on how miracles relate to magic and whether the two are identical. Indeed, the same problem arises when one tries to delimit ancient medicine from both miracle and magic; at times all three realities overlapped in Greek and Roman culture.[28] Fortunately, our concern here is not with a universally valid or cross-cultural definition of magic, but rather with the relation of reports of Jesus' miracles to examples of magic in the Greco-Roman world. Granted this restricted focus, I will intentionally adopt a pragmatic approach that will stay close to the concrete data. In other words, I will purposely avoid the temptation to construct some grand model abstracted from and supposedly applicable to widely different cultures. Instead I will concentrate on comparing two particular collections of Greco-Roman literature: the four canonical Gospels and the collections of Greek magical papyri.[29]

It must be emphasized that for now we are interested in these two collections solely as literature. Only further down the road (in Chapter 19) can we move to the question of what, if any, historical settings or events the Gospels may mirror. Right now we are dealing with the texts only as literary products. The question we are addressing to these two literary collections is what light they can shed on the relation of miracle to magic. More precisely, our question will be: Does a comparison of the Gospel miracle stories and the magical papyri suggest some sort of typology that can do justice to the messy mixture of the miraculous and the magical that we find in the ancient world?

B. IDEAL TYPES FROM THE GOSPELS AND THE PAPYRI

In my opinion, the approach that comes closest to describing accurately the complicated relationship of miracle and magic in these two bodies of literature is neither total identification of miracle and magic nor complete differentiation of one from the other. Rather, as one reads these two collections, the image that naturally comes to mind is that of a sliding scale, a spectrum or continuum of characteristics.[30] At one end of the spectrum lies the "ideal type" of miracle, at the other end lies the "ideal type" of magic. In reality, individual cases may lie at different points along the spectrum between the two ideal types.[31]

What characteristics would make up the two ideal types of miracle and magic? More importantly—since we have seen that in the Greco-Roman world the use of the word "magic" was often determined by a writer's social location and polemical stance—are these ideal types anything more than figments of an imagination engaged in apologetics and polemics? Or are these types based on solid data in the texts? In my judgment, the two extreme types I label "miracle" and "magic" do have a concrete basis in the texts of the Gospels and the magical papyri. To test this claim, we will begin with the Gospel miracles and then turn to the magical papyri.

I propose that there are certain common tendencies in the Gospel stories that move in the direction of the ideal type I call "miracle," even though not all the tendencies are found in every miracle story and elements of magic are sometimes present. To support this point, let us examine one miracle story in the Gospels that approaches closely to what I consider the ideal type of miracle: the raising of Lazarus in John 11.[32]

From the start and running throughout the whole narrative, the vocabulary of the story sets up both (1) a context of interpersonal love among Jesus, Lazarus, Mary, and Martha (note the verbs for loving in 11:1–5,11,35–36, especially *phileis* in vv 3 and 36 and *ēgapa* in v 5), and (2) a context of personal faith in God and in Jesus (*pisteuō* ["to believe"] throughout vv 15,25–27,40,45). The petitioners are quite insistent, yet they know that they cannot coerce the miraculous powers of Jesus (vv 3,21–22); they are not clients paying for a service and therefore entitled to demand results. Even when Jesus apparently rejects their request and so fails to save Lazarus, Martha reaffirms her disappointed yet persevering faith (11:22). Almost from the start of the story, the reader is informed that, in reality, Jesus has permitted the whole drama of initial disappointment and final miracle to occur because the miracle has a goal beyond the individual benefit (new life) conferred on Lazarus. The miracle is meant to be both a revelation of God's glory leading to faith and a sign pointing forward to Jesus' own life-giving death and resurrection (vv 4,9–15,25–27,40,45). Indeed, the raising of Lazarus from the dead paradoxically precipitates Jesus' own death (11:45–53; 12:9–11). Granted this heavy theological freight, the terse nature of the story's climax is all the more striking. When Jesus finally does perform the miracle that betokens his perfect union with his Father (vv 41–42) and carries such fateful consequences, he raises Lazarus to life with a single laconic command: "Lazarus, come forth" (11:43).

My point here is not whether all or part of the Lazarus story is historical. My focus is rather on this text as it stands in a literary work called a Gospel. And my point is that to judge the question of miracle and magic in this literary work one must look beyond merely formalistic considerations of literary genre, structure, and technical words for miracles (e.g., *teras* and *sēmeion*). One must also consider the context[33] and content of this story and many others like it in the Gospels, especially the healing miracles (the raising of Lazarus being, as it were, an extreme example of healing).

What significant elements of context and content in the Lazarus story find echoes in many other Gospel miracles, especially those of healing? First of all, it is fair to say that the context of many of these stories within a given Gospel is one of a personal religious relationship between Jesus and the recipient(s) of his miracles. At least implicitly, the context of miracles in the Gospels is one of faith, trust, or discipleship.[34] At times, other motifs are added: the audience responds with worship and praise of God or Jesus; alternately, the recipient of the miracle becomes an unofficial missionary, spreading the news of Jesus' miracle to others. To put it abstractly: in one way or another, the petitioner, recipient, or audience of the miracle enters into a personal relationship with the divinity or the divinity's envoy, both of whom are conceived of in highly personal terms.

Concretely, this element of personal religious relationship can vary from story to story and from evangelist to evangelist. For example, Luke tends more than Mark to see faith as a result produced by a miracle.[35] Yet even in Mark the theme of faith or some other religious response can vary in placement and emphasis. Sometimes the faith of the petitioner(s) is mentioned at the beginning or in the middle of the story (e.g., the people who lower the paralytic through the roof in Mark 2:5; Jairus, who is encouraged by Jesus to believe in 5:36), other times at the end of the story (the woman with the hemorrhage in 5:34). The personal relationship of faith or trust need not be recorded by using one particular word for faith (e.g., *pistis*) in the story. Nothing could bespeak more poignantly the personal trust of the leper begging for healing in Mark 1:40–45 than his terse profession of faith: "If you wish, you can make me clean" (v 40). But action often speaks louder than theological words. The persistence of the petitioner (e.g., the Syrophoenician woman in 7:24–30) or the fact that the recipient of the cure follows Jesus (Bartimaeus in 10:48) or goes forth to proclaim what God and Jesus have done for him (the Gerasene demoniac in 5:17–20) all speak eloquently of faith, trust, discipleship, and even mission. Interestingly, in cases where faith or some other personal attitude is implicit in Mark, it tends to be made explicit in the revisions of Matthew and Luke.[36]

To be sure, not every miracle story in the Gospels contains an explicit reference to some personal religious response to Jesus. Sometimes, the personal relationship runs primarily in the other direction, with Jesus seizing the initiative because he is moved with mercy (e.g., the two multiplications of loaves in Mark 6:34; 8:2). Still, in various ways, all four evangelists make generalizing or programmatic statements indicating that miracles are meant to lead one toward faith and that those who refuse to take the lead are culpable. Emphatic in this matter is the Fourth Evangelist, who concludes both the first half of his Gospel (the end of Jesus' public ministry in 12:37–43) as well as the second half (20:30–31, following the risen Jesus' appearance to Thomas) with progammatic statements on the role of "signs" (Jesus' symbolic miracles) in leading people to faith. In 12:37, the Evangelist complains that "although he [Jesus] did so many great signs, they [the Jerusalem crowds] did not believe in him." In 20:30–31, the Evangelist tells his audience: "Now Jesus performed many other signs in the presence of his disciples that have not been written down in this book. But these [signs] have been written down in order that you may believe that Jesus is the Messiah, the Son of God." Thus, John stresses twice in his Gospel that not just this or that sign performed by Jesus but the signs of Jesus as a whole and by their very nature are intended to help people come to faith in him.[37] Those who do not allow the signs to function as they should—for signs do not automatically or magically produce faith—are culpable.

An intriguing variation on this theme of culpability for not believing in the face of miracles is found in Mark. After the first multiplication of loaves and Jesus' walking on the water, we are told that the disciples in the boat are beside themselves with astonishment "because they did not understand about [the multiplication of] the loaves, for their hearts were hardened" (Mark 6:51). Then, after the second multiplication of loaves, Jesus rebukes these same disciples for their continued lack of understanding and hardness of heart (8:14–21). He questions them on how many baskets of bread they collected after each multiplication of loaves. They can give precise statistics about the empirical events, and yet they remain in the dark about the events' deeper meaning. The pericope ends with Jesus' sad and censuring reply, which takes the form of a terse rhetorical question: "Do you not yet understand?" Jesus' rebuke makes sense only if the two multiplications of loaves (and by implication, Jesus' other miracles that have met with both astonishment and lack of understanding) were geared to giving the disciples the insight of faith, if only they would see with their inner eyes.

That Jesus' miracles are meant to lead people to faith—but not cause it automatically—is also presumed by Matthew and Luke. For example, both record Jesus' reply to John the Baptist, who has asked Jesus: "Are you the one who is to come?" Jesus answers by listing the various types of miracles he has performed, miracles that fulfill Isaiah's depiction of the time of Israel's salvation. Jesus then appends a cryptic warning to the Baptist not to refuse to believe in him: "And happy is the one who is not scandalized [i.e., impeded from believing] because of me" (Matt 11:2–6 par.). The same sort of warning, though put more strongly, is conveyed by the woes Jesus pronounces on the cities of Galilee for refusing to believe in him: "For if the miracles [*dynameis*, "mighty deeds"] performed in you had been performed in Tyre and Sidon, they would have long ago repented in sackcloth and ashes" (Matt 11:21 ‖ Luke 10:13). For all the differences in theological outlook, the underlying stance here in Matthew and Luke is the one also found in John and Mark: Jesus' miracles can help well-disposed people come to faith in him, and refusal to believe in the face of his miracles is culpable.

In short, all these negative statements in John, Mark, Matthew, and Luke arise from a positive presupposition that pervades the Four Gospels: all the miracles of Jesus aim at bringing people to faith, repentance, and discipleship. Those who refuse to let the miracles work as Jesus intends are guilty of disbelief. Thus, even the short miracle stories and the summaries of Jesus' miracles are brought within an overarching context: the interpersonal religious relationship between Jesus and the recipients of his miracles. The lengthy, detailed example of the raising of Lazarus simply spells out what is implied in the Gospels as a whole.

This emphasis on interpersonal relationship with Jesus has a natural corollary in the Gospel miracle stories. With few exceptions, the miraculous power of Jesus that heals or saves is not seen as some impersonal force to be harnessed or tapped, whether Jesus wills to use it or not. Neither is it the power of a

capricious divinity or demon who must be cajoled or coerced by lengthy esoteric spells, incantations, concoctions of recipes, amulets, charms, or invoca-
tions of secret names of the gods. If one agrees with Aune that "extraordinary
events which are categorized as magic should properly consist of the perceived
results of ritualistic procedures which are believed to effect desirable goals,"[38]
one must disqualify most of the Gospel narratives of Jesus' miracles as magic.
Most of them do not represent Jesus as engaging in anything that can reasonably be called ritual—certainly not ritual of the kind that we see in the magical papyri.

Moreover, the Gospel miracles are performed with a grand overriding purpose. Put simply, the miracles of Jesus in the Gospels are presented as signs
and realizations of the gracious power of the God of Israel, acting in the end
time to save not only individuals but Israel as a whole through his agent Jesus.
The miracles are performed mostly for actual or potential followers, as the
circle of disciples widens.

Let me stress again that here I am speaking only of the picture portrayed in
the literary works called Gospels, taken as a whole; the question of original
historical events will be taken up later. All I am claiming at the moment is that
in the Gospels a particular type, configuration, or pattern of religious attitudes
and actions is reflected, a type that has a distinct profile that should not be
haphazardly mixed with other types. The Lazarus story in particular helps us
to formulate what one end of the spectrum of miracle-to-magic might look
like.

The characteristics of the other end of the spectrum can be culled from
general tendencies often found in the Greco-Roman magical papyri, dating
from the 2d or 1st century B.C. to the 5th century A.D.[39] To take one famous
specimen: in the Paris Magical Papyrus (*PGM* IV), lines 3007–85,[40] we find a
"recipe" for an exorcism that is literally a recipe; the oil of unripe olives is
mixed with herbs and fruit pulp and then boiled in colorless marjoram while
the magician/exorcist recites an almost unpronounceable list of names of many
gods of different nations. Another list of divine names is then inscribed on a
sheet of tin that is hung around the patient. A still longer list (including "the
god of the Hebrews, Jesus" [*kata tou theou tōn Hebraiōn Iēsou*]) is then recited
by the magician as he faces the patient and proceeds to garble OT stories,
Jewish traditions, and Egyptian words. Sometimes simply a string of vowels
or nonsense syllables adds to the mysterious nature of the formulas. Foreign
languages, names, and practices (notably Jewish ones like not eating pork) are
jumbled together; the syncretistic nature of this piece of late Roman magic is
pronounced.[41] While the linguistic and cultural mishmash may be extreme in
this particular text, the same pattern of strange recipes, long chains of divine
names, or strings of nonsense syllables appears on almost every other page of
the papyri collections of Karl Preisendanz and Hans Dieter Betz.

The reason for the multiplication of words, divine titles, and ritual observances from many races and religions is highly pragmatic: whatever works!
Significantly, we regularly find in the magical texts "advertising slogans,"

added by editors to recommend a particular spell: "This really works," or "If it does not work, try this other spell."[42] The rationale for the multiplication of names and meaningless syllables is thus clear: one or another of the magic words or actions, it is hoped, will push the right button and open the door to the desired effect. Since the magician may not know which of the buttons is the right one, he presses as many as possible. When the right button is pushed, the desired effect will occur. It is all a matter of using the right words, actions, and materials. Whether the power harnessed by the correct technique is thought of in personal or impersonal terms is of secondary importance; permanent commitment to or personal love for one particular deity is hardly a prominent issue in most of the texts.[43]

The desired effects of magic rituals in the papyri range from the serious and beneficent goal of exorcism, through the relatively pedestrian or self-centered goals of winning a horse race, obtaining money, curing a runny nose, exterminating bedbugs, obtaining a lover, or achieving an erection, to the sinister purpose of doing harm to another, especially a rival in business, love, or legal action. One is reminded of Bronislaw Malinowski's view of magic: it is inherently pragmatic, a specific means to a specific end.[44] In all this, the person petitioning the magician for help was basically a client, who most likely paid for the magician's professional services. Indeed, in one sense the Greco-Roman magician was the skilled technician of the day, the expert who was hired to implement his or her special technology (magic) when ordinary means did not avail or speedy results were desired. In general, a magician, especially from the Greek religious milieu, was "a one-man show," although at times he might have an apprentice.[45] One does not find in the magical papyri the thought of founding or cultivating a community of believers or disciples.

These, then, are the two extremes that can be distilled from two different bodies of Greco-Roman literature, the Four Gospels and the collections of magical papyri. They are, as I have said, the extremes at the two ends of a spectrum. There are many gray areas in between—and that holds true not only when we start from the magical end of the spectrum and move toward miracles. Some of the miracle stories of the Gospels also display elements of magic. Perhaps the clearest example is the Marcan form of the story of the woman with the hemorrhage (Mark 5:24b–34), who "sneaks up" behind Jesus and touches his garment without his seeing her.[46] The woman is "automatically" cured, as it were, by a surge of electric current coming from the cloak of Jesus. At the moment of the cure, Jesus is unaware of who is touching him or what exactly is happening; he only feels power go forth from him. It is fair to say, though, that such automatic and anonymous healings are atypical of the Gospel miracles.[47] Moreover, even in the Marcan version of the story, implicit in the woman's action is her faith in Jesus' power to heal; and Jesus concludes the episode by identifying her faith as what has really saved her.

It is telling, though, that even in the 1st century A.D. another evangelist (namely, Matthew) apparently sensed some difficulty in the magical presentation of Mark. Matthew modifies the order of events so that the woman is not

said to be immediately cured simply by touching Jesus' cloak. Instead, as she touches the cloak, Jesus immediately turns around, sees her, understands the situation, and proclaims that her faith has saved (i.e., healed) her (Matt 9:22). Matthew concludes the episode by emphasizing that it was from that moment (of Jesus' proclamation of healing by faith) that the woman was in fact healed. Thus, faith in Jesus rather than some automatic electric charge from his garment is extolled as the conduit of healing and salvation.[48]

On the other side of the spectrum, some of the formulas in the magical papyri take on the tone of personal prayer to a personal deity. For example, despite the pervasive magic and the usual string of divine names and nonsense syllables, the description of the mystical ascent of the soul in the so-called *Mithras Liturgy* (*PGM* IV. 479–829) within the Paris Magical Papyrus seems to reflect a deeply felt personal spirituality.[49] Outside the magical papyri, this emphasis on the personal relationship of the suppliant praying to a beneficent deity can be found elsewhere in pagan literature, even when the same document also plays with magic.

For example, in Apuleius' prayer to Isis in his picaresque novel *Metamorphoses (The Golden Ass)*, we see magic passing over into personal religion (though the syncretistic multiplication of divine names remains).[50] Indeed, this "passing over" is part of the book's message. Toward the end of the story, not only is the hero of the novel, Lucius (who is probably a "stand-in" for Apuleius), converted from an ass back to a human form. His physical transformation is also symbolic of his conversion from dabbling with dark and harmful magic to a whole-hearted, life-changing commitment to Isis, as revealed in her mystery cult. What is remarkable here is that it is not a Christian apologist but the pagan Apuleius, the defender of an acceptable sense of "magic" in his *Apology*, who implies in his *Metamorphoses* that there is a fundamental difference between magic and the worship of the savior-goddess Isis, who can work the definitive wonder of personal transformation for her devotee. One form of religious experience is depicted by Apuleius as essentially—and experientially—higher and purer than the other.[51] Thus, the two types, miracle and magic, can be found in paganism as well as in Christianity—indeed, even in the same author.

In short, it is not an arbitrary exercise in apologetics to distinguish these two extreme types of more-than-human power in the ancient world. They are present, with many variations and degrees of difference, in two significant bodies of religious literature of the Greco-Roman period: the Gospels and the magical papyri.[52] And there is a real difference between the two types. Despite the contrasting theologies and literary styles of the Four Evangelists, the canonical Gospels do in general represent or tend toward the type I have called miracle. In constructing this typology, there is no covert attempt on my part to make the stories of Jesus' miracles totally different from miracle stories found in pagan and Jewish literature. Some of the latter (notably in the Jewish material) tend toward the miraculous rather than the magical end of the spectrum as well. The point of constructing this spectrum or continuum is to illustrate a valid, phenomenological difference between the ideal types miracle and magic. I am not claiming that the stories of Jesus' miracles have a monopoly on the former type.

C. Listing the Characteristics of the Types

Having looked at some concrete examples from the Gospels and the magical papyri, we can begin to form a list of the characteristics common to each type. Obviously, since they make up ideal types, these characteristics are found in individual cases only to varying degrees. That is why there is a spectrum of possibilities lying between the two extremes. Still, we can say that in general the typology of miracle, as reflected in the Gospels, involves the following elements:

(1) The usual overarching context for a religious miracle is that of an interpersonal relationship of faith, trust, or love between a human being and a deity (and/or his agent).

(2) The person in need, a worshiper or disciple rather than a business client, requests of God or his envoy a healing or some other benefit. Alternately, in some stories the envoy (i.e., Jesus) seizes the initiative to instill or foster faith in those in need.

(3) Jesus usually grants the miracle with a terse but intelligible set of words spoken in his own language,[53] at times accompanied by a symbolic gesture (touching, use of spittle), at times not.[54] Put negatively: there are no lengthy incantations, endless lists of esoteric names and unintelligible words, amulets, charms, or recipes of foodstuffs to be boiled.

(4) With few exceptions, the miracle takes place because the personal will of the miracle-worker responds to the urgent request of the petitioner or to the patent, unspoken need of some afflicted person. Put negatively: there is no idea that the petitioner can use coercive power to force the miracle-worker to perform a miracle against his will. Nor does the miracle-worker in turn coerce the deity to obtain a request, whether the deity wishes to accede or not. A basic supposition of the Gospel miracle stories is that God's hand is not to be forced.

(5) Specifically, all miraculous activity takes place within the overarching Gospel context of Jesus' obedience to his Father and to the mission he has been given. Indeed, Jesus' own prayer for rescue in Gethsemane is put under the rubric of "not what I will but what you will [be done]"—and so his request for rescue is not granted.

(6) Another overarching context is also characteristic: as the miracles now stand in the Gospels, they are not simply discrete acts of divine power granting benefits to individual petitioners. They are understood as symbols and partial concrete realizations of the kingdom of God, who comes to save his people Israel in the end time through the ministry of Jesus.[55] Both eschatology and community belong to the overall pattern of Gospel miracles.

(7) Jesus' miracles do not directly punish or hurt anyone. This contrasts with the Greek magical papyri, which include spells for causing sickness or

insomnia, preventing marriages, silencing opponents, fomenting strife between friends or marriage partners, and getting rid of enemies.

The type at the other end of the spectrum, which I label magic, is practically the reverse mirror image of this description. Again, I emphasize that I speak of an ideal type, abstracted from many examples in the Greek magical papyri. Not every individual text exhibits all the characteristics. Moreover, the typology is meant to reflect the striking characteristics of these particular magical papyri vis-à-vis those of the Gospel narratives. No universally valid or cross-cultural definition of magic is intended.

(1) In the ideal type, magic is the technical manipulation of various (often impersonal) supernatural forces or the coercion of a deity in order to obtain a desired concrete benefit.[56] A striking example is given in a spell found in *PGM* XIII. 760–821. The spell begins with a summons to the god, who is addressed with flattering titles that identify him with the ocean and proclaim his power over all the elements of the universe. As in most of the spells, a string of divine names (Egyptian, Hebrew, and Aramaic) and nonsense vowels is used in the invocation. Then the magician proceeds:

> Enter my mind . . . and do for me all the things my soul desires. For you are I, and I [am] you. *Whatever I say [i.e., command] must take place, for I possess your name as a unique amulet [literally: phylactery] in my heart,* and no flesh . . . will prevail against me; no spirit will oppose me in battle . . . because of your name, which I possess in my soul. . . . [Give] me health, well-being, abundance of goods, fame, victory, strength, the ability to make people love me. Restrain the eyes of all my adversaries. . . .[57]

There follows an even longer string of divine names and nonsense vowels. This characteristic pervades most of the magical papyri, though some texts do exhibit a tone of supplication and genuine prayer.[58]

(2) Contrary to most definitions of a miracle, which usually speak of an effect transcending all human power, and contrary to almost all of the Gospel miracles, the benefits sought by magic are sometimes relatively petty and moreover obtainable by human means: e.g., winning a horse race or a lover.

(3) For the magician, each request was basically a discrete case. Hellenistic magicians did not usually operate within an overarching context such as salvation history or the eschatological drama, with each wonder symbolic of and tending toward the supreme wonder to come.[59]

(4) Likewise, the magician did not usually operate within a fairly stable circle of disciples or believers, a circle often widened by the wonders he performed. Emile Durkheim sees here an "essential" difference between magic and religion (which belongs to a group and makes for the group's unity). Durkheim asserts: "*There is no Church of magic.* Between the magician and the individuals who consult him . . . there are no lasting bonds which make them members of the same moral community. . . . The magician has a clientele and not a Church, and it is very possible that his clients have no other relations

between each other, or even do not know each other; even the relations which they have with him are generally accidental and transient."[60] While this distinction may not hold for all religions and all magic in every time and place, it does capture well a basic difference between the picture of Jesus in the Gospels and the image of the magician suggested by the magical papyri.[61]

(5) Especially typical of the spells in the magical papyri is the multiplication of names of various deities and strings of nonsense syllables (both are capitalized in the citation below). Perhaps nothing makes one feel more the difference in tone and spirit between the spells of the Greek magical papyri and the Gospel miracles than to read through a collection like Betz's *The Greek Magical Papyri in Translation* and to encounter regularly spells like "A EE ĒĒĒ IIII OOOOO YYYYY ŌŌŌŌŌŌŌ, come to me, Good Husbandman, Good Daimon, HARPON KNOUPHI BRINTANTĒN SIPHRI BRISKYLMA AROUAZAR [BAMESEN] KRIPHI NIPOUMICHMOUMAŌPH."[62] At times this sort of spell fills most of a page. The dictum of Malinowski seems verified here: "The most important element in magic is the spell. The spell is that part of magic which is occult, . . . known only to the practitioner."[63] Kee comments on the reason for heaping up meaningless names and syllables in the spells: "The origins or initial meaning of neither act nor formula is of significance: central alone is efficacy. Failure is attributed to imprecision in rite or pronouncement. The formulae are repeated and gradually expanded by accretion, so that they end up by becoming completely unintelligible. So long as they work, that does not matter."[64] The terse, intelligible commands of Jesus, often spoken before an audience, stand out in stark contrast.[65]

(6) This last point emphasizes in turn the element of the secret, esoteric nature of the magic seen in the papyri. Mauss has claimed of magic in general: "It is private, secret, mysterious and approaches the limit of a prohibited rite."[66] That may be too sweeping a claim if one is describing magic of every time and place, but it does seem to hold true in general of the magic reflected in the papyri. While Mark and perhaps his tradition before him surrounded some (though not all) of Jesus' miracles with an aura of secrecy, this Marcan motif does not seem to have been essential to early Christians' conception of Jesus' miracles. All Four Gospels—including Mark—know of many miracles that Jesus performed in full public view, and Matthew in particular regularly eliminates the element of secrecy from the Marcan stories he edits.[67]

As I readily admit, what I have just described are two extremes. There are gray areas in both bodies of literature and blurred lines along the spectrum. But I think that the two ends of the spectrum, miracle and magic, are clearly rooted in the major tendencies of the two types of literature. Therefore I hold that there is an objective basis for designating Jesus' supposed wonders "miracles" instead of "magic," even though in a few cases magical traits may enter into some of the miracle stories. So too, traits of a personal faith in a personal deity who works miracles may at times be found in the magical papyri or in Greco-Roman narratives about magic. But variations within and commingling between the two types do not abolish the basic validity of the two types themselves. In general, most of the stories of Jesus' extraordinary deeds in the Gospels tend toward the ideal type of miracle, and many examples in the Hellenistic magical papyri tend toward the ideal type of magic. Hence I do not agree with the attempts of Morton Smith and John Dominic Crossan to label Jesus a magician and to describe his miracles as magic. In what follows I will continue to speak of Jesus' "miracles" in the sense outlined here.

D. Final Remarks on Jesus as Magician

Apart from all these detailed arguments about definitions and types, there is a simple, commonsense reason for not applying the label of "magician" to Jesus. Just as a matter of fact, although the NT knows the vocabulary of "magician" (the noun *magos*, Acts 13:6,8; the participle *mageuōn*, 8:9) and "magic" (*mageia*, Acts 8:11; *perierga*, 19:19),[68] these words are never applied in the NT to Jesus or his activities. Jesus never uses it as a self-designation. Neither his disciples during his lifetime nor the early church during the rest of the 1st century ever used it among the many titles and descriptions applied to Jesus. Nor, most significantly, did the adversaries of Jesus or of the early church in the decades immediately after his crucifixion attack him with the precise charge of magic.[69]

The absence of a direct charge of magic is noteworthy, since a large number of other accusations against Jesus are recorded in the Gospels: he was in league with Beelzebul (Mark 3:22 parr.), he broke the Sabbath (Mark 3:1–6; John 5:16; 9:16), he blasphemed (Mark 2:7 parr.; 14:64 parr.), he was a deceiver (Matt 27:63), he claimed to be the king of the Jews (Mark 15:2 parr.), he claimed to be the Messiah, the Son of God, and the Son of Man (Mark 15:61–62 parr.), he misled the Jewish people and forbade payment of taxes to Caesar (Luke 23:2), he created a dangerous situation in which the Romans might intervene and do away with Jewish self-governance and even the temple (John 11:48). To be sure, many of these accusations—especially the more overtly christological ones—mirror polemics in and against the early church rather than against the historical Jesus. All the more telling, therefore, is the absence of any charge of magic in the list. Historians and social scientists may equate certain accusations (e.g., being in league with the devil or being a deceiver who led the Jewish people astray) with being a magician (or, alternately, a witch); but that is a move made by modern scholars engaging in model-building at a high level of abstraction.[70] It does not reflect the precise vocabulary and immediate reaction of Jesus' fellow Jews in his own day or in the decades immediately following his death.

In fact, the earliest extant documentation for the application of the precise word "magician" (*magos*) to Jesus is Justin Martyr's *First Apology* (30.1) and his *Dialogue with Trypho* (69.7).[71] The exact date of the composition of these two works is not certain, but most probably they both were written during Justin's residence in Rome, ca. A.D. 150–65. The statements of Trypho the Jew in the *Dialogue* supposedly represent what a Jew said to Justin during a conversation a decade or two before (ca. 133–34). But it is difficult to judge to what extent the *Dialogue* is a reliable report of a real conversation and to what extent it mirrors Justin's theological creativity. In any case, no document reporting the charge that Jesus was a magician can be dated before the middle of the 2d century A.D. The next work containing such an accusation is the *True Discourse* of the pagan Celsus (and his supposed Jewish source), who used the charge of magic against Jesus ca. A.D. 178.[72] Thus, as far as our documentary evidence goes, the charge that Jesus was a magician is a phenomenon that is not attested until the middle and late 2d century.

Moreover, when we focus on the Gospel miracle stories in particular, we notice that as a general rule only certain miracles engender fierce opposition, and that for two precise reasons: (1) in the case of some—but certainly not all—exorcisms, they are thought to be worked in league with demonic powers; (2) some of the healing miracles, because they are done on the Sabbath, are viewed as works violating the Sabbath. Nowhere in the Gospels is there any idea that the miracles as a whole and in themselves—simply because they are miracles—are objectionable and a reason for deadly opposition.[73] The frequent choruses of praise after healing miracles create just the opposite impression. All this coheres well with the absence in the NT of a general charge that Jesus was a magician or practiced magic.[74] It may be, however, that when miracles are joined together with other aspects of Jesus' message and ministry, they do prove to be an "aggravating factor," especially in the eyes of the authorities.

Having surveyed the preliminary problems, both modern and ancient, involved in treating miracle stories, we can at last turn directly to the Four Gospels and attempt to classify and evaluate historically their accounts of Jesus' miracles.

NOTES TO CHAPTER 18

[1] The rejection of any sort of miracle by the Epicurean tradition is rooted in two fundamental positions: (1) the gods, being happy and immortal, do not concern themselves with human beings or their world, which the gods did not create; (2) in the physical world nothing new is ever created out of nothing, and nothing existing is ever destroyed into nothingness; thus, the universe has always been and will always be as it is now. For key texts in the very limited material that survives from Epicurus himself, see his *Letter to Menoeceus*, 10. 123, in Diogenes Laertius, *Lives of Eminent Philosophers* (LCL; 2 vols.; ed. R. D. Hicks; Cambridge, MA: Harvard University; London: Heinemann, 1925) 2. 648–51 (see also his total rejection of divination, from his short epitome, ibid., 10. 135 [pp. 660–61]); and his *Letter to Herodotus*, ibid., 10. 38–39 (pp. 566–69). On this see A.-J. Festugière, *Epicure et ses dieux* (Paris: Presses Universitaires de France, 1968) 71–100; Howard Jones, *The Epicurean Tradition* (London/New York: Routledge, 1989) 22–62.

For Cicero's rejection of miracles (with particular reference to "portents," i.e., terrifying monsters born of humans or animals), see his *De divinatione*, 2. 60–61: "For whatever comes to be, of whatever sort it is, necessarily has a cause from nature, so that, even if its existence is unusual, it nevertheless cannot exist outside of the course of nature *(praeter naturam)*. . . . nothing happens which cannot happen; and, if what could happen has happened, it should not be called a portent. . . . what could not happen has never happened, and anything that could happen is not a portent; hence a portent simply does not exist." For a critical text, see Arthur Stanley Pease (ed.), *M. Tulli Ciceronis De divinatione libri duo* (Darmstadt: Wissenschaftliche Buchgesellschaft, 1963) 450–52. As Pease points out (pp. 9–13, 36–37), *De divinatione* is a rationalistic critique of divination and popular superstition in general. Interestingly, its main argument did not have wide impact until it was taken up by the English Deists (and also Voltaire). Like the Deists, Cicero was interested in destroying superstition (at least among the educated upper class) while maintaining true belief in God or the gods and the traditional religious observances deemed necessary for the welfare of the state. In this he differed from the radical materialism and Epicureanism of the poet-philosopher Lucretius in his *De rerum natura* ("On the nature of things"), which rejects religion of all sorts. On all this, see R. J. Goar, *Cicero and the State Religion* (Amsterdam: Hakkert, 1972) 96–104; John E. Rexine, *Religion in Plato and Cicero* (New York: Greenwood, 1968) 33–52; Remus, *Pagan-Christian Conflict*, 35–36.

[2] See, e.g., Robin Lane Fox, *Pagans and Christians* (New York: Knopf, 1986) 102–67, esp. 118–19. Naturally, this insight should not be pushed to the extreme: ancient Mediterranean peoples did have a sense of what events were normal, regular, and to be expected as opposed to those that were extraordinary or unheard of. See the sober remarks of Remus, *Pagan-Christian Conflict*, 7–26.

[3] On the contribution of the history-of-religion school to the study of magic and the NT, see Aune ("Magic in Early Christianity," 1508), who mentions as leading lights A. Dieterich, R. Reitzenstein, A. Deissmann, W. Heitmüller, F. Preisigke, and O. Bauernfeind. A brief overview of the contributions of the history-of-religion school to the debate over the supposed Greco-Roman concept of a "divine man" *(theios anēr)* miracle-worker is given by Gail Paterson Corrington, *The "Divine Man." His Origin and Function in Hellenistic Popular Religion* (American University Studies; Series VII, Theology and Religion Vol. 17; New York/Berne/Frankfurt: Lang, 1986) 1–58. For a classic expression of the history-of-religion ap-

proach to christology and the tradition of Jesus as miracle-worker, see Wilhelm Bousset, *Kyrios Christos* (Nashville/New York: Abingdon, 1970, German original 1913) 98–106. Typical is the general statement that introduces his treatment of miracles (p. 98): "We are still able to see clearly how the earliest tradition of Jesus' life was still relatively free from the miraculous." Besides OT miracle stories, Bousset draws parallels to the Gospel miracles from such sources as the Talmud and the wine miracle of the Dionysus cult on the island of Andros.

[4] Bultmann, *Geschichte*, 233–60; Dibelius, *Formgeschichte*, 66–100 (where the miracle stories are called *Novellen*, "short stories" or "tales"; rabbinic and pagan analogies to various genres of Gospel material are collected on pp. 130–78).

[5] On the two points I make here, see Kee, *Medicine, Miracle and Magic*, 75–78.

[6] So rightly Richardson, *Miracle-Stories*, 28; van der Loos, *The Miracles of Jesus*, 120.

[7] So Harold Remus, "Does Terminology Distinguish Early Christian from Pagan Miracles?" *JBL* 101 (1982) 531–51 (with the bibliography cited there). Remus points out in particular that there is (1) no great difference in meaning between *teras* ("portent," "wonder") and *sēmeion* ("sign") and (2) no great difference in the way pagans and Christians used the terms. The same holds true for *dynameis* ("acts of power"). For further problems of ancient terminology, see Remus's *Pagan-Christian Conflict*, 48–72.

[8] From the books and articles on miracles already listed above, see especially Wilson, *Magic and the Millennium*; Hull, *Hellenistic Magic*; Smith, *Jesus the Magician*; Aune, "Magic in Early Christianity," 1507–57; Remus, *Pagan-Christian Conflict*; Kee, *Miracle in the Early Christian World*; idem, *Miracle and Magic*; Schoedel and Malina, "Miracle or Magic?" 31–39; Yamauchi, "Magic or Miracle?" 89–183; Crossan, *The Historical Jesus*, 137–67, 303–32. For magic in ancient Greek and Roman culture, see the various essays in Christopher A. Faraone and Dirk Obbink (eds.), *Magika Hiera. Ancient Greek Magic and Religion* (New York/Oxford: Oxford University, 1991); in this volume note in particular Hans Dieter Betz, "Magic and Mystery in the Greek Magical Papyri," 244–59; and C. R. Phillips III, "*Nullum Crimen sine Lege*: Socioreligious Sanctions on Magic," 260–76. To Betz's article may be added two of his other essays on the Greek magical papyri: Hans Dieter Betz, "The Formation of Authoritative Tradition in the Greek Magical Papyri," *Jewish and Christian Self-Definition. Volume Three. Self-Definition in the Greco-Roman World* (ed. Ben F. Meyer and E. P. Sanders; Philadelphia: Fortress, 1982) 161–70; idem, "Introduction to the Greek Magical Papyri," *The Greek Magical Papyri in Translation Including the Demotic Spells* (ed. Hans Dieter Betz; Chicago/London: University of Chicago, 1986) xli–liii. The three articles by Betz supply an abundant bibliography on the problem of magic, especially in the Greco-Roman world. More general works on magic that may be consulted to gain a sense of the range of definitions and interpretations of magic in different historical periods and different cultures include Robert-Léon Wagner, "*Sorcier*" et "*Magicien*" (Paris: Droz, 1939); Kurt Seligmann, *Magic, Supernaturalism and Religion* (New York: Pantheon, 1948); Keith Thomas, *Religion and the Decline of Magic* (New York: Scribner's Sons, 1971); Marcel Mauss, *A General Theory of Magic* (New York: Norton, 1972); Richard Kieckhefer, *Magic in the Middle Ages* (Cambridge: Cambridge University, 1989), esp. 1–42.

[9] For most of the 20th century, the classical collection of Greek magical papyri

has been the edition of Karl Preisendanz, *Papyri Graecae Magicae* (2 vols.; Leipzig: Teubner, 1928, 1931). A new edition, edited by Albert Henrichs, appeared in 1973–74: Karl Preisendanz, *Papyri Graecae Magicae. Die Griechischen Zauberpapyri* (Sammlung Wissenschaftlicher Commentare; 2d ed.; ed. Albert Henrichs; Stuttgart: Teubner, 1973–74). Various corrections and additions have been made in the second edition. In particular, the second volume of the second edition is much expanded, with material originally planned for a third volume included. It is this second edition that I have used in the present work. More accessible to many readers will be the volume edited by Betz, *The Greek Magical Papyri in Translation*. While it does not give the texts in their original languages, it has the advantage of including Greek and demotic texts not found in the Preisendanz volumes. ("Demotic" is the stage of the Egyptian language that immediately preceded Coptic and that is known from documents written in demotic characters [a simplified form of Egyptian hieratic writing], dating from the 8th century B.C. to the 3d century A.D.) For a brief history of modern research on the Greek magical papyri, see Betz, "Introduction," xlii–xliv. As Betz notes (p. xli), the collections we now possess probably represent only a small part of all the magical documents that once existed in the Greco-Roman world. Beyond these written documents, magic is attested by many other types of materials: e.g., symbols and inscriptions on gemstones and on bowls.

[10] See Aune, "Magic in Early Christianity," 1519; E. R. Dodds, *Pagan and Christian in an Age of Anxiety* (New York/London: Norton, 1965) 37–101; Helmut Koester, *Introduction to the New Testament. Volume One. History, Culture, and Religion of the Hellenistic Age* (Philadelphia: Fortress; Berlin/New York: de Gruyter, 1982) 379–81; Everett Ferguson, *Backgrounds of Early Christianity* (Grand Rapids: Eerdmans, 1987) 177–86. For the survival of pagan magic in the West after the fall of the Roman Empire and for Christianity's struggle with it, see Kieckhefer, *Magic in the Middle Ages*; Michel Rouche, "The Early Middle Ages in the West," *A History of Private Life. I. From Pagan Rome to Byzantium* (ed. Paul Veyne; Cambridge, MA/London: Harvard University, 1987) 519–36; Karen Louise Jolly, "Magic, Miracle, and Popular Practice in the Early Medieval West: Anglo-Saxon England," *Religion, Science, and Magic in Concert and in Conflict* (ed. Jacob Neusner, Ernest S. Frerichs, and Paul V. M. Flesher; New York/Oxford: Oxford University, 1989) 166–82. There is not complete agreement on why interest in magic increases in the later Roman Empire. The supposition that this reflects the irreversible decline and decay of Roman culture and society is common, but is challenged by Peter Brown in "Sorcery, Demons and the Rise of Christianity: From Late Antiquity into the Middle Ages," *Religion and Society in the Age of Saint Augustine* (New York: Harper & Row, 1972) 119–46. Brown sees the source of the increase of accusations against supposed "sorcerers" in the malaise of the governing classes of the Empire, as "newly arrived" groups rising from the lower classes threatened those accustomed to holding power at court. This situation of uncertainty and conflict in the "new" society of the mid-4th century helped increase interest in and charges of magic. In all this speculation one important caveat must be voiced: the greater number of magical papyri and other witnesses to magic in the later Empire may be due at least in part to accidents of preservation.

[11] Moreover, the extant magical papyri obviously reflect a long-standing tradition. On this, see Susan R. Garrett, "Light on a Dark Subject and Vice Versa: Magic and Magicians in the New Testament," *Religion, Science, and Magic in Concert and in Conflict* (ed. Jacob Neusner, Ernest S. Frerichs, and Paul V. M. Flesher;

New York/Oxford: Oxford University, 1989) 142–65, esp. 162 n. 19: "There are
. . . strong indications that many of the texts [of the magical papyri] have been
copied one or more times, so that it is reasonable to assume that the core of the
traditions in them dates back to a much earlier period." On the subject of magic
in the Lucan corpus, see Susan R. Garrett, *The Demise of the Devil. Magic and the
Demonic in Luke's Writings* (Minneapolis: Fortress, 1989).

[12] See Fox, *Pagans and Christians*, 36–37. Betz ("Introduction," xli) notes that the
extant texts of the Greek magical papyri from Greco-Roman Egypt reach back as
far as the 2d century B.C. and forward as far as the 5th century A.D.
    On magic in the ancient Near East in general and in the OT in particular, see
J. A. Scurlock and Joanne K. Kuemmerlin-McLean, "Magic," *Anchor Bible Dictionary* (6 vols.; New York: Doubleday, 1992) 4. 464–71. On Jewish magic, see P. S.
Alexander, "Incantations and Books of Magic," in the revised Schürer, *The History
of the Jewish People*, 3. 342–79. Unfortunately, most of the written evidence for
Jewish magic in this period is later than the 1st century A.D. It is also unfortunate
that Alexander automatically equates any report of exorcism with magic
(pp. 342–43). In my opinion, Aune ("Magic in Early Christianity," 1520) is correct
in rejecting J. Trachtenberg's claim (*Jewish Magic and Superstition* [New York:
Behrman, 1939]) that a distinctive form of Jewish magic did not exist until the
post-Talmudic period. A short survey of indications of Jewish magic in the Hebrew
Bible and at the turn of the era can be found in the old classic by Ludwig Blau,
Das altjüdische Zauberwesen (Budapest: Landes-Rabbinerschule, 1898) 18–20. For the
use of magic in Diaspora Judaism, see Jack N. Lightstone, *The Commerce of the Sa-
cred. Mediation of the Divine among Jews in the Graeco-Roman Diaspora* (Brown Judaic
Studies 59; Chico, CA: Scholars, 1984), especially Chapter 2, "Magicians and Di-
vine Men," pp. 17–56. For magic and superstition in the rabbinic literature, see
Judah Goldin, "The Magic of Magic and Superstition," *Aspects of Religious Propa-
ganda in Judaism and Early Christianity* (University of Notre Dame Center for the
Study of Judaism and Christianity in Antiquity 2; ed. Elisabeth Schüssler Fiorenza;
Notre Dame/London: University of Notre Dame, 1976) 115–47; Jacob Neusner,
"Science and Magic, Miracle and Magic in Formative Judaism: The System and
the Difference," *Religion, Science and Magic in Concert and in Conflict* (ed. Jacob
Neusner, Ernest S. Frerichs, and Paul V. M. Flesher; New York/Oxford: Oxford
University, 1989) 61–81. For the influence of rabbinic lore in Hellenistic magical
and gnostic material, see Daniel Sperber, "Some Rabbinic Themes in Magical Papyri," *JSJ* 16 (1985) 93–103. For magical texts from the Cairo Genizah fragments
preserved at Cambridge University, see Peter Schäfer, "Jewish Magic Literature in
Late Antiquity and Early Middle Ages," *JJS* 41 (1990) 75–91. Some later developments can be found in Gershom G. Scholem, *Major Trends in Jewish Mysticism* (3d
rev. ed.; New York: Schocken, 1961, originally 1941); Moshe Idel, "Jewish Magic
from the Renaissance Period to Early Hasidism," *Religion, Science and Magic in
Concert and in Conflict*, 82–117. For the *Sepher ha-razim* (containing texts of Jewish
magic from the 3d and 4th centuries A.D.) as well as for amulets and magic bowls
with Aramaic incantations (from the 4th to the 7th centuries A.D.), see Kee, *Medicine, Miracle and Magic*, 112–15; also Lightstone, *The Commerce of the Sacred*,
23–31. The *Sepher ha-razim* has been translated into English by Michael A. Morgan, *Sepher Ha-Razim. The Book of Mysteries* (SBLTT 25; Pseudepigrapha Series 11;
Chico, CA: Scholars, 1983).

[13] An interesting synthesis of contemporary literary (structural) criticism, form
criticism, and sociological analysis can be found in Theissen's *Urchristliche Wun-*

dergeschichten. For two essay-long and trenchant reviews, see Hendrikus Boers, "Sisyphus and His Rock. Concerning Gerd Theissen, *Urchristliche Wundergeschichten,*" *Early Christian Miracle Stories* (Semeia 11; ed. Robert W. Funk; Missoula, MT: Scholars, 1978) 1–48; and Paul J. Achtemeier, "An Imperfect Union: Reflections on Gerd Theissen, *Urchristliche Wundergeschichten,*" ibid., 49–81.

[14] Typical of this type of work is Hull, *Hellenistic Magic*; Smith, *Jesus the Magician*; Aune, "Magic in Early Christianity"; Kee, *Miracle in the Early Christian World*; idem, *Medicine, Miracle and Magic.*

As soon as one seeks to appropriate the insights of the social sciences, a whole range of basic methodological questions arises that cannot be adequately dealt with here. Two points, however, should be mentioned in passing. (1) It is sometimes claimed that true sociological analysis is value-free, bias-free, and totally objective. I think that today such claims are rightly treated with more than a little skepticism; see, e.g., the remarks of Betz, "Magic and Mystery," 245–46. Granted the historical and social nature of human understanding, total objectivity is not to be had, although it is a goal to be pursued. As I pointed out in *A Marginal Jew,* 1. 4–6, one can try to exclude bias by clearly enunciating and employing criteria of judgment and by then inviting other scholars to point out where one's guard has slipped. (2) The precise stance of the social sciences toward the claims of faith, religion, and theology will vary from author to author. Hence disparate views of social scientists via-à-vis religious faith need to be distinguished. It is one thing for a social scientist to prescind from the claims of faith and religion for methodological reasons. In such a case faith-claims are not directly denied; they are simply not taken into consideration because they do not fit into the methodological framework in which the social scientist works and forms judgments. It is another thing for a social scientist to claim full competence to examine, judge, and accept or reject faith-claims as part of his or her proper area of research. It is still another thing for a social scientist to employ as a postulate of his or her work that there simply is no divine or transcendent reality beyond empirical investigations and that all faith-claims are simply masks or tools of various social, economic, and political interests. As is no doubt clear by now, I reject the last two approaches as unwarranted biases.

[15] Jacob Neusner ("Introduction," *Religion, Science, and Magic in Concert and in Conflict* [ed. Jacob Neusner, Ernest S. Frerichs, and Paul V. M. Flesher; New York/ Oxford: Oxford University, 1989] 3–7, esp. 4–5) puts it succinctly: "A convention of the history of religion in the West, well-established in a variety of studies, is that one group's holy man is another group's magician: 'what I do is a miracle, but what you do is magic.'" This echoes the famous bon mot of Robert M. Grant (*Gnosticism and Early Christianity* [2d ed.; New York/London: Columbia University, 1966] 93): ". . . in polemical writing, your magic is my miracle, and vice versa. . . ."

[16] For Crossan's presentation, see *The Historical Jesus,* 137–67, 303–32; for Aune's, see "Magic in Early Christianity," 1523–39. The impression must not be given that these authors agree on all points. Crossan joins the description magician to that of an itinerant Jewish preacher with traits similar to those of a Greco-Roman Cynic philosopher. While Aune affirms that Jesus used magical techniques in his healings and exorcisms, he thinks that "messianic prophet" is a more adequate description of Jesus' sociological role than "magician." Aune's view that Jesus was a messianic prophet legitimated by magic in a "millennial movement" marked by "deviant behavior" should have received more substantiation than he gives it

(pp. 1527, 1538–39). In particular: (1) The application of the label "millennial movement" to the group Jesus gathered around him needs greater nuance in the light of Jesus' complex teaching on eschatology, which we have seen in Chapters 15 and 16 of this volume. Aune is too quick to lump together Jesus, Theudas, Judas the Galilean, an unnamed Samaritan who tried to gather his followers at Mt. Gerizim, an unnamed Egyptian prophet who sought to gather his followers on the Mount of Olives, and other "impostors and deceivers" described summarily by Josephus. It is questionable whether all these people can be equally put under the same rubric, namely, leaders of millennial movements displaying social deviance and miraculous activity. In particular, one should note that, in some of the cases adduced, Josephus' narratives do not state that the would-be leaders actually performed or were thought to have performed miracles. Rather, the narratives state that they promised some future sign or signs to their followers. (2) "Messianic prophet" is too vague a term to be useful unless the troublesome and multivalent label "messianic" is explained in detail; cf. Wilson, *Magic and the Millennium,* who explains on pp. 484–85 why he has avoided both "millennial" and "messianic" in his work.

As for Morton Smith's position, Alan F. Segal ("Hellenistic Magic: Some Questions of Definition," *Studies in Gnosticism and Hellenistic Religions* [Gilles Quispel Festschrift; ed R. van den Broek and M. J. Vermaseren; Leiden: Brill, 1981] 349–75) comments (p. 369): "A defense against the charge of magic is not only characteristic of the polemics of the church fathers and evangelists, it goes back to the earliest traditions of the church. But it does not prove that Jesus was a magician. The early charge of magic against Jesus is not so much clear proof that Jesus was a magician as a clear example of the social manipulation of the charge of magic. When Jesus is accused of magic, it is his credentials as miracle-worker that are under scrutiny. . . . There is no evidence that Jesus wished to claim the title of magician." One may question, though, whether one should speak of "a defense against the charge of magic" by the evangelists when in fact they do not express any charge against Jesus with the vocabulary of *mageia* or *magos*.

[17] Crossan, *The Historical Jesus,* 305.

[18] So, e.g., Aune, "Magic in Early Christianity," 1509, 1516; likewise, Crossan ("The Historical Jesus," 138), whose definition of magic remains vague: "magic renders transcendental power present concretely, physically, sensibly, tangibly, whereas ritual renders it present abstractly, ceremonially, liturgically, symbolically." One wonders, for instance, whether the highly ritualized religious sacrifice and eating of conquered enemies among certain tribes (e.g., the Aztecs) was experienced by them as abstract and merely symbolic. The ritual strikes one as remarkably concrete, physical, sensible, and tangible. Some scholars simply reject a distinction between ritual and magic by collapsing the latter into the former; on this approach see Hans H. Penner, "Rationality, Ritual, and Science," *Religion, Science, and Magic in Concert and in Conflict* (ed. Jacob Neusner, Ernest S. Frerichs, and Paul V. M. Flesher; New York/Oxford: Oxford University, 1989) 11–24, esp. 12–13.

[19] Aune ("Magic in Early Christianity," 1518–19) observes that in the Roman Empire "most of the terms for magical practitioners were always used in a pejorative sense . . . though the term *magos* carried with it a certain oriental mystique and so could be understood in both a positive and negative way. With the lone exception of *magos* in Mt. 2:1ff., these terms invariably carry a pejorative connotation in the New Testament and early Christian literature." See also Remus, *Pagan-Christian Conflict,* 54–55; as Re-

mus notes, *magos* ("magician"), *mageia* ("magic"), and related words almost always have a negative connotation in extant Christian sources of the 2d century A.D. On the negative use of magic in the polemics of Celsus and Origen, see Eugene V. Gallagher, *Divine Man or Magician? Celsus and Origen on Jesus* (SBLDS 64; Chico, CA: Scholars, 1982); see, e.g., pp. 41–52.

[20] *Apology*, 25: "Nam si . . . Persarum lingua magus est qui nostra sacerdos, quod tandem est crimen. . . ." ("For if 'magician' is simply the Persian word for what we in our language call a priest, what crime, then, is it . . . ?") For a critical text, see Rudolf Helm (ed.), *Apulei Platonici Madaurensis opera quae supersunt. Vol. II Fasc. 1. Pro se de magia liber (Apologia)* (2d ed.; Leipzig: Teubner, 1959) 29–30. One problem with evaluating the *Apology* is that it is supposedly Apuleius' defense speech when he was on trial for allegedly having tricked a rich widow into marrying him by using magic. Hence Apuleius' defense of magic may be necessitated by the special circumstances of the trial, making a virtue of necessity. All this presumes that the defense oration reflects a real trial and is not, as some have speculated, a rhetorical exercise in which the novelist and philosopher defends himself against critics in general. Against the idea of a merely rhetorical exercise is Remus, *Pagan-Christian Conflict*, 69–70.

[21] This double meaning, "dignified priestly tribe" from Media and "quack," was known in Greece from the 5th century B.C. onwards, according to Arthur Darby Nock, "Paul and the Magus," *The Beginnings of Christianity. Part I. The Acts of the Apostles. Vol. V. Additional Notes to the Commentary* (ed. Kirsopp Lake and Henry J. Cadbury; Grand Rapids: Baker Book House, 1979, originally 1933) 164–88, esp. 164–65. On Apuleius' distinction between the two possible meanings of magic, see Segal, "Hellenistic Magic," 361–62. Segal notes that Greek authors went out of their way to emphasize that the Magi, i.e., the "clergy" of Persia, did not practice magic in the pejorative sense (p. 361 n. 37).

[22] See the examples in Remus, "Does Terminology Distinguish Early Christian from Pagan Miracles?" 551 and n. 140. Remus phrases his point with due discretion: "Even a word so generally pejorative in usage as *mageia/magia* ["magic"] is a term of honor in some texts and some social settings" (p. 551). The same thing could be said of "white supremacy" and "racial purity" in the United States today: fortunately, most people would view the terms negatively, though in certain texts and social settings they would be held in honor. Hence it is hardly surprising that "magic" is always used positively in the Greek magical papyri. Surprisingly, though, even in these papyri *mageia* "occurs only infrequently and mostly in connection with definitions" (Betz, "The Formation of Authoritative Tradition," 163).

[23] This is a constant theme of Remus, *Pagan-Christian Conflict*; see, e.g., 73–94; see also Gallagher, *Divine Man or Magician?*; Schoedel and Malina, "Miracle or Magic?" *passim*.

[24] Nock ("Paul and the Magus," 169) notes that "in the ordinary colloquial language of educated men," the words magic and magical have retained from ancient Greece and Rome a "rather contemptuous connotation . . . so that they customarily afford terms of abuse for religious ceremonies which are regarded as superstitious." Nock then goes on to observe that students of the history of religion use magic in a clearer and narrower sense: "the attempt to divert the course of nature by methods which to our science appear to be of a non-rational kind, or which to the user appear to rest on some hidden and peculiar wisdom. . . ." Contrary to some scholars today, Nock holds that this sense of magic is to be distinguished from both science and religion. In his

view, though, ancient Greeks and Romans did not clearly distinguish "a sphere of magic in contrast to the sphere of religion" (p. 170).

[25] One is surprised to see the blanket claim of Jan de Vries ("Magic and Religion," *History of Religions* 1 [1962] 214–21): "It is *generally agreed*, of course, that the two [magic and religion] are fundamentally opposed" (p. 214, emphasis mine). On p. 221 de Vries explicitly rejects the view of G. van der Leeuw that "magic is religion." The approach of van der Leeuw is echoed in the judgment of Jonathan Z. Smith ("Good News Is No News: Aretalogy and Gospel," *Christianity, Judaism and Other Greco-Roman Cults. Studies for Morton Smith at Sixty* (SJLA 20; 4 vols.; ed. Jacob Neusner; Leiden: Brill, 1975) 1. 21–38, esp. 23: "One of the more important insights [about magic] was suggested by the French Sociological School which argued that magic was not different in essence from religion, but rather different with respect to social position." Despite his disagreement with this approach, de Vries does admit that "religion and magic go through the ages side by side as conflicting twin brothers" (p. 214). Emile Durkheim (*The Elementary Forms of the Religious Life. A Study in Religious Sociology* [Glencoe, IL: The Free Press, 1974, originally 1915] 42–43) holds that, while magic and religion are related to each other, they must nevertheless be distinguished. He draws the line of demarcation by holding that religious beliefs belong to a group and create its unity, while magic does not unite individuals who believe in magic into a group leading a common life. As distinct from sociologists and anthropologists, theologians and exegetes tend to take a darker view of magic. For example, in his "Magie und Aberglaube an den Anfängen des Christentums," *TTZ* 83 (1974) 157–80, Norbert Brox lumps magic together with superstition and defines it as the "constantly threatening decadence and ever-present perversion of religion and also of Christian faith" (p. 157). In Brox's defense, it must be remembered that he is writing from the perspective of Christian faith in a theological journal. Since *A Marginal Jew* is pursuing as much as possible a consensus statement, in what follows I will avoid such evaluative labels as "decadence," "decay," "perversion," and "evil" when speaking of magic.

[26] Segal, "Hellenistic Magic," 349–75, esp. 349; similarly, Garrett, "Light on a Dark Subject," 144. A brief overview of various approaches to magic in 20th-century scholarship can be found in de Vries, "Magic and Religion," 214–21. Another compact survey of theories (including those of scholars like Frazer, Malinowski, Mauss, Evans-Pritchard, and Lévi-Strauss) can be found in Nur Yalman, "Magic," *International Encyclopedia of the Social Sciences* (18 vols.; New York: Macmillan/Free Press/Collier, 1968–79) 9. 521–28. Like many others, Yalman notes the various, at times conflicting, theories and definitions of magic and concludes: "Magic, then, is not a uniform class of practices and beliefs which can be immediately discerned in every society" (p. 522).

Thus, even among themselves, social scientists of the 20th century have not been of one mind as to the proper definition of and the proper approach to magic. In the view of Aune ("Magic in Early Christianity," 1510–16), the period before World War II was dominated by the presupposition that magic was a decadent cultural phenomenon easily separable from religion. After World War II one could sense a change in the scholarly atmosphere: magic was investigated with greater sympathy, and the study of magic and religion became respectable. See also the remarks of Mary Douglas on the shift in the way social scientists view magic and miracle in her *Purity and Danger. An Analysis of Concepts of Pollution and Taboo* (London/Boston: Routledge & Kegan Paul, 1966) 58–72. Influential in the shift were social scientists like E. E. Evans-Pritchard; among his works are *Witchcraft, Oracles and Magic among the Azande* (Oxford: Clarendon, 1937), esp. 387–544 on magic; idem, *Theories of Primitive Religion* (Oxford: Clarendon, 1965); idem, "The Morphology and Function of Magic," *Magic, Witchcraft and Curing* (ed.

John Middleton; Garden City, NY: The Natural History Press, 1967) 1–22. Evans-Pritchard held that "to try to understand magic as an idea in itself, what is the essence of it, as it were, is a hopeless task" (*Theories of Primitive Religion*, 111); it can be understood only in relation to empirical activities and in relation to other beliefs as a part of a system of thought.

Also rejecting a simplistic definition of magic, but preferring the approach of a continuum, with the two ideal types of religion and magic at the two ends, was William J. Goode, "Magic and Religion: A Continuum," *Ethnos* 14 (1949) 172–82; the same material can be found in his *Religion Among the Primitives* (Glencoe, IL: The Free Press, 1951) 50–55. A different approach was represented by Bronislaw Malinowski, who distinguished between religion, which is a system of beliefs concerned with the fundamental issues of human existence (death, immortality, the rulings of providence, etc.), and magic, which is a combination of ritual, act, and spoken spell that has pragmatic goals (e.g., obtaining good weather or a bountiful harvest); on this see his "A Scientific Theory of Culture," *A Scientific Theory of Culture and Other Essays* (Chapel Hill, NC: University of North Carolina, 1944) 26; idem, "Sir James George Frazer: A Biographical Appreciation," ibid., 198–201; idem, "Magic, Science and Religion," *Magic, Science and Religion and Other Essays* (Boston: Beacon; Glencoe, IL: The Free Press, 1948) 50–71, esp. 51: ". . . magic . . . [is] a body of purely practical acts, performed as a means to an end."

In recent decades exegetes have sought to apply various theories of magic to the treatment of the Gospel miracles. Not all the undertakings have been equally successful. In particular, the attempt by Hull (*Hellenistic Magic*, 45–72) to distinguish between a "magical miracle" and an "eschatological (or, alternately, a religious) miracle" is hopelessly muddled and useless. The weakness of his exegesis of the Synoptic Gospels only makes matters worse. For critiques of Hull, see Aune, "Magic in Early Christianity," 1543; Kee, *Medicine, Miracle and Magic*, 117–18; Garrett, "Light on a Dark Subject," 148–50.

All in all, there is nothing completely new in this modern-day debate over the proper understanding of magic. Remus (*Pagan-Christian Conflict*, 52–72) shows that the struggle to differentiate miracle (or true religion) from magic was going on between pagan and Christian writers as far back as the 2d century A.D. Remus highlights well the fact that the word "magic" was often used simply to stigmatize an adversary's religious position and that social conditioning had a great deal to do with what one identified as magic (pp. 73–94).

[27] So Betz ("Magic and Mystery," 246), reflecting the view of Sigmund Mowinckel. Independently this view has been developed by Rosalie and Murray Wax, "The Magical World View," *JSSR* 1 (1961) 179–88.

[28] See the examples in Kee, *Medicine, Miracle and Magic*, 38–39, 42, and 46. The great physician Galen (A.D. 129–99) stands out as being almost completely free of magical tendencies (pp. 62–63).

[29] In this concentrated focus on two literary collections my treatment differs from many other studies, which discuss the problem of miracle and magic either in a very wide cross-cultural perspective or at least in the context of ancient Christian literature in general. The ultimate goal of *A Marginal Jew*, the quest for the historical Jesus, determines this concentration on the canonical Gospels. It must also be stressed that in this present section of Chapter 18 we are dealing with the Gospels in their final literary forms, for the sake of comparison with another literary collection, the Greek magical papyri. Only in Chapter 19 will we try to move back to the time of the historical Jesus. The same basic observation must be made about the other term of our com-

parison. Just as our focus is not on all of ancient Christian literature but only the Four Gospels, so too in the case of Hellenistic magic our focus is not on all possible sources of information (charms, amulets, cursing tablets, references throughout Greco-Roman novels and histories, etc.) but only the collections of the Greek magical papyri. On the other sources of information, see Aune, "Magic in Early Christianity," 1516–17. In Segal's view ("Hellenistic Magic," 351), the magical papyri constitute "the easiest place to see the whole paradox" of the interweaving of religion and magic in Hellenistic culture, with the distinction between the two depending at times purely on the social context.

[30] I had already decided on the approach of a continuum with an ideal type at either end of the continuum before I read the similar proposal put forward by Goode in his "Magic and Religion," 172–82; and his *Religion Among the Primitives*, 50–55. Since our suggestions are similar, I should note important differences as well. (1) Goode is interested in comparing and contrasting *religion* and magic, not *miracle* and magic. His broader concern means that some of his descriptions of the "religion" end of the continuum as contrasted with the "magic" end would not fit my more restricted concern with miracles. For example, Goode claims that magic has fewer cult activities and a simpler structure than religion and that the practitioner of magic is freer in deciding whether or when the magical process is to start. Obviously, these contrasts do not hold true when one is comparing magic with miracles in particular rather than with religion in general. (2) Some of Goode's claims about magic do not seem to hold in any case (e.g., that a lesser degree of emotion is expected at the magical end of the continuum) and have not been taken up in my list of the characteristics of miracle and magic. (3) Goode is interested in the very broad project of finding a way that social anthropology can distinguish in general between magic and religion on the basis of concrete criteria. I have purposely kept to the much more limited project of seeking objective characteristics that distinguish the Gospels' reports of Jesus' miracles from the magic exhibited in the Greek magical papyri.

[31] So Goode, "Magic and Religion," 176, 178. On the development and refinement of the notion of ideal type by Max Weber, see Kee, *Miracle in the Early Christian World*, 44–46. In offering what is admittedly a rough typology at best, I am comforted by the words of Wilson, *Magic and the Millennium*, 10: "There are, then, no definitive typologies, no correct terms. The typology employed here is offered only in the hope that types of this kind may illumine some relations in a diverse body of phenomena in new ways: that it has its own limitations and blindspots one cannot doubt."

[32] This miracle story is unusually long, but its very length helps to highlight typical tendencies that can be found in varying degrees in many other Gospel miracles as well. The story's length also provides a better comparison-and-contrast with lengthier examples of Hellenistic magic, such as the Paris Magical Papyrus.

[33] I think that Aune ("Magic in Early Christianity," 1526–28) dismisses too quickly the question of whether difference in context may help distinguish miracle from magic. By way of contrast, I stress that here I am reading the individual miracle stories within the context of a given Gospel, the literary composition that lies before us as a whole.

[34] Heinz Joachim Held ("Matthäus als Interpret der Wundergeschichten," in Günther Bornkamm—Gerhard Barth—Heinz Joachim Held, *Überlieferung und Auslegung im Matthäusevangelium* [WMANT 1; 5th ed.; Neukirchen-Vluyn: Neukirchener Verlag, 1968] 263) observes: "In the Synoptic tradition, the terminology of faith is at home first of all in the miracle stories. One can easily get an overview of this in the Gospel of Mark. Namely, if one takes away the passages that betray the linguistic usage

of the Christian church (Mark 1:15; 9:42; 16:11ff.), what is shown is that, with a few exceptions (Mark 11:31; 13:21; 15:32) the word-family *pistis/pisteuein* appears only within or (as in Mark 11:22ff.) in very close connection with a miracle story. Matthew's Gospel exhibits a very similar state of affairs. . . . Already this overview shows how the terminology of faith in the early tradition appears predominantly in the context of the miracles. That holds true first of all for its occurrence in the narrative material. But the sayings tradition also knows this connection between faith and miracle" (translation mine).

[35] On this see Paul J. Achtemeier, " 'And He Followed Him': Miracles and Discipleship in Mark 10:46–52," *Early Christian Miracle Stories* (Semeia 11; ed. Robert W. Funk; Missoula, MT: Scholars, 1978) 115–45, esp. 133–35.

[36] A prime example is the story of the Syrophoenician woman who asks for the exorcism of her daughter. In Mark 7:29, Jesus finally "caves in" to the woman's persistence by saying: "Because of this word [i.e., your humble yet persistent reply to my rebuffs], go; the demon has gone forth from your daughter." Mark 7:30 then records in detail that the woman went home and found her daughter healed. Matt 15:28 ends the story quite differently. The first half of Jesus' reply becomes quite specific. Instead of Mark's vague "because of this word," Jesus says: "O woman, great is *your faith!*" By comparison, the actual promise of healing in the second half of Jesus' reply is laconic and almost overshadowed by the main point of faith: "Be it done to you as you wish." The report of the healing is likewise terse and generic: "Her daughter was healed at that hour." Thus, Matthew has pointedly shifted the climax of the story to the theme of the woman's faith as expressed in her persistent petition. On all this, see Held, "Matthäus als Interpret der Wundergeschichten," 155–287, esp. 168–71, 182–89, 263–84. On Luke, see Achtemeier, " 'And He Followed Him,' " 133–34: "More than any other evangelist, Luke appends to miracle stories references to the fact that those who had observed the miracles, or who had benefited from them, gave praise to God, . . . an attitude which belongs to the Lukan understanding of faith. . . . For Luke, miracles constitute a clearly legitimate basis for discipleship."

[37] For too long it has been a dogma among some exegetes that in the Gospels—or at least in Mark and John—there is no positive relationship between miracles and coming to faith. Such a position arises more from modern theologians' problems with miracle stories than with the data in the Gospel texts. For a healthy alternative to the Bultmannian way of interpreting signs in the Fourth Gospel, see Marianne Meye Thompson, *The Humanity of Jesus in the Fourth Gospel* (Philadelphia: Fortress, 1988) 63–81, esp. 80: "In the Fourth Gospel the purpose of Jesus' signs is to evoke faith. John 2:11; 12:37; and 20:30–31 make clear this connection between seeing signs and faith. Where the signs do not produce faith (9:16; 11:47–53; 12:37), the fault lies neither with the insufficiency of signs nor with the inadequacy of the faith they produce, but rather with the individuals who stubbornly refuse to see." See also Mussner, *Die Wunder Jesu,* 69–72.

[38] Aune, "Magic in Early Christianity," 1522. Even when Jesus uses the touch of his hand or (rarely) spittle in healing, one must ask whether the gesture is thought to be necessary to effect the cure, especially since the same Gospels contain stories that portray Jesus performing similar healings without these symbolic gestures.

[39] A point I have already mentioned should be reemphasized here: the purpose of the comparison undertaken in the main text is to examine two literary corpora of the Greco-Roman period and to see whether their similarities and contrasts can generate a useful typology with regard to miracle and magic for the Greco-Roman period. To be

sure, one methodological problem should not be overlooked: while the Gospels all belong to the second half of the 1st century A.D., the magical papyri we possess range over roughly seven centuries, with a good number of them coming from the later Roman Empire. However, the problem of dating is not so important for our present project, since we are engaged in constructing ideal types, not in arguing for causal relationship or literary influence. I stress, therefore, that I am not using the magical papyri "to offer what pass for historical explanations of events or phenomena which date from centuries earlier," a procedure Kee (*Miracle in the Early Christian World*, 288) rightly censures.

[40] Besides the Greek and German texts in Preisendanz (*Papyri Graecae Magicae*, 1. 170–73) and the English text in Betz (*The Greek Magical Papyri in Translation*, 96–97), one can find photographs of the document (dating from roughly A.D. 300), the original text, and a German translation in Deissmann, *Licht vom Osten*, 216–25. An English translation with notes is available in C. K. Barrett, *The New Testament Background: Selected Documents* (rev. ed.; San Francisco: Harper & Row, 1987) 34–37. The reader is advised that the usual way of citing the Greek magical papyri is with the siglum *PGM* (= *Papyri Graecae Magicae*), then the number of the papyrus manuscript in Roman numerals, and then the number(s) of the line(s) in Arabic numerals. The enumeration is according to the volumes of Preisendanz.

[41] Aune ("Magic in Early Christianity," 1519) wisely observes that the syncretism in the magical papyri simply reflects the larger phenomenon of increasing syncretism in the religious cults of the Roman Empire from the 2d to the 5th centuries A.D. Since our material comes from Hellenistic and Roman Egypt, it is not surprising that the major components of the cultural mix are Greek and Egyptian. The Jewish elements come from a Hellenistic Judaism of syncretistic bent, not directly from Israelite religion as enshrined in the Hebrew OT. The relatively few Christian features probably come via this syncretistic Hellenistic Judaism. Betz ("Magic and Mystery," 249) notes: "Christian magic rapidly expanded about the sixth century A.D., transforming and largely—but not totally—replacing the older material then classified as 'pagan.' "

[42] Betz, "Magic and Mystery," 248. As Betz points out, the magical papyri show at times some concern about the propriety of coercing the gods. On the whole, though, this concern is subdued in the magical papyri; it surfaces fully in the Neoplatonists and the Church Fathers. Betz states that, for the most part, the papyri were merely concerned with whether the magic worked.

[43] With respect to the deities who are mentioned, what is striking is the great emphasis on the gods and goddesses of the underworld, as well as the evident fascination with the elements of the physical universe, suitably deified.

[44] This pragmatic view is attributed specifically to the magical papyri by Kee, *Miracle in the Early Christian World*, 37; see the concrete examples he gives in his *Medicine, Miracle and Magic*, 108–11.

[45] For the magician as a "one-man show," see Betz, "The Formation of Authoritative Tradition," 161. However, one must be cautious in making sweeping statements. As Betz notes elsewhere ("Introduction," xlvi), "some of the magicians writing and using the spells may have been associated with temples of Egyptian and Greek deities. According to Egyptian practice, the magician was a resident member of the temple priesthood." Even here, though, there is no thought of creating a new circle of disciples.

[46] On the "magical-magnetic power to heal, transmitted through the body," see Haenchen, *Der Weg Jesu*, 207. As Hull bluntly puts it (*Hellenistic Magic*, 136), "in Mark

the woman expects magic and gets it." Aune ("Magic in Early Christianity," 1536) is even more emphatic: "The ideas expressed in the story of the woman's healing do not border on magic, they are of the essence of Graeco-Roman magical notions." Lane (*Mark*, 193) strains to mitigate the magical tone of this incident by claiming—quite contrary to the indications in the text—that it was the personal relationship between Jesus and the woman that released power. Indeed, says Lane, Jesus sought out the woman because he could not allow her "to recede into the crowd still entertaining ideas tinged with superstition and magic." Perhaps Jesus should have sought out Mark as well.

[47] I stress the word *Gospel* in the phrase "Gospel miracles." Some of the miracles in Acts seem to slide more toward the magical end of the spectrum: e.g., Peter's shadow heals those laid out in the streets as he passes by (Acts 5:15), and handkerchiefs (*soudaria*) and aprons (*simikinthia*) that had touched Paul's skin heal the sick (19:12). The reactions of exegetes to these two narratives are predictable. Some pass over the problem of magic in silence (e.g., Bruce in his NICNT commentary on Acts). On the other side of the great divide, Haenchen (*Die Apostelgeschichte*, 201–2, 497–98) sees here twin evils: (1) a flight into fantasy that transforms the true Pauline conception of a suffering apostle into a triumphant Hellenistic "divine man" (a questionable label for miracle-workers in the 1st century A.D.); and (2) a falling away into the horrors of early Catholicism, which changes a theology of the cross into a theology of glory. (On the questionable nature of many of the assumptions of the Bultmannian school in dealing with the theology of Luke vis-à-vis the theology of Paul, see Fitzmyer, *The Gospel According to Luke*, 1. 3–29.)

More sober in her evaluation than Haenchen is Elisabeth Schüssler Fiorenza, "Miracles, Mission, and Apologetics: An Introduction," *Aspects of Religious Propaganda in Judaism and Early Christianity* (University of Notre Dame Center for the Study of Judaism and Christianity in Antiquity 2; ed. Elisabeth Schüssler Fiorenza; Notre Dame/ London: University of Notre Dame, 1976) 1–25, esp. 12–13: "In ancient literature it is very difficult to distinguish the category of miracle from that of magic. They go hand in hand. In Acts 19:11–20 Luke links miracles and magic closely to each other. His summary statement about the great miraculous powers of Paul includes magical elements (19:11f.)." Magical traits can also be seen in the story of the miraculous "executions" of Ananias and Sapphira in Acts 5:1–11; see Brox, "Magie und Aberglaube," 160.

The story of Ananias and Sapphira raises the possibility that there is a correlation between magical traits in Acts and another characteristic difference between the miracles of the Gospels and those of Acts. The Four Gospels are totally free of miracles that directly punish people. In contrast, in Acts Ananias and Sapphira are both struck dead because they lie about the sale of a piece of property (Acts 5:1–11), Saul the future Apostle is temporarily struck blind for fighting against the gospel (9:8–9), Saul/Paul the Apostle strikes the magician (!) Bar-Jesus (Elymas) blind for the same sin (13:11), and the sons of Sceva suffer for their attempt to exorcise an evil spirit in the name of Jesus (19:13–18). On the magical and punitive character of some of the miracles in Acts, see Kee, *Miracle in the Early Christian World*, 211, 215–17. On p. 285 Kee notes that the number and vehemence of punitive miracles increase in the later apocryphal Gospels and Acts. For a sympathetic reading of Acts 13:6–11 (the blinding of Bar-Jesus) that tries to understand why Luke would not see Paul's action as magic but rather the defeat of magic, see Garrett, "Light on a Dark Subject," 152–59. Garrett stresses the need to attempt to understand the viewpoint of the ancient narrator of or participants in such incidents, which in the ancient world remained open to both magical and nonmagical interpretations.

A conclusion that is sometimes drawn from this increase of magical or punitive overtones in the apostles' miracles in Acts as compared with Jesus' miracles in the Gospels is that, from the beginning, stories about Jesus in the Gospel traditions enjoyed more of a normative quality and were less open to wholesale recasting and invention than stories that circulated in the early church about various apostles. While there may be some truth in this, the objection of Paul J. Achtemeier ("Jesus and the Disciples as Miracle Workers in the Apocryphal New Testament," *Aspects of Religious Propaganda in Judaism and Early Christianity* [University of Notre Dame Center for the Study of Judaism and Christianity in Antiquity 2; ed. Elisabeth Schüssler Fiorenza; Notre Dame/ London: University of Notre Dame, 1976] 149–86) must be pondered: why did the canonical tradition exercise no such restraining force on the sayings of Jesus? Achtemeier concludes that the meager increase of Jesus' miracles in the apocryphal Gospels (apart from Infancy Gospels), as compared with the notable increase of new miracle stories told of the apostles in the apocryphal Acts, "remains a mystery within the development of Christian tradition in the second and third centuries" (p. 177). Perhaps one can suggest a certain type of proportionality in the controlling force of the early Christian tradition: just as the stories of the apostles' miracles in Acts were less constrained by a generally known normative tradition than were the stories of Jesus' miracles in the Gospels, so too the words and speeches of the apostles in Acts were more open to pure creation than were the words of Jesus in the Gospels.

[48] For Matthew's redactional changes in the story, see Held, "Matthäus als Interpret der Wundergeschichten," 204–7; cf. Hull, *Hellenistic Magic*, 136–37.

[49] For a translation of and commentary on the so-called *Mithras Liturgy*, see Marvin W. Meyer, *The "Mithras Liturgy"* (Missoula, MT: Scholars, 1976); alternately, Betz, *The Greek Magical Papyri in Translation*, 48–54 (the translation is by Meyer). Note, for instance, the exalted spirit of the climax of the initiation (lines 719–22): "O Lord, while being born again, I am passing away; while growing and having grown, I am dying; while being born from a life-generating birth, I am passing on, released to death—as you have founded, as you have decreed, and have established the mystery." For the classical debate between Albrecht Dieterich and Franz Cumont on the nature of this text, see Betz ("Magic and Mystery," 252), who favors the view of Dieterich that the text does reflect an actual Mithras liturgy. On the other hand, Segal ("Hellenistic Magic," 355 n. 20) thinks that the debate has never been satisfactorily resolved. For Segal's comments on the Mithras Liturgy, see ibid., 354–55.

[50] *Metamorphoses* 11.2; for the Latin text with English translation, see J. Arthur Hanson (ed.), *Apuleius. Metamorphoses* (LCL; 2 vols.; Cambridge, MA/London: Harvard University, 1989) 2. 292–95. Even with the multiplication of divine names there is a difference from many of the magical papyri: the names that the anti-hero Lucius invokes as he prays to the "Queen of Heaven" are all well-known deities in the Greco-Roman world (Ceres, Venus, Phoebus' sister [= Artemis], and Proserpina); there are no strings of nonsense syllables.

[51] On the *Metamorphoses* as "Apuleius' full view of magic *per se*," see Segal, "Hellenistic Magic," 362–64. On p. 364 Segal asserts: "Apuleius' final understanding of 'magic' [in the *Metamorphoses*] is negative. Magic represents the world under the power of blind chance, a world in which Lucius had been enslaved until the grace of the goddess saved him." See also Kee, *Miracle in the Early Christian World*, 131–41; on p. 145 he notes that, unlike Diodorus Siculus (active in mid-1st century B.C.), who portrays Isis primarily as a healer, in neither Apuleius nor Plutarch (before A.D. 50–after 120) do we hear of healing miracles performed by Isis. "Her role is rather that of a life-orienter. Her functions are cosmic and mystical rather than practical and immediate, though in Apuleius's case there are certain practical benefits."

[52] I stress here that the comparison is between the four canonical Gospels on the one hand and documents containing pagan magic on the other. The same contrast would not necessarily hold if the two points of comparison were pagan magic and the official religious cults of paganism. As Fox remarks (*Pagans and Christians*, 36), "In antiquity, magic was itself a religious ritual which worked on pagan divinities. . . . [conventional pagan] cults, too, [like magic,] compelled their gods with symbols and aimed to work on them for beneficial ends."

[53] It is sometimes claimed that Mark's use of the Aramaic phrases *talitha koum* in the raising of the daughter of Jairus (5:41) and *ephphatha* in the healing of the deaf and mute man (7:34) reflects the magical practice of using unintelligible or foreign words to create a mysterious atmosphere of esoteric, secret knowledge. Needless to say, this would not hold on the level of the hypothetical historical events, where Aramaic would have been the common language spoken by Jesus' audience. But even on the level of Mark's redaction, in both cases the Evangelist supplies a Greek translation ("little girl, . . . arise," "be opened"), which naturally dispels any atmosphere of esoteric knowledge or secrecy. Mark likewise provides Aramaic words with Greek translations on the two occasions when Jesus prays during the Passion Narrative (*abba* ["Father"] in 14:36; and *elōi elōi lema sabachthani* ["my God, my God, why have you forsaken me?"] in 15:34). These are examples of intense prayer, not magic. Taken together, all these cases indicate a high point of emotion and drama in the narrative, not magical practices. They are in no way parallel to the lengthy strings of divine names and nonsense syllables of some Hellenistic magical texts. Hence I think Aune ("Magic in Early Christianity," 1534–35) is wrong when he suggests that *talitha koum* or *ephphatha* was probably preserved by Mark "for the purpose of guiding Christian thaumaturges in exorcistic and healing activities. In early Christianity, therefore, these Aramaic phrases may have functioned as magic formulas." If these Aramaic phrases were so important in this regard, it is surprising that not only Matthew but even Luke drop them from their versions of Mark's stories. That various words of Jesus appear in later centuries in, e.g., Christian charms and amulets hardly proves anything about the intention of Jesus or the evangelists. From the beginnings of the Christian church, and certainly throughout the patristic period, magic was a phenomenon in Christianity as in other Greco-Roman religions; see Brox, "Magie und Aberglaube," 157–80.

[54] Jesus' use of spittle (Mark 7:33; 8:23; John 9:6) is sometimes cited as an indication of magic; so Aune, "Magic in Early Christianity," 1537–38. But this point is not so clear as some think. (1) The exact sense of the spittle in the two Marcan stories is a bone of contention among present-day scholars. While Aune considers it magical, Yamauchi ("Magic or Miracle?" 137–40, esp. 139) claims that spittle was thought to have medicinal properties by physicians of the period: "There is . . . considerable evidence that [in the Greco-Roman world] spittle was commonly used to treat eye diseases." However, this claim is disputed by Howard Clark Kee ("Magic and Messiah," *Religion, Science, and Magic in Concert and in Conflict* [ed. Jacob Neusner, Ernest S. Frerichs, and Paul V. M. Flesher; New York/Oxford: Oxford University, 1989] 121–41, esp. 138), who states that no case of spittle as a medical means of healing has been preserved from the Hellenistic or Roman period. Kee says that spittle as a medium of healing is likewise absent from the Jewish and Greek magic materials that derive from this period: the Greek magical papyri, the Aramaic incantation bowls and amulets, and the *Sepher harazim*. What then is the point of the spittle? Kee observes that in the Torah (Lev 15:8 and Num 12:14) spittle—which is never a means of healing in the Hebrew Scriptures—is instead defiling. Kee therefore thinks that the two Marcan passages present the action of Jesus as a challenge to the purity laws. "Jesus is seen in this material as radically

redefining covenantal participation, so the ritual purity as understood in the developing Pharisaic tradition of that period is sharply challenged . . ." (p. 139). To all these scholarly opinions one may add a further observation and question. In Tacitus' account of how Vespasian, while in Alexandria, cured a blind man with spittle, Vespasian takes action only after consulting physicians about the gravity of the illness and a possible cure. Does this imply that the use of spittle by Vespasian was part of the physicians' advice? In any case, whether the use of spittle in the two Marcan stories is to be considered part of a symbolic action of healing by a miracle-worker, or part of a magical ritual performed by a magician, or a symbolic challenge to certain purity laws as defining God's people must be judged on the larger grounds of content and context, not on the mere fact of the use of spittle. (2) In the magical papyri, the various ingredients in a recipe or amulet must be used exactly as prescribed; otherwise, the magic will not work. This is hardly the thought of the Marcan tradition, since among all his many cures Jesus uses spittle only twice. In particular, Mark hardly considers spittle a necessary component of a cure for blindness, since the Marcan Jesus just as easily cures the blind Bartimaeus without it (Mark 10:46–52). Indeed, not even Jesus' touch is deemed necessary in this case; a terse command is sufficient. (3) The case of John 9:6 is not really *ad rem*. Unlike the two cases in Mark, Jesus does not apply his spittle directly to the affected organs of the afflicted person. Rather, Jesus spits on the ground to make clay with his saliva. In other words, Jesus uses his spittle not directly to heal the beggar's blindness but rather for the pedestrian purpose of making clay that he then smears on the man's eyes (the covering of clay apparently symbolizing the impediment of blindness, to be washed away). As the story in John 9 repeatedly stresses, it is the combination of Jesus' symbolic action of smearing the clay on the man's eyes, his order to go and wash in the pool of Siloam, and the actual washing by the obedient beggar that brings about the miraculous cure. Thus, unlike the two cases in Mark, the spittle in John 9:6 does not directly constitute Jesus' act of healing. (4) A larger methodological question lies behind these particular cases: Are all symbolic actions of a person who performs miracles *ipso facto* to be considered magic? Unless one allows the content and context of the Gospel miracle stories to be ignored in favor of a mechanical formalism, the answer must be no. A still larger question that cannot be discussed here opens up the underlying problem of the critic's philosophical and theological viewpoint: Are the categories of the incarnational, the sacramental, and the symbolic really the same thing as the category of the magical?

[55] This fusion of the eschatological and the miraculous in Jesus' ministry is one reason why it is not easy to apply Bryan Wilson's typology of new "deviant" religious movements to Jesus' public career (see *Magic and the Millennium*, 18–30, esp. 22–26). Among the seven types of "response to the world" that distinguish new religious movements according to Wilson, four are potentially important for the study of the historical Jesus: (1) the conversionist response, in which salvation comes by a profoundly felt transformation of the self, a transformation wrought by God alone; (2) the revolutionist response, which awaits from God a sudden, imminent act that will destroy (or profoundly shake) the old world and create (or recreate, or restore) another; (3) the reformist response, which holds that evil in the world may be dealt with according to supernaturally given insights about the way in which social life should be amended; (4) the thaumaturgical response, which takes the form of magical healings, rescues, and oracles granted by God. As Wilson notes, the revolutionist and thaumaturgical responses are in theory polar opposites. The revolutionist response aims at a group and looks to the imminent future. The thaumaturgical response aims at conferring concrete benefits now on particular individuals. In reality, the thaumaturgical response may both precede and follow a revolutionist movement, which may also have thaumaturgical traits. In the

case of Jesus, however, his ministry was both profoundly thaumaturgical and profoundly eschatological (alias "revolutionist" or "millennial") at the same time. To complicate matters more, Jesus' eschatology was both present and future, the miracles both partially realizing the kingdom now and pointing to its full realization soon.

But that is not all. In his call to discipleship, in his demand for a new mode of living God's will, in his teaching of various concrete ethical imperatives to his disciples (e.g., radical love and forgiveness, rejection of divorce), Jesus gave his ministry some of the aspects of both a conversionist and a reformist movement (though these elements are in a sense secondary to the major emphasis on eschatology in his preaching and miracles in his activity). To sum up: I think it unwise to seize upon any one type within Wilson's seven possibilities and squeeze Jesus into it. The desire to do so may explain in part the tendency of some to delete future eschatology (e.g., Crossan) or morality (e.g., Smith) from Jesus' message: it makes sociological pigeonholing much easier.

[56] On the question of coercion in the Greek magical papyri, Kee ("Magic and Messiah," 127) remarks: "The power of the magic is dependent on the forcefulness of the orders to the divine powers, with the instructions expressed by the most forceful verbs: *horkizō, epitassō, exorkizō*. There is never anything humble about the requests addressed to supernatural agents. Yet it is the cosmic rulers that are involved. . . ."

In the main text I speak of "the technical manipulation of . . . forces or the coercion of a deity" in preference to the formulation of Aune ("Magic in Early Christianity," 1515), who suggests the following as one criterion for judging religious activity to be magic: "Goals sought within the context of religious deviance are magical when attained through the management of supernatural powers in such a way that results are virtually guaranteed." Putting aside the question of magic/miracles and "religious deviance" for consideration in a later note, I think that the phrases "management" and "virtually guaranteed" are too vague to be truly helpful. Interestingly, even Crossan, who otherwise agrees to a great degree with Aune, urges that the language of guarantee be dropped (*The Historical Jesus*, 309).

In particular, we may ask what qualifies as "virtually guaranteed"? Let us take a concrete case from the OT. Yahweh promises the people Israel both a huge number of descendants and the promised land. To be sure, Israel is to keep Yahweh's covenant and walk in all his ways. But Yahweh's commitment to Israel is prior to any response from Israel and perdures through all of Israel's infidelities. The blessings of the covenant are not virtually but absolutely guaranteed; Yahweh is absolutely faithful to his promises, though individual generations of Israelites may be punished or even exiled from the land for their disobedience to the covenant. After punishment or exile, Yahweh always restores his people, as he will (according to apocalyptic hopes) in the end time. Does this absolutely guaranteed result of Yahweh's faithfulness to Israel in their covenant relationship, celebrated and renewed in all sorts of ritual, qualify as magic? I do not think so, because one must take into account both context and content before one can decide whether a particular religious phenomenon is magical. The overarching context of this covenant is Yahweh's free, gracious choice of entering into a personal relationship with Israel and Israel's free response (at least at times) of trust in and obedience to Yahweh. Thus, the "guarantee" issues from a promise freely made by a personal deity to human beings and freely received in trust by the human beings. Wherever in religion the "guarantee" arises and operates within such an interpersonal context of faith, trust, and obedience, the result should not be considered magical.

[57] PGM XIII. 793–806; Greek text in Preisendanz, *Papyri Graecae Magicae*, 2. 123. The translations (and obviously the emphasis) is my own. Another English translation, by Morton Smith, can be found in Betz, *The Greek Magical Papyri in Translation*, 191.

This tendency of the magic in the papyri to coerce the deity to grant concrete personal benefits is similar to that noted by Kee (*Medicine, Miracle and Magic*, 96) in Apuleius' presentation of magic in his *Metamorphoses*, though in the latter the tone is perhaps darker still: "The dominant features of Apuleius' narratives are of the sort that deal in coercion and achievement of personal goals—largely destructive and retaliatory— rather than healing."

[58] See, e.g., *PGM* XXI and LXXVII. Hence I agree with those who refuse to make coercion or lack of coercion of the deity *the* sole criterion for labeling an event magic or miracle. In my typology it is only one characteristic among many, and it may be present in varying degrees or even absent in individual cases. In contrast, de Vries ("Magic and Religion," 214) seems to make the audacity of seeking to coerce supernatural powers *the* hallmark of magic as opposed to religion: ". . . the act of the magician constitutes an audacity, since he coerces to his service what his community regards as venerable" (p. 221). The aspect of coercion is also stressed by Kee, *Miracle in the Early Christian World*, 62–63 (although his appeal to Mauss should be modified, since Mauss [*A General Theory of Magic*, 21] acknowledges that magic may supplicate as well as coerce); Kee makes the same point in his *Christian Origins in Sociological Perspective* (Philadelphia: Westminster, 1980) 65–66. Much more careful is Goode ("Magic and Religion," 177–78), who not only lists eleven different distinguishing characteristics of magic (of which coercion or manipulation is only one) but also stresses that he is talking of coercion or manipulation as one variable on a continuum. He simply claims that the manipulative attitude is found most strongly at the magical pole of the continuum, while concrete cases will actually fall somewhere between the two poles.

[59] Kee (*Miracle in the Early Christian World*, 86–87) makes a similar observation about the cures attributed to the healing god Asklepios before the 2d century A.D., as they are recorded on tablets at his shrine in Epidauros: "There is no suggestion that the healing had any meaning outside of itself; it is not a pointer to a spiritual transformation or a promise of anything transcendent." Kee suggests that a change took place in the 2d century A.D.: elites like Aelius Aristides (A.D. 118–ca. 180) began to seek from Asklepios not only physical healing but also the meaning of life or an experience of salvation (pp. 88–104).

[60] Durkheim, *The Elementary Forms of the Religious Life*, 44; the emphasis is in the original.

[61] Kee ("Magic and Messiah," 131), speaking of the Greek magical papyri, the *Sepher ha-razim*, and Aramaic amulets and incantation bowls, observes a basic difference from the messianic hopes of postbiblical Jewish literature and of early Christian writings: "Also absent [in the magical material] are any expressions of concern for the welfare or the future of the covenant people. Indeed, the focus of interest is in every case the welfare of the petitioning individual, not the community of which he or she is presumably a member." Likewise absent from these magical materials is any eschatological hope of the coming rule of God that will defeat the powers of evil once and for all.

[62] *PGM* I. 27–29; see Betz, *The Greek Magical Papyri in Translation*, 3. The accompanying recipe is as intriguing as the spell: two of the magician's fingernails, all of the hair from his head, a falcon drowned in the milk of a black cow (after Attic honey is mixed with the milk). Unintentionally hilarious is the directive: "Take the milk with the honey and drink it before the rising of the sun, and there will be something divine in your heart." The subsequent invocation to the deity alludes to the story of Ra-Atum's creation of the gods by masturbation. While this particular papyrus is from the 4th or 5th century A.D., the same basic pattern of strings of divine names or nonsense

syllables can be found in papyri from the 1st and 2d centuries A.D.; see, e.g., *PGM* XVI. 1–75 or LVII.1–37.

[63] Malinowski, "Magic, Science, and Religion," 54.

[64] Kee, *Miracle in the Early Christian World*, 213.

[65] Here I disagree with Aune's judgment about Jesus' exorcisms ("Magic in Early Christianity," 1531–32): "The great gulf which some New Testament scholars would place between 'the powerful word of the Son' and 'magical incantations' is simply nonexistent. The short authoritative commands of Jesus to demons in the gospel narratives are formulas of magical adjuration." Aune likewise considers the healing commands of Jesus to be "magical formulas of adjuration" (p. 1534).

In reply to Aune's view of Jesus' exorcisms, the following observations may be made: (1) In the face of the massive differences between the terse command of Jesus and the lengthy recipes, manipulations, and spells of the magical papyri, Aune shrugs his shoulder and says: ". . . such a contrast is quantitative, not qualitative." Anyone who reads through Betz's *The Greek Magical Papyri in Translation* will see that it is both. One reason for the length of the material in the papyri is the need to describe the complicated recipes to be concocted, the lengthy string of divine names and nonsense syllables to be recited, and the various ritual actions to be performed. There is something more than mere quantity at stake here; a whole conception of what exorcism is all about and how it operates is being reflected. To take only the spell: the magician must try all sorts of names and combinations of syllables because he does not know which one may press the right button and achieve the desired effect in a particular case. The whole conception of divine (or superhuman) power, its mode of operation, and the relation of human beings to it that is reflected in these papyri is qualitatively different from the conception presupposed by the Gospel narratives. Moreover, the basic conception reflected in the magical papyri is no doubt much older than the documents, no matter what the precise length of any given spell. Although older spells may tend to be shorter, even in the 1st century A.D. we already have a lengthy chain of spells of *PGM* XVI.1–75, with the typical strings of divine names. See also *PGM* LVII.1–37, from the 1st or 2d century A.D., which exhibits both strings of divine names and nonsense syllables. (2) Ultimately, Aune's evaluation of the Gospel exorcisms stems not so much from his analysis of individual texts of the Gospels or the papyri as from his prior identification of miracle and magic.

[66] Mauss, *A General Theory of Magic*, 24; de Vries ("Magic and Religion," 217) objects that this does not hold true of all magic. Other authors prefer to approach magic by way of illegality rather than secrecy. Relying on the work of Morton Smith and Peter Brown, Jonathan Z. Smith has claimed that illegality is "the one universal characteristic of magic"; see his "Good News Is No News," 21–38, esp. 23. Actually, this does not seem to hold true of ancient Greek law; see Phillips, *"Nullum Crimen sine Lege,"* 260–76, esp. 261–63. Similarly, until the 4th century A.D. Roman law subjected specific unsanctioned religious activities to legal sanctions, "but there appears no omnibus definition [of magic as illegal]" (p. 263). One problem was that ancient Romans, like modern sociologists, did not possess a single clear definition of magic agreed upon by all. Wide discretion was left to the individual magistrate. As a matter of fact, formal acts of repression were relatively infrequent (p. 265). Phillips concludes with a methodological caution (p. 269): "Instead of looking for legal repression of ancient magic, we could more accurately—and hence profitably—look for legal repression of unsanctioned religious activity, some but by no means all of which might be magical in the ancient view." Taking a somewhat different tack, Segal ("Hellenistic Magic," 356) ob-

serves that, while magic is always discussed in a negative context in Roman laws, "a consensus was established early which viewed harmful acts (and only harmful acts) of magic as criminal." What was proscribed was magic that hurt others ("witchcraft" in that sense); "presumably, what we call 'white' or non-aggressive magic was no crime" (p. 358). By this definition, Jesus' miracles of exorcism, healing, feeding, and sea-rescue, even if judged to be magic, would not be criminal by the standards of Roman law.

Eschewing the claim that illegality is an essential characteristic of magic, Aune ("Magic in Early Christianity," 1515) thinks a more adequate formulation would run like this: "Magic is universally regarded as a form of deviant behavior." Accordingly, Aune proceeds to define magic as "that form of religious deviance whereby individual or social goals are sought by means alternate to those normally sanctioned by the dominant religious institution." Since Aune sees no objective distinction between miracle and magic, his sweeping definition runs into trouble on a number of grounds. (1) The 2d-century pagan religious figure Alexander of Abonuteichos was considered a deviant and socially unacceptable magician or wizard by the influential writer and satirist Lucian. Yet Alexander enjoyed favor and patronage from the high and the mighty in the Roman imperial government. (2) In the patristic, medieval, and modern Catholic Church sainted priests, bishops, and popes are said to have worked miracles, sometimes specifically as warrants for the orthodoxy of their views. How can these miracles of hierarchs of the orthodox religious establishment—miracles that, in Aune's view, do not differ objectively from magic—be examples of deviant behavior? And what does it mean in this case to say that magic/miracle is a "means alternate to those normally sanctioned by the dominant religious institution" when as a matter of fact the Catholic Church demands a number of miracles as prerequisites for canonization as a saint? Like many other attempts to find one definition of magic that will encompass all examples in all religious traditions, Aune's definition looks good as theory but fails when applied to concrete cases. This is one reason why I have purposely narrowed my focus to two concrete literary corpora (the Four Gospels and the Greek magical papyri) and have waived any attempt to construct a definition of magic valid for all times, places, and religions.

One might add that the objections I have raised against defining miracle/magic in terms of illegality or deviant behavior opposed to the established religious powers undermines Crossan's whole approach to miracle/magic in his *The Historical Jesus*. For instance, on p. 305 he makes a claim pivotal to his whole reconstruction of the historical Jesus as a magician: ". . . magic is to religion as banditry is to politics. As banditry challenges the ultimate legitimacy of political power, so magic challenges that of spiritual power." One wonders what all the miracle-working authority figures from the Emperor Vespasian to Pope St. Pius X would make of this. Indeed, one need not go so far afield; Crossan's antiestablishment, subversive view of magic seems to founder on the place of the magician in Diaspora Judaism of the Roman period, if Lightstone is correct in his evaluation. According to Lightstone (*The Commerce of the Sacred*, 56), "when for any number of reasons the Sanctuary remains remote, demons and Holy Men thrive, as in the Greco-Roman Diaspora. Thus Judaic 'magicians' do not constitute a fringe element removed from the institutional centre of the Diaspora community. Quite the contrary, he [*sic*] often set up shop in the synagogue itself, along with the community's courts and senate." Crossan's whole project falters precisely on the point of an adequate understanding of miracle and magic.

[67] Miracles in Mark that are performed in public include Jesus' first exorcism in Capernaum (1:21–28); his healing of many people at the door of the house of Simon (1:32–34); the healing of the paralytic (2:1–12); the healing of the man with the withered hand (3:1–6); the healing of many by the Sea of Galilee (3:7–12); the healing of the

woman with the hemorrhage (5:25–32, within the story of the raising of the daughter of Jairus, which is performed before a select group); the feeding of the five thousand and later of the four thousand (6:30–44; 8:1–10); the healing of many in the region of Gennesaret (6:53–56); the healing of the boy with the unclean spirit (9:14–29); and the healing of Bartimaeus (10:26–52). The fact that in some cases Jesus forbids the exorcised demons to speak or reveal who he is does not negate the public nature of the words and/or deeds that accomplish the exorcism. There is no idea of Jesus' trying to conceal his "technique" or "spells."

[68] There is also the special case of the more technical sense of *magoi* as "Magi" or "astrologers" from the East in Matthew's Infancy Narrative (Matt 2:1,7,16 *bis*).

[69] Hence one does not know what to make of the claim by Lightstone, *The Commerce of the Sacred*, 55: "The labelling, then, of someone a 'magician' and something as demonic seems akin. . . . That perhaps is why Jesus' detractors in the Gospels may either label him a magician or, alternatively, one possessed by the Devil." Where "in the Gospels" do his detractors ever label him a magician?

[70] For an interpretation of the accusation of being in league with Beelzebul in Matt 12:24 as an accusation of witchcraft, see Bruce J. Malina and Jerome H. Neyrey, *Calling Jesus Names. The Social Value of Labels in Matthew* (Sonoma, CA: Polebridge, 1988) 3–32. As the authors stress, the essay in question, "Jesus the Witch," is dealing with the text of Matthew's Gospel as it stands, and not explicitly with the quest for the historical Jesus. One should also note that social scientists no more agree on a single definition of witchcraft than they do on a single definition of magic. On witchcraft see also Tzvi Abusch, "The Demonic Image of the Witch in Standard Babylonian Literature: The Reworking of Popular Conceptions by Learned Exorcists," *Religion, Science, and Magic in Concert and in Conflict* (ed. Jacob Neusner, Ernest S. Frerichs, and Paul V. M. Flesher; New York/Oxford: Oxford University, 1989) 27–58; Nachman Ben-Yehuda, "Witchcraft and the Occult as Boundary Maintenance Devices," ibid., 229–60, esp. 233–44.

[71] In this regard, it is remarkable to notice how free Morton Smith is with both his translations and his evidence when mounting his case for Jesus as a magician. For instance, when translating Justin Martyr, Smith (*Jesus the Magician*, 54) blithely supplies the word "magician" when Justin (*Dialogue with Trypho* 108.2) speaks of the Jewish accusation that Jesus was a *planos*, a "deceiver," i.e., a person who led people astray. Now *planos* can mean "magician" when the context makes that meaning clear, but the range of *planos* is much broader than "magician." Therefore, something in the larger context of the passage being translated must justify the precise translation "magician." Now the immediate context of Justin's remarks in the *Dialogue with Trypho* 108.2 is Matthew's story of the guarding of Jesus' tomb and the lie concocted by the high priests after the resurrection (Matt 27:62–66; 28:11–15), especially the statement of the high priests: "Sir, we remember that this deceiver [*planos*] said while still alive . . ." (Matt 27:63). In context, the word *planos* need mean nothing more than "a liar." Nothing daunted, Smith likewise translates *planos* in Matt 27:63 as "magician," despite the fact that nothing in the immediate context favors such a choice. This is translation at its most tendentious. Worst of all, it obscures the fact that Justin is quite sparing in applying *magos* and *magikos* to Jesus, even when reporting Jewish accusations. An inspection of Edgar J. Goodspeed (ed.), *Index Apologeticus, sive clavis Justini Martyris operum aliorumque apologetarum pristinorum* (Leipzig: Hinrichs, 1912) 167, shows that in the *Dialogue* and in the *First and Second Apologies* Justin used the adjective *magikos* 8 times and the noun *magos* 16 times. However, he uses these two words almost entirely of the Wise

Men of Matthew's Infancy Narrative, Egyptian and other pagan magicians (such as the
ones who opposed Moses), the Christian "heretics" Simon and Menander, and demons
and fallen angels. Only in two passages (*Dialogue* 69.7 and *First Apology* 30.1) does he
use these words of accusations aimed at Jesus. Hence the loose translations by Smith
skew data that should be presented with great precision. In his *Dialogue with Trypho*
69.7, Justin, having just listed the various types of miracles Jesus performed, laments
that "those who saw these very things happen said that they were a magical vision, for
they even dared to say that he [Jesus] was a magician and one who led the people
astray" (*hoi de kai tauta horōntes ginomena phantasian magikēn ginesthai elegon. kai gar
magon einai auton etolmōn legein kai laoplanon*). For the Greek text with French
translation and notes, see Georges Archambault (ed.), *Justin. Dialogue avec Tryphon*
(2 vols.; Paris: Picard, 1909) 1. 338. In his *First Apology* 30.1, Justin takes up the
objection of those who suggest that "the person we call Christ, who was [simply] a
man among men, performed by magical skill the miracles that we narrate" (*ton par'
hēmin legomenon Christon, anthrōpon ex anthrōpōn onta, magikē technē has legomen
dynameis pepoiēkenai*). For the Greek text with Latin translation and notes, see Gerard
Rauschen (ed.), *Florilegium Patristicum. Fasciculus Alter. S. Justini Apologiae Duae* (2d
ed.; Bonn: Hanstein, 1911) 58.

[72] For Celsus and the debate he unleashed about Jesus as a magician, see Remus,
Pagan-Christian Conflict, 105–58; Robert L. Wilken, *The Christians as the Romans Saw
Them* (New Haven/London: Yale University, 1984) 94–125; Kee, *Medicine, Miracle
and Magic*, 120–25; and the whole of Gallagher, *Divine Man or Magician?* Gallagher
(p. 46) points out that Celsus' main purpose in calling Jesus a magician was to
impugn his social, moral, and intellectual status and so deny him the dignity of a
true philosopher.
As I have indicated already, I think that Morton Smith (*Jesus the Magician*) lumps
together too much disparate material, too many different categories, and too many
widely separated sources, without due concern for dating and historical reliability, to
create his portrait of the historical Jesus as a magician. In particular, the use he makes
of both Josephus and the rabbinic material is open to serious question; see *A Marginal
Jew*, 1. 56–88, 93–98. For a critique of Smith's use of his sources, see Kee, *Miracle in
the Early Christian World*, 211 n. 69; idem, *Medicine, Miracle and Magic*, 115–17; Garrett,
"Light on a Dark Subject," 144–48. Garrett astutely remarks of Smith's methodology:
"Smith's 'social type [of magician],' abstracted 'with the eye of historical faith' from the
'many different patterns' of ancient holy men, is an analytic category biased so as always
to favor the opinion of the accusers. In subsuming all wonder-workers under this heading [of magician], Smith precludes any chance of understanding the point of view of
sympathizers."

[73] The closest we come to such an idea is the deliberation of the high priests and the
Pharisees (!) in John 11:45–53, especially v 47: "Therefore the high priests and the
Pharisees held a meeting [*synedrion*] and said: "What are we to do? For this fellow keeps
on performing numerous signs." The passage is clearly a Johannine creation, suffused
with Johannine theology and irony: the miracle of raising the dead Lazarus to life will
occasion the life-giving death and resurrection of Jesus. The placement of the Pharisees
within the group plotting Jesus' death shows the late nature of the material; the Pharisees are absent from all the earliest passion traditions.

[74] An interesting side point arises here: Jesus could be accused by his opponents of
using the power of the prince of demons without any talk about "magic" surfacing.
This simply underlines the point that there was no inextricable link between the two;
Jewish magic did not necessarily involve being in league with Satan or his minions (the

latter being a much more serious matter). As Lightstone points out (*The Commerce of the Sacred*, 56), Jewish magicians were quite capable in some cases of setting up shop in the Diaspora synagogue itself, "along with the community's courts and senate." I think it highly unlikely that this would have been allowed if the synagogue members equated the magician's practice of magic with being in league with Satan or his hosts. To be sure, some magicians in some cases might invoke Satan or some equivalent evil power; but magic and Satan did not necessarily go together. That was true in the ancient world, just as it is obviously true for people who claim to be magicians today.

EXCURSUS ON PARALLELS TO THE GOSPEL MIRACLES

(An Excursus to Chapter 18)

In Chapter 18 I briefly touched on the question of Greco-Roman parallels to the miracles of Jesus reported in the Four Gospels. The precise evaluation of such parallels would require a volume of its own. In fact, in recent decades various authors have dedicated whole books to the question of one or more such parallels to the Gospels. For example, Gerd Petzke has written both a whole volume and a scholarly essay involving comparisons between Apollonius of Tyana and the Gospel traditions of Jesus (1970, 1975), while Gerd Theissen's treatment of *The Miracle Stories of the Early Christian Tradition* (1974) is rich in comparative material from many different traditions.[1] Howard Clark Kee took up the question of Greco-Roman parallels in his *Miracle in the Early Christian World* (1983) and returned to it in his later *Medicine, Miracle and Magic in New Testament Times* (1986). My intent in this excursus is not to review every problem that these and other works raise. Rather, I wish simply to highlight a few questions about certain figures and terms that often appear in discussions of the Gospel miracles of Jesus.

I. PAGAN TRADITIONS ABOUT APOLLONIUS OF TYANA[2]

Scholars disagree on how much can be said with fair certitude about the "historical" Apollonius. No one seems to doubt the existence of this teacher, preacher, and philosopher whose life extended over most of the 1st century A.D. He was active for a good part of the second half of the 1st century, lived at least into the reign of the Emperor Domitian (A.D. 81–96), and died probably during the reign of the Emperor Nerva (96–98), though the early years of the 2d century are also possible.[3] He came from the city of Tyana in Cappadocia (present eastern Turkey). Granted the syncretistic tendency of Greek and Roman philosophy in the early centuries A.D., it is no wonder that, while Apollonius stood basically in the neo-Pythagorean tradition, elements of Stoicism, Cynicism, and Platonism can also be seen in the traditions about him that have come down to us. In his wide-ranging travels,[4] he showed himself—at least according to later reports—to be not only an ascetic philosopher but also a reformer of cult and morals who was interested in restoring ancient cultic practices where they had fallen into desuetude. He was also intent on learning various mystical and esoteric traditions from holy men of far-flung regions. He seems to have held an exalted concept of the supreme God who needs no sacrifices.

How much of this description can be applied to the historical Apollonius is still debated among scholars. At any rate, by the time we come to Philostratus' life of Apollonius, written in the first part of the 3d century A.D., we find many miracles attributed to Apollonius. His detractors, not surprisingly, denounced him as a magician who used his secret arts for sinister purposes. In the view of Ewen Lyall Bowie, the agreement of various sources that Apollonius did play the role of prophet and miracle-worker makes this role one of the few aspects of him that can be affirmed with a high degree of probability.[5]

An attempt to say anything more precise about Apollonius entangles the scholar in a complicated problem of sources. Put most simply, the problem of sources comes down to the fact that we have almost total silence about Apollonius (apart from a few scraps, such as a passing negative reference in the 2d-century satirist Lucian of Samosata) until we come to Philostratus' work.[6] The person, purpose, and sources of Philostratus thus become all-important. Philostratus was born on the island of Lemnos ca. A.D. 172.[7] He studied rhetoric at Athens and then went on to Rome. Acquiring a reputation as a sophist, he entered the literary and philosophical circle of the Empress Julia Domna,[8] the wife of Septimius Severus (reigned A.D. 193–211) and the mother of Caracalla (reigned 211–17). A Syrian and a daughter of a priest of Emesa, Julia Domna had an ecumenical and eclectic interest in philosophy and religion. In keeping with this interest she asked Philostratus to write a biography of Apollonius, which is usually referred to as the *Life of Apollonius (Vita Apollonii)*.[9]

Supposedly Philostratus had at his disposal a number of sources: (1) Julia Domna is said to have given the author a diary or collection of memoirs, written by a disciple and traveling companion of Apollonius called Damis, who was alleged to hail from Nineveh in Assyria. (2) Maximus, an admirer of Apollonius, is said to have written a history of the philosopher's career. (3) There were various collections of letters of Apollonius in circulation; Philostratus' collection does not seem to coincide with the collection that has come down to us. There are serious problems of authenticity with the extant letters. Robert J. Penella, who has edited a critical text of the letters, judges that at least some of the letters that have come down to us "can be condemned [as falsifications] or at least seriously suspected on historical grounds."[10] The best he can say about some of the other letters is that they contain "nothing inherently implausible" (including a letter in which Apollonius claims to have sedated a satyr).[11] (4) Apollonius wrote several treatises, none of which has survived. (5) Philostratus is said to have journeyed to Tyana and to other cities connected with the philosopher's career to cull surviving traditions. (6) There was also a work, in four volumes, by a pagan named Moiragenes. Again, it has not come down to us, although Origen mentions it in his *Contra Celsum* (6.41) and indicates that Moiragenes called Apollonius a philosopher and a magician.[12]

Philostratus' *Life of Apollonius*, in eight books, was probably not published until after the death of Julia Domna, hence some time around A.D. 217–20. One of the purposes of the *Life* seems to have been to rehabilitate the reputation of Apollonius as a divinely guided philosopher and sage. If we may judge from the polemics of the sophist Euphrates in the 1st century and of Lucian and (presumably) Moiragenes in the 2d century, Apollonius was viewed instead by many of the educated class as a fraud and a magician (see, e.g., *Life* 1.2). Such an apologetic purpose need not exclude, however, the rhetorical intent of a sophist to display his talent and entertain a cultured audience.

The struggle over the status of Apollonius continued after Philostratus. Around the end of the 3d century A.D., Hierocles, a provincial governor of lower Egypt under Diocletian, wrote a work to demonstrate that Apollonius was as great a sage, miracle-worker, and exorcist as Jesus Christ. The church historian Eusebius composed a treatise in reply; he accused Apollonius of being a charlatan. Any miracle/magic Apollonius did perform was by means of evil spirits. Controversy over Apollonius continued into the time of Julian the Apostate.

But the "definitive" work on Apollonius remained Philostratus' *Life of Apollonius.* It is a large, sprawling, meandering piece of literature, combining the features of a Greco-Roman novel or "romance" with those of popular biographies of philosophers.[13] In the *Life* Philostratus employed many of the rhetorical devices known to sophists of his time: supernatural portents, short dialogues on popular issues of the day, colorful archaeological lore, magic and/or miracles, rapid scene changes, descriptions of fabled far-off lands, travelogues, and erotic episodes (often with homoerotic overtones). Imaginary "official" letters, inscriptions, and edicts help to create the illusion of sober history. Still, the supernatural atmosphere is all-pervading. Apollonius performs numerous miracles and exorcisms, enjoys powers of precognition, telepathy, and the ability to move suddenly from place to place. He finally disappears from earth and reappears later on from the next world to convince a doubting disciple that the soul is immortal.

The historical worth of the traditions enshrined in Philostratus' *Life* is still debated among scholars. Petzke, in his book-length comparison of the traditions about Apollonius with those about Jesus in the Gospels, is relatively confident about his quest for the "historical" Apollonius. He judges that in the case of both Apollonius and Jesus one can distinguish the "historical" figure, the oral traditions beginning in his life and continuing after his death, and the initial scattered written forms that led up to larger written works, culminating in the *Life of Apollonius* on the one hand and the Gospels on the other.

Petzke's method is clear, his work painstaking, and his form-critical analysis of the *Life of Apollonius* penetrating. Nevertheless, some nagging problems remain:

(1) Petzke does not seem to appreciate sufficiently the problem of the different situation of the sources in the two cases of Jesus and Apollonius. Despite his careful use of sources about Apollonius outside of the *Life*, it remains true that we know very little about Apollonius before Philostratus' work. Hence we are faced with a serious gap of information between the time of Apollonius' death toward the end of the 1st century A.D. and the composition of the *Life* ca. 217–20. This contrasts sharply with the case of Jesus. Some 20 to 30 years after Jesus' death we have the epistles of Paul, giving a few facts about Jesus'

life and death and a great amount of data about the missionary efforts of his disciples in the intervening decades and the faith in him that they propagated. By 40 years after Jesus' death there is a full-blown Gospel (Mark) and probably a lengthy collection of his sayings (Q), plus developing oral traditions that will finally find a berth in the Gospels of Matthew, Luke, and John in the next generation or two. Thus, in a little over a generation after Jesus' death all the major facts and teachings of his life were fixed in writing, and by the end of the second or third Christian generation almost everything we know about Jesus had been written down. The contrast with the century-long gap in the case of Apollonius is stark. Petzke tries to bridge the gap somewhat by stressing that Philostratus did use a number of different traditions. Petzke leaves open the question of the diary of Damis. If, instead, we decide with a number of recent studies that both Damis and his diary are inventions of Philostratus, the gap between the historical Apollonius and the *Life* appears almost un-bridgeable.

(2) The parallel between the historical Apollonius and the historical Jesus that Petzke sets up is made possible by opting for the meager portrait of the historical Jesus common in the Bultmannian tradition on the one hand, while allowing a fairly confident assessment of the traditions about Apollonius on the other.[14] A more confident assessment of the Jesus traditions and more skepticism about the historical value of the Apollonius traditions would have yielded notably different results.

(3) Petzke has a good grasp of the material in the *Life of Apollonius;* his understanding of the Gospel material at times leaves something to be desired.

(4) The parallel created between the *Life* and the Gospels tends to play down the large blocks of material in the *Life* that have no equivalent in the Gospels: travelogues, natural history, long excursuses on the exotic and eso-teric, the customs of foreign courts, etc.

It is not surprising, therefore, that some scholars are not convinced by Petzke's conclusions. For example, in his *Miracle in the Early Christian World,* Howard Clark Kee has called into question the historical reliability of many of the traditions in the *Life.*[15] In this he follows critics like E. R. Dodds, John Ferguson, and Martin Hengel;[16] and he can find further support in the doubts of Ewen Lyall Bowie and Maria Dzielska. The heart of the problem is the supposed diary of Damis. Kee thinks that Philostratus invented both Damis and his diary as literary conventions. According to Kee, "the material allegedly drawn from Damis is so full of historical anachronisms and gross geographical errors that one could not have confidence in Damis as a reporter if there actu-ally were a diary."[17] Kee then proceeds to give a list of egregious errors that lead him to the conclusion that Philostratus either invented most of his mate-rial or borrowed it in eclectic fashion from earlier classical authors. "In any case, what Philostratus reports tells us a great deal about the author and his time—that is, at the turn of the third century—but provides no unassailable evidence about Apollonius and his epoch."[18]

Kee's arguments are impressive and become all the more so when put alongside those of Bowie. Bowie examines in detail a number of historical scenes in the *Life of Apollonius:* Apollonius' encounters with the Parthian king Vardanes, his dealings with the philosopher Musonius Rufus, the portrait of the philosopher Demetrius the Cynic, and Apollonius' meeting with the Emperor Vespasian in Alexandria.[19] In each case the account in the *Life of Apollonius* is either patently wrong or at least highly improbable. Bowie, like Kee, comes to the conclusion that Damis and his diary are simply inventions of Philostratus. Bowie even suggests that educated Greek readers of the time would have recognized these novelistic techniques for what they were.[20] All this should make one very leery of citing the *Life of Apollonius* as a reliable report about what exactly a miracle-worker similar to Jesus was doing in the 1st century A.D.

Moreover, if it be true that the *Life* is largely Philostratus' invention, a further intriguing question arises: could it be that some of the stories of Apollonius' miracles and exorcisms were drawn from the Christian Gospels? That pagan authors knew and used the Gospels (in polemical fashion) as early as the 2d century A.D. is clear from Celsus and the famous physician Galen.[21] By the first part of the 3d century it would hardly be surprising that educated authors within the philosophical-religious circle of Julia Domna would have some nodding acquaintance with the Gospels. Indeed, we are told in a 4th- or 5th-century work (the not-always-reliable *Scriptores Historiae Augustae*), that the later Severan Emperor Severus Alexander (reigned 222–35) kept in his private chapel statues of various holy men and forebears, including Apollonius, Christ, Abraham, Orpheus, and Alexander the Great.[22]

Now, I am not claiming that Philostratus issued the *Life* as a "counterblast" to the Gospels, a position rejected by F. C. Conybeare, though still accepted by some scholars.[23] I suggest instead that, in the ecumenical and eclectic climate of the circle of Julia Domna, Philostratus possibly borrowed some miracle stories from the Gospels to help him flesh out his portrait of Apollonius as a great philosopher and miracle-worker. It was only about a century later, in a work by Hierocles, the governor of Bithynia (303–307) and subsequently of Egypt, that Apollonius was made out to be a direct rival of Jesus. While admittedly there is no way of proving that Philostratus used the Gospels, it would help explain some curious phenomena: e.g., the story of Apollonius resuscitating a young Roman bride who has died in the very hour of her marriage (*Life of Apollonius* 4.45) looks suspiciously like a conflation of the Gospel stories of the raising of the daughter of Jairus (Mark 5:21–43) and the raising of the son of the widow of Nain (Luke 7:11–17). However, since many of the motifs are found in other ancient miracle stories as well, no firm proof is possible.[24]

Be that as it may, the upshot of this short survey is clear: the serious questions that arise about the sources and historical reliability of the *Life of Apollonius* make it difficult to speak in any detail of the 1st-century Apollonius as a parallel figure to Jesus of Nazareth. The miracle stories in the *Life* are indeed useful for ahistorical, synchronic comparisons of literary patterns found in miracle stories of different times and places; as a basis for historical judgments about 1st-century figures they are very shaky.

II. JEWISH TRADITIONS ABOUT ḤONI THE CIRCLE-DRAWER AND ḤANINA BEN DOSA

Geza Vermes has made the intriguing suggestion that Jesus of Nazareth should be understood as one of a number of popular Galilean holy men or *ḥăsîdîm* who were noted for their powerful spontaneous prayers, the miracles that often answered their prayers, and practical acts of kindness. They were not, however, famous for either their teaching on the Mosaic Law or their punctilious observance of the finer points of the Law. Hence, as freewheeling posssessors of special power not transmitted by the usual conduits of religious authority, they stood in tension vis-à-vis both the temple officials in Jerusalem and the Pharisees zealous for the Law. The pattern of popular miracle-workers in northern Palestine, "men of deed" in conflict with traditional leaders of the people, naturally conjured up memories of Elijah and Elisha, to whom these holy men may have looked for inspiration. Besides Jesus, says Vermes, the two examples of such "charismatic" Galilean holy men known from rabbinic sources are Ḥoni the Circle-Drawer (1st century B.C.) and Ḥanina ben Dosa (1st century A.D.). Vermes's suggestion has been enthusiastically adopted by a number of recent scholars, including Crossan.

If we did have reliable access to the "historical" Ḥoni or Ḥanina, the typology suggested by Vermes would indeed be valuable. However, as with Apollonius, so with Ḥoni and Ḥanina, the devil is in the details of the sources. Despite the attempts of Vermes and others to sift the sources carefully, in the end one must admit that all the written sources are later than Jesus, and almost all of them centuries later. I would venture to claim that, beyond the fact that around the turn of the era there existed two Jews in Palestine named Ḥoni and Ḥanina, both of whom were famous for having their prayers answered in extraordinary ways, nothing definite can be said. Let us examine the evidence in each case.

Ḥoni makes his first appearance in literature under the Greek form of his name, Onias, in Josephus' *Jewish Antiquities*. At least, that seems to be the case, though the identification of the Onias mentioned in passing by Josephus and the Ḥoni of later rabbinic literature is not absolutely certain.[25] At any rate, in Book 14 of the *Jewish Antiquities*, written ca. A.D. 93–94, Josephus briefly mentions a certain Onias, "a just man and beloved of God, who once during a drought prayed that God would bring the drought to an end. Listening to [Onias' prayer], God caused rain to fall" (*Ant.* 14.2.1 §22). Because this event apparently made Onias famous for his efficacious prayers, during a civil war one group of Jews, led by Hyrcanus II, tried to force Onias to curse the other side, led by Aristobulus II. Onias refused to curse the other group, which included priests besieged in the Jerusalem temple, and he was accordingly stoned to death (§23–24). Josephus then goes on to describe how the followers of Hyrcanus II were punished by God for the murder of Onias. The mention of the civil war places Onias' death ca. 65 B.C.

A few points should be noted about Josephus' account. Not unlike John the Baptist and some other religious figures in the *Antiquities*, Onias surfaces suddenly, displays some remarkable and admirable characteristics, and then disappears forever because he is unjustly put to death. Onias' murder ca. 65 B.C. places his activity, such as it was, in the first half of the 1st century B.C. It must be emphasized that nothing in Josephus' story connects Onias with Galilee; indeed, the only indication of place is Jerusalem, where he dies. Even more to be emphasized is the fact that Onias' fame is tied to a single (*pote*, "once") incident in which his prayer for rain during a drought proves efficacious. There is no claim of any other case of extraordinary response by God to his prayer. Still more to be emphasized is the question whether Onias can be called a "miracle-worker" because once his prayer for rain was immediately answered by God. Josephus' formulation stresses that God, not Onias, caused the rain to fall (*ho theos hysen*) in answer to Onias' prayer. If God's immediate answer to prayer in a time of grave need automatically made the person praying a miracle-worker, the history of religion would see a vast explosion of names in the ranks of miracle-workers. I could supply a few names from personal experience. Lest categories like miracle-worker become hopelessly fuzzy, I would suggest that we take the phrase miracle-*worker* at face value and reserve it for someone who is more actively involved in *working* the miracle instead of simply petitioning God for some extraordinary benefit.

The next we hear of Onias, now Ḥoni in the Hebrew, is in the Mishna, redacted somewhere around the end of the 2d or beginning of the 3d century A.D.[26] In the tractate *Taʿanit* 3:8 we find the Onias/Ḥoni tradition developed "with much embellishment," as Schürer puts it,[27] into the sole miracle story about Tannaitic figures (i.e., teachers up to ca. A.D. 300) in the Mishna. In this version, people ask Ḥoni to pray for rain during a drought. However—here we have a surprising twist to the story—Ḥoni's prayer is at first not answered. Nothing daunted, Ḥoni proceeds to draw a circle and stand within it (hence his title, "the Circle-Drawer," *mĕʿaggēl* in the Hebrew text). Interceding for all the "children" of God who have had recourse to him, Ḥoni dares as a favorite son ("a son of the house") to put God on notice: with an oath using God's "great name," he swears that he will not step outside the circle until God sends rain. A few drops begin to fall. Ḥoni complains that this is too little. When God responds with violent torrents, Ḥoni again complains, and it begins to rain moderately. After more than enough has fallen, the Jews finally ask Ḥoni to pray that the rain cease. The great figure Simeon ben Shetaḥ (active ca. 80 B.C.) tells Ḥoni that he (Simeon) would like to excommunicate him for such effrontery toward God, but he knows it would do no good. God grants Ḥoni whatever he asks in prayer, just as an indulgent father grants a spoiled son whatever he asks.

We have come a long way from the Onias of Josephus' account, and even as early as the Mishna the Ḥoni tradition has probably passed through several stages of development.[28] The enduring core of the story is that Onias/Ḥoni is known for his efficacious prayer for rain in time of drought. The mention of Simeon again places Ḥoni in the first half of the 1st century B.C., and geographical references in the story intimate that he is in Jerusalem. Once again, nothing is said about Galilee.

But a great deal has changed. From one incident in the past (the "once" of Josephus' story is preserved) we have moved to a general truth about the efficacy of Ḥoni's prayer that is demonstrated in the one incident recounted in *Taʿanit*: even if God at first resists, Ḥoni can get whatever he asks for in prayer by being persistent to the point of insolence. Against the background of Greco-Roman magic, the drawing of and standing in a circle and Ḥoni's oath, taken in the name of God's "great name," could be understood as magical, though the general context is rather one of a graphic demonstration of persistent and trusting prayer in a gracious God who acts like a loving father toward his favorite son. In any case, the miraculous atmosphere of the story is more palpable than in Josephus' version. In the Mishna, Ḥoni can presumably in any instance obtain whatever he wants from God in prayer, provided he is persistent, even impudent (e.g., using the circle and the oath), in the manner of a good-natured but spoiled child importuning his father. Ḥoni can even have God regulate the amount of rain from moment to moment.

In other words, Ḥoni has come closer to being not just a person who prays efficaciously but a miracle-*worker*, though the miracle is still a matter of his praying with infallible efficacy to God, who then sends the rain in the requested doses. The increase of the miraculous element—which might be interpreted as magic, given the hint of coercion—may be why the tradition has attracted to itself a certain tone of diffidence and censure:[29] i.e., the initial refusal by God at the beginning of the story and the rebuke of Simeon at the end. The slightly negative tone that has crept into the tradition contrasts sharply with the account of Josephus, who has nothing but praise for Onias.

At the same time, the very fact that Simeon, a prominent Pharisee, could threaten Ḥoni with excommunication implicitly puts Ḥoni in the company of the Pharisees (and in the eyes of later tradition in the company of the rabbis). The agenda for the subsequent treatment of Ḥoni in rabbinic literature is already set: if Ḥoni is to become more explicitly a miracle-worker, in some way or other he must also be "rabbinized," i.e., assimilated to rabbinic views and piety, to make him acceptable to the leaders of post-A.D. 70 Judaism. As William Scott Green has pointed out, "rabbinization" is precisely what we see in the subsequent versions of the Ḥoni story in rabbinic sources.[30]

In fact, while *Taʿanit* 3:8 is the only miracle story in the Mishna involving a Tannaitic figure, later on in the Babylonian Talmud the rabbi in general becomes a figure endowed with extraordinary powers, including the power to bring rain or cause a drought by his prayers. Such powers, however, were seen as the natural result of knowing and mastering the Torah. This "rabbinization" of the miraculous is clear when the Ḥoni story is retold with expansions in the Babylonian Talmud's tractate *Taʿanit* 23a: the miraculous/magical element is diminished, Scriptural warrant (Hab 2:1) is given for Ḥoni's drawing of a circle, Ḥoni is given the title "rabbi" (a further story makes him the greatest teacher of his time), the focus is more firmly on God as the giver of the rain, and the Sanhedrin confirms Ḥoni's action, which is emphatically identified as prayer.[31] The rabbinization of Ḥoni is fairly complete.

To return from the end of the tradition history of "Rabbi Ḥoni" to its humble beginnings: all we can say with any probability about the "historical" Onias/Ḥoni is that he lived in the first half of the 1st century B.C., perhaps in Jerusalem, and was noted for an occasion when he prayed in a time of drought and God sent rain. Even this meager statement has to rest on two accounts written over one (Josephus) or two (the Mishna) hundred years after the event. There is no basis in the early tradition for constructing a Galilean charismatic miracle-worker.[32] In fact, as Green wisely observes, the very attempt to draw any historical material from the rabbinic material for a portrait of the "historical" Ḥoni is nigh impossible. After reviewing previous attempts to claim that *Taʿanit* 3:8 has a 1st century B.C. provenance and can be proven to enjoy historical veracity, Green remarks that the "distinguishing feature of this pseudocritical approach is its credulity."[33] I need not repeat here what I said above with respect to the difference between the nature and dating of the sources for Apollonius of Tyana and the nature and dating of the sources for Jesus. Mutatis mutandis, the same holds true for the nature and dating of the sources for Ḥoni.

I would also claim that the same holds true for the other well-known miracle-worker of rabbinic literature, Ḥanina ben Dosa. I realize that this flies in the face of two detailed studies on the Ḥanina tradition by Geza Vermes, but the critique of Vermes's work by Sean Freyne emboldens me to demur.[34] Vermes himself begins his study by admitting that rabbinic reports about Ḥanina ben Dosa do not belong to historiography proper, "a literary genre completely alien to talmudic and midrashic writings."[35] Moreover, dating rabbinic traditions remains a difficult problem. Despite his own warnings, Vermes does attempt to create a profile of the historical Ḥanina from various rabbinic reports, some of which are quite late.[36]

Unlike Onias/Ḥoni, Ḥanina does not enjoy even a passing mention in Josephus or any other source from the 1st century A.D. He first appears in the Mishna. Since Ḥanina was probably active in the 1st century A.D., most likely before A.D. 70,[37] a certain symmetry exists between himself and Ḥoni when it comes to written sources naming them. Just as Josephus wrote the *Antiquities* over a hundred years after Ḥoni died, so the Mishna was redacted over a hundred years after the most likely dating of Ḥanina's public life. In each case, the wide gap between original event and first written attestation—again, not unlike the gap between the historical Apollonius and Philostratus' *Life of Apollonius*—must give one pause.

When we look at the three traditions about Ḥanina preserved in the

Mishna, we see that we are a little better informed than we were by the Ḥoni-tradition in the Mishna—though not by much. The first text that concerns us, in the mishnaic tractate 'Abot (3:10–11),[38] contains three ethical sayings of a general nature. They emphasize that fear of sin takes precedence over wisdom, that practicing good deeds takes precedence over wisdom, and that kindness toward other human beings determines one's relationship with God. Like Ḥoni, Ḥanina is not presented in the rabbinic literature debating or ruling on intricate legal questions—although, unlike Ḥoni, even in his first appearance in the Mishna Ḥanina already carries the title "Rabbi."[39]

The second text in the Mishna involves a much-disputed phrase in the tractate Soṭa. Soṭa 9:15 begins with a list of great rabbis and students. The text laments how with the death of each figure a certain virtue ceased: "When Rabbi Meir died there were no more makers of parables, when Ben Azzai died there were no more diligent students. . . ." In the eighth place in the list we find: "When Rabbi Ḥanina ben Dosa died the men of deed ceased." The problem here is that scholars do not agree on the exact meaning of the phrase "men of deed [ʾanšê maʿáśeh]." With an eye to Ḥanina's role as miracle-worker in other rabbinic texts (e.g., in m. Ber. 5:5), some scholars interpret "men of deed" here to mean miracle-workers. Still, almost all the other rabbis and students listed in m. Soṭa 9:15 are praised for their learning and/or moral virtues. Hence in the immediate context "men of deed" could easily refer to a person dedicated to kindly deeds to others or in general to zealous and punctilious observance of the Torah.[40] There is no sure way of deciding the issue, and so it is unwise to make any argument depend on this text.

The third mishnaic text, in the tractate Berakot, is the key one. In m. Ber. 5:5 we read: "It is told concerning Rabbi Ḥanina ben Dosa that when he prayed for the sick he used to say: This one will live and this one will die. They said to him: How do you know? He replied: If my prayer is fluent in my mouth, I know that he [the sick person] is favored; if not, I know that [his illness] is fatal."[41] For all the dissimilarity from the Ḥoni-tradition in the Mishna (e.g., Ḥanina is given the title "rabbi" and pronounces wisdom sayings), here we meet with a basic similarity between Ḥoni and Ḥanina. Both are known as men whose prayer has exceptional power of one sort or another.[42] In the case of Ḥoni, the prayer's power was straightforward; with some persistence, Ḥoni could obtain from God whatever he requested—in particular, rain.

The case of Ḥanina's prayer is more subtle. m. Ber. 5:5 does not claim that Ḥanina's prayer had any special power to heal. This is important to note: the text does not say that Ḥanina was a healer, miraculous or otherwise. Rather, when Ḥanina prayed over the sick, he could tell from the way his spontaneous prayer flowed with ease or difficulty on the tongue whether God would grant his request for healing.[43] It is not the healing power of Ḥanina's prayer that is miraculous, but rather the special knowledge, granted him through a sign, of whether his prayer for healing will be answered.[44] Strictly speaking, therefore, his text deals with Ḥanina's gift of precognition at prayer, not with any miraculous power of his to heal, exorcise, or *work* other miracles. The upshot of all this is that none of the three texts in the Mishna explicitly and unambiguously presents Ḥanina as a miracle-*worker* in the more rigorous sense of that term (i.e., a human person who directly performs a miracle by giving certain commands or using certain gestures). Given the Mishna's silence about miracle-working rabbis, we should not be surprised that Ḥanina ben Dosa is not really an exception.

I stress the lack of explicit and unambiguous reference to real miracle-working in the Mishna's portrait of Ḥanina ben Dosa because to a certain extent this pattern of God working a miracle in answer to the holy man's prayer persists even as miracle stories increase rapidly in the Babylonian Talmud. Suddenly we hear of all sorts of miraculous events attributed to Ḥanina—especially in connection with his powerful prayer. At the same time, as was the case with Ḥoni, there is a clear attempt to make the world of miracles safe for rabbinism by connecting Ḥanina's miracles with great rabbis, rabbinic doctrine, and rabbinic piety, or alternately by adding critical remarks. Ḥanina heals the son of Rabban Gamaliel at a distance by saying a prayer (*b. Ber.* 34b; also *y. Ber.* 9d). His prayer likewise heals the son of the greatest figure of the Jamnia movement, Rabbi Joḥanan ben Zakkai (also in *b. Ber.* 34b). From a distance Ḥanina is able to tell (presumably while praying) when the daughter of a ditch-digger who has fallen into a pit is brought up to safety (*b. B. Qam.* 50a; cf. *b. Yebam.* 121b).[45] Building on a general story in the Mishna about how the *ḥăsîdîm* were so attentive at prayer that they would not interrupt their prayer even if a snake were wound around their heel (*m. Ber.* 5:1), the Tosefta and the Palestinian Talmud both apply the story to Ḥanina (*t. Ber.* 3:20; *y. Ber.* 9a; cf. *b. Ber.* 33a). Not only does Ḥanina not stop praying and not suffer any harm when a snake bites him, Ḥanina's disciples—note that according to the Tosefta's version Ḥanina now has disciples like every great rabbi—find the snake dead at the opening of its hole!

Ḥanina apparently became a magnet for miracle stories in the later talmudic tradition.[46] In a series of miracle stories preserved in Aramaic in *b. Taʿan.* 24b–25a—stories even Vermes admits are "mostly secondary elaborations"[47]—Ḥanina has God stop and start rain (shades of Ḥoni!), makes the ill-fitting joists of a house join together, and turns vinegar into oil for a Sabbath lamp. Bread miraculously appears in the empty oven of Ḥanina's wife. In response to Ḥanina's prayer a mysterious hand supplies a missing leg for a golden table. He proves that his goats do not destroy property by having them come home one evening with bears on their horns. The goats turn out to carry the same marks that were previously borne by the hens Ḥanina sold to buy the goats. Ḥanina's table collapses when his wife uses borrowed spices which were not tithed. When stolen, Ḥanina's pious donkey refuses to eat or drink until it is allowed to return home. These later stories display a notable increase in folkloric and bizarre elements, and correspondingly prayer is less prominent.[48]

Despite the fact that many of the traditions about Ḥanina ben Dosa do not find any literary attestation earlier than the two Talmuds, Vermes suggests that in some of the statements attributed to Ḥanina we may possess genuine sayings of "a remarkable personality living in first-century Palestine," sayings that "constitute the most direct insight we possess into the Ḥasidic mind and outlook." That Vermes can make this claim when discussing sayings attributed to Ḥanina in the *Pirqe Rabbi Eliezer* (*Pirqe R. El.* 29, 31) leaves one speechless. This work apparently originated in the 8th or 9th century A.D.; while it uses older tradition, it is not basically "a compilation like other midrashim, but . . . the creative achievement of a personal author."[49] Ultimately, Vermes' acritical use of sources undermines his whole argument.

In the last analysis, all we can say with fair probability about the "historical" Ḥanina is that he was a Palestinian Jew who lived in the 1st century A.D., that he was noted for praying over the sick, and that he enjoyed the reputation of having precognition as to the results of his prayers for healing. That he lived in Galilee has no written attestation before the two Talmuds.[50] Poverty and asceticism are likewise not attested in the earliest written traditions.

From our survey of rabbinic texts about Ḥoni and Ḥanina ben Dosa three major points emerge:

(1) The dating of the sources reflects a situation very different from the dating of the earliest Jesus material. Written sources (Mark and Q) containing numerous stories and sayings about Jesus' miracles existed a little over one generation after Jesus' death. During the same period, the oral traditions about Jesus' miracles that would find written form within another generation or two in Matthew, Luke, and John were already developing. In contrast, the earliest written attestation of miracle stories connected with Ḥoni and Ḥanina—each having only one miracle story connected with him in the earliest sources—comes in each case over a century after the events narrated. I emphasize that this is not said to show that Jesus' miracles did happen and Ḥoni's or Ḥanina's did not; that would be a totally illogical and unwarranted conclusion. Rather, I wish simply to call attention to the difference in the nature of the sources, a difference too often glossed over in academic eagerness to heap up an undifferentiated pile of parallels. If our goal is reasonable historical reconstruction, the nature and dating of sources do make a difference.

(2) In comparing Gospel and rabbinic miracle stories, more care needs to be taken with our categories and descriptions. To be sure, as we have seen, miracle stories occur in the rabbinic literature as well as in the Gospels, and Vermes has rightly underlined parallel elements. And yet there are important differences in content as well as sources. Jesus, Ḥoni, and Ḥanina may all be called miracle-workers in a broad sense, but that broad sense calls for more careful differentiation. In almost all cases in the Gospels, Jesus directly *works* a miracle by giving a command and/or by using a gesture. As a general rule, he does not first turn aside to God in prayer, who then unfailingly accedes to Jesus' request by performing the miracle in question. While there is one clear case where the miracle happens "automatically" or "magically" (the woman with the hemorrhage in Mark and Luke), in almost all other cases Jesus know-

ingly and freely *works* the miracle himself. He is in this strict, rigorous sense a miracle-*worker*.

Not so Ḥoni and Ḥanina, especially in the earliest traditions. In the Onias/Ḥoni-story in Josephus and in the Ḥanina story *m. Ber.* 5:5, what is central is the holy man's prayer to God. Neither holy man directly *works* a miracle. Josephus' Onias, on one occasion, had his prayer for rain during a drought answered by God. The Mishna's Ḥanina enjoys God-given knowledge as to whether God will answer favorably his prayer for healing.[51] That is it, for the earliest traditions about each man.[52] Even when the rabbinic tradition begins to expand or multiply miracle stories about these two holy men, the emphasis usually remains on the miraculous power of their prayer to God. Alternately, in some stories God preserves the holy men from danger without any prior knowledge or action on their part. Only in some late traditions does Ḥanina in particular take a more active role as a miracle-*worker*. Perhaps early rabbinic Judaism, under siege by a hostile pagan world and leery of mystical, magical, or gnostic tendencies that could threaten strict monotheism, was wary of presenting miracle-workers as autonomous agents who could directly perform miracles by their own power.

(3) Neither Ḥoni nor Ḥanina is characterized as a Galilean by the earliest traditions.[53] Indeed, by implication, Onias/Ḥoni seems to be active in or about Jerusalem. Thus, the claim that Ḥoni and Ḥanina belong along with Jesus to the type of the Galilean charismatic miracle-worker and holy man is not sustained by the earliest sources. Moreover, the earliest sources do not supply lengthy blocks of teaching from either Ḥoni or Ḥanina that would parallel the various teachings of Jesus.

It is not my purpose here to deny in principle that a group of charismatic miracle-workers and holy men might have existed in Galilee at the turn of the era. I simply point out that the earliest traditions about Ḥoni and Ḥanina ben Dosa do not support such a contention. This is not meant to deny the interest in miracles in Palestine at the time of Jesus. Indeed, Qumran is one witness that the opposite is true.

III. MIRACLES BY INDIVIDUAL HUMANS IN THE DEAD SEA LITERATURE

Two notable cases of miracles of healing and/or exorcism, performed by human beings, are narrated in the literature found at Qumran. As we saw in Chapter 16, exorcism, one of the most typical miracles Jesus performed, was an object of interest in some of the documents preserved at Qumran (though not necessarily composed there). In the *Genesis Apocryphon*, Pharaoh and all his men are afflicted with an evil spirit, which manifests itself in a plague and other physical sufferings. Abram prays for Pharaoh and lays hands on his head. As a result, the plague is removed from him and the evil spirit is "rebuked," i.e., commanded to depart. Pharaoh is cured.

As noted in Chapter 16, there are interesting parallels here with the miracles of Jesus.[54] In his exorcisms Jesus is said to "rebuke" (*epitmaō*) the demons, the Greek verb being an equivalent of the Aramaic *gʿr* in 1QapGen 20:28–29. Some of Jesus' healings are performed with a touch or hand gesture, as is the healing performed by Abram. In fact, the *Genesis Apocryphon* is the first instance in Jewish literature in which the laying on of hands is used for healing; the gesture does not occur in the OT or rabbinic literature for this purpose.

Yet at the same time there are notable differences between the account of the healing of Pharaoh in the *Genesis Apocryphon* and the Gospel miracles of Jesus. The story of Pharaoh in the *Genesis Apocryphon* is a story of demonic obsession rather than of demonic possession: the demon afflicts Pharaoh's body from without, instead of entering into Pharaoh and taking over both his body and his psyche. Notice how Pharaoh begs for a cure from Abram instead of trying to ward him off, as a true demoniac would in the Gospels. Perhaps the closest analogy to the cure of Pharaoh would be Luke's version of Jesus' cure of Simon Peter's mother-in-law, where a simple cure of a fever in Mark 1:30–31 takes on the tone of an exorcism (Luke 4:39: "he *rebuked* [*epetimēsen*] the fever," as though it were a fever-demon). Another difference between the cure in the *Genesis Apocryphon* and Jesus' miracles is that, while Jesus uses touch at times to heal, he does not use the laying on of hands in the case of exorcisms (there is no touch from Jesus in Luke 4:39). The one exception is the case of diabolical obsession presented by Luke in 13:10–17, Jesus' healing of a crippled woman on the Sabbath. The interpretation of a healing in terms of exorcism and the use of the laying on of hands in Luke 13:10–17 may both be redactional contributions of Luke. In any event, Jesus certainly does not lay on hands in clear cases of diabolical possession.

A second case of exorcism in the face of diabolical obsession is found in the very fragmentary *Prayer of Nabonidus*. King Nabonidus of Babylon is afflicted by God with an "evil disease" (4QPrNab 6) and prays to God. A Jewish exorcist from among the exiles (perhaps Daniel) forgives Nabonidus' sins in God's name; from the fragmentary text we may also infer that Nabonidus is cured through the Jew's prayer. The connection of healing with forgiveness of sins provides a striking parallel to Jesus' forgiving and healing of the paralytic in Mark 2:1–12 parr. In the case of Jesus' miracle, however, the note of exorcism is lacking (though some exegetes, wrongly in my view, wish to read it into Mark's story).

Obviously, a further difference in both the Pharaoh and Nabonidus stories is that the authors of these works were not claiming to recount miracles that had been worked in the recent past. They were engaged in midrash, i.e., literature about literature, a homiletic expansion of and reflection on stories in Scripture that seek to make them relevant to the present-day concerns of the community. Mark, by comparison, speaks of miracles that he claims were performed by Jesus some four decades before the Evangelist wrote his Gospel.

No one, I think, would feel a need to inquire about the historical events supposedly lying behind the cure of Pharaoh in the *Genesis Apocryphon* or the cure of Nabonidus in the *Prayer of Nabonidus*. The quest for the historical Jesus and the sources at our disposal do demand that at least the question be raised in the case of the Nazarene.

IV. MIRACLES BY HUMAN BEINGS IN JOSEPHUS

One is hardly surprised to find that the works of Josephus are no stranger to the miraculous.[55] But miracles in the strict sense, as distinct from portents, omens, prophecies,[56] dreams, and visions, and especially miracles worked by human beings, are by no means evenly distributed among Josephus' works. Since we are interested in particular in miracles performed by humans, there is little to cause us to tarry in Josephus' *Life* or his *Against Apion*. Even his *Jewish War* is characterized mostly by portents, omens, prophecies, dreams, and visions.[57] The most fertile area for our investigation is, not surprisingly, his largest work, *The Jewish Antiquities*, which naturally recounts, though with some remarkable changes, the great signs and miracles worked by Moses, Elijah, and Elisha.

When it comes to Josephus' treatment of miracles, there is a fascinating tug-of-war in *The Antiquities* between the two great influences on Josephus: his Jewish-Palestinian heritage, which received a definitive Pharisaic coloration after the quest of his teenage years (or so he claims in his *Life*),[58] and Greco-Roman culture, with the conventions of its historiography and the rationalism of its philosophy.[59] On the basic question of whether God does work miracles, Josephus' Jewish heritage regularly wins out.[60] In *The Antiquities* miracles occur particularly to authenticate the mission of a prophet as truly sent by God (e.g., *Ant.* 2.13.1 §280; 2.13.2–3 §283–84),[61] as opposed to false prophets—especially numerous, in Josephus' view, during the last decades before the catastrophe of A.D. 70—and pagan magicians. Indeed, the authenticating quality of a miracle is what causes it in certain instances to be a called "a sign" (*sēmeion*).[62] Such a miracle exists not for its own sake but in order to point beyond itself to the greater saving action of God in the future, as he guides history on its appointed path by his providence (*pronoia*) and power (*dynamis*). In its essence, a true miracle is a manifestation, (*epiphaneia* or *emphaneia*), a making present and revealing, of God's providence and power in sacred history.[63]

In Moses' contest with the Egyptian magicians before Pharaoh in the Book of Exodus (7:8–13), Moses' miraculous feats, while similar in appearance to that of the magicians, are pointedly declared by Josephus not to be magic (*Ant.* 2.13.3 §284–86). For Moses' miracles are not human achievements performed by knowledge of secret techniques and forces, forces that nevertheless remain on the human plane. Moses' miracles proceed directly from the infinitely greater power and providence of God, who accomplishes them as part of his guidance of history for the sake of his chosen people. Here two important points are made: (1) Josephus sees the need to distinguish miracles performed by Jewish heroes from pagan magic and thinks such a distinction can be made.[64] (2) As in the later rabbinic literature, part of the strategy for preventing Jewish miracles from becoming magic is to insist that God alone works the miracle; the human being supposedly performing the miracle is at best a mere instrument, who displays his dependence on God by lengthy prayer before the miracle is accomplished (e.g., Moses' prayer to God at the Red Sea in *Ant.* 2.16.1 §334–37).[65] Pagan miracles are performed by human wonder-workers, who regularly show no direct dependence on a particular god working through them to perform a particular feat.

As far as one can tell from his written affirmations, Josephus accepted the reality of the biblical miracles he recounted.[66] To be sure, there are a number of "rationalistic formulas" in *The Antiquities*, phrases that seem at first blush to express doubt in or indifference to the reality of the miracles just narrated. At times Josephus appears to throw responsibility for the incredible event back on the sacred text, or he allows that the astounding occurrence may have happened by accident, or he ends the narrative with a rhetorical shrug of the shoulders, such as "but, with respect to these events, let each one believe what he thinks best." All three rhetorical techniques are found together in *Ant.* 2.14.5 §347–48).[67]

But initial impressions can be deceiving. In fact, Josephus appeals to the witness of Scripture (which he clearly affirms to be inspired) precisely to bolster his argument in a culture that revered what was ancient and sacred (see *Ag. Ap.* 1.8 §42–43; cf. 2.30 §218–19). At times he even reinforces the argument from Scripture by claiming that "archaeological proof" of the narrative in question is still available.[68] Elsewhere he makes clear that he rejects the idea that miracles are just the fortunate results of chance, for everything, in his view, happens by God's providence (*Ant.* 4.3.2 §47; 10.11.7 §277–80). As for rhetorical shrugs of the shoulder, they are not restricted to accounts of miracles (e.g., *Ant.* 8.10.3 §262, of the sack of Jerusalem by Shishak) and should not be read as expressions of personal skepticism on the part of Josephus. They rather mirror his situation as a Jewish apologist in the Greco-Roman world: he knows he is dealing with a largely skeptical pagan audience. Accordingly, he politely makes allowances for the mind-set of his hearers, who will not always accept his interpretation of events. Here we simply have a typical expression of the diplomacy and tolerance shown by Jews of the Hellenistic Diaspora—a member of which Josephus had long since become—when faced with the philosophical or religious sensitivities of their vastly more numerous hosts. Moreover, his rhetorical shrugs were already set conventions in pagan Greco-Roman historiography and should be read as such in Josephus.[69] As a matter of fact, Josephus uses such bows to his audience even when he recounts the theophany at Sinai, during which God gave the Law to Israel (*Ant.* 3.5.2 §81), an event Josephus hardly doubts.[70]

None of this is meant to deny that Josephus was affected by the cultural atmosphere of philosophical rationalism in which he lived the latter part of his life. Just as he will sometimes heighten the miraculous element of a story (so, e.g., in the account of the lions devouring the enemies of Daniel the seer in *Ant.* 10.11.6 §260–61),[71] so in other instances he will attempt a rationalistic explanation of a miracle (e.g., Moses' feat of sweetening bitter water in *Ant.* 3.1.2 §8, or the flocks of quail and the manna that provide food for the hungry Israelites on their desert march in 3.1.5–6 §25–32). Still, such rationalizing does not characterize Josephus' primary approach to biblical miracles.[72] Although Josephus may strike us as inconsistent or ambiguous in his treatment of miracles,[73] he himself may not have felt any great tension between an overall acceptance of miracles and rationalizing explanations in some cases, since both strict miracles and happy accidents were understood by him as expressions of God's providence and power at work for his people.

When Josephus comes to narrate the history of his own century, he is still willing to adorn the tragic events leading up to the destruction of Jerusalem in A.D. 70 with all sorts of portents, prophecies, and visions.[74] Indeed, he himself becomes most conveniently the prophet of Vespasian's future ascent to the imperial throne (*J.W.* 3.8.3 §351–54, 3.8.9 §400–402). But what happens if we focus instead on miraculous *deeds* performed by *human beings?* In contrast to Josephus' treatment of the OT period, any collection of miracles performed by a single named individual, such as a Moses or an Elijah, disappears.

It cannot be stressed too much that when Josephus polemicizes against "false prophets" [*pseudoprophētai*] and "charlatans" [*goētes*] like Theudas (*Ant.* 20.5.1 §97–98) or the unnamed Egyptian (*Ant.* 20.8.6 §160–70; cf. *J.W.* 2.13.5 §261–62), he presents them as *promising* the people signs of deliverance. Shortly before the final storming of Jerusalem a "false prophet" promises "signs of deliverance" and persuades many desperate Jews to flee to the temple (*J.W.* 6.5.2 §285). Josephus likewise speaks in more general terms of "deceivers," who enticed people into rebellion by promising them that if they followed them into the wilderness, there God would show them "the signs of deliverance" (*J.W.* 2.13.4 §259; cf. *Ant.* 20.8.6 §167–68). In A.D. 73 a weaver called Jonathan persuaded the Jews of Cyrene to follow him into the wilderness, so that there he could show them "signs and apparitions" (*J.W.* 7.9.1 §437–42). All of these popular leaders, whatever their precise agenda, are sometimes referred to by scholars as "sign prophets." In one sense that is correct, since they all promise "signs" or the equivalent thereof. But the phrase "sign prophets" can easily lead the unwary reader astray. Josephus never says that any of these "deceivers" actually performed miracles. Strictly speaking, they do not belong under the rubric of "miracle-worker."[75]

Thus, Jesus of Nazareth stands out as a relative exception in *The Antiquities* in that he is a named figure in 1st-century Jewish Palestine to whom Josephus is willing to attribute a number of miraculous deeds (*Ant.* 18.3.3 §63: *paradoxōn ergōn poiētēs*). That Josephus did not transform 1st-century religious figures into miracle-workers in an irresponsible fashion is shown not only by his presentation of the "sign prophets" but also by the intriguing contrast between Jesus and the Baptist in Book 18 of *The Antiquities*. The Baptist receives the longer and more laudatory notice (18.5.2 §16–19), but without benefit of miracles, while Jesus is presented as both miracle-worker and teacher. The distinction implied in Josephus is mirrored perfectly in the Four Gospels and given explicit articulation in John 10:40–41.

When we do finally find an individual Jewish miracle-worker in *The Antiquities'* narrative of Palestine of the 1st-century A.D. to set alongside Jesus, the comparison and contrast are instructive. When Josephus does mention by name a particular Jewish miracle-worker (i.e., Eleazar), it is hardly by accident that he is an exorcist. Exorcism seems to have been a Jewish specialty around the turn of the era. After boasting of Solomon's powers in this regard, Josephus adds: "And this ability to cure [by exorcism] remains a very strong power among us [Jews] even to this day" (*Ant*. 8.2.5 §45–46). He then proceeds to tell of an exorcism he himself witnessed by a Jew named Eleazar (*Ant*. 8.2.5 §46–48). Thus, the fact that exorcism is prominent among the types of miracles performed by Jesus places him squarely in the Jewish-Palestinian milieu of the 1st century A.D.

At the same time, though, the contrasts between the exorcisms of Jesus in the Gospels and Eleazar's exorcism are striking. Jesus' exorcisms are performed, as far as we can tell, for and in the presence of the ordinary Galilean population, with perhaps some pious elites looking on at times and criticizing. In contrast, Eleazar's exorcism is performed in the presence of the Emperor-to-be Vespasian. Jesus' exorcisms—taking exorcism in the strict sense of involving a demoniac suffering from diabolical possession, not diabolical obsession or some demon-caused illness—always take place simply by a bare word of command. No imposition of hands, magical paraphernalia, or incantations are used. In contrast, Eleazar performs an exorcism by using a ring with special roots under its seal. He puts the ring under the possessed man's nose; when the man smells the root, Eleazar is able to draw out the demon through the man's nostrils. He then commands the demon never to return by invoking the name and incantations of King Solomon, the Jewish exorcist *par excellence*.[76] Finally, to prove that the demon has left the man, he orders the demon, upon exiting, to overturn a basin of water he had set up. On the sliding scale from miracle to magic, we are definitely slipping with Eleazar toward magic, if we have not already arrived.

I stress that neither these nor any other remarks in this excursus should be taken as a denial of the real parallels that exist between the Gospel miracles and other miracle stories recounted in Greco-Roman literature, both pagan and Jewish. The thrust of my comments is simply to emphasize that a correct use of the parallels brought forward by history-of-religion research demands a proper appreciation of points of contrast as well as points of comparison.

V. VESPASIAN AND MIRACLES

In the historical works of Tacitus and Suetonius, many portents, omens, and
dreams adorn the lives of the Roman emperors (more properly, *principes*) of
the 1st century A.D. Presenting an emperor as someone consciously engaged
in miracle-working was quite another matter. In Tacitus and Suetonius the
one grand example—indeed, for all practical purposes the only example[77]—of
a story of a 1st-century emperor consciously performing a miracle of healing
is an account about Vespasian during his stay at Alexandria (A.D. 69–70), while
he was on his way to Rome to take up the imperial throne at the end of the
civil war unleashed by the suicide of Nero. Being the first Roman emperor
who was not from the founding Julio-Claudian line (if we may ignore the ill-
fated Galba, Otho, and Vitellius), Vespasian (reigned A.D. 69–79) had a problem of legitimacy, especially since he could be seen as just another rebellious
military upstart (à la Galba, Otho, and Vitellius), snatching the throne vacated
by Nero. As we have already seen, prophecies, omens, and miracles were all
useful ways of obtaining legitimacy in the Greco-Roman world; and so, not
surprisingly, Vespasian is presented by Roman authors as surrounded by them.
Suetonius, in his *Lives of the Twelve Caesars* (*Vespasian* 4 §5),[78] recounts the
belief, widespread in the Orient, of world-rulers who were to come from Judea. The Jews mistakenly took the prophecy to refer to themselves, when it
actually pointed to Vespasian, who paradoxically was in Judea at the time to
put down the Jewish rebellion. In a passage that is difficult to interpret,
Suetonius tells us that, when Vespasian consulted the oracle of the god of
Carmel in Judea, the lots were very favorable (*Vespasian* 5 §6).[79] Suetonius then
repeats Josephus' story of his prophecy of Vespasian's rise to the imperial
throne. This agreed with omens that supposedly had been observed in Rome.
Legitimacy was on its way.

But there is nothing like a miracle story to give one indisputable legitimation, which Vespasian particularly needed as he traveled from Judea via Alexandria to Rome. In *Vespasian* 7 §2–3, Suetonius emphasizes that Vespasian, even
after he received the news at Alexandria that Vitellius had been killed, still
lacked "authority and a certain majesty," since he was an *arriviste* of humble
origins. In Alexandria, however, his entourage apparently arranged to give him
what he lacked.[80] Two men, one blind and one lame, came to Vespasian while
he was seated on his tribunal. They informed him that the god Serapis had
promised them in a dream that Vespasian could cure their infirmities if he
would spit on the blind man's eyes and touch the lame man's leg with his heel.
(In Tacitus' version of the story [*Histories* 4.81], the spittle is to be applied to
the cheeks [or possibly, the eyelids] as well, and the second man has a paralyzed
hand instead of an infirmity of the leg.)[81]

Vespasian, says Suetonius, hardly believed that such an attempt at performing a healing miracle would meet with success. Indeed, he hesitated even to try. (Tacitus goes further: Vespasian laughed at the men and treated them with contempt.) But his entourage—one suspects because they had arranged the whole drama—persuaded him to attempt both healings, not accidentally in the presence of a large crowd. (Tacitus suggests that Vespasian was moved to hope for success by the flattery of his courtiers. Physicians were brought in to give their prognosis as to whether the illnesses could be overcome by human help ["ope humana"]. The doctors thought that there was some hope for restoration of both eyes and hands by the application of the proper treatment. For apparently the eyesight had not been totally lost and could be restored "if the obstacles were taken away." The joints in the hand could be restored if proper pressure were applied to them. Vespasian finally makes a Blaise-Pascal type of wager: if he succeeds, the glory is his; if not, the two men will suffer the ridicule. Believing in his luck and smiling as the crowd went wild, Vespasian acceded to the request.) Needless to say, the two men were healed; Tacitus emphasizes that both cures are attested in his own day by eyewitnesses.

The healing of a blind man with spittle provides an intriguing parallel with two stories of Jesus' healing with spittle in Mark (the deaf and dumb man in 7:31–37 and the blind man in 8:22–26; cf. John 9:6). It confirms what we have seen already: spittle was considered a healing agent in the ancient world. Jesus also healed the lame, though not by touching their limbs with his heel. That, however, is the extent of any parallel. The arranged street-theater of the Emperor's healing powers, not a regular part of a Roman Emperor's *curriculum vitae*, apparently struck even Vespasian as strange, if not comical. He tolerates the drama for the sake of the political propaganda he may gain from it. Like Vespasian, Suetonius can hardly restrain a smile. His ironic and skeptical account, as well as Tacitus' rationalizing manner of supplying a medical explanation of what happens, belongs to a different world than the Gospel miracles. Indeed, Tacitus' account is, strictly speaking, no miracle story at all. He stresses that Vespasian inquires of the doctors (conveniently at hand) whether human means can effect the cure. They reply in the positive, describing the necessary treatment, which Vespasian proceeds to administer.[82] Be our vantage point modern or ancient, this hardly qualifies as a miracle.

VI. PROBLEMS OF TERMINOLOGY: "DIVINE MAN" AND "ARETALOGY"

Those readers acquainted with recent scholarly discussion of NT miracles and christology, especially in Mark's Gospel, may be surprised that my treatment in Chapter 18 does not use the term "divine man" *(theios anēr* or *theios anthrōpos)* for Jesus as miracle-worker and does not refer to collections of miracle stories in the Gospels as "aretalogies."[83] Such terms have been bandied about in NT research, especially in the history-of-religion school and its successors, for a good part of the 20th century. Despite their wide use, notably in debates over Mark's Gospel from the 1960s onward,[84] the terms suffer from some major difficulties, especially when employed in the quest for the historical Jesus: (1) The terms were not used with one precise meaning prior to or during the time of Jesus. (2) The terminology does not reflect the Greek words actually used to describe Jesus and his miracles in the NT. (3) In 20th-century exegesis, the terms have often been connected with highly speculative theories about pre-Christian pagan and Jewish missionaries with "divine-man" traits, the development of various streams of christology in the NT (including a "divine-man" christology in competition with the other types), and the tension between collections of Gospel miracles and the theologies of the final redactors of the Gospels.[85] (4) Even today scholars do not always use the terms with the same understanding.

(A) In the case of the phrase "divine man," scholars cannot point to one clear and coherent concept—or collection of concepts—connected with the phrase "divine man" that was current in Greco-Roman literature before or during the time of Jesus. To construct their concept of a "divine man," scholars of the 20th century have culled ideas from a vast array of Greek and Roman works from Homer up until the writings of the late Roman Empire. While the vague constant in the phrase "divine man" is divine power as revealed or embodied in some human being, the exact human referent ranges widely over priest-kings of Asia Minor and Egypt (including kingly magicians and lawgivers), monarchs whose vast power on earth was believed to extend over nature itself (especially the Roman Emperors), and various kinds of prophetic philosophers (including ecstatics, magicians, miracle-workers, apostles, hero-sages, founders and leaders of religious groups, shamans, and charlatans). In many of the reconstructions, scholars rely heavily on works like *The Death of Peregrinus* and *Alexander or the False Prophet* by Lucian, the satirist of the 2d century A.D., and *The Life of Apollonius* by Philostratus, the rhetorician of the 3d century A.D. Lucian almost certainly knew the Christian Gospels, and Philostratus probably did as well.

Using the vast range of literature belonging to the classical Greek, Hellenistic, and Roman periods, Ludwig Bieler in particular linked the "divine man" concept with miracle-working, which he considered the chief means of legitimating the divine character of both the *theios anēr* and his teaching. Both Bieler's creation of a synthetic picture of the divine man and his intense focus on miracle-working have been criticized by some recent scholars. For instance, David Lenz Tiede strongly rejects the idea that there was a fixed concept of the divine man in the Hellenistic world.[86] The criticism Tiede aims at Bieler could be repeated of some current authors as well: ". . . Bieler aggregated so many features into his composite portrait of the 'typical divine man' that it would be difficult to find any hero in antiquity to whom at least several of these qualities were not attributed, and it is perhaps as difficult to find a pre-third century A.D. portrayal of any figure which supplies its hero with Bieler's complete catalog of the characteristics of the 'divine man.' "[87]

Tiede grants that the phrase "divine man" expressed a commonly held "propagandistic intent of documenting the glorious features or even divine stature" of a charismatic figure honored in a particular tradition.[88] However, the particular features that verified this divine status varied according to the given tradition or stage of the tradition. Amid the many variations, Tiede distinguishes two main tendencies in the Greco-Roman way of viewing the divine man. Sophisticated writers standing in a philosophical tradition tended to base the divine status of a charismatic figure on his wisdom and possession of virtue, which made him a paradigm for moral edification. The same basic philosophical portrait is found in the depiction of Moses by Philo and Josephus. Perhaps the most striking example of the "elastic" nature of the attribute "divine" in a philosophical context is the fact that Epicurus, noted for his battles against superstition and popular conceptions of the gods, was honored as "divine" even during his lifetime because "a man could be said to be divine to the degree that his life was tranquil and untroubled."[89] In sharp contrast to this philosophical conception of divinity, heroes of popular romantic legends, who also appear at times in magical material, were extolled as divine mainly for their miraculous powers. In the later Roman Empire these two reasons for viewing people as divine—philosophical wisdom and spectacular wonder-working—were merged by authors like Philostratus, though such fusion met with resistance (as is seen in the satires of Lucian).[90]

Since it is often claimed that Hellenistic Judaism was the funnel or corridor through which ideas about "divine men" passed from Greco-Roman paganism into early Christianity, scholars like Carl H. Holladay have investigated in detail the portrait of the divine man supposedly drawn by Hellenistic-Jewish authors around the turn of the era. Holladay has shown that, contrary to oft-made scholarly claims, Philo and Josephus do not stress the image of miracle-worker but rather that of wise philosopher, lawgiver, and king in their presentations of Moses as "divine."[91] Interestingly, Josephus uses "divine man" only once, when he describes Moses as a wise lawgiver who prescribed the arrangement of the tabernacle in the wilderness in order to give it cosmic significance.[92] Despite his greater openness to recasting biblical narratives in Greek philosophical terms, even Philo uses "divine man" only rarely and never of Moses or any other Jewish hero.[93] More to the point, Philo never uses "divine man" for a miracle-worker or in a context of miracle-working. As a matter of fact, in comparison with the biblical narratives, Philo plays down Moses' activity as a miracle-worker.

The upshot of this research is clear: in the Greco-Roman world prior to and around the time of Jesus, miracle-working was not a necessary component of the concept or collection of concepts represented by the phrase "divine man." In other words, in the period before and during Jesus' lifetime, there was no clear and coherent concept of a God-like miracle-worker regularly tied to the phrase "divine man."[94]

To all this one may add a commonsense observation similar to the one I made above about calling Jesus a magician *(magos)*, a usage totally absent from the NT. The simple fact of the matter is that nowhere in the NT is Jesus ever called a "divine man." Indeed, not only is that exact phrase never used of Jesus, it never occurs at all either in the Septuagint or in the NT. Furthermore, the adjective *theios* ("divine") is never predicated of Jesus in the NT in any context or combination of words describing his earthly ministry or his performance of miracles. In fact, this adjective, so important to Hellenistic philosophical and theological writings, appears only three times in the NT, never directly modifying "Jesus" or an equivalent title.[95] All three occurrences have a high-sounding philosophical ring alien to the Gospel stories of Jesus.

In Acts 17:29, in his great speech to the Areopagus, the Lucan Paul argues against pagan worship of idols by stating: "We should not imagine that the Divinity [*to theion*, the adjective used as an abstract substantive] is similar to gold or silver or stone. . . ." 2 Pet 1:3 proclaims how "his divine power has bestowed upon us everything necessary for life and godliness." It is unclear from the context whether "his" refers to God the Father or to Jesus Christ. If the latter, the reference is to the risen Christ; and in any event, the divine power is engaged in calling people to faith, not in working miracles. In the very next verse (2 Pet 1:4), the ultimate goal of this exercise of divine power is said to be to make believers "sharers in the divine nature." It is not by accident that all three of these occurrences of the word "divine" are found in two late NT documents that are intent on expressing the Christian message in a vocabulary and style acceptable to a cultured Greco-Roman audience. In all three cases there is not even an indirect reference to the miracles Jesus worked during his public ministry.

The basic problem I have been underlining throughout these remarks, namely, the lack of fixed content tied to a fixed title, is acknowledged by Gail Peterson Corrington in her monograph *The "Divine Man."* Nevertheless, she thinks that "divine man" is still a useful category if we employ it as an "ideal type" of sociology, a type that allows for fluidity in definition. One can appreciate the new approach that treating "divine man" as an ideal type opens up. However, it still leaves us, as far as the historical Jesus is concerned, with a "fluid" concept, varying in content from case to case, that at least in the early 1st century A.D. was not especially tied to the phrase "divine man." What benefit a fluid concept bereft of any particular identifying label brings to a discussion of the historical Jesus or NT christology is not clear to me.[96] Hence I do not think that putting the label of "divine man" on this protean concept and then using it as an analytic tool for understanding the Jesus of history is helpful to the goals of *A Marginal Jew*—or, for that matter, to any quest for the historical Jesus.[97] That is not to say that other scholars may not find the label useful in other contexts. I have simply wished to explain to my readers why it is not employed in this work.

(B) My view of the term "aretalogy" is similar. Once again, the term is not univocal, is not widely attested in the literature that concerns us, and has no direct basis in the Greek vocabulary of the NT. All this runs counter to the naive supposition, still encountered at times, that "aretalogy" obviously and univocally means "miracle story" or a cycle of miracle stories, such as we find in the Four Gospels. Things are by no means so simple.[98]

The word "aretalogy" does not occur frequently in ancient Greco-Roman literature. We find it only once in the LXX, in Ben Sira 36:16 (19): "Fill Zion with the telling of your wondrous deeds" (where the Hebrew text [36:14] has: "Fill Zion with your glory").[99] Interestingly, the word does not occur in those sections of Ben Sira that scholars today might call "aretalogical," e.g., chap. 24 (in which divine Wisdom praises herself and her works) and chap. 43 (in which Ben Sira praises the awesome power of God displayed in creation). "Aretalogy" never occurs in the NT or in early Christian literature in general. The word is found in a pseudonymous collection of the 4th century A.D. called *Manetho the Astrologer*, 4:444–77. In his work on geography, Strabo *may* (the text is uncertain) refer to "aretalogists," people who in a cultic context apparently recited the mighty deeds performed by the god Serapis.[100] Two inscriptions from Delos (ca. 1st century B.C.) mention an *aretalogos*, some functionary connected with the worship of Isis; among other things he interpreted dreams.

Latin authors sometimes took over the Greek word in a pejorative or at least profane sense: e.g., someone who told fantastic and miraculous stories (so Juvenal in his *Satire 15*).[101] In Suetonius' life of Augustus (*Augustus* 74) it seems to carry the general sense of a storyteller at a dinner party.[102] Lucian in the 2d century A.D. (in *Philopseudes*) and Porphyrion in the 3d century also employ the word-field of aretalogy in a satirical or pejorative sense. In short, the use of aretalogy/aretalogist in the Greco-Roman world is neither frequent nor univocal. Morton Smith suggests that the word "aretalogist" came from popular speech, and so its usage in antiquity was somewhat inconsistent. Consequently, "aretalogy," what an aretalogist did, was likewise vague.[103]

To move from the Greek and Latin words to the various literary works that have been labeled "aretalogy" by modern authors: the first thing that we must realize is that "aretalogy" signifies no one literary genre.[104] It is applied to at least three different types of literature, each of which could in principle be composed in either prose or poetry. Tiede sums up what all of these works have in common in a terse definition: a propagandistic recitation of praise.[105] One type of "aretalogy" is found in various inscriptions and texts (including Apuleius' *Metamorphoses*) in which the goddess Isis proclaims her virtues or powers in the first person—although the words *aretai* and *aretalogia* do not occur in such texts. In these propagandistic texts, written with a view to competing with other Hellenistic cults, Isis praises herself as the goddess who has instituted and preserved the order of the world. While Isis is hailed as a healer in other religious texts, she does not praise herself for that quality in these supposed "aretalogies."

A second type of aretalogy is the formal account of the life, deeds, and sayings of a great wise man, philosopher, or teacher, often with Socrates as the primary model. In such accounts the virtues *(aretai)* of the wise man are held up for imitation by a particular philosophical school.

From this aretalogy of the wise man must be distinguished the third type of aretalogy, that of the miracle-working figure. For example, the *aretai* (in the sense of the miracles) of the healing-god Asclepius were recited in a cultic context. It is from this third possible meaning that scholars derive the common use of "aretalogy" for a miracle story. But, as Kee stresses, even in the cases where an aretalogy tells of the healing or saving act of a divinity, it has no one fixed literary form. Nor, most importantly, is such an aretalogy used of human beings with an eye to divinizing them; it is always a report of what a god or goddess has done.[106]

Hence, in the period prior to or during Jesus' lifetime, there is no basis for equating an aretalogy with a biography of a *theios anēr*, marked by miracle-working. If one wants instead to define aretalogy quite modestly as a collection of miracle stories featuring a human miracle-worker, one is free to do so, though there is no basis for this in ancient usage. In any case, one must beware of moving beyond this modest usage to grand theories of pagan aretalogies paralleling the aretalogies that supposedly formed the basis of the Four Gospels and presented Jesus as a "divine man."

Simply from the vantage point of the Gospel texts (or the NT texts in general), there is likewise no basis for using "aretalogy" as a technical term for miracle stories involving Jesus. Like *theios*, *aretē* ("virtue" or "strength") never occurs anywhere in the Four Gospels. The Gospels do have a number of words to designate Jesus' miracles (e.g., *dynamis, sēmeion, teras, paradoxon*), but *aretē* is not one of them. Phil 4:8 uses the word in its popular-philosophical sense of "virtue," good human quality, or excellence. 1 Pet 2:9 uses it of the mighty and glorious works of God (not Jesus), or perhaps of the praise of such works; but these mighty works appear to be the creation of God's people and its call to faith rather than any specific miracles. 2 Pet 1:3 also speaks of God calling us by (or possibly, "to") his own glory and goodness (*aretē*, possibly "excellence," "magnanimity," or "might").[107] In 2 Pet 1:5 *aretē* occurs twice, both in the moral sense of "virtue" or "magnanimity." As with *theios*, we have only a few occurrences of the word *aretē*, all outside the Gospels; in none of the five occurrences is there any reference to miracles performed by the earthly Jesus. The infrequent use of the word, its total absence from the Gospels, and the lack of any connection to Jesus' miracles (to say nothing of a *theios anēr* Christology!) leads me to avoid speaking of the Gospel miracle stories, or the Gospels as a whole, in terms of "aretalogies."[108] Needless to say, others are free to use such terminology if they find it helpful. Personally, I find it—as well as "divine man"—obfuscating instead of clarifying.

As we come to the end of this excursus on ancient parallels to the Gospel miracles, I wish to emphasize an important point: this excursus does not intend to deny or minimize the importance of pagan and Jewish parallels in the study of the Gospel miracles. My one concern has been to stress that, if we employ such parallels for a better understanding of the Gospel miracles, we must take into account differences as well as similarities. If this excursus has focused on differences, the reason is that all too often comparative studies ignore or play down the differences in favor of the similarities. The focus of this excursus in no way aims at suppressing the many and obvious similarities, which are widely acknowledged and often examined. In sum, the goal of this excursus has been solely to restore a balance that is often lacking.

NOTES TO EXCURSUS TO CHAPTER 18

[1] Gerd Petzke, *Die Traditionen über Apollonius von Tyana und das Neue Testament* (SCHNT 1; Leiden: Brill, 1970); idem, "Die historische Frage," 180–204. See my remark on the latter work in *A Marginal Jew*, 1. 190 n. 34.

[2] Besides the works of Petzke and Kee, for the sketch of Apollonius in the text I am indebted to the information given by David R. Cartlidge and David L. Dungan, *Documents for the Study of the Gospels* (Philadelphia: Fortress, 1980) 205–8.

[3] These are the commonly accepted dates. However, Maria Dzielska (*Apollonius of Tyana in Legend and History* [Problemi e ricerche di storia antica 10; Rome: L'erma, 1986] 185) prefers A.D. 40–ca. 120. This is due to the fact that Dzielska largely rejects the presentation of Philostratus because of "the extent of fabrication, fiction, and historical falsity contained in this book [i.e., the *Life of Apollonius*]." She may indeed be correct about Philostratus, but whether the fragmentary documents of the pre-Philostratean tradition can support her alternate portrait of Apollonius is debatable. For her arguments in favor of the later dating, see her *Apollonius of Tyana*, 32–38.

[4] Once again, Dzielska (*Apollonius of Tyana*, 83–84) takes a revisionist view, claiming that Apollonius' activity was confined to a few cities in the eastern end of the Roman Empire. According to Dzielska, Apollonius was not well known in his own lifetime and remained unknown in the West until the second half of the 4th century A.D., except for a small circle in the court of the Severan emperors.

[5] Ewen Lyall Bowie, "Apollonius of Tyana: Tradition and Reality," *ANRW* II/16.2 (published 1978), 1652–99, esp. 1686. But just before and after this judgment Bowie issues caveats: "The state of the evidence is such that no certainty is attainable about the Ur-Apollonius and only arguments from probability can be applied" (pp. 1685–86). Indeed, even granted that the historical Apollonius was a prophet and miracle-worker, "that any one of the tales of miracle and prophecy is authentic can rarely be established" (p. 1687).

[6] Scholars argue over the possibility that individual letters or other fragments might come from the historical Apollonius. For instance, Dzielska (*Apollonius of Tyana*, 129) thinks that a fragment of the work *On Sacrifices* does come from Apollonius: "Ostensibly, it is the only historically accurate fragment of Apollonius' work which has persisted till our times. . . ." However, not all critics agree with this estimation. For instance, Bowie ("Apollonius of Tyana," 1961) remains suspicious of the work.

[7] On the problem of distinguishing this Philostratus, usually called Flavius Philostratus, from two other figures with the same name, see Petzke, *Die Traditionen*, 1–5.

[8] On the circle of Julia Domna—and on how relatively little we know about it and its members—see G. W. Bowersock, *Greek Sophists in the Roman Empire* (Oxford: Clarendon, 1969) 101–9. Bowersock thinks that her circle was made up of lesser philosophers and sophists; great men were lacking.

[9] The standard edition in English is F. C. Conybeare (ed.), *Philostratus. The Life of Apollonius of Tyana* (LCL; 2 vols.; London: Heinemann; Cambridge, MA: Harvard University, 1912). It is from pp. vii–x of the introduction that I take the summary of the sources Philostratus is supposed to have used; cf. *Life of Apollonius* 1.3.

[10] Robert J. Penella, *The Letters of Apollonius of Tyana. A Critical Text with Prolegomena, Translation and Commentary* (Mnemosyne Supplementum 56; Leiden: Brill, 1979) 24–25. Penella goes on to list likely cases of forgery on p. 25. On p. 28 he adds: "Spurious letters in the *Vita Apollonii* were either invented by Philostratus or inherited by him from an earlier fabricator. A motive for their invention is easy to divine." He concludes his treatment of authenticity on p. 29 with the observation: "There is a good chance, then, that if there are fabricated letters in the separately transmitted collection and in Stobaeus, at least some of them were made in the fourth or early fifth century, an age of intensified admiration for and controversy about Apollonius." Dzielska (*Apollonius of Tyana*, 190) considers the letters to be "mostly apocryphal."

[11] Penella, *The Letters of Apollonius of Tyana*, 24. This statement, however, comes right after the following admissions: "We lack adequate and sure information on the historical Apollonius. There is no canon of Apollonius's writings of certain authenticity to compare stylistically with the letters. For most of the letters we must be content with stating probabilities and setting forth tentative lines of argumentation."

[12] Moiragenes' work is sometimes presumed to have been hostile to Apollonius, but Bowie ("Apollonius of Tyana," 1672) argues that the statements of neither Philostratus nor Origen necessitate such a judgment.

[13] On the *Life of Apollonius* as basically a novel, see Bowie, "Apollonius of Tyana," 1663–64.

[14] See the strong note of skepticism in the treatment of the criteria of historicity (Petzke, "Die historische Frage," 182–84) and in the treatment of the miracle traditions in the Gospels (pp. 198–204). If such a skeptical approach were applied uniformly to all ancient sources, the whole of ancient history would be one big black hole in the academic universe.

[15] See Kee, *Miracle in the Early Christian World*, 256–65, esp. 256–57 and n. 11 for the authors who doubt the existence of Damis' diary. Lane Fox (*Pagans and Christians*, 253) says simply: "The real Apollonius cannot be untangled from the admiring legends. . . ."

[16] E.g., Dodds (*Pagan and Christian in an Age of Anxiety*, 59) states flatly: "Neither a fictitious romance like Philostratus' *Life of Apollonius* nor an artificial allegory like Hermas's *Shepherd* tells us much about real *prophetai*." Martin Hengel (*Nachfolge und Charisma* [BZNW 34; Berlin: Töpelmann, 1968] 30) thinks that Damis is "presumably an invention of the author" Philostratus. John Ferguson (*The Religions of the Roman Empire* [Ithaca, NY: Cornell University, 1970] 181–82) does not doubt the existence of a 1st-century historical figure called Apollonius who played some part in the Pythagorean revival. But "it is now almost impossible to disentangle fact from fiction in our records of him. . . . Philostratus professed to have discovered an old document by one Damis as his source, but such discoveries are the stock-in-trade of historical romances, and we can place no credence upon Damis." Similarly, Frederick Copleston, *A History of Philosophy: Volume I. Greece and Rome. Part II* (Garden City, NY: Image Books [Doubleday], 1962, originally 1946) 193: "The story given by Philostratus about the Memoirs of Apollonius by his disciple Damis . . . is probably a literary fiction. . . . it is practically impossible to say exactly what sort of a man the historic Apollonius actually was." It is perhaps telling that, when Bowersock mentions the *Life of Apollonius* in his book *Greek Sophists*, he refers to it simply as the "Apollonius novel" (p. 5).

[17] Kee, *Miracle in the Early Christian World*, 256. Dzielska (*Apollonius of Tyana*, 190) likewise considers the diary "a literary fiction but concocted, as it seems, with a full awareness." Indeed, Dzielska suggests that "together with Julia Domna, . . . he [Philostratus] created Damis the Syrian from Nineveh to whom, as to a most faithful pupil of Apollonius, he attributed the authorship of the history of Apollonius' life that he made up himself" (pp. 190–91). The reason for this invention, says Dzielska, is that Apollonius was little-known in the Greco-Roman world before his death. With not much information at his disposal, Philostratus had to invent Apollonius anew, as it were. "Thus, using his literary imagination, he [Philostratus] turned a modest Cappadocian mystic into an impressive figure, full of life, politically outstanding, and yet also preposterous" (p. 14).

[18] Kee, *Miracle in the Early Christian World*, 257. After surveying briefly the opinions of various scholars, Penella (*The Letters of Apollonius of Tyana*, 1 n. 3) inclines "to regard Damis's memoirs as a pre-Philostratean fabrication."

[19] Bowie, "Apollonius of Tyana," 1653–62.

[20] Bowie, "Apollonius of Tyana," 1663–64.

[21] On the reactions of Galen and Celsus to Christianity, see Wilken, *The Christians as the Romans Saw Them*, 68–93 and 94–125 respectively.

[22] The text is found in the *Scriptores Historiae Augustae*, in *Alexander Severus* 29.2: Severus Alexander is said to have kept in the sanctuary of his Lares ". . . et divos principes sed optimos electos et animas sanctiores, in quis Apollonium et, quantum scriptor suorum temporum dicit, Christum, Abraham et Orpheum et huiuscemodi ceteros habebat ac maiorum effigies. . . ." (". . . both the divinized emperors—but only the best ones having been chosen—and especially holy souls, among whom he had Apollonius and, according to what a writer of his own period claims, Christ, Abraham, and Orpheus, and others of this type, as well as images of his ancestors"). According to 31.5, the chapel also had a statue of Alexander the Great. For the Latin text and an English translation, see David Magie (ed.), *The Scriptores Historiae Augustae* (LCL; 3 vols.; London: Heinemann; New York: Putnam's Sons, 1924) 2. 234.

[23] Conybeare, *Philostratus. The Life of Apollonius of Tyana*, xv. Some scholars continue to propose that Philostratus was consciously attacking the Christian Gospels or at least Christian preaching; so, e.g., Vincent M. Scramuzza and Paul L. MacKendrick, *The Ancient World* (New York: Holt, Rinehard and Winston, 1958) 693: "She [Julia Domna] inspired a muddle-minded philosopher, Philostratus, to write a pagan counterblast to the Christian Gospels, the *Life of Apollonius of Tyana*. . . ." See also Ferguson, *The Religions of the Roman Empire*, 181–82: "Julia Domna . . . encouraged . . . Philostratus to write a heroic life of Apollonius, no doubt to counterweigh the increasingly insistent propaganda of the Christians." Copleston (*A History of Philosophy*, 193) tries to strike a moderate note: "There are indications that Philostratus knew and utilised the Gospels, Acts of the Apostles and Lives of the Saints, but it remains uncertain how far it was his conscious intention to substitute the ideal of a 'Hellenistic Christ' for the Christian Christ: resemblances have been greatly exaggerated."

[24] Petzke (*Die Traditionen*, 130) rejects any dependence on the Gospels (he considers only the Lucan parallel). He points instead to the classical story of Alcestis, raised up by Hercules, and also to a resurrection story in a work by Apuleius (*Florida* 19).

[25] For misguided attempts to identify Onias with the Qumran Teacher of Righteousness, see the literature cited in the revised Schürer, *History of the Jewish People*, 1. 235 n. 6.

[26] Perhaps nowhere do we see Vermes's strange disregard for the dating of sources more than in his treatment of Onias/Ḥoni in *Jesus the Jew*, 69–72. He first discusses the mishnaic Ḥoni, then takes up Josephus' Onias, and remarks: "The shift from the almost openly critical presentation of Ḥoni in the Mishna to the fully sympathetic portrayal in Josephus for the benefit of a Hellenistic audience is worthy of remark." On Vermes's views in general, see Hershel Shanks, "Escape and Rescue," *Bible Review* 10/3 (June, 1994) 30–37.

[27] Schürer, *History of the Jewish People*, 1. 235 n. 6.

[28] For a careful tracing of the tradition history of Ḥoni in the rabbinic sources, see William Scott Green, "Palestinian Holy Men: Charismatic Leadership and Rabbinic Tradition," *ANRW* II/19.2 (published 1979), 619–47. He employs the method developed by Jacob Neusner for discerning different layers in a given rabbinic tradition.

[29] Green ("Palestinian Holy Men," 634–35) thinks that the account has "a decidedly magical character" and that "the root" of the story, "the core of the Ḥoni-narrative, is an account of an ancient Jewish magical rite." One should note that Green is speaking here of a primitive form of the story, shorn of the emphasis on prayer and the caveats that limit or criticize Ḥoni's power in the final form of the story. Green also honestly admits that "no exact parallel to Ḥoni's rite appears in either primary or secondary sources on ancient magic" (p. 635). Here we run into the old problem of defining the characteristics of magic. Green takes Ḥoni's personal intimacy with God that is at the root of his astounding trust and daring to be a sign of magic; other scholars might take such a close personal relationship with God to be the very opposite of magic.

Whether the story about Onias/Ḥoni ever circulated without the context of prayer and piety seems doubtful to me because of the earlier version seen in Josephus. Green notes the differences between the stories in the Mishna and Josephus, but only to affirm that "we cannot assume that Josephus here refers to the mishnaic account of Ḥoni's rain-making." That the accounts are not identical is obvious; that the Mishna's story has not grown out of something like Josephus' story is not so obvious. I think it is telling that Green begins his treatment of Ḥoni with a detailed analysis of the Mishna and the variant in the Tosefta, and only then goes back to Josephus. It seems to me that proper methodology demands looking at Josephus first and then asking ourselves what has happened to the Ḥoni-tradition between Josephus' writing of the *Antiquities* at the end of the 1st century A.D. and the redaction of the Mishna at the end of the 2d.

[30] Green, "Palestinian Holy Men," 628–39. Green thinks that the similar story told of an anonymous *ḥāsîd* in the Tosefta tractate *Taʿanit* 2:13 is not an alternate version of the Ḥoni story. Rather, the Ḥoni and the *ḥāsîd* stories are "two different stories which share a common literary structure that probably derives from another source" (p. 632). I would suggest an alternate possibility: the Tosefta version is a further "rabbinization" of the tradition, replacing Ḥoni with a *ḥāsîd*, removing any suggestion of magic (e.g., drawing and standing in the circle), making prayer the direct and sole reason for the rain, and inserting scriptural warrants.

[31] Green, "Palestinian Holy Men," 644–45. Crossan (*The Historical Jesus*, 146–

47) notes that it is in the context of these rain-making stories in the Babylonian Talmud (*b. Ta'an.* 23ab) that God is twice referred to as *'abbā'*—the only two times this occurs in rabbinical literature. Crossan states that "God is *addressed* as 'Abba'" in these two passages (emphasis mine), a claim that is technically not correct. In the first case, *'abbā'* is the address of a petulant son asking his father to bathe him first in warm and then in cold water; this situation of a spoiled son indulged by his father is compared to Ḥoni's relationship with God. In the second case, Ḥanan ha-Nehba, the grandson of Ḥoni, addresses God as "Lord of the World." He then beseeches God to grant rain for the sake of the school children who have come to him and begged, "Abba, Abba, give us rain." As in the first case, Ḥanan speaks in terms of a comparison: he asks God to have mercy on children who cannot distinguish between the father [*'abbā'*] who gives rain and the father [*'abbā'*] who does not.

[32] One is puzzled by Crossan's summary statement about Ḥoni (*The Historical Jesus*, 147): "He was probably a peasant, but his magic was too powerfully present and had moved, at least by the story of his death, from the Little into the Great Tradition." How, from the earliest form of the story in Josephus—or how even from the historical kernel that might be extracted from the later expansion of the tradition in the Mishna—do we get to a peasant and a magician? This may be a case of the desired goal of an author dictating the results of his research.

[33] Green, "Palestinian Holy Men," 627.

[34] For the attempt to sketch the "historical" Ḥanina ben Dosa, see Geza Vermes, "Ḥanina ben Dosa. A Controversial Galilean Saint from the First Century of the Christian Era," *JJS* 23 (1972) 28–50 and 24 (1973) 51–64. A summary of Vermes's position can be found in his *Jesus the Jew*, 72–78. For trenchant criticism of Vermes's views, which in my opinion undoes what Vermes tries to do, see Sean Freyne, "The Charismatic," *Ideal Figures in Ancient Judaism. Profiles and Paradigms* (SBLSCS 12; ed. John J. Collins and George W. E. Nickelsburg; Chico, CA: Scholars, 1980) 223–58.

[35] Vermes, "Ḥanina ben Dosa" (1972), 28.

[36] See especially Vermes, "Ḥanina ben Dosa" (1972), 57–64; Freyne ("The Charismatic," 223–24) pointedly waives any such attempt. On p. 228 Freyne comments on his own approach: "As mentioned in the introduction, this approach is not burdened by the impossible task of determining how the traditions relate to the historical person [of Ḥanina]." Freyne (p. 227) notes that Vermes's way of arranging the data "can easily lead to treating the material as potentially biographical, a trap Vermes falls into only too often in his apparent desire to establish good parallels between the historical Jesus and the historical Hanina." Crossan (*The Historical Jesus*, 148–56) falls into the same sort of trap, with the added problem that he engages in a highly speculative reordering of the sources that ignores the chronology of the written witnesses in favor of a hypothetical trajectory that traces the rabbinization of Ḥanina (p. 149).

It is significant that in one of the most detailed studies of the Ḥanina-traditions in recent years, Baruch M. Bokser ("Wonder-Working and the Rabbinic Tradition: The Case of Ḥanina ben Dosa," *JSJ* 16 [1985] 42–92) purposely concentrates on how the image of Ḥanina was developed and adapted to various Jewish needs in various times and places in Late Antiquity. It is not by accident that he spends a good deal of his time on the Palestinian and Babylonian Talmuds. When Bokser mentions in passing the attempts of Vermes and Freyne to discern and situate the original meaning of the Ḥanina-tradition and the men of deed in the 1st century, he quickly adds: "But . . . we must be wary of overinterpreting the evidence. . . ." When one looks at the different ways in which various critics dissect the later traditions about Ḥanina, one declaring one snippet of tradition to be early or even historical, another another, Bokser's call for wariness is well taken.

[37] For the question of dating, see Vermes, "Ḥanina ben Dosa" (1973) 59–61. Even on this main point attestation is weak and arguments are circumstantial. Freyne ("The Charismatic," 242) says simply: "We have made no attempt to date the historical Ḥanina, though the pre-70 period suggested by both Vermes and Neusner does seem to be a more plausible context for his activity as a man of deed."

[38] Different editions of the tractate ʾAbot use different systems of enumeration. Here I follow the enumeration of the Danby edition of the Mishna (which is also that of the Neusner edition); Vermes throughout his article cites this text as ʾAbot 3:9–10.

[39] Freyne ("The Charismatic," 235) is skeptical of any teaching tradition from Ḥanina: ". . . the amount of sayings attributed to Hanina in the tradition is minimal and despite the ascription to him of the title Rabbi, the absence of any legal rulings in his name must be decisive. He never was considered to have been a teacher and this observation could cast doubts on the authenticity of even those few sayings that do appear in his name." On p. 241 he remarks: "In Hanina's case, though his rabbinization had been progressively developing, it had never been completely carried through to the point that Halakhic teaching could be attributed to him." See also Bokser ("Wonder-Working," 42): ". . . the Mishnah, Tosefta, Babylonian and Palestinian Talmuds, and several later midrashim narrate his [Ḥanina's] wonder-working activities but attribute to him no halakhic teachings."

[40] For the Hebrew text, a German translation, and commentary on *m. Soṭa* 9:15, see Hans Bietenhard, *Die Mischna. Sota* (Berlin: Töpelmann, 1956) 174. Vermes ("Ḥanina ben Dosa" [1972], 38) lists A. Büchler, G. Alon, and S. Safrai among the scholars who oppose interpreting "men of deed" as miracle-workers. Vermes himself favors the "miraculous" interpretation, although he admits the possibility of interpreting the phrase in terms of charitable works and promotion of public welfare. In all this, Vermes appears to be interpreting the Mishna in the light of the Talmuds. Freyne ("The Charismatic," 224–27) not only emphasizes the uncertainty of what "men of deed" means but also objects to Vermes's easy equation of the men of deed with the *ḥăsîdîm*. For the latter point Freyne depends on the research of Dennis Berman, "Hasidim in Rabbinic Traditions," *Society of Biblical Literature 1979 Seminar Papers* (SBL Seminar Papers Series 17; 2 vols.; ed. Paul J. Achtemeier; Missoula, MT: Scholars, 1979) 2. 15–33, esp. 16–17. On this point, Crossan (*The Historical Jesus*, 148–49) follows Freyne and Berman. Berman ("Hasidim," 16) summarizes the rabbinic concept of a *ḥāsîd* thus: "The hasid . . . is kind and merciful, but still more he is completely selfless, sinless and devout . . . . in his zeal to fulfill the Law he goes beyond the norm. A quality of exuberance and extreme piety pervades the rabbinic hasid traditions. However, the hasid is never characterized as a martyr or an ascetic." Berman (p. 17) points out that, while a *ḥāsîd* might be a miracle-worker, the two social roles were distinct; one did not necessarily entail the other. It should also be noted that, while Ḥanina is often numbered among the men of deed, only twice is he called a *ḥāsîd*, and both texts are late.

[41] The translation is the one supplied by Vermes, "Ḥanina ben Dosa" (1972), 29. The translation in the Neusner edition (done by Tzvee Zahavy and Alan J. Avery-Peck) of the Mishna formulates Hanina's response slightly differently, but with the same basic meaning: "If my prayer is fluent, then I know that it is accepted [and the person will live]. But if not, I know that it is rejected [and the person will die]." The Hebrew text

(with vocalization added) of the key clause "if my prayer is fluent in my mouth" is *'im šāgĕrâ tĕpillātî bĕpî*. The verb *šāgar* means "run, flow"; hence the sense is that the prayer is spoken easily and smoothly, without hesitation or mistakes.

[42] The fact that Josephus' presentation of Onias and the Mishna's presentations of Ḥoni and Ḥanina all agree on the central importance of prayer makes Crossan's attempt (*The Historical Jesus*, 148–56) to banish prayer from the earliest Ḥanina-traditions highly unlikely.

[43] As Vermes ("Ḥanina ben Dosa" [1972], 29) observes, this precise point of the Ḥanina-tradition in *m. Ber.* 5:5 does not really fit the larger context, where the point at issue is the importance of reciting a fixed prayer smoothly and without error.

[44] Hence I do not agree with Vermes's claim ("Ḥanina ben Dosa" [1972], 30): "The ecstatic prayer to which it [the Ḥanina logion] refers belongs to an account of charismatic healing." As his article soon shows, Vermes is reading this mishnaic text through the lenses of texts from the Babylonian Talmud and other later works. Nothing in the mishnaic text, taken by itself, speaks of "charismatic healing."

[45] I think Vermes ("Ḥanina ben Dosa" [1972], 33) is correct in taking the mention in the story of a first, a second, and a third hour as a reference to the hours that Ḥanina spends in prayer, "first reassuring the messengers that the girl was safe, and then asserting that she was completely out of danger." Crossan (*The Historical Jesus*, 150), who sees no reference to prayer, really has no explanation for the mention of the three successive hours. I think Crossan likewise misses the point of the story when he states that "it is not clear whether Hanina miraculously saved her or miraculously announced that she had been normally saved by others." Nothing in the text gives the slightest indication that Ḥanina himself has saved her; only a firm determination to make Ḥanina a miracle-*worker* can read such an interpretation into the text. Rather, once one grants that the successive hours are hours of prayer, one sees that the story bears a similarity to the early tradition about prayer being fluent in Ḥanina's mouth (*m. Ber.* 5:5): through his charismatic prayer Ḥanina is granted miraculous knowledge of whether the people he is praying for are or will be safe.

[46] Freyne ("The Charismatic," 228) remarks: "The largest single body of items associated with Hanina comes in the category of what can loosely be described as miracle stories."

[47] Vermes, "Ḥanina ben Dosa" (1972), 39.

[48] Bokser ("Wonder-Working," 71–72) discerns a difference in the way Ḥanina is depicted in the Palestinian and the Babylonian Talmuds. In the former he represents the pious individual respected by people and protected, even supernaturally, by God. In the latter he is an example of leaders helping the community and teaching ethical lessons. The Babylonian Talmud also includes more wondrous acts of Ḥanina than does the Palestinian Talmud.

[49] Strack and Stemberger, *Introduction to the Talmud and Midrash*, 357.

[50] For the relevant texts, see Vermes, "Ḥanina ben Dosa" (1973), 58.

[51] Freyne ("The Charismatic," 232) observes of the whole Ḥanina-tradition: "It seems safe to suggest that a constant underlying recollection is that of Hanina's reputation for powerful prayer of a mysterious nature which . . . suggests intimate knowledge of the divine action rather than miraculous powers which he himself possessed."

[52] Freyne ("The Charismatic," 243–44) stresses that there is no basis for ascribing

to Ḥanina a wandering charismatic healing ministry or the role of eschatological bringer of salvation ascribed to Jesus in the Gospels.

[53] While Freyne remains skeptical about most of the material in the later Ḥanina-traditions, he seems willing to allow that Ḥanina was active in the Galilean countryside ("The Charismatic," 244). I do not see a sufficient basis for this historical judgment. Here I agree with Crossan (*The Historical Jesus*, 157), who observes that the evidence for placing Ḥoni and Ḥanina in Galilee "is very doubtful."

[54] For the question of similarities yet differences between the Qumran documents and the exorcisms in the Synoptic Gospels, see Kirchschläger, "Exorzismus in Qumran?" 135–53.

[55] For books and articles on the miraculous in Josephus, see Louis H. Feldman, *Josephus and Modern Scholarship (1937–80)* (Berlin/New York: de Gruyter, 1984); the bibliography for "demons" is found on p. 429, "magic" on pp. 429–30, "dreams" on p. 430, and "miracles" on pp. 477–80. On pp. 478–80 the ever-reliable Feldman gives a synopsis and critique of major works on miracles in Josephus. Important articles on the subject include Gerhard Delling, "Josephus und das Wunderbare," *NovT* 2 (1958) 291–309; George MacRae, "Miracle in *The Antiquities* of Josephus," in C. F. D. Moule (ed.), *Miracles. Cambridge Studies in Their Philosophy and History* (London: Mowbray, 1965) 129–47; H. R. Moehring, "Rationalization of Miracles in the Writings of Flavius Josephus," *Studia Evangelica Vol. VI* (TU 112; ed. Elizabeth A. Livingstone; Berlin: Akademie, 1973) 376–83; Otto Betz, "Das Problem des Wunders bei Flavius Josephus im Vergleich zum Wunderproblem bei den Rabbinen und im Johannesevangelium," *Josephus-Studien. Untersuchungen zu Josephus, dem antiken Judentum, und dem Neuen Testament* (Otto Michel Festschrift; ed. Otto Betz, Klaus Haacker, and Martin Hengel; Göttingen: Vandenhoeck & Ruprecht, 1974) 23–44; Karl Heinrich Rengstorf, "*sēmeion*, etc.," *TDNT* 7 (1971) 200–269, esp. 223–25; idem, "*teras*," *TDNT* 8 (1972) 113–26, esp. 121–22. Feldman (*Josephus and Modern Scholarship*, 479) considers MacRae's article "the most satisfactory treatment of the subject."

[56] On the question of prophecy in Josephus, see Louis H. Feldman, "Prophets and Prophecy in Josephus," *JTS* 41 (1990) 386–422.

[57] When MacRae ("Miracle," 132) touches on "prophecy, dreams, omens, apparitions of the dead, and the like, experienced by pagans as well as by Jews, which are intended to reveal the future to men," he claims that Josephus does not regard them "as miracles . . . but rather as part of the normal processes by which God governs the world." On Josephus' treatment of portents in relation to the fall of Jerusalem in A.D. 70, see S. V. McCasland, "Portents in Josephus and in the Gospels," *JBL* 51 (1932) 323–35.

[58] On possible Sadducean influences on Josephus' treatment of miracles (e.g., his restraint in speaking of angels, especially outside of OT narratives that he recounts), see Delling, "Josephus und das Wunderbare," 308–9.

[59] Both of the two great cultural influences can be felt in the *Proemium* to *The Antiquities*.

[60] So emphatically Delling, "Josephus und das Wunderbare," 294–96.

[61] On this see Delling, "Josephus und das Wunderbare," 296–98; Betz, "Das Problem des Wunders," 27–30.

[62] Betz ("Das Problem des Wunders," 28) distinguishes in Josephus between a miracle performed to answer a prayer that God rescue believers in danger or need (e.g., at

the Red Sea) and the miracle that is properly called a "sign." The latter is usually not requested but is rather performed in accordance with God's command, even for those who do not want it (e.g., Pharaoh in the contest between Moses and the Egyptian magicians). Even though seen, the miraculous sign must be believed because it points forward to a saving event still in the future, which alone will fully confirm the sign given in the present (p. 31). The sign thus provokes a division in the audience between believers and unbelievers. One can see why Betz treats the Fourth Gospel's concept of "sign" in this same article (pp. 34–44).

The "sign" regularly has a legitimizing function for the prophet who performs it (so Moses before Pharaoh). Hence Josephus does not use *sēmeion* for Elijah and Elisha (so Betz, "Das Problem des Wunders," 30). This emphasis on the legitimizing function of the sign may reflect Josephus' preoccupation with the "false prophets" who promised signs to the Jews in the decades before the catastrophe of A.D. 70.

[63] On the distinctive vocabulary of Josephus for miracles (especially his use of *epiphaneia*), see MacRae, "Miracle," 142–47; and Rengstorf, "*sēmeion*, etc.," 223–25. Betz ("Das Problem des Wunders," 26) emphasizes how for Josephus a miracle manifests God's powerful and providential guidance of history. The emphasis on divine providence *(pronoia)* probably reflects Stoic influence as mediated through Hellenistic Judaism of the Diaspora. Significantly, in a single sentence in his *Life* (2 §12), Josephus both affirms his adherence to the Pharisaic movement from his nineteenth year and compares the Pharisees to the Stoics. On this see Feldman, *Josephus and Modern Scholarship*, 479.

[64] On this see Moehring, "Rationalization of Miracles," 377.

[65] Betz suggests this link between the rabbis and Josephus in his "Das Problem des Wunders," 24–25. For Betz, the definition of a genuine "sign" for Josephus is that it participates in God's power and in his plan that directs history (p. 29). The truth of such a sign is ultimately confirmed in the future events toward which it pointed. On the relation between prayer and miracles and on human beings as merely God's instruments in performing miracles, see Delling, "Josephus und das Wunderbare," 298, 308.

[66] I purposely include the restriction "as far as one can tell from his written affirmations," since it is obviously impossible to know the innermost religious thoughts of Josephus, who was nothing if not a survivor who had survived more than once through dissembling. It is in this sense that I agree with the judgment of Grant, *Miracle and Natural Law*, 184: "Of course, in view of Josephus' frequent employment of the technique of the Hellenistic romance we cannot be entirely certain that he actually accepted any of these [miracle] stories as true. On the other hand, no evidence exists which definitively proves that he rejected them."

[67] See Delling, "Josephus und das Wunderbare," 298–301; MacRae, "Miracle," 137; Moehring, "Rationalization of Miracles," 376, 378, 381.

[68] See Moehring, "Rationalization of Miracles," 376.

[69] H. St. John Thackeray (*Josephus. The Man and the Historian* [The Hilda Stich Stroock Lectures; New York: Jewish Institute of Religion, 1929] 57–58) makes a number of questionable assertions about Josephus' "rationalization" of miracles. (1) He affirms that the apparently skeptical formula (e.g., "but in these matters let each person believe what he judges best") not only conforms to the contemporary convention of Greco-Roman historiography (which is certainly true) but more specifically comes from Dionysius of Halicarnassus (historian active in Rome ca. 30–8 B.C.) as Josephus' "immediate model." Shaye J. D. Cohen (*Josephus in Galilee and Rome. His Vita and*

Development as a Historian [Columbia Studies in the Classical Tradition 8; Leiden: Brill, 1979] 39) rejects this claim of Thackeray; Cohen points out that the formula goes back to Herodotus and Thucydides and had long since become a commonplace in Hellenistic-Roman historiography. (2) Thackeray claims that the apparently skeptical formula shows that Josephus did not want to commit himself to a statement that the miracles he narrated were literally true. The evidence I adduce in the main text tells against such a position.

[70] Delling, "Josephus und das Wunderbare," 305–6.

[71] See Betz, "Das Problem des Wunders," 26. Hence Thackeray (*Josephus. The Man and the Historian,* 98) is not correct when he claims that "for miraculous events in the O. T. narrative he [Josephus] *constantly* suggests rationalistic explanations . . ." (emphasis mine). Moehring ("Rationalization of Miracles," 378) tries to prove that some passages in which Josephus at first glance appears to emphasize the miraculous element turn out on closer analysis to be rationalizations too. However, Moehring seems at times to confuse two different things, both of which are present in Josephus: (1) "rationalization" in the sense of reducing the miraculous and (2) the tendency to supply a "sufficient cause" for the startling event, a cause not present in the original biblical story. Sometimes Josephus supplies the latter precisely by heightening the miraculous element. This is not to deny that at times Josephus does use rationalization; but Moehring (p. 381) seems to exaggerate when he states: "Whenever possible, Josephus tries to find a rational explanation for the events." More moderate in his judgment is Feldman (*Josephus and Modern Scholarship,* 478), who corrects the presentation of Delling ("Josephus und das Wunderbare") with the comment: "Josephus, on the whole, tends to downgrade miracles, as we see especially when we compare, for example, his view of Abraham and Moses as talented generals with the rabbinic portraits of these leaders" as prevailing because of God's miraculous assistance.

[72] As Delling ("Josephus und das Wunderbare," 306–7) observes, Josephus, unlike such Alexandrian theologians as Philo, was not interested in the systematic-philosophical understanding of how miracles take place vis-à-vis the laws of nature.

[73] Cohen (*Josephus in Galilee and Rome,* 39) judges: "His [Josephus'] inconsistent attitude towards miracles has been noted already: he can omit, transcribe without comment, transcribe with the apology that every reader should decide for himself on the veracity, or rationalize. . . ." Perhaps we should not be too surprised that Josephus strikes us as ambiguous on miracles; in thought as well as in life Josephus was a very ambiguous man. Then again, he was not the only person, ancient or modern, to be ambivalent about the subject.

[74] See McCasland, "Portents," 323–35.

[75] See the treatment of these "prophets" who were leaders of popular prophetic movements in Richard A. Horsley and John S. Hanson, *Bandits, Prophets, and Messiahs. Popular Movements at the Time of Jesus* (Minneapolis: Seabury/Winston, 1985) 161–72. Moehring ("Rationalization of Miracles," 383) speaks too loosely when he refers to "the way Josephus rejects the miracles claimed on behalf of messianic pretenders like Theudas." First of all, it should be engraved in stone that, apart from the case of Jesus of Nazareth, there is no clear proof in the literature of the Greco-Roman period that any Jew prior to Bar-Kochba (Simon Ben-Kosiba) claimed to be or was generally held by his followers to be the Messiah. Jews like Theudas or the unnamed Egyptian should not have the predicate "messianic" attached to them. Morton Smith surprisingly falls into this mistake ("Prolegomena to a Discussion of Aretalogies, Divine Men, the Gos-

pels and Jesus," *JBL* 90 [1971] 174–99, esp. 180): "From the first century . . . we hear of many messianic prophets in Palestine." Secondly, Moehring's statement could easily be taken to mean that Theudas and those like him performed or claimed to perform miracles and thus were able to entice people to follow them. As far as we know from Josephus, Theudas and leaders like him did not perform or claim to perform miracles prior to the great "eschatological" event they predicted, which obviously was meant to reenact some primordial event in Israel's history, e.g., the exodus, the desert wandering, the crossing of the Jordan, or the capture of Jericho.

[76] On all this, see the comments on Matt 12:28 ‖ Luke 11:20 in Chapter 16.

[77] David Lenz Tiede (*The Charismatic Figure as Miracle Worker* [SBLDS 1; Missoula, MT: Scholars, 1972] 91–92) calls this instance "singular" and "unique." On p. 92 he observes: "But meteorological and zoological prodigies aside such stories of a miracle working ruler are highly exceptional in first century Rome." Tiede suggests that this exceptional case may be tied to its special venue, i.e., Egypt, where there was a particular tradition of a "divine king" with miraculous powers.

[78] See J. C. Rolfe (ed.), *Suetonius* (LCL; 2 vols.; Cambridge, MA: Harvard University; London: Heinemann, 1917) 2. 288 (*Divus Vespasianus* 4 §5): "Percrebruerat Oriente toto vetus et constans opinio esse in fatis ut eo tempore Iudaea profecti rerum potirentur" ("Throughout the whole of the East there had spread an old and persistent belief: destiny had decreed that at that time men coming forth from Judea would seize power [and rule the world]").

[79] See John Nicols, *Vespasian and the Partes Flavianae* (Historia, Einzelschriften 28; Wiesbaden: Steiner, 1978) 71 and n. 15: the god may be the local Ba'al venerated on Mt. Carmel.

[80] P. A. L. Greenhalgh (*The Year of the Four Emperors* [New York: Harper & Row, 1975] 246) comments: "In Alexandria he [Vespasian] was able to make up to some extent for his mortal birth by indicating divine favor through a series of miracles. . . . Such marvels went down very well in the East. For Roman consumption he felt that something more tangible and businesslike was required. . . ." See also Barry Baldwin, *Suetonius* (Amsterdam: Hakkert, 1983) 287.

[81] I place the variations of and additions to the story found in Tacitus in parentheses. For Tacitus' text, see Clifford H. Moore (ed.), *Tacitus* (LCL; 5 vols.; Cambridge, MA: Harvard University; London: Heinemann, 1931–37) 3. 158–61. A third version of the story, which is only a passing reference, is given by Cassius Dio in his *Roman History* 65.8 (written in Greek in the first half of the 3d century A.D.). For the text from Cassius Dio, see Ernest Cary (ed.), *Dio's Roman History* (LCL; 9 vols.; London: Heinemann; New York: Macmillan, 1914–27) 8. 270–71. Cassius Dio agrees with Tacitus in locating the second man's infirmity in his hand rather than in his leg.

[82] Tacitus' account could be read in a straightforward fashion, but a number of commentators consider it ironical and sarcastic. So, e.g., Ronald Syme (*Tacitus* [2 vols.; Oxford: Clarendon, 1958] 1. 206) considers the cure of the two men by Vespasian one concrete example of a stylistic tendency of Tacitus: "Tacitus sometimes resorts to sarcasm or a ferocious humour. . . . Irony is all-pervasive, not only in detail or comment, when a brief phrase quickly discloses some supreme incongruity, but in the setting of whole transactions." Similarly G. E. F. Chilver and G. B. Townend, *A Historical Commentary on Tacitus' Histories IV and V* (Oxford: Clarendon, 1985) 83–84; the authors consider the use of the subjunctive in the verb "ostenderetur" in *Histories* 4.81 ("multa miracula evenere, quis caelestis favor et quaedam in Vespasianum inclinatio numinum

ostenderetur") a sign of Tacitus' ironical attitude toward the two miracles: ". . . certainly the indicative would imply T.'s acceptance of the miracles."

83 For a summary of scholarly views on "divine man" in the 20th century, see Corrington, The "Divine Man," 1–58; cf. Clyde Weber Votaw, The Gospels and Contemporary Biographies in the Greco-Roman World (FBBS 27; ed. John Reumann; Philadelphia: Fortress, 1970, originally 1915); Ludwig Bieler, ΘΕΙΟΣ ANHP. Das Bild des "göttlichen Menschen" in Spätantike und Frühchristentum (2 vols.; Darmstadt: Wissenschaftliche Buchgesellschaft, 1967, originally 1935, 1936); Tiede, The Charismatic Figure; Carl H. Holladay, Theios Aner in Hellenistic-Judaism: A Critique of the Use of This Category in New Testament Christology (SBLDS 40; Missoula, MT: Scholars, 1977) 1–45. For aretalogies see Morton Smith, "Prolegomena to a Discussion of Aretalogies, Divine Men, the Gospels and Jesus," JBL 90 (1971) 174–99; Tiede, The Charismatic Figure, 1–13; Howard C. Kee, "Aretalogy and Gospel," JBL 92 (1973) 402–22.

84 Perhaps the most famous example from the 1970s was Theodore J. Weeden, Sr., Mark—Traditions in Conflict (Philadelphia: Fortress, 1971).

85 On this see Holladay, Theios Aner, 237–42; cf. Moses Hadas and Morton Smith, Heroes and Gods: Spiritual Biographies in Antiquity (New York: Harper & Row, 1965); Helmut Koester, "One Jesus and Four Primitive Gospels," HTR 61 (1968) 203–47, esp. 230–36 on the divine man; Hans Dieter Betz, "Jesus as Divine Man," Jesus and the Historian (Ernest Cadman Colwell Festschrift; ed. F. Thomas Trotter; Philadelphia: Westminster, 1968) 114–33; James M. Robinson and Helmut Koester, Trajectories through Early Christianity (Philadelphia: Fortress, 1971). Notice how the concept of the divine man is introduced in the essays of Koester and Betz with no sense that there is any need to establish its existence in the 1st century A.D.; it is simply taken for granted.

86 See, e.g., Tiede, The Charismatic Figure, 238, 240: "To a large extent, the thrust of this study has been a negative evaluation of the interpretative significance of the generalized portrait of the theios anēr which has been extensively defended by Ludwig Bieler, among others. . . . Even the fact that the whole range of traditions may still be extant for a given figure does not permit the view that a general image which is the sum of its diverse parts is of primary interpretative value for assessing a particular text. The general image may only exist in the mind of the modern scholar who can assemble all of the available traditions about a particular hero and view them together." While stressing the importance of Bieler's work, Smith ("Prolegomena," 191) notes that the author is somewhat careless, the references are sometimes in error, the texts sometimes misinterpreted, and the choice of sources sometimes questionable.

87 Tiede, The Charismatic Figure, 246. Tiede then adds the telling observation: "The image of Jesus as a 'divine man' that Bieler assembled was also a composite portrait, composed of features drawn from all four gospels and other early Christian sources." That in a nutshell is why the "divine man" typology is not useful for the quest of the historical Jesus.

88 Tiede, The Charismatic Figure, 289.

89 Tiede, The Charismatic Figure, 48–49.

90 Tiede, The Charismatic Figure, 99.

91 A point of division between Tiede and Holladay is the proper evaluation of the Jewish apologist Artapanus, who portrays Moses as the great benefactor and bringer of culture to the Egyptians (including the worship of animals!). Artapanus is certainly a more openly syncretistic author than is either Philo or Josephus. Tiede (The Charismatic

Figure, 146–77) points out the miraculous and magical elements in Artapanus' portrait of Moses. Holladay (*Theios Aner,* 199–232) instead stresses that Artapanus never uses the term "divine man," that Artapanus attributes miraculous power to God and his name and not to Moses himself, and that Artapanus shows restraint by having the Egyptians rather than Moses perform the more questionable actions in the narrative (e.g., Moses is deemed worthy of honor befitting a god by the Egyptian priests). One of the problems in this debate is that we have only fragments of Artapanus' work, and so any definitive judgment is difficult, if not impossible.

[92] On the passage in question (*Ant.* 3.7.7 §179–80), see Holladay, *Theios Aner,* 47–102.

[93] Holladay, *Theios Aner,* 104. Not surprisingly, *theios* in Philo shows great elasticity. It can mean "incorporeal," "immortal," or "sinless" (pp. 194–95). Often Philo will use the adjective *theios* as a substitute for the genitive construction *tou theou* ("of God") found in the Septuagint: so, e.g., *ho theios logos* ("the divine word") instead of *ho theou logos* ("the word of God") (pp. 188–89). All the more striking, therefore, is Philo's refusal to substitute "divine man" for the OT's "man of God." Indeed, Philo rarely applies *theios* to an individual human being in any sense. Both his Platonic dualism and his OT creation-faith prevented Philo from thinking that a concrete human being made up of body and soul could ever become truly divine.

[94] With regard to Hellenistic-Jewish authors, Holladay concludes (*Theios Aner,* 236–37): "Our investigation has shown that there is even less reason . . . to use the expression *theios aner* as an equivalent of 'miracle worker.' In none of the four instances where *theios aner* occurs in the sources examined does the expression carry this meaning. Apart from the expression *theios aner* itself, in those passages where 'language of deification' was employed, there was no visible tendency to authenticate such claims by appeals to miracles or miracle traditions." The fact that there was no fixed concept of a "divine man" in the 1st century A.D., especially in Hellenistic Judaism, renders highly questionable the leaps of logic performed by scholars like Smith as he presumes the existence of such a fixed concept ("Prolegomena," 192): "Of course, Jewish Christians identified the divine man as Jesus, put him in a Jewish world, and used him for Jewish purposes, but this does not tell us where they got the divine man." Where indeed?

[95] The abstract noun *theiotēs* ("deity," "divine nature," "divinity") occurs once of God the Creator as revealed in his creation in Rom 1:20. The variant abstract noun *theotēs* occurs of the glorified, "cosmic" Christ in Col 2:9, without any reference to miracle-working. It is perhaps symptomatic of the philological-theological situation in the NT that the three clearest cases of "God" (*theos*) being applied to Christ occur in the context of his preexistence and incarnation (John 1:1,18) and his resurrection (John 20:28), not in the context of the miracles he performs during the public ministry. Even when the adversaries of the Johannine Jesus accuse him of making himself equal to God (John 5:18) after he cures the paralytic in 5:1–9, the precise grounds of the accusation are not the miracle in itself but rather the breaking of the Sabbath that the miracle supposedly entailed (5:16) and Jesus' vindication of his right to act so on the Sabbath (5:17). The situation is similar in the healing of the man born blind in John 9 and the reference back to it in 10:33.

[96] Needless to say, the questions at issue here are not to be decided solely by the presence or absence of the precise phrase "divine man." Yet simply as a matter of fact it is that title that scholars have made the focus of their hypothetical reconstructions and wide-ranging claims about Greco-Roman religious figures in general and the portrait of Jesus in the Gospels in particular. The remarks of Holladay (*Theios aner,* 7) are

apropos here: "The issues arising out of the *theios aner* expression are broader than the term itself, but whatever else the term does it serves as a focal point at which these issues meet; in fact, it acts as a kind of prism into which certain questions can be focused, the resultant diffraction serving to expose more vividly the inner fabric of the questions. . . ."

[97] Even Betz ("Jesus as Divine Man," 128) admits: "In general, we can say with certainty that the historical Jesus did not conceive of himself as a Divine Man in the Hellenistic sense." Betz then goes on, however, to claim that certain traits of Jesus' ministry, if translated into Hellenistic concepts, "would come out as traits characteristic of the Hellenistic Divine Man" (p. 129). For a prime example of the uncritical and unquestioned use of "divine man" to explain both the adversaries of Paul and the supposed critique of miracles in Mark, see Petzke, "Die historische Frage," 199–200.

[98] What follows is a synopsis of the information found in Tiede, *The Charismatic Figure*, 1–13; and Kee, "Aretalogy and Gospel," 402–22.

[99] The Greek text reads *plēson Siōn aretalogias sou;* the Hebrew text reads *ml' sywn 't hwdk.*

[100] The text in question (*Geography* 17.1.17) in the LCL edition of Strabo states that "others [record] the powers [or: powerful deeds] of the oracles there": *alloi de aretas tōn entauthai logiōn.* In the textual note accompanying this reading the editor observes that manuscripts CDF*h* read *aretalogiōn,* manuscript *x* reads *aretologiōn,* and manuscript *i* reads *tetratologiōn.* See Horace Leonard Jones (ed.), *The Geography of Strabo* (LCL; 8 vols.; London: Heinemann; New York: Putnam's Sons, 1932) 8. 64.

[101] In *Satire 15,* line 16, Juvenal says that when Ulysses narrated a tale, he moved some to anger and perhaps others to laughter, "like a lying storyteller" (*ut mendax aretalogus*). For the Latin text and an English translation, see G. G. Ramsay (ed.), *Juvenal and Persius* (LCL; Cambridge, MA: Harvard University; London: Heinemann, 1969) 290.

[102] The Latin text in question (*Augustus* 74) is ". . . interponebat [Augustus] ac frequentius aretalogos" ("[Augustus] frequently introduced [into his dinner parties] tellers of marvelous tales"; see Rolfe (ed.), *Suetonius,* 1. 238–39.

[103] Smith, "Prolegomena," 175.

[104] Smith ("Prolegomena," 195–96) tries to get around the problem by declaring that aretalogy is a case in which a literary genre is defined by its content, not its literary form. Yet Smith himself cannot maintain this dubious claim consistently. On p. 196 he suggests: "The important question is whether or not those literary forms which, because of their distinctive content, modern critics have agreed to call aretalogies, so influenced either Jesus or his followers that many traditions about him, and eventually, the Gospels themselves were automatically cast in similar forms." Realizing, perhaps, that he has naturally slipped back into talking about "forms"—which is what one naturally does when one is talking about literary genres—Smith continues unconvincingly: "Here 'form' is evidently being used in the Platonic sense of 'essential structure' . . . " —whatever that means, which is by no means evident. This is an embarrassing case of damage control. Things become even wilder when Smith proposes that a primitive aretalogy lies behind Mark 1–10, beginning with Jesus' baptism, continuing with his miracles, and ending with his transfiguration, all of which "might have been composed even during Jesus' lifetime" (p. 197).

[105] Tiede, *The Charismatic Figure,* 1. Whether religious "propaganda" is always the

context or intent of an aretalogy may be debated. Sometimes the context may be the joyful celebration of divine power or deeds in the cult of a believing community, without any intention to engage in propaganda or apologetics.

[106] Kee, "Aretalogy and Gospel," 404.

[107] Bauer's *Wöakrterbuch* (6th ed. edited by Kurt and Barbara Aland, col. 213) claims that 2 Pet 1:3 "surely" carries the sense of a manifestation of divine power or a miracle. Even if that be the case, the reference is to the "miracle of grace and faith," not to miracle in the sense that we are using it in this chapter of Jesus' public ministry. However, Frederick W. Danker ("2 Peter 1: A Solemn Decree," *CBQ* 40 [1978] 64–82, esp. 69, 72) has pointed out the echoes of the "benefactor-language" of Hellenistic decrees in 2 Peter; hence he prefers words like "magnanimity," "nobility," "generosity" to translate *aretē* in both v 3 and v 5.

[108] Even Smith ("Prolegomena," 178–79) admits: ". . . the collections of miracle stories which circulated in the Graeco-Roman world do not seem, as *collections*, to have been similar in literary form to the canonical Gospels." Hence Smith appeals to Damis' reported "memoirs" or diary, supposedly lying behind Philostratus' *Life of Apollonius*. If the view espoused above be true, namely, that Damis' diary is an invention of Philostratus, then the lack of real parallels in the 1st century A.D. to the literary genre of the canonical Gospels is all the more striking.

CHAPTER 19

THE HISTORICITY OF JESUS' MIRACLES: THE GLOBAL QUESTION

I. THE GLOBAL QUESTION OF HISTORICITY

At long last we come to the miracles of Jesus as narrated in the Four Gospels. As I emphasized throughout Chapter 17, when it comes to the miracles of Jesus, the focus of my historical quest is—and must be—a narrow one. I do not claim to be able to decide the theological question of whether particular extraordinary deeds done by Jesus were actually miracles, i.e., direct acts of God accomplishing what no ordinary human being could accomplish. As I have indicated, I think that such a judgment ("this particular act is a miracle performed directly by God") goes beyond what any historian can legitimately assert within the limits of his or her own discipline.

Rather, my quest seeks to remain within the realm of what, at least in principle, is verifiable by historical research. Hence I ask: Given the fact of the many miracle stories present in the Four Gospels, are there reasons for thinking that at least the core of some of these stories goes back to the time and ministry of Jesus himself? In other words, did the historical Jesus actually perform certain startling, extraordinary deeds (e.g., supposed healings or exorcisms) that were considered by himself and his audience to be miracles? Or did such reports come entirely from the creative imagination of the early church, as it remembered the deeds of Jesus in the light of such OT figures as Elijah and Elisha and as it proclaimed these deeds in a highly competitive religious "marketplace" that extolled Jewish and pagan miracle-workers? Was it the missionary needs of the early church that created Jesus' miracles and read them back into a miracle-free ministry of the historical Jesus?

Such a scenario was suggested by a number of questers in the 19th century and by some historians of religion in the early 20th century. The judgment of Wilhelm Bousset in his highly influential work *Kyrios Christos*, published in 1913, may stand for many others: "We are still able to see clearly how the earliest tradition of Jesus' life was still relatively free from the miraculous."[1] Actually, such a miracle-free Jesus has been the holy grail sought by many questers from the Enlightenment onwards. It has been reinvented at various times by American thinkers from Thomas Jefferson to present-day popularizers, who share Jefferson's ignorance of historical-critical exegesis but lack his brilliance.[2] That a depiction of Jesus minus miracles runs completely counter to the empirical data in the Gospels makes no difference to a public that enjoys regularly remaking Jesus in its own image and likeness.[3]

Bultmann and his followers were not so uncritical. They did not completely deny the presence of alleged miracles in the ministry of the historical Jesus, but miracles were definitely pushed to the sidelines in their presentations of the Nazarene.[4] It is against the background of this tendency to sweep embarrassing miracles under the Heideggerian rug that the reaction of scholars like Morton Smith and E. P. Sanders can be appreciated. As I have suggested above, many of Smith's claims about "Jesus the magician" are questionable. But Smith and Sanders are certainly correct in censuring an overemphasis on the words of Jesus to the neglect of his striking deeds, including his supposed miracles. Even before we get to the application of the criteria of historicity, the sheer massiveness of the miracle traditions in the Four Gospels makes sweeping them under a respectable modern carpet unacceptable.

It is difficult to give precise statistics on how many separate miracle stories there are in the Gospels, since scholars do not always agree on which pericope should be counted as a separate story and which pericope is just a literary parallel or variant of a story present in another Gospel. At any rate, the numerical overview supplied by David E. Aune gives a good sense of the enormous and all-pervading presence of miracles in the Four Gospels.[5] According to Aune's tally (which does not count parallels separately), there are accounts of six exorcisms, seventeen healings (including three stories of raising the dead), and eight so-called nature miracles (namely, the stilling of the storm, the feeding of the five thousand, the feeding of the four thousand, the walking on the water, the cursing of the fig tree, the coin in the fish's mouth, the miraculous catch of fish, and the changing of water into wine at Cana).[6] Many of these accounts have one or more parallels in other Gospels.

To the full narratives of miracles many other Gospel verses referring to miracles can be added. The Synoptics give a number of summary statements about Jesus' miracle-working, thus creating the impression that many more miracles were performed than are narrated in the text.[7] There are also allusions to individual miracles that are not narrated in full: e.g., we are told only in passing that Jesus cast seven demons out of Mary Magdalene (Luke 8:2; cf. Mark 16:9).[8] In commissioning his disciples, Jesus gives them the power to exorcise and/or heal (Matt 10:1 parr.); other passages mention in passing that the disciples performed or failed to perform miracles (Luke 9:6; 10:17–20; Mark 3:15; 9:18,28,38). In addition to his miracle-working, Jesus demonstrates more-than-human knowledge of the past, present, and future (e.g., John 1:48; Mark 2:8; 14:12–16). Besides all the narrative material, there are various sayings in which Jesus comments on his miraculous activity and indicates its ultimate significance within his overall message and ministry. Finally, the accusation by some of his adversaries that his exorcisms show that he is in league with Beelzebul is a backhanded admission that he performed deeds not easily explained by ordinary human means.

The mere recitation of this catalogue is not meant to be a proof that all of the items listed here are historical. The summary accounts of Jesus' wonder-working activity and various references to his more-than-human knowledge no doubt come from the evangelists, and certain full-length stories may indeed be Christian creations. But the enormous amount of data does serve to give one an initial, healthy suspicion of any attempt to dismiss or play down such a large (and to some academicians embarrassing) corpus of material with an airy wave of the existentialist hand. At first glance, the material seems simply too mammoth and omnipresent in the various strata of the Gospel tradition to be purely the creation of the early church. To move beyond mere general impressions, though, we must apply the criteria of historicity to the miracle traditions.[9]

II. THE CRITERIA OF HISTORICITY AND THE GLOBAL QUESTION

Before employing the criteria on individual narratives or sayings, we should first apply them to the miracle traditions of the Gospel taken as a whole to answer the global question: Did the historical Jesus perform extraordinary deeds deemed by his contemporaries as well as by himself to be miracles? As we shall see, the criteria of multiple attestation and coherence will be of pivotal importance in providing an answer to this question, while the other criteria will simply give secondary support.

(1) The single most important criterion in the investigation of Jesus' miracles is the criterion of *multiple attestation of sources and forms.* (a) As for multiple *sources,* the evidence is overwhelming. Every Gospel source (Mark, Q, M, L, and John), every evangelist in his redactional summaries, and Josephus to boot affirm the miracle-working activity of Jesus.[10] Indeed, each Gospel source does so more than once, and some do it repeatedly.

To take Mark as a prime example: by Alan Richardson's count, some 209 verses of a total 666 (counting up through Mark 16:8) deal directly or indirectly with miracles.[11] That is a little over 31 percent of the total material in the Gospel. Indeed, if one takes just the first ten chapters of the Gospel (i.e., omitting the Passion Narrative in the broad sense of the term), some 200 out of 425 verses deal directly or indirectly with miracles, in other words, 47 percent.[12]

Mark apparently inherited miracle stories from many different streams of first-generation Christian tradition.[13] We find blocks of miracle stories (e.g., the stilling of the storm, the exorcism of the Gerasene demoniac, and the raising of the daughter of Jairus with the healing of the woman with the hemorrhage in 4:35–5:43), individual miracle stories surrounded by other types of material (e.g., the demoniac boy in 9:14–29), miracle stories embedded in larger cycles of stories (e.g., the two multiplications of loaves within the so-called "bread section" of Mark [6:7–8:21]),[14] and individual miracles perhaps already embedded in a primitive pre-Marcan passion tradition (e.g., the healing of the blind Bartimaeus in 10:46–52; the cursing of the fig tree in 11:12–14,20–25).

The style and tone of the miracle stories are hardly uniform. Some of the narratives are remarkably long and circumstantial (e.g., the Gerasene demoniac, the demoniac boy); others are quite laconic (e.g., the healing of Simon Peter's mother-in-law in 1:30–31). A few give names of persons and places (Jairus, who asks that his sick daughter be healed; Bartimaeus, the blind beggar near Jericho), but the majority name neither the petitioner(s) nor the beneficiary nor the exact location of the miracle. Mark also includes displays of Jesus' miraculous knowledge (e.g., the prediction of future events and the end of the world throughout chap. 13; the prediction of the betrayal by Judas and the denial by Peter in 14:18–21,29–31).

Although Mark contains much less discourse material than Matthew, Luke, or John, he does at times present Jesus speaking about miracles: the Beelzebul dispute (3:20–30), the commissioning of his disciples to perform cures and exorcisms (6:7,13), and the question about the exorcist who uses Jesus' name although he is not a disciple (9:38–40). When one looks at this vast array of disparate streams of miracle traditions in the first Christian generation, some already grouped in collections, some still stray bits of material, Mark alone—writing as he does at the end of the first Christian generation—constitutes a fair refutation of the idea that the miracle traditions were totally the creation of the early church after Jesus' death.

Mark, however, does not stand alone in his testimony to the Gospel miracle tradition. Quite different in form and content from Mark is the Q tradition, which is made up almost entirely of sayings. But even Q contains one miracle story, the healing of the centurion's servant (Matt 8:5–13 par.), which has a distant parallel in the story of the healing of the royal official's son in John 4:46–54. Various sayings of Jesus also testify to Q's knowledge of his miracles: e.g., the references to exorcism in the Beelzebul dispute (Matt 12:22–32 par.), the list of various miracles (notably omitting exorcisms) in Jesus' reply to the Baptist (Matt 11:5–6 par.), and the woes spoken against the cities of Galilee that did not believe Jesus despite his miracles (Matt 11:20–24 par.). Given its great emphasis on eschatological prophecy, Q, not surprisingly, highlights Jesus' knowledge of the future in various eschatological prophecies and parables. The Q version of the missionary discourse shows Jesus commissioning his disciples to perform miracles in imitation of his own ministry (Matt 10:8 ‖ Luke 10:9).[15]

The special traditions of both Matthew and Luke likewise know of miracles performed by Jesus during his public ministry.[16] Miracles unique to Matthew are relatively few: e.g., Peter finding the coin in the mouth of the fish (Matt

17:27) and Peter walking on the water (Matt 14:28–31).[17] The special Lucan tradition has notably more examples: the miraculous catch of fish (5:1–11; cf. John 21:1–14), the raising of the widow's son at Nain (7:11–17), the exorcism of seven demons from Mary Magdalene and the healing of other women (8:2–3; cf. Mark 16:9), the healing of the bent-over woman (13:10–17), the healing of the man with dropsy (14:1–6), the cleansing of the ten lepers (17:11–19), and perhaps Jesus' escape from his murderous townspeople (4:29–30).

Since I judge John's Gospel to be literarily independent of the Synoptics, his distinct miracle tradition must be given separate treatment as an important witness. Most of the same types of miracle stories are present, some with parallels in the Synoptics: healings, including a healing from a distance (the royal official's son), raising the dead (Lazarus), and nature miracles (multiplication of loaves, walking on the water, changing water into wine). Exorcisms, however, are remarkably absent, perhaps because of John's particular theological outlook.[18] John's theological outlook also dictates that the miracles with parallels in the Synoptics become even more massive and overwhelming (e.g., healing a man who was *born* blind; raising Lazarus after he has been in the tomb for four days). John's high christology also emphasizes Jesus' miraculous knowledge of the past, present, and future, as well as his corresponding ability to control both conversations and the flow of events (notably in the Passion Narrative).

Yet despite the strong Johannine language and theology that pervade the miracle stories of the Fourth Gospel, source and form criticism indicate that behind the present Gospel pericopes lie earlier, more primitive forms of the miracle stories.[19] Indeed, some of the miracle stories have preserved the basic length and form that their parallels have in the Synoptics: e.g., the healing of the royal official's son, the multiplication of loaves, and the walking on the water. In other words, John's miracle stories were not created out of whole cloth by the Evangelist, as the stories that have a parallel in Mark or Q clearly demonstrate.[20]

Finally, there is the independent attestation of Josephus in the authentic core of his *Testimonium Flavianum* (*Ant.* 18:3.3 §63–64): "At this time [i.e., the rule of Pontius Pilate as prefect of Judea] there appeared Jesus, a wise man. For he was a doer of startling deeds, a teacher of people who receive the truth with pleasure. And he gained a following both among many Jews and among many of Gentile origin." As we saw in Volume One,[21] there is a careful development of thought in this presentation. Josephus first gives Jesus the generic title of "wise man" (*sophos anēr*). Then he unpacks that title by enumerating what would be its major components in the eyes of a Greco-Roman audience: (1) Jesus worked "startling deeds" (*paradoxa*), a word Josephus also uses of the miracles worked by the prophet Elisha (*Ant.* 9.7.6 §182).[22] (2) Jesus taught people who were searching for the truth. (3) Jesus' miraculous deeds and powerful teaching attracted a large following of both Jews and Gentiles. In short, Jesus was a charismatic leader whose special powers of miracle-working and teaching were acknowledged and ratified by his followers. Apart from the idea of attracting many Gentiles during his lifetime, this bundle of assertions gives exactly the same configuration of Jesus' ministry as do the Gospels. Rarely does attestation of Gospel tradition by multiple literary witnesses reach out to encompass so many different sources, including a non-Christian one. But such is the case here, and the attestation includes a reference to Jesus' alleged miracles.

(b) As our inventory of sources has already revealed, the multiple attestation of Jesus' miracles involves not only multiple sources but also *multiple literary forms*. The narratives comprise three major literary forms: exorcisms, healings (including stories of raising the dead), and nature miracles.[23] Alongside these narratives and the evangelists' summary statements about miracles stand various references to miracles in the sayings tradition. These sayings about miracles reflect in turn a number of different form-critical categories: e.g., the parable of the strong man (Mark 3:27 parr.); the dispute story in which Jesus answers the charge of being in league with Beelzebul with two conditional sentences (Matt 12:27–28 parr.), one a rhetorical question, the other a declaration of fact; Jesus' mandate to his disciples within the missionary discourse to heal and exorcise (Mark 6:7,13; Luke 10:9 par.); sayings that display Jesus' miraculous knowledge of past, present, and future (John 4:17–18,21; 2:23–25); general biographical statements that summarize his own activity in terms of miracle-working (Luke 13:32; Matt 11:5–6 par.), and his instruction concerning the exorcist who is not one of his disciples (Mark 9:38–40).

In short, multiple sources intertwine with multiple forms to give abundant testimony that the historical Jesus performed deeds deemed by himself and others to be miracles. If the multiple attestation of sources and forms does not produce reliable results here, it should be dropped as a criterion of historicity. For hardly any other type of Gospel material enjoys greater multiple attestation than do Jesus' miracles.

(2) The multiple attestation of both sources and forms, of both narratives and sayings, naturally leads to the next criterion: *coherence*. Our initial inventory of narratives and sayings has made it clear that we have here a grand example of various actions and sayings of Jesus converging, meshing, and mutually supporting each other. For instance, the various narratives of exorcisms cry out for some explanation. What do these strange events mean within the larger context of Jesus' ministry? In the sayings material of both Mark and Q the answer is given. The exorcisms are dramatic presentations and partial realizations of God's eschatological triumph over Satan and the powers of evil through the actions of Jesus. They are a preliminary experience of the future kingdom of God, already present and victorious to some degree in Jesus' ministry (Mark 3:27 parr.; Luke 11:20 par.). Similarly, the various narratives of healing, especially prominent in the Marcan and the special L traditions, receive their interpretation in a Q saying, Jesus' response to the Baptist: the miracles fulfill the prophecies of Isaiah concerning the time of Israel's definitive salvation. Hence they are also an implicit call to believe in the message

and mission of the miracle-worker (Matt 11:5–6 par.). If we turn to John's Gospel, we see a similar pattern, though the material there is often quite different. Even though the symbolic "signs" (i.e., miracles) and the lengthy discourses in the Fourth Gospel may come at least in part from different Johannine sources, certain discourses comment perfectly on certain signs (e.g., the bread of life discourse in 6:34–51 vis-à-vis the multiplication of loaves in 6:1–15).

What is remarkable in all this is how deeds and sayings cut across different sources and form-critical categories to create a meaningful whole. This neat, elegant, and unforced "fit" of the deeds and sayings of Jesus, coming from many different sources, argues eloquently for a basic historical fact: Jesus did perform deeds that he and some of his contemporaries considered miracles.

The argument from coherence may be approached from another angle as well, namely, the success of Jesus in gaining large numbers of followers. All Four Gospels as well as Josephus speak of the large following that Jesus attracted, and all Four Gospels agree with Josephus in identifying the powerful combination of miracles and teaching as the cause of the attraction. Morton Smith was right to emphasize Jesus' miracles as a major reason why so many people flocked to him,[24] though he was wrong to play down or ignore the power of Jesus' teachings to draw people as well. In this, Smith seems to have momentarily overlooked the case of John the Baptist. After all, John the Baptist was able to attract many followers simply by his fiery eschatological preaching and his special rite of baptism, without the added support of miracles.

Yet there was a notable difference between the long-term impact of the Baptist and that of Jesus. After the Baptist's death, his followers did not continue to grow into a religious movement that in due time swept the Greco-Roman world. Followers remained, revering the Baptist's memory and practices. But by the early 2d century A.D. any cohesive group that could have claimed an organic connection with the historical Baptist seems to have passed from the scene. In contrast, the movement that had begun to sprout up around the historical Jesus continued to grow—amid many sea changes—throughout the 1st century and beyond. Not entirely by coincidence, the post-Easter "Jesus movement" claimed the same sort of ability to work miracles that Jesus had claimed for himself during his lifetime. This continued claim to work miracles may help to explain the continued growth, instead of a tapering off, of the group that emerged from Jesus' ministry. In short, while miracles are not strictly necessary to explain the success of Jesus in attracting many followers, his execution at the hands of Pilate, and the ongoing success of the church in attracting more followers, the presence of the miraculous in the mission of both Jesus and the early church coheres well with Jesus' temporary and the church's permanent success.

(3) As we might expect from all that we saw in the section on miracles and ancient minds, the criterion of *discontinuity* is useful only to a very limited degree. In the Greco-Roman world, there were many traditions about miracles

in both pagan and Jewish literature. Hence the bare idea that Jesus worked miracles is hardly discontinuous with surrounding pagan and Jewish culture.

Yet some aspects of the Gospel miracle traditions do stand out as unusual, not to say unique. (For substantiation of what I say here, see the excursus at the end of Chapter 18.) First of all, the early dating of the literary testimony to Jesus' miracles, i.e., the closeness of the dates of the written documents to the alleged miracles of Jesus' life, is almost unparalleled for the period. The common opinion of scholars places the writing of both Mark and the hypothetical Q document somewhere around A.D. 70. Thus, only about 40 years separates the supposed events from their being fixed in writing.

By way of comparison, we know very little about the 1st-century pagan miracle-worker Apollonius of Tyana prior to the writing of his biography by Philostratus in the early 3d century. To complicate matters further, the question of whether Philostratus had access to a firsthand source as he claimed (i.e., the diary of Damis, a disciple of Apollonius) or whether Philostratus simply created a good deal of the material himself is still debated by scholars. As I indicate in the excursus, invention by Philostratus seems the more likely solution.

Likewise, Jewish holy men (*ḥăsîdîm*) from Galilee, like Honi the Circle-Drawer and Hanina ben-Dosa, have miracles attributed to them in the rabbinic literature. Thus, they might supply intriguing parallels to traditions of Jesus as a Galilean holy man and miracle-worker. Such, at least, has been the contention of scholars like Vermes and Crossan. The problem is that such holy miracle-workers are only fleetingly mentioned in the Mishna, the earliest rabbinic corpus, which was written some 200 years after Honi lived.[25] No indication that these holy men came from Galilee exists in the earliest stages of the traditions. The traditions then develop further into the Talmuds (5th–6th centuries), but the historical value of these later traditions is extremely doubtful.

Moreover, the nature of these stories in the rabbinic sources is notably different from the miracle stories in the Gospels. The usual rabbinic context is that a holy man is asked to pray for some blessing (e.g., rain or a healing). His prayers are then regularly or infallibly answered.[26] This is not exactly the same thing as Jesus curing diseases, exorcising demons, raising the dead, or calming a storm with a mere word or touch. In other words, in the earliest rabbinic traditions, Honi and Hanina are not, strictly speaking, miracle-*workers*. Then, too, the emphasis on faith (e.g., "your faith has saved you"), which is found in many Gospel miracle stories of healing or exorcism or in their larger context, is for the most part lacking in pagan or Jewish parallels.[27]

Still more to the point: the overall configuration, pattern, or *Gestalt* of Jesus as popular preacher and teller of parables, *plus* authoritative interpreter of the Law and teacher of morality, *plus* proclaimer and realizer of the eschatological kingdom of God, *plus* miracle-worker actualizing his own proclamation has no adequate parallel in either the pagan or the Jewish literature of the time. As I have already suggested, when the prickly question of the "uniqueness" of Jesus is raised, his uniqueness is best discussed not in terms of any individual aspect of his ministry taken in isolation but rather in terms of the total configuration of his words and deeds. If the criterion of discontinuity applies at all to the miracles of Jesus, it is only in this larger context or configuration.

It should be noted that a few Greco-Roman writers do stand fairly close to at least some of the supposedly miraculous events they narrate: Josephus, Suetonius, and Tacitus. In none of their works, though, do these authors focus upon any one miracle-worker for an extensive narrative of his miracle-working activity. For instance, Josephus recounts all sorts of miracles, prodigies, portents, and prophecies in his voluminous writings. Yet, when dealing with the 1st century A.D., there is no detailed treatment of any one miracle-worker's career. In particular, one should observe that the various Jewish "sign prophets" who gather followers in Palestine with promises of deliverance and who therefore call Rome's wrath down upon their heads, are said by Josephus to promise their supporters signs and wonders in the near future. Josephus never says that the sign prophets themselves actually perform such signs before the Roman authorities intervene.

As for Suetonius and Tacitus, their most famous narrative of miracle-working is the half-humorous account of Vespasian in Alexandria, as he is journeying back to Rome to assume the role of emperor. Vespasian is asked by a blind man and a man with a maimed foot (or hand) to heal them both. At first Vespasian refuses, but after consultation with his entourage and with doctors, who hold out some hope for a cure in both cases, Vespasian finally decides to give it "the old college try." He seems to engage in a sort of Blaise-Pascal wager: he cannot lose anything by the attempt, and he might gain something. The two men are healed. Suetonius and Tacitus seem to tell the whole story with a twinkle in their eyes and smiles on their lips, an attitude probably shared by Vespasian. The whole event looks like a 1st-century equivalent of a "photo opportunity" staged by Vespasian's P.R. team to give the new emperor divine legitimacy—courtesy of the god Serapion, who supposedly commanded the two men to go to Vespasian. Again, both in content and in form, we are far from the miracle traditions of the Four Gospels—to say nothing of the overall pattern of Jesus' ministry, into which his miracles fit.

(4) Like the criterion of discontinuity, the criterion of embarrassment applies only to a very limited degree. The Mark and Q versions of the Beelzebul dispute (Mark 3:20–30; Matt 12:22–32 par.) indicate that at times Jesus' exorcisms exposed him to the charge of being in league with the devil, a charge he proceeds to rebut with various arguments. It seems unlikely that the church would have gone out of its way to create such a story, which places Jesus—to say the least—in an ambiguous light. That the charge was made only on some specific occasion(s) may be reflected in the fact that it is not present in all exorcism stories and is never applied to Jesus' miracles in general.

(5) To what extent does the criterion of Jesus' rejection and execution support the tradition that he was thought to work miracles? To answer that question adequately we will have to wait until we treat the historical problems

surrounding Jesus' arrest, trial(s), and crucifixion.[28] A few general points, though, may be made here. Some scholars look to Jesus' miracles as a major explanation of why he was finally executed.[29] Magic, so the explanation goes, was illegal in the Roman Empire, and so the miracles of Jesus, a nonconformist often in conflict with religious authorities, would naturally take on the air of illegality, a sort of religious banditry that attacked the authority and legitimacy of the Jerusalem priests and their temple. Paul Hollenbach even goes further and combines acritical exegesis with various sociological and psychological theories to maintain that it was Jesus' exorcisms in particular that led the public authorities to consider him dangerous to the status quo and so execute him: ". . . Jesus' first exorcism led inevitably to his crucifixion."[30]

Now, it is true that, in principle, magic was illegal in the Roman Empire. However, what exactly qualified as magic was not spelled out in extensive detail by the laws of the time. In practice, a great deal was left to the discretion of the local magistrates. As a rough rule of thumb one can say that only "black magic," i.e., those secret arts used to harm others, usually would be punished if brought to the attention of the authorities. Those engaged in more benign practices were ordinarily left unmolested.[31] Since the Gospels record no miracle of Jesus that directly harms or punishes a person,[32] indeed since the Gospel miracles are almost entirely beneficent in their effects, it is difficult to see how deeds like healing the sick and freeing people from the power of demons could be considered criminal. The one possible exception, as we have seen, was the practice of exorcism, which caused some Jews—we cannot say historically who or how many—to accuse Jesus of being in league with Beelzebul.

Significantly, when we examine the various traditions of Jesus' trial(s) and the different charges laid against him, there is practically no indication that miracles were the main reason for his condemnation and execution.[33] This is all the more curious, since all the evangelists are at pains to tie their Gospels together as literary works having coherent plots by signaling early on in their stories that Jesus' miracles caused various parties to plot his death (e.g., Mark 3:6; Matt 12:14; more mildly, Luke 6:11; John 5:18, with increasing vehemence throughout the rest of the public ministry).[34] Yet, when we finally do come to the arrest and trial(s) of Jesus, we hear nothing about miracles as a reason for execution. In the various versions of Jesus' trial(s), we hear of some accusations that are more directly christological and possibly Christian (he claims to be the Messiah, the Son of God, the Son of Man [Mark 14:61–62 parr.]), some accusations that are more directly political and aimed at gaining Pilate's attention (he claims to be the King of the Jews and thus a rival to Caesar, he stirs up or corrupts the people by his teaching, he forbids payment of taxes to Caesar [Mark 15:2 parr.; Luke 23:2–3]), and some inquiries that are simply vague (the high priest interrogates Jesus about his teaching and his disciples [John 18:19]). Interestingly, nowhere in the widely varying versions of Jesus' trial(s) and the charges brought against him is there a single explicit word about his miracles.[35]

This has to strike us as very strange after our survey of the massive presence of miracles in each Gospel's picture of Jesus' public ministry and after we have seen that the evangelists themselves assert early on in their stories that certain groups seek Jesus' death because of some miracle he has performed. In a way, there is a curious sense of disconnectedness between a major element of the narrative of the public ministry (i.e., the miracles, at times unleashing plans to kill Jesus) and the accusations against Jesus at his trial(s). Hence, at least at this stage of our inquiry, and simply on the basis of the varying ways in which all Four Gospels describe the trial(s) of Jesus, we can find no evidence suggesting that Jesus' miracles, taken by themselves, constituted the major reason why Jesus was arrested, condemned, and crucified.

In my opinion, though, we should leave open the possibility that the miracles were an "aggravating circumstance" leading to Jesus' death. This is not the place to engage in detailed argumentation about who was involved in Jesus' arrest and trial(s) and why. For the moment, and simply for the sake of argument, I accept as historical the point on which Josephus in his *Testimonium Flavianum* agrees with all Four Gospels (*Ant.* 18.3.3 §64): ". . . Pilate, because of an accusation made [or possibly: an indictment brought] by the leading men among us, condemned him to the cross. . . ." That is to say, Pilate, who as the Roman prefect of the province of Judea had supreme power of life and death over provincials, exercised it by crucifying Jesus. He did so after "the leading men [literally: the first men] among us," no doubt the high priest and other officials around him, including perhaps some of the lay aristocrats, brought some charge or indictment against Jesus to Pilate's attention.

That Joseph Caiaphas the high priest and Pilate the prefect would have worked hand in glove in solving the problem named Jesus is hardly surprising. It was no accident that the remarkably long tenures in office of both rulers roughly coincided: Caiaphas from A.D. 18 to 36 and Pilate from 26 to 36.[36] Caiaphas enjoyed the longest tenure of any Jewish high priest in the 1st century A.D., and Pilate was either the longest or the second-longest ruling prefect of Judea.[37] Their cagey cooperation, beneficial to both rulers if not always to their subjects, was one of the more successful examples of Rome's attempt to govern local populations in the East through their native aristocracies, with ultimate power naturally kept in Roman hands.[38]

But, if Caiaphas and the aristocratic rulers around him in Jerusalem brought accusations against Jesus before Pilate, why did they do so? As opposed to whatever was the wording of the accusation they presented to Pilate (probably something to do with claiming to be "the King of the Jews"), what was the real reason why they found Jesus disturbing and wished to be rid of him? A detailed discussion must be left to a later chapter, but for the moment I would simply offer the following hypothesis.

I think it is a basic mistake to ask what was *the* reason why Caiaphas wanted Jesus arrested and executed. I propose that Jesus was arrested for no one reason but rather for a convergence of reasons. Here we come back to the point I made above: the importance of keeping in mind the total configuration, pattern, or *Gestalt* of Jesus' ministry. The "imploding" reasons that moved Caia-

phas to action no doubt included: Jesus' proclamation that the definitive kingdom of God was soon to come and would put an end to the present state of
affairs in the world in general and Israel in particular, when Israel would be
restored to its glory and reconstituted as the twelve tribes in the end time; his
claim to teach authoritatively the will of God for people's lives, even when this
seemed in individual instances to run counter to provisions in the Law of Moses; his ability to attract a large following, and perhaps his decision to form a
stable inner circle of 12 disciples, representing the 12 patriarchs and the 12
tribes of a restored Israel; his practice of a special rite of baptism to admit
persons into his group of disciples; and his freewheeling personal conduct that
expressed itself in table fellowship with toll collectors and sinners.

Taken together, this was disturbing enough. If one adds to this volatile mix
the likelihood that at least some of Jesus' followers believed him to be descended from King David[39] and that they therefore took him to be the Davidic
Messiah expected by some pious Jews, and if one allows further that Jesus had
at times spoken at least in veiled fashion of his own future role in the eschatological drama, perhaps even using special titles or self-designations, the mix
becomes positively explosive. If one then accepts the basic historicity of the so-
called triumphal entry into Jerusalem (Mark 11:1–11 parr.) and the so-called
cleansing of the temple (actually a prophetic sign of its coming destruction,
Mark 11:15–19 parr.), we have the match set to the barrel of gasoline. If one
proceeds to add to all this the fact that Jesus performed actions deemed to be
miracles, actions meant to be both a partial realization of the coming kingdom
and a legitimation of his claim on Israel, actions that would naturally stir up
great excitement among the people, the miracles would take on—in the eyes
of the aristocratic priest-rulers in Jerusalem—a much more ominous and dangerous coloration than they would have if seen in isolation. I suggest, therefore, that it may have been as an aggravating circumstance rather than as the
major cause that the miracles played a part in leading Jesus to Calvary.

With this, all five primary criteria of authenticity have been canvassed.
When we turn to the secondary criteria, we quickly see that they offer only
spotty support at best. A few points, though, are worth noting. For instance,
while most miracle stories in the Gospels have been schematized and generalized by the time they reach the evangelists and therefore present us with anonymous persons acting in nameless settings, a few of the stories retain traces of
their original Aramaic language and local Palestinian color. For example, two
of the rare cases of Jesus' words being preserved in Aramaic occur in Marcan
miracle stories: *talitha koum* ("little girl, arise"), spoken to the daughter of
Jairus (Mark 5:41), and *ephphatha* ("be opened"), spoken when Jesus heals the
deaf man with a speech impediment (7:34).

Similarly, there are a few exceptions to the general rule that in the full-
length miracle stories the only actors who regularly have names are Jesus and
his closest disciples.[40] Apart from the disciples who belong to the circle of the
Twelve, petitioners and recipients of miracles are usually anonymous. Hence
people like Jairus, the ruler of the synagogue (Mark 5:22), Bartimaeus the blind

beggar on the road from Jericho to Jerusalem (Mark 10:46), and Lazarus of Bethany (John 11:1) stand out in the normally faceless and nameless miracle stories of all Four Gospels. The mentioning of their names is especially remarkable when one considers some of the lengthy, detailed miracle stories, at times with geographical names attached, that do not preserve the name of the recipient of the miracle: e.g., the lengthy stories of the Gerasene demoniac (Mark 5:1–20 parr.), the demoniac boy and his distraught father (Mark 9:14–29 parr.), and the man born blind, who dominates the narrative throughout the whole of John 9. Likewise, it is surprising that petitioners with relatively high social status, e.g., the centurion in Matt 8:5 par. and the royal official in John 4:46, are not mentioned by name, even though the venue of their petitions (Capernaum and Cana respectively) are.

Needless to say, the mere fact of individuals being named does not guarantee the story's historicity; one must allow for legend-building in the Gospel tradition. Indeed, as E. P. Sanders has long since pointed out, one cannot speak globally of *the* tendencies of the Synoptic tradition; tendencies such as lengthening and shortening the tradition, adding or dropping proper names, in fact go in both directions.[41] However, in the very limited compass of the miracle stories of the four canonical Gospels, there does seem to be a pronounced tendency not to preserve proper names of petitioners or recipients except for the twelve disciples. Indeed, what is especially remarkable, in the light of the increase of proper names in later Christian legends, is that no such tendency to add proper names exists in the Synoptic miracle stories as we move from the narratives in Mark to their parallels in Matthew and Luke. Matthew, in particular, tends to omit the names Mark has. Hence one should take seriously the unusual characteristic of the presence of proper names in a few of the Gospel miracle stories.

For instance, in the Synoptic Gospels, the only individual who is directly named as the petitioner for a healing or exorcism of another person is Jairus, "one of the rulers of the synagogue" (Mark 5:22).[42] The fact that "one of the rulers of the synagogue" (*heis tōn archisynagōgōn*) is put in such a favorable light may itself be significant. Matthew, for whom "the synagogue" has come to represent the Jewish adversaries of the Christian church, pointedly drops not only the petitioner's proper name but also his specific office; he becomes simply and vaguely "a ruler" (*archōn heis*, Matt 9:18).[43] Mark, and apparently the tradition before him, as yet felt no difficulty in presenting a leader of a synagogue, known by name, who requests and receives a particularly astounding miracle from Jesus.

To move from petitioner to beneficiary: Bartimaeus is the only recipient of a healing or exorcism in the full-length miracle stories of the Synoptics who is directly named. As a matter of fact, he also represents the rare conjunction of a personal name and a place name (Jericho, which Jesus has just left as he travels up to Jerusalem for the fateful Passover of his death). The conjunction of personal name, place name, and at least a rough time designation (near the Passover of Jesus' death) is otherwise unheard of in the Synoptic miracle stories. The only miracle story in John's Gospel that is similar in this respect is the raising of Lazarus, where the recipient (Lazarus), the petitioners (Martha and Mary), the place (Bethany), and the time (roughly close to the Passover of Jesus' death) are all indicated. With this one exception, the miracle stories in John are as anonymous (especially with regard to the name of the beneficiary) as most of the Synoptic examples.[44] All in all, then, there is an amazing scarcity of personal names in the Gospels' miracle stories, even when the narratives are otherwise lengthy and detailed. Thus, the few times the name of a petitioner or recipient of a miracle is mentioned may point to a historical remembrance. But at best this is a secondary and supporting criterion; no argument for historicity can be built on it alone.

III. CONCLUSION TO THE GLOBAL QUESTION

To sum up: the historical fact that Jesus performed extraordinary deeds deemed by himself and others to be miracles is supported most impressively by the criterion of multiple attestation of sources and forms and the criterion of coherence. The miracle traditions about Jesus' public ministry are already so widely attested in various sources and literary forms by the end of the first Christian generation that total fabrication by the early church is, practically speaking, impossible. Other literary sources from the second and third generation—M, L, John, and Josephus—only confirm this impression. The criterion of coherence likewise supports historicity; the neat fit between the words and deeds of Jesus emanating from many different sources is striking.

In contrast, the other primary criteria (discontinuity, embarrassment, rejection and execution) supply at best only partial or weak arguments. Similarly, the secondary criteria of Aramaic usage, Palestinian color, and tendencies of the miracle tradition within the Four Gospels give at best only "after-the-fact" support. That is to say, granted the weighty and convincing evidence from the criteria of multiple attestation and coherence, the other criteria all point in the same direction of historicity. Put negatively, none of the other criteria runs counter to the two decisive criteria; all give at least weak backing.

The curious upshot of our investigation is that, viewed globally, the tradition of Jesus' miracles is more firmly supported by the criteria of historicity than are a number of other well-known and often readily accepted traditions about his life and ministry (e.g., his status as a carpenter, his use of 'abbā' in prayer, his own prayer in Gethsemane before his arrest). Put dramatically but with not too much exaggeration: if the miracle tradition from Jesus' public ministry were to be rejected *in toto* as unhistorical, so should every other Gospel tradition about him. For if the criteria of historicity do not work in the case of the miracle tradition, where multiple attestation is so massive and coherence so impressive, there is no reason to expect them to work elsewhere.

The quest would simply have to be abandoned. Needless to say, that is not the conclusion we have reached here.

Having answered the global question of historicity, we now turn to the much more difficult question: the historicity (in the modest sense defined above) of all the individual miracle stories in the Four Gospels.

NOTES TO CHAPTER 19

[1] Bousset, *Kyrios Christos*, 98.

[2] The first printed edition of the fuller compilation of Jefferson's excerpts from the Four Gospels was Thomas Jefferson, *The Life and Morals of Jesus of Nazareth* (Washington, DC: Government Printing Office, 1904). The edition has a short introduction to the history of the work by Cyrus Adler. For present-day research, though, one should go to Dickinson W. Adams (ed.), *Jefferson's Extracts from the Gospels. "The Philosophy of Jesus" and "The Life and Morals of Jesus"* (Princeton: Princeton University, 1983). In his helpful introduction (pp. 3–42), Dickinson points out that many people confuse two different works of Jefferson, his earlier and shorter "The Philosophy of Jesus," compiled in 1804, and the later and more elaborate "The Life and Morals of Jesus," written in 1819–1820. The first compilation, "The Philosophy of Jesus," has unfortunately disappeared, though Dickinson is able from various sources to offer a hypothetical reconstruction on pp. 60–105. It focused on the moral precepts of Jesus, while the longer cento, "The Life and Morals of Jesus," "gives attention to the details of his career as well as of his doctrine" (p. 30). One guiding principle of both compilations— witnessing to the heavy influence of Enlightenment rationalism on Jefferson's religious positions—was that all miracles were to be excised. This leads to some decisions about the inclusion or exclusion of material that strike anyone schooled in historical-critical exegesis as curious. In "The Life and Morals of Jesus," for example, parts of the Lucan Infancy Narrative (basically chap. 2) are kept, including the journey to Bethlehem for the census and the visit of the 12-year-old Jesus to the temple, but with all the miraculous elements excluded. Some instances of prophecy apparently did not fall under the ban of the miraculous, since Jesus still prophesies imminent and distant events. Strange to say, we find a passing reference to Jesus' mighty deeds (*dynameis*), which in the language of the Synoptics means his miracles. Sometimes the introduction or "setup" to a miracle is kept, while the miracle itself is omitted (so, e.g., John 9:1–3, the introduction to the healing of the man born blind, with John 10:1, the beginning of the Good Shepherd discourse, immediately following). In a way, it is fitting that in our own day Stephen Mitchell harks back to Jefferson's digest of the Gospels when he presents his own truncated Jesus in *The Gospel According to Jesus. A New Translation and Guide to His Essential Teaching for Believers and Unbelievers* (New York: HarperCollins, 1991). For all the differences between the two—Mitchell's Jesus reflects an intriguing mix of Asian religions and San Francisco Bay Area New Ageism—they both demonstrate what happens/when Jesus is tailored to one's personal wishes and the *Zeitgeist* instead of being studied with the use of historical-critical criteria that allow for some control and check of claims on the level playing field of scholarly investigation.

[3] Blomberg ("Concluding Reflections on Miracles and *Gospel Perspectives*," *Gospel Perspectives. The Miracles of Jesus. Volume 6* [ed. David Wenham and Craig Blomberg; Sheffield: JSOT, 1986] 443–57, esp. 446) thinks that "the nineteenth-century liberal quest for a miracle-free layer of Christian tradition has been all but abandoned." That may indeed be true of responsible exegetes, but some authors are ruled more by the laws of Madison Avenue than by the laws of evidence.

[4] In his early *Jesus and the Word* (originally published in 1926), Bultmann spent some 5 pages (pp. 123–28) out of 154 pages (according to the pagination of the English translation) on "belief in miracles." Actually, little more than a page is devoted to Jesus' performance of miracles. The rest of the section is given over to

Bultmann's theological observations about Jesus' idea of God as remote yet near, the omnipotence of the miracle-working God who is nevertheless always active in the everyday world, and universally valid propositions about God versus God's omnipotence as "I experience this power in my own life" (p. 126). Thus, most of the treatment is really a mini-treatise of systematic theology in an existentialistic and dialectical mode. Bultmann's depiction of the historical Jesus becomes even more bereft of miracles in the sketch of Jesus' message that opens his *Theology of the New Testament* (2 vols.; London: SCM, 1952, 1955, originally 1948–53) 1. 3–32; there is not even a separate section on the question. One reason for this relative absence of miracles in Bultmann's portraits of Jesus can be seen in the titles of his treatments: *Jesus and the Word* and "The Message of Jesus." The specific deeds of Jesus tend to disappear behind the "naked word" of Jesus' message—which is characteristic of Bultmann's whole theological program.

This tendency to give short shrift to Jesus' miracles is likewise found in post-Bultmannians like Herbert Braun, who in his *Jesus of Nazareth. The Man and His Time* (Philadelphia: Fortress, 1979, originally 1969) devotes some 3 pages (pp. 28–31) out of 137 pages to Jesus' miracles. Hans Conzelmann may have set a record in this regard by dedicating one paragraph (plus scattered passing references) to miracles in his article on Jesus in the 3d edition of *Die Religion in Geschichte und Gegenwart* (1959); the English translation by John Reumann (*Jesus* [Philadelphia: Fortress, 1973]) comes to 96 pages of text (the paragraph on miracles is on p. 55). Even though the "new quest" for the historical Jesus produced a more expansive and confident treatment in Günther Bornkamm's *Jesus of Nazareth* (New York: Harper & Row, 1960, originally 1956), the proportion of pages given over to Jesus' miracles is still remarkably small. There is no separate section that deals with miracles; out of a text of 231 pages, only some 3 pages, within a section on "faith and prayer" (pp. 129–37), treat directly of Jesus' miracles (pp. 130–33). An even more skeptical attitude toward the Gospel tradition of Jesus' miracles can be seen in Gerd Petzke's "Die historische Frage nach den Wundertaten Jesu, dargestellt am Beispiel des Exorzismus Mark. IX. 14–29 par," *NTS* 22 (1975–76) 180–204, esp. 198–204; this attitude stems in turn from his hypercritical approach to the question of the criteria of historicity (pp. 182–84).

It is interesting to note that in this regard Martin Dibelius differed from Bultmann and many of his followers. In the 122 pages of his short sketch *Jesus* (Sammlung Göschen 1130; 4th ed.; ed. Werner Georg Kümmel; Berlin: de Gruyter, 1966, originally 1939), Dibelius dedicates a whole chapter (pp. 62–73) to Jesus' miracles, understood as "signs of the kingdom." One wonders if it is specifically against Bultmann's approach that Dibelius writes: "But, to be sure, he [Jesus] *has* taken action, he has intervened in the realm of illness as in the realm of unrighteousness and has fought against the way this world runs. He has not only spoken of the coming kingdom of God, but he has also brought its promises as well as its demands near to human beings—by his action, by his judgment, admonition, and healing" (p. 72).

[5] One should remember that, at this point in his treatment, Aune is counting not separate historical events but separate literary accounts.

[6] What follows is the full enumeration Aune ("Magic in Early Christianity," 1523–24 nn. 67, 68, and 69) supplies, divided according to traditional form-critical categories (with slight editorial modifications and corrections introduced):
(A) six exorcisms: (1) the demoniac in the synagogue (Mark 1:23–28 ∥ Luke 4:33–37); (2) the Gerasene (or Gadarene) demoniac (Mark 5:1–20 ∥ Matt 8:28–34 ∥

Luke 8:26–39); (3) the daughter of the Syrophoenician (or Canaanite) woman (Mark 7:24–30 || Matt 15:21–28); (4) the demoniac boy and his father (Mark 9:14–29 || Matt 17:14–21 || Luke 9:37–43); (5) the dumb demoniac (Matt 9:32–34); (6) the blind and dumb demoniac (Matt 12:22–23 || Luke 11:14–15; cf. Mark 3:22). Some might count only five exorcisms because they consider Matt 9:32–34 to be simply a redactional variant, a shadowy twin or doublet of Matt 12:22–24.

(B) seventeen healings: (1) Peter's mother-in-law (Mark 1:29–31 || Matt 8:14–15 || Luke 4:38–39); (2) the leper (Mark 1:40–45 || Matt 8:1–4 || Luke 5:12–16); (3) the paralytic (Mark 2:1–12 || Matt 9:1–8 || Luke 5:17–26); (4) the man with the withered hand (Mark 3:1–6 || Matt 12:9–14 || Luke 6:6–11); (5) the daughter of Jairus (Mark 5:21–24,35–43 || Matt 9:18–19,23–26 || Luke 8:40–42,49–56); (6) the woman with the hemorrhage (Mark 5:25–34 || Matt 9:20–22 || Luke 8:43–48); (7) the deaf mute (Mark 7:31–36); (8) the blind man near Bethsaida (Mark 8:22–26); (9) blind Bartimaeus (Mark 10:46–52 || Matt 20:29–34 [cf. the doublet in Matt 9:27–31] || Luke 18:35–43); (10) the young man at Nain (Luke 7:11–17); (11) the woman bent over (Luke 13:10–17); (12) the ten lepers (Luke 17:11–19); (13) the man with dropsy (Luke 14:1–6); (14) the paralytic by the pool (John 5:1–9); (15) the raising of Lazarus (John 11); (16) the man born blind (John 9); (17) the centurion's servant (Matt 8:5–13 || Luke 7:1–10 || John 4:46–54). Some might count John 4:46–54 separately.

(C) eight so-called nature miracles: (1) the stilling of the storm (Mark 4:35–41 || Matt 8:23–27 || Luke 8:22–25); (2) the feeding of the five thousand (Mark 6:32–44 || Matt 14:13–21 || Luke 9:10–17); (3) the feeding of the four thousand (Mark 8:1–10 || Matt 15:32–39); (4) walking on the water (Mark 6:45–52 || Matt 14:22–33 || John 6:16–21); (5) the cursing of the fig tree (Mark 11:12–14,20–26 || Matt 21:18–22); (6) the coin in the fish's mouth (Matt 17:24–27); (7) the miraculous catch of fish (Luke 5:1–11; cf. John 21:1–14); (8) changing water into wine (John 2:1–11).

A number of difficulties are masked by this neat schema. (1) Since Mark and Matthew obviously consider the feeding of the five thousand and the feeding of the four thousand as different events in their narratives, they are counted as separate accounts from a literary point of view. The common opinion is that actually they are variants of the same basic tradition or event, with the two variants perhaps already being enshrined in two parallel cycles of stories prior to Mark. For the position favoring two variants in the pre-Marcan tradition, see Kertelge, *Die Wunder Jesu*, 127–50; Koch, *Die Bedeutung*, 99–112; for the opposite view that the feeding of the five thousand is Mark's redactional composition based on the traditional story of the feeding of the four thousand, see Robert M. Fowler, *Loaves and Fishes* (SBLDS 54; Chico, CA: Scholars, 1981). (2) Another difficulty in counting the miracle stories according to the three traditional categories of form criticism (exorcisms, healings, and nature miracles) is that the redaction of a particular evangelist may move a story from one category to another. For instance, the healing of Simon Peter's mother-in-law belongs to the category of healing miracles in Mark 1:30–31; but Luke's redaction pushes it in the direction of an exorcism (Luke 4:38–39: Simon's mother-in-law was "restrained" or "in the grip of" a high fever; "standing over her, he [Jesus] *rebuked* the fever and it left her"). On this see van der Loos, *The Miracles of Jesus*, 552; Schürmann, *Das Lukasevangelium*, 1. 252; Fitzmyer, *The Gospel According to Luke*, 1. 548. (3) A third difficulty is the problem of where to put accounts of raising the dead. Here they have been counted with healing miracles as extreme examples of healing; that is the form they most clearly re-

semble. But it would be conceivable to place them among nature miracles instead. So as not to complicate this initial overview, for the time being I will leave accounts of raising the dead in the category of healings. However, for the sake of clarity, I will treat the miracles of raising the dead as a distinct category when we come to the detailed analysis of individual narratives. (4) A fourth and massive difficulty is the very validity of the category "nature miracles." As will become clear when this subject is treated in detail, I do not think that "nature miracle" constitutes a valid category. Moreover, at least one of the "miracles" listed in that category is never narrated as such (i.e., the coin in the fish's mouth). Once again, in the main text I accept the traditional classification for the moment so as not to present the reader with too many complications in the initial overview and inventory of Gospel miracles.

⁷ Aune's list ("Magic in Early Christianity," 1524 n. 70) of summaries includes (with some editorial modifications): (1) Mark 1:32–34 ‖ Matt 8:16 ‖ Luke 4:40–41; (2) Mark 1:39 ‖ Matt 4:23–24 [cf. the parallel statement in Matt 9:35]; (3) Mark 3:10–12 ‖ Luke 6:17–19 [cf. Matt 12:15–16]; (4) Mark 6:55–56 ‖ Matt 14:35–36. Since the notices are often very brief, it is difficult at times to know what should be considered the parallel of what.

⁸ Luke 8:2–3 first speaks in general of "some women who had been healed of evil spirits and illnesses." Then the passage mentions in particular "Mary called the Magdalene, from whom seven demons had come forth." Verse 3 then continues: "and Joanna, the wife of Chuza, Herod's steward, and Susanna, and many other [women]. . . ." Presumably Joanna and Susanna had been cured by Jesus, but whether the cure concerned demonic possession or just physical illness is not specified. Also, whether the "many other" women are to be understood likewise as beneficiaries of Jesus' exorcising or healing power is not completely clear from the loose syntax of the text. Fitzmyer (*The Gospel According to Luke*, 1. 697–98) takes the "some" of v 2 and the "many others" of v 3 to refer to the same group of women cured by Jesus, and he is probably right.

It is possible that various references to Jesus' escape from the hostile attacks or intentions of his enemies (e.g., Luke 4:29–30; John 7:44; 8:20) should also be taken as miraculous, but the matter is not clear in the texts.

⁹ See the explanation of the criteria of historicity in *A Marginal Jew*, 1. 167–95.

¹⁰ The reader will notice that certain alleged witnesses are absent from my list: the *True Discourse* (*Alēthēs logos*) of the pagan polemicist Celsus, the Jewish interlocutor in Justin Martyr's *Dialogue with Trypho*, and various passages in the rabbinic literature (the latter two sources are cited as witnesses, e.g., by Mussner, *Die Wunder Jesu*, 29–30). In all these later documents we supposedly find references to Jesus performing miracles, usually in the form of an accusation that he practiced magic. If these accusations represented truly independent testimony about Jesus of Nazareth, they would indeed be useful in an argument from multiple attestation of sources. However, as I argued in Volume One of *A Marginal Jew* (93–98, 223–25), what is said about Jesus in these documents, dating from roughly the middle of the 2d century and later, most probably reflects knowledge of and reaction to the Christian Gospels or Christian oral proclamation. There is no solid evidence that what Celsus or the rabbinic sources say about Jesus goes back by way of an independent stream of tradition to the historical Jesus. Indeed, in the case of the rabbinic texts, scholars have questioned whether the wonder-worker referred to in the passages usually cited was originally Jesus of Nazareth, or whether such an identi-

fication was made secondarily. The failure to take the problem of independent sources seriously greatly weakens the whole argument of Morton Smith in his *Jesus the Magician.*

[11] Richardson, *Miracle-Stories,* 36; similarly, Paul J. Achtemeier, "Person and Deed. Jesus and the Storm-Tossed Sea," *Int* 16 (1962) 169–76, esp. 169.

[12] Even if we adopt the more stringent mode of counting used by Kertelge (*Die Wunder Jesu,* 40), the results are still impressive. Kertelge includes in his count only individual, full-dress narratives of Jesus' miracles occurring during the public ministry in Mark's Gospel. He does not include narratives that have some miraculous features, but are not in his view full-fledged miracle stories (e.g., the finding of the ass for Jesus to ride on as he enters Jerusalem in 11:2–6; the cursing of the fig tree in 11:12–14,20). Granted these restrictions, all the Marcan miracle stories occur in the first ten chapters of the Gospel. They take up 156 verses; if one adds the 13 verses of the summary accounts, two-fifths of Mark 1–10 is made up of miracle stories.

[13] On tradition and redaction in the Marcan miracle stories, see Kertelge, *Die Wunder Jesu,* 45–49; Koch, *Die Bedeutung,* 8–41. While both authors accept the idea of pre-Marcan miracle stories that Mark took over and redacted, Kertelge is more open to the possibility, even probability, of pre-Marcan collections of miracle stories. For instance, he holds that the miracle stories in Mark 4–5 "were probably already transmitted as a unit prior to Mark" (p. 90). In contrast, Koch thinks that sufficient indications of written collections of miracle stories in the pre-Marcan tradition are lacking (pp. 30–39). I find Kertelge's arguments more persuasive. The probability of pre-Marcan collections has received great support from the work of Paul J. Achtemeier; see, e.g., "Toward the Isolation of Pre-Markan Miracle Catenae," *JBL* 89 (1970) 265–91; "The Origin and Function of the Pre-Marcan Miracle Catenae," *JBL* 91 (1972) 198–221; " 'He Taught Them Many Things': Reflections on Marcan Christology," *CBQ* 42 (1980) 465–81.

[14] Mark 6:7–8:21 is called the "bread section" because most pericopes in this section of Mark have at least a passing reference to a loaf or loaves of bread (*artos*), a word that is rare elsewhere in the Gospel. Before the bread section begins, the word for a loaf of bread (*artos*) occurs only in Mark 2:26 and 3:20. Once the bread section begins, *artos* occurs 18 times: 6:8,37,38,41(*bis*),44,52; 7:2,5,27; 8:4,5,6,14(*bis*),16,17,19. After the bread section concludes, *artos* never appears again in Mark's Gospel, with the sole exception of Jesus' symbolic action with the bread at the Last Supper (14:22). The first multiplication of loaves marks the beginning of the bread section, the second multiplication of loaves its center, and Jesus' reminder to the disciples about the two multiplications its conclusion. The strange trait of the constantly repeated *artos* may reflect a mnemonic device in the oral stage of the tradition, though a redactional technique or theological program of Mark cannot be excluded. For the view that the bread section came to Mark in a relatively fixed form (simpler than the redactional forms we have in our Gospels, but with the majority of the pericopes already in their present order), see Lucien Cerfaux, "La section des pains (*Mc* VI,31—VIII,26; *Mt* XIV,13—XVI,12)," *Synoptische Studien* (Alfred Wikenhauser Festschrift; Munich: Zink, 1953) 64–77, esp. 64; cf. Ernst Lohmeyer, *Das Evangelium des Markus* (MeyerK 1/2; 17th ed.; Göttingen: Vandenhoeck & Ruprecht, 1967) 121.

[15] The agreement of Matthew and Luke in joining the two themes of the disciples' performing miracles and their proclaiming the kingdom (Matt 10:7–8 ‖ Luke 10:9) argues for some mention of miracle-working by the disciples in the Q form of the

missionary discourse. Unfortunately, the differences between Matthew and Luke make a sure reconstruction of the Q text difficult. Laufen (*Die Doppelüberlieferungen*, 221–24) argues for the Lucan wording as the original Q form: ". . . and heal the sick in it [i.e., the city you enter] and say to them: 'The kingdom of God has drawn near to you' "; similarly, Schulz, *Q. Die Spruchquelle der Evangelisten*, 406–8. Kloppenborg (*The Formation of Q*, 116) makes the interesting observation: "More importantly, Q [= Luke] 10:9 . . . associate[s] the display of the miraculous with the manifestation of the kingdom"; see also p. 248. A stronger formulation of this insight is given by Sato (*Q und Prophetie*, 312), who notes how Luke 10:9 par. depicts a prophetic symbol that communicates the reality it symbolizes. Those healed are immediately told the eschatological interpretation of their healing: "The kingdom of God has drawn near to you"; similarly, Polag, *Die Christologie der Logienquelle*, 50. See also Boring, *The Continuing Voice of Jesus*, 208–9. Lührmann (*Die Redaktion der Logienquelle*, 59) thinks that Mark's emphasis on exorcisms in the missionary discourse (Mark 6:7,13) is more original than Q's emphasis on healings.

[16] Because our concern is the question of the miracles reputed to have been performed by the historical Jesus during his public ministry, the special traditions of the Infancy Narratives of Matthew and Luke are not considered here.

[17] It may not be totally accidental that some of the miracles unique to Matthew feature Peter, either positively or negatively. I do not include here miracles in Matthew that seem derived not from special tradition but rather from Matthew's redactional activity. For example, the healing of the two blind men in 9:27–31 seems to be a pale reflection of Mark's story of Bartimaeus, which has as its more direct Matthean parallel the healing of two blind men on the road from Jericho to Jerusalem in Matt 19:29–34. Some might prefer to put Peter's walking on the water into this category of Matthean redactional creations.

[18] Two possible reasons for the omission of exorcisms by John are: (1) John's high christology of the eternal Word made flesh would sit uneasily with Jesus engaging in sometimes lengthy battles and negotiations with demons (who, after all, are only minions of Satan, Jesus' true adversary); (2) John's realized eschatology sees Jesus' exaltation and death on the cross as the grand cosmic exorcism that once and for all casts Satan out of the world that he once controlled. Notice the exorcism-language in Jesus' prediction of his death in John 12:21: "Now shall the ruler of this world be cast out (*ekblēthēsetai exō*)."

[19] See, e.g., the different reconstructions of the earlier form(s) of the Lazarus story in Wilhelm Wilkens, "Die Erweckung des Lazarus," *TZ* 15 (1959) 22–39, esp. 25–29; Schnackenburg, *Das Johannesevangelium*, 2. 398–402; W. Nicol, *The Sēmeia in the Fourth Gospel. Tradition and Redaction* (NovTSup 32; Leiden: Brill, 1972) 37–39, 109–10; Werner Stenger, "Die Auferweckung des Lazarus (Joh 11, 1–45). Vorlage und johanneische Redaction," *TTZ* 83 (1974) 17–37, esp. 19–28; Jacob Kremer, *Lazarus. Die Geschichte einer Auferstehung. Text, Wirkungsgeschichte und Botschaft von Joh 11, 1–46* (Stuttgart: KBW, 1985); von Wahlde, *The Earliest Version of John's Gospel*, 116–23; Fortna, *The Fourth Gospel and Its Predecessor*, 94–109. As the reader might expect, these exegetes do not agree among themselves on the exact reconstruction of a pre-Johannine source of the Lazarus story. Kremer (*Lazarus*, 108) in particular remains doubtful about whether the wording of the pre-Johannine source can be abstracted from the present Gospel. But, in a sense, that is not the important point. As Kremer himself goes on to assert (p. 109), there are sufficient indications in the text to affirm that the tradition about Lazarus is not a pure creation of the early church or a historicizing of the parable

of Lazarus and the rich man (Luke 16:19–31), but rather goes back to an extraordinary event that took place during the ministry of Jesus. As we shall see, the one exception to my claim that John has not simply created miracle stories is the first Cana miracle.

[20] That Jesus performed miracles during his public ministry is also affirmed by Peter's missionary sermons in Acts 2:22; 10:38. This may be put down simply to Luke's knowledge of the miracle traditions in Mark, Q, and L. However, those who think that Luke drew upon a special source for the missionary sermons in Acts would see here another independent witness to Jesus' miracle-working activity. Wilckens (*Die Missionsreden der Apostelgeschichte*, 109) thinks that Acts 10:38 is a Lucan composition and does not reflect any source beyond the Third Gospel. Schneider (*Die Apostelgeschichte*, 2. 63), however, judges it most likely that Peter's speech to Cornelius in 10:34–43 reflects a traditional missionary sermon to Jews or at least the basic structure of such a sermon. As for Acts 2:22–23, Wilckens (p. 126) insists that the present formulation and theology is Lucan, but allows that Luke has taken up some traditional motifs. More strongly in favor of pre-Lucan Christian tradition in Acts 2:22 and 10:38 is Mussner, *Die Wunder Jesu*, 31–32 (see the further literature cited there).

[21] *A Marginal Jew*, 1. 56–88, esp. 61–62 and 81.

[22] The word *paradoxa* is used only once in the NT, of the miracle of Jesus' healing of the paralytic in Luke 5:26.

[23] For convenience' sake and for the time being, I retain this traditional division of Gospel miracles into three form-critical categories; this division is used by many scholars, including notably Aune, "Magic in Early Christianity," 1523–24. For the sake of clarity, though, I will treat miracles of raising the dead as a distinct category when we come to the detailed examination of individual pericopes. The whole concept of one category called "nature miracles" will demand further probing when we come to an examination of such miracles in detail.

Bultmann's overall division of miracle stories consists simply of healings and nature miracles, exorcisms being subsumed under the former (*Geschichte*, 223–33). Yet when he comes to listing Jewish and pagan parallels, he uses a fourfold division: exorcisms, "other healings," raising the dead, and nature miracles (ibid., 247–53)—a division that I will adopt for my separate chapters. The same four types, though without a strict enumeration as four, are found in Dibelius's treatment of "tales" (*Novellen*) in his *Die Formgeschichte des Evangeliums*, 66–100. The problems connected with these and other form-critical classifications of the Gospel miracles are discussed by Kertelge, *Die Wunder Jesu*, 40–45. Obviously, no matter what the mode of classification and division adopted, we are dealing to a certain degree with convenient conventions.

A much more exhaustive catalog of "persons" or "characters" (e.g., miracle-worker, sick person), "motifs" (e.g., the coming of the miracle-worker, description of the distress, resistance of the demon, touch of the miracle-worker), and "themes" (form-critical categories for the pericope as a whole) has been drawn up by Theissen in his *Urchristliche Wundergeschichten*, 11–128. He distinguishes six "themes": exorcisms, healings, epiphany (the divinity is seen not simply in his activity or effects but in person; hence, Jesus walking on the water), rescue miracles (e.g., the stilling of the storm), gift miracles (e.g., the feeding of the five thousand, changing water into wine), and rule miracles (miracles that enforce sacred demands, e.g., the healings on the Sabbath and the consequent disputes).

Since my purpose in this chapter is a summary overview of all the Gospel miracles and not a detailed theoretical study in form, redaction, or literary criticism, I do not tarry here over the question of which form-critical categories are best. The three traditional ones will serve our purposes well enough for the moment. As I have indicated, I will sort out miracles of raising the dead as a distinct category when we come to detailed analysis of individual narratives. The question of whether there is such a category as "nature miracles" will be treated when we take up the stories usually lumped under that label. As for the basic grid or form of a miracle story, the generic structure of the miracle stories sketched by Kertelge (*Die Wunder Jesu*, 44) is easily adapted to the details of individual stories: (1) the exposition or setup, i.e., the circumstances that lead up to the miracle (e.g., the description of the desperate situation or pressing need, the request for help or healing, the approach of Jesus or the petitioner, the audience); (2) the intervention of the miracle-worker (usually a word, sometimes a touch or other gesture), along with attestation and confirmation of the miracle; (3) the result of the miracle, often expressed in terms of the impression made on bystanders (e.g., astonishment, bewilderment, a "choral conclusion" of praise) and/or the spread of the report of the miracle and Jesus' fame. In some stories, the confirmation of the miracle seems to belong instead to the third part.

[24] See, e.g., Smith, *Jesus the Magician*, 8–20.

[25] Vögtle ("The Miracles of Jesus," 97–98) remarks on the stories of Jewish miracle-workers of the Roman period: "It must be said that apart from practices connected with exorcism . . . we hear next to nothing of miracle workers and specific miracle stories from Jewish Palestine in the time of Jesus and his disciples. Jewish tradition first tells of scribes who perform miracles from the period around A.D. 70 onwards and especially in the second and subsequent centuries." Even here, one may question whether it is best to speak of "*scribes* who *perform* miracles . . ." (emphasis mine). For the reasons for questioning this phrasing, see the excursus at the end of Chapter 18.

[26] Vögtle ("The Miracles of Jesus," 99) comments on the rabbinic miracles: ". . . perhaps more striking still, the supposed miracles such as healings, raisings of the dead, and punishment miracles are regarded as answers to prayer or else as the results of occult knowledge and complicated magical practices. This can be seen particularly in charms uttered over the sick-bed and in exorcisms."

[27] See the remarks of Perrin (*Rediscovering the Teaching of Jesus*, 130–42) and his comparison of the Gospel miracle stories with pagan and Jewish parallels. Speaking of the pagan Hellenistic miracle stories, Perrin remarks that the use of "faith" in the Gospel miracle stories "is not only completely absent from these stories, it is also without parallel anywhere in the Hellenistic literature" (p. 134). Perrin likewise claims that the emphasis on faith is "completely missing" in the rabbinic stories of exorcism. "Power over the demons is an attribute of a particular rabbi, or it is granted in answer to prayer or as a reward for a meritorious act. . . . the same thing is true if all types of miracle stories [in the rabbinic literature] are considered" (pp. 135–36). The use of "faith" in the Gospel miracle stories should also be distinguished from the specific Christian use of "faith" for faith in the God who raised Jesus from the dead or faith in the Lord Jesus Christ. In the miracle stories, faith seems to carry the simpler sense of belief in Jesus' power to heal or exorcise; it is never specified as faith "in Jesus."

[28] I purposely use the word "trial(s)" to indicate the uncertainty of scholars over whether Jesus had one or more trials. Indeed, the question can be raised whether we should speak of "trials" at all rather than of some more informal sort of judicial hearing(s). Hence the use of the term "trial(s)" here is to be understood as studied ambiguity, not as an attempt to solve the problem early on.

[29] See, e.g, Crossan's equation of magic with banditry (*The Historical Jesus*, 305) and

his view (dependent on Jonathan Smith) that the temple and the magician were characteristic antinomies of Late Antiquity (pp. 354–55). Crossan begins his chapter on Jesus' death and burial by stressing that Jesus the itinerant magician fits this antinomy vis-à-vis the temple localized in Jerusalem. Thus, "no matter . . . what Jesus thought, said, or did about the Temple, he was its functional opponent, alternative, and substitute" (p. 355). Even apart from the question of the illegality of magic in the Roman Empire, this may be too sweeping a generalization. Not all miracle-workers or magicians in the Greco-Roman world were necessarily opposed to traditional temples. Perhaps one of the more likely traditions about Apollonius of Tyana, an itinerant miracle-worker of the 1st century A.D., is that he had an antiquarian interest (not unlike the Emperor Claudius) in restoring proper cultic usages in temples.

[30] Paul W. Hollenbach, "Jesus, Demoniacs, and Public Authorities: A Socio-Historical Study," *JAAR* 49 (1981) 567–88; the quotation is from p. 583. Hollenbach's uncritical use of texts from the Four Gospels leaves one breathless. Most of the texts are treated like videotape replays of historical events (including the words of the demoniacs as well as the words of Jesus), with practically no questions of form, source, and redaction criticism—to say nothing of the criteria of historicity—being treated. Even the plain statements of certain texts are garbled. For example, on p. 582 Hollenbach speaks of the Pharisees (considered public authorities in early 1st-century Galilee!) accusing Jesus of witchcraft and being a demoniac. As evidence Hollenbach cites Mark 3:22, which speaks not of Pharisees but of "the scribes who had come down from Jerusalem." Such arbitrary use of Gospel texts is common throughout the article. Various sayings of Jesus (e.g., Luke 13:31–33), taken as historical without any argumentation, are declared to come from particular times and places in Jesus' ministry, as though Karl Ludwig Schmidt had never shown in his *Der Rahmen der Geschichte Jesu* that the temporal-spatial framework of the Gospel narratives of the public ministry is largely a redactional creation. Unfortunately, this sort of carelessness in treating the texts of the Gospels—to say nothing of a lack of methodological rigor—is typical of the whole article. Equally problematic is the mixture of political, sociological, and psychological theories to explain why the public authorities would view Jesus' exorcisms in particular as a danger to public order, when other Jews were also performing exorcisms. Hollenbach never notices that his theory about exorcisms being a major cause of Jesus' execution runs into a glaring difficulty if one takes the Gospel texts and scene-settings as literally as he does: all the exorcism stories are set in Galilee, the region of Tyre, or the region of the Decapolis. None is ever reported as taking place in Judea in general or Jerusalem in particular; yet it is the cooperation of the Judean officials Caiaphas and Pilate that brings Jesus to execution in Jerusalem, not in Galilee. Given Hollenbach's presuppositions and mode of reading Gospel texts, it is hard to believe that the major motivating force leading Judean officials to put Jesus to death was his performance of exorcisms, which never occurred in their jurisdiction.

[31] On the question of the illegality of magic, see Phillips, "*Nullum Crimen sine Lege,*" 260–76; Segal, "Hellenistic Magic," 356–58. As noted above, Alexander of Abonuteichos, a famous "magician" of the 2d century A.D., had patrons among the high and mighty in Roman government—including, if we may trust Lucian, the Emperor Marcus Aurelius.

[32] My formulation is carefully chosen: ". . . the Gospels record no miracle of Jesus that directly harms or punishes a person. . . ." In two cases one presumes—though the narrative never speaks of or reflects upon the problem—that some owner of property was indirectly injured by having a piece of property destroyed as the result of a miracle. The two cases are (1) the herd of about 2,000 swine, into which the demons that had

possessed the Gerasene demoniac enter, causing the swine to rush into the Sea of Galilee and perish (Mark 5:11–13 parr.), and (2) the fig tree that withers after Jesus curses it for having no fruit when he was hungry (Mark 11:12–14, 20–26 par.). While the two stories raise many intriguing questions for form and redaction critics, to say nothing of theologians concerned with social justice, they hold no great interest for scholars in quest of the historical Jesus. Exegetes of various stripes, who differ notably among themselves in attempts to reconstruct hypothetical original events behind the present stories, concur in the view that both anecdotes (i.e., the drowning of the swine and the cursing of the fig tree) do not go back to the historical Jesus, at least in their present form. Rather, they represent later legendary developments or reinterpretations of earlier tradition. For a brief treatment of both stories, see Vögtle, "The Miracles of Jesus," 103–4.

I will take up both cases in detail in subsequent chapters on exorcisms (for the swine incident) and the so-called nature miracles (for the cursing of the fig tree). For the time being, the following observations may suffice. A useful catalog of opinions on the "swine saga" in the story of the Gerasene demoniac can be found in John F. Craghan, "The Gerasene Demoniac," *CBQ* 30 (1968) 522–36, esp. 522–24. Various literary and form-critical considerations (tensions and reduplications within Mark 5:1–20, the disruption of the ordinary form-critical contours of an exorcism story, differing vocabulary, midrashic and symbolic motifs) argue for an earlier form of the story of the Gerasene demoniac without the swine saga. Those who favor the secondary nature of the swine saga include Craghan, "The Gerasene Demoniac," 526, 533 (a "midrashic" element); Pesch, *Das Markusevangelium*, 1. 284, 292–93; Guelich, *Mark 1–8:26*, 273, 282. Bultmann (*Geschichte*, 224–25), on the other hand, thinks that the story of the Gerasene demoniac is basically all of a piece, but that it is probably an anecdote taken over by Christians and attributed to Jesus. Similarly, Dibelius (*Die Formgeschichte des Evangeliums*, 86–87) suggests that the story originally told of a Jewish exorcist in a pagan country and was later transferred to Jesus. Trying to hold on to the historicity of the whole of Mark 5:1–20, Taylor (*The Gospel According to St. Mark*, 282–83) has recourse to the "psychologizing" or "rationalistic" solution of Johannes Weiss: the paroxysm of the demoniac as he was being exorcised frightened the swine into a stampede. Whatever one thinks of such an attempt to save the swine saga for history, the upshot is still the same as far as we are concerned: the anecdote of the demons asking and Jesus allowing them to enter the swine (with the swine's destruction resulting from Jesus' permission of the transfer) is still a secondary interpretation of the original event. On all this, see my treatment of the Gerasene demoniac below.

As for the cursing of the fig tree, even Taylor (*The Gospel According to St. Mark*, 458–59), who is generally so favorable to historicity, admits that "many modern commentators deny the historical character of the incident." He allows one of two possible origins to the anecdote: (1) the narrative grew out of the parable of the unfruitful fig tree in Luke 13:6–9 or some similar parable that was transformed into a factual story (a possibility allowed by Bultmann, *Geschichte*, 246; similarly Dibelius, *Die Formgeschichte des Evangeliums*, 103; Vögtle, "The Miracles of Jesus," 103; Günther Bornkamm, "*Pneuma alalon*. Eine Studie zum Markusevangelium," *Geschichte und Glaube. Zweiter Teil. Gesammelte Aufsätze Band IV* [BEvT 53; Munich: Kaiser, 1971] 21–36, esp. 22 n. 3); or (2) "in primitive Christian tradition a popular legend came to be attached to a withered fig tree on the way to Jerusalem." For the possibility that the story originally belonged to another setting and has secondarily been transferred to the present Marcan context, see Wendy J. Cotter, " 'For It Was Not the Season for Figs,' " *CBQ* 48 (1986) 62–66, esp. 63 and n. 7. Jeremias (*New Testament Theology*, 87) attempts to avoid the basic difficulty of the story by seeking refuge in his favorite escape hatch, a mistranslation of the Aramaic. According to Jeremias, Jesus originally said: "No one *will* ever eat fruit from you again [because the end will have come before it is ripe]" as an announcement of the nearness of the end; but this prophecy was transformed in the later tradition into a curse. In contrast, Haenchen's trenchant judgment does not mince words (*Der Weg Jesu*, 381): "Here if anywhere we are in the realm of a later legend." Among serious historical-critical exegetes of the present day Pesch (*Das Markusevangelium*, 2. 189–201) stands in the minority by maintaining the historicity of the event as narrated. His curious position is an unfortunate corollary of his insistence on an extensive pre-Marcan Passion Narrative that supposedly stems from the Jerusalem church and is historically quite reliable. Witherington (*The Christology of Jesus*, 173–75) joins Pesch in upholding the historicity of the event, but sees it as a prophetic-symbolic action, something that Pesch denies. Pesch and Witherington really have no answer to the observation that nowhere else in the Four Gospels does the Jesus of the earthly ministry utter a curse or perform a punitive or intentionally destructive miracle, while such phenomena proliferate in the Christian apocrypha (e.g., the *Infancy Gospel of Thomas*). It is telling that even such a zealous defender of the historicity of Jesus' miracles as van der Loos (*The Miracles of Jesus*, 688–98) concludes that we have here a story that arose out of various OT texts and/or words of Jesus.

Both stories seem to be symbolic, at least in their present redactional forms: (1) The precise rationale for the swine saga is disputed among exegetes, but in my view the point is that Jesus outwits the demons of Gerasa at their own game. He seems at first to accede to their request to transfer to the swine, which would allow them to remain in the largely pagan region of the Decapolis. However, the demons wind up being tricked. Even the swine, unclean animals according to Jewish purity laws, cannot abide the presence of the demons and so rush to destroy themselves (and, symbolically, consign the demons to the great abyss of chaos, their proper home) in the sea. Thus, the story of the exorcism of one disturbed Gentile becomes a symbol of the expulsion of the power of evil from Gentile territory. Mark's community would probably see in the anecdote a symbol of the gospel of Jesus Christ triumphing over and expelling the powers of darkness from the Gentile world (so Craghan, "The Gerasene Demoniac," 532–36; Pesch, *Das Markusevangelium*, 1. 293–94; Guelich, *Mark 1–8:26*, 283). (2) Framing as it does Mark's account of the "cleansing" (i.e., the symbolic prophecy of the destruction) of the Jerusalem temple, the cursing of the fig tree symbolizes, in the eyes of Mark and his community, the fate that awaits the temple and its authorities because of their failure to respond to Jesus' call by producing the "fruits" of faith and repentance (cf. Mark 1:15), despite a great show of religious activity (symbolized by the leaves). Crossan (*The Historical Jesus*, 357), along with many other critics (e.g., Bornkamm, "*Pneuma alalon*," 22 n. 3), is quite right to see this symbolism in the story, at least on the Marcan level; Pesch is unconvincing and unrepresentative in denying it. If, from the time of their initial formulation, these two stories were weighty symbols of the destiny of the Gentiles and the Jerusalem temple respectively, it is no wonder that the concrete, pragmatic question of the injury done to the owner of the swine or the fig tree never surfaced in the Gospel tradition.

[33] I stress that here I am simply examining the various accounts of Jesus' trial(s) in the Four Gospels as they stand, with no attempt to reconstruct what exactly was the historical course of events between Jesus' arrest and his crucifixion. All I wish to point out here is that none of the accounts of Jesus' trial(s) gives any reason for thinking that his miracles were a major motivating force for his arrest and execution.

[34] For the important part that controversies arising from healing stories play in this

connection, see Anitra Bingham Kolenkow, "Healing Controversy as a Tie between Miracle and Passion Material for a Proto-Gospel," *JBL* 95 (1976) 623–38.

[35] As I have already noted, the closest we get to the idea that a miracle of Jesus is the immediate cause of his death is the aftermath of the Lazarus story in John 11:45–53; 12:10–11. Yet even in this case (1) as soon as the second half of the Gospel (the so-called Book of Glory or Book of the Passion) begins in chap. 13, the raising of Lazarus as the precise motivating force for Jesus' arrest and death disappears; (2) the statements in 11:45–53; 12:10–11 are suffused with Johannine theology; I doubt that many critics would want to use them to reconstruct the historical causes of Jesus' arrest and execution. Brown (*The Gospel According to John*, 1. 430) states that "while the basic story behind the Lazarus account may stem from early tradition, its causal relationship to the death of Jesus is more a question of Johannine pedagogical and theological purpose than of historical reminiscence; and this explains why no such causal connection is found in the Synoptic tradition. A miracle story that was once transmitted without fixed context or chronological sequence has been used in one of the later stages in Johannine editing as an ending to the public ministry of Jesus." A similar position on the causal connection found in John is held by Schnackenburg (*Das Johannesevangelium*, 2. 446–47, 464), who remarks on John 12:10–11: "The brief statement belongs not to a historical report but only to the dramatic presentation" (p. 464).

[36] What appears to be the family tomb of the high priest Joseph Caiaphas was discovered in 1990 by Israeli archaeologists digging in the Peace Forest located south of the Old City of Jerusalem. For a report on the burial cave, see Zvi Greenhut, "Burial Cave of the Caiaphas Family," *BARev* 18/5 (1992) 28–36; for a report on the relevant inscriptions, see Ronny Reich, "Caiaphas [*sic*] Name Inscribed on Bone Box," ibid., pp. 38–44, 76. Two ossuaries (rectangular boxes containing bones placed there for secondary burial) are involved. The more simply designed ossuary has the name Caiaphas inscribed on its narrow side. The inscription is made up of only three letters: *qp'*, probably = *Qafa'*. The second ossuary, the most beautifully decorated in the burial cave, bears two inscriptions with some form of the name Caiaphas. On the narrow side of the ossuary is found: *yhwsp br qp'*, probably = Joseph son of Qafa'. In this inscription the family name is spelled exactly as it was on the other ossuary, i.e., with only three letters. The undecorated long rear side of this second ossuary has the other form of basically the same inscription, but this time with a *yod* (or possibly a *waw*) in the family name: *yhwsp br qyp'*, probably = Joseph son of Qayafa'. Reich (p. 41) observes that this inscription does not necessarily indicate that Caiaphas was Joseph's father. "Caiaphas" could have been simply a family nickname, acquired by some ancestor and then passed down in the family. Since "Joseph" and "Simon" seem to have been the two most popular Jewish names among Palestinian males of the period, a prominent person named Joseph would find a family nickname a useful specification. Reich also suggests that the remains of a man about 60 years old found in the highly decorated ossuary are those of Joseph Caiaphas. (As an aside, it may be noted that the NT refers to this person only as Caiaphas; fittingly, it is Josephus who tells us that Caiaphas' proper name was Joseph [*Ant.* 18.2.2 §35; 18.4.3 §95].) For other reports of the discovery, see *The New York Times*, pp. A1 and A10, and *The Washington Post*, p. A3, both for August 14, 1992. See also James H. Charlesworth, "Caiaphas, Pilate, and Jesus' Trial," *Explorations* 7/1 (1993) 3–4.

[37] The longest ruling prefect/procurator may have been Pilate's predecessor, Valerius Gratus (ruled A.D. 15–26). However, since the exact dates of assuming and leaving the post of prefect are not absolutely certain in the case of either Valerius Gratus or Pontius Pilate, the matter remains unclear. On the importance of the high priest as the

middleman between the Roman prefect and the Jewish people, see Sanders, *Judaism. Practice and Belief*, 321–25; on p. 323 Sanders states flatly: "The most successful high priest during the Roman period was Joseph Caiaphas. . . ." Sanders goes on to observe that "the impression given by Josephus is that during the periods of direct Roman rule the high priests tried to be honest brokers, mediating between the prefect or procurator and the people" (p. 326). Richard Horsley (*Jesus and the Spiral of Violence* [San Francisco: Harper & Row, 1987] 9–15) sees in Rome's use of the Jewish high priest and the indigenous aristocracy a typical example of how an imperial power rules in a "colonial" situation. However, Horsley's picture of the situation in Palestine between the removal of the Jewish ethnarch Archelaus (A.D. 6) and the accession of King Agrippa I (reigned over the reconstituted kingdom of Herod the Great A.D. 41–44) may be too negative. As the lengthy tenures of Caiaphas and Pilate indicate (not to mention the still lengthier reign of Herod Antipas from 4 B.C. to A.D. 39), the system—however oppressive and intolerable by our 20th-century standards—basically worked from A.D. 6 to 41—at least by 1st-century standards.

[38] Naturally such a statement goes against the received opinion of Pilate as political monster and Caiaphas as corrupt cleric. Such portraits owe more to the religious sensitivities of Jews and Christians than they do to a sober analysis of the complex political and religious situation of early 1st-century Palestine. In his book *Judaism. Practice and Belief*, Sanders has rendered scholarship a great service by questioning the commonly received presumptions (1) that the priestly aristocracy in Jerusalem was entirely corrupt, hated by the people, impotent vis-à-vis other groups, and dominated by the Pharisees, (2) that all the Roman prefects were incompetent monsters, and (3) that all Palestinian Jews were constantly on the brink of revolt from A.D. 6 to 41. In this, Sanders supplies a good antidote to the exaggerations in Horsley's *Jesus and the Spiral of Violence* and Martin Goodman's *The Ruling Class of Judea. The Origins of the Jewish Revolt against Rome A.D. 66–70* (Cambridge/New York: Cambridge University, 1987). Needless to say, no scholar wants to go to the opposite extreme and propose Pilate for canonization (although that has been done in some Eastern churches!). Nevertheless, attempts at a more balanced assessment of Pilate can be found in recent works like Brian C. McGing, "Pontius Pilate and the Sources," *CBQ* 53 (1991) 416–38; cf. the magisterial study of Jean-Pierre Lémonon, *Pilate et le gouvernement de la Judée. Textes et monuments* (EBib; Paris: Gabalda, 1981).

[39] For the reasons for thinking that the idea of Jesus' Davidic descent goes back to his own lifetime, see *A Marginal Jew*, 1. 216–19.

[40] My formulation is carefully chosen. (1) In a few instances people are named in a passing reference (so Mary Magdalene, Joanna, the wife of Chuza, and Susanna, recipients of Jesus' exorcisms and/or healings in Luke 8:2–3), but do not appear in any full-length miracle story. (2) In certain stories some or all of the twelve disciples are prominent as petitioners or recipients. So, for instance, one presumes that Simon, Andrew, James, and John (listed in Mark 1:29 as entering the house of Simon) are to be included in the understood subject "they" when we are told that "they speak" to Jesus about Simon's mother-in-law in Mark 1:30 (cf. Luke 4:38). The disciples in general are petitioners and/or recipients in the nature miracles of the stilling of the storm and the walking on the water. They also act as go-betweens and presumably share in the benefit of the multiplication of loaves (in John 6:7–8, Philip and Andrew, "the brother of Simon Peter," are singled out). Simon Peter is singled out in a number of miracles, notably nature miracles and notably in Matthew: he is empowered (initially) to walk on the water with Jesus (Matt 14:28–31) and is instructed by Jesus to find the coin for the temple tax in the mouth of a fish (Matt 17:27; the actual carrying out of this command

is never narrated). Simon Peter is also the focus of the story of the miraculous catch of fish in Luke 5:1–11 (cf. John 21:1–14).

⁴¹ See E. P. Sanders, *The Tendencies of the Synoptic Tradition* (SNTSMS 9; Cambridge: Cambridge University, 1969).

⁴² The absence of "Jairus by name" (*onomati Iaïros*) in the Codex Bezae and some manuscripts of the Old Latin, plus other more dubious considerations (e.g., the name Jairus is not repeated in the narrative and is lacking in the Matthean parallel), led Bultmann (*Geschichte*, 230), Schmidt (*Der Rahmen der Geschichte Jesu*, 147), and Taylor (*The Gospel According to St. Mark*, 287) to suggest that these words were either a later interpolation in Mark 5:22 or a secondary addition to the oral tradition that Mark received. A lengthy and convincing refutation of the view that these words are not original in the text of Mark is given by Metzger, *Textual Commentary*, 85–86 (cf. Guelich, *Mark 1–8:26*, 290 n. c); the textual evidence is overwhelmingly in favor of keeping *onomati Iaïros*. The presumption that the presence of a proper name is ipso facto a sign of a secondary expansion of the original form of a story is called into question by the vast majority of Synoptic miracle stories, especially when one compares the Matthean and Lucan versions to the Marcan ones.

⁴³ Luke follows Mark in keeping both the proper name and the specific office, though in place of Mark's *heis tōn archisynagōgōn* he has the clearer and simpler *archōn tēs synagōgēs* in Luke 8:41, while keeping Mark's *archisynagōgou* in Luke 8:49 ‖ Mark 5:35. The title seems to refer to a lay leader, probably elected, who made arrangements for the synagogue service and saw to the maintenance of the building.

⁴⁴ Since we are dealing throughout with the quest for the historical Jesus, the question of the resurrection of Jesus, the resurrection appearances, and any miracles accompanying them lies outside the scope of our inquiry. As noted above, Jesus' resurrection and his resurrection appearances do not fall under the working definition of miracle adopted in the first section of this chapter. In any case, it seems reasonable to suppose that the stories concerning the resurrection and the resurrection appearances had a different sort of tradition history than did the miracle stories connected with the public ministry.

CHAPTER 20

JESUS' EXORCISMS

I. PROLOGUE TO THE INVENTORY: THE VARIOUS TYPES OF JESUS' MIRACLES

As we have seen, several criteria of historicity make it very probable that the historical Jesus claimed to perform and was thought by both followers and enemies to have performed miracles. Put more concretely, Jesus undertook to perform such extraordinary actions as healing the sick and exorcising demoniacs; and both he and his followers considered the successful results of these actions to be miracles (in the language of our Greek Gospels: *dynameis* [mighty deeds], *sēmeia* [signs], *terata* [wonders], *paradoxa* [astounding deeds], and *thaumasia* [wondrous deeds]).

It is one thing to be able to make this *global* assertion. It is quite another to descend to particular types of miracles and individual miracle stories and to render judgments on their historicity. Obviously, it is easier to speak of the historicity of *types* of miracles. That is to say, Jesus did "this sort of thing": e.g., he was thought by at least some of his contemporaries to have given sight to the blind, to have exorcised demoniacs, even to have raised the dead. The reason it is easier to make these global assertions is the multiple attestation of these *types* of miracles in both narratives and sayings. It is much more difficult to take up an individual story of healing or exorcism and claim historicity for the specifics of its narrative.

By now the reasons for the difficulty of judging *individual* miracle stories should be obvious. On the one hand, the miracles of Jesus were narrated according to the motifs, themes, and forms customary in the Greco-Roman world. A particular story that was not only historical but also quite unusual could easily take on, in the course of oral transmission, the conventional contours of the literary form we call miracle story, the specific features of the historical event being lost in the process. On the other hand, storytellers in the early church and the curious audiences they catered to could foster the opposite tendency: the introduction of actors with names, the location of events in familiar places, and the addition of colorful details to enliven the narrative.

Moreover, as the church in general and the evangelists in particular used the miracle stories as symbols of the salvation Jesus had brought, traits that served this symbolic function would either be heightened or created. For instance, some of the details of the stories of the multiplication of loaves may reflect the traditions about Jesus' Last Supper and about the church's eucharist. In some cases, the whole miracle story may have grown out of a dramatization of a saying or parable of Jesus. Candidates sometimes suggested as examples of this dramatizing process are the changing of water into wine at Cana, the cursing of the fig tree, and the raising of Lazarus.

A further problem with judging individual miracle stories, especially those involving a healing, is that the description of the illness or other difficulty presented to Jesus is often vague. We hear of "paralyzed" men who cannot walk, a man with a "withered" hand, a woman "bent over," a woman with a flow of blood, "lepers," "blind men," and so forth. What the precise pathology of each condition was, what its cause was, how serious or irreversible it was, and whether the cure Jesus worked was permanent are not stated.[1] One remembers from our quick glance at the medical board at Lourdes how difficult it is to judge claims of inexplicable cures even when medical evidence and personal interviews are available to 20th-century doctors. What is the historian or exegete to do when faced with a chasm of 20 centuries and almost no reliable medical descriptions—especially when there is no evidence as to whether the cured person suffered a relapse at a future date?

In addition, even when the pathology in the Gospel story seems relatively clear, interpreting the incident may be complicated by the cultural and scientific gap that separates us from the 1st century. For instance, the story of the possessed boy in Mark 9:14–29 lists symptoms that make it likely that the boy suffered from epilepsy. However, not only is the exact type of epilepsy debatable, more importantly the chief actors in the drama—Jesus, his disciples, and the boy's father—as well as the evangelists consider the case to be one of demonic possession, and not simply one of physical illness. Thus, even as we approach a story that seems easier to handle because of its concrete description of the affliction, we must remember that the modern scientific worldview we automatically take with us is light-years away from the worldview of Jesus and the evangelists, who shared the cultural belief that the boy's sufferings were caused by a demon. Even in those rare cases where the medical problem in the Gospel story is relatively clear, we must constantly remind ourselves how different our modern mental horizon is from that of Jesus or the evangelist.

For all these reasons, it is easier to discuss the types of miracles Jesus claimed to perform or was thought to perform than to judge the historicity of an individual account of miracle-working, especially as regards the narrative's details. This is hardly a new or controversial insight; even conservative or moderate scholars, who accept the general historicity of the tradition that Jesus worked what were thought to be miracles, are diffident about individual stories.[2] In the following overview we will therefore group the miracle stories of the Gospels according to types, in order to study general patterns as well as to probe individual narratives. Even if we cannot always reach a sure judgment about an individual story,[3] our survey may highlight some interesting patterns of distribution among the miracle stories as a whole: e.g., what types of miracles did Jesus regularly perform or claim to perform and, by way of contrast, what types of miracles are relatively rare in the Gospel tradition? As regards the individual miracle stories, the reader should remember that our goal is a very limited one: a search for hints that the story either goes back to Jesus or was invented by the early church. Accordingly, the literary artistry and redactional theology with which the evangelists have clothed these stories, while important in other contexts, are not the direct object of this rapid overview of the data.[4]

II. THE EXORCISMS

Our treatment of exorcisms will differ slightly from our study of the other miracle traditions for a simple reason: we have already examined the question of Jesus' exorcisms at length in Chapter 16.[5] Hence, in the present chapter I will try as much as possible to remain strictly focused on one task: assessing the possible historical elements in individual cases. In addition to the sayings of Jesus dealing with exorcisms and to the summaries of Jesus' activities that mention exorcisms in passing, the Synoptic Gospels present seven distinct instances of Jesus' performance of an exorcism. That there should be seven individual "specimens" of a very specific type of miracle, namely, exorcism, supports the view that exorcisms loomed large in Jesus' ministry.

At the same time, caution is advised because the narratives of exorcism are not evenly distributed among the various Gospel sources. As already noted, John's Gospel contains no exorcism story, though the absence of exorcisms is most likely due to John's particular theological stance. In the Synoptics, almost all of the full-dress stories of exorcism come from the Marcan tradition. A short narrative of exorcism seems to have stood in Q as the introduction to the Beelzebul controversy (Matt 12:22–24 ‖ Luke 11:14). The special L tradition of Luke's Gospel supplies no separate example of a full story of exorcism, though it makes a passing reference to Jesus' exorcism of Mary Magdalene (echoed in Mark 16:9).[6] The special M tradition of Matthew's Gospel has one very brief exorcism story, but it is probably a redactional creation of Matthew. Granted this limited number of sources, one may conclude that, when it comes to exorcisms, multiple attestation of *forms* is as important as multiple attestation of *sources*: Q sayings join Marcan sayings and Marcan narratives in providing multiple attestation for the existence of exorcisms in the ministry of the historical Jesus.

A. THE DEMONIAC IN THE SYNAGOGUE AT CAPERNAUM (MARK 1:23–28 ‖ LUKE 4:33–37)[7]

This story is used by Mark as part of a paradigmatic scene: the first full day of Jesus' ministry in Capernaum, fittingly placed on a Sabbath.[8] Indeed, for Mark it is the true beginning of Jesus' *public* ministry, period. Hence the scene summarizes a good deal of Jesus' ministry, especially from chap. 1 to chap. 6 of the Gospel. Jesus with his disciples enters a synagogue on the Sabbath (1:21), his teaching—and especially its unique authority, so different from that of the scribes—astonishes his audience (v 22), Jesus frees a man from a demon that knows Jesus' true identity and that is therefore silenced (vv 23–27), Jesus' fame spreads (v 28), Jesus heals an individual sick person (vv 29–31), and Jesus engages in healing many sick people and exorcising many demoniacs (vv 32–34).

Granted the paradigmatic and generalizing nature of 1:21–34, a unit perhaps welded together by Mark,[9] it would be unwise to press the details of the first exorcism in the Gospel, the exorcism of the demoniac in the Capernaum synagogue. In particular, the themes of the demon's knowledge of Jesus' true identity, his crying out of a christological title,[10] and Jesus' command to be silent may all be expressions of Mark's theology of the messianic secret.[11]

Perhaps the most that can be said about the historicity of this exorcism is that it does represent in a global way the fact that Jesus probably did perform one or more exorcisms at Capernaum. The reason for putting forth this claim lies not so much in Mark 1:23–28 taken by itself as in various references throughout all Four Gospels to Jesus' activity—including his miracle-working activity—in Capernaum. That Jesus was active in Capernaum, perhaps even making it his "home base" in Galilee, is supported by multiple attestation of both sources and forms. Mark has Jesus entering Capernaum in 1:21; 2:1; and 9:33. The first two references introduce miracle stories, all three contexts present Jesus teaching, and all three contexts have Jesus exercising his ministry in someone's house in Capernaum. Both Matthew and Luke follow Mark's basic view of things,[12] Matthew going so far as to make Jesus' move to Capernaum an object of prophecy (4:12–17) and to call Capernaum "his [Jesus'] own city" (9:1). John's Gospel gives independent support to this depiction of Capernaum as Jesus' home base in Galilee. His testimony is all the more important because his presentation of Jesus' ministry is much more focused on Jerusalem and Judea than on Galilee, the locale emphasized by the Synoptics. Yet John presents Jesus—as well as his mother, his brothers, and his disciples—descending from Cana to Capernaum after his first sign (2:12). Curiously, the presence of Jesus' mother, brothers, and disciples (or at least a receptive audience) all together in Capernaum coincides with Mark's depiction of an otherwise different incident in Mark 3:20–35.

Just as Matthew and Luke agree in locating the Q story of the healing of the centurion's servant in Capernaum (Matt 8:5–13 ‖ Luke 7:1–10),[13] so John likewise connects the equivalent story of the healing of the royal official's son with Capernaum. As in Q the story recounts a healing at a distance. Since John is prone to making miracles even more miraculous, it may be a specifically Johannine touch that Jesus is farther away than in the Synoptics—in Cana, to be precise (thus providing at the same time a neat inclusion with the first Cana miracle of John 1:1–11). This is not the only appearance of Capernaum in John's Jerusalem-centered Gospel. In John 6, although neither the initial story of the multiplication of loaves nor the account of Jesus' walking on the water demands it, John places the subsequent discourse on the bread of life in Capernaum, pointedly in the synagogue (6:59). John thus agrees with Mark in portraying Jesus as active in Capernaum, where both his teaching and his miracles find a home.

All the more significant, then, is the Q saying in which Jesus excoriates certain cities of Galilee for not repenting despite the miracles (*hai dynameis*) he had worked in them. After upbraiding the otherwise unmentioned Chorazin and Bethsaida,[14] Jesus reserves his fiercest rebuke for Capernaum: "And you, Capernaum, shall you be exalted to heaven? You shall go down to Hades!" (Matt 11:23 || Luke 10:15). Capernaum's climactic place in Jesus' denunciation (a dubious distinction) suggests what all Four Gospels intimate: among the towns of Galilee, Capernaum was the chief beneficiary of Jesus' Galilean ministry. All the more, then, is Capernaum guilty. Of special importance is the fact that the saying focuses upon the inexcusable nature of the impenitence of the three towns in view of the miracles Jesus performed in them. As we have seen in our inventory of Gospel miracles, exorcisms were prominent among Jesus' miracles in general, and so it is no great logical leap to take the Q saying as implying that Jesus worked exorcisms in Capernaum.

In short, multiple attestation argues for the pivotal place of Capernaum in Jesus' Galilean ministry and for the performance of miracles, including exorcisms, there. Hence, while Mark 1:23–28 cannot be pressed in its details, it is historically reliable in the sense that it serves as a global representation of "the sort of thing" Jesus did during his ministry in Capernaum.

B. THE GERASENE DEMONIAC (MARK 5:1–20)

One of the few things the story of the Gerasene demoniac has in common with the story of the demoniac in the Capernaum synagogue is a place-name. Otherwise, this lengthy, sprawling story resembles more the story of the possessed boy of Mark 9 in its rambling, sometimes incoherent, yet concrete and bizarre narrative. The many problems, tensions, and even contradictions within the story no doubt reflect a complicated, decades-long evolution of a simpler narrative into the baroque account that lies before us in Mark 5:1–20.[15] What exactly the earliest form of the story looked like is hard to say. Still, we have a few clues as to what may be original in the narrative and what may be later additions.

To begin with, it is not all that common for one of Jesus' miracles to be connected with the name of a pagan city in pagan territory. The only other example is the exorcism of the daughter of the Syrophoenician woman (Mark 7:24–30), which takes place in "the region of Tyre"—a much vaster and vaguer territory than the region around the Decapolis city of Gerasa. Moreover, as we shall see below, as far as form-critical categories are concerned, the story of the Syrophoenician woman belongs along with the healing of the centurion's servant to the category of healings at a distance rather than to the category of exorcism stories, since it lacks most of the usual motifs and themes of a narrative of exorcism. Hence, the exorcism of the Gerasene demoniac is the only true exorcism story that is connected with a pagan city. More specifically, this exorcism is the only miracle directly connected with one of the cities of the Decapolis (a group of Hellenistic cities with mostly pagan populations in the region of southern Syria and northeastern Palestine).[16] This may suggest—though hardly proves—that an exorcism of Jesus did take place somewhere in the environs of the pagan city of Gerasa and that the unusual venue of the exorcism helped anchor it in the oral tradition.

I hasten to add, however, that there is a problem with the designation "Gerasenes." The ancient manuscripts of the Gospels of Matthew, Mark, and Luke have a bewildering variety of place-names at the beginning of this story: Gerasenes, Gadarenes, Gergesenes, Gergesines, and Gergystenes. Later scribes apparently had their own ideas about where the miracle ought to be located and changed the text accordingly. In the view of the distinguished text critic Bruce M. Metzger, the most likely reading in Mark (on whom Matthew and Luke depend for their versions of the story) is "region of the Gerasenes," and I accept this judgment as the most probable position.[17]

If "the region of the Gerasenes" is the original reading in Mark, the evolution of this strange story may help explain why a change of venue was felt necessary at a later date in the story's retelling. As I have noted in Chapter 19, it is likely that the incident of the demons entering into the pigs, who then rush over or down a precipice into the Sea of Galilee and drown (Mark 5:11–13) is an easily detachable and probably secondary accretion to the original form of the exorcism story.[18] Without the panicky pigs and their dip in the deep, the environs of Gerasa, a city some 33 miles southeast of the Sea of Galilee, create no problem for the story.

However, once the incident of the swine running over or down a cliff into the Sea of Galilee was added to the story at some later date, Gerasa, roughly 33 miles southeast of the Sea, simply did not fit, even if one were willing to stretch the sense of "the *region* of the Gerasenes." Other cities of the Decapolis, along with their "regions," were much closer to the Sea of Galilee—including Gadara, which, though not without its own geographical problems, lay at a more convenient five-to-six miles from the sea. Still better was Gergesa, on the east bank of the Sea. Finding even Gadara too improbable, the Church Father Origen championed Gergesa, and it was probably Origen's influence that accounts for "Gergesenes" appearing in some manuscripts.

In brief, "Gerasenes" as the original reading in Mark easily explains the change to "Gadarenes" or "Gergesenes." If one of the latter two had been the original reading, one would be hard pressed to explain how "Gerasenes" wound up in many early and excellent manuscripts.[19] Now, the decision that "Gerasenes" is the original reading has interesting consequences for determining the primitive content of the story. Since the story most likely arose on Palestinian soil or adjoining territory, and since presumably the native storyteller would have known that Gerasa was nowhere near the Sea of Galilee, our decision that "Gerasenes" belongs to the earliest form of the story confirms the view that the original story of the Gerasene demoniac did not include the incident of the pigs rushing into the Sea of Galilee. In other words, what has often been claimed on form-critical grounds (namely, that the pig-incident is secondary) is likewise supported by our text-critical decision that the primitive story was located near Gerasa—from which not even possessed pigs can jump into the Sea of Galilee.[20] Since the self-destructive pigs do not belong in the original story, we may dispense with rationalizing theories about how the swine were panicked into stampeding by the paroxysms of the demoniac in the throes of his exorcism.[21]

Even apart from the secondary swine, it is difficult to say how much of the story may be pressed for historical facts. The gruesome description of the demoniac's alienation from self, neighbor, and God is truly gripping (Mark 5:2–10), but for that very reason one must reckon with the possibility of a powerful imagination making a powerful theological as well as narrative point.[22] Certainly, as the story stands in Mark, it serves the theological purpose of symbolizing the bringing of the healing, liberating message of the Christian gospel to the unclean Gentiles, a mission undertaken proleptically by Jesus himself.[23]

This overarching theological program must make us leery about accepting various details in the story as historical data. In particular, despite the fascination of critics with the dialogue between Jesus and the demoniac, notably the latter's declaration, "my name is Legion, for we are many," one must not be carried away by the almost hypnotic power of the exchange.[24] If throughout this volume we have been cautious in designating any sentence as the *ipsissima verba Jesu* (the exact words of Jesus), a fortiori we must be skeptical about declaring any sentence the *ipsissima verba* of a demoniac. Even if one wants to see in the name "Legion" a reference to the Roman occupation that tormented the indigenous population—a dubious mixture of political and psychological theories in any event—such interpretations are best kept to the level of Mark's redaction.[25] To suggest that we have here exactly what a "historical" demoniac said to the historical Jesus on a specific occasion strains credulity.

This holds true not only of the name Legion but also of the demoniac's designation of Jesus as "Son of the Most High God." According to Mark's theory of the "messianic secret" (better: "the Son secret"), no human being can know and proclaim in faith that Jesus is the Son of God before the ultimate act of mysterious revelation that is Jesus' death on the cross. Only then can a human being—pointedly, an outsider, a Gentile centurion involved in Jesus' execution—proclaim the truth: "Truly this man was Son of God" (Mark 15:39). Before that, only God, speaking from heaven at Jesus' baptism and transfiguration, and the demons as they are exorcised—hence, only supernatural beings—can voice the truth of Jesus' divine sonship. The dialogue between Jesus and the demoniac in Mark 5:6–7 fits this pattern perfectly and so must be viewed as a theological program rather than a historical record.

In the end, despite the lengthy and detailed story before us in Mark 5:1–20,

the historical residue, if any, is small. A preliminary and global reason for suspecting some underlying historical tradition is the complicated, many-layered nature of the story that received final formulation in Mark's Gospel sometime around A.D. 70. The various additions and expansions to the core narrative suggest an evolution over several decades, which in any case brings us back close to the time of Jesus.[26] Moreover, curious linguistic details in the story may point in the direction of historicity. The word "Gerasenes," which, as we have seen, is the original reading in Mark, occurs only here in the whole of the Bible. Still more curious is the fact that "Decapolis" in Mark 5:20 probably represents the earliest occurrence of the word in the whole of ancient literature.[27] If early Christian imagination were making up this story out of whole cloth and simply needed some location for Jesus' exorcism, it is odd that it hit upon the double philological rarity of the territory of the Gerasenes in the Decapolis. The sheer oddity of the geographical designation—unparalleled in the Bible and early Christian tradition—may reflect a singular historical event. It could be that the unique connection of one of Jesus' miracles with a particular pagan city in the Decapolis, at a good distance from the Sea of Galilee and Jesus' customary area of activity, may have stuck in the collective memory of Jesus' disciples precisely because of the exorcism's unusual venue.

Franz Annen, who has dedicated so much labor to this pericope, offers a further reason why he thinks some event in Jesus' ministry lies behind the story of the Gerasene demoniac. In seeking a plausible "setting in life" (*Sitz im Leben*) for the story, Annen suggests that it was formulated by first-generation Christian Jews who favored a mission to Gentiles and who were locked in controversy over this point with more conservative Christian Jews who opposed such a mission. The mission-minded Christians would have used the story of the Gerasene demoniac as an argument against their opponents: we are only continuing what Jesus began. Annen points out that the argument would have made sense and would have been useful against the opponents only if both groups of first-generation Palestinian Christian Jews knew and accepted the fact that Jesus had indeed performed an exorcism in the region of Gerasa. To have invented such a story out of thin air would hardly have provided an effective debating point against the opponents of the Gentile mission. Annen's suggestion is attractive, but it depends upon prior acceptance of his view of the story's *Sitz im Leben*.

All in all, the linguistic oddities noted in the story, plus the possible *Sitz im Leben* that Annen sketches, incline me to the view that an exorcism performed by Jesus near Gerasa lies at the basis of the Gospel narrative in Mark 5:1–20. I readily admit, though, that there is no hard proof in the matter. Beyond this, I doubt that much can be said about the historical event; too many layers of literary activity and theological imagination have been superimposed.[28]

C. THE POSSESSED BOY (MARK 9:14–29 PARR.)

The story of the possessed boy[29] reminds us of the Gerasene demoniac in its length, its rambling, not to say incoherent, presentation, and some of its graphic, concrete details.[30] Whether Mark 9:14–29 results from the conflation of two different versions of the same event or from the slow evolution of one story is debated by critics.[31] At any rate, in the Marcan version we are again dealing with a pericope that is the result of a complicated literary history. To take the present Marcan form as a videotape replay of some original event would be the height of naïveté.[32]

Perhaps one approach to detecting historical tradition behind Mark's story is to observe where it diverges notably from the basic form-critical pattern of exorcism stories,[33] a pattern seen in other direct encounters of Jesus with a demoniac, notably the stories laid in Capernaum and near Gerasa. In their general contours, all three stories reflect the basic form:

(a) Jesus arrives on the scene;

(b) the demoniac confronts him or is brought to him;

(c) in the stories of the Gerasene demoniac and the possessed boy, there are detailed descriptions of the demoniac's pitiful and frightening condition;

(d) in the Capernaum and Gerasa stories, the demon tries to ward off Jesus: he shouts out Jesus' true identity as a sort of apotropaic device to control him;

(e) refusing to be warded off, and sometimes after initial questioning, Jesus rebukes (*epitimēsen*) the demon and commands him to "come out" (*exelthe*);

(f) the story narrates the fact of the demon's exit, often amid paroxysms, convulsions, or some sort of general upset;

(g) sometimes a separate statement about the well-being of the former demoniac is made to confirm the results;

(h) usually the reaction of bystanders (awe, fear) is part of the conclusion of the story.

While the story of the possessed boy in Mark 9:14–29 fits this pattern well, there are a few remarkable differences that contribute to the murky and halting movement of the narrative:

(a) Unlike other exorcism stories, this one is bracketed by references to the failure of Jesus' disciples to perform the requested exorcism (Mark 9:18 + 28–29). This is striking even within Mark's Gospel, which is not overly fond of the disciples, since Mark elsewhere (even later in chap. 9!) affirms that the disciples can perform exorcisms by Jesus' own mandate (6:7,13; 9:38–39).

(b) Jesus' interlocutor is not the demon possessing the demoniac, as in the Capernaum and Gerasa stories, but rather the distraught father of the boy.[34] Since the demon is said to cause speechlessness (v 17) and deafness (v 25),[35] obviously the boy cannot take part in the conversation (cf. the exorcisms of the speechless demoniac in Matt 9:32–34 and the blind demoniac who is also speechless in 12:22–24).

(c) Instead of a supernatural struggle between Jesus and the demon we see a passionate psychological—one might almost say "pastoral"—struggle. It is a struggle between Jesus, who (only in this exorcism story) demands faith as a condition for the exorcism, and the loving father at his wit's end, who finally cries out: "I believe, help my unbelief" (v 24).[36]

(d) When the father first petitions Jesus for help in v 22 ("If you can do anything, help us"), Jesus replies, apparently with some indignation, in v 23: "What do you mean, 'If you can . . .'? All things are possible to the one who believes!" Depending upon how we interpret Jesus' reply in v 23, we may see here a unique reference in the Gospels to the faith Jesus *has*, a faith he identifies as the source of his power to work miracles. It is also possible, though, that v 23 presents Jesus reacting sharply to the father's hesitant faith in v 22 by challenging him to full faith; hence the father's moving reply in v 24.[37] In any event, we have the unusual case of Jesus demanding faith as a condition for an exorcism,[38] as well as the possibility—unique within the Four Gospels and indeed the NT—that Jesus speaks of his own faith as the source of his miracles.

(e) What is most distinctive of this story is the almost clinical nature of the detailed description we receive of the boy's affliction (vv 17–18, 20–22): impeded speech, seizures, being dashed down on the ground, foaming at the mouth, grinding of teeth, and becoming rigid. Even as the boy is brought to Jesus, he goes into convulsions, falls to the ground, rolls about, and foams at the mouth. The father recounts that the boy has been afflicted in this way from childhood and has often fallen into fire or water. All in all, the boy seems to have suffered from some form of epilepsy,[39] a point not missed by Matthew, who applies to him the unusual verb *selēniazetai* (literally, "moonstruck"), which reflects the ancient belief that such fits were caused by the moon.[40] Needless to say, while we moderns recognize the problem as epilepsy, both Mark and all the actors in the story, including Jesus, think in terms of a demon and its expulsion.

None of this in itself guarantees historicity. Mark obviously uses the material to develop some of his own favorite themes: the growing conflict between Jesus and his disciples, the victory of Jesus over the demonic powers, and the need of faith (and prayer, which Mark awkwardly tacks on in v 29).[41]

Nevertheless, the pre-Marcan story of the possessed boy certainly went through a lengthy and complicated evolution in the oral tradition before it reached Mark's hands and so may even reach back as far as the life of Jesus. In particular, the divergences from and additions to the usual form of an exorcism story may point to a special and memorable encounter between Jesus and the father of an epileptic child during the public ministry. Instead of the pure form of an exorcism story, we find a mixture of exorcism story, regular healing story (with perhaps a touch of a story of raising the dead), and a pronouncement story (Jesus' saying on the power of faith). As Pesch points out in his analysis, some of the regular motifs of an exorcism or healing story are strangely out of place in Mark 9:14–27.[42] A good number of elements in the narrative (the failure of the disciples to exorcise, the father pleading for his son, the clear description of epilepsy, Jesus' demand for faith prior to the exorcism, and possibly Jesus' reference to his own faith as the source of miracles) are untypical of exorcism stories in the Gospels. In fact, some elements are unique. Moreover, in stark contrast to the other major stories of exorcism in Mark's Gospel, no christological title appears (cf. "Jesus of Nazareth . . . the holy one of God" in 1:24; "Jesus, Son of the Most High God" in 5:7; "Lord" in 7:28). The father simply addresses Jesus with the hardly surprising title of "teacher" (9:17). No specific christological concern is in evidence. In addition, the Greek of the story contains a number of Semitisms; the narrative may have existed originally in Aramaic.[43] With all these indicators pointing in one direction, I incline to the view of Pesch and many other commentators that some historical remembrance from the ministry of Jesus lies behind the present story.

More than this cannot be said. It is perhaps worth noting, though, that even Karl Ludwig Schmidt, the master of dissolving the Marcan narrative framework to discover pre-Gospel units, thought that this strange story did go back to some "real tradition and—one may add—real remembrance and history."[44]

D. THE MUTE (AND BLIND?) DEMONIAC (MATT 12:22–23a || LUKE 11:14)

In Matt 12:22–23a || Luke 11:14 we have what is probably the only narrative—however brief—of an exorcism in Q.[45] Needless to say, Q knows of Jesus' exorcisms, as the saying about the divided kingdom (Luke 11:17–18), the question about exorcism performed by the followers of Jesus' adversaries (Luke 11:19), the saying about exorcism by the finger of God (Luke 11:20), and the parable of the strong man (Luke 11:21–22 parr.) show. But here we have the sole Q narrative of exorcism. A narrative in Q is a rarity in any case, and the only other narrative of a miracle in Q is the healing of the centurion's servant (Matt 8:5–13 || Luke 7:1–10).

Befitting Q, the narrative is laconic in the extreme and apparently exists merely to introduce the Q version of the Beelzebul controversy.[46] Hence one might ask whether this story is purely a literary product of the author(s) of Q, created as a narrative introduction to a dispute over Jesus' exorcisms.[47] While that is possible, the unusual nature of the brief narrative gives one pause. The recipient of the exorcism is a demoniac who is also mute, or at least suffering from some sort of speech impediment (*kōphos*)[48]—as well as being blind in Matthew's version. Interestingly, a demoniac who is both blind and mute is unique in the Gospel tradition. If one were to judge that the Matthean picture of the demoniac as both blind and mute represents the original Q form, perhaps the unparalleled combination of a blind and mute demoniac could be used to argue for the historicity of this exorcism.[49]

However, most critics judge that Luke represents the form of the story closer to Q, at least when it comes to the absence of the motif of blindness.[50] Even if this be true, one should note that the only other examples of exorcism stories with a mute demoniac are the redactional creation of Matthew in Matt 9:32–33, a doublet that takes the theme of muteness from our Q story here (see below), and the story of the epileptic boy who had a "mute and deaf spirit" (Mark 9:25: *to alalon kai kōphon pneuma*).[51] In the latter case, the theme of (probably temporary) muteness is no doubt occasioned by the fits of epilepsy, and in our short Q story there is no indication of anything like epilepsy.

In other words, in these other two cases there are clear reasons for the presence of the motif of muteness in the text (Matthew's copying from his Q

model or the symptoms of an epileptic attack). No such reason is apparent in the narrative in Luke 11:14. It is by no means clear why the author(s) of Q would have created a story about a *mute* demoniac when all they needed was an introduction to a dispute occasioned by the exorcism of a demoniac; the motif of muteness immediately disappears after Luke 11:14 and never surfaces during the subsequent dispute. Though this reasoning is admittedly tenuous (given the wisp of a narrative), I think it more probable that the exorcism narrated in Luke 11:14 was not a creation of the author(s) of Q but was originally connected with at least some of the sayings material that now makes up the Beelzebul dispute. Lacking further data, I grant that this hardly proves the historicity of the single-verse narrative, though I see no countervailing reasons for denying historicity.

All in all, though, the question of the historicity of this introductory exorcism is much less important than the valuable Q sayings on exorcism that follow it, sayings that we have already examined in Chapter 16. Presumably, some exorcism or exorcisms occasioned these sayings, whether or not it is the particular exorcism that stands in Q as their introduction.

E. The Exorcism of a Mute Demoniac (Matt 9:32–33)

This brief story is widely seen by commentators as a redactional creation by Matthew on the model of the Q tradition that he also uses in Matt 12:22–23.[52] The reason for this recycling lies in the complex and beautiful structure Matthew has fashioned in chaps. 8–9 of his Gospel to enshrine his cycle of nine miracle stories.[53] Matthew carefully divides his collection of miracle stories into three groups of three (8:1–17; 8:23–9:8; 9:18–34), with some "buffer" section on discipleship in between each group (8:18–22; 9:9–17; 9:35–38). Apparently, by the time Matthew comes to his ninth miracle, he has exhausted his stock of miracle stories (drawn from Mark, Q, and M traditions). He fills out his final trio of miracles by creating in 9:32–33 a weak mirror image of the exorcism that unleashes the Beelzebul controversy in chap. 12.[54] If this explanation is correct, there is obviously no point in asking about a distinct historical tradition behind this particular formulation of an exorcism story.

F. The Reference to Mary Magdalene (Luke 8:2)

In a Lucan summary of Jesus' ministry that introduces the events of chaps. 8–9, Luke mentions Jesus' entourage. The entourage is made up of the Twelve "and some women who had been cured of evil spirits and diseases, [in particular] Mary called the Magdalene [i.e., from the town of Magdala],[55] out of whom seven demons had come, and Joanna, the wife of Chuza, the steward of Herod [Antipas], and Susanna, and many other women, who ministered to him out of their own resources" (Luke 8:2–3). This loosely written and rambling sentence leaves it unclear whether besides Mary Magdalene any of the other women had experienced an exorcism as distinct from the cure of an illness.

The distinction may not be all that important to Luke, since he narrates some stories of physical healing with exorcistic language (e.g., Simon's mother-in-law and the woman who had been bent over for 18 years). In any event, Mary Magdalene is said to have been liberated from a most severe case of demonic possession, the severity being underscored by the number seven.[56] Though the exorcist is not named, Luke obviously presupposes it to be Jesus, since in the context the exorcism explains Magdalene's devotion to and support of Jesus and the Twelve.

What can be said about the historical reliability of the information in 8:2?[57] On the one hand, the summary of Luke 8:1–3, taken as a whole, is probably a Lucan composition, replete with Greek words and phrases typical of Luke.[58] Moreover, the mention of Magdalene during the public ministry fits Luke's interest in women and his desire for witnesses who can testify to events of Jesus' public ministry as well as to his death and resurrection.[59] On the other hand, in the view of Fitzmyer, the words "out of whom seven demons had come" sound like "a stereotyped, inherited phrase."[60] At the very least, the phrase seems to suppose a fuller narrative to which it only alludes.

If we grant that the idea that Jesus exorcised Magdalene is pre-Lucan, can anything be said in favor of its historicity? In my opinion, one cannot appeal to the criterion of multiple attestation of sources. Luke 8:2 is the only clearly independent source for this idea. The brief mention in the "longer ending" of Mark's Gospel (16:9: "Mary Magdalene, out of whom he [Jesus] had cast seven demons") reflects, in my view, knowledge of Luke's Gospel (see in addition the references to the Lucan Emmaus account in Mark 16:12–13 and to the Lucan ascension in 16:19). Still, noted scholars like Rudolf Pesch and Joseph Hug maintain that Mark 16:9 represents independent tradition; so the argument from multiple attestation may be cogent to some.[61]

In my view, a better argument can be mounted from the criteria of embarrassment and coherence. All Four Gospels present Mary Magdalene as a chief witness to the crucifixion and burial of Jesus (Mark 15:40–41,47 parr.) and as the chief or only witness to the empty tomb (Mark 16:1–8 parr.). The Matthean and Johannine traditions even depict her as receiving a resurrection appearance from Jesus (Matt 28:8–10; John 20:11–18) before Jesus appears to the assembled group of male disciples. It seems unlikely that the early Christian tradition would have gone out of its way to cast doubt on the reliability of such a pivotal figure by recasting her—for no apparent reason—as a former demoniac. What purpose would have been served by such an invention? The vulnerability of a female witness who was a former demoniac was not lost on male critics of the Gospels, from Celsus in the 2d century to Ernest Renan in the 19th.[62] In addition, we may argue from the criterion of coherence that an exorcism by Jesus, freeing Magdalene from a severe disorder, would explain perfectly her intense dedication to him, even to the point of following him to his crucifixion, death, and entombment. If we may accept Luke 8:2 as basically historical, we receive a further bit of information about Jesus' exorcisms: at

least some of the recipients of these exorcisms, notably Magdalene, became loyal and lasting disciples—which only stands to reason in any case.

G. The Story of the Syrophoenician Woman (Mark 7:24–30 ‖ Matt 15:21–28)[63]

This story shares traits with a number of other types of Gospel miracle stories. Insofar as it involves an exorcism of a pagan in non-Jewish territory, it is reminiscent of the Gerasene demoniac of Mark 5:1–20. Yet, unlike the account of the Gerasene demoniac, this narrative lacks most of the motifs of a regular exorcism story (e.g., confrontation between Jesus and the demoniac, struggle of the demon to ward off Jesus, Jesus' rebuke and command to come out, the amazement of the crowd). Despite the theme of exorcism at the beginning and end of the story (Mark 7:25b,26b,29b–30), the heart of the narrative is a thrust-and-parry dialogue between Jesus and the Syrophoenician woman, who is begging for the healing of her possessed daughter (vv 27–28,29a).[64] Hence the one exorcism story that this narrative somewhat resembles is that of the possessed boy of Mark 9, since in each case a distraught parent begs Jesus for the exorcism of a possessed child, only at first to be rebuffed. Yet in Mark 9 the possessed boy actually meets Jesus and is "on stage" for almost the whole of the drama. In Mark 7, the possessed girl never comes into direct contact with Jesus and appears "on stage" only very briefly at the end of the story, after she has already been healed.

On the whole, the greatest similarities to the story of the Syrophoenician woman are to be found in the two other Gospel miracle stories involving healing at a distance: the healing of the centurion's servant (Matt 8:5–13 ‖ Luke 7:1–10) and the healing of the royal official's son (John 4:46–54, probably the Johannine variant of the healing of the centurion's servant).[65] In all three cases, (a) the person petitioning for the healing is a representative interceding for a beloved absent person who is suffering; (b) the dialogue, which is at the heart of the story, deals with some difficulty that might make one think that Jesus will not grant the request; (c) the dialogue reaches a climax in some word or deed that expresses the trust the petitioner has in Jesus' promise of healing, a promise that is given as Jesus sends the petitioner away; and (d) the fact of the healing is affirmed by the narrator at the end of the story. In this genre, the dialogue between the petitioner and Jesus, rather than Jesus' performance of the healing, stands at the center of the story.

On the one hand, the story of the Syrophoenician woman[66] resembles that of the centurion's servant in that in each story a Gentile dares to ask the Jewish wonder-worker (in both instances addressed with faith as "Lord" [kyrie]) for a miracle, one that turns out to be performed at a distance. On the other hand, the story of the Syrophoenician woman resembles that of the royal official's son in that in both cases Jesus seems at first to reject the request, but the petitioner persists in the face of discouragement and so winds up dismissed with the promise that the beloved child is well.[67]

The story of the Syrophoenician woman fits well into Mark's redactional framework,[68] since it is preceded by the dispute about clean and unclean in 7:1–23. Having just declared all food clean, Jesus now acts out the breaking down of the religious barrier separating Jew from Gentile.[69] But even apart from Mark's redactional framework, the story of the Syrophoenician woman carries the heavy freight of later Christian theology, specifically a theology of mission. As all Four Gospels and Paul agree (Rom 15:8–9), during his earthly ministry Jesus undertook no programmatic mission to the Gentiles as a group. But in a few exceptions made for special cases (the centurion, the Syrophoenician, the Gerasene demoniac), the future offer of salvation to the Gentiles is foreshadowed by the symbols of healing and exorcism. Indeed, in Jesus' affirmation (7:27) that it is only right that the children (= the Jews) *first* be fed to the full with the bread (= the gospel message of salvation), we seem to hear a variation on the theme of Paul's dictum, "first to the Jews" (Rom 1:16), a dictum turned into narrative in the Acts of the Apostles. Granted this theological allegory of salvation history, which lies at the very heart of the story of the Syrophoenician woman (i.e., in the dialogue with Jesus), it becomes difficult to maintain that this story's core is historical.[70] In this I think the story of the Syrophoenician woman differs from those of the Gerasene demoniac and the centurion's servant. To be sure, the latter two stories were open to Christian application to the mission to the Gentiles after Easter and they were so used.[71] But the clearly Christian theme of the mission "first to the Jews and then to the Gentiles" does not lie so blatantly at the very heart of these two stories and is not so clearly verbalized in their primitive forms as it is in the story of the Syrophoenician woman.

Admittedly, this decision about the historicity of an individual miracle story is not absolutely certain. Some arguments could be mounted in favor of historicity. The story contains a number of unusual concrete details that might argue for a striking event that stuck in the disciples' memory:[72] e.g., a pagan Syrophoenician woman in the region of Tyre,[73] a woman interceding for a demoniac daughter. These precise elements occur nowhere else in the Gospel tradition.

More significantly, nowhere else in the Gospel tradition does Jesus address a sincere petitioner with such harsh, insulting language. Christian exegetes would probably have decried the use of "dogs"[74] to designate Gentiles as shocking and intolerable if it had appeared in a Gospel story on the lips of a Pharisee instead of on the lips of Jesus. Some critics have suggested that the brutality of Jesus' initial address to the woman may be one reason why Luke omitted the story.[75] That a pre-Marcan storyteller created a scene in which Jesus used such offensive language may seem unlikely to many. To others it may simply be a reminder that the sensitivities of first-generation Christians may have been different from ours and that the views of Christians on the nascent Gentile mission may have been more diverse than we imagine. Weighing all the pros and cons, it seems to me that the story of the Syrophoenician woman is so shot through with

Christian missionary theology and concerns that creation by first-generation Christians is the more likely conclusion.[76]

Looking at our seven cases, we must admit how meager the data and therefore how fragile our judgments are. If, however, one is pressed to judge whether some historical core lies behind the stories of exorcism in the narrative sections of the Gospel, the following positions are, in my view, the most likely: (1) The story of the possessed boy and the brief reference to Mary Magdalene's exorcism probably go back to historical events in Jesus' ministry. I tend to think the same is true of the story of the Gerasene demoniac, though in this case the arguments are less probative. (2) In its present form, the exorcism of the demoniac in the Capernaum synagogue may be a Christian creation, but it probably represents "the sort of thing" Jesus did during his ministry in Capernaum. (3) The brief story of the exorcism of a mute (and blind?) demoniac in the Q tradition (Matt 12:24 ‖ Luke 11:14–15) is difficult to judge. It could go back to some historical incident, or it could be a literary creation used to introduce the Beelzebul controversy. (4) In contrast, it seems very likely that the story of the mute demoniac in Matt 9:32–33 is a redactional creation of Matthew to fill out his schema of three groups of three miracle stories in chaps. 8–9 of his Gospel. (5) The story of the Syrophoenician woman is probably a Christian creation to exemplify the missionary theology of the early church.

In the stories that seem to have some historical basis, the modern reader will no doubt want to press the question further: what exactly did happen to these tormented people? Once again, the various members of our mythical committee locked up in the Harvard Divinity School library will have different answers. A conservative Christian might wish to maintain the reality of demonic possession and Jesus' performance of true exorcisms. However, even a scholar with such a worldview would have to admit that the case of the possessed boy in Mark 9 points to epilepsy rather than demonic possession.[77] Moderate or liberal Christians would probably join other members of the committee in seeing most or all of the instances of "possession" as various types of mental or psychosomatic illnesses. One could go on to conjecture about how the charismatic personality of Jesus could have had a positive impact on these troubled people, but here one begins to lose all ability to verify hypotheses. Psychiatry is difficult enough to practice when the patient is next to the doctor on the couch. When the patient is some 20 centuries away, diagnosis is nigh impossible.[78] Moreover, purely psychological explanations may not be sufficient in a case like epilepsy. In any event, as I have stressed in the first section of this chapter, a decision that in any of these exorcisms a true miracle has taken place—in other words, that God has directly acted beyond all human potentiality to heal a particular individual—goes beyond what any scholar can say on purely historical grounds.

NOTES TO CHAPTER 20

[1] Sometimes even the length of the illness is not stated, though at other times it is for the sake of stressing the serious or incurable nature of the malady: e.g., the woman bent over for eighteen years (Luke 13:10–17), the woman who suffered a flow of blood for twelve years (Mark 5:25–34), the man who was paralyzed for thirty-eight years (John 5:1–9), and the man born blind (John 9:1). In the stories of the daughter of Jairus and the son of the widow of Nain, death has taken place the very day of the resuscitation (Mark 5:35; Luke 7:12), while Jesus arrives at Bethany four days after Lazarus' burial (John 11:39).

[2] See, e.g., Fridrichsen, *The Problem of Miracles,* 26–27; Richardson, *Miracle-Stories,* 128–30; Meyer, *The Aims of Jesus,* 154–55, 158.

[3] Granted the enormous difficulty of the material, one can sympathize with those critics who accept the global historicity of Jesus' miraculous activity but who prefer to think that the individual miracle stories are all creations of the early church, which remembered that Jesus did "these types of things." For the debate between those who think that we can affirm the historicity of at least some individual miracle stories (e.g., Franz Mussner in his *Die Wunder Jesu*) and those who in general are doubtful about such an affirmation (e.g., Reginald H. Fuller in his *Interpreting the Miracles* and Rudolf Pesch in his *Jesu ureigene Taten?*), see Franz Annen, *Heil für die Heiden. Zur Bedeutung und Geschichte der Tradition vom besessenen Gerasener (Mk 5,1–20 parr.)* (Frankfurter Theologische Studien 20; Frankfurt: Knecht, 1976), 192. Yet even among the skeptics, some make distinctions. Fuller, for instance, asks whether certain miracle stories that look like "ideal scenes" were created out of nothing. He replies: "Is it not more likely that the early Christians drew upon their store of *generalized memory* about Jesus? If these stories originated in the Palestinian community, this is more than likely. The dumb demoniac, the withered hand, the bent woman, and the dropsical man—all of these will not be stories of what Jesus actually did on a specific occasion, but will represent the *kind* of thing he used to do. Yet we would not rule out the possibility that occasionally a *specific* memory of an actual incident has been preserved." Fuller mentions the paralytic, the Syrophoenician woman, and the centurion of Capernaum as candidates. The possibility that there may be some candidates moves me to supply a brief examination of the individual miracle stories in what follows. If nothing else, certain patterns among the types of miracle stories will arise and may prove helpful.

[4] For detailed considerations of the individual miracle stories in the Gospels, see van der Loos, *The Miracles of Jesus,* 339–698; and Latourelle, *The Miracles of Jesus,* 70–237. It should be noted that both works have a strongly conservative and apologetic tone to them. Van der Loos, in particular, seems innocent of the problems raised by source and redaction criticism. Strange to say, despite his extremely conservative approach the results remain meager and vague. For a more critically informed approach, see the volume edited by Xavier Léon-Dufour, *Les miracles de Jésus* (Parole de Dieu; Paris: Editions du Seuil, 1977). For the grand form-critical surveys, see Bultmann, *Geschichte,* 223–60; and Dibelius, *Formgeschichte,* 66–100.

[5] For overall treatment of the subject with bibliography, see Twelftree's *Jesus the Exorcist.*

[6] As noted already, Luke gives some healing stories an air of exorcism: e.g., Pe-

ter's mother-in-law (4:38–39) and the woman who was bent over for eighteen years (13:10–17).

[7] In the Marcan miracle stories, I do not engage in detailed analysis of the redactional changes made in Mark's text by Matthew and/or Luke, since such changes are not relevant to the question of historicity. For Matthew's treatment of the miracle stories in his Gospel, see Heinz Joachim Held, "Matthäus als Interpret der Wundergeschichten," Günther Bornkamm, Gerhard Barth, and Heinz Joachim Held, *Überlieferung und Auslegung im Matthäusevangelium* (WMANT 1; 5th ed.; Neukirchen-Vluyn: Neukirchener Verlag, 1968) 155–287. For Luke's treatment of the miracle stories in his Gospel, see Ulrich Busse, *Die Wunder des Propheten Jesus. Die Rezeption, Komposition und Interpretation der Wundertradition im Evangelium des Lukas* (FB 24; Stuttgart: KBW, 1977).

For major exegetical questions concerning Mark 1:23–28, see Joshua Starr, "The Meaning of 'Authority' in Mark 1, 22," *HTR* 23 (1930) 302–5; David Daube, "*exousia* in Mark 1:22 and 27," *JTS* 39 (1938) 45–59; D. F. Hudson, "*hōs exousian echōn*," *ExpTim* 67 (1955–56) 17; Franz Mussner, "Ein Wortspiel in Mk 1,24?" *BZ* 4 (1960) 285–86; Ulrich Luz, "Das Geheimnismotif und die markinische Christologie," *ZNW* 56 (1965) 9–30 (= "The Secrecy Motif and the Marcan Christology," *The Messianic Secret* [Issues in Religion and Theology 1; ed. Christopher Tuckett; Philadelphia: Fortress; London: SPCK, 1983] 75–96); A. W. Argyle, "The Meaning of *exousia* in Mark 1:22, 27," *ExpTim* 80 (1968–69) 343; Robert H. Stein, "The 'Redaktionsgeschichtlich' Investigation of a Markan Seam (Mc 1:21f.)," *ZNW* 61 (1970) 70–94; Peter von der Osten-Sacken, "Streitgespräch und Parabel als Formen markinischer Christologie," *Jesus Christus in Historie und Theologie* (Hans Conzelmann Festschrift; ed. Georg Strecker; Tübingen: Mohr [Siebeck], 1975) 375–94, esp. 376–77; D. Dideberg and P. Mourlon Beenaert, " 'Jésus vint en Galilée.' Essai sur la structure de *Marc 1*, 21–45," *NRT* 98 (1976) 306–22; Otto Bächli, " 'Was habe ich mit Dir zu schaffen?' Eine formelhafte Frage im A.T. und N.T.," *TZ* 33 (1977) 69–80; Pierre Guillemette, "Mc 1,24 est-il une formule de défense magique?" *ScEs* 30 (1978) 81–96; Ernest Best, *The Temptation and the Passion: The Markan Soteriology* (2d ed. [originally SNTSMS 2]; Cambridge: Cambridge University, 1990) 68, 116.

[8] On the paradigmatic nature of "the day in Capernaum," see von der Osten-Sacken, "Streitgespräch," 376 (citing Julius Wellhausen as the source of the insight). See also Pesch, *Das Markusevangelium*, 1. 116–36; Guelich, *Mark 1–8:26*, 53–67; Paul J. Achtemeier, " 'He Taught Them Many Things': Reflections on Marcan Christology," *CBQ* 42 (1980) 465–81, esp. 478–80. Possibly Mark has taken a story of exorcism and framed it with references to Jesus' authoritative teaching to create a balance between exorcism and teaching.

[9] The exact extent of Marcan redaction must remain speculative; for attempts at distinguishing tradition and redaction, see Best, *The Temptation and the Passion*, 68; Stein "The 'Redaktionsgeschichtlich' Investigation," 87–89.

[10] The question of the precise meaning and function of the demon's words has been a source of debate since the seminal work of Otto Bauernfeind, *Die Worte der Dämonen im Markusevangelium* (BWANT 3/8; Stuttgart: Kohlhammer, 1927). Bauernfeind's use of parallels from Philo and notably from the magical papyri to interpret the demons' cries as formulas of apotropaic magic has not gone unchallenged; see, e.g., Bächli, " 'Was habe ich mit Dir zu schaffen?' " 77–78; Guillemette, "Mc 1,24," 81; Koch, *Die Bedeutung*, 56–61. Favorable to Bauernfeind's in-

terpretation is James M. Robinson, *The Problem of History in Mark* (SBT 21; London: SCM, 1957) 36–37; on the exorcisms in general, see pp. 33–42.

[11] It is true that similar motifs can be found in non-Christian exorcism stories, as Theissen has pointed out in his *Urchristliche Wundergeschichten.* But the question must always be how a given motif functions in a given literary work. In Mark, these motifs seem to function as part of what is vaguely called "the messianic secret"—though the precise meanings of the Marcan "secret" are debated among scholars; for a sampling of views, see Christopher Tuckett (ed.), *The Messianic Secret* (Issues in Religion and Theology 1; Philadelphia: Fortress; London: SPCK, 1983). Especially worthwhile are the essays by Ulrich Luz, "The Secrecy Motif and the Marcan Christology," 75–96; James D. G. Dunn, "The Messianic Secret in Mark," 116–31; and Heikki Räisänen, "The 'Messianic Secret' in Mark's Gospel," 132–40.

Moreover, one common word in Synoptic miracle stories is not found in Jewish and pagan parallels, namely, the verb *epitimaō* (literally, "rebuke"). From a number of Qumran documents (*Genesis Apocryphon,* the *War Scroll,* and the *Hodayoth*) we see that the Hebrew and Aramaic equivalent (the root *gʿr*) carries the sense of speaking "the commanding word, uttered by God or by his spokesman, by which evil powers are brought into submission, and the way is thereby prepared for the establishment of God's righteous rule in the world" (so Howard Clark Kee, "The Terminology of Mark's Exorcism Stories," *NTS* 14 [1967–68] 232–46, esp. 235). Kee sees this usage rooted in the OT use of *gʿr* and continued in the intertestamental literature. It is with this eschatological sense that the Gospels speak of Jesus "rebuking" the demons. As Kee points out, the *epitimaō* terminology is lacking in the exorcism stories of Philostratus and Lucian of Samosata, as is the eschatological/apocalyptic context.

[12] In Luke 4:23, the townspeople of Nazareth ask Jesus to perform in his hometown the kind of miracles he has already performed in Capernaum. Since I think that the whole of Luke 4:16–30 is Luke's creative redaction of Mark 6:1–6, Luke 4:23 may simply reflect Luke's knowledge of Capernaum's importance in Mark and Q. On the difficult source question in Luke 4:16–30, see *A Marginal Jew,* 1. 269–70.

[13] I think that the agreement indicates that the location in Capernaum was already in the Q tradition. Still, the matter is not certain. Matthew and Luke may have hit upon the same location by coincidence. What town in Galilee that Jesus visited would provide a more likely place for the house and entourage of a centurion?

[14] Unmentioned, that is, anywhere else in the Q document as best we can reconstruct it. As a matter of fact, Chorazin is never mentioned elsewhere in the NT (though it does occur in rabbinic literature); Bethsaida appears again (usually in passing) in Mark 6:45; 8:22; Luke 9:10; and John 1:44.

[15] See the list of tensions in Rudolf Pesch, "The Markan Version of the Healing of the Gerasene Demoniac," *Ecumenical Review* 23 (1971) 349–76, esp. 350–51 (this article is available in a fuller, reworked form as *Der Besessene von Gerasa. Entstehung und Überlieferung einer Wundergeschichte* [SBS 56; Stuttgart: KBW, 1972]); Latourelle, *The Miracles of Jesus,* 112. On the complicated tradition history, see Pesch, *Das Markusevangelium,* 1. 284, 292–93. For treatment of individual points and further bibliography, see (besides Pesch) Campbell Bonner, "The Technique of Exorcism," *HTR* 36 (1943) 39–49; T. A. Burkill, "Concerning Mk. 5,7 and 5,18–20," *ST* 11

(1957) 159–66; Harald Sahlin, "Die Perikope vom gerasenischen Besessenen und der Plan des Markusevangeliums," *ST* 18 (1964) 159–72; C. H. Cave, "The Obedience of Unclean Spirits," *NTS* 11 (1964–65) 93–97; Craghan, "The Gerasene Demoniac," 522–36; John Bligh, "The Gerasene Demoniac and the Resurrection of Christ," *CBQ* 31 (1969) 383–90 (quite fanciful); G. Schwarz, " 'Aus der Gegend' (Markus V. 10b)," *NTS* 22 (1975–76) 214–15 (lacking a sense of source and redaction criticism); Annen, *Heil für die Heiden*; Jean Calloud, Georges Combet, and Jean Delorme, "Essai d'analyse sémiotique," Léon-Dufour (ed.), *Les miracles de Jésus*, 151–81; Louis Beirnaert, "Approche psychanalytique," ibid., 183–88; Jean-Noël Aletti, "Une lecture en questions," ibid., 189–208; J. Duncan M. Derrett, "Contributions to the Study of the Gerasene Demoniac," *JSNT* 3 (1979) 2–17 (highly imaginative).

[16] Despite frequent affirmations that the Decapolis was a "league" or "confederation," no such claim can be substantiated from the ancient sources, literary or epigraphic. The name "Decapolis" indicates that originally the geographical group consisted of ten cities, but the number varied later on. Scythopolis was the only city in the group west of the Jordan River. On all this see S. Thomas Parker, "The Decapolis Reviewed," *JBL* 94 (1975) 437–41.

[17] Metzger (*A Textual Commentary*, 84) gives three reasons for preferring "Gerasenes": (1) the evidence of superior texts of both the Alexandrian and the so-called "Western" traditions; (2) the probability that "Gadarene" in some Marcan manuscripts represents an assimilation to what is the original reading in the Matthean parallel (Matt 8:28), Matthew's Gospel being the predominant Synoptic Gospel in the patristic period; (3) the probability that "Gergesenes" is a correction, "perhaps originally proposed by Origen." Metzger thinks that the strange reading of codex W ("Gergystenes") simply represents a scribal idiosyncrasy. See also his comments on Matt 8:28 (pp. 23–24). For a similar but fuller treatment of the question of "Gerasene" and its variants, see Annen, *Heil für die Heiden*, 201–6.

[18] Various form-critical observations point in the direction of the pig-incident's secondary nature. For example, as Pesch ("The Markan Version," 366–67) observes, one must distinguish in exorcism stories between the *apopompē*, the mere expelling of the demon without worrying about where it will go next, and the *epipompē*, the banishment of the demon to a new specified abode (e.g., animals, objects, distant places—including the sea). One also regularly finds in exorcism stories the motif of the demon's plea for some concession from the exorcist. But Pesch notes a peculiarity of Mark 5:1–20: "Clearly the concept of the *epipompe* in Mk. 5.12 is by no means unusual. But the combination of the plea for a concession and the *epipompe* is unusual. Usually the demoniac pleads for an *epipompe*, and the demons for a concession (in exchange for a strict *epipompe*). It is the amalgamation and combination of the two which constitutes the distinctiveness of the Markan narrative." One might go one step further in this form-critical observation. While an *epipompē* is by no means unusual in non-Christian exorcism stories, it is not present in the Gospel exorcisms, with the exception of Mark 5:1–20. This too may be an indication that, form-critically, the pig incident is a secondary addition, representing perhaps an assimilation to a pagan form of the exorcism story.

Some scholars would also argue for the secondary nature of the pig-incident by using the criteria of historicity. For example, in his exhaustive study of the story of the Gerasene demoniac, Annen (*Heil für die Heiden*, 192) concludes that the "swine episode" is the only motif in the story that is strictly speaking "improbable" from a historical point of view. Annen's major argument at this point is from the criterion of coherence: in the Gospel material that has a good chance of being historical, Jesus nowhere performs a destructive miracle that injures people (here the owner[s] of the pigs) and that seems to indulge in the spectacular simply for the sake of the spectacular.

[19] This argument combines two basic arguments of text criticism: (1) the reading that can explain the rise of the other variants is to be preferred; and more specifically (2) *lectio difficilior potior:* the more difficult reading is the better reading. Needless to say, this second argument, like any other in text criticism, has its limitations; see Kurt Aland and Barbara Aland, *The Text of the New Testament* (2d ed.; Grand Rapids: Eerdmans; Leiden: Brill, 1989) 281.

[20] Some critics argue the wrong-way round, supposing that the pig-incident is original to the story and then using the incident to decide the story's venue. See, e.g., John McRay, "Gerasenes," *The Anchor Bible Dictionary* (6 vols.; New York: Doubleday, 1992) 2. 991: "[If we reject Gerasa and Gadara as candidates,] this leaves Gergesa, modern El Koursi, on the E[ast] bank of the sea [of Galilee] as the only reasonable possibility, if any credence is to be given to the geographical statements of the gospels." One needs to distinguish here between the original form of the Gospel story and its final redactional form.

[21] Such a hypothesis is still found in a commentary as recent as Mann, *Mark*, 280. Two problems face the rationalizing approach, according to Pesch ("The Markan Version," 349) and Derrett ("Contributions," 5): (1) when panicked, pigs, unlike horses or cattle, do not usually stampede in groups but rather scatter; (2) pigs can swim. The unnatural behavior of the pigs may be intended by the ancient storyteller, who naturally believed in demonic possession, to demonstrate their possession by wild, destructive demons (consider what the demons had been doing to the poor man!). But the pigs' behavior makes no sense in a modern rationalizing explanation.

[22] Even if we take the description at face value, all we can be sure of is that Jesus was facing a profoundly disturbed individual. Precise diagnoses over the chasm of 2,000 years (e.g., the demoniac was a paranoid schizophrenic) are speculative at best.

[23] Annen (*Heil für die Heiden*, 185–86) thinks that this theological message was already contained in the pre-Marcan story.

[24] All this is said within the context of our particular historical-critical project of the quest for the historical Jesus. This powerful story can have tremendous hermeneutical potential when other methods of interpretation are applied to it. For interpretations of the pericope and allied materials in a "postmodern" literary framework, see Robert Detweiler and William G. Doty, *The Daemonic Imagination. Biblical Text and Secular Story* (American Academy of Religion Studies in Religion 60; Atlanta: Scholars, 1990).

[25] The exact meaning of "Legion" in the story—apart from the obvious sense of a large number—is still disputed among scholars. For various opinions, see Lane, *The Gospel According to Mark*, 184–85. Highly questionable is the interpretation of Hollenbach ("Jesus, Demoniacs, and Public Authorities," 581), who not only takes "My name is Legion" as a historical response of a demoniac speaking to Jesus but also proceeds to see the response as the "oblique aggressive strategy" of an oppressed native against an invading "colonial" power (i.e., Rome with its legions). Supposedly the tension between the demoniac's hatred for his Roman oppressors and "the necessity to repress this hatred in order to avoid dire recrimination drove him mad. But his very madness permitted him to do in a socially acceptable manner what he could not do as sane, namely express his total hostility to the Romans; he did this by identifying the Roman legions with demons." This in turn explains why the townspeople ask Jesus to leave

after the exorcism. By healing the demoniac Jesus had brought "the man's and the neighborhood's hatred of the Romans out into the open, where the result would be disaster for the community." After all, "the man evidently was a loudmouth (Mark 5:20)." Apart from the uncritical treatment of a Marcan miracle story as a videotape replay of a historical event in the life of Jesus, and apart from questionable analogies between French colonials in Algeria in the 20th century and Rome as a "colonial" power in Palestine in the 1st century A.D., Hollenbach never faces a serious objection to his whole interpretation. The story of the Gerasene demoniac is set in the Decapolis near the city of Gerasa, a hellenized and largely pagan city. Indeed, the whole story (pigs included) suggests that apart from Jesus and his disciples all the actors are pagans, not Jews. Now hellenized pagans in Palestine and environs were on the whole hostile to Palestinian Jews and looked to Roman forces to protect and support them against their Jewish adversaries. Moreover, the hellenized pagans of Gerasa may have been viewed as "colonials" by the Jews, since there was a tradition that the city had been settled by veterans of Alexander the Great. As the revised Schürer notes (*The History of the Jewish People*, 2. 150), "as a Greek city it [Gerasa] would certainly have been friendly towards Rome." Given this history instead of ahistorical sociological theories, one is hard-pressed to imagine that the Roman legions looked oppressive to the hellenized pagans of Palestine and surrounding regions (including Gerasa), as opposed to their Jewish neighbors.

[26] Pesch (*Das Markusevangelium*, 1. 292–93, 282) suggests three distinct stages in the growth of the story, which in his view was completed before Mark took it over and incorporated it into his Gospel without any changes. As to whether the kernel of the story goes back to the historical Jesus, Pesch remains undecided, though he seems to lean toward a negative answer ("The Markan Version," 370–71).

[27] Parker ("The Decapolis Reviewed," 438) states: "The use of the term ["Decapolis"] in the Gospel of Mark is apparently the earliest reference in ancient literature." The qualification "apparently" is prudent. The next attestation Parker mentions is in Pliny's *Natural History*, which was completed somewhere around A.D. 77. There is also a reference in Josephus' *Jewish War*, a work translated into Greek and published in that form some five to ten years after the destruction of Jerusalem in A.D. 70. Hence, it is likely that Mark's use is prior literarily to that of Pliny or Josephus; but, since all these dates are approximate (the publication of Mark's Gospel being placed usually ca. A.D. 70), certainty is not to be had. Perhaps more to the point is the fact that, in any case, "Decapolis" was a relatively and surprisingly rare geographical designation in the literature of the 1st century A.D.

[28] It may be that various OT texts have influenced the way the story was told as it was passed down in the oral tradition and finally redacted by Mark; Isa 65:1–5 and the account of the drowning of Pharaoh's troops in the Reed Sea are favorite candidates for midrashic influence. One must admit, however, that the suggestions of Sahlin ("Die Perikope"), Cave ("The Obedience"), and Derrett ("Contributions") appear at times as fanciful as the pig-incident itself.

[29] Often called the "lunatic" boy because of Matthew's use of the rare verb *selēniazo-mai* (literally, "to be moonstruck") in 17:15. In general, Matthew reduces greatly both the length of the story and the emphasis on the demonic element; the noun *daimonion* occurs only in v 18. Some critics argue for the antiquity and reliability of the story by pointing out that it occurs in the same place in all three Synoptics: between the transfiguration and the second prediction of the passion. But since Matthew and Luke are simply following Mark's story line here, no conclusions about the historical framework as distinct from the narrative framework can be drawn.

[30] For the tensions within the story as it now stands, see Koch, *Die Bedeutung*, 115; Pesch, *Markusevangelium*, 2. 86 n. 1; Latourelle, *The Miracles of Jesus*, 152. Pesch notes how the tensions and repetitions have led to all sorts of hypotheses about literary sources, most of them mutually contradictory. For an attempt to see an overarching structure and to understand the pericope as Marcan composition and theology, see Friedrich Gustav Lang, "Sola Gratia im Markusevangelium. Die Soteriologie des Markus nach 9,14–29 und 10,17–31," *Rechtfertigung* (Ernst Käsemann Festschrift; ed. Johannes Friedrich, Wolfgang Pöhlmann, and Peter Stuhlmacher; Tübingen: Mohr [Siebeck]; Göttingen: Vandenhoeck & Ruprecht, 1976) 321–37.

[31] Influential in propagating the view that two miracle stories were joined together to form 9:14–27 (in his opinion, before Mark) was Bultmann, *Geschichte*, 225–26. Also in favor of two stories secondarily combined are Held, "Matthäus als Interpret der Wundergeschichten," 177; Günther Bornkamm, "*Pneuma alalon*. Eine Studie zum Markusevangelium," *Geschichte und Glaube. Zweiter Teil. Gesammelte Aufsätze Band IV* (BEvT 53; Munich: Kaiser, 1971) 21–36; Paul J. Achtemeier, "Miracles and the Historical Jesus: A Study of Mark 9, 14–29," *CBQ* 37 (1975) 461–91, esp. 476–78; Koch, *Die Bedeutung*, 115–18 (espousing the view that Mark himself combined the two stories, pp. 118–21); Latourelle, *The Miracles of Jesus*, 151. Against distinguishing two different stories later woven together are Roloff, *Das Kerygma*, 144; Kertelge, *Die Wunder Jesu*, 174–75; Wolfgang Schenk, "Tradition und Redaktion in der Epileptiker-Perikope Mk 9:14–29," *ZNW* 63 (1972) 76–94, esp. 93; Gerd Petzke, "Die historische Frage nach den Wundertaten Jesu, dargestellt am Beispiel des Exorzismus Mark. IX. 14–29 par," *NTS* 22 (1975–76) 180–204, esp. 186–88; Howard, *Das Ego Jesu*, 87–90 (with lengthy lists of authors on each side of the question); Pesch, *Markusevangelium*, 2. 88. While I incline to the view that one basic story has undergone development in the tradition before being redacted by Mark, I admit that a firm decision is not possible; hence I do not make my treatment depend upon the details of any one hypothesis about the oral and literary evolution of the narrative.

I should note as an aside that Walter Schmithals rejects both the two-sources and one-source-with-expansions approach to explaining the formation of the narrative of the epileptic boy; see his "Die Heilung des Epileptischen (Mk. 9,14–29). Ein Beitrag zur notwendigen Revision der Formgeschichte," *Theologia Viatorum* 13 (1975–1976) 211–33. Indeed, Schmithals rejects the whole evolutionary model for narrative material in Mark suggested by traditional form criticism. According to Schmithals, miracle stories, apophthegms, and legends in Mark's Gospel result from the clothing of theological statements with narrative forms; this creative work was done by a theological teacher of the first Christian generation, perhaps with a school around him. Using this questionable model, Schmithals proceeds to read the story of the epileptic boy as an allegory of a humanity totally fallen under the power of evil. In effect, the story is read through the lenses of Paul, Augustine, and Luther, with no apologies on Schmithals's part. The whole exercise is idiosyncratic and highly imaginative. Another author who goes his own way is Xavier Léon-Dufour, who rejects any explanation of differences among the three Synoptics that relies on the view that two of the Synoptists depended on the third. For his own complicated explanation, which relies heavily on oral tradition, see "L'épisode de l'enfant épileptique," *Etudes d'évangile* (Parole de Dieu; Paris: Editions du Seuil, 1965) 184–227.

[32] For an uncritical interpretation of Mark 9:14–27 as the narrative of an eyewitness (e.g., Peter), see John Wilkinson, "The Case of the Epileptic Boy," *ExpTim* 79 (1967–68) 39–42.

[33] While it is true that the present form of the story in Mark reflects more than one

form-critical category, nevertheless the overarching form is that of a miracle story, more specifically an exorcism story; see Bornkamm, *"Pneuma alalon,"* 25. Roloff (*Das Kerygma*, 143–52) fails to take this point seriously—which is only the first of many problems in his highly speculative theory of the evolution of the narrative.

[34] The initial presence of the "scribes" (only in Mark's version, v 14) is curious; perhaps for Mark they provide a cross-reference to the scribes in the Beelzebul dispute (3:22). In any case, since they immediately disappear, never speak to or about Jesus, and play no part in the rest of the story, they probably do not belong to the earliest form of the tradition. In this I differ notably from Schenk ("Tradition und Redaktion," 79), who maintains (*contra* Bultmann) that the scribes originally played the role of the unsuccessful exorcists, precisely at the spot where now in v 18b the disciples stand. This theory is taken up by Pesch (*Markusevangelium*, 2. 84), who holds that in the original form of the story the argument at the beginning of the narrative was between the crowd and the scribes, who had just failed to perform the requested exorcism (v 14). Jesus' rebuke about the unbelieving generation (v 19) would thus have been aimed originally at the scribes. Supposedly a later reworking of the story introduced the disciples as the failed exorcists and so pushed the scribes to the margin of the narrative. Pesch proceeds to give his exegesis of the entire pericope from this angle, referring only briefly to the present form of the story. In my view, this makes a great deal hang by a very thin and speculative thread. One need only compare his approach with that of Roloff (*Das Kerygma*, 145–46), who just as adamantly insists on understanding the evolution of the pericope on the theory that the failure of Jesus' disciples is already in the oldest stratum of the tradition. On this whole question one may consult with profit Kertelge (*Die Wunder Jesu*, 176), who points out possible redactional links between the introductory verse (9:14) and other passages in Mark: e.g., *syzēteō* ("argue, dispute") appears already in 8:11 (of the Pharisees arguing with Jesus) and 9:10 (of the disciples arguing among themselves about the resurrection); the scribes have just been mentioned in 9:11. Part of the methodological problem in deciding among various scholarly analyses of Mark 9:14–27 is that particularly in the core of this story it is hard to distinguish between pre-Marcan tradition and Marcan redaction. In my opinion, Schenk is much too confident in his claim to be able to distinguish word-by-word and verse-by-verse between Mark and his source(s) by using word-statistics; in this I agree with Petzke ("Die historische Frage," 188), though his own reconstruction (pp. 188–89) remains problematic.

[35] As Pesch notes (*Markusevangelium*, 2. 88), both disabilities are explainable by the epilepsy from which the boy suffers. Bornkamm's insistence (*"Pneuma alalon,"* 29) that the inability to hear or speak is a permanent illness needs more of a basis than the text supplies; his position seems to be determined by his desire to see a stark contrast in Mark's juxtaposition of the stories of transfiguration and demonic possession between divine power and human impotence.

[36] Perhaps in their desire to tidy up the sprawling Marcan narrative, both Matthew and Luke omit the dialogue between Jesus and the boy's father on the subject of faith in Mark 9:21–24. Roloff's claim (*Das Kerygma*, 146–47) that Matthew and Luke had access to a special source for the story, a claim that he bases partly on their omission of Mark 9:21–24, ignores the common tendency of Matthew in particular to omit the concrete details of Marcan miracle stories. On Matthew's redaction, see Held, "Matthäus als Interpret der Wundergeschichten," 177–82. On the various reasons why both Matthew and Luke would have abbreviated Mark's account, see Achtemeier, "Miracles and the Historical Jesus," 473–74; Petzke, "Die historische Frage," 197–98; Bornkamm, *"Pneuma alalon,"* 31–32.

[37] For different interpretations of the "all things are possible to the one who be-

lieves," see van der Loos, *The Miracles of Jesus*, 400; Held, "Matthäus als Interpret der Wundergeschichten," 179–80. Held takes the interesting view that originally Jesus was speaking about his own faith as the source of his power to work miracles, but that Mark understood the saying to refer to the faith of the person asking for the miracle. For similar views, see Lohmeyer, *Das Evangelium des Markus*, 190–91; Gerhard Barth, "Glaube und Zweifel in den synoptischen Evangelien," *ZTK* 72 (1975) 269–92, esp. 278–82. Barth makes the telling point that in Mark 9:22 (the father's cry for help), *ei ti dynę boēthēson hēmin* means "if you can do anything [i.e., to heal my son], help us." The *dynę* refers here to the miracle-worker's power to heal. When therefore in the next verse (v 23) Jesus retorts with *panta dynata tǭ pisteuonti* ("all things can be done by the one who believes"), the word *dynata* naturally refers to the power to work a miraculous healing, as did the *dynę* in the previous verse. The flow from v 22 to v 23 thus argues strongly for taking v 23 as referring to the faith of the miracle-worker.

Other exegetes who with various nuances incline to this view include Pesch (*Markusevangelium*, 2. 92), who interprets the present Marcan text as referring to Jesus' own faith; and Kertelge (*Die Wunder Jesu*, 178), who thinks that the connection between v 19 and v 23 seems to demand this interpretation. Achtemeier ("Miracles and the Historical Jesus," 480–82) likewise interprets the dialogue as referring to Jesus' own faith.

Roloff (*Das Kerygma*, 150–51) takes the opposite view: the faith in question is that of the petitioner. Others who share this position include Lang ("Sola Gratia," 323–24), who claims that all other occurrences of faith (*pistis*) in Marcan miracle stories refer to the faith of the recipient of the miracle; Schenk ("Tradition und Redaktion," 90), who considers the whole dialogue on faith to be Mark's redactional creation; and Petzke ("Die historische Frage," 192), who thinks instead that the material is probably pre-Marcan. To be sure, in this whole debate one must ask whether it is probable that a lively exchange within a miracle story has preserved a saying of the historical Jesus. It is sobering to note that, despite their differences, Roloff, Schenk, Petzke, and Achtemeier all think that the dialogue between Jesus and the father is a secondary addition. Yet, if we should decide that the interpretation of Pesch and Kertelge is correct (i.e., that the faith Jesus speaks of is his own), a saying of Jesus that speaks of his own faith as the source of his miracles would certainly satisfy the criteria of embarrassment and discontinuity: it is unique within the Four Gospels (see Petzke, "Die historische Frage," 198).

[38] Schenk ("Tradition und Redaktion," 89) stresses how out of place talk of faith is in an exorcism story; similarly Roy Yates, "Jesus and the Demonic in the Synoptic Gospels," *ITQ* 44 (1977) 39–57, esp. 47.

[39] Van der Loos (*The Miracles of Jesus*, 401) speaks of "a surprising unanimity" in the diagnosis, though he notes (p. 405) that F. Fenner prefers the designation "hysteria," however that be defined. Wilkinson ("The Case," 41), however, claims that some of the symptoms do not correspond to fits of hysteria; he is emphatic that the boy suffered from *le grand mal* epilepsy. Petzke ("Die historische Frage," 189–90) supplies various ancient descriptions of epilepsy and notes how closely they coincide with the symptoms described by Mark.

[40] Not surprisingly, in the ancient world this influence of the moon on epileptics was understood in both natural and supernatural ways; see van der Loos, *The Miracles of Jesus*, 403; and the excursus on epilepsy in the ancient Greco-Roman world in Petzke, "Die historische Frage," 189–90.

[41] The redactional tacking-on of a moral lesson on prayer, which has no anchorage

in the story proper, is a sure sign of Mark's redaction of a pre-Marcan narrative for his own purposes; see Petzke, "Die historische Frage," 194–96. On the importance of prayer, including prayer for miracles, in Mark's theology, see Sharyn Echols Dowd, *Prayer, Power, and the Problem of Suffering: Mark 11:22–25 in the Context of Markan Theology* (SBLDS 105; Atlanta: Scholars, 1988). While Pesch (*Markusevangelium*, 2. 96–97) agrees that the verses on prayer (9:28–29) are secondary to the original miracle story, he suggests that they were already added to the tradition by the time it came to Mark. This fits in with Pesch's view of Mark as a conservative redactor and especially with his position espousing a lengthy pre-Marcan "Passion Narrative" that reaches all the way back to Mark 8:27–33 (see 2. 1–25). For what I consider cogent arguments that Mark himself has appended 9:28–29, see Karl-Georg Reploh, *Markus—Lehrer der Gemeinde* (SBM 9; Stuttgart: KBW, 1969) 211–21. In the view of Koch (*Die Bedeutung*, 125–26), the still larger redactional context of Mark 8–10 places the exorcism within the themes of the epiphany of Jesus in his miracles and his journey toward death and resurrection. Curiously, the desire to use and expand upon this story of the possessed boy seems to have stopped with Mark. Unlike some other miracles in the Gospels, the apocryphal Gospels and Acts show no interest in using or developing this story; on this point see Achtemeier, "Miracles and the Historical Jesus," 473.

[42] Pesch, *Markusevangelium*, 2. 95.

[43] See Pesch, *Markusevangelium*, 2. 95 n. 38.

[44] Schmidt, *Der Rahmen der Geschichte Jesu*, 227. A similar view is taken by Achtemeier at the end of his lengthy and careful analysis ("Miracles and the Historical Jesus," 491): "Jesus did heal a young lad in a way identified in his world as casting out a demon, and any historical picture of Jesus that does not include his activity as exorcist will be a distortion."

What I have presented in the main text is, in my view, the best one can say about the historicity of this story. Latourelle (*The Miracles of Jesus*, 151–54) tries to heap up further arguments, but most will not stand close critical inspection. Both his work and that of van der Loos suffer from a lack of clarity about their positions on the Synoptic problem and hence on the use of the criterion of multiple attestation of sources (multiple versions do not automatically equal multiple sources). Both works also suffer from a strong apologetic tone, marked by claims that are not supported by evidence. Consider, for instance, Latourelle's closing claim about the story of the possessed boy (p. 154): "This much is certain: the healing of this boy, who was truly ill, is permanent, whereas modern medicine could not eliminate every possibility of a relapse." Where in this or other Gospel miracle stories are we given assurances that relapses did not occur at a later date?

[45] Lührmann, *Die Redaktion*, 32; Kloppenborg (*Q Parallels*, 92), who lists various opinions and judges: "The agreements between Matt 12:22–23; 9:32–33 and Luke 11:14 against Mark in relating an exorcism of a dumb demoniac, with mention of his speaking and the astonishment of the crowd, indicate that 11:14 is indeed from Q." See also Busse, *Die Wunder des Propheten Jesus*, 278–82.

[46] Sato, *Q und Prophetie*, 82.

[47] See Kloppenborg, *The Formation of Q*, 122: "Whether it [the miracle story in Luke 11:14] served as the occasion for the pronouncement from the beginning, or whether it was supplied in a pre-Q stratum of tradition can no longer be determined."

[48] The range of meanings of *kōphos* is wide; the word can signify "deaf" or "mute" or both. Since in this Q story both Matthew and Luke present the cure in terms of the

demoniac's ability to speak, without any reference to a restored ability to hear, *kōphos* probably means only "mute." Practically, though, in the ancient world, especially among peasants lacking sophisticated medical treatment, being deaf from birth would probably entail muteness or extreme difficulty in speaking in any case.

As an aside, it may be noted that, while certain other stories of healing in Mark— especially 7:31–37 (a deaf and mute man [*kōphon kai mogilalon*]) and 8:22–26 (the blind man at Bethsaida)—may carry some exorcistic overtones, neither the noun "demon" nor the exorcistic command "come out" (*exelthe*) appears. Strictly speaking, such narratives are not exorcism stories.

[49] Whether the Matthean form of the miracle is the original Q version must remain an open question. The combination of demoniac-mute-blind could come from a running together of two separate stories in Matt 9:27–31 (the healing of two blind men) and 9:32–33 (the healing of a mute demoniac). Yet the latter story is itself most probably a weak mirror image of Matt 12:22–23. Deciding which evangelist gives us the original vocabulary of the Q story is still more difficult. Luke speaks in usual exorcistic terms of the demon "coming out" (*daimoniou exelthontos*, Luke 11:14). Although Matthew begins the narrative by referring to a demoniac (*daimonizomenos*), the exorcistic terminology immediately disappears as he speaks of Jesus *healing* the blind and mute man, with no mention of the demon "coming out." Since the crowd then responds with a marveling question ("Could this possibly be the Son of David?"), Matthew's version may reflect his own theology of the merciful Son of David, who heals the "nobodies" of Israel and "outsiders" (cf., e.g., Matt 15:22; 20:30,31; 21:14–15). Since both the Matthean and Lucan texts immediately continue with Jesus' adversaries claiming that Jesus "casts out demons by the power of the prince of demons," Luke's vocabulary of exorcism is probably original in the Q narrative. Moreover, Davies and Allison (*The Gospel According to Saint Matthew*, 2. 334) point out that the Matthean version of the story is marked by typically Matthean vocabulary. For a detailed examination of the Greek vocabulary of both versions of the story, see Laufen, *Die Doppelüberlieferungen*, 126–27.

[50] Schulz (*Q. Die Spruchquelle der Evangelisten*, 204) holds that the Q form of the exorcism was probably identical to Luke 11:14. Against this view is Laufen (*Die Doppelüberlieferungen*, 127), who thinks, nevertheless, that the motif of blindness is a Matthean addition. Laufen gives his hypothetical reconstruction of the Q text on p. 131; significantly, he chooses to paraphrase the opening clause of Luke 11:14 in German ("Jesus trieb einen Dämonen aus, der stumm war") because he thinks that the Q text at this point cannot be reconstructed with fair certitude.

[51] Here *kōphos* obviously means "deaf" as opposed to "mute."

[52] So Latourelle, *The Miracles of Jesus*, 168; Meier, *Matthew*, 98–100. Davies and Allison (*The Gospel According to Saint Matthew*, 2. 138) remark: "This exceedingly concise and comparatively unremarkable pronouncement [?] story . . . is a redactional doublet of 12.22–3." As noted above, Matt 9:32–33 may reflect the model found in Q more than Matt 12:22–23a does, since, like Luke 11:14, Matt 9:32–33 depicts the demoniac simply as mute, not as both blind and mute (as in Matt 12:22).

[53] On this point see Meier, *Matthew*, 79–80: "Often commentators speak of ten miracle stories in chaps. 8–9. . . . But this is to misunderstand Mt's pattern. The stories of the healing of the woman with a hemorrhage and the raising of the dead girl were already woven together by Mk into one long pericope, and Mt cuts that pericope to its bare bones. It is better to count nine miracle *stories* or pericopes, though there are admittedly more than nine miracles. In fact, there are really more than ten, since by

common consent the healings at evening (8:16) are counted together with the healing of Peter's mother-in-law (8:14–15). As far as Mt's pattern goes, there are nine pericopes." This pattern has been adopted by Davies and Allison, *The Gospel According to Saint Matthew*, 1. 67 n. 35, 2. 1–4.

[54] Ending his catena of nine miracles with the cure of two blind men and then the healing of a mute demoniac also allows Matthew to have Jesus be scrupulously exact when he describes his miraculous activity to the disciples of John the Baptist in 11:2–6: "The blind see . . . the deaf [*kōphoi*] hear . . ." (11:5). Because of the reference forward to Matt 11:5, *kōphon* in 9:32 probably means both "mute" and "deaf."

[55] Apart from the name Mary Magdalene, the town of Magdala is not mentioned in the NT, Josephus, or sources contemporaneous with them. Fitzmyer (*The Gospel According to Luke*, 1. 697) suggests that Magdala may be the town of Tarichaeae in Galilee mentioned by Josephus (e.g., *J.W.* 2.13.2 §252), "not far from Tiberias on the west coast of Lake Gennesaret" (i.e., the Sea of Galilee). On this see also Marshall, *The Gospel of Luke*, 316.

[56] The symbolic number seven simply expresses fullness, completeness, or intensity. There is no need to engage in speculation about the Babylonian idea of seven evil spirits, the seven planets, or phases of the moon (see van der Loos, *The Miracles of Jesus*, 410–11). Obviously, the generic and symbolic reference to a severely disturbed psychological state hardly allows a precise diagnosis, such as schizophrenia, multiple personalities, or the ever-popular and all-purpose "hysteria."

[57] It goes without saying—or should—that Mary Magdalene is not to be equated with either the "sinful woman" of Luke 7:36–50 or the Mary of Bethany from the Johannine tradition (John 11–12). This is a commonplace in exegesis today; see, e.g., Raymond F. Collins, "Mary (Person)," *The Anchor Bible Dictionary* (6 vols.; New York: Doubleday, 1992) 4. 579–82, esp. 580. Indeed, even in 20th-century Roman Catholic exegesis this view is nothing new; see the 1929 monograph of Peter Ketter, *Die Magdalenen Frage* (Trier: Paulinus, 1929) 15, 33, 55.

[58] E.g., *kai egeneto en tŌ . . . kai autos, kathexēs, diodeuō, euaggelizomai,* and *astheneia*; on this see Fitzmyer, *The Gospel According to Luke*, 1. 695. Martin Hengel ("Maria Magdalena und die Frauen als Zeugen," *Abraham unser Vater. Juden und Christen im Gespräch über die Bibel* [Arbeiten zur Geschichte des Spätjudentums und Urchristentums 5; Otto Michel Festschrift; ed. Otto Betz, Martin Hengel, and Peter Schmidt; Leiden/Cologne: Brill, 1963] 243–56, esp. 245 n. 4, 247) strongly affirms the redactional nature of Luke 8:1, but he is equally strong in holding (rightly, in my opinion) that Luke 8:2–3 and Mark 15:40 represent two ancient pieces of tradition of entirely different origin and that the former cannot simply be derived by Lucan redaction from the latter.

[59] On this see Schürmann, *Das Lukasevangelium*, 1. 446; and Marshall, *The Gospel of Luke*, 315. Schürmann even suggests that the mention of three women here (as in Mark 16:1 and Luke 24:10) reflects the law of Deuteronomy concerning the sufficient number of witnesses for valid testimony (Deut 19:15). The important missionary role of certain women in the early church may also be shining through the Lucan text here. Hengel ("Maria Magdalena," 248) sees in the list of three female witnesses a phenomenon also observed in the list of Peter, James, and John as the inner core of the Twelve in the Synoptics and the list of James, Cephas, and John as the three pillars of the Jerusalem community in Gal 2:9. Accordingly, Hengel suggests that the list of three women, with Mary Magdalene always first, may indicate authority or prestige in the early Christian community. In a somewhat different direction, François Bovon ("Le

privilège pascal de Marie-Madeleine," *NTS* 30 [1984] 50–62) claims to see a certain "official disdain" for Magdalene in canonical and "orthodox" writings of the 1st and early 2d century A.D., while gnostic and "heretical writings" tend to exalt her role. In my opinion the latter point is much clearer in the sources than the prior.

[60] Fitzmyer, *The Gospel According to Luke*, 1. 695. Schürmann (*Das Lukasevangelium*, 1. 448) speculates about a possible source dealing with Jesus and women, reflected in Luke 7:11–17,36–50; 8:2–3.

[61] Pesch (*Das Markusevangelium*, 2. 544–46) prefers to explain Mark 16:9 in terms of a knowledge of various pre-Lucan traditions, which Luke later incorporated into his Gospel. A similar position is defended by Joseph Hug, *La finale de l'évangile de Marc (Mc 16, 9–20)* (EBib; Paris: Gabalda, 1978) 164. Hug, however, is cautious in his formulation: "It is not certain that this feature [i.e., the exorcism of seven demons from Magdalene] has been borrowed from Luke 8:2; the different formulation . . . could indicate that it is a question of borrowing a tradition about the women, elements of which Luke has used in various places." But is independence of the canonical Gospels likely if, as Hug suggests, Mark 16:9–20 was written in the second third of the 2d century? That the vocabulary and style in Mark 16:9–20 are different from that of the canonical Gospels is hardly telling. If a 2d-century author has meshed and compressed resurrection traditions of Matthew, Luke, and John into a mere twelve verses, it is not surprising that he speaks with his own vocabulary and style. Personally, I find it too much of a coincidence that such a short passage as Mark 16:9–20 should have at least three striking parallels to specifically Lucan material. Hence I concur with Lane (*The Gospel According to Mark*, 604), who considers the events in Mark 16:9–20 "brief extracts from the resurrection reports in Matthew, Luke and John."

[62] For Celsus' attack on Magdalene's credibility, see Origen's *Contra Celsum*, 2.55. For a critical Greek text and French translation, see Marcel Borret, *Origène. Contra Celse. Tome I (Livre I et II)* (SC 132; Paris: Cerf, 1967) 414–15: *tis touto eide; gynē paroistros, hōs phate, kai ei tis allos tōn ek tēs autēs goēteias* ("Who saw this [i.e., the resurrection appearances]? A frenzied woman, as you say, and perhaps some other [Peter?] of those attached to this magical quackery . . ."). For Renan's observations on Mary Magdalene at the empty tomb, see Ernest Renan, *The Life of Jesus* (New York: Brentano's, 1863) 295–96. On the whole question of Magdalene and the resurrection appearances, see Gerald O'Collins and Daniel Kendall, "Mary Magdalene as Major Witness to Jesus' Resurrection," *TS* 48 (1987) 631–46, esp. 631–32.

[63] For basic discussion and further bibliography on the pericope, see Roy A. Harrisville, "The Woman of Canaan. A Chapter in the History of Exegesis," *Int* 20 (1966) 274–87; T. A. Burkill, "The Syrophoenician Woman: The Congruence of Mark 7:24–31," *ZNW* 57 (1966) 23–37; idem, "The Historical Development of the Story of the Syrophoenician Woman (Mark vii:24–31)," *NovT* 9 (1967) 161–77; idem, "The Syrophoenician Woman: Mark 7,24–31," *Studia Evangelica IV. Part I* (TU 102; ed. F. L. Cross; Berlin: Akademie, 1968) 166–70 [basically the same text as pp. 172–77 of the article in *NovT* 9]; Barnabas Flammer, "Die Syrophoenizierin. Mk 7,24–30," *TQ* 148 (1968) 263–78; W. Storch, "Zur Perikope von der Syrophönizierin," *BZ* 14 (1970) 256–57; Alice Dermience, "Tradition et rédaction dans la péricope de la Syrophénicienne: Marc 7,24–30," *RTL* 8 (1977) 15–29; Gerd Theissen, "Lokal- und Sozialkolorit in der Geschichte von der syrophönikischen Frau (Mk 7:24–30)," *ZNW* 75 (1984) 202–25 [= Gerd Theissen, "The Story of the Syrophoenician Woman and the Border Region between Tyre and Galilee," *The Gospels in Context. Social and Political History in the Synoptic Tradition* (Minneapolis: Fortress, 1991) 61–80].

[64] One is astounded to read the judgment of Harrisville, "The Woman of Canaan," 276: "In Mark's version, the emphasis is clearly upon the healing itself and not upon the exchange between Jesus and the woman." In fact, the exchange between Jesus and the woman is so important that Bultmann (*Geschichte*, 38) labels the story an apophthegm: "The miracle is not really narrated here for its own sake; rather, the attitude of Jesus as it develops in the conversation is the main point. And indeed what lies before us is a kind of dispute story [*Streitgespräch*], in which this time however Jesus . . . is the one who is overcome." Using equivalent terminology, Taylor (*The Gospel According to St. Mark*, 347) says that "the narrative is more akin in form to the Pronouncement-story than to the Miracle-story," although he goes on to state that the narrative has not taken on the full form of a pronouncement story. Harrisville may have been led to make his dubious claim at least in part by his unlikely—and in the article unsubstantiated—view that Mark is here dependent on Matthew; for a defense of Marcan priority in this story, see Davies and Allison, *The Gospel According to Saint Matthew*, 2. 542–43.

[65] See Pesch, *Das Markusevangelium*, 1. 386.

[66] On Mark's designation of the woman as "a Greek, a Syrophoenician by birth," see *A Marginal Jew*, 1. 295. "Greek" (*Hellēnis*) is probably meant to designate her as a pagan (here it probably does not mean "Greek-speaking"); "Syrophoenician" indicates that she stems from an ethnically mixed group. Theissen ("Lokal- und Sozialkolorit," 210–11) makes a great deal (too much, in my opinion) hang on his interpretation of *Hellēnis* as a Greek-speaking woman, integrated into Greek culture, who belonged to the upper class. Not a little imagination is being mixed here with a wealth of cultural, economic, political, and social data.

"Canaanite" (Matt 15:22) is a redactional substitution by Matthew, who conjures up the idea of the ancient indigenous enemies of Israel in the Holy Land; on this explanation (as well as five others), see Davies and Allison, *The Gospel According to Saint Matthew*, 2. 547.

[67] Some exegetes would claim that all three stories share these last two motifs (Gentile petitioners and initial rebuff) equally. But in my view (1) there are no grounds in John's narrative for turning a royal official of Herod Antipas in Galilee into a Gentile. In fact, in John's Gospel, during the public ministry Jesus never interacts directly with a person who is explicitly designated a Gentile. Supposing that the royal official is a Gentile is a prime example of reading John through the lenses of the Synoptics. (2) While the words of Jesus to the centurion in Matt 8:7 could be taken as an indignant question ("Am I supposed to come [to your house] and heal him?"), it is more probable that the sentence should be taken as a gracious assent to the request ("I shall come and heal him"). (a) This ties in better with the previous story (Matt 8:2–4), where Jesus breaks the Mosaic Law by touching a leper to cure him. (b) Moreover, only when Jesus' words are taken to express compliance with the request does the centurion's humble reply in v 8 understandably cause such great amazement on Jesus' part (v 10). (c) Gundry (*Matthew*, 143) makes another telling point: ". . . if it were a question of coming into a Gentile's house, we should have expected *elthōn* [in v 7] to be more than the mere participle it is, and perhaps have expected to read 'into your house.' But the stress falls on healing. Not till the response of the centurion does the stress fall on entry into his house." For the position that v 7 is a question, see Davies and Allison, *The Gospel According to Saint Matthew*, 2. 21–22; scholars defending both sides of the question are listed there. For the position that v 7 is a statement, see (besides Gundry) Meier, *Matthew*, 83–84; Grundmann, *Das Evangelium nach Matthäus*, 251–52. For a fuller treatment of this question, see Chapter 21, Section V.

[68] On this see Burkill, "The Syrophoenician Woman: The Congruence of Mark 7:24–31," 28–35.

[69] The story of the Syrophoenician woman may look forward as well as backward in the Marcan framework. For instance, Jesus' words to the Syrophoenician woman about taking bread and being filled (7:27) are echoed later on in the second multiplication of loaves (8:6, *labōn artous* ["taking bread"]; and 8:8, *echortasthēsan* ["they were filled"]). For a detailed study of signs of Marcan redactional activity in the story, see Dermience, "Tradition," 15–29. Dermience goes so far as to suggest (p. 28) that the whole story may be a creation of Mark, who drew traditional material from the double-story of the raising of the daughter of Jairus and the healing of the woman with the hemorrhage. Needless to say, if this view, which is not widely held, should be true, any question of a historical core vanishes. At any rate, the heavy amount of Marcan style and vocabulary that Dermience sees in the narrative should make us wary about declaring particular details historical or erecting some grand sociological or psychological analysis on weak foundations.

[70] Burkill ("The Syrophoenician Woman: Mark 7,24–31," 166–70) sketches a hypothetical four-stage development of the story. He suggests that in the first stage a primitive form of the story arose as a dramatization of the truth that Jesus the Messiah had been appointed to minister exclusively to the chosen people, the Jews. A second stage then supposedly gave the story a more universalistic thrust. Stage three involved Mark's modest redactional touches, while stage four was Matthew's redaction. While not impossible, the first two stages of this reconstruction are highly speculative.

Some commentators have suggested that the story of the Syrophoenician woman echoes bits of the story of the prophet Elijah's visit to the widow of Zarephath in the region of Sidon (1 Kgs 17:7–24). But themes from this OT story are not so dominant as to justify seeing it as the major source of the Gospel pericope. In this I agree with Guelich (*Mark 1–8:26*, 385); and Davies and Allison, *The Gospel According to Saint Matthew*, 2. 545. For more positive views on the supposed parallel, see Grundmann, *Das Evangelium nach Markus*, 154; Kertelge, *Die Wunder Jesu*, 152; and J. D. M. Derrett, "Law in the New Testament: The Syro-Phoenician Woman and the Centurion of Capernaum," *NovT* 15 (1973) 161–86, esp. 162–74. I find the supposed allusion to Judg 1:7 (Storch, "Zur Perikope," 256–57) even more questionable.

[71] A prime example of this is Matthew's insertion of the Q prophecy of the coming of "many from east and west" to the eschatological banquet (Matt 8:11–12 ‖ Luke 13:28–29) into the separate Q context of the story of the centurion's servant (Matt 8:5–13 ‖ Luke 7:1–10).

[72] Yet, strictly speaking, the disciples are not present in this Marcan story; they are added by Matthew.

[73] Theissen ("Lokal- und Sozialkolorit," 221) takes a cautious and vague stand in favor of historicity: "In principle it cannot be excluded that the story has a historical core: an encounter of Jesus with a hellenized Syrophoenician woman. Still, one should not speculate on it here."

[74] The diminutive form *kynarion* (literally, "puppy") is typical of popular Hellenistic Greek in general (note the diminutive *thygatrion*, "little daughter," in v 25 and then the regular form *thygatros* in v 26) and should not be seen as a "softening" or "humorous" touch. For an attempt to soften the insult by another route, see Flammer, "Die Syrophoenizerin," 465. On the clear harshness of the epithet, see Burkill, "The Historical Development," 170.

[75] See Burkill, "The Syrophoenician Woman: The Congruence of Mark 7:24–31," 25.

[76] For arguments in favor of historicity, see Latourelle, *The Miracles of Jesus*, 173–75; Davies and Allison, *The Gospel According to Saint Matthew*, 544–45.

[77] For example, Yamauchi ("Magic or Miracle?" 128–31) refers freely to the possessed boy of Mark 9 as "the epileptic boy" and complains of fundamentalistic sects who do serious damage by insisting that cases of epilepsy should be exorcised. Yet he waffles on the question of whether the epileptic symptoms described in Mark 9 may be seen as the result of demonic possession. Yamauchi seems to be caught in an embarrassing situation. On the one hand, he notes how enlightened physicians like the anonymous author of the Hippocratic treatise *On the Sacred Disease* denounced magicians who resorted to incantations to cure epilepsy; the anonymous author's explanation is a purely physiological one (pp. 112–13). On the other hand, Yamauchi is faced with the fact that Jesus treats what seems to be a case of epilepsy in Mark 9 by commanding that the demon causing the illness depart from the boy and never return. To claim that Jesus is just pretending to think that a demon is present and is just pretending to perform an exorcism goes against the natural sense of this text and every other exorcism text in the Gospels. If one accepts that the "possessed boy" is really an epileptic and that enlightened physicians in the Greco-Roman world recognized this affliction as a physical disease, one must face the consequences of this in assessing the cultural mind-set of Jesus. For the continuation of the conflict between a natural and a demonic explanation of epilepsy in the exegesis of the church (heavily influenced by Origen), see Franz Joseph Dölger, "Der Einfluss des Origenes auf die Beurteilung der Epilepsie und Mondsucht im christlichen Altertum," *Antike und Christentum. Kultur- und religionsgeschichtliche Studien* (5 vols.; Münster: Aschendorff, 1929–36) 4. 95–109. One can only be astounded when Wilkinson ("The Case," 42) tries to maintain the possibility that what is correctly diagnosed as epilepsy may nevertheless be the result of demonic possession. As a rule I prescind in this book from questions of present-day pastoral concern, but in this case I must protest against such irresponsible exegesis, which could do incalculable harm to innocent people.

[78] On this see Joachim Gnilka, "Psicologia del profondo ed esegesi," *RivB* 38 (1990) 3–12. The difficulty of applying any psychiatric approach to the exorcism stories of the Gospels is exemplified in Hollenbach's article, "Jesus, Demoniacs, and Public Authorities," 567–88. The particular views on mental illness, psychiatry, society, and political power espoused by Hollenbach are influenced by such "anti-psychiatrists" as Thomas Szasz. Though these views enjoyed a certain vogue for a decade or two, they have come in more recently for heavy criticism; see, e.g., Paul R. McHugh, "Psychiatric Misadventures," *The American Scholar*, Autumn (1992) 497–510. We are reminded once again that nothing ages quicker than relevance. The quest for the historical Jesus is speculative enough without highly questionable psychiatric theories being thrown into the mix.

CHAPTER 21

JESUS' HEALINGS

For all their difficult and even bizarre nature, the exorcism stories we have examined at least have the advantage of a unified focus. When we turn to the stories in which Jesus heals various kinds of illnesses or other bodily afflictions,[1] we are confronted with a wide range of vague pathologies that are not easily brought under a few neat headings. Nevertheless, at the risk of oversimplifying, I think that the heterogeneous material in the Gospel stories of healing can be conveniently divided into four major categories.

(1) Depending on whether or not we include Matthew's version of the cure of the centurion's servant, there are four or five distinct miracle stories in the Gospels about people suffering from paralyzed, withered, or crippled parts of their bodies.[2] The sources represented are Mark, L, and John—and Q, if we include the Matthean version of the centurion's servant. In addition, there is a general reference in a Q logion to the lame walking (Matt 11:5 || Luke 7:22).

(2) There are three distinct stories involving blindness, plus a general reference to the blind seeing in the Q logion already mentioned. Besides Q, the sources represented are Mark and John.

(3) There are two cases of leprosy, one in Mark and one in the L tradition, plus a general reference in the already cited Q logion.

(4) Finally, there is a catch-all category for various physical afflictions that occur only once each. These add up to five separate instances, or six if we include Luke's version of the centurion's servant (Luke 7:1–10, with the distant parallel of the royal official's son in John 4:46–54).

This general inventory immediately makes a few points clear. First, even apart from exorcisms, there is wide multiple attestation of sources and forms for Jesus' ministry of healing the sick and infirm. References to Jesus' healing activity—indeed, whole stories—are found in almost every Gospel source: Mark, Q, L, and John.[3] Second, while it is perfectly correct to say that Jesus was a 1st-century Jewish exorcist, that is hardly an adequate description of him, even from the limited vantage point of miracle-working. In the Gospels there are 6 exorcism stories, plus the reference to Mary Magdalene in Luke 8:2. In contrast, there are some 15 distinct stories of healing, plus the general Q list in Matt 11:2–6 || Luke 7:18–23.[4] Needless to say—as should be clear from my treatment of the exorcisms—I am not arguing that every Gospel story

of healing has a historical core that goes back to Jesus. Rather, the point that I am making here is the simple one that, if we judge the general tradition of Jesus as exorcist to have some historical basis, we should be open to forming the same judgment about the tradition of Jesus as healer of illnesses and physical infirmities. In its narratives, the Christian sources of the first and second generation remembered Jesus even more clearly as a healer of bodily ills than as an exorcist.

In the inventory that follows we are interested not in a complete exegesis of the various pericopes but only in possible signals of material going back to Jesus. As with our study of the exorcism stories, we must be prepared for meager results. The criteria of historicity work well when applied to large blocks of narrative about which we can make general statements. An individual, short miracle story, handed down orally over a generation or two with stylized formulas and within a set genre, does not offer all that much on which to base a judgment of historicity. The best we can do is point out certain concrete or curious details, as well as traits that diverge from the general form of miracle story or from the redactional tendencies of the evangelist.

I. THE PARALYZED AND THE CRIPPLED

A. MARK 2:1–12

Under the general rubric of paralyzed or crippled people, we have the peculiar story of the paralyzed man (*paralytikos*) who must be let down to Jesus through a torn-up roof because the entrance to the house is obstructed by a huge crowd. Presumably the friends of the paralytic used ropes attached to his pallet or mat to lower him through the roof to the spot in the house where Jesus was. The story is a complicated one, in which the basic elements of a miracle story are meshed with elements foreign to a simple miracle story: Jesus' surprising declaration that the paralytic's sins are forgiven, the reaction of the scribes ("He blasphemes!"), Jesus' ability to read the scribes' thoughts, his argument implying that his visible miraculous power to heal the paralytic is evidence for his invisible power to forgive sins, and the first occurrence in Mark of Jesus' self-designation "the Son of Man."

The convergence of so many unusual motifs in a narrative that might have been originally a simple story about the healing of a paralytic has given rise to endless theories about the stages of tradition and redaction. Was there originally one story that was gradually expanded, or were there two stories, a miracle story and a controversy dialogue, that were secondarily meshed?[5] Often the unusual motifs that are foreign to the genre of miracle story are declared to be secondary additions, though one must be careful about deciding a priori that the "purest" form of a story must be the earliest form. What is of interest to us, though, is the bare fact that by the time the story of the paralytic had reached Mark (or possibly a pre-Marcan collection of dispute stories reflected in Mark 2:1–3:6),[6] i.e., by the end of the first Christian generation, the story had already gone through so many stages of development. When we add to this the striking and (in the NT) unparalleled event of four men carrying the paralytic on a mat up to the flat roof of the house where Jesus is (presumably by way of an outside staircase), digging through the mud-and-thatch roof of a Palestinian house,[7] and lowering the paralytic on his pallet down to Jesus, I am inclined to think that some event in the public ministry stuck in the corporate memory precisely because of its strange circumstances. Moreover, if one should allow that Jesus' assurance that the man's sins were forgiven formed part of the original story, this element would make the narrative practically unique among the miracle stories of the Gospels.

B. JOHN 5:1–9

Some might want to bolster the argument for the historicity of Mark 2:1–12 by invoking the criterion of multiple attestation. In their view, the story of the cure of the sick man by the pool of Bethesda (or Bethzatha) in John 5:1–9 is actually an alternate version of the cure of the paralytic man in Mark 2:1–12. We would thus have two independent sources for the same incident, a relative rarity when it comes to miracle stories. But are the Marcan and Johannine narratives alternate versions of the same event? To be sure, the parallels between the two stories are intriguing: in each story a man who is in some way or other paralyzed is healed by a word of Jesus and then obeys Jesus' command to take up his pallet or mattress (the late and vulgar Greek word *krabattos*) and walk. Moreover, in each story Jesus seems to draw a connection between the man's sins and the paralysis he suffers.

Yet, as René Latourelle points out, the few precise verbal parallels are probably due to the stereotypical formulas used in the genre of miracle stories: "Same sickness, same formula."[8] Indeed, in how many different ways could a brief account of the healing of a paralytic be told? Much more significant are the many differences between the two stories: Mark's picture of an unroofed house in Capernaum versus John's scene of the pool of Bethesda near the Sheep Gate in Jerusalem;[9] likewise, the label "paralytic" (*paralytikos*) applied to the man in Mark 2 versus its absence in John 5, where the man is simply said to have an "illness" (*astheneia*). The man in Mark 2 is helped by four friends while the man in John 5 is alone and helpless. In John 5 Jesus seizes the initiative in offering to cure the sick man, who instead of evincing great faith makes excuses. In contrast, the friends of the man in Mark 2 have a faith that will brook no obstacle in getting to Jesus. In Mark 2 there is no connection with a Sabbath; it is Jesus' declaration that the man's sins are forgiven that unleashes a theological dispute. In John 5 the healing takes place on the Sabbath; it is this, not the forgiveness of sins, that leads to a theological conflict involving a plot to kill Jesus. Further, in John 5 Jesus' statement connecting the man's illness with his sins is not made in the miracle story proper but later on, when Jesus finds the healed man in the temple and warns him to avoid future sin lest something worse befall him. In Mark 2 Jesus' declaration about forgiveness lies at the heart of the story as it now stands.

Hence, despite some similarities with Mark 2:1–12, I think it best to treat John 5:1–9 as a distinct story. But does this distinct story reflect some historical incident in Jesus' ministry? The precise topography of the miracle (illuminated in the 20th century by excavations in Jerusalem) certainly supports such a position. The Copper Scroll from Qumran has given us the first confirmation outside of John 5 (and to a degree Josephus) that there was an area of Jerusalem called Bethesda or Bethzatha, an area that had pools that people could enter.[10] The archaeological digs near the church of St. Anne in Jerusalem have revealed both two large pools and a number of smaller pools near them, north-north-east of the temple area.[11] Scholars may debate which of the pools is referred to in John 5:2, but the knowledge of their location and their connection with a cult of healing shows remarkable acquaintance with the details of life in Jerusalem in the pre-A.D. 70 period. Moreover, the curious attitude and actions of the sick man in John 5 hardly fit the stock character of many stereotyped miracle stories. The man is initially ambivalent about the healing (5:6–7). After being cured he expresses no gratitude to Jesus; indeed, he does not even bother at first to find out who has healed him. When Jesus subsequently seeks him out in the temple, he responds to Jesus' warning not to sin by compliantly reporting Jesus to the authorities. The man then disappears from the story and from the Gospel. An indication that at the very least the story is not simply a creation of the Evangelist is the fact that he has to "tack on" the motifs of Sabbath and sin (5:9b,14) to a story that originally lacked them—and still lacks them in the miracle story proper.[12]

All this inclines me to the view that behind the present form of John 5:1–9 stands some historical event from the life of Jesus. It hardly strains credulity to suppose that during Jesus' ministry there was more than one person in Palestine suffering from some form of bodily paralysis. In fact, if one holds that Jesus' ministry lasted for more than one year[13] and that—as most religiously inclined Palestinian Jews would—Jesus regularly went up to Jerusalem for the great pilgrimage feasts, one would be surprised if the famed miracle-worker from Nazareth performed no miracles in and around the Holy City. What is surprising instead is that, granted the great emphasis John's Gospel gives to Jesus' ministry in Jerusalem, the Fourth Gospel has only two full-blown miracles set in Jerusalem proper: this healing in John 5 and the healing of the man born blind in John 9. Despite his intense focus on the Jerusalem ministry, John has not gone out of his way to flesh out that ministry with a large number of miracle stories.

C. MARK 3:1–6

The cycle of dispute stories in Mark 2:1–3:6, a cycle begun with the paralytic in Capernaum (2:1–12), concludes with the healing of a man with a withered (*exērammenēn*) hand, i.e., a paralyzed or crippled hand (3:1–6). The vague description does not allow us to decide whether we are dealing with a physical deformity from birth, the result of an accident, or some disease like rheumatoid arthritis. In any case, just as the cycle of Mark 2:1–3:6 begins with the mixed form of miracle-plus-dispute story (the paralytic whose sins are forgiven), so it ends with a similar mixed form, though in 3:1–6 the connection between the miracle and the (implied) dispute is closer and more organic.[14]

The healing of the man with the withered hand takes place in a synagogue on the Sabbath. This setting provides the occasion for an implicit argument—actually only Jesus speaks—between Jesus and his unnamed adversaries on the lawfulness of curing on the Sabbath. In Mark's mind, the adversaries are probably to be identified with the Pharisees mentioned in 2:24. For, at the end of the story in Mark 3:1–6—and thus at the end of the whole cycle of dispute stories—we read what is probably a redactional creation of Mark to close out the whole complex: "And going out the Pharisees immediately took counsel with the Herodians against Jesus on how to destroy him" (3:6).[15] Mark is consciously linking this final story of the cycle with the first one, which raised the charge of blasphemy (2:7), the charge on which Jesus will finally be condemned to death (14:63–64).[16] No doubt Mark also sees the cure of the withered hand on the Sabbath as confirmation of what Jesus affirms at the end of chap. 2: the Son of Man is Lord even of the Sabbath (2:28). All of these redactional manipulations by Mark (or by a pre-Marcan editor of the cycle) point to earlier material that was inherited and reworked.

"Earlier material," however, does not automatically translate into a historical incident.[17] To bolster the historicity of the narrative, some commentators point to the verisimilitude of the legal argumentation—in the form of rhetorical questions—that Jesus employs to justify his healing: "Is it licit to do good on the Sabbath or evil? To save a life or to kill [it]?" (3:4).[18] In my view, though, using the legal argumentation in v 4 to prove the historicity of the story is questionable strategy. First of all, scholars disagree among themselves as to whether this legal dispute belongs to the earliest stage of the story. Moreover, exegetes like Robert Guelich maintain that the legal dispute as it now stands in the story is formulated with a view to the christological concerns of the early church.[19] Indeed, it does seem that, in the final form of the pericope, the focus of the narrative is more christological than legal (halakic): the emphasis is on the supreme authority of Jesus the Son of Man, who is Lord of the Sabbath but who nevertheless will be put to death on the charge of blasphemy.

But, for the sake of argument, let us suppose that behind the present form of Mark 3:1–6 lies some sort of miracle story that included a quarrel about Sabbath observance. Even then we would be hard-pressed to maintain that a deadly or even simply a serious quarrel over Sabbath observance could have arisen out of Jesus' cure as related in Mark 3:1–6. Like most other Jews of 1st-century Palestine, Galilean peasants no doubt observed the basic rules of the Sabbath: no secular everyday work, no buying and selling, no lengthy journeys, no lighting or extinguishing of a fire, no cooking, no medical treatment of illnesses outside of life-or-death situations, and no military activity except in cases of self-defense. But ordinary Galilean peasants probably did not worry about the fine points over which special religious groups quarreled.

And quarrel they did. As E. P. Sanders observes, not only were there differences of interpretation of Sabbath rules that distinguished Essenes, Pharisees, and Sadducees from one another, even the Pharisees apparently differed among themselves on various points.[20] For instance, the debates between the House of Shammai and the House of Hillel on the observance of Sabbath and festival days as preserved in the Mishna may well go back to the pre-A.D. 70 period. Thus, to be a pious Pharisee who carefully kept the Sabbath according to stringent rules did not automatically mean that one was in agreement with every other Pharisee on all of these rules. More importantly, no one group of pious Jews seems to have thought that it could or should impose its special Sabbath rules on any other group. In this limited sense, religious pluralism extended even to Sabbath observance. Further still, Galilean peasants who did not belong to any stringent pious group would probably not have been terribly upset over minor acts to aid the sick on the Sabbath. The Mishna itself gives evidence that some rabbis found ways of getting around the strict rule that medicine was not to be practiced on the Sabbath. As Sanders notes, "these [rules prohibiting medical treatment and the ways around them] are the discussions of the strict, and we may suppose that most people would be more tolerant of minor cures."[21]

Even more to the point, in Mark 3:1–6 Jesus *performs no action* to cure the man's withered hand. He only speaks two commands: "Stand up before the assembly. . . . Stretch out your hand." According to Mark 3:5, as soon as the man stretched out his hand, it was healed. All this stands in contrast to some other Sabbath-healing stories, where at least Jesus touches the person to be healed (Luke 13:13 [the bent-over woman]; 14:4 [the man with dropsy]). If we take the story in Mark 3:1–6 at face value, Jesus literally *does* nothing—that is, he performs no action—and so in no sense can he be said to break the Sabbath by working.[22] Thus, it is incredible that Pharisees or anyone else would seek to put Jesus to death for the event described in Mark 3:1–6.[23] It is also difficult to believe that any group of Jews could or would accuse Jesus of breaking the Sabbath when all Jesus did was to speak a few words that brought healing to a crippled hand. Consequently, I do not think that the Sabbath controversy, as it is presented in Mark 3:1–6, goes back to a historical event in Jesus' ministry; and to substitute some other Sabbath controversy that would be more believable involves us in pure conjecture.

Granted, it remains possible that on some Sabbath, when Jesus was in a synagogue, he cured a man's crippled hand and that this cure evolved through decades of controversy between Jews and Christians into the story we now have in Mark 3:1–6. Yet we must admit that, shorn of the Sabbath controversy, the brief and bland miracle story we are left with lacks those signs of concreteness, peculiarity, or singularity that might make us suspect historical tradition going back to Jesus. Still, none of these considerations positively proves that the basic miracle story is unhistorical. Hence, in my opinion, the historicity of the miracle story in Mark 3:1–6 is best left in the limbo-category of not clear (*non liquet*).[24]

D. LUKE 13:10–17

The cure of the bent-over woman is a story unique to Luke, hence an L tradition. Its placement, style, and vocabulary are typically Lucan. Luke positions the story during the great journey of Jesus to Jerusalem that occupies chaps. 9–19 of his Gospel. The partial assimilation of this healing story to an exorcism, the theme of glorifying God and rejoicing over the glorious works of Jesus, plus a number of phrases that imitate the language of the Greek OT all reflect the redactional activity of Luke.[25] Indeed, some critics have suggested that what we have here is Luke's reworking of the L story of the cure of the man with dropsy (Luke 14:1–6). But, apart from the fact that in each story Jesus defends his healing on the Sabbath with an *a minori ad maius* argument (the rabbinic *qal waḥomer*), drawn from humane acts allowed on the Sabbath, the two stories are quite different: the woman is in a synagogue; she has been stooped over for eighteen years;[26] her infirmity is attributed to an evil spirit or Satan; after the cure the "ruler of the synagogue" (not identified as a Pharisee) tells the congregation not to come to the synagogue for cures on the Sabbath; Jesus likewise addresses the congregation to rebut the ruler; and the whole crowd rejoices at the end of the story. In contrast, in Luke 14:1–6 Jesus is in the house of a leader of the Pharisees for a Sabbath meal; Jesus addresses not a crowd but rather the lawyers and the Pharisees prior to his cure of the man with dropsy; and both before and after the cure his enemies remain silent. What these two stories have in common is the hybrid genre of a miracle story laced with traits of a dispute story or pronouncement story focusing on an *a fortiori* argument—a genre we have already seen elsewhere (e.g., Mark 2:1–12). In itself, the hybrid nature of the narrative tells us nothing about what may be historical, invented, or derived from another story.

A few details of the narrative of the bent-over woman in Luke 13:10–17 are curious and may at least point to pre-Lucan tradition. Despite Luke's great redactional interest in the Pharisees as dialogue partners of Jesus, the adversary in the story is called simply "the synagogue ruler." No Pharisees appear on the scene. The detail that the woman was afflicted for eighteen years certainly serves to stress the severity and incurable nature of the ailment, but the precise number eighteen comes out of nowhere and does not seem motivated by any particular theological agenda.[27] These concrete details may point to pre-Lucan tradition and even to tradition stemming from the historical Jesus, but they hardly prove the case.

As for the dispute about the Sabbath, Sanders remarks that the story of the bent-over woman in Luke 13 has more verisimilitude than the story of the man with the crippled hand in Mark 3. In Luke 13:13 Jesus lays hands on the afflicted woman. At least in the eyes of the punctilious this could be thought to be a "work" of healing performed on the Sabbath, thus violating the Law.

In contrast, in Mark 3:5 the mere word of Jesus heals the man, and so the charge of violating the Sabbath makes no sense there. At the same time, Sanders wisely remarks with regard to Luke 13:10–17 that verisimilitude does not automatically equal historicity: "I doubt that we can find out just what Jesus did on each occasion that he healed, or just who said what to him about it."[28] Balancing this insight with the few concrete details that serve no theological purpose, I think we are faced with a situation similar to that of the story of the man with the withered hand in Mark 3:1–6: *non liquet*.[29]

E. THE CENTURION'S SERVANT (MATT 8:5–13 PARR.)?

We would have a fifth instance of Jesus curing a paralyzed person if we decided to take up at this point Matthew's version of the story of the centurion's servant (Matt 8:5–13 parr.). However, there is a reason for not doing so. Only in Matthew's account are we told that the servant lies at home paralyzed (*paralytikos*) and in extreme pain (v 6). This description is lacking in both the Lucan parallel (Luke 7:1–10) and in the distant parallel in John, the story of the cure of the royal official's son (John 4:46–54). In both Luke and John the problem is rather that the slave or son is near death from a grave but unspecified illness (Luke 7:2; John 4:46–47). This striking agreement of both the Lucan form of the Q story and the Johannine tradition over against Matthew inclines me to treat the story in a later category, namely, various *types* of healing that are attested only once in the Gospels. The primitive form of the story of the centurion's servant seems to have dealt with Jesus curing at a distance a servant or son who was near death.[30] Treating this story separately will respect its individuality much better than putting it into the category of the healing of paralytics, with which it has little to do in either form or content.

F. "THE LAME WALK" (MATT 11:5 PAR.)

The four or five stories about paralytics that we have just reviewed all come from the narrative traditions of Mark, John, and L—plus Q if we include Matt 8:5–13. To this multiple attestation of sources we can add multiple attestation of forms, since at one point in the sayings tradition of Q Jesus lists the healing of the lame as a type of miracle prominent among his powerful works. The saying in question occurs in the Q story of John the Baptist sending messengers to Jesus to inquire: "Are you the one who is to come?" We have examined this pericope (Matt 11:2–6 ‖ Luke 7:18–23) at length in Chapters 13 and 16 of this book, when treating the Baptist's relationship to Jesus and Jesus' statements on realized eschatology. There we saw good reason for accepting the core of the pericope as historical. There is no need to repeat the analysis of the pericope here. All that need be said is that, when Jesus desired to sum up in a few words his miracle-working activity, "the lame walk" (*chōloi peripatousin*) stood out in his mind as one of the five types of miracles that especially characterized his ministry of healing—which in turn symbolized and partially realized God's coming rule and kingdom. The generalizing plural "the lame walk" correlates well with the prominence of four or five Gospel narratives dealing with paralyzed or crippled people. Whatever our judgment about this or that individual story, this type of miracle is firmly rooted in the earliest traditions of Jesus' ministry.

II. THE BLIND

A. BARTIMAEUS (MARK 10:46–52 PARR.)

In Mark's account, the blind beggar Bartimaeus is healed by Jesus as the latter leaves Jericho on the last stage of his fateful journey up to Jerusalem and the cross.[31] In the rush to probe historical elements in this story, one should not ignore the pivotal place it holds in the structure of Mark's Gospel. What has been called "the great central section of Mark's Gospel" (8:22–10:52) is carefully framed by two stories of Jesus curing blindness: the blind man at Bethsaida (8:22–26) and Bartimaeus outside Jericho (10:46–52). As we shall see later on, Jesus heals the blind man at Bethsaida in two stages, a point that may have deep symbolic meaning for Mark. For immediately after this healing, Peter, who up until now has been totally blind to the true identity of Jesus, has his inner sight partially healed. Near Caesarea Philippi, Peter, representing the disciples in general, makes a partial breakthrough to the truth: he at least sees that Jesus is the Messiah (8:29), however inadequate his conception of Messiah may be.[32] Peter, however, is still blind to the complementary truth, the second stage of sight, that Jesus is the suffering, dying, and rising Son of Man. Despite Jesus' three subsequent predictions of his passion (8:31; 9:31; 10:32) and God's confirmation in the transfiguration that Jesus is his Son (9:7), even Peter, James, and John remain blind to what Jesus' resurrection from the dead as Son of Man might mean (9:9–13). Even after the detailed third prediction of the passion, James and John are so blind that they promptly proceed to ask for seats of honor in the kingdom (10:35–45). All Jesus can promise is a share in his death, the ransom for the many (10:45).

It is at this point in Mark's narrative that the healing of Bartimaeus takes place. Corresponding to the healing at Bethsaida, it foreshadows the second stage of the healing of the disciples' inner sight, this time fully. Fittingly, then, unlike the lengthy healing of the blind man at Bethsaida, which demanded a lengthy two-stage procedure involving spittle, Jesus heals Bartimaeus with a simple declaration: "Go, your faith has saved you." Not only does Bartimaeus see immediately and fully, more importantly for Marcan symbolism he follows Jesus "on the way," that is, on the way of the cross, the way the disciples followed in fear (10:32), the way every true disciple must follow (8:34).[33]

Though it forms the end of the great central section, the Bartimaeus story is also connected literarily and theologically with what follows.[34] "Son of David," Bartimaeus' somewhat startling address to Jesus, is echoed in the very next pericope, the triumphant entry into Jerusalem (11:1–11) when the crowd cries out: "Blessed is the coming kingdom of our father David" (11:10). By way of inclusion, the Son of David theme comes back at the end of the verbal sparring between Jesus and his opponents in Jerusalem, when Jesus himself raises the question of how the Messiah can be the Son of David when King David supposedly addresses him as "Lord" in Ps 110:1 (Mark 12:35–37). Transposed into the theme of "Messiah" and "King of the Jews (or Israel)," the Son of David theme resurfaces during the Sanhedrin and Roman trials, as well as during the mockery of Jesus on the cross (14:61; 15:2,12,18,26,32).[35]

In a deeper sense, though, the healing of Bartimaeus' sight has as its ultimate correlative the scenes at Jesus' death and at the empty tomb. It is only when the centurion sees the dead Jesus on the cross—just as the temple veil is rent—that he sees the ultimate truth: the crucified Jesus is revealed as the Son of God: "This man truly was God's son" (15:39). For the first time in the Gospel, a human being can say in faith that Jesus is the Son of God; only the "theophany" of the cross makes this vision of faith possible. Then, at the empty tomb, the young man in white (a heavenly envoy) proclaims the Easter kerygma that the crucified Jesus of Nazareth has been raised from the dead. Significantly, the last spoken words of any character in Mark's story are: "But go, tell his disciples and Peter, 'He goes before you into Galilee; there you will see him, as he told you'" (16:7). Thus, just as the healing of the blind man at Bethsaida prefigures the partial healing of Peter's inner sight at Caesarea Philippi, so the healing of Bartimaeus, just before the Passion Narrative in the wider sense begins, prefigures the full healing of Peter's blindness after Jesus' death and resurrection. Along with the other disciples, he will finally see that Jesus the Messiah is also necessarily Jesus the crucified and risen Son of Man. Only then will he see and understand Jesus as Son of God.[36]

Considering this heavy theological freight that the healing of Bartimaeus carries, we would be naive to treat the story as a videotape replay of an event in A.D. 30. Yet at the same time there is much in the story that points to primitive tradition, however much reworked by Christian theology.[37] First of all, as I noted when treating Jesus' miracles in general, it is unusual for any direct recipient of a miracle—outside of the group of the Twelve—to be named. Indeed, Bartimaeus is the only example in the whole of the Synoptic tradition.[38] One might simply shrug this off as a legendary accretion if one did not notice that throughout all four canonical Gospels there is almost an unspoken rule that direct recipients of Jesus' miracles, outside of the Twelve, are not named. Bartimaeus is the only exception in the Synoptic tradition, and Lazarus the only example in John's Gospel. Far from manifesting a tendency to add proper names to miracle stories, Matthew and Luke both omit the name of Bartimaeus in their retellings of Mark 10:46–52. The sobriety of the four canonical Gospels in this regard is remarkable when compared to the lush imagination of apocryphal Christian Gospels and Acts from the 2d century onwards. Lengthy and detailed narratives like the exorcisms of the Gerasene demoniac or the epileptic boy in Mark or the healing of the man born blind in John seem to cry out for names for the principal actors, but in vain. Bartimaeus stands alone in the Synoptic tradition in general and in Mark's Gospel in particular. Indeed, apart from Jesus, the Twelve, and Jairus, Bartimaeus is the only actor in Mark's Gospel who is named prior to the Passion Narrative. We thus have a certain argument from discontinuity, in this case discontinuity vis-à-vis the Synoptic Gospels and the traditions behind them.

But that is not all. The Aramaic substratum and Palestinian milieu of this story rise to the surface more than once. The very fact that Mark—or a pre-Marcan collector of miracle stories—goes out of his way to tell his audience that the name Bartimaeus (*bar Tim'ai*) is really a patronymic meaning "son of Timaeus" suggests that Mark is writing for an audience made up largely of Gentiles who need some clarification, while the name needed no such explanation for the first hearers of the story.[39] That the story originated in Aramaic-speaking Palestine is also implied by the way Bartimaeus addresses Jesus when he gropes his way to him: "Rabbouni," Aramaic for "my master" or "my teacher" (appearing elsewhere in the NT only in John 20:16). From Bultmann onwards, some critics have seen tension between the two different types of address (Son of David and teacher) that Bartimaeus uses; the tension is then employed to separate tradition from redaction.[40] However, as we shall see below, this whole approach rests on a misunderstanding of the meaning of "Son of David" in this story.

Then, too, the scene reflects Palestinian geography and Jewish customs perfectly. For those Galilean Jews on pilgrimage to Jerusalem who consciously avoided the territory of the hostile Samaritans, and who therefore traveled through Herod Antipas' Perea on the east side of the Jordan, Jericho (just west of the Jordan) was the last way station and gathering point for pilgrims as they began the trek up to Jerusalem (slightly less than 20 miles away) on the steeply ascending Roman road.[41] In this story, Bartimaeus is truly "well situated," since he has stationed himself on the road leading out of Jericho in order to beg alms of the Jewish Passover-pilgrims as they began their ascent to the Holy City. The days before Passover were a special time for giving alms to the poor. Bartimaeus, condemned to be a beggar by his blindness, wisely chooses not to beg amid the bustle and confusion of Jericho itself but rather on the road outside the city, the road all pilgrims journeying to Jerusalem must travel.

There is a still more important element of the story—perhaps the most important—that points in the direction of very early tradition. Since there is good reason for seeing this story as pre-Marcan, one must explain why, detached from the larger Marcan framework, Bartimaeus should cry out to Jesus twice with the (for the Marcan tradition) unusual title "Son of David." In no other miracle story in Mark does this title appear.[42] Indeed, outside of those Gospel parallels and redactional creations dependent on this story (plus a few redactional insertions by Matthew), "Son of David" occurs in no other miracle story in the Four Gospels.[43] In short, apart from the Bartimaeus episode and passages dependent upon it, "Son of David" is alien to the earliest Christian traditions about Jesus' miracles. As a direct address to Jesus, it is also alien to the rest of Mark's Gospel.[44] Actually, there is nothing surprising about its relative absence. The title was not at home in the earliest Christian narratives of Jesus' miracles because in the Judaism of the time there seems to have been no direct connection made between King David, his royal heir who was to reign on his throne as the Messiah of the end time, and the power to perform miracles of healing.[45]

But that does not mean that the connection of Jesus as Son of David with miracle-working is necessarily a secondary Christian combination.[46] The connection of miracles of healing with the title "Son of David" is more convoluted than might first appear. By the 1st century A.D., King Solomon—who was the only individual reigning monarch to be called Son of David in the OT[47]—had acquired a reputation in Jewish circles as a great exorcist and healer. As we have already seen, Josephus recalls how he himself witnessed the Jew Eleazar perform exorcisms in the presence of Vespasian with the help of roots prescribed by Solomon, the invocation of Solomon's name, and the use of incantations Solomon had composed (*Ant.* 8.2.5 §46–49). Josephus recounts this story in the context of extolling Solomon, who had received from God the skill to combat demons in order "to help and heal human beings." For that purpose Solomon composed incantations to relieve illnesses (*Ant.* 8.2.5 §45). This tradition of Solomon as exorcist and healer is likewise reflected in the apocryphal *Testament of Solomon*. Although it may be as late as the 3d century A.D. and was no doubt put into final form by a Christian, the traditions about Solomon underlying the *Testament* go back, in the opinion of many critics, to Judaism around the turn of the era.[48]

It is against this Jewish background that the blind Bartimaeus' appeal to Jesus as "Son of David," i.e., as miraculous healer, makes sense. Indeed, the combination of Jesus as wise teacher, exorcist, and healer would make the address "Son of David" [= a latter-day miracle-working Solomon] natural to a fellow 1st-century Jew in need of healing, all the more so if some idea about Jesus' being of Davidic descent circulated among the common people of the day. Moreover, if this is the meaning of "Son of David" in the mouth of Bartimaeus, there is no necessary "collision" (as Bultmann and Burger claim) between a Solomonic figure and a teacher addressed as "Rabbouni."

What is significant for our investigation is that such a picture of Jesus as a latter-day Solomon precisely in his capacity as exorcist and miracle-worker is almost nonexistent in the final forms of the canonical Gospels. Apart from (1) a mention in Jesus' genealogy in Matthew, (2) passing references to Solomon's great wisdom, and (3) allusions to his relation to the Jerusalem temple, Solomon is practically absent from the NT, never being mentioned outside of the Gospels and Acts. John 10:23 and Acts 3:11; 5:12 simply speak of "Solomon's portico" in the temple, while Acts 7:47 states the well-known fact that Solomon built the first temple. Besides the two references to Solomon in the Matthean genealogy of Jesus (Matt 1:6–7), Matthew, along with Luke, names Solomon only in two Q traditions: (1) the comparison of Solomon's glorious array with the lilies of the field (Matt 6:29 ‖ Luke 12:27) and (2) the picture of

Solomon as *the* great wise man, consulted by the Queen of Sheba—with the pointed conclusion: "Behold, something greater than Solomon is here" (Matt 12:42 ‖ Luke 11:31).[49] It is telling that, of the four evangelists, Mark alone has not a single reference to Solomon, while no direct reference to Solomon anywhere in the NT connects him with the title "Son of David" or with exorcisms and healings. For the evangelists, as for the Christian traditions before them, belief in Jesus' resurrection and exaltation at God's right hand, interpreted as the royal enthronement of the Davidic Messiah, had given the idea of descent from David and the general idea of Davidic messiahship a completely different thrust.[50]

Hence the isolated allusion to the Son of David as a Solomonic miracle-worker in the Bartimaeus story is most probably not a product of Christian theology but a relic of how some Palestinian Jews with infirmities actually looked upon this particular Jewish miracle-worker and teacher of wisdom, who was believed to be of Davidic descent. From the vantage point of their own needs, these Jews afflicted with illnesses pictured him not so much as a reigning king upon a throne à la David as rather a miraculous healer à la Solomon. In my view, then, this extremely primitive "Jewish christology," which was not developed further by the early Christian tradition of the first generation,[51] most probably goes back to the time of Jesus himself. The sole clear example preserved for us is the story of Bartimaeus.

No one of the considerations I have offered, taken by itself, establishes the historicity of the Bartimaeus incident. As I pointed out in Volume One of *A Marginal Jew*,[52] a single example of Palestinian or Aramaic background does not prove that a story or saying goes back to the historical Jesus. However, in the case of the Bartimaeus incident, we have the unusual convergence of an impressive number of elements pointing to historicity: the only case in the Synoptics of the naming of the direct recipient of a miracle performed by Jesus; the tying of this named individual to a precise place (the road outside Jericho leading up to Jerusalem),[53] to a precise time of year (shortly before Passover), and to a precise period of Jesus' ministry (his final journey up to Jerusalem along with other Passover pilgrims); the occurrence of two Aramaic phrases within one story (*bar Tim'ai* and *rabbouni*); and most of all, an archaic conception of Jesus the miracle-worker as a "Son of David" like Solomon the miracle-worker. All these elements join in supporting a judgment that the story is basically historical. If Bartimaeus was a resident of Jericho, and especially if he did actually follow Jesus up to Jerusalem, it is hardly surprising that the earliest Christian communities in Jerusalem and Judea would have preserved this story from one of their earliest members and most notable witnesses.[54] While these considerations do not add up to strict proof, they do suggest that the Bartimaeus story is one of the strongest candidates for the report of a specific miracle going back to the historical Jesus.

B. THE BLIND MAN OF BETHSAIDA (MARK 8:22–26)[55]

In this short yet detailed miracle story, unnamed people bring a blind man to Jesus after he has arrived at Bethsaida, a city situated on the northeast shore of the Sea of Galilee and slightly east of the Jordan River.[56] Jesus leads the man by hand "outside the town," spits into the man's eyes, places his hands on him, and asks: "Do you see anything?" The man indicates that he has regained partial vision by saying that he can see men in the distance, but they look like trees walking around.[57] Jesus again places his hands on the man's eyes, whereupon the man sees perfectly, even at a distance.[58] Jesus then sends the man home with the order not to enter the town.[59]

Obviously, this story sounds strange on any reading. It apparently sounded strange even to Matthew and Luke, who both omitted the story in their Gospels. For those engaged in the quest for the historical Jesus the healing at Bethsaida poses a special riddle, since it contains strong signals both of historical tradition and of creativity on the part of the early church. To be fair to both sides, we shall look first at the indications of editorial activity by Mark or a pre-Marcan collector of miracle stories and then at the hints of an event originating in the life of the historical Jesus.

As the story now stands in Mark's Gospel, there are plentiful signs of the reshaping of the material either by the Evangelist or by the collector(s) of the tradition he inherited. It is probable that even in the pre-Marcan tradition, the story of the healing of the blind man at Bethsaida had already been shaped as a "twin narrative" of the story of the healing of the deaf-mute now found in Mark 7:32–37.[60] As Taylor has demonstrated in detail, the parallels in both structure and vocabulary between the two stories are striking,[61] so much so that some critics have suggested that the two narratives sprang from a single event or tradition.[62] Yet, as Taylor also admits, the differences between the two stories are also numerous and impressive. At any rate, we can feel fairly sure that a great deal of "contouring" of the tradition took place before Mark incorporated it into his Gospel.

Mark's major contribution to the story's message was the pivotal position he gave it within the overarching structure of his Gospel.[63] Mark has endowed the healing of the blind man in 8:22–26 with a Janus-like quality. On the one hand, the healing looks back. It marks the end of the two-part "bread section" (where the key word stitching the pericopes together is *artos* [bread]), a section that stretches from Mark 6:30 to 8:21. The first part of the "bread section" begins with the multiplication of loaves for the five thousand (6:30–44) and ends with the healing of the deaf-mute (7:32–37). The second part of the "bread section" begins with the multiplication of loaves for the four thousand (8:1–10) and ends with the healing of the blind man (8:22–26), just after Jesus has excoriated his disciples for being blind to the mystery of his own person, a mystery that he has tried to reveal to them through the two multiplications of loaves (8:14–21).

At the same time, the healing at Bethsaida also looks forward, as we saw when we examined the Bartimaeus story. The healing of the blind man at Bethsaida, which takes place in two stages, symbolizes the two-stage healing of the spiritual vision of Jesus' disciples: first with Peter's confession that Jesus is the Messiah at Caesarea Philippi (8:27–30) and finally with the full vision of

Jesus as Son of Man and Son of God, a vision made possible only by his death on the cross and resurrection (cf. Mark 9:9–13; 15:39; 16:6–7).[64] It could be, then, that Matthew and Luke omit the Bethsaida story not so much out of embarrassment that Jesus used saliva or initially failed to work a full cure as out of rejection of Mark's theological agenda, with its heavy emphasis on the increasing blindness of the disciples to the mystery of Jesus' true nature as Son of God, crucified and risen.

In addition to the strong theological coloration of the story, those who question the narrative's historicity would claim that even the concrete traits and oddities of the story need not argue for its origin in the life of Jesus. To be sure, the story pinpoints a location for the miracle, an unusual one at that: Bethsaida. However, Bultmann claims that the story's opening—and only—mention of Bethsaida, a fairly large city rebuilt by the Herodian tetrarch Philip, is not original to the narrative, since it clashes with the story's repeated designation of the venue of the miracle as a *kōmē*, a village or small town.[65] Instead of being signs of historicity, the two-stage healing and the use of saliva could be signs of the assimilation of a miracle story about Jesus to the techniques and tools of miracles and/or magic in the Greco-Roman world at large, especially as reflected in the magical papyri. Possibly the listing of the stages of healing, the use of saliva, and the question asked of the blind man by Jesus are all meant as instructions to Christian miracle-workers attempting to replicate their master's feat. The story could thus have functioned not unlike some of the "recipes" found in the Greek magical papyri.[66] In short, skeptical critics question whether there are all that many signs of historical tradition in the Bethsaida story.

Yet the defenders of a historical core to the story are not without a reply. The name Bethsaida is not so easily dismissed as not being original to the narrative. While the names of certain cities were probably attached to some miracle stories from the beginning (Capernaum, Gerasa, and Jericho are the other great examples in Mark), many miracle stories apparently floated in the oral Synoptic tradition, free of any precise location in a city or town. They remained without venue when the Synoptic Gospels came to be written.[67]

More to the point, Bethsaida as the locus of Jesus' miracle enjoys a certain kind of limited multiple attestation by sources and forms. On the one hand, Bethsaida is mentioned in this Marcan miracle story, along with a passing reference in Mark 6:45.[68] On the other hand, Bethsaida appears again in a Q saying (Matt 11:20–24 ‖ Luke 10:12–15) in which Jesus denounces three Galilean cities (Chorazin, Bethsaida, and Capernaum) for not believing in him despite the fact that he had worked miracles in their midst.[69] The Q tradition thus emphasizes Bethsaida as a major locus of Jesus' miraculous activity, yet the earliest Synoptic tradition has no record of any particular miracle performed there by Jesus—except for Mark's story of the healing of the blind man. Hence two separate first-generation Christian sources (Mark and Q), using two different literary forms (narrative and a saying of woe), agree on

Bethsaida as a venue of Jesus' miraculous activity. This agreement tends to argue against Mark's arbitrary insertion of the name into this story.

Moreover, Bultmann's objection that the status of Bethsaida as a city clashes with the story's references to it as a town (*kōmē* in Mark 8:23,26) is hardly telling, since in the NT "there is no sharp distinction between *polis* [city] and *kōmē* [town]."[70] In fact, if one wishes to press the point, recent archaeological investigations suggest that, when the tetrarch Philip created his Roman city of Bethsaida-Julias a little inland from the Sea of Galilee, the old fishing village of Bethsaida continued to operate on the shore of the Sea as the port of the Roman city. Since the Marcan narrative presents Jesus as arriving at Bethsaida by boat (Mark 8:10,13,14–22), the natural understanding of the text is that the Bethsaida of the story is the fishing village. Whether or not Mark (or the pre-Marcan storyteller) knew or cared about this, in any event Bultmann's objection does not hold. There is no solid reason for dismissing Bethsaida as the original location of the tradition.[71]

The most striking arguments for historicity come, however, from the criteria of embarrassment and discontinuity. Since Matthew and Luke, each in his own way, represent the disciples as obtuse at least to the mystery of Jesus' passion, they would not necessarily be adverse to a miracle story symbolic of Jesus' gradual gift of spiritual sight to his followers. Consequently, embarrassment over the at-first unsuccessful healing with saliva may well be the major reason both evangelists dropped this story from their Gospels. One does not have to be overly sensitive to be disturbed by a story in which Jesus does not simply apply saliva to the blind man's eyes with his hand but instead directly spits into the blind man's eyes.[72] Significantly, the only other miracle story that both Matthew and Luke omit from their Marcan tradition is the healing of the deaf-mute, a miracle in which Jesus also uses saliva. While used as a healing agent in medical, miraculous, and magical contexts, saliva was certainly open to a magical interpretation, all the more so since the healing gestures of spitting and the laying on of hands are not immediately and fully successful. The fact that Jesus must ask the "patient" what effect his healing gesture has had ("Do you see anything?"), that the patient gives a description of his partial sight in a way reminiscent of a story in the Greek healing sanctuary of Epidauros,[73] and that Jesus must remedy the matter by giving a second "application" of his "treatment" makes Jesus look like either a primitive doctor or a magician—the two not always being distinguished in the ancient world.

These concrete details meet not only the criterion of embarrassment but also that of discontinuity—in this case, discontinuity from other miracle stories in the NT. The use of saliva as a direct instrument of healing is found only once elsewhere in the NT, namely, in the story of the deaf-mute in Mark 7:33.[74] And even there Jesus does not directly spit into the person's face as he does in 8:23. To put it as delicately as possible: having Jesus spit in a person's face does not seem to fit any stream of christology in the early church. Moreover, nowhere else in the NT does Jesus' healing action fail to have its full effect immediately and therefore need to be repeated.

Not as significant, though still noteworthy, is the absence in Mark 8:22–26 of a number of common motifs found in Gospel miracle stories. There is no mention of faith on the part of the blind man or his helpers either before or after the miracle. Indeed, there is no reaction whatever from anyone. The healed man neither glorifies God nor thanks Jesus nor spreads the news of his healing nor seeks to follow Jesus. There is no larger audience to be astonished, bewildered, shocked, or moved to praise. A "choral conclusion" is totally lacking. Even Jesus' order that the blind man go home without entering the town does not quite fit the usual Marcan command to be silent. Strictly speaking, Jesus simply tells the man to avoid the town on his way home. He does not order the man to say nothing to his family or friends once he reaches home.[75] The ending of the story, not unlike the story as a whole, is idiosyncratic, even for Mark. As a matter of fact, the story has a number of words not found elsewhere in Mark's Gospel; it is hardly a pure Marcan composition.[76] A final oddity is that the only words that Jesus speaks in direct address in the whole story are not the words of healing but rather the physician-like inquiry, "Do you see anything?"—an element unparalleled in any other miracle story told of Jesus in the Gospels.

In my view, then, the many oddities in the narrative, including elements that are embarrassing or discontinuous, tilt the balance of judgment in favor of the historicity of the core of the story. However much the story may have been "worked up" in the oral tradition and "exploited" by Mark's redactional theology, most probably Jesus did heal a blind man in or around Bethsaida.

C. THE MAN BORN BLIND (JOHN 9:1–41)[77]

As it now stands in John's Gospel, the story of the man born blind ranks alongside the healing of the paralyzed man at the pool of Bethesda (5:1–47) and the raising of Lazarus (11:1–44) as one of the three miracle stories that, with their ramifications, take up most or all of a chapter in the Fourth Gospel. The lengthy narratives-plus-dialogues form superb pieces of literary and theological art that clearly reveal the fine hand of the Fourth Evangelist.[78] Still, in each of the three cases, form criticism can discern the nucleus of a primitive miracle story within the complex structure created by John. This is especially true of chaps. 5 and 9, where the miracle stories proper are clearly (and for the form critic, conveniently) situated at the beginning of the chapters (5:1–9 for the paralyzed man at Bethesda; 9:1–7 for the man born blind). The primitive miracle story of the raising of Lazarus is more integrated into the lengthy narrative-plus-dialogue that John or his immediate source has constructed; hence the original miracle story behind chap. 11 takes more effort to isolate.[79]

The isolation of the original miracle story behind the healing of the man born blind in chap. 9 is much easier. As form criticism has abundantly shown, almost all Gospel stories of healing boil down to the bare bones of three steps: (1) the presentation of the problem (Jesus' encounter with the sick person, with some description of the nature and/or length of the illness); (2) the act of healing (usually involving a word and/or gesture of Jesus); (3) the affirmation and/or demonstration of the healing, with reactions from bystanders (e.g., the mute person speaks, the paralyzed person walks, the crowd is amazed).[80]

This entire pattern is found in the first seven verses of John 9: (1) Jesus comes upon the man born blind (v 1); (2) Jesus uses gestures (spitting, smearing mud on the blind man's eyes in v 6) and a command ("Go, wash in the pool of Siloam" in v 7a) to heal him; and (3) after obeying Jesus' command to wash, the blind man sees (v 7b).[81] Everything that follows in chap. 9 recounts not the miracle story itself but the growing debate over the reality of the miracle and the claim that, in healing the blind man, Jesus broke the Sabbath. Significantly, the fact that the healing took place on the Sabbath is not mentioned until v 14, at the beginning of a "hearing" before the Pharisees. Most probably a secondary addition to the miracle story, the motif of the Sabbath acts as a springboard for the evolving controversy that fills the rest of chap. 9: the controversy over who Jesus, a healer yet Sabbath-breaker, really is. There is no need to go into this controversy material, not only because it is not part of the miracle story in the narrow sense of the word, but also because this controversy material is suffused with Johannine theology, reflecting in particular the painful break of John's church from the Jewish synagogue.[82]

When we turn to the miracle story proper (9:1–7), we notice that the "bare bones" of the form of a healing miracle are not spread out evenly across all seven verses of 9:1–7 but are found only in vv 1 + 6–7. A further observation that correlates neatly with this insight from form criticism is that vv 2–5 contain dialogue that is not typical of a miracle story but that is stamped instead with the theological thought and vocabulary of John. Jesus' disciples, who conveniently and suddenly appear in vv 2–5, who just as conveniently disappear from the rest of the chapter,[83] and who conveniently voice erroneous opinions begging for correction, ask Jesus whether the blind man's sins or those of his parents caused him to be born blind (v 2). Jesus replies by redirecting the focus of the story from the *cause* of the man's blindness to its ultimate *purpose* in the plan of God: "that the works of God might be revealed in him" (v 3). Having sounded the typical Johannine theme of the revelation of God working in Jesus, Jesus then inculcates the urgency of doing the works "of him who sent me" (i.e., the Father) while it is day (i.e., while the public ministry lasts), before the "night" of Jesus' passion and death puts an end to the work of his ministry (v 4). All this leads up to the grand christological revelation of Jesus' true nature, echoing 8:12 but now ominously restricted by the hint of the coming hour of crucifixion: "While I am in the world, I am the light of the world" (v 5). The Evangelist then deftly uses a brief connecting phrase ("having said this") to return to the basic story of the healing. Thus, the vocabulary, style, and theological content of vv 2–5 are all perfectly Johannine and can be bracketed from 9:1–7 without the loss of any essential part of the miracle story.[84]

Indeed, the bare lines of the miracle story stand out all the more clearly once the theological dialogue of vv 2–5 is omitted. Hence it is likely that vv 1 + 6–7 represent the primitive core of the healing of the man born blind.

Granted, it may be that the present theological dialogue in vv 2–5 replaced some initial conversation between Jesus and the blind man, or that the original ending of the miracle story contained a reaction from bystanders that has been obscured or replaced by the doubts and questions of the blind man's neighbors in 9:8–12. But we may feel fairly sure that in 9:1 + 6–7 we have the heart of the earliest attainable version of this miracle story: "And passing along [Jesus] saw a man blind from birth.[85] He spat on the ground, made mud from the spittle, and smeared the mud on his eyes. And he said to him: 'Go, wash in the pool of Siloam.' He [i.e., the blind man] therefore went and washed and came [back] seeing."[86] At the very least, then, the healing of the man born blind is not a creation of the Evangelist. In fact, the whole of chap. 9 is such a huge and complicated work of literary and theological art that we must suppose that a number of stages of tradition and redaction lie between the primitive miracle story embedded in 9:1 + 6–7 and the monumental tract of Johannine theology that is chap. 9.

The original healing story bears similarities to other stories of healing that circulated in the oral tradition, but 9:1 + 6–7 does not appear to be a second-ary creation patterned on these other stories. True, it contains motifs found in various miracle stories (e.g., healings connected with Jesus' spittle, a healing connected with a pool, the healing of a blind beggar), but the very spread of these motifs over different stories from different streams of the oral tradition suggests that John 9:1 + 6–7 is not dependent on any one story.[87]

Granted that the core miracle story in John 9:1,6–7 is an independent tradi-tion that is much earlier than the composition of John's Gospel, are there any signs of its going back to Jesus? We may begin with a preliminary and global observation already made above: despite the focus of the Fourth Evangelist—and apparently a good part of his tradition—on the city of Jerusalem as the setting of Jesus' ministry, the Johannine tradition is remarkably restrained in setting only two miracle stories in the city proper: the paralyzed man at Bethesda (5:1–9) and the healing of the man born blind. In other words, for all its heavy emphasis on the city of Jerusalem, the Johannine tradition shows a surprising sobriety in not multiplying miracles there.

More positively, the miracle in John 9:1 + 6–7, like other Johannine stories set in and around Jerusalem, shows knowledge of—and more importantly, takes for granted—the topography of pre-A.D. 70 Jerusalem. The pool of Si-loam, at the southwest corner of the eastern hill of biblical Jerusalem, near the point where the Kidron Valley meets the Tyropean Valley, is not introduced or explained when it is mentioned in John 9:7; it is just there.[88] Besides being mentioned in Josephus, the existence of Siloam in pre-A.D. 70 Jerusalem is attested by a mention in the Copper Scroll found at Qumran (3Q15 10:15–16). At the very least, this nonchalant mention of the pool of Siloam in John 9:7 points to very early tradition at home in a community that knew pre-A.D. 70 Jerusalem well, since the area of Siloam seems to have been destroyed by the Romans in A.D. 70 and was probably not rebuilt until the time of Emperor

Hadrian in A.D. 135.[89] Within the NT, Siloam as the name of a pool is unique to this passage of John.[90]

Besides being unique to this Gospel, the reference to the pool of Siloam fits nicely into the Gospel's larger context. In chaps. 8–9 of the Gospel, Jesus has been discoursing in the Jerusalem temple during the feast of tabernacles. Now, according to the Mishna, on each day of this feast a solemn procession descended from the temple to Siloam to draw out water that was brought back to the temple and poured out on the altar of holocausts.[91] If the cure of the blind man took place during or at the end of the feast of tabernacles, Jesus' choice of the pool of Siloam for the symbolic washing would have clear motivation. However, even in the present form of the Fourth Gospel it is not certain that the Evangelist intends a connection between the cure of the blind man in chap. 9 and the feast of tabernacles in chaps. 7–8.[92] Whether any connection between the feast and the healing existed in the original miracle story is even more problematic. Still, the basic point remains: the mention of the pool of Siloam is unique in the miracle traditions of the Gospels and in the NT as a whole.

Another element in the healing of the man born blind that is unique within the miracle stories of the Gospels—and indeed the whole of the NT—is the use of Jesus' spittle to make mud or clay to "anoint" the eyes of the blind man. Scholars often make reference to the two uses of spittle in Mark: the healing of the deaf-mute (7:31–37) and the healing of the blind man at Bethsaida (8:22–26). But in both of the Marcan miracles the spittle is used as a direct agent of healing, while in John 9 it is merely the means by which Jesus makes the mud that he then smears on the blind man's eyes, mud that in turn is washed away by the blind man in the pool of Siloam. Apparently the mud is meant to symbolize the blindness that is "washed away" when the blind man obeys Jesus' command to wash in Siloam. Hence, far from being parallel to the use of spittle in the two Marcan miracles, this use of spittle by Jesus in John 9:6 is discontinuous with the entire miracle tradition in the Four Gospels.

Likewise unique is the exact way in which Jesus effects the cure: first he spits on the ground to make mud, then he smears the mud on the eyes of the blind man, then he orders the blind man to wash in a pool. The story intimates that it is the washing in the pool, in obedience to Jesus' command, that cures the man's blindness.[93] Nothing is expressly said about the man's faith (or any petition by him for healing) prior to or immediately following upon the miracle.[94] The blind man's obedience must suffice for an expression of faith. In short, the precise way in which Jesus brings about this healing is discontinuous with the entire miracle tradition in the Gospels.

The odd elements of discontinuity, the taken-for-granted knowledge of Jerusalem's topography, and in general the lengthy tradition history that apparently lies behind the present form of John 9 converge to form an argument for the historicity of the primitive tradition. I admit once again that certitude is not to be had in such matters. It is conceivable that the primitive story was invented by a Christian community resident in Jerusalem before A.D. 70. Still, on the whole, I think it more likely than not that Jesus healed a blind man in Jerusalem under the curious circumstances related in 9:6–7. Whether the man was "blind from birth" (9:1) cannot be decided. It could be that the tendency of John's Gospel to heighten the miraculous element in miracle stories has given us the only healing of a man specifically said to be born blind. Then, too, a man blind from birth supplies a convenient symbol of a humanity born into a world of spiritual darkness. Granted these theological tendencies in the Fourth Gospel, no decision can be made on the historicity of the detail that the man was born blind.

D. "THE BLIND SEE" (MATT 11:5 ‖ LUKE 7:22)

In addition to the *narratives* of the healing of Bartimaeus, the blind man at Bethsaida, and the man born blind, we also have a *saying* of Jesus mentioning the healing of the blind, namely the famous Q saying in Matt 11:5 ‖ Luke 7:22: "Blind people see and lame people walk; lepers are cleansed and deaf people hear; dead people are raised and poor people have the good news preached to them." We have already seen the reasons for accepting this saying as authentic. Hence the fact that Jesus claimed—and was thought by others—to give sight to the blind is supported both by multiple attestation of sources (Mark, Q, and John)[95] and by multiple attestation of forms (miracle stories about Jesus and a saying of Jesus). In addition, as I have tried to show in the individual treatments, the claim to basic historicity on the part of the stories about Bartimaeus and the man at Bethsaida are quite strong, while the claim for the story about the man born blind is fairly strong. All in all, the tradition that Jesus healed the blind stands alongside the tradition that he worked exorcisms as one of the best attested miracle traditions in the Four Gospels.

III. PERSONS AFFLICTED WITH "LEPROSY"

When we come to the stories of Jesus healing "lepers," the difficulties of rendering a historical judgment increase for three reasons. First, the number of stories about curing lepers is smaller than that of any of the types of miracle stories (exorcisms, healings of the paralyzed, healings of the blind) that we have treated so far. There are only two full narratives recounting the cure of leprosy: the healing of the leper in Mark 1:40–45 parr. and the healing of the ten lepers—including the grateful Samaritan—in Luke 17:11–19 (a story unique to Luke). If one were to agree with the critics who assign the healing of the ten lepers to Luke's creative reworking of Mark 1:40–45 or to a pure creation by Luke, the number of narratives would be reduced to one. And even this Marcan narrative is viewed by some critics as a creation of the early church. In any event, the number of independent stories narrating the cure of leprosy by Jesus is quite small.

Nevertheless, I do not think the case hopeless. As I shall indicate below, it is more likely that Luke 17:11–19 represents an independent tradition, not just a creative redaction of Mark 1:40–45 or a pure invention of Luke. When we add to these two stories the passing reference to the cleansing of lepers in the Q saying of Matt 11:5 par., we have multiple attestation of both sources and forms for the basic affirmation that Jesus healed—or was thought to have healed—lepers during his own lifetime.[96] Naturally, this does not guarantee the historicity of the two particular stories before us, but at least there is no a priori reason to be more skeptical about the tradition of Jesus' healing leprosy than about other types of his miracles.

The second difficulty we face is that, more than some other types of healings by Jesus, his healing of lepers has met with skepticism even among critics who are not themselves hardened skeptics. For instance, Rudolf Pesch, who on the whole is quite accepting of the basic historicity of the Marcan tradition, is strongly opposed to the historicity of the narratives involving the cure of leprosy.[97] One of Pesch's major objections, especially to the Marcan story, is that it depicts Jesus as the eschatological prophet and echoes the miracles attributed to the OT prophets Elijah and Elisha. Pesch argues that such a portrait of Jesus as the miracle-working eschatological prophet must come from early Christian theology, not from the historical Jesus. But it is precisely here that Pesch's objections are vulnerable to counterattack. From all that we have seen in these two volumes of *A Marginal Jew*, nothing seems clearer than that (1) Jesus acted and was thought of as a Jewish prophet during his lifetime; (2) Jesus' prophetic message was strongly eschatological, naturally casting Jesus in the role of "a" or "the" eschatological prophet; (3) Jesus distinguished himself from many other prophetic figures of the period (e.g., John the Baptist and the "sign prophets") by claiming to perform numerous miracles of healing, some of which would almost inevitably remind pious Jews of the miracles of Elijah and Elisha, the only OT prophets especially noted for miracle-working.

Hence what Pesch labels as purely early Christian theology—the picture of Jesus as miracle-working eschatological prophet—is firmly rooted in the tradition that goes back to Jesus' own lifetime. Needless to say, such an idea was seized upon and developed further in the early church, but its existence in a particular narrative does not ipso facto prove that such a narrative is a pure creation of the church. More specifically, that the Marcan story of Jesus' cure of a leper reflects such a picture of Jesus does not automatically prove Pesch's contention that the account is simply a Christian creation.

A third difficulty is that we are not at all sure of the exact meaning of "leper" or "leprosy" in these Gospel stories.[98] When used today, "leprosy" usually refers to what is known as Hansen's disease, caused by the bacillus *mycobacterium leprae*. In English Bible translations the word "leprosy" has traditionally been used in the OT to render the Hebrew noun *ṣāraʿat*, but that convention is technically misleading. In Leviticus 13–14, the major OT legislation on the subject, *ṣāraʿat* refers to types of fungal growth or mold in fabrics and houses as well as to various skin infections in human beings. Leviticus 13 does not describe the lesions on human skin with sufficient clarity to make a precise medical judgment, but the symptoms described by Leviticus suggest that the various skin conditions are not leprosy in the modern sense. The word *ṣāraʿat* probably includes such conditions as psoriasis, eczema, and vitiligo. In fact, it is doubtful that Hansen's disease (i.e., leprosy in the modern scientific sense) existed in the ancient Near East at the time that the priestly legislation in Leviticus was codified (roughly, in the 6th century B.C.).[99] Only after the time of Alexander the Great (died 323 B.C.) do we have firm evidence of Hansen's disease in the ancient Near East. It is possible that by Jesus' day "leprosy" (Greek *lepra*) had come to include Hansen's disease. However, the NT reflects the terminology and prescriptions of the OT legislation and so may well be referring to the types of skin diseases depicted in the OT. Leprosy thus presents us with a concrete example of a more general truth: the Gospel stories of healing do not usually allow a precise and detailed diagnosis of the diseases that are claimed to be cured by Jesus. We must bear this in mind as we turn to the three relevant Gospel texts referring to Jesus' cure of "leprosy."

A. MARK 1:40–45 (PARR.)

The story of Jesus' healing of an individual leper is a curious mixture of a standard form-critical pattern, little additions stressing the attitudes and emotions of the two actors, and redactional touches by Mark.

The healing story in Mark 1:40–45, which lacks personal and place-names[100] as well as a strong connection with the larger context of chaps. 1–2, follows the basic form-critical outline of a miracle story:[101] (1) the petitioner *approaches* Jesus, requesting a healing (v 40); (2) Jesus accedes, *healing* the petitioner with a touch and a word (v 41); the fact and immediacy of the cure are then affirmed (v 42); (3) in the special case of leprosy, the *confirmation* of the cure is foreshadowed rather than narrated as Jesus orders the petitioner to present himself before a priest for a declaration that he is clean and for the prescribed sacrifice.[102] The sacrifice will seal the reintegration of the formerly ostracized leper into the ordinary social and religious life of Israel (v 44).[103] Notable in the skeletal structure of Mark 1:40–44 is the repetition of the key words "cleanse" and "cleansing" (*katharizō, katharismos*) in vv 40,41,42, and 44; the repetition binds the elements of the basic story (vv 40–44) tightly together.[104] The tightness of the core of the miracle story contrasts with the somewhat wordy and meandering conclusion in v 45.

Filling out the basic story are a few details emphasizing the attitudes and emotions of both parties. The leper is described as "pleading," "kneeling,"[105] and uttering a moving yet terse profession of trust in Jesus' gracious will and power: "If you want, you can make me clean" (v 40). Responding with strong emotion[106] and dramatic gesture, Jesus takes up the key words of the petition in an even-more-terse reply (only two words in the Greek): "[I do] want [to], [be] clean" (v 41). Then with sternness bordering on anger (*embrimēsamenos*, literally, "snorting," "puffing"),[107] Jesus immediately sends (literally, "drives") the man away, giving him the double charge both to say nothing to anyone and to go to a priest for a declaration of cleanness and the prescribed sacrifice (vv 43–44).

Whether or not the details of the actors' emotions come from Mark or from his tradition, most likely the lengthy and overloaded conclusion of the story is at least partly due to his additions to the traditional structure of a miracle story.[108] The third element of a traditional miracle story, the confirmation, demands in the case of leprosy that the healed person go to a priest, so that the cure can be officially confirmed and "activated" by admitting the former leper back into Israelite society. Mark surrounds this traditional element (located in v 44b) with his characteristic dialectic of the mysterious hiddenness yet unavoidable manifestation of God's power in Jesus' healings. On the one hand, in v 44a Jesus typically—and somewhat unrealistically—orders the man to say nothing to anyone;[109] on the other hand, in v 45a the man blatantly disobeys the order by spreading the news of his cure far and wide.[110] The result in v 45b is that Jesus can no longer appear openly in town (the subsequent context in Mark 2:1 suggests that Capernaum in particular is in mind), but must stay in deserted, out-of-the-way places. The paradox is complete when in v 45c Mark adds by way of conclusion to the story that Jesus' isolation only has the effect of drawing people to him from every side. This puzzling interplay between the secrecy or privacy desired by Jesus and the unavoidable publicity that his actions occasion is Mark's personal signature at the end of what is apparently a traditional story.[111] The ending in vv 44–45 is cumbersome and overburdened precisely because the Marcan double motif of hiddenness-yet-revelation (vv 44a + 45) is inserted on either side of the traditional element of the necessary confirmation of the miracle by a priest (v 44b).

The unwieldy addition by Mark to an otherwise terse, schematic miracle story indicates that at the very least Mark 1:40–45 is not a purely Marcan creation.[112] But that may be all that can be said with fair assurance. Shorn of the Marcan conclusion, and perhaps also of the expressions of emotion by the leper and Jesus, the narrative exemplifies the bare bones of what would be needed to tell the story of the cleansing of a leper. As we have already seen, this stereotypical outline, isolated by form criticism, tells neither for nor against the historicity of the story. We must examine the remaining Gospel passages to see if they can add further weight to Mark's testimony.

B. LUKE 17:11–19

The story of Jesus' healing of ten lepers is a narrative unique to Luke's Gospel.[113] In both structure and theology it is more complex than the account in Mark 1:40–45. Indeed, be it the question of the story's proper title, its literary category and historical origins, or its theological message, critics disagree on what this pericope is and is about. Titles range from "The Ten Lepers" to "The Grateful Samaritan" to the all-inclusive "The Ten Lepers and the Grateful Samaritan." As for form-critical categories, the story has been called a biographical apophthegm (so Bultmann), a personal legend about Jesus (so Dibelius), simply a miracle story (so many other critics), and even the tongue-twisting "imitation of a prophetic narrative with the characteristic of surpassing the model" (so Wilhelm Bruners).[114] Scholars likewise disagree on whether the story is totally a creation of Luke, represents a Lucan redaction of some earlier story in the L tradition (possibly dependent in turn on the Marcan tradition behind Mark 1:40–45), or actually goes back through stages of tradition and redaction to the historical Jesus. Not surprisingly, all these disagreements result in further disagreements on the theological point or points of the story.

As always, one must start with the text as it stands. The structure of the story falls into two clear parts.[115] In part one (17:11–14), we have a concise miracle story in which, by a mere word, Jesus heals ten lepers who beg him for mercy. The major difference from the cleansing of the leper in Mark 1:40–45 is that the lepers are not healed instantaneously but rather while they are in the process of fulfilling Jesus' command, i.e., while they are on their way to present themselves before priests for an official declaration that they are free of leprosy. The cleansing "on the way" unleashes part two of the narrative (vv 15–19), which is the more important part theologically. One of the men reacts to the recognition of his cure by praising God and returning immediately to Jesus, whom he thanks with a prostration. Only at this late stage of the story does Luke show the card up his sleeve: "And he [the one grateful leper] was a Samaritan." Jesus responds with three rhetorical questions, which raise the issues of ethnic differences and differences in gratitude: "Were not ten cleansed? The nine, where [are they]? Has no one been found to return and give glory to God except this foreigner?" The three questions are then followed by a declaration Jesus makes at the end of a number of other miracle stories: "Arise and go; your faith has saved [sesōken, also with the meaning of "healed"] you."

The two-part structure of the story may explain why views on its form-critical category have differed so much. No one category can cover, umbrella-like, the entire narrative. Perhaps it is best simply to acknowledge that we have here a pericope that combines two forms in succession: (1) a concise miracle story recounting how Jesus cured ten lepers with a mere command (vv 11–14); and (2) an apophthegm (vv 15–19), i.e., a short narrative that acts as a frame or a "setup" for a pithy and powerful pronouncement by Jesus (hence, Vincent Taylor's category, "pronouncement story").[116]

The theology of the story is more complicated than its two-part literary form might at first suggest. Obviously the greatest weight falls on the final, climactic pronouncements of Jesus. But even they bear more than one theological message. We easily detect the clear opposition between the effusive gratitude of the one leper, expressed to both God and Jesus, and the attitude of the other nine lepers, who quite literally take their miraculous healing "in stride." This opposition is deepened by the juxtaposition of the grateful Samaritan ("this foreigner," who would be despised by most Jews as a half-breed schismatic) and the blasé nine, understood in the narrative to be Jews. For Luke, all this foreshadows his account in Acts: many Jews reject the gospel while many Samaritans—as well as many Gentiles—accept it (see Acts 8:5–25; contrast 7:54–8:3). This wider Lucan theme is hinted at in the somewhat clumsy opening verse that sets a puzzling geographical scene: Jesus is on his way to Jerusalem, the city of destiny (we are in the "great journey narrative" of Luke 9–19), and is—inexplicably—"passing through the midst of Samaria and Galilee." The thematic opposition runs still deeper, though. All ten lepers are "cleansed" (*ekatharisthēsan*, v 14) and "healed" (*iathē*, v 15); they receive the physical miracle conferred by Jesus' word of command, with which they comply. But the nine who do not return to Jesus to express their gratitude receive *only* a physical healing—and that is their loss. Only the grateful Samaritan is described as having faith (*pistis*), and Jesus declares that his faith has brought him not only physical healing but also salvation (*sesōken* in v 19, with its full sense of "saved"). It is one thing to be healed by Jesus; it is another to see in that healing a token of the saving action of God at work in Jesus, respond in faith to that token with praise and gratitude, and so be assured of salvation by Jesus.[117]

Although these observations sum up most of the major theological points made by the narrative, one should not completely ignore the message conveyed by the first half of the story. As one would expect, the miracle story proper emphasizes the power of Jesus to heal those who appeal to him for mercy (which all ten lepers sincerely do). Jesus' power is magnified in this particular episode insofar as he purposely delays the miracle until the lepers are on their way to the priests. In this way he performs a miracle at a distance, tests the lepers' trust in his power to cure them,[118] and—from the angle of literary criticism—provides the "setup" for the second half of the pericope. In sum, then, the theology of Luke 17:11–19 is much denser and richer than a first reading might intimate.

Our most immediate concern, however, is the question of tradition and redaction. What is the origin of this story? Among scholars one finds almost every position imaginable. Bultmann considers Luke 17:11–19 to be merely a variant of Mark 1:40–45; it represents an "ideal scene."[119] A different yet allied approach is taken by Pesch.[120] Behind Luke 17:11–19 with its slight Lucan redaction lies an L tradition. However, this L tradition was formulated on the basis of Mark 1:40–45 and the OT model of the cure of the Syrian leper Naaman by the prophet Elisha in 2 Kings 5.[121] Hence, while not purely a Lucan creation, the story was created by the early church and does not go back to Jesus. Taking a more radical view, Bruners judges that Luke 17:11–19 is totally a creation of Luke, who is imitating the Naaman story in 2 Kings 5 even as he has Jesus surpass the OT miracle.[122] Finally, conservative critics like van der Loos and Latourelle hold that the basic event behind Luke 17:11–19 goes back to Jesus.[123]

How can one begin to adjudicate such a variety of views? First of all, this broad range of opinions on the story's origins can serve to warn us that we are not dealing with as simple a narrative as might first appear. We have already seen that it is no easy matter to sum up in a few words the complex theological message—or better messages—contained in a mere nine verses. The very fact that these nine verses contain so many different theological insights operating on various levels or in various parts of this story highlights the question of whether Luke composed this story on his own, in a single solitary act of creation. The multi-layered narrative, which seems to point in so many directions at the same time, may indicate instead that Luke has redacted an L tradition he has received, thus producing a very complicated piece of literature.

This possibility becomes a probability when one considers the strange phrases, unusual words, and various tensions that can be discerned in these nine verses. So many striking phenomena in so short a compass make it difficult to sustain the view that Luke 17:11–19 is purely a creation of Luke, a literary whole cast at one time. If Luke himself invented the story on the basis of various OT and NT models, one must struggle to answer two outstanding questions:

(1) Why does Luke create confusion right at the beginning of the pericope by going out of his way to set the scene—or rather, not set the scene—with the unintelligible phrase *diērcheto dia meson Samareias kai Galilaias*, literally, "he was passing through the middle of Samaria and Galilee" (v 11)? Attempts to emend or explain away the words are legion, and understandably so.[124] The prepositional phrase *dia meson* (in the accusative case) occurs nowhere else in the NT or the LXX; it is certainly not Lucan redactional style. What "through the middle of Samaria and Galilee" can mean when Samaria lies south of Galilee and when Luke has already stated that Jesus has left Galilee and has entered Samaritan territory on his way up to Jerusalem (9:51–56) is unclear. Conzelmann's suggestion that Luke, writing "from abroad," is ignorant of the exact geographical locations of Galilee, Samaria, and Judea has rightly won widespread acceptance, but does not solve the entire problem.[125] Conzelmann claims that after Jesus is rebuffed by a Samaritan village in 9:52–55, he returns to Galilee and journeys through Galilee to Judea and Jerusalem. This interpretation is by no means certain. As Luke begins the great journey narrative with the solemn statement at 9:51–52, he apparently intends to close off the period of the Galilean ministry (4:14–9:50). He makes it clear in 9:51–52 that Jesus is entering Samaritan territory in order to travel up to Jerusalem; he never "revokes" this impression by making an explicit statement anywhere in chaps. 9–19 that Jesus reenters Galilee.[126]

The main point for us, though, is that, whatever the explanation of the present text in Luke 17:11, it is much easier to conceive of Luke writing this geographical muddle ("through the middle of Samaria and Galilee") if he took it over or redacted it from some previous tradition. Why he would have taken pains to create this geographical mess (paralleled nowhere else in the great journey narrative) if he were writing freely is difficult to explain.[127]

(2) Some words and phrases in the nine verses of Luke 17:11–19 never

occur elsewhere in the NT or at least in Luke-Acts. Apart from the geographical puzzle in v 11 (with wording witnessed nowhere else in the Bible), the list of unusual locutions includes "leper" (*leproi*) used as an adjective modifying a noun (v 12, "men" [*andres*]); the verb "meet" (v 12, *apantaō*, elsewhere in the NT only in Mark 14:13); "from a distance" (v 12, *porrōthen*, which occurs again only in Heb 11:13); the address to Jesus as "master" (*epistata*) when placed in the mouths of people who are not disciples and when joined directly to the name Jesus as "Jesus Master" (v 13, *Iēsou epistata*);[128] and the word "foreigner" (*allogenēs*, v 18, found nowhere else in the NT).

To be sure, some of the special features of this story may be due to the influence of the vocabulary of the Septuagint in general and the Naaman story in 2 Kings 5 in particular. But Luke had no monopoly on the Septuagint in early Christianity; such "biblical Greek" might have been a characteristic of Luke's special tradition as well. Indeed, if what we call the L tradition was the tradition that developed over decades in Luke's own church, it may well be that some traits we consider signs of Luke's redaction were actually traits he inherited from his L tradition. Granted, no one consideration is all that probative, but the convergence of a number of curious locutions in this short narrative that has so many different layers of theological meaning inclines me to the view that Luke is reworking for his own purposes an L tradition he has inherited.

Was this L tradition simply created by the early church on the pattern of the pre-Marcan story seen in Mark 1:40–45? Bultmann and Pesch think so, but the structure and content of Luke 17:11–19 are notably different. Instead of the usual pattern of a miracle story as seen in Mark 1:40–45 (modified, admittedly, by the special needs of a story about lepers and by Mark's redactional concerns at the end of the story), we have in Luke a two-part narrative that is first miracle story and then apophthegm. As the story now stands, the venue is some strange middle ground or border area between Samaria and Galilee instead of the Galilee of Mark 1:40–45; the persons who are cured comprise ten lepers as opposed to Mark's one; the key figure is a Samaritan leper as opposed to Mark's Jewish leper; in Luke's story the lepers—unlike the bold leper in Mark 1:40–45—carefully observe the law by keeping their distance from Jesus; in Mark's story the cure takes place instantaneously and by Jesus' touch, while in Luke 17 the cure is delayed, at a distance, and merely by Jesus' word; in Mark the leper responds by spreading the news abroad, while in Luke the grateful leper responds by returning to Jesus to express his gratitude. One may justly ask: Is there anything common to Mark 1:40–45 and Luke 17:11–19 beyond the essential words and motifs that would have to be present in any Gospel story of Jesus curing a leper? Granted all the striking differences (be they traceable to 2 Kings 5 or not), I see no reason to reduce Luke 17:11–19 to a mere variant of Mark 1:40–45.[129] At the very least, I think that the L tradition, independently of the Marcan tradition, contained a story of Jesus healing lepers.[130]

C. CONCLUSIONS ON THE HEALING OF LEPROSY

What does all this come to? Admittedly, not much. However, I do think that what we have seen makes it likely that three independent traditions—Mark, L, and Q (Matt 11:5 par.: "lepers are cleansed")—all affirm that during his ministry Jesus was thought to have cured lepers. In other words, the criterion of multiple attestation of sources and forms (narratives in Mark and L, a saying of Jesus in Q) supports the claim that the picture of Jesus cleansing lepers goes back to the life of Jesus himself and is not purely a creation of the early church.[131] However, the relatively sparse evidence does not allow us to go further. In light of the many difficult questions that surround the tradition and redaction of Mark 1:40–45 and Luke 17:11–19, I would not want to make any claims about the details of the two accounts. In short: contrary to Pesch, I think that Mark, Q, and L do allow us to state that during his ministry Jesus claimed to heal lepers and was thought by other people to have done so. But beyond that the data do not permit us to go.

IV. VARIOUS HEALINGS OF WHICH ONLY ONE INCIDENT IS REPORTED

Throughout this treatment of *types* of miracle stories (e.g., healings of the crippled, healings of the blind), I have been stressing that historical judgments are tenuous at best. Still, a few factors have allowed us to grope our way tentatively through the stories of exorcisms, the healing of the crippled, the healing of the blind, and the healing of lepers. Each *type* of miracle in this list (1) was represented by more than one distinct incident or story in the Gospel tradition and (2) was attested by more than one literary source (Mark, Q, M, L, and John) or form (a narrative about Jesus and a saying of Jesus). However meager, these data opened the way for reasoned argumentation, the probing of theories, and judgments enjoying some degree of probability.

As we come to our fourth category of healings, which is really a "catchall" or "umbrella" category, we must recognize a shift in the situation. With one exception (the healing of the centurion's servant or royal official's son), this catchall category includes various types of miracles of healing that have two discouraging characteristics: (1) there is only one occurrence of each type of healing;[132] and, as a natural corollary, (2) each type is witnessed in only one independent source.[133] When we remember the significant role that the criterion of multiple attestation has played in our survey of miracle stories up until now, we immediately appreciate what a limiting, not to say crippling, factor the lack of multiple stories or multiple forms is. Given this severe restriction, we must be open to the possibility that we will have to assign the frustrating judgment of *non liquet* ("not clear") to some if not all of the stories in our catchall category. It may turn out that, because of the lack of data, no clear decision can be made one way or the other in most or even all of the cases. This decision should not be viewed as a diplomatic way of saying the accounts do not go back in some form to the historical Jesus, anymore than it should be taken as a covert judgment of historicity. *Non liquet* means *non liquet*, no more, no less. Often both liberal and conservative scholars are understandably unhappy with a decision not to decide, but sometimes the fragmentary state of our sources leaves us no other option.

Five miracle stories are candidates for this decision not to decide: (A) The healing of the fever of Peter's mother-in-law (Mark 1:29–31 parr.); (B) the healing of the woman with a hemorrhage (Mark 5:24–34 parr.); (C) the healing of the man with dropsy (Luke 14:1–6); (D) the healing of the deaf man with a speech impediment[134] (the "deaf-mute" in Mark 7:31–37); (E) the healing of the ear of the high priest's slave (Luke 22:50–51). Still, while the lack of multiple cases or multiple sources makes any firm judgment of historicity extremely difficult, we should not automatically jump to a decision of *non liquet* for all the stories, as though there were no differences among them. A brief review of the five stories shows that a judgment about an account's historicity may be possible in some cases, though not in others.

A. PETER'S MOTHER-IN-LAW (MARK 1:29–31 PARR.)

The healing of the fever of Peter's mother-in-law (Mark 1:29–31 parr.) is one of the shortest miracle stories in the Gospels.[135] Mark's version, which takes up all of three verses (two verses, if one omits the scene-setting v 29), contains 44 words (27 words, if v 29 is omitted). In their redactional activity both Matthew and Luke reduce the wordage even further. Obviously, one is not left with a great deal of data to deal with. As we saw when we studied the story of the exorcism of the demoniac in the Capernaum synagogue, this brief miracle story is part of a larger unit probably put together by Mark or a pre-Marcan author. The larger unit presents a typical or ideal "day in Capernaum," which reaches from Mark 1:21 to 1:32 (or even 1:39). The artificial overarching framework should make us leery of confident judgments about historicity.

At the same time, one cannot ignore the striking, almost paradoxical, combination of brevity and detailed concreteness in the story of the healing of Peter's mother-in-law. Within the compass of three verses we are given (1) a precise time (the Sabbath after the close of the synagogue service, around the time of the main Sabbath meal), (2) a precise place (the house of Simon Peter in Capernaum), (3) a precise audience (Simon Peter, his brother Andrew, and the two sons of Zebedee James and John), and (4) the most unlikely of subjects, who appears out of nowhere and immediately disappears: Peter's mother-in-law. Not surprisingly in an androcentric culture, the male disciples of Jesus rather than the woman lying in bed with the fever appeal to him for help. The miracle itself is narrated in the shortest space possible: taking the woman's hand, Jesus raises her up;[136] the fever leaves her; and she begins serving the Sabbath meal to the group.[137]

The brevity yet concreteness of the story may persuade some that the story does reflect a specific Sabbath-day healing by Jesus in Capernaum. In particular, the unexpected concrete detail of the sufferer being Peter's mother-in-law is arresting.[138] Nowhere in the Four Gospels is it ever directly mentioned that Peter is married; only in this story, and with no further explanation, do we hear of his mother-in-law. Reciprocally, while saying nothing about Peter's mother-in-law, Paul mentions in passing in 1 Cor 9:5 that Peter has a wife whom he takes along on his missionary journeys. Some critics might want to see here a curious, indirect type of multiple attestation—though only of the mother-in-law, not of her cure! In all this, though, we should recall from our initial treatment of the criteria of historicity the point that vivid, concrete narration is not of itself a proof of historicity.[139] Otherwise, a vividly narrated and realistic novel could qualify as history. Hence my judgment on the historicity of this miracle story is *non liquet*, though I am willing to take a firm stand in favor of the existence of Peter's mother-in-law.

B. The Woman with the Hemorrhage (Mark 5:24–34 parr.)

Our second case, the woman suffering from a hemorrhage (Mark 5:24–34 parr.), is unusual in that in the present texts of the Gospels it forms part of a larger narrative, the raising of the daughter of Jairus (Mark 5:21–43 parr.). In fact, in the Marcan version the story of the woman with a hemorrhage plays a necessary role in the story. In Mark 5:23 (though not in Matt 9:18, where the girl is dead from the start), Jairus begs Jesus to come and cure his sick daughter, who is close to death. In Mark, the incident of the woman with a hemorrhage delays Jesus on the way. As a result, Jesus is still speaking to the woman when news arrives that in the meantime the daughter has died (Mark 5:35). Some conservative critics suggest that the intrinsic literary connection in Mark reflects a real-life historical connection: the healing of the woman did take place while Jesus was on his way to Jairus' house. The connection was there from the beginning.[140]

That may well be, but one has to face the possibility that the connection between the two miracle stories is purely a literary connection, the product of Mark or a pre-Marcan source. After all, the connection between the two stories is of a particular kind. One story is not simply tacked on to the end of the other. Rather, the story of the woman is inserted into the middle of the story of Jairus' daughter, resulting in a configuration that is variously called "dovetailed," "sandwiched," "intercalated" or simply A-B-A'. Similar configurations can be seen elsewhere in Mark's Gospel, including the opposition to Jesus from his family and Jerusalem scribes (3:20–35), the cursing of the fig tree and the cleansing of the temple (11:12–25), and the trial by the Sanhedrin and the denial by Peter (14:53–72). Once again, some critics might want to argue that the narratives in these pericopes likewise follow the order of historical events,[141] but the presence of a set style of storytelling in Mark warns us that we cannot take that position for granted. Moreover, some would see the strange coincidence that the woman was ill for twelve years (5:25) and that the daughter of Jairus was twelve years old (5:42) as a sign of a conscious attempt by some author or storyteller to stitch the two stories together.[142] In any event, the story of the woman with a hemorrhage is self-contained and does not need the surrounding story of Jairus' daughter; the former is perfectly intelligible without the latter.

Even taken by itself, the narrative of the woman with a hemorrhage is most unusual for a Gospel miracle story. No other miracle story in the Gospels centers on the delicate question of a gynecological problem (perhaps chronic uterine hemorrhage), which would be not only a sensitive private matter for the woman but also a constant source of ritual impurity according to the laws of Leviticus. Hence her dilemma: with popular religious ideas that smack of magic, she believes that to be healed she must physically touch Jesus or at least his clothing; yet to do so would constitute the brazen act of a ritually unclean woman communicating her uncleanness to a holy man whom she otherwise does not know. Her solution is stealth. She sneaks up behind Jesus in the surging crowd, touches his cloak without his seeing her (v 28), and is immediately cured. According to Mark, Jesus senses healing power streaming from his body, almost as though it were an electric current. Thus, a magical conception of miracle-working is attributed by the narrative to Jesus as well as to the woman (v 30). This sense of his own power flowing from him does not, however, tell Jesus who has touched him or why. He has to inquire after the identity of the person and look around to find her, while his bewildered disciples tell him in hardly polite terms that it is absurd in the press of the crowd to look for a single person who touched him. The frightened woman comes forward and tells the whole story. Jesus responds with a phrase found at the conclusion of a number of miracle stories: "Your faith has saved [sesōken, also "healed"] you," to which Jesus adds: "Go in peace and be healed of this illness." In the Marcan narrative, the final words of Jesus serve to deflect somewhat the magical tone of the story by stressing the woman's faith as the source of healing and highlighting the concluding command of Jesus ("be healed") as the surety that the cure is permanent.

Surprisingly, champions of the basic historicity of this story come from opposite camps. Those who wish to classify Jesus as a magician find in this story a star witness. Conservative scholars, caught in exegetical straits, must maintain the story's historicity while trying to downplay or explain away the magical element.[143] Perhaps we need to remind ourselves that we have before us not a videotape replay of what happened in A.D. 28 but a Christian composition, a carefully written miracle story, flowing from an evangelist's pen somewhere around A.D. 70. The story, including its magical aura, is first, last, and always the product of Mark's literary activity. One becomes even more cautious when one remembers that the two other Gospel miracles often cited as having magical overtones are both unique to Mark: the healing of the deaf-mute (7:31–37) and the healing of the blind man at Bethsaida (8:22–26). It is often claimed that Mark has preserved Jesus' magical practices, which other evangelists suppressed. That may well be. But, at least in theory, one must entertain another possibility, namely, that Mark or his tradition was especially given to narrating miracle stories in magical terms. In other words, magical elements in a story no more automatically guarantee historical reporting than does vividness of narration. Granted the fact that the story of the woman with a hemorrhage is sui generis in the Gospel tradition and that we have no multiple attestation or even remote parallel for it in the Gospels, it too, in my opinion, must fall into the category of *non liquet*.

C. THE MAN WITH DROPSY (LUKE 14:1–6)

Our third intractable case is a story unique to Luke (Luke 14:1–6), the healing of the man with dropsy (*hydrōpikos*, i.e., edema).[144] Though the precise afflic-tion (dropsy) is found only in this narrative, the story is similar in form and message to other accounts of Jesus' healings on the Sabbath, healings that unleash controversy and opposition (e.g., the man with the withered hand in Mark 3:1–6; the bent-over woman in Luke 13:10–17). Hence we have here a mixture of a miracle story and a dispute story (a particular form of an apo-phthegm), the miracle story providing the occasion for—and thus being subor-dinate to—the dispute. Since, however, I am classifying the Gospels' miracle stories of healing according to types of ailments and not according to more detailed form-critical categories (e.g., apophthegm, dispute story), I treat the case of the man with dropsy separately; he clearly does not come under cases of paralyzed or crippled limbs.

Luke 14:1–6 differs from Mark 3:1–6 and Luke 13:10–17 not only in the specified ailment but also in the setting of the story: it is located not in a synagogue but in the home of a Pharisee, who has invited Jesus to eat with him on the Sabbath. The event is without precise time or place; we are within Luke's meandering narrative of the great journey up to Jerusalem (chaps. 9–19). Once Jesus enters the house, he is subject to hostile observation by his adversaries (cf. Mark 3:2 || Luke 6:7). It is unclear whether the man with dropsy is thought of as a guest, someone who has wandered in looking for a cure, or a person purposely "planted" at the meal to entrap Jesus. Before he works the miracle, Jesus confronts the lawyers and the Pharisees with the basic question of whether it is lawful to heal people on the Sabbath. Thus the major concern of the pericope is put "up front." When his adversaries remain silent, Jesus takes hold of the man, heals him (nothing is said about a healing word), and sends him home.

Jesus then resumes the implicit dispute with his adversaries by answering his previous question with a rhetorical question (v 5): "If your son or ox fell into a well, which of you would not immediately pull him [or it] out, [even] on the Sabbath?" Jesus appeals to common sense and ordinary experience by way of an *a pari* argument.[145] Emergency situations call for "immediate" (v 5: *eu-theōs*) merciful assistance, even on the Sabbath. Almost everyone would agree that this would hold in the case of the son or the ox in the well;[146] Jesus sees his healing as justified by the same rule of immediate merciful assistance.

A judgment about the historicity of this story is extremely difficult for a number of reasons. The precise word for the physical suffering involved, dropsy (*hydrōpikos*), is never mentioned again anywhere in the OT or NT, and there is no indication of what illness the dropsy is a symptom. While the story may go back to a special L tradition, in its present state it shows signs of heavy Lucan redaction.[147] In fact, Busse thinks that the miracle story proper is a creation of Luke himself.[148]

Parallels to individual verses can be found in other Sabbath dispute stories. The prime example is v 5: "If your son or ox fell into a well, which of you would not immediately pull him [or it] out, [even] on the Sabbath?" This logion is remarkably similar to Matt 12:11 (Matthew's version of the Marcan story of the man with the withered hand), though in Matt 12:11 it is a *sheep* that falls into a *pit*. The vocabulary of Matt 12:11 differs from that of Luke 14:5, and Matthew's version argues *a fortiori*: "How much more important is a human being than a sheep?"[149] Jesus' concise question in Luke 14:3b ("Is it lawful to heal on the Sabbath, or not?") is similar to the longer one in Mark 3:4 ‖ Luke 6:9 ("Is it lawful on the Sabbath to do good or to do evil, to save a life or kill [it]?"), but again the vocabulary is different. Not surprisingly, Bultmann considers Luke 14:1–6 simply a variant of the cure of the man with the withered hand in Mark 3:1–6.[150] If we think in terms of variations and growth within the oral tradition instead of just mechanical literary copying by the Synoptists, that is certainly a possibility. However, if we try to go beyond the question of variant versions of the same story and raise the possibility of similar events in the life of Jesus, there is the persistent historical question we have already seen when treating the other stories of healing on the Sabbath: would Jesus' cure by a mere touch have been considered a grave violation of the Sabbath by most Jews of the time? Probably not.[151]

Still, the question of historicity is not so easily settled. Luke 14:1–6 does have characteristics that mark it off from all other stories of healing on the Sabbath: the healing takes place in the house of a Pharisee, not in a synagogue, and in the context of a meal. Dropsy as the ailment cured is unparalleled in the rest of the Bible. Jesus heals not with a word but with a touch. No opposition to Jesus is voiced, Jesus' reaction to his adversaries is not as fierce as elsewhere, and no hostile action is planned against Jesus. Thus, the question of Luke 14:1–6 being a mere variant of other stories of healing on the Sabbath is not such an open-and-shut case as might first appear. Again, I prefer a judgment of *non liquet*.

D. THE DEAF-MUTE (MARK 7:31–37)

The fourth type of miracle with no exact parallel elsewhere in the Gospels is the healing of the deaf-mute (Mark 7:31–37). As it now stands, the miracle is situated by Mark toward the end of a rather confusing itinerary: Jesus has gone

north from Galilee into the territory of Tyre and Sidon and has then returned
to the Sea of Galilee by traveling through the midst of the Decapolis region.
At least, that is the best sense one can make of the strange geographical references in Mark 7:31. Mark may be combining various geographical designations
from his sources, or betraying his ignorance of Palestinian geography, or both.

In any case, the itinerary is probably more theological than geographical:
having declared all foods clean (and therefore having torn down a major barrier between Jews and Gentiles in 7:19), the Marcan Jesus now passes through
various Gentile regions, bringing healing and food (symbolically, the salvation
proclaimed by the gospel) to pagans and thus foreshadowing the Christian
mission.[152] Marcan theological concerns are also clear in the messianic-secret
motif: Jesus takes the deaf-mute away from the crowd for the sake of privacy
(v 33) and (fruitlessly) enjoins silence on all (v 36). The "choral conclusion" in
v 37 is likewise an expression of Marcan theology (or that of his source). Here
Jesus is acclaimed as accomplishing the new creation that fulfills the prophecies
of Isaiah about the last days: "He has done all things well [cf. Gen 1:31]; he
has made both the deaf to hear and the mute to speak [cf. Isa 35:5–6]."

On a larger scale, this miracle story fits within the great "bread section" of
Mark 6:30–8:21, where Jesus struggles to bring spiritual sight to his obtuse
disciples.[153] Within this overall framework, the healing of the deaf-mute is
paired with the healing of the blind man at Bethsaida (Mark 8:22–26) to form
two similar symbolic representations of the (at least partial) healing of the
disciples' inner deafness and blindness. As I mentioned in my treatment of
Mark 8:22–26, the healing of the blind man at Bethsaida may have already
been shaped as a "twin narrative" of the deaf-mute in the pre-Marcan tradition. In any event, there are many striking parallels between the two stories.

If one prescinds from all this Marcan redactional theology (some of the
theology being present perhaps already in Mark's source), are there any signals
of early tradition that might be traced back to Jesus? There are, and the signals
are similar to those discussed above in my treatment of the blind man at Bethsaida. One difference, though, should be noted. While the story of the blind
man was anchored concretely in Bethsaida, the story of the deaf-mute, once
stripped of the Marcan redactional framework, is bereft of specific time, place,
or named actors.

Still, there are indications that we are dealing here not with a pure creation
by Mark but with some tradition Mark has inherited. An initial signal is the
significant number of words in the seven verses of this miracle story that never
occur anywhere else in Mark's Gospel.[154] Then there are the unusual, even
bizarre, elements in the narrative that make it stand out from the ordinary
pattern of miracle stories in the Gospels in general and in Mark in particular.
Specifically, the healing of the deaf-mute, perhaps even more than the healing
of the blind man at Bethsaida, is replete with ritual or symbolic actions of Jesus
that could be interpreted as magic. This may explain why this story and the
healing at Bethsaida are the only two Marcan miracles that are omitted by
both Matthew and Luke.

Jesus' ritual-like gestures include (1) putting his fingers into the man's ears (symbolic of opening them so that the man can hear), (2) placing his own saliva on the man's tongue (symbolic of loosening the "bond" of the tongue so that the man can speak), (3) looking up to heaven (probably a gesture of prayer), (4) sighing or groaning deeply (*estenaxen*, seen by some as expressing the inner "arousal" of the charismatic's miracle-working powers), and (5) the command "be opened" (given by Mark both in the Aramaic *ephphatha* and in Greek translation).

Certainly no other miracle story of comparable length in the Gospels carries so many accoutrements of the symbolic or the ritual or the magical (depending on one's interpretive point of view). As we saw in the case of the healing at Bethsaida, in the ancient world saliva was used as a healing agent in medical, miraculous, or magical contexts. In Mark 7:31–37, the combination of the saliva with the other symbolic gestures could easily suggest a magical interpretation—though if Jesus' glance up to heaven and his sigh are both seen as expressions of prayer and supplication to God, the saliva can be placed more at the "miracle" as opposed to the "magical" end of the spectrum of religious experience.[155] Still, it apparently smacked enough of the magical to make both Matthew and Luke uncomfortable.

One can therefore say that the presence of saliva satisfies to a certain degree the criteria of embarrassment and discontinuity insofar as, in all Four Gospels, only this healing and that of Bethsaida depict Jesus performing a cure by the direct application of saliva.[156] Likewise unique to this healing of the deaf-mute is the insertion of Jesus' fingers into the man's ears. Also unparalleled elsewhere in the NT is the combination in one story of Jesus' gazing up to heaven and his sighing. The only other times that Jesus gazes up to heaven while working a miracle are when he gives thanks over the loaves and fish he is about to distribute to the five thousand (Mark 6:41 ‖ Matt 14:19 ‖ Luke 9:16) and when he prays to the Father just before raising Lazarus from the dead (John 11:41).[157] In the immediate context of giving thanks (*eulogēsen*) before feeding the five thousand, Jesus' gesture of looking up to heaven is obviously one of prayer. That is expressly the case in John 11:41, where the words of Jesus' prayer of thanksgiving to the Father immediately follow the gesture of raising his eyes. Hence prayer may well be the sense of Jesus' looking up to heaven in Mark 7:34 as well. In fact, given the literary parallel between "looking up to heaven he pronounced a blessing [or: gave thanks]" (*anablepsas eis ton ouranon eulogēsen* in Mark 6:41) and "looking up to heaven he sighed" (*anablepsas eis ton ouranon estenaxen* in Mark 7:34), the sighing is probably best taken as an expression of prayer as well.[158]

A final element that is unique within the Gospel stories of miraculous healing is that a command of Jesus is given in Aramaic: *ephphatha*, "be opened." Only a few Aramaic words of Jesus are preserved in the Gospels, and besides *ephphatha* the only Aramaic words that Jesus speaks in a miracle story are found in the story of the raising of the daughter of Jairus from the dead (*talitha koum* in Mark 5:41). Thus, Mark 7:31–37 is the only miracle *of healing* that contains Aramaic spoken by Jesus.[159]

In short, the healing of the deaf-mute stands out among Gospel miracle stories because it contains within a brief compass a number of words or phrases, describing key actions of Jesus as he heals, that are unique or highly unusual in accounts of Jesus' miracles. Some of these unusual words and actions obviously caused even Christians unease, witness the omission of the story by Matthew and Luke. To be sure, the lack of any other Gospel story concerning a deaf-mute and the lack of any specific location for this story in the tradition make one wary of a firm judgment. Nevertheless, I think that one could reasonably use the criteria of embarrassment and discontinuity to argue that this story reflects some event in the life of Jesus, though I can well understand why others might prefer to stay with a vote of *non liquet*. At the very least, one can draw a general conclusion from this Marcan narrative plus the reference in Q to the deaf receiving the power to hear (Matt 11:5 par.). The multiple attestation of sources and forms supplied by these two passages indicates that during his ministry Jesus claimed that he empowered the deaf to hear.

E. THE EAR OF THE SLAVE OF THE HIGH PRIEST (LUKE 22:49–51)

The fifth case of a unique type of miracle that lacks any sort of multiple attestation in the Gospels is found in Luke's Gospel: the healing of the ear of the slave of the high priest as Jesus is arrested in Gethsemane (Luke 22:49–51).[160] In itself, the story of the unfortunate slave of the high priest is an intriguing study in the history and growth of Gospel traditions. All Four Gospels have the basic story: as Jesus is being arrested in Gethsemane (actually, the Mount of Olives in Luke's Gospel and the "garden" in John's Gospel),[161] someone strikes the slave of the high priest and cuts off his ear. That, however, is the only point on which all Four Gospels agree. Each then goes its separate way, with some curious minor agreements between John and Matthew on one hand and John and Luke on the other (Mark 14:47 || Matt 26:51–54 || Luke 22:49–51 || John 18:10–11). In my view, this mélange of agreements and disagreements is best explained by a combination of literary reworking of Mark by Matthew and Luke, independent development in the Johannine tradition, and possibly contacts between the Matthean, Lucan, and Johannine traditions in the oral stage.

As we might expect, laconic stark Mark has the shortest and most puzzling version of the story. Mark 14:47 baldly informs us without preparation or subsequent comment: "One of the bystanders, drawing the sword, struck the servant of the high priest and cut off [literally: took away] his ear." What should be underlined here—because even some commentators misrepresent Mark on the matter—is that Mark does *not* say that the person drawing the sword was a disciple of Jesus.[162] The vague phrase in the Greek is *heis de tōn parestēkotōn*, "one of those standing by."[163] When Mark uses the phrase "the bystanders" (*hoi parestōtes*) in his Gospel (14:69,70; 15:35,39), he never employs it of Jesus' disciples in general or of the Twelve in particular. He always uses it of other persons and groups who are "on stage," sometimes in active roles. Designated by this vague phrase, they are never given proper names.[164]

In contrast, from 14:10 onwards Mark always refers to the immediate followers of Jesus as "the Twelve" (*hoi dōdeka* in 14:10,17,20,43) or "the disciples" (*hoi mathētai* in 14:12,32). When a single disciple is involved in a significant action, he is named: Judas in 14:10,43; Peter (or Simon) in 14:29,33,37; Peter, James, and John in 14:33. Given this precision from the beginning of Mark's Passion Narrative, it would be strange for Mark at this critical juncture to refer to one of the twelve disciples, Peter in particular (cf. John 18:10), as "one of the bystanders." In light of Mark's consistent style throughout the Passion Narrative, the hazy designation "one of the bystanders" most likely refers to some member of the otherwise faceless "crowd" (*ochlos*, v 43) that has come with Judas to arrest Jesus. So at the start of this Synoptic tradition about ear-amputation in Gethsemane, we have nothing but a nameless figure, probably a member of the crowd arresting Jesus, cutting off the ear of an anonymous slave of the high priest—apparently accidentally amid the confusion—with no further development or happy denouement for the hapless slave. Mark's point may be one of grim irony: at his arrest, Jesus' disciples were unprepared and ignorant bunglers (witness the young man who flees naked in vv 51–52), but so were his enemies.[165]

Since the work of Donald Senior,[166] it has generally been granted that Matthew had no extended source for his Passion Narrative beyond the Gospel of Mark. The story of the anonymous swordsman in Gethsemane proves to be a case in point. The changes and additions in Matt 26:51–54 are readily explicable as the work of Matthew theologizing on Mark. The unnamed bystander now becomes "one of those with Jesus." This specification is hardly surprising for anyone who has traced Matthew's redactional additions to Mark from the beginning of the Passion Narrative. In the first part of his Passion Narrative, Matthew emphasizes the theme of the relation of Jesus to his disciples and vice versa even more than Mark does. Regularly Matthew will insert the preposition "with" (*meta* or *syn*) to stress Jesus' desire to be with his disciples and to have them spiritually with him during the great crisis of his arrest and passion (see, e.g., Matt 26:29,37,38; contrast Mark). But they consistently fail to be "with" him in the deepest sense, in vigil and prayer (Matt 26:40; cf. Mark 14:37). In 26:51 Matthew shows with sad irony how one of those who failed to be with Jesus in vigil and prayer now tries to be one "with" him by using violence, the very thing Jesus forbade in the Sermon on the Mount (5:38–48).

The Matthean Jesus shows his total command of the situation—a theme throughout Matthew's Passion Narrative that brings him at times close to the tone of the Fourth Gospel—by ordering the sword to be sheathed.[167] In an insertion typical of Matthew, Jesus seizes upon even this melee at his arrest to teach his disciples. He instructs them about nonviolence (v 52), his unbroken relation to and protection by his heavenly Father (v 53), and the necessity to fulfill the Scriptures by his passion (v 54). Thus, Matthew's version of the story of the amputated ear—an ear that apparently remains amputated—is completely explainable on the grounds of Matthew's own redactional interests.[168]

Luke agrees with Matthew in making the swashbuckling swordsman a disciple, though he expresses the idea differently from and a little less clearly than Matthew. Luke 22:49 tells us that, as soon as Judas betrays Jesus with a kiss, "those around him [Jesus], seeing what was about to happen, said: 'Lord, shall we strike with a sword?' " Not waiting for an answer from Jesus, "one of them [*tis ex autōn*] struck the slave of the high priest and cut off his right ear" (v 50).

Jesus responds to this unsolicited violence both with his words and with a deed. First (v 51a), he issues a laconic order to his disciples: "Let it be even to this [extent]." This cryptic command seems to enjoin an end to violent resistance and a patient endurance of Jesus' arrest. Fitzmyer paraphrases it as "Let events take their course—even to my arrest."[169] We have here an echo of an earlier scene specific to Luke at the Last Supper. In Luke 22:35–38 Jesus contrasts the relatively peaceful and protected time the disciples enjoyed during his public ministry with the crisis of fierce opposition that is about to break in both upon himself and upon them. Speaking metaphorically, Jesus enjoins the disciples to take special care and watch out for themselves: "But now let him who has a purse carry it, and likewise his traveling bag. And let him who does not have one sell his cloak and buy a sword" (22:36). As usual, the disciples fail to grasp Jesus' metaphorical speech. Taking his words literally, they confidently display their weapons: "Lord, behold, here are two swords." Jesus shows his disdain for their misunderstanding with a curt: "Enough of that!" (v 38, *hikanon estin*). Both the disciples' misguided trust in weapons and Jesus' peremptory rejection of such means of protection are replayed at the arrest in 22:49–51. One of the swords displayed at the Last Supper is zealously and foolishly put to use, and Jesus immediately commands an end to such futile attempts at defense.

Then (v 51b), Jesus turns from the needs of his disciples to the need of the slave: "Touching the ear he healed him." Judging from the Marcan source, which seems to be the only extended source Luke had for his Passion Narrative, we are justified in concluding that the whole incident of the healing of the ear is a Lucan creation.[170] In addition to the Lucan vocabulary and style that pervade the pericope, such a redactional touch fits in perfectly with Luke's theological tendencies, which highlight Jesus the merciful healer, Jesus the defender of the marginalized of society, and Jesus the compassionate teacher of forgiveness. The Lucan Jesus who earlier healed another slave (the slave of the centurion in 7:1–10) is also the Lucan Jesus whose last words include a prayer to the Father for the forgiveness of the enemies who have arrested, condemned, and crucified him ("Father, forgive them, for they know not what they do" in 23:34). That the healing as well as the forgiving action of Jesus should continue into the Passion Narrative (and perhaps provide one theological interpretation of what the passion of Jesus is all about) is perfectly in accord with the rest of Luke's Gospel.[171] Hence it seems likely that the healing of the servant's ear comes not from earlier tradition but from Luke's creative hand.

This conclusion is confirmed by a quick glance at John's version of the story.[172] The impulse to create legend, unleashed by the kernel of this intriguing story as it circulated in early Christian tradition, reached its logical conclusion in John—at least as regards the identity of the wielder of the sword.[173] As we saw, both Matthew and Luke, apparently independently of each other and with different wording, made of the Marcan bystander in the crowd a foolishly overzealous and misdirected disciple. The Fourth Evangelist, or the Johannine tradition before him, pushed this natural tendency to "Christianize" the anonymous swordsman for parenetic purposes to the extreme by identifying the swashbuckler with Simon Peter.

This identification is especially useful for John's Passion Narrative, since Peter last appeared in the Gospel at the beginning of the lengthy Last Supper discourses, when Jesus predicted that Peter would deny him three times (13:36–38). Because there is no prayer or "agony" in the garden in John's Passion Narrative, there is no part for Peter to play before the arrest scene. Hence Peter needs to be reintroduced to the reader and put on the stage at some point during the arrest, since he has to be present to follow Jesus to the house of Annas, where he will deny Jesus three times. Identifying the swordsman as Peter is the literary ploy the Fourth Evangelist employs to pick up the "Petrine" narrative thread that has been dropped since Jesus predicted Peter's triple denial back in 13:36–38. It also gives Jesus a definite addressee in 18:11 for both his command to sheathe the sword and his rhetorical question, filled with Johannine theology: "Shall I not drink of the cup that the Father has given me?"

Peter's display of spiritual obtuseness in wielding the sword (18:10–11) also prepares the reader for the greater spiritual disaster of his denial of Jesus (18:15–18,25–27).[174] The Fourth Evangelist explicitly and cleverly ties together the two scenes by making the third questioner of Peter during his triple denial a relative of the slave whose ear Peter cut off (18:26). The third questioner is thus able to say with both credibility and personal animus: "Didn't I see you in the garden with him [i.e., Jesus]?" Implied in all this is that the third questioner, more than those who have preceded him, would be in a particularly good position to recognize Peter, since he was with his relative and fellow-slave in the garden at Jesus' arrest. All these neat connections between Peter at the beginning of the Last Supper (when Jesus predicts Peter's triple denial), Peter at Jesus' arrest in the garden, and Peter at the climax of his triple denial lead me to think that the identification of Peter with the amputating swordsman was not even in the Johannine tradition but is simply a literary and theological invention of the Evangelist, tying the Peter-material smoothly together and preparing for Peter's triple denial.[175]

The upshot of all this is that a comparison of the four Gospel accounts as well as an examination of Lucan composition in 22:49–51 make it most probable that the healing of the ear of the high priest's slave is a creation of Luke himself and therefore has no claim to go back to the historical Jesus.

Our survey of the five miracle stories that are unique in the type of malady healed and that lack multiple attestation has produced mixed results. In the stories of Peter's mother-in-law, the woman with a hemorrhage, and the man suffering from dropsy, our initial suspicions were confirmed. The data are simply too meager to reach any judgment except *non liquet*. While some critics might take the same approach to the story of the deaf-mute, I incline to the view that some event lying behind the present story goes back to Jesus. My firmest judgment is the negative one on the healing of the ear of the high priest's slave. While there can be no absolute certitude in the matter, I feel fairly certain that the story is a Lucan creation.

V. THE SPECIAL CASE OF THE CENTURION'S SERVANT (MATT 8:5–13 PARR.)

As I indicated when I started examining the five cases of various healings of which only one incident is reported in the Gospels, I have purposely kept the healing of the centurion's servant (or the royal official's son in John's Gospel) separate from the five cases just treated.[176] For various reasons it is a special case that presents special difficulties. At the root of a great deal of the difficulty is the peculiar nature of the source or sources. The story of the centurion's servant is witnessed, with some notable variations, in both Matthew and Luke (Matt 8:5–13 ‖ Luke 7:1–10); hence it qualifies as a Q tradition[177]—indeed, the only miracle story in Q that is developed at length.[178] The story of the royal official's son in John 4:46–54 is held by most, but not all, scholars to be a variant of the primitive tradition that lies behind the Q story. If it is a true variant of the same tradition, we have multiple attestation of sources; if not, there is only one source each for the Q and Johannine stories respectively.

We face another difficulty when we try to classify this miracle under the rubric of a particular kind of illness or physical affliction that Jesus cures. Even if all the versions reflect one basic story or event, the wide variation among the three versions leaves us in doubt about what ailment was afflicting the servant or the son. Matthew speaks of a paralysis that tortures the servant, but does not indicate that the case is at the moment life-threatening.[179] Luke and John agree that the servant or son is close to death, but do not say what is causing this grave crisis. At the end of his story, John adds the detail of a fever. Obviously we are dealing in all three versions with a healing miracle, but what is being healed we do not know.

Also bewildering are the various parallels, almost all partial rather than full, between this servant/son story and other Gospel miracle stories. Matthew's mention of paralysis reminds us of other accounts of the cure of paralyzed or crippled limbs. However, the one word "paralyzed" is about all the Matthean story has in common with the stories of paralysis that we have already reviewed. John's mention of fever calls to mind the cure of Peter's mother-in-law, but again the mere word is about the only significant element that the two stories share. The idea of a father begging Jesus to heal his child, who is close to death, reminds us of how the Marcan and Lucan versions of the raising of the daughter of Jairus begin (Mark 5:23 ‖ Luke 8:42).[180] But then the stories proceed very differently, with Jesus' physical presence being key to the raising of the daughter of Jairus, while our present story of the servant or son emphasizes the motif of healing at a distance.

Indeed, a major element of the servant/son story that is lacking in *all* these parallels is that the healing takes place at a distance. This motif links the servant/son story instead with the healing of the daughter of the Syrophoenician woman (Mark 7:24–30 ‖ Matt 15:21–28).[181] Other similarities between the two stories can be seen as well: in both cases the beneficiaries are Gentiles (if we ignore for the moment John 4); in at least some of the versions of the two stories, Jesus at first seems to rebuff the request for the healing; and in the end he is won over by the humble pleading of the parent or official. Differences exist, however, between these two stories: the Syrophoenician woman encounters Jesus in the region of Tyre and Sidon, outside of Galilee, and the miracle is strictly speaking an exorcism rather than the healing of an illness, especially a life-threatening illness. Moreover, if one does not read Matthew's version of the story of the centurion's servant to include an initial rebuff by Jesus in Matt 8:7—and I do not—an important parallel to the story of the Syrophoenician woman disappears from the Q version of the healing of the servant (Luke has no hint of a rebuff by Jesus).[182]

Likewise lacking the elements of a Galilean venue and an initial rebuff is the story of the healing of the ten lepers in Luke 17:11–19. To be sure, the ten lepers are strictly speaking healed at a distance (i.e., while they are on their way to show themselves to priests), and the story does compare the Jewish lepers unfavorably with the one grateful Samaritan leper. Still, all ten lepers (unlike the centurion's servant, the royal official's son, or the Syrophoenician woman's daughter) do speak to Jesus face to face (though naturally at a distance) and do not employ an intermediary or intercessor. Insofar as Jesus' command ("Go, show yourselves to the priests"), which is spoken directly to the ten lepers, can be considered the healing word (with a sort of delayed effect), the healing is not "at a distance" in quite the same sense that it is in the stories of the Syrophoenician woman or the centurion. In short, our present story of the centurion's servant or the royal official's son has many partial parallels with other Gospel miracle stories, but an exact parallel with none. Hence its separate treatment here.

Two basic questions we must examine are (1) whether the Q story of the centurion's servant and the Johannine story of the royal official's son are simply alternate versions of the same primitive tradition (and possibly the same event); and (2) whether John's version is literarily dependent on Matthew and/

or Luke. To answer these questions, one must weigh carefully the many simi-larities-yet-differences among the three versions.

The basic similarities among all three stories are obvious: (1) In all three the ailing servant or son is in Capernaum, where the centurion or royal official presumably has his home. (2) The centurion or royal official asks Jesus for a miraculous healing of his servant/son. (3) Jesus gives an initial response to the petitioner (or, in Luke's version, to a group of intermediaries, inasmuch as Jesus accompanies them). (4) Reacting to Jesus' response, the petitioner makes a still more moving plea to Jesus. (5) Jesus responds to this plea by healing the servant or son at a distance. (6) At the end of the pericope, the reality of the healing is affirmed by the narrator or confirmed by characters in the story.

Within this basic grid there are many divergences among the three evange-lists. Yet in most cases the divergences can be explained either as the results of the redaction of a particular evangelist, pursuing his own theological interests, or as perfectly understandable variations of the early tradition as it developed in its oral stage.

(1) *The venue of the miracle.* Most probably the earliest tradition located the entire action in Capernaum. Being at the northwestern corner of the Sea of Galilee and located on the Galilean side of the border between the tetrarchy of Herod Antipas and the tetrarchy of Herod's half-brother Philip, Capernaum was the site of toll stations and a military garrison. A number of royal officials or military officers in the service of Herod Antipas would have been natural fixtures in Capernaum.

In John's Gospel, Jesus is located instead in Cana of Galilee, whither the royal official must journey from Capernaum to ask for the miracle. This change in venue is probably due to the redaction of the Fourth Evangelist. On the one hand, the distance between Jesus and the person he heals is thus in-creased and the display of Jesus' miraculous powers heightened. Such a height-ening of the miraculous is a common characteristic of miracle stories in John.[183] On the other hand, placing Jesus at Cana neatly connects his second Galilean "sign" with his first, performed at the wedding feast at Cana in 2:1–11. This point is underscored by the similarity of the concluding formulas John uses in 2:11 and 4:54.[184] The first part of John's presentation of the public ministry is thus carefully encased in an *inclusio* of the first and second Galilean signs. It may well be, then, that the placing of Jesus at Cana in 4:46–54 is the work of the Evangelist and that, in the earliest tradition, the only place-name connected with the miracle was Capernaum.

(2) *The designation of the petitioner.* Matthew and Luke agree on calling the petitioner a centurion (*hekatontarchos* in Matthew, *hekatontarchēs* in Luke), while John speaks more vaguely of a *basilikos*, traditionally translated as "a royal official." Actually, there is no necessary contradiction between the two words. The adjective *basilikos* ("royal") was used at times of people of royal blood, but more often of persons serving a king as ambassadors, officials, scribes, or courtiers.[185] More to the point, in Josephus *basilikoi* in the plural is used fre-quently for soldiers or troops of various monarchs, including Herodian rulers

and the Roman emperor.[186] Thus, it is not impossible that *basilikos* in John 4:46,49 refers to a centurion. Still, one wonders why John would have used the vague designation *basilikos* if he had meant a centurion in particular, since he is not ignorant of various Roman military terms.[187]

As the name suggests, a centurion[188] commanded a *centuria*, a company of soldiers technically numbering 100. In fact, the number varied greatly throughout the history of the Roman Empire, depending on time, place, and circumstances. At times a *centuria* could number between 30 and 60 men. While some centurions came from the equestrian order, most of them were ordinary soldiers who through years of effort and proven ability rose through the ranks. Centurions exercised more than strictly military duties; at times they could serve in special capacities such as watchmen, policemen, overseers of building projects, judges who set the boundaries of communities, and diplomatic representatives of the emperor or the provincial governor before foreign princes. Be it with regard to their rank, their pay, their social origins, or their precise functions, the centurions did not form a neat, homogeneous group in the army about which generalizations can easily be made.

Modern readers sometimes take for granted that the designation "centurion," when used of a soldier in the ancient Mediterranean world, always refers to a member of the Roman army. We must remember, however, that Matthew, Luke, and John all place the healing of the son or servant in Galilee, which during the ministry of Jesus was part of the tetrarchy of Herod Antipas and therefore was not under the direct control of a Roman prefect, as was Judea. Antipas maintained and controlled his own army within the borders of his tetrarchy of Galilee-Perea;[189] Roman legions would intervene only in case of an emergency. Hence, if some actual event lies behind our Gospel story and if that event did in fact involve a centurion at Capernaum in Galilee, he would not have been a member of the Roman army and probably not a Roman himself. If the centurion of the Q tradition was a historical figure, he could have been either a Jew or a Gentile (e.g., a Syrian). While the majority of Galileans at the time of Antipas was most probably Jewish, there was a strong Gentile minority.[190] Herod the Great had had both Jews and Gentiles in his armed forces,[191] and presumably his son Antipas would not have changed a military policy that worked. A similar openness to both Jews and Gentiles would probably have marked Antipas' "civil service." Thus, the ethnic origin of the centurion (or, alternately, the royal official) remains ambiguous when we try to probe the earliest attainable tradition or a hypothetical historical event.

However, no such ambiguity attends the stories as they now stand in Matthew and Luke, or even in John. Both Matthew and Luke, in various ways, make clear that the centurion is a Gentile. Both evangelists recount the centurion's acknowledgment that he is not worthy to have Jesus come under his roof (Matt 8:8 || Luke 7:6) and Jesus' astonished exclamation that the centurion's great faith surpasses anything Jesus has found in Israel (Matt 8:10 || Luke 7:9). As we saw when we examined future eschatology in the teaching of Jesus, Matthew makes this scene clearly programmatic by inserting a separate Q saying about many (= the Gentiles) coming from east and west to recline with the patriarchs at the banquet in the kingdom of heaven, while the sons of the kingdom (= unbelieving Israelites) will be cast out (Matt 8:11–12).[192] Luke emphasizes the Gentile origin of the centurion by having a delegation of Jewish elders intercede with Jesus for him on the grounds that the centurion "loves our nation and personally built the synagogue for us" (Luke 7:5). This Jewish delegation, as well as a second delegation sent by the centurion from his house, may well be a Lucan creation.[193] In Luke's overall composition, the centurion may be intended to prefigure the pious and generous centurion Cornelius, who converts to Christianity in Acts 10.

Matters are not quite so clear in John, who does not specify the ethnic origin of the royal official. Yet the overall redactional theology of John makes it likely that the Fourth Evangelist understands the official to be a Jew.[194] In many ways the Fourth Gospel is the most "Jewish" of Gospels, notably in that John does not allow Jesus to interact directly during the public ministry with anyone who is clearly a Gentile. The closest Jesus comes to such contact is with the Samaritans (a people of mixed ethnic and religious origins), who probably prefigure in John's mind the future Gentile mission (John 4:1–42).[195] In John's Gospel, even more than in Matthew's, Jesus' ministry is limited to Israelites. While Matthew allows a few prophetic exceptions (the centurion in 8:5–13 and the Canaanite woman in 15:21–28), John is adamant: no Gentile speaks directly to Jesus during the public ministry.

That is the point of a crucial scene at the end of the public ministry: Gentiles who have come up to Jerusalem to worship during Passover ask to see Jesus (John 12:20–26). Despite the intercession of the two disciples with Greek names (Philip and Andrew), Jesus never accedes to the request. He instead sees the desire of the Gentiles to come to him as an indication that the "hour" of his "glorification," of his death and resurrection, has now arrived (v 23). Only if, like the grain of wheat, he goes down into the earth in death, will he yield a rich harvest, i.e., the ingathering of the Gentiles (v 24). Only the "lifting up" of the Son of Man on the throne of the cross will make Jesus a cosmic magnet attracting all the Gentiles to the unity he is about to create: " 'And I, if I be lifted up from the earth [on the cross], will draw all people to myself.' Now he said this signifying by what death he was about to die" (vv 32–33). The same point is made by the Evangelist in 11:52: Jesus was about to die "not only for the nation [of Israel], but also in order that he might gather into one the children of God [scattered throughout the world]." For John, only the outpouring of the Spirit from the crucified and risen Christ makes possible this bringing of the Gentiles into the saving unity created by Jesus' death and resurrection.

Given this theological schema, it is natural to suppose that the otherwise unidentified royal official in the service of the tetrarch of Galilee counts in the mind of John as a Jew. The whole story in John 4:46–54 traces how the royal official moves from a vague initial trust in Jesus as a miracle-worker (provided Jesus follows the official's directions and comes in person to the bedside of the dying boy) to unconditional trust in Jesus' all-powerful word that can heal at a distance. It is only at the end of the story that John says absolutely: "He [the royal official] and his whole household *believed*." The tone is very much that of one of the conversion stories in the Acts of the Apostles: John presents the royal official and his household as coming to full faith in Jesus—but in this case during the public ministry. Thus, granted John's theological framework, which allows no Gentile to interact directly with Jesus during the ministry, it is difficult to see the royal official as being—in John's mind—anything but a Jew. At the very least, to read the Gentile petitioner of Matthew's or Luke's story into John is uncritical harmonization.[196]

We notice, then, that both Q's presentation of the "centurion" as a Gentile and John's (implicit) presentation of the "royal official" as a Jew serve the theological goals of the respective writers. Neither presentation can claim to be a theologically neutral reporting of the original event. The reason for the divergence between Q and John may be that the primitive tradition that lies behind both versions of the story gave no indication of the petitioner's ethnic or religious background. The earliest attainable tradition apparently spoke simply of some official or officer at Capernaum (who would have been in the service of Herod Antipas). The specification of the petitioner as either a Gentile centurion or a Jewish royal official may well have been a later development in the Q and Johannine traditions respectively. Granted the independence of John from the Synoptics, there is no reason to give automatic preference to Q's Gentile centurion if one is seeking to reconstruct an original historical event lying behind the various traditions.[197]

(3) *The designation of the person who is healed.* The three evangelists differ notably in their designation of the suffering person on whose behalf the centurion or royal official petitions Jesus for a miracle. From the beginning of his story Luke clearly calls the suffering person a slave (*doulos*) of the centurion (Luke 7:2,3,10), though he also has the centurion refer to the sufferer as "my servant" (*ho pais mou* in v 7). Clearly, then, in Luke's version, *pais* means "boy" in the sense of a servant, not in the sense of a son.

John employs the exact opposite usage. From the beginning of his story John makes clear that the suffering person is the royal official's son (*huios* in 4:46,47,50,53). But in his renewed and poignant appeal to Jesus in v 49, the official employs instead the word *paidion*, the diminutive form of *pais*: "Lord, come down before my little boy dies." As a perfect foil to Luke's usage, John even employs *pais* once, in v 51, obviously in the sense of son, not servant: "His servants met him [i.e., the royal official], saying that his boy [*ho pais autou*] was alive."

Matthew both completes and yet explains this verbal confusion: throughout his version of the story (8:5,8,13), Matthew refers to the suffering person only with the ambiguous word *pais* ("boy" in the sense of servant or son?). This ambiguity is usually lost in English translations of Matt 8:5–13; perhaps in some cases the translators never even considered the alternatives. Instead, because they mentally place Matthew's version of the Q story alongside Luke's, translators (perhaps unconsciously) tend to assimilate Matthew's vocabulary to

Luke's and so translate Matthew's *pais* as "servant" or "slave," when in fact it could just as easily mean "son," as it does in John's version.[198]

Nothing in Matthew's version, taken by itself, resolves the ambiguity[199]— and here we may have the root reason for at least part of the differences in the three versions of the story. It is possible that the earliest Q and Johannine versions of the healing story in Greek used only the ambiguous *pais.* The word occurs at some point in all three versions of the story we now have; that is not true of *huios, doulos,* or *paidion.* In fact, in the only verse of the story where the wording of Matthew and Luke is practically identical, the word used for the sufferer is *pais:* "Say but the word and my *pais* will be healed" (Matt 8:8 ‖ Luke 7:7). Most probably, then, the primitive form of this tradition about the centurion or royal official spoke throughout only of the man's *pais.*[200] As the tradition developed both orally and in writing, it was interpreted differently by different groups. John's Gospel represents those who took *pais* to mean son, and Luke's Gospel represents those who took it to mean servant or slave, while Matthew's Gospel alone preserves the original ambiguity.

The ambiguity of *pais* in the Greek versions of the story may reflect a similar ambiguity in a still earlier Aramaic stage of the narrative. The Aramaic word *talyā'* (or possibly the Hebrew word *na'ar*) means "boy" in the sense of either servant or child (son). It could be, then, that an ambiguous *talyā'* in the original Aramaic story led to an ambiguous *pais* in the Greek translation, which in turn led to the different interpretations in Luke ("servant") and John ("son"). Alternately, *talyā'* in the original Aramaic story could have occasioned various Greek translations from the start, with *pais, doulos,* and *huios* arising as alternate ways of rendering into Greek the Aramaic form that existed from the earliest days of the church.

Our examination of the basic differences-yet-agreements among Matthew, Luke, and John on the venue, petitioner, and recipient of the miracle makes three conclusions highly probable. First, there is enough similarity in form and content to affirm that all three versions reflect the same primitive tradition (and perhaps even some originating event in the life of Jesus).[201] Second, the independence of John from the Synoptics, which I have espoused along with most recent commentators on John's Gospel,[202] seems confirmed once again. The curious crazy quilt of similarities and differences between John on the one hand and Matthew and Luke on the other is best explained by John's redaction of an independent tradition he had received from his own source, written or oral. To explain John's text as simply a creative redaction of Matthew and/or Luke (Frans Neirynck would include Mark in the mix as well) would involve John in a literary process that would be highly erratic, eclectic, and eccentric— some might even say unintelligible.[203] We would have to imagine the Fourth Evangelist spreading out copies of Mark, Matthew, and Luke in front of him on his desk and proceeding to pick out a verse here and a verse there from each of the Synoptics, at times without any discernible reason or pattern. The path that connects Luke's centurion pleading for a sick slave to John's royal official pleading for a sick son is much more likely the path of similar but independent oral traditions.

Third, there is the question of the historicity of the core tradition lying behind the versions of the story we have in Matthew, Luke, and John. The core tradition does meet the criterion of multiple attestation of sources—indeed, in a unique way. For the only time in the catalogue of Gospel miracle stories, a fully developed miracle story is attested in both Q and John. That two such diverse sources, which otherwise have relatively little in common, should agree on the core of a miracle story is itself a striking datum.

Redaction-critical studies of John's Gospel are practically unanimous in the judgment that the story of the royal official in John 4:46–54 is not a creation of the Fourth Evangelist. Rather, the Evangelist seems to have gone out of his way to connect the story secondarily with Cana (to create an *inclusio* with the first Cana miracle) and to have inserted into the story the intrusive v 48, which criticizes a superficial faith that demands miracles on its own terms. Trimmed of the Evangelist's additions, the story reaches back into the pre-Gospel tradition of the Johannine community. Some critics assign it to the hypothetical "sign source" or "sign Gospel" that the Fourth Evangelist supposedly used.[204] Be that as it may, the very existence of this miracle story in the Johannine tradition prior to the Gospel is sufficient reason for supposing that its alternate version in Q (the story of the centurion's servant/son) was likewise not a creation of the redactor of the Q document.[205] The Q version similarly reaches back into a tradition prior to the redaction of Q, and hence into the early days of the church.

In my opinion, one may also appeal to the criteria of discontinuity and embarrassment, at least with respect to one small point in the core tradition from Q. The Q story presents us with the only occasion in the miracle stories of all Four Gospels when Jesus is said to be "surprised," "astonished," or "marveling" (*ethaumasen*, Matt 8:10 par.).[206] This motif, which strongly emphasizes Jesus' humanity, is understandably lacking in the version of the story found in John, the Gospel that fiercely defends Jesus' divine origins. Indeed, it is not surprising that throughout all Four Gospels—with the notable exceptions of Matt 8:10 par. and Mark 6:6—references to Jesus' being astonished are simply absent.

A secondary criterion of historicity supports the primary criteria of multiple attestation, discontinuity, and embarrassment. The tradition that probably lies behind Q is notable for the large number of Semitisms it contains. Uwe Wegner has examined this point at length. Although he himself admits that some of his examples of Semitisms are not certain, he rightly claims that the pre-Q tradition has a good chance of having existed in an Aramaic form before it was translated into Greek.[207] To this linguistic observation can be added another consideration, drawn from the Palestinian milieu: the Q and Johannine traditions, for all their differences, are both anchored in Capernaum, a border town where such figures as a centurion or an official of Antipas' bureaucracy would naturally be functioning.

None of these considerations, especially when taken in isolation, can prove the historicity of the core tradition. Thus I can well understand why some scholars might prefer to repeat once again the judgment of *non liquet.* However, in my view the combination of a number of significant factors argues for a different judgment: (1) The basic story enjoys a unique type of multiple attestation from Q and John, pointing to a tradition that goes back to the earliest days of the church. (2) There are indications of a Semitic substratum underlying the earliest Greek tradition. (3) One is struck by the independent agreement of the Q and Johannine versions on the venue of Capernaum, which squares perfectly with the content of the story.[208] (4) There is also the slight element of discontinuity and embarrassment with respect to Jesus' being surprised or astonished. Taken together, these considerations make it seem more probable that behind the primitive tradition lies a historical event from the public ministry of Jesus.

With all the differences between the Q and Johannine versions—to say nothing of the differences between Matthew and Luke—a summary account of the event must remain distressingly vague. While Jesus was present in or approaching Capernaum, an official or officer of Herod Antipas, possibly a centurion stationed at Capernaum, asked Jesus for the cure of a "boy" in his household—whether the "boy" was a slave or a son is not clear.[209] Jesus acceded to the request by healing the "boy" at a distance. That, I think, is all that can be said with any probability. The further details in each version of the story and the various pieces of dialogue between Jesus and the petitioner may derive from the repeated retelling of the story in the early church or from the creativity of the evangelists. In particular, I would not want to claim historicity for any specific part of the dialogue between Jesus and the petitioner, especially since the dialogue differs notably in John's version as opposed to Q's.[210]

VI. CONCLUSION

To summarize: various criteria of historicity suggest that the historical Jesus performed certain actions during his public ministry that both he and some of his contemporaries thought were miraculous healings of the sick or infirm. Major *types* of such healings involved persons with paralyzed limbs, persons suffering from blindness (or some impairment of vision), persons suffering from various skin ailments ("leprosy"), and persons who were deaf and/or mute. Individual stories that have a good chance of going back to some event in the life of the historical Jesus—however much they may have been reworked and expanded by Christian theology—include the stories of the paralyzed man let down through the roof (Mark 2:1–12 parr.), the paralyzed man by the pool of Bethesda (John 5:1–9), the blind Bartimaeus begging near Jericho (Mark 10:46–50 parr.), the blind man of Bethsaida (Mark 8:22–26), the blind man who washed in the pool of Siloam (John 9:1–7), a deaf-mute (Mark 7:31–37), and the servant or son of a royal official (possibly a centurion) of Antipas (Matt 8:5–13 par.; John 4:46–54). One notices that persons suffering from some sort of bodily paralysis or some sort of impairment of vision loom large among these candidates.

The details of these illnesses—their origin, exact nature, duration, and indeed the permanency of their cure—are now lost to us. No doubt each member on our hypothetical committee locked up in the Harvard Divinity School library would interpret these events in the life of Jesus according to his or her own worldview. Believers would be at least open to the idea that Jesus actually performed miracles of healing in these cases, while nonbelievers might think in terms of psychosomatic illnesses susceptible to such influences as hypnosis, the impact of a strong charismatic personality, or autosuggestion.[211] Be that as it may, we must now turn our attention to miracle stories where hypnosis and autosuggestion are less cogent explanations: the raising of the dead.

NOTES TO CHAPTER 21

[1] Intending as usual the kind of "low-level" interpretation sought throughout this volume, I stay as close as possible to the language and mode of presentation of the individual healing stories. Since the Gospel healing stories do not make neat distinctions in their vocabulary for healing (e.g., *iaomai, therapeuō, sōzō*), I do not engage in neat distinctions between curing and healing, or between disease and illness. Such distinctions belong not to our initial quest for reliable historical data but to a later stage of inquiry, conducted in the light of the social sciences. For an analysis of Marcan healing stories that employs the social sciences, see John J. Pilch, "Healing in Mark: A Social Science Analysis," *BTB* 15 (1985) 142–50.

[2] This count does not include parallel versions of the same basic story. The case of the centurion's servant is problematic because Matthew, but not Luke (or John in his distant parallel), says that the servant is paralyzed (Matt 8:6). On this pericope, see Section V below.

[3] It is likely that healings unique to Matthew's Gospel are redactional creations modeled on traditional miracle stories: e.g., the healing of the two blind men in Matt 9:27–31 (modeled on the Bartimaeus story in Mark 10:46–52) and the healing of a mute demoniac in 9:32–34 (modeled on the Beelzebul controversy in the Q tradition in Matt 12:22–23 ‖ Luke 11:14).

[4] I say "some" to allow for slight differences in counting because of disagreement over what constitutes a distinct story as opposed to a Synoptic parallel or a purely redactional creation. Moreover, in this count I do not include short summaries of Jesus' activity, some of which at least are redactional creations. In my view, almost all of such summaries are products of the evangelists. For the opposite view, that at least some summaries come from the tradition, see Guelich's remarks on Mark 3:7–12 in his *Mark 1–8:26*, 142–51.

[5] The problem is a classic one; see, e.g., William Wrede, "Zur Heilung des Gelähmten, Mk 2,1ff.," *ZNW* 5 (1904) 354–58; Ingrid Maisch, *Die Heilung des Gelähmten. Eine exegetisch-traditionsgeschichtliche Untersuchung zu Mk 2,1–12* (SBS 52; Stuttgart: KBW, 1971); Christian P. Ceroke, "Is Mk 2,10 a Saying of Jesus?" *CBQ* 22 (1960) 369–90; Richard T. Mead, "The Healing of the Paralytic—A Unit?" *JBL* 80 (1961) 348–54; Hans-Josef Klauck, "Die Frage der Sündenvergebung in der Perikope von der Heilung des Gelähmten (Mk 2,1–12 parr)," *BZ* 25 (1981) 223–48. Decisions about the original unity of the story do not divide neatly down the lines of conservative versus liberal. For example, both Bultmann (*Geschichte*, 12–14, 227) and Taylor (*The Gospel According to St. Mark*, 191) favor the idea that the miracle story originally existed apart from the discussion of forgiveness of sins. However, while Taylor would allow that both stories (healing and discussion of forgiveness) go back to events in Jesus' life, Bultmann thinks that the material on forgiveness was composed as an insert into the miracle story. For reasons for thinking that the miracle story once existed by itself, see Latourelle, *The Miracles of Jesus*, 93–95. Curiously, Dibelius, contrary to the view that most exegetes hold of this pericope, thinks that it represents his category of "paradigm" with considerable purity (*Formgeschichte*, 40).

[6] On the theory of some sort of pre-Marcan collection behind Mark 2:1–3:6, see Dewey (*Markan Public Debate*, 181–93), who holds that the present elegant concentric pattern is Mark's creation, but that he drew upon a pre-Marcan collection that included 2:3–12. James D. G. Dunn ("Mark 2.1–3.6: A Bridge Between Jesus and

Paul in the Question of the Law," *NTS* 30 [1984] 395–415) thinks that in a very early stage of the tradition a unit made up of 2:15–3:6 was formed, with 2:1–12 being added at a later stage, though still quite probably at a stage prior to Mark's composition. Guelich, on the other hand, does not think that 2:1–12 was already part of a pre-Marcan collection of dispute stories; he supposes instead that Mark himself chose to make this pericope an introduction to a traditional complex found in 2:15–28 (*Mark 1–8:26*, 81–96). Taylor (*The Gospel According to St. Mark*, 91–92) takes the intriguing view that the collection of Mark 2:1–3:6 was created by Mark himself some time before he wrote his Gospel.

[7] Some have seen in the stratagem of digging through the roof and lowering the paralytic an attempt to hide the house's door from the demon responsible for the illness, so that after its expulsion through the roof (which will then be closed up) it will not know how to return; so Hedwig Jahnow, "Das Abdecken des Daches (Mc 2,4/Lc 5,19)," *ZNW* 24 (1925) 155–58 (relying on two Indian magical texts); Bultmann, *Geschichte*, 237; Kertelge, *Wunder*, 77; Otto Böcher, *Christus Exorcista: Dämonismus und Taufe im Neuen Testament* (BWANT 5/16; Stuttgart: Kohlhammer, 1972) 72. This "pan-demonic" approach to the miracle stories of the Gospels lacks solid basis in the text; see Guelich, *Mark 1–8:26*, 83. Jahnow's argument, to which later exegetes often appeal, rests on very slight and distant parallels from India; moreover, one must suppose that in the pre-Marcan tradition the real reason for the uncovering of the roof had been forgotten or suppressed and a specious one (the large crowd blocking the doorway) had been invented. All this strains credulity.

[8] Latourelle, *The Miracles of Jesus*, 218.

[9] On the many problems of the Greek text in John 5:2, see Brown, *The Gospel According to John*, 1. 206; Metzger, *A Textual Commentary*, 208. The name of the pool or area is variously given in the Greek manuscripts as Bethesda (favored by Brown), Bethsaida, and Be(t)zatha. In a passage in the Copper Scroll found at Qumran (3Q15 11:11–13) a "Bet 'Ešdatayin" is mentioned "in the pool at the entrance to its smaller basin" (unfortunately, the reading is not certain). Brown suggests that the name of the pool was "Bet 'Ešdâ," the form in the Copper Scroll being a dual form because there were two basins.

A larger question is how one should translate John 5:2, in which a substantive has to be understood. While I have supplied "gate" after "sheep," Brown prefers to supply "place" with the name Bethesda: "Now in Jerusalem, by the Sheep Pool, there is a place with the Hebrew name Bethesda." Perhaps more in keeping with archaeological findings, which have located a number of pools in the area north of the temple, would be to supply "pool" with both "sheep" and "Bethesda." As Brown observes, "in any case, John is speaking of the area northeast of the Temple where the sheep were brought into Jerusalem for sacrifice; and the name of this region and/or its pool was Bethesda."

[10] In Josephus we find the place-name "Bezetha" (other spellings occur in various manuscripts). It is used of (1) a hill north of the temple and the fortress Antonia and of (2) the quarter of the city built on this hill (recently populated in the 1st century A.D.); see Josephus, *J.W.*, 5.4.2 §149, 151; 5.5.8 §246; see also 2.15.5 §328; 2.19.4 §530. Nothing is said in these passages that connects "Bezetha" with healing pools.

[11] On the excavations near the church of St. Anne that seem to have uncovered the pools referred to in John 5:2, see, e.g., Joachim Jeremias, *Die Wiederentdeckung*

von Bethesda. Johannes 5, 2 (FRLANT 41; Göttingen: Vandenhoeck & Ruprecht, 1949) (= *The Rediscovery of Bethesda. John 5:2* [Louisville: Southern Baptist Theological Seminary, 1966]); Brown, *The Gospel According to John,* 1. 207; A. Duprez, "Probatique (Piscine)," *DBSup,* 8. cols. 606–21; Murphy-O'Connor, *The Holy Land,* 29–31; James F. Strange, "Beth-zatha," *Anchor Bible Dictionary* (6 vols.; New York: Doubleday, 1992) 1. 700–701. Murphy-O'Connor notes that the high priest Simeon built two large pools ca. 200 B.C. to supply water to the Jerusalem temple (see Sir 50:3). "Towards the middle of the next century caves east of the pools were adapted to serve as small baths," their function being either religious or medicinal, probably both (Murphy-O'Connor, *The Holy Land,* 29). The two large pools fell into disuse during the reign of Herod the Great, but they continued to fill with water during the winter rains and may have been used to wash the animals brought for sacrifice in the temple. As one way of explaining the scribal confusion in the Greek manuscripts of John 5, Strange ("Beth-zatha," 701) suggests the possibility that the northeast quarter of the city bore the name Bethzetha or Bethzatha, while the pool was called Beth Ḥesdaʾ ("house of mercy"). The area was certainly a healing sanctuary dedicated to the god Serapis or Asclepius by the time of the Emperor Hadrian (reigned A.D. 117–38), who transformed Jerusalem into a pagan city, Aelia Capitolina. The area may have already been a healing sanctuary at the time of Jesus, though this is not certain.

Scholars differ on the identification of the pool depicted as the site of Jesus' miracle in John 5:1–9. Brown identifies John's pool of five porticoes with the double pool of Simeon, which was supposedly divided by a central partition, with colonnades on the four sides and on the partition; similarly, Strange, "Beth-zatha," 701. However, Murphy-O'Connor notes that the double pool was taken out of commission "when Herod the Great (37–4 B.C.) dug the Pool of Israel closer to his new temple." Duprez ("Probatique," 619) thinks that the sick waited for a cure not at the two large pools but rather in the smaller baths; in his view, it is here that the miracle of John 5:1–9 occurred. Accordingly, Duprez is doubtful about the contention that five porticoes surrounded the two large pools. In any case, the story in John 5:1–9 shows a remarkable knowledge of the topography of pre-A.D. 70 Jerusalem, and the remark of the sick man in 5:7 is noteworthy in presupposing but not explaining the nature of the pool(s) as a healing sanctuary. A later scribe apparently felt the need for some further explanation and so added 5:4, which tells of an angel who descended at times into the pool and stirred up the waters, thus conferring healing power on them. On the text-critical question, see Brown, *The Gospel According to John,* 1. 207; Metzger, *A Textual Commentary,* 209. In Brown's opinion, "this ancient gloss [while not being an original part of the text of John's Gospel] . . . may well reflect with accuracy a popular tradition about the pool." The opinion of Duprez ("Probatique," 619) and Latourelle (*The Miracles of Jesus,* 219) that v 4 is original in the text of John's Gospel is highly unlikely.

[12] On the absence of the Sabbath-motif in the original story, see Eduard Lohse, "Jesu Worte über den Sabbat," *Judentum, Urchristentum, Kirche* (Joachim Jeremias Festschrift; BZNW 26; ed. Walther Eltester; Berlin: Töpelmann, 1960) 79–89, esp. 79–80.

[13] For considerations in favor of this position, see *A Marginal Jew,* 1. 403–6.

[14] Pesch, *Das Markusevangelium,* 1. 189.

[15] Since the vast majority of exegetes agree that Mark 3:6 is a redactional creation of Mark (or possibly the pre-Marcan editor of the cycle of dispute stories),

there is no need to concern ourselves with historical questions such as the identity of the Herodians and the reasons the Pharisees would be willing to collaborate with them against Jesus. For a summary of views on the Herodians, see Guelich, *Mark 1–8:26*, 138. For the minority view, that v 6 belongs to the earliest form of the story, see Roloff, *Das Kerygma*, 63–66.

[16] As soon as we decide that 3:6 represents Christian storytelling, the question of the historicity of the dispute motif in 3:1–6 is necessarily raised. As I have already noted, Mark 3:1–6, though a mixed form like 2:1–12, is much more integrated and "organic" in its composition than 2:1–12; the dispute element cannot be easily disengaged from the rest of 3:1–6. In particular, 3:6, on the level of the final composition of the story, has an ironic connection with the precise formulation of Jesus' rhetorical question: ". . . to save a life or to kill?" The intended irony on the part of the Christian storyteller is that Jesus "saves" a life on the Sabbath by healing the man's crippled hand (a symbol of the fullness of life Jesus proclaims and brings), while the Pharisees respond to the life-giving power of Jesus displayed on the Sabbath by plotting on the Sabbath to kill him. If, then, we consider 3:6 not to reflect one precise event in the actual ministry of the historical Jesus in A.D. 28–30, this raises serious questions about the historicity of the rhetorical question in 3:4 and hence of the form of the dispute as it now appears in Mark 3:1–6. But what is Mark 3:1–6 without the element of the dispute story? Once one unravels 3:6, which in turn unravels 3:4, one wonders what is left of the ball of yarn that is 3:1–6.

[17] Sometimes critics will bring up the similarity of language between this miracle and the punishment-miracle recounted in 1 Kgs 13:4–6 (LXX 3 Kgdms 13:4–6): King Jeroboam's hand withers when he stretches it out against a prophet of doom, and then it is restored when the prophet prays to the Lord. But the similarity is simply one of a few words (*ekteinō, tēn cheira autou, xērainō*) and nothing more. The context and sense are completely different. No decision for or against the historicity of the miracle in Mark 3:1–6 can be made to rest on these sparse verbal parallels.

[18] Pesch (*Das Markusevangelium*, 1. 195) makes what is in my opinion a dubious historical claim and argument when he affirms: "The word of Jesus in v 4, which is certainly original, is in its formulation tied to the situation, so that the healing of the crippled hand must also count as material handed down in the tradition."

[19] Guelich, *Mark 1–8:26*, 134–37.

[20] See E. P. Sanders, *Jewish Law from Jesus to the Mishnah. Five Studies* (London: SCM; Philadelphia: Trinity, 1990) 6–23; also Eduard Lohse, *"sabbaton,* etc.," *TDNT* 7 (1971) 1–35, esp. 24. For a response to Lohse and some reflections on the methodological problems involved in discussing Jesus' view of the Sabbath (with abundant bibliography), see Frans Neirynck, "Jesus and the Sabbath. Some Observations on Mark II, 27," *Jésus aux origines de la christologie* (BETL 40; new expanded edition; ed. Jacques Dupont; Leuven: Leuven University/ Peeters, 1989) 227–70.
Sanders gives an overview of the development of and debates over rules for observance of the Sabbath from the OT to the Mishna. Since our immediate concern in this chapter is miracle stories rather than legal disputes in the Gospels, I refer the interested reader to Sanders's treatment for details of controversies over Sabbath regulations.
On the extreme strictness of the Essenes see Josephus, *J.W.* 2.8.9 §147: they

are stricter than all other Jews in abstaining from work on the Sabbath, even to
the point of not defecating on the Sabbath. The *Damascus Document* likewise lays
down lengthy and stringent prohibitions for the Sabbath, including not talking
about work to be done the next day or not drawing out a newborn animal that has
fallen into a cistern or a pit (CD 10:14–11:18; cf. Matt 12:11; Luke 14:5). Unfortunately, the text is partially corrupt just at the point where the case of a man who
has fallen into a pit is discussed; it is not clear whether use of a ladder or rope to
help him out is allowed (see the translations of Vermes, *The Dead Sea Scrolls in English*, 95; and Dupont-Sommer, *The Essene Writings from Qumran*, 153 n. 5). Similar stringency can be found in the *Book of Jubilees;* see esp. *Jub.* 50: 6–13. As for
the Sadducees, we are poorly informed on their views of Sabbath observance. One
might infer from the Mishna that, while not as severe as the Essenes, they were
stricter than the Pharisees in that they did not allow the theoretical joining ("fusion") of a number of houses to allow the carrying of vessels from place to place
on the Sabbath; this is the rabbinic institution of the ʿerûb. On differences between
Pharisees and Sadducees on this point, see *m. ʿErub.* 6:2 (though the attribution of
the text is disputed). Differences over Sabbath observance between the House of
Shammai and the House of Hillel (both belonging to the Pharisaic tradition) can
be found in *m. Šabb.* 1:6; they also differed on the proper observance of festival
days.

[21] Sanders, *Jewish Law*, 13.

[22] For the list of the 39 works forbidden by rabbinic interpretation of the Sabbath, see *m. Šabb.* 7:2; various works are then treated in detail from *m. Šabb.* 11:1
onwards. On the relation of observance of the Sabbath and the observance of festival days, see *m. Beṣa* 5:1–2. For the principle that danger to life creates an exception to the rules forbidding medical treatment on the Sabbath (a principle perhaps
alluded to in Mark 3:4), see *m. Yoma* 8:6. If Rabbi Mattithiah ben Heresh is so lenient that he allows medicine to be dropped into a man's mouth simply because
the man has a pain in his throat—all on the grounds that there is doubt whether
life is in danger—it is difficult to imagine that 1st-century Jews in Galilee would
become very upset over Jesus' healing with a mere word. As Sanders (*Jewish Law*,
21) puts it, "talking is not regarded as work in any Jewish tradition, and so no
work was performed." It is remarkable how many exegetes simply take for granted
that the pericope depicts Jesus breaking the Sabbath prohibition of work, without
ever raising the question of whether Jesus performs any physical action in the
story; see, e.g., Dunn, "Mark 2.1–3.6," 408: Jesus performs "an unnecessary healing in breach of the Sabbath. . . ."

[23] If we could take *m. Šabb.* 7:1 as reflecting pre-A.D. 70 Pharisaic views, we
would be sure that, among Pharisees, inadvertent transgressions of the Sabbath
were atoned for simply by sin-offerings. Even though one cannot be certain about
this particular point, the general conclusion of Sanders (*Jewish Law*, 19, 22) seems
sound: "In any case there is no reason to think that Pharisees sought the death
penalty for minor transgressions of the sabbath. . . . The plot in Mark 3.6, as most
scholars recognize, is editorial, put here by the person who collected the sequence
of conflict narratives in Mark 2.1–3.5. The story itself reveals no actual conflict
over the sabbath."

[24] Consequently, I do not agree with Pesch (*Das Markusevangelium*, 1. 195–96) that
"the text [of Mark 3:1–6] is an important and reliable source for the ministry, self-
understanding, and impact (opposition) of Jesus." Nor do I find the four reasons he

gives cogent. In particular, his argument from Semitisms in the text supports the idea of an earlier Aramaic form of the story with a Palestinian provenance; a pure creation by Mark seems excluded. This in itself, however, hardly proves the story's origin in Jesus' ministry. Still, Lohse ("Jesu Worte über den Sabbat," 84) thinks that of all the Gospel stories connected with disputes about the Sabbath, Mark 3:1–5 is the one most likely to reflect an event in the ministry of the historical Jesus. Yet even here he admits that the individual details of the conflict cannot now be reconstructed. Moreover, Lohse's argument for the authenticity of Mark 3:4 is questionable. He claims that healings on the Sabbath never occurred in the primitive Christian community, which was still bound by reverential ties to the Mosaic Law (p. 85). On what grounds can we make such an assertion about what kinds of miracles the "primitive community" did or did not perform?

[25] See Busse, *Die Wunder des Propheten Jesus*, 289–304, especially the detailed analysis of vocabulary and style on pp. 294–98.

[26] Once again, the description is too vague to give a precise diagnosis. In dependence on J. Wilkinson ("The Case of the Bent Woman in Luke 13:10–17," *EvQ* 49 [1977] 195–205), Fitzmyer (*The Gospel According to Luke*, 2. 1012) suggests that the ailment is *spondylitis ankylopoietica*, causing a fusion of spinal joints.

[27] It is sometimes pointed out that in Luke 13:4, in a pericope that is separated from the cure of the bent-over woman by the parable of the barren fig tree (13:6–9), there is a passing reference to 18 people who were killed by the fall of a tower in Siloam. The two occurrences of the same numeral may help explain why the two pericopes wind up close to each other in the Lucan narrative and perhaps already in the pre-Lucan tradition. But there is nothing to indicate that one story borrowed the numeral from the other; see Fitzmyer, *The Gospel According to Luke*, 2. 1010; see also Busse, *Die Wunder des Propheten Jesus*, 294.

[28] Sanders, *Jewish Law*, 20.

[29] For the theory that Luke 13:10–17 is a Christian creation based on the originally independent logion in 13:15, see Bultmann, *Geschichte*, 10; Lohse, "Jesu Worte über den Sabbat," 81; idem, "*sabbaton*," 25; and in a slightly different way, Dibelius, *Formgeschichte*, 94–95. More positive on historicity is Roloff, *Kerygma*, 67–69 (denying that 13:15 is the origin of the pericope); Marshall, *The Gospel of Luke*, 557. In favor of at least 3:15 as an authentic saying of Jesus is Martin Hengel, "*phantē*," *TDNT* 9 (1974) 53.

[30] Why Matthew would have introduced the term *paralytikos* into the story of the centurion's servant is by no means clear. It is curious, though, that there is a clear divide in the Gospel between Matthew's use of "paralyzed" (*paralytikos*) before chap. 11 and his use of "lame" (*chōlos*) from chap. 11 onwards. The word *paralytikos* occurs in Matthew only in 4:24; 8:6; 9:2(*bis*),6, while *chōlos* occurs only in 11:5; 15:30–31; 18:8; 21:14.

[31] For general treatments of the Bartimaeus story and the title "Son of David," see Bultmann, *Geschichte*, 288; Dibelius, *Formgeschichte*, 49–50; van der Loos, *The Miracles of Jesus*, 422–25; Latourelle, *The Miracles of Jesus*, 155–61; Kertelge, *Die Wunder Jesu*, 179–82; Roloff, *Das Kerygma*, 121–26; Loren R. Fisher, " 'Can This Be the Son of David?' " *Jesus and the Historian* (Ernest Cadman Colwell Festschrift; ed. F. Thomas Trotter; Philadelphia: Westminster, 1968) 82–97; Vernon K. Robbins, "The Healing of Blind Bartimaeus (10:46–52) in the Marcan Theology," *JBL* 92 (1973) 224–43; Klaus Berger, "Die königlichen Messiastraditionen des Neuen Testaments," *NTS* 20 (1974) 1–44; Dennis C. Duling, "The Promises to David and Their Entrance into

Christianity—Nailing Down a Likely Hypothesis," *NTS* 20 (1974) 55–77; idem, "Solomon, Exorcism, and the Son of David," *HTR* 68 (1975) 235–52; idem, "The Therapeutic Son of David: An Element in Matthew's Christological Apologetic," *NTS* 24 (1978) 392–410; idem, "Matthew's Plurisignificant 'Son of David' in Social Science Perspective: Kinship, Kingship, Magic, and Miracle," *BTB* 22 (1992) 99–116; Evald Lövestam, "Jésus Fils de David chez les Synoptiques," *ST* 28 (1974) 97–109; Koch, *Die Bedeutung,* 126–32; Pesch, *Das Markusevangelium,* 2. 167–75; Paul J. Achtemeier, " 'And He Followed Him': Miracles and Discipleship in Mark 10:46–52," *Early Christian Miracle Stories* (Semeia 11; ed. Robert W. Funk; Missoula, MT: Scholars, 1978) 115–45; W. R. G. Loader, "Son of David, Blindness, Possession, and Duality in Matthew," *CBQ* 44 (1982) 570–85; Michael G. Steinhauser, "Part of a 'Call Story'?" *ExpTim* 94 (1982–83) 204–6; idem, "The Form of the Bartimaeus Narrative (Mark 10.46–52)," *NTS* 32 (1986) 583–95.

[32] On the proper understanding of Peter's confession in Mark's theology, see Raymond E. Brown, Karl P. Donfried, and John Reumann (eds.), *Peter in the New Testament* (Minneapolis: Augsburg; New York: Paulist, 1973) 68–69. Jack Dean Kingsbury rightly defends the view that Mark sees Peter's confession as "correct" but "insufficient"; see his *The Christology of Mark's Gospel* (Philadelphia: Fortress, 1983) 92–98. As Kingsbury points out, Peter's confession is presented as the antithesis to wrong views about Jesus (John the Baptist, Elijah, or a prophet), correctly summarizes all of Jesus' activity in the first half of Mark's Gospel, and coincides with Mark's own proclamation of Jesus as Messiah in 1:1. Hence I reject the negative evaluation of Peter's confession that has been urged by Weeden (*Mark. Traditions in Conflict,* 52–69) and many American critics since him.

[33] Achtemeier (" 'And He Followed Him,' " 115) goes so far as to claim that the literary form of the Bartimaeus story is not that of a miracle story but of a "call story," such as is found in Luke 5:1–11; see also Roloff, *Das Kerygma,* 126; and Steinhauser in his earlier study, "Part of a 'Call Story'?" 204–6. In my view, the Bartimaeus story does contain the basic motifs of a miracle story, while lacking the all-decisive command of Jesus: "[Come,] Follow me." Jesus calls Bartimaeus to him for healing; he does not explicitly call him to follow as a disciple. Hence I would prefer to say that, by his redactional positioning and editing of the story, Mark uses a miracle story as an example of discipleship. Robbins ("The Healing," 226–27) stresses the interweaving of christology and discipleship in the story as "the two sides of the same coin."
    Differing from Achtemeier, Steinhauser ("The Form," 583–95) tries to understand the Bartimaeus narrative as a call story modeled on the form of OT call stories of such figures as Gideon (Judg 6:11b–17) and Moses (Exod 3:1–12). But the form Steinhauser sketches is extremely broad; it could fit almost any theophany, angelophany, or annunciation of birth. Moreover, Steinhauser has difficulty making the Bartimaeus narrative fit the suggested pattern (see, e.g., his treatment of "the objection" and "the commission" on pp. 586–87).

[34] For the Bartimaeus story as both concluding and beginning sections of the Gospel of Mark, see Robbins, "The Healing," 235–36.

[35] I am not claiming here that these various titles all meant the same thing or were necessarily interconnected in early Judaism or early Christianity. What I am claiming is that on the redactional level Mark intended a connection.

[36] Hence I reject the claims of authors like Weeden and Crossan that Peter and the Twelve (or alternately the Jerusalem church and the relatives of Jesus) are rejected at the end of Mark's Gospel.

[37] That the story in Mark 10:46–52 is not a purely Marcan creation but has some tradition behind it is so generally recognized that I do not belabor the point. After surveying the evidence, Achtemeier (" 'And He Followed Him,' " 119) concludes that "aside from the introduction and conclusion, Mark has reproduced the story pretty much as he received it, including the title, 'son of David'. . . ." For various signs of tension and unevenness in the Marcan text that argue for a tradition that is being redacted, see, e.g., Roloff, *Das Kerygma*, 122; Robbins, "The Healing," 230–36 (though I do not agree with all of his arguments). In my opinion, among the signals that point to pre-Marcan tradition are the syntactically overloaded sentence beginning the story (v 46), the unusual naming of the recipient of the miracle, the presence of two Aramaic words in one story, the unique occurrence of "Son of David" as a direct address to Jesus in Mark's Gospel, and the unusual use of words and motifs that are found elsewhere in Mark (e.g., it is the crowd, not Jesus, who rebukes [*epetimōn*, v 48] and issues a command to be silent).

[38] Strictly speaking, Jairus is not the direct recipient of one of Jesus' miracles, since he asks for the cure of his daughter (Mark 5:23 parr.). Bultmann (*Geschichte*, 228) reflects his own presupposition (a very questionable one, in my opinion) when he takes for granted that the proper name Bartimaeus must be a sign of a secondary tradition. This in turn reflects a deeper and still more questionable presupposition, namely, that the "pure" forms of miracle stories are chronologically the earliest forms, and any deviation from the pure form is due to later additions. In a similar vein, Dibelius (*Formgeschichte*, 49–50) struggles with the appearance of the name Bartimaeus in what he considers a paradigm "of the less pure type" by suggesting that originally a "genuine," pure paradigm recounted the healing of a nameless blind man and that later on this man was identified with a well-known blind man from Jericho who might have been a disciple of Jesus. Dibelius does not inform us as to whether the blind man known as Bartimaeus was at some point cured of blindness and if so how. The underlying problem of the approach of both Bultmann and Dibelius is a certain literary romanticism that supposes that the "pure" forms must always be chronologically earlier and that more complicated forms must always be secondary creations. I do not think that such a presupposition will hold up to rigorous testing; one need only think of Matthew's handling of some of Mark's miracle stories. Indeed, in his editing of Mark's version of the Bartimaeus story, Matthew "purifies" the form in that he drops the proper name, as does Luke. Roloff (*Das Kerygma*, 121) takes the exactly opposite tack from Bultmann and Dibelius by stressing the concrete details of the story as indications of early tradition. It is regrettable that Christoph Burger uncritically takes over Bultmann's judgments in his treatment of Mark 10:46–52; see his *Jesus als Davidssohn. Eine traditionsgeschichtliche Untersuchung* (FRLANT 98; Göttingen: Vandenhoeck & Ruprecht, 1970) 43.

[39] For various attempts to explain "Bartimaeus" as something other than a patronymic, see Taylor (*The Gospel According to St. Mark*, 447–48), who judges a patronymic to be the most likely explanation. It is difficult to imagine that even Hellenistic Jews of the Diaspora would have been ignorant of the meaning of the Aramaic *bar* as the sign of a patronymic. It is possible that the explanation of the Aramaic name in Greek already existed in the Greek version of the story before it came to Mark. Roloff (*Das Kerygma*, 122) points out that the order of words in 10:46 (*ho huios Timaiou Bartimaios*, "the son of Timaeus, Bartimaeus") is not the usual order used by Mark when he explains an Aramaic word in Greek. He customarily gives the Aramaic word first and then follows it with an explanatory *ho estin* (*methermēneuomenon*) (see 3:17; 5:41; 7:11,34; also his explanation of various terms with *ho estin* in 12:42; 15:16,42). The explanation

may therefore come from a pre-Marcan editor of miracle stories or possibly of a primitive passion tradition. This is much more likely than Taylor's suggestion (p. 448) that the explanation is a scribal gloss, a theory for which there is no textual evidence in the earliest and best manuscripts.

[40] Bultmann, *Geschichte*, 228; Burger, *Jesus als Davidssohn*, 43.

[41] The Jericho involved in this story is "Roman Jericho," also referred to as "Herodian Jericho" or "NT Jericho." Its location is the archaeological site known as Tulul Abu el-ʿAlayiq, where remains of Hasmonean and Herodian palace complexes have been unearthed. This Roman Jericho is to be distinguished from the Jericho made famous by the Book of Joshua in the OT; it is located at Tell es-Sultan, about eight miles north-northwest of the Dead Sea, on the west side of (and set back from) the Jordan River. Roman Jericho is situated about a mile south-southwest of OT Jericho. For basic archaeological and historical data, see T. A. Holland and Ehud Netzer, "Jericho," *Anchor Bible Dictionary* (6 vols.; New York: Doubleday, 1992) 3. 723–40. For a description of the Roman road from Jericho to Jerusalem that Jesus would have traveled—a road that rose from Jericho at 770 feet below sea level to Jerusalem at 2,500 feet above sea level—see Jack Finegan, *The Archeology of the New Testament. The Life of Jesus and the Beginning of the Early Church* (Princeton: Princeton University, 1969) 86–87.

[42] In fact, the only other place in Mark's Gospel where "Son of David" appears is in the learned question Jesus poses during his last days in Jerusalem: "How do the scribes say [i.e., how can they claim, or on what grounds do they claim] that the Messiah is the Son of David?" (Mark 12:35).

[43] Sometimes scholars uncritically start their investigation of the NT's use of "Son of David" with Matthew's Gospel, which should rather be a terminus of the investigation, since Matthew increases and exploits occurrences of "Son of David" for his own theological purposes. On Matthew's use of "Son of David," see Duling, "The Therapeutic Son of David," 392–410; idem, "Matthew's Plurisignificant 'Son of David,' " 99–116; Loader, "Son of David," 570–85; Jack Dean Kingsbury, "The Title 'Son of David' in Matthew's Gospel," *JBL* 95 (1976) 591–602. Kingsbury rightly observes that "Matthew is the only evangelist who displays a strong interest in this title" (p. 601). However, Kingsbury asserts that "Son of David" has a much more limited scope in Matthew than many German redaction critics (e.g., Georg Strecker, Reinhart Hummel, Rolf Walker, Alfred Suhl, Christoph Burger, Alexander Sand, and Günther Bornkamm) would allow (p. 591).

[44] Hence I find unlikely Robbins's attempt to explain its presence here as a result of Marcan redaction ("The Healing," 233–36); see also Duling, "Solomon," 252. Jesus-as-Son-of-David is simply not a major christological concern of Mark, and I think that the Davidic notes struck in Mark 11:10 and 12:35–37 come to Mark from his tradition. Thus I consider it improbable that Mark would have created the only instance in his Gospel of a direct address to Jesus as "Son of David," when there was no precedent for such a title in his tradition. For the presence of "Son of David" in the pre-Marcan form of the story, see Achtemeier, " 'And He Followed Him,' " 119.

[45] See Burger, *Jesus als Davidssohn*, 44, 46.

[46] Because both Roloff (*Das Kerygma*, 124) and Robbins ("The Healing," 234) think only in terms of the Jewish tradition of a political Son-of-David Messiah reigning on his father's throne (à la *Psalms of Solomon* 17) or of the mainstream-Christian understanding of Jesus as descended from David (e.g., in the Infancy Narratives or in the

early confessional formula of Rom 1:3–4), they have difficulty conceiving of the cry as an original element of the story. This is also a serious failing in Burger's treatment of Mark 10:46–52 (*Jesus als Davidssohn*, 42–46). In his chapter on the Jewish background of the "Son of David" title and christology, Burger never takes up the question of the image of Solomon and Jewish traditions about him as an exorcist and healer that are found, e.g., in Josephus and the *Testament of Solomon*. Hence Burger approaches Mark 10:46–52 with the rigid paradigm of the Son of David as a monarch reigning on David's throne, a figure that 1st-century Judaism did not associate with miracles. It is not surprising that he therefore considers Bartimaeus' cry of "Son of David" in conflict with his cry of "Rabbouni" and finally a Christian insertion into the story.

[47] It is important to realize that "Son of David" was not a widely used designation (a better word than "title" in this context) in the OT. Apart from one occurrence with reference to Absalom (2 Sam 13:1), all other uses of "Son of David" are relatively late in the OT and refer only to Solomon (1 Chr 29:22; 2 Chr 1:1; 13:6; 30:26; 35:3; Prov 1:1; Qoh 1:1); see Fisher, " 'Can This Be the Son of David?' " 90. The nearly complete restriction of "Son of David" to Solomon in the OT is significant in light of the subsequent tradition history both of "Son of David" in the Synoptics and of the image of Solomon as an exorcist and magician.

[48] So, e.g., Lövestam, "Jésus Fils de David," 101. This position becomes all the more interesting when one notices that the *Testament of Solomon* 20:1 actually has a petitioner cry out to Solomon: "King Solomon, Son of David, have mercy on me" (cf. Mark 10:47). However, the full text of this verse is contained in only one manuscript (H); and the many Christian traits in the present form of the *Testament* make it impossible to decide whether we have here an echo of the Christian Gospels or an authentic Jewish tradition. Duling ("Solomon," 243) is more ready than Berger ("Die königlichen Messiastraditionen," 6–8) to see Christian influence in the cry. In this Duling may well be right. As is often the case, Berger shows a great knowledge of ancient texts and traditions, but is not sufficiently critical in his mixing of early and late texts and his decisions about what constitutes an independent tradition. Duling goes on to observe (p. 249) that, within the ambit of intertestamental literature mentioning Solomon, only the *Testament of Solomon* has Solomon *addressed* as "Son of David" as Jesus is addressed in the Gospels. In exorcism stories one cannot document the absolute use of "Son of David" as a title or its use in direct address before Christianity. Unfortunately, Berger is not as careful as Duling in distinguishing various metaphors of Davidic descent from the designation "Son of David."

For the development of the image of Solomon as exorcist and magician in the period of early Judaism and early Christianity, see Fisher, " 'Can This Be the Son of David?' " 82–85; and more extensively Duling, "Solomon," 244–49. As most writers on the subject point out, the earliest reference to Solomon as having knowledge of the spirit world may be Wis 7:20: divine Wisdom taught Solomon knowledge of, *inter alia*, the natures of animals, the dispositions of beasts, and *pneumatōn bias*. Berger ("Die königlichen Messiastraditionen," 5), along with a number of other critics and some modern translations (*RSV, JB*), interprets the Greek phrase as meaning the powers of spirits. However, such a translation is not certain. In the context of Solomon's encyclopedic knowledge of the natural world, "powers of winds" is also a possible translation, and in fact the *NAB* translates the phrase in this way (similarly the *NEB* and the variant in the margin of the *RSV*).

[49] Since, however, the statement about Solomon is—at least in its context in Q—part of Jesus' reply to his adversaries' request for a sign, the "wisdom" of Solomon might include his power to perform miracles, especially exorcisms. On this see Lövestam,

"Jésus Fils de David," 104. While this is possible, one should notice the exact wording of the passage involving Solomon (Matt 12:42 par.): ". . . she [the Queen of Sheba] came from the ends of the earth to *hear* the wisdom of Solomon." The stress on "hearing" indicates that what is in view is his wise speech (proverbs, parables, discourses on nature, etc.).

[50] On all this see Duling, "The Promises to David," 55–77. I agree with him that in general the Christian use of the *title* "Son of David" (as distinct from references to the fulfillment of Yahweh's promise to David to raise up seed after him, seed that would be Yahweh's son and would be established on David's throne [see 2 Sam 7:11–16]) is relatively late in NT christological formulations. However, I do not think that this is true of the use of "Son of David" by Bartimaeus. It reflects not later Christian beliefs in Jesus as the royal Davidic Messiah enthroned at God's right hand by the resurrection (or begotten by the power of the Holy Spirit in the virgin Mary, who was espoused to Joseph, a son of David), but rather Jewish belief in an exorcist-like-Solomon.

[51] By speaking of the "early Christian tradition of the first generation," I purposely exclude the later redactional expansion of "Son of David" references by Matthew. Even apart from the question of dating, Matthew's increased references to Jesus as the Son of David do not move in the direction of a Solomon typology.

[52] *A Marginal Jew*, 1. 178–80.

[53] Even Robbins ("The Healing," 238), who concentrates on Mark's redactional theology in the passage, admits that the placement of the Bartimaeus story precisely at the end of chap. 10 of the Gospel probably reflects the fact that the story was firmly tied to Jericho in the tradition.

[54] See Achtemeier, " 'And He Followed Him,' " 124: "It is possible that the healing of blind Bartimaeus may also have functioned originally as the account of how he became a disciple of Jesus."

[55] For various views on this story, see Bultmann, *Geschichte*, 227–28; Dibelius, *Formgeschichte*, 82–84; Taylor, *The Gospel According to St. Mark*, 368–73; van der Loos, *The Miracles of Jesus*, 419–22; R. Beauvery, "La guérison d'un aveugle à Bethsaïde," *NRT* 90 (1968) 1083–91; Kertelge, *Die Wunder Jesu*, 161–65; Roloff, *Das Kerygma*, 127–31; Pesch, *Markusevangelium*, 1. 415–21; E. S. Johnson, "Mark VIII.22–26: The Blind Man from Bethsaida," *NTS* 25 (1978–79) 370–83; J. Duncan M. Derrett, "Trees Walking, Prophecy, and Christology," *ST* 35 (1981) 33–54; J. I. Miller, "Was Tischendorf Really Wrong? Mark 8:26b Revisited," *NovT* 28 (1986) 97–103; J. M. Ross, "Another Look at Mark 8:26," *NovT* 29 (1987) 97–99; Latourelle, *The Miracles of Jesus*, 179–85; Guelich, *Mark 1–8:26*, 428–36.

[56] The original Bethsaida was a small fishing village on the northeast shore of the Sea of Galilee. The Greek spelling *Bēthsaïda* suggests that the Aramaic name was *bêt ṣaidā'*, "house of hunting" or possibly "house of fishing" (see Fitzmyer, *The Gospel According to Luke*, 1. 765). Philip, son of Herod the Great and tetrarch of a collection of regions including Gaulanitis, Batanaea, Auranitis, Paneas, and Trachonitis (cf. Luke 3:1, which also mentions the politically defunct Iturea), built up Bethsaida, increased its population, and granted it the status of a city. He called it "Julias" in honor of Julia, the daughter of Caesar Augustus (*Ant.* 18.2.1. §28). Since Julia fell into disgrace and was banished in 2 B.C., it is supposed that the founding and naming of Bethsaida-Julias preceded that date. Putting together data from both Josephus and the NT, James F. Strange ("Beth-saida," *Anchor Bible Dictionary* [6 vols.; New York: Doubleday, 1992] 1. 692–93) suggests that Roman Bethsaida was about one-eighth of a mile east of the

Jordan River, but that there was a port of anchorage on the Sea of Galilee. In Strange's view, the excavation called et-Tell (1.7 miles to the north-northeast of the Sea of Galilee) represents the acropolis of the Roman city, while two sites originally on the shore of the Sea but now partly underwater, el-Araj and el-Mis'adiyye, are remnants of the fishing village of Bethsaida. There is some disagreement among scholars as to whether Bethsaida strictly speaking belonged to the territory of Trachonitis or Gaulanitis. To add to the confusion, John 12:21, Pliny in his *Natural History*, Eusebius, and Jerome all refer to Bethsaida as being in Galilee, but they are probably speaking loosely from a geographical rather than a political point of view.

[57] As Johnson rightly observes ("The Blind Man from Bethsaida," 376–77), *anablepsas* in 8:24a means "regaining his sight," not "looking up." What follows in the Greek of v 24b is confused, perhaps reflecting an Aramaic construction, but the basic sense is clear enough; for different explanations of the wording, see Guelich, *Mark 1–8:26*, 433. The essential point is that the man has regained his sight well enough to make out men moving in the distance, but the blurred images look more like trees moving around than men. This fits in with Jesus' having led the blind man away from the men who had brought him (v 23a). Presumably the narrative in v 24 depicts the blind man peering into the distance to see his erstwhile helpers.

[58] The Greek verb *dieblepsen* in v 25b means in context "he saw clearly." The additional statement *kai eneblepen tēlaugōs hapanta* underlines the complete and perduring nature of the cure: "he kept on [imperfect tense] seeing [or: staring intently at] all things clearly [even at a distance]." See Johnson, "The Blind Man from Bethsaida," 378.

[59] This reading involves an intricate text-critical question. For the ending of Mark 8:26 UBSGNT[3] lists eight different readings, which however can be reduced to two basic alternatives: (1) "Do not enter the town" (Sinaiticus, Vaticanus, and Washingtonianus); or (2) "Do not speak to anyone in the town" (Old Latin manuscript k). Most other manuscripts show some conflation of these two choices. See Metzger (*Textual Commentary*, 98–99) for the reason for favoring the first reading, "which is supported by early representatives of the Alexandrian, Caesarean, Eastern, and Egyptian text-types . . ." (p. 99). The substitution of the prohibition "Do not speak to anyone in the town" may stem from (1) the difficulty of imagining how a man who—as the Christian scribe supposes—lives in Bethsaida could go home without entering the town (but Mark never says that the blind man *lived* in Bethsaida), and (2) the tendency to assimilate this command of Jesus to other commands in Mark to remain silent. Actually, the difference of the command "Do not enter the town" from the commands to be silent that are found elsewhere in Mark is one reason for judging the former to be original; the tendency of the scribes would be to assimilate the unfamiliar type of command to the more familiar form. This point is missed by Ross, "Another Look," 99. In favor of a reading slightly different from but basically identical to the one I espouse, see Miller, "Was Tischendorf Really Wrong?" 97–103.

[60] Guelich (*Mark 1–8:26*, 429) suggests that Mark found the two stories paired in the tradition and that they may have been composed by the same author or community.

[61] See Taylor, *The Gospel According to St. Mark*, 368–69. As Taylor observes, "both cures [of the deaf-mute and of the blind man at Bethsaida] are wrought in privacy or semi-privacy; in each case spittle is used and the laying on of hands; restoration is accomplished with some difficulty or in stages; and, finally, in each instance a charge to maintain secrecy is imposed." Taylor proceeds to outline in two columns the verbal parallels between the two Greek texts.

[62] Bultmann (*Geschichte*, 228), for instance, suggests that the healing of the blind man in Mark 8:22–27 is to be judged a "variant" of the healing of the deaf-mute in 7:32–37.

[63] On what follows, see Latourelle, *The Miracles of Jesus*, 180–81; Beauvery, "La guérison," 1083–85. In his desire to maintain the basic historicity of Mark 8:22–26, Roloff (*Das Kerygma*, 129–31) too quickly dismisses the symbolic use Mark has made of the story by incorporating it into his redactional framework. Historicity and symbolism need not be mutually exclusive terms.

[64] To use the distinctions of contemporary literary (or narrative) criticism: the full healing of the disciples' (spiritual) sight does not occur within the "plotted time" of the Gospel. But Mark's narrative does end in chap. 16 with a prophecy made by a heavenly messenger, the young man in white: "He [Jesus] goes before you [the disciples and Peter] into Galilee; there you *shall see* him" (16:7). Speaking as he does for God, the young man voices a prophecy that is no doubt to be understood by the reader as having been fulfilled, despite the apparent failure of the women to act on their commission (16:8). Hence the disciples' sight is restored in the "story time" of the Gospel, though not in its "plotted time." On the distinction between plotted time and story time, see Norman R. Petersen, *Literary Criticism for New Testament Critics* (Philadelphia: Fortress, 1978), esp. Chapter 3, "Story Time and Plotted Time in Mark's Narrative," 49–80.

[65] Bultmann, *Geschichte*, 227; so also Roloff, *Das Kerygma*, 128.

[66] So Dibelius, *Formgeschichte*, 84.

[67] Notice the difference here from John's Gospel, where almost all miracles receive a precise location: the wedding feast at Cana, Jesus' miraculous knowledge of the Samaritan woman displayed at the well of Sychar, the healing of the paralyzed man at the pool in the Bethesda (or Bethzatha) region of Jerusalem, the feeding of the five thousand (located not in but in relation to the city of Tiberias, with the complementary discourse on the bread of life delivered at Capernaum), the healing of the man born blind in Jerusalem (in connection with the pool of Siloam), and the raising of Lazarus at Bethany near Jerusalem.

[68] The only other occurrence of Bethsaida in a Synoptic narrative is Luke 9:10, where Luke associates the city with the multiplication of loaves for the five thousand. Fitzmyer (*The Gospel According to Luke*, 1. 765) rightly explains this strange relocation of the feeding story as Luke's reworking of Marcan material for his own purpose. The only other appearances of Bethsaida in the NT are two passing references in John's Gospel. Both John 1:44 and 12:21 serve to inform the reader that the disciple Philip comes from Bethsaida, the hometown—we are told only in John—of Andrew and Peter. These passing references support the view that along with the new Roman city of Bethsaida-Julias, built a little further inland by the tetrarch Philip, the old fishing village of Bethsaida, with perhaps more of a Jewish population, continued to exist. It is probably this fishing village that is meant as the setting of Mark 8:22–26.

[69] Matthew 11:20 introduces the Q logion by saying: "Then he [Jesus] began to excoriate the cities in which most of his miracles [*hai pleistai dynameis*] had taken place, because they had not repented." The peculiar presence in the saying of the town of Chorazin, otherwise unattested as a locus of activity either by Jesus or by the early church, is in itself an argument for the logion's authenticity.

[70] Hermann Strathmann, "*polis*, etc.," *TDNT* 6 (1968) 516–35, esp. 530. Even the cosmopolitan Luke is capable of calling Nazareth, Capernaum, and Bethlehem as well as Jerusalem a *polis* (4:29,31; 2:4; 22:10). In Luke 5:17 the sweeping nature of Luke's statement suggests that *kōmē* stands for "city" as well as "town" and "village": "And

sitting there were Pharisees and teachers of the law who had come from every *kōmēs* of Galilee and Judea and Jerusalem." Guelich (*Mark 1–8:26*, 432) takes a different approach to the problem, arguing that *organizationally* Bethsaida remained a village under the tetrarch Philip. But are we to suppose that Mark or his tradition knew about such a political nicety? In any event, I agree with Guelich that the designation *kōmē* need not be seen as standing in tension with the mention of Bethsaida.

[71] Along with many other critics, Guelich (*Mark 1–8:26*, 431) assigns the mention of Bethsaida to Mark. Guelich's argument rests on redactional considerations: Bethsaida is part of the itinerary that Mark has mapped out for Jesus from 7:24 to 8:21. Guelich suggests that Mark may have taken the name Bethsaida from 6:45, where, after the first multiplication of loaves, Jesus orders his disciples to get into the boat and go ahead of him to Bethsaida. Actually, one could just as easily read the borrowing and redactional composition of Mark the other way round: if Mark knew that he was going to use a miracle story located at Bethsaida to conclude the "bread section," he might have "signaled ahead" the destination in an earlier attempt by the disciples to cross the Sea of Galilee—a destination they never reach until 8:22. As indicated above, I agree that Mark has situated 8:22–26 at this point in his narrative for the sake of his redactional theology; in this I concur with Guelich. But I do not see why this consideration necessarily argues in favor of the word Bethsaida being a Marcan invention in 8:22.

[72] That is the natural sense of the Greek text in 8:23: *kai ptysas eis ta ommata autou, epitheis tas cheiras autọ, epērōta auton . . .* ("and spitting into his eyes, placing [his] hands on him, he asked him . . ."). Notice that there is mention of Jesus laying his hands on the man only after it is said that Jesus spat into his eyes. Nothing suggests—and the order of words argues against the idea—that Jesus touched his fingers to his own mouth, moistened them with his saliva, and then applied the saliva to the blind man's eyes with his hand. While slightly less disconcerting to us moderns, such a scenario is hardly a literal or faithful translation of *ptysas eis ta ommata autou*. The presentation of this healing is thus more "violent" than that of the healing of the deaf-mute, where in 7:33 Jesus is described as *ptysas hēpsato tēs glōssēs autou*, which suggests that Jesus spat on his own fingers and then touched the tongue of the deaf-mute with his moistened fingers.

[73] The frequently cited text can be found in Taylor, *The Gospel According to St. Mark*, 371.

[74] *Not* in John 9:6–7, where Jesus spits on the ground (not in the eyes of the blind man) to form clay, which he then applies to the blind man's eyes, while ordering the blind man to wash in the pool of Siloam. The clay thus symbolizes the impediment of blindness, which the washing ordered by Jesus removes. Thus, in John 9 the saliva of Jesus does not function directly to heal the infirmity as it does in Mark 7:32–37 and 8:22–26.

[75] Such an illogical order would not be beyond Mark. At the end of the raising of the daughter of Jairus, just before Jesus orders some food to be given to the twelve-year-old girl, he commands that "no one is to know [about] this" (5:43). How the parents are to keep the news of the resurrection of their dead daughter from the crowd of mourners that Jesus has just thrown out of the house (5:38–40) is a question not posed by Mark, so intent is he on his redactional theme of the secrecy and mystery that surround Jesus. On 8:26 as possibly reflecting pre-Marcan tradition, see Roloff, *Das Kerygma*, 128–29.

[76] Words that occur nowhere else in Mark include *epilambanomai, ekpherō, omma,*

dendron, diablepō, and *tēlaugōs.* The verb *ptyō* occurs in Mark only here and in the "twin" story of the deaf-mute (7:33); the adverb *tēlaugōs* occurs nowhere else in the NT or the LXX. Granted, any author in the NT has a certain number of *hapax legomena* in his work. But it is strange that so many *hapax legomena* occur in concentrated form in a single Marcan story only five verses long—all the more so when one considers the many verbal and structural parallels that this story has with Mark 7:32–37. As a matter of fact, all the *hapax legomena* are concentrated in the three verses that make up the core of the story (vv 23–25). This fact alone argues against Marcan composition or heavy Marcan redaction. Indeed, one might use the same argument against the idea that the story was created by the editor responsible for the pre-Marcan collection of miracle stories that the Evangelist apparently used.

[77] For basic treatments of the pericope and its hypothetical source, see Dodd, *Historical Tradition in the Fourth Gospel,* 181–88; van der Loos, *The Miracles of Jesus,* 425–34; Brown, *The Gospel According to John,* 1. 367–82; Karlheinz Müller, "Joh 9,7 und das jüdische Verständnis des Šiloh-Spruches," *BZ* 13 (1969) 251–56; Schnackenburg, *Das Johannesevangelium,* 2. 304–11; Günter Reim, "Joh 9—Tradition und zeitgenössische messianische Diskussion," *BZ* 22 (1978) 245–53; J. Louis Martyn, *History & Theology in the Fourth Gospel* (rev. ed.; Nashville: Abingdon, 1979) 24–36; Thomas Louis Brodie, "Jesus as the New Elisha: Cracking the Code," *ExpTim* 93 (1981–82) 39–41; Michel Gourgues, "L'aveugle-né (Jn 9). Du miracle au signe: typologie des réactions à l'égard du Fils de l'homme," *NRT* 104 (1982) 381–95; Bruce Grigsby, "Washing in the Pool of Siloam—A Thematic Anticipation of the Johannine Cross," *NovT* 27 (1985) 227–35; Latourelle, *The Miracles of Jesus,* 224–28; John Painter, "John 9 and the Interpretation of the Fourth Gospel," *JSNT* 28 (1986) 31–61; Robert Tomson Fortna, *The Fourth Gospel and Its Predecessor* (Philadelphia: Fortress, 1988) 109–13; Urban C. von Wahlde, *The Earliest Version of John's Gospel* (Wilmington, DE: Glazier, 1989) 109–12; Jeffrey L. Staley, "Stumbling in the Dark, Reaching for the Light: Reading Character in John 5 and 9," *The Fourth Gospel from a Literary Perspective* (Semeia 53; ed. R. Alan Culpepper and Fernando F. Segovia; Atlanta: Scholars, 1991) 55–80.

[78] For a treatment of these three miracle stories from the viewpoint of modern narrative criticism, see R. Alan Culpepper, *Anatomy of the Fourth Gospel. A Study in Literary Design* (Philadelphia: Fortress, 1983) 137–42. Culpepper highlights the parallels between the paralyzed man in chap. 5 and the man born blind in chap. 9. So too does Staley, "Stumbling in the Dark," 55–80.

[79] On this point see Fortna, *The Fourth Gospel and Its Predecessor,* 112.

[80] These three steps are laid out in simple form by Rudolf Bultmann in his classic "The Study of the Synoptic Gospels," 11–76, esp. 37–39, available in Rudolf Bultmann and Karl Kundsin, *Form Criticism. Two Essays on New Testament Research* (New York: Harper & Row [Harper Torchbooks], 1962). These three steps are taken over and applied to John 9:1–7 by Martyn, *History & Theology,* 24–26. The numerous possible expansions of this basic grid are investigated by Theissen in his *Urchristliche Wundergeschichten,* 57–83. Theissen calls the various elements that can be found within the grid "motifs." On pp. 81–83 Theissen shows how all the possible motifs might fit together within the larger structure of a miracle story. He prefers a four-part division in which my "presentation" is divided into an "introduction" (the coming of the various actors) and an "exposition" (including any initial dialogue). Theissen's "middle" and "conclusion" are roughly equivalent to my categories of "act of healing" and "affirmation/demonstration," although he puts the basic affirmation of the healing in the "middle," a position that in some cases does seem preferable. These theoretical differences are of no great importance for the essential point I make in the main text.

[81] Some critics would include v 8 or vv 8–9 (the amazement and doubt of the man's neighbors as well as the man's own affirmation that he is the former blind man) as a sort of demonstration of the fact of the miracle as well as an initial reaction to the miracle by others (though in this case not by bystanders who witnessed the act of healing). It may be that the original story ended with some sort of demonstration or reaction that has been obscured by John's editing of the larger composition; see Martyn, *History & Theology*, 25–26.

[82] Besides the typically Johannine language and style, John's hand can be seen in (1) the depiction of the Pharisees as a juridically competent body with the authority to expel *any* Jew (including rulers, cf. 12:42) from the synagogue; (2) the expression of this state of affairs in 9:22 by a compound adjective apparently created by John (*aposynagōgos*, "cast out of the synagogue"), an adjective that appears in no other book of the NT; (3) John's "realized eschatology," expressed in the idea that Jesus the Son of Man passes judgment not on a future "last day" but on the "last day" of decision that is right now, in the moment of belief or unbelief; (4) the theme of Jesus as the light of the world, who not only gives the blind man both physical sight and the insight of faith but also passes judgment on the Pharisees, who despite their physical sight plunge further and further into spiritual blindness (9:40–41). In particular, John's depiction of the Pharisees and their authority over Judaism reflects the realignment of power-structures in Judaism after the First Jewish War and the destruction of Jerusalem in A.D. 70. It is therefore not accidental that the Fourth Gospel, among the last NT books to be written, is the first piece of Greek literature to use the adjective *aposynagōgos*. John is reflecting a new religious situation, one that did not hold true during the time of Jesus' ministry. All this is true, whether or not *aposynagōgos* and the procedure it encapsulates represent the *birkat ha-minim*, the "blessing [actually, cursing] of heretics," the twelfth benediction in the great synagogal prayer The Eighteen Benedictions (the *Shemoneh Esreh*). On this question see Martyn, *History & Theology*, 37–62; cf. Reuven Kimelman, *"Birkat Ha-Minim* and the Lack of Evidence for an Anti-Christian Jewish Prayer in Late Antiquity," *Jewish and Christian Self-Definition. Volume Two. Aspects of Judaism in the Graeco-Roman Period* (ed. E. P. Sanders, A. I. Baumgarten, and Alan Mendelson; Philadelphia: Fortress, 1981) 226–44.

[83] The disciples of Jesus have not appeared as actors in the narrative of John's Gospel since the end of chap. 6. They do not appear again as actors until the beginning of the Lazarus story in chap. 11. For the disciples in 9:2 as an addition of the Fourth Evangelist, see Fortna, *The Fourth Gospel and Its Predecessor*, 113.

[84] On this see, e.g., Martyn, *History & Theology*, 26 n. 14; Latourelle, *The Miracles of Jesus*, 225; Fortna, *The Fourth Gospel and Its Predecessor*, 109–11; von Wahlde, *The Earliest Version of John's Gospel*, 111. For Johannine style and vocabulary, esp. in vv 3b–5, see Schnackenburg, *Das Johannesevangelium*, 2. 304–7. Surveys of the views of scholars as to which verses in 9:1–7(8) existed in the primitive version of the story can be found in Reim, "Joh 9," 245; Latourelle, *The Miracles of Jesus*, 226. Dodd (*Historical Tradition*, 185–88) thinks that the pre-Johannine miracle story encompassed 9:1–7 minus v 5 and the etymology of Siloam in v 7 (though he admits John may have reshaped the dialogue material in vv 2–4). A similar view of 9:1–7 is held by Reim, who thinks, however, (echoing Bultmann) that the traditional material behind John 9 continued through a good deal of the rest of the chapter; a fair amount of tradition behind John 9 is also seen by von Wahlde. Haenchen (*John 2*, 41) takes a somewhat extreme view of the matter: he thinks that the source included the whole of chap. 9 with the exception of vv 4–5 and probably 39–41. For a critique of Haenchen that supports a source made up of vv 1–3 + 6–11, see Painter, "John and the Interpretation of the Fourth Gospel,"

31–34. Schnackenburg (p. 309) prefers a primitive story made up of vv 1–3a + 6–7; Fortna (pp. 109–10) favors vv 1 + 6–8. These variations on the insight that in 9:1–7 we have the core of the primitive miracle story plus some Johannine redaction do not affect the basic argument I make in the main text.

[85] While we cannot be sure that the miracle story began exactly in this way in the earliest tradition, there is nothing improbable in a beginning like *kai paragōn* ("and passing along"); see Dodd, *Historical Tradition*, 181. The verb *paragō* (as a participle or an indicative verb) occurs in the introductions to a number of stories in the Synoptics, including miracle stories: Mark 1:16 (the call of the first four disciples); 2:14 (the call of Levi); Matt 9:27 (the healing of two blind men); 20:30 (the healing of two blind men outside of Jericho). Moreover, *paragō* occurs nowhere else in John's Gospel; it is hardly a sign of Johannine redaction.

[86] The interpretation of the name of Siloam in v 7a by way of a folk-etymology as "the One Sent" (*ho apestalmenos*, i.e., Jesus, the one sent by the Father) betrays the hand of the Evangelist or his immediate source; see Fortna, *The Fourth Gospel and Its Predecessor*, 111–13; Latourelle, *The Miracles of Jesus*, 226. However, as Dodd (*Historical Tradition*, 184) points out, the name Siloam itself, minus its theological interpretation, probably stood in the pre-Johannine tradition and so called forth the inventive interpretation of the Evangelist. Probably the same hand that inserted the theological dialogue in 9:2–5, with its reference to the Father as the "one who sent me [Jesus]," inserted the interpretation of the pool's name as "the One Sent." The symbolism is clear: by washing in the One Sent a humanity that was spiritually blind from birth receives spiritual sight from the light of the world. Thus, on the level of Johannine editing, the story does seem to have baptismal overtones. Here I agree with Brown against Schnackenburg; see also Grigsby, "Washing," 227–35. On the possible ways of reading the Hebrew *šlḥ* and the midrashic connection of it with Gen 49:10 (even as early as Qumran), see Müller, "Joh 9,7," 251–56; Schnackenburg, *Das Johannesevangelium*, 2. 308–9.

[87] On this, see Dodd, *Historical Tradition*, 185; Schnackenburg, *Das Johannesevangelium*, 2. 309–10; Painter, "John and the Interpretation of the Fourth Gospel," 34. The use of spittle by Jesus is restricted elsewhere to two miracles in Mark (the deaf-mute in 7:31–37 and the blind man at Bethsaida in 8:22–26). But there the spittle is a direct agent of the healing; that is not the case in John 9:1 + 6–7, where it is simply used to make mud. The healing of a blind beggar is found in the Bartimaeus story (Mark 10:46–52), but there Bartimaeus, not Jesus, seizes the initiative by begging for a cure in the face of opposition from the crowd. A pool also occurs in the story of the healing of the paralyzed man at Bethesda (John 5:1–9), but there the pool pointedly plays no part in the healing. In addition, various stories of Jesus healing on the Sabbath and thus occasioning opposition from Jewish leaders can be found in the Synoptic tradition. But there the Sabbath motif is integral to the story, while in John 9 (as in John 5) the motif seems to have been added at a later stage of the tradition to provide a springboard to a dispute that was not originally part of the miracle story. In sum, the primitive form of the story of the man born blind is not derived from any single miracle story found elsewhere in the Gospels. This coheres with a position held by *A Marginal Jew* (1. 44) from the start, namely, that the Fourth Gospel is not dependent literarily on the Synoptic Gospels. For a defense of the independence of this particular miracle story from the Synoptics, see Brown, *The Gospel According to John*, 1. 378–79. For a sustained defense of the overall independence of John's Gospel from the Synoptics, see D. Moody Smith, *John among the Gospels* (Minneapolis: Fortress, 1992).

[88] Siloam in Hebrew is *šilôaḥ*; the "waters of Shiloah [= Siloam]" are mentioned in Isa 8:6.

[89] See Josephus (*J.W.* 6.7.2 §363), describing the destruction of Jerusalem by the Romans in September of A.D. 70: "On the next day, the Romans . . . set ablaze all [of the city] as far as Siloam." On this see Murphy-O'Connor, *The Holy Land*, 101.

[90] Outside of John 9:7,11, the name "Siloam" occurs in the NT only in Luke 13:4, which refers without explanation to eighteen people "who were killed when the tower in Siloam fell upon them." Fitzmyer (*The Gospel According to Luke*, 2. 1008) states: "This undoubtedly refers to a tower that formed part of the old (first) wall of ancient Jerusalem, which according to Joseph . . . turned from the east southward 'above the fountain of Siloam.' Nothing more is known about a tower there. . . ."

[91] See *m. Sukk.* 4:9. Brown (*The Gospel According to John*, 1. 327) interprets the text as referring to the fountain of Gihon, the source of the water that flowed into the pool(s) of Siloam. Gihon was situated in the Kidron Valley on the southeast side of the temple hill. Actually, as archaeological investigations have shown, there was more than one pool in the area of Siloam. On the distinction between the Lower Old Pool and the Upper Pool (shown today to tourists as the Pool of Siloam), see W. Harold Mare, "Siloam, Pool of," *Anchor Bible Dictionary* (6 vols.; New York: Doubleday, 1992) 6. 24–26.

[92] Gourgues ("L'aveugle-né," 381) argues that, at least on the level of the Evangelist's composition, the healing of the blind man does take place during the feast of tabernacles, since there is no indication of a change of time before 10:22, the feast of Hanukkah.

[93] There may be an allusion—though, granted, a remote one—to the cure of the leprosy of Naaman the Syrian, who at the command of Elisha the prophet washed seven times in the Jordan River (2 Kgs 5:10–14). Brodie ("Jesus as the New Elisha," 39–41) sees a much closer and more detailed parallel to this Elisha story, but many of his examples of similarity between John 9 and 2 Kings 5 are farfetched. Interestingly, scholars must strain for such distant allusions because the Moses and Elijah-Elisha traditions—the largest blocks of material containing man-worked miracles in the OT— contain no healing of a blind person. One might appeal to the healing of the blind Tobit; but the healing of Tobit's blindness by the medicine brought by his son Tobiah is attributed a number of times in the text to the angel Raphael; see Tob 3:17; 12:3,14. However, the opening of the eyes of the blind is a notable theme in passages in which the OT prophets speak of an eschatological future: e.g., Isa 29:18; 35:5; 42:7.

Commentators also compare the healing of the man born blind to other miracles in which Jesus heals at a distance (the daughter of the Syrophoenician woman, the centurion's servant [or the royal official's son], and the ten lepers). But in all these cases it is merely the word of Jesus that heals; the use of the concrete symbols seen in John 9 (the making of mud, the smearing on the eyes, washing it off in the pool) is unique in the Gospel stories of a cure at a distance. Moreover, unlike the other cures at a distance, in John 9 Jesus does come into direct contact with the afflicted person; only later does the cure take place at a distance.

[94] As Brown (*The Gospel According to John*, 1. 372) notes, this contrasts with most of the stories of the healing of the blind in the Synoptics, where a request is made by or on behalf of the blind. An important difference from the two healings with spittle in Mark is pointed out by Dodd (*Historical Tradition*, 183): the afflicted in the Marcan stories remain basically passive, while active cooperation and obedience are demanded of the man born blind as essential elements of the cure. Dodd goes on to observe that active cooperation in miracle stories is not a trait proper to the Fourth Gospel alone and hence need not be seen as a redactional element.

[95] The special M tradition of Matthew's Gospel probably should not be added to the list as another independent witness. As we have seen, the healing of two blind men in Matt 9:27–31 is most likely a doublet of Matt 20:29–34 (= the Bartimaeus story in Mark 10:46–52). Likewise, the passing reference to the cure of the blind and the lame by Jesus (Matt 21:14–15) after the triumphal entry into Jerusalem and the cleansing of the temple is almost certainly a Matthean addition to the Marcan narrative. As Gundry (*Matthew*, 413) remarks, "Verses 14–17 [in chap. 21] are largely distinctive and exhibit Matthew's favorite diction and habit of alluding to the OT."

[96] We will be considering only those passages that directly claim that Jesus healed leprosy. Passages that mention leprosy or a leper but are not relevant to this limited goal include the following: (1) In his missionary charge to his twelve disciples in Matt 10:8, Jesus says not only "heal the sick" (similarly Luke 9:2; cf. Mark 6:13) but also "raise the dead, cleanse lepers. . . ." That Jesus empowered his disciples to cure lepers certainly implies that he claimed to exercise the power himself. But this reference to curing lepers is probably due to Matthew's redaction of the missionary discourse. In Matt 10:8 Matthew enumerates specific types of miracles, while the Marcan and the Lucan forms of the missionary discourse lack any equivalent list. Matthew's list serves to link up the missionary discourse both with the preceding cycle of nine miracle stories in chaps. 8–9 (which includes the cleansing of a leper in 8:1–4) and with the subsequent story of the question of John the Baptist in 11:2–6 (v 2: "John, hearing in prison of the works of the Messiah . . ."; v 5: "the blind see and the lame walk, lepers are cleansed and the deaf hear . . ."). The pattern is obviously created by Matthew. Hence Matt 10:8 is of no use in the quest for the historical Jesus. (2) In his "inaugural sermon" in the synagogue at Nazareth (Luke 4:27), the Lucan Jesus refers to the cure of the leper Naaman the Syrian by the prophet Elisha (2 Kgs 5:1–14). No claim is made in this passage about Jesus doing the same, though no doubt Luke sees a connection between Jesus the miracle-working eschatological prophet and the great miracle-working prophets Elijah and Elisha. Moreover, one must reckon with the possibility that the whole scene is Luke's creative redaction of Mark 6:1–6 (see Meier, *A Marginal Jew*, 1. 269–71). (3) Mark has a passing and puzzling reference to "Simon the leper," the host of the meal at which Jesus is anointed at Bethany (Mark 14:3 = Matt 26:6; Luke omits the Marcan story but has an anointing in Galilee in the house of Simon a Pharisee, who is not called a leper [Luke 7:36,40]). Mark 14:3 could mean that Simon was a former leper cured by Jesus (so, as a possibility, Grundmann, *Das Evangelium nach Markus*, 276; rejected by Pesch, *Das Markusevangelium*, 2. 331); but, as so often, laconic Mark leaves us guessing. Other possibilities include: (a) Simon was a former leper who had recovered his health, but not by a miracle of Jesus; (b) "leper" is simply an insulting sobriquet; (c) the house formerly belonged to a leper named Simon; (d) "leper" represents a mistranslation of the Aramaic ("potter"? "the pious"? "the Essene"?). The multiplication of theories reflects the lack of hard evidence.

To increase the multiple attestation of stories about Jesus curing a leper, some authors cite the narrative in *Egerton Papyrus 2* (so Latourelle, *The Miracles of Jesus*, 89). However, as we have seen (Meier, *A Marginal Jew*, 1. 119), the story of the leper in *Egerton Papyrus 2* may instead represent an imaginative retelling of Luke 17:11–19, with traits from elsewhere in the Synoptics (e.g., a mention of an inn may come from the Parable of the Good Samaritan). The author of *Egerton Papyrus 2* may well have been working from the memory of what he had heard read and preached upon during Christian worship rather than from a text in front of him. On this see Pesch, *Jesu ureigene Taten?*, 107–13.

[97] Pesch has dedicated the major portion of a monograph to this point; see his *Jesu*

ureigene Taten?, 35–134. He summarizes his views in *Das Markusevangelium*, 1. 140-49. Pesch argues in particular against the claims of Franz Mussner, who in his *Die Wunder Jesu* argues strongly for the historicity of the two Synoptic stories of the cleansing of lepers. I think that Pesch is correct in criticizing many of the conclusions of Mussner (e.g., that Jesus' healing of the leper in Mark 1:40–45 is an "anti-Pharisaic" or "anti-rabbinic" miracle performed in anger against the injustice done the poor leper by the legalistic leaders of Israel). Mussner claims that all this highlights the "unique" nature of the miracle of Jesus, who provides the leper with proximity to God, from which he was excluded by being excluded from the Jerusalem temple. Jesus pointedly cures the leper by breaking the Mosaic Law, i.e., by touching the leper to cure him. Pesch is correct: all this reads into the Greek text of Mark 1:40–45 a great deal that simply is not there.

[98] For a treatment of "leprosy" in the Bible, see David P. Wright and Richard N. Jones, "Leprosy," *Anchor Bible Dictionary* (6 vols.; New York: Doubleday, 1992) 4. 277–82.

[99] I am well aware that there is great debate among scholars as to the time of the codification of the priestly legislation. Estimates range from the 8th or 7th century down to the 6th or 5th century. In any event, while I lean toward a 6th-century dating for the *codification* of the material, I readily admit that much of the material contained in the priestly code may go back in some form to the preexilic period.

[100] Even the proper name Jesus is lacking; the only exception is the passing reference to Moses (v 44) when Jesus directs the healed man to offer the sacrifice prescribed by Leviticus. As we shall see, the use of only pronouns for the two actors occasions a slight problem of interpretation in v 45.

[101] See, e.g., Koch, *Die Bedeutung*, 73.

[102] So Pesch, *Jesu ureigene Taten?*, 71; Koch, *Die Bedeutung*, 73.

[103] For prescriptions detailing the separation of the leper from ordinary life, see Lev 13:45–46; and the comments on them by Josephus in *Ag. Ap.* 1.31 §281–83; cf. *J.W.* 5.5.6 §227; *Ant.* 3.11.3 §261 and §265–68. The great concern Jews had about "leprosy" in persons, clothing, and houses can be seen in the entire tractate of the Mishna devoted to the question: *Nega'im* (translated by Danby as "Leprosy-Signs"). Thus, the basic stance of Israel vis-à-vis leprosy remained essentially the same from OT times through the 1st century A.D. (the Synoptic Gospels, Josephus) to the Mishna (end of 2d century A.D.).

[104] Various attempts have been made to translate *katharizō* as "declare clean" instead of "make clean." In other words, Jesus the layman is asked to assume (or usurp) the role of a levitical priest in declaring the leper clean. Such an explanation does violence to the core of the miracle story as it stands, for (1) 1:42 clearly says that "the leprosy departed from him," and therefore the immediately following *kai ekatharisthē* can mean only "and he was made clean"; (2) as can be seen from other miracle stories, the stretching out of Jesus' hand is understood as a curative gesture. On all this, see Taylor, *The Gospel According to St. Mark*, 185. Others, following Johannes Weiss, find the meaning "declare clean" not in the present text of Mark but in the historical event or the earlier form of the story behind the Marcan text; for one such attempt, see C. H. Cave, "The Leper: Mark 1. 40–45," *NTS* 25 (1978–79) 245–50. Cave fails to supply any sure documentation that Jewish laymen in Galilee during the time of Jesus would have been asked or would have attempted to declare lepers clean in the absence of a priest. More to the point, Cave gives no cogent explanation of how or why such a nonmiraculous

story was passed down in the early Christian tradition until such time as it was transformed into a miracle story.

[105] The originality of the reading "and kneeling" (*kai gonypetōn*) is disputed, since the manuscript evidence is divided and the verse seems overloaded. *UBSGNT*[3] gives the reading a "D" (very uncertain) rating and puts it in the main text but in brackets. Such weighty witnesses as Vaticanus, Bezae, and Washingtonianus omit it; yet other important manuscripts, such as Sinaiticus and Koridethi have it. Perhaps one of the best arguments for originality is that both Matthew and Luke have equivalent (though differently worded) expressions at this point in the text: *prosekynei* ("he prostrated himself in worship," Matt 8:1) and *pesōn epi prosōpon* ("falling on his face," Luke 5:12). Both Taylor (*The Gospel According to St. Mark*, 187) and Pesch (*Das Markusevangelium*, 141) argue for retaining the phrase; on the whole question, see Metzger, *A Textual Commentary*, 76.

[106] Here too there is a problem of choosing between two starkly different readings in the description of Jesus' emotion in 1:41: "moved with compassion" (*splagchnistheis*) or "angered" (*orgistheis*). An odd aspect of the debate is that most critical editions of the Greek NT place *splagchnistheis* in the main text, while many commentators on Mark's Gospel (e.g., Taylor, Pesch, Guelich) prefer "angered" when they interpret the text. This split corresponds to the divergence between "internal" and "external" arguments. The "external" argument stresses that the vast majority of ancient manuscripts favor "moved with compassion," while "angered" is supported only by Bezae, a few Old Latin manuscripts, and Ephraem (yet all Syriac versions support "moved with compassion"). On the other hand, "internal" considerations favor "angered": (1) It is the more difficult reading and the one more likely to have been changed to the opposite reading by later Christian scribes for reasons of piety. (2) It seems to correspond better in tone to the likewise difficult participle in v 43 *embrimēsamenos* (literally, "snorting," "puffing"). (3) The participle is omitted by both Matthew (8:3) and Luke (5:13)—an omission much more understandable if the participle referred to anger rather than to mercy. Still, such considerations are not conclusive: (1) Mark 3:5 and 10:14 present Jesus as angry or indignant, yet later scribes did not correct the text. (2) The strange *embrimēsamenos* in v 43 may have been the very factor that caused some scribes to supply a correlative *orgistheis* ("angered") in v 41. (3) Some critics suggest that the alternate readings are due to confusion over two similar-sounding words in Aramaic.

Then, too, there is the whole problem of explaining what "angered" means in this context. Opinions vary widely (see, e.g., Guelich, *Mark 1–8:26*, 74): Jesus is angry because the leper breaks the Mosaic Law by approaching him and exposing him to possible defilement; Jesus is angry at the injustice done to this poor man by a legalistic system that has ostracized him; Jesus is angry at the power of evil (or the devil) seen in the man's illness and ostracism; Jesus is stirring up the charismatic powers within himself that enable him to perform the miracle. The list could go on. Since the text-critical question is far from settled, since the meaning of *orgistheis* (if accepted as the original reading) is far from clear, and since most importantly I think it very doubtful that a historian should take either *orgistheis* (alternately *splagchnistheis*) or *embrimēsamenos* as a reliable description of the original historical event, I do not make anything of these participles in my consideration of the story's historicity.

[107] The verb *embrimaomai* in v 43 (literally, "to snort") takes on the metaphorical meaning of "to scold," "to rebuke," "to warn sternly," "to be furious with," "to be indignant at." That some strong negative emotion is indicated is clear; but, as with *orgistheis* in v 41 (if that be the original reading), the reason for the strong negative emotion is by no means obvious, and explanations vary widely among commentators;

see, e.g., Guelich, *Mark 1–8:26*, 74–75. Since this emotional reaction occurs after the healing, explanations based on Jesus' anger at the leper's illegal approach, or anger at the power of evil in the world, or the stirring up of Jesus' miraculous power within himself all fall by the wayside. Some suggest that Jesus already senses that the leper will not obey his order not to tell others, but nothing in the text or parallel texts in Mark suggests this. Relying on E. E. Bishop, Jeremias (*New Testament Theology*, 92 n. 1) suggests that the participle represents "the oriental sign-language for a command to be silent": "while the hand is placed on the lips, air is blown in puffs through the teeth. . . ." Stretching a point, Kee ("Aretalogy and Gospel," 402–22, esp. 418) tries to make *embrimaomai* equivalent to the Aramaic *gĕʿar* ("to rebuke") as a term for bringing a demon under control; the following phrase in Greek, *exebalen auton*, would then mean not that Jesus drove away the man but that he expelled the demon causing the evil. That this introduces the note of possession into a story that has not mentioned it and that the expelling of the demon would take place after the man is emphatically said to be cured of the leprosy make this solution highly unlikely—even apart from the doubtful explanation of *embrimaomai*. As with *orgistheis*, so with *embrimēsamenos*: in the face of the vast array of debatable interpretations, and more importantly in the face of serious doubt that this participle can be taken to report the exact emotion of Jesus in the original historical situation, I refrain from using the word when weighing the question of historicity. This approach is a fortiori necessary if one agrees with Koch (*Die Bedeutung*, 76–77) that v 43 is probably Marcan redaction.

[108] Koch (*Die Bedeutung*, 74–75) stresses the difficulty of distinguishing tradition from redaction in Mark 1:40–45, but thinks that the clearest case of Marcan redaction is v 45. He points to (1) Mark's interest in the spreading of the report about Jesus, seen already in 1:28, and (2) the dialectic between people coming to Jesus and the futile withdrawal of Jesus depicted in Mark's summary and transitional statements in 3:7–12 and 6:30–33.

[109] For v 44a as redactional, see Koch, *Die Bedeutung*, 75–76.

[110] The lack of a noun for the leper or Jesus in v 45 (everything is expressed with pronouns) makes the meaning less than pellucid. But by analogy with Mark's other stories of healing where the healed person disobeys Jesus' command to be silent, v 45a ("but he, going out [*ho de exelthōn*], began to proclaim much and spread the word") most likely refers to the leper, while v 45b ("so that he could no longer come openly into a city") clearly refers to Jesus. The attempt to make *ho de exelthōn* in v 45a refer to Jesus is forced; it is expecting too much to demand that the reader connect it with *exēlthen* in 1:35 and *exēlthon* in 1:38, both in the preceding story.

[111] See the similar case of the story of the deaf and mute man (Mark 7:31–35), concluded by vv 36–37: the more Jesus commands silence, the more people make the miracle known.

[112] While commentators disagree on the exact extent of Marcan redaction, there is widespread agreement that Mark 1:40–45 is not a purely Marcan creation but rather a traditional story taken over by Mark with some redactional additions. Even Pesch (*Jesu ureigene Taten?*, 76–87), who considers the story a pure invention of the early church and not a reflection of some event in the life of Jesus, thinks that the tradition antedates Mark, whose redactional additions are minimal.

[113] For a full-length study of the relevant questions, see Wilhelm Bruners, *Die Reinigung der zehn Aussätzigen und die Heilung des Samariters Lk 17,11–19* (FB 23; Stuttgart: KBW, 1977); his treatment of introductory questions can be found on pp. 9–123. Other

substantive discussions can be found in Pesch, *Jesu ureigene Taten?*, 114–34; Busse, *Die Wunder des Propheten Jesus*, 313–27. See also Bultmann, *Geschichte*, 33; Dibelius, *Formgeschichte*, 117–18; van der Loos, *The Miracles of Jesus*, 494–503; Otto Glombitza, "Der dankbare Samariter. Luk. xvii 11–19," *NovT* 11 (1969) 242–46; Hans Dieter Betz, "The Cleansing of the Ten Lepers (Luke 17:11–19)," *JBL* 90 (1971) 314–28; Grundmann, *Das Evangelium nach Lukas*, 334–37; Ernst, *Das Evangelium nach Lukas*, 482–84; Marshall, *The Gospel of Luke*, 648–52; Fitzmyer, *The Gospel According to Luke*, 2. 1148–56; Latourelle, *The Miracles of Jesus*, 199–203.

[114] My English rendering is an attempt to paraphrase but hopefully not misrepresent the concise German phrase of Bruners: "nachgeahmte prophetische Erzählung mit überbietendem Charakter" (*Die Reinigung*, 118–22).

[115] See Pesch, *Jesu ureigene Taten?*, 124; Betz, "The Cleansing," 317. I do not agree with Betz's view that the story means to correct a common interpretation of miracles as identical to the experience of Christian salvation. Betz claims that the first part of the story, the miracle proper, is meant to be a satirical parody of a story of the healing of a leper, such as we find in Mark 1:40–45 (pp. 324–28). Modern concerns about miracles are creeping into the exegesis here.

[116] See the remarks by Fitzmyer, *The Gospel According to Luke*, 2. 1150–51.

[117] Hence the title of Bruners's monograph: all ten lepers receive physical cleansing from leprosy (*Reinigung*), but only the Samaritan receives the fullness of healing that is also salvation (*Heilung*). See also Fitzmyer, *The Gospel According to Luke*, 2. 1152; he rightly criticizes Betz ("The Cleansing," 324–28), who pushes the distinction between physical cleansing and full salvation too far by making the distinction part of an early-Christian polemic about miracles.
Along with the key word *pistis* in v 19 ("faith" in the full Christian sense), the "conversion" or "coming to faith" of the Samaritan may be symbolized by the fact that he alone "sees" (*idōn* in v 15) that he is cured (with the eyes of faith) and therefore "turns around" to return to Jesus with praise and thanksgiving (*hypestrepsen*, the physical turning being symbolic of conversion). Since the climactic "your faith has *saved* [and not just cleansed] you" is essential to the two-part structure and two-part message of the story, I do not think that the declaration is awkward or misplaced at the end of the whole narrative or that it has to be attributed to the redactional pen of Luke. On this point I agree with Roloff (*Das Kerygma*, 157–58), Marshall (*The Gospel of Luke*, 652), and Bruners (*Die Reinigung*, 293–95) against Pesch (*Jesu ureigene Taten?*, 121–22), Ernst (*Das Evangelium nach Lukas*, 484), and Fitzmyer (*The Gospel According to Luke*, 2. 1156).

[118] While only the Samaritan leper is said to have the "faith" that saves (*pistis* in the full Christian sense), all ten lepers must be presumed to have had some initial trust in Jesus as a miracle-worker; otherwise one cannot explain their obedience to Jesus' command to go and show themselves to the priests. See Fitzmyer, *The Gospel According to Luke*, 2. 1154–55.

[119] Bultmann, *Geschichte*, 33: "The story of Mark 1:40–45 is therefore used to create an ideal scene. . . ."

[120] Pesch, *Jesu ureigene Taten?*, 114–27. To a great degree, Pesch's position is an elaboration of the terse statements of Bultmann.

[121] In the MT the story is designated 2 Kgs 5:1–27; the equivalent enumeration in the LXX (used by some commentators) is 4 Kgdms 5:1–27.

[122] Also in favor of a Lucan creation is Busse, *Die Wunder des Propheten Jesus*, 319–23.

While elements of the Naaman story in 2 Kings 5 are certainly present (Naaman and the Samaritan are foreigners healed by an Israelite holy man, there is a delay in the healing and the healing is indirect, and the foreigner returns to the holy man to give thanks), the parallels can be overplayed. After all, we are dealing in 2 Kings 5, Mark 1, and Luke 17 with an Israelite miracle-worker performing the extraordinary miracle of cleansing a leper; parallels in vocabulary and motifs naturally arise from the form-critical category the three stories share. In fairness one should also notice the differences between Luke 17:11–19 and 2 Kings 5: (1) While Luke elsewhere mentions Elisha the prophet cleansing Naaman (Luke 4:27), there is no explicit reference to Elisha or Naaman here. (2) While elsewhere in Luke Jesus is hailed as a prophet for his Elijah-like or Elisha-like miracles (7:16), he is not so hailed here; cf. Fitzmyer, *The Gospel According to Luke*, 2. 1150–51. (3) While there is a delay in the performance of the miracle in 2 Kings 5 and Luke 17:11–19, the delay is of a different nature and for a different ostensible reason in Luke. (4) While 2 Kings 5 ends in a punitive miracle (the greedy servant Gehazi has Naaman's leprosy transferred to him and his descendants), no such punitive miracle connected with healing occurs here or anywhere else in the Gospel tradition. For a brief summary of similarities to 2 Kings 5, see Pesch, *Jesu ureigene Taten?*, 127; a much more detailed treatment is given by Bruners, *Die Reinigung*, 103–20; cf. 297–306. Inner-Lucan contacts include 4:27; 5:12–16; 9:51–55; 10:29–37; Acts 8. One might also point to two other miracle stories in the great journey narrative that are developed in the direction of apophthegms: the bent-over woman (13:10–17) and the man with dropsy (14:1–6). In short, it would be a mistake to explain Luke 17:11–19 simply in terms of one source or influence.

[123] Van der Loos, *The Miracles of Jesus*, 494–503; Latourelle, *The Miracles of Jesus*, 201–2. The suggestion, mentioned in passing by Grundmann (*Das Evangelium nach Lukas*, 335), that originally the story of the grateful Samaritan was simply a parable (e.g., like the parable of the good Samaritan) has not been taken up by most critics, and understandably so. There is nothing in the Lucan text or in a plausible tradition history based on the Lucan text to point in that direction.

[124] For a survey of proposed solutions, see Bruners, *Die Reinigung*, 149–63; Pesch, *Jesu ureigene Taten?*, 117–19. That *dia meson* is the original reading (the *lectio difficilior*, witnessed by [apparently] papyrus 75, Vaticanus, Sinaiticus, and Codex Regius) is admitted today by almost all commentators; on the textual question see *Die Reinigung*, 50–53. To be precise, *dia meson Samareias kai Galilaias* involves two distinct problems: (1) *dia* with the accusative usually has a causative meaning; the idea of "through" is usually expressed by *dia* with the genitive. However, there are rare cases of *dia* + the accusative in the sense of "through" in classical Greek poetry and Hellenistic Greek prose; see Fitzmyer, *The Gospel According to Luke*, 2. 1153. There is no other clear case of this usage in the NT, and certainly not in Luke-Acts. (2) The larger problem is that it makes no sense geographically to say that Jesus was passing through the middle of Samaria and Galilee on his way up to Jerusalem. Commentators often interpret the phrase to mean that Jesus was traveling (from west to east?) along the border between Samaria and Galilee; yet Pesch (*Jesu ureigene Taten?*, 118 n. 13) questions whether this translation of *dia meson Samareias kai Galilaias* is philologically possible. Even more pressing is the question whether it is possible given Luke's presentation of Jesus' journey to Jerusalem, solemnly announced and begun in 9:51–56. See the discussion below.

[125] Conzelmann, *The Theology of St Luke*, 68–71. Conzelmann suggests that Luke "appears to think of Galilee as inland, but adjoining Judaea, and of Samaria as being to the north of Judaea . . ." (p. 70). This is not impossible. But to make this theory work Conzelmann must interpret 9:51–55 and what follows as meaning that, after being

rejected at the border of Samaria, Jesus "returns to Galilee, where he continues his ministry, now in the context of the journey; then he goes to Judaea, which is also an old sphere of activity . . ." (p. 71); similarly, Marshall, *The Gospel of Luke*, 404. The problem with this approach is that nothing in 9:51–55 or in the following narratives explicitly states that Jesus ever returned to Galilee after entering Samaria. Indeed, with the exception of our problematic 17:11, Galilee is never mentioned during the whole of the great journey narrative, though admittedly individual stories would fit better in either Galilee or Perea. In contrast, Samaria or Samaritans are mentioned in Luke 9:52; 10:33 (in the parable of the good Samaritan); 17:11; and 17:16. The natural sense of the flow of the narrative is that, once the Galilean ministry comes to an end in 9:51–52, "Jesus goes from Galilee or the country of the Jews to Jerusalem not *via* Perea (as in Mark and Matthew), but he heads instead for the city of destiny [i.e., Jerusalem] through the land that symbolizes opposition, Samaria . . ." (Fitzmyer, *The Gospel According to Luke*, 1. 824). This is not to deny that Luke has a somewhat confused sense of the geography of Palestine and the rulers of individual sections thereof (hence the reference to Herod Antipas in 13:31–32); but, in my view, nothing in chaps. 9–19 justifies Conzelmann's escape hatch of a return to Galilee after 9:51–55.

[126] One plausible explanation of how the present reading arose is given by Pesch, *Jesu ureigene Taten?*, 118–19: The presence of nine Jews in the group of ten lepers plus the presence of the phrase "of Galilee" in the description of the region may suggest that originally the tradition told of a cleansing of a group of lepers by Jesus in Galilee. Luke has added "of Samaria and" to the statement of venue because he has chosen to place the story of the ten lepers in the great journey narrative, i.e., after Jesus leaves Galilee and enters Samaria. Pesch also suggests (perhaps less cogently) that Luke keeps the reference to Galilee because the next pericope (17:20–37) begins with a question posed by the Pharisees.

[127] Pesch (*Jesu ureigene Taten?*, 118) rightly observes: "The idea that he [Luke] is responsible for the positioning of both [place-]names (in the order Samaria—Galilee) cannot be made plausible." This is one of the major problems of Bruners's thesis that Luke created the whole of 17:11–19; Bruners never adequately explains why Luke, with no impetus from the tradition, would have invented such a strange and indeed unintelligible phrase as *dia meson Samareias kai Galilaias*. Glombitza ("Der dankbare Samariter," 244–46) gives a bizarre interpretation of the geographical phrase by mixing allegory worthy of the patristic age with existentialistic meditations worthy of Bultmann. The phrase "through the middle of Samaria and Galilee" is taken to express the stand that Jesus takes between the various fronts of this world. Christian existence moves not on the level of this-worldly programs (e.g., various messianic expectations); rather it is life lived in totally individual responsibility, a life lived by the individual as one-who-receives. Similarly, Jesus stands between Samaria's expectation of a messiah as a Moses *redivivus* and Israel's expectation of a messiah as the Davidic king, prophet, and high priest. Glombitza's article is a sober reminder to all hermeneutists of how odd existentialistic interpretation looks a quarter-of-a-century later. Nothing ages faster than relevance. The "cutting edge" of scholarship at any given moment often turns out to be the sharp cliff of Gerasa, off of which academic lemmings keep hurling themselves.

[128] Luke alone has people address Jesus as "Master" (*epistatēs*); indeed, he alone uses the word in the NT. Hence what is un-Lucan here is not the word but rather its presence in the mouths of people who are not formal disciples and who use it together with the proper name Jesus. The strange combination may arise from Lucan redaction of L material. For disciples addressing Jesus with the vocative form *epistata*, see Luke

(*ēgeiren autēn kratēsas tēs cheiros*), the symbolism of Jesus raising up the believer may be intended.

[137] Serving the meal functions first of all within the form-critical structure of a miracle story as the demonstration of the cure. Some (e.g., Latourelle, *The Miracles of Jesus*, 81) would also see in the verb *diakoneō* ("to serve") a symbolic reference to service in the ecclesial community. But granted the context of a woman in her home on the Sabbath after the synagogue service, the idea of serving the Sabbath meal is quite natural; seeing some further symbolic meaning may be reading too much into the spare text. Moreover, *diakoneō* with a clear sense of service to the ecclesial community is of its nature rare in the Four Gospels; perhaps Luke 22:26–27 provides the only example. Instead of reading a great amount of symbolism into the text (e.g., Peter's house symbolizes the church), one should rather focus on the terse and sober nature of the story. Specific Christian and christological concerns and titles are lacking, as is the common motif of astonishment or "choral" acclamation concluding a miracle story of healing. The spare narrative plus the unusual concrete details move Pesch (*Das Markusevangelium*, 1. 131–32) to argue for the historicity of the story. In my view, these considerations, minus multiple attestation, are not sufficient to form a judgment on the matter.

[138] However, one should not push this point too far. One is at a loss to understand Latourelle's apologetic argument for the historicity of the story (*The Miracles of Jesus*, 83): ". . . why keep this mention of Simon's 'mother-in-law,' a figure who elicits no special sympathy? . . . We know, moreover, that women, even those in the group of disciples, were not particularly esteemed (Lk 24:11); yet the recipient of this miracle is not only Peter's mother-in-law, but a 'woman.' " How's that again?

[139] Meier, *A Marginal Jew*, 1. 180–82.

[140] So Cranfield, *The Gospel According to Saint Mark*, 182; Taylor, *The Gospel According to St. Mark*, 289; and apparently Robert H. Gundry, *Mark. A Commentary on His Apology for the Cross* (Grand Rapids: Eerdmans, 1993) 266–88. This also seems to be the stance of Mann (*Mark*, 284), who, following Taylor, claims that the "unique" (!) placing of an episode within an episode "suggests that it rests upon a very early tradition." (Actually, what is unique here is the intercalation of two *miracle* stories in Mark.) The episode has, says Mann, "the air of an unreconstructed oral tradition . . . vividly recalled by an eyewitness." Not surprisingly, Bultmann (*Geschichte*, 228–29) holds that the intertwining of the two stories does not go back to the original events. What is surprising is that Schmidt (*Der Rahmen der Geschichte Jesu*, 148) claims that the dovetailing of the two accounts is an accurate recollection of what happened.

It should be emphasized that not all conservative critics maintain that the intertwining of the two stories mirrors historical occurrence. Lane (*The Gospel According to Mark*, 189) quite rightly (as opposed to Mann's erroneous claim) points out that "the structural device of intercalating one incident within another is paralleled by other instances in which Mark uses the device of anticipation." On Marcan intercalation, see my remarks below in the main text. Guelich (*Mark 1–8:26*, 291–92) is especially helpful in laying out all the differences in style and content that make it unlikely that the two miracles were originally narrated together—to say nothing of their having occurred together. Guelich also reviews the debate over whether the two stories were already joined in a pre-Marcan miracle source or were intercalated for the first time by Mark himself. Those who favor a connection in the pre-Marcan source (e.g., Bultmann, ibid., 228; Dibelius, ibid., 220; apparently Guelich, ibid., 292) might argue that the incident of the woman with a hemorrhage supplies the necessary element of delay, allowing

Jairus' daughter to die before Jesus arrives at her house; it also heightens the suspense of the narrative as a whole. Yet Mark displays the technique of intercalation in nonmiraculous stories as well; hence the question cannot be resolved with certitude. Fortunately, the question of the origin of the intercalation does not affect decisively the basic problem of the historicity of each story taken by itself.

[141] So Gundry, *Mark*, 288.

[142] Guelich (*Mark 1–8:26*, 296–97) says guardedly: "She [the woman with a hemorrhage] had suffered for 'twelve years,' another perhaps less than coincidental point of contact with the Jairus story. . . ." I think it more likely, though, that the presence of the number 12 in each story is a mere coincidence. It is possible that the presence of this number in both stories was one of the factors that over time brought the two stories together in the oral tradition or in the pre-Marcan collection of miracle stories. In favor of the presence of the number 12 being purely coincidental in the two stories is Schmidt, *Der Rahmen der Geschichte Jesu*, 148; and Gundry (*Mark*, 284), who notes that there is no demonstrable theological symbolism in either mention of the number and that the points of reference (the woman's years of suffering, the age of the child) are quite different.

[143] In dealing with the faith of the woman with a hemorrhage, Lane (*The Gospel According to Mark*, 193) theologizes thus: "By an act of sovereign will God determined to honor the woman's faith in spite of the fact that it was tinged with ideas which bordered on magic." Aune ("Magic in Early Christianity," 1536) brusquely replies: "The ideas expressed in the story of the woman's healing do not border on magic, they are of the essence of Graeco-Roman magical notions."

[144] Dropsy or edema is not so much an illness in itself as rather a symptom of a serious illness. Fitzmyer defines edema as "an abnormal accumulation of serous fluids in connective tissues or cavities of the body accompanied by swelling, distention, or defective circulation" (*The Gospel According to Luke*, 2. 1041).—On Luke's placement of the story within his redactional framework, see Busse, *Die Wunder des Propheten Jesus*, 313–15.

[145] Fitzmyer (*The Gospel According to Luke*, 2. 1041) prefers to call this an argument a pari rather than a fortiori "because a human being (a child) is already part of the comparison." The phrase "a son or an ox" in v 5 struck ancient scribes as well as modern commentators as strange; hence there are a number of textual variants as well as modern emendations. But "a son or an ox" has strong early attestation (papyrus 45, papyrus 75, Alexandrinus, Vaticanus, and a good deal of the later Koine text-tradition) and is also the *lectio difficilior*, all the other textual readings being obvious attempts to make the verse read more smoothly. See Metzger, *Textual Commentary*, 164.

[146] I say "almost everyone" because there seems to have been some dispute over this very issue among observant Jews around the turn of the era. The Essene group or groups that stand behind the *Damascus Document* took an extreme view: "No one is to help an animal give birth on the Sabbath day. [Even] if the animal drops its newborn into a cistern or a pit [or alternately: even if the newborn falls into a cistern or a pit], no one is to draw it out on the Sabbath" (CD 11:13–14). In Luke 14:5 as well as in Matt 12:11 Jesus is presented as taking the diametrically opposite point of view and presupposing that his audience would agree with him. Apparently on this issue Jesus, the common people, and the Pharisees would have basically united. The Mishna, redacted at the end of the 2d century A.D., records a view more lenient than that of the *Damascus Document* at least with regard to giving help to an animal giving birth: "They

may not deliver the young of cattle on a Festival-day, but they may give help to the dam" (m. Šabb. 18:3 in Danby's translation; Neusner's translation renders the second clause: ". . . but they help out"). While Jesus is dealing with the question raised in the *Damascus Document* rather than the one in the Mishna, one may surmise that on the *hălākâ* in question he stands on the same side as the humane tradition enshrined in the Mishna, reflecting probably the approach of at least some of the Pharisees. Yet at other times, e.g., on the question of divorce, Jesus was apparently closer to the radical or extreme view of the Essenes, or at least some of them.

Here we have an initial warning not to take a simplistic view of "Jesus and the Law"—a subject to which we must return in a later chapter. It would seem that on some issues Jesus would have struck many Jews of his day as "humane" and "liberal" (e.g., Sabbath observance); on other issues he would have struck them as extremely strict (e.g., divorce). One can only guess that perhaps some Jews of Jesus' day (to say nothing of Christians since) might have wished Jesus to have been more stringent on the former and more lenient on the latter question. In any case, sweeping assertions about Jesus and the Law should be carefully avoided. Individual cases must be judged on their own merits.

Apart from the major issues here, there is a curious minor point: the agreement-and-disagreement in wording between CD 11:13–14 on the one hand and Luke 14:5 ‖ Matt 12:11 on the other. CD 11:13–14 mentions falling into a cistern (*bôr*) or a pit (*pahat*); Luke 14:5 speaks of falling into a well (*phrear*), while Matt 12:11 speaks of falling into a pit (*bothynos*). The coincidence is striking. But, rather than engage in highly dubious speculation about connections in the oral or written stages of the Qumran and NT material, I think it more likely that the same Palestinian agrarian milieu, acquainted with recurring problems of this type—plus the religious concern of pious Jews about proper interpretation and observance of the law in concrete cases (*hălākâ*)— would lead at times to such coincidences of issues and even of wording. There were just so many different types of holes in the ground that young animals could fall into. Moreover, a *phrear* can also mean a pit or a shaft; and the Hebrew *gēb* (pit or ditch), while usually rendered by *bothynos* in the LXX, is rendered once by *phrear*. This is not surprising, since a cistern is simply a pit dug and equipped for the special purpose of catching and retaining rainwater.

The similarities yet differences between Luke 14:5 and Matt 12:11 are more puzzling still. Some have suggested that both evangelists lifted a saying from Q and inserted it into different-yet-similar stories about healing on the Sabbath. More likely, I think, is a stray oral tradition (possibly going back to an actual saying of Jesus) that was known in variant forms by Matthew and Luke. But I am leery of engaging in speculation about Aramaic wordplays (*bĕʿîrāʾ* [ox, cattle], *bêrāʾ* [well, pit], and *bĕrāʾ* [son]), as does Lohse ("Jesu Worte über den Sabbat," 86–87).

[147] Neirynck ("Jesus and the Sabbath," 227–70, esp. 230) thinks that Luke 14:1–6 is "almost completely due to Lukan redaction. The dependence of Lk XIV upon Mk III, 1–6 is especially relevant and attempts to reconstruct a Q passage are based on a false evaluation of the similarities with the Matthean redaction of the pericope of the man with the withered hand (XII, 9–14)." Critics like Lohse ("Jesu Worte über den Sabbat," 79–89, esp. 81) and Roloff (*Das Kerygma*, 66–69) consider Luke 14:1–6 to have been created by the early Christian community (i.e., a *Gemeindebildung*), though Lohse (p. 84) allows that a saying like Luke 14:5 may go back to the historical Jesus. Lohse claims that the formulation of the rhetorical question (*tis ex hymōn*) has no precise rabbinic parallel and reflects Jesus' characteristic style; he sees in this a sign of a genuine word of Jesus. Fitzmyer (*The Gospel According to Luke*, 2. 1038–40) examines all the arguments

for and against the historicity of Luke 14:1–6, but makes no final judgment on the matter.

[148] Busse, *Die Wunder des Propheten Jesus*, 305–7; but he considers the stray logion in 14:5 traditional material, as is seen from a comparison with Matt 12:11 and Luke 13:15 (pp. 308–10).

[149] Note that Luke 14:5 has to argue a pari instead of a fortiori, since the example offered for consideration includes "a son."

[150] Bultmann, *Geschichte*, 10.

[151] See above for my remarks on Mark 3:1–6 and Luke 13:10–17. Admittedly, Luke 13:10–17 and 14:1–6 would supply slightly more of a basis for objections from punctilious observers of the law, since in the two Lucan stories Jesus touches the person to be healed, while in Mark 3:1–6 he literally *does* nothing, effecting the cure simply by a command. Actually, in Luke 14:4 all we are told is that Jesus, "taking hold [of the man], healed him." Sanders (*Jewish Law*, 22) seems not to consider Jesus' act of taking hold of the man equivalent to work in any sense of the word. In any event, as Sanders rightly points out (ibid., 18–23), it is unlikely that ordinary Jewish peasants would have been greatly disturbed by minor acts of kindness or aid to the sick on the Sabbath.

[152] On the problem of the geographical references, see Guelich, *Mark 1–8:26*, 391–92.

[153] On the "bread section" and Mark's theology, see the treatment of the healing of the blind man at Bethsaida above.

[154] Words occurring only here in Mark's Gospel include *mogilalon* ("speaking with difficulty," only here in the NT), *apolambanō* ("take aside"), *daktylos* ("finger"), *stenazō* (only here in the Four Gospels), *ephphatha* (only here in the NT), *dianoigō* ("open"), *anoigō* ("open"), *desmos* ("bond," "fetter"), *orthōs* ("rightly," "correctly"), *hyperperissōs* ("beyond all measure," only here in the NT). In addition, *ptyō* occurs again in Mark only in the similar miracle story of the blind man at Bethsaida (Mark 8:23; the only other occurrence in the NT is in the healing of the man born blind in John 9:6); *anablepō* occurs again in Mark only in the feeding of the five thousand (6:41). In short, this is a remarkably large amount of non-Marcan vocabulary for one compact seven-verse story (actually, six verses if one omits Jesus' itinerary in v 31).

[155] For the distinction between miracle and magic along the sliding spectrum or continuum of religious experience, see above in Chapter 18.

[156] As already noted, the action of Jesus in John 9:6 is not quite the same, since Jesus spits on the ground to form clay or mud that he then applies to the blind beggar's eyes as a symbol of the blindness that keeps him from seeing, a blindness that he subsequently washes away in the pool of Siloam. Hence, there is no *direct application* of the spittle to the man's face as the agent effecting the healing.

[157] The terminology is different in John 11:41: *ēren tous ophthalmous anō* (literally: "he raised [his] eyes upwards").

[158] The difficulty in interpreting the sighing is that the verb *stenazō* ("to sigh" in 7:34) never occurs again in the NT in the context of a miracle story, though other verbs of emotion such as *embrimaomai* or *orgizō* ("to snort" in John 11:38, "to be angry" in Mark 1:41 [Codex Bezae]) appear at times in miracle stories. In these latter cases some critics see the arousal of the supernatural power of the charismatic miracle-worker, but this is far from certain.

[159] The usual view among exegetes is that *ephphatha* represents a relic from the Aramaic form of the Jesus tradition and perhaps from an actual word of the historical Jesus. However, a revisionist view is championed by Fred L. Horton, Jr., in his article "Nochmals *ephphatha* in Mk 7:34," *ZNW* 77 (1986) 101–8. Horton suggests that *ephphatha* (and likewise *talitha koum* in Mark 5:41) is a magical word, similar to those seen in the Greek magical papyri, and was inserted secondarily into the Greek text of the miracle story by a redactor. As I indicated when treating the ancient problem of miracles, what stands out for any reader of ancient texts is the massive difference between the magical formulas preserved in the corpus of Greek magical papyri and the miracle stories of the Gospels. Horton must gloss over these differences by appealing to the fact that the Gospel miracle stories come from an earlier century than the Greek magical papyri (though that is not true of *all* the papyri) and from a Palestinian milieu. But Horton's own admission that the two Aramaic phrases in the Marcan miracle stories are syntactically meaningful while the Semitic words in the magical papyri are not is a fatal weakness to his own position, a weakness that no amount of special pleading and hypothesis-building can overcome. He cannot explain away—or create genuine parallels between—the two different types of literature.

Against Horton's position, a number of points may be noted about *ephphatha* and *talitha koum* in particular: (1) Horton suggests, without any proof, that *ephphatha* and *koum* existed in the 1st century A.D. as magical commands well-known to the Greek speaking world. Horton then has to suppose that by a remarkable coincidence the pre-Marcan (?) redactor happened to be dealing with two miracle stories that just happened to contain the commands "be opened" and "arise," commands that thus coincided with the Aramaic magical commands in circulation. To make all of this work, Horton also has to suppose that in the story of the daughter of Jairus the redactor happened to know enough Aramaic to supply *talitha* along with *koum*, while ignoring the authoritative "I say to you." This is to pile one unlikely hypothesis on top of another. (2) The two phrases *ephphatha* and *talitha koum* cannot be identified with various unintelligible foreign words or strings of nonsense syllables found in the magical papyri and some pagan miracle stories. This is all the more evident if one takes the usual view that the Aramaic phrases reflect the time when the whole stories circulated in Aramaic form. When the Gospel stories of the deaf-mute and the daughter of Jairus circulated in the Aramaic tradition, the Aramaic words were, needless to say, *not* foreign words and were immediately intelligible. When the Aramaic phrases were retained in these two miracle stories when the stories were translated into Greek, care was taken to include a Greek translation of the Aramaic words. Therefore, even in the Greek text, the Aramaic words were never some unintelligible mumbo-jumbo. There is no evidence that the Greek miracle story ever circulated without a Greek translation of the Aramaic phrase. (3) The word *ephphatha* is the only case of an Aramaic word appearing in a Marcan miracle of healing. If, according to Horton, some otherwise unidentified redactor wished to introduce magical Aramaic formulas into Christian miracle stories, why did he do so only here? (4) The Marcan tradition equally retains Aramaic phrases of Jesus outside of miracle stories: the prayer beginning with *'abbā'* in Gethsemane (Mark 14:36) and the cry of desolation on the cross *elōi elōi lema sabachthani* (Mark 15:34). Both are translated into Greek, and neither can be considered a magical formula. In short, there is no proof that either *ephphatha* or *talitha koum* was ever considered a magical formula in first-generation Christianity. Most likely, when, during the first-generation, the Aramaic miracle stories were being translated into Greek, different stories were translated by different people in different places. Most translators chose not to keep any Aramaic in their translations; one or a few translators did, probably for dramatic effect and emphasis on the climactic word of Jesus in the story. The same reason may explain the retention of *'abbā'* and the cry of desolation.

[160] One must be careful in one's phrasing here: it is the *miracle of the healing* of the slave's ear that is witnessed only in Luke. The incident of the *cutting off* of the ear is found in all Four Gospels and enjoys multiple attestation by both Mark and John. For a detailed commentary on all four accounts of the cutting off of the ear, see Raymond E. Brown, *The Death of the Messiah. From Gethsemane to the Grave. A Commentary on the Passion Narratives in the Four Gospels* (2 vols.; New York: Doubleday, 1994) 1. 264–81.

[161] For the sake of convenience, scholars usually speak in generic fashion of the place of Jesus' arrest as Gethsemane. One should remember, though, that the place-name Gethsemane occurs only twice in the whole of the NT: once in Mark 14:32, as Mark introduces the story of Jesus' prayer at Gethsemane, and once in Matthew's parallel to Mark, Matt 26:36. Luke (who speaks of the Mount of Olives, e.g., in 22:39) and John (who speaks of a garden, e.g., in John 18:1) never use the word Gethsemane.

[162] For a list of critics who try to take the swordsman as a disciple and the question-able nature of their arguments, see Gundry, *Mark*, 878–79. One is astounded to read in Latourelle's *The Miracles of Jesus*, 203 (emphasis mine): "Mark tells us that *one of the twelve* 'drew his sword.' . . . Matthew says the *same thing* in the *same words.* . . ." Both affirmations are simply false.

[163] Many Greek manuscripts include a *tis* ("someone"), which seems redundant after *heis* ("one"); hence the Codex Bezae tries to improve the text by reading simply *kai tis*. Lagrange (*Evangile selon Saint Marc*, 394), followed by Taylor (*The Gospel According to St. Mark*, 559), suggests that *heis tis* indicates that the narrator knows the name of the assailant ("a certain man known to me"). While possible, this meaning is by no means necessary here; it seems based more on the desire of Lagrange and Taylor to harmonize Mark and John.

[164] On this see Pesch (*Das Markusevangelium*, 2. 401). In most cases, the participle *parestōtes*, along with the definite article, acts as a noun: "the bystanders." A special case is 15:39, where the participle does not function alone as a substantive but rather mod-ifies *ho kentyriōn*, the centurion who has been standing near the cross, facing the cruci-fied Jesus. Even though the person is designated more precisely in this case, he is not given a proper name and is certainly not to be numbered among the formal disciples of Jesus during the public ministry.

[165] This, at least, is what I think Mark's redactional point is. That in the early oral tradition the blow was understood as a defensive act by a sympathizer of Jesus is possi-ble, though hardly provable.

[166] Donald P. Senior, *The Passion Narrative According to Matthew* (BETL 39; Leuven: Leuven University, 1975). I would allow more than Senior does for the influence of stray oral traditions, but I agree with him that Matthew had no extended source be-sides Mark.

[167] The explicit command to sheathe the sword is the only notable parallel that is unique to Matthew and John. While English translations sometimes make the two versions of the command sound almost identical, the Greek texts of the two commands are quite different: *apostrepson tēn machairan sou eis ton topon autēs* (Matt 26:52, "return your sword into its place") and *bale tēn machairan eis tēn thēkēn* (John 18:11, "put the sword into the scabbard"). As Dodd correctly asserts (*Historical Tradition*, 79), neither here nor elsewhere in the story do we find sufficient grounds "for inferring that the story of the assault on the slave was derived from the Synoptic Gospels. . . . It is impossible to treat any one of the Synoptics as the primary source of the Johannine version of the narrative, since he is sometimes closer to one and sometimes to another of the three."

[168] See Senior's detailed explanation of Matthew's additions to Mark in *The Passion Narrative According to Matthew*, 128–48; more concisely, Meier, *Matthew*, 327–28. As Senior observes (p. 129): "It is one of Jesus' disciples (not just a bystander) who strikes with the sword [in Matthew's version], hence the admonition of Jesus in vs. 52–53 applies to the Christian community, those 'with Jesus.'"

[169] Fitzmyer, *The Gospel According to Luke*, 2. 1451. The Greek phrase (*eatō heōs toutou*) is difficult to render literally; it means roughly "let him [or: it] (be) as far as [or: up to] this." According to Bauer (*Wörterbuch* [6th ed.], col. 428), another way of rendering the phrase would be: "Stop! No more of this!"

[170] Fitzmyer (*The Gospel According to Luke*, 2. 1447–48) compares the Lucan with the Marcan scene of the arrest (Mark 14:43–52 || Luke 22:47–53) and concludes that the differences in Luke are all explicable as redactional alterations of the Marcan story. On p. 1448 he examines the Lucan style and vocabulary of the pericope in detail. In my view, Fitzmyer's argumentation is more cogent than that of Grundmann (*Das Evangelium nach Lukas*, 413) and Marshall (*The Gospel of Luke*, 834), who maintain that Luke is combining Mark with another independent source. As I have indicated in Volume One of *A Marginal Jew* (p. 420), I do not accept the theory that Luke is using in addition to Mark a non-Marcan pre-Lucan Passion Narrative. On such a question one should apply Occam's razor: entities are not to be multiplied without necessity. For a defense of such a pre-Lucan Passion Narrative, see Vincent Taylor, *The Passion Narrative of St Luke. A Critical and Historical Investigation* (SNTSMS 19; ed. Owen E. Evans; Cambridge: Cambridge University, 1972); cf. Joachim Jeremias, "Perikopen-Umstellungen bei Lukas?" *Abba*, 93–97. For the view that Luke is basically redacting Mark's Passion Narrative with a view to his own theology and style, see Marion L. Soards, *The Passion According to Luke. The Special Material of Luke 22* (JSNTSup 14; Sheffield: JSOT, 1987); for reasons for rejecting the Proto-Luke hypothesis in general, see Fitzmyer, *The Gospel According to Luke*, 1. 89–91.

This is not to deny that at times Luke may have known and used stray oral traditions or that there may have been some "cross-fertilization" of Lucan and Johannine traditions in their oral stage; see Brown, *The Gospel According to John*, 2. 812. This is how some critics prefer to explain certain minor agreements between Luke and John in this pericope: e.g., the specification of the amputated ear as the right (*dexion*) ear (Luke 22:50 || John 18:10). In this they may well be right. Nevertheless, we should remember that the "right" side or member of any part of the body was usually considered the more important or prestigious, and therefore the addition of "right" to emphasize the damage done could have been a spontaneous development of both the Lucan and Johannine traditions. (On damage to the right side of the body as more serious and shameful, see Pierre Benoit, *The Passion and Resurrection of Jesus Christ* [New York: Herder and Herder; London: Darton, Longman and Todd, 1969] 43–44. This basic insight is sometimes expanded to suggest that the assailant intended to maim symbolically the high priest through his representative, the slave, and so render the high priest incapable of performing his sacred functions; for a critique of this approach, see Haenchen, *John 2*, 166.) As a matter of fact, we have one clear case of Luke, apparently on his own, adding the specification "right" to a Marcan tradition. In Mark 3:1, Mark speaks of a man with a withered hand, whom Jesus will cure on the Sabbath. In the parallel pericope, as he redacts Mark's story, Luke makes the withered hand a "right" hand (Luke 6:6).

[171] Fitzmyer's comment is apposite (*The Gospel According to Luke*, 2. 1449): "Jesus thus uses the moment of his arrest as the occasion for manifesting his healing power even toward one of those who is among his enemies. It betokens the symbolic value of

his passion; through his arrest and death will come forgiveness. As God's agent he reverses the evil done by human beings." See also Brown, *The Death of the Messiah*, 1. 281. Strange to say, it is this coherence with Luke's theological presentation of Jesus that Latourelle invokes in his weak defense of the healing's historicity. Even then, Latourelle concludes: "If the story of this healing were an isolated incident in the Gospel [which, as far as the precise type of healing is concerned, it is], I would have trouble accepting it. In the context of the life of Jesus, however, I think simply that it is not impossible" (*The Miracles of Jesus*, 204). That something is not impossible is hardly a proof—or even an argument—that it actually happened.

[172] That John's version of the story is literarily independent of the Synoptics is convincingly defended by Dodd, *Historical Tradition*, 77–80. His position, accepted by many contemporary interpreters (e.g., R. E. Brown), is superior to more complicated theories, e.g., that of Anton Dauer (*Die Passionsgeschichte im Johannesevangelium* [SANT 30; Munich: Kösel, 1972]), because Dodd's approach adequately explains all the relevant data in a simple fashion. Dauer, by comparison, proposes a complicated hypothesis, which at the same time remains distressingly vague. According to Dauer, the Fourth Evangelist drew the scene of Peter wielding the sword from a source that was an independent passion tradition; but this source in turn depended on the three Synoptic Gospels not directly but indirectly, through the oral traditions the Synoptic Gospels unleashed. This seems an attempt to have it both ways. For a critique of Dauer's theory, see M. Sabbe, "The Arrest of Jesus in Jn 18, 1–11 and its Relation to the Synoptic Gospels. A Critical Evaluation of A. Dauer's Hypothesis," *L'évangile de Jean. Sources, rédaction, théologie* (BETL 44; ed. M. de Jonge; Gembloux: Duculot; Leuven: Leuven University, 1977) 203–34. While I agree with Sabbe that Dauer's theory is unnecessarily complicated, I do not agree that the proper solution is John's dependence on Mark. Here Sabbe follows the basic approach of Neirynck, "John and the Synoptics," ibid., 73–106.

[173] The impulse to embroider a simple story with legendary details may also be verified in the proper name "Malchus" that the Fourth Gospel bestows on the earless slave in 18:10. However, one must be careful not to be too apodictic here. (1) Gospel traditions can move in both directions, at times inventing proper names for later versions of a story, at other times dropping the names present in the earlier version; on this see Dodd, *Historical Tradition*, 79–80. Haenchen (*John 2*, 166) misses this point. (2) At times the Fourth Gospel does preserve surprising nuggets and tidbits of what seems to be reliable historical tradition. (3) One objection to seeing the name Malchus as a later invention is that the natural tendency would be to identify a nameless actor in the drama with someone known to the audience. Instead, the name Malchus never occurs elsewhere either in the LXX or in the NT. Yet Malchus was a well-known name at the time; it appears five times in Josephus and is found in Palmyrene and Nabatean inscriptions. For a detailed treatment of the name as well as fanciful theories about it, see Brown, *The Gospel According to John*, 2. 812. Dodd (ibid., p. 80) seems to feel more strongly about the presence of the name Peter in the tradition than he does about the presence of Malchus, but in the end he remains undecided about both. I take a different point of view. While definitely judging that the name of Peter is secondary in the tradition of the swordsman, I would not absolutely exclude the possibility that Malchus was in fact the name of the hapless slave, though I think it highly improbable. Looking at the creative imagination at work in the growth of the Synoptic versions of the story, I suspect that similar creativity was operative in the Johannine tradition. In fact, as I will explain below, I think that the identification of the swordsman with Peter is the work of the Fourth Evangelist.

[174] So rightly Haenchen, *John 2*, 165.

[175] Here I differ with Schnackenburg (*Das Johannesevangelium*, 3. 256), who thinks instead of Johannine tradition. He is not alone in this view. Despite differences in detail, both Fortna (*The Fourth Gospel and Its Predecessor*, 149–54) and von Wahlde (*The Earliest Version of John's Gospel*, 133–37) think that their hypothetical primitive Gospel, which supposedly lay behind the Fourth Gospel, contained this incident with the names of both Peter and Malchus. Though admitting that the double name "Simon Peter" is typical of the Fourth Evangelist, Schnackenburg favors the theory of Johannine tradition rather than a redactional creation because he can see no reason why the Evangelist would have inserted Peter's name into this text. A similar line of reasoning is taken by Dauer (*Die Passionsgeschichte*, 44), who claims that there are no theological, apologetic, or polemical reasons why the Fourth Evangelist should have introduced Peter's name at this point. It is interesting that Dauer does not think of mentioning literary reasons. I think that the literary considerations I present in the main text supply a sufficient reason.

[176] To avoid confusion as I begin the treatment of these complicated traditions, I speak globally of the "centurion's servant" in the versions of Matthew, Luke, and Q. As we shall see, it is not absolutely clear whether Matthew and Q before him used *pais* in the sense of servant (slave) or boy (son). I use "centurion's servant" and "royal official's son" simply as set conventions to distinguish the story of the Q tradition from that of the Johannine tradition.

[177] For a survey of opinions on which verses come from Q, see Kloppenborg, *Q Parallels*, 50. For speculation on the context of the story in the Q document, see Lührmann, *Die Redaktion der Logienquelle*, 57; Kloppenborg, *The Formation of Q*, 117.

[178] The bare bones of a Q story of the exorcism of a mute demoniac are preserved in Matt 12:22–23 (cf. Matt 9:32–33) ‖ Luke 11:14 as the introduction to the lengthy dispute on whether Jesus is in league with Beelzebul. Schulz (*Q. Die Spruchquelle der Evangelisten*, 240 and n. 430) tries to explain this relative absence of miracle stories in Q with an appeal to the now-shopworn claims about a *theios anēr* christology in Mark's miracle stories.

That the story of the centurion's servant or royal official's son should be categorized as a miracle story is sometimes denied by scholars. For example, in his treatment of the healing of the centurion's servant, Dibelius (*Formgeschichte*, 245, 261 n. 3) suggests that only the dialogue was original, while the narrative parts were later additions; hence the tradition circulated originally as one of the words of Jesus. Similarly, Bultmann (*Geschichte*, 39, 223) discusses the tradition in an appendix to his treatment of Jesus' apophthegms, since the story is supposedly narrated not in the style of a miracle story but in the style of an apophthegm: the miracle is totally at the service of Jesus' pronouncement. Fitzmyer (*The Gospel According to Luke*, 1. 649) concurs in Bultmann's judgment.

Yet other scholars still consider the story of the centurion's servant to be a miracle story, specifically a story of a miraculous healing: e.g., Theissen (*Urchristliche Wundergeschichten*, 318, where it is listed under healings) and Roloff (*Das Kerygma*, 155–56, where it is treated under the heading of Jesus' miracles). As Wegner observes (*Der Hauptmann*, 340), the story does in fact have many of the major motifs found in a Gospel miracle story: the coming of the miracle-worker (Matt 8:5a), the appearance of the petitioner (v 5b), the description of the affliction (v 6), the petitioner's request and expression of trust (vv 6,8–9), marveling (v 10, but here Jesus, not the crowd, marvels), the dismissal of the petitioner by the miracle-worker (13a), the miracle-worker's promise that the healing has taken place or will take place (v 13b), and the confirmation of the miracle (v 13c).

Nevertheless, as Wegner also correctly notes (ibid., pp. 341–43), the story is not *just* a miracle story. The narrative elements are extremely terse, a large part of the story is taken up with the words of Jesus and the centurion, and the climax of the story is reached when Jesus expresses his surprise and admiration in v 10 (which overshadows the actual word of healing in v 13b and the confirmation of the healing in v 13c). What we have here therefore is a mixed form, partaking of both miracle story and apophthegm (pronouncement story); hence Wegner and Kloppenborg (*The Formation of Q*, 118) prefer to speak of an "apophthegmatic [or: apophthegmatized] miracle story." The words of Jesus and the centurion are indeed emphasized, but this does not make the form of a miracle story simply disappear. One is reminded of the similar mixed form of healings on the Sabbath.

The variant form of the story in John 4:46–54 is closer to the set pattern of a miracle story (as analyzed by form critics), but the verbal exchanges do underline the question of faith and the movement of the official to full faith. I would therefore consider it a mixed form as well. The fact that the mixed form of miracle-story-plus-theological-dialogue is found in both the Q and Johannine forms of the tradition argues against any attempt (e.g., by Dibelius; Lührmann, *Die Redaktion der Logienquelle*, 57; Kloppenborg, *The Formation of Q*, 120; Sato, *Q und Prophetie*, 82) to claim that either a simple narrative or just the dialogue without a narrative framework was the original form of the tradition. One must beware of the presupposition that a "pure" or simple form of a story must always be chronologically earlier in the history of the tradition. For example, let us suppose for a moment that at times Jesus did make memorable statements on the occasion of working miracles. The accounts of such occasions would naturally be "mixed forms" from the very beginning, and any simplification (e.g., dropping the memorable saying from the miracle story, omitting the miracle story and preserving only the memorable saying) would be secondary. A telling warning against presuming that pure forms are always earlier is Busse's judgment (*Die Wunder des Propheten Jesus*, 151) that Luke's redacted form of the centurion story comes closer to the proper form of a miracle story than does the original Q version.

[179] Schürmann (*Das Lukasevangelium*, 1. 391 n. 14) points out that, without the mention of the servant or son being near death, Matthew's version has no adequate explanation of why the sufferer is not brought to Jesus, as are many other ill people in the Gospel miracles (e.g., Mark 2:1–12). Hence it may be that the element of the sufferer being near death belongs to the earlier tradition (reflected in both Luke and John), which Matthew has modified at this point.

[180] To heighten the degree of the father's faith, Matthew has the girl dead at the start of the story; hence the father's initial petition (that his daughter be raised to life) shows tremendous faith from the very beginning of the narrative (Matt 9:18).—One could multiply examples of how one trait, motif, or phrase from a particular miracle story can also be found in the story of the centurion's servant. This obvious fact, which arises largely from the shared grid of Synoptic miracle stories, should not lead us to adopt the extreme view of E. Wendling ("Synoptische Studien. II. Der Hauptmann von Kapernaum," *ZNW* 9 [1908] 96–109), who claims that Matthew basically created the story of the centurion's *paralyzed* servant under the influence of the healing of the *paralytic* in Mark 2:1–12 (as well as other Marcan miracle stories). Hence the story would not come from Q; Luke would be dependent for it on Matthew, although Wendling admits Luke's independent use of Q elsewhere. Wendling gives us a highly imaginative tour de force rather than a credible Synoptic source theory.

[181] As we have already seen it is probably Matthew's redactional activity that changes the designation "Syrophoenician" to "Canaanite."

[182] Hence I do not agree with Bultmann's view (echoed by other commentators) that the story of the centurion's servant is simply a variant of the story of the Syrophoenician woman (*Geschichte*, 39). For doubts about Bultmann's view, see Schürmann, *Das Lukasevangelium*, 1. 397; Fitzmyer, *The Gospel According to Luke*, 1. 649. Even stranger is Schulz's claim (*Q. Die Spruchquelle der Evangelisten*, 241) that the Q story of the centurion's servant shows influence from the Marcan story of the Syrophoenician woman. I find it odd that someone would argue for the two-source theory of Synoptic relationships and then adopt a view (i.e., a connection between Mark and Q) that could undermine the very arguments that established the theory.

As part of the argument for a close parallel between the story of the Syrophoenician woman and the story of the centurion's servant, many commentators read Matt 8:7 as an indignant question on Jesus' part: "Am I supposed to come and heal him [i.e., the centurion's servant]?" On this reading, Jesus is offended by the daring suggestion that he ignore the rules of Jewish purity and enter a Gentile's house. The Gentile centurion then responds with great humility, acknowledging that he is unworthy to have Jesus enter his house and professing his faith that the physical presence of Jesus is not necessary. Having authority over illness the way the centurion has authority over his soldiers and his slaves, Jesus need only issue a command from a distance, and the servant will be healed (v 8). This interpretation of v 7 is certainly possible and is defended at length by Wegner, *Der Hauptmann*, 375–80 (depending on the classic arguments of Theodor Zahn); see also Davies and Allison, *The Gospel According to Saint Matthew*, 2. 21–22; and Held, "Matthäus als Interpret der Wundergeschichten," 184. Along with Wegner, Schulz (*Q. Die Spruchquelle der Evangelisten*, 242 n. 447) gives a list of major exegetes who accept this interpretation, as well as a few who do not.

A summary of the arguments in favor of taking Matt 8:7 as a question would run as follows: (1) The emphatic *ego* ("*I* come") in 8:7 makes no sense in a statement, but fits in perfectly with an indignant question ("Am *I* to come . . . ?"). (2) The statement of the centurion in v 8 truly expresses astounding faith only as an answer to an apparent rebuff. If the centurion is replying to an affirmation and assent on Jesus' part, v 8 is difficult to understand in the flow of the narrative. Why did not the centurion make the point expressed in v 8 clear in his initial request in v 6? Why did he not express his humility, his trust, and his faith that Jesus' physical presence was not necessary when he first made his request? (3) If v 7 is Jesus' firm assent to the centurion's request, why does not Jesus proceed to act according to this assent rather than according to the suddenly affirmed humility and alternate suggestion of the centurion in v 8? (4) All admit that the story of the centurion's servant has as its closest Synoptic parallel the only other clear example in the Synoptics of a healing at a distance, namely, the story of the healing of the daughter of the Syrophoenician woman (or Canaanite woman in Matthew). In the latter story, the element of Jesus' apparent refusal of the woman's request is clear (Mark 7:27; Matt 15:23,26 sounds even more severe). It is reasonable to expect this element in the parallel story of the centurion's servant as well—all the more so when Jesus seems to rebuff the royal official in John 4:48. (5) In the context of Matthew's redactional theology, during this earthly life Jesus is sent only to the lost sheep of the house of Israel (15:24) and sends his twelve apostles only to the same limited group (10:6). The unrestricted, universal mission is proclaimed only in Matt 28:16–20, after the death-resurrection of Jesus. Could Matthew with any consistency present the earthly Jesus, who fulfills the Law and the prophets (5:17), as being ready and willing to enter a Gentile's house on a religious mission?

While these combined arguments are weighty, there are some counterarguments to be considered: (1) For the reader who is following Matthew's Gospel in the order of its narrative, the immediate context of the healing of the centurion's servant (Matt 8:5–13) is not the healing of the Canaanite's daughter (15:21–28) but rather the preceding healing of a leper (8:1–4). In the latter story Jesus accedes at once to the plea of the outcast leper (who, analogous to the Gentile centurion, is not fully integrated into the worshiping community of Israel) and even breaks the Mosaic Law as he touches the leper to heal him. It is strange that the freewheeling Jesus of Matt 8:3 should suddenly become so scrupulous in 8:7. On this see Ernst Haenchen, "Johanneische Probleme," *ZTK* 56 (1959) 19–54, esp. 24. (2) Only if we understand 8:7 to mean Jesus' ready assent to come to the centurion's house does the response of the centurion in v 8 receive its full weight as a startling expression of humble faith. Verse 8 is not a desperate attempt by a rebuffed person to bargain for a second type of miracle after his request for a first type has been rejected. Rather, v 8 is an astonishing, humble waiving of the favor Jesus has voluntarily offered. One should notice that the centurion said nothing about Jesus' coming to his house in his initial petition in v 6; that idea came from Jesus alone. All this highlights the humble, trusting faith that causes Jesus to marvel. Most of Jesus' audience is never satisfied; they always want more by way of miracles, miracles according to their own tastes and specifications. The centurion is willing to take even less than Jesus offers, so sure is he that a mere word from Jesus at a distance is enough. It is this contrast between the never-satisfied demands of most of Israel and the humble faith of a Gentile who is so readily satisfied that the Matthean Jesus underscores in v 10. (3) If v 7 were an indignant question, the cause of the indignation would be the centurion's undue expectation that Jesus would *come* into a Gentile's *house*. Yet *elthōn* ("coming") is a mere participle in v 7, "into your house" does not appear, and the whole structure of the sentence puts the emphasis on the positive idea of healing (the main verb *therapeusō* rather than the participle *elthōn*). Not until the centurion's response in v 8 is the idea of coming into the centurion's house explicitly mentioned. On this point see Gundry, *Matthew*, 143. (4) Some exegetes support the idea of a rebuff in Matt 8:7 by appealing to a supposedly parallel rebuff of the royal official by Jesus in John 4:48. The appeal may not be cogent. In fact, the "parallel" may not prove anything, especially with respect to the underlying tradition of Q or John, since both verses may be redactional creations of the two evangelists. If that be the case, the supposed parallel would indicate nothing about the basic tradition behind the present stories, nor would one text necessarily throw any light on the meaning of the other text. In the case of Matthew, although Wegner (*Der Hauptmann*, 149–57, 270) argues that 8:7 existed in the Q tradition (despite any parallel in the Lucan version of the story), Davies and Allison (*The Gospel According to Saint Matthew*, 2. 21 n. 50) point out that the vocabulary and style of v 7 are strongly Matthean and may well be redactional. As for the supposed parallel in the Fourth Gospel, John 4:48 is often thought by commentators to be an insertion by the Fourth Evangelist into a traditional story, since (a) v 48 is strangely intrusive, suddenly jumping for the length of a single verse into the 2d person plural ("Jesus said *to him*, 'Unless *you* [plural!] see signs and wonders, you will not believe"), when everything before and after it is in the 2d person singular; (b) Jesus' strong reaction does not seem sufficiently motivated by what has just preceded in the story; (c) it does not fit neatly with the ending of the story (the official does come to full faith as a result of Jesus' sign). On all this see Brown, *The Gospel According to John*, 1. 195–96; Schnackenburg, *The Gospel According to St John*, 1. 469; Haenchen, "Johanneische Probleme," 30; idem, *John 1*, 234–35; von Wahlde, *The Earliest Version of John's Gospel*, 93; Fortna, *The Fourth Gospel*, 62–63. What is significant here for anyone seeking to track down historical tradition is that the whole question of whether Matt 8:7 is an assent or a rebuff in the form of a question may well be beside the point, since any such rebuff probably does not belong to the earliest form of the story. (5) If Matt 8:7 were an indignant question, Matthew could have made the point much more clearly by beginning Jesus' response with the negative interrogative *mē*, which shows that the speaker expects the answer "no." (6) More generally, arguments from Matthew's redactional theology of Jesus and the law often rest on questionable understandings of the law in Matthew's Gospel.

All in all, then, I incline to the view that Matt 8:7 is best understood as a declaration rather than a question. In any event, though, what we have seen here makes it unlikely that Matt 8:7 reflects the earliest attainable tradition and possibly the original historical event. In general, I am wary of trying to reconstruct the dialogue that would have been connected with the original event behind the Q and Johannine traditions. Wegner (*Der Hauptmann*, 427) is more confident, but at the price of ignoring John in favor of the Q version of the tradition when it comes to historical reconstruction. Since John's presentation of the dialogue material is so different from Q's, I think it wise to be modest in one's claims and waive any attempt to reconstruct the statements supposedly made during the historical encounter.

[183] See, e.g., the immediate arrival of the disciples' boat at the far shore after Jesus walks on the water (John 6:21), the healing of a man *born* blind (9:1, cf. v 32; never said of any blind person healed in the Synoptic Gospels), and the raising of Lazarus after he was dead and in the tomb for *four days* (11:17,39; Jairus' daughter and the son of the widow of Nain were both raised to life on the day of their death, before entombment). The idea that only John's "sign source" had a positive attitude toward miracles and that the Evangelist himself is cool or hostile toward the miraculous will not stand up to close scrutiny. John is certainly hostile to interest in miracles solely for their spectacular nature or the material benefits they confer; the superficial faith based on such interest is no true faith at all. But John is positive about the value of miracles when they are allowed to function properly as "signs," pointing the well-disposed beyond the signs to the one signified by them, the life-giving Jesus. On all this see Marianne Meye Thompson, *The Humanity of Jesus in the Fourth Gospel* (Philadelphia: Fortress, 1988) 53–86; and Udo Schnelle, *Antidocetic Christology in the Gospel of John* (Minneapolis: Fortress, 1992) 74–175.

[184] The idea that the placing of Jesus at Cana at the beginning of the story of the royal official's son stems from the creative hand of the Fourth Evangelist is suggested by many commentators on John's Gospel; see also Fitzmyer, *The Gospel According to Luke*, 1. 648. Some scholars (e.g., Schnackenburg, *The Gospel According to St John*, 1. 470; Fortna, *The Fourth Gospel*, 58–59) offer an intriguing suggestion: in John's "sign source" or "sign Gospel" some form of John 2:12, which reports the descent of Jesus from Cana to Capernaum, may have led immediately into the story of the healing of the royal official's son at Capernaum. Perhaps in the source the royal official went out to meet Jesus while he was still on the road to Capernaum. All this naturally remains very speculative; von Wahlde (*The Earliest Version*, 92 n. 60) disagrees with Fortna and claims that even in John's source Jesus was situated at Cana.—While John obviously intends the second "Cana sign" to point back to the first, the theme of Jesus as the life-giver points forward to the next major section of the Gospel, with the idea of giving life extremely prominent in chaps. 5–6. On this point, see André Feuillet, "The Theological Significance of the Second Cana Miracle," *Johannine Studies* (Staten Island, NY: Alba House, 1964) 39–51, esp. 44–51.

[185] For a survey of the meanings of *basilikos*, see Wegner, *Der Hauptmann*, 57–60, with the attached references to Greco-Roman literature. My remarks on the meaning of "royal official" and "centurion" are heavily dependent on Wegner's treatment.

[186] See, e.g., *J.W.* 1.1.5 §45 [the soldiers of the Seleucid monarch Antiochus IV

Epiphanes]; 2.3.4 §52 [Roman troops]; 2.17.5–6 §423 and 426 [troops of Herod Agrippa II]. Even though Herod Antipas was strictly speaking a mere tetrarch and not a king, the common people apparently referred to him loosely as king (*basileus*), witness Mark 6:14. Mark's "king" is carefully corrected by Matthew to "tetrarch" (*tetraarchēs*) in Matt 14:1; but the lack of a real distinction for the common people is reflected in Matthew's reversion to Mark's "king" in Matt 14:9. Hence there would be nothing surprising in having an official or soldier of Herod Antipas referred to as *basilikos*.

[187] Although John never uses any of the words for "centurion" (*hekatontarchos*, *hekatontarchēs*, or *kentyriōn*), he speaks of a *speira* (a Roman cohort of 600 men or a maniple of 200 men) in 18:3,12, a *chiliarchos* (literally, a captain or officer over 1,000 men, but also designating a Roman military tribune commanding a cohort of 600 men) in 18:12, and the *praitōrion* (originally, the tent in a military camp where the Roman praetor had his headquarters) in 18:28.

[188] There is no need here to go into a detailed review of every occurrence of "centurion" in the NT; for a quick overview, see Wegner, *Der Hauptmann*, 66–69. Outside of this Q miracle story, a centurion is mentioned in the Gospels only in connection with the death of Jesus (Mark 15:39 || Matt 27:54 || Luke 23:47) and his burial (Mark 15:44–45). In these passages the centurion is obviously an officer overseeing a company of soldiers charged with the execution of criminals. All other NT references to centurions occur in the Acts of the Apostles, mostly notably in Acts 10, which narrates the angelic vision given to the centurion Cornelius at Caesarea, leading to his conversion by Peter. All other references in Acts occur in chaps. 21–27, in connection with Paul's arrest in Jerusalem, imprisonment in Caesarea, and journey to Rome. In these last cases, the centurion basically functions as a policeman and guard.

[189] Freyne (*Galilee from Alexander the Great to Hadrian*, 94 n. 33) remarks: "According to *Ant* 18:251f, Agrippa [i.e., Herod Agrippa I, writing to the Roman Emperor Caligula] accused Antipas of having equipment for 70,000 foot-soldiers, and the latter admitted to the charge. While the number is unlikely there is nothing improbable about Antipas having a private army in view of the war with the Nabataeans."

[190] Hoehner (*Herod Antipas*, 54) speculates that "perhaps only southern Galilee was predominantly Jewish" at the time of the Hasmonean ruler Alexander Jannaeus (103–76 B.C.). But he thinks that by the time of Jesus "Galilee seems to have been quite thoroughly Judaized," though he admits it is not possible to give an exact proportion. While Hoehner therefore rejects the view of J. H. Moulton that Gentiles were in the majority in Galilee at the time of Antipas, he nevertheless grants that "a large element of the population was Gentile" including Egyptians, Arabians, Phoenicians, and Greeks. Freyne (*Galilee from Alexander the Great to Hadrian*, 22–50) emphasizes that there is no proof that Galilee ever lost its Jewish identity under the Seleucids and therefore had to be completely re-Judaized by the Maccabees and Hasmoneans.

[191] See the revised edition of Schürer, *The History of the Jewish People*, 1. 315: "Herod [the Great] possessed a dependable army of mercenaries composed of numerous Thracians, Germans and Gauls." In n. 315 the author adds: "The army also included substantial levies from both the Jewish and the non-Jewish inhabitants of his kingdom. . . ." While Abraham Shalit (*König Herodes. Der Mann und sein Werk* [Berlin: de Gruyter, 1969] 168–70) thinks that Herod the Great increased the percentage of Gentile soldiers in his army, he suggests that the majority of soldiers were still Jewish (see p. 170 n. 86). In contrast, Schürmann (*Das Lukasevangelium*, 1. 391) opines that Antipas' troops would have been mainly Gentile.

[192] Ernst (*Das Evangelium nach Lukas*, 238) is among the few contemporary exegetes

who claim that Luke has dropped from the traditional story the prophecy about many coming from east and west. For the reasons for seeing Matt 8:11–12 as Matthew's insertion of a distinct Q logion into the story of the centurion, see Wegner, *Der Hauptmann*, 3–5. In a nutshell: (1) it is easy to see why Matthew would insert the prophecy here, while it is difficult to see why Luke would have dropped it, only to introduce it later on (Luke 13:28–29) as a logion loosely connected with its context during the great journey section of his Gospel. (2) There is a slight tension between the polemical threat of Matt 8:11–12 and the surrounding narrative context. (3) The introductory formula "I say to you" in Matt 8:11 strikes one as very awkward after almost the same introductory formula has been used in the previous verse (v 10: "Amen I say to you"), especially since there is no indication of a change of audience.

[193] So Busse, *Die Wunder des Propheten Jesus*, 147–48, with n. 1 on pp. 148–49; Robert A. J. Gagnon, "Statistical Analysis and the Case of the Double Delegation in Luke 7:3–7a," *CBQ* 55 (1993) 709–31. For arguments pro and con, see Kloppenborg, *Q Parallels*, 50. The overall question of whether Matthew or Luke preserves the more original form of the Q story is of no great concern to my investigation, since in my opinion only the bare bones of an account that would lie behind both the Q and Johannine versions of the story could be a candidate for a judgment of "historical." The details of any individual account, including the dialogue between the petitioner and Jesus, must drop out of consideration.

However, I think that Schulz (*Q. Die Spruchquelle der Evangelisten*, 236–40) and Fitzmyer (*The Gospel According to Luke*, 1. 648–49) make a good case for the position that, apart from the redactional insertion in Matt 8:11–12, Matthew's version of the story is closer to the Q form than is Luke's version. In particular: (1) Matthew and John agree that the petitioner comes to Jesus and speaks face-to-face with him; neither knows anything of the two Lucan delegations. (2) As we shall see below, Matthew's ambiguous *pais* (which can mean "boy" in the sense of either servant or son) may be primitive, explaining the opposite interpretations of Luke ("servant") and John ("son"). (3) The second of Luke's delegations has an awkward "feel" to it in the story. If the centurion went to all the trouble of sending a formal delegation to Jesus, and if from the beginning he used the mechanism of a delegation because he felt too unworthy to have Jesus enter his house (as the centurion affirms through his second delegation in Luke 7:7), why did he not instruct the first delegation to make this declaration and so obviate the need for a second delegation? The switch from third-person narrative by the first delegation ("he is worthy") to first-person confession of the centurion conveyed through the second delegation ("I am not worthy") also looks suspicious. Indeed, the whole two-part pattern of Jews confidently proclaiming worth and Gentiles confessing lack of worth may be part of Luke's theological message (cf. Acts 10:34–35; see Schulz, ibid., 237–38; also Fitzmyer, ibid., 650, though on p. 652 he thinks it more probable that the second delegation was also made up of Jews [but then why does the centurion send these "friends" "from his house"?]).

On balance it is easier to understand why Luke, with his interest in the problem of Jewish-Gentile relations in Acts, would have inserted the double delegation than why Matthew would have omitted it. Still, it remains possible that the element of the double delegation had already become incorporated into Luke's copy of Q (i.e., Q^{Lk}) before it was redacted by him; so Sato, *Q und Prophetie*, 55; against this view is Busse (*Die Wunder des Propheten Jesus*, 150), who attributes all additions to the basic Q story to Luke himself. In any event, I give no detailed consideration to such Lucan elements, since in my view they contribute nothing to the question of a historical tradition going back to Jesus. For the view that Luke rather than Matthew has preserved the earlier form of the story or at least has not invented the double delegation himself, see Schürmann,

Das Lukasevangelium, 1. 395–96; Rudolf Pesch and Reinhard Kratz, *So liest man synoptisch. III. Wundergeschichten. Teil II. Rettungswunder—Geschenkwunder—Normenwunder—Fernheilungen* (Frankfurt: Knecht, 1976) 77–83, esp. 77–80.

[194] Ernst Haenchen ("Faith and Miracle," *Studia Evangelica I* [TU 73; ed. Kurt Aland et. al.; Berlin: Akademie, 1959] 495–98) thinks that in the Johannine tradition prior to the writing of the Fourth Gospel the royal official was thought of as a Jew.

[195] See, e.g., the story's differentiation of Samaritans from Jews (John 4:9,20–22) and the overcoming of that differentiation in the grand climactic chorus of the Samaritans, using for the only time in the Fourth Gospel language very much at home in the Greco-Roman world (4:42): "This is truly the savior of the world."

[196] Yet that is what some commentators on John do; see, e.g., Marsh, *The Gospel of St John*, 235; Feuillet, "The Theological Significance," 45 (though with hesitation). Marsh cannot defend himself merely by saying that he thinks that John knew the Synoptics and used them. If John had before him the accounts of Matthew and Luke, which go out of their way to emphasize the Gentile nature of the centurion as a major theological element in the story, John's total silence about the petitioner's Gentile origins would make it all the more likely that John is pointedly changing the Synoptic story to make it fit his own theological schema, in which Gentiles do not directly interact with Jesus during the public ministry.

[197] Unfortunately, this is often what happens. Even Wegner, who uses John's version early on as an independent witness to the tradition (*Der Hauptmann*, 36–37), ends up reconstructing the historical event purely in terms of the Gentile centurion of the Q tradition (p. 419).

[198] See the remarks of van der Loos in *The Miracles of Jesus*, 532 n. 1.

[199] Apart from the story of the centurion, Matthew knows and uses both meanings of *pais:* "boy" or "children" (in the plural) in 2:16, 17:18; 21:15; and "servant" in 12:18; 14:2.

[200] So Schulz, *Q. Die Spruchquelle der Evangelisten*, 236 and n. 400.

[201] This is the opinion of many recent scholars: e.g., Haenchen, "Johanneische Probleme," 30; Latourelle, *The Miracles of Jesus*, 136. Dodd (*Historical Tradition*, 194) offers this position as a possibility, but admits he hesitates because of what he considers the strong formal parallels between the story of the royal official's son in John and the story of the Syrophoenician woman's daughter in Mark. As I have indicated above, I am not as impressed by the supposed parallels between the story of the centurion/royal official story and the story of the Syrophoenician woman as are some.

[202] See Meier, *A Marginal Jew*, 1. 44. This view, which many Johannine scholars (e.g., Haenchen, "Johanneische Probleme," 30) maintain in their exegesis of the story of the royal official's son, is also espoused by commentators on other Gospels who treat the Matthean or Lucan form of the story; see, e.g., Fitzmyer, *The Gospel According to Luke*, 1. 648; cf. Latourelle, *The Miracles of Jesus*, 136–37.

[203] For a detailed study of John's version in relation to Matthew's and Luke's, see Wegner (*Der Hauptmann*, 32–37), who criticizes Neirynck's attempt to explain John's narrative as a creative reworking of Synoptic sources. Criticism of Neirynck's overall approach to the question of John's use of the Synoptics can also be found in Jürgen Becker, "Das Johannesevangelium im Streit der Methoden (1980–84)," *TRu* 51 (1986) 1–78, esp. pp. 22–23. For Neirynck's position, see Frans Neirynck, "John and the Synoptics," *L'évangile de Jean: Sources, rédaction, théologie* (BETL 44; ed. M. de Jonge; Gem-

bloux: Duculot; Leuven: Leuven University, 1977) 73–106; idem, *Jean et les Synoptiques* (Leuven: Leuven University, 1979). For other presentations defending John's independence of the Synoptics in the story of the centurion/royal official, see Brown, *The Gospel According to John*, 1. 192–94; Dodd, *Historical Tradition*, 188–95.

[204] So both Fortna (*The Fourth Gospel and Its Predecessor*, 58–65) and von Wahlde (*The Earliest Version*, 92–94), though understandably the two scholars differ on details of wording in the hypothetical Gospel that supposedly stands behind our Fourth Gospel.

[205] Individual linguistic phenomena also argue in favor of the story's existence prior to its being taken into the Q document. For example, *kyrie* ("sir" or "Lord") used as an address for the earthly Jesus (as opposed to the risen Lord or judge of the world on the last day) is found only here in Q. On this, see Schulz, *Q. Die Spruchquelle der Evangelisten*, 242.

[206] The only other time in the Four Gospels that Jesus is said to be astonished (*thaumazō*) is Mark 6:6, when Jesus marvels at the unbelief of the townspeople of Nazareth. Otherwise, *thaumazō* always describes the reaction of other people, never of Jesus. There is an intriguing point here: the only thing that surprises Jesus (as he is presented in all Four Gospels) is the unbelief of Israel and the belief of Gentiles; he apparently was expecting just the opposite.

[207] Wegner, *Der Hauptmann*, 409–19; also Schulz, *Q. Die Spruchquelle der Evangelisten*, 242 n. 440. Some of Wegner's individual claims, such as what is characteristic of Jesus' own style of speaking, are not very cogent; but the overall inventory of possible Semitisms is impressive.
As I indicated above, I think that Wegner is correct in claiming that Matthew rather than Luke is closer to the wording of Q in this story (ibid., 269–76); so too J. Duncan M. Derrett, "Law in the New Testament: The Syro-Phoenician Woman and the Centurion of Capernaum," *NovT* 15 (1973) 161–86, esp. 174. Wegner accordingly cites the Q text by the verse-numbers of the Matthean text, a refreshing change from the convention of citing Q always by the chapter- and verse-numbers in Luke. Such a convention, when it turns into an unexamined tradition, can inadvertently import some questionable presuppositions into the reconstruction and exegesis of Q.

[208] Even Schulz (*Q. Die Spruchquelle der Evangelisten*, 242), who is otherwise noncommittal or skeptical about the historicity of the Q tradition, opines that, since the geographical designation of Capernaum is so firmly anchored in the tradition, one may perhaps accept the idea that the tradition arose in Galilee. To cite another critic not noted for his naïveté: Haenchen ("Faith and Miracle," 494) thinks that it would be "precipitate" to call the tradition behind Matt 8:5–10,13 an "ideal scene," as Bultmann does.

[209] Latourelle (*The Miracles of Jesus*, 136) claims that the oldest elements of the story behind both the Q and Johannine traditions included a *pagan* resident of Capernaum whose *son* was sick. I do not see how one can establish with sufficient probability that the earliest form of the story spoke expressly of a pagan rather than of a Jew and of a son rather than of a servant.

[210] Here I would differ with Wegner, who tries to salvage the substance if not the exact wording of the exchange between Jesus and the petitioner (*Der Hauptmann*, 419–28). In my opinion, Wegner's attempt reflects his concentration on the Q version of the story to the relative neglect of the Johannine version. If John's version is given due

emphasis, one becomes less certain whether any part of the dialogue in either version can be declared historical.

[211] Some nonbelievers might want to venture more daring explanations: e.g., trickery on the part of Jesus, on the part of the supposedly sick person, or on the part of both working in collusion.

CHAPTER 22

RAISING THE DEAD

I. THREE INITIAL OBSERVATIONS ON THE STORIES OF RAISING THE DEAD

Hardly any type of miracle clashes more with the skeptical mind-set of modern Western culture than that of raising the dead. Even Jesus' exorcisms pale in comparison. For many critics, the automatic response to the Gospel stories of Jesus' raising the dead is to attribute all of them to the symbolic imagination of the early church. Scholars usually judge these stories to be graphic depictions of the church's belief that the risen Jesus has conquered the powers of evil, the ultimate evil being death. The implied corollary of this line of argument is that it is a waste of time to inquire about the origins of these stories in the public ministry of the historical Jesus. They are products, pure and simple, of the early church.

While this position is perfectly understandable, one may question whether it takes into consideration three important points.

(1) First, what a person at any given time in history considers possible or probable is affected by the prevailing culture, the "everybody-knows-that-this-is-so" feeling investigated by the sociology of knowledge. We all tend to accept certain things as given and certain presuppositions as obvious, not because we have exhaustively examined them but because everybody around us—especially authority figures and experts—seems to take them for granted. It is within this overarching context of the possible, the plausible, and the probable that we then engage in individual acts of knowing and form judgments about what is true or false, real or unreal.

Hence it takes a leap of the imagination for the sophisticated modern American to understand that large segments of the ancient Mediterranean world would have considered it at least possible or plausible that a great holy man or god-like figure might raise the dead to life. Yet such was the case.[1] Among pagans, stories of the dead (or the apparently dead) being restored to life are told by Pliny the Elder, Apuleius, Lucian (in a mocking vein), and Philostratus (in a hesitant vein). The OT gives the examples of Elijah and Elisha (1 Kgs 17:17–24; 2 Kgs 4:18–37; cf. 2 Kgs 13:20–21) in stories that contrast sharply with the skepticism or hesitation of some Greco-Roman accounts. Early

Christianity, from the story of Peter raising Tabitha onwards (Acts 9:36–43),[2] continued the tradition for Christian saints down through the patristic and medieval periods. As we have already seen, later rabbinic literature increasingly associated famous rabbis with miracle-working powers. While raising the dead was not prominent among such miracles, a few accounts are preserved.[3]

When, therefore, Jesus' disciples—be it only after Easter or before as well—recounted stories of Jesus raising the dead, such accounts, while unusual and astounding, were not completely unheard of in the ancient Mediterranean world. Neither Jesus nor his followers would have considered the idea of a holy man raising the dead as outlandish as many modern critics would. At the same time, one must note that stories of raising the dead are relatively rare among accounts of Jesus' miracles, as they are among miracles attributed to other famous figures of the Greco-Roman era or the Bible.

(2) A second point to be taken into account is that, although the stories of Jesus raising the dead are relatively rare within the whole corpus of Gospel miracles, they are neatly spread over a number of different literary sources instead of being concentrated in one source. The three Gospel stories that depict Jesus raising the dead are found in the Marcan tradition (the raising of the daughter of Jairus, Mark 5:21–43), the special L tradition (the raising of the son of the widow of Nain, Luke 7:11–17), and the Johannine tradition (the raising of Lazarus, John 11:1–46). As we shall see, in each case the story shows signs of being not the creation of the evangelist but rather an earlier tradition redacted by him. To these three narratives one must add a saying of Jesus, namely, his reply to the disciples sent by John the Baptist in the Q tradition: "The blind see and the lame walk, lepers are cleansed and the deaf hear, *the dead are raised*, and the poor have the good news proclaimed to them" (Matt 11:5 par.). The criterion of multiple attestation of sources and forms is therefore adequately met: the sources lying behind Mark, Luke, John, and Q all agree that Jesus raised the dead during his public ministry. Many a word and deed of Jesus in the Four Gospels lack attestation this widely based.

(3) This leads to a third point—actually, a reminder of an observation made when we first started investigating the Gospel miracle stories. As we test the various miracle stories, what exactly are we trying to establish? Are we trying to prove that at some time around A.D. 30 God actually worked certain miracles through Jesus of Nazareth? As we have already seen, that is a *theo*-logical claim; it lies beyond what any historian working purely by the rules of historical research could ever establish. Rather, what we are asking as we apply the criterion of multiple attestation as well as other criteria is whether some of the Gospel miracle stories are not simply creations of the early church but actually go back to various events in the life of Jesus, however those events be evaluated and however much they may have been reinterpreted by later Christian tradition. We have already seen that certain miracle stories do appear to have roots in Jesus' public ministry, e.g., the healing of the blind Bartimaeus. What we seek to establish in such cases is that certain miracle stories in the Gospels rest upon actual events in Jesus' life, events in which he, his disciples, and the

people helped by him *thought* that he had performed miracles. Whether such miracles were actually the result of various "natural forces" (autosuggestion, hypnosis, or even collusion in deception) is beyond our power to investigate today.

This basic approach, which we have applied to Gospel stories of exorcism and healing, is also valid for stories about Jesus raising the dead. At best, all that one can hope to establish is that some of these stories may go back to events in the life of Jesus, events that he and/or his disciples interpreted as the raising of the dead to life. The agnostic—and perhaps even some of the believers on our hypothetical committee in the Harvard Divinity School library—might explain such events in the light of the poor state of medical knowledge at the time. Comas or other types of "suspended animation" could easily be mistaken for death, especially since, for ordinary people in Palestine, burial occurred very swiftly after death was thought to have taken place. Alternately, one could suppose—as is sometimes done in the interpretation of the raising of the daughter of Jairus[4]—that Jesus' healing of a person close to death was elaborated in the post-Easter Christian tradition to the point where it was transformed into a story of Jesus raising the dead. Then, too, the agnostic might not exclude the possibility of a staged event, while a believer might want to leave open the possibility of a true miracle.[5]

Whatever the actual explanation, all that a historical investigation like ours can hope to ask (and perhaps decide) is whether a particular story of Jesus' raising a person from the dead is purely a creation of the early church or whether it goes back to some event—whatever that event may have been—in the public ministry. If the story does go back in some way to Jesus' ministry, then the possibility arises that a *belief* that Jesus raised the dead already existed among his disciples during his lifetime. That is the extent of what historical-critical research, operating at a distance of some 1900 years from the creation of these Gospel stories, can hope to establish.

II. THE CONTENT AND FORM OF THESE STORIES

Even the label for these miracle stories—namely, "raising the dead"—needs clarification. Two very different types of events in the Gospels share the Greek vocabulary of "raising up" (*egeirō, anistēmi*). Both types of events are accordingly called "resurrections" by critics, but the one label applied to both types is open to misunderstanding. Both the content and the literary form of the two types are quite different.

(1) One type of "raising" takes place during Jesus' public ministry, when he supposedly raises to life people recently deceased.

(a) As far as *content* is concerned, these acts of raising the dead refer to the restoration of dead persons to the ordinary earthly life they formerly enjoyed. Quite literally they "come *back*" to the old mortal life they possessed prior to death, with all its ordinary human activities, requirements, and restrictions, the ultimate restriction being the necessity to die again at some future date. Being raised is only a temporary reprieve, not a permanent exemption, from the inevitable death sentence common to all humanity.[6]

The return to ordinary life is intimated in various ways in each story of raising the dead. The twelve-year-old daughter of Jairus reacts to being raised to life by walking around the room, and Jesus proceeds to order her parents to give her something to eat (Mark 5:42–43). The son of the widow of Nain sits up and speaks and Jesus gives him back to his mother—and thus to the whole of his old life (Luke 7:15). Lazarus comes forth from the tomb still bound by his burial cloths and face cloth (John 11:44), a symbol that he will need them again at a future date (contrast the burial cloths and face cloth left behind by the risen Jesus in his tomb in John 20:6–7).[7] The ordinary Palestinian life to which Lazarus is restored is graphically represented by the feast at which both he and Jesus recline in John 12:1–2. In these three cases, then, "being raised" means being brought *back* to the old life one had exited through death.

(b) Corresponding to this common content is a common type of narrative, very similar in *form* to that of miracle stories of healing: (i) the encounter between Jesus and the sorrowing person (sometimes a petitioner), with a depiction of the doleful circumstances that move Jesus to act;[8] (ii) the word and/ or gesture of Jesus that raises the dead, along with the confirmation of this miraculous event by the actions of the person raised; (iii) the reaction of the bystanders: amazement, praise, or faith. The Gospels thus treat these acts of raising the dead as extreme examples of healing.[9] Thus, in these stories, being raised from the dead is very much connected with and conceived of in terms of physical life in this present world. The dead person is "healed" of the ultimate "sickness," death, and is thus restored to his or her former healthy life.

(2) Quite different in both content and form is the presentation of the resurrection *par excellence* in the NT, the resurrection of Jesus from the dead.[10]

(a) In *content* it is different basically because Jesus' own resurrection is not conceived of in terms of his "coming back" to the earthly life he once had. In this the Gospels agree with Paul's affirmation in Rom 6:9–10: "Christ, having been raised from the dead, will never die again; death no longer has dominion over him. For the death that he died, he died to [the domain of] sin once and for all, but the life that he lives he lives in [the domain of] God." In other words, the resurrection of Jesus is portrayed in the Gospels not as a return to his former mortal life but as a passing through and beyond death into the fullness of eternal life in God's presence. Having entered into a radically new type of existence, the risen Jesus is not subject to the restrictions of this world of time and space—an idea graphically depicted by his appearing and disappearing at will.

Another difference in content is that, during the public ministry, Jesus himself was the agent who raised dead people to life. In contrast, the NT usually attributes Jesus' own resurrection (or exaltation) to the action of God the Father.[11] One of the earliest Christian formulas proclaiming the resurrection

simply stated that "God [the Father] raised Jesus from the dead" (cf. the variations on this theme in 1 Thess 1:10; Gal 1:1; 1 Cor 6:14; 15:15; 2 Cor 4:14;
Rom 8:11; 10:9; Col 2:12; Eph 1:20; 1 Pet 1:21; Acts 2:24,32; 3:15; 4:10; 5:30;
10:40; 13:33–37; 17:31).[12] In light of this, the various NT statements in the
passive voice (e.g., "Christ was raised from the dead") should, in general, be
understood to have God the Father as the implied agent.[13]

(b) As the proclamation of Jesus' own resurrection differs in content from
the narratives of his raising people from the dead during his public ministry,
so it differs as well in literary form. The most striking difference is that there
simply is no narrative form for Jesus' own resurrection. The event of Jesus'
rising from the dead is never directly narrated. In this the canonical Gospels
differ markedly in their sobriety from the later apocryphal gospels, such as the
2d-century Gospel of Peter.[14]

To be sure, the canonical Gospels have two types of post-resurrection narratives: the finding of the empty tomb and Jesus' appearances to chosen witnesses. But the resurrection itself is never narrated. It is simply prophesied
beforehand (e.g., Mark 8:31) and proclaimed after the fact (e.g., Mark 16:6).
In this the Gospels do not really differ all that much from the epistles of Paul,
who recalls the primitive creedal formulas that affirm but do not describe the
resurrection of Jesus (e.g., 1 Cor 15:4).

All these distinctions are made simply to stress that in what follows I will
be speaking directly of "raising the dead" only in the first sense, i.e., bringing
the dead back to life, a feat that Jesus is said to have accomplished during his
public ministry. Because of the built-in limitations of the quest for the historical Jesus, the question of Jesus' own resurrection from the dead does not come
within the purview of the quest.[15]

I will now take up in turn the raising of Jairus' daughter (Marcan tradition),
the raising of the son of the widow of Nain (Lucan tradition), the raising of
Lazarus (Johannine tradition), and finally the Q logion mentioning Jesus' acts
of raising the dead. In each case I will be focusing on the question of whether
the basic tradition goes back in some form or other to the public ministry of
the historical Jesus.[16]

III. THE MARCAN TRADITION: THE RAISING OF THE DAUGHTER OF JAIRUS (MARK 5:21–43 ‖ MATT 9:18–26 ‖ LUKE 8:40–56)

A. MARK'S REDACTION OF THE TRADITIONAL STORY

The vast majority of critics agree that the earliest written version of the story
available to us is the one preserved in Mark's Gospel. Redaction criticism has
shown how Matthew abbreviated and Luke rewrote the story to fit each evangelist's theological agenda.[17] Since neither Matthew nor Luke shows any indication of possessing independent tradition about the raising of the daughter of

Jairus, I will restrict my comments to Mark. The Matthean and Lucan texts are important for those investigating the redactional theologies of the evangelists, but they offer no help to those inquiring about historical tradition behind the present story.[18]

As we have already seen when treating the story of the woman with the hemorrhage (Mark 5:24–35), which is dovetailed with the story of Jairus' daughter in the present form of Mark's Gospel, the two stories probably existed independent of each other in an earlier stage of the tradition. Most likely, it was either Mark or the pre-Marcan redactor of the cycle of miracle stories preserved in Mark 4:35–5:43 who inserted the story of the woman with the hemorrhage into the story of the raising of Jairus' daughter.[19] (For the sake of brevity, the latter story will be referred to hereafter simply as "the Jairus story.")

If we extricate the Jairus story from the story of the hemorrhaging woman, can we discern any redactional touches added when the two stories were joined? Verse 21, which recounts Jesus' arrival on the shore of the sea after the story of the stilling of the storm is a bridge-verse and therefore most likely redactional.[20] Another likely candidate for a redactional addition would be most of 5:24, which comes right after Jairus' petition to Jesus (5:22–23) and the beginning of their journey to Jairus' house: "And there was following him [Jesus] a great crowd, and they kept pressing upon him." This sentence acts as a convenient bridge to the story of the woman who is able to touch Jesus undetected because of the crowd (5:25–27).[21]

Another change may have occurred at the end of the story of the hemorrhaging woman, but here the change may have been one of meaning rather than of wording. In 5:35 we are told that "while he was still speaking," messengers come from the synagogue ruler's house, announcing the daughter's death. In the present form of Mark's Gospel, "while he was still speaking" refers to Jesus speaking to the woman he has just healed. It is just possible, though, that when the earlier form of the Jairus story was a separate unit in the oral tradition, "while he was still speaking" described Jairus, who was still making his plea to Jesus when the sad news of his daughter's death arrived.[22] In other words, originally v 35 ("while he was still speaking . . .") would have followed immediately upon v 23, in which Jairus is begging Jesus to come and lay his hands on the girl to heal her. In this hypothesis, all of v 24 (including "and he [Jesus] went with him [Jairus]") drops out of the original Jairus story; the redactor has created the whole of v 24 as the bridge to the story of the hemorrhaging woman.

Another addition that Mark may have made to the traditional story is the presence in 5:37 + 40 of his favorite trio of disciples, Peter, James, and John, whom he also places at the "secret epiphanies" of Jesus' transfiguration (9:2) and his agonized prayer in Gethsemane before his arrest (14:33). Still, on the whole, Mark's additions or other changes to the traditional form of the Jairus story do not seem to have been massive. In fact, when the story of the hemorrhaging woman and the few redactional bridge-verses of Mark are removed, what is left of the Jairus story (vv 22–23,35–37a,38–43) makes almost perfect sense as a self-contained miracle story. There is virtually no further need for rewording, cutting, or adding verses.

I say "almost perfect sense" and "virtually no further need" because there is one disruption at the end of the Jairus story that may betray the redactional hand of Mark. At the end of a miracle story it is quite common to have first some confirmation of the reality of the miracle (e.g., the lame man gets up and walks, the mute man speaks) and then a reaction from the crowd (e.g., astonishment or an acclamation of praise). Compared with this pattern, the ending of the Jairus story strikes the reader as overloaded, redundant, and even self-contradictory.[23]

Instead of going into the child's death-chamber alone, as Elijah and Elisha are said to do when they raise dead youths to life (1 Kgs 17:19,23; 2 Kgs 4:33, 36–37; cf. Peter in Acts 9:40), Jesus purposely takes along the father and mother of the child (plus Peter, James, and John in Mark's redaction). Obviously they are present as witnesses, not helpers. When Jesus raises the child to life, v 42ab tells us that "immediately the young girl stood up and began walking around (for she was twelve years old)."[24] The girl's physical activity no doubt counts as the confirmation of her being raised from the dead. Verse 42c continues with the reaction of the bystanders: "And they were beside themselves with astonishment [literally, "they were astonished with great astonishment"]." The reader might well expect the miracle story to end here with the reaction of the audience (and perhaps with a reference to the story spreading abroad), as many miracle stories do in Mark (e.g., 1:27–28; 2:12; 3:6; 4:41; 5:17,20; 6:51–52; 7:37).

But the story does not end in v 42. Verse 43a proceeds to sound the secrecy motif that is characteristic of Mark's Gospel: "And he gave them a strict command that no one should know this." Despite the loose usage of some commentators, one should not use the label "messianic secret" for this command. Unlike most of the exorcism stories (e.g., 1:24–25,34; 3:11–12; 5:7), the miracle stories of healing in Mark do not threaten to trigger a direct revelation of Jesus' secret identity as Son of God, but only his miraculous power to heal. At the end of some—but not all—of Mark's miracle stories, it is the general aura of mystery surrounding Jesus that is emphasized when Jesus commands the participants to remain silent about the miracle just worked.[25] That we have such a command here is clear from the wording: ". . . that no one should know this," i.e., the miracle of raising the girl, not the identity of Jesus as Son of God (contrast the exorcisms in 1:24–25,34; 3:11–12; 5:7).

The upshot of all this is that in 5:43 Mark, as is his wont, has inserted a command of silence at the end of a miracle story; but here, more than anywhere else in the Gospel, the command makes no sense. After all, the messengers from Jairus' house had announced the death of the girl in the presence of the whole crowd, before Jesus left the crowd behind (vv 35–37). By the time Jesus arrives at Jairus' house, a group of mourners, probably family and friends, has already gathered, bewailing the girl's death and then laughing at Jesus when he announces that the girl is not (definitively) dead (vv 38–39).[26] In the face of such public knowledge of the girl's death, the absolute command of silence is absurd. With the mourners still outside the house and the once-dead girl running around the room and munching on food, the idea that the parents could keep her being raised to life a secret even for a relatively short time is ludicrous.[27] Clearly, Mark is so intent on his theological theme of secrecy and "secret epiphanies" that he does not care about the narrative's verisimilitude at this point. All the more bewildering is the final sentence on which the whole story ends (v 43b): "And he [Jesus] told them to give her something to eat." Whether this second command is meant to be a second confirmation of the reality of the girl's being restored to bodily life (ghosts do not eat ordinary food), a sign of Jesus' practical concern for the girl's welfare while her parents are frozen with astonishment, or both is disputed among critics.[28] In any event, it comes awkwardly after the Marcan command for silence and seems out of place—possibly another sign of Mark's intrusive and disruptive hand at the end of the story.

One obvious corollary of all these considerations is that Mark himself has not created the Jairus story out of whole cloth. The meshing of two different miracle stories that probably once enjoyed independent existence, the need to create a bridge between the two stories in 5:24, the awkward insertion by Mark of his beloved theme of secrecy into a story where it makes no sense—plus Jesus' Aramaic command, *talitha koum*, which must be translated into Greek for Mark's audience—all indicate a previous tradition Mark has inherited and edited. If, as scholars like Kertelge and Pesch think, there was a pre-Marcan redactor who formed the cycle of miracle stories now found in Mark 4:35–5:43, the Jairus story would have existed as a separate unit still earlier, before the pre-Marcan collection was made.

B. THE BASIC FORM AND CONTENT OF THE TRADITIONAL STORY

The exact wording of the earliest form of the Jairus tradition cannot be reconstructed with certainty, especially since the preservation of Jesus' command in Aramaic (*talitha koum*) points to an Aramaic original. Still, the overall form and content of the story seem clear enough. The primitive narrative would have had the basic three-part structure of a miracle story, but with the initial encounter greatly expanded to allow for the transition from a story of healing to a story of raising the dead:[29]

(1) The initial *encounter* turns into a lengthy "setup."

(a) In the initial encounter proper (5:22–23), "one of the synagogue rulers,"[30] named Jairus, comes to Jesus, falls down at his feet, and begs him: "My little daughter is at the point of death. Come, lay your hands on her, that she may recover and live."[31]

(b) In 5:35–36, a story of healing begins to make the transition to a story of raising the dead. While Jairus is still speaking, messengers come from his house, announcing his daughter's death and indicating that any further appeal to Jesus is futile. But Jesus encourages Jairus to continue believing and sets out with him for the house.[32]

(c) Before the miracle proper takes place, Jesus narrows down the circle of witnesses (5:38–40). When they arrive at the house, Jesus perceives the uproar of people weeping and lamenting. Upon entering the house he says: "Why do you create this uproar and weep? The child is not dead but asleep." When they laugh at him in derision, Jesus throws them all out. Then he takes the mother and father and enters the chamber where the child is.

(2) The *miracle proper* with its confirmation is then narrated (5:41–42ab). Taking the hand of the child, Jesus says: "*Talitha koum* [little girl, arise]." And immediately the little girl gets up and starts walking around.[33]

(3) The final part of the story is the *reaction* of the bystanders, namely, the parents (5:42c): they are greatly astonished.

Whether Jesus' command that the girl be fed (5:43b) was part of the original story is difficult to say. The double confirmation (walking and eating) is odd; some would explain v 43b as an addition made when the original story of healing was turned into a story of raising the dead.[34] Since, in my opinion, the Jairus story was from the start a narrative about raising the dead, v 43b was probably present from the beginning. Its presence is explainable by the special nature of a miracle of raising the dead—the only such miracle in Mark. That the girl gets up and walks around indicates that she is—at least in some sense— alive. But is she perhaps a ghost or some preternatural creature? The eating of ordinary food may be meant to demonstrate that this is the very same girl who just died, now returned to her former human life.[35] Hence the double confirmation, walking and eating. Possibly Mark's insertion of his secrecy motif (5:43a) disturbed the connection and order of the two types of confirmation; admittedly, though, any position on such a question of detail must remain highly speculative.[36]

In any event, what stands out in this reconstruction is the long first part (the extended "encounter" section), in which a miracle of healing gradually becomes a miracle of raising the dead. Possibly the original form of the story had a briefer first part, which was gradually expanded as the story was retold. Still, all three Gospel stories of raising the dead, for all their differences, share one clear trait that distinguishes them from the Elijah-Elisha stories as well as from Peter's raising of Tabitha in Acts 9:36–43: no one ever thinks of asking— —or dares to ask—Jesus from the start for a miracle of restoring life to the dead.[37] For the petitioners, that is simply beyond the realm of the possible. Hence it is reasonable to suppose that, even in its primitive form, the Jairus story involved some transition in its first part (the encounter) from Jairus' petition that Jesus heal a sick girl to Jesus' determination to raise up a dead girl. Whether the transition was managed with notably fewer words than we now have in Mark 5:22–23,35–36,38–40 we cannot say.

C. A STILL EARLIER FORM OF THE STORY?

In my view, we have arrived at the earliest form of the Jairus story attainable by critical means. In fairness, though, I should note that scholars like Kertelge,

Pesch, and Rochais think that we can push back still further to a radically simpler story, namely, a miracle story of healing that had not yet been transformed into a story of raising the dead. While their theories differ in detail, the basic thrust of their reconstruction is the same. After Jairus' petition for a healing in the encounter proper (5:22–23) and Jesus' departure with him (v 24a), the story proceeded immediately to Jesus' arrival at Jairus' house (there are no messengers and no news of an intervening death). At the house Jesus sees a crowd already assembled and making a din (v 38). Throwing them all out, he enters with the parents into the chamber where the child is (v 40). Taking the (sick, not dead) child's hand, he raises her up (v 41). The young girl immediately stands up and begins to walk around. The parents are greatly astonished.[38]

Such a reconstruction is certainly possible, but in my opinion the arguments put forward in its favor are not convincing.[39] For example, Kertelge bases his reconstruction on a supposed similarity between the Jairus story and the story of the centurion's servant. Yet a comparison of the two stories would uncover many more dissimilarities than similarities. Kertelge's parallels between the two stories are tenuous at best.[40]

Pesch constructs an even more detailed and complicated tradition history. He attempts to show how the symbolic meaning of the name Jairus ("he [God] will enlighten" or "he will awaken") and the OT pattern of the Elijah-Elisha stories of raising the dead influenced a primitive story of healing to become a story of raising the dead.[41] Granted, any reconstruction of the tradition history of the Jairus story must remain speculative, but Pesch's theory is open to many objections.

(1) Pesch's argument about Jairus' name is not particularly strong. To begin with, it is somewhat precarious to base a tradition history of this miracle story even partially on the symbolic meaning of Jairus' name, since we are not sure of the exact meaning of "Jairus" ("enlighten" or "awaken"?).[42] Moreover, many Jewish names in the ancient world were "theophoric," i.e., in abbreviated fashion they expressed faith or hope in some particular action of God. For example, Isaiah means "Yahweh saves," Ezekiel means "God strengthens," and John (= Joḥanan) means "Yahweh is gracious."[43] If one so desired, one could easily think up correlations between the names and the religious careers of Isaiah, Ezekiel, and John the Baptist. This would hardly prove that their names had somehow generated their particular messages or careers. Similarly, the ordinary Hebrew name Jairus, which is well attested in the OT,[44] is in no way unusual in having a theological meaning. The supposed correlation between its meaning and the idea of raising the dead hardly proves that the name Jairus helped transform a story of healing into a story of raising the dead. In fact, one may wonder about the exact relevance of *Jairus'* name if, as seems likely, its proper explanation is "he [God] will enlighten." It takes more than a small leap of the imagination to get from the synagogue ruler bearing this name to Jesus raising the synagogue ruler's daughter from the dead.[45] Indeed, one wonders how Mark's audience, which has to have Aramaic words like *tali-*

5:5; 8:24 (bis), 45; 9:33,49; cf. Fitzmyer, *The Gospel According to Luke*, 2. 1154. Glombitza ("Der dankbare Samariter," 242–43) claims that the use of *epistata* by all ten lepers shows that Luke thinks of the ten as belonging to the circle of disciples in the widest sense. This is difficult to sustain in light of the fact that, while the story presumes that all ten lepers have some vague, initial trust in Jesus as a miracle-worker, only the Samaritan, who returns to give thanks, is declared by Jesus to have the faith that saves. How could Luke conceive of people as disciples of Jesus in any meaningful sense if they did not have the faith that saves?

[129] Marshall (*The Gospel of Luke*, 649) adds the helpful observation that, because in general Luke avoids doublets in his narrative material, it is unlikely that he created 17:11–19 from Mark 1:40–45, since he has already taken over the Marcan story in Luke 5:12–16; similarly, Latourelle, *The Miracles of Jesus*, 199. As Marshall (ibid.) comments, "the theory that this story [in Luke 17:11–19] is a variant of the Marcan one appears to have no stronger basis than the questionable assumption that there can originally have been only one story of the cure of a leper." It is surprising to see that Pesch's whole argument for the dependence of Luke 17:11–19 on Mark 1:40–45 comes down to the presence in both stories of Jesus' command to the leper(s) to show himself/ themselves to the priest(s) (*Jesu ureigene Taten?*, 126–27). Actually, the command would be almost unavoidable in a miracle story that presented Jesus curing leprosy in a 1st-century Palestinian situation. Especially since the command has a different position and a slightly different function in Luke's story—a function that makes perfect sense there—there is no basis for the claim that Jesus' command in Luke 17:14 proves that the Lucan story is dependent on the Marcan one.

[130] Betz ("The Cleansing," 321) suggests that behind the present Lucan story there lay the oldest layer of the tradition (a healing of ten lepers, of whom only one returns to give thanks) plus a second layer (introducing the anti-Jewish note that the one thankful leper was a Samaritan); Luke then added certain touches when he redacted the tradition. As Fitzmyer rightly notes (*The Gospel According to Luke*, 2. 1151), this reconstruction, while not impossible, remains "quite speculative."

[131] Contrary to Latourelle (*The Miracles of Jesus*, 199), I do not include in this list of independent witnesses *Egerton Papyrus 2*, since I judge it to be dependent on the Synoptic tradition. For my reasons, see *A Marginal Jew*, 1. 118–20, 149 nn. 39 and 41. Curiously, while Pesch (*Jesu ureigene Taten?*, 107–9, 120) thinks that *Egerton Papyrus 2* reflects a further development of the Synoptic tradition even after the writing of the Gospels (the Gospels being recalled from memory), he nevertheless suggests that the author of the papyrus knew the pre-Lucan version of Luke 17:11–19. This strikes me as an unnecessary complication of a basically correct hypothesis. The knowledge of the special L material seen in the papyrus is most easily explained by reminiscences of the actual Gospel of Luke.

[132] When I speak of "one occurrence" of a *type* of miracle, I am prescinding from Synoptic parallels that are literarily dependent, e.g., on Mark. For example, the story of the healing of the woman with the hemorrhage, while present in all three Synoptics, "occurs" only once according to this mode of classification.

[133] This point is often missed by Latourelle in his argumentation about the historicity of the miracle stories. For example, in his treatment of the healing of Peter's mother-in-law, Latourelle appeals to "multiple attestation" (*The Miracles of Jesus*, 83). In fact, while all three Synoptics have the story, both Matthew and Luke are clearly dependent on Mark, and so there is no multiple attestation of sources. One of the weaknesses of Latourelle's whole approach is his oscillating and erratic position on the

sources of the Gospels. Gospel relationships seem to be defined in any given narrative depending on the usefulness of a theory to Latourelle's apologetic purpose.

[134] The adjective *mogilalos* (Mark 7:32) occurs only here in the NT and only once in the LXX (Isa 35:6 for the Hebrew *'illēm*). The literal sense of *mogilalos* is "speaking with difficulty" or "having a speech impediment." It can also carry the more general sense of "mute," and that seems to be the sense in LXX Isa 35:6, since the other OT examples of *'illēm* in the MT (Exod 4:11; Isa 56:10; Hab 2:18; Ps 38:14; Prov 31:8) most likely mean "mute," "speechless."

Since in Mark 7:31–37 the man, when cured, is said to speak correctly, clearly, or normally (*elalei orthōs* in v 35), the literal sense seems to be the one intended in 7:32: because of his deafness, the man had not learned to speak in a normal and clear fashion. The only objection to this line of reasoning is that the choral conclusion to the miracle praises Jesus for making the deaf to hear and the mute [*alalous*, "those without speech"] to speak. This choral conclusion, though, is expressed in the generalizing plural and harks back to OT prophecy. Moreover, if the core of the narrative in 7:31–37 goes back to some event in the life of Jesus, the stylized choral conclusion, typical of the literary form of a miracle story, is almost certainly secondary, a theological reflection of the early church or of Mark. Philology aside, I refer in what follows to the "deaf-mute" purely for the practical reason of brevity.

[135] For a study of the pericope, see Xavier Léon-Dufour, "La guérison de la belle-mère de Simon-Pierre," *Etudes d'évangile* (Parole de Dieu; Paris: Editions du Seuil, 1965) 124–48. The usefulness of Léon-Dufour's study is limited by his unusual view of the Gospel sources: Matthew and Luke both depend on pre-Synoptic traditions that have only an indirect relation to Mark; no two Synoptists are directly dependent on the third as their source.

A word should be said about the common title of the pericope: "the healing of Simon's mother-in-law." Technically, a fever is not an illness to be healed but only a symptom of an illness (e.g., malaria). However, in this case as in the case of the man with dropsy, the Gospel texts reflect the popular mentality of the time when they speak of Jesus healing what we would consider symptoms. Since I must begin my discussion by exegeting the text as it stands, I retain the Evangelists' way of speaking.

Different from the story of Peter's mother-in-law is the story of the royal official's son in John 4:46–54. In John the major problem for which Jesus' help is requested is an unnamed illness that is about to cause the death of the official's son. The story revolves around the father's fear that his son is about to die and Jesus' promise that "your son lives" (v 50). Only at the end of the story, when the father asks his servants when the son got better, do the servants mention, as a way of specifying the hour of improvement, that it was at the seventh hour of the previous day that the *fever* left the boy. Here the fever is mentioned as a symptom of the deadly illness, the illness itself being the object of the official's request and Jesus' healing action. Hence, instead of ranging John 4:46–54 alongside the story of Peter's mother-in-law, I will reserve discussion of it until I treat what is more properly its parallel, the Q story of the centurion's servant.

[136] Here one must allow for the possibility of symbolism in the narrative. The two other miracles in Mark in which Jesus is said to take a person's hand both involve some sort of "resurrection" or restoration to life of an apparently dead person: the daughter of Jairus (Mark 5:41, *kratēsas tēs cheiros*) and the epileptic boy (9:27, *kratēsas tēs cheiros*), who is said after his exorcism to "become like a dead man" or "a corpse" (*hōsei nekros*). Hence when we are told in 1:31 that Jesus "raised her up by taking hold of her hand"

tha koum translated for it, could be expected to catch the pun Pesch discerns when in v 36 Jesus tells Jairus not to fear but only to believe. Pesch claims that Jesus is urging Jairus to believe *in the meaning of Jairus' own name:* God will awaken (= raise from the dead) his daughter through Jesus.[46] This is more than a little farfetched.

(2) Pesch makes the erroneous claim that the Jairus story has an otherwise unattested trait: it is a story of raising the dead in which a petitioner first asks for the healing of a sick person and then the death of the sick person is announced.[47] Here Pesch is mistaken. The independent Johannine tradition also has a story of a sick person whose relatives petition Jesus for a miracle of healing and who dies before Jesus arrives: the raising of Lazarus. One can understand why Pesch would not want the story line of the Jairus narrative surfacing in another, independent stream of Gospel tradition. After all, are we to suppose that, by a happy coincidence, in two separate Gospel sources a story about healing changed into a story about raising the dead? In the view of critics who have explored the tradition history of the Lazarus story, this does not seem to be the case for the Johannine tradition. As far back as they can trace the story, it is a story about raising a dead person to life.[48] There is no positive reason for thinking the same is not true of the Jairus story. Moreover, this theory of transformation from a story of healing will not work for all the NT stories of raising the dead. It is not applicable at all to the story of the widow of Nain, which opens with the son's body about to be buried.

(3) The OT parallels of the raising of the dead performed by the prophets Elijah and Elisha are also invoked by Pesch as influences that helped transform the Jairus story from one of healing to one of restoring the dead to life. Yet Pesch must admit that the allusions to the Elijah-Elisha stories in the Jairus story remain for the most part unclear and indirect.[49] That is putting it mildly, for at some crucial points the Elijah-Elisha parallels are not parallels at all. Especially crucial for the Jairus story—as well as the Lazarus story—is the pattern of moving from an initial petition for healing the sick to a miracle of raising the dead. In the Elijah-Elisha stories of raising the dead, the sick person has already died when the petitioner first asks the prophet for help (1 Kgs 17:17–18; 2 Kgs 4:20). From the beginning of the Elijah-Elisha stories the problem is a death that has already occurred, and from the beginning the petitioner dares to request—or at least intimate—that the prophet bring the dead back to life. In this, as in a number of other traits, the Elijah-Elisha stories are closer to Peter's raising of Tabitha in Acts 9:36–43.[50]

(4) All this brings us to a further objection. If the name Jairus and the supposed Elijah-Elisha parallels are really not all that cogent as explanations for the transformation of the Jairus story into a story of restoring the dead to life, Pesch is left with an unanswered question. Why is it that, amid all the Marcan stories of healing—indeed, amid all the miracles in all Four Gospels—such a transformation from a healing story to a story about raising the dead occurred only once? And why precisely in the case of the daughter of Jairus? Would not the stories of the healing of Peter's mother-in-law or the Syro-

phoenician's daughter—to take but two examples—have lent themselves just as easily to such a transformation? Why the restraint of the Marcan tradition, as well as the other Gospel traditions?

Behind all these individual objections stands the ultimate problem with the theory that the Jairus narrative was originally a story of healing that was transformed into one of raising the dead: there is no positive evidence for such a transformation in the text we have before us. Why, then, is the theory so popular? I suspect that some critics have in the back of their minds a further, distinct question: What really happened? What event lies behind this story? But that is a different question, distinct from the question of how to trace the earlier stages of the story in the Christian tradition. A common methodological error in Gospel studies is to confuse the question of the stages involved in handing on a Christian *story*, oral or written, with the further question of the original *event* in the life of Jesus, if indeed one existed.

The reader will have noticed by now that, each time I have treated a miracle story at length, I have first examined the text as it stands and tried to trace the earlier stages of the story in the Christian tradition, and only then turned to the question of a possible event in the life of Jesus. If we focus upon the *story* of the raising of the daughter of Jairus and its tradition history, it seems to me that nothing in the story argues strongly that it was originally a *story* of healing rather than of restoring the dead to life. To be sure, it is not impossible that historically, in the life of Jesus, the originating event was an act of healing. But as far as we can trace back the Christian story in the Gospel tradition, the story seems to have been one of raising the dead. Just as we acknowledge that at times important changes occurred between the earlier and later stages of a Christian story about Jesus, so we must allow the possibility that important transformations may have taken place between the time of the originating event in the life of Jesus and the earliest form of the Christian story available to us.

D. DOES THE STORY GO BACK TO JESUS' MINISTRY?

Having sketched what seems to be the earliest form of the Jairus story available to us, we can move to the further question: Are there any signs of this tradition having roots in the life of Jesus? Are there any signals in the text that the story may go back to some event (whatever that event may have been) in the public ministry?

There are some striking linguistic phenomena that at least make the question worth asking. As we saw when we did a global survey of the miracle stories, in the Synoptic Gospels—and in this they differ markedly from some of the later apocryphal gospels—there is a strong tendency not to mention the proper names of the petitioners or beneficiaries of miracles (other than the twelve disciples) in full-length miracle stories. To be more precise, in all three Synoptic Gospels Jairus is the only individual (apart from the twelve disciples) who is directly named as the petitioner for a healing or exorcism of another person.[51]

Also striking, in the view of the church's struggles with the Jewish synagogue during the 1st century, is the designation of this singularly favored petitioner as "one of the synagogue rulers" (*heis tōn archisynagōgōn* in Mark 5:22). Not only does Matthew drop the proper name Jairus but more pointedly he changes the man's status to the vague description of "a ruler" (*archōn heis* in Matt 9:18). Contrary to the distaste evinced by Matthew, Mark and his source apparently saw no difficulty in presenting a leader of the synagogue as a successful petitioner for a healing miracle. The mentioning of Jairus by name—as well as Bartimaeus, the only named beneficiary of a miracle in Mark's Gospel—is also remarkable in that the petitioners and beneficiaries in other lengthy miracle stories of the Four Gospels (e.g., the Gerasene demoniac, the distraught father of the demoniac boy, the man born blind of John 9) almost cry out to be named, but are not. The same holds true of petitioners of high social status, such as the centurion of the Q document and the royal official of the Johannine tradition. In short, the curious and largely unparalleled naming of the petitioner of a miracle at least invites us to examine the question of possible historical tradition more closely.

Another striking linguistic phenomenon is that Mark gives Jesus' climactic command, "Young girl, arise," in Aramaic (*talitha koum*) as well as in Greek translation (*to korasion . . . egeire*).[52] As we saw in Volume One, Aramaic was the language Jesus regularly used in addressing his fellow Palestinian Jews; but only a few traces of his Aramaic words have been preserved in our Four Gospels.[53] In fact, *talitha koum* and *ephphatha* ("be opened" in the story of the deaf-mute in Mark 7:34) are the only cases of Jesus' Aramaic words of command appearing in miracle stories of the Four Gospels. At the very least, then, our Greek Gospels do not attempt to create an artificial air of ancient tradition by regularly inserting Aramaic phrases into Gospel narratives in general or miracle stories in particular.[54]

That *talitha koum* is not some secondary attempt by a learned scribe to inject a feeling of historical reality into the later Greek stage of the Jesus tradition is shown by Jesus' use of the technically incorrect form of the verb *koum* for "little girl, arise." Strictly speaking, *koum* is the masculine-singular form of the imperative; the feminine-singular imperative would be *koumi*. Scholars suggest that, at the time of Jesus, popular speech either simply used the masculine for the feminine form or failed to pronounce the final, unaccented *i* of the feminine form—which comes down to the same thing.[55] Hence, Jesus, reflecting popular rather than learned usage, employed the set form *koum*, which almost had the force of an indeclinable interjection or adverb. Not surprisingly, later scribes intervened in the Marcan text to change the incorrect *koum* to *koumi* in some manuscripts, but the original form in Mark's text is undoubtedly *koum*.[56] It may well be a trace of the popular Aramaic Jesus actually spoke as opposed to the correct Aramaic some scribes wished he had spoken.

In addition to this Aramaic phrase, the Greek text of the Jairus story displays a number of other Semitisms, i.e., examples of word usage, grammar, and syntax that are unusual or impossible in proper Greek but are common in Semitic languages and therefore reflect an underlying Semitic text that has been translated woodenly into Greek. After an extensive analysis of the Greek text of the Jairus story in Mark, Gérard Rochais detects about six candidates for Semitisms in the narrative. Some of his candidates are debatable, but at least a few are probably true Semitisms.[57] Thus, not only *talitha koum* in Mark 5:41 but also other signs of a Semitic substratum point to an early stage of this story when it circulated in Aramaic in Palestine.

This does not in itself prove that the story reflects an originating event in the life of Jesus. If nothing else, though, it confirms that the story had a remarkably long life in the oral and written tradition: from Mark's redaction it reached back, probably through a collection of miracle stories in Greek, to a still earlier stage as an individual story in the Greek oral tradition,[58] and prior to that to an existence as an Aramaic story circulating in Palestine. Given that Mark's Gospel was probably written somewhere around A.D. 70, this lengthy tradition history, reaching back to the early Aramaic tradition about Jesus current in Palestine before A.D. 70, at the very least situates the Jairus story closer in time and place to the historical Jesus than is the case with a number of other Gospel stories.

Another sign of the very early nature of the pre-Marcan form of the Jairus story is the startling absence of any christological title or explicit christological statement in what must count as the greatest type of miracle story imaginable. The closest one gets to a christological title is the actually dismissive reference to Jesus by the messengers who announce the daughter's death (5:35): "Why bother the teacher any further?" The subliminal message here is that Jesus is only a teacher, and death marks the limit of whatever power he may have. This absence of christological titles, which is still seen in Mark's version, is modified only slightly by Luke, who introduces the characteristically Lucan title "Master" (*epistata*) in Peter's address to Jesus in Luke 8:45. On the whole, though, both the Matthean and Lucan redactions of the Jairus story follow Mark's lead in not adding major christological titles to a story that apparently lacked them from the beginning.

This dearth of christological titles stands out all the more when one compares the Jairus story with the other two Gospel narratives of raising the dead. In the raising of the son of the widow of Nain, Luke has a typical choral acclamation at the narrative's conclusion (7:16): "*A great prophet* has arisen among us, and God has visited his people [to save them]." Much greater is the difference between the Marcan version of the Jairus story and John's narrative of the raising of Lazarus. In keeping with the high christology of the Fourth Gospel, the raising of Lazarus supplies the context in which Jesus proclaims that he is the Resurrection and the Life and Martha professes her faith in him as the Messiah and Son of God who has come into the world (John 11:25,27). Actually, this effusive exaltation of the miracle-worker is almost what we might expect in a story where the hero performs the ultimate feat of raising the dead to life. What is strange is rather the lack of any such christological confession in the Jairus story, a lack that again points in the direction of early tradition. Indeed, the Jairus story, taken by itself, does not even contain any pointer toward or thematic connection with Jesus' own resurrection—a connection that John's story of Lazarus is at pains to make.

Beyond these various indications of very early tradition, the Jairus story also contains elements that relate to the criteria of embarrassment and discontinuity. To be sure, many Gospel stories indicate that Jesus met with disbelief, rejection, and hostility at the hands of various audiences. Yet it is startling to hear in Mark 5:40 that, just before he is about to raise the dead to life, the all-powerful miracle-worker is laughed to scorn (*kategelōn*) by the bystanders. Nowhere else in the Gospels is Jesus the object of this verb,[59] and in no other miracle story, even where Jesus meets with disbelief, is he made the direct object of this kind of scornful laughter.

Another highly unusual and surprising element follows right upon the scornful laughter: in Mark's Gospel Jesus himself throws all the mocking bystanders out of the house (*autos de ekbalōn pantas*).[60] Significantly, Matthew changes this embarrassing statement into the passive voice ("when the crowd had been thrown out"), thus avoiding the picture of Christ as bouncer. Luke simply omits the whole scene of the mourning bystanders and so obviates the problem of Jesus personally throwing the mourners out of the house. As with the mocking laughter of the mourners, so with the forceful physical reaction of Jesus throwing them out: no other miracle story in the Gospels has anything quite parallel.

We arrive at an observation made a number of times already in our survey. None of the considerations listed above establishes by itself that the Jairus story goes back to some event in the life of Jesus. Yet the convergence of all the considerations in one miracle story—its lengthy tradition history, the unusual mentioning of the petitioner's name and his status as a synagogue ruler, the indications of a Semitic substratum and especially the striking *talitha koum*, the absence of any christological title or affirmation, and the elements of embarrassment and discontinuity—incline me to the view that the Jairus story does reflect and stem from some event in Jesus' public ministry. In other words, the story is not an invention of the early church pure and simple, however much it may have been expanded and reinterpreted by Christian faith.

But, if some historical event lies behind the Jairus story, what was it? What did Jesus do that triggered this narrative? Here we reach the limits of the knowable, and pure speculation takes over. As I have already indicated, it is possible that the daughter of Jairus was actually the recipient of one of Jesus' miracles of healing; but, since she was so close to death, the enthusiastic followers of Jesus early on, even during his own lifetime, transformed the event into a story of raising the dead. Other scholars suggest the possibility that the girl was unconscious or had lapsed into a coma from which Jesus roused her. In such a case, the event might have been hailed by the disciples as an act of raising the dead from the very beginning. In favor of this view is a point that I have already stressed: critics cannot produce solid reasons for thinking that the Jairus story ever circulated as a story of healing before it was supposedly changed into a story of restoring the dead to life.

A very different solution would remain a possibility for agnostics, namely, that the whole event was staged by Jesus and his followers as a way of gaining credibility, renown, and more disciples. On the opposite end of the ideological spectrum, some Christian believers would leave open the possibility of a true miracle of raising the dead. Many believers would also allow for the possibility that one of Jesus' acts of healing, when put into narrative form by his disciples, was transformed into an account of raising the dead.

When it comes to these explicitly agnostic or Christian explanations, we should remember what we saw in our treatment of the modern problem of miracles, as exemplified by the investigations done at Lourdes. The judgment that "this apparently miraculous event could not possibly be a miracle, no matter what" and the judgment that "this particular event is truly a miracle worked by God" are both affirmations that flow from one's overarching world-view rather than from examining the data of an individual incident. Both decisions, being of a philosophical or theological nature, go beyond what historical research, especially when applied to 2,000-year-old narratives, can ever affirm by its own rules of evidence and reasoning. As I have emphasized repeatedly, all that our investigation of the Jairus story—and all the other miracle stories of the Gospels—can hope to establish is that certain stories, rather than being pure creations of the early church, do go back to some action of the historical Jesus. In my view, such is the case with the story of Jairus' daughter, but one must be content with this admittedly vague affirmation.

IV. THE LUCAN TRADITION: THE RAISING OF THE SON OF THE WIDOW OF NAIN (LUKE 7:11–17)

A. THE PLACE OF THE MIRACLE WITHIN LUKE'S LARGER STORY

The story of the raising of the son of the widow of Nain (hereafter: the Nain story) is a unit unique to Luke's Gospel. Hence it is important to begin our analysis by appreciating its place within Luke's entire literary work and theology. After the Sermon on the Plain (6:20–49, Luke's version of the Q sermon used by Matthew to create his Sermon on the Mount), Luke continues Jesus' Galilean ministry with a series of incidents that display the merciful, saving action of God at work in Jesus' own actions. Jesus' miracles, which Luke has mentioned repeatedly in his account of the early days of the ministry (4:31–41; 5:12–26; 6:6–11), are now resumed with a special "slant."

First, Jesus heals at a distance the slave of a Gentile centurion and takes the occasion to praise the centurion's humble, trusting faith in comparison with what he has found in Israel (7:1–10). Then, simply because he is moved with compassion, Jesus (pointedly called "the Lord" by Luke) restores a dead son, an only child, to his weeping mother, a widow (7:11–17).[61] The crowd responds with an acclamation expressing its awe: a great prophet has arisen in their midst, and God has "visited" his people (7:17). This idea of God "visiting" his people Israel to save it through the ministry of Jesus is unique to Luke's Gospel within the NT.[62]

But not all are so easily impressed by this merciful visitation. Apparently puzzled by all this healing, life-giving activity with no fiery judgment in sight, John the Baptist asks through his envoys whether Jesus is "the stronger one," the fiery judge whose fearsome appearance John had prophesied back in 3:15–17: "Are you the one to come?" (7:19). Jesus replies by declaring that his miracles and his proclamation of good news to the poor (cf. 6:20–23) are the fulfillment of God's promise of salvation to Israel, especially as spoken by the prophet Isaiah (7:22). Significantly, the list of miracles in 7:22 culminates in the affirmation that "the dead are raised," pointing back to the immediately preceding story set in Nain.[63]

Clearly, Luke has placed the two miracle stories of the centurion's servant and the widow's son just before the Baptist's question to provide Jesus with a clear basis for his reply.[64] The Lucan Jesus then proceeds to emphasize a contrast: for all the differences between the Baptist and himself, the common people (including the despised toll collectors) have readily accepted both John and Jesus, while the Pharisees and the lawyers have scoffed at God's merciful plan of salvation (7:29–30), thus excluding themselves from it.[65]

These opposite responses to Jesus, manifested by the self-satisfied Pharisees on the one hand and by the ordinary people willing to confess their sins on the other, are then acted out at the end of chap. 7.[66] A sinful woman bathes Jesus' feet in her tears of repentance, while the proper Pharisee, who is Jesus' host at table, wonders how Jesus could be a prophet and still allow such a woman to touch him (7:36–39).[67] Jesus shows that he is indeed a prophet by replying to the Pharisee's unspoken objection with a parable. The parable, about two debtors who owe very different sums and who are both forgiven their debts, emphasizes the nexus between great forgiveness and great love. At the end of his parable Jesus declares that the woman's sins are forgiven because of her great love.[68] The astonished guests at the meal ask: "Who is this who even forgives sins?" Ignoring the question, Jesus concludes the scene (and chap. 7) by saying to the woman what he also says at the end of a number of miracles of healing: "Your faith has saved you; go in peace" (7:50). Miracles of healing and miracles of forgiveness are thus tied together as concrete manifestations of God's visitation of his people through Jesus.

To sum up: Luke is obviously developing a number of important theological themes in this chapter. God is graciously "visiting," i.e., coming to and acting upon, his people to bring them salvation through the ministry of Jesus. God's sick and sinful people receive this salvation appropriately enough through physical healing, the raising of the dead, and finally the spiritual equivalent of healing the sick or raising the dead, the forgiveness of sins. This salvation is offered especially to the poor, the marginalized, and the despised of society:

the widow bereft of children,[69] the sinful woman despised by the Pharisee, and even the slave of a Gentile centurion. In stark contrast, the smug Pharisees and lawyers laugh at God's saving plan as manifested in Jesus and so fail to be touched by it.

The failure to believe on the part of the Jewish leaders, as opposed to the common people, is balanced by the hint that the people God is visiting will no longer be restricted to the Jews. The Gentile centurion's faith, along with the healing of his servant at a distance, points forward to a time when the gospel message will reach out to the distant Gentiles, who—as the Acts of the Apostles will recount—will receive it with faith and so be incorporated into God's people.[70] Thus is the prophecy of Isaiah, recalled at the beginning of the Baptist's ministry, fulfilled: "And all flesh will see the salvation of God" (Isa 40:5, cited in Luke 3:6).[71] There may even be a hint of this breaking down of borders in the conclusion of the Nain story: "And this report about him [Jesus] spread throughout the whole land of the Jews and all the surrounding territory."[72]

Such is the vision of salvation history implied in Luke 7. As is clear from this chapter, Luke's christology never stands as a theme by itself, but is rather a function of this vision of salvation history.[73] In this time of the fulfillment of God's saving promise to Israel, Jesus undertakes a healing ministry among God's people similar to but greater than the ministries of the great prophets and miracle-workers once active in Galilee, Elijah and Elisha.[74] In healing the sick, raising the dead, proclaiming good news to the poor, and forgiving a repentant Israel its sins, Jesus transcends his prophetic types, just as he transcends even John the Baptist. Without a qualm Luke can have Jesus extol the Baptist as "more than a prophet" (7:26), as the eschatological messenger prophesied by Malachi (7:27), yes, even as the greatest human being ever born of woman (7:28). Luke has no fear of rivalry because, for Luke, Jesus surpasses all these glorious categories. He is "the Lord" without qualification, the Lord who raises the dead with a mere word (7:13–14). He is the super-prophet who can forgive sins and declare sinners saved (7:48–50). He is the proclaimer of good news who, by a miracle of healing at a distance, begins to reach out to believing Gentiles who call upon him as "Lord" (7:6), thus associating them with "the poor" of Israel, those Israelites who repent and believe, who are forgiven and raised from the dead.

In short, Luke has carefully located the Nain story within his larger theological composition. It both contributes to the greater whole and receives theological depth from its surroundings. From Luke's overarching vision let us now descend to the Nain story in particular.

B. TRADITION AND REDACTION IN THE NAIN STORY

Once we realize how well the Nain story fits Luke's literary and theological purposes, the question naturally arises: Did he create the story himself?[75] This question needs clarification. We need not suppose that Luke had to create the story with no building blocks to work with. In composing the Nain narrative,

Luke could have easily drawn upon other stories about raising the dead in both the Jewish and the Christian traditions. Indeed, at first glance one might argue that almost every element of the Nain story can be explained on the basis of other stories of raising the dead: the Elijah and Elisha stories in the Books of Kings, the Gospel story of the raising of the daughter of Jairus, and possibly even the story of Peter raising Tabitha in Acts.

(1) The Elijah-Elisha cycles in the Books of Kings supply the basic picture of an itinerant prophet from northern Israel, active in Galilee, who was famous for miracles, including raising the dead.

(a) The major OT parallel is found in 1 Kgs (= LXX 3 Kgdms) 17:7–24. Elijah encounters a widow (*chēra*) in distress at the gate (*pylōn*) of the city (*polis*) of Zarephath. Similarly, Jesus encounters a widow (*chēra*) in distress at the gate (*pylē*) of the city (*polis*) of Nain.[76] The widow of Zarephath has a son, apparently her only child (see 1 Kgs 17:12 in the Hebrew text; the LXX reads instead the plural "my children"). According to the story, when her only son died, Elijah restored him to life, "and he gave him to his mother" (*kai edōken auton tē mētri autou*, 17:23 in the LXX). The exact same Greek words occur in the exact same order in Luke 7:15, when Jesus, having raised the son to life, gives him back to his mother, the widow of Nain.[77] The Elijah story ends with the widow acclaiming Elijah as a "man of God" who has the true word of God in his mouth. In other words, the miracle causes her to recognize Elijah as a true prophet, just as Jesus' miracle causes the crowd to acclaim him as a great prophet.

(b) In 2 Kgs (= LXX 4 Kgdms) 4:8–37, a married woman in the city of Shunem in southern Galilee becomes a benefactress of the prophet Elisha. In return, Elisha promises the woman, who up to now was barren, that she will bear a son. In due time the promise is fulfilled, but later on the young son suddenly dies. After Elisha initially fails to raise the son merely by sending his servant to lay his staff on the boy, the prophet comes in person and raises the boy to life. Admittedly, this story does not supply as close a parallel to the Nain story as does 1 Kgs 17:7–24. Its one contribution is the setting in the city of Shunem in lower Galilee, not far from the town of Nain. Some critics opine that the setting of the Elisha story in Shunem suggested to the author of Luke 7:11–17 the venue of Nain nearby.

(2) From Mark's Gospel Luke naturally knew the story of the raising of the daughter of Jairus, which he takes over in Luke 8:40–42,49–56. Because Luke stays much closer to Mark's version of the Jairus story than does Matthew, his redactional changes are all the more interesting. Salient among them is the specification that Jairus' child is his *only* daughter (*thygatēr monogenēs* in 8:42), *monogenēs* being the adjective that Luke also applies to the son of the widow of Nain (*monogenēs huios* in 7:12).[78] Luke's desire for parallelism and pathos in these two stories is clear.[79]

The parallels do not end there. In both cases people are weeping at the death of the only child, and in both cases Jesus bids the person(s) weeping to stop (*mē klaie* in 7:13; *mē klaiete* in 8:52).[80] At both Nain and in the house of

Jairus, the raising of the dead takes place in the presence of the parent(s) as well as some other people. This contrasts with both the Elijah and the Elisha stories, in which the prophets are alone in a room when they raise the dead to life. Only afterwards does the OT prophet either bring the boy to the mother or the mother to the boy. Finally, the life-giving command of Jesus to the deceased son of the widow of Nain in Luke 7:14 ("Young man, I say to you, arise") is a perfect parallel to his command to Jairus' daughter in Mark 5:41 ("Little girl, I say to you, arise").[81]

(3) The story of Peter raising Tabitha from the dead (Acts 9:36–43) contains many similarities to the Elijah-Elisha stories; indeed, they may have been its chief source. Still, a few elements of the Tabitha story are closer to the Jairus story and the Nain story.[82] As in these two Gospel stories, and unlike the Elijah-Elisha stories, Peter directly addresses the deceased with a peremptory command that effects the miracle: "Tabitha, arise" (*Tabitha, anastēthi* in Acts 9:40). There is a further parallel that only the Nain and Tabitha stories share. In each story, the reaction of the deceased to the peremptory command is that he or she sits up (*anekathisen* in Luke 7:15 and Acts 9:40, the only two times the verb *anakathizō* is used in the NT).[83]

From this survey of texts we may conclude that it is conceivable that Luke created the Nain story out of the building blocks of other stories of revivification known to him. The disparate building blocks would have been selected and put together according to Luke's vision of Jesus as the merciful Lord, the prophet like—but greater than—Elijah, a "great prophet," mighty in word and work, through whom God has definitively "visited" his people Israel. This is a possible scenario, but is it the most probable? While it has its advantages—e.g., it does not postulate an otherwise unknown source—it must also face a number of objections.

(1) While our survey of the various stories of raising the dead at Luke's disposal is at first glance impressive, it glosses over many differences. We can compose the Nain story from our list of texts only by abstracting bits and pieces eclectically from all the various stories, while leaving the core of each story behind.

The many differences between the Nain story and the Elijah-Elisha stories are striking. (a) In the Elijah-Elisha stories, the pathos of each narrative is based upon the fact that the prophet has known the woman and her son for some time; he has helped the woman and she has helped him. This pathos is all the more powerful in the Elisha story, where the prophet has apparently brought about the miraculous birth of the son for the sterile mother. This detailed background of each story of raising the dead also has the effect of making the mother of the resuscitated son a full flesh-and-blood character, a major actor in each story. It is only by the mother's fierce importuning, indeed, reproaching of the prophet that he is moved to act.

In contrast, Jesus and the beneficiaries of the Nain miracle have never met before; the story has no extended "setup." We do not trace the history of the son from health through sickness to death; he is already dead at the beginning of the story. The widow takes no initiative vis-à-vis Jesus; indeed, there is no indication that she knows who he is. Hence there can be no petition and no mention of faith in Jesus or his power. For his part, Jesus acts simply because he feels compassion at the sight of a widow bereft of her only son (*idōn autēn . . . esplagchnisthē* in Luke 7:13).

(b) The whole manner in which the miracle is worked is different. In the OT stories, the deceased son is lying in a room in the house, not being carried on a bier to his grave. The prophet works alone in the room, with even the parent(s) excluded. Both Elijah and Elisha first pray to God and then stretch themselves out over the child (Elijah three times, Elisha twice) to reanimate the body by a sort of prophetic version of CPR. In contrast, the whole Nain story takes place in public, at the city gate. Instead of being a lone prophet, Jesus is accompanied by his disciples and a large crowd. To stop the bier on which the dead son is being carried to his grave, Jesus touches the bier, but he does not touch the son before the miracle. Without any prayer or physical manipulations, Jesus effects the raising of the dead simply with a brief, authoritative command: "Young man, I say to you, arise" (Luke 7:14). The acclamation or act of reverence that follows upon the miracle comes not from the mother in particular, as in the OT stories, but from "all." The Nain story then concludes with a statement that the story (or more precisely: the acclamation of the miracle-worker) spread far and wide, a motif lacking in the two raising-of-the-dead stories of the Elijah-Elisha cycles.

(2) The differences between the Nain story and the Jairus story are also clear. Jairus comes to Jesus with a petition that implicitly shows an incipient faith, a faith that is challenged to grow during the story; there is no petition and no mention of faith in the Nain story. More significantly, the Jairus story begins with the daughter being gravely ill; only during the course of the story does the daughter die and the miracle become one of restoring the dead to life. As we saw above, this factor has led some critics to suggest—wrongly, in my view—that the Jairus story was originally a story about a healing miracle, which only in the course of time became a story of raising the dead. Such a suggestion about the Nain story is hardly feasible. The whole movement of the narrative springs from its starting point: Jesus feels compassion at the sight of the widow bewailing her only son on his bier as he is carried to burial. The attendant circumstances of the two miracles are almost entirely different: the raising of Jairus' daughter before the restricted audience of her parents and three of Jesus' disciples versus the raising of the dead man in public before *two* large crowds (see Luke 7:11–12); the mockery of Jesus by the mourners in Jairus' house versus the reverent awe and acclamation of the crowd in Nain; the command that no one is to know about the restoration of the daughter to life versus the spread of Jesus' fame in and outside of Israel.[84] The basic idea that Jesus raises the child of a bereaved parent is all that the two stories have in common. Even here there is a remarkable difference: the father, Jairus, is—by way of exception—named, while the widow—as is usual for the petitioner in Gospel miracle stories of healing—is not.

(3) As we have seen, the story of Peter raising Tabitha finds its major parallels in the Elijah-Elisha stories, which, in turn, are notably different from the Nain story. Peter is summoned by believers, who at least implicitly are requesting that he raise the deceased Tabitha to life. Like the OT prophets, Peter is alone with the corpse in the chamber of death and prays to God for a miracle. Unique among the raising-of-the-dead stories we have seen is the insistence on Tabitha's good works and the implicit plea from the Christian widows that she be allowed to continue her support of them. The one common element here is the need of a widow or widows for support. But while this motive for the miracle is mentioned in the Tabitha story, it is only surmised by critics in the Nain story, without anything being explicitly said about it in the text. There are a few other elements that the Tabitha story shares with the Nain story: the resurrected person is said to "sit up" (*anekathisen*), and the story spreads, though in Acts 9:42 only throughout "the whole of [the town of] Joppa." Peter's command to rise is given in direct speech ("Tabitha, arise"), but Jesus' command in the Nain story is closer to that of the Jairus story.

In the case of the Tabitha story, beyond all these individual parallels there is one global observation: Luke seems at pains in Acts to supply continuity between the Jesus of the public ministry and his "successors" (i.e., the apostles and other church figures) by contouring stories about members of the early church so that they reflect the paradigmatic story of Jesus.[85] Hence it is more probable, for example, that Luke fashioned the trial and execution of Stephen in Acts 6–7 to mirror the passion of Jesus than that Luke refashioned the narrative about Jesus' death to make it reflect Stephen's.[86] The same thing can be said about Peter's raising of Tabitha. Its assimilation to the Jesus tradition Luke knew and used is more likely than the reverse.[87]

This survey of the many dissimilarities leaves us with a curious picture, if we wish to claim that Luke himself made up the Nain story, drawing its elements from other written stories about raising the dead. We would have to imagine Luke at his writing table with the texts of 3 Kingdoms, 4 Kingdoms, and Mark's Gospel spread out before him—the Tabitha story being an improbable source, especially in written form. We would further have to imagine Luke proceeding in a strange and eclectic manner, plucking one detail from one story and another detail from a second story, all the while leaving the substance and major circumstances of each story behind and creating a story that was actually like none of the models he used.[88]

In addition to this argument against a pure creation by Luke—an argument that proceeds in negative fashion—there are a number of elements in the Nain story that argue positively for some special pre-Lucan source of Jesus tradition (L). These elements seem to demand such a source, since they cannot be derived from stories about raising the dead in either the OT or Mark's Gospel.

(1) The most obvious element that cannot be derived from other stories of restoring the dead to life is the concrete venue of Nain. To claim that it is occasioned by Elisha's miracle of raising the dead at Shunem in 2 Kgs 4:8–37 is an act of exegetical desperation.[89] Shunem was a border town in the hill

territory of Issachar in southern Galilee. Overlooking the Plain of Jezreel, it stood near the hill of Moreh.[90] Nain, in the Plain of Jezreel, was located on the northern slope of the hill of Moreh, roughly five to six miles southeast of Nazareth, and to the northeast of Shunem. Thus, both Shunem and Nain were towns in southwestern Galilee, but there is no reason why the name of one would suggest the name of the other. There were many towns in southern Galilee better known than Nain. Why either Shunem or some other well-known town of Galilee would not have been chosen by Luke if he had simply created the Nain story under the influence of the Elijah-Elisha stories cannot be explained.

As a matter of fact, except for the single verse of Luke 7:11, the Galilean town called Nain is never mentioned in the OT, the NT, the pre-Christian pseudepigrapha, Philo, Josephus, or the Mishna.[91] How did Luke, who does not appear as well informed about Palestinian geography as some of the other evangelists, know about the existence of the obscure southern Galilean town of Nain?[92] Further, how did he know that it was a walled town—as recent archaeological excavations have shown—and therefore had a gate?[93] The very specificity of Nain militates against the theory that Luke has created the whole story. The name, and presumably at least the core of the unusual story attached to it, probably came to Luke from his special tradition (L).

(2) Other elements of the story may also point to a pre-Lucan tradition. Rochais, in particular, argues that the Greek text shows signs of a Semitic substratum.[94] Whether the examples he brings forward are probative is debatable. For instance, the paratactic style of narrative in 7:11–17 (i.e., the constant use of simple sentences joined by "and" instead of the use of subordinate clauses)[95] is not an ironclad proof of a Semitic source. The paratactic style could be explained either as popular Hellenistic Greek or as Luke's conscious imitation of Septuagint Greek with its Semitic, "biblical" feel. Nevertheless, while either explanation is theoretically possible, as a general rule Luke the stylist tends to eliminate parataxis when he edits Mark's material.[96] It would be strange for him to employ it if he were creating the narrative of 7:11–17 on his own.

Some other aspects of the text also seem to argue for a Semitic substratum––at least at first glance. For instance, Luke ends the Nain story by saying that the acclamation of Jesus "spread throughout the whole of the Jewish land and all the surrounding territory" (7:17). Now the Greek verb often translated as "spread" in this verse is *exerchomai*, literally "to go out." Rochais claims that in ordinary Greek *exerchomai* does not usually carry the sense of a report spreading to various places. In biblical Greek it can acquire that sense because it is used to translate Semitic verbs that can mean both "go out" and "spread." Possible candidates would include the Hebrew verb *yāṣāʾ* and the Aramaic verb *nĕpaq*.[97] However, one could argue that Luke is once again imitating the Semitic-flavored Greek he finds in the LXX, a type of Greek we find in NT authors even when they are not writing with some specific Semitic text before them. For instance, not only does Paul cite a Psalm text (Rom 10:18 = LXX

Ps 18:5) that contains *exerchomai* in the sense of news spreading, he also uses *exerchomai* in this way when he is writing on his own (1 Thess 1:8; 1 Cor 14:36). Similarly, in changing Mark's command to be silent at the end of the Jairus story, Matthew, composing on his own, uses *exerchomai* to state that "this report of the miracle spread [*exēlthen*] throughout that whole region" (Matt 9:26; cf. Mark 5:43). One might counter this argument with a point we have just seen: when Luke rewrites Mark's miracle stories, he tries to improve Mark's Greek vocabulary and style by moving away from Semitisms toward more normal Greek. That is certainly the case in his redaction of Mark's version of the Jairus story.[98] It would be strange, then, if, when composing another raising-the-dead story like the Jairus narrative, Luke should fail to pursue the good Greek style he evinces in redacting Mark.[99] In the end, though, one must admit that the various examples cited by Rochais demonstrate only the possibility of a Semitic source behind the Nain story; they do not prove its existence.[100]

(3) Another possible indication of Luke's redaction of a pre-Lucan story is the apparent attempt he makes to modify or recast the christology of the Nain story. As we have seen, the story concludes with the acclamation of Jesus as *a* (not *the*) great prophet.[101] While Luke accepts that designation as true (especially if one understands it as he does: the eschatological prophet mirroring yet surpassing Elijah and Elisha), the designation is not entirely adequate for a Christian evangelist writing toward the end of the 1st century A.D. For Luke, Jesus is above all Messiah, Lord, and Son of God, and he is such from the virginal conception onwards (Luke 1:32–35,43; 2:11). For an evangelist with this kind of christology, to have the account of such an astounding miracle as raising the dead define Jesus simply and solely as "a great prophet" (as apparently the pre-Lucan tradition did) is insufficient. It must be taken up into a larger vision.

It is therefore not by accident that here, for the first time in his Gospel, Luke himself refers to Jesus in his *third-person narrative* (as opposed to sayings material) with the simple, absolute title "the Lord" (*ho kyrios*). Luke sums up the wellspring of the entire action of the story in 7:13: "And seeing her [the widow], the Lord was moved with compassion." Here at 7:13 Luke begins a string of narrative references to the earthly Jesus as the Lord that will continue throughout his Gospel. The important point is that this *regular* use of "the Lord" for the earthly Jesus in Gospel narrative is a trait unique to Luke; no other NT Gospel (or Gospel source, as far as we can tell) employs it. Thus, there is good reason to see here the redactional hand of Luke, making sure that the climactic affirmation about Jesus in 7:16 ("a great prophet") is not taken as the only or adequate designation of the one who raises the dead.[102]

(4) Finally, there is a general observation about Luke's mode of composing his Gospel that argues against the Nain story's being a pure invention by him. On the whole, in composing his Gospel from various sources, Luke tends to avoid narrative doublets, i.e., two very similar stories or two variants of the same story.[103] For example, while Matthew takes over from Mark both versions

of the multiplication of loaves, Luke includes only the first. Faced with both the Marcan story of a woman from Bethany anointing Jesus' head at the beginning of the Passion Narrative and a special L tradition about a penitent woman anointing Jesus' feet sometime during the public ministry in Galilee, Luke chooses to include the second story but omit the first. Given this tendency, and given the fact that only a chapter later Luke will take over Mark's story of the raising of Jairus (8:40–56), it seems unlikely that Luke would have gone out of his way to create a narrative doublet of a miracle of raising the dead. In fact, Luke's Gospel stands out as the only canonical Gospel that includes two narratives recounting how Jesus raised the dead. The existence of two different stories in two different sources appears to be a much more probable explanation for Luke's departing from his usual mode of writing than does the theory of his free composition of the Nain story.

Once again, we are faced not with one clear-cut and all-deciding argument, but rather with converging lines of probability. On balance, the many different considerations listed above, both positive and negative, argue in favor of Luke's redaction of a special L tradition rather than a free creation of 7:11–17. Since I do not think that we can imagine Luke's special L tradition to have been a single document or source (à la the Q document), the ultimate origin and nature of the Nain story must remain highly speculative. The anchoring of the story in the obscure Galilean town of Nain (now shown by archaeology to have had a gate), as well as the presence of some possible Semitisms in the text, argues for the origin of the story among Jewish Christians in Palestine.

C. DOES THE STORY GO BACK TO JESUS?

Can the story be traced back further, into the ministry of the historical Jesus? Here I am less confident than I was in the case of the Jairus story. We must face the fact that this story is witnessed only in Luke's Gospel, which in my view was written toward the end of the 1st century A.D.[104] Although the Nain story existed before the Gospel was written, there is very little we can say about a hypothetical tradition history. While I have argued that the story was not simply created out of the Elijah-Elisha stories or the Marcan story of Jairus' daughter, the influence of these narratives on the Nain story cannot be denied. The most obvious case is the word-for-word repetition of LXX 3 Kgdms 17:23 ("and he gave him to his mother") in Luke 7:15. Jesus' command to the son of the widow in Luke 7:14, which is parallel to his command to the daughter of Jairus in Mark 5:41, is also a good candidate for literary influence. Hence it is understandable that a careful critic like Rochais should have concluded, with some hesitation, that the Nain story is simply "a christological elaboration of the narrative of the resurrection worked by Elijah at Zarephath."[105] What, then, is to be the final judgment? It is interesting to note that, when weighing his decision, Rochais points out that the concrete location of Nain is one of the most serious arguments in favor of historicity. In fact, in my opinion, Rochais never does give an adequate explanation of how the name of this obscure town became attached to what he sees as a Christian reworking of the Elijah story in 1 Kings 17.[106] To this concrete nugget of the town's name there may be added a much more general observation: the various sources of the canonical Gospels do not show any tendency or interest in multiplying miracle stories in which Jesus raises the dead. The Marcan, Lucan, and Johannine traditions each knew of only one story, and the evangelists make no attempt to create such stories on their own. Still, in view of the paucity of evidence one way or the other, I can readily understand why some scholars may prefer a judgment of *non liquet* or even Rochais's judgment of unhistorical. Nevertheless, given the anchoring of Luke 7:11–17 in the otherwise unheard-of town of Nain plus this general tendency of the traditions of the Four Gospels, I incline (with some hesitation) to the view that the story goes back to some incident involving Jesus at Nain during his public ministry.

V. THE JOHANNINE TRADITION: THE RAISING OF LAZARUS (JOHN 11:1–45)

A. THE PLACE OF THE MIRACLE WITHIN JOHN'S LARGER STORY

The raising of Lazarus is the last and greatest of the "signs" performed by the Johannine Jesus.[107] For a number of reasons the Fourth Evangelist has purposely placed the Lazarus story at the culmination of the public ministry. He has given it links both backward and forward to connect it with the overall structure of his Gospel.

Looking *backward*, we see that he has carefully arranged the miraculous "signs" of Jesus to create a careful crescendo both in literary style and theological message.[108]

(a) From a *literary* point of view, John has moved (1) from short, relatively isolated miracle stories of a Synoptic character (the changing of water into wine at Cana [2:1–11], the healing of the royal official's son [4:46–54]) (2) to short miracle stories that begin to be integrated into larger literary wholes because they are the starting point for lengthy theological dialogues and monologues (the healing of the paralyzed man at the pool of Bethesda [5:1–9], the multiplication of loaves along with the walking on the water [6:1–15,16–21], the healing of the man born blind [9:1–17]) (3) to the final miracle story of Lazarus, where theological dialogue does not come after the miracle story but is rather woven into it.[109] Throughout the Lazarus narrative Jesus delivers mini-discourses on typically Johannine themes: the glory of God, light and darkness, resurrection and life, and his union with his Father.

(b) From a *theological* point of view, each of the earlier signs was conveying to some degree the message clearly proclaimed by this final sign: Jesus is the giver of life.[110] The life he gives is not ordinary human life; it is *zōē*, God's own life, eternal life, communicated right now to believers who accept Jesus as the savior signified by the signs he performs. The sign itself may involve, on the surface level, various physical benefits: giving abundant wine at a marriage feast that has run dry, restoring a sick boy to life, raising up a paralytic so that he can walk, giving bread and fish to a hungry crowd, bestriding the waters of chaos and death to come to his disciples in difficulty, or giving sight to a man born blind. Yet in all these signs there is a common underlying element. In every sign Jesus gives, on the physical level, some sort of fuller, more joyful, or more secure life to people whose lives were in some way constricted, saddened, or threatened.

Unfortunately, many participants in the stories never see beyond the physical level, never "see" the sign in the deepest sense of seeing (cf. John 6:2,14,26). For John, the real point of each sign is not to be found, let alone exhausted, in the physical gift conferred on the surface level. John uses the word "sign" precisely to emphasize that the gift of fuller human life on the physical level is not an end in itself but only a symbol, pointing beyond itself to the fullness of divine life that Jesus offers the believer: "I have come that they may have life (zōē, divine life, eternal life), and have it in abundance" (John 10:10). Fittingly, Jesus gives this interpretation of the whole reason for his mission in 10:10, after he has performed the penultimate sign of the public ministry, the healing of the man born blind in chap. 9. Jesus will now proceed to his last sign, the raising of Lazarus in chap. 11, where the gift of human life in the face of death is no longer simply symbolized or given in part. It is now given directly and in full on the physical level. It therefore qualifies as the greatest, most striking symbol of the divine life that Jesus offers the believer.

(2) Just as the raising of Lazarus is the culmination of all that has gone before, so it also points *forward*. Indeed, it unleashes, in a most ironic and paradoxical way, all that follows in the Gospel. This is true from both a literary and a theological point of view.

(a) In a *literary* sense, the raising of Lazarus unleashes what follows by pushing the plot forward to its inexorable conclusion; it moves the Gospel story from Jesus' public ministry to his death and resurrection. In John's story of Jesus, unlike the Synoptic presentation, it is not the "cleansing" of the temple and the last verbal clashes with his enemies in Jerusalem that bring Jesus to his trial and death. Instead, the Fourth Evangelist places the cleansing of the temple at the beginning of the public ministry; this makes way for the raising of Lazarus as the immediate cause of Jesus' arrest and execution.[111]

No sooner is the Lazarus miracle over than it precipitates a meeting (*synedrion*) of "the high priests and the Pharisees."[112] They must decide what to do with this sign-worker who could attract such a following that the Romans might intervene and destroy the Jewish state and the Jerusalem temple (John 11:47–48). Caiaphas, the high priest in that fateful year, gives the *realpolitik* advice that it is better that one man die for the people than that the whole nation perish (11:49–50).[113] The scene ends with John remarking: "Therefore from that day onwards they planned to kill him" (11:53). The great irony in this chain of causality is that Jesus is to be put to death because he has raised the dead to life. Yet it is precisely by his death that Jesus will pour out the

Spirit (= divine life) on believers. So addicted is John to this grand irony that
he cannot resist a final touch: Lazarus, the man raised from the dead, must
likewise be put to death because he is a most inconvenient witness, leading
many to faith in Jesus the life-giver (12:9–11).

(b) With these last observations we have already turned toward the second,
theological dimension of the story: the raising of Lazarus unleashes the future
in a theological sense as well. As we saw when we compared the theological
presentation of Jesus' miracles of raising the dead with the theological presentation of his own resurrection on Easter, the raising of Lazarus involves for its
beneficiary only a reprieve from a death that must take place at a future date.
Lazarus is brought *back* to his old, ordinary human life, with its built-in death
warrant. Appropriately, he comes forth from his tomb still bound by his burial
cloths, which he will need again. In other words, for all its wonder, the raising
of Lazarus, taken in itself, remains on the level of "sign," a physical benefit
whose ultimate importance lies not in itself but in what it points toward: the
resurrection of Jesus, who will leave his burial cloths behind in his tomb, since
he will never need them again. As C. H. Dodd puts it, the raising of Lazarus
is Jesus' victory *over* death (i.e., Lazarus' death), which symbolizes and points
forward to Jesus' victory *through* death (i.e., his own death).[114] Passing through
death on the cross, Jesus will not come *back* but will rather move forward and
ascend into the fullness of divine life, a life that he will then bestow on those
who believe in him.

Thus, the raising of Lazarus points forward graphically to the gift of divine
life in all its stages: in Jesus' own resurrection, in the gift of divine life that the
risen Jesus gives all believers right now through the Spirit, and in the gift of
divine life that Jesus will give believers definitively when he raises them up on
the last day (11:21–27; cf. 5:24–29). The resurrection of Jesus on Easter Sunday, the spiritual resurrection of every believer in the moment of coming to
faith, and the bodily resurrection of believers on the last day: all three interre-
lated events are symbolized by the raising of Lazarus, which is thus the most
theologically dense as well as the last of the signs of the public ministry.[115]

B. TRADITION AND REDACTION IN THE LAZARUS STORY

1. Can We Get at the Underlying Tradition?

Granted that the Lazarus story is carefully redacted to fit a pivotal point in the
Johannine narrative, and granted that it is suffused with typically Johannine
vocabulary and theology, is there any hope of discerning what tradition lay
behind the Evangelist's composition? To be sure, in view of the strange inconsistencies, tensions, and reduplications that run through John 11:1–45, most
commentators allow that the Evangelist has reworked some earlier miracle
story. But specifying what exactly that traditional story said is no easy matter.

So difficult is the task that some scholars simply despair of distinguishing
tradition from redaction in chap. 11. C. H. Dodd spoke for more than one

critic when he wrote in 1963: "To attempt to reconstruct the story [of the raising of Lazarus] as it may have been handed down in pre-canonical tradition would be idle. John has worked it over too thoroughly."[116] Yet even Dodd held that behind the Evangelist's composition there did stand some sort of tradition; he simply thought that we can no longer specify what it looked like, especially since it probably remained "fluid and unformed."

While other critics agree with Dodd that the task is formidable, many think that some rough approximation of the pre-Johannine story of Lazarus can be discerned from various signals in the present text.[117] Proponents of Dodd's skepticism might smile as they survey the many disagreements among critics who have tried to reconstruct the primitive story. But, then, disagreements are to be expected in such hypothetical reconstructions. What is more impressive is the basic agreement of many critics on a minimal core text, to which some scholars then add a few verses here and there.[118] That over decades exegetes from very different backgrounds should concur more or less on a core text may indicate that the project of reconstructing the tradition behind John 11:1–45 may not be as hopeless as Dodd thought.

What may indeed be hopeless is any attempt to reconstruct the primitive tradition word for word. To this extent, Dodd is correct: John has so thoroughly reworked the tradition with his own vocabulary, style, and theology that an exact word-for-word reconstruction of the story he inherited is impossible. But such a precise reconstruction is not necessary for our purposes; we have not usually demanded or achieved it in dealing with the Synoptic miracle stories. All we need ask is whether it is possible to discern which elements or blocks of material would have likely existed in the pre-Johannine story. The general contours and flow of the narrative are all we need recover and all we can reasonably hope to recover.

To do this, we shall first give a general overview of the literary contours of John 11:1–45, noting patterns and peculiarities that strike us immediately; then we shall seek to articulate criteria that will help us distinguish traditional material from John's redaction; then we shall try to apply these criteria to the Lazarus story; finally, using the results of the criteria along with other helpful observations, we shall try to reconstruct a rough approximation of the tradition the Evangelist redacted—always with the understanding that the exact wording of such a tradition is beyond our grasp.

2. The Contours of the Text

Before we articulate the criteria for detecting the Evangelist's additions to the tradition he received, we should first survey the basic structure and content of John 11:1–45 as it now stands in the Gospel:[119]

I.   The Introduction to the Story: The Dual Problem of Lazarus' Illness and Jesus' Delay (vv 1–6)

v 1:   Initial problem: Lazarus from Bethany is sick; his two sisters:
            Mary and Martha
v 2:   (Parenthetical identification of Mary as the one who
            anointed "the Lord")
v 3:   Sisters send Jesus message that Lazarus is sick
v 4:   Jesus' puzzling reply: this sickness will have as its ultimate
            result not death but the *glory* of God and his Son
v 5:   (Parenthesis: narrator insists that Jesus did love *Martha, her
            sister,* and Lazarus)
v 6:   Creation of further problem and tension: Jesus stays where
            he is for two days

II. Jesus' Two Dialogues with His Disciples (vv 7–16)
     vv 7–10:   First dialogue with disciples: Jesus: "*Let us go* into Judea
                again." Disciples object that only recently Jews tried to stone
                him; Jesus replies with metaphors of light and darkness
     vv 11–16: Second dialogue with disciples: Jesus announces that Lazarus
                sleeps, then explains to literalistic disciples that Lazarus is
                dead; Jesus rejoices over this because it will cause disciples
                to *believe*; Jesus: "*Let us go* to him." Thomas' response: "*Let
                us go* to die with him."

III. The Arrival at Bethany and the Two Encounters with the Sisters (vv
     17–32)
     v 17:   Jesus comes and finds Lazarus four days in the tomb
     v 18:   (Parenthesis: explanation of the location of Bethany)
     v 19:   Many of the Jews had come out to comfort the sisters
     vv 20–26: Jesus' (first) encounter with *Martha*; Martha's gentle rebuke
                and yet continued faith in Jesus and in a hope of future resur-
                rection; Jesus' declaration: "I am the resurrection and the
                life," along with a double promise of future and present res-
                urrection for the believer; Martha *believes*; "You are the Mes-
                siah, the Son of God who is to come into the world."
     vv 27–32: Jesus' encounter with *Mary*: Martha summons Mary, who
                comes to Jesus and repeats Martha's gentle rebuke

IV. With Strong Emotion Jesus Comes to the Grave (vv 33–39a)
     v 33:   Seeing everyone weeping, Jesus is deeply moved
     vv 34–35: At Jesus' request people show him to the grave, where he
                weeps
     vv 36–37: The Jews note his deep love for Lazarus, yet wonder why
                a person who opened the eyes of the blind could not have
                prevented Lazarus' death
     v 38:   Again deeply moved, Jesus comes to the tomb, a cave with a
                stone in front of it
     v 39a: Jesus orders the stone to be removed

V. Jesus' (Second) Encounter with *Martha* (vv 39b–40)

    v 39b: Martha objects that there will be a stench

    v 40:   Jesus: If you *believe* you will see the *glory* of God

VI. The Raising of Lazarus (vv 41–44)

    v 41a: The stone is taken away

    vv 41b–42:   Jesus' prayer, giving thanks to the Father in order that the bystanders may *believe*

    v 43:   Jesus cries out: "Lazarus, come forth!"

    v 44:   Lazarus comes forth, feet and hands bound, head covered; Jesus orders him untied

VII. Reaction(s) (vv 45–46)

    v 45:   Positive: many of the Jews who had come *to Mary* believe in Jesus

    v 46:   Negative: some report the miracle to the Pharisees (transition to the meeting of high priests and Pharisees to plan Jesus' death in vv 47–53)

Even before we list and apply our criteria for distinguishing tradition from redaction in John 11:1–45, certain points strike us immediately from the outline above. First, we cannot help but compare this story's lengthy and intricate structure with the simple three-part structure found in most miracle stories: (1) initial problem with attendant circumstances and petition for help; (2) miracle worked by word and/or action with confirmation of the reality of the miracle; (3) reaction(s) and/or conclusion. When we compare this tight structure with the sprawling narrative of 11:1–45, what we notice right away is that the second and third parts of the form of a simple miracle story correspond to the relatively terse statements of vv 43–44 (miracle and its confirmation: Jesus cries out, Lazarus comes forth, his bonds are untied, and he is set free) and vv 45–46 (reactions: some believe, some report the event to Jesus' enemies).

Thus, the lengthening of the traditional structure of a miracle story has occurred entirely in the first of the three parts, i.e., the setup that recounts the initial problem, along with the circumstances surrounding Jesus and the petitioner and any further problems that threaten to impede the miracle. Indeed, the first part of the traditional structure has grown to such gargantuan proportions that it encompasses everything that I have labeled parts I–V in the outline above. Not by sheer coincidence, it is especially in parts I–V, which correspond to part one of the traditional form of a miracle story, that we see what is unique to the Lazarus story among the sign-stories of the Fourth Gospel: the interweaving of a number of mini-dialogues or discourses within the ongoing narrative of the miracle. Clearly, if the Evangelist (or the final redactor) has added material, it must have been especially in this striking elongation of the first part of a traditional miracle story (vv 1–40, out of a total of 45 verses).

A second observation is that 11:1–45 is held together by a number of key words and phrases that reappear at various points in the story, sometimes creating an *inclusio*, a stylistic technique typical of the Fourth Evangelist.[120] For example, at the very beginning and end of the story, Mary is mentioned either ahead of Martha or alone (v 1 + v 45). But almost immediately, the narrator brings Martha to the fore by speaking in v 5 of "Martha and her sister"; Mary's name is not even mentioned. This prepares the way for Martha's dominant role in the rest of the story (vv 20–28,39–40), which vastly overshadows Mary's (vv 31–32) in theological importance. All the stranger, then, is the mention of Mary alone at the end of the story (v 45).[121] Another phrase that forms a neat *inclusio* is Jesus' exhortation "Let us go," which both introduces his first dialogue with his disciples, about going into Judea (vv 7–10), and concludes his second dialogue with them, about going to Lazarus (vv 11–15). Thomas then reinforces this *inclusio* by echoing Jesus with his own "let us go" in v 16.

Two theological terms that act as leitmotifs and also help form a grand *inclusio*, both in the story and in the first half of the Gospel, are "glory" and "believe." In v 4 Jesus announces that Lazarus' illness has as its ultimate goal the glory of God (*doxēs tou theou*) and of his Son. Indeed, in v 15 Jesus can even rejoice at his absence from Bethany, which has caused Lazarus' death, because it will give the disciples an opportunity to believe (*hina pisteusēte*). One is reminded of what is certainly the Evangelist's own comment at the end of the first sign at Cana, the changing of water into wine (2:11): "[Jesus] revealed his *glory*, and his disciples *believed* in him." This connection between belief and glory, first sounded at 2:11, is now echoed in the Lazarus story—a grand *inclusio* in the whole "Book of Signs" (John 1–12).

The themes of belief and glory continue throughout the Lazarus story. In vv 25–26, Jesus assures Martha: "The one who *believes* in me, even if he dies, shall live; and everyone who is living and *believing* in me shall never die." Jesus then pointedly adds the searching question: "Do you *believe* this?" Martha replies with her great christological confession of faith (v 27). Nevertheless, her faith still does not seem complete, at least with respect to Jesus being the resurrection and the life right now. She objects when Jesus orders Lazarus' tomb opened, and Jesus responds by conveniently putting together the two great themes and thus forming another *inclusio* (v 40): "Did I not tell you that, if you *believed*, you would see the *glory of God* [*tēn doxan tou theou*]?"

The theme of belief persists to the very end of the story. Just before he raises Lazarus, Jesus prays publicly to the Father in order to move the bystanders to *believe* in his mission (v 42). The whole narrative ends with a fine example of John's dualism: some *believe* in Jesus (v 45), while others express their unbelief by reporting the event to the Pharisees (v 46). What strikes one in all this is that the author who created this sprawling narrative also took pains to keep it tied together with various leitmotifs, some of which are used to form an *inclusio*. All the more interesting and puzzling, then, are those passages where the narrative meanders and becomes repetitive (e.g., vv 33–38).

With this initial overview and these preliminary observations as a guide, let us now turn to the task of articulating and applying criteria that can help us detect the hand of the Evangelist in the individual verses of John 11:1–45.

3. Criteria for Discerning the Evangelist's Hand

While lengthy lists of criteria have been developed for identifying the editorial work of the Evangelist (or at times the final redactor) in the Gospel as a whole,[122] I think four criteria in particular are useful in dealing with the Lazarus story:

(1) In its most primitive form, the Lazarus story probably circulated as an independent and isolated unit. Therefore, references in the present text backward and forward to other events in the Fourth Gospel come from the Evangelist or the final redactor. To put the same point slightly differently: in John 11:1–45, those parenthetical remarks, asides, or clarifications by the narrator that demand a knowledge of other individual incidents in John's Gospel do not belong to the primitive tradition, since they would not make sense in the isolated unit.

(2) Discourse material placed in the mouth of Jesus that enunciates in a nutshell major theological themes of the Fourth Gospel, especially when such themes are found in more developed form in other discourses of Jesus in the Gospel, are most likely the work of the Evangelist. There is a particular reason for thinking that this is true in the Lazarus story. As we have already seen, the Evangelist has carefully arranged the structure of the public ministry so that the first two signs of Jesus lack any notable amount of interpretive discourse, the next couple of signs act as springboards for lengthy discourses, while the last sign, the raising of Lazarus, instead melds the discourse material into the sign. This neat pattern spanning chaps. 2–11 is hardly an accident; it is certainly the work of the Evangelist. Hence at least the present positioning of the mini-discourses of Jesus, "blended" as they are into the flow of 11:1–45, comes from John.

(3) The magnificent dramas of Jesus and the Samaritan woman at the well (chap. 4), the healing and subsequent "trial" of the man born blind (chap. 9), and the Lazarus story itself (chap. 11) show that the Evangelist is a superb writer of suspenseful narratives. Therefore, various signs of awkwardness or confusion in the text—e.g., literary sutures or seams that stand out, interruptions in the flow of the text, clumsy repetitions of the same basic statement, tensions between verses—may intimate that the Evangelist is grappling with and reworking a tradition not of his own making.

(4) The heavy presence of the vocabulary and literary style that redaction critics have identified as typical of the Evangelist may signal a phrase or sentence that is of his own making. This last criterion in particular must be used with care, since on the whole the vocabulary and style of the Fourth Gospel (and, in a looser sense, of the Johannine Epistles as well) are remarkably uniform.[123] This criterion is best used by way of confirmation: if we judge certain verses to be John's own work on the grounds of the other criteria, the notable

presence of characteristically Johannine language and style can give further support to the judgment.

4. Using the Criteria to Distinguish Tradition from Redaction

As much as possible, I shall apply the four criteria in order. At times, however, the analysis of certain verses will demand the application of more than one criterion at a time. Accordingly, the use of a particular criterion will sometimes have to be anticipated in the discussion.

(a) *The first criterion: references backward and forward to other events in the Gospel do not belong to the primitive tradition.* There are a number of clear candidates.

(i) No sooner has the narrative started in 11:1 than v 2 stops the narrative to identify Mary, the sister of Lazarus (v 1), as the woman who "anointed the Lord with myrrh and wiped his feet with her hair. . . ." The reference is not just to some vague tradition about a woman who anoints Jesus, but to the specifically Johannine story of the anointing at Bethany contained in John 12:1–8. No other form of the anointing story in the Four Gospels fits the description of John 11:2. Mark and Matthew speak only of an anonymous woman at Bethany anointing Jesus' *head* with myrrh (Mark 14:3–9 ‖ Matt 26:6–13). Luke, who omits the anointing at Bethany before the passion, recounts how a sinful woman in Galilee washed Jesus' *feet* with her *tears*, wiped them dry with her hair, and *then* anointed his feet with myrrh (Luke 7:36–50). The curious order of first applying myrrh to Jesus' feet and then wiping the feet with one's hair is found only in John 12:1–8. The proleptic reference in 11:2 therefore presupposes the composition of John's Gospel in general and of John 12:1–8 in particular, for the anointing story would not have been in a "sign source" that was by definition a collection of miracle stories. Moreover, since the Evangelist regularly avoids using "the Lord" (*ho kyrios*) for Jesus in his third-person narrative of the public ministry, some scholars suggest that the use of "the Lord" here may betray the hand of the final redactor (cf. John 21:7,12).[124]

(ii) Another possible insertion by the Evangelist is the dialogue between Jesus and his disciples in 11:7–8. When in 11:7 Jesus, after a delay of two days, suggests that he and the disciples go *again* into Judea, the disciples reply in v 8: "Rabbi, just recently the Jews [*hoi Ioudaioi*] were seeking to stone you. And are you going there again?" Verse 7 already presupposes a previous journey of Jesus into Judea, as well as the fact that he is not there now. This whole geographical pattern of journeys to and from Judea is part of the overall framework of John's Gospel, but nothing in the Lazarus story suggests it before v 7.

More to the point, the reply of the disciples in v 8 clearly refers back to what has just transpired in the latter part of chap. 10. There, in the Jerusalem temple (and hence in Judea), Jesus declares "I and the Father are one" (10:30). In response, "the Jews [*hoi Ioudaioi*, i.e., the hostile authorities in Jerusalem, a typical Johannine usage] again picked up stones in order to stone him [Jesus]"

(10:31). After Jesus rebuts their charge of blasphemy, they try once again to seize him, but he escapes their grasp and departs to the other side of the Jordan (10:39–40). It is there that, according to the framework of the Fourth Gospel, the events of 11:1–16 take place, though nothing in the first six verses of the Lazarus story, taken by itself, would inform the reader of the location and setting within the larger plot. Hence, the whole exchange between Jesus and his disciples in 11:7–8 presupposes the wider story of the Gospel and comes from the Evangelist.

This conclusion is supported by the use of *hoi Ioudaioi* in 11:8 to mean the hostile authorities in Jerusalem. As we have seen, that is also the meaning of *hoi Ioudaioi* in 10:31, and it is a meaning of the phrase typical of the Evangelist throughout the Gospel. In contrast, when *hoi Ioudaioi* occurs in the rest of the Lazarus story, it never carries this fiercely hostile meaning. Rather, the meaning is the relatively neutral one of Jews from Jerusalem who come to Bethany to comfort the bereaved sisters (vv 18–19). So far are they from being irrevocably hostile to Jesus that *many* of them wind up believing in him because of the miracle (v 45; cf. 12:9–11).[125]

(iii) If 11:7–8 comes from the Evangelist, the same can probably be said of v 16 as well. There Thomas remarks with glum resignation after Jesus insists on going to Lazarus: "Let us go also that we may die with him." The "let us go" (*agōmen*) in v 16, echoing Jesus' "let us go" in v 15, forms an *inclusio* with Jesus' "let us go" (*agōmen*) in v 7. More to the point, the prospect of dying with Jesus presupposes the danger of execution mentioned in v 8; ultimately, it refers back to chap. 10.

That v 16 is meant to be an *inclusio*, reaching back to vv 7–8, is supported by the fact that it does not flow logically from the second dialogue between Jesus and his disciples in vv 11–15. In the second dialogue, the topic is not Jesus' desire to go to *Judea* and the danger of being killed that such a journey might involve (as in vv 7–10). Rather, the topic is Jesus' desire to go to the "sleeping" *Lazarus* for the purpose of "waking" him—a metaphor that the disciples take literally and that Jesus then has to explain in terms of death. Nothing in vv 11–15 intimates that going to Lazarus involves any danger of death. Moreover, in the present context Thomas' exhortation "Let us die *with him* [*met' autou*]" is confusing. The sense of the whole passage demands that "with him" refer to Jesus, but in v 15 and v 17 the pronoun "him" (*auton*) refers in each case to Lazarus. Verse 16 is obviously not at home in its present setting. In my opinion, it belongs to the same block of material as vv 7–8, an addition by the Evangelist. Later on we will return to the problem of vv 9–10 and 11–15.[126]

(iv) A final candidate for being an addition by the Evangelist is the reaction of the Jews in vv 36–37 to the sight of Jesus crying (v 35). As is usual with Johannine dualism, even the relatively neutral crowd is split in its estimation of Jesus as he cries. In v 36, some of "the Jews" say: "Behold, how much he [Jesus] loved him [Lazarus]!" In v 37, others counter: "Could not this fellow, who opened the eyes of the blind, prevent this man from dying?" Verse 37 clearly refers back to the story of the man born blind, which occupies the whole of chap. 9 and which likewise splits the Jewish bystanders into two "opinion-groups" (9:8–9). Hence v 37 is an addition by the Evangelist; the reference to healing the blind man would make no sense when the Lazarus story was a separate piece of tradition circulating as an independent unit.[127] Since in 11:36–37 the "center of gravity" in the exchange among the Jews lies with the criticism voiced in v 37, and since the sympathy expressed in v 36 seems to exist mainly as a "setup" for v 37, v 36 is probably an addition as well.

To sum up, the first criterion suggests that 11:2, 11:7–8,16, and 11:36–37 are additions by the Evangelist (or the final redactor), who thus ties the discrete unit of the Lazarus story to his larger narrative, specifically to the events in chaps. 9 and 10 prior to the Lazarus story and to the anointing at Bethany that will follow it in chap. 12. In doing this the Evangelist already shows himself to be a skillful editor. Instead of inserting references to events scattered throughout the Gospel, he creates references to events in the chapters immediately preceding and following the Lazarus story, thus implanting the story into the flow of the plot as it moves toward the end of the public ministry.

(b) *The second criterion: mini-discourses or dialogues that announce major theological themes that John develops elsewhere in his Gospel probably come from the Evangelist.* In a sense, this second criterion is a variation on the first. The first criterion focuses on references to events narrated elsewhere in the Gospel; the second criterion focuses on theological themes that are only briefly touched upon in the Lazarus story, but receive greater attention elsewhere in the Gospel. As we have already seen, one reason for suspecting that these mini-discourses or dialogues are secondary is the overall pattern of the Gospel as shaped by the Evangelist: from miracles with no subsequent discourses to miracles followed by explanatory discourses to the final miracle with explanatory discourses melded into the narrative.

(i) Judged by this second criterion, vv 9–10 are a primary candidate for being an addition of the Evangelist. First of all, once we take away vv 7–8 (the dispute over whether or not to go back to Judea in the face of mortal danger), vv 9–10 lose their reason for being in the text. They are the theological explanation Jesus gives for seizing the present moment to return to Judea despite the danger of death: "Are there not twelve hours of daylight? If anyone walks in the daylight, he does not stumble, for he sees the light of this world [i.e., the sun]. But if anyone walks at night, he stumbles, for the light is not in him."

If we had only the Lazarus story, this explanation by Jesus of his desire to return to Judea would be quite puzzling. It comes out of nowhere, does nothing, then disappears, not to be taken up again in the rest of the Lazarus story. But within the context of the whole Gospel it makes sense, for it refers to the "law of the hour," the divine "must" that governs Jesus' actions. As long as the "hour" of his passion and death was still far off, Jesus purposely avoided being captured by his enemies. But now time is running out. The "hour" approaches, and he must work rapidly before the night of his death comes. Jesus makes exactly the same point at the beginning of his previous miracle, the healing of the man born blind. Just before he heals the man, he enunciates the law of the hour to his disciples (9:4): "We must work the works of him who sent me while it is day [or: while there is daylight]. Night is coming, when no one can work." The Evangelist thus introduces the last sign with an explanation very similar to the one with which he introduced the previous sign: the law of the hour, the divine imperative to make soteriological hay while the sun shines.[128]

This, at least, is the immediate meaning of Jesus' words when taken as the justification of his desire to go back to Judea in spite of possible death. However, for those who know the whole Gospel, the metaphors of light and darkness work at a second, deeper level. As opposed to the sun, which Jesus pointedly calls "the light of *this* world," Jesus himself is the true "light of the world," as he likewise proclaims in 9:5 (cf. 8:12): "As long as I am in the world, I am the light of the world." Just as he must seize the day, so must those whom he calls to faith. Humans must seize the opportunity of walking in his light, of believing in him and becoming his disciples, while he is still among them and still offering them his revelation (= shining his light). If they fail to believe, they will find themselves stumbling spiritually in the darkness of ignorance and sin once Jesus departs this world. As Pilate will find out during the Roman trial, the law of the hour involves a second law: the law of "too late." God's gracious offer of revelation, of saving truth, is not always and everywhere available. A set time of grace is granted to each individual. If the individual lets the chance to accept the light slip away, it will then be too late. This theme, only intimated in 11:9–10, is enunciated by Jesus in his very last words to the Jerusalem crowd as his ministry ends (12:35–36): "For [only] a little while longer the light is in your midst. Walk while you have the light, lest the darkness overtake you. The one who walks in darkness does not know where he is going. While you have the light, believe in the light, that you may become sons of light."

Thus, 11:9–10 provides a clear case of a phenomenon we shall see elsewhere in chap. 11: certain theological statements make sense only if the reader knows the theological pronouncements of Jesus elsewhere in the Gospel. This is especially true of vv 9–10, for they represent the "intrusion" of particular metaphors into a story in which they are otherwise absent. The metaphors of light and darkness, day and night, are certainly at home in John's Gospel as a whole. But they are not at home in the Lazarus story. Verses 9–10 are the only place in the Lazarus story where these metaphors appear. They surface suddenly at this point only to disappear for the rest of the story.[129] The bulk of the Lazarus story is dominated instead by the key dualistic metaphors of life and death, not light and darkness.

In short, the dependence of 11:9–10 on vv 7–8 (already judged to be an addition by the Evangelist), the intelligibility of vv 9–10 only in the context of other statements made by Jesus in chaps. 9 and 12, and the lack of connection between the key metaphors of light and darkness in vv 9–10 and the rest of the Lazarus story all argue for an addition made by the Evangelist. Once again we see that the Evangelist is intent on connecting this discrete story of Lazarus with what precedes and follows it in his Gospel.

(ii) If vv 9–10 make sense only in the larger theological framework of the Gospel, the great dialogue between Jesus and Martha in vv 21–27 encapsulates that theological framework in a nutshell and raises it to new heights. John 11:21–27 is one of the theological masterpieces of the Gospel, all the more so because it is a theological masterpiece in miniature.[130]

In v 21, the grieving Martha meets Jesus with an ambiguous statement that mixes a gentle reproach with persevering faith: "Lord, if you had been here, my brother would not have died." But—implies Martha—Jesus did not heed her plea, he failed to come in time, and so her brother did die. With a firm "nevertheless" of faith, Martha adds: "But even now I know that whatever you ask God, God will give you." Martha struggles to reaffirm her faith in Jesus, but her words cannot escape the irony that suffuses John's Gospel. On a superficial level, what she says sounds like a poignant and touching affirmation of faith; and yet, on the deeper level of the high christology of the Fourth Gospel, it is hopelessly inadequate. Her faith remains faith in Jesus the miracle-worker, who may indeed be able to pray to God to obtain a healing, but whose power is obviously limited by the greater, irreversible power of death.

"I know," says Martha bravely—and, as so often in the Fourth Gospel, when people affirm what they know, they actually betray their ignorance (cf. 9:24,29,41; and contrast Martha's "I believe" in 11:27). What she thinks she knows is that Jesus the miracle-worker has the power to ask God to work miracles on this side of the grave. Jesus will pointedly do the opposite just before he raises Lazarus. In v 41–42, instead of offering a prayer of petition he will offer a prayer of thanksgiving, and instead of praying to "God" he will thank his "Father."

In v 23, Jesus counters Martha's ambiguous faith with an ambiguous promise: "Your brother shall rise." Naturally, the Johannine Jesus means this word of comfort in a most immediate and literal sense: he is about to raise Lazarus from the dead. Martha, however, still thinking on a "surface level"—which includes an eschatology that knows only of a future resurrection—takes Jesus to be expressing the Jewish (and Christian) hope of a resurrection on the last day (v 24). "I know," she says, still not knowing, "I know he shall rise at the resurrection on the last day."

In the manner typical of the Fourth Evangelist, Jesus now breaks through the ambiguity created by his own initial statement by clarifying its deeper sense in vv 25–26. At this point we reach one of the theological climaxes of the Fourth Gospel. To understand this climax, we must remember that John's Gospel is unique among the books of the NT in that it grounds its whole theology in an explicit affirmation of the eternal preexistence of the Son of God who becomes flesh as Jesus of Nazareth. In John's Gospel there is a christological "implosion"; all sorts of distinct theological themes collapse into the person of Jesus Christ.

The whole process of salvation centers on his person. In the Son of God, the Word, was life ($z\bar{o}\bar{e}$, God's own life) from all eternity; through the incarnation that eternal, divine life has entered into human history and has become available right now to all who believe in the Son (1:4,12–14). This eternal life is therefore not just some future good: "He who believes has eternal life" (5:24)—now, in the moment of believing. Here we touch on the center of John's theology: high christology produces realized eschatology. Because the Word has become flesh, the last day has become the present moment.

This nucleus of John's theology, this nexus between a high christology of preexistence-incarnation and a realized eschatology that places the last day in the present moment of belief, receives no more succinct expression in the whole of the Gospel than in Jesus' reply to a Martha who can think only in terms of Jesus the miracle-worker and of future eschatology.[131] Smashing the low christology and purely future eschatology that Martha has enunciated, Jesus replies to her future hope with a present proclamation: "I am the resurrection and the life." All the dramatic events of the last day envisioned by Jewish apocalyptic—resurrection from the dead, eternal life in heaven—have collapsed into the present moment and into the person who dares to say simply: "I am." In effect, Jesus says to Martha: "Martha, the resurrection you are looking for is looking at you."

Frequently throughout the Fourth Gospel, Jesus' majestic "I am" with some metaphor attached begins a discourse of revelation, in which he uses the dominant metaphor of the discourse to expatiate on the saving goods he bestows even now on the believer. For instance, the bread of life discourse begins with the revelation "I am the bread of life" and is immediately followed by the double promise: "The one who comes to me shall never hunger, the one who believes in me shall never thirst again" (6:35). The Evangelist follows the same pattern in the mini-discourse of revelation in 11:25b–26. Continuing the double revelation of himself as the resurrection and the life, Jesus makes a double promise, encompassing both future and realized eschatology: (1) "The one who believes in me, even if he dies, shall live" (v 25b). Even the believer faces the prospect of physical death, but physical death will not have the last word. As Martha had hoped, there will be a resurrection on the last day. Beyond her hopes, Jesus will symbolize and anticipate that final resurrection of the body by raising her brother Lazarus in a few minutes. (2) The still deeper truth that undergirds this hope of future eschatology is the abiding truth of realized eschatology (v 26): "And the one who is living and believing in me shall never die." The believer who possesses God's own life, eternal life, in the present moment will never experience a rupture in or end to that life, even in the face of physical death. In brief, this incredibly concise summation of the christology and eschatology of the Fourth Gospel most assuredly comes from the hand of the Evangelist. While keeping to the pattern of his great revelation discourses (I am + metaphor + promise of saving benefit to those who believe), John sums up everything he has to say in those discourses in a mini-discourse of two verses.

The Fourth Evangelist is intent on presenting his unique theology not as some idiosyncratic brainstorm but as the genuine, legitimate interpretation of the earliest creeds of the church. Hence throughout his Gospel his special christology is tied to and equated with the traditional christological titles of primitive Christianity. So it is here. When challenged to accept Jesus' revelation of himself as the resurrection and the life Martha replies in v 27: "Yes, Lord, I have come to believe that you are the Messiah, the Son of God, who is to come into the world."

Messiah and Son of God are two of the earliest titles given by the church to Jesus (cf. the traditional formulas Paul quotes in 1 Thess 1:9–10; 1 Cor 15:3–5; Rom 1:3–4). Significantly, Matthew presents Simon Peter making almost the same profession of faith in Matt 16:16 that Martha makes here in John 11:27. The Fourth Evangelist places these traditional titles in Martha's mouth to show that they are equivalent to his own theological definitions of Jesus (e.g., the resurrection and the life; the way, the truth, and the life; the bread of life; the Word made flesh). Needless to say, John understands the more traditional christological titles within the framework of his christology of preexistence and incarnation. It is not by accident that Martha adds to the traditional titles of Messiah and Son of God the further qualification of "he who is to come into the world" (*ho eis ton kosmon erchomenos*), which stresses the ideas of preexistence and incarnation.[132]

Thus, Martha, rather than Peter, becomes the grand spokesperson of the christological faith of John's Gospel. The Evangelist hammers home this point by repeating Martha's traditional formulation of christology at the very end of his Gospel (20:31). As he explains his reason for writing the Gospel, he echoes 11:25–27: "These signs [including the sign of Lazarus] have been recorded that you may *believe* that Jesus is *the Messiah, the Son of God,* and that by *believing* you may have *life* in his name." In all probability, therefore, the theological dialogue between Martha and Jesus in vv 21–24, Jesus' mini-discourse of revelation in vv 25–26, and Martha's profession of faith in v 27 all represent a dense and profound composition of the Evangelist, announcing the ultimate meaning of the Lazarus story within the context of the whole Gospel.[133]

(iii) If Martha has proven to be a theological tool of the Evangelist in 11:21–27, it may be that she returns in that role just before the actual raising of Lazarus.[134] When in v 39a Jesus orders the stone to be taken away from the entrance to Lazarus' tomb, Martha suddenly reappears in v 39b to object that there will be a stench from the four-day-old corpse. For all her faith, Martha apparently still does not appreciate the full import for the present moment of the truth that Jesus is the resurrection and the life. That is to say, she does not understand that he has the power to "embody" that great truth in a concrete, physical sign by raising Lazarus to life. It is Jesus' turn to issue a gentle rebuke to Martha (v 40): "Did I not tell you that, if you *believed,* you would see the *glory of God?"*

As I have already noted, in 11:40 the Evangelist is purposely creating an *inclusio*—in fact, more than one kind of *inclusio.* On the one hand, there is the grand *inclusio* between this, the last sign of the public ministry, and the first of

Jesus' signs in chap. 2. At the end of the first sign, the changing of water into wine at Cana, we surely hear the Evangelist's own voice and theological interpretation in the concluding comment of 2:11: Jesus "revealed his glory and his disciples believed in him." While John creates an *inclusio* between the first and second signs at Cana (see 4:54), he pointedly does not repeat this sentence linking glory and belief. In fact, nowhere else in the public ministry are these two key words brought together in a single sentence during a narrative of one of Jesus' signs—until we reach the last sign and 11:40. Now, for only the second time in the Gospel, belief and glory are brought together in a single sentence within the context of one of Jesus' signs.

On the other hand, the statement of Jesus in 11:40 creates a smaller *inclusio* as well; his promise points back to his own statements on glory and belief at the beginning of the Lazarus story. The very first "theological" interpretation Jesus gives of the whole Lazarus story is found in v 4b, when Jesus gives his response to the news that Lazarus is sick: "This sickness is not [meant to end in] death, rather [it has occurred] for the sake of the *glory of God*, in order that the Son of God may be glorified through it." Although the Johannine Jesus knows from the start that Lazarus will die of this illness, he confidently asserts that death will not be the definitive result of the illness. Rather, the illness (along with the temporary event of Lazarus' death) has been permitted for the sake of a greater good, the revelation of God's glory, which in turn brings eternal life to those who believe. The typical Johannine theology in v 4b is expressed in a literary style likewise characteristic of John: negative statement followed by an ellipsis introduced by "but" (*alla*) and formulated as a purpose clause introduced by *hina* ("in order that").[135] Verse 4b is consequently judged by the vast majority of critics to be an addition by the Evangelist. Not surprisingly, the first "theological" interpretation of the whole story, placed conveniently at the story's beginning, is John's own work.

The same judgment seems to hold true for the last "theological" interpretation Jesus gives of Lazarus' illness (and now his death) just before he leaves for Bethany, namely, the emphasis on believing in v 15. Having announced Lazarus' death to his bewildered disciples in v 14, Jesus makes an astounding statement in v 15: "And I rejoice on your account that I was not there [at Bethany to heal Lazarus], in order that you may *believe*." Thus, the revelation of glory and its connection with belief not only form the grand *inclusio* between chap. 2 and chap. 11; they also form an *inclusio* between Jesus' initial interpretation of Lazarus' sickness and death, given to his disciples in 11:4–15, and his final interpretation of the whole event, given to Martha in 11:40.[136]

To sum up: in view of this carefully worked out pattern of cross-references, I think that the Evangelist's hand can be found in (1) Jesus' joining of faith and God's glory in 11:40 (probably along with Martha's objection to opening the tomb in v 39b, which occasions Jesus' remark), (2) Jesus' initial interpretation of Lazarus' illness in v 4b in terms of God's glory, and (3) his interpretation of Lazarus' death in terms of the disciples' faith in v 15. A further confirmation of the editorial nature of vv 39b–40 is that, once this second encounter between Martha and Jesus is removed, the narrative flows smoothly and succinctly from Jesus' order to take away the stone (v 39a) to the compliance of the bystanders (v 41a).

(iv) One may draw an additional conclusion from the view that v 4b comes from the Evangelist. What immediately follows in v 5 seems to be a parenthetical comment meant to ward off the misapprehension that Jesus was not deeply concerned about Lazarus and his siblings. Rather, says v 5, "Jesus loved [the imperfect tense of the Greek verb stresses duration] Martha and her sister and Lazarus." If this clarification in v 5 was written to offset what might seem to be cool detachment on Jesus' part in v 4b, and if v 4b comes from the Evangelist, then logically so does v 5, which depends upon v 4b for its meaning in the flow of the story.[137]

(v) One further corollary of all this is that by now so much of 11:4–16 has been assigned to the Evangelist's creativity that it seems reasonable to suppose that 11:4–16 as a whole is the Evangelist's contribution. An observation that supports this suggestion is that the disciples of Jesus play no role in the action of the story. They appear suddenly in 11:7, after being "off stage" since 9:2. Significantly, they appear briefly at the beginning of chap. 9 for the same reason that they appear briefly at the beginning of chap. 11: to act as theological foils for Jesus. They voice objections, questions, and misunderstandings of Jesus' statements so that Jesus may develop his theological pronouncements further. In both chap. 9 and chap. 11, as soon as the disciples fulfill this role of theological foil, they disappear. From 11:17 onwards we hear only of Jesus interacting with Martha, Mary, the Jews, and Lazarus. The disciples have vanished. Thus, in chap. 11 as in chap. 9, they play no part in the story proper. They might almost be compared to a sort of Greek chorus: they help along the theological commentary on the action, but never act themselves.

Most likely, then, in both chap. 9 and chap. 11 the disciples are the literary instruments of the Evangelist, introduced by him into the stories in order to clarify the theology underlying the narrative. In particular, the typically Johannine vocabulary and style of vv 11–15 make it likely that Jesus' second dialogue with his disciples was also composed by John.[138] Hence I would venture the opinion that most of 11:4–16, from the initial theological comment of Jesus down to the final glum comment of Thomas, is the creation of the Evangelist. Still, it may be that some individual verses that appear necessary to the narrative (e.g., v 6: Jesus stays where he is for two days) belonged to the traditional story prior to its incorporation into the Fourth Gospel.

(c) *The third criterion: signs of contradiction, tension, clumsy repetition, interruptions in the flow of the text, or confusion in the text may indicate the hand of the Evangelist reworking tradition.* Precisely because the Lazarus story, like the dramas of the Samaritan woman at the well (chap. 4) and the man born blind (chap. 9), is on the whole so well written, clumsy repetitions, interruptions in the flow of the text, or other types of literary awkwardness stand out and demand some explanation.

(i) For example, we have already seen under the second criterion that v 5, which assures the reader of Jesus' love for Lazarus and his sisters, may well be an addition by the Evangelist. The third criterion reinforces that impression in that the parenthetical remark in v 5 does not fit smoothly into the flow of the presentation.

(ii) Another parenthetical remark that interrupts the flow of the story is v 18. Here the narrator stops for a moment in order to turn to the audience and explain that Bethany was near Jerusalem, the distance between them being about two miles. This parenthetical remark is instructive in more than one way. First of all, in this case the strongest reason for thinking that v 18 may be secondary lies outside of any of the four criteria. As C. H. Dodd, Raymond Brown, and other commentators have stressed, the oldest stratum of the Johannine narrative seems to come from Palestine and indeed at times from the environs of Jerusalem, whose topography appears to be well known in some of the Gospel's stories.

However, if this be true, and if in particular some primitive form of the Lazarus story did circulate among Christians living in the environs of pre-A.D. 70 Jerusalem, then the geographical information in v 18 would obviously be unnecessary in the story's earliest form. Such an explanatory parenthesis would become necessary only when the story began to be told outside the environs of Jerusalem. It may be, then, that, while v 18 does not belong to the earliest stratum of the story, it was added fairly early on, before the story was edited by the Fourth Evangelist. All this brings up a second point: in dealing with the Fourth Gospel, we should not think simply in terms of a pre-Johannine tradition and then redaction by the Evangelist. If the Lazarus story ultimately comes from a Palestinian milieu and circulated for a good many decades before it was incorporated into the Fourth Gospel (perhaps being collected with other miracles into a "sign source" along the way), then we must allow for a number of stages in the process of handing down the oral and written tradition contained in John. A verse like v 18 could have been part of the story as it reached the Evangelist and yet not have belonged to the earliest form of the story.

(iii) The place in the Lazarus story where repetitions prove most awkward and puzzling is in the "bridge" section that moves Jesus from his encounter with Mary (v 32) to his arrival at the tomb (v 38), namely vv 33–37. The chief problem in these verses is the multiplication and repetition of references to Jesus' deep emotions. The precise reason for Jesus' emotional reaction at this point is unclear, and scholars offer differing interpretations: e.g., the weeping of Mary and the Jews moves Jesus in a very human way to share their emotions and tears; the unbelief betokened by all this weeping moves him to anger and emotional distress; his direct confrontation with the Satanic power of death, typified in Lazarus' death, moves him to anger and combat with the demonic forces; or the miracle-worker must stir up his spirit within to prepare himself to perform a mighty miracle.

Whatever the precise reason, the present text seems overloaded and even repetitious in its references to Jesus' deep feelings. In v 33 we are told that he "groaned" (*enebrimēsato*, literally: "snorted") in spirit and "was deeply disturbed" (*etaraxen heauton,* literally: "he disturbed himself"). In v 35, Jesus weeps. Then in v 38 we are told: "Then Jesus, again groaning within himself (*embrimōmenos en heautǭ*) came to the tomb." The double use of the verb "to groan" (*embrimaomai*), each time with the reflexive pronoun or its equivalent (i.e., "in spirit"), is a striking repetition of the same thought. Some authors also suggest that the double statement in v 33 ("he groaned in spirit and was deeply disturbed") may represent alternate translations of the same Aramaic word or phrase.[139] This is a prime example of a case where we cannot hope to guess the exact wording of the earliest tradition. All we can do is surmise that originally the tradition may have contained a single statement that Jesus was deeply moved (or possibly: very angry) as he came to the tomb.

In brief, while one might argue about other awkward, disruptive, or repetitious statements in the text, the best candidates for additions according to the third criterion are v 5, v 18, and some of the statements about Jesus' emotions in vv 33–38.

(d) *The fourth criterion: the heavy presence of vocabulary and style typical of the Evangelist can help confirm the results obtained by applying the first three criteria.* Put negatively, this criterion states that we should be leery of candidates that do not display stylistic traits characteristic of the Fourth Evangelist. I have already noted in passing some cases where the indications of the other three criteria are bolstered by the typically Johannine vocabulary and style of the verses in question. The same kind of philological support for my conclusions can be found in all the verses I have isolated as John's own composition. I will not bore the reader with all the particulars here; the data on Johannine words and style in 11:1–45 can easily be found in the works of Bultmann and Rochais.[140] The important point is that verses suspected of being additions by the Evangelist on other grounds are confirmed as such by an examination of their vocabulary and style.

5. Drawing Some Further Conclusions

The application of the four criteria has given us a rough idea of which verses of the Lazarus story most likely come from the Evangelist. When we look at the results, are any further conclusions suggested?

Rochais makes one suggestion that seems highly plausible. Once we have decided that Martha has been used by the Evangelist as a mouthpiece for certain theological views and that her two encounters with Jesus (vv 21–27 and vv 39–40) are creations of the Evangelist, the likelihood arises that her very presence in the story is a secondary element. A number of scattered curiosities in the story suddenly become explainable if this is true.

(a) As already noted, the very beginning and end of the story highlight Mary, not Martha, even though Martha is the more prominent sister within the story. Mary is mentioned before Martha in v 1 (Martha being identified as "her sister"), and the whole story ends with the strange wording of v 45:

"Therefore many of the Jews who had come out *to Mary* and had seen what he [Jesus] had done, believed in him."

(b) It almost seems that the Evangelist is at pains to reverse this tendency and to prepare for the dominant role of Martha when he writes in v 5: "Jesus loved Martha *and her sister* and Lazarus." It is remarkable that, while Mary was named before Martha in v 1, here not only is Martha placed first, but Mary is not even named, although Lazarus as well as Martha are. We have seen from the criteria that v 5 is probably an addition of the Evangelist as he tries to ward off the false impression that Jesus is indifferent to the plea of the sisters for their sick brother. Verse 5 therefore gives us the Evangelist's priorities, which include highlighting Martha instead of Mary—precisely what happens in vv 21–27 and 39–40.

(c) Once Jesus' encounter with Martha in vv 21–27 is removed, the briefer encounter of Jesus with Mary in vv 29 + 32 makes sense. If one reads the complete text of John 11:1–45, Mary's truncated repetition of what Martha has already said more fully and forcefully ("Lord, if you had been here, my brother would not have died") seems anticlimactic and superfluous. If, instead, we omit the character of Martha and her encounter with Jesus in vv 21–27, Mary's encounter with Jesus makes good dramatic sense.[141] Mary voices her grief and disappointment in a gentle rebuke mixed with ongoing faith in Jesus the miracle-worker. Her lamentation, along with the lamentation of the Jews who had accompanied her to Jesus, moves Jesus deeply and prompts him to ask where the grave is. Omitting the variant descriptions of Jesus' emotions as well as the second encounter with Martha (vv 39–40), we move expeditiously from Mary's lament (v 32) to Jesus' emotional response (v 33), his movement to the grave (vv 34,38), his order to remove the stone (v 39a), and then the miracle proper (vv 43–44a), plus confirmation (the rest of v 44) and reaction (v 45).

It may well be that the presence of the short, touching encounter of Mary with Jesus suggested to the Fourth Evangelist the possibility of a longer, theologically denser encounter with Martha. The result was theological richness, but not without a certain disruption in the flow of the story. What was originally a short, poignant encounter between Mary and Jesus became somewhat bathetic in the final text.

The upshot of all this is that the removal of the two encounters with Martha, suggested by the application of the criteria, receives further confirmation from other phenomena in the text that make much more sense once Martha is excised. Her complete disappearance would demand that her name also be dropped from verses that mention her alongside Mary and that "bridge verses" that serve to introduce her or connect her with Mary's activity should likewise be omitted. In practice this would mean that (1) her name would be dropped from vv 1 and 19; (2) references to "sisters" would be changed to the singular; and (3) bridge verses that tell of Martha's coming to Jesus (vv 20,30b) or to Mary (v 28) would be omitted. Admittedly, in any such operation one is dealing with greater and lesser probabilities, and it is not always clear whether a half-verse here or there should be retained (e.g., 20b).

Nevertheless, a certain confirmation of the whole process emerges as we finish our detailed analysis and ask what picture results from the various omissions suggested by the four criteria and these further observations. Since we were not constantly looking at the "big picture" as we examined individual verses, it would be possible to wind up with a jumble of verses that made no sense or lacked literary coherence. Instead, while we must naturally remain uncertain about some fine points of the reconstruction (since the presence or absence of some verses remains debatable), on the whole the pared-down pericope that emerges from all the omissions makes sense, fits the form-critical category of a Synoptic-like miracle story very well, and supplies a reasonable starting point for all the theological expansions the Fourth Evangelist brought to his tradition.

6. The Resulting Reconstruction of the Pre-Gospel Tradition

We are now in a position to try to bring the results of our various criteria and observations to bear on the task of reconstructing the hypothetical source John used in composing the Lazarus story. The verses that—in whole or in part—belonged to the pre-Gospel tradition used by the evangelist were probably vv 1,3,6, [possibly 11–14,15d], 17, [18–]19, [20b], 29[–30a], 31–34,38–39a, 41a, 43–45.[142] I place in brackets those verses whose status is unclear. For the most part, they are verses that add further details to the bare story. Perhaps they were added at a later stage of the evolving tradition, but before John edited it. The uncertainty about the bracketed verses is a healthy reminder that the best we can hope for is a rough approximation of John's source, not a word-for-word reconstruction that is equally reliable in all its parts.

Putting these results together, we arrive at the following hypothetical text of the primitive tradition:

Once there was a sick man, Lazarus of Bethany, the town [in which] Mary his sister [also lived]. His sister sent [a message] to Jesus, saying: "Lord, behold, he whom you love is sick." When Jesus heard that he was sick, he then remained in the place where he was for two days.

[Possible secondary addition in the tradition: After this he said to his disciples: "Lazarus our friend is asleep, but I am going to wake him." The disciples said to him: "Lord, if he is asleep, he will recover." But Jesus had spoken about his death; but they thought that he was speaking about the repose of sleep. Then Jesus said to them plainly: "Lazarus is dead. But let us go to him."][143]

When Jesus came [to Bethany], he found him already four days in the tomb. Many of the Jews had come to Mary to comfort her over her brother. [Mary was sitting at home.] When she heard [that Jesus had come], she arose quickly and came to him. [Jesus had not yet come into the town.] When the Jews who were with her in the house and were comforting her saw that Mary had quickly arisen and went out, they followed her, thinking that she was going to the tomb to weep there.

When Mary came to the place where Jesus was, seeing him she fell at his feet, saying to him: "Lord if you had been here, my brother would not have died." When he saw her weeping and the Jews who had come with her weeping, Jesus groaned in spirit. And he said: "Where have you laid him?" They said to him: "Lord, come and see."

Jesus came to the tomb. It was a cave, and a stone lay over its entrance. Jesus said: "Take the stone away." They therefore took the stone away. In a loud voice Jesus shouted: "Lazarus, come forth." The dead man came forth, [with his feet and hands bound with burial cloths, and his face wrapped in a handkerchief.][144] Jesus said to them: "Untie him and let him go." Now many of the Jews who had come to Mary and had seen what he had done believed in him.

I have stressed a number of times that this reconstruction is only a rough approximation and that, quite understandably, different scholars take out or put in a verse here and there. One source of these disagreements is the probability that, prior to its inclusion in the Fourth Gospel, the Lazarus story existed in a "fluid" state, as Dodd puts it. Over the decades various amplifications would have been added; hence I enclose some verses in brackets to indicate that they may not have belonged to the earliest form of the story and yet may have been added before the editorial work of the Evangelist. Similarly, one cannot be dogmatic about the exact wording of the pre-Gospel tradition. In a given verse, what are now pronouns may have originally been proper names, and vice versa; various connecting phrases may have dropped out or been added along the way.

Still, I think this rough approximation has some validity. It has been arrived at not capriciously but by the application of certain reasonable and clearly articulated criteria. A post-factum confirmation of the reconstruction's basic validity may also be had by comparing the text I propose with the alternate reconstructions offered by major commentators on the Lazarus story. Throughout my own process of creating this hypothetical reconstruction, I purposely did not take any one model from the commentators as my guide. I tried as much as possible to go my own way. At the end of the process, however, the core of my reconstruction essentially coincides with the core text that lies at the heart of most of the other reconstructions, despite all the disagreements over individual verses that might be added to this core. Almost everyone agrees that to the basic or "core" story of the Evangelist's source belonged at least vv 1,3,6, possibly parts of 11–15,17–18 (also 19?), parts of 33–39, and 43–44 (also 45?).

One must also keep in mind that some differences of opinion arise because some scholars are intent on reconstructing a fixed written text that existed in a "sign source" or a whole "Sign Gospel" just prior to the Evangelist's redaction of the text, while others think in terms of an evolving oral tradition and still others seek to reconstruct the earliest available form of the oral tradition. In light of this, it is hardly surprising that a scholar like Fortna, who holds to a "Sign Gospel," proposes a fairly long text, while a scholar like Schnackenburg, who does not hold such a theory, suggests a relatively short text. Yet even these two scholars, representing the two ends of the spectrum of reconstructions, agree on most of the "core" text.

One must also allow for the fact that a verse as it now stands in the text may be a formulation composed by John and yet be a replacement for some earlier, similar statement in the pre-Gospel form of the story. For example, many commentators are wary of accepting v 45 as the original ending of the story: "Therefore many of the Jews who had come to Mary and had seen what he had done believed in him." When one notices that the key verb "believe" (*pisteuō*) is (1) a favorite verb of the Evangelist[145] and (2) occurs elsewhere in 11:1–45 only in those verses that probably come from the hand of the Evangelist (vv 15,25–27,40,42), one can well understand why many commentators prefer to end the pre-Gospel tradition at v 44 (or even v 43).

At the same time, the reaction of bystanders is a regular element at the conclusion of a miracle story. More specifically, all stories of raising the dead in both the OT and the NT end with some sort of reaction by the "audience," be it prostration in homage, astonishment, praise, or belief. It would be very strange if the pre-Gospel form of the Lazarus story had contained no reaction whatever. Hence I leave v 45 in my reconstruction as the representative of the motif of the bystanders' reaction, even though I realize that some other verb than "believe" may have been used to indicate that reaction. Still, even the reaction of belief would not be impossible in the pre-Gospel tradition. After all, the Evangelist did not have a monopoly on the verb *pisteuō*, and he no doubt shared many words and phrases with the tradition he inherited. Moreover, the story of the raising of Tabitha in Acts 9 ends with a reaction similar to John 11:45: "And many believed in the Lord [= Jesus]" (Acts 9:42).[146]

Another problem with any reconstruction is that one can never be sure to what degree the beginnings and endings of verses that were already in the tradition were modified by the Evangelist when he inserted his own additions. For instance, the end of v 1, as it now stands in John's Gospel, is awkward: "Now there was a sick man, Lazarus from Bethany, from the town of Mary and Martha, her sister." Part of the confusion in the text may be due to the addition of both the name of Martha (plus her identification as Mary's sister) and the further identification of Mary as the one who anointed the Lord (v 2). The beginning of v 3 would also have been altered to make it speak of both sisters: "The sisters sent to him, saying. . . ." It may be that, before all these additions were made, v 1 introduced Lazarus and his condition while v 3 introduced Mary with her message: "Now there was a sick man, Lazarus from Bethany. His sister Mary sent a message to Jesus, saying. . . ." Other readjustments are possible at various points throughout the text (e.g., pronouns that were originally proper names). But such readjustments must remain speculative, and fortunately they do not affect the rough approximation that is our goal.

7. A Still Earlier Version of the Lazarus Tradition?

My suggested pre-Gospel text stands somewhere between the lengthy text of Fortna and the terse text of Schnackenburg. While I think that my reconstruction has a good chance of reflecting the pre-Gospel Lazarus story at some stage of its development, one may question whether it represents the earliest form of the tradition. Wilkens, Rochais, and Kremer all offer hypothetical reconstructions of a severely pruned tradition that supposedly lay behind the source the Evangelist knew. For instance, Rochais offers a Synoptic-like primitive tradition that is so abbreviated that all the characters except Jesus are anonymous.[147]

That there may have been a very brief story at the origin of the tradition, comprising little more than parts of vv 1,3,7,15,17,32,38–39,41,43–45 is possible. In addition, it may well be that, in this earliest form, there was no mention of "many of the Jews," but only of "many [people]," understood to be the townspeople of Bethany. However, to reconstruct the wording of the earliest version, Rochais must take for granted some presuppositions that are by no means certain, namely: (1) that the Lazarus story existed in fixed written form in the sign source John used, (2) that we can know the style and theology of the author of the sign source, and (3) that we can use this knowledge to discern what words were in the most primitive version. On these points I remain doubtful. I do not think it certain that the Lazarus story was fixed in writing in a sign source, and I would not venture to state what the stylistic traits and theology of the writer of the sign source were.[148]

In particular, I would question Rochais's idea that in the most primitive version of the story both the sick man and the woman who petitions Jesus were anonymous. To begin with, Rochais must struggle to explain why, out of all the possible candidates, the names "Lazarus" and "Mary" should have been chosen post factum for the two anonymous characters. I find his complicated explanation of how all this came about highly speculative.[149] More to the point, though, we saw in our global survey of Jesus' miracles that, except in the case of the immediate disciples of Jesus, the general tendency of the Synoptic Gospels was to keep or make the beneficiary or petitioner of a miracle during the public ministry anonymous. To be precise: apart from the immediate disciples, the only named recipient of a miracle during the public ministry is Bartimaeus, and the only named petitioner is Jairus. The rare presence of a proper name, taken along with other observations about the two miracle stories, led us to judge it likely that the two names went back to certain historical events in the life of Jesus.

A parallel situation is seen in John's Gospel. Again, with the exception of Jesus' immediate disciples, miracle stories belonging to the public ministry almost never name the beneficiary or the petitioner. This holds true even in cases where we would have expected a name. For instance, in the first Cana miracle (2:1–11) not only the chief steward and the bridegroom but even "the mother of Jesus" remain nameless. If any miracle story cries out for a name, it is the story of the man born blind. The plucky beggar who receives his sight from Jesus dominates the whole of John 9 and, from a literary point of view, is the most fully realized "character" in all of the Gospel miracle stories. He alone may be said to have a completely developed personality. And yet he remains anonymous.

Like Bartimaeus in Mark, so Lazarus in John is the only beneficiary of a miracle during the public ministry who is named (in spite of the fact that he never speaks); and like Jairus in Mark, so Mary in John is the only petitioner who is named. The Lazarus story is also unique in John as the Bartimaeus story is unique in Mark in that the beneficiary's name is linked in the story to a place-name. This "going against the grain" of the entire miracle tradition of the Four Gospels, this "discontinuity" with the rest of the canonical miracle stories of the public ministry, inclines me to think that the names of Lazarus, Mary, and Bethany were original to the tradition, however short and Synoptic-like it was in the beginning. The major objection to such a position comes from the possibility of borrowing or contamination from the special Lucan tradition, to which we must now turn.

8. Influence from the Lucan Tradition?

Those who think that the Lazarus story does not go back to any historical event in the life of Jesus, as well as those who claim that the earliest tradition of the story contained, apart from Jesus, only anonymous characters, have some explaining to do. Specifically, these critics must explain how or why the names Lazarus and Mary were chosen out of all possible names and then were connected, out of all the miracle stories circulating in the Johannine tradition, with the story of Jesus raising a dead man to life.[150]

The usual route is to appeal to two special "L" traditions in Luke's Gospel: (1) the parable of Lazarus and the rich man (Luke 16:19–31), which presents a sympathetic character called Lazarus who dies, and which ends with the al-most bitter remark that "they will not be convinced even if someone rises from the dead"; and (2) the story of Jesus' visit to the house of Martha and Mary (Luke 10:38–42), where Martha busies herself with serving at table while Mary sits at Jesus' feet to hear his word. Other traditions found in Luke's Gospel are also invoked at times: e.g., the story of the anonymous woman who washes and anoints Jesus' feet in Galilee (Luke 7:36–50), as well as the connections that this story may have (through oral or written tradition) with John's account of Mary of Bethany anointing Jesus' feet (John 12:1–8). But the major sources for the Lazarus story are usually sought in the parable of Lazarus and the rich man and the story of Jesus' visit to Martha and Mary.[151]

(a) At first glance, the parable of Lazarus and the rich man seems a promis-ing source. True, it apparently circulated only within the stream of special tradition available to Luke, but the Gospels of Luke and John display some fascinating cases of "cross-fertilization" or "contamination" between their two streams of special traditions.[152] One cannot help but be struck by the fact that Lazarus of Bethany in John 11–12 and the poor man of the parable in Luke 16 are the only two persons in the NT who bear the name Lazarus. It is likewise a striking phenomenon that, just as Lazarus is the only named beneficiary of a sign performed by the Johannine Jesus, so Lazarus is the only named character in any of the Gospel parables.

The narratives in both the Lucan parable and the Johannine miracle story offer still more intriguing parallels. One reason why a number of parallels can exist between such two dissimilar literary forms (parable and miracle story) is that, unlike many parables attributed to Jesus, the parable of Lazarus and the rich man comprises a fairly extensive narrative that communicates an example or a warning. In this it is not unlike the parable of the good Samaritan.[153] In other ways it is reminiscent of another long parable unique to Luke, the parable of the prodigal son. Each parable has two parts, and each part reaches its climax in a solemn pronouncement by an authority figure (the father of the prodigal son in 15:24,32 and Abraham in 16:25–26,31).[154] The similarity in form, structure, and tone may indicate that these and other special "L" parables shared a process of formation in a particular early-Christian milieu to which Luke had access.

With all this in mind, let us take a closer look at the two halves of the parable of Lazarus and the rich man.[155] In the first half of Luke's parable (16:19–26), the poor beggar Lazarus suffers throughout life with no relief, while the rich man at whose gate Lazarus is wont to lie in misery feasts sumptuously every day. Both die, only to find that their lots in the next world are completely reversed. Lazarus is now consoled in the bosom of Abraham (a metaphor for a place of comfort within the abode of the dead),[156] while the rich man suffers fiery torment in his place of torture, set at a great distance from the bosom of Abraham. The rich man apparently still thinks of others as servants of his needs, since he pleads with "Father Abraham" to send Lazarus with a little water to quench his terrible thirst. Abraham replies first by simply reaffirming the fact of the total reversal of the earthly lots of the two men and then by disclosing that any passage from his bosom to the place of torment or vice versa is impossible. The first half of the parable thus ends with Abraham confirming the irreversible and unbending nature of the reversal of the two men's fates. With reference to our special concern about the parable being a possible source of John 11:1–45, the result is clear and simple, though not overwhelming: the first half of the Lucan parable supplies us with a sympathetic figure named Lazarus who dies.

Perhaps more important for the parable's supposed status as a source of the Johannine story of Lazarus is the second half of the parable (16:27–31). Realizing that his own terrible fate is irreversible and without relief, the rich man now pleads with Abraham to send Lazarus to his five brothers, who are still living. Lazarus—whom the rich man still considers his lackey—is to give them a solemn, eyewitness warning (*diamartyrētai*) about what awaits them, and so prevent them from ending up in the same place of torture after death. Abraham coolly rebuffs the request for special spiritual warnings for the rich by observing: "They have Moses and the prophets [i.e., the Hebrew Scriptures]; let them listen to them [and the warnings they contain]." The desperate rich man persists, insisting that if only someone would come to them from the dead, then they would repent (*metanoēsousin*). The second half of the parable ends with Abraham's stern reply: "If they do not listen to Moses and the prophets, they will not be convinced even if someone rises from the dead."

From the second half of the parable, then, we garner the themes of (1) Lazarus coming back from (or rising from) the dead as a means of calling the obdurate to repentance and (2) the grim observation that, even if this should happen, the obdurate people targeted for the warning would still not be persuaded. Is not this what happens in John 11:1–46? Lazarus does rise from the dead (11:44), and still some people who witness the event do not believe, but rather report Jesus to the Pharisees (11:46). Looking at each narrative as a whole, we can detect another curious parallel: in both Luke and John Lazarus is a named character, yet he never acts or speaks for himself; he is always talked about by others.[157] The action revolves around him, but he never initiates action or dialogue. Here, then, say some critics, is the likely source of the Johannine story of the raising of Lazarus, or at least the source of the name Lazarus for a character who rises from the dead only to meet with disbelief.

While this argument has some merit, I do not consider it all that convincing. To begin with, it focuses on a few parallels between the Lucan parable and the Johannine miracle story, while ignoring the vast differences. The Lazarus of the parable is a poor beggar covered with sores, without family or material support, who experiences nothing but evil during his life. None of this is true of the Lazarus of John's Gospel, who is well-off enough to have a house shared with his family and, when he dies, a cave tomb sealed with a stone. Apart from his sickness and death, no mention is made of any hardship; in fact, in John 12:1–8 Lazarus' sister Mary pours ointment worth 300 denarii (almost a whole year's income for a day laborer) on Jesus. Moreover, at the heart of the Lucan parable lies the sharp contrast between the destitute Lazarus and the bon-vivant rich man, whose lots are reversed after death. John's miracle story lacks any character who functions as the antithesis to Lazarus, and the theme of the reversal of fates in the next world is completely absent. Indeed, except for the setup of the first three verses, Luke's parable takes place entirely in the abode of the dead, while John's narrative is set firmly in this world.

One could continue picking out individual elements of contrast or simply non-connection between the Lucan parable and the Johannine miracle, but the basic point is clear: if it were not for (1) the name of Lazarus in each story and (2) the theme in the last verse of the parable of someone rising from the dead only to meet with disbelief, it would not have occurred to anyone to connect these two Gospel pericopes. In fact, even the second motif of rising from the dead would have hardly been sufficient to make the connection if the name of Lazarus had not been present in each story. Just how probative are these two parallels?

(i) The presence of the name Lazarus in each story is at first glance impressive. Yet the name Eleazar or Lazar(us) (a shortened form of Eleazar) was one of the most common names for Jewish men in Palestine around the turn of the era.[158] Granted the large following Jesus had during his ministry, it would have been surprising if one or another of his followers had not been named Lazarus. Hence what is problematic is not the presence of the name Lazarus in a Gospel narrative concerning a disciple of Jesus. Though very rare, there are at least a few other cases in which proper names of beneficiaries or petitioners occur in Gospel miracle stories.

What is absolutely unparalleled and demands an explanation is the occurrence of a proper name in a parable. If the name Lazarus was original in John's miracle story because it did refer to some actual disciple of Jesus, we can at least entertain the possibility that the name might have passed over secondarily into the Lucan parable.[159] But if we champion the reverse movement of the tradition history (i.e., that the name was original in the parable and secondarily passed over into the miracle story), then we are hard pressed to explain the origin of the unparalleled phenomenon of a named character in one—and only one—of Jesus' parables.

Explanations have been offered, but in my view none of them explains very much. Commentators point out that the name Lazarus (= Eleazar) means "God helps" in Hebrew. That is true, but it is not relevant to the question we are asking. The name Eleazar would fit just as well a number of characters in other parables of the "L" tradition, e.g., the man set upon by the robbers in the parable of the good Samaritan or the humble toll collector in the parable of the toll collector and the Pharisee. Then, too, many other names would have fit the poor beggar Lazarus equally well or even better: Johanan (= Yahweh has been gracious), Daniel (= God is my judge), Simeon (= Hear, [O God]!)—one could go on indefinitely with most of the "theophoric" names of men in the OT. If one wanted to derive a proper name from the parable's own language, Menaḥem (= consoler) or Tobit (= the goodness [of Yahweh]) would echo Luke 16:25 with its mention of "being consoled" and "good things" much better than does the name Lazarus.

There is a further and larger problem in this whole approach. Our starting point for interpreting this parable must be the Greek text as written by Luke for an obviously Greek-speaking and largely Gentile audience. How is this audience supposed to know that Lazarus means "God helps"? If this point were so important to the understanding of the parable, would not a translation be given—as, e.g., in the case of "Akeldama" ("Field of Blood") in Acts 1:19?[160] In short, to observe that Lazarus means "God helps" in no way explains why a personal name should have been attached to *this* parable of Jesus rather than to any other and why *this* particular name should have been deemed more suited to the story of Luke 16:19–31 than many other likely candidates. Other solutions offered by scholars fare no better. For instance, attempts to explain Lazarus by way of the Eliezer (notice the different name) who is Abraham's steward in Gen 15:2 border on pure fantasy.[161] In the end, the name Lazarus in the Lucan parable is more of a problem than a way toward a solution.[162]

(ii) What, then, of the other connection between the parable and John 11:1–45: the mention at the end of the parable of someone rising from the dead, only to meet with disbelief (Luke 16:31)? Unfortunately, to evaluate this argument properly we have to examine some of the murky speculation surrounding the origin and development of Luke 16:19–31. A number of scholars have suggested that the two parts of the parable of Lazarus and the rich man did not originally belong together. As Bultmann and many others since have pointed out, the two parts of the parable make two very different points: (1) vv 19–26 emphasize the irrevocable reversal of lots of the rich and the poor in the next life: the pampered rich will suffer eternal torment, while the suffering poor will receive eternal consolation; (2) vv 27–31 emphasize that, if the obdurate will not listen to the Scriptures' call to repentance, even a messenger returning from the dead will not be able to persuade them to change.[163] Either point could easily be made without the other. Indeed, the first half of the parable is completely self-contained and could stand alone; if a short introduction were supplied, the same would be true of the second half.[164]

This is not to say that the two halves of the parable do not basically cohere in their present form. Dupont has shown convincingly how Luke's redactional hand has shaped the present form of the parable and brought it into contact with the other parts of chap. 16.[165] Yet the differences between the two halves remain palpable, especially when read against the background of the literature of the ancient Near East. Indeed, each half reflects a different type of Near Eastern folktale. The first half of the parable has a famous parallel in a story that circulated in Egyptian demotic in the 1st century A.D.: a rich man is tormented in the next world while a poor man is honored.[166] Variant forms of the same tradition, stressing the reversal of one's status after death, appear in later rabbinic literature. The second half of the parable, with its theme of a messenger coming back from the dead to warn the living to change their lives, is also found in later Jewish literature. My point here is not that any of these Egyptian or Jewish stories was a direct source for either Jesus or Luke. Rather, my point is that the two halves of the parable seem to reflect two different streams of Near Eastern folklore, and so, not surprisingly, they reflect the different themes that the two different streams conveyed.

The differences are not exhausted in the two different ideas: reversal of the lot of poor and rich after death, and the effectiveness of a messenger returning from the dead to warn the living. The "moral" tone of the two halves of the Lazarus parable are strikingly different. While commentators often seek to read a clear moral tone or moral criterion into the first half of the parable, I think their efforts are mistaken. There is no explicit moral criterion or exhortation present. In 16:25 Abraham does not explain the *reason* for the reversal of the rich man's earthly status; he simply affirms the obvious *fact* of the reversal as though it were something to be expected: "Son, remember that you received good things in your life, and Lazarus likewise received evil; but now he is being consoled while you are being tormented." That is clearly the case, but no reason for its being the case is given. The first half of the parable never says that the rich man was evil or that Lazarus was pious or good.[167] Granted, such ideas may be inferred from the rich man's failure to care for Lazarus lying at his gate and from the OT's regular affirmations that God champions the cause of the neglected poor. But notice: to arrive at this moral message we must read into the first half of the parable the exhortations of the OT, Jesus, Luke, or later rabbinic material.[168] Taken by itself, the first half of the parable never makes this moral point and never appeals to it as the reason for the reversal.

Quite different is the explicit moral tone of the second half of the parable. Unlike the first half, the second half speaks with a clearly moral vocabulary. The purpose of sending a messenger from the dead is to have the five brothers "repent"—no doubt, of their sinful ways that could bring them to the place of torment already inhabited by their brother. Only here does one find any intimation that evil behavior is what causes one to come to the place of torment. Correspondingly, we hear nothing in the second half about the five brothers being rich, though undoubtedly they are thought to be so. But wealth is no longer the point. The point inculcated in the second half is not that the rich will suffer a reversal of fortune in the next life; the point is rather that an evildoer who does not repent will be punished—something that holds true of rich and poor alike.

Hence the theme of reversal, like the theme of wealth, disappears because it is not relevant to the message of the parable's second half. What determines one's fate beyond the grave is whether one listens to the moral exhortation of Moses and the prophets and accordingly repents of one's evil deeds. If a person refuses to be called to repentance by God's word in Scripture, then not even a messenger from the dead will succeed in persuading such an obdurate person to change. Thus, the parable's second half has a moral focus and emphasis that is foreign to the first half. Taken together, the different basic themes of the two halves, their different folkloric backgrounds, and this difference in moral tone suggest that the two halves of Luke 16:19–31 were brought together relatively late in the Gospel tradition. At the very least, the parable's present shape, vocabulary, and theological thrust certainly betray the redactional hand of Luke.[169] If it be true that the parable's two halves were melded into their present form relatively late in the development of the Gospel tradition, then the influence of the parable on the Johannine tradition of the raising of Lazarus becomes problematic. Without the existence in the early Christian tradition of a single unit that combined the story of Lazarus on earth with the theme of Lazarus rising from the dead only to meet with disbelief, the claim that the parable of Luke 16:19–31 was a source for John 11:1–45 becomes doubtful.

But even if we put aside all the problems involved in the tradition history of the Lucan parable, any theory claiming that the parable influenced the pre-Gospel story of Jesus raising Lazarus must face a major difficulty: the last verse of the parable. The parable of Lazarus and the rich man might never have been suggested as a source for John's story of Lazarus if the present form of the parable did not end with Abraham's stern prediction (16:31): "If they do not listen to Moses and the prophets, they will not be convinced even if someone rises from the dead." Yet the theory that Luke 16:31 in particular influenced the formation of John's story of Lazarus suffers from a number of weaknesses.

First of all, what Abraham bitterly predicts does not prove true according to the story in John's Gospel. As John 11:1–45 now stands, the primary reaction that is "up front" in the story is that "*many* of the Jews . . . believed in him [Jesus]" (John 11:45). Only in the next verse, which is the transition to the next scene rather than the proper ending of the Lazarus story, do we hear that "*some* of them [the Jews] went off to the Pharisees and told them what Jesus had done" (11:46). John's emphasis on the *many* who do believe stands in direct contradiction to Abraham's prediction.

This objection to the supposed influence of Luke 16:31 on the Johannine story of Lazarus becomes all the more pressing when we notice that almost none of the reconstructions of the pre-Gospel story of the raising of Lazarus includes 11:46 as part of the tradition the Evangelist received. Verse 46 is most likely an addition made by the Evangelist to create a bridge to the next scene, the meeting of the high priests and the Pharisees, who discuss what to do with Jesus. If John 11:46 is not original to the story a severe blow is dealt to the theory that Luke 16:31 was a source of the traditional Johannine story of Lazarus. If the traditional story ended with belief as the general reaction to the raising of Lazarus, then it flatly contradicted the ending of the Lucan parable. The supposed tradition history becomes stranger and stranger.

To all this I would add another objection to the theory of the influence of the final verse of the parable on the Johannine miracle story, an objection based on the Lucan vocabulary and style of v 31. In my opinion, the present wording of Luke 16:31 is a product of the Evangelist himself. It may even be that v 31 was never part of the traditional parable of Lazarus and the rich man, even after the two halves were joined together to form our present parable; v 31 may be completely a creation of Luke.

An initial reason for this suspicion is that there is a certain tension in wording and concepts between vv 27 and 30 on the one hand and v 31 on the other as the parable draws to a close. In 16:27, when the rich man seeks to spare his brothers the damnation he now suffers, he asks Abraham to "send" Lazarus "to the house of my father" to warn them. Lazarus, quite comfortable in the bosom of Abraham, is obviously thought of as a messenger who comes back temporarily from the dead in some sort of vision or dream to deliver his warning, and who then obviously returns to his eternal happiness. In v 30, the rich man accordingly speaks in general terms: "If someone *goes* to them from the dead [*ean tis apo nekrōn poreuthȩ̄ pros autous*]. . . ."

Yet in the final verse of the parable there is a marked shift in language and imagery. Now the hypothetical reason for sinners being converted is that "someone" (notice how Lazarus has dropped out of the picture from v 30 onwards) *rises* from the dead. Within the story world of Luke's parable, it makes no sense to think of Lazarus "rising from the dead" as the Johannine Lazarus does—or, for that matter, as Jesus does on Easter Sunday. The Lucan Lazarus is already settled in his final resting place of eternal bliss. His mission is accordingly conceived of in terms of "going" to the five brothers in some sort of monitory apparition, all the more frightening because it is the apparition of a dead man, coming back for a moment from the abode of the dead.

Hence our suspicions are aroused when, in the last verse of the parable (a place especially open to a redactor's intervention), the vocabulary and thought-world suddenly change in a way that would remind a Christian of the kerygma of Christ's resurrection (16:31): "If someone rises from the dead [*ean tis ek nekrōn anastē*]. . . ."[170] I think that one must reckon here with a relatively late modification of a parable that originally did not speak in such terms. I suggest that Luke himself modified the ending of the parable to introduce an allusion to Jesus' resurrection and its failure (as seen in the Acts of the Apostles) to move the majority of the Jews to accept the Christian call to repentance.

The shift in thought and imagery from vv 27–30 to v 31 is not the only reason for suspecting Luke's hand; v 31 also displays vocabulary characteristic of Luke. Luke uses the verb *anistēmi* ("to raise" or "rise," the verb in v 31) more than any other author in the NT. Of the roughly 108 uses of the verb in the NT, two-thirds (72) occur in Luke–Acts.[171] In contrast, the entire Pauline corpus (both authentic and pseudepigraphic letters) uses the verb only 5 times, only once of the resurrection of Jesus. Matthew uses the verb only 4 times (never of the resurrection of Jesus or the dead in general), John only 8 times.

The shift to the vocabulary of *anistēmi* at the end of the parable would therefore fit Luke's style and even his way of modifying his tradition, for he makes a similar change in a Marcan tradition that he takes over in Luke 9:8 (cf. Mark 6:15). In reporting one of a number of popular opinions about who Jesus is, Mark uses the phrase "a prophet like one of the prophets [of old]"; Luke changes that to "some prophet from among the ancient [prophets] has risen *[anestē]*." This is not an accident; Luke repeats the change in 9:19 (cf. Mark 8:28). The sense is remarkably similar to that of 16:31: a person who has died and gone to the next world has come back on a mission that startles and upsets people.

One can reinforce the case for Luke's hand in v 31 by observing that the verb used to predict that "they will not be convinced" (*peisthēsontai*, from *peithō*) is also characteristic of Luke; he uses it more than any other author in the NT.[172] Dupont notes other Lucan stylistic traits in v 31 as well: Luke's use of the set phrases "Moses and the prophets" (vv 29,31), "but he said" (*eipen de*), and "someone from" (*tis ek*).[173] Kremer goes even further: for him, the whole dialogue over unbelief (vv 27–31), loaded as it is with Lucan characteristics, was apparently formulated by Luke.[174]

Nevertheless, I prefer to focus on what seems to me the clearest case of Lucan redaction: v 31. When we put together (1) the sudden shift of imagery and thought in v 31, (2) the position of v 31 as the parable's final verse, which delivers the parable's "punch line," (3) Luke's unrivaled penchant among NT writers for *anistēmi* (including a redactional change in 9:8 similar to the usage of 16:31), (4) the Lucan character of the verb *peithō*, and (5) the other Lucan traits in v 31 pointed out by Dupont, I think it probable that at the very least the wording in v 31 is due to Luke's hand. Indeed, it may be that the whole ending of the parable as we now have it is Luke's composition. Since, in my view, Luke wrote his Gospel roughly around the time John the Evangelist was also active (toward the end of 1st century A.D.), it is difficult to imagine that a redactional formulation of Luke in 16:31 influenced or gave rise to the traditional Johannine story of the raising of Lazarus. The latter would have been in circulation for some decades before the Fourth Gospel (and probably the Third Gospel) was written.

This argument, I admit, does not enjoy ironclad certainty. But when one considers in tandem the problem of explaining the origin of the name Lazarus in the parable of Luke 16:19–31, the possibility that the parable originally circulated as two distinct stories, perhaps even in the early Christian tradition, and the possibility that the key mention of rising from the dead in the last verse was a redactional formulation of Luke, one begins to appreciate that explaining the Johannine story of Lazarus by way of the Lucan parable is a classic case of explaining the obscure by the more obscure.

After all, despite disagreements over details, there is a rough consensus among most commentators on the contours of a pre-Gospel Johannine tradition that told how Jesus raised Lazarus from the dead. Reaching any consensus on the tradition history of the Lucan parable of Lazarus and the rich man is, in my opinion, much more difficult, if not impossible. Personally, I suspect that the Lucan parable did not attain its present form before Luke wrote his Gospel, and so I remain very doubtful about the parable's influence on the Johannine miracle story.[175] If there is any "cross-fertilization," I think it more likely that the pre-Gospel Johannine tradition of Jesus raising Lazarus from the dead may have helped confer the name Lazarus on the originally anonymous poor man of the Lucan parable.[176]

(b) As for the Lucan story of Jesus visiting Mary and Martha (Luke 10:38–42), it may indeed have had some influence by way of the oral tradition on the story of the anointing of Jesus in the Fourth Gospel (John 12:1–8)—and so indirectly on John's redaction of the Lazarus story. But, as we have seen, it is likely that Martha's role in John 11:1–45 is due to John's own hand and that originally the Lazarus story spoke only of the dead man Lazarus and his sister Mary of Bethany. The insertion of Martha into the Lazarus story of John 11, the identification of the woman who anoints Jesus in chap. 12 with the Mary of Bethany mentioned in chap. 11, and the passing reference to Martha and Lazarus in the anointing story (12:1–2) may all come from the Evangelist. Hence I see no reason for thinking that the Lucan story of Martha and Mary had any significant impact on the pre-Gospel Johannine tradition about the raising of Lazarus.[177] The Lucan story of Martha and Mary has no Lazarus, and apparently the early Johannine form of the Lazarus story had no Martha.

9. Conclusion

The upshot of this lengthy disquisition is that the Fourth Gospel's story of Jesus raising Lazarus from the dead is not a pure creation of John the Evangelist but rather goes back to a miracle story circulating in the Johannine tradition before the Gospel was written. It is highly unlikely that the presence of the name Lazarus in the story is to be explained from the Lucan parable of Lazarus and the rich man. As far back as we can reconstruct the Johannine tradition behind John 11:1–45, Lazarus, Mary, and Bethany seem to be fixed elements in the story. At the same time, one must be cautious about making historical claims; the tradition passed through many decades and many modifications before it came to the Evangelist.

In the end, I find myself adopting a position similar to the one I hold with regard to the Lucan story of the raising of the son of the widow of Nain. The signs of a lengthy tradition history and the anchoring of the event in a set place (plus in the Johannine tradition the presence of the proper names of the principal actors, something contrary to the general tendency of the miracle traditions in all Four Gospels) incline me to think that the Lazarus story ultimately reflects some incident in the life of the historical Jesus.[178] As in the other stories of raising the dead, the question of what actually happened cannot be resolved by us today. It is possible that a story about Jesus healing a mortally ill Lazarus grew into a story of raising the dead.[179] However, there is no indication in the tradition histories suggested by most present-day scholars that the story of Lazarus ever existed as a story of healing rather than a story of restoring the dead to life.[180] I think it likely that John 11:1–45 goes back ultimately to some event involving Lazarus, a disciple of Jesus, and that this event was believed by Jesus' disciples even during his lifetime to be a miracle of raising the dead.[181] In other words, the basic idea that Jesus raised Lazarus from the dead does not seem to have been simply created out of thin air by the early church.

A final observation on arguments about the historicity of the Lazarus story: Once we appreciate how a short and isolated story about Jesus raising Lazarus grew over decades into the huge theological masterpiece of John the Evangelist, we can understand why the silence of the other evangelists provides no solid proof that the raising of Lazarus cannot go back to an event in the life of Jesus. In the early tradition, the raising of Lazarus was not a major cause of Jesus' arrest and passion; that connection is a creation of the Fourth Evangelist. Nor did the earliest form of the story in the tradition carry such impressive literary and theological weight; it was much more Synoptic-like in appearance. Finally, just as John does not seem to have known the Synoptic Gospels, so it seems that the Synoptists did not know the special Johannine tradition. Indeed, even if they had known the primitive story of Lazarus, the three Synoptists, who already had at their disposal the story of the daughter of Jairus and (in the case of Luke) the story of the son of the widow of Nain, would not have been in dire need of yet another story about raising the dead. In short, the silence of the Synoptic Gospels about the raising of Lazarus says nothing one way or the other about the ultimate historicity of the tradition.

VI. THE Q TRADITION: JESUS AFFIRMS THAT "THE DEAD ARE RAISED" (MATT 11:5 ‖ LUKE 7:22)

In previous chapters we examined Jesus' miracles of giving sight to the blind, enabling the lame to walk, cleansing lepers, and curing the deaf. At the conclusion of our treatment of each category, we returned to a key saying of Jesus preserved in the Q tradition (Matt 11:4–5 ‖ Luke 7:22): "Go tell John [the Baptist] what you have seen and heard: the blind see, the lame walk, the lepers are cleansed, the deaf hear, the dead are raised, and the poor have the good news preached to them."[182] This Q saying has great importance for each kind of miracle it lists. Because of this logion, not only do we have various *narratives* from different *sources* attesting to these various kinds of miracles, we also have a *saying* of Jesus attesting to them, a saying taken from a basically non-narrative source, the Q document. Thus, for these categories of miracles—as well as for exorcisms—we have not only multiple attestation of sources (e.g., Mark, Q, L, John) but also multiple attestation of forms (a saying of Jesus as well as a narrative about Jesus).[183]

The same can be said about miracles of raising the dead. Besides the narratives in Mark, L, and John, we have the reference to the dead being raised in Matt 11:5 par. Thus, not only is the claim that Jesus performed such a miracle made by four different sources (Mark, L, John, and Q), it is also made in two different literary forms (narrative and saying). Moreover, the saying-form found in Matt 11:5 par. is definitely not a secondary phenomenon derived from narratives of Jesus raising the dead. As a matter of fact, the Q document has no narrative of Jesus restoring the dead to life; hence the Q saying in Matt 11:5 par. is hardly a distillation of other Q material on the subject. Independent of any narrative, this Q tradition preserves the idea, enshrined in a statement supposedly made by Jesus himself, that he raised the dead.

I must emphasize once again that I am not claiming here that this multiple attestation of sources and forms proves that Jesus did actually raise the dead. Rather, it demonstrates something else: the early church did not invent the picture of Jesus raising the dead out of thin air. The multiple attestation of sources and forms argues strongly that the *claim* that Jesus raised the dead— whatever we think of the truth of that claim—goes back to the public ministry and to Jesus himself. Apparently early Christians believed that Jesus had raised the dead because his disciples believed it during the public ministry.

Those who reject this conclusion usually try to remove the embarrassing evidence of the early Q saying one way or another. Three major approaches to neutralizing the Q logion can be distinguished:

(1) Some critics assert that the whole of Matt 11:5–6 par. is not a saying of the historical Jesus but rather a product of the first-generation Christian church.[184] Early on in this volume, when we examined in Chapter 13 all the Gospel material in which John the Baptist and Jesus interacted, we saw the reasons why this Q saying (indeed, the core of the whole Q tradition in Matt 11:2–6 par.) should be accepted as authentic. There is no need to repeat all the arguments here in detail. In a nutshell, the pericope may be judged basically historical for the following reasons:[185]

(a) The core of the question of the Baptist ("Are you the one to come [*ho erchomenos*], or should we look for another?") uses terminology that is suggestive of eschatological hopes but does not employ any set messianic title used by Judaism at the turn of the era or by Christians in their earliest days.

(b) The pericope, like the Q material in general, does not presume that the Baptist once believed in Jesus and is now questioning his former faith. Rather, up until now nothing has indicated that the Baptist ever accepted Jesus as "the one to come." Hence John's question is a very real and vital one for himself and his circle as he tries to evaluate a former disciple whose message and ministry have diverged so sharply from his own expectations. To accept Jesus would mean a recasting of much of his own vision.

(c) Jesus' reply uses none of the christological titles of the early church. Indeed, Jesus shifts the spotlight away from any title that would define his own person and toward the effects of his ministry on Israel: healing and good news to the poor, the fulfillment of Isaiah's vision for the last days. His answer remains allusive rather than direct.

(d) Behind Jesus' concluding beatitude in Matt 11:6, "Happy is the one who is not kept from believing because of me [literally: who is not scandalized in me]," lies a discreet but urgent appeal to John to overcome his disappointed hopes and to accept Jesus' ministry as the way God is bringing Israel's history to its promised consummation. As in every beatitude, the promise of happiness involves an implied threat of unhappiness if one does not follow the right path.

(e) The whole pericope ends abruptly with this entreaty clothed in a beatitude along with the implied threat to one who does not follow the direction of the beatitude. We are not told whether John ever accepted Jesus' argument, Jesus' ministry, and Jesus as "the one to come." Far from being propaganda to convert the Baptist's followers to the Jesus movement, this pericope ends with an embarrassed silence on the subject of the Baptist's reply to Jesus' appeal.

In all this, the church's kerygma of cross, resurrection, and parousia has had no impact on the Baptist's question, Jesus' answer, and the non-answer of the Baptist that ends—or rather, fails to end—the pericope. In view of all this, those who would claim that Matt 11:2–6 par. is simply an invention of the early church must bear the burden of proof. All indications point to a tradition rooted in the ministry of the historical John and the historical Jesus.

(2) There is a second approach to neutralizing the impact of Matt 11:5 par.

According to this approach, while parts of Matt 11:5 par. may be authentic, the reference to the dead being raised is a secondary element added to the saying by the early church. One may reply that, if this is so, the secondary element must have been added very early on, since the reference to the dead being raised was present in the two versions of Q known independently to Matthew and Luke. But why would the authors or bearers of the tradition in the Q document add the reference to raising the dead, when the Q document contains no narrative of Jesus raising the dead and no other saying referring to such an action on his part? As has been already noted, the reference to raising the dead in Matt 11:5 par. can hardly be chalked up to some sort of distillation or précis of Q material found elsewhere when this is the only time in the Q document that Jesus' miracles of raising the dead are mentioned. Why the bearers of the Q tradition would have added such a reference to an already existing list of miracles is by no means clear.

It is sometimes claimed that the secondary nature of the reference to raising the dead can be seen from a certain discontinuity in the saying. Some of the other miracles mentioned in Matt 11:5 par. echo prophecies in the Book of Isaiah, but the raising of the dead does not. Hence, the argument runs, "the dead are raised" does not belong to the original form of the saying. Now while it is true that the references to the blind seeing, the lame walking, and the deaf hearing do echo Isa 35:5–6 and 42:18, leprosy as well as raising the dead is not represented in the prophecies. Moreover, the section of the Book of Isaiah labeled by modern scholars "The Apocalypse of Isaiah" (Isaiah 24–27) does celebrate God's destruction of the power of death (Isa 25:6–8; 26:19).[186] Since the other miracles mentioned in Matt 11:5 par. do not always echo word-for-word the exact phrases found in the Isaian passages, we need not demand a word-for-word citation in the case of raising the dead.[187] And certainly we should not demand that all the prophecies be located in one section of the Book of Isaiah, since the promise of good news being proclaimed to the poor is found much later on, in Isa 61:1.

Furthermore, if the early bearers of the Q tradition were manufacturing or making additions to the list of miracles in Matt 11:5 par., one might ask why they did not include the more frequent and prominent miracle of exorcism, which, unlike raising the dead, is witnessed in Q both by a short narrative and by various sayings (Matt 12:22–30 par.).

One may also argue against the idea that "the dead are raised" is a later addition by appealing to the rhythmic structure of the Q saying as we now find it. When he examines Matt 11:5–6 par. in the context of the speech-patterns of Jesus, Joachim Jeremias finds a two-beat rhythm typical of the authentic sayings of Jesus. To be precise: Jeremias finds the pattern of six lines with two beats each (three lines plus three lines) followed by one three-beat line as a conclusion.[188] Personally, I am leery about using an argument from rhythm to prove that Jesus spoke a particular saying.[189] However, Jeremias's argument does have a limited use here, inasmuch as it shows that the Q saying as it now stands is rhythmically a self-contained unit, undisturbed by a supposed secondary addition. There is no reason for thinking that "the dead are raised" is a later gloss on the original form of the saying.

(3) The third approach to neutralizing the Q saying is first to admit that the whole of Matt 11:5 par. comes from Jesus and then to maintain that Jesus originally meant the words metaphorically. That is to say, while Matthew and Luke take the saying as referring to Jesus' miracles, the historical Jesus was in fact speaking of the spiritual benefits of his ministry, understood as the dawning of the consummation of the world. By proclaiming good news to the poor Jesus made the spiritually blind see, the spiritually lame walk, and the spiritually dead rise to new life. While this interpretation of Matt 11:5 is popular among some conservative critics who wish to save the authenticity of the saying without having to contend with the disturbing picture of a historical Jesus who claims to raise the dead,[190] their solution suffers from a number of difficulties:

(a) In this solution, the whole of Matt 11:5 par. was circulating throughout the first Christian generation because it came from Jesus. But during that same period, large numbers of pre-Marcan miracle stories (and I would maintain some pre-Lucan and pre-Johannine miracle stories) were also circulating. As we have seen, at least some of these miracle stories most probably originate in Jesus' ministry, as does Matt 11:5. Prominent among these early miracle stories were pre-Marcan, pre-Lucan, and pre-Johannine accounts of Jesus healing people suffering from various types of sight impairment, paralysis, skin diseases, and hearing impairment—as well as accounts of Jesus raising the dead. Indeed, the pre-Marcan tradition alone, certainly belonging to the first Christian generation, knew of each of these categories.

Hence it strains one's imagination to suppose that, with all these miracle stories in circulation in the first Christian generation, the Q list would ever have been understood in a purely metaphorical sense. It is not just Matthew or Luke who would have taken the list of Jesus' actions literally; Christians from the very beginning of the Q tradition would naturally have understood it that way. In other words, granted Jesus' reputation as a miracle-worker, a reputation that goes back to the public ministry, how was any audience hearing this terse saying supposed to know that the language of Jesus the miracle-worker was at this point simply metaphorical? This question is just as pertinent to the audience hearing Jesus speak these words for the first time as it is for an audience listening to the Q tradition in the early church. Needless to say, one can escape this difficulty by attempting a Solomonic solution, i.e., by claiming that the first four verbs in Matt 11:5 par. are to be taken literally, but that the reference to the dead being raised should instead be taken metaphorically. Such a distinction among the "wonders" listed is without any basis in the text and is highly artificial.

(b) In addition, we might well ask: Where else in the sayings of Jesus—or in narratives about Jesus—do we find a long list of Jesus' miraculous actions employed in a purely metaphorical sense? Even when an individual term is used metaphorically (a favorite being the image of "seeing" or "hearing"), the context makes the metaphorical or spiritual sense perfectly clear. Indeed, granted the early and widespread tradition of Jesus working miracles, the context would have to make this metaphorical sense crystal clear if it wanted to avoid hopeless confusion. Moreover, any danger of misunderstanding is usually obviated because the metaphorical usage often denies what the miracle stories affirm: namely, that people react to Jesus by (re)gaining their sight or hearing. For example, in passages like Mark 4:12 and John 9:39–41, Jesus berates his audience for *not* seeing or hearing, i.e., for not understanding his mission and message.[191] The metaphorical or spiritual sense is obvious from the larger context.

(c) Completely different from the context of these metaphorical uses is the context of Matt 11:5 par. Here the context is the puzzlement and doubts that the Baptist suffers about a former disciple named Jesus. As I argued in Chapter 13, the embarrassment that the Baptist doubts Jesus and the greater embarrassment that the Baptist is never said to overcome his doubts argue for the context being historical. In his own ministry the Baptist had proclaimed the imminent coming of a fierce judge who would condemn the wicked to fiery punishment. Jesus, the former disciple who winds up surpassing his master in the range and impact of his ministry, has based his success instead on a message of mercy, forgiveness, and healing—a message he embodies in miracles of healing.

This is not what John expected or promised, and so John poses his question: "Are you the one to come, or should we look for another?" Is Jesus the one who is to play the decisive role in the denouement of Israel's eschatological drama, despite the fact that his ministry runs counter to what John had foreseen? As so often, Jesus deflects attention from any attempt to define his own person and toward the actions and effects of his ministry: his miracles and his proclamation of good news to the poor. These, he intimates, are the concrete signs indicating that the promises of Israel's prophets are now being fulfilled––however contrary this may be to the way John saw things. Jesus ends his list with a poignant appeal, veiled in a beatitude but obviously aimed at John (Matt 11:6 par.): "And happy is the one who is not kept from believing because of me." This message and these miracles of mercy must not be allowed to become a stumbling block to the Baptist, who had expected sterner stuff.

Granted this context, does a purely metaphorical interpretation of giving sight to the blind, hearing to the deaf, and life to the dead make all that much sense? With his fiery proclamation of imminent judgment the Baptist obviously wanted to open the eyes of the spiritually blind to their impending doom and to open the ears of the spiritually deaf to the message that would save them from God's wrath. Both the Gospels and Josephus affirm that in fact the Baptist succeeded to a notable degree in doing so. Hence giving sight to the blind and hearing to the deaf, when taken metaphorically, could apply to John's ministry just as well as to Jesus'. If Jesus were using the words of Matt 11:5 par. in a metaphorical sense, they would not sufficiently differentiate Jesus' ministry from John's or intimate the reason for the difference. If instead they are understood literally, they highlight the miracles as the point at which

Jesus' ministry diverged from John's (John 10:41: "John worked no sign"), as the means by which Jesus publicly surpassed John in power and popular appeal, and as the concrete evidence that Jesus' disconcerting message and ministry were the culmination of God's plan for Israel in the last days. If Jesus meant his words metaphorically, it is hard to see the cogency of the argument he addressed to John. If he meant his words literally, the argument's thrust is clear, whether or not John was ever convinced by it. In short, there is no solid reason for claiming either that Matt 11:5 par. is a creation of the early church or that Jesus' words were originally intended in a purely metaphorical sense. This includes his assertion that "the dead are raised."

I suspect that behind this whole debate on Matt 11:5 par. lies a deeper problem: the perennial desire to make Jesus seem "reasonable" or "rational" to post-Enlightenment "modern man," who looks suspiciously like a professor in a Religious Studies Department at some American university. Perhaps the attempt to see Jesus simply as a Cynic-Stoic philosopher or as an early type of Jewish rabbi active among the common people is the present-day, sophisticated version of the Enlightenment's quest for the reasonable, rational Jesus, the teacher of morality created by Thomas Jefferson's scissors. The results of this chapter, as of the previous chapters on miracles, are a salutary reminder that the historical Jesus does not square with the view of many a post-Enlightenment academic as to what is reasonable, rational, or desirable in religion.

Unless we wish to throw the criteria of historicity overboard in favor of a protean Jesus who always confirms the religious predilections of every individual, the criteria impose on us the picture of a 1st-century Palestinian Jew who performed startling actions that both he and at least some of his audience judged to be miraculous deeds of power. To Jesus' mind these acts—including what he claimed to be acts of raising the dead—both proclaimed and actualized, however imperfectly, the kingdom of God promised by the prophets. To excise these acts from the ministry of the historical Jesus is to excise a good deal of what he was all about.

Having examined three major categories of miracles (exorcism, healing, and raising the dead), we must now turn to what is perhaps the most troublesome category of all, the so-called nature miracles. As we shall see, the first problem is that the category of nature miracle may not be a valid category at all.

NOTES TO CHAPTER 22

[1] For a summary treatment of the examples that follow, see van der Loos, *The Miracles of Jesus*, 559–66.

[2] Whether Paul's rescue of Eutychus, who falls asleep during Paul's sermon and then tumbles out of a third-story window (Acts 20:7–12), is meant by Luke to be a raising of the dead or simply the restoration of a person almost dead is not absolutely clear. Most recent commentators hold that Luke presents it as a true raising of the dead; so Haenchen, *Apostelgeschichte*, 517–20; Conzelmann, *Acts of the Apostles*, 169–70; F. F. Bruce, *The Book of the Acts* (NICNT; Grand Rapids: Eerdmans, n.d.) 407–9; Schneider, *Apostelgeschichte*, 2. 283–88; Fitzmyer, "Acts," *NJBC*, 758.

[3] Two examples preserved in the Babylonian Talmud (note therefore the relatively late date of final composition) are *b. Meg.* 7b and *b. ʿAbod. Zar.* 10b. Translations may be found in I. Epstein (ed.), *The Babylonian Talmud. Seder Moʿed. Megillah* (London: Soncino, 1938) 38 (translation by Maurice Simon); idem, *The Babylonian Talmud. Seder Nezikin. ʿAbodah Zarah* (London: Soncino, 1935) 52–53 (translation by A. Mishcon). The tone of the two stories is folkloric and even comedic. For example, in *b. Meg.* 7b, Rabba and Rabbi Zera drink to the point of inebriation at their celebration of the feast of Purim. Under the influence of the drink, Rabba kills Rabbi Zera. The next day he prays on his behalf and thus brings him back to life. Next year, Rabba invites Rabbi Zera to join him again for the Purim celebration, but Rabbi Zera replies: "A miracle does not take place on every occasion [literally: at every hour]." The editor of the Soncino edition interprets the Aramaic verb *šḥṭ* as meaning that Rabba "cut the throat" of Rabbi Zera "apparently without killing him." The correlative verbs in the story, *šḥṭ* and *ḥyy*, make this interpretation unlikely. A variant of the story in *b. ʿAbod. Zar.* 10b, involving the Roman Emperor Antoninus (a generic fictitious name, perhaps referring here to the Emperor Caracalla) and some disciple of Judah ha-Nasi, can be found in *Lev. Rab.* 10, 111ᵈ (= 10:4); for an English translation, see H. Freedman and Maurice Simon (eds.), *Midrash Rabbah. Leviticus* (London/New York: Soncino, 1939) 125. Interestingly, while the translator (J. Israelstam) admits that the original text literally speaks of raising the dead, the English translation softens this to reviving a dying man.

[4] See Rudolf Pesch, "Jairus (Mk 5, 22/Lk 8, 41)," *BZ* 14 (1970) 252–56; idem, *Markusevangelium*, 1. 295–314, esp. 312–14; Gérard Rochais, *Les récits de résurrection des morts dans le Nouveau Testament* (SNTSMS 40; Cambridge: Cambridge University, 1981) 110–12, 163–64.

[5] We are left with something of a methodological puzzle here. Even before examining the evidence of a particular miracle story in the Gospels, the agnostic is unalterably committed to one of the following explanations: (1) the story is a pure invention of the early church; (2) the story represents a parable Jesus told or a parabolic action he performed, which was later transformed by the Christian tradition into a miracle; (3) something Jesus did that is explainable by natural means (e.g., alleviating a psychosomatic illness by hypnotic suggestion) was interpreted as a miracle by the people of that time; or (4) the story reflects an actual event in the life of Jesus, namely, a fraud perpetrated by Jesus and/or the person supposedly helped. An educated believer trained in the historical-critical method would be open to accepting the first three explanations in individual cases, while at the same time being open to the possibility of a real miracle in other cases. It would all de-

pend on the evidence of the particular case. The methodological question thus arises: which investigator is truly open-minded? If neither investigator is willing to accept all the options listed above as real possibilities, is either completely open-minded?

[6] Hence the raising of the dead recounted in such a story is sometimes referred to as a "resuscitation." I avoid the word "resuscitation" because of possible confusion with its common meaning today: the act of reviving someone from *apparent* death or from unconsciousness. In the Gospel *stories* (whatever may have been true of the original event, if there was one), the death is thought to be real and irreversible by any and all human means.

[7] On this see James P. Martin, "History and Eschatology in the Lazarus Narrative. John 11.1–44," *SJT* 17 (1964) 332–43, esp. 342. This cross-reference between the Lazarus story and the empty tomb story seems intended by the Fourth Evangelist. Even apart from the obvious connection in content (a dead man who had been carefully wrapped in burial cloths comes forth from a sealed tomb), there is a twofold connection: (1) the Evangelist stresses that Lazarus' resurrection is paradoxically the reason why Jesus is put to death (John 11:46–53); and (2) the word "facecloth" (*soudarion*, a Latin loan-word meaning literally "sweatcloth" or handkerchief) occurs in each story after the formerly dead man leaves his tomb. John 11:44 (the Lazarus story) and 20:7 (the empty tomb story) are the only two places where *soudarion* occurs in John's Gospel. Indeed, there are only two other occurrences of the word in the whole of the NT, both Lucan: Luke 19:20 and Acts 19:12; neither refers to death or burial.

[8] The petition for the miracle, a common element in miracles of healing, takes on a different form in stories of raising the dead. Quite understandably in view of the stupendous nature of the miracle involved, the petitioner usually does not directly request a restoration of the dead to life. In the Marcan and Lucan versions of the raising of the daughter of Jairus, Jairus starts off by asking Jesus to heal his daughter, who is near death (Mark 5:23 ‖ Luke 8:42). However, insofar as Jairus continues to conduct Jesus to his house even after the death of his daughter has been announced and the messengers suggest that he bother Jesus no further, implicitly Jairus' petition becomes one for raising the dead. In keeping with his radical abbreviation of Mark's story and his emphasis on the encounter between the petitioner's word of faith and Jesus' word of healing, Matthew boldly rewrites Mark to make the father ask for a raising of the dead from the very beginning of the story (Matt 9:18)—so great is the father's faith!

Similar to Mark and Luke, John begins the story of the raising of Lazarus with a petition of Martha and Mary that Jesus heal their sick brother Lazarus (John 11:1–3); Lazarus, like the daughter of Jairus, then dies during the story while Jesus delays coming. The case of the son of the widow of Nain is somewhat different from all the other Gospel stories of raising the dead. Jesus is moved with compassion by the doleful scene of a widow bereaved of her only son (Luke 7:12–13) and takes the initiative in comforting her by raising him.

Despite all these variations, there is still a common element in what moves Jesus to act. In each of the three stories, Jesus' act of raising the dead is in some sense a response to and reversal of the mourning of the bystanders. In the Jairus and Lazarus stories, the response is more one of anger or distress; in the Nain story, it is clearly and solely compassion.

[9] The reader will remember that early on, when I presented a global overview

of the Gospel miracles, I let stand the common mode of classifying a miracle of raising the dead as a form of healing. While that is defensible on form-critical grounds, I think that, because of the special content of a miracle of raising the dead, entailing as it does special problems, the accounts should be treated separately. Theoretically, one might also argue that raising the dead is actually a type of "nature miracle," since, technically speaking, in such cases Jesus would be acting on what is for the moment inanimate matter. But, at least as far as literary form is concerned, the Gospel stories take the tack that a miracle of raising the dead is simply a miracle of healing pushed to the limit. On this point, see the observation of Theissen in his *Urchristliche Wundergeschichten*, 98 n. 25: "Miracles of raising the dead belong to [the category of] healings: (1) almost all ancient raisings of the dead by miracle workers can be understood as the awaking of persons [only] apparently dead; and (2) the typical motifs are the same: the transmission of power takes place by touching." While I agree with Theissen's basic point on classification, his reasons are open to question: (1) his first reason confuses historical with literary questions; and (2) the raising of Lazarus is not accomplished by touching but only by Jesus' stark command: "Lazarus, come forth" (John 11:43). In recognition of the fact that miracles of raising the dead share something with both healings and nature miracles, I place my treatment of raising the dead between the other two types of miracles.

[10] To undertake a full study of the form and content of the NT texts about the resurrection of Jesus would take us too far afield. My concern here is simply a basic contrast between NT texts that recount Jesus' miracles of raising others from the dead during his public ministry and the NT texts that deal with Jesus' own resurrection on Easter Sunday. For an introduction to the many problems connected with the NT texts dealing with Jesus' own resurrection, see Hans F. von Campenhausen, *Der Ablauf der Osterereignisse und das leere Grab* (Sitzungsberichte der Heidelberger Akademie der Wissenschaften, philosophisch-historische Klasse; 3d ed.; Heidelberg: Winter, Universitätsverlag, 1966; 1st ed. 1952); Hans Grass, *Ostergeschehen und Osterberichte* (4th ed.; Göttingen: Vandenhoeck & Ruprecht, 1970; 1st ed. 1956); Karl Lehmann, *Auferweckt am dritten Tag nach der Schrift* (QD 38; Freiberg/Basel/Vienna: Herder, 1968); P. de Surgy et al., *La résurrection du Christ et l'exégèse moderne* (LD 50; Paris: Cerf, 1969); C. F. Evans, *Resurrection and the New Testament* (SBT 2/12; London: SCM, 1970); Ulrich Wilckens, *Auferstehung* (Themen der Theologie 4; Stuttgart/Berlin: Kreuz, 1970); Günter Kegel, *Auferstehung Jesu—Auferstehung der Toten* (Gütersloh: Mohn, 1970); Reginald H. Fuller, *The Formation of the Resurrection Narratives* (New York: Macmillan; London: Collier-Macmillan, 1971); Xavier Léon Dufour, *Resurrection and the Message of Easter* (London: Chapman, 1974); Pheme Perkins, *Resurrection* (Garden City, NY: Doubleday, 1984); Hans Kessler, *Sucht den Lebenden nicht bei den Toten. Die Auferstehung Jesu Christi in biblischer, fundamentaltheologischer und systematischer Sicht* (Düsseldorf: Patmos, 1985); Gisbert Greshake and Jacob Kremer, *Resurrectio Mortuorum. Zum theologischen Verständnis der leiblichen Auferstehung* (Darmstadt: Wissenshaftliche Buchgesellschaft, 1986).

[11] The one great exception here is the Gospel of John, which hammers home its high christology of preexistence and incarnation of the divine Word by insisting that Jesus raised himself to new life after his death. For example, the Johannine Jesus makes the point repeatedly in the Good Shepherd discourse (John 10:17–18): "I lay down my life [for my sheep] that I may take it up again. No one takes it

from me, but I lay it down of my own accord. I have power to lay it down, and I have power to take it up again."

[12] On this see Kegel, *Auferstehung Jesu*, 11–29, esp. 14–15. In some cases (e.g., 2 Cor 4:14) God the Father is referred to indirectly by the solemn hymnic or liturgical phrase *ho egeiras* ("the One who raised"), but the larger context makes it clear that the agent referred to is God the Father.

[13] I say "in general" because in NT Greek (being part of the larger phenomenon of koine or Hellenistic Greek) the passive voice at times takes on the sense of the middle voice, notably in the aorist tense. Hence a statement like *Christos ēgerthē* could by itself be translated either as "Christ was raised" or "Christ rose." However, given the large number of texts that explicitly state that God the Father raised Christ from the dead, passive forms like *ēgerthē* are best understood as true passives unless the context indicates otherwise. On this see Zerwick, *Graecitas biblica*, 76 (#229–31).

[14] On the *Gospel of Peter* see Meier, *A Marginal Jew*, 1. 116–18.

[15] On this see Meier, *A Marginal Jew*, 1. 13, 197, 201 n. 2.

[16] For general surveys of the material to follow, see Rochais, *Les récits de résurrection;* Murray J. Harris, " 'The Dead Are Restored to Life': Miracles of Revivification in the Gospels," *Gospel Perspectives. The Miracles of Jesus. Volume 6* (ed. David Wenham and Craig Blomberg; Sheffield: JSOT, 1986) 295–326.

[17] As throughout this study, I presume the two-source theory of Synoptic relationships; on this see Meier, *A Marginal Jew*, 1. 41–45. In my view, the two major alternative theories, the complicated Benoit-Boismard theory and the Griesbach hypothesis (Mark is a conflation of Matthew and Luke), both fail to explain the data of the Jairus story adequately. For a critique of the Benoit-Boismard source theory as applied to this story, see Rochais, *Les récits de résurrection*, 100–104. Mann's attempt to explain the Gospel of Mark on the basis of the Griesbach hypothesis breaks down when he comes to treat the Jairus story. Indeed, he tacitly admits as much (*Mark*, 282–84): "The wealth of detail [in Mark's account] . . . makes for a very distinct personal reminiscence from an eyewitness. Comparison with Matthew and Luke demonstrates that the evangelist [Mark], while adhering to Matthew's order, drew upon his own sources. . . . Mark's independence of Matthew and Luke seems to be underlined by his use of the historic present in *came* [in Mark 5:22] whereas the others use the aorist." Mann has to admit this sort of thing so often in his commentary that the commentary paradoxically becomes a refutation of the Griesbach hypothesis.

[18] For Lucan and Matthean redaction of the Marcan story, see Rochais, *Les récits de résurrection*, 74–99. For Matthew's redaction see Held, "Matthäus als Interpret der Wundergeschichten," 168–71 (see also 204–7 for the hemorrahaging woman); for Luke's redaction see Fitzmyer, *The Gospel According to Luke*, 1. 742–50.

[19] So Bultmann (*Geschichte*, 228–29) and many other critics after him. For the reasons for this position, see the treatment of the woman with the hemorrhage in Chapter 21. Gundry (*Mark*, 266–88) and Latourelle (*The Miracles of Jesus*, 122) represent the strongly conservative position that seeks to maintain that the interlocking of the two events reflects historical facts. However, various signals in the text (e.g., the different Greek style of each story, which is a self-contained unit) seem to argue for different origins in the tradition; on this see Guelich, *Mark 1–8:26*, 291–93; Fitzmyer, *The Gospel According to Luke*, 1. 743.

In the Jairus story as in other Marcan miracle stories, Kertelge (*Die Wunder Jesu*, 110–20) and Pesch (*Markusevangelium*, 295–314) favor the idea of a large pre-Marcan collection of miracle stories, which Mark has handled in a very conservative fashion, intervening seldom. Koch (*Die Bedeutung*, 65–68) instead favors the view that, while Mark is using previous tradition, he is the one responsible for the present collection. Thus, a good deal of what Kertelge and Pesch attribute to the pre-Marcan redactor of the miracle stories Koch attributes to Mark himself. Obviously, who exactly is responsible for various redactional traits is not of great concern when one is raising the question of the ultimate historicity of the tradition.

Kertelge (p. 112) points to the various common words and motifs shared by the two stories: each story speaks of an ill woman who is addressed or referred to as "daughter" (*thygatēr* or *thygatrion*); the hemorrhaging woman has been suffering for *twelve* years, while Jairus' daughter is *twelve* years old; in both stories someone (Jairus, the hemorrhaging woman) "falls down" before Jesus; both stories have petitioners who seek healing, expressed by the verb *sōzō*; both stories exemplify the theme of faith; and both use the verb "fear" (*phobeomai*) of the petitioner. Whether we see here the literary skill of the pre-Marcan redactor joining the two stories (as Kertelge thinks), or accidental similarities that helped draw the two stories together in the oral tradition, or perhaps something of both phenomena, remains debatable.

[20] Rochais (*Les récits de résurrection*, 39–48) spends the better part of a chapter establishing this point against Schmidt (*Der Rahmen*, 146) who considers v 21 a "summary report," a remnant of some itinerary of Jesus. While Schmidt suggests that v 21 was probably already joined to v 22 in the tradition, he does not think that v 21 was part of the original Jairus story.

[21] My point is that the present position and formulation of Mark 5:24bc in the Jairus story are probably redactional; some mention of the crowd that makes the secret approach of the woman possible would have been part of the primitive form of the story of the hemorrhaging woman. On this see Kertelge, *Die Wunder Jesu*, 111.

[22] Pesch (*Markusevangelium*, 1. 306) mentions this as a possibility. Rochais (*Les récits de résurrection*, 60) instead proposes that the phrase comes from Mark, who thus creates a transition from the story of the hemorrhaging woman back to the Jairus story; transitional phrases like *eti autou lalountos* are well known in both the OT and the NT (see ibid., 218 n. 24). Guelich (*Mark 1–8:26*, 300) suggests that it comes from the redactor of the pre-Marcan collection of miracles. If Rochais or Gundry is correct, then the redactional change is not simply one of meaning but one involving the addition of a phrase.

[23] On this see Koch, *Die Bedeutung*, 65–67.

[24] The exact reason why the girl's age is mentioned and why it is mentioned precisely at this late (and awkward) stage of the story is debated among scholars. Gundry (*Mark*, 275) points out that the story has regularly used diminutives of the girl (*thygatrion*, *paidion*, *korasion*), and so the reader could easily form the false impression that the girl was an infant too young to walk. Hence the appropriateness of mentioning her age here as an explanation of the statement that the girl was walking about.

[25] This command is sometimes broken (e.g., 1:44–45; 7:36–37), though nothing is said about its being broken at the end of the Jairus story or at the end of the healing of the blind man at Bethsaida (8:26). In this breaking of Jesus' command of silence, Mark 1:44–45 and 7:36–37 (in miracles of healing) differ notably from the exorcism stories in which Jesus successfully imposes silence on the demons. On this whole problem see the various essays in Christopher Tuckett (ed.), *The Messianic Secret* (Issues in Religion and Theology 1; Philadelphia: Fortress; London: SPCK, 1983); the essays by Ulrich Luz, James D. G. Dunn, and Heikki Räisänen are especially helpful.

[26] In Mark 5:39 Jesus tells the mourners to stop crying and gives this reason: "The child is not dead [literally with the Greek aorist: "did not die"], but is sleeping." This riddle-like (*māšāl*-like) statement of Jesus, playing with the opposite-yet-similar images of death and sleep, has sparked a great deal of scholarly debate, with strongly contrasting opinions:

(1) Some scholars take Jesus' *māšāl* quite literally (always a questionable procedure with a *māšāl*). Supposedly Jesus knew that the girl was simply unconscious or in a coma, which the mourners had mistaken for death. Taylor (*The Gospel According to St. Mark*, 285–86, 295) takes this approach, but with some nuance. He admits that the versions of the story in Matthew and Luke explicitly rule out such an interpretation and that Mark himself probably understands the story as narrating a raising of the dead, but he maintains that the text of Mark is itself ambiguous and need not be understood as narrating a raising of the dead. There are a number of problems with any such explanation (see Guelich, *Mark 1–8:26*, 301–2): (a) As Rochais (*Les récits de résurrection*, 64–65) notes, Jesus has just arrived on the scene and is still standing outside the girl's room when he tells the mourners that the girl is not dead. How did Jesus know what was the true state of the girl, when others who had seen her state (e.g., the messengers) had judged that she was dead? Are we to substitute a minor miracle of precognition plus modern medical knowledge for a major miracle of raising the dead? (b) If the girl is in a death-like coma, how does Jesus, lacking all modern medical means, rouse her from it so easily? (c) In this explanation, the Marcan Jesus enjoys surprisingly enlightened, not to say modern, medical knowledge. Yet this is the same Marcan Jesus who considers a case of epilepsy to be demonic possession (Mark 9:14–29). (d) The underlying methodological problem in this approach is that some critics are jumping immediately from the written text of Mark back to a hypothetical historical event, without making the necessary distinction between the present state of Mark's text and the various stages of the tradition. The story we find in Mark's text must first be read and interpreted on its own terms before any theories about original events are launched. Even many critics who hold that the primitive form of the Jairus story spoke of Jesus healing a sick girl admit that the present form of the Marcan story intends to portray a raising from the dead; so, e.g., Kertelge, *Die Wunder Jesu*, 113; Pesch, *Markusevangelium*, 1. 312–14; Rochais, *Les récits de résurrection*, 110–12. As a matter of fact, the present state of the Marcan text, precisely as theological literature, is not as ambiguous as Taylor claims. The ever-increasing dramatic tension of the story—from the initial report of Jairus that the girl is *in extremis* (Greek: *eschatōs echei*, at the point of death), through the fatal delay caused by the hemorrhaging woman, the report of the messengers that the girl has died, the encounter with and mockery by the mourners, and the narrowing down of the audience, to the climactic words of Jesus in Aramaic and the utter astonishment of the audience—argues for something more than another story of healing. To have the story begin with the girl at the point of death and to end with Jesus rousing her from a trance-like sleep or coma is from a literary as well as a theological point of view incredibly bathetic. The position of the Jairus story both within the pre-Marcan collection of miracles and in the Gospel of Mark, namely as the "finale" and climax of a whole series of miracles (4:35–5:43), likewise argues for the Jairus story being understood as the supreme miracle of raising the dead. But if Mark 5:39 does not deny that at the moment the girl is physically dead, what does Jesus' cryptic remark mean? Scholars still differ.

(b) Some speak in general terms of a euphemism, for to call death a sleep was a well-known euphemism in the ancient world (and in many other cultures). The euphemism rests on the obvious similarity between the two states: the prone state of a still body that does not sense what is going on around it. But this explanation misses the point of

Jesus' statement; his two-part assertion does not identify death with sleep but rather opposes the two. Moreover, part of the intention of anyone using the well-known euphemism of calling death sleep would be to soften or gloss over the glaring difference between sleep and death: sleep is a transitory state, while death is permanent. Jesus' statement that the girl is sleeping is not a euphemism in this sense.

(c) Put more properly, Jesus is taking a well-known euphemism and twisting it to a different end (on this see Gundry, *Mark*, 273–74). The frightening difference of death, the very essence of death as opposed to sleep, is its inexorable permanence. Now, a Pharisaic Jew might have understood Jesus' twisting of the euphemism in terms of a general eschatological hope: the girl's death can be seen as transitory sleep because on the last day God will raise the girl to eternal life. But Mark's story is concerned with something more specific and immediate. In the Marcan story as it stands in this Christian Gospel, Jesus knows that he is about to raise the girl from what, apart from his saving presence, would be the terrible permanence of death. The good news Mark means to proclaim by the Jairus story is that, in the presence of Jesus, not only must demons flee and sickness give way, but even death loses its permanent grip on human beings. In Mark 5:39 death is declared mere sleep not because of a cagey medical diagnosis or a comforting euphemism or a general eschatological hope but because Jesus wills in this particular case to make death as impermanent as sleep by raising the girl to life. On all this see Cranfield, *The Gospel According to Saint Mark*, 188–89; Lane, *The Gospel According to Mark*, 196–97. One must realize that Jesus' assertion in 5:39 expresses first of all the Christian faith that suffuses Mark's narrative. Whether or not the historical Jesus ever made such an assertion in such circumstances, and what the assertion would have meant if he had made it, is quite another question, one that I do not think the present narrative allows us to decide (see Albrecht Oepke, "*katheudō*," *TDNT* 3 [1965] 436). One must be very careful about citing theological dialogue in a miracle story as the *ipsissima verba Jesu*, or in this case even using the dialogue to create an earlier form of the story that contained only a miracle of healing.

[27] Gundry (*Mark*, 276–77) strains to make the command to keep the miracle a secret plausible and indeed part of the traditional story. He argues that the command is not impossible "*if* [emphasis mine] its purpose is not to keep the raising permanently secret, but to keep it secret only long enough to allow a getaway by Jesus." Both the idea of a briefly observed secret and the idea of Jesus making a "getaway" are read into a story that mentions neither. Mark's absolute formulation in v 43a ("and he strictly charged them that no one should know this") hardly invites the understood proviso "for a short time." Moreover, Gundry is arguing about what was in the traditional story before Mark; nothing in the traditional story hints of any "getaway" by Jesus. This is the sort of novel-writing that gave the 19th-century quest for the historical Jesus a bad name.

[28] Koch (*Die Bedeutung*, 65–66) favors the mention of food as another demonstration of the miracle's reality, a demonstration that Guelich (*Mark 1–8:26*, 304) considers redundant and assigns to the pre-Marcan redactor of the miracle cycle. Pesch (*Markusevangelium*, 1. 311–12) also sees the food as a demonstration; the doubling of the demonstration is seen as arising from the fact that an earlier story of healing a mortally sick girl has been turned into a story of raising a girl from the dead. Latourelle (*The Miracles of Jesus*, 123) instead interprets the command to give the girl something to eat in terms of Jesus' concern for the girl when her parents are still too confused to think of her needs. Gundry (*Mark*, 276–77) makes the unlikely suggestion that Jesus uses the command to feed the girl as a delaying tactic, so that he can get away before the crowd outside discovers that the girl has been raised from the dead.

[29] A careful distinction must be made here: the present form of the Jairus story moves

from an initial petition for a miracle of healing to the actual performance of a miracle of raising the dead. But one cannot automatically conclude that this transition in the present narrative mimics perfectly the history of the development of the story in the oral tradition. In other words, the transition from healing to raising the dead in the present narrative does not necessarily prove that in the early Christian tradition the story was originally and solely about healing and only over the course of time became a story about raising the dead. Only a detailed study of the story's form and tradition history can make such a position probable.

[30] In the NT the compound noun *archisynagōgos* ("synagogue ruler [or: president]") is used only by Mark and Luke (Mark 5:22,35–36,38 [N.B.: only in the Jairus story]; Luke 8:49; 13:14; Acts 13:15; 18:8,17). Luke also uses the phrase *archōn tēs synagōgēs*. As Wolfgang Schrage notes (*"synagōgē* etc.," *TDNT* 7 [1971] 845), "there is abundant testimony to *archisynagōgoi* in literature and inscriptions from all parts of the Roman world." No doubt in the fluid situation in Judaism around the turn of the era the exact structure of local synagogue governance varied from place to place. It seems that the *archisynagōgos* sometimes was counted among the *archontes tēs synagōgēs* and sometimes was differentiated from them. Functional differentiation and multiplication of offices are to be expected in large cities as opposed to small towns. Most commentators take the *archisynagōgos* to be the person (usually an esteemed layman elected to the position) who was in charge of presiding over the conduct of synagogue worship and assigning functions within it to various people; he was also responsible for erecting and maintaining the synagogue building. However, Taylor (*The Gospel According to St. Mark*, 287) thinks that the term could simply mean a prominent member of the synagogue who exercised some form of leadership.

The precise meaning of Mark's phrase *heis tōn archisynagōgōn* ("one of the synagogue rulers") is disputed. (1) If *heis* ("one") is taken as a Semitism and therefore equivalent to an indefinite pronoun with a partitive genitive, the whole phrase could simply mean "a [or: a certain] synagogue ruler." In favor of a true Semitism here is Elliott C. Maloney, *Semitic Interference in Marcan Syntax* (SBLDS 51; Chico, CA: Scholars, 1981) 127–30. (2) If, however, *heis* is taken with the full force of a numeral, the phrase might indicate that Jairus was one of a group of rulers presiding over a particular synagogue. Acts 13:15 (*apesteilan hoi archisynagōgoi pros autous* [Paul and Barnabas in Pisidian Antioch]) suggests that at least some synagogues had more than one presiding officer. One wonders, though, whether a town or village of Galilee (as opposed to a city like Pisidian Antioch) would have had more than one "synagogue ruler." On balance, Maloney, who is very stringent in his application of criteria for detecting true Semitisms, is probably right that this is a Semitism.

[31] The phrase "that she may recover and live" is literally "that she may be saved [*sōthē*] and live [*zēsē*]." A number of commentators (e.g., Guelich, *Mark 1–8:26*, 296) suggest that the two verbs are alternate translations of one Aramaic verb *ḥăyā'*, which can mean both "to live" and "to recover." While this is possible, the two verbs make perfect sense in the Greek story as it stands. The girl is so sick that she is at the point of dying; hence the act of healing her or making her recover would also have the effect of bringing her back from near death and assuring her of continued life. The two verbs express distinct ideas and are not simply redundant. On this see Taylor, *The Gospel According to St. Mark*, 288 n. 1. Moreover, the use of both *sōzō* ("to save," also "to heal") and *zaō* ("to live") lends itself nicely to a symbolic interpretation of the whole story.

[32] Roloff (*Das Kerygma*, 154) points out that Jesus' exhortation not to fear in the face of death but only to believe plays no part in what follows and is not referred to in any subsequent verse. Roloff draws the conclusion that this exhortation is part of the oldest

stratum of the tradition. If he is correct that vv 35–36 are part of the original narrative, then the story was a story about raising the dead from the beginning. Another critic who highlights the absolute demand for faith by Jesus in v 36 is Santos Sabugal, "La resurrección de la Hija de Jairo (Mc 5,21–24a. 35–42 par.)," *Estudio Agustiniano* 26 (1991) 79–101, esp. 97. Sabugal claims that the imperative *pisteue*, without any specification of the personal object of faith or its effects, is unique in the NT.

A famous exegetical conundrum is whether *parakousas* in Mark 5:36 means that Jesus "overheard" what the messengers said or "ignored" what they said. Either meaning is possible, and Gundry (*Mark*, 272) points out that in a sense both meanings could be intended here. However, Guelich (*Mark 1–8:26*, 291 n. 1) argues strongly for "ignored" on the basis of the word's meaning elsewhere in the LXX and the NT. But as Guelich himself intimates, a decision one way or the other makes no great difference to the Jairus story as a whole—a fortiori when one is inquiring about the earliest form of the story in the Aramaic tradition and a possible historical event lying behind it.

[33] Whether the enigmatic explanation "for she was twelve years old" was part of the earliest tradition is difficult to decide. If Gundry (*Mark*, 275) is right that the explanation is meant to correct the possible misconception that the girl, who is regularly referred to in the Greek text with diminutives (*thygatrion, paidion, korasion*), was an infant too young to walk, the explanation was formulated with a view to the present Greek text and so may well have been absent in the original Aramaic. Since Mark seems to be responsible for a number of other enigmatic or awkwardly placed clauses of explanation introduced by *gar* ("for"), he may have introduced the explanation here as well; cf. 11:13 ("for it was not the season for figs," in the cursing of the fig tree); 16:4 ("for it [the stone in front of Jesus' tomb] was very large"); and 16:8 ("for they [the women fleeing from the empty tomb] were afraid"). If one adopts this hypothesis, then it is possible that Mark purposely took over the number 12 from the story of the hemorrhaging woman to provide another verbal link between the two stories; however, this is far from certain.

[34] So Pesch, *Markusevangelium*, 1. 311–12. While Pesch allows that a double confirmation makes sense in a story of raising the dead, he suggests that the double confirmation is especially understandable if the walking about comes from the primitive story of healing and the eating was added when the story was transformed into a story of raising the dead.

[35] So Bultmann, *Geschichte*, 229. This seems to be the (apologetic) point of the risen Jesus eating fish in Luke 24:41–43: the risen Jesus has a true body; he is not a ghost.

[36] Theissen (*Urchristliche Wundergeschichten*, 152) sees no problem in the double confirmation of the miracle; the raising of the dead is such an extraordinary miracle that more than one confirmation makes sense. The true difficulty, says Theissen, comes from the order of motifs at the end of the story (vv 42–43). He suggests that the original order in the story was first the eating of food, which then gave the girl the strength to walk around, at which the audience expressed astonishment.

[37] The closest one comes in the NT to a request for a miracle of raising the dead is in the story of Peter raising the dead Tabitha in Acts 9:36–43, and even there the request is more implied than explicit.

[38] For this precise reconstruction, see Rochais, *Les récits de résurrection*, 110–11. A lengthy reconstruction of the stages by which the supposed story of healing changed into the present story of raising the dead is offered by Pesch, *Markusevangelium*, 1. 312–14. Kertelge (*Die Wunder Jesu*, 113) offers a short sketch of a hypothesis that leans

heavily on the dubious premise that the Jairus story is similar to the Q story of the centurion's servant. Pesch himself (p. 312 n. 59) finds difficulty with Kertelge's approach.

[39] See the remark of Schürmann, *Lukasevangelium*, 1. 497.

[40] For example, Kertelge (*Die Wunder Jesu*, 113) points to the fact that both narratives share certain common words like "come," "house," and "faith." Such ordinary words, which appear in one way or another in many miracle stories, will hardly carry the heavy burden of establishing that the earliest form of the Jairus story was a healing story similar to the healing of the centurion's servant. What strikes one instead is the basic difference between the two stories: (1) the extraordinary element in the Q story is that Jesus heals the servant (or son) of a Gentile centurion at a distance, while contrasting the Gentile's faith favorably with what he has found in Israel; (2) the extraordinary element in the Jairus story is that what starts out as a healing miracle winds up as a raising of the dead, as Jesus accedes to the plea of a Jewish synagogue ruler by coming to his house to raise his daughter to life. In short, what impresses one most is that in many ways the two stories are polar opposites.

[41] Interestingly, Pesch seems more open to Kertelge's theory in his earlier article entitled "Jairus" (published in 1970) than he does in his treatment in the first volume of his Mark commentary (published in 1976), which modifies the position he took in the article. In what follows, I argue with Pesch's position as laid out in his commentary.

[42] The more common explanation of the name is based on the Hebrew root *y'yr* ("he will enlighten"; so Claudia J. Setzer, "Jairus," *Anchor Bible Dictionary*, 3. 615), but some favor the root *y'yr* ("he will awaken"; see S. Sandmel, "Jairus," *IDB* 2. 789).

[43] In the abbreviated form of the nouns and verbs found in proper names, it is often difficult to know the exact tense and mood intended; hence a name like Jairus could be variously translated as "he will enlighten," "may he enlighten," or "let him enlighten."

[44] It is found in Num 32:41; Deut 3:14; Josh 13:30; Judg 10:3,4,5; 1 Kgs 4:13; 1 Chr 2:22–23; Esth 2:5; and LXX 1 Esdr 5:31. In all these texts (except obviously LXX 1 Esdr 5:31) the Hebrew form of the name is *yā'îr*, "he [God] will enlighten" (*not* "he will awaken"). The LXX form is *Iaïr*, except in Esth 2:5 and 1 Esdr 5:31, where we have the declinable form found in the NT: *Iaïros*. The name is also found on an ostracon of the Ptolemaic era and in Josephus' *The Jewish War*, where a certain Jairus is the father of Eleazar, the commander of the garrison at Masada (*J. W.* 2.17.9 §447). On this see Rochais, *Les récits de résurrection*, 56. By way of comparison, *yā'îr* as a Hebrew proper name of a person does not appear in the OT except as a marginal correction (qěrê) of the MT reading *yā'ûr* (kětîb) in 1 Chr 20:5.

[45] With a slight exegetical smile, Rochais (*Les récits de résurrection*, 57) remarks that, if one engaged in such imaginative exegesis, then one would have expected the person raised by Jesus in John 11 to be called Jairus ("may God awaken") and the father begging for help for his daughter in Mark 5 to be called Lazarus ("God helps").

[46] Pesch, *Markusevangelium*, 1. 307. If, as seems likely, the proper meaning of "Jairus" is "he [God] will *enlighten*," the supposed pun in Mark 5:36 seems even more improbable.

[47] Pesch, *Markusevangelium*, 1. 131.

[48] See, e.g., Bultmann, *Das Evangelium des Johannes*, 301; Dodd, *Historical Tradition*, 228–32 (with hesitation about whether a tradition history can be sketched in this case); Brown, *The Gospel According to John*, 1. 428–29; Schnackenburg, *Johannesevangelium*, 2.

428–33; Nicol, *The Sēmeia in the Fourth Gospel*, 37–39, 109–10; Haenchen, *John 2*, 67–72; Fortna, *The Fourth Gospel*, 94–95; von Wahlde, *The Earliest Version*, 116–17. See also the special studies of Wilkens, "Die Erweckung des Lazarus," 25–29; Stenger, "Die Auferweckung des Lazarus," 19–28; Kremer, *Lazarus*, 108–9 (with hesitation about whether the wording of the pre-Johannine source can be reconstructed). As we shall see when we come to the treatment of the Lazarus story, I do not think that the narrative of the raising of Lazarus derived either from John's copying of the Synoptic stories of raising the dead or from the Lucan parable of the rich man and Lazarus. But even if one of these two unlikely theories were correct, the Lazarus story would still have seen the light of day as a story of raising the dead, not of healing.

[49] Pesch, *Markusevangelium*, 1. 313. Pesch thinks that the unclear and indirect allusions to the Elijah-Elisha stories show that the Jairus story was originally one of healing. This line of argument presupposes that, if the Jairus story had been from the beginning a story of raising the dead, allusions to the Elijah-Elisha stories would have been clear and direct. Why anyone should grant such a presupposition is unclear to me.

[50] See, e.g., Haenchen, *Apostelgeschichte*, 285–86.

[51] As I pointed out earlier, when treating the global question of the historicity of miracles in Chapter 19, there is no solid basis for denying that the original Greek text of Mark's Gospel contained the name Jairus in 5:22. Its absence in the Codex Bezae and in some manuscripts of the Old Latin is hardly sufficient reason to doubt its originality when every ancient Greek manuscript except Bezae contains it. For a defense of the originality of Jairus in 5:22, see Metzger, *Textual Commentary*, 85–86; Guelich, *Mark 1–8:26*, 290 n. c; Rochais, *Les récits de résurrection*, 56–57 (although I think that Rochais's suppression of *onomati* before *Iaïros* in 5:22 as a later scribal addition is unnecessary).

[52] Rochais (*Les récits de résurrection*, 66–67) gives a good survey of the variant readings of *talitha koum* in the Greek manuscripts and ancient versions. The reading *tabitha* in Codex Wahingtonianus and a few other manuscripts obviously comes from a confusion with the woman named Tabitha, whom Peter raises from the dead in Acts 9:36–40. More difficult is the odd reading *rabbi thabita* in Codex Bezae. Rochais favors the view of Julius Wellhausen that the original wording in the story was *rabitha*, the Aramaic word *rĕbîtaʾ* signifying "young girl." Rochais suggests that this original wording was later corrected to *talitha*, which has the same basic meaning. All this is to make a great deal depend upon the somewhat idiosyncratic Codex Bezae, which has more than one unlikely variant in this story.

The Greek translation of the Aramaic is notable for more than one reason. (1) The phrase *to korasion* (literally: "the little girl") is a perfect example of the Greek definite article plus the nominative of the noun used to render the determined (or emphatic) state of an Aramaic noun used as a vocative (here: *talyĕtāʾ*, spelled in Greek *talitha*). The same usage is seen in *abba, ho patēr* in Mark 14:36. (2) The translator apparently wished to emphasize the authority of this most powerful of Jesus' declarations; hence he adds *soi legō*, "I say to you," which is not represented in the Aramaic phrase. The placement of the *soi* ("to you") first in the added phrase is emphatic. Perhaps it underlines the astounding fact that Jesus dares to address his command to someone who at the moment is dead and who now will no longer be dead precisely because of the words Jesus speaks. (3) Rochais (p. 68) thinks that the added phrase also emphasizes the enigmatic character and secret power that the Aramaic words would have for a reader who did not know Aramaic. I must confess that I do not see the basis for this last point.

As I indicated above when treating *ephphatha* in the healing of the deaf-mute in

Chapter 21, there is no basis for the opinion of critics like Bultmann, Dibelius, Hull, and Horton that *ephphatha* or *talitha koum* were meant to function as magical formulas similar to the unintelligible foreign words and nonsense syllables in the Greek magical papyri. When the Gospel miracle stories were still in Aramaic, there were no foreign words to create a sense of mystery or magic, and the translators of the stories into Greek took care to equip the Aramaic words of Jesus with Greek translations so that they would be immediately intelligible. I find especially strange the suggestion of Dibelius (*Formgeschichte*, 80–81) that the retention of *talitha koum* was meant to be part of the technical instruction to Christian miracle-workers on how to repeat Jesus' miracles. Not only must one wonder whether the Christian miracle-workers in the first Christian generation were performing so many miracles of raising the dead that they needed instructions on the most effective techniques patterned on the methods of Jesus; one must also note that, when we do read of *one* account of raising the dead in Acts, namely, that of Peter raising Tabitha (Acts 9:36–43), the narrative conforms more to the OT stories of Elijah and Elisha raising the dead than to the Jairus story. And Aramaic formulas are nowhere to be seen.

[53] Meier, *A Marginal Jew*, 1. 264–68.

[54] The wording of this last phrase is carefully chosen: note the words "Aramaic" and "narrative." The evangelists do at times add the *Hebrew* word "amen" to some of Jesus' *sayings*, but in this they seem to be simply imitating a striking mode of speech employed by Jesus himself.

[55] See Dalman, *Grammatik*, 321 n. 1.

[56] See Metzger, *Textual Commentary*, 87.

[57] For his analysis see Rochais, *Les récits de résurrection*, 54–73, 104–12. Besides *talitha koum* Rochais judges the following phrases to be Semitisms: *heis tōn archisynagōgōn* ("one of the synagogue rulers," i.e., a synagogue ruler) in v 22; the construction *hina elthōn epithēs* ("coming lay your hands . . . ," reflecting an original Aramaic "come and lay your hands") in v 23; *thorybos* ("uproar," "din" as the object of a verb "to see") in v 38 as the equivalent of the Aramaic *hmwn*; the construction *ton patera tou paidiou kai tēn matera* in v 40 ("the father of the child and the mother," instead of "the father and the mother of the child"); *kai exestēsan ekstasei megalē* ("and they were amazed with great amazement") in v 42; and possibly *dounai phagein* ("to give [her something] to eat") as the equivalent of the aphel form of the verb *ʾkl* in v 43. Not all his examples are equally convincing, since some of the constructions are both possible and perfectly intelligible in Greek. This criticism is even more valid for the lengthy list compiled by Sabugal, "La resurrección," 90–94. Maloney (*Semitic Interference*, 95, 77, 127–30, 136–37, 162, 188–89) is much more reserved about supposed Semitisms in the Jairus story, although he accepts *heis tōn archisynagōgōn* (v 22: *heis* used as an indefinite pronoun with a partitive genitive) and *to korasion* (v 41: definite article plus noun in nominative in place of the vocative in direct address) and is willing to consider the cognate dative *ekstasei megalē* (v 42) as a possible candidate. In any case, there do seem to be at least a few other Semitisms besides *talitha koum* in the Jairus story.

[58] One might distinguish even further in the Greek stage of the tradition: the Jairus story may have existed in Greek first apart from the story of the hemorrhaging woman and then meshed with it before it was taken into a pre-Marcan collection of miracle stories. Obviously, one cannot be dogmatic about these various hypothetical stages of the tradition.

[59] The same holds true of the simple form of the verb, *gelaō*.

[60] To be sure, *ekballō* (literally, "to throw out") can have in Hellenistic Greek the milder sense of "send out," "send away." This seems to be the sense in Acts 9:40, when Peter sends out (*ekbalōn*) of the room all the Christians mourning Tabitha. However, (1) since Jesus' action in Mark 5:40 is his immediate response to the hostile reception by the mourners of the girl and (2) since Mark, for the only time in the story, uses the emphatic nominative *autos de* to emphasize Jesus as subject of the action, the stronger sense of the verb seems justified here. This is the view of Bauer (*Wörterbuch* [6th ed.], 478), who puts Mark 5:40 under the literal sense of throwing or driving out "more or less forcibly."

[61] Luke Timothy Johnson (*The Literary Function of Possessions in Luke-Acts* [SBLDS 39; Missoula, MT: Scholars, 1977] 97–98) suggests that, by putting these two miracles together, Luke is intentionally recalling Elisha's cure of the foreign military leader Naaman of his leprosy (= the cure of the slave of the Gentile centurion) and Elijah's raising of the son of the widow of Zarephath (= the raising of the son of the widow of Nain). If this is so, then the miracles in Luke 7 would also refer back to Jesus' allusion to these Elijah and Elisha stories in his inaugural sermon in the synagogue at Nazareth (Luke 4:25–27). With refreshing honesty, Johnson admits that the equivalence he is suggesting is a "rough" one. In any case, there seems to be a conscious desire on Luke's part to surpass the healing of the centurion's servant with a still greater miracle, that of raising the dead. On this see Busse, *Die Wunder des Propheten Jesus*, 161–62.—One might also observe that in adjacent chapters (2 Kings 4 and 5) Elisha both heeds a mother's plea to restore her son to life and cleanses Naaman of his leprosy.

[62] Johnson (*The Literary Function*, 98) rightly observes that the two parts of the crowd's acclamation in 17:16 actually express a single idea; Johnson sees thematic connections with Luke 1:68; 19:44; Acts 7:23; cf. Luke 24:19. Speaking of God's "visiting" (Hebrew verb *pāqad*) his people either to save or to punish them is a rich tradition in the OT and the intertestamental literature, including the *Damascus Document* at Qumran, where God's visitation is connected with the Messiah of Aaron and Israel (CD 19:10–11). But the language of "visitation" passes over into the NT in only a limited way.

When it carries the weighty theological sense of God's intervention in history to save or punish, the Hebrew verb *pāqad* is regularly rendered in the LXX by the verb *episkeptomai* ("to look upon," "to have regard to," "to care for," "to visit"). In the LXX the verb describes "the act in which the Lord in a special incursion into the course of life of individuals or of a people, mostly Israel, makes known to them His will either in judgment or in grace. . . . The visitation takes place when God draws near to His people in its sin and distress, and shows Himself to be the Lord of history" (Hermann W. Beyer, "*episkeptomai*, etc.," *TDNT* 2 [1964] 599–622, esp. 602; see further Rochais, *Les récits de résurrection*, 36–38). Luke is the NT author who uses *episkeptomai* the most (7 out of 11 occurrences). Apart from the author of Hebrews (2:6), who uses the verb when citing Ps 8:5, Luke is the only NT author who makes God the subject of *episkeptomai*, thus reflecting the strictly *theo*-logical usage of the LXX. Indeed, in Luke's Gospel, God, acting through Jesus, is the only subject of the verb *episkeptomai* (human subjects predominate in Acts). In the context of the Third Gospel, especially its Infancy Narrative, what God does through Jesus in the Nain story is seen as the fulfillment of the prophecy of Zechariah in his canticle the *Benedictus*: God "has visited and wrought redemption for his people"; the rising sun "will visit us from on high *to shine on those who sit in darkness and the shadow of death*" (Luke 1:36,43). This is exactly what Jesus does at Nain. Thus, with that wonderful genius for compound nouns which only German exegetes have, Busse (*Die Wunder des Propheten Jesus*, 174) fittingly calls Luke 7:11–17 a "christological-theological epiphany-story."

The LXX also uses the derived noun *episkopē* of God's visitation of his people, usually in the sense of punishment, but sometimes in the sense of pardon as well. While *episkopē* occurs some 47 times in the LXX, it appears only 4 times in the NT. Not surprisingly, only Luke uses it to refer to God's visiting Israel through Jesus: ". . . because you did not recognize the time of your visitation" (Luke 19:44). 1 Pet 2:12 also uses the noun of God's visitation, but in reference to the day of judgment at the end of time. The upshot of all this is that, within the NT, only Luke in his Gospel uses "visitation" terminology of Jesus' ministry. (The allied verb *episkopeō* is not used in the NT in this strictly theological sense of God's visiting his people.)

[63] On this see Charles H. Talbert, *Reading Luke. A Literary and Theological Commentary on the Third Gospel* (New York: Crossroad, 1982) 78. When in 7:18 Luke says that John's disciples reported to him "about all these things," the phrase "all these things" encompasses everything Jesus has been saying and doing, notably his proclamation of beatitude to the poor in the Sermon on the Plain and the two miracles of 7:1–17. In particular, Talbert (p. 246) sees the miracle at Nain as having a legitimating function, attesting to Jesus as the one through whom God works. On the "validating" power of miracles in Luke, see Paul J. Achtemeier, "The Lucan Perspective on the Miracles of Jesus: A Preliminary Sketch," *JBL* 94 (1975) 547–62, esp. 552–53. As Rochais (*Les récits de résurrection*, 18–19) points out, there was a practical reason why Luke chose to put the Nain story rather than the Jairus story right before Jesus' reply to the envoys of the Baptist. Mark's version of the Jairus story ends with Jesus prohibiting any divulging of the daughter's restoration to life, and Luke basically maintains this ending to the story. Hence, the Nain story, which ends with the spread of the acclamation of Jesus as a great prophet who has raised the dead, fits Jesus' reply to the envoys much better.

[64] See Conzelmann, *The Theology of St. Luke*, 191. This "evidence" for Jesus' argument is supplemented by Luke with a reference to Jesus' healing activity taking place even as the Baptist's envoys arrive: "In that very hour he [Jesus] healed many of sicknesses and afflictions and evil spirits, and he gave many blind people [their] sight" (Luke 7:21). Obviously this is Luke's insertion into the Q tradition (cf. Matt 11:2–4). In a sense, along with the two miracle stories of 7:1–17, it is Luke's equivalent of the cycle of nine miracle stories that Matthew arranges in Matthew 8–9 to provide a basis for Jesus' reply to the Baptist in Matt 11:5.

[65] On this point see Johnson, *The Literary Function*, 100–101. On p. 124, he states: "Instead of having all the people [of Israel] reject Jesus, he [Luke] as much as possible pictures the ordinary people as positive and accepting both of Jesus and the Apostles. The rejection is carried out by the leaders." Here as elsewhere in *A Marginal Jew* I must ask the reader to distinguish carefully between the polemical remarks the Christian evangelists make against the Pharisees (and other Jewish groups) and the attempt at a sober historical description of the Pharisees and other Jewish parties that will appear in Volume Three. My attempts to summarize a given evangelist's theological evaluation of the Pharisees must not be taken as my own view of what historically was the case.

[66] See Johnson, *The Literary Function*, 102.

[67] Note here the contrast between the acclamation of the crowd confessing Jesus to be "a great prophet" who even raises the dead (7:16) and the skepticism of the Pharisee, who takes Jesus' acceptance of the sinful woman as a sign that he is not a prophet even in the "low" sense of someone who enjoys special knowledge (7:39).

[68] However, one might construe the pivotal verse (7:47) to mean instead that the fact

that the woman loves much (*ēgapēsen* taken as a Greek aorist representing a Semitic perfect tense with present meaning) is proof that her sins have been forgiven. The precise connection between the parable of the two debtors and Jesus' declaration that the woman's sins are forgiven—a forgiveness that is in some way related to her great love—is disputed among exegetes and theologians; in brief, the debate turns on the two possible meanings of *hoti* in v 47: "because" or "considering that." In a larger sense, the debate turns on the theological presuppositions that Christian exegetes bring to a text that may not have had their questions in mind. See the different approaches considered by Schürmann, *Lukasevangelium*, 1. 434–42; Marshall, *Luke*, 313; Fitzmyer, *The Gospel According to Luke*, 1. 686–87. It may well be that *hoti* meant "because" in the primitive form of the story but then took on the meaning of "considering that" when the parable of the two debtors was inserted secondarily, switching the relationship between forgiveness and love. In any event, since I am simply interested in the general flow of thought in the overarching context, it is not necessary for my purpose to try to decide such detailed points of exegesis.

[69] In his Gospel, as in Acts, Luke displays a special concern for the socially disadvantaged, in particular women, and, within the circle of women, widows. Robert F. O'Toole (*The Unity of Luke's Theology. An Analysis of Luke-Acts* [Good News Studies 9; Wilmington, DE: Glazier, 1984] 126) maintains: "Widows, more disadvantaged than other women, were particular favorites of Luke." As O'Toole observes (p. 35), the widow of Nain is in especially desperate straits: having already lost her husband, she is now bereft of her only son, her main means of financial support and legal representation in the public forums of a patriarchal society.

[70] It must be stressed that, in Luke's theological vision, the Gentiles have not replaced Israel; rather, they have been incorporated into Israel without any complete rupture in salvation history. As Johnson (*The Literary Function*, 123) puts it: "For Luke, the notion of a break, of an hiatus in the working out of God's plan was unthinkable. In order for the Gentiles now to enjoy the promises that were made in the first place to Israel, those promises had to have found fulfillment within Israel and been extended in a continuous line to the Gentiles. The Gentile Church, in a word, was not seen by Luke as the replacement of Israel, but as an extension of the true and believing Israel." Although they do not articulate this understanding of Israel in exactly the same way, both Paul in Romans 11:17–24 (the allegory of the wild and cultivated olive trees) and the author of the Epistle to the Ephesians are on the same "theological wavelength" as Luke.

[71] Significantly, while all Four Gospels cite Isaiah 40 with reference to John the Baptist, only Luke continues the citation down to Isa 40:5 (in Luke 3:6), thus including a reference to universal salvation.

[72] On this translation, see Rochais, *Les récits de résurrection*, 28. The Greek of Luke 7:17 contains a number of problems. The phrase *ho logos houtos* (literally: "this word") probably makes a precise reference back to the crowd's acclamation of Jesus (*peri autou*) in v 16. It is this acclamation of Jesus as a great prophet through whom God is visiting his people that spreads *en holē tē Ioudaią* (literally: "in all of Judea"). In Luke, however, the noun *Ioudaia* can often mean not Judea as opposed to Galilee but rather the whole land of the Jews, the Holy Land or Palestine (see Luke 1:5; 4:44; 6:17; 23:5; Acts 2:9; 10:37; also possibly Acts 1:8). In view of the adjective *holos* ("whole") modifying *Ioudaia* and the lack of any mention of Galilee, "the land of the Jews" is the most likely meaning here in Luke 7:17 (so Schürmann, *Lukasevangelium*, 1. 29 n. 12; Busse, *Die Wunder des Propheten Jesus*, 165, 172, 175; some hesitancy is expressed by Fitzmyer, *The Gospel*

According to Luke, 1. 660). If this translation is correct, then "all the surrounding territory" (*pasē tē perichōrō*) necessarily refers to Gentile territory. Thus, the theme of Jesus' activity (or the report thereof) reaching out to the Gentiles, which was struck in the previous story of the centurion's servant, is continued in the Nain story. In any event, Conzelmann's claim (*The Theology of St. Luke*, 46) that "Luke probably imagines that Nain is situated in Judaea" has no solid basis in this particular text or in Lucan usage in general.

[73] Eric Franklin (*Christ the Lord. A Study in the Purpose and Theology of Luke-Acts* [Philadelphia: Westminster, 1975] 7) puts the point this way: ". . . Luke's understanding of Jesus . . . [is] determined by his belief that Jesus was the climax of God's activity in Israel." Johnson (*The Literary Function*, 173 and passim) articulates the same basic insight from a different vantage point when he states that the whole narrative of Luke-Acts is dominated by a literary pattern that he labels "The Prophet and the People."

[74] On this point see Augustin George, "Le miracle dans l'oeuvre de Luc," Xavier Léon-Dufour (ed.), *Les miracles de Jésus selon le Nouveau Testament* (Parole de Dieu; Paris: Seuil, 1977) 249–68, esp. 252–53; also Félix Gils, *Jésus prophète d'après les évangiles synoptiques* (Orientalia et biblica lovaniensia 2; Louvain: Publications universitaires, 1957) 26–27. On the various ways in which Luke clothes Jesus in the mantle of Elijah throughout the Third Gospel and Acts, see Jean-Daniel Dubois, "La figure d'Elie dans la perspective lucanienne," *RHPR* 53 (1973) 155–76, esp. 168; also Rochais (*Les récits de résurrection*, 32–35), though some of the allusions to Elijah that Rochais detects are questionable. In a more general vein, see Barnabas Lindars, "Elijah, Elisha and the Gospel Miracles," C. F. D. Moule (ed.), *Miracles. Cambridge Studies in Their Philosophy and History* (London: Mowbray; New York: Morehouse-Barlow, 1965) 63–79. Donald K. Campbell ("The Prince of Life at Nain," *BSac* 115 [1958] 341–47, esp. 344) also sees in the acclamation of the crowd a possible allusion to the prophecy of Deut 18:15–18, in which Moses promises the people that God will raise up "a prophet like me" (cf. Acts 3:22–23; 7:37).

The application of the title of "prophet" to Jesus in Peter's kerygmatic speech of Acts 3:22–23 and in Stephen's defense in Acts 7:37 is important for understanding Luke's approach to christology. It demonstrates that Luke evaluates "prophet" positively as a christological title and is willing to present the early Spirit-filled Christians as proclaiming Jesus under this title. This poses a serious objection to the thesis of Jack Dean Kingsbury (*Conflict in Luke. Jesus, Authorities, Disciples* [Minneapolis: Fortress, 1991] 50–53) that Luke considers "prophet" to be a false title when applied to Jesus, a title that is antithetical to his true title of Messiah (as well as Lord and Son of God). Now it is true that in Luke 9:19–20 the Evangelist opposes Peter's confession of Jesus as "the Messiah of God" to the crowds' view that Jesus is John the Baptist, Elijah, or one of the ancient prophets who has risen from the dead. But this is not to deny that Jesus is a prophet in any sense; it is to deny that he is a particular prophet, namely, one of the prophets of the old dispensation who exercised his ministry, died, and now has risen from the dead (or, in the case of Elijah, who did not die, returned from heaven). Jesus is not one of the old prophets who has come back "recycled." This does not mean, though, that he is not a prophet in any sense of the word. Hence in 9:19–20 Luke is not totally rejecting the crowd's acclamation in 7:16 that Jesus is a great prophet. Indeed, this precise title, "a great prophet," is never used of anyone else in Luke-Acts, including John the Baptist. True, John is called "great" by the angel Gabriel in Luke 1:15 and "a prophet" by his father Zechariah in 1:76, but the two designations are never brought together as a single title applied to John. Only Jesus receives this title; and while not entirely adequate, it is not entirely false. It expresses one aspect of

Jesus that Luke subsumes under the grander and more pivotal titles of Lord, Christ, Son of God, and Son of Man.

[75] Interestingly, this methodologically prior question is rarely treated by commentators. Almost immediately most exegetes will declare the Nain story a special L tradition and proceed to try to distinguish the original L tradition from Luke's redaction. But if the Nain story fits so snugly into Luke's redactional framework and if Lucan vocabulary and stylistic traits (including use of LXX phrases) can be seen throughout the pericope, the careful investigator must first ask whether Luke himself created the whole pericope. Only if that does not seem the most likely hypothesis can one then turn to the question of the existence, the extent, and the origin of a special L tradition. This is the procedure that will be followed here.

[76] Note the similarity in wording with which each widow is introduced into the narrative: *kai idou ekei gynē chēra* (3 Kgdms 17:10) and *kai autē ēn chēra* (Luke 7:12), which in turn is quite similar to the phrase Luke uses in 2:37 to introduce the prophetess Anna (*kai autē chēra*). As Rochais points out (*Les récits de résurrection*, 24), some elements in the wording of the Nain story stand closer to the MT than to the LXX, notably the idea that the widow has only one son (so both the MT and Luke), and not a number of children (so the LXX). Rochais draws the conclusion that the primitive form of the Nain story was formed in a Jewish milieu that knew and used the Hebrew form of the story. This may well be true, but we must remember two points: (1) One must not overemphasize the dependence of the Nain story on the Elijah story of 1 Kgs 17:17–24. As we shall see, in many places the Nain story diverges from the Elijah story, and at times the Nain story agrees against the Elijah story with other stories of raising the dead. The only point at which the Nain story parallels the Elijah story word-for-word to any great extent is Luke 7:15c = 1 Kgs (LXX 3 Kgdms) 17:23b. (2) We have no way of knowing whether the author(s) of the primitive form of the Nain story may have been acquainted with a Greek translation of 1 Kings that varied at points from what we call the Septuagint. However, no variants in the Greek text of 3 Kgdms 17:17–24 (as recorded in *The Old Testament in Greek. Volume II. The Later Historical Books. Part II. I and II Kings* [ed. A. Brooke, N. McLean, and H. St. J. Thackeray; Cambridge: Cambridge University, 1930] 276–77) bring the Elijah story notably closer to the Nain story. This is all the more remarkable when one recalls that, with few exceptions, the copies of the Greek OT that we possess are the products of Christian scribes.

[77] Whether the LXX allusions in the story already stood in the tradition or were added by Luke is debated among commentators; for the latter view, see Busse, *Die Wunder des Propheten Jesus*, 168, 173.

[78] The parallelism of expression extends even to the dative of possession that follows in each case: *tē̜ mētri autou* in 7:12 and *autō̜* in 8:42. This desire for parallelism may explain the awkward succession of Greek words in 7:12: *exekomizeto tethnēkōs monogenēs huios tē̜ mētri autou*. The *autō̜* in 8:42 flows more easily since it follows the copulative verb *ēn*.

[79] For patterns and parallels throughout Luke-Acts, see Charles H. Talbert, *Literary Patterns, Theological Themes, and the Genre of Luke-Acts* (SBLMS 20; Missoula, MT: Scholars, 1974). On pp. 39 and 43 he points out that the raising of the son of the widow in 7:11–17 follows upon a story of healing (the centurion's servant, which emphasizes the theme of faith), just as the raising of the daughter of Jairus (8:49–56) follows upon a story of healing (the hemorrhaging woman, which emphasizes the theme of faith).—In the case of Luke 7:11–17, Luke's desire for patterns and parallels extends

even beyond his stories of raising the dead. The idea of the child of the distressed parent being an *only* child (*monogenēs*) is also inserted by Luke into his version of the Marcan story of the possessed (= epileptic) boy; cf. Mark 9:17 and Luke 9:38. Obviously, Luke has imported the idea of an *only* child into both the Jairus story and the story of the possessed boy. Whether the idea that the widow's son in Luke 7:11–17 is an only child is the invention of Luke or a traditional datum that Luke extended to the two Marcan stories to create another parallel and pattern is debatable.

[80] Luke again sharpens the parallel by changing Mark's rhetorical question "Why are you making a din and weeping?" (Mark 5:39) to the laconic command "Stop weeping" (Luke 8:52), which parallels the "Stop weeping" of Luke 7:13 perfectly.

[81] Luke 7:13 in the Nain story is closer to the Marcan form of the Jairus story: compare *neaniske, soi legō, egerthēti* (Luke 7:13: "Young man, I say to you, arise") and *to korasion, soi legō, egeire* (Mark 5:41: "Little girl, I say to you, arise"). The Lucan form of the command to Jairus' daughter is abbreviated: *hē pais, egeire* (Luke 8:54: "Child, arise").

[82] On the Tabitha story in general, see Rochais, *Les récits de résurrection*, 147–61. Rochais thinks that some story about Peter raising Tabitha may have circulated in the oral tradition, but that Luke himself composed the written form of the story by combining elements from Elisha's raising of the son of the woman of Shunem in 2 Kings 4 and the Jairus story in Mark 5.

[83] The sitting up involves another parallel as well. In each case the sitting up is accompanied by some other physical action that demonstrates that the formerly deceased person is now alive. In Luke 7:15, the young man "sat up and began to speak." In Acts 9:40, Tabitha "opened her eyes and, seeing Peter, sat up." On the parallel between the Nain and the Tabitha stories, see Talbert, *Literary Patterns*, 19–20.

[84] This last point of comparison must remain hypothetical, since the command of silence most probably comes from Mark and reflects his theme of the "messianic secret." Luke keeps the command of silence with some modification (Luke 8:56). Matthew, who regularly insists that revelation "go public," substitutes a notably different ending: "And this report spread throughout that whole district" (Matt 9:26). Whether there was any statement about the report of the miracle spreading in the pre-Marcan form of the Jairus story is difficult to judge. Most likely the story ended with the double confirmation of the miracle by the child both walking and eating.

[85] This point is made in different ways throughout both Talbert's *Literary Patterns* and Johnson's *The Literary Function*. See also the comment of Charles H. Talbert in his *What Is a Gospel? The Genre of the Canonical Gospels* (Philadelphia: Fortress, 1977) 107–8: "Luke-Acts contains an extensive succession narrative as part of its story of the founder's life [i.e., the "life" of Jesus in Luke's Gospel]. In this, it belongs together with those Graeco-Roman biographies of philosophers which also included succession material within the life of the hero. . . . Christian and pagan alike attempted to answer the matter [i.e., the question of where the true tradition is to be found in the present time] by means of a succession principle."

[86] On the echoes of Jesus' trial and death in Stephen's, see Haenchen, *Apostelgeschichte*, 227; Bruce, *Acts*, 165–72; Schneider, *Apostelgeschichte*, 1. 433–34, 477–78; Conzelmann, *Acts of the Apostles*, 48, 60. Some of the connections would be clearer to the modern reader than to an ancient reader who knew only Luke's works, since certain elements from the early gospel tradition of Jesus' trial and death are used by Luke not in the Passion Narrative of his Gospel but only in his account of Stephen's "passion."

[87] So Schürmann, *Lukasevangelium*, 1. 497.

[88] Rochais (*Les récits de résurrection*, 19–21) holds that one element of the Nain story that does not appear in any of the other biblical stories of raising the dead is found in some pagan accounts of curing the sick or raising the dead (e.g., Asclepius in an Epidauros inscription, Asclepiades of Prusa as described by Pliny the Elder and Apuleius, a Chaldean who prevents the burial of a young girl [as recounted by Iamblichus], and Apollonius of Tyana raising the daughter of a Roman noble [as recounted by Philostratus]): the miracle-worker happens to meet the funeral procession on the road. I am doubtful, though, that we can speak, as Rochais wishes to do, of a distinct literary genre marked by this element. Even the few cases he brings forward are drawn from different literary categories, and the content is hardly the same in all cases. To take three examples: (1) The inscription from Epidauros can be found in *CIG*, 4. 229, inscription no. 952. In a few lines the inscription tells how a woman with a stomach ailment at first failed to receive a healing dream at the shrine of Epidauros. But later, as she was being carried on a stretcher, the god Asclepius met her, ordered the stretcher to be put down, and healed the woman of her ailment. (2) Pliny the Elder in his *Natural History* 7.37 §124 praises Asclepiades of Prusa, a doctor who practiced in Rome in the 2d century B.C.; for text and translation see H. Rackham (ed.), *Pliny. Natural History* (LCL; 10 vols.; London: Heinemann; Cambridge, MA: Harvard University, 1942) 2. 588–89. Pliny mentions, among many notable achievements, how the doctor brought a man back from death (or: from his funeral obsequies) and preserved his life. The entire Latin text consists simply of "relato e funere homine et conservato." If we did not have the full story from Apuleius, we would hardly know what to make of this. It does not contribute anything to the definition of a literary genre. (3) Apuleius gives us a full narrative of the Asclepiades incident in his *Florida*, chap. 19; for text and translation see Paul Vallette (ed.), *Apulée. Apologie. Florides* (Paris: Les Belles Lettres, 1924) 167–68. One day Asclepiades is coming back to the city from his country house. Outside the city but near the city walls he sees a large funeral, with a huge crowd standing around a funeral pyre, where a supposedly deceased man is about to be cremated. Out of curiosity, Asclepiades goes over to the funeral pyre and discovers that the supposed corpse still has vital signs. To the chagrin of some of the man's heirs Asclepiades calls off the cremation and restores the man to health. In this case it is not quite true that a miracle-worker meets a funeral procession, which he stops in order to raise the dead. In this case a doctor walks over to a cremation about to take place and by a medical examination determines that the man is still alive.

Pace Rochais, one cannot form any sort of distinct literary genre out of such disparate material. The only story that is close to the Nain story is Philostratus' account of Apollonius raising the daughter of a Roman noble; but even in this case Philostratus leaves open the possibility that the girl was merely in a coma. Moreover, Philostratus wrote the story in the first half of the 3d century A.D. and may have known some of the Gospel miracle stories.

[89] Fitzmyer (*The Gospel According to Luke*, 1. 656) calls the attempt to derive the mention of Nain from the Elisha story at Shunem "very tenuous."

[90] See G. W. Van Beek, "Shunem," *IDB*, 4. 341–42; Elizabeth F. Huwiller, "Shunem," *Anchor Bible Dictionary*, 5. 1228–29.

[91] The earliest literary references we have for Nain after Luke are Origen (ca. A.D. 200), Eusebius of Caesarea (4th century A.D.), and *Gen. Rab.* 98:12 (redacted ca. 5th century A.D.); see James F. Strange, "Nain," *Anchor Bible Dictionary*, 4. 1000–1001. Ancient Nain is generally identified by scholars with the modern Arab village of Nein,

[102] So Rochais, *Les récits de résurrection*, 25; Busse, *Die Wunder des Propheten Jesus*, 171. Some critics reject the idea of a modification or correction by Luke; so, e.g., Johnson, *The Literary Function*, 98 n. 3, against Schürmann, *Lukasevangelium*, 1. 403. (For other arguments for and against "the Lord" being in the L source, see Marshall, *Luke*, 285–86.) It is perhaps telling that Johnson unconsciously changes the crowd's acclamation to "*the* great prophet" (emphasis mine) instead of Luke's "a great prophet" (*The Literary Function*, 99–100). It may have been the lack of specificity on the part of the phrase *prophētēs megas* in the climactic acclamation of 17:16 that moved Luke to introduce for the first time in his Gospel the simple and absolute use of *ho kyrios* for Jesus in his third-person narrative. Interestingly, while Luke and other NT authors employ the term "prophet" as one designation for Jesus, the precise phrase "great prophet" never occurs again in the NT. Hence I would disagree with Busse (ibid., 169), who thinks that the basic acclamation of the crowd in 7:16c existed in the tradition but that Luke added the adjective "great."—Another possible indication that Luke has added *ho kyrios* to the Nain story is the presence of *kyrie* as an address to Jesus in the previous Q story of the centurion's servant (Luke 7:6). Luke may have purposely created a redactional link here, moving from an address of Jesus as "Lord" that was already in the Q tradition (cf. Matt 8:8) to a redactional use of "Lord" for Jesus in his own third-person narrative.

[103] On the complicated question of doublets in Luke, see Fitzmyer, *The Gospel According to Luke*, 1. 81–82. Those doublets that do occur in Luke are all limited to one, two, or at most three verses from sayings material. Except for his two stories of raising a dead child to life, Luke contains no doublet of a full story.

[104] Obviously, if one thinks that Luke's Gospel was written some decades earlier, this problem would not loom so large. Marshall (*Luke*, 34–35), for instance, thinks that "a date not far off AD 70 appears to satisfy all requirements"; he even allows for the possibility of Luke's Gospel being written in the early sixties.

[105] Rochais, *Les récits de résurrection*, 30. With some variation in emphasis, Fuller (*Interpreting the Miracles*, 64) speaks instead of a popular pagan tale that was secondarily Christianized by a number of traits drawn from the Elijah-Elisha stories. Fuller's approach is questionable in that he appeals to Philostratus' famous story about Apollonius of Tyana raising to life the daughter of a Roman nobleman. The usefulness of this parallel for making any decisions about the source and historicity of Luke 7:11–17 is highly dubious for a number of reasons. (1) Philostratus' *Life of Apollonius* was not published until about A.D. 217–220. (2) Its supposed major source, a diary of Apollonius' disciple Damis, may be a fabrication of Philostratus. (3) Learned pagans of the 2d century A.D. (e.g., Celsus and Galen) already knew and used the Christian Gospels. There would therefore be nothing strange about a philosophical writer in the religiously syncretistic imperial court of the early 3d century knowing and perhaps drawing upon Gospel stories. If there is any influence between Luke 7:11–17 and the story about Apollonius raising a young girl, the line of influence might well run from Luke's Gospel to Philostratus. (4) With the typical moderate rationalism, not to say skepticism, of a learned pagan, Philostratus leaves open the question of whether the girl was really dead or simply in a comatose state. This is hardly the way Luke presents the Nain story. (5) Philostratus says that Apollonius whispered something indistinct (i.e., something that could not be heard by bystanders) over the girl. In both the Nain and Jairus stories, Jesus addresses the deceased quite plainly in the hearing of others. As I have noted, the *talitha koum* of the Jairus story would have been intelligible to the original Aramaic-speaking audience and was carefully translated to make it plain to a later Greek-speaking audience. When it comes to the words spoken, there is nothing

here of the esoteric that we find in the account of Philostratus. On all this, see the "Excursus on Parallels to the Gospel Miracles" above; and Fitzmyer, *The Gospel According to Luke*, 1. 657.

[106] See Rochais, *Les récits de résurrection*, 30–31.

[107] Many commentators on John's Gospel discern precisely seven "signs" (i.e., miracles) of Jesus that are depicted in a full-length narrative: the changing of water into wine at Cana, the healing of the royal official's son at Cana, the healing of the paralyzed man at the pool of Bethesda, the multiplication of loaves, the walking on the water, the healing of the man born blind, and the raising of Lazarus from the dead. While this observation is in a certain sense correct, two warnings are in order: (1) While the Evangelist pointedly counts the first and second signs (both at Cana) to create an *inclusio* for the first part of the public ministry (2:11; 4:54), he does not continue the count. Hence, we cannot be sure, e.g., that he counted the walking on the water as a sign distinct from the sign of the multiplication of loaves. (2) The Evangelist does not explicitly designate each of the seven miracles as a *sēmeion* (the cure of the paralyzed man and the walking on the water are not so designated), and there are passing references to other signs that Jesus performs that are not narrated in detail (e.g., 2:23; 6:2; 12:37; 20:30). This blasé attitude toward the exact number of signs (or of full-blown narratives of signs) makes one wonder whether the exact number of seven signs was all that important to the Evangelist. At the very least, the number 7 does not have the structural importance for the Gospel of John that it has for the Revelation of John; one must avoid reading the numerical structures of the latter into the former. On this see Brown, *The Gospel According to John*, 1. CXXXIX-CXLIII. In any event, the raising of Lazarus is certainly the last and greatest of the signs of Jesus that John narrates, whether or not it is in the Evangelist's mind the seventh.

[108] Along with Raymond E. Brown and many other exegetes, I hold that the word "sign" (*sēmeion*), when used in John's Gospel of an act of Jesus, always means something miraculous. It is therefore a more narrow category than "work" (*ergon*), which includes more than the signs. The works of Jesus are everything he does to accomplish the "work" of salvation, the all-inclusive work that the Father wills to bring to completion by sending the Son into the world and exalting him on the cross. Thus, the works of Jesus can encompass both words and deeds (see John 14:10). Fittingly, therefore, the wider term *ergon* is used more often in John's Gospel than is *sēmeion* (27 times versus 17 times) and occurs more often on the lips of Jesus when he describes what he does. Indeed, Jesus himself speaks only twice of "signs," once in a negative sense (4:48) and once in an ambiguous sense (6:26; cf. 6:2,14). In contrast, he often speaks of his "work" or "works" in a positive sense. On all this see Brown, *The Gospel According to John*, 1. 525–32; cf. Thompson, *The Humanity of Jesus*, 53–86; Schnelle, *Antidocetic Christology*, 74–175. Since the "signs" Jesus performs are always and only miraculous actions in the physical order whose benefits are immediately visible to the participants or the audience, I do not think that it conforms to John's mode of speaking to call Jesus' death and resurrection the last and greatest sign, for two reasons: (1) John himself does not apply the word "sign" to Jesus' death and resurrection; rather, the vocabulary of "exaltation," "glorification," "ascending," "returning to the Father," and "going away" are the privileged words. In fact, after being widely used in chaps. 2–12 (in the "Book of Signs"), the word *sēmeion* disappears from the Gospel for the whole of the narrative and sayings material of the Last Supper, the passion, and the resurrection (chaps. 13–20, the "Book of Glory"). The word *sēmeion* returns only in the summarizing and concluding statement of the Evangelist (20:30). (2) To call Jesus' death-resurrection a "sign" is to miss the point that a sign performed by Jesus is a miraculous benefit on the physical

level whose very meaning is to point beyond itself to the deeper, saving benefits Jesus offers. The death-resurrection is not such a miraculous benefit on the physical level that points beyond itself; it is the saving action, the ultimate "work," to which all the signs were pointing. Therefore, in my opinion, John's thought and vocabulary militate against even the "compromise" solution proposed by authors like Marsh (*The Gospel of St John*, 577), namely, that the death-resurrection is both a sign and the reality to which all the signs point.

[109] On this point see Wilhelm Wilkens, "Die Erweckung des Lazarus," *TZ* 15 (1959) 22–39, esp. 33; also Werner Stenger, "Die Auferweckung des Lazarus (Joh 11, 1–45)," *TTZ* 83 (1974) 17–37, esp. 28; W. Nicol, *The Sēmeia in the Fourth Gospel. Tradition and Redaction* (NovTSup 32; Leiden: Brill, 1972) 37.

[110] On "life" in John's Gospel see the excursus in Schnackenburg, *Das Johannes-evangelium*, 2. 434–45.

[111] Brown (*The Gospel According to John*, 1. XXXVII, 118, 414, 427–30) even suggests that in both editions of his Gospel the Fourth Evangelist placed the cleansing of the temple at the end of the public ministry and that it was only the final redactor who introduced the raising of Lazarus as the immediate cause of Jesus' arrest and death, thus occasioning the transposition of the cleansing of the temple to its present position at the beginning of the ministry. In my view, the Johannine tradition did indeed know of the cleansing of the temple as an event at the end of Jesus' ministry. But, since, in my opinion, the editorial work of the final redactor of the Fourth Gospel was quite limited, I think it more likely that the Evangelist himself made the transposition of the cleansing to the beginning of the ministry; on this see Schnackenburg, *The Gospel According to St John*, 1. 342–44.

[112] Since the noun *synedrion* lacks the definite article in 11:47, I prefer the generic translation "meeting [to take counsel]" to the more specific "[the] Sanhedrin." Opinions on this point differ: Brown (*The Gospel According to John*, 1. 438–39) translates the word as "the Sanhedrin" and sees here the technical sense of Sanhedrin; Bauer (*Wörterbuch* [6th ed.], col. 1568) makes a slight distinction in holding that it means an official session held by the members of the Sanhedrin; while Schnackenburg (*Das Johannes-evangelium*, 2. 447 n. 2), seeing a closer connection with secular Greek usage, understands it in the generic sense of "a council session" and claims that this is the only occurrence of the word in this sense in the NT. In any case, the picture of the high priests and the Pharisees acting as equal partners in calling together an official meeting, be it of the Sanhedrin or not, is hardly an accurate reflection of the Jewish power structure in Jerusalem in the thirties of the 1st century A.D.

[113] The reference to Caiaphas being high priest "that year" (11:49) does not mean that the Evangelist had the mistaken notion that the high priest held office only for one year—an odd idea for someone who seems to know the OT fairly well. Rather, the phrase "that year" refers to the fateful year of Jesus' death; so Gottlob Schrenk, "*hieros*, etc.," *TDNT* 3 (1965) 221–83, esp. 270; Brown, *The Gospel According to John*, 1. 439–40 (cf. BDF, 100, §186 [2]); Schnackenburg, *Das Johannesevangelium*, 2. 449; *contra* Bultmann, *Das Evangelium des Johannes*, 314 n. 2. Needless to say, the whole line of causality in John 11 and in particular the scene of the high priests and the Pharisees (!) calling a meeting to decide on Jesus' death because he has raised Lazarus to life are a theological construct of the Evangelist. The earliest passion traditions behind the Passion Narratives of the canonical Gospels do not mention the Pharisees in connection with Jesus' arrest and trial. John's theology, and in particular his irony, are also evident in Caiaphas' fear that, unless something is done about Jesus, the Romans will destroy the Jewish

state and its temple. Here, too, in John's view, Caiaphas unwittingly prophesies what will in fact happen, not in spite of but because of the action the leaders take. On this see Schnackenburg, ibid., 2. 448–49.

[114] Dodd, *The Interpretation of the Fourth Gospel*, 363, 368.

[115] For a full-scale treatment of the raising of Lazarus in all its exegetical, theological, and historical aspects, see Jacob Kremer, *Lazarus. Die Geschichte einer Auferstehung* (Stuttgart: KBW, 1985).

[116] Dodd, *Historical Tradition*, 232.

[117] For example, Bultmann (*Das Evangelium des Johannes*, 301 n. 4) first expresses his doubts about whether any clear results can be achieved. Nevertheless, he proceeds to list some criteria for distinguishing tradition from redaction and to suggest the verses in which pre-Johannine tradition is most likely to be found.

[118] For overviews of various attempts at reconstructing a source behind John 11:1–45, see, e.g., Schnackenburg, *Das Johannesevangelium*, 2. 398–402; Haenchen, *John 2*, 67–72; von Wahlde, *The Earliest Version*, 118 n. 110. It is helpful to lay out and compare the theories of some major scholars as to which verses were in the Evangelist's source:

Bultmann:	vv 1, 3, 5–6, 11–12, 14–15, 17–19, 33–39, 43–44
Nicol:	vv 1–3, 6,11–15, 17–19, 28–39, 43–44
Wilkens:	vv 1, 3–4, 11–15, 17, 32b–34, 38–39a, 41–44
Schnackenburg:	vv 1, 3, 6, 17–18, 33–34, 39a, 43–44
Fortna:	vv 1, 2c–3, 7, 11, 15c, 17–18, 32–34, 38–39a, 41, 43b, 44–45
von Wahlde:	vv 1, 3, 6, 11–15a, 17–20, 28–39, 43–45
Rochais:	vv 1–3, 4a, 6b, 7a, 11b, 12, 14, 15d, 17, 32–33, 35, 34, 38bcd, 39a, 41ab, 43bc–45
Kremer:	vv 1, 3, 5–7, 11–12, 14–15, 17–21, 28–30, 32–34, 38–39, 41, 44

(I do not include in the list the atypical view of Haenchen [*John 2*, 71] who suggests that all the Evangelist added to the Lazarus story in his source was vv 23–27.) While Bultmann, Fortna, Rochais, and Kremer all construct a fairly extensive source, Schnackenburg reduces John 11:1–45 to a small core. It is hardly conceivable that a narrative could be shorter than Schnackenburg's reconstruction and still be identified as the Evangelist's source for the Lazarus story. One should note, however, that, while many commentators propose a more extensive source than Schnackenburg's, at times they suggest that only parts of some of the verses they list were in the source used by the Evangelist (so, e.g., Rochais). Moreover, their suggestions are made with varying degrees of probability. For example, Bultmann offers his list of verses with the cautious codicil: ". . . in which [verses] one might primarily find the text of the source." At times scholars also rewrite individual verses and sometimes change their order (again, Rochais). Scholars like Wilkens and Rochais also distinguish between what was in the sign source that the Evangelist used (the verses given above) and a still more primitive version of the story. Given all the variations, one might be tempted to cut the Gordian knot by simply accepting the least common denominator (i.e., by including in the source only those verses agreed upon by almost all the critics). But I think it important that the reader see why certain verses have a much better claim than others to be included in the pre-Gospel tradition. Hence I will present my own reconstruction and the reasons for it. When I am finished, I will then compare my results with some of the previous reconstructions.

[119] For the sake of precision, I use here a more detailed structural analysis of the

narrative than the simple three-part division of a miracle story common to form critics: (1) initial circumstances with petition, (2) miracle-working word and/or gesture with confirmation of the reality of the miracle, and (3) various reactions and/or conclusion. The lengthy Lazarus story especially lends itself to a more detailed analysis. For various attempts to analyze the story's structure, see, e.g., Bultmann, *Das Evangelium des Johannes*, 301; Brown, *The Gospel According to John*, 1. 419; Schnackenburg, *Das Johannesevangelium*, 2. 397. I have made my outline more detailed than theirs in order to highlight certain particulars in individual blocks of material. My results are somewhat similar to those of Kremer (*Lazarus*, 23–28), though there are also notable differences. See also Mark W. G. Stibbe, "A Tomb with a View: John 11.1–44 in Narrative–Critical Perspective," *NTS* 40 (1994) 38–54.

[120] I do not include in this short list the obvious concatenation of references to death and life, since this is to be expected in any story of raising the dead. I will examine John's main statements about life, death, and resurrection in my exposition of the story below.

[121] On this see Nicol, *The Sēmeia*, 37.

[122] Notable in this work have been Fortna (*The Fourth Gospel and Its Predecessor*) and von Wahlde (*The Earliest Version*), both of whom hold that the Evangelist is working not simply with various disparate sources but with a whole primitive Gospel, a sort of Fourth Synoptic Gospel. Put very simplistically, this source is more or less the Fourth Gospel minus the lengthy discourse material. Fortna explains his method and criteria on pp. 1–11 of his work; von Wahlde, on pp. 26–65 of his. One difference between my approach and theirs should be underscored from the start. Since I do not think that the Evangelist had a whole primitive gospel in front of him, indeed, since I am not even completely sure about a single document that we can call a "sign source" (i.e., a single document containing a primitive form of the Johannine miracle stories), I consider any references in the Lazarus story backwards or forwards to other events in the Fourth Gospel as signs of the editorial work of the Evangelist or the final redactor. The original, isolated miracle story could not have contained such cross-references.

[123] On the fairly uniform nature of John's vocabulary and style, see Eugen Ruckstuhl, *Die literarische Einheit des Johannesevangeliums* (Freiburg: Paulus, 1951); Eduard Schweizer, *Ego eimi. Die religionsgeschichtliche Herkunft und theologische Bedeutung der johanneischen Bildreden* (FRLANT 56; 2d ed.; Göttingen: Vandenhoeck & Ruprecht, 1965; original 1939); Brown, *The Gospel According to John*, 1. XXXI–XXXII. Ruckstuhl and Schweizer supply lengthy lists of words and stylistic traits typical of the Fourth Evangelist.

[124] The third-person usage of *ho kyrios* in the narrative of the public ministry is to be distinguished from three other usages of *kyrios* that are employed by the Evangelist: (1) the vocative *kyrie*, which is commonly addressed to Jesus during the public ministry (e.g., John 4:11,15,19,49); (2) sayings material in which Jesus is referring to himself as viewed by others (13:13–14, at the Last Supper), and (3) the Evangelist's use of *ho kyrios* of the risen Jesus in chap. 20. There are a few other places in the Fourth Gospel where *kyrios* is used of Jesus in third-person narrative during the public ministry (4:1; 6:23), but in these passages the correct reading of the Greek text is uncertain because of disagreements among manuscripts.—I say in the main text that the presence of "the Lord" in 11:2 *may* betray the hand of the final redactor, for (in my opinion) we do not possess any extensive narrative from the final redactor besides chap. 21. Therefore, we cannot be sure that he would also have used *ho kyrios* of Jesus during the public ministry.

In any event, I think that the clear reference in 11:2 to the specifically Johannine version of the anointing in 12:1–8 (which would not have been in a "sign source" that was a collection of miracle stories) demands the hand of the Evangelist or the final redactor; similarly, Kremer, *Lazarus*, 83. Hence I cannot agree with Rochais (*Les récits de résurrection*, 123), who assigns it to the sign source the Evangelist used.

[125] It is important to distinguish the meaning of *hoi Ioudaioi* in 11:8 from its meaning in the rest of the Lazarus story. Since v 8 represents the most characteristic, not to say idiosyncratic, meaning of *hoi Ioudaioi* in John's Gospel (i.e., the authorities in Jerusalem who are hostile to Jesus), and since v 8 is by almost universal agreement of the commentators assigned to the Evangelist, it becomes difficult, as Rochais (*Les récits de résurrection*, 115–18) wishes to do, to assign the uncharacteristic, relatively neutral sense of *hoi Ioudaioi* in the rest of the Lazarus story to the Evangelist as well. The untypical sense of *hoi Ioudaioi* (inhabitants of Jerusalem who come out to comfort Mary at Bethany and who are at least partially open to belief in Jesus) in the body of the Lazarus story argues for its presence in the source the Evangelist used. Nevertheless, it remains possible that this typical use of *hoi Ioudaioi* may have been introduced into the Lazarus story in some stage in the oral tradition and that in the earliest stage the comforters of Mary were simply designated with a vague *polloi* ("many"), probably to be taken as the townspeople of Bethany.

[126] On all this see Rochais, *Les récits de résurrection*, 114–15. Rochais treats and excises all of 11:7b–11a,16 in one fell swoop. I think that vv 9–10 must be considered under a different criterion than vv 7–8. In the end, though, the result will be basically the same; we both judge most of vv 7–10 to be secondary.

[127] It might be objected that the reference to opening the eyes of the blind man in 11:37 could be taken as a global reference to Jesus' various miracles of healing the blind and therefore need not refer back to chap. 9 in particular. Two observations may be made: (1) An ambiguous English translation of John 11:37 (e.g., "who opened the eyes of the blind") could create the false impression that the clause refers to miracles of healing many blind people. The Greek of 11:37, however, has the adjective *typhlos* ("blind") in the singular with the definite article: *ho anoixas tous ophthalmous tou typhlou*, "he who opened the eyes of the blind man"—clearly referring to the man born blind in chap. 9. (2) Unlike the Synoptics (e.g., Matt 9:27–31; 11:5 par.; 20:29; 21:14), John's Gospel has only one story of Jesus healing a blind man. Moreover, John is perfectly capable of referring globally to healings of blind people (in the plural) when he wants to. See 10:21: "A demon cannot open the eyes of blind people [*typhlōn*], can he?" Notice that in this case, the speakers (the "Jews" in Jerusalem) are not referring to a number of specific miracles of Jesus but are rather raising a hypothetical, global question about what a demon could or could not do. In contrast, the concrete reference in 11:37 to what Jesus has done speaks of only one blind man.

[128] On grounds of vocabulary, style, and content, both Bultmann and Schnackenburg hold that 9:4 comes from the Evangelist; see Bultmann, *Das Evangelium des Johannes*, 250–51; Schnackenburg, *Das Johannesevangelium*, 2. 309.

[129] The Greek word *hēmera* does occur again in 11:6,17,24, but not in the metaphorical and dualistic sense of spiritual (day)light as opposed to spiritual night or darkness.

[130] Rochais (*Les récits de résurrection*, 119) remarks that "it is hardly necessary to prove that vv 23–27 come from the principal author of the Gospel." Rochais lists all the words, phrases, and stylistic traits of these verses that are characteristic of the Fourth Evangelist. This kind of argument falls under our fourth criterion, but it should at least be noted here. See also Kremer, *Lazarus*, 84–85.

[131] On the complex theology articulated in Jesus' first encounter with Martha in John 11, see Martin, "History and Eschatology," 337–40.

[132] It is difficult to translate *ho eis ton kosmon erchomenos* properly into English; "he who is to come into the world" is simply an expedient convention. The present participle *erchomenos*, like any Greek participle, does not express time either absolutely or in relation to the main verb. In the Gospels *ho erchomenos* begins to become a quasi-title of Jesus ("the coming one," i.e., the one whose coming fulfills the prophecies and hopes of Israel). In John 11:27, *ho erchomenos* should not be taken as referring to some future event of coming (e.g., the parousia, an event that is hardly visible on the mental horizon of the Fourth Evangelist). As so often in the Fourth Gospel, *erchomai*, when used theologically of Jesus, refers to his coming into this world by the incarnation (e.g., 1:9,11; 12:46; 18:37). Hence, despite the fact that *ho erchomenos* is the present participle, "he who has come into the world" would be an acceptable translation in the context of John's Gospel.

[133] On all this, see Stenger, "Die Auferweckung des Lazarus," 28–32.

[134] On these verses, see Rochais, *Les récits de résurrection*, 119–20. On p. 118 Rochais sums up the role of Martha in the Lazarus story thus: "It is through the character of Martha that the Evangelist expresses his theological thought."

[135] See, e.g., the Evangelist's addition to the prologue of the Gospel in 1:8, where he explains the true function of John the Baptist: "He [John] was *not* the light, *but* [he came] in order that he might bear witness concerning the light." Similar constructions may be found in John 1:31; 9:3; 13:18 (but with the negative particle more distant); 14:31; 15:25 (the negative idea is contained in the idea of hating). On this see Rochais, *Les récits de résurrection*, 118.

[136] At first glance, there is a notable difference, not to say a contradiction, between Jesus' two interpretations at the two ends of the Lazarus story. In 11:15, the clause "in order that you may believe" seems to imply that belief will follow upon and be nourished by the great sign of raising Lazarus, which reveals the glory of God (cf. v 4). In 11:40, however, belief seems to be demanded as a necessary condition laid down prior to the miracle: "Did I not tell you that, if you believed, you would see the glory of God?" Still, the difference may be more apparent than real. Both the disciples and Martha believe in Jesus prior to the miracle. Indeed, the disciples are said to believe from 2:11 onwards; and Martha proclaims her faith with a Johannine creedal formula in 11:27, prior to the miracle. Nevertheless, Martha's objection in v 39 shows that her faith is not yet perfect—a state of affairs that Thomas' glum resignation in v 16 shows to be true of the disciples as well, and something that the Gospel shows to be true of the disciples even as late as the Last Supper (e.g., 13:8–11,36–38; 14:5–11; 16:29–32). Hence both the disciples and Martha are in process: they are on their way from an initial faith toward a perfect faith. On the way, the raising of Lazarus both demands some initial faith on their part if they are to profit from the revelation of God's glory and at the same time leads them to still greater faith. The story of the healing of the royal official's son (4:46–54) is a model of John's idea of growth in faith.—As will be noted below, most if not all of the uses of the verb "to believe" (*pisteuō*) in the Lazarus story can be traced to the editorial hand of the Evangelist.

[137] This seems to be the interpretation of Haenchen, *John 2*, 57. I admit, however, that this is not the only possible reading of the flow of thought. Brown (*The Gospel According to John*, 1. 423) prefers to read v 5 with v 6, though he agrees that the function of v 5 is to ward off the impression that Jesus is indifferent to Lazarus' fate. Perhaps as

the text now stands v 5 looks both backwards and forwards as it tries to forestall a misunderstanding of Jesus' strange words (v 4) and inaction (v 6). For example, Schnackenburg's division of the Lazarus story joins v 5 to v 4; at the same time he points out how the affirmation in v 5 makes Jesus' inaction in v 6 all the more surprising (*Das Johannesevangelium*, 2. 405). A similar approach is taken by Kremer, *Lazarus*, 57. Taking a different tack, Bultmann (*Das Evangelium des Johannes*, 302 n. 7) thinks that, while v 4 comes from the Evangelist (which is my major point), v 5 existed in the source and followed immediately upon v 3. In my opinion, the succession of v 3 + v 5 does not make good sense, to say nothing of a smooth narrative.

[138] On the Johannine vocabulary and style in vv 11–15, see Rochais, *Les récits de résurrection*, 121–22.

[139] So Rochais (*Les récits de résurrection*, 127), following Black, *An Aramaic Approach*, 240–43. Black, however, admits with refreshing honesty that, although the Semitic construction (ʾethʿazaz bĕruḥa) he espouses is found in later Christian Syriac, it "has not yet been found in Jewish Palestinian Aramaic or Palestinian Syriac."

[140] See the detailed philological analysis of Bultmann, *Das Evangelium des Johannes*, 300–313; Rochais, *Les récits de résurrection*, 114–24.

[141] Rochais (*Les récits de résurrection*, 119) argues for the primitive nature of John 11:32 from the similar motif in Mark 5:22 (falling at the feet of Jesus in supplication) and from the similarity of Mary's reproach to that of the women speaking to Elijah or Elisha in 1 Kgs 17:18 and 2 Kgs 4:28. Rochais concludes that Martha's reproach in John 11:21 is a secondary formulation modeled upon the more original reproach spoken by Mary in 11:32.

[142] Rochais (*Les récits de résurrection*, 123) represents an unusual position in that he posits a fairly long text in the sign source and yet has the text skip entirely from v 17 to v 32. The closest to his approach on this point is Wilkins.

[143] I remain uncertain as to whether some part of this second dialogue of Jesus with his disciples existed in the pre-Gospel tradition. Rochais (*Les récits de résurrection*, 123) suggests that the tradition contained the following pared-down version of the dialogue: "Then after this he said to his disciples: 'Lazarus our friend is asleep.' The disciples said to him: 'Lord, if he is asleep, he will recover.' Jesus said to them: 'Lazarus is dead. But let us go to him.' " Rochais goes on to emphasize the parallels between this tradition and Jesus' statement that the dead daughter of Jairus is only asleep in Mark 5:38–39. There are other scattered parallels between the Jairus story in Mark and the Lazarus story, but nothing that goes beyond what one would expect from two early Christian miracle stories about Jesus raising the dead that circulated in the oral tradition.—Whatever its source or sources, the narrative of the raising of Lazarus has been so reshaped in a Johannine milieu and according to a Johannine theology of signs that comparisons with the OT and Synoptic stories of raising the dead are of very limited use; on this see Jacob Kremer, *Lazarus. Die Geschichte einer Auferstehung* (Stuttgart: KBW, 1985) 38–50.

[144] It may be that these curious details, which make the miracle of raising the dead man a miracle twice over, were added by the Evangelist as a contrast to Jesus' empty tomb (20:6–7), in which the burial cloths are left behind, the message being that Jesus will never need them again. However, it remains possible that these details in 11:44 stood in the pre-Gospel tradition as part as the confirmation of the reality of the miracle. If that be the case, their presence in the Lazarus story might have suggested to the Evangelist the counterpoint of 20:6–7.

[145] In this case the statistics are quite impressive: *pisteuō* is used 98 times in John's Gospel versus 11 times in Matthew, 14 times in Mark, and 9 times in Luke.

[146] A comparison of the two reactions in Greek is interesting, especially since there is no reason to think that the Fourth Evangelist knew the text of Acts:

John 11:45 *polloi . . . episteusan eis auton* [= Jesus]
Acts 9:42 *episteusan polloi epi ton kyrion* [= Jesus]

[147] Rochais, *Les récits de résurrection*, 124–29. Similar suggestions are made by Wilkens, "Die Erweckung," 22–39, esp. 27; Kremer, *Lazarus*, 88–89 (reporting the view of Jürgen Becker). Wilkens's early traditional narrative includes vv 1,3,17, 33–34,38–40,43–44. Unlike Rochais, Wilkens retains the name Lazarus in the earliest available form of the story. The short, Synoptic-like pericope offered by Kremer includes vv 1,3,17,38–39,41,43–44; this version maintains the names of Lazarus, Mary, and Martha in v 1.

[148] In particular, I think some commentators on John's Gospel are too quick to contrast the theology of miracles in the hypothetical sign source with the theology of miracles championed by the Fourth Evangelist. Even in the case of an entity that we know existed and that we still possess (i.e., the Fourth Gospel), articulating precisely the subtle and complicated view that the Evangelist has of Jesus' signs is no mean task. To do the same thing with the hypothetical sign source—if it ever existed—is an extremely difficult undertaking, to say nothing of the final step of comparing the two views.

[149] Rochais, *Les récits de résurrection*, 125–26.

[150] See, e.g., Rochais, *Les récits de résurrection*, 125.

[151] On all this see Haenchen, *John 2*, 69. Haenchen rightly emphasizes that, if one is to make anything of these parallels, one must think in terms of mutations in the oral tradition, not of John's copying erratically from various passages in Luke's Gospel.

[152] One caveat should be noted, however: almost all the most striking cases of this "cross-fertilization" of the two traditions occur in the narratives of Jesus' death and resurrection.

[153] Modern critics refer to such a narrative that conveys an example or warning to its audience as a *Beispielerzählung*; see, e.g., Bultmann, *Geschichte*, 193. While these refinements are useful for modern scholars, one must remember that for Jesus' audience such a narrative would have fallen under the general category of *māšāl* and that the evangelists would have no doubt labeled it as another *parabolē* (as indeed the writer of the Codex Bazae did in the case of the parable of Lazarus and the rich man). On this see Fitzmyer, *The Gospel According to Luke*, 2. 1125–26.—On the similarity of the parable of Lazarus and the rich man with the parables of the good Samaritan and the prodigal son as examples of the "tale type" of parable, see Christopher F. Evans, "Uncomfortable Words—V. 'If they do not hear Moses and the prophets, neither will they be convinced if someone should rise from the dead' (Lk 16:31)," *ExpTim* 81 (1969–70) 228–31, esp. 228.

[154] On the two parts or "tiers" of the parable, see Evans, "Uncomfortable Words," 228–29; Jacques Dupont, *Les béatitudes* (EBib; 3 vols.; Paris: Gabalda, 1969 [vols. 1 and 2], 1973 [vol. 3]) 3. 173; A. Feuillet, "La parabole du mauvais riche et du pauvre Lazare (Lc 16, 19–31) antithèse de la parabole de l'intendant astucieux (Lc 16, 1–9)," *NRT* 101 (1979) 212–23, esp. 216.

[155] For the precise question I am treating, see Jacob Kremer, "Der arme Lazarus. Lazarus, der Freund Jesu. Beobachtungen zur Beziehung zwischen Lk 16, 19–31 und John 11, 1–46," *A cause de l'évangile. Etudes sur les Synoptiques et les Actes* (LD 123; Jacques Dupont Festschrift; Paris: Cerf, 1985) 571–85. Since my purpose is to compare the Lucan parable of Lazarus with John's narrative of Lazarus, I do not engage here in a detailed exegesis of the parable, which contains a number of fascinating conundrums. For basic exegesis, see Jeremias, *The Parables of Jesus*, 182–87; Grundmann, *Das Evangelium nach Lukas*, 324–30; Ernst, *Das Evangelium nach Lukas*, 471–77; Marshall, *Luke*, 632–39; Fitzmyer, *The Gospel According to Luke*, 2. 1124–34. Further material can be found in A. O. Standen, "The Parable of Dives and Lazarus, and Enoch 22," *ExpTim* 33 (1921–22) 523; J. Renié, "Le mauvais riche (Lc., xvi, 19–31)," *Année théologique* 6 (1945) 268–75; N. Rimmer, "Parable of Dives and Lazarus (Luke xvi. 19–31)," *ExpTim* 66 (1954–55) 215–16; R. Dunkerley, "Lazarus," *NTS* 5 (1958–59) 321–27; Jean Cantinat, "Le mauvais riche et Lazare," *BVC* 48 (1962) 19–26; K. Grobel, " '. . . Whose Name Was Neves,' " *NTS* 10 (1963–64) 373–82; C. H. Cave, "Lazarus and the Lukan Deuteronomy," *NTS* 15 (1968–69) 319–25; Evans, "Uncomfortable Words," 228–31; J. Duncan M. Derrett, "Dives and Lazarus and the Preceding Sayings," *Law in the New Testament* (London: Darton, Longman & Todd, 1970) 78–99; Otto Glombitza, "Der reiche Mann und der arme Lazarus," *NovT* 12 (1970) 166–80; Dupont, *Les béatitudes*, 3. 60–64, 111–12, 162–82; F. Schnider and W. Stenger, "Die offene Tür und die unüberschreitbare Kluft," *NTS* 25 (1978–79) 273–83; Feuillet, "La parabole du mauvais riche," 212–23.

[156] The metaphor of the "bosom" obviously connotes intimacy (e.g., a child lying on a parent's lap). The Jewish roots of the image might also include the OT references to a dying person "going to" his fathers or being "gathered to" his kindred (e.g., Gen 15:15; 49:33). The further idea of intimacy as a guest reclines on the bosom of the host at a banquet may also be present (cf. John 13:23). To suggest, though, that the image is that of the "messianic banquet" (so Marshall, *Luke*, 636) is to push the metaphor beyond the immediate context. Besides, the eschatology presupposed in the parable seems to be one of punishment or reward immediately after the death of the individual; this does not fit well with a messianic banquet at the end of the present age. Still, one must be cautious about any decision in such a matter since, as most commentators note, the eschatological ideas reflected in the parable are not consistent and do not intend to convey any formal and fixed doctrine about an afterlife. This is not surprising, since Jewish ideas on the subject at the turn of the era were quite fluid.

[157] Hence a number of exegetes claim that the main character in the parable is not Lazarus but the rich man; accordingly, they give the parable titles like "the parable of the evil rich man." On this see Feuillet, "La parabole du mauvais riche," 216.

[158] On the problem of the disappearance of the initial letter aleph in Eleazar, which results in the shortened form Lazar (Lazarus in Latin), see Joseph A. Fitzmyer, "The New Testament Title 'Son of Man' Philologically Considered," *A Wandering Aramean. Collected Aramaic Essays* (SBLMS 25; Missoula, MT: Scholars, 1979) 143–60, esp. 149–51; for a different view of the phenomenon, see Geza Vermes, *Jesus the Jew* (Philadelphia: Fortress, 1973) 189–90. Fitzmyer notes the appearance of the name Eleazar in such varied contexts as a bill of divorce found at Murabbaʿat, a Jerusalem ossuary, and the text of 1QapGen 22:34. At a much later date (ca. the first half of the 5th century A.D.), the Palestinian Talmud often truncates Eleazar to produce Lazar or Liezer.

[159] See the reconstruction of the earliest form of the parable in Kremer, *Lazarus*, 104. Kremer suggests that the primitive parable consisted only of a short narrative

(Luke 16:19–23), without any dialogue and without a proper name for the poor beggar. If this be the case, and if one thinks in terms of a "cross-fertilization" of the Johannine and Lucan traditions, then a pre-Gospel Johannine tradition about the raising of Lazarus would be the likely candidate for the source of the name in the Lucan parable. This is also Kremer's thesis in "Der arme Lazarus," 571–85. I should stress, though, that this theory of the name drifting from the Johannine miracle story to the Lucan parable is not to be confused with the highly imaginative (indeed, novel-like) theory of Dunkerley, "Lazarus," 321–27. Rejecting form criticism (to say nothing of redaction criticism), Dunkerley naively equates the redactional settings of the Lucan parable of Lazarus and the Johannine story of Lazarus with two historical settings, which he then proceeds to harmonize. After Jesus receives the news of Lazarus' illness, his disciples urge him to heal Lazarus and thus create a sensation that would turn the tide of opinion in his favor. Jesus tells the parable of Lazarus (taking the name from the historical situation of his sick friend) to warn his disciples that disbelief would continue even in the face of a resurrection. Yet, later on, faced with the grief of Lazarus' sisters, and wishing to demonstrate to his disciples the truth of his parable, Jesus proceeds to raise Lazarus. This is fantasy rather than exegesis.

[160] It is strange to see how authors who espouse a "synchronic" or structuralist approach to this Lucan parable nevertheless appeal to knowledge of the meaning of the Hebrew name Eleazar by the audience to solve a difficulty in the text; see, e.g., Schnider and Stenger, "Die offene Tür," 273–83. One sees in this structuralist analysis one of the dangers of the method: intent on finding bipolar oppositions or correspondences everywhere, interpreters begin to read into the text what is simply not there.

[161] One of the most fanciful examples of this approach is found in Derrett, "Dives and Lazarus," 78–99, esp. 86–87; see also Cave, "Lazarus," 323. Derrett is very erudite and completely uncritical. He ranges freely from the OT through the Jesus tradition and Luke's Gospel (with little or no concern about Luke's redactional language, theology, and literary composition) to later rabbinic material, notably the classical midrashim. In Derrett's "method," anything and everything may be read into the parable text from another source of a different time period. This is learning without learned controls, resulting in a historical Jesus hardly distinguishable from the redactional text of Luke's Gospel.

[162] Kremer (*Lazarus*, 92) mentions another theory to explain the development of the tradition. According to this theory, Mary the sister of Lazarus was identified by the Fourth Evangelist with the anonymous Marcan woman who anointed Jesus at Bethany before his passion (John 11:1–2; 12:1–8; cf. Mark 14:3–9). Now in Mark 14:3, the man in whose house the anointing takes place is called "Simon the leper." (Is it purely a coincidence that the Pharisee in Luke's story of the anointing in Galilee is also called Simon [Luke 7:40]?) Perhaps Simon was called "the leper" because Jesus had healed him of leprosy; in this connection we should remember that from the OT through to rabbinic times, healing leprosy was equated with raising the dead. Hence it is possible that in another stream of early Christian tradition Simon, whom Jesus cured of leprosy, underwent a transmutation into Lazarus, whom Jesus raised from the dead. The farfetched nature of this theory can serve as a model of the lengths to which scholars will go when they do not have an explanation for something. In the end, this theory still does not explain how the name Lazarus became attached to the story; for that the theory has to turn to the Lucan parable of Lazarus and the rich man.

[163] On Bultmann's formulation of the two points (with which not all would agree), see his *Geschichte*, 193, 212.

[164] As already noted, Kremer (*Lazarus*, 104) thinks that the primitive form of the first half of the parable included only vv 19–23; everything else was added in stages at a later date.

[165] Dupont, *Les béatitudes*, 3. 162–82; see also Feuillet, "La parabole du mauvais riche," 212–23.

[166] See Grobel, " '. . . Whose Name Was Neves,' " 373–82; for a critical assessment of various supposed sources of the Lucan parable, see Fitzmyer, *The Gospel According to Luke*, 2. 1126–27.

[167] On the lack of explicit moral criteria or judgments in the first half of the parable, see Dupont, *Les béatitudes*, 3. 174–78. It must be stressed that this is true of the first part of the parable *read by itself*. Dupont emphasizes that, within the context of the redaction of the whole of chap. 16, Luke uses the parable to inculcate the proper use of wealth by the rich to make friends among the poor and so prepare for a happy reception of the rich into the "everlasting dwellings" after death (cf. 16:9). To be sure, the element of moral responsibility is supplied by the second half of the parable of Lazarus and the rich man; but it is significant that one must wait until the second half for any moral tone that links up with the major concern of the rest of chap. 16 (the parable of the "unjust steward" [16:1–8] with the logia attached to it [16:9–13], Jesus' denunciation of the Pharisees who mock his teaching because they love money [16:14–15], and the references to the "law and the prophets" [16:16–18]). See also Feuillet, "La parabole du mauvais riche," 212–23.

[168] This is what Derrett does in his "Dives and Lazarus," 85–92.

[169] See the detailed study of Lucan vocabulary and style in the individual verses by Dupont, *Les béatitudes*, 3. 173–82.

[170] So Dupont, *Les béatitudes*, 3. 63–64, 179.

[171] I say "roughly" because there are text-critical problems in some relevant passages; hence, e.g., some critics count 107 occurrences in the NT and 71 occurrences in Luke. To appreciate the unusual nature of Luke's frequent use of *anistēmi*, both in secular contexts and in passages referring to Jesus' resurrection and the resurrection of the dead in general, one should compare him to other NT authors. To begin with, the majority of NT books never use the verb. Apart from Luke, almost all NT authors who use *anistēmi* do so only sparingly; and some who use it never or almost never use it of the resurrection of Jesus. For example, Matthew uses the verb 4 times, but always in a context that does not refer to Jesus' resurrection or the act of the dead rising either in this life or at the end of time. The only passage that comes close is Matt 12:41: "The men of Nineveh will arise at the [last] judgment with this generation and condemn it." But here the act of rising refers to the judges at a trial rising from their seats to pass judgment. Equally surprising is Paul in his undisputed epistles. He uses the verb only 4 times, 2 of which are quotations from the OT and do not refer to the resurrection of the dead. The only time he uses the verb of Christ's resurrection is in 1 Thess 4:14, where he seems to be citing an early Christian formula of faith. It is probably the influence of that formula on the flow of his argument that leads him to use the verb of the resurrection of Christians in 1 Thess 4:16, the only time he does so. The only occurrence of the verb in the deutero-Paulines is in Eph 5:14, where the reference is to the spiritual resurrection of the Christian through faith and baptism. The 2 occurrences in the Epistle to the Hebrews have nothing to do with the resurrection of the dead. Even the Gospel of John, which uses the verb 8 times, restricts all but 1 (20:9) of the occurrences to 2 key passages: the bread of life discourse in chap. 6 (vv 39–40,44,54)

and the raising of Lazarus in chap. 11 (vv 23–24,31). Mark is the only NT writer besides Luke who uses *anistēmi* to a significant extent (17 times, though 1 case is in the secondary ending, 16:9); his usage includes references to the resurrection of the dead. Luke takes over some of Mark's uses in connection with raising the dead in this world (e.g., Jairus' daughter in Luke 8:55 ‖ Mark 5:42) and in connection with Jesus' own resurrection (the third passion prediction in Luke 18:33 ‖ Mark 10:34). Significantly, Matthew takes over neither use from Mark. But Luke also adds to Mark's use of *anistēmi* referring to the resurrection of the dead; see the example of Mark 6:15 in the main text.

[172] Luke uses *peithō* 4 times in his Gospel and 17 times in Acts, for a total of 21. The historical Paul comes closest to Luke since he uses *peithō* 19 times. Mark and John do not use the verb at all, and Matthew uses it 3 times.

[173] Dupont, *Les béatitudes*, 3. 179. Note especially Luke's tendency to use "Moses and the prophets" instead of the traditional phrase "the law and the prophets"; see Luke 24:27,44; Acts 26:22; 28:23. Sometimes additional words are included in the formula: e.g., "all the prophets" in Luke 24:27. Sometimes "law" is joined to "Moses": "in the law of Moses and the prophets and the Psalms" in Luke 24:44; and "the law of Moses and the prophets" in Acts 28:23. With the exception of John 1:45, where the phrasing is a bit awkward ("We have found him of whom Moses wrote in the law—and the prophets [wrote]"), no other author in the NT uses the phrase in place of "the law and the prophets."

[174] Kremer (*Lazarus*, 104 n. 176) points to the phrase "Moses and the Prophets," the verb *diamartyromai* (10 out of the 15 occurrences are Lucan, with no use in the other Gospels), the verb *metanoeō* (17 out of 34 uses are Lucan, while Matthew uses it 5 times, Mark twice, and John not at all), and the theme of the rejection of the call to repentance issued by the one who rises from the dead (pointing forward to the Acts of the Apostles). As Kremer points out in his separate article ("Der arme Lazarus," 578–79), such a convergence of Lucan traits is not evident in the earlier part of the parable (though there are some; see Dupont, *Les béatitudes*, 3. 173–78). While these observations on non-Lucan and Lucan traits are impressive, I think it better to argue from the more limited but more verifiable position that Luke's hand is surely found in 16:31.

[175] Similarly, Wilkens, "Die Erweckung," 29 n. 15.

[176] So Kremer, *Lazarus*, 104–5; idem, "Der arme Lazarus," 572, 584–85.

[177] Kremer (*Lazarus*, 91–92) gives greater weight to the influence of the Lucan story of Martha and Mary.

[178] While some critics would retain the name of Lazarus in the primitive tradition of the story, they consider the references to Mary and Bethany to be secondary; on this see Kremer, "Der arme Lazarus," 571–85. While I tend to think that all three names— Lazarus, Mary, and Bethany—were in the primitive tradition, I would grant that the name Lazarus is anchored in the story in a way that the other two names are not. As I have argued above, unlike the names Mary and Bethany, the name Lazarus cannot be logically derived from other Gospel passages, including the Lucan parable of Lazarus and the rich man.

[179] On this suggestion, see Kremer, *Lazarus*, 105–7. Rochais (*Les récits de résurrection*, 134) thinks instead that the Lazarus story may not go back to any event in the life of Jesus; it may simply be Christian preaching in narrative form, giving dramatic shape to the church's faith in Jesus the Messiah and its hope in the resurrection of the dead.

[180] Rochais's attempt at a reconstruction of the most primitive form of the tradition

would be an exception to the general rule. However, almost no critic omits the name Lazarus from the source that the Fourth Evangelist directly used.

[181] This view is similar to that of Schnackenburg, *Das Johannesevangelium*, 2. 433; Kremer, *Lazarus*, 107–8. Kremer rightly emphasizes that such a judgment aims directly only at what the disciples around Jesus *thought* had taken place and what they told others about Jesus even during his public ministry. Obviously, the disciples did not have our modern ability (or even the ability of an ancient doctor like Galen) to discern the difference between apparent and clinical death.

[182] I should note a liberty I take in the translation. The Greek text does not have the definite article before each of the adjectives; I supply it for the sake of smooth English style. The definite article should not be taken to mean that *all* the blind see, or *all* the lame walk. Perhaps a more accurate translation would read: "Blind people see, lame people walk. . . ." But this is ungainly; hence I employ the definite article plus the adjective used as a substantive (except for the noun "lepers").

[183] While exorcisms are not mentioned in Matt 11:5 par., they are discussed in sayings of Jesus preserved in the Beelzebul controversy (Mark 3:22–27 ‖ Matt 12:22–30 ‖ Luke 11:14–23), which itself is represented in both the Marcan and the Q traditions. Thus exorcisms likewise enjoy multiple attestation of both sources and forms.

[184] While Bultmann (*Geschichte*, 22) takes the nuanced view that Matt 11:2–6 is a church composition encapsulating an authentic saying of Jesus in vv 5–6, Kloppenborg (*Formation*, 107) holds that "the entire pronouncement story is a post-Easter creation, arising in the effort to attract Baptist disciples into the Christian fold." For a full survey and evaluation of scholarly opinions of Matt 11:2–6 par., see the treatment in Chapter 13.

[185] On the basic historicity of the pericope, see Kümmel, *Promise and Fulfilment*, 109–11.

[186] Scholars debate whether these verses were added by a later redactor of the Book of Isaiah and whether their original meaning referred to the national restoration of Israel or to the resurrection of the dead at the end of time. For example, Otto Kaiser (*Isaiah 13–39* [OTL; Philadelphia: Westminster, 1974] 201) thinks that 25:8a (Yahweh "will destroy death forever") is an addition by a later redactor, but that it correctly interprets the previous verse with reference to the abolition of death itself. Kaiser (pp. 210, 215–20) likewise thinks that 26:19 ("your dead shall live, their corpses shall rise") is a later addition to the text and speaks of the hope of the resurrection of the body on the last day. For a similar view of 25:8a, see R. E. Clements, *Isaiah 1–39* (NCB; Grand Rapids: Eerdmans; London: Marshall, Morgan & Scott, 1980) 208–9. However, Clements interprets 26:19 of national restoration rather than of individual resurrection; hence he does not consider the verse a later gloss. In any case, by the time of the 1st century A.D., the disputed verses were in the text of the Book of Isaiah and were obviously open to an apocalyptic interpretation.

[187] As a matter of fact, in LXX Isa 26:19 the vocabulary of "the dead are raised" is present, though not in so concise a way as in Matt 11:5 par. LXX Isa 26:19 reads *anastēsontai hoi nekroi, kai egerthēsontai hoi en tois mnēmeiois* ("the dead shall rise, and those in the tombs will be raised"). One might almost see Matt 11:5 as a terse combination of the two clauses in its simple *nekroi egeirontai*.

[188] See Jeremias, *New Testament Theology*, 20–21. In the Greek text Jeremias finds the following pattern:

1. | *typhloi anablepousin,* | [the blind see] |
    | *chōloi peripatousin,* | [the lame walk] |
    | *leproi katharizontai.* | [lepers are cleansed] |

2. | *kai kōphoi akouousin,* | [and the deaf hear] |
    | *nekroi egeirontai,* | [the dead are raised] |
    | *ptōchoi euaggelizontai.* | [the poor have the good news preached to them] |

3. | *kai makarios estin hos ean mē skandalisthę̄ en emoi.* |
    | [and happy is the one who is not scandalized in me] |

[189] See my remarks in *A Marginal Jew*, 1. 179.

[190] So, e.g., Jeremias, *New Testament Theology*, 103–5.

[191] Each of these examples is instructive. In Mark 4:12, the larger context is understanding or not understanding the parables of Jesus, as the subsequent verse (4:13), with its use of verbs for knowing and understanding (*oidate, gnōsesthe*), makes clear. Mark 4:12, moreover, is a word-for-word citation of Isa 6:9–10; this makes the reference to the rejection of the prophet's message even clearer. John 9:39–41 is more intriguing in that the literal miracle of giving sight to the man born blind in 9:1–7 occasions the metaphorical use of "blind" (*typhlos*) of the Pharisees, who, by way of Johannine irony, apply the metaphor to themselves in v 40. The vocabulary of "seeing" likewise develops throughout the chapter from the physical sight that the blind man receives in the miracle (vv 1–7) to the full sight of faith that he receives in vv 35–38.

CHAPTER 23

THE SO-CALLED NATURE MIRACLES

I. "NATURE MIRACLE" AS A QUESTIONABLE CATEGORY FOR THE GOSPELS

When we examined the categories of Gospel miracles labeled exorcisms, healings, and raising the dead, there was no major problem about defining each category. Casting out a demon from a possessed person, healing a sick person of his or her illness, and raising a dead person to life are all clear concepts, however incredible they may be to "modern man." In the Four Gospels, each category has a fairly stable literary form, a common vocabulary, and common content. When necessary, it is even possible to distinguish subcategories within a given category. For example, in the Gospels, healing the crippled, giving sight to the blind, and cleansing lepers are all distinct subcategories (each containing a number of individual stories) within the category of healing. These subcategories likewise enjoy common form, vocabulary, and content.

This is not the case with the catchall category that is traditionally called the "nature miracles" of the Gospels. So variegated are the form, language, and content of these stories that one may rightly question whether, within the Four Gospels, "nature miracles" constitute a single intelligible category like exorcisms, healings, or raising the dead. The idea of a nature miracle is anything but clear and distinct à la Descartes. To be more precise: any attempt to present "nature miracle" as a discrete and uniform category in the Gospels must face four serious objections:

(1) The label itself contains a major problem: "nature." From the beginning of Part Three of this volume, I have tried as much as possible to avoid the language of "nature" and the "natural." The vocabulary of "nature" involves two significant difficulties. On the one hand, if one wants to use the term accurately, one must first engage in and come to terms with the weighty disputes in philosophy and theology over the proper definition of the concept "nature." On the other hand, the exegete must beware of importing into the world of the OT and the NT an idea of a self-contained and self-regulating universe that is more at home in some schools of Greek philosophy or in Newtonian physics than in the miracle stories of the Gospels.

(2) Beyond the problem of an abstract definition of "nature," there is the

more specific problem of defining a "nature miracle" as opposed to exorcisms, healings, and raising the dead. One common way of defining a nature miracle is to say that it recounts the miracle-worker's power over or ability to change inanimate matter, as opposed to his power over living persons. This does not seem a valid distinction, since the category of raising the dead (sometimes assimilated to the category of healing) directly concerns the miracle-worker's power over the inanimate matter of a corpse. Hence power over inanimate matter cannot be the essential characteristic that distinguishes a nature miracle from other categories of miracles.

At the same time, some miracles usually placed under the rubric of nature miracle are not concerned simply with inanimate matter. For example, let us suppose for the sake of argument that Jesus actually walked on the Sea of Galilee. When he did this, his miraculous power touched and changed the abilities of his own living body to perform certain actions, and not just the quality of the water in the Sea of Galilee. Once again, the clear and uniform status of the category "nature miracle" becomes questionable.

(3) The group of stories usually labeled "nature miracles" lacks any common form beyond the most basic grid of a miracle story, and even that grid is strained at times to the breaking point. As we have seen, the basic three-part form of a miracle story comprises (a) the *setup* or initial situation: the initial problem, sickness, or need that may occasion a petition for help or Jesus' initiative, along with various attendant circumstances and an audience; (b) the *miracle proper*: the words and/or actions of Jesus that heal the person or meet the need, along with an attestation of the occurrence of the miracle, plus some event or circumstance that confirms the miracle's reality; (c) the *conclusion*: often the audience's amazement, consternation, wondering question, acclamation, praise, belief (and unbelief), and/or the spread of the story and Jesus' fame.

These three basic components admit of numerous variations, but in many of the "nature miracles" one or another major component practically disappears.

(a) In the *setup*, quite often the motif of a petition is simply absent. To be sure, sometimes it is absent in other miracle stories: without any request, Jesus seizes the initiative by healing some illness (e.g., the paralyzed man and the man born blind in John 5 and 9) or raising the dead (the son of the widow of Nain in Luke 7:11–17). Yet even in these examples Jesus is responding to the dire or pressing need of someone other than himself. In some of the "nature miracles," even this element is lacking. For instance, the most primitive form of the story of Jesus walking on the water probably did not present the disciples as being in danger (as in the story of the stilling of the storm). By walking on the water, Jesus simply displays himself in divine majesty because he wishes to do so. No urgent need of another person is being met.

Likewise, in the cursing of the fig tree, no one besides Jesus feels a need, and Jesus' hunger can hardly be called a pressing or dire need—a need that in any event is scarcely met by cursing the fig tree and thus causing it to wither! In the story of the temple tax in Matt 17:24–27, the collectors of the tax ask whether Jesus pays the temple tax at all, not whether he will pay it at that instant (v 24, cf. v 25). Hence there is no dire or pressing need. Even if one construes the question of the collectors as a request for payment forthwith, the request is anything but a petition for a miracle; and the coin for payment could easily have been supplied by means other than a miracle—which is never narrated anyway.

(b) Strange to say, some of the "nature miracles" lack what in other miracle stories constitutes the *miracle proper*, i.e., the word and/or action of Jesus that effects the miracle. For example, in the feeding of the multitude,[1] Jesus' prayer over and actions upon the bread and fish are simply the usual actions of a host at a solemn Jewish meal. Nothing indicates that Jesus' words and actions are thought to effect the miracle. (If anything, they are mentioned in the Gospel narratives to evoke parallels with the Last Supper and the Christian eucharist.) Not surprisingly, therefore, older commentators debated whether the "multiplication" of loaves and fish was thought to have taken place in the hands of Jesus or in the hands of his disciples. The point is that, unlike stories of exorcism or healing, little or nothing is said about exactly when and how the miracle is effected. To take another example: *that* Jesus walks on the water is the essence of this particular nature miracle; but nothing is said about any word or gesture of Jesus that makes his walking on the water possible.

(c) Sometimes the *conclusion* typical of a miracle story, be it the reaction of the onlookers or the spread of the report of the miracle, is lacking. For example, in the story of the temple tax (Matt 17:24–27), the narrative ends abruptly with Jesus' command to Peter to go fishing to find sufficient money to pay the tax (v 27). All the Synoptic versions of the feeding of the multitude lack a conclusion typical of a miracle story. Nothing is said either of the astonished crowd's acclamation or the spread of the story. Only in John's redaction of the traditional story is a reaction on the part of the crowd supplied (John 6:14–15). When one stops to think about it, one realizes that, in the Synoptic version of the feeding of the multitude, the initial petition requesting a miracle, the word and gesture of Jesus that effect the miracle proper, and the usual conclusion are all absent.

Yet not even these departures from the basic form of a miracle story help us group the so-called nature miracles into a single uniform category of dissidents or "un-miracle stories," for some of the nature miracles do follow the basic form fairly closely. For instance, the stilling of the storm has all three major components; and to a certain degree so does the cursing of the fig tree, if we put together Mark's two halves of the story (Mark 11:12–14,20–21 ∥ Matt 21:18–20).[2] So the inconsistency is complete: the so-called "nature miracles" are not even consistent among themselves in their departure from the basic form of a miracle story.

(4) Along with disparate forms, there is great variety in content and accordingly vocabulary. Only what Gerd Theissen calls the "gift miracle" allows a few nature miracles to come together under a single umbrella. Theissen defines a gift miracle as one in which material goods are provided in a surprising

way; these miracles confer larger-than-life and extraordinary gifts, especially goods that have been transformed, multiplied, and heaped up.[3] The common content of Jesus directly or indirectly giving food (or drink) to people in need unites the wine miracle of Cana and the feeding of the multitude—and to a lesser extent the miraculous catch of fish.

The miraculous catch of fish differs from the two stories that clearly belong to the category of gift miracle insofar as—at least in the Lucan form of the story—the professional fishermen were not in immediate need of food for themselves and would presumably have sold most of the fish they caught instead of personally eating such a vast amount.[4] Actually, in the story as it stands in Luke, the whole point becomes moot because Jesus immediately bids the fishermen follow him and thus effectively leave behind the gift of fish they have just now miraculously received (Luke 5:11: "leaving all things"; cf. John 21:19–20). In light of this it is understandable that, in the Lucan form of the story, no hint of actual consumption forms part of the story of the miraculous catch (unlike the Cana miracle and the feeding of the multitude). A still more distant cousin to a true gift miracle is the story of the temple tax in Matthew 17, which does not really qualify form-critically as a miracle story at all. In particular, despite the claims of some exegetes, it should not be included in the category of gift miracle.[5]

Therefore, only two miracles, the wine miracle at Cana and the feeding of the multitude, really fit snugly under the umbrella of the gift miracle. This is the best one can do to create a single category that encompasses a number of the so-called "nature miracles."[6] In the end, one has to admit that most of the "nature miracles" are actually sui generis within the Four Gospels, each constituting as it were its own category. Hence, although the traditional label "nature miracle" had a heuristic value when we attempted an initial overview and inventory of the miracle stories in the Gospels, defining a single category of "nature miracle" proves, upon closer inspection, unworkable and untenable.

II. ALTERNATE CATEGORIES

What categories, then, would be more helpful in reflecting the complexity of the data? Perhaps the critic who deals best with this confusing array of idiosyncratic miracle stories is Theissen, who breaks down the unworkable category of nature miracles into a number of more specific classifications.[7] Adapting and adding to his approach, I prefer to distinguish four categories of miracles performed by Jesus that may serve to take the place of the unwieldy category of "nature miracle":

(1) We have already examined the concept of the *gift miracle* (especially the gift of food). As we have seen, the two miracles that properly belong here are the wine miracle of Cana and the feeding of the multitude. The miraculous catch of fish bears some resemblance to these two, but has some notable differ-

ences as well. The story of the temple tax really does not fit this category; it is not a miracle story at all.

(2) In the strict sense of the word, an *epiphany miracle* is a miracle in which the divinity of a person becomes visible not only in what the person effects or in the phenomena surrounding him but in the very person himself.[8] The only pure example among the miracles performed by Jesus during the public ministry is Jesus' walking on the water.[9]

(3) A *rescue miracle* involves a rescue either from a turbulent sea or from imprisonment. In the public ministry we meet only the case of a sea rescue. The one pure example in the Gospels is the stilling of the storm.

(4) A *curse miracle* (also called a punitive miracle or a miracle of destruction) effects some harm or destruction intended by the miracle-worker by the mere speaking of a wish or order. In the public ministry the only example is the cursing of the fig tree by Jesus.

Looking at this lineup, we should immediately hear a warning bell ringing in our minds. When we undertook our initial overview and inventory of miracle stories in the Gospels, we saw that the Gospels contain (apart from literary parallels) six exorcisms, fourteen healings, and three stories of raising the dead. These categories are attested by a number of different Gospel sources and, in many cases, by both narrative and saying. Indeed, within the category of healings we find subcategories such as curing cripples, conferring sight on the blind, and cleansing lepers, each of which in turn is attested by a number of stories coming from different sources as well as by the two different forms of narrative and saying.

The contrast with the four categories listed above could hardly be starker. With the exception of the gift miracle, each category has only one incident, and even the gift miracle has only two proper specimens. Especially problematic is the situation of the sea rescue miracle and the curse miracle. Besides being represented by only one Gospel story, each category is found in only one source and one literary form. Thus, the criterion of multiple attestation of sources and forms, which was pivotal both in our overview and in our detailed analysis of exorcisms, healings, and raising the dead, is simply "inoperative" for sea rescue and curse miracles. To be blunter: since multiple attestation proved to be the single most important criterion for evaluating the three major categories of miracles, its inapplicability to the case of sea rescue and curse miracles casts a serious question mark over any attempt to establish some historical basis for these miracle stories in the ministry of Jesus. I say this not to decide the whole problem in one fell swoop; but obviously a closer inspection of these stories would have to produce serious grounds for affirming a historical core, if the initial negative impressions these stories give are to be overcome.

The case of the epiphany miracle is not all that much better. Again, it is represented by only one story, the walking on the water, which occurs in only one literary form. However, the story does enjoy multiple attestation of sources (Mark 6 and John 6) and so deserves more careful attention than the first two categories.

The remaining category, the gift miracle, is the only one that contains a number of miracle stories. But, as we have already seen, the relevant stories can effectively be reduced to two: the Cana wine miracle and the feeding of the multitude. The temple tax story is simply not a miracle story. The miraculous catch of fish, besides diverging in some respects from the two main gift miracles, may well be a story of a post-resurrection appearance of Jesus (as it is in John 21) retrojected into the beginning of his public ministry (where it stands in Luke 5). If it was originally a post-resurrection narrative, then by definition it falls outside of the ambit of the quest for the historical Jesus as defined in *A Marginal Jew*.

The wine miracle at Cana does qualify as a true gift miracle, but it too suffers from having no multiple attestation of sources or forms; it is a solitary incident witnessed only by the Johannine tradition. The only gift miracle that enjoys multiple attestation of sources (though not forms)[10] is the feeding of the multitude, found in both the Marcan and Johannine traditions. In fact, the tradition of the feeding of the multitude stands apart from all other miracle stories in that it is the only one present in all Four Gospels. Still, when it comes to multiple attestation of sources, this preeminence boils down to being attested in both the Marcan and the Johannine traditions. Despite this limited attestation, though, the feeding of the multitude is better attested than any other so-called "nature miracle" and so deserves closer scrutiny than the others.[11]

The upshot of all this is that, lacking as they do more than one concrete narrative and in most cases any multiple attestation of sources and forms, most of the so-called "nature miracles" pose grave problems for anyone trying to establish some historical basis for them. I shall examine each story in turn to see if the problems are insurmountable. Since these stories do not belong to one precise category or subform within the larger category of miracle stories, any grouping or order of treatment must be somewhat arbitrary. For convenience' sake, I shall first consider the two miracles that are almost universally assigned to the creativity of the early church, even by many Christian apologists who would otherwise defend the historicity of the Gospel miracles: Peter's finding of a coin in the mouth of a fish and Jesus' cursing of a fruitless fig tree.

The next group to be taken up consists of three stories enjoying at least superficial similarities. All three concern Jesus' relationship with his disciples, who are portrayed as experiencing some need while they are in their boat on the Sea of Galilee. In each case the difficulty of the disciples is resolved by the miraculous words of Jesus: the sudden catch of fish after a fruitless night of toil, Jesus' walking on the water, and Jesus' stilling of the storm. Nevertheless, despite the apparent similarities of the three stories, we shall find that they belong to different categories.

Finally, we shall examine the only two stories that do share a common category: the water-into-wine miracle at Cana and the feeding of the five (or four) thousand. Both of these miracles qualify as gift miracles involving nourishment.

In this whole process it should be emphasized that my decisions have been and will be reached not on the basis of an a priori philosophical judgment (e.g., that such miracles did not happen because they simply could not happen) but rather on the basis of the same criteria of historicity that have been applied to the Jesus tradition in general and to other categories of miracle stories in particular. If some of the stories now under consideration are judged to be creations of the early church, such a judgment will be made on the basis of the criteria of historicity and not on the basis of philosophical presuppositions. That is why these stories are treated at such length: as far as possible, I try to ensure that the decision made in each case is based on the evidence, not on ideological bias.

III. THE STORY OF THE TEMPLE TAX (MATT 17:24–27)[12]

Often, for the sake of completeness, the story of the temple tax is included in an inventory of Gospel miracle stories, usually under the category of "nature miracles."[13] Yet this pericope is not, by form-critical standards, a miracle story, and strictly speaking no miracle is narrated. Actually, this story, unique to Matthew's Gospel and marked by Matthean vocabulary, style, structural connections, and theological concerns,[14] is so idiosyncratic that it is difficult to assign it to any form-critical category. Perhaps it is best classified as a kind of scholastic dispute story or pronouncement story.[15]

As it stands, the pericope (Matt 17:24–27) is carefully constructed in two parallel parts, the second concluding with a rhythmic, parallel saying of Jesus. In the first part (17:24–25a), (a) after Jesus and his disciples *come into* Capernaum, (b) the collectors of the temple tax (paid with a coin called the didrachmon) *ask Peter a question* ("Does your master not pay the didrachma?"),[16] (c) to which *Peter responds* ("Yes"). In the second half (17:25b–26c), (a) after Peter *comes into* the house, (b) Jesus *asks Peter a question* ("From whom do the kings of the earth receive tolls or head taxes? From their sons or from others?"), to which *Peter responds* ("From others"). At the end of this parallel structure Jesus makes the pronouncement that is the climax and point of the whole dispute story (17:26d): "Therefore the sons are free," i.e., exempt from any and all taxes. The theological point is clear: Jesus and his disciples are exempt from paying the temple tax.

Granted this structure, simply from a form-critical point of view the final verse of the pericope (v 27) seems to stand outside of the two-part pattern. Rather than being part of the parallel structure of the pericope, it has its own rhythmic parallelism. After enunciating a new theological principle governing action (v 27a: "but lest we scandalize them"), Jesus issues an order made up of four clauses, each beginning with an aorist participle, which is then followed by an aorist imperative (or, in one case, an equivalent future tense):

Participle	+	*Command*
going to the sea		throw in a hook
the fish coming up first		take
and opening its mouth		you will find a stater [= two didrachma]
taking it		give [it] to them for me and you.

Thus, from a purely form-critical and structural point of view, Jesus' *prediction* of a miracle in which Peter is the agent (and not a *narrative* of a miracle in which Jesus is the agent) stands outside (1) the form of the dispute story, which reaches its climax in the pronouncement of Jesus at the end of v 26, and (2) the parallel structure of the dispute story, with the prediction of v 27 having its own intricate parallel structure instead.

Turning from purely formal and structural analysis to a consideration of the content of the story, we notice immediately that not only the vocabulary, style, and architectonic composition but also the theological concerns are very much those of Matthew. Matthew has carefully chosen this story to be the last narrative of the fourth major section of his account of the public ministry (13:54–18:35).[17] In this fourth section Matthew has emphasized the widening breach between Jesus and the Jewish authorities and, correspondingly, the increasing role of Peter and his fellow disciples as Jesus invests them with authority to teach and discipline (see, e.g., 15:1–20; 16:1–12,13–20; cf. 18:15–20). Throughout this fourth section Matthew highlights ecclesiological themes, notably those centered on the person of Peter (14:28–31; 15:15; 16:16–19; 17:24–27; cf. 18:21); and so he fittingly concludes the fourth section with the discourse on church life and order (chap. 18). Not by accident, the only times the word "church" (*ekklēsia*) appears in the Four Gospels is in this section of Matthew (16:18; 18:17 [*bis*]).

The temple tax story must be understood within the ecclesiological context that Matthew creates.[18] The collectors automatically address their question about Jesus' payment or nonpayment to Peter, the leader of the Twelve, who has been invested with the power to bind and loose (16:19).[19] Impetuously Peter responds with a yes; as the Matthean form of the story turns out, Jesus will "back up" Peter's yes in a most unusual way. In both halves of the Matthean version of the story, Peter's answer turns out to be correct, thanks to the guidance of Jesus. Since Peter has not really understood the import of his first answer, in the second half Jesus privately instructs Peter (whom he commissioned to instruct others in Matt 16:18–19) with a homely similitude or *māšāl*, proposed as a question. Peter gets the point: as a general rule, earthly kings do not tax their own sons, but only other people in their kingdoms.[20] The implied analogy is that God the supreme King—and Father—does not tax his own sons. Jesus then draws the conclusion, which is the central point and key pronouncement of the whole pericope: the sons are free, i.e., exempt from paying the tax.

This principle must be understood first of all in the context of Matthew's theology. Matthew's whole christology can be summed up in the one word "Son": Jesus is the Son of God, the Son of Man, and *the* Son, period. The disciples who obediently hear his word and so do the will of his Father become his brothers and sisters (12:49–50) and are therefore sons and daughters of the Father (6:9–15), "sons of the kingdom" (13:38,43).[21] As Jesus the Son is free from paying the temple tax, so are all those disciples who become sons and daughters of his Father through him. This is the major point of the scholastic dialogue, which also serves as an instruction for Peter, the leader of the disciples.

Hence theologically as well as structurally the story reaches its high point in Jesus' pronouncement on freedom. Yet the story does not end there, for throughout his Gospel Matthew is concerned that Christian freedom not degenerate into license and "lawlessness" (*anomia*, e.g., Matt 7:23). If Christian love means freedom, it also means a responsibility to one's neighbor, the chief responsibility being the obligation of not "scandalizing," i.e., not impeding someone from coming to faith in Jesus and not causing a fellow believer to fall away from faith.[22] This obligation is summed up in the story's second theological concern, introduced by Matthew at the beginning of the final verse (v 27a): "But lest we [you and I, Peter] scandalize them [the Jews with our freedom]. . . ." The obligation to avoid scandal is a major theme of the discourse on church life and order that follows immediately (18:6,8,9). Jesus thus acts out his injunctions to avoid scandal by voluntarily providing the temple tax. With a humorous and folkloric touch, Matthew emphasizes the voluntary nature of Jesus' action by having him provide the money not from the common purse or some rich supporter but from the fortuitous and fortunate find of the exact amount needed in the mouth of a fish.[23]

At the same time, v 27 makes a typically Matthean point about the important position of Peter within the Twelve. While the collectors had asked only about Jesus' payment, Jesus predicts that the philanthropic fish will harbor in its mouth just enough money to pay the tax for Jesus and for Peter: "Give [the stater] to them *for me and for you* [2d person singular!]." Conveniently, the fish contains the coin called a stater, which equals two didrachma, just enough to cover Jesus and Peter.[24]

Besides making an ecclesiological point in v 27, Matthew also creates a smooth and significant bridge to the beginning of his discourse on church life and order in chap. 18. At the equivalent point of Mark's Gospel, the thread of which Matthew has been following fairly closely throughout his Gospel's fourth major section, the disciples quarrel about who is the greatest among them (Mark 9:33–34). In Mark, no precise cause of the quarrel is mentioned. Matthew, who likes logical and temporal links, supplies the necessary connec-

"a site which fits the biblical evidence," according to W. H. Morton, "Nain," *IDB*, 3. 500. The Nain referred to by Josephus (*J. W.* 4.9.4–5 §511, §517) cannot be identified with Luke's Nain, since Josephus' Nain was situated along the border of Idumea.

[92] In saying this I do not mean to grant that Luke is as muddleheaded about Palestinian geography as Conzelmann claims he is in *The Theology of St. Luke*. On this, see Freyne, *Galilee from Alexander the Great to Hadrian*, 364–67. Still, many scholars would admit that Mark and John seem better informed about Palestinian geography than Luke. Hence one can only be bemused when Bultmann (*Geschichte*, 230) claims that "perhaps" the name Nain stems from Luke. Bultmann's whole treatment of the Nain story is a startling exercise in unproven assertions. For instance, we are informed that the fact that the mother of the resurrected person is a widow is "typical." Since the only other biblical story of raising the dead that features a widowed mother is the Elijah story of 1 Kings 17, what "typical" means here is not clear. It certainly does not refer to the most famous parallel in pagan literature, Philostratus' story of Apollonius raising the daughter of a Roman noble (*Life of Apollonius*, 4. 45), since the daughter's father is mentioned in the story and the daughter's mother is not.

[93] Earlier biblical reference works have stated that no archaeological indication of walls or a gate has been found at Nain (Nein); so, e.g., Marshall, *Luke*, 284 (with proper cautions about inadequate archaeological investigation). However, "a survey by the University of South Florida in 1982 confirmed that the topography apparently includes a ruined and eroded circular wall around the city, . . . which would have required a gate as in Luke 7:11" (Strange, "Nain," 1001). Remains of a cemetery have been found outside the settlement proper.

[94] Rochais, *Les récits de résurrection*, 21–30, summarized on p. 29. Besides the paratactic style, Rochais lists (1) the designation of the widow's son as her "only" son, a detail that agrees with the Hebrew but not the Greek form of 1 Kgs 17:12; (2) the clause *kai autē ēn chēra* ("and she was a widow") in Luke 17:12, which corresponds to a circumstantial clause in Aramaic; (3) *exēlthen ho logos* in Luke 17:17 in the sense of a story spreading. As so often in these matters, it is not any single phenomenon but rather all these indicators crowded together in one short story that may form a cogent argument for some Semitic substratum.

[95] One might observe that the style is not completely paratactic: a subordinate clause introduced by *hōs* begins v 12, and the circumstantial participles *idōn* and *proselthōn* introduce vv 13 and 14 respectively. But, on the whole, it is true that the pericope is marked by parataxis. Not surprisingly, Rochais (*Les récits de résurrection*, 24) claims that Luke supplied the *hōs de ēggizen* clause, replacing an earlier paratactic construction that read *kai ēlthen*. At this point, the argument is in danger of becoming circular: any phrase that is not sufficiently "Semitic" is rewritten to make it Semitic.

[96] See Fitzmyer, *The Gospel According to Luke*, 1. 107–8. One may ask, though, why Luke does not eliminate the parataxis in the supposed L source of 7:11–17 if he often does eliminate it in his Marcan source. While there can be no certain answer, one might observe that the Q material in Luke often has a more Semitic flavor to it than does the Matthean version of the same material. Possibly, when it came to recasting his sources in standard Greek, Luke was more interested in his main narrative source (Mark) than he was in either Q or L. For Luke's stylistic tendencies in editing Mark's miracle stories, see Achtemeier, "The Lucan Perspective," 548–49.

[97] For this metaphorical meaning of the Hebrew verb *yāṣāʾ* ("go forth"), see MT Ps 19:5 (taking the verb with its second subject, *millēhem* ("their words")); cf. Mic 4:2; Esth

1:17. The literal and metaphorical meanings of the Aramaic verb *nĕpaq* are illustrated back-to-back in Dan 2:13–14. In 2:14 the chief executioner *goes out* (from the king's presence) to kill the wise men of Babylon because in v 13 a royal decree *has gone out* (i.e., has been issued) to that effect. In both cases the Aramaic *pĕ'al* perfect of *nĕpaq* is used. Rochais (*Les récits de résurrection*, 29), relying on Matthew Black (*An Aramaic Approach to the Gospels and Acts* [3d ed.; Oxford: Clarendon, 1967] 136) points to *Lev. Rab.* 27 as a case in which *nĕpaq* carries the sense of news or fame spreading.

[98] So, e.g., Ernst, *Das Evangelium nach Lukas*, 279; Marshall, *Luke*, 341.

[99] Other stylistic traits of the Nain story are also used by some scholars to argue against Luke's free composition or copying from the Elijah-Elisha stories of the LXX. For example, in Luke 7:12, when Jesus is said to approach the "gate" of the city, the Greek word used for "gate" is the feminine noun *pylē*. Interestingly, the word for gate used both in the story in which Elijah meets the widow of Zarephath (LXX 3 Kgdms 17:10) and in the only other passage in Luke's Gospel where "gate" appears (the parable of Lazarus and the rich man) is not *pylē* but the alternate form of the word, the masculine noun *pylōn*. One might argue that the different form of the word indicates neither borrowing from the Elijah story nor free composition of a Gospel story. However, while this is an interesting observation, it is hardly an airtight argument, since in Acts Luke uses both forms of the word for gate.

[100] The reader will notice one approach I do not take: arguing for the existence of an L source by distinguishing in the Nain story between the words and phrases that must come from Luke's hand and the words and phrases that must have stood in some prior tradition. Distinguishing between the L source and Lucan redaction is difficult in any pericope of the Third Gospel, and especially difficult in the Nain story. One is not surprised to find experts in Luke's Gospel divided in their judgments about exactly how much Luke himself contributed to the Nain story. Hence I think it wiser to abstain from an analysis that claims to be able to distinguish Lucan redaction from L tradition on a word-to-word or phrase-to-phrase basis. For attempts to carry out such an analysis, see Rochais, *Les récits de résurrection*, 21–30; Busse, *Die Wunder des Propheten Jesus*, 162–72. One may compare and contrast their conclusions with those of Fitzmyer, *The Gospel According to Luke*, 1. 655–60; Marshall, *Luke*, 283–87; and Dibelius, *Formgeschichte*, 71–72. Perhaps what is most significant for our purposes is that, despite differences on individual points, all these scholars are agreed that Luke 7:11–17 represents an L tradition that Luke redacted. Busse (pp. 172–75) may well be right: the reason why it is so difficult to decide the exact wording of the L tradition is that Luke has thoroughly redacted the tradition, adapting it to the language of the LXX and heightening its dramatic power.

[101] In my view, Oscar Cullmann (*The Christology of the New Testament* [Philadelphia: Westminster, 1959] 30) is quite right in emphasizing the lack of the definite article here: "This indicates that the remark of the crowd does not point to *the* eschatological Prophet; that prophet does not need the description 'great.' Jesus is simply placed in the prophetic category, a category in which also others have belonged." I do not think that Ferdinand Hahn (*The Titles of Jesus in Christology* [London: Lutterworth, 1969; German original 1963] 379) can adequately counter Cullmann's observation by appealing to Luke 24:19,21. Instead of a general acclamation by the people of Nain, 24:19,21 give us a definition of Jesus by two of his disciples on Easter Sunday—a definition that is in Luke's redaction purposely hazy and confused because the disciples still lack the full revelation of the Risen One. Hence the two passages should not be put on the same level as saying the same thing; both speakers and contexts are quite different.

tion by having the other disciples suddenly appear on the scene with their question of who is the greatest just after Jesus has spoken of supplying exactly enough tax money to cover only himself and Peter. The ecclesiological reason for the jealous question of the other disciples becomes clear.[25]

Often in Matthew's Gospel, the Evangelist's redactional changes and additions to Mark serve both theological and structural aims. So it is in 17:27. The single verse emphasizes a number of Matthew's theological concerns: Jesus' moral teaching on avoiding scandal, the consequent waiving of freedom in voluntary acts of love for others, Jesus' foreknowledge and control of events (an important theme in the approaching Passion Narrative), and Peter's special position as the recipient of Jesus' instruction and care. But the same verse serves a structural function as well by giving the reason for the envy of the other disciples, which in turn unleashes both their question about greatness and the whole discourse of chap. 18.

Given the significant amount of Matthew's particular vocabulary and stylistic traits, his care in creating a structure that also serves his theology, his characteristic concerns about Son-christology, the place of Peter in the church, the relation of Jesus' followers to Jews and Jewish observances, the obligation to avoid scandal, and finally the deft redaction of Mark in order to provide a bridge to chap. 18 *via* the special treatment given Peter in 17:27, it seems evident that 17:24–27 is either entirely or predominantly the work of Matthew himself. Some scholars, such as Robert Gundry, opt for the view that Matthew has created the entire pericope; if that be the case, obviously any question of a tradition about a miracle that goes back to the public ministry of Jesus is moot.[26]

However, while I grant that the pericope as it stands is a composition thoroughly shaped by Matthew's literary techniques and theological concerns, I think a number of considerations favor the view that some sort of scholastic dispute about whether Jewish Christians should pay the temple tax lies behind Matthew's composition. (1) Since Matthew wrote his Gospel somewhere around A.D. 85–90, it seems improbable that he would have gone out of his way to create an entirely new dispute story about the temple tax, which had ceased to be paid to the temple after its destruction in A.D. 70. After that date, the Romans forced the Jews instead to pay a tax to the temple of Jupiter Capitoline in Rome. The question of whether Jewish Christians should voluntarily comply with the payment of the temple tax would thus not be a real question for Matthew. There would be no reason for him to create the story out of thin air.[27] At the same time, if the story already existed in his church, we have already seen the theological uses to which he could bend it. (2) The pericope does contain some words and usages that are unique either in the NT as a whole or at least in Matthew's Gospel.[28] This points in the direction of tradition that has been redacted by Matthew. (3) The structural and theological analysis suggests that the scholastic dispute story may have originally ended with v 26.[29] Verse 27 supplies both a corrective point and further theological insights from Matthew, who is concerned about balancing freedom with avoiding scandal, about the special place of Peter in the community, and about a smooth transition to the discourse of chap. 18.

Hence, before A.D. 70 some sort of pre-Gospel tradition about the payment of the temple tax by Jewish Christians may have circulated in Matthew's church (probably the church at Antioch), a church heavily Jewish in its origins and with Jewish members even in Matthew's day.[30] Indeed, even the skeptical Bultmann thinks that vv 25–26 may have been traditional (M) material that originally referred to some other matter than the temple tax, though Bultmann does not venture to guess what the original topic may have been.[31] Even on this reading, though, v 27, which contains not a narrative but only a prediction of a miracle, is most likely a secondary addition to the original story, an addition probably made by Matthew himself when he was inserting the scholastic dispute story into the architectonic structure of his Gospel. In short, the miracle of the fiscally philanthropic fish, which in fact is never actually narrated since Matthew loses all interest in it as soon as the prediction serves its theological and structural function, has no claim to go back to the time of Jesus.[32]

IV. THE CURSING OF THE FRUITLESS FIG TREE
(MARK 11:12–14,20–21 ‖ MATT 21:18–20)[33]

A. INITIAL OBSERVATIONS ON METHOD

If the coin in the fish's mouth is the most curious Gospel miracle that is *not* narrated, the cursing of the fruitless fig tree may be the most curious one that is. The story occurs in Mark in two parts: Jesus curses the fruitless fig tree (11:12–14) and then proceeds to the "cleansing" of the temple (11:15–19); early the next day, Jesus and his disciples see that the fig tree has withered completely (11:20–21). Matthew takes over the story of the fig tree (Matt 21:18–20), but puts Mark's two pieces together as one event that occurs the morning after the cleansing of the temple.[34] Inasmuch as the tree shrivels instantly at Jesus' imprecation, the element of the dramatic and the miraculous is heightened in Matthew's version.[35] While Luke follows the basic order of Mark in narrating the first days of Jesus in Jerusalem, he pointedly omits the cursing of the fig tree, perhaps because he found the story puzzling or distasteful, perhaps because he had already sounded a similar theme in his parable of the unproductive fig tree (Luke 13:6–9), or perhaps for both reasons.[36] There is no story in John that is at all similar to the cursing of the fig tree. In short, the story has attestation in only one source, Mark.

It is strange to see how many commentators, when faced with Mark's fruitless fig tree, immediately rush to calculations about what sort of fruit might or might not have been present on a fig tree on the Mount of Olives in early April and to speculation about what state of mind the historical Jesus might have been in the morning after his triumphal entry into Jerusalem.[37] A leap is made to the historical situation of A.D. 30 as though Mark 11:12–14,20–21 gave us a videotape replay of what had gone on and as though no one had ever heard of form, source, and redaction criticism. From all we have seen so far, including what we have just seen from Matthew's story of the temple tax, the first rule of exegesis must be: begin by examining a given pericope within the literary and theological context of its Gospel, and only then, through form, source, and redaction criticism plus the criteria of historicity, test to see if anything can be discerned about an originating historical event in the life of Jesus. We must first ask what Mark meant to communicate to his audience by his literary and theological composition in chap. 11 of his Gospel. Whether Mark or his audience knew what the precise state of fig trees on the slopes of the Mount of Olives would be in early April is beyond our ken and perhaps beside the point. Our best approach, therefore, is to begin with an inspection of the structure and content of Mark 11, putting aside for the moment questions of sources and earlier tradition.

B. OVERVIEW OF THE STRUCTURE AND CONTENT OF MARK 11

Mark clearly divides the five major components of chap. 11 by content, indications of time, and verbs of motion:

(1) *The entry into Jerusalem* (11:1–11): As Jesus *draws near to Jerusalem* by way of Bethany, Bethphage, and the Mount of Olives, he expresses his royal messianic authority by commandeering an ass on which to ride into Jerusalem (with an allusion to the meek, just, and saving king who comes to Zion in Zech 9:9; cf. 14:4).[38] The jubilant crowd pays him homage with garments, branches, and Hosannas echoing Ps 118:25–26. In parallel phrases they bless both Jesus "who comes in the name of the Lord" and "the coming kingdom of our father David." Not by accident, in the immediately preceding pericope, the cure of the blind Bartimaeus (10:46–52), Jesus was hailed as the Son of David. After all this theological "buildup," it strikes the reader as strange that Mark's pericope of the triumphal entry into Jerusalem, instead of reaching a climax with the cleansing of the temple (as in Matthew and Luke), ends with puzzling abruptness and bathos: "He *came into Jerusalem, into the temple.* And having looked around at everything, since the hour was already late, he *went out to Bethany* with the Twelve."

(2) *The cursing of the fig tree* (11:12–14): The next day, while they *were coming from Bethany,* Jesus felt hungry. Seeing at a distance a fig tree with leaves, *he came* to see whether he could find anything on it. And *coming* to it, he found nothing but leaves. Mark adds mysteriously at this point: "For it was not the season for figs" (v 13). In response, Jesus says to the tree: "Henceforth may no one ever eat fruit from you!"[39] Mark concludes the pericope with the observation that "his disciples *heard* [Jesus utter this curse]," thus preparing for Peter's remembering about the fig tree the next day (in the second half of the story, vv 20–21).

(3) *The "cleansing" of the temple* (11:15–19): This forms the central pericope of chap. 11.[40] Jesus *comes to Jerusalem* once again. *Coming into the temple,* he

begins to drive out those buying and selling in the temple. In justification he cites Isa 56:7 and Jer 7:11: "My house shall be called a house of prayer for all the nations, but you have made it a den of thieves." Mark observes that the high priests and the scribes *heard* Jesus utter this prophetic critique of the temple,[41] thus setting up the challenge to Jesus' authority on the next day, in the last pericope of chap. 11 (vv 27–33). Once again, when it grows late, Jesus and his disciples *go out of the city.*

As a number of commentators have seen, in Mark's redactional vision this central pericope of vv 15–19 is not a "cleansing" of the temple in the sense of a demand for reform and purification.[42] Rather, at least in Mark's theology, it functions as a prophecy in action, symbolizing the rejection and destruction of the temple, which Jesus will directly announce when he leaves the temple for the last time in 13:2: "Not one stone [of the temple] shall be left upon another; it shall be completely pulled down."

(4) *The discovery that the cursed fig tree has withered* (11:20–25): This fourth pericope obviously picks up on the second (vv 12–14). *Passing by* in the early morning (presumably of the next day), Jesus and his disciples see the fig tree withered (literally: "having been dried up") from its roots. In other words, overnight the tree cursed by Jesus has suddenly withered away completely. Remembering what Jesus said the previous day, Peter remarks to him: "Rabbi, behold the fig tree that you cursed has withered." The reader might expect either that the pericope, having made clear its connection with vv 12–14, would end here, or perhaps that Jesus would speak about the fig tree as a symbol of the barren and rejected temple, doomed to destruction. Instead, Jesus replies in vv 22–25 with teaching about faith and mutual forgiveness as conditions for having one's prayer—even prayer for the impossible— unfailingly answered by God.[43]

(5) *The challenge to Jesus' authority* (11:27–33): Jesus again *comes into Jerusalem. In the temple* the chief priests, scribes, and elders (echoing the makeup of the Sanhedrin that will condemn him to death in 14:53–65)[44] *come to* him, demanding to know by what authority he does "these things." Since Jesus has done nothing in the temple since driving out the buyers and sellers and quoting the prophetic critique of the temple, what the Sanhedrin members must be challenging is his prophetic action in the temple the previous day. In reply, Jesus cleverly unmasks their own lack of legitimate teaching authority by asking whether John the Baptist's authority was divine or human in origin. When the religious politicians realize that either answer would be damaging to them, they refuse to give an opinion on one of the most significant religious figures of their time. Having revealed the emptiness of their authority, which they cannot or will not use when faced with a forthright question, Jesus indicates his rejection of their claim to authority by refusing to answer their question about his own authority. Then, as chap. 12 opens ("and he began to speak to them in parables"), Jesus goes on the offensive with the dark parable of the evil tenants of the vineyard, a parable that the authorities recognize to be aimed at themselves.

C. THE MEANING OF THE CURSING OF THE FIG TREE IN THE CONTEXT OF MARK 11

Granted this larger context, what is the meaning for Mark of the strange incident of the cursing of the fig tree that withers by the next day? As it stands, Mark's text seems to offer two interpretations of the curse miracle: (1) one interpretation is created by the overall structure of the chapter and of the larger context of Mark 11–15; (2) the other interpretation is created by the words of Jesus (vv 22–25) that follow upon Peter's verification of the power of Jesus' curse. The first, or structural, interpretation arises from the fact that the author positions the pericope narrating Jesus' curse (vv 12–14) just before the cleansing of the temple (vv 15–19) and the pericope narrating the verification of the curse's power (vv 20–21) immediately after the cleansing.[45]

To understand what this enfolding of the cleansing of the temple within the story of the fig tree might mean to Jews and early Christians, one must appreciate the OT background of the imagery the author uses.[46] The OT, especially in its prophetic books, is replete with the symbolic use of trees or plants in general and of the fig tree and its fruit in particular to depict the scenario of God's coming to judge Israel, particularly in an eschatological context. *Both* the backdrop of the OT texts that speak of God's rejection of the bad figs in Israel (or more generally of his blasting of a bad tree) *and* the structural connection with the story of the cleansing of the temple must be borne in mind if Jesus' cursing of the fig tree is to be interpreted correctly. Especially when read in the light of the relevant OT texts, the author's careful dovetailing of the pericopes in 11:12–21 (curse of tree—cleansing of temple—verification of curse) indicates how he intends the two stories to interpret each other. Jesus' curse of the fig tree and his cleansing of the temple are two prophecies-in-action, both foretelling (and beginning to set in motion) God's eschatological judgment on the Jerusalem temple.

Besides looking back at the OT context, one must also look forward to Mark's subsequent narrative of Jesus' last days in Jerusalem, as well as his passion and death, if one is to appreciate fully this "structural" interpretation of the cursing of the fig tree. The cursing of the fig tree and the cleansing story it surrounds must be read within (1) Mark's overall depiction of Jesus' final clashes with the Jerusalem authorities and his final departure from them and the temple to the Mount of Olives (11:27–13:1); (2) Jesus' eschatological discourse, which begins with a prophecy of the temple's destruction (13:2), goes on to speak of its desolation (13:14), and moves to a hortatory conclusion that employs the metaphor of the fig tree putting forth leaves as a sign that summer (the eschatological harvest) is near (13:28–29); (3) the mention at Jesus' trial of his supposed prophecy about destroying the Jerusalem sanctuary "made by [human] hands" and within three days building another "not made by hands" (14:58); (4) the mockery at the cross, which recalls Jesus' supposed threat to destroy the sanctuary (15:29); and (5) the rending of the veil of the sanctuary as soon as Jesus dies (15:38). Within this overarching context that repeatedly sounds the theme of the temple's rejection and destruction as the end draws near, the "structural" interpretation of the cursing of the fig tree as a symbol of God's judgment on the temple must be judged to be primary. Not only does the story of the curse and its effect stand on either side of the cleansing of the temple; the story of the curse begins a theme that resounds throughout Mark 11–15.

This is not to say, however, that the verses on faith, prayer, and forgiveness (11:22–25) that immediately follow upon Peter's discovery of the curse's effect (11:20–21) are foreign bodies that have nothing to do with the context. The striking power of the words that Jesus speaks to the fig tree conjures up for Mark a chain of associations, expressed in a chain of Jesus' sayings. Mark uses the curse miracle as an occasion for exhorting his audience to faith, prayer, and forgiveness. The Marcan Jesus, who has just worked the curse miracle, makes a promise to his disciples—and through them to Mark's fellow Christians. The words of prayer spoken by these Christians, who like Jesus face great opposition from the powers that be, will have an efficacy equal to his words, provided that their words of prayer are spoken with faith (v 22) in the God for whom nothing is impossible (vv 23–24) and in a spirit of mutual forgiveness (v 25).

To be sure, this theme of the power of faith-filled prayer has links with other passages of Mark, including the reference to the failure of the Jerusalem temple to be a house of prayer for all the nations in 11:17. Nevertheless, one must admit that 11:22–25 as a unit is not as well integrated into the immediate context of Mark 11 and the larger context of Mark 11–15 as is the story of the cursing of the fig tree.[47] In particular, the stipulation that forgiveness is a necessary condition for having one's prayers heard (v 25) strikes the reader as a strange commentary on Jesus' destructive curse of a tree that symbolizes the temple. Obviously, as Mark exhorts Christians in v 25 to forgive as they pray, Mark does not think of the Christians' prayers as involving curses. Even prior to any analysis of sources and redaction, the reader cannot help but feel some tension here.

The sense of tension grows as one recalls that, throughout his Gospel, Mark rarely if ever presents Jesus' miracles as the direct results of Jesus' prayer to God or his faith in God. Yet 11:22–24 apparently makes Jesus' powerful curse of the fig tree a paradigm of the power of faith-filled prayer, despite the fact that this curse miracle, like most of the miracle stories in Mark, says nothing about Jesus praying or believing. One senses the Evangelist straining to make a connection between Jesus' sayings on faith and forgiveness (11:22–25) and Jesus' curse of the fig tree (11:12–14, 20–21) that is far from smooth or self-evident.

Up until this point, for methodological reasons I have purposely kept my observations on the level of Mark's composition and structure, without raising the question of possible sources and their redaction by Mark. Even on this level, we begin to see the problem of assessing the cursing of the fig tree as a historical event. It is attested in only one source (Mark), and there it fits snugly into the redactional structure and theological intent of the author. In this it already stands out from the less integrated sayings on faith, prayer, and forgiveness in 11:22–25.

D. TRADITION, SOURCES, AND REDACTION IN MARK 11

1. The Sources of Mark 11:22–25

Our initial impression of tension, gained from a survey of Mark's ordering of the material, is confirmed once we begin to look at the possible sources of chap. 11. We find that our sense that Jesus' sayings in 11:22–25 are not totally integrated into the Marcan context corresponds to the fact that, far from being attested only in Mark, the sayings are also witnessed, in one form or another, in Q, in the special tradition of Matthew, and even in distant parallels in Paul and John.

(1) A variant form of the saying on the power of prayer (Mark 11:22–23) to move a mountain (or alternately, a sycamore tree) is found in Q material (Matt 7:19–20 ‖ Luke 17:6) and more distantly in Paul's remark on the power of faith to move mountains in 1 Cor 13:2. Obviously, this saying, perhaps rooted in a popular proverb, circulated widely and independently of any larger context in first-generation Christianity (Mark, Q, and Paul).[48]

(2) Mark 11:24 makes an amazing promise: "All things whatsoever you pray and ask for, believe that you have [already] received [it], and it shall be yours [or: it shall be done for you]." This promise has no exact parallel beyond what Matthew copies from Mark in Matt 21:22. But the same basic promise of Jesus to his disciples that what they pray for they will certainly receive is voiced with the same Greek verb (*aiteō*) in various sayings of Jesus in Q and John— and, outside the sayings of Jesus, in the Epistle of James and the First Epistle of John. In fact, the promise Jesus speaks in Mark 11:24 finds a vague parallel three separate times in the words of Jesus in the Last Supper discourses of John's Gospel (14:13–14; 15:7; 16:23). John 15:7b provides even a partial parallel in the structure of the saying: "Whatsoever you wish, ask [for it], and it shall be done for you [or: it shall be yours]."[49] Clearly, we are dealing in these examples not with common literary sources but rather with similar yet independent streams of the oral tradition of Jesus' sayings, sayings that circulated without a set context.

(3) Mark 11:25, which makes the forgiveness "of your Father in heaven" dependent on Christians' forgiveness of one another when they pray, is the most intriguing saying of the three, since it parallels a special M saying that Matthew appends to his version of the Lord's Prayer: "For if you forgive people their transgressions, your heavenly Father will likewise forgive you yours" (Matt 6:14). Mark 11:25 has the substance of this saying, though not the exact wording: "And when you stand to pray, forgive anyone against whom you may have some grievance, that your Father in heaven may likewise forgive you your transgressions." Despite the Matthean-sounding "your Father in heaven," this

saying does not prove that Mark knew Matthew's Gospel; rather, he knew a stray saying of Jesus that also entered into the M tradition that Matthew drew upon. As a matter of fact, a key word in this saying is no more characteristic of Matthew than it is of Mark. Both forms of the saying use the noun *paraptōma* ("transgression"), a word that occurs nowhere else in Mark or Matthew. It is probably not even accurate to say that Mark knew the M tradition. He just happened to know this particular stray saying of Jesus, which in a slightly different form was also preserved in the M tradition and placed by Matthew in a different context, his commentary on the Our Father.

Hence what we already suspected on the basis of the structure and flow of thought in Mark 11 is now confirmed by source criticism. At the end of the story of the cursing of the fig tree Mark has brought together disparate sayings of Jesus from various sources, sayings that he ties together by the catchwords "believe" and "pray." These sayings also found their way into the traditions of Q and Matthew, and in vaguer forms into the traditions known to Paul and John. Mark draws together these stray sayings and introduces them at v 22 of chap. 11 for a specific purpose: to give the basically "dogmatic" message of the curse miracle (Jesus prophesies the destruction of the temple with a word-and-deed of power) a parenetic application as well (the prayer of Christians is guaranteed to have an equally powerful effect).

Thus, the tension we felt at a first reading of Mark 11:20–25 is confirmed and explained by an analysis of the sources. The sayings that make up the catechesis on prayer, faith, and forgiveness come from various sources; therefore the ending of the Marcan curse miracle is not their original setting or context. In fact, these stray logia apparently floated without a set context in the sayings tradition of first-generation Christianity before they wound up in the traditions of Mark, Q, and Matthew. Hence most likely it is Mark himself who has put these sayings together and placed them at this precise point in chap. 11 for his own parenetic purposes.[50] In this the sayings of 11:22–25 are not unlike the various sayings that make up the catechesis of 9:42–50 (or even 9:33–50), which is likewise created by Mark out of stray logia strung together by catchwords, and which likewise briefly interrupts the flow of the narrative.[51]

As one might expect, the succession of dovetailed pericopes in Mark 11 actually flows more smoothly when Mark's catechesis on faith is removed: the triumphal entry looks forward to the cleansing of the temple, the cursing of the fig tree looks forward both to the cleansing and to the discovery of the withered tree the next day, the cleansing of the temple resumes the triumphal entry and looks forward to the challenge to Jesus' authority the next day, the discovery of the withered fig tree the next day completes the story of the cursing and interprets the cleansing of the temple, and the challenge to Jesus' authority picks up on his authoritative act of cleansing the temple the day before. Dovetailing or "intercalation" is a hallmark of Mark and apparently of some of the narrative traditions he inherited.[52] Indeed, chap. 11 provides a striking example of double dovetailing, as the succession of the three main events (entrance into Jerusalem—cleansing of the temple—challenge to Jesus' authority) is melded with the two-part story of the cursing of the fig tree. Structurally, the loose chain of sayings in the catechesis on faith and prayer only gets in the way of the double intercalation that is the backbone of the chapter's whole narrative. One is therefore not surprised to learn from source criticism that they are a secondary addition by Mark.

2. The Existence of a Pre-Marcan Complex Behind Chap. 11

These two insights, that the chain of sayings in 11:22–25 is inserted into a previously existing composition and that this prior composition displays the intercalation typical of Mark and at least some of his narrative sources, make a further conclusion about the sources of chap. 11 very likely. If Mark is responsible for an insertion (vv 22–25) that slightly disrupts the flow of thought and narrative in chap. 11, presumably the carefully ordered material he disrupted existed before him. In other words, prior to Mark's insertion of 11:22–25, there existed an ordered narrative composed by some pre-Marcan author. This pre-Marcan narrative contained, in an intercalated pattern, the stories of the triumphal entry, the cursing of the fig tree, the cleansing of the temple, the verification of the effect of the curse on the tree, and the challenge to Jesus' authority.

There is an additional indication that the story of the cursing of the fig tree was already part of this pre-Marcan narrative complex that Mark took over. It is the puzzling parenthetical comment in the story of the cursing of the tree (v 13e): "For (*gar*) it was not the season for figs." Whatever the meaning of this clause, it is typical of the enigmatic *gar* ("for") clauses that Mark inserts into or appends to traditional material that he takes over and redacts in his Gospel. The most famous of these *gar* clauses is the one that ends the Greek text of Mark (16:8): "For they were afraid." In some of Mark's narratives his *gar* clauses create difficulty either because they are laconic and enigmatic (so in 16:8) or because they seem awkward or out of place in the story, i.e., they appear to explain a statement made somewhere else in the pericope.[53]

A prime example of an awkwardly placed *gar* clause occurs in the story of the finding of the empty tomb (16:1–8). In 16:4 the women coming to the tomb see that the stone in front of the tomb has been rolled away, "for (*gar*) it was very large." This clause at the end of v 4 obviously does not explain why the stone had been rolled away or why the women saw that it had been rolled away. According to the flow of thought, the *gar* clause actually belongs with v 3, where the women wonder on the way to the tomb: "Who will roll the stone away from the entrance to the tomb for us?" The reason why they are anxious about this question is that they cannot perform this feat for themselves (cf. *hēmin*, "for" or "by ourselves"), "for the stone was very large." In other words, the reason given at the end of v 4 really belongs at the end of v 3.

Since, as most commentators admit, an earlier form of the story of the empty tomb lies behind the present Marcan narrative in 16:1–8,[54] it is not difficult to imagine what has happened. Mark has inserted a parenthetical clause (a *gar* clause) to explain the women's difficulty, but—not being the best of Greek stylists—he has inserted it clumsily in the wrong place.[55] I would suggest that something similar may have happened at the end of 11:13. Again a *gar* clause seems to have been inserted secondarily, creating confusion rather than clarity. It has caused countless commentators to ask the obvious question: If it was not the season for figs, why did Jesus bother looking for any?[56]

My purpose here is not to debate the precise meaning of 11:13e, though it is an intriguing point that has created a flood of literature.[57] My point is that this enigmatic and perhaps poorly placed *gar* clause joins other signals in the text to persuade us that Mark has redacted a previously existing story of the cursing of the fig tree. In all probability, even prior to Mark's editorial work, the story of the curse miracle already existed in a dovetailed pattern within a narrative complex made up of the stories of chap. 11 minus the sayings in vv 22–25. In other words, it is a pre-Marcan author of the first Christian generation who is responsible for the intercalated stories Mark has taken over and redacted in chap. 11.

3. The Sources of the Pre-Marcan Author

Is it possible to move back farther in time and ask what this pre-Marcan author received from his tradition and what he created? Can we know anything about the literary units he was able to use as his building blocks? Here things must obviously become more speculative; but one important factor allows us to suggest a probable hypothesis: the parallel but independent tradition of John's Gospel. Outside of his Passion Narrative and the cycle of stories in chap. 6 (the feeding of the multitude, the walking on the water, the request for a sign, sayings about bread, and Peter's confession of faith), John's Gospel shares very few narratives and story lines with Mark's Gospel. By the time we reach Mark 11, however, we are approaching the Passion Narrative; indeed, some would say that we are already in the Passion Narrative in the wide sense of the word.[58] And so we need not be surprised to find in John's Gospel independent parallels to some of the pericopes of Mark 11.

Anyone acquainted with the Fourth Gospel is not startled to discover that the pericopes in John that parallel material in Mark 11 are not put together in the same order as in Mark. One of the fascinating features of the Fourth Gospel is that it often has scattered throughout its narrative events that stand together in the Synoptics.[59] Such is the case here. John's Gospel does contain accounts of Jesus' triumphal entry into Jerusalem, the cleansing of the temple, and a challenge from the Jerusalem authorities in response to the cleansing; but they do not occur together in one chapter and in the Marcan order.

The one event that is positioned roughly at the same place in both Mark and John is the triumphal entry (Mark 11:1–11 || John 12:12–19).[60] But John does not have the cleansing of the temple follow upon the triumphal entry. John's account of the cleansing of the temple occurs at the beginning of the public ministry (John 2:13–22) instead of at its end, as in Mark 11:15–17.

John's narrative of the cleansing clearly bears his theological fingerprints. Motifs unique to John's narrative of the cleansing include: (1) the occurrence of the first of three Passovers (mentioned in chaps. 2, 6, and 11–19), which serve to structure and color the whole of John's presentation of the public ministry; (2) the interpretation of the death and resurrection of Jesus as the destruction and raising up of the temple of his body (2:19–21); and (3) the fuller understanding of Scripture and of Jesus' ministry that only the events of Jesus' final Passover can give to his disciples (2:22).

Despite all these Johannine characteristics, the basic elements found in the Marcan account of the cleansing of the temple are present in John's account as well: close to Passover, Jesus comes to Jerusalem with his disciples (John 2:13,17 = Mark 11:1,15), enters the temple (2:14 = Mark 11:11,15), drives out the merchants and the money-changers (2:15 = Mark 11:15), and rebukes the authorities for perverting the holy "house" of the temple into a place of business (2:16 = Mark 11:17). In both versions, the account ends with the citation of Scripture to interpret Jesus' action (2:17 = Mark 11:17). Thus, the cleansing of the temple in Mark 11:15–17 clearly parallels the same event in John 2:13–17 step by step.

What we may not see so clearly and quickly is that the final pericope in Mark 11, the challenge of the Jerusalem officials to Jesus' authority after the cleansing (11:27–33), is also paralleled in John. In Mark 11 the challenge is a separate story, placed on the next day and separated from the cleansing by the verification of the curse miracle (11:20–25). This tends to obscure somewhat the link between the cleansing and the challenge to Jesus. Yet the challenge to Jesus in Mark 11:27–33 obviously harks back to the cleansing in 11:15–19. At the end of the story of the cleansing Mark notes that the high priests and the scribes heard Jesus' critique and sought to destroy him (11:18). This hostility is picked up in 11:27–33, when the officials challenge Jesus in the temple with the question (v 28): "By what authority do you do these things?"

The equivalent confrontation in John is narrated not as a separate event on a different day, but as the conclusion of the story of the cleansing (2:13–22) in 2:18–22. As soon as the relevant Scripture verse is cited about the temple "house" (2:17), "the Jews" (John's set term for the hostile authorities in Jerusalem) challenge Jesus in the temple with the question: "What sign do you show us [to justify or legitimize the fact] that you do these things?" Remarkably, in both Mark and John this question about Jesus' right or authority to cleanse the temple ends with a clause containing the same Greek words: *tauta poieis* ("you do these things").

This is a good reminder that, for all the redactional differences, we are dealing with the same basic story. In both Mark and John, after and because of the cleansing, the Jerusalem officials challenge Jesus to give some proof of his authorization, some explanation or reason why "you do these things." In both narratives Jesus answers not directly but enigmatically, with either a counter-question or a riddle-like saying. Since this close logical link between the cleansing of the temple and the challenge to Jesus is found independently in both Mark and John, the parallel suggests that originally the challenge to Jesus followed immediately upon the cleansing of the temple—the order that John's narrative preserves.[61]

The upshot of this analysis is that, for all the differences in order and language, Mark and John both witness to a very early complex of narrative material that recounted Jesus' entry into Jerusalem, his cleansing of the temple, and the challenge to his action that the Jerusalem authorities then pose.[62] Thus, all three major building blocks of Mark 11 were present in the primitive tradition that the pre-Marcan author knew and used. What is equally significant is what apparently was not present in the earliest discernible tradition that narrated these three events. While John shows full knowledge of the triumphal entry, the cleansing, and the subsequent challenge to Jesus' authority, he shows no trace of the story of the cursing of the fig tree. Indeed, since Matthew is dependent on Mark for his version of the story, no independent version of this miracle story can be found anywhere else in the Four Gospels.[63] This suggests that, while the earliest tradition of Jesus' last days in Jerusalem knew of the successive events of entry, cleansing, and challenge, it did not contain any tradition about the cursing of the fig tree. In the primitive Gospel tradition entry, cleansing, and challenge followed immediately upon one another, with no intercalation of other events.

Yet it is difficult to conceive of the cursing of the fig tree circulating as an isolated story. Its whole raison d'être is to interpret the cleansing of the temple, which in turn interprets the curse miracle. One is hard-pressed to imagine what function or meaning the cursing of the fig tree would have apart from the climactic final days of Jesus in Jerusalem, when he is facing the fatal hostility of the temple authorities—and more specifically what function or meaning it would have apart from the cleansing of the temple.

Hence, I suggest that the most probable sketch of the history of the tradition in Mark 11 is as follows. In the beginning, quite early on in the first Christian generation, the stories of Jesus' triumphal entry, his cleansing of the temple, and the temple officials' challenge to his authority were told as a single block of material, a narrative unit in which one story followed immediately upon the other. Perhaps we have here an early sign of a primitive yet already expanding Passion Narrative, reflected in different ways in both Mark's and John's tradition. As the passion tradition developed, a pre-Marcan author sought to emphasize that the cleansing of the temple was not an act of reform and purification but rather a prophetic judgment on the temple.[64] He accomplished this by creating the story of the cursing of the fig tree and wrapping it around the account of the cleansing. By mutual interpretation, the two intercalated stories made clear that Jesus was not urging the temple's reform but pronouncing the temple's doom.

E. THE HISTORICITY OF THE CURSE MIRACLE IN MARK 11:12–14, 20–21

We have concluded from our study of the composition and sources of Mark 11 that (1) the curse miracle of vv 12–14, 20–21 is an interpretation of the cleansing story and that (2) this interpretation was created by a pre-Marcan author as he developed the earliest traditions about Jesus' entry into Jerusalem, his cleansing of the temple, and the challenge to his authority. It remained for Mark himself to give the curse miracle a parenetic as well as a "dogmatic" meaning by tacking on the chain of sayings on faith, prayer, and forgiveness in 11:22–25. In short, the story of the cursing of the fig tree has no claim to go back to the public ministry of the historical Jesus. It is a *theologoumenon*, a theological idea or affirmation put into the form of an apparently historical narrative.[65] It was created by the composer of a block of pre-Marcan tradition to illuminate the meaning of the cleansing of the temple.

Is this conclusion drawn from composition, source, and tradition criticism confirmed by the criteria of historicity? As a matter of fact, the conclusion that Mark 11:12–14,20–21 does not come from the historical Jesus is supported by two primary criteria of historicity, discontinuity and coherence. To refresh the memory of the reader: (1) According to the criterion of discontinuity, those words or deeds of Jesus that are *discontinuous* with the OT and Judaism before him and with Christianity after him are likely to be historical. (2) According to the criterion of coherence, those words or deeds of Jesus that *cohere* with other words and deeds of his already judged to be historical on other grounds may well be historical. Interestingly, the cursing of the fig tree runs diametrically counter to these two criteria.

Curse miracles or punitive miracles are known both to the OT and to later Christian literature. Yet, with the exception of Mark 11:12–14,20–21 (along with the Matthean parallel), they are completely absent from the miracles of Jesus' public ministry as recounted in the Four Gospels. In the OT, punitive miracles include the ten plagues of Egypt, culminating in the slaughter of the first-born (Exod 7:14–12:30); the destruction of the Egyptian army in the Reed Sea (Exod 14:23–31); the withering of the hand of King Jeroboam (1 Kgs 13:1–5); the destruction of King Ahaziah's soldiers by fire from heaven at the order of Elijah (2 Kgs 1:9–12); the destruction of the small boys by bears because of the curse of Elisha (2 Kgs 2:23–24); the infliction of leprosy on the servant Gehazi at the order of his master Elisha (2 Kgs 5:27); the infliction of leprosy on King Uzziah for having presumed to offer incense in the temple (2 Chr 26:16–21, expanding on the tradition in 2 Kgs 15:5); and the scourging of Heliodorus in the temple (2 Macc 3:22–30).[66]

In the NT, the Acts of the Apostles shows how stories of punitive miracles began to grow in Christianity outside of the Four Gospels. In Acts Luke recounts the death of Ananias and Sapphira (Acts 5:1–11), the blinding of Saul/Paul (9:1–9), and the blinding of Bar-Jesus/Elymas (13:6–12). When we return to the apocryphal literature of the 2d century A.D., we find that the child Jesus, presented as a divine brat, becomes a worker of punitive miracles in the *Infancy Gospel of Thomas*.[67] Elsewhere in the apocryphal Gospels and Acts it is the miracles of apostolic figures rather than of Jesus that proliferate, including some punitive miracles.[68]

Hence, in the case of punitive miracles, a glaring discontinuity exists between almost the entire canonical tradition of Jesus' miracles and the only curse miracle found in the Four Gospels: Mark 11:12–14,20–21 (along with Matthew's redaction of the Marcan story in Matt 21:18–20). It is a miracle that is in perfect continuity with punitive miracles in the OT, the Acts of the Apostles, and the NT apocrypha, but a miracle that lacks coherence with the other miracles of Jesus in the Four Gospels.[69] Thus, the criteria of discontinuity and coherence converge with our analysis of the tradition history of the cursing of the fig tree to form a fairly firm judgment: in all likelihood, Mark 11:12–14,20–21 does not go back to the historical Jesus.[70] It is a creation of an early Christian author who took up the tradition of punitive miracles seen in the OT and so presaged the multiplication of such miracles in the Acts of the Apostles, the apocryphal Gospels and Acts of the 2d century, and later Christian literature. We may have here an intriguing case of Christianity being in continuity with the OT rather than with Jesus the Jew.[71]

V. THE MIRACULOUS CATCH OF FISH (LUKE 5:1–11 ‖ JOHN 21:1–14 [+ 15–19])[72]

When it came to judgments about historicity, both the Matthean story of the coin in the mouth of the fish and the Marcan story of the cursing of the fig tree suffered from having attestation in only one source. In itself, presence in only one source did not prove that either story was unhistorical. But when we added to this basic problem other difficulties (e.g., the coin miracle is never actually narrated, the curse miracle is the only punitive miracle of Jesus in the public ministry), a decision against historicity became the more probable judgment.

At first glance, the miraculous catch of fish seems to be in a better position. It has multiple attestation of sources: it is found in both the special Lucan tradition (L, in Luke 5:1–11) and the Johannine tradition known to the final redactor of the Fourth Gospel (John 21:1–14, plus the further tradition in vv 15–19).[73] Moreover, if we categorized the catch as a gift miracle, it would not, unlike the cursing of the fig tree, stand alone in its category; the feeding of the multitude and the wine miracle of Cana also qualify as gift miracles.[74]

Things, however, are never as simple as they first appear. The Lucan and Johannine versions of the catch of fish are replete with problems of tradition, source, and redaction criticism, not to mention numerous problems of interpretation in individual verses. For our purposes, though, two problems are pivotal:

(1) Luke places the catch toward the beginning of Jesus' public ministry (5:1–11); it coincides with the initial call of Peter, James, and John to follow Jesus. In the Fourth Gospel, the miracle occurs in the so-called epilogue of the Gospel (chap. 21) probably added by the final redactor after the Evangelist's death. In John 21, the miraculous catch is part of a post-resurrection appear-

ance of the risen Jesus to a group of seven disciples, including Peter and the sons of Zebedee. The appearance is connected with a mysterious breakfast by the Sea of Tiberias and a triple confession of Peter's love for Jesus that symbolically undoes Peter's triple denial of Jesus during the latter's trial. All these differences pose the first question: do Luke 5 and John 21 reflect two versions of the same basic story, or do we have here two different stories or incidents that are superficially similar?[75]

(2) If we decide that we are dealing with the same story or incident, we must face a second question: who preserved the original setting of the story, Luke or John? In other words, has the Lucan tradition retrojected a post-resurrection story into the public ministry, or has the Johannine tradition taken a story of the public ministry and turned it into a resurrection appearance?[76]

In my opinion, if we can solve these two major questions, the question of historicity that is the focus of this chapter will likewise be solved.

A. Do Luke 5:1–11 and John 21 Preserve the Same Basic Story?

The major differences between the Lucan and Johannine stories are obvious and need not be belabored. The Lucan story occurs toward the beginning of Jesus' public ministry and involves the call of those first disciples who will in due time form the core of the twelve apostles: Peter, James, and John. There is no indication that they have previously followed Jesus.[77] The catch of fish takes place after Jesus has used Peter's boat to teach the crowds standing on the shore of the Lake of Gennesaret (5:1–3).[78] When Peter's boat cannot handle the huge catch to which Jesus directs him, another boat carrying Peter's partners comes to help. Peter reacts to the miracle with a confession of sin and a plea that Jesus leave him. Jesus brushes aside Peter's fear and calls him and the sons of Zebedee to follow him.

In contrast, the Johannine story occurs after the resurrection—and, in the present form of John's Gospel, after Jesus has twice appeared to the disciples assembled in Jerusalem and after the Gospel seems to come to a conclusion in 20:30–31. In chap. 21, Jesus, at first unrecognized, appears on the shore of the Sea of Tiberias (= the Sea of Galilee, the Lucan Lake of Gennesaret) only after the disciples have embarked to go fishing (21:4). There are no crowds, there is only one boat, and Jesus never gets into the disciples' boat. When Peter recognizes Jesus from afar with the help of the beloved disciple, Peter swims to meet him (contrast the Lucan Peter asking Jesus to depart from him). When the disciples come to shore with their great catch, Jesus mysteriously supplies them with bread and fish already lying on a charcoal fire (21:9). The disciples have breakfast (v 12), at the end of which Jesus thrice asks Peter whether Peter loves him, Peter thrice replies affirmatively, and Jesus thrice charges Peter to feed his sheep (vv 15–17). Jesus concludes the dialogue with a call to Peter to follow him (v 19).

Despite all these differences, I agree with exegetes like Raymond E. Brown and Joseph A. Fitzmyer that we have here two alternate versions of the same basic story.[79] Behind the individual differences, many caused by the different redactional contexts and theologies of the two Gospels, one discerns the clear grid of the same story:[80]

1. A group of fishermen, among whom Peter is the chief actor, has spent the night fishing but has caught nothing (Luke 5:2–5; John 21:2–5).[81] Now daylight has come, and Jesus is on the scene.

2. With apparently supernatural knowledge, Jesus directs Peter and his colleagues to cast their nets into the water once again, with the explicit (John) or implicit (Luke) promise that now they will have success (Luke 5:4; John 21:6).

3. Peter and his colleagues trust and obey Jesus' command, with the result that many fish are caught (Luke 5:6; John 21:6).

4. The effect of the large number of fish on the nets is mentioned. In Luke, the nets are in danger of being torn asunder (Luke 5:6).[82] John instead mentions that, despite the great number of fish, the nets were not torn asunder (21:11). The ultimate result is the same, though: in spite of the extraordinary number of fish, and contrary to what one might expect, the nets are not torn to pieces with the resultant loss of the catch (Luke 5:7; John 21:8,10–11).

5. Peter is the only named disciple who reacts in a dramatic fashion to the miraculous event (Luke 5:8; John 21:7). In Luke he proclaims his sinfulness and begs Jesus to depart; in John he jumps overboard and swims to Jesus on shore. To be sure, in John 21 the beloved disciple recognizes Jesus' presence before Peter acts. But the vast majority of commentators hold that the Johannine author has added the beloved disciple, his hero and the source of his tradition, to the original story.[83] Indeed, one can see that, even in the final form of the story, the beloved disciple remains a marginal figure, being mentioned in 21:1–19 only in v 7. In any case, here as elsewhere in the Fourth Gospel the beloved disciple is never named.

6. In the third-person narrative in which the author directly speaks to his audience, Jesus (even the risen Jesus of John's narrative) is referred to simply as "Jesus"; Peter and Peter alone directly addresses Jesus as "Lord" (Luke 5:8; John 21:15–17).[84]

7. The other fishermen share in the action of catching the fish (Luke 5:6–7; John 21:6,8), but neither on sea nor on land do they (apart from the beloved disciple in John 21:7) say anything once the miracle begins.

8. At the end of each story, Jesus directly or indirectly issues a summons to Peter to follow him, with the verb *akoloutheō* ("follow") occurring in Luke 5:11 and John 21:19.

9. The abundant catch of fish symbolizes in each story the future missionary work and the resultant success of Peter and the other disciples. A further idea symbolized in each story is that the disciples, left to themselves in the night of this world, are doomed to failure. With Jesus' help and direction, they are granted startling success.

10. The same Greek words are used for many verbs and nouns in the two stories: e.g., embark (*embainō*), disembark (*apobainō*), follow (*akoloutheō*), net

(*diktyon*), fish (*ichthys*), a large number of fish (*plēthos* [*tōn*] *ichthyōn*), boat (*ploion*), night (*nyx*), and the sons of Zebedee (*hoi* [*huioi*] *tou Zebedaiou*). Since both stories are concerned with fishing, some of the agreements in vocabulary may be coincidental.

11. In both stories, at the moment when he reacts to the miraculous catch, Peter is referred to as "Simon Peter" (Luke 5:8; John 21:7). This point is especially remarkable because this is the only time in the Third Gospel that Luke uses the double name, while it is the regular way in which the redactor refers to Peter in John 21:1–14.

Looking at both the overall agreement in the basic content of the two narratives and some of the striking agreements in small details, I think it clear that we are dealing here with two alternate versions of the same story and not two different stories that are superficially similar.[85]

B. HAS LUKE OR JOHN PRESERVED THE ORIGINAL SETTING OF THE STORY?

Since Luke 5 and John 21 contain the same basic story, which has developed in different ways in the two Gospel traditions, the question naturally arises: Which Gospel has preserved the original setting of the story?[86] It is not surprising to see scholars stressing the difficulty of making a decision in the matter; no less a critic than Rudolf Bultmann felt constrained to change his mind on the subject during the course of his career.[87] Nor is it a question of "liberals" versus "conservatives." Along with the earlier Bultmann, scholars like Dibelius, Agnew, Dietrich, and Schürmann maintain that Luke's setting (the beginning of the public ministry) is prior, while, along with the later Bultmann, scholars like Grass, Smith, Klein, Marrow, Kasting, Brown, and Fitzmyer consider John's setting (a post-resurrection appearance) to be the original one.[88] There is no party line here.

Is there any way of adjudicating the claims of the two positions? In my view, when placed in the balance, the arguments of scholars like Klein, Brown, and Fitzmyer are weightier:

1. The single most impressive argument is what we might call the general flow of the Gospel tradition from a post-resurrection setting to a pre-resurrection setting.[89] Put simply: we have a number of convincing candidates for material that originally stood in a post-resurrection context (or material that was originally understood to be a saying of the risen Lord), material that was then secondarily retrojected into the framework of Jesus' earthly life and ministry. For example, many Catholic as well as Protestant exegetes today accept the likelihood that Jesus' famous charge to Peter at Caesarea Philippi (Matt 16:18–19: "You are Peter and upon this rock I will build my church . . .") derives from a tradition of a post-resurrection appearance of Jesus to Peter.[90] Something similar could be said of Jesus' empowering the local church to admit or excommunicate members with the "power of the keys" (Matt 18:15–18).[91] In our survey of sayings about the kingdom of God, we saw reasons for thinking that the sayings of Jesus that proclaim the coming of the

kingdom within the lifetime of some members of his audience (Mark 9:1; 13:30; Matt 10:23) were actually words of comfort spoken by Christian prophets to their communities during the first Christian generation. In due time these sayings were presented as prophecies that Jesus had spoken during his ministry.

To take another example: at least some of Jesus' lengthy discourses in John's Gospel are now deemed by scholars to be Christian homilies, which developed sayings or deeds of Jesus into a type of Christian midrash. This is the case, e.g., with the bread of life discourse in John 6. It follows upon and interprets the traditional story of the feeding of the multitude in terms of John's high christology. In John 6:34–58, Jesus himself is the bread of life that has come down from heaven. The post-Easter, Christian tone is especially clear in the last part of the discourse (John 6:53–58), which emphasizes in graphic language the presence of Christ in the eucharist: "He who eats my flesh and drinks my blood has eternal life. . . . for my flesh is real food, and my blood is real drink" (vv 54–55). A Christian homily on the eucharist has in the course of the Johannine tradition become a homily of the earthly Jesus, teaching in the synagogue at Capernaum (6:59).[92]

This retrojection of post-Easter material into the earthly life of Jesus is not restricted to sayings. As we have already seen, it is often claimed that some Gospel miracles did not originate in Jesus' public ministry but rather arose as creations of the early church, which then located these miracle stories in the ministry of Jesus to teach a particular lesson. For instance, in the chapter on exorcisms I judged the story of the Syrophoenician woman's daughter to be a creation of the early church, which placed it in the context of Jesus' earthly life in order to foreshadow the breaching of the wall between Jew and Gentile that Jesus' word and work would bring. Other scholars might nominate Jesus' walking on the water or his transfiguration as an example of this process of retrojection, though other scholars would dispute whether the transfiguration belongs to this category.[93]

Examples could be multiplied at will. The important point here is that, in contrast to this general flow of material from a post-Easter origin into the public ministry of Jesus, in the canonical Gospels there is no proof of a general flow in the opposite direction, i.e., a flow of the historical words and deeds of Jesus into a post-resurrection context. The church retrojected, it did not project. Indeed, putting aside for a moment the disputed case of John 21:1–14, I dare say that in the Four Gospels there is not one example of a story of Jesus' post-resurrection appearances that has a claim to be originally material from the public ministry, material that the church later projected into a post-Easter context.

All this only stands to reason. The early church had more than sufficient reason to retroject post-Easter material into the public ministry. By so doing, her life, teaching, worship, and mission were grounded in, legitimated by, and given an organic connection with the earthly Jesus, who was thus clearly identified with the risen Lord. What would move the church to take precious material about Jesus' earthly ministry and shift it into a post-resurrection context? What theological goal would be served? It is not by accident that we have many plausible candidates for material that was retrojected, but not one clear candidate for material that was projected.

2. While, in my judgment, this first argument is almost sufficient of itself to decide the question óf the original setting of Luke 5:1–11 ‖ John 21:1–14 (+ vv 15–19), some detailed observations about the two texts can give further support to this global argument:

(a) The reaction of Peter in Luke 5:8 to the miraculous catch of fish is startling and unusual in stories that depict Jesus calling people to discipleship during the public ministry: "Seeing [the miracle], Simon Peter fell on his knees before Jesus saying: 'Depart from me, for I am a sinful man, O Lord.'" Granted, to explain this reaction one could appeal to the general air of theophany that this miracle enjoys: it is the first revelation to Peter of Jesus' divine power. Amazement, terror, and a sense of one's own unworthiness and sinfulness are common reactions to theophanies inside and outside the Bible.[94] One sees it especially in the call of Isaiah (Isa 6:5–7). But is this sort of general observation really relevant to the particular case of Luke 5:1–11? Simply as a matter of fact, nowhere else in the Gospels is a concrete confession of one's sinfulness the first and most prominent reaction of a person who meets the earthly Jesus and is called by him to discipleship and/or ministry. Even in the case of ostensibly sinful people like Levi/Matthew (Mark 2:13–17 parr.), the reaction of the disciple who is called is not a confession of sins. Indeed, in Mark 2:13–17 Levi apparently reacts by throwing a party.[95] The same basic observation could be made about the reaction to or acclamation of the miracles Jesus works in the Gospels; they do not first of all call forth in the recipients or spectators a confession of sinfulness.[96]

Hence the motif of Peter's initial reaction to the revelation of Jesus, namely, that he is a sinner, demands some further explanation. The context and flow of John 21 supply this. After the miraculous catch of fish, Jesus asks Peter three times whether Peter loves him, and three times Peter professes his love. From patristic times onward this scene has been rightly recognized as a reversal of Peter's triple denial of Jesus during the latter's trial.[97] To be sure, the precise formulation of Peter's triple confession of love in John 21:15–17 is very much a product of the Johannine author's creativity. But it does point up the sort of context that would make Peter's sudden confession of his sinfulness after the miraculous catch of fish perfectly intelligible: a meeting between the risen Jesus and the chief disciple who denied him during the Passion.

These observations are connected with another intriguing point: behind Luke 5:1–11 ‖ John 21:1–17 we may have some remnants of a primitive tradition narrating the initial resurrection appearance of Jesus, i.e., the appearance granted to Peter. The appearance to Peter is highlighted in one of the earliest Christian creeds we possess (1 Cor 15:3–5) and is also mentioned in Luke 24:34. Yet, while we have stories of appearances of Jesus to Mary Magdalene, to the two disciples on the road to Emmaus, and to the group of eleven disci-

ples (the Twelve minus Judas), we have no full story of what 1 Cor 15:5 claims
was the first of all appearances, the appearance to "Cephas" (= Peter).

However, we may have the remnants of such a story contained within the
account of the miraculous catch of fish. This would explain a number of puzzling aspects in the Johannine version in particular: why Peter is the focus of
the story, why he has gone back to his old trade of fishing (Jesus has died and
Peter expects nothing further), why he is the only actor who speaks to Jesus,
why the miracle moves from failure to success, why the miracle consists of an
event symbolizing a widespread (worldwide?) mission, why Jesus is not with
the disciples when the story begins, why the disciples do not at first recognize
Jesus, and why the miracle culminates in a conversation between (only!) Peter
and Jesus that involves both Peter's sinfulness and Jesus' overriding call to
Peter to follow him in his mission.

(b) If Luke received a story about an initial post-resurrection appearance of
Jesus to Peter that involved a catch of fish in the Sea of Galilee, and if Luke
wanted to use this story within the intended framework of his Gospel, he had
to transform this story into a call story placed at the beginning of the public
ministry.[98] In his unique view of the events of Easter Sunday, Luke has all the
resurrection appearances take place in and around Jerusalem on that one day,
a day that culminates with Jesus ascending to heaven (Luke 24:50–53). That
such a schema is Luke's own artificial arrangement, invented to suit his literary
and theological purposes, is made clear by Luke himself. After penning chap.
24 of his Gospel, Luke blithely opens his second volume, the Acts of the Apostles, with Jesus still appearing to his disciples on earth for forty days after the
resurrection. Only at the end of this forty-day period does Jesus ascend to
heaven (Acts 1:6–11). No attentive reader can miss the sharp contrast between
the scenario in Acts 1 and the restriction of appearances to Easter Sunday and
the environs of Jerusalem in Luke 24.

Within the literary straitjacket of Luke 24, there was no room for a quick
excursion up to Galilee for an appearance of Jesus to Peter while the latter was
fishing. If the story of the miraculous catch was to be used by Luke at all, it
had to be used as an event in the public ministry. Once that was decided, where
else could it be used except partly in place of and partly in conjunction with
Mark's tradition of the call of the first four disciples while they were fishing in
the Sea of Galilee (Mark 1:16–20)?[99] This placement would naturally appeal
to Luke, the evangelist with the keenest interest in human emotions and psychology, since the miraculous catch provides a motive for following Jesus that
the terse account in Mark 1:16–20 lacks.[100] In other words, if we grant that
the miraculous catch of fish was originally a resurrection appearance, we can
readily divine why Luke would have made it part of the beginnings of the
public ministry instead. If, however, it was originally a story about the earthly
ministry of Jesus, we are hard-pressed to explain what would have prompted a
Johannine author to transform it into a resurrection appearance and then insist
on tacking it onto an already completed Gospel.

(c) Paradoxically, a further argument in favor of the catch of fish being originally a post-resurrection story is the interpretation given Luke 5:1–11 by Schürmann, who strenuously defends the opposite view, namely, that the placement of the catch in the earthly life of Jesus represents the original setting of the story. Despite his theoretical position, Schürmann is constantly forced by his own careful exegesis of Luke 5:1–11 to understand the story in what is equivalently a post-resurrection context. In Luke 5:1–11, says Schürmann, Jesus is seen as the exalted Lord, who is summoning Peter not to some initial discipleship but to his future vocation as an apostle.[101] Accordingly, Schürmann considers Luke's use of the double name "Simon Peter" in v 8 an anticipation of Simon's later apostolic office and activity in the church. From the beginning of the Lucan pericope, Jesus is depicted as the majestic Lord present in the midst of his people; at the same time, the boat from which Jesus teaches in 5:3 gives Jesus that distance from the crowd which befits his majesty. According to Schürmann, Christian faith already sees in this story the Jesus who is Lord, the Jesus who is exalted in the heavenly world, whence he speaks his word to the church. Peter's address to Jesus as "Lord" in 5:8 reinforces the theme of Jesus' transcendent majesty.

It is telling that Schürmann gives the following interpretation of Peter's confession of his sinfulness: "The pericope also knows about [Peter's] subsequent fall (Luke 22:33–34,54–62) and conversion (Luke 22:32,61–62; cf. John 21:15–19); hence he [Luke] chooses for his narrative the words 'I am a sinful man'. . . ."[102] When Simon falls down before Jesus, the latter speaks like a heavenly being appearing to mere mortals: "Fear not!" Schürmann comments that Jesus addresses Peter in the same way that "he will one day address people as the Risen and Exalted One (Matt 28:10; Rev 1:17)."[103] All in all, I can imagine no better argument in favor of the position that Luke 5:1–11 is derived from a post-resurrection appearance, an appearance that has been subsequently reworked to meld with and partially substitute for Mark's story of the call of the first disciples. As Schürmann willy-nilly indicates, the original post-Easter setting still shines through Luke's adaptation of the story.

(d) A final argument may be fashioned from form criticism. The unusual setting of this miracle story in a post-resurrection context may help explain its strange form, which defies easy classification. Theissen tries to place the miraculous catch among the "gift miracles" or miracles of divine provision.[104] The other full examples of this type are the feeding of the multitude and the wine miracle at Cana. However, the miraculous catch is basically different from these two miracles. In these two stories, the direct purpose of Jesus' miraculous provision of loaves and fish in the wilderness and of wine at Cana is to meet the real and immediate physical needs of people lacking food or drink. As soon as the food or drink is supplied by Jesus, it is eaten or drunk. Any symbolic sense rests upon the literal one of supplying food to satisfy people's physical hunger and thirst.

Not so with the miraculous catch of fish. So primary is the symbolic theme of the call to ministry that the "practical" theme of supplying fish to be actually eaten evaporates. In Luke 5:11, the disciples, who have been supplied by Jesus with the fish they were seeking, immediately leave "all things"—including, presumably, the catch—to follow Jesus. In John 21, the disciples do engage in a sort of mystical breakfast with Jesus, a meal with eucharistic overtones (21:12–13). But it is not clear that the meal uses the fish just caught. The flow of the narrative in 21:8–13 is somewhat confused, probably because the story of the miraculous catch has been joined to another story about table fellowship with the risen Lord. But apparently, at least in the present form of the narrative, Jesus himself supplies the bread and fish for the breakfast (21:13): "Jesus comes and takes the bread [that was already on the shore with him when the disciples arrived; cf. v 9] and gives it to them, and likewise the fish [already lying on the charcoal fire when the disciples arrived on shore]."[105] In any event, Peter, the beloved disciple, and presumably the other disciples leave behind their catch to follow Jesus after the breakfast (21:19–20). Nothing is said of the use or disposal of the one hundred and fifty-three fish just caught. Thus, the form of "gift miracle" has been absorbed into the more dominant form of a post-resurrection appearance that confers an apostolic commission—another sign, even in Luke 5, of the original setting of the story.[106]

Consequently, I think that the preponderance of evidence favors the view that in the miraculous catch of fish we have a story of a post-resurrection appearance that in the Lucan tradition has been turned into a call story at the beginnings of Jesus' public ministry. Since the quest for the historical Jesus as defined in *A Marginal Jew* is concerned only with the empirically verifiable life of Jesus up until his death, and since our investigation of his miracles is concerned specifically with whether any miracle stories go back to incidents in the public ministry, a story about a post-resurrection appearance automatically drops out of consideration. This is not to pass any judgment on the reality of such an appearance; it is simply to observe that the material does not fall under the narrow limits of our study.

I should note that some critics take a quite different approach to the tradition history of the miraculous catch, though the practical conclusion of their position winds up the same as mine. Instead of seeing the origins of John 21:1–14 ‖ Luke 5:1–11 in a story of a post-resurrection appearance, some scholars suggest that the story was spun out of Jesus' summons to his disciples as recorded in Mark 1:17 (or, alternately, Luke 5:10): "Come, follow me, and I will make you fishers of men [i.e., *anthrōpōn*, human beings]."[107] While I doubt that such a one-liner in the Marcan tradition is the source of a lengthy miracle story in the Johannine tradition, the adoption of this theory would make no difference in the final result of our investigation. In either scenario (post-resurrection appearance or saying turned into miracle story), the story of the miraculous catch of fish does not go back to a startling action of the historical Jesus that his disciples or audience interpreted as a miracle during the public ministry.

VI. THE WALKING ON THE WATER (MARK 6:45–52 ‖ MATT 14:22–33 ‖ JOHN 6:16–21)[108]

A. THE SOURCES

The story of Jesus walking on the water is often compared to the story of the miraculous catch of fish in John 21:1–14 or to the appearance of the risen Jesus in Luke 24:36–49.[109] Some suggest that the story of the walking on the water and John 21:1–14 both arose as accounts of the risen Jesus appearing to his disciples, who were in a boat on the Sea of Galilee, while he was walking by or on the sea. Both stories also enjoy attestation in two different Gospel sources, one of them being John.

There the similarities end. The two independent sources for the walking on the water are Mark and John;[110] this automatically pushes the origin of the story back at least into the first Christian generation. Matthew basically follows Mark, though he inserts into the story the additional incident of Peter trying to walk to Jesus across the water (Matt 14:28–32a). For reasons that are probably more literary than theological, Luke simply omits the story.[111]

What is especially intriguing about the independent agreement between Mark and John is that it extends not just to this one story but to a whole primitive pattern or grid of stories about Jesus' ministry in Galilee. The grid stretches from the feeding of the multitude to Peter's confession of faith. As I have already noted when treating other Marcan miracle stories (e.g., the blind man of Bethsaida), most of Mark 6–8 comprises a double cycle of stories, dubbed by some critics "the bread section" of Mark's Gospel. The bread section, in which most of the pericopes contain some mention of "bread" (*artos*), extends from Mark 6:30 to 8:21. The first part of the bread section begins with the feeding of the five thousand (6:30–44) and ends with the healing of the deaf-mute (7:32–37). The second part of the bread section begins with the feeding of the four thousand (8:1–10) and ends with the healing of the blind man of Bethsaida (8:22–26), just after Jesus has excoriated his disciples for being blind to the mystery of his own person, a mystery that he has tried to reveal to them through the two feedings (8:14–21). The healing of the blind man then leads into the story of Peter's confession of faith at Caesarea Philippi, where the spiritual sight of the disciples is partially healed (like the first stage of the healing of the blind man of Bethsaida): Peter confesses that Jesus is the Messiah (8:29).

For our purposes, what is significant about the bread section is that not just the two feeding stories but a whole succession of events is repeated in the two parts of the section. In the first section (6:30–7:37), the story line progresses (1) *from* a miraculous feeding (of five thousand) (2) *through* a crossing of the Sea of Galilee by Jesus and his disciples (the walking on the water), an arrival on the other side and a dispute with Jewish leaders that involves the key word "bread" (3) *to* miracles of healing. In the shorter second section (8:1–26), the story line again progresses (1) *from* a miraculous feeding (of four thousand) (2) *through* a crossing of the Sea of Galilee by Jesus and his disciples, an arrival on the other side, a dispute with Jewish leaders who demand a sign from heaven, and conflict between Jesus and his disciples over bread (3) *to* a miracle of healing. At the culmination of the double cycle comes Peter's confession of faith in Jesus as Messiah at Caesarea Philippi. It would appear that Mark, who loves "duality" large and small, knew two versions of an early catechetical pattern recounting Jesus' ministry in Galilee and incorporated both versions—with a good deal of his redactional theology added—into his account of the Galilean ministry as it approaches its climax.

What makes this idea of a pre-Marcan "bread cycle" or pattern of events in the Galilean ministry likely is that John 6, the only chapter in the Fourth Gospel totally dedicated to Jesus' activity in Galilee, seems to reflect this same primitive pattern. Apparently, when the Fourth Evangelist, whose traditions were rooted mostly in Jerusalem and Judea, wanted to create a relatively long account of Jesus' ministry in Galilee, he had to reach back to a traditional pattern well-known in 1st-century Christianity.[112] Once again, the story line moves (1) *from* a miraculous feeding of the crowd (which also mentions in passing Jesus' healing of the sick) (2) *through* a crossing of the Sea of Galilee by Jesus and his disciples (the walking on the water), an arrival on the other side, a dispute with the crowd (which develops into John's stock group, "the Jews") about their demand for a sign (a demand involving the key theme of "bread"), and conflict between Jesus and his disciples, (3) *to* a climactic confession of faith by Peter in Jesus as the Holy One of God (this time at Capernaum). To be sure, decades of ongoing tradition as well as redactional changes by Mark and John have given the first bread section, the second bread section, and John 6 each its own character; the parallels are by no means perfect. Nevertheless, the basic grid is still detectable beneath the many variations on the theme.

As far as the story of the walking on the water is concerned, the significance of this analysis is twofold: (1) the walking on the water was known independently to both the Marcan and Johannine traditions; (2) early on in both traditions it had become attached to the story of the feeding of the five thousand as its immediate sequel.[113] Whatever else may be said about the walking on the water, it cannot be made to disappear by waving that famous verbal magic wand of exegetes, "a late legend." Be it a legend or a historical event, the story of Jesus walking on the water did not develop relatively late in the Gospel tradition. Sometime in the first Christian generation it already stood attached to the feeding of the five thousand.

Having seen that the story enjoys multiple attestation of sources (but not forms), let us compare and contrast the two independent versions Mark and John offer, with a view to asking what a more primitive form of the story might have looked like.

B. THE STORY IN MARK AND JOHN

1. Mark's Version of the Story (6:45–51)

Mark's story is told largely from the viewpoint of Jesus.[114] Immediately after the collection of twelve baskets full of fragments from the feeding of the five thousand, Jesus—without any explanation—forces his disciples to get into the boat that had brought them to the site of the feeding and to go before him to Bethsaida (v 45). After Jesus says farewell to the crowd and dismisses them, he goes off to the mountain to pray (v 46). In the evening, the boat is out on the sea, while Jesus is alone on the land (v 47). (Mark has thus set up the basic problem of the separation of Jesus from his disciples, which will now be remedied by the epiphany of Jesus). In v 48, Jesus sees that, as they try to row to their destination, the disciples are straining at the oars, since the wind is blowing against them.

Sometime between 3 and 6 a.m. ("about the fourth watch of the night"),[115] Jesus performs the central and defining action of the pericope: he comes to the disciples by walking upon the sea. Mark emphasizes Jesus' purpose in performing this miracle by stating in v 48d that "he wished to pass by them." The use of the phrase "to pass by someone" in OT narratives of theophany illuminates the point Mark is making in v 48d: Jesus wished to reveal himself to his disciples in all his divine majesty and power by demonstrating his dominion over the unruly forces of wind, sea, and waves. He acts toward them as Yahweh or Yahweh's personified divine Wisdom acts in the OT.

However, while all the disciples see Jesus walking on the water, they mistake him for a ghost (perhaps the night is thought to impede their vision), and so they cry out in terror (vv 49–50a). In response to their misconception and fear, Jesus adds his revealing word to his revealing action by speaking a formula reminiscent of OT theophanies (v 50c): "Have courage, it is I [literally in Greek: "I am," egō eimi], fear not." Jesus then enters the boat and the wind dies down (v 51ab).[116] The typical Marcan reaction on the part of the disciples is total astonishment, "for they did not understand [the mystery of who Jesus is] on the basis of [epi] the [miracle of the] loaves, but their heart was hardened" (vv 51c–52).[117]

Both content and structure make clear what is the main point of Mark's presentation: it is the epiphany of Jesus, revealed in divine power before his disciples.[118] Jesus' action of walking on the sea is quite literally the center of the pericope: 64 words precede the central statement of the narrative ("and he comes to them, walking on the sea; and he wished to pass by them") and 64 words follow it. To be sure, one should not overemphasize this exact balance in the word count, since (1) most likely Mark was not keeping an exact count of words as he composed his narrative, and (2) text-critical decisions could alter the exact number of words in either half of the pericope (e.g., ēn palai in v 47 and ek perissou in v 51). Nevertheless, the main point is clear. In Mark's composition, Jesus' act of walking on the water to reveal himself in divine majesty and power to his disciples stands at the very center of the story, while his solemn self-revelation (v 50: *egō eimi*) stands a little further along in the text as the verbal climax.[119] Simply on structural grounds alone, his epiphany on the sea cannot be brushed aside as a secondary point in favor of some other theme, such as the rescue of the disciples from danger or their lack of understanding.

In fact, as we can already see, strictly speaking there is no grave danger from which the disciples are clamoring to be rescued. Unlike the story of the stilling of the storm (Mark 4:35–41), the walking on the water does not depict either a fierce storm swamping the disciples' boat with waves (4:37) or the panicky disciples crying out to Jesus in fear for their lives (4:38). Rather, in 6:49 they cry out in terror at the sight of Jesus, not at the sight of the waves. The only difficulty the disciples face is a contrary wind, which makes the rowing difficult and the going slow. When Jesus enters the boat, his mere presence—and not some spoken command as in Mark 4:39—makes the wind die down. Presumably, this in turn makes the rowing easier and the going swifter; but so far is this point from being a major concern of the story that it is never mentioned. Hence, this story should not be called a "sea-rescue epiphany."[120] It is an epiphany of Jesus pure and simple. There is no rescue of the disciples, because there is no serious danger from which the disciples need to be rescued.

Will this analysis—not sea rescue but epiphany—hold true for John 6:16–21 as well?

2. John's Version of the Story (John 6:16–21)

a. The question of John's use of his source. In agreement with Schnackenburg and many other critics, I think that John's version of the story is on the whole more primitive than Mark's.[121] This in itself is a good reminder that tradition history is tricky business. It may seem strange that John's Gospel, written toward the end of the second Christian generation, should preserve some material in an earlier form than Mark's Gospel, written at the end of the first Christian generation. But the date of a Gospel's composition by no means guarantees the age or state of the various traditions it contains. In fact, the walking on the water is probably not the only case in which John's Gospel retains tradition in an earlier form than the Synoptics do; one need only think of John's dating of the Last Supper and Jesus' death. An important corollary of this needs to be emphasized: when using the criterion of multiple attestation of sources, one should not automatically presume that a source written down in the first generation is always more reliable than a source written down in the second.

The primitive nature of John's version of the walking on the water is seen not simply in the notably shorter narrative (87 words versus 139 words) but more importantly in the lack of typically Johannine theological commentary or symbolism (cf. Mark's theological commentary in Mark 6:51–52). It is odd that, on the whole, "John the Divine" gives us a less theologically interpreted narrative than does Mark.[122] At best, the Evangelist's hand can be found in the mention in v 17 of darkness (a favorite symbol of evil), the parenthetical remark that Jesus had not yet come to the disciples (also v 17), and the heightening of the miraculous in v 21 (as soon as the disciples try to take Jesus into the boat, the boat immediately reaches the shore to which the disciples had been heading). However, even these examples are not certain: some of them could have existed already in the Evangelist's tradition, especially if we think in terms of a written sign source.[123] The connection between the feeding of the five thousand and the walking on the water in Mark and probably Mark's source makes it practically certain that the two miracles were also already connected in John's source as well.

Indeed, the early traditional connection between the two miracles in John's source may have been a major reason why John bothered to keep the walking on the water.[124] In a certain sense, it gets in the way of the typically Johannine flow of thought that moves from sign through dialogue to monologue. In chap. 6 the sign of the feeding of the five thousand in 6:1–13 could have easily been made to flow directly into the dialogue between Jesus and the crowd in 6:26–33, which then flows into Jesus' monologue on the bread of life in 6:34–58. The walking on the water may provide an interlude, but it is an interlude that is disruptive:[125] (1) it causes a second miracle to follow immediately upon a first, without any theological dialogue or monologue intervening (a most un-Johannine ordering of material); and (2) it necessitates some awkward maneuvering in 6:22–25 to get Jesus and his well-fed audience back together again. One senses an interruption of the smooth flow from sign to dialogue to monologue that John would have constructed if left to himself.

Perhaps John was willing to take over the walking on the water relatively unchanged from his source because its basic theme, the revelation of Jesus in divine majesty, was so congenial to his high christology and theology of revelation. John's theology of revelation depicts Jesus in the terms and metaphors of the personified Wisdom of God described in the OT; Jesus *is* the revelation or Word of God made flesh. In a sense, the whole of John's Gospel is the story of an epiphany, the epiphany of the Word in the flesh, with Jesus' glory being ever more fully revealed until the climax of the death-resurrection, his ultimate glorification. For this reason John would probably have found it hard to pass over one of the few miracle stories in the entire Gospel tradition that narrated a specific epiphany of Jesus during the public ministry.

No doubt the presence of the solemn formula *egō eimi* at the climax of the epiphany made the story especially attractive to John. Granted, on the surface level of the narrative, *egō eimi* in John 6:20 means exactly what it means in Mark 6:50: "It is I," or in colloquial English, "It's me." Within the narrative, Jesus is first of all assuring his frightened disciples with a formula of self-identification: "It is I, the Jesus you know and trust; therefore, there is no reason to fear." That is obviously the sense in Mark, who explicitly says that the disciples have mistaken Jesus for a ghost. It is also the most likely "surface meaning" in the flow of John's narrative as well. The disciples have been separated from

Jesus for some hours, they do not know where he is, and they certainly do not expect to see him walking toward them across the water. Thus, the need for self-identification.

However, the OT language of theophany, the picture of Jesus bestriding the rough waters of the sea like God or God's Wisdom, and most of all John's use of *egō eimi* as a formula of divine revelation elsewhere in his Gospel join together to create a secondary resonance.[126] For John, the Jesus who walks on the turbulent sea is the eternal Word made flesh, divine Wisdom who bestrode the waves of chaos in the OT. Hence Jesus' "I am" echoes the divine name of Yahweh revealed in Exod 3:14–15 and the formula of revelation regularly used in Deutero-Isaiah. Indeed, given the overarching context of Jesus' *egō eimi* in John's Gospel, the surface meaning of "It is I" almost necessarily resonates with the deeper meaning of "I am."[127]

It was perhaps this double meaning in particular that proved irresistible to the Evangelist most addicted to double meanings. This double meaning, as well as the overall theme of the epiphany of the divine in the human, may have moved John to take over from his source a narrative that disrupted the smooth flow he would have preferred. These considerations, which led John to preserve in his text what he otherwise might have dropped, may help explain why he left the story in a relatively primitive state and did not expand or suffuse it with a great deal of his own theological concepts, vocabulary, or commentary. He is much more interested in the connection between the feeding of the multitude with bread and the bread of life discourse, and therefore he wishes to proceed to the main point of chap. 6 as quickly as possible. John tolerates the interruption caused by the walking on the water for the sake of the epiphany it supplies; but he does not allow it to expand to the point of derailing the major thrust of chap. 6.

b. *The content of John's story as compared with Mark's.* At the end of the feeding of the five thousand, when Jesus perceives that the enthusiastic crowd wants to seize him and make him king, Jesus withdraws by himself to a mountain (6:15). John's story of the walking on the water therefore begins differently than Mark's. In John 6:16–17a, instead of Jesus being on the scene and forcing his disciples to get into the boat, the disciples have apparently been abandoned by Jesus. (This is in keeping with the fact that, in contrast to Mark's version, John's story is told largely from the viewpoint of the disciples, not Jesus.)[128] Having nothing better to do, the disciples go down to the shore and embark for Capernaum (not Mark's Bethsaida). One should no more try to harmonize the two versions of why the disciples get into the boat and leave without Jesus than one should try to harmonize the two contradictory destinations.

John's penchant for theological symbolism may be responsible for the remark in v 17b that darkness (*skotia*) had already fallen. He is probably also responsible for the curious remark in 17c: "And Jesus had not yet come to them." At first hearing, this statement might create the impression that the disciples were expecting Jesus to come to them across the water. Rather, the parenthetical explanation is an aside by the Evangelist to the reader. Such parenthetical asides, which look either forward or backward in the narrative, are found elsewhere in John's Gospel (e.g., 12:33; 18:14). When these asides blithely refer to events still to come in the narrative, they may be an indication that the Evangelist presupposes that his audience already knows the basic story (see, e.g., 11:2).

Like Mark 6:48, John 6:18–19 explains that the disciples were having difficulty making headway because of the wind. The difficulty in John is described in greater and more dramatic detail (v 18): "The sea was being whipped up by a fierce wind that was blowing." Nevertheless, the weather conditions are not said to put the disciples in any danger.[129] Rather, as in Mark, the conditions make rowing difficult and the going slow. Despite all the time they have been separated from Jesus, they have traveled only about three or four miles ("25 or 30 stadia" in v 19). They are making progress, but the progress is painfully slow. This, and not danger to life or limb, is the disciples' problem. Thus, the depiction of the situation is remarkably similar to Mark's; and, as in Mark, there is no "sea rescue" because there is no danger from which to be rescued.[130]

It is after the disciples have rowed three or four miles that they see Jesus walking on the sea and coming close to the boat (6:19). In this core of the story John's account is very similar to Mark's, although John's narrative is tighter and briefer. In both versions, the disciples' reaction is fear; but John, unlike Mark, does not say that the disciples thought Jesus was a ghost. In John, Jesus' words of revelation are almost the same as in Mark (John 6:20 ‖ Mark 6:50): "But he says to them, 'It is I [the ambiguous egō eimi], fear not.' " All that is lacking is the initial exhortation present in Mark 6:50: "Have courage."

It is immediately after Jesus' word of revelation that John diverges totally from Mark and offers a very different—and a very abrupt—ending to his story. Mark's ending is much more typical of a miracle story: (1) Mark narrates the resolution of the problem: the separation from Jesus is overcome by Jesus' climbing into the boat to be with his disciples, and his presence causes the troublesome wind to die down (6:51ab). (2) Mark notes the great amazement of the witnesses to the miracle (6:51c). (3) Mark concludes the whole story with his own redactional theology, stressing the disciples' lack of understanding of who Jesus is, despite his miracles (6:52).

In contrast, John brings the story to such a speedy conclusion that some exegetes are at a loss to explain the final verse (6:21): "Then they [the disciples] wished to take him [Jesus] into the boat, and immediately the boat was at the shore toward which they were going." While it is unclear whether the disciples achieved their goal of getting Jesus into the boat, the point is really moot. No sooner do they want to do so than the boat is immediately—and hence miraculously—at the far shore (in John's story, Capernaum's shore), which the disciples had been laboring so long and so hard to reach.[131] Since, because of the strong wind, the disciples had been able to row only three or four miles from the near shore, their immediate arrival at the far shore can only be read as a second miracle added to (and flowing from?) the first (i.e., Jesus' walking on the water).[132]

There is a hint of this miracle-on-top-of-a-miracle in Mark, insofar as the contrary wind dies down as soon as Jesus enters the boat. We need not be surprised that this hint of the miraculous, if it existed in the pre-Marcan tradition, becomes a full-blown miracle in John. As a rule, in the Johannine tradition the miraculous tends to be heightened as compared to the Synoptics. (For instance, only in John's Gospel does Jesus heal a man *born* blind and raise a man dead *four days in the tomb*.) Hence, while in Mark the dying down of the wind no doubt helps the disciples row to their destination more quickly, in John there can be no question of the wind dying down or the disciples rowing at a swifter pace. Such events would be superfluous because the boat is miraculously and instantaneously transported to its destination. Such is the power of the epiphany of the Word made flesh as he declares *egō eimi*. In the face of such an epiphany, it would be unthinkable that the disciples would continue their mundane rowing, however speedy, and so arrive at the far shore by ordinary means. Clearly, the fingerprints of John's high christology are all over the concluding verse of his narrative.[133]

C. THE PRIMITIVE VERSION OF THE STORY

Having reviewed the contents of John's story and the salient points at which it agrees or disagrees with Mark, what can we conclude about a primitive form of the story, a form that existed prior to the redaction of Mark and John? I doubt that we can reconstruct such a primitive version word for word, especially in the conclusion, where Mark, Matthew, and John all diverge. Nevertheless, the agreements between Mark and John, plus the places where their redactional hands are evident, allow us to suggest the basic content of the primitive story. Like any miracle story, it has three main parts: (1) the setup and attendant circumstances, (2) the word and/or deed of Jesus effecting the miracle, (3) the reaction of the bystanders, further results of the miracle, and/ or conclusion.

1. The Setting and Attendant Circumstances. (a) Temporal and geographical setting: In both the pre-Marcan and the pre-Johannine tradition, the story was already tied to the feeding of the five thousand. This connection placed the walking on the water within the context of a high point in Jesus' Galilean ministry. Needless to say, the very nature of the walking on the water placed it more precisely at and on the Sea of Galilee (in John, also known as the Sea of Tiberias). Disagreements over the location of the feeding of the five thousand in the various Gospels as well as disagreements over the destination of the disciples in the boat make a more exact geographical location impossible, despite many attempts by exegetes to harmonize the accounts.[134]

(b) The Initial Action of Jesus: In both stories, but in very different ways, some initial action of Jesus is the catalyst for the disciples' departure—and in that sense for the problem of separation that Jesus must then overcome by his

not occur in a theophany. However, similar images of God walking on the deep and dominating the unruly waters of chaos do occur in God's magnificent speech to Job when the former appears to the latter in a theophany, speaking "out of the whirlwind" (Job 38:1). When he created the world, God alone was able to shut up the deep and set limits to its waves (38:8–11).[138] Indeed, God alone, and no puny human like Job, was present at creation to enter into the sources of the sea and to *walk upon* the deep waters of the abyss (38:16: the words *peripateō* ["walk"] and *thalassa* ["sea"] occur in the LXX of this verse). Here we have the imagery and language of Job 9:8b in the context of a theophany—in fact, in the mouth of God describing his act of creation, an act that infinitely separates him from all mortals.

3. Similar images in the context of a terrifying theophany can be found in Hab 3:15. Again, the key image of "trampling upon" (*dārak ʿal*) is used of God displaying his power over creation as he battles the enemies of his people Israel: "You trampled [or: tread] on the sea [with] your horses." The LXX translates freely here: God is said to cause his horses to ride into the sea, though the overall thrust of the imagery is the same.

4. With the Habakkuk passage we see the imagery of God the Creator, treading upon and controlling the waters of chaos, now being used as a metaphor for the salvation of his people Israel. This metaphor of salvation is clearer when the imagery of God walking on or through the sea, which has its home in creation theology, is explicitly applied to God's salvation of Israel as he led it through the Reed Sea at the exodus. Ps 77:20 praises God for that feat: "In [or: through] the sea was your way, and your path in the many waters, and [i.e., but] your footprints were not known [i.e., seen]." The deliverance at the Reed Sea is depicted in vv 17–21 with the imagery of a theophany of the Creator God, whose power is directly experienced in the sea even though he himself cannot be directly seen. The God who controls the raging sea makes it possible for his people to cross it.

5. A more starkly mythological picture of Yahweh defeating the chaos monster of the sea, i.e., drying up the Reed Sea so that Israel might pass through at the exodus, is used with great poetic power in Isa 51:9–10. Such imagery is typical of Deutero-Isaiah, who regularly connects the themes of creation and redemption, both being divine triumphs over the powers of chaos.[139] Such is the point of the imagery Deutero-Isaiah employs as he begins a promise of salvation in 43:16: "Thus says Yahweh, who provides in the sea a way, and in mighty waters a path." Practically the same language is used of God in Wis 14:3.

6. Especially important for John's version of the miracle of Jesus' walking on the water is a remarkable tendency of the OT wisdom tradition. In a number of passages it transfers to the personified Wisdom of God the imagery of God the Creator walking on or through the primordial waters or making a way for Israel through the Reed Sea. (a) For instance, in Proverbs 8 divine Wisdom describes herself as the craftsman or architect who worked alongside God at creation, assisting him when he set limits for the sea (Prov 8:29; cf. Job

38:8–11). (b) In dependence on Proverbs 8, Ben Sira writes a poem in Sirach 24 in which Wisdom speaks her own praises, praises that include her presence at creation and the fact that "on the deep abyss [of the primordial sea] I *walked* [*periepatēsa*]; over the waves of the sea . . . I held sway" (Sir 24:5–6). (c) In line with this tradition, the Wisdom of Solomon transfers to the Wisdom of God Yahweh's saving act of leading Israel through the waters of the Red Sea and guiding it through the desert by the theophany of the pillar of fire (Wis 10:17–18): "She made them [Israel] pass through the Red Sea, and she led them through the great water."

This tendency to attribute to divine Wisdom the imagery used elsewhere of the God who dominates the waters of the sea as he creates the world and redeems Israel is extremely important to John's high christology and to the miracle of 6:16–21 in particular. A great characteristic of the Fourth Gospel is that it applies to Christ much of the OT speculation about divine Wisdom active in creation and redemption.[140] Thus, in 6:16–21 John may well see Jesus as the Wisdom of God incarnate, once again walking upon the deep abyss and holding sway over the waves of the sea.

7. Clearly, then, the story of Jesus' walking on the water in Mark and John echoes various OT passages that depict God displaying his power over the waters of chaos at creation and the exodus, scenes often described with the language of a theophany. That Mark in particular wishes to evoke the OT idea of a theophany as Jesus bestrides the sea seems evident from his at first puzzling statement in 6:48: "Jesus comes to them, walking on the sea, and he wished to *pass by them* [*parelthein autous*]."

This cryptic conclusion to v 48 has led to a flurry of explanations, one more unlikely than the next.[141] (a) Some want the verb "he wished" (*ēthelen*) to equal an auxiliary verb with the sense of "he was about to"; but no such meaning of the verb *thelō* is witnessed elsewhere in the NT. (b) Others take the phrase as a description of what the disciples *thought* Jesus was going to do; but this explanation suddenly and illegitimately switches the story's perspective to the disciples' point of view, while the rest of the narrative in Mark is told from Jesus' point of view. Moreover, the text plainly says that Jesus did wish to pass by them. (c) Others interpret the phrase to mean that Jesus wanted to test the disciples' faith; but the wording at the end of v 48 would be an odd way of expressing this idea. (d) Others try to interpret the phrase in light of Mark's messianic secret: Jesus wishes to withdraw from the disciples and remain incognito in the way that he withdraws elsewhere into secrecy in Mark's Gospel. Yet it strikes one as extremely strange that Jesus would—spontaneously and for no reason beyond his own desire—initiate a terrifying theophany in which he would act like Yahweh bestriding the sea, and that he would parade his transcendent majesty in front of his disciples—only then to withdraw coyly in order to keep under wraps his messianic secret after he has unveiled a divine one. (e) Finally, some try to get around the difficulty by suggesting that "and he wished to pass by them" actually means "*for* he wished to pass by them," the Greek *kai* ("and") sometimes introducing an explanation, especially in Semitic

Greek. Actually, this final interpretation can be fitted into what is the best explanation of the phrase.

We have already seen that the motif of God dominating the chaotic sea was often connected in the OT with a theophany. It need not surprise us, then, that the strange phrase "to pass by" is likewise best understood against the background of OT theophanies. A prime example is Yahweh's appearance to Moses at Sinai in Exod 33:18–34:6. Moses begs to see Yahweh's divine glory. Yahweh agrees, promising in 33:19 to make "all my goodness *pass before* [or: by] you." The Hebrew text uses the verb *ʿābar* ("to pass by"), for which the LXX naturally employs the equivalent verb *parerchomai*, the same verb Mark uses in 6:48 ("he wished to *pass by* them"). The same construction occurs again in Exod 33:22. Yahweh fulfills his promise by coming down in a cloud, standing with Moses, and proclaiming his sacred name Yahweh. In this theophany, the last phrase describing Yahweh's movements vis-à-vis Moses is found in 34:6: "And Yahweh passed before him [literally: "passed before his face"] and proclaimed: 'Yahweh, Yahweh, a God merciful and gracious.'" The LXX translates the Hebrew statement literally, using again the verb *parerchomai*.

There is a remarkable correspondence here between Exodus and Mark. Yahweh comes down to Moses, stands with him, "passes before [or by] him," and proclaims his identity in a solemn formula that also reassures. In Mark Jesus comes to the disciples, walking on the sea, wishes to "pass by them," and finally proclaims his identity in a solemn formula that also reassures: "Have courage. It is I; fear not." Clearly, in such a context the verb *parerchomai* ("pass by") refers to an epiphany in which Yahweh or Jesus wills to draw close to someone so as to be seen in transcendent majesty, to proclaim his identity, and to give reassurance. The action of "passing by" has nothing to do with withdrawing from others' view so as to protect one's transcendence and mystery.

The Sinai theophany granted to Moses is not the only OT theophany that uses this terminology of "passing by." When Yahweh "recycles" the Sinai theophany for Elijah in 1 Kgs 19:11, Yahweh promises Elijah that he "will pass by" (the Hebrew participle *ʿōbēr*; the LXX reads the future tense of the verb: *pareleusetai*). In Gen 32:31–32, the LXX version of the story of Jacob wrestling with the angel states that the face of God "passed by" (*parēlthen*). In Dan 12:1, the LXX version of the prophecy of the coming of the angel Michael at the end of time is expressed in terms of Michael "passing by" (*pareleusetai*).[142] The conclusion from all this is clear: the verb *parerchomai* in Mark 6:48 intends to present Jesus' walking on the water in terms of an OT epiphany. Granted this, one might indeed take the *kai* ("and") at the beginning of the clause in the sense of "for": "Jesus comes to them, walking on the water, *for* he wished to pass by them [i.e., reveal himself to them in an epiphany]."

8. As with OT theophanies and angelophanies, this epiphany of Christ in all his power and majesty frightens the audience. Jesus responds to his disciples' fear with a classic OT formula of self-identification and reassurance: "It is I [or: I am]; fear not." As we have already seen, while the "surface meaning"

of *egō eimi* in the Gospel narrative is "It is I," the many OT allusions in the
story (especially to the Creator God's domination of the waters of chaos in a
context of theophany) intimate a secondary, solemn meaning: the divine "I
am." Ultimately this solemn utterance goes all the way back to Yahweh's revelation of himself to Moses in the burning bush, with the mysterious proclamation *ehyeh ăšer ehyeh* ("I shall be what I shall be," "I am what I am," or "I am
who am"), a proclamation that serves as the explanation of the name Yahweh
(Exod 3:14–15). The LXX translation of Yahweh's self-proclamation in Exod
3:14 was the fateful *egō eimi ho ōn* ("I am the One who is"), a rendering open
to the metaphysical speculation of Hellenistic Jews like Philo.

Within the Hebrew Bible, it was Deutero-Isaiah in particular who seized
upon the mysterious explanation of the mysterious name in Exod 3:14–15. He
"recycled" it to articulate *both* Yahweh's transcendence, uniqueness, and mystery *and* his nearness as the Creator and Savior God, the redeemer of a sinful
and exiled Israel. In Isa 43:1–13, Deutero-Isaiah gives a splendid summation
of the theological riches he attaches to the simple yet majestic proclamation:
"It is I, I Yahweh" (or: "I am he, I Yahweh"). In this passage, the formula
of divine self-revelation is connected with the command "fear not," with a
recollection of passing through water at the exodus, and the promise of a new
act of revelation and salvation, to which Israel must be a witness:

v 1: Fear not (LXX: *mē phobou*), for I have redeemed you.
v 2: When you pass through the water, I will be with you; the rivers shall not
      overwhelm you.
v 3: For I am Yahweh, your God.
v 5: Fear not, for I am with you.
v 10: You are my witnesses . . . to know and believe in me and understand that
      it is I [or: I am he] (MT: *ʾănî hûʾ*; LXX: *egō eimi*).
      Prior to me no god was formed, and after me there shall not be [any].
v 11: [It is] I, I Yahweh (MT: *ʾānōkî ʾānōkî yahweh*; LXX: *egō ho theos* ["I am
      God"]).
      There is besides me no Savior.

The pregnant and enticing use of terse formulas like *ʾănî hûʾ* and *ʾānōkî
yahweh* provided fodder for theological speculation among the later rabbis, just
as the LXX translations did for Philo and the later Fathers of the Church,
notably Justin Martyr and Origen. But this much is clear from the usage of
Deutero-Isaiah himself: the emphasis on such phrases as "I am he," "I am,"
and simply "I" hammer home the message that Yahweh is the one, true, only,
transcendent God, who has revealed himself to Israel in past acts of "creative
redemption" and who will do so again. It is precisely this revelation of the one,
transcendent, all-powerful God, the God who can simply say "I am," that is
the reason why his audience should "fear not."

9. When one puts together all these OT motifs connected with (1) God
dominating and walking upon the waters of chaos as he creates and saves, (2)

the setting of such mighty acts in the context of a theophany, and (3) the divine self-revelation of "It is I, fear not" (proclaimed by Yahweh, the one, true, transcendent God), the application of all these motifs to Jesus in the brief miracle of the walking on the water is nothing less than astounding. It must be especially astounding for anyone accustomed to charting the development of NT christology via a neat progression from a pre-Synoptic "low christology" of Jesus the prophet and teacher, endowed with special power from God, to John's "high christology" of the eternal Word made flesh. Such tidy evolutionary schemas should always be suspect, and in reality they simply do not mirror the complexity of NT christology. As a matter of fact, some relatively early texts already reflect a high christology: e.g., the pre-Pauline hymn in Phil 2:6–11 probably existed in Aramaic and may go back to the first or second Christian decade.[143] In contrast, some relatively late texts are surprisingly low: e.g., a fair amount of Luke's Gospel presents Jesus as a good, prayerful man through whom God's power flows.

Instead of engaging in artificial rectilinear patterns of development, we should recognize that, once the early Christians believed that Jesus had been raised from the dead, a theological explosion was set off that assured both creativity and disorder for the rest of the 1st century A.D. When it comes to understanding NT christology, it is best to recite this mantra: in the beginning was the grab bag. The next couple of centuries would be taken up sorting out the grab bag. Many early Christians were quite content to make both "low" and "high" affirmations about Jesus, with no great concern about consistency, systematization, or synthesis. Hence we need not be surprised to find in a pre-Marcan and pre-Johannine miracle story a presentation of Jesus that basically depicts him as Yahweh bestriding the waters of chaos in a theophany and proclaiming his identity with the words of Yahweh in Deutero-Isaiah: "It is I [or: I am]; fear not." The same Mark who takes over this portrayal of Jesus has no difficulty in speaking of Jesus' inability to heal people because of their unbelief or of Jesus' ignorance of the date of the parousia. In the beginning was the grab bag.

As we at last turn to a decision about the historicity of the walking on the water, we will see how this lengthy excursus on the OT background will prove useful in making an informed judgment.

E. THE DECISION ABOUT HISTORICITY

I am well aware that some critics will think this exploration of the historicity of the walking on the water a waste of time. Their judgment is made, however, not on strictly historical grounds but on the basis of a philosophical or theological a priori, a version of Bultmann's incantation that "modern man cannot believe in miracles." We have already seen how that claim has been empirically falsified by a Gallup poll. Any claims for or against historicity must proceed not by invoking a philosophical bias but by using the same criteria of historicity by which the rest of the Jesus material (e.g., sayings, parables) is judged.

I stress that the question I am asking is a historical, not a philosophical or theological one, and a quite limited one at that. I am simply inquiring whether the story of the walking on the water goes back to some incident in the life of Jesus (whatever that incident may have been), or whether it is simply a creation of the early church. In the present case, the claim that the story goes back to some event in Jesus' ministry is not entirely without merit. The story enjoys double attestation of sources (though not forms). It obviously existed in both the pre-Marcan and pre-Johannine traditions, and in that early stage of the tradition it was already connected with the story of the feeding of the five thousand. Such early material cannot be dismissed out of hand without a serious examination, which is what I have tried to provide.

At the end of the examination, though, I think that the decision must go against historicity, despite the multiple attestation of sources. Two considerations in particular weigh heavily against historicity:

1. The criteria of discontinuity and coherence, used in tandem, tell against historicity. By now, we have surveyed almost all the miracles of Jesus in the Four Gospels. Almost all the miracles that have some claim to go back to an event in Jesus' life have two things in common: (a) These miracles seek to help a person in dire need or mortal danger: e.g., the gravely ill, the blind, the paralyzed, lepers ostracized from society, and demoniacs deprived of a normal, peaceful life. (b) These miracles focus on helping the person in need and on proclaiming the coming of God's kingdom; they do not focus on Jesus' person and status or seek his self-glorification. When Jesus does speak of the purpose of his miracles, he sees them as signs of the kingdom of God already present in some way (Luke 11:20 par.), signs that the prophecies and hopes of Israel for the end time are now being fulfilled (Matt 11:2–6 par.).

To be sure, all this implies something about Jesus the miracle-worker, the sign-giver, the bearer of the kingdom, but the "something" usually remains implied. In connection with his miracles Jesus speaks of himself in veiled, parabolic terms as the one stronger than Satan, the one who is despoiling Satan by performing exorcisms (Mark 3:27 parr.). In other words, almost all the miracles examined so far and judged to go back to some incident in Jesus' ministry *cohere* with this other-centered, healing focus.

In contrast, the walking on the water fails to cohere with this tendency; indeed, it is diametrically opposed to it. Here is where our extended study both of the content of the miracle and of its OT background is decisive. We have seen that the walking on the water is not a "sea rescue" or any other type of miracle that has its raison d'être in helping others in dire need or mortal danger. True, the contrary wind (Mark 6:48 ‖ John 6:18–19) makes rowing difficult for the disciples and their progress across the Sea of Galilee painfully slow. But this is hardly dire need or mortal danger, and in any case speeding up the boat is not the main point of this miracle story. Rather, the main point of the story is an epiphany in which Jesus *wills* to reveal himself (Mark 6:48: *kai ēthelen parelthein autous*) in his transcendent majesty and power, bestriding the sea and proclaiming "It is I; fear not" in the grand manner of the Yahweh of

Job and Deutero-Isaiah. To play down the essential element of Jesus' astounding epiphany, decked out with the trappings of an OT theophany, in favor of a supposed rescue of the disciples that consists merely in expediting the progress of a boat is the exegetical equivalent of straining out the gnat and swallowing the camel.

Thus, the walking on the water does not cohere with the miracle stories that have a good chance of going back to some event in Jesus' ministry. Indeed, this miracle story is emphatically discontinuous with them. Instead, it is continuous with the christology of the early church, especially with an early thrust toward high christology that tended to associate Jesus with Yahweh or to make Jesus the functional equivalent of Yahweh. The seeds of such an idea are already present in the pre-Marcan and pre-Johannine story of the walking on the water, and they bear abundant fruit in John's full-blown theological vision a generation or two later. Judging therefore by what the story coheres with and with what it is discontinuous, I think that the walking on the water is most likely from start to finish a creation of the early church, a christological confession in narrative form.

2. The second consideration that argues against historicity flows from the first and is allied to it. In a broad sense, any miracle Jesus was thought to have performed possessed for the believing audience a certain "epiphanic" quality insofar as the miracle made God's presence and power palpable and effective in ordinary human life. Likewise, many Gospel accounts of Jesus' miracles are permeated with the "atmosphere" of the OT; they contain echoes or allusions to particular OT stories (e.g., Moses, Elijah, Elisha) or prophecies (especially from the Book of Isaiah). But with the walking on the water we notice a substantive difference.

The difference in the walking on the water is that the elements of epiphany and of OT allusions have moved to center stage and have become the very stuff of the narrative. In stories like the walking on the water Jesus is becoming the very epiphany of God; what the OT texts said of God displaying his power in theophany is being applied directly to Jesus in his public ministry. When the OT material, especially the OT portrayal of Yahweh, enters so massively into a NT miracle story, we have a fairly good indication that we may be dealing with a theological creation of the early church.

To say that the story of the walking on the water was created by the early church leaves many questions unanswered, perhaps unavoidably so. Why was the pericope created? What were its function and setting in the early church? These questions of *Sitz im Leben* are both legitimate and easy to raise, but I doubt whether we have sufficient indications in the text or in the history of early Christianity to answer them. Noting various contacts with the miraculous catch of fish in John 21:1–14 or the resurrection appearance in Luke 24:36–49, some authors suggest that the walking on the water was originally a story of a post-resurrection appearance.[144]

Such a theory has a certain amount of plausibility. Similar to John 21:1–14, the story of the walking on the water is situated by the Sea of Galilee. The disciples are bereft of Jesus and are in difficulty. Jesus appears to them, but at first they do not recognize him. He reassures them of his identity and calms their fears. All these elements fit neatly into the pattern of a post-resurrection appearance, especially Dodd's "concise" type.[145] However, the element of commissioning the disciples is lacking in the story of Jesus' walking on the water.

An explicit commissioning of the disciples does appear in the post-resurrection appearance of Luke 24:36–49, along with the motifs of the disciples' being afraid because they think Jesus is a spirit and Jesus' reassurance that "it is I myself" (v 39, *egō eimi autos*). Still, one objection to seeing the walking on the water as a parallel to either post-resurrection appearance remains: the basic setting, a frightening theophany amid the mighty forces of wind and sea—not to mention the essential point of Jesus' walking on the sea—does not fit the post-resurrection appearances preserved in the Four Gospels. Nevertheless, the possibility of an origin in a post-resurrection appearance cannot be totally excluded.

As an alternate theory, I would venture a suggestion that must remain very tentative and speculative. We have seen that, as far back as we can trace the tradition history, the story of Jesus' walking on the water was always connected with the feeding of the five thousand.[146] The connection is pre-Marcan and pre-Johannine. I would suggest that the connection is original in the sense that the walking on the water never existed as an isolated pericope. In other words, when the early church created the story of the walking on the water, it was created precisely as a narrative comment on the feeding of the five thousand, an example of "doing theology" by story. I am moved to make this suggestion because we have already seen in this chapter one likely example of such a process, namely, the cursing of the fig tree. In my view, it too never existed in isolation but was created by the early church as a theological commentary on the story of the "cleansing" of the temple. One obvious difference strikes us immediately: of its nature, the walking on the water did not lend itself to Marcan intercalation, with one half of the story preceding the feeding of the five thousand and the other half following. The Marcan as well as the Johannine tradition had to have the miraculous commentary on the feeding story follow it.

If all this be true, what sort of commentary on the story of the feeding does the walking on the water offer? It is commonly held by exegetes that the various versions of the feeding story were understood by the early church to prefigure not only the Last Supper but also the Christian celebration of the eucharist. This would help explain why this feeding story enjoys the unique privilege of being the only miracle present in all Four Gospels—and present twice in Mark and Matthew (i.e., the feeding of the five thousand and its alternate version, the feeding of the four thousand). Unlike most miracle stories, the feeding of the multitude spoke directly to what the local church did on a regular basis. I would suggest, therefore, that from the beginning the walking on the water was a way in which the early church drew out certain theological implications or commented on certain theological aspects of the eucharist. Quite understandably, the early church did this not by way of speculative systematics but by telling a further symbol-laden story replete with OT allusions, as was the feeding story itself. It is a question of a symbolic story interpreted by another symbolic story.

Put in this context, the walking on the water can be seen in a new light. As is often noted by scholars investigating NT christology, many of the "high" christological statements in the NT, especially the early ones, seem to have had their original setting in Christian worship. It is not by accident that affirmations of Christ's preexistence or divine status are found most notably in early Christian hymns: Phil 2:6–11; Col 1:15–20; and the core of John 1:1–18. It was in experiencing Christ's presence in worship rather than in speculative affirmations about him that the earliest "high" christology took shape. This may help explain why so early a narrative as the walking on the water reflects a surprisingly high christology: it is actually a symbolic representation of one way in which the church experienced the risen Christ in its celebration of the eucharist.

In other words, the eucharistic symbolism that begins in the story of the feeding of the five thousand continues into the story of the walking on the water. The first story reflects what the Christian "crowds in the wilderness" of this world experience when the risen Jesus once again gives thanks, breaks bread, and gives it to those who have followed him and are hungry because they lack their own resources. What I am suggesting is that, to a small church struggling in the night of a hostile world and feeling bereft of Christ's presence, the walking on the water likewise symbolized the experience of Christ in the eucharist.[147] Once again, with all the power of Yahweh bestriding the chaos of a rebellious creation, Jesus reveals himself in a secret epiphany to his frightened, beleaguered disciples, telling them: "It is I; fear not."[148] The story of the walking on the water reflects the fact that, for the early church, the eucharist was the ritualized experience of an epiphany of the risen Jesus, coming to a small group of believers laboring in the night of this present age; once again he gave courage and calmed fears simply by announcing his presence.[149]

I offer this hypothesis as one possibility among several, and I do not want to insist upon it. Whether or not one finds it plausible as an original *Sitz im Leben* for the story, the basic point remains firm: a number of considerations make it likely that the story of the walking on the water is a creation of the early church and does not go back to an incident in Jesus' public ministry. A positive corollary of this decision is that several exegetical blind alleys need not be explored. In particular, we may dismiss as beside the point various attempts by rationalists to explain the miracle in a "natural way": e.g., by suggesting that Jesus was standing on the shore of the sea (or on a promontory over the sea, or in the shallow part of the sea) and that his frightened disciples, struggling against the wind in the dark, mistakenly thought that they saw him walking on the sea.[150] How the disciples could have seen Jesus standing on the shore in the dark of night if they were "in the middle of the sea" (as Mark puts it) or if they had traveled some three or four miles (as John says) is a question that creates even more amusing theories. If instead we accept the most probable hypothesis, that the whole story is a creation of the early church, we are spared such intellectual acrobatics.

We are likewise spared a debate over whether Matthew's special material about Peter's walking on the water (Matt 14:28–32a) goes back to any historical event. Obviously, if the basic story of Jesus' walking on the water is a church-creation, the story of Peter doing likewise is a fortiori to be explained in the same way. Whether the story about Peter was already present in Matthew's special tradition (e.g., as an oral expansion on Mark's text) or whether Matthew himself created it as a further ecclesiological comment on a christological (and possibly even eucharistic) story is an intriguing question that need not be answered here.[151]

VII. THE STILLING OF THE STORM (MARK 4:35–41 ‖ MATT 8:23–27 ‖ LUKE 8:22–25[152])

A. THE PLACE OF THE STORY IN MARK'S GOSPEL AND ITS POSSIBLE SOURCE

Mark's account of the stilling of the storm stands at a turning point in the first part of his Gospel.[153] Almost the whole of chap. 4 of Mark is taken up with Jesus' first discourse, the parable discourse (4:1–34). Starting at 4:35, the stilling of the storm marks the end of this collection of parables and the beginning of a collection of miracle stories: the stilling of the storm (4:35–41), the exorcism of the Gerasene demoniac (5:1–20), and the raising of the daughter of Jairus, which is meshed with the healing of the woman with a hemorrhage (5:21–43).

Early on in the Gospel, in his account of Jesus' first day of ministry in Capernaum (1:21–28), Mark emphasized the connection between the authority of Jesus' teaching word and the authority of his miracle-working word (1:27). Mark now gives a lengthy example of that same nexus by juxtaposing the parable discourse (4:1–34) with the miracles performed on and around the Sea of Galilee (4:35–5:43).

It may well be that Mark 4:35–5:43 represents a pre-Marcan collection of three (or four) miracle stories that formed something of a didactic cycle in early Christian tradition.[154] The four stories can be seen as moving progressively from Jesus' power over the demonic forces present in wind and waves through his direct power over the demons present in a tormented man to his power over disease and death in the case of two women.[155] The stories of 4:35–5:43 are connected geographically by Jesus' moving back and forth across the Sea of Galilee. The stories are also connected "internally" by their literary style and theological tone, which to a large degree distinguish them from the miracle stories of the first three chapters of Mark.[156] Contrary to some of the miracle stories in Mark 1–3, there is no mention of Jesus' teaching within this cycle of miracle stories (contrast 1:21–28; 2:1–12; 3:1–6; 3:7–12). In 4:35–5:43 the miracle itself stands at center stage; it does not occur to bolster or accompany Jesus' teaching.

Not surprisingly, then, since these miracle stories exist for their own sake, they are told with much greater liveliness and with more of an eye to colorful (even irrelevant) detail than the miracle stories in Mark 1–3.[157] It is hardly by accident that the cycle of 4:35–5:43 encompasses only "big" miracles with a certain "massive" character: a storm whipping up the Sea of Galilee and threatening to destroy Jesus and his disciples is suddenly stilled; an entire "legion" of demons is cast out of a wild man, with the result that two thousand swine rush into the sea and drown; a dead girl is brought back to life right after a woman who had suffered from a hemorrhage for twelve years and who had only gotten worse at the hands of many doctors is healed simply by touching Jesus' garments. This massiveness is seen even in the length of the stories: 20 verses for the Gerasene demoniac and 22 verses for the meshed stories of Jairus' daughter and the hemorrhaging woman. Even the relatively short story of the stilling of the storm (7 verses) spends an inordinate 4 verses on the detailed "setup" of the miracle.[158]

In short, we seem to be dealing with a pre-Marcan collection that had already taken on certain specific narrative traits prior to Mark. To be sure, the four stories show various Marcan additions; but the redactional touches themselves point to a tradition on which Mark is working, a chain of stories that were already collected before Mark inserted them into his overarching framework. Whether the pre-Marcan collection extended further, encompassing either more miracle stories or the parable discourse as a first half of the collection, is debated among critics; here hypotheses become much more tenuous.[159] Also quite speculative is the attempt to decide in every case whether a secondary element inserted into the primitive form of a miracle story was added by Mark or by the pre-Marcan editor of the collection. Since we are concerned with discerning the earliest form of the story, the question of which editor or redactor added a particular verse or phrase is not relevant to our project.

B. THE STORY'S CONTENT AND FORM-CRITICAL CATEGORY

Having appreciated the overarching Marcan context, we now focus on the narrative of the stilling of the storm. That it belongs to the general form-critical category of a miracle story is clear from its makeup:[160]

(1) The *setup*, including the attendant circumstances and the (implicit) petition, is narrated in great detail, describing at length the problem that Jesus is called upon to solve. In v 35, as evening comes on, Jesus seizes the initiative and marks the end of the parable discourse by commanding the disciples to cross the Sea of Galilee with him.[161] In v 36, the disciples leave the crowd that served as the audience for the parable discourse and take Jesus as he is, sitting in the boat.[162] Verse 36 ends with the cryptic information that "other boats were with him [or, less likely: with it, i.e., the boat]." These boats disappear

from the story as soon as they are mentioned. They are a prime candidate for being a relic of pre-Marcan tradition.[163]

In v 37, the pressing problem that calls forth Jesus' miracle is introduced: a fierce wind storm that whips up the sea to the point that waves are crashing into the boat, which is already filling up. In the first of a number of sharp contrasts in the story, v 38 stops the action for a moment to depict Jesus, in the midst of this possibly fatal storm, sleeping on a cushion in the stern of the boat.[164] The second sharp contrast is provided by the frightened disciples, who wake up Jesus with a harsh question that is really a panic-ridden rebuke. Acting as the functional equivalent of the usual petition for a miracle, their brusque rhetorical question asks: "Teacher, are you not concerned that we are perishing?"

That the question carries the tone of complaint and rebuke can hardly be denied. Still, one should not speak here of total despair.[165] The disciples' question is indeed rhetorical and needs to be examined carefully. It is expressed not with the negative particle *mē*, which would indicate that a negative answer is expected (no, Jesus is not concerned). Rather, it is introduced by the negative particle *ou*, which presupposes an affirmative answer (yes, Jesus is concerned).[166] Moreover, with an assurance that seems to be illogical to us—but then, we are in a miracle story—the disciples presuppose that, although Jesus has been asleep during the storm, they can take for granted that he is aware of the danger and is concerned about it. Their complaint is basically that he has not shown his concern by doing something to help them. This implies that the disciples, however vaguely, think that Jesus could do something to help them. All in all, it is a very strange type of petition for a miracle, though it fits well with the other tensions and contrasts in the story. The panic and rudeness of the disciples hardly betoken faith in Jesus (see v 40), yet the question does presuppose that the disciples have had some experience of this "teacher," whose authoritative word also works miracles—though up until now in Mark, only miracles of exorcism and healing.

(2) Compared with the lengthy setup, the narration of the *miracle proper* (v 39), along with the affirmation of the miraculous event's occurrence, takes up only one verse. In v 39, the awakened Jesus "rebuked the wind and said to the sea: 'Be quiet, be muzzled.'" Two verbs in the Greek text make up all there is to the miracle-producing command of Jesus; the remainder of the verse narrates the miracle's occurrence: "And there came a great calm." Precisely because the miracle proper is so concise, the verbs used in reporting Jesus' command are all the more striking. Jesus "rebuked" (*epitimēsen*) the wind; the verb *epitmaō* ("rebuke") is used at times elsewhere in Mark to describe Jesus' exorcisms (Mark 1:25; 3:12; 9:25). In addition, Jesus uses the colorful metaphor "be muzzled" in commanding the sea to be quiet. The same verb is used in the first exorcism Jesus performs, as he commands the demon (1:25): "Be muzzled, and come out of him." By implication, at least in the Marcan context, Jesus "exorcises" the demonic powers creating the turbulence on the sea just as he exorcises them when they create turbulence in possessed people.[167] Verse

39 then concludes with the affirmation that this exorcism of wind and waves results in a "great calm," which corresponds perfectly to the "great storm" in v 37.

(3) The concluding *reaction and acclamation* (vv 40–41) contains a surprising and somewhat intrusive element. As the sequel to the affirmation of the miracle one would expect some sort of reaction (great fear) and acclamation ("Who is this . . . ?") on the part of the spectators. All this is present in v 41. But first the miracle-worker interrupts the smooth flow of the story to its typical conclusion. In v 40, Jesus addresses to his disciples a rebuke in the form of a double rhetorical question, thus matching and countering their rebuke, likewise spoken in the form of a rhetorical question (v 39). The rebukes spoken by the disciples and by Jesus correspond in content as well as in form. In his rebuke, Jesus asks rhetorically: "Why are you cowardly? Do you not yet have faith?" In effect, Jesus' question is responding to theirs. A simple petition for a miracle would not of itself have been a sign of cowardice or unbelief.[168] But the disciples addressed Jesus not with an ordinary petition but with a rude rhetorical question complaining about his apparent lack of concern for their survival. That is why their conduct and question deserve to be branded by him as cowardly and unbelieving.

The "not yet" in Jesus' question is intriguing, for it looks both backward and forward.[169] It looks back to the disciples' previous experience of Jesus' powerful word displayed in teaching and miracles, an experience that should have produced faith by now, but has not. Yet all is not lost. The same "not yet" also looks forward with expectation to some future moment when the disciples will have faith. We will see more of this "not yet" of Mark later on in his Gospel.

Once the (literarily disruptive) rebuke of Jesus is voiced, the miracle story receives a typical conclusion. The manifestation of miraculous power calls forth "great fear" (note the link words: great storm—great calm—great fear). In itself, this reverential fear is the proper response to a miracle and is not to be equated with the disciples' cowardice.[170] Then, as is fitting in a story already marked by the disciples' rhetorical question and Jesus' double rhetorical question, the narrative ends with a final question addressed by the disciples to themselves: "Who then is this, that even the wind and the sea obey him?" The sense of tension or contrast that has pervaded the story is thus maintained to the end. The disciples cannot identify Jesus by a clear title or label (v 41c: "Who then is this?"), and yet they do correctly describe him as the mighty miracle-worker who commands both wind and sea (v 41d). The positive element here is that they have moved beyond an estimation of him that could result from Mark 1–3: merely as an exorcist and healer.[171] Yet obviously, for Mark, this description of Jesus is not enough. The disciples should see revealed in this miracle the Messiah (8:29) and Son of God (15:39), the full and only adequate description of Jesus (1:1). But for the moment, their experience of Jesus' miracle generates only another rhetorical question. In keeping with Mark's messianic secret, it is the demon at Gerasa, not the disciples, who will supply the correct answer in the next story: Jesus is "the Son of the most high God" (Mark 5:7).[172]

C. IS THE STORY A "SEA-RESCUE EPIPHANY"?

From all that we have seen, the stilling of the storm certainly fits the category of miracle story; all three main parts are clearly present. What subcategory it belongs to is disputed. A number of exegetes, stressing the "epiphanic" quality of the stilling of the storm, suggest that, as in the case of the walking on the water, we have some sort of combination of a sea rescue and an epiphany.[173] Once again, I must disagree. In my opinion, the walking on the water is an epiphany, but not in the strict sense a sea rescue, since the disciples are not in mortal danger. In contrast, I think that the stilling of the storm is a sea rescue (the disciples are in mortal danger), but it is not in the strict sense an epiphany.[174]

I say "in the strict sense," because all of Jesus' miracles have a certain "epiphanic" quality about them.[175] In one way or another all of them reveal something of a divine presence and power suddenly appearing and acting in the earthly realm. Accordingly, many of Jesus' miracles cause fear or astonishment among the spectators, and a number of them point indirectly to the special nature of Jesus and the mystery of his person. For example, the story of the raising of the son of the widow of Nain concludes with all the spectators being seized with fear (*phobos*). They then give voice to a choral acclamation that defines the mystery of Jesus' person in terms of a prophet through whom God has momentarily become present and palpable to his people through his saving power (Luke 7:16): "A great prophet has arisen among us, and God has visited his people." This last clause obviously casts the light of epiphany on the story, but I would not for that reason classify this particular miracle of raising the dead as an epiphany story. Similarly, Jesus' miracles in the Fourth Gospel in one way or another reveal his "glory," as the conclusion of the water-into-wine miracle at Cana makes clear (John 2:11): "He revealed his glory, and his disciples believed in him." Nevertheless, to classify all the miracles of John's Gospel as epiphanies in the strict form-critical sense would be to ignore the specific nature of each. To be sure, in the Fourth Gospel the wine miracle of Cana reveals Jesus' glory and is in that sense epiphanic; but that does not alter the form-critical classification of that "sign" as a gift miracle.

What, then, is required for an epiphany miracle "in the strict sense"? Form critics may debate the details of a definition, but in my view the essential elements must include the absence (or invisibility) of the divine or heavenly figure at the beginning of the story, his or her sudden and frightening appearance in great power and majesty at a certain moment in the story, and usually some statement by the figure that reveals his or her true identity and willingness to help. All this is verified in Jesus' walking on the water. He is absent from the disciples as they struggle in their boat against the wind, he suddenly appears before them as he comes to them walking on the sea with divine power and majesty, and he speaks his solemn, revelatory "I am, fear not."

This basic core of an epiphany miracle is to a large extent lacking in the stilling of the storm. Jesus is present with his disciples in the boat from the beginning of the story to its end,[176] he is never transformed in appearance, and the words he speaks (first to the wind and the waves, then to the disciples) are not self-identifying or self-revelatory formulas.[177] At the end of the stilling of the storm the Marcan disciples are still capable of asking: "Who is this?" Despite their continued and indeed increased obtuseness, they do not ask that specific question at the end of Mark's version of the walking on the water; it would be out of place at the end of an epiphany.[178] Hence, for all the supposed "epiphanic" atmosphere, the stilling of the storm is not an epiphany in the strict form-critical sense. It is plainly a sea-rescue miracle, but not a sea-rescue epiphany.

D. Tradition and Redaction

Since we have only Mark's story, on which Matthew and Luke depend,[179] it is difficult to distinguish tradition from redaction, especially since there may have been some editing done by the pre-Marcan collector of the miracle stories. Nevertheless, on the one hand we can discern the bare grid of the sea-rescue miracle story, while on the other hand some redactional additions of Mark seem fairly clear.

The most primitive grid of the story of the stilling of the storm coincides neatly with the three major elements of a miracle story, which in this case also coincide neatly with the three appearances of the word "great." (1) A *great* storm (v 37, the threatening problem of the setup) is resolved by (2) Jesus' word of command, which produces a *great* calm (v 39, the miracle proper with the affirmation of its occurrence), (3) which in turn calls forth *great* fear on the part of the disciples (v 41, reaction and choral acclamation). I think it hardly accidental that the three "greats" represent respectively the three form-critical building blocks of the setup, the miracle proper, and the reaction.[180] They were probably a useful mnemonic technique in the earliest oral tradition. Without the statements tied to the three "greats" there is no miracle story; with them the core of the miracle story is narrated.

How much more of the present Marcan text belonged to the primitive miracle story is hard to say. Needless to say, the story grew in telling and retelling. Perhaps at some point in the oral tradition the story was a longer and more circumstantial narrative in which such details as the "other boats" of v 36 played a meaningful role. Now this detail remains a relic, a sign that Mark did indeed work with a tradition instead of merely inventing the story out of whole cloth.

As far as Mark's editorial hand is concerned, the best candidates for redactional intervention are the correlative rhetorical questions we have already noticed. The rude, unedifying remarks of the disciples to Jesus are typical of

Mark's Gospel, as are the corresponding sharp rebukes of Jesus, which at times portray the disciples as without faith and no better than blind outsiders. As most commentators observe, Jesus' double blast at the disciples as cowardly and—more significantly—as *still* without faith fits Mark's depiction of the disciples as well as his theme of the "messianic secret" perfectly. As Jesus tries more and more to reveal his true nature to the disciples, they prove to be more and more obtuse, as can be seen at the conclusion of the walking on the water. Jesus' censure of the disciples reaches a high point in Mark 8:14–21, after the second multiplication of loaves: "Do you *not yet* understand or comprehend? Are your hearts [so] hardened? Having eyes do you not see, and having ears do you not hear? . . . Do you *not yet* comprehend?" Since almost all commentators see the heart of Jesus' rebuke to the disciples in 8:17–21 as Mark's own redactional judgment, and since this Marcan composition ends with a telling rhetorical question marked by *oupō* ("not yet"), it is all but certain that the very similar rhetorical question in 4:40 ("Do you *not yet* [*oupō*] have faith?") is likewise Marcan redaction.

Now, if Jesus' rhetorical question-plus-rebuke in 4:40 is Mark's addition to the story, so too, most likely, is the correlative rhetorical question-plus-rebuke uttered by the disciples in v 38.[181] This line of reasoning may be taken one step further. Since Mark's contributions to this story apparently took the form of rhetorical questions—first by the disciples, then by Jesus—one wonders whether the quasi-acclamation of the disciples at the end of the story is also Mark's formulation, since it too takes the form of a rhetorical question that the disciples ask themselves.[182] Fittingly, this final rhetorical question emphasizes the tension between the disciples' experience of Jesus the miracle-worker ("even the wind and the sea obey him") and their lack of understanding of who he really is ("Who is this?"). The tension between intimate experience of Jesus' power and lack of understanding of his true nature is a great theme of Mark's portrayal of the disciples. Hence, while the primitive story may have had some type of concluding choral acclamation, the present formulation may well come from Mark's hand.

E. OT BACKGROUND

As with Jesus' walking on the water, so too with the stilling of the storm, a full understanding of the miracle story demands a consideration of the OT passages that seem to be echoed or alluded to in the Gospel narrative.

(1) In our study of the walking on the water we reviewed a number of OT texts that speak of Yahweh's dominion over the powers of chaos, specifically over the rebellious sea. Yahweh imposes on the sea its proper limits and orders it to be still. Similar statements, often in the same OT contexts, are made of Yahweh's power over the wind. While Jesus' stilling of the storm is not an epiphany in the strict sense that his walking on the water is, both stories present Jesus wielding the awesome power over the chaotic forces of creation that the OT reserves to Yahweh or his divine Wisdom.[183]

(2) More specifically, the stilling of the storm echoes, with a certain type of paradoxical reversal, the initial chapter of the Book of Jonah. In Jonah 1, Jonah the prophet is on board a ship (LXX: *ploion*, the word used in Mark 4:35–41 for the boat) when Yahweh sends a great wind and a mighty storm on the sea, thus bringing the vessel close to shipwreck. The emphasis in the Hebrew text of Jonah 1:4 on the *great* wind and the *great* storm that Yahweh sends is reminiscent of the "great storm of wind" in Mark 4:37.[184] While in Jonah 1:5 the fearful sailors try everything from prayer to their pagan gods to throwing the cargo overboard, Jonah is blissfully asleep in the ship's hold (*katheudō*, the verb for sleeping employed in Jonah 1:5, is likewise used for Jesus in Mark 4:38). In Jonah 1:6 the ship's captain comes to Jonah and rebukes him with a rhetorical question for sleeping in the midst of the storm: "Why are you sleeping?" He urges Jonah to arise and call upon his God with the hope that "God will spare us and we shall not *perish* [LXX: *apolōmetha*; cf. Mark 4:38: *apollymetha*]." When the sailors finally heed Jonah's request to throw him overboard since he is the guilty party causing the storm, they first pray that they may not *perish* for what they do. When they throw Jonah overboard, "the sea ceased from its raging."[185] The sailors respond by fearing the Lord even more. Indeed, the Hebrew text literally says (Jonah 1:16): "And the men feared a great fear"— which is repeated word for word in Mark 4:41: "And they feared a great fear."[186]

Needless to say, much in the Jonah story differs from the Marcan story: most notably, Jonah is a disobedient prophet who is fleeing from Yahweh. Yahweh responds by sending the storm as punishment and obstacle; the sailors avert the punishment only by tossing Jonah overboard. Still, the similarity of many of the themes and some of the phrases is striking: the prophet and the crew together in a boat that is threatened with sinking by a "great" storm of wind, the prophet peacefully asleep as the storm rages and the crew panics, the use of a rhetorical question to urge the prophet to do something to keep the crew from "perishing," the sudden cessation of the raging storm once the prophet rouses himself and issues a command (the command being quite different in the two stories), and finally the description of the crew responding to the calm by "fearing a great fear."

The use of the Jonah story in the Gospel miracle story is naturally meant to be paradoxical; to the Christian writer, the fulfillment in Jesus both transcends and reverses the events in the Book of Jonah. The christological message of the Gospel story is vaguely reminiscent of the Q saying in Matt 12:41 || Luke 11:32: "And behold, there is something greater than Jonah here."[187] Instead of the disobedient prophet we see the eschatological prophet, who is totally obedient to God's will. As Messiah and Son of God, Jesus need not pray to Israel's God, as the ship's captain urges Jonah to do—to say nothing of appeasing an angry God. Rather, with the power that the OT ascribes to Yahweh and that Yahweh exercises in Jonah 1, Jesus stills the wind and sea with two words of command. The startling christology of the story of the stilling of the storm, a christology just as startling as that of the walking on the water, combines the role of Jonah the prophet of Yahweh and the role of Yahweh the stiller of the storm in one person, Jesus. Like the walking on the water, the stilling of the storm reminds us that some surprising cases of "high christology" (Jesus in the place of and acting as Yahweh, the Lord of creation) receive early symbolic expression in a few of the pre-Marcan miracle stories.[188]

(3) A third OT passage that may stand behind the Gospel miracle is Psalm 107, in which Yahweh is thanked for redeeming those in trouble, including those in ships on the sea (vv 23–32).[189] At Yahweh's command the storm wind (literally: "the wind of a storm") arises, and the waves of the sea are lifted high (v 25). The crew cries out to Yahweh in the midst of their affliction, and he rescues them from their distress (v 28). He makes the storm calm down, and the waves grow still (v 29). In short, what Yahweh does to save the crew of the ship on the sea in Psalm 107 Jesus does to save his disciples in the ship on the Sea of Galilee. This divine power over the sea is also described in Ps 104:7: "At your *rebuke* [LXX: *epitimēseōs*] they [the waters of the deep] flee, at the sound of your thunder they take to flight." This idea of rebuking the sea occurs likewise in Jesus' majestic command to the elements (*epetimēsen* in Mark 4:39). Strictly speaking, the rebuke is addressed to the wind rather than to the sea, though the exorcism-like command to the sea ("Be quiet, be muzzled") is no doubt also considered part of Jesus' rebuke.[190]

F. THE QUESTION OF HISTORICITY

The narrative of the stilling of the storm is already at some disadvantage because, unlike the walking on the water, it does not enjoy multiple attestation of sources. It is found only in the Marcan source, Matthew and Luke being directly dependent on Mark for their versions of the story. To be sure, the stilling of the storm is similar to the walking on the water in two notable ways, but these similarities only make the case for historicity more difficult: (1) There is a large and pervasive use of OT stories, motifs, and phrases in the Marcan miracle story. (2) More significantly, these OT elements serve the purpose of putting Jesus in the place of Yahweh as the sovereign of the cosmos, the one who reduces the raging wind and sea to silence with a mere word of rebuke. In other words, as in the walking on the water, so in the stilling of the storm, a heavy presence of OT themes serves the purpose of articulating symbolically an early form of "narrative high christology." Other Christian elements have entered into the telling of the story: e.g., the presence of the theme of Yahweh or Jesus "rebuking" the wind and waves may have occasioned the assimilation of the stilling of the storm to a sort of cosmic exorcism. Moreover, in the last stage of redaction Mark has adapted the story to his particular theology of the messianic secret and the obtuseness of the disciples.

From a certain point of view, the criterion of discontinuity from the Jesus tradition and continuity with early church tradition might also be invoked to argue against historicity. As B. M. F. van Iersel and A. J. Linmans point out, the stilling of the storm "is the only miracle story in which Jesus' disciples are saved from distress."[191] Perhaps one might sharpen and clarify this observation by stating that this is the only Gospel miracle in which people who already follow Jesus as their master are rescued by him from mortal danger. Hence the stilling of the storm, under this aspect, is discontinuous from the rest of the Gospel miracle tradition. Yet it is certainly continuous with the tradition of miracles worked in the life of the early church, as recorded in the Acts of the Apostles (to say nothing of the later apocryphal Acts). For example, Peter is rescued from prison and no doubt from mortal danger by an angel of the Lord (Acts 12:6–19, esp. v 11); Paul and his companions have their lives preserved by God despite shipwreck (Acts 27:13–44, esp. vv 23–25). Thus, a miracle in which God or Jesus acting as God preserves the followers of Jesus from mortal danger fits the miracle tradition originating in the early church more than it fits any miracle tradition that can claim to go back to Jesus' public ministry. Weighing all these considerations, I think that there is little in the tradition of the stilling of the storm that does not bear the imprint of the post-Easter Christian church and its theology.[192]

Needless to say, no one questions the historical fact that Jesus crossed the Sea of Galilee in a boat with his disciples and probably did so with some frequency. Nor does anyone question the existence of frequent violent storms that suddenly descend upon the basin-like Sea of Galilee from the surrounding mountains, especially from the south.[193] The question is rather the occurrence of the specific stilling of a storm by Jesus as recounted in Mark 4:35–41. In itself, it would be rash to claim a priori that such an event would be simply impossible. In fact, such a claim is contradicted by the recording of similar acts of calming storms, supposedly performed by charismatic healers and wonder-workers, even in the modern period of history. For example, it is reported that the revivalist preacher Aimee Semple McPherson commanded a strong wind to cease when it was disrupting her first tent meeting, held in Mount Forest, Ontario, Canada, in August 1915; the wind duly ceased.[194] Naturally, one can put this down to a happy (for Aimee) coincidence or to her "sixth sense" that the storm was about to pass. The same thing could be suggested in reference to Jesus in Mark 4:35–41.[195] Sudden calms following sudden storms were and are by no means unusual on the Sea of Galilee. Indeed, a famous Jewish quester for the historical Jesus, Joseph Klausner, relates that he himself experienced a similar sudden storm followed by a sudden calm on the Sea of Galilee in the spring of 1912.[196]

But all this does not get us beyond the realm of mere possibility. Our examination of Mark's redactional theology in the text, the heavy presence of OT themes and phrases serving a surprisingly early high christology of the church, the similarity all this bears to the walking on the water, the lack of multiple attestation of the miracle, and the miracle's continuity with the miracle tradition of the early church rather than the miracle tradition that has a claim to go back to Jesus' public ministry oblige us to conclude that the more probable opinion—though not an absolutely certain one—is that the stilling of the storm is a product of early Christian theology.[197]

VIII. THE CHANGING OF WATER INTO WINE AT CANA
(JOHN 2:1–11)[198]

A. BASIC FORM AND CONTENT OF THE STORY

Even within the compass of Gospel miracle stories, which pose many a riddle to the interpreter, the story of Jesus changing water into wine at Cana (John 2:1–11) is especially puzzling.[199] To be sure, in some ways it seems like a straightforward miracle story—a gift miracle, to be precise. Like any standard miracle story, it has the three elements of (1) a setup (vv 1–6, opening circumstances, the need, and the petition), (2) the miracle proper (vv 7–9a, the meeting of the need by Jesus), and (3) the concluding reaction (vv 9b–11, confirmation of the miracle's reality, a quasi-acclamation of the wonder, and belief in the miracle-worker).[200]

More specifically, the wine miracle resembles in some ways the only other gift miracle in the public ministry, the feeding of the multitude:[201]

(1) The *setup*: (a) In each story Jesus is faced with the need for nourishment experienced by a group that goes far beyond his immediate circle of disciples (John 2: the guests at the wedding; John 6: the crowd that has followed him).[202] (b) The theme of need is emphasized in a dialogue between Jesus and another character in the story (John 2: his mother; John 6: his disciple Philip). (c) The unpromising material that Jesus will use to meet the need is then introduced into the narrative (John 2: six stone water jars and the water to fill them; John 6: five loaves and two fish). (d) Jesus' initial response is to order others to do something that seems to have no relation with meeting the need (John 2: the servants are ordered to fill the jars with water; John 6: the disciples are ordered to make the crowd recline on the grass).

(2) The *miracle proper*: The actual moment and manner in which the miracle is accomplished are never narrated; there is a "veiled" aspect to each story.

(3) *The conclusion*: Each story concludes with a statement that confirms the fine quality or great quantity of the nourishment Jesus provides (John 2: best wine kept until now; John 6: twelve baskets of fragments collected).

B. THE DIFFERENT, ALLUSIVE NATURE OF THE STORY

Despite the rough parallels noted above, the wine miracle of Cana has many characteristics that set it apart from most or all other miracle stories in the Gospels. What strikes one immediately is that the story has an indirect, allusive character throughout. Three key elements of a miracle story (the petition in the setup, the miracle-working word and/or deed of Jesus, and the acclamation) are all narrated in an indirect, puzzling, or ironic way.

(1) Instead of a clear petition, we hear only the laconic observation of Jesus' mother (v 3): "They have no wine."[203] It is not surprising that commentators

differ over whether the mother is thought simply to be making an observation, vaguely asking Jesus for help, or specifically requesting a miracle. As with so much of this story, there is ellipsis and silence where we would want further explanations. Commentators are forever trying to fill in the gaps, an effort that often misses the story's point and distorts its emphasis.[204]

(2) The miracle proper is narrated in an even more indirect fashion than the feeding of the multitude, where Jesus' act of taking the food, giving thanks, and distributing it at least depicts Jesus engaged in a solemn, prayerful manner over the food. In the wine miracle of Cana all Jesus does is give two orders to the servants: fill the jars with water (v 7); draw off some of the liquid and bring it to the headwaiter (v 8). In effect, Jesus does nothing and says nothing directly over the water. The servants are the ones who perform the central actions during which, one supposes, the transformation of the water into wine is thought to take place. The fact of the transformation is then mentioned only in passing in v 9: "When the headwaiter had tasted the water-become-wine. . . ."

(3) The concluding acclamation is likewise indirect and allusive. A miracle story often ends with an acclamation of Jesus or astonishment at his wonderful deed, stated in no uncertain terms. Here, in a quasi-acclamation,[205] and with no little irony, the happy but ignorant headwaiter praises the fine quality of the wine to the bridegroom (v 10): "You have kept the fine [or: best] wine until now." Here we should note a difference from the feeding of the multitude: in John 2:10 it is the quality, not the quantity, of what Jesus has provided that is emphasized at the end of the story. The miracle of the loaves and fish is a miracle involving the multiplication of the same food stuff; the miracle at Cana is a miracle of the transformation of one element (ordinary water) into another (fine wine), the quantity remaining the same. More importantly, though, and totally in keeping with Johannine irony, the person extolling the quality of the wine in 2:10 does not realize that he is acclaiming a miracle. In contrast, the crowd that has been miraculously fed with the loaves and fish respond by acclaiming Jesus as the true prophet-king who has come into the world (6:14–15).[206]

If the story of the Cana miracle ended with the quasi-acclamation in 2:10, we might think that no one except the servants knew of Jesus' miracle. However, the summarizing conclusion of the narrator (v 11) informs us that in this first of his signs Jesus "revealed his glory and his disciples believed in him." Even in these concluding words John's laconic story remains terse to the point of bemusement. We are not told how the disciples, who have not been mentioned since v 2, knew of the miracle when the headwaiter did not. In any event, the narrator deftly concludes the story by supplying a double reaction to the miracle: the acclamation of the ignorant headwaiter, spoken to the anonymous bridegroom, and the belief of the disciples, directed to Jesus.[207]

This allusive, veiled character of the Cana miracle is not the only characteristic that sets this miracle story apart. It is the only miracle story of the public ministry in which Jesus' mother is involved.[208] It is also the only miracle story that places Jesus at a marriage and involves wine. While the Fourth Evangelist underscores it as the first (and in some sense the paradigm or archetype) of Jesus' signs, it is absent not only from the beginning of the ministry in the Synoptics but also from the whole range of the Synoptic miracle tradition. Unlike some of the other Johannine miracles (the feeding of the multitude, the walking on the water, the miraculous catch of fish), it does not enjoy multiple attestation of sources. Indeed, unlike the healing of the blind man in chap. 9 and the raising of Lazarus in chap. 11—and thus unlike every other miracle story in John—it lacks any kind of parallel miracle story in the Synoptics.[209] Within the Four Gospels, the wine miracle of Cana truly stands a lone.

C. ISOLATING THE JOHANNINE TRAITS OF THE STORY

This strange similarity to, yet difference from, the rest of the Gospel miracle tradition, the laconic, allusive nature of the story, the puzzling exchange between Jesus and his mother, and the obvious presence of Johannine theology expressed in symbols (yet how far should the symbolism be pressed?) make this story especially difficult to interpret and trace back to earlier tradition. What one exegete declares an addition of the Fourth Evangelist, another exegete judges to be part of a signs source or Signs Gospel that the Evangelist supposedly used. Behind the signs source (a written collection of miracle stories) or Signs Gospel (a sort of fourth Synoptic Gospel, without the great discourses of John) would presumably lie a still more primitive form of the Cana story, circulating independently in the oral tradition. But did such a primitive stage ever exist, and what would the story have looked like in its early oral stage?

Faced with so many different questions and conflicting opinions, perhaps the best we can do is repeat the procedure we adopted when treating the raising of Lazarus in John 11: we shall try to isolate those stylistic and theological traits that most likely come from the hand of the Evangelist. As we saw in the Lazarus story, we can identify fairly easily those elements of the story that presume the larger literary and theological context of John's Gospel (or at least the larger context of a sizable source), elements that therefore would not go back to a primitive isolated story and any historical event lying behind it. Even if some commentators would prefer to assign these "Johannine traits" to a signs source or Signs Gospel that the Fourth Evangelist used, such traits would still be the products of the author who redacted such a source, as opposed to a primitive tradition going back to Jesus' public ministry.

Elements in the story that presuppose the larger literary and theological context of the Gospel and therefore the Evangelist's hand include the following:[210]

(1) The first and most obvious element that presupposes some larger literary unit is the opening phrase of 2:1: "And on the third day. . . ." This beginning of the Cana story makes sense only within the larger context of the preceding events in chap. 1 of the Gospel. Indeed, "on the third day" completes a pattern of counting days that begins in 1:29, when John the Baptist bears witness to Jesus as the Lamb of God: "On the next day [tē epaurion]. . . ." The

same words occur in 1:35 ("On the next day" two disciples of the Baptist follow and stay with Jesus) and 1:43 ("On the next day" Jesus summons Philip to follow him to Galilee and encounters Nathanael). Thus the phrase "on the third day" picks up the conclusion of Jesus' encounter with Nathanael, where Jesus promises Nathanael that he will see greater things (1:50), in fact, an epiphany of the Son of Man (1:51). In the immediate context, therefore, "on the third day" completes the story of the gathering of the first disciples.[211] The promise that the disciples will see the heavenly Son of Man in all his glory receives its first and partial fulfillment in the first sign at Cana (2:11): "This beginning of the signs Jesus performed at Cana of Galilee, and he revealed his glory, and his disciples believed in him." The Cana story is thus something of a pivot. It completes the call of the first disciples (a beginning of sorts), even as it signals the beginning of Jesus' signs. We will explore this dual role of Cana at greater length below.

Not surprisingly, other meanings are often read into the phrase "on the third day" in 2:1. For instance, many authors see a veiled reference to the resurrection.[212] The fact that in 2:4 Jesus speaks of his "hour" that has not yet come (i.e., the hour of his passion and glorification) gives some support to this view. Moreover, in the next pericope, the cleansing of the temple, Jesus predicts that he will raise up the destroyed temple (a metaphor for his crucified body) "in three days" (2:19; cf. vv 21–22). However, there is a major obstacle to adopting this interpretation of "on the third day" as referring to the resurrection: John's Gospel, unlike some other NT writings, nowhere refers to Jesus' resurrection with the set phrase "on the third day." One would have thought that, if John wanted his readers to catch an allusion to the resurrection in 2:1, he would have used "on the third day" in connection with the resurrection somewhere else in his Gospel.

Perhaps the most ambitious and also controversial interpretation of "on the third day" is that of M.-E. Boismard.[213] In his view, from the first appearance of the Baptist in 1:19, the Fourth Evangelist has been carefully constructing a pattern of seven days of progressive revelation that reaches its climax in the first Cana miracle. Boismard claims that the Evangelist intended to underline the parallelism between the first creation of the world in seven days, accomplished by the preexistent Word (John 1:1–5), and the new creation accomplished by Jesus the Word made flesh (1:3,17), also depicted symbolically in seven days: namely, in 1:19–2:11.

While this neat parallelism is attractive, it is not without its difficulties. The exegete must strain to find a pattern of seven days laid out in John 1:19–2:11. The first day of the Baptist's witness (1:19–28) is not explicitly counted as such; the same can be said of the supposed fourth day, on which Simon Peter comes to Jesus (1:40–42). The day or days between Jesus' encounter with Nathanael are neither counted nor narrated as such, but are simply inferred from "on the third day" in 2:1 (understood inclusively). It is no wonder that various scholars count the first Cana miracle as either the sixth or the eighth day instead of the seventh day.[214] The mode of computation is by no means clear.

Moreover, so as not to leave one of the days of the new creation empty, Boismard quite arbitrarily places Jesus' encounter with Nathanael (1:47–51) on the
sixth day, when in fact the Gospel narrative seems to place it on the same day as
Jesus' summons to Philip (1:43–46), which Boismard counts as the fifth day.[215]

Hence I find the best and simplest explanation of "on the third day" to be
the first I mentioned: it connects the Cana story with the gathering of the first
disciples in general and with Jesus' promise to Nathanael in particular. Whatever further symbolic references the phrase may or may not have, its basic
function as a link backwards to chap. 1 marks it out as a contribution of the
Evangelist.

(2) The references to "the mother of Jesus" (2:1,3–5) reflect both the manner of speaking and the overarching theological vision of the Evangelist.

(a) The Fourth Evangelist's manner of speaking about Jesus' mother is
striking and unique in the NT. Among those NT authors who mention the
mother of Jesus, only John steadfastly refuses to mention her proper name,
Mary. She is always and only "the mother of Jesus" (2:1,3) or "his mother"
(2:5,12; 6:42; 19:25–26 [sometimes without "his" being expressed in the
Greek]) or finally "your mother" (19:27, as Jesus entrusts his mother to the
care of the beloved disciple).[216] That the Fourth Evangelist should have been
ignorant of the proper name of Jesus' mother seems hardly credible. He knows
the name of Joseph, Jesus' putative father (1:45; 6:42), and he mentions by
name a number of women standing by Jesus' cross (19:25)—though in that
group the mother of Jesus remains curiously unnamed. Indeed, the fact that
"his mother" can occur in the same verses in which "his father" and the other
women at the cross are mentioned by name (6:42; 19:25) makes it all but certain that, for whatever theological or symbolic reason, the Fourth Evangelist
purposely suppresses the name of Jesus' mother and refers to her only by a
phrase that begins to look like some sort of formula or title.

(b) This impression of some sort of stylized, symbolic reference to and
function of Jesus' mother in the Fourth Gospel is reinforced by the way Jesus
addresses his mother. When he responds to her observation in v 3 about the
lack of wine, he asks in v 4: "What is that to me and to you, *woman*?[217] My
hour has not yet come." To be sure, the use of "woman" as a mode of address
is not a sign of disrespect or angry rebuff, for Jesus uses it elsewhere when
addressing women in the Fourth Gospel, all of whom he is calling to initial
faith or a deeper faith: the Samaritan woman at the well in 4:21; Mary Magdalene by the empty tomb in 20:15; and (in a later addition to the Fourth Gospel)
the woman caught in adultery in 8:10. Yet, outside of John's Gospel, it is unheard of in either the OT or the NT that a son should address his biological
mother with the unadorned title "woman."[218] When we put this strange mode
of address together with the Evangelist's avoidance of Mary's proper name in
favor of the formal phrase "the mother of Jesus," the natural conclusion is that
the Evangelist intends to convey some sort of symbolic relationship between
Jesus and his mother.[219]

(c) Moreover, it is highly significant that, within the Fourth Gospel, both miracle. In Mark, without explanation Jesus forces the disciples to leave before he says farewell to and dismisses the crowd. Only after that does Jesus go up the mountain to pray. In John, because Jesus perceives the desire of the crowd to seize him and make him king, he withdraws by himself to the mountain (nothing is said about prayer). The crowd simply disappears from the narrative, and the abandoned disciples, after apparently waiting around for a while, leave by boat on their own initiative when evening comes on. The common thread is that, because of some initial action of Jesus, the disciples leave in a boat without him, while he goes up a mountain by himself. To borrow some terms from structuralism: at the beginning of the narrative Jesus sets up a bipolar opposition (disciples harassed on sea—Jesus alone on land) that is then overcome or mediated by Jesus' epiphany.

2. The Miracle Proper: The word and deed of Jesus effect an epiphany that overcomes the separation. Separated from Jesus and rowing at night in the face of a strong wind, the disciples make painfully slow progress across the sea. Suddenly, out of the darkness they see Jesus walking toward them on the sea. As elsewhere in the Bible, the typical reaction of those receiving the epiphany is fear, just as Jesus' response to their fear is the typical word of identification, revelation, and comfort: "It is I [or: I am], fear not." It is noteworthy that here, at the heart of the story, John and Mark agree closely.

3. The Reaction of the Audience and the Conclusion of the Story: Here nothing certain can be said beyond the obvious fact that the plight of the disciples is resolved: they are reunited with Jesus, whose presence expedites their arrival at their destination. Beyond that basic and (one might say) necessary conclusion to this miracle story of epiphany, each evangelist goes his own way.

Mark first has the wind die down, which presumably lets the disciples row speedily to the far shore (though that point is not dwelt on). He then concludes the story with his characteristic theme of the disciple's amazement and lack of understanding. At this point Matthew blithely contradicts Mark, since the First Evangelist does not hold to the messianic secret but rather prefers to have revelation go public. Accordingly, after the wind dies down, "those in the boat" (a generalizing phrase that allows the listening audience to take part) worship Jesus (Matthew uses his favorite verb *proskyneō* for "worship") with a choral profession of faith: "Truly you are God's Son." This acclamation anticipates the confession of faith of Peter at Caesarea Philippi (16:16) and more precisely the confession of the centurion and his companions at the cross (27:54). As we have seen, John takes a totally different tack: the very presence of Jesus immediately and miraculously brings the boat to the far shore.

Since each ending is typical of the theology of each evangelist, nothing certain can be said about the ending of the primitive tradition beyond the obvious: by walking on the water in a majestic epiphany Jesus reunites himself with his harassed disciples, who then reach the far shore with their master.

In sum, the basic content of the primitive story is fairly clear: After the feeding of the five thousand, and in response to some initial action of Jesus, the disciples get into the boat and start to cross the Sea of Galilee without him. As darkness comes on, they are rowing in distress on the sea, making little headway because of the strong wind against them, while Jesus is alone on the land on a mountain. Suddenly the disciples see Jesus walking toward them on the sea. They are frightened, but Jesus tells them: "It is I [*egō eimi*], fear not [*mē phobeisthe*]." Jesus is reunited with his disciples, who now reach the far shore without difficulty. We have here a concise miracle story belonging to the form-critical category of epiphany, the only epiphany miracle Jesus performs in the public ministry.[135]

D. THE OT BACKGROUND TO THE EPIPHANY MIRACLE

I have noted already how the story of Jesus walking on the water uses vocabulary and themes found in OT epiphanies as well as in representations of God or God's Wisdom displaying divine power over the unruly waters of chaos. It will help us to appreciate better the origin of this Gospel miracle if we examine more closely and distinguish among the various ways in which these motifs of God's epiphany and God's power over the sea are expressed in the OT.

1. Of most direct concern are those passages where God or God's personified Wisdom walk on or through water in a display of majesty and power. In the Masoretic Text (MT) of the Book of Job, God the Creator is described poetically as the one who, at creation, "tread upon [or: trampled upon] the high places [or: back] of the sea" (9:8b). The phrase "tread upon" or "trample upon" (*dôrēk ʿal*) is a metaphor suggesting God's dominance and power over the sea, which in ancient Near Eastern mythology was often depicted as the monster of chaos, the principle of evil, disorder, and death that opposed the creator god(s).[136]

This passage in Job is especially significant for the story of Jesus' walking on the water because almost the exact same phrase is used for the action of walking on the sea in both the Greek Septuagint (LXX) translation of Job 9:8b and in Mark 6:48 ‖ John 6:19. LXX Job 9:8b describes God the Creator as *peripatōn . . . epi thalassēs* ("walking on [the] sea").[137] Mark 6:48 describes Jesus as *peripatōn epi tēs thalassēs* (the same phrase, but with the definite article used before the noun for "sea"). John 6:19 has the same phrase as Mark, with the participle put into the accusative case to fit the syntax of his sentence: *peripatounta epi tēs thalassēs*. The LXX has somewhat "demythologized" the description of God by having the Lord "walk" instead of "tread" or "trample" and by omitting the imagery of the "back" or "heights" of the sea. Instead, the LXX says that the Lord walks on the sea "as on dry ground" (*hōs ep' edaphous*). Thus, in language and imagery the LXX is closer than the MT to the Gospel depiction of Jesus walking on the water. In any event, the image of God the Creator walking on the sea as on dry ground conveys his unlimited power over the sea and indeed over all the forces of creation—a power humans do not have. The same imagery is applied to Jesus in the Gospel miracle.

2. One should note, though, that the description of God in Job 9:8b does

the person of Mary and this peculiar combination of the title "the mother of Jesus" (or "his mother") and the address "woman" occur only in the first Cana miracle and at the cross. In other words, the Fourth Evangelist has carefully introduced and limited "the mother of Jesus" to two pericopes at the beginning and at the end of Jesus' public life: the "sign" at Cana marking the beginning of his public ministry and a scene at the cross just before his death.

That this positioning seeks more than just literary balance is clear from the theological correspondence between the two scenes. At Cana, the reason why Jesus distances himself and his intention from his mother's implied request is that "my hour has not yet come." In John's Gospel, while phrases like "*an* hour is coming and is now here" can refer in a general fashion to the realized eschatology that Jesus' incarnation and revelation introduce into the world (e.g., 4:21,23; 5:25), the more precise phrases "my hour," "his hour," "the hour," and "this hour" (i.e., the hour of Jesus) regularly refer to Jesus' "glorification" by his death on the cross (7:30; 8:20; 12:23,27; 13:1; 17:1).[220]

Thus the Evangelist has carefully constructed a theological cross-reference in the first Cana miracle.[221] The mother of Jesus is kept in a sense at arm's length ("What is that to me and to you?") because the decisive hour of the cross is not at hand (2:4). In keeping with this theological schema, she disappears from the narrative of John's Gospel after 2:12 (unlike the unbelieving brothers of Jesus in 7:3–10) until the hour of the cross.[222] Then in a dramatic scene (19:25–27) just before the death of Jesus, she is brought back on stage, referred to as "his mother," addressed by him as "woman," and confided by him to the care of the beloved disciple—and thus symbolically to the tradition and memory of the Johannine community. This depiction of the mother stands in stark contrast to the brothers of Jesus, who are never brought back on stage for "rehabilitation" after their negative portrayal as unbelievers in 7:3–10.

The upshot of all this is that the curious way in which Mary is referred to and addressed in the first Cana miracle, the way Jesus distances himself from her for the time being, and the way he points forward to her place at the cross all make sense only within the larger composition of John's Gospel. In other words, Mary's mode of being referred to and addressed, her theological and symbolic function, and her dialogue with her son in the first Cana miracle all seem to stem from the Evangelist composing the Gospel as a whole, and not from the tradition.

(3) This theological function of Jesus' mother in the Cana story ties in with a larger theological pattern that also seems to be the work of the Evangelist. Most commentators spend great energy trying to solve the puzzle of why, although Jesus seems at first glance to refuse Mary's implied request for help (2:4), Mary immediately instructs the servants to do whatever Jesus tells them (v 5), and Jesus then dutifully proceeds in vv 7–8 to provide the miraculous help he seemed to refuse his mother in v 4.

At times, this tension in the story between Jesus' initial refusal and his eventual granting of the request is explained as a result of the tension between the tradition the Evangelist has received and his own redaction of the story.[223]

While such an explanation cannot be dismissed lightly, the whole strange succession of events may be explained more easily on the basis of a literary and theological pattern the Evangelist employs elsewhere in his Gospel.[224] To understand this pattern, we must remind ourselves that, according to the high christology of John's Gospel, Jesus always knows everything and maintains the initiative in all events—even his passion and death—thus displaying his divine sovereignty and control. Hence in a number of John's miracle stories, Jesus seizes the initiative and performs the miracle when no one has made a request or even thought in terms of a miracle to be performed by him: so the paralytic man by the pool in 5:1–9, the feeding of the multitude in 6:1–15, the walking on the water in 6:16–21, and the man born blind in 9:1–7.

However, there are three stories in which someone at least implicitly asks for a miracle: the mother of Jesus at Cana in 2:3 ("they have no wine"), the royal official pleading for his sick son in 4:47 ("he asked that he [Jesus] come down and heal his son"), and Mary and Martha pleading for the sick Lazarus in 11:3 ("Lord, behold, he whom you love is sick"). It is hardly by accident that it is in these three miracle stories that we notice a particular Johannine pattern that safeguards the sovereign initiative and control of Jesus. In each of these three stories:

(a) A petitioner makes an implied or explicit request for a miracle.

(b) Jesus at first seems to refuse the request for his miraculous intervention abruptly and unfeelingly. In this way he keeps control of the flow of events and shows that whatever he will do he will do according to the "timetable" and purpose of his mission, which is ultimately controlled by his Father's will (cf. 4:34; 5:30; 6:38–40; 7:2–10).

(c) The petitioner, being a person who is basically well-disposed to Jesus and open to his challenge of faith, is not put off by the apparent refusal but in one way or another persists in his or her request, thereby implicitly affirming faith in the Jesus who appears to be disappointing the petitioner.[225]

(d) In the end, in response to this persistent faith, Jesus does accede to the request, but each time in a more spectacular and amazing way than the petitioner could possibly have imagined. Jesus thus makes clear that, when he does grant the miraculous favor, he does so on his own terms, at his own time, with a superabundant generosity the petitioner could not have expected, and with a special theological symbolism that far transcends the original intention of the petitioner.

We can see this pattern worked out in all three of the Johannine miracle stories that begin with petitions:

In the first Cana miracle, we have already observed the elements of the pattern: (a) In v 3, Mary makes the implied request: "They have no wine." (b) In v 4, Jesus seems to refuse the request: "What is that to you and to me, woman? My hour has not yet come." (c) In v 5, in the face of this apparent refusal, Mary persists in believing that Jesus will do something to help; hence she tells the servants: "Do whatever he tells you." (d) In vv 7–8, Jesus does accede to the request, but with a superabundant gift of fine wine that symbolizes the irruption into the present moment of the final age, overflowing with the wine of the messianic banquet and thus transcending the ritual institutions of Judaism, symbolized by the water of purification that has been transformed into wine.

The same basic pattern can be seen in the story of the royal official's son, when Jesus is again at Cana. (a) In 4:47, the official begs Jesus to come down from Cana to Capernaum to heal his son before he dies. (b) In v 48, Jesus appears to refuse in a most unfeeling and brusque manner: "Unless you [plural] see signs and wonders, you will not believe." (c) In v 49 the official persists in pleading (and so implicitly believing): "Lord, come down before my little boy dies." (d) In v 50, Jesus accedes to the request in a way that goes beyond the father's expectations. Instead of coming down to heal the boy (presumably by his touch), Jesus simply heals the boy at a distance by saying: "Go; your son lives." Thus, the healing is done on Jesus' terms and at the time he chooses, with the result that the miracle is all the more spectacular for being performed at a distance. Moreover, by emphasizing the theme of life ("your son *lives*"), this miracle story conveniently sounds the theme of life that will dominate the next section of the Fourth Gospel, beginning in chap. 5.

The pattern is found for a third time in the raising of Lazarus, though this time in a more diffuse form, since the interpretive discourse material has been woven into the narrative of the sign. Still, the basic outline is clear enough. (a) In 11:3, Mary and Martha make an implicit request by sending Jesus the message: "Lord, behold, the one you love is sick." Like the veiled petition of Jesus' mother in 2:3, the implicit request is expressed as a terse declarative sentence, informing (!) Jesus of a pressing need. (b) In 11:4, Jesus seems to ignore or put off the request, remarking that the apparently mortal illness will not really lead to death (as the ultimate result). Jesus then purposely stays on where he is for two more days (v 6), thus allowing Lazarus to die and thus giving what would appear to be the definitive refusal of any help. But in fact Jesus is simply following the "timetable" set for him by the salvific will of his Father (vv 7–16). (c) Despite this apparently definitive rebuff, Martha persists in believing in Jesus; indeed, prodded by Jesus' revelation of himself as the resurrection and the life, she rises to new heights of belief in him as the Son of God come into the world (vv 21–27). (d) After a final challenge to Martha to believe in what seems impossible after Lazarus has been four days dead in the tomb, Jesus raises the dead man to life (vv 39–44). Once again, Jesus asserts his initiative in the face of a petition, follows a divine instead of a human timetable, and in the end bestows a miracle beyond the petitioner's wildest expectations: instead of the healing of a sick man, the restoration of a dead man to life after four days in the tomb. The miracle symbolizes Jesus' own coming death and resurrection (which, according to John, is paradoxically occasioned by the Lazarus miracle) as well as his power to give eternal life to all who believe, both now and on the last day.

We see, then, that in 2:1–11 not only (1) the way in which Jesus' mother is referred to and functions theologically in the story vis-à-vis the later story of

Jesus' crucifixion but also (2) the very pattern of request—apparent refusal—persistent faith—and final bestowal of the miracle in an unexpected way all bear the fingerprints of the Evangelist's creative hand. The first five verses of the story, as well as the structure of the story as a whole, would appear to be largely or wholly the Evangelist's creation.

(4) A fourth element in 2:1–11 seems very typical of the Evangelist's theology, namely, the way the miracle itself is presented and a symbolic meaning is attached to it. (a) The miracle is spectacular and massive, as are many of Jesus' miracles in John. They often surpass in sheer quantity and quality equivalent stories in the Synoptics. The Synoptics know of healings of blind people (e.g., Bartimaeus in Mark 10:46–52 parr.), but only the Johannine Jesus heals a man specifically said to be *born* blind (chap. 9). The Synoptics know of miracles of raising the dead (e.g., the daughter of Jairus in Mark 5:21–43 parr.), but only the Johannine Jesus raises a man already four days in the tomb (Lazarus in chap. 11). The Synoptic Jesus heals a woman suffering from a hemorrhage for 12 years (Mark 5:25–34 parr.) and a woman crippled for 18 years (Luke 13:10–17), but the Johannine Jesus heals a man paralyzed for 38 years (5:1–9). The Synoptic Jesus walks on the water toward his disciples in a boat; but when the Johannine Jesus does this, the boat is suddenly and miraculously at the far shore whither it was headed. In short, anything the Synoptic Jesus can do, the Johannine Jesus can do better; this is a typical trait of the Fourth Gospel.

We find this same physical massiveness and a spectacular quality in the first Cana miracle. Standing in the house at Cana are six stone water jars, each holding two or three measures (= about sixteen to twenty-four gallons). Jesus therefore provides a wedding feast that is already a good ways along[226] with something like one hundred forty-four gallons of fine wine. The physically massive, spectacular, and overflowing nature of the miracle fits John's tendencies perfectly.

(b) As usual in John, the physical reality portrayed (in this case, the overabundant supply of fine wine at a wedding feast) symbolizes a higher, spiritual, eschatological reality. We need not search far in the OT to understand the symbolism. As plentiful wine at harvest time (the end of the year) is a natural symbol of "joy at the end," so naturally the OT prophets used the imagery of abundant wine to symbolize the joy of the "final days," when Yahweh would reverse the sinful and sad condition of his people (see Amos 9:13–14; Isa 25:6–7; Jer 31:12–14).[227] The same theme is found in the OT pseudepigrapha, including the pre-Christian passage in *1 Enoch* 10:19. Indeed, the *Syriac Apocalypse of Baruch*, written roughly around the same time as the Fourth Gospel, revels in exuberant descriptions of the massive amount of wine available in the end time: "And on one vine will be a thousand branches, and one branch will produce a thousand clusters, and one cluster will produce a thousand grapes, and one grape will produce a cor of wine" (*2 Apoc. Bar.* 29:5).[228]

(c) Not surprisingly, in addition to the theme of Yahweh supplying wine and joy to Israel at the end time, we also find the related OT image of Yahweh, the true husband of Israel, rejoicing with his bride at the wedding banquet of the end time (Isa 54:4–8; 62:4–5).[229] Interestingly, in such prophetic passages of the OT it is always Yahweh, and not some human "messianic" figure, who is depicted as the bridegroom or husband of Israel (see also Hosea 1–2; Jer 2:2; 3:1–12; Ezekiel 16; 23). It is rather in the NT that we find the messianic figure of Jesus taking the place of Yahweh as the bridegroom wedded to the people of God in the last days. The Book of Revelation, a writing in some sense within the Johannine ambit of theology,[230] rejoices over "the wedding feast of the Lamb [the slain and risen Jesus]" (Rev 19:9). Accordingly, the bride of the Lamb is the church, who calls upon her bridegroom (Jesus the Lamb) to come (19:7; 22:17). Similarly, in his parable of the wise and foolish virgins (Matt 25:1–13), Matthew presents Jesus as the bridegroom coming to his people at the parousia. Matthew also turns the Q parable of the great feast (cf. Luke 14:15–24) into an eschatological wedding banquet, which God the King arranges for his son (Matt 22:1–14). We have seen already how an early metaphor about a joyful wedding was turned by the Christian tradition into a reference to the presence and then absence of Jesus the bridegroom because of his passion and death (Mark 2:19–20). The Epistle to the Ephesians, while not using the precise term "bridegroom," makes the union of Christ and his church the archetype and example of the love between husbands and wives in Christian marriage (Eph 5:22–33). Hence, the transferral of the bridegroom imagery from Yahweh to the Messiah seems in the 1st century A.D. to be very much a piece of Christian theology. It is significant that the vast majority of passages where Jesus is explicitly said to be a bridegroom or is placed at a wedding come from the second Christian generation (Ephesians, Matthew, Revelation, and the Gospel of John).[231]

Interestingly, despite all this bridegroom imagery, the only time in the Gospels that a historical figure in the narrative directly refers to Jesus as the bridegroom of Israel is in John's Gospel. In 3:27–30, John the Baptist firmly rejects the complaints of his jealous disciples over the great success of the upstart Jesus, whose "career" the Baptist had helped "launch." John reminds his disciples that he is only a witness to the Messiah, not the Messiah himself (v 28). Then, obviously referring to the Messiah and his people Israel, John says (v 29): "He [Jesus] who has the bride [Israel] is the bridegroom. The friend [i.e., John the Baptist] of the bridegroom, who stands by and listens to him, rejoices greatly because of the voice of the bridegroom."[232]

In light of this direct identification of Jesus with the bridegroom of Israel in John 3:29 (as well as the allied imagery in the Book of Revelation), it seems likely that the first Cana miracle also means to conjure up the idea of Jesus the bridegroom coming to claim his bride Israel at a wedding feast.[233] The messianic wedding feast, which both Matthew and the Book of Revelation place at the parousia, John sees being realized from the very beginning of Jesus' ministry; this is typical of John's realized eschatology.

This emphasis on the symbolism of Jesus as the bridegroom may illuminate what is otherwise a puzzling feature of the first Cana miracle. We have seen that the headwaiter supplies a quasi-acclamation of Jesus' fine (eschatological) wine at the end of the miracle (2:10). Strangely, though, Jesus seems to have disappeared from the scene. Instead, the headwaiter addresses his praise to an anonymous bridegroom (*ton nymphion* in v 9), who up until now has played no part in the story and who suddenly appears at its climax to receive the headwaiter's acclamation: "Everyone [*pas anthrōpos*] serves the good wine first. . . . But *you* [emphatic in the Greek] have kept the good wine *until now*."[234] The "until now" echoes the realized eschatology of John; *now*, in this time of the incarnation and revelation of the Son of God on earth, *now* the abundant wine of the end time is being poured out at the messianic wedding feast.[235] Granted the symbolic sense of this final acclamation with its "until now," and granted the messianic symbolism of the bridegroom elsewhere in John and the NT,[236] I think it likely that the silent bridegroom to whom the climactic acclamation is addressed is meant by the Evangelist to symbolize Jesus. Of him it can be truly said: "*You* have kept the best wine [a Semitism: the positive adjective "good" for the superlative] of God's own life *until now*," until these eschatological days of your incarnation, when you reveal your glory in your signs and your disciples believe in you (v 11).

(d) The description of the happy but ignorant headwaiter betrays the Evangelist's hand in another way as well. We are told in v 9 that the headwaiter "did *not know whence* the water-become-wine was [i.e., where the wine had come from], but the servants who had drawn the water *knew*." In itself, this detail makes for typically Johannine irony. But there is something more deeply theological in this detail. Elsewhere in the Gospel the key word "whence" (*pothen*) serves as a sort of code word for Jesus' divine origin from the heavenly world.[237] In John's theology, Jesus has come down from heaven in the incarnation (his "whence"), and he will return there by way of the cross (his "whither"). To know Jesus' true origin (his "whence"), and hence his divine nature and gift, is equivalent to believing and to having eternal life; not to know it is to stand already condemned. Hence the weighty words—and implied threat—of Jesus as he confronts his adversaries in the temple during the feast of Tabernacles: "Even if I bear witness concerning myself, my witness is true [or: valid], for *I know whence* I have come and *whither* I am going. But you *do not know whence I come and whither I go*."

Once again, the first Cana miracle shows itself to be the "beginning" in more ways than one. For the first time in the Gospel the dualistic theme of knowing and not knowing is combined with the theme of the "whence" of the divine gift Jesus gives. As elsewhere in the short narrative of 2:1–11, central theological themes of John's christology and soteriology are touched upon ever so briefly for the first time. They will be developed at greater length in what follows this "beginning."

(e) The overall Johannine message of the first Cana miracle thus begins to fall into place. In the "now" of the end time, inaugurated by the incarnation of the Son of God, Jesus is able to hold the eschatological marriage feast in which he, the messianic bridegroom, comes to claim his bride Israel.[238] The superabundant gift of God's life (= the Spirit) is poured out lavishly for believers under the symbol of the massive quantity of fine wine. Within this context of eschatological abundance and fulfillment, the stone water jars of v 6 may play their symbolic role as well. Since the Evangelist stresses that the water in these jars served for Jewish ritual purification, and since it is the water in these jars that Jesus pointedly changes into his abundant and fine wine (the gift of God's life in the end time), the transformation of the water into wine may symbolize for the Evangelist the replacement of Judaism by Christianity.[239]

This suggestion does not appear all that cogent when the first Cana miracle is read in isolation. But read precisely as the *beginning* of Jesus' signs, it introduces a whole series of his actions and discourses that stress the replacement of the Jewish religion. In chaps. 2–4, Jesus in principle replaces the Jerusalem Temple with his (crucified and risen) body (2:13–22) and the sanctuaries of Jerusalem and Gerizim with worship in Spirit and in truth (4:20–26). In chaps. 5–10, Jesus proceeds to replace Jewish observances and feasts: the Sabbath along with its rest (5:1–18), Passover along with the manna (6:1–58), Tabernacles along with its water and light (7:1–9:41), and Hanukkah along with its dedication of the altar (10:22–39). What replaces them is simply the gift of divine life and light that Jesus brings and is. This theme of replacement is struck not only in the events following upon the first Cana miracle; we hear it already in the programmatic pronouncement on the relation between the old and new order made toward the end of the Gospel's Prologue (1:17): "For the law was given through Moses; grace and truth came through Jesus Christ."

Given this larger context, which the first Cana miracle introduces, the changing of water meant for Jewish purification into the fine wine of the eschaton seems to fit into this Johannine theme of the replacement of Judaism by Christianity. This obviously polemical theme makes perfect sense toward the end of the first century, when John's church, originally at home within the Jewish synagogue, has undergone a traumatic break with Judaism and is now articulating its new identity as a separate people.[240] In theological retrospect, this painful break is now seen by the Evangelist to be the work of Jesus himself, who symbolically accomplishes the replacement of Judaism by the church during his incarnate life.

(5) Having seen the Johannine theology that pervades the narrative in 2:1–10, we can easily recognize the hand of John in the summary concluding statement in v 11, which points both forward and backward in his overarching theological composition.[241] Verse 11a, translated literally, tells us that "this beginning of the signs Jesus performed in Cana of Galilee." It should be emphasized that John does not say, as translations often put it, "Jesus performed this as the first of his signs." Rather, John pointedly uses the noun *archē*, "beginning," which he also employs to begin the whole Gospel: *en archē* . . . in the beginning. "Beginning" is a very important term for the whole Johannine tradition, not only for the Gospel but also for the First Epistle of John. In 1 John 1:1–3, the Prologue of the Gospel is echoed, but with a notable difference: "What was *from the beginning*, what we have heard, what we have seen . . . concerning the word of life . . . that we announce to you." Here the

beginning is not the beginning of creation but rather the beginning of the authentic Johannine tradition, rooted in the beginning of Jesus' public ministry as witnessed by his first disciples—in other words, what is portrayed in the gathering of the first disciples in the first chapter of the Gospel.[242] As Jesus says at the Last Supper in John 15:27: "And you will bear witness, for you have been with me *from the beginning*." This "beginning," this gathering and forming of disciples, has reached a certain climax and turning point in the first Cana miracle of John 2:1–11. For the first time, Jesus works a miraculous sign in the presence of his disciples.

But this sign is not just the "first" in a purely numerical sense. It is also the beginning—not just in the sense of the culmination of the beginning seen in the gathering of the community of disciples narrated in chap. 1 but also in the sense of the beginning of a series of signs that will spell out in ever greater detail the abundant, overflowing gift of divine life succinctly symbolized in this first sign. The first sign is the *archē* almost in the sense of the archetype of all the signs to come.[243] All those signs will gradually, progressively reveal the glory that the Word had with the Father before the world existed (17:5; cf. 12:41), the glory that begins to shine forth in Jesus from the incarnation onward (1:14), the glory that is first revealed to the disciples at Cana (2:11), the glory that shines ever brighter throughout the public ministry with its various signs (e.g., 11:40, in the raising of Lazarus), the glory that leaves behind all signs as it blazes forth in the reality of Jesus' definitive glorification, his death on the cross (12:23,27–33; 17:1–5), the glory that penetrates the believing community and so makes it one even as the Father and the Son are one (17:22), the glory that the disciples will see fully when they are reunited with Jesus in heaven (17:24).[244]

The purpose of this first Cana sign and all the signs that reveal Jesus' "glory" (i.e., his union of life and love with the Father, a union that is offered to all who accept his revelation) is to bring his disciples to ever deeper faith (v 11c): ". . . and his disciples believed in him." Here the idea of the first Cana miracle as the culmination of all that has happened in the narrative of chap. 1 reaches its clearest expression. As the first disciples are drawn to Jesus from 1:35 onward, they address Jesus with ever higher titles: rabbi (v 38), the Messiah (v 41), the one of whom Moses in the law and the prophets wrote, Jesus the son of Joseph, from Nazareth (v 45), the Son of God and King of Israel (v 49). Yet Jesus sees none of this as enough. Chap. 1 ends with his promise that the disciples will *see* still greater things, indeed, the Son of Man upon whom the angels ascend and descend (an evocation of Jacob's ladder in Gen 28:12; Jesus is the definitive conduit of revelation).

Interestingly, amid all these christological affirmations in chap. 1, the Evangelist never states directly in his narrative that the recently gathered group of disciples has come to *believe* in Jesus. The closest we come to that is Jesus' gently ironic question to the eager Nathanael at the end of chap. 1 (v 50): "Because I told you that I saw you under the fig tree, do you *believe*? Greater things than these shall you *see*."[245] This promise seems to receive its "first" fulfillment in the first Cana sign; hence the Evangelist's first use of the verb "believe" for the group of the disciples Jesus has gathered.[246] Having seen his glory revealed in the first sign, "his disciples *believed* in him." One appreciates, then, how 2:11 fits perfectly as a pivot, both closing out the gathering of the first disciples who now believe and at the same time beginning the series of signs that will progressively reveal Jesus' glory and lead the disciples to deeper faith.

A final indication that 2:11 comes from the Evangelist's hand is its role in structuring the first section of the public ministry, from chap. 2 to the end of chap. 4. John 2:11 is clearly picked up and echoed at the end of the second Cana miracle, the healing of the royal official's son, when the Evangelist concludes the healing by saying (4:54): "Now this second sign Jesus performed, coming from Judea into Galilee." The first two signs narrated at length thus form a neat *inclusio*, sandwiching together the first part of the public ministry. Many commentators think that this enumeration of the first two signs already existed in the signs source, since in the present Gospel there are mentions of other signs of Jesus intervening (2:23; 3:2), signs performed in Jerusalem. Hence, reason the commentators, the enumeration of the healing of the royal official's son is not in the present form of the Gospel the second sign; the enumeration must stem from the signs source.

While that may be true, the reasoning is not airtight. Strictly speaking, the Evangelist says in 4:54 that the healing is the second sign Jesus performed *as he came from Judea into Galilee.* That Jesus had just come into Galilee was also true of the first sign at Cana, but this specific geographical context is not affirmed of any other signs mentioned before the healing of the royal official's son. Moreover, such intervening signs (2:23; 3:2) are mentioned only in passing and are not narrated. In contrast, this healing of the son, like the wine miracle, is performed right after Jesus has come into Galilee (and to Cana in particular) and qualifies as a full miracle story. Hence, I do not think it necessary to invoke a signs source to explain the enumeration in 4:54. Rather, I think both 2:11 and 4:54 are creations of the Evangelist, forming a clear *inclusio* to structure the first part of the public ministry. That is why *only* the first two signs are clearly enumerated, while the other signs in chaps. 1–12 are not; the first two signs play a particular role in structuring the first section of the public ministry in the Fourth Gospel.[247]

In short, from start to finish, John 2:1–11 is pervaded with Johannine theological concepts and literary patterns. It fits snugly and functions smoothly within the overarching literary and theological structure of the Gospel. Certainly, the impression one gets is that the pericope seems to be for the most part, if not entirely, the creation of the Evangelist—or, as some would claim, of the Johannine "circle" or "school" whose work he inherited.

D. SECONDARY HISTORICAL CONSIDERATIONS

The impression that 2:1–11 was created by John or by the school whose work he took over is also supported by various secondary observations from historical criticism. A number of elements in the story create historical difficulties.

(1) Chief among them is the figure of the person I have called the "head-waiter," in Greek *architriklinos*. In the Greco-Roman world, the *architriklinos* was the chief slave who was responsible for managing a banquet. Such a definition is partially verified in John 2:1–11 insofar as the *architriklinos* of vv 9–10 functions as both the head of a group of servants at the feast and the mediator between them and the bridegroom. But in vv 9–10 this headwaiter seems to interact with the bridegroom more as a friend. Having tasted the fine wine that he thinks has been "held back" until now, he calls over the bridegroom and gently chides him in a humorous fashion. To this extent he approaches the position of the Greek *symposiarchos*, the "toastmaster," "president of the drinking-party," or "master of the feast," who was certainly not a mere servant waiting on the guests. The equivalent Roman figure was the *arbiter bibendi*, the "master of drinking" or "toastmaster," who was one of the guests chosen to preside at the meal and, needless to say, especially over the drinking.

The basic problem here is that in the Jewish Palestine of Jesus' time we can find no evidence for the complicated figure of John's *architriklinos* at wedding banquets. The few parallels brought forward from rabbinic literature are both chronologically later and not truly equivalent.[248] To be sure, in the second century B.C. Ben Sira already knows of a person who presides at a dinner (Sir 32:1: *hēgoumenon* in the Greek translation; we lack the original Hebrew at this point). From Ben Sira's exhortations (Sir 32:1–2), it is clear that this president is chosen from among the guests to oversee the arrangements of the meal; he is the equivalent of the *symposiarchos* or the *arbiter bibendi*.[249] Ben Sira warns that the president must not let the honor make him haughty; rather, he should look after the other guests before himself. Clearly the "headwaiter" of John 2:1–11 does not fit this description, since he is not a guest or the best man at the wedding, but rather the head of the servants; yet he enjoys an unusual level of familiarity and friendship with the bridegroom. Moreover, the usual place of a *symposiarchos* was at the communal meal of some voluntary association or club, not at a Jewish family celebration such as a wedding. Faced with the complex figure of the Johannine *architriklinos*, Brown suggests that "in the telling of the story [of John 2:1–11] the functionary [the headwaiter] has taken on some of the aspects of the *arbiter bibendi*."[250]

In any event, as he is portrayed in John 2:1–11, the "headwaiter" does not seem to represent any historical functionary in 1st-century Jewish Palestine. One might appeal to the inroads that Hellenistic culture had made in Palestine by the time of Jesus.[251] But we are situated at a wedding in a peasant hill-town in Galilee, not in Jerusalem or even Sepphoris. The appeal to inroads from Hellenistic culture seems strained, especially when Jewish sources do not reflect this particular inroad, though they reflect many others.

(2) A similar problem arises from the supposedly well-known rule or saying the headwaiter quotes to the bridegroom (2:10): "Everyone [*pas anthrōpos*] puts out first the good [or: best] wine, and when they [the guests] get drunk, the poorer wine." He then goes on to contrast this rule of action with the contrary action of the bridegroom ("but *you* . . ."). Despite the impression created by v

10, we can find no such universal custom, rule, or proverb about hosts and guests in ancient Greco-Roman or Jewish society.[252] Moreover, one is hard pressed to see how this rule, if it existed, could have applied to a peasant wedding in a hill-town in Galilee. Such a wedding went on for many days (various Jewish sources speak of seven days),[253] and people naturally came and went without much ado. The imagined rule or custom presupposes instead a fixed group of people who might or might not notice the change in the quality of wine served to them over a certain period of time.

One cannot avoid the impression that this supposed rule or custom, which would not really fit the situation of a marriage feast in a Galilean hill-town, has actually been created *ad hoc* by the Evangelist for his theological purposes. It alludes in allegorical fashion to the "good wine" of Jesus' revelation being kept to the end time, after the OT economy has run its course. If this is the case, obviously the whole exchange between the dubious figure of the head-waiter and the perhaps allegorical bridegroom has been constructed as an expression of Johannine theology—to be specific, a theology of replacement.

(3) Other elements of the story are somewhat surprising, though not historically impossible. It is strange that both Mary and Jesus, guests at a wedding in a town not their own, proceed without further ado to give orders to the servants, Jesus' orders being especially demanding and puzzling, if not outright bizarre. Likewise strange for a house in a small hill-town in Galilee would be the large number of massive stone water jars within or right outside the house. In general, one wonders about the large number of servants (for many would be needed to fulfill Jesus' command in any speedy fashion) under the direction of a headwaiter. Is this a likely scenario in a Galilean hill-town? Has perhaps a Greco-Roman urban setting familiar to the Evangelist been imported into this story?

E. CONCLUSION

In sum, when one adds these historical difficulties to the massive amount of Johannine literary and theological traits permeating the whole story, it is difficult to identify any "historical kernel" or "core event" that might have a claim to go back to the historical Jesus. Put another way: if we subtract from the eleven verses of the first Cana miracle every element that is likely to have come from the creative mind of John or his Johannine "school" and every element that raises historical problems, the entire pericope vanishes before our eyes verse by verse.[254] Many critics would assign the origin of the story to the Johannine "school" or "circle" lying behind the Gospel. I prefer the view that the story is a creation of the Evangelist himself, using a number of traditional themes.[255]

This is not to question the fact that there was a town called Cana of Galilee (though rival towns have coveted the honor),[256] or that Jesus might well have visited such a town, or that Jesus might well have attended a wedding feast during his public ministry (though no such event is recorded elsewhere in the

Four Gospels). But if we are asked whether there are sufficient indications that at Cana of Galilee the historical Jesus actually performed some astounding deed involving water and/or wine, a deed that the disciples with him considered a miracle, the answer must be negative.

IX. THE FEEDING OF THE MULTITUDE
(MARK 6:32–44 PARR.)[257]

A. THE UNIQUE NATURE OF THIS MIRACLE STORY

The story of Jesus' feeding of the multitude with a few loaves and fish has a number of unique characteristics. To begin with its form-critical classification: the story of the feeding of the multitude is the only gift miracle of multiplication in the Four Gospels, as opposed to the first Cana miracle, which is the only gift miracle of transformation. There is a further difference in comparison with the Cana miracle: in John 2:9, the transformation of water into wine is explicitly stated (though almost as an afterthought): "When the headwaiter tasted *the water-become-wine* [*to hydōr oinon gegenēmenon*]. . . ."[258] In contrast, one has to infer from the result of the feeding miracle what is never explicitly asserted: that at some point, be it when Jesus gave thanks or when he broke the bread or when he and his disciples distributed it, the bread (as well as the fish) was multiplied. It is typical of gift miracles that the miracle proper is narrated in a "veiled" or indirect way.[259]

More important for our purposes is the unique kind of attestation the feeding of the multitude enjoys. This miracle is the only one recounted in all Four Gospels, and the only one recounted twice (i.e., in two variant forms) in both Mark and Matthew. The first Marcan account, the feeding of the five thousand with five loaves and two fish, is found in Mark 6:32–44, with parallels in Matt 14:13–21 and Luke 9:10b–17.[260] The second Marcan account, the feeding of the four thousand with seven loaves and "a few fish," is found in Mark 8:1–10, with a parallel in Matt 15:32–39. The story of the feeding of the multitude in John 6:1–15 is closest to the first Marcan story, since it also speaks of feeding five thousand with five loaves and two fish. However, John's version has some characteristics in common with the second Marcan story, and even one or two characteristics in common with the Matthean and Lucan versions, which depend on Mark.[261]

Clearly, the task of comparing and contrasting different versions of the same miracle story is uniquely complicated in this case. While one must remain open to the possibility of a stray independent tradition in Matthew or Luke also appearing in John, the question of multiple attestation of *sources* (as opposed to the simple phenomenon of multiple versions of a story) basically boils down to the problem of the two versions of the story in Mark 6 and 8 and their relation to the version in John 6.[262] Two major questions must be asked:[263] (1) Is John's version literarily independent of Mark's versions in particular and the

Synoptics' versions in general? (2) Do the versions in Mark 6 and 8 represent two different versions circulating in the pre-Marcan tradition, or is one Marcan version really a creation by Mark, reshaping for his own purposes the traditional version he received from his source?

B. Is John's Version Independent?

As I noted at the beginning of Volume One of *A Marginal Jew*, most of the major commentators on John's Gospel in the 20th century have held that the Fourth Gospel is literarily independent of the Synoptics.[264] In Volume Two, we have seen this view confirmed a number of times when analyzing individual pericopes (e.g., the healing of the royal official's son, the walking on the water). The feeding of the multitude provides exegetes with a superb test case, since it is the only miracle appearing in all Four Gospels, including two versions in Mark and Matthew.

Two commentators on John's Gospel who have undertaken detailed comparisons of the Synoptic and Johannine versions of the story are Raymond E. Brown and C. H. Dodd.[265] Brown is especially helpful in that he supplies a four-page chart detailing every element of the feeding story in each Gospel version, along with a comparison of Jesus' actions over the loaves and fish with his actions over the bread and wine at the Last Supper. Brown distinguishes five discrete elements in the setting of the feeding story, five more in the dialogue between Jesus and his disciples, and four more in the actual miracle and its aftermath. What results from a comparison of all the individual elements in the story is a crazy quilt of similarities and differences between the Synoptics (especially Mark) and John. John's version is closest to Mark 6, but it also contains some intriguing agreements with Mark 8 as opposed to Mark 6, and there is a strange echo of Matthew's version of the second feeding.[266] Moreover, even when John agrees with a particular Synoptic version (e.g., Mark 6), the Greek vocabulary and phrasing are sometimes different.[267]

The upshot of the comparisons and contrasts is clear: if John depends on the Synoptics for his story of the feeding, then we must imagine him spreading out the texts of most of the Synoptic versions on his writing desk and then choosing one phrase from one version and then another phrase from another version, without much rhyme or reason.[268]

Still more, the erratic and haphazard use that John would have had to make of the Synoptics to produce his version is not the only reason for thinking that he is literarily independent of them. There is also the curious fact that, if John knew Mark 6 (the version to which he stands closest), then he purposely omitted some of the elements of Mark's story that would have served the Fourth Evangelist best in conveying his own theological message. A prime example is the reference to an isolated, desolate, or "wilderness" place (*erēmos topos*), which occurs three times in the larger context of Mark's narrative of the first feeding (6:31,32,35).[269] This detail would fit in perfectly with John's bread of life discourse, which follows upon and symbolically explains the feeding in

CHART COMPARING THE MULTIPLICATION IN JOHN AND THE SYNOPTICS

	I FIRST SYNOPTIC ACCOUNT: MK 6:32–44 MT 14:13–21 LK 9:10–17	II SECOND SYNOPTIC ACCOUNT: MK 8:1–10 MT 15:32–39	JOHANNINE ACCOUNT 6:1–15
Setting			
#1	MK–MT: goes in a boat to a *desert* place. LK: withdraws to Bethsaida (contrast with Mark 6:45).	MK: no localization; but 7:31 mentions Decapolis region near the Sea of Galilee. MT: passing along the Sea of Galilee.	Crosses the Sea of Galilee (to Tiberias?); see 6:22–24. It is somewhere across the Sea from Capernaum (6:17). For *desert* theme see 6:31.
#2	MK–MT: see a large crowd as he lands. LK: the crowds follow him.	MK: a large crowd is with him. MT: a large crowd came to him (30). BOTH: crowd(s) have been there three days.	v 2: a large crowd keeps following. v 5: sees a large crowd coming toward him.
#3	MK: no healings mentioned; he teaches. MT–LK: he heals the sick in the crowds.	MK: new story seemingly unconnected with previous healing of deaf-mute. MT (30–31): crowds had brought afflicted whom he healed; they had seen and wondered.	The crowd had seen the signs he was performing on the sick.
#4	MK–MT: only after the multiplication does Jesus go off to/climb up (*anabainein*) the mountain to pray (Mk 6:46; Mt 14:23). ALL: the twelve disciples/apostles are with him.	MT (29): Jesus climbs up (*anabainein*) the mountain and sits down there. BOTH: the disciples are with him.	Jesus goes up (*anerchesthai*) the mountain and sits down there. with his disciples.
#5	MK–MT: In #10 both mention grass; MK says "green grass," implying springtime.		Near Passover; thus springtime.

Dialogue	Synoptic I	Synoptic II	John
#6	ALL: The disciples take initiative. Mk–Mt: worried about the late hour. ALL: They urge Jesus to send the people away to buy food for themselves.	Jesus takes initiative, worried about feeding the crowd that has been with him three days and will faint if he sends them away.	Jesus takes initiative, worried about feeding the crowd.
#7a	ALL: Jesus answers by telling the disciples themselves to feed them.	The disciples answer by asking: "Where are we to get bread in the desert to satisfy such a crowd?" (Mt).	Jesus asks Philip: "Where shall we ever buy bread for these people to eat?"
7b	Mk: They say, "Shall we go and buy 200 denarii worth of bread and give it to them to eat?" Lk (13): ". . . unless we are to go and buy food for all these people."		Philip replies, "Not even with 200 denarii could we buy loaves enough to give each of them a mouthful."
#8	Mk: Jesus asks them, "How many loaves have you? Go and see." They find out. ALL: "We have five loaves and two fish [*ichthys*]." Mt: Jesus says, "Bring them here to me."	BOTH: Jesus asks them, "How many loaves have you?" They say, "Seven— Mt: and a few small fish [*ichthydion*, but *ichthys* in 36]." Mk (later in 7): They have a few small fish (*ichthydion*).	Andrew tells Jesus, "There is a lad here who has five barley loaves and a couple of dried fish [*opsarion*] but what good is that for so many?"
#9	ALL: There are about 5000 men Mt: besides women and children. (only Lk, like Jn, mentions the number at this point; Mk–Mt mention it at the end of the account.)	Mk: There are about 4000. Mt: There are about 4000 men besides women and children. (Both mention the number at the end of the account.)	The men number about 5000.

	SYNOPTIC I	SYNOPTIC II	JOHN
Multi-plication			
#10	MT: He orders the crowds to take a place (*anaklinein*) on the grass. MK: He commands them all to take places (*anaklinein*) by companies on the green grass. So they sit down in groups by hundreds and fifties. LK: He says to his disciples, "Get them to take places [*kataklinein*] in groups of about fifty each." And they do so and make all take their places.	He directs the crowd to sit down (*ana-piptein*).	Jesus says, "Get the people to sit down [*anapiptein*]." There is plenty of grass there; so they sit down.
#11	See special chart for Jesus' action over the loaves and the fish.		
#12	And they all eat and are satisfied.	And they all eat and are satisfied.	—just as much as they want. When they have enough,
#13	ALL: And they take up (*airein*) 12 baskets (*kophinos*) of the fragments. MT–LK: of what is left over. MK: and of the fish. MK–MT: And those who have eaten (MK: the loaves) are about 5000 (MT: the loaves) men = #9.	And they take up (*airein*) 7 hampers (*spyris*) of the fragments that are left over. There are about 4000 (MT: who have eaten) = #9.	he tells his disciples, "Gather up [*synagein*] the fragments that are left over so that nothing will perish." And so they gather 12 baskets (*kophinos*) full of fragments left over by those who have been fed with the 5 barley loaves.

SPECIAL SUBDIVISION OF THE CHART: Comparison of Jesus' actions over the loaves in the multiplication accounts with the eucharistic action over the bread at the Last Supper (Mk 14:22; Mt 26:26; Lk 22:19; 1 Cor 11:23–24)

	Synoptic Multiplication I	Synoptic Multiplication II	Johannine Multiplication	Last Supper
#11a	And taking the five loaves and the two fish (ichthys),	Mt: He takes the seven loaves and the fish (ichthys), Mk: And taking the seven loaves,	Jesus then takes the loaves;	Mk-Mt-Lk: And taking bread, Paul: He takes bread;
11b	and looking up to heaven,			
11c	he pronounces a blessing (eulogein)	and giving thanks (eucharistein),	and giving thanks (eucharistein),	Mk-Mt (over bread): and blessing (eulogein), Lk-Paul (over bread) and ALL over wine: and giving thanks (eucharistein),
11d	and breaks (the loaves)	he breaks		he breaks
11e	and gives (the loaves) to the disciples (didonai)	and gives to the disciples (didonai)	he gives them around (diadidonai)	Mk-Mt-Lk: and gives to them/the disciples (didonai).
11f		Mk: to set them out. And they set them out before the crowd. Mt: and the disciples give them to the crowds.	to those sitting there;	
11g	Mk (only): And he divides the two fish (ichthys) among them all.	Mt: see #11a Mk: And they have a few small fish (ichthydion); and blessing (eulogein) them, he tells them to set them out.	and the same with the dried fish (opsarion).	Action over the wine.

(charts courtesy of Raymond E. Brown)

John 6. In John 6:31, the well-fed crowd provides Jesus with the theme of his discourse when they recall from the Book of Exodus how "our fathers ate manna *in the wilderness* [*en tę erēmǭ*]. . . ."[270] Jesus' discourse takes off from the launching pad of this theme; and, ironically, later on in the discourse Jesus hurls the same theme back at his opponents with a negative twist: "Your fathers ate manna *in the wilderness* and they died" (6:49). It seems incredible that John would have taken over various minor details from Mark 6 (e.g., the presence of grass on which the crowd can recline, noted in Mark 6:39 and John 6:10) while omitting three times a phrase that would have tied in perfectly with a key theme of his bread of life discourse.

Dodd takes a slightly different path in reaching his conclusion,[271] but the conclusion is basically the same: the feeding of the multitude in John 6 is best explained by a tradition similar to but not literarily dependent on the versions of the story preserved in Mark 6 and 8. As we shall see, this initial decision about sources has an important repercussion when we come to evaluate the relationship between the two versions of the feeding story in Mark 6 and 8.

C. The Relationship Between the Two Marcan Versions of the Feeding Story

The problem of the relationship between the two versions of the feeding of the multitude in Mark (6:32–44; 8:1–10) is unique among the miracle stories of his Gospel. To be sure, Mark has a large number of stories about exorcisms and healings, stories that are naturally similar to one another in varying degrees because of common content and literary form. But in general such miracle stories do not resemble one another so closely that they convey the impression of being alternate forms of the same basic story and possibly the same basic historical event.

The possibility of being alternate versions of the same story does arise in the case of the two feeding miracles for a number of reasons:[272]

(1) A detailed examination of the two Marcan versions shows that both the content and the structure of the stories are strikingly similar, at times practically identical.

(2) As is often pointed out, the disciples in the second version of the feeding miracle (8:1–10) seem completely and inexplicably unaware of the possibility that Jesus might perform a miracle of multiplying loaves and fish, even though they experienced such a miracle back in chap. 6 under similar conditions.

(3) As we have just seen, the independent version of the feeding story in John 6:1–15 contains elements of both the first and the second Marcan versions. This points in the direction of one early but fluid oral tradition, which subsequently bifurcated in the pre-Marcan tradition, producing two versions of the same basic story.

(4) One may add an observation from the Q material: the two versions of the healing of the centurion's servant (or son) in Matt 8:5–13 and Luke 7:1–10 differ from each other just as much as the two Marcan versions of the feeding

of the multitude. Yet practically no serious exegete today would posit two different events behind the Matthean and Lucan versions of the healing story. Indeed, as we saw when we treated this miracle story, many critics would consider John 4:46–54 a third form of the same healing story, despite the large number of differences from the Matthean and Lucan versions, differences far greater than those between the two Marcan versions of the feeding story.

As for the second point (the disciples' unawareness of the possibility of Jesus performing another feeding miracle), one might try to see this strange inconsistency as Mark's way of emphasizing the disciples' obtuseness, blindness, and lack of faith. Yet that does not seem to be the theological point Mark wants to make as he narrates the second feeding miracle (8:1–10). The story contains no rebuke of the disciples by Jesus for their faulty memory or faulty faith. When, soon afterwards (8:17–21), Jesus does rebuke them with respect to the feeding miracles, it is not because of their faulty recollection of his miracles. As a matter of fact, the disciples' ability to remember the bare facts of the two miraculous feedings is quite good. It is their inability to understand the deeper, symbolic meaning of the miracles that Jesus rebukes.

Hence, even taking into account Mark's redactional view of the disciples, their amnesia about Jesus' previous feeding miracle when faced with a very similar problem is difficult to comprehend. The most likely explanation is that Mark has incorporated two versions of the same story into his narrative.[273] This is supported by the fact that John knows of only one story, which has similarities to both of the Marcan versions. As I noted when discussing the healing of the blind man of Bethsaida, and as exegetes as diverse as Dodd and Haenchen have suggested, the two feeding stories may have been part of two alternate yet similar cycles of oral traditions about Jesus' Galilean ministry.[274] The two cycles, both of which have been incorporated by Mark into chaps. 6–8, may have been tied together in the oral stage of the tradition by the use of the keyword "bread," employed as a mnemonic device.

One possible objection to this theory of two alternate versions of the feeding miracle circulating in the pre-Marcan tradition is the counterclaim that Mark derived only one version of the feeding miracle from his tradition and then proceeded to create a second version of the story, based on the first version but with some variations.[275] This theory has been proposed by various exegetes, and at first glance it seems possible if not probable. In practice, though, it does not work when one looks more closely at the texts of both Mark 6:32–44 and Mark 8:1–10, especially when compared with the independent version in John 6:1–15.

(1) The theory clearly does not work if one tries to show that Mark 8:1–10 is simply Mark's rewriting of the first feeding miracle in 6:32–44.[276] While Mark 8:1–10 is the shorter and sparer of the two stories, it also contains a surprising number of words and phrases that occur only here in Mark.[277] This is the opposite of what one would expect if Mark were creating in chap. 8 his own abbreviated version of the traditional story he inherited and placed in chap. 6. Moreover, if Mark 8:1–10 were totally the Evangelist's own creation,

one might expect some typically Marcan rebuke of the obtuse disciples. Instead, as was just noted, Mark's redactional comment on the disciples' failure vis-à-vis the feeding miracles is found in a subsequent and obviously redactional pericope (8:14–21). Indeed, with all its non-Marcan vocabulary, the second feeding miracle, when compared with 8:14–21, looks anything but redactional.

This impression is all the more compelling when we notice in Mark 8:1–10 a few striking similarities to John's version of the story, similarities not found in Mark 6:32–44. For example, the Johannine-sounding question of "whence?" (*pothen*) occurs in both Mark 8:4 and John 6:5.[278] Then, too, Jesus' prayer over the bread is described with the participle "giving thanks" (*eucharistēsas*) in both Mark 8:6 and John 6:11; in contrast, Mark 6:41 uses a finite verb stating that "he said a blessing" (*eulogēsen*). These and similar phenomena, when taken together, make the idea of Mark reworking 6:32–44 to produce 8:1–10 highly unlikely.

(2) Yet the opposite suggestion, that the first version of the feeding miracle in Mark 6:32–44 is a Marcan creation based on 8:1–10,[279] likewise labors under many difficulties. The main difficulty stems from the widely accepted position I noted above, namely, that John's version of the feeding story is independent of Mark's. If one admits that John 6:1–15 is not literarily dependent on Mark, and if one then tries to claim that Mark 6:32–44 is simply Mark's redactional reworking of Mark 8:1–10, one runs into massive problems in trying to explain all the agreements that Mark 6:32–44 shares with John 6:1–15 as opposed to Mark 8:1–10. Let us suppose for a moment that Mark is reworking a story about Jesus feeding four thousand with seven loaves and a few fish, a feeding that produces seven baskets of leftovers (as in Mark 8). How is it that Mark accidentally manufactures a redactional creation that just happens to coincide with John 6 and not with Mark 8 at key points in the story: e.g., five thousand people fed with five loaves and two fish, the sum of two-hundred-denarii-worth of bread mentioned by a disciple, and twelve baskets of leftovers (with even the same Greek word for "baskets" in Mark 6 and John 6, as opposed to Mark 8)?[280]

As a matter of fact, Mark 6:32–44 rather than Mark 8:1–10 has the greatest number of parallels with the independent version in John 6:1–15. Hence the theory that Mark 6 is a Marcan redactional creation based simply on Mark 8 is untenable. The upshot of all our comparisons is not only that John 6 is an independent version of the feeding miracle but also that Mark 6 and Mark 8 represent two alternate versions of the feeding miracle, both of which circulated in the pre-Marcan tradition of the first Christian generation.

D. THE PRIMITIVE FORM OF THE STORY

Commentators argue at great length over which elements should be assigned to tradition or redaction in the feeding stories of Mark 6, Mark 8, and John 6.[281] Some redactional traits are fairly clear. For example, John's redactional hand can be seen in his great care to assure the reader in 6:6 that, even when Jesus asks Philip for information, he already knows what he will do. Other redactional interventions (e.g., the mention of Passover in John 6:4) are more debatable.[282] The simplest and surest way of distilling the essential elements of the primitive feeding story is to list the elements present in at least two, and preferably all three, of the stories. Since John represents an independent tradition at greater distance from Mark's tradition than Mark 6 would be from Mark 8, agreements between John 6 and one of the Marcan versions should be given preference.[283]

Employing the usual three-part division of miracle stories,[284] I think the primitive version of the feeding of the multitude would have contained the following elements:

(1) *The Setup* (the temporal and geographical setting, the introduction of the actors, and the need to be met):

(a) the setting: on the shore of the Sea of Galilee (an uninhabited, "desolate" place?);[285]

(b) the actors: Jesus, his immediate disciples, and a large crowd that has followed him because of the miracles he has performed;[286]

(c) the dialogue presenting the problem: in an exchange involving questions and answers, Jesus and his disciples broach the subject of the lack of food for the crowd and the apparent impossibility of meeting the need of such a large group (in the desolate area in which they find themselves?).[287] Two hundred denarii would be needed to buy sufficient bread (or in John: such an amount would not suffice). After checking, the disciples tell Jesus that five loaves and two fish are available.[288] The inadequacy of these supplies in the face of so many people is obvious.

(d) Jesus' command, conveyed by the disciples, that the crowd recline on the grass brings the setup to an end and provides the bridge to the miracle proper.[289]

(2) *The Miracle Proper* (the words and/or deeds that effect the miracle, plus the simple assertion of the miracle's occurrence):

(a) Jesus takes the five loaves and, giving thanks, he breaks them and gives them to the disciples to distribute.[290] He does likewise with the fish.

(b) All eat and are filled.

(3) *The Conclusion* (the confirmation or proof that the miracle has really taken place):

Twelve baskets full of leftover bread are collected after five thousand people have eaten.[291]

[Possible further conclusion: Jesus dismisses the crowd (so Mark's versions) or the crowd acclaims Jesus (so John's version).][292]

E. THE QUESTION OF HISTORICITY

Even some exegetes who maintain that, during his public ministry, Jesus performed what were thought by his contemporaries to be miracles of exorcism and healing doubt that the feeding of the multitude goes back to any event in Jesus' lifetime.[293] One reason for this position is that many commentators see in the feeding miracle massive influence from OT miracle stories (especially Elisha feeding one hundred people with twenty barley loaves in 2 Kgs 4:42–44), from the accounts of Jesus' actions over the bread and wine at the Last Supper, and from the regular repetition of the eucharistic words and actions of Jesus in early Christian worship. It is from such sources, say many critics, that the story of Jesus feeding the multitude arose in the early church. In my view, each of these sources has indeed left its mark on the various versions of the story—though on some versions more than on others. It remains to be seen, however, whether these Jewish and Christian influences can be credited with creating the Gospel miracle story out of whole cloth.

Surely the clearest OT parallel to the story of Jesus feeding the multitude is the miracle of feeding attributed to the prophet Elisha in 2 Kgs 4:42–44. While the Elijah-Elisha cycle knows of other miracles involving the gift or multiplication of food (oil or meal), none comes as close to the Gospel story as does the story of Elisha and the twenty barley loaves.[294] In 2 Kgs 4:42–44, a man comes from Baalshalisha, bringing Elisha an offering of twenty loaves of barley bread.[295] Elisha orders his servant to give the bread "to the people that they may eat" (4:42). His servant objects: "How can I give this to a hundred men?" Elisha repeats his command and appends a short prophecy: "For thus says Yahweh: 'They shall eat and there will be some left over'" (v 43). The servant obeys and the prophecy is fulfilled (v 44).

The parallels with the Gospel narratives of the feeding of the multitude are obvious.[296] (1) *The prophet's apparently impossible order*: a prophet orders his servant to feed a large group of people with a relatively small amount of bread; exact numbers (twenty loaves and one hundred men) are given. (2) *Bread plus some other foodstuff*: although the Hebrew text is not clear, some other foodstuff is mentioned alongside the bread, but it does not figure in the rest of the story. (3) *The objection from his assistant*: the prophet's servant, who does not understand what is about to happen, protests, thus emphasizing the impossibility of satisfying one hundred people with twenty loaves (and hence emphasizing the magnitude of the miracle about to occur). (4) *The prophet's insistent command*: overriding his servant's objection, the prophet insists that his order be carried out. (5) *The miracle and its confirmation by way of surplus*: when the order is obeyed, the people are fed and some of the bread is left over. Since the point of the Gospel miracle, if derived from 2 Kgs 4:42–44, would be that "one greater than Elisha is here,"[297] the number of people fed would naturally be increased in the Gospel story (from one hundred to four or five thousand), and the number of loaves on hand would naturally be decreased (from twenty to seven or five).

At the same time, one must observe that there are many differences between the Elisha and the Gospel feeding miracles.[298] (1) There is no precise geographical or temporal setting to the Elisha story, unlike the Gospel scenes (e.g., by the Sea of Galilee, near Passover, in the late afternoon). (2) In 2 Kgs

4:42–44, we hear nothing of a crowd following the prophet. (3) Indeed, who exactly the hundred people are and where they have come from is unclear in this very concise story. (4) In any event, in the Elisha story there is no indication that these people are suffering from great hunger, lack food, or are unable to get food by ordinary means. (5) The miracle story in 2 Kings really begins with the surprising, peremptory command of Elisha, with no preparation, background, or motivation in the narrative. In contrast, a discussion between Jesus and his disciples "sets up" the problem of the people's lack of food before any concrete food appears on the scene. (6) In the Gospels, the disciples are the ones who supply or locate the little food available, and they do so only after the story is under way. (7) Jesus first commands the crowd to recline on the grass, then he performs the ritual observed by the head of a Jewish household for beginning a formal meal; all this is lacking in the Elisha story—as are, of course, the fish. In particular, the central actions of Jesus that some commentators see as allusions to the Last Supper and the Christian eucharist have no parallels whatever in the Elisha story. (8) The questions and objections of Jesus' disciples precede his actual order to give the food to the crowd; there is no resistance once Jesus issues his order, which introduces the miracle proper. (9) While we are tersely informed that there were leftovers from Elisha's meal, these are not counted, as opposed to the twelve or seven baskets of bread left over in the Gospel narratives. (10) The basic structure of the short Elisha story is that of prophecy-and-fulfillment; not so the Gospel story.

One might point out other parallels that some versions of the Gospel story have with the Elisha story, but such parallels are not necessarily part of the most primitive form of the Gospel miracle of feeding. For example, the detail that the bread is barley (*krithinos*) bread is found only in John's version (6:9,13) of the Gospel story; the same Greek adjective *krithinos* occurs in the LXX translation of the Elisha story. While this mention of barley might be a remnant from the primitive form of the Gospel story preserved in John (it would be a mistake to presume that John's version is in every aspect late and secondary), it is also possible that John's tradition recognized and wished to highlight the similarities between Elisha's and Jesus' miracles.[299] There is also another possible explanation of why John's tradition might have added the specification of *barley* loaves. John alone mentions that the miracle takes place near Passover, and Passover is the time of the barley harvest. Hence John's precision that the bread was barley bread might simply be his way of emphasizing his beloved Passover symbolism.[300] In short, not every parallel we can detect between the present Gospel versions of Jesus' feeding of the multitude and the Elisha story necessarily goes back to the primitive form of the Gospel story. While the Elisha story does share a number of basic elements with the primitive Gospel story, there is much in the Gospel miracle not found in and not derivable from 2 Kgs 4:42–44.

The other major texts suggested as sources for the Gospel feeding miracle are the various forms of Jesus' words and actions over the bread and wine at the Last Supper, as recounted in the Synoptics and reenacted in early Christian eucharists. To be sure, not all commentators agree that the feeding miracle has been affected by or alludes to the Last Supper and/or the Christian eucharist.[301] At the very least, one must admit that whatever allusions may be present in the feeding story are more apparent in some versions than in others. For example, among the two Marcan and the one Johannine versions, the overtones of the Last Supper seem most apparent in the structure of the second Marcan story. One may compare Jesus' actions in Mark 8:6–7 with his actions at the Last Supper:

MARK 8:6–7	LAST SUPPER[302]
over the bread	*over the bread*
AND TAKING the seven loaves of BREAD,	AND TAKING the loaf of BREAD,
GIVING THANKS,	GIVING THANKS,
HE BROKE [them]	HE BROKE [it]
AND GAVE [them] TO HIS DISCIPLES. . . .	AND GAVE [it] TO THE DISCIPLES [or: to them]

over the fish[303]	*over the cup*
AND PRONOUNCING A BLESSING OVER THEM[304] [i.e., a few fish]	GIVING THANKS [in some traditions over the bread: PRONOUNCING A BLESSING]
he commanded them also to be set out, AND THEY ATE. . . .	he gave it to them, AND THEY ALL DRANK. . . .

What is especially intriguing in the second Marcan version is the careful delay of any mention of the fish until the Evangelist is ready to depict a second parallel action of Jesus, namely, pronouncing a blessing over the fish. On the one hand, this causes the bread to dominate the story from beginning to end. On the other hand, the double action over the bread and then over the fish, each with its own mention of "giving thanks" or "pronouncing a blessing," resembles closely the basic structure of the actions over the bread and over the wine at the Last Supper. In the Marcan version of the Last Supper (Mark 14:22–23), Jesus first "pronounces a blessing" [*eulogēsas*] over the bread and then "gives thanks" [*eucharistēsas*] over the wine, with the very same participles (though in reverse order) that are used in Mark 8:6–7.[305]

The parallel with the Last Supper narrative is not quite as clear in the first Marcan version of the feeding miracle, and still less clear in John 6. More to the point, those exegetes who reject a reference to the Last Supper in any version of the feeding miracle stress that the actions of Jesus over the bread and fish simply reflect the thanksgiving to God that the head of a Jewish household pronounced over the bread that he broke as he began a formal meal.

While there is some truth to this claim,[306] it does not take into account a number of factors:

(1) The reason Mark 8:1–10 is so significant in the debate is that here the tradition has apparently been carefully formulated to provide a balanced pattern of "giving thanks" and then "pronouncing a blessing" over the two elements of food. This sort of parallel "thanksgiving" or "blessing" over first the bread (the main foodstuff of the meal in this case) and then over some side dish or secondary food (i.e., pieces of dried and salted fish) does not fit the ordinary ritual observed by a host at a formal Jewish meal, but does match the narrative of Jesus' parallel "thanksgivings" or "blessings" over the bread and the wine at the Last Supper.[307] The neat coordination of the blessing and the thanksgiving in Mark 8:6–7, which does not seem to belong to the earliest form of the feeding story, is thus most easily understood as an assimilation of the feeding miracle to Jesus' actions at the Last Supper.

(2) Moreover, there is the question of the larger context within which any version of the feeding miracle would have been understood by Christians, whether they were reading it in a written Gospel or listening to it proclaimed as an independent unit in the early oral tradition. Within the context of the Synoptic Gospels, it really misses the point to say that the actions of Jesus over the bread (and the fish) are simply those of a Jewish host at a formal meal. Within the framework of any given Gospel, which is a fixed web of linguistic cross-references, one must ask: where else in this Gospel does Jesus perform the actions he performs over the bread in the feeding miracle? Put that way, the question answers itself. In any of the Synoptic Gospels, the only occasion outside the feeding miracle when Jesus acts as the host of a meal, takes bread, gives thanks or pronounces a blessing, breaks the bread, and gives it to his followers is the Last Supper.[308]

The question of Gospel context yields a similar answer in John's Gospel, at least in its present canonical form. In the narrative of Jesus feeding the multitude, the actions of Jesus over the bread do not echo perfectly those of the Synoptic Jesus at the Last Supper, and in John's Gospel there *is* no institution of the eucharist at the Last Supper. Nevertheless, in the present form of John 6 the feeding of the multitude (6:1–15) is clearly aimed at introducing the bread of life discourse (6:35–58), which culminates in a clearly eucharistic section (6:51–58): "The bread that I shall give is my flesh for the life of the world. . . . If you do not eat the flesh of the Son of Man and drink his blood, you do not have life in you. . . . This is the bread that has come down from heaven."[309] In the context of John 6 read as a whole, with one of the most explicit statements of eucharistic theology in the NT (6:51–58), it is difficult to see how in v 11 the picture of Jesus taking bread, "giving thanks" (*eucharistēsas*), and sharing the bread with "those reclining" (as at table) would not conjure up for Christians the idea of the eucharist they celebrated.[310]

(3) One might grant all this on the level of the written Gospels and yet object that the isolated story of the feeding miracle, when it was still circulating in the early oral tradition, would not have had such an overarching interpretive

context and therefore would not have created in the listener's mind a connection with the eucharist. I think, however, that even on the level of the oral tradition in the first Christian generation, the argument from the larger context holds.

After all, in Christian oral catechesis and in Christian worship, in what connection or in what context did Christians regularly hear about Jesus taking bread, giving thanks, breaking it, and giving it to his disciples? It was not the feeding miracle that the Christians heard proclaimed week after week in their Christian worship. It was rather Jesus' words and actions over the bread and wine at the Last Supper that the Christians recalled and celebrated regularly—witness the fixed tradition Paul taught the Corinthians in the early fifties (1 Cor 11:23–26), a tradition he himself learned in the thirties or forties, a tradition that was repeated in variant forms in the communities Mark, Matthew, and Luke knew. Granted that ongoing oral context, I find it difficult to believe that any version of the miracle of the feeding of the multitude could have been told in a first-generation Christian community without reverberating with eucharistic echoes.

(4) A small confirmatory point may be added to these major considerations. Although the feeding miracle concerns the multiplication of loaves *and* fish, in every version of the Gospel story the fish, in one way or another, recede into the background.[311] The spotlight is kept mostly on the bread, probably because the bread rather than the fish offers a direct cross-reference to the Last Supper and the eucharist. Indeed, as we have already seen, in the second Marcan narrative of the feeding miracle (8:1–10), the one that has the clearest eucharistic references, the story speaks from start to finish almost entirely of loaves of bread or leftover pieces of bread (*artoi* or *klasmata*). In only one verse (8:7) are "a few fish" mentioned, and there apparently only because the separate mention of the fish and of Jesus' pronouncing a blessing over them provides an artfully designed balance: Jesus' coordinated actions over two types of food (bread and fish) mirror his coordinated actions over the bread and the wine at the Last Supper.

In summation: as regards the influence of the Elisha miracle and the Last Supper tradition on the Gospel stories of Jesus feeding the multitude, I take a "middle" position. On the one hand, I reject the views of those exegetes who exclude any influence of the Elisha story or the Last Supper tradition on the Gospel narratives of the feeding. The parallels are simply too clear. On the other hand, I do not find the parallels so massive and all-pervasive that the origin of the story of the feeding miracle can be fully explained simply by appealing to the Elisha story or the Last Supper tradition.[312]

To be sure, both of these have influenced the present forms of the Gospel feeding miracle. But, especially if we look back at what was probably the primitive form of the story of Jesus feeding the multitude, the core of the story is not explicable simply on the grounds of either the Elisha miracle or the Last Supper narrative.[313] For instance, both the specification of the loaves as *barley* loaves in John 6:9,13 and the clearest parallel to the Last Supper tradition in

Mark 8:6–7 are probably later developments in the tradition of the Gospel story. Moreover, neither the Last Supper tradition nor the Elisha story can account for the presence of fish alongside the bread. As we have seen, the fish tend to be increasingly downplayed in most of the Gospel versions of the feeding story; they are a primitive element rather than a later development in the tradition. (Indeed, in my opinion, there is no explanation for their presence in all the versions of the story short of some originating event in the life of Jesus.[314]) In brief, the earliest form of the feeding miracle available to us does not seem to have been as suffused with Elisha or Last Supper motifs as some of the later versions we now possess, and some of the elements of the earliest form (notably the fish) are not explicable on the grounds of the Elisha and Last Supper traditions. Rather, as it was retold in early Christian tradition, the account of Jesus feeding the multitude was refracted through the lenses of the Elisha and the Last Supper stories; but those stories do not seem to have created the Gospel feeding miracle out of whole cloth.

If, then, the Elisha miracle or the Last Supper/eucharistic tradition cannot fully explain the origin of the story of Jesus feeding the multitude, are there any positive indications that some historical event in Jesus' public ministry may lie behind the early Christian narrative? Two criteria of historicity come into play here:[315]

(1) When compared to most Gospel miracle stories, the feeding of the multitude is supported by an unusually strong attestation of multiple sources.[316] It is not only attested independently in both Mark and John, it is also attested by two variant forms of the tradition lying behind Mark's Gospel. This suggests a long and complicated tradition history reaching back to the early days of the first Christian generation. Prior to Mark's Gospel there seem to have been two cycles of traditions about Jesus' ministry in Galilee, each one beginning with one version of the feeding miracle (Mark 6:32–44 and Mark 8:1–10). Before these cycles were created, the two versions of the feeding would have circulated as independent units, the first version attracting to itself the story of Jesus' walking on the water (a development also witnessed in John 6), while the second version did not receive such an elaboration. Behind all three versions of the miracle story would have stood some primitive form.

(2) Besides this multiple attestation of sources, we should also consider another criterion, one that does not always arise in the consideration of miracle stories: the criterion of coherence. In both parables and other sayings, Jesus regularly spoke of the coming kingdom of God under the image of a banquet. The intriguing thing here is that this emphasis on a banquet or a festive meal as an image of the kingdom was not simply a matter of words Jesus spoke; banquets and festive meals played an important part in Jesus' actions as well. Quite apart from the feeding miracle, Jesus is attested in both Gospel sayings and non-miraculous Gospel stories to have been noteworthy for his presence at festive meals and banquets, a remarkably non-ascetic habit considered scandalous by some (Mark 2:15–17 parr. cf. Luke 15:1–2; 19:1–10; Matt 11:18–19 || Luke 7:33–34).[317] His offer of table fellowship to all, including social and

religious "lowlifes" like toll collectors and "sinners,"[318] was meant to fore-shadow the final eschatological banquet and to give a foretaste of that banquet even during his public ministry (cf. Matt 8:11–12 ‖ Luke 13:28–29; Mark 14:25 parr.).

It is within this greater context and regular habit of Jesus' public ministry, a habit that culminated with what was literally the *Last* Supper among a great number of "suppers," that one may try to understand the origin of the story of the feeding miracle. In my opinion, the criteria of both multiple attestation and coherence make it likely that, amid the various celebrations of table fellow-ship Jesus hosted during his ministry, there was one especially memorable one: memorable because of the unusual number of participants, memorable also because, unlike many meals held in towns and villages, this one was held by the Sea of Galilee. In contrast to Jesus' other "kingdom meals," bread and fish rather than bread and wine (cf. Matt 11:18–19 par.; Mark 14:22–25) would be the natural components of such a meal at such a spot. Connected from the beginning with Jesus' eschatological message, this special meal of bread and fish, shared with a large crowd by the Sea of Galilee, would be remembered and interpreted by the post-Easter church through the filter of the Last Supper tradition and the church's own celebration of the eucharist.

What, more precisely, happened at this memorable meal of fellowship among Jesus and his followers by the Sea of Galilee has been a subject of great speculation, some highly imaginative, by modern exegetes.[319] Some have suggested that Jesus and his disciples shared what little food they had with others, thus prompting the rest of the crowd (especially the rich among them) by their good example to a similar sharing of their supplies until all were fed.[320] Truly imaginative is the suggestion of other critics that Jesus had supplies of food hidden in a cave, whence his disciples passed him helpings to distribute to the crowd. Albert Schweitzer gave his own twist to these attempts at recon-struction, emphasizing the tense eschatological expectation of both Jesus and his followers. In this highly charged atmosphere, Jesus gave everyone in the crowd a morsel of bread as a symbol of the heavenly banquet about to come; the meal was thus "the antitype of the messianic feast . . . a sacrament of redemption."[321]

To be honest, our sources do not allow us to specify the details of the event, especially since we must allow for the influence of both the Elisha miracle story and the Last Supper tradition on the retelling of the story in subsequent Christian decades.[322] However, despite our galling inability to be specific, I think the criteria of multiple attestation and of coherence make it more likely than not that behind our Gospel stories of Jesus feeding the multitude lies some especially memorable communal meal of bread and fish, a meal with eschatological overtones celebrated by Jesus and his disciples with a large crowd by the Sea of Galilee. Whether something actually miraculous took place is not open to verification by the means available to the historian. A decision pro or con will ultimately depend on one's worldview, not on what purely historical investigation can tell us about this event.[323]

With this study of the story of Jesus feeding the multitude, we come to the end of our survey of the so-called "nature miracles" of the Four Gospels. In the last analysis, nothing binds these widely diverse stories together, not even the probability that none of them goes back to some event in the life of Jesus. For a while, as we inched through our survey, it might have seemed that at least one link, that of non-historicity, would bind all the "nature miracles" together. But now even that common link has been broken by the story of Jesus feeding the multitude, a story that, in my view, does go back to some especially memorable meal of the public ministry. Once again, and for the last time, the common category called "nature miracles" is seen to be an illusion.

X. SUMMING UP THE GOSPEL MIRACLES[324]

It has been a prolonged, wearisome trek through the exorcisms, the healings, the miracles of raising the dead, and the various miracle stories wrongly classified as "nature miracles." The road has indeed been long and dusty. No doubt some scholars would consider such an inventory of all the miracle stories in the Four Gospels wrongheaded from the start, at least for a volume engaged in the quest for the historical Jesus.

The paradox here is that many of the scholars who would object to this inventory of the Gospel miracles would not deny that Jesus was known as a miracle-worker during his lifetime and that the great emphasis on miracles in the Four Gospels reflects this reputation. Such critics would probably have no great problem with the brief chapter in which I gave a global overview of the Gospel miracles and argued from various criteria of historicity that the image of Jesus as exorcist and healer goes back to the activity of the historical Jesus. It is when I turn from global assertions to evaluations of individual miracle stories that such critics object. At that point they feel that the material is too meager or dubious for any serious judgment of historicity to be made.

Having sifted through the whole of this recalcitrant material, I can well sympathize with their viewpoint. It is a great temptation simply to make the general assertion that the historical Jesus was considered a miracle-worker by his contemporaries—and then waive any attempt to evaluate the historicity of individual miracle stories. In such a "strategic compromise," the global assertion is thus accepted, but individual stories are dismissed as most likely creations of the early church, with no basis in the life of Jesus.

However, despite its initial appeal, there is a serious methodological problem in such an approach. As we saw in our global survey of Gospel miracles, the single most important criterion for judging that the historical Jesus was viewed as a miracle-worker by his contemporaries was the criterion of the multiple attestation of sources. In other words, a major reason for accepting the global assertion that the historical Jesus performed actions considered miracles by his followers was the convergence of so many different miracle stories from so many different sources. But what if each miracle story in turn—or the sum total of miracle stories taken together—is judged to have no basis in the life of the historical Jesus? In such a case, is not the global assertion that Jesus was considered a miracle-worker left dangling in midair, with no concrete foundation? It was to come to grips with this problem that I conducted my inventory of the individual miracle stories of all Four Gospels.

I should remind the reader once again of the goal of this inventory. The goal is *not* to decide whether certain events in the life of Jesus were truly miracles; that is a decision no historian can make on purely historical grounds. Rather, the goal is to decide whether some of the miracle stories in the Gospels go back to and reflect (in however an imaginative way) events that actually occurred in Jesus' lifetime, events that Jesus' contemporaries (or in some cases subsequent believers) considered miraculous. Such a modest goal should not be considered a priori impossible in the case of the miracle stories, just as it would not be considered a priori impossible in a study of the "triumphal entry" into Jerusalem or the "cleansing" of the temple.

Our inventory has at least one positive result: it reminds us that no one theoretical approach to the Gospel miracle stories is sufficient to explain the whole complex collection. Admittedly, this insight runs counter to a desire entertained by many different ideological camps: a desire for one simple solution that explains everything neatly. Staunch conservative believers hold that all the miracles of Jesus actually took place just as they are narrated. Thoroughgoing rationalists claim that the miracle stories report more or less what actually happened, except that the events can be explained in a natural rather than supernatural way. Champions of a mythic or symbolic explanation, be they followers of David Friedrich Strauss or Carl Jung, see the miracles as pure creations of the early church expressing its faith in symbols, with no particular event in the life of Jesus providing a concrete basis for the narrative.

Our inventory suggests that no one theory can explain all the miracle stories in the same way and with equal aplomb. (1) In some cases (e.g., the cursing of the fig tree), the story appears to have been created whole and entire by the early church to symbolize a religious teaching; it has no historical basis in an individual action of the historical Jesus. (2) In other cases (e.g., the healing of the blind Bartimaeus), the story most likely has a historical foundation: Jesus' contemporaries actually witnessed an event they believed to be a miracle, a miracle whereby Jesus gave a blind man his sight. (Needless to say, even if we think that a particular blind man named Bartimaeus, encountering Jesus near Jericho, did suddenly gain his sight, this historical judgment—paralleled by historical reports from healing shrines like Lourdes—is not to be confused with the theological judgment that such an event constituted a true miracle.) (3) The miracle story of the feeding of the multitude may be based on a symbolic meal that the historical Jesus celebrated with a large crowd by the Sea of Galilee, a meal that perhaps was interpreted as miraculous only later on by the early church.

It is with these caveats in mind that I now summarize the results of the inventory. The types of miracles most widely attested in the Gospels are exorcisms and healings. Of the seven references to individual exorcisms in the Synoptics, the story of the (epileptic?) boy in Mark 9:14–29, the brief reference to Mary Magdalene's exorcism (Luke 8:2), and possibly (though here I feel less certain) the core of the story of the Gerasene demoniac (Mark 5:1–20) go back—sometimes through a number of layers of later Christian interpretation—to events in Jesus' ministry. That Jesus performed exorcisms is also supported by the Q tradition (Luke 11:20 par. in particular and Luke 11:14–23 par. in general).

The many different types of healing stories found in the Gospels can be assigned to four basic categories: (1) four stories about people suffering from paralyzed, withered or crippled parts of their bodies; (2) three stories involving the blind; (3) two stories of people suffering from "leprosy"; and finally (4) a catchall category for various physical afflictions that occur only once each (six separate instances). Most of these four categories are also attested in a Q saying of Jesus (Matt 11:5 par.). The overall attestation of the figure of Jesus as healer of physical infirmities and illnesses is thus even stronger than the attestation of his activity as an exorcist.

To take up the four categories in turn: among the four stories of physical paralysis, I think that two stories, the paralyzed man let down through the roof (Mark 2:1–12 parr.) and the paralyzed man by the pool of Bethesda (John 5:1–9), go back to the historical Jesus. The Q saying in Matt 11:5 par. likewise supports the tradition of Jesus empowering the lame to walk.

The three stories involving the blind form a most unusual case, for I judge that all three stories (Bartimaeus [Mark 10:46–52], the blind man at Bethsaida [Mark 8:22–26], and the man born blind in Jerusalem [John 9]) reflect events in Jesus' ministry. This is the only instance where I think that all the stories in a particular subcategory go back to Jesus' ministry. The same Q saying in Matt 11:5 par. supports this tradition as well. That Jesus was thought to give sight to the blind is apparently one of the most strongly supported traditions about the healing activity of the historical Jesus.

The two stories about Jesus healing people afflicted with some skin disease ("leprosy") are much more difficult to evaluate. Neither the story in Mark (1:40–45 parr.) nor the story in Luke (17:11–19), by itself, argues strongly for or against historicity. The best I can say is that, since three independent traditions (Mark, Q, and L) all speak of Jesus cleansing lepers, I incline to the view that Jesus was thought by his contemporaries to have cured lepers. But I do not feel sure enough to decide whether either story is based on a particular historical event.

Not surprisingly, most of the variegated stories in the fourth, "catchall," category fall into the twilight zone of *non liquet*, since each story represents the single occurrence of a particular type of healing, a type of healing moreover witnessed (with one exception) in only one independent source. The only story that has a solid claim to go back to the ministry of the historical Jesus is the healing of the "boy" of the centurion (or royal official of Herod Antipas) in

Capernaum (Matt 8:5–13 ‖ Luke 7:1–10 ‖ John 4:46–54). While a single incident, this story, by way of exception, enjoys multiple attestation of sources (Q and John).

Moving beyond miracles of exorcism and healing, we run into a curious state of affairs with the next type of miracle. Though the very idea of raising the dead would strike many moderns as bizarre, the tradition that Jesus brought the dead back to life enjoys remarkably strong multiple attestation in the sources: Mark, John, L, and Q. Although this material is especially difficult to judge, I venture to suggest that the story of Jairus' daughter (Mark 5:21–43 parr.) goes back to some event in Jesus' ministry. Whether that event was originally viewed by Jesus' disciples as a miracle of raising the dead or simply as a healing that was only later reinterpreted as raising the dead is hard to say. Even more tenuous must be any judgment on the raising of the son of the widow of Nain (Luke 7:11–17). While I incline to the view that it goes back to some event in Jesus' ministry, I can well understand why others would prefer to assign it entirely to the early church. The same can be said for John's story of the raising of Lazarus (John 11:1–46). We find ourselves in a position similar to that of the tradition about the healing of persons suffering from "leprosy." Historical judgments about individual stories are extremely difficult, but the multiple attestation of both sources and forms (once again Matt 11:5 par. comes into play) argues that even during his lifetime Jesus was thought by his disciples to have raised the dead.

Summarizing our judgments about the mélange of stories incorrectly labeled "nature miracles" is much easier. With the sole exception of the feeding of the multitude, all these stories appear to have been created by the early church to serve various theological purposes. In contrast, the multiple attestation of sources and the coherence of the story with Jesus' habit of holding joyful meals fraught with eschatological significance argue for a historical basis to the feeding of the multitude. The story seems to go back to some especially memorable and symbolic meal Jesus celebrated with a large crowd by the Sea of Galilee.

In sum, the statement that Jesus acted as and was viewed as an exorcist and healer during his public ministry has as much historical corroboration as almost any other statement we can make about the Jesus of history. Indeed, as a global affirmation about Jesus and his ministry it has much better attestation than many other assertions made about Jesus, assertions that people often take for granted. Looming large in the Gospels and no doubt in his actual ministry, Jesus' miracle-working activity played an integral part in his being able to attract attention, both positive and negative. His miracle-working activity not only supported but also dramatized and actuated his eschatological message, and it may have contributed to some degree to the alarm felt by the authorities who finally brought about his death. Any historian who seeks to portray the historical Jesus without giving due weight to his fame as a miracle-worker is not delineating this strange and complex Jew, but rather a domesticated Jesus reminiscent of the bland moralist created by Thomas Jefferson.

NOTES TO CHAPTER 23

[1] I use the generic phrase "the feeding of the multitude" to cover the different versions of the Gospel stories of Jesus feeding the five thousand and the four thousand.

[2] Jesus' hunger (Mark 11:12 par.) must take the place of the pressing or dire need of another person, and the fact that the disciples hear Jesus' curse (11:14) and that the next day they see the tree withered must count as the attestation and confirmation of the miracle. Peter's remembrance of the curse (11:21) may count as the reaction of the bystanders. Matthew (Matt 21:18–20) reformulates the story along more traditional form-critical lines: unlike Mark, he makes the curse, the instantaneous withering, and the immediate reaction of the disciples all one event in one pericope. Moreover, he supplies in his own third-person narrative an attestation of the instantaneous effect of the curse (Matt 21:19, hence not just a statement of what the disciples see, as in Mark); and the disciples as a group are said to be amazed (*ethaumasan*, v 20) and to exclaim over the instantaneous miracle, thus creating a formal and typical reaction. On Matthew's redaction see Held, "Matthäus als Interpret der Wundergeschichten," 276–77.

[3] Theissen, *Urchristliche Wundergeschichten*, 111.

[4] I concentrate here on the Lucan form of the story (Luke 5:1–11) because it is presented as part of the public ministry of Jesus, while the Johannine form (John 21:1–14) is presented as a post-Easter appearance of the risen Jesus to his disciples.

[5] For example, Richard Bauckham ("The Coin in the Fish's Mouth," *Gospel Perspectives. The Miracles of Jesus. Volume 6* [ed. David Wenham and Craig Blomberg; Sheffield: JSOT, 1986] 219–52) complains on pp. 233–34 that Theissen "fails to note that the coin in the fish's mouth" belongs to the category of gift miracles. As I shall show below in the exegesis of Matt 17:24–27, the story of the temple tax is neither a gift miracle nor a rule miracle.

[6] Hence I think Bauckham ("The Coin," 234) is too enthusiastic when he claims that "as a class" the gift miracles are "remarkably well attested in the [Gospel] tradition." In my view, only the feeding of the multitude and the wine miracle of Cana qualify strictly speaking as gift miracles; and only the feeding of the multitude enjoys multiple attestation of sources, though not of forms.

[7] Theissen, *Urchristliche Wundergeschichten*, 90–125; note that Theissen uses the term "theme" for what many other critics would call a "(sub-)form," "genre," or "Gattung."

[8] Theissen, *Urchristliche Wundergeschichten*, 102; as Theissen notes, in the broader sense every miracle is an epiphany, an appearance of the heavenly or the divine in the visible, earthly realm.

[9] Unlike Theissen, I would count neither the audition and vision after the baptism of Jesus nor his transfiguration as an *epiphany miracle* performed by Jesus. (1) The events after the baptism can hardly be thought of as miracles performed or effected by Jesus; he is rather the recipient of a vision. Indeed, in Mark's story (Mark 1:10–11), the earliest written version of the tradition we have, Jesus *alone* receives the vision, which thus remains a private communication from God the Father to the one he designates his Son. Such an event does not meet the definition of miracle with which we have been operating from the beginning of the third

part of this volume, a definition that demands that the extraordinary event be perceivable in principle by any interested and fair-minded observer. While the matter
is not entirely clear, Luke (3:21–22) seems to maintain Mark's idea that the vision
is granted to Jesus alone. Matthew, who emphasizes the public nature of revelation,
extends at least the heavenly voice to an unspecified larger group by having the
voice say (Matt 3:17): "This is [not the Marcan and Lucan "you are"] my beloved
Son." In any event, we are dealing with a theophany or a "vision that interprets"
(*Deute-Vision,* the term used by Lentzen-Deis in his *Die Taufe Jesu,* 195–289), a vision that Jesus receives, not an epiphany miracle worked by Jesus for others to see.
(2) The same point basically holds true of the transfiguration (Mark 9:2–10 parr.).
Again we are dealing with an esoteric vision, not a miracle performed by Jesus that
in principle would be perceivable by any and all bystanders. Matthew specifically
labels the transfiguration a "vision" (*to horama*), which picks up on the *ōphthē* and
ha eidon of Mark's narrative (Mark 9:4,9). The esoteric nature of the vision is emphasized not only by its restriction to the inner circle of Peter, James, and John
but also by Jesus' command that the disciples tell the vision to no one before his
resurrection. (3) A further difficulty in treating both Jesus' baptismal theophany
and Jesus' transfiguration is that in each case the full narrative of the esoteric vision is clearly attested by only one Gospel source. (a) Granted, I suspect that the
Q document also contained a narrative of Jesus' baptism along with the subsequent
theophany. But I must admit that many exegetes reject this position and that at
any rate it is not possible to reconstruct what exactly the Q document might have
contained. (b) As regards the transfiguration, we have only the Marcan tradition,
which both Matthew and Luke redact for their purposes. On this point I am ultimately not convinced by the carefully argued thesis of Barbara E. Reid (*The Transfiguration: A Source- and Redaction-Critical Study of Luke 9:28–36* [CahRB 32; Paris:
Gabalda, 1993]), who maintains that, in addition to Mark, Luke had access to a
non-Marcan source for his narrative of the transfiguration. In my view, the differences between the Marcan and Lucan narratives are best explained by Lucan redaction of the Marcan text. Thus, with only one source for each esoteric vision,
the question of historicity is very difficult to treat. That Jesus and/or his disciples
experienced spiritual visions during the public ministry is perfectly possible in principle. Whether these accounts of specific visions on specific occasions reflect the
original subjective experiences of Jesus and his disciples or whether they are simply
vehicles of interpretation employed by the early church is something I see no way
of deciding with certitude. A similar judgment could be made with respect to the
temptation of Jesus.

[10] In Mark 8:19–20 the Marcan Jesus reminds his disciples in almost catechetical
fashion of the two incidents of feeding the multitude in Mark 6:30–44 and 8:1–9.
These statements are almost universally granted by critics to be redactional creations of Mark. For example, Pesch (*Das Markusevangelium,* 1. 411) thinks that for
vv 18b–21 any other explanation than Mark's redaction is hardly possible. He
points to the presentation of the two feedings as two distinct events in a particular
narrative flow and to the recapitulation of each narrative with a precise reference
to the vocabulary used in each story for the baskets (*kophinous* and *spyridōn*). Similar views on the redactional nature of Mark 8:19–20 are expressed by Taylor, *The
Gospel According to St. Mark,* 363–64, 367; Grundmann, *Markus,* 164; Guelich,
Mark 1–8:26, 419; Mann, *Mark,* 334. Gundry (*Mark,* 410–16) is in a very small
minority among contemporary Marcan critics in trying to counter the arguments
of the commentators who are in favor of Marcan redaction. In the end, even Gundry (p. 413) must admit that his observations "do not prove the traditional origin

of vv 13–14,16–21. . . ." It is difficult not to see Mark's redactional hand in this summary. With this catechetical repetition Mark is operating both theologically (as he emphasizes his theme of the messianic secret and blindness of the disciples to it) and literarily (as he summarizes the climax of the first half of the Gospel and prepares for the second half).

[11] The better attestation (compared with the story of the walking on the water) stems from the fact that within the pre-Marcan tradition the story of the feeding already circulated in two different versions, the feeding of the five thousand and the feeding of the four thousand.

[12] For treatment in the standard commentaries see Grundmann, *Das Evangelium nach Matthäus*, 409–11; Meier, *Matthew*, 195–98; Gundry, *Matthew*, 355–57; Davies-Allison, *Matthew*, 2. 737–49. Other useful literature includes J. Duncan M. Derrett, "Peter's Penny," *Law in the New Testament* (London: Darton, Longman & Todd, 1970) 247–65 (published in an earlier form in *NovT* 6 [1963] 1–15); H. W. Montefiore, "Jesus and the Temple Tax," *NTS* 11 (1964–65) 60–71; van der Loos, *The Miracles of Jesus*, 680–87; Neil J. McEleney, "Mt 17:24–27—Who Paid the Temple Tax? A Lesson in Avoidance of Scandal," *CBQ* 38 (1976) 178–92; Richard J. Cassidy, "Matthew 17:24–27—A Word on Civil Taxes," *CBQ* 41 (1979) 571–80; W. Horbury, "The Temple Tax," *Jesus and the Politics of His Day* (ed. Ernst Bammel and C. F. D. Moule; Cambridge: Cambridge University, 1984) 265–86; Bauckham, "The Coin," 219–52.—Basic Jewish sources for our knowledge of the temple tax include Exod 30:11–16 (the foundational law that specifies a half-shekel from every male 20 years of age and older); Neh 10:33 (where the tax is changed to a third of a shekel; cf. 2 Chr 24:5); Philo (*On the Special Laws* 1.14 §77); Josephus (*Ant.* 18.9.1 §312; *J.W.* 7.6.6 §218); and the Mishna Tractate *Šeqalim*. For an attempt to trace the history of the temple tax, see Horbury, "The Temple Tax," 277–82. Horbury thinks that the temple tax, understood as an annual tax of a half-shekel paid by all Jewish males 20 years of age and older for the support of the temple liturgy, was of comparatively recent origin, was strongly advocated by the Pharisees, but was not as widely accepted in Palestine as is sometimes supposed. Horbury (p. 282) goes so far as to suggest that, besides the Jewish priests and the Qumran sectarians, "there were many who, for whatever reason, in practice did not pay."

[13] So, e.g., van der Loos, *The Miracles of Jesus*, 680–87 (where "the account of the stater" is placed within the overarching category of "nature miracles," pp. 590–698).

[14] The suggestion that the *Epistle of the Apostles* 5 (written around the middle of the 2d century A.D.) preserves an independent form of the tradition behind Matt 17:24–27 is rightly rejected by Horbury, "The Temple Tax," 265 n. 1; Bauckham, "The Coin," 235–36. The text is obviously a cento cataloguing miracles found in all Four Gospels. The story of finding the coin in the fish has become pale and generalized, losing the specific traits of Peter's special role (instead: "we, his disciples"), the nature of the tax as the temple tax, the precise (and unusual) location of the coin in the fish's *mouth*, and the stater (which becomes the more common denarius). For the text, see H. Duensing, "Epistula Apostolorum," Edgar Hennecke–Wilhelm Schneemelcher, *Neutestamentliche Apokryphen* (2 vols.; 4th ed.; Mohr [Siebeck], 1968, 1971) 1. 126–55, esp. 128–29.—On the Matthean vocabulary, style, and theology of the pericope, as well as non-Matthean traits, see Grundmann, *Das Evangelium nach Matthäus*, 409–11; Strecker, *Der Weg der Gerechtigkeit*, 200–201;

Meier, *Matthew*, 196–98; Gundry, *Matthew*, 355–57; Horbury, "The Temple Tax," 266–68 (with a dubious appeal to the Koine text tradition to lessen the elegant Greek style of Matthew's redaction). I agree with Bauckham ("The Coin," 229, 247) that a merely mechanical use of word statistics does not of itself prove the presence of Matthew's heavy redactional hand, let alone, as Gundry claims, a purely Matthean creation. It is rather the convergence of Matthean vocabulary, style, theology, and carefully constructed structural connections, all in a short pericope of only four verses, that argues in favor of heavy Matthean redaction, though not necessarily for a Matthean creation out of thin air.

[15] Bultmann (*Geschichte*, 35) and Davies-Allison (*Matthew*, 2. 738) call it a scholastic dialogue; Dodd (*Historical Tradition*, 227) calls the pericope's present form a pronouncement story; Horbury ("The Temple Tax," 266) says that it combines characteristics of a disputation (*Streitgespräch*) with those of a miracle story; Dibelius denies that the story of the coin in the mouth of the fish is a personal legend, though it resembles one (*Formgeschichte*, 97, 103, 113 n. 2); Bauckham ("The Coin," 225) thinks that it is "most comparable with those controversy stories whose climax is a miracle" (but in Matt 17:24–27 is the miracle, rather than Jesus' pronouncement on freedom, the true climax?). Theissen (*Urchristliche Wundergeschichten*, 114) puts it in the category of a "norm miracle" (or "rule miracle"), and more specifically a norm miracle that grounds or supports some norm or rule. Such a label may indeed fit stories like Mark 2:1–12; 3:1–6, where a miracle is actually narrated as the legitimation of some key pronouncement or teaching of Jesus. But that is not the case in Matt 17:24–27: the miracle is never narrated, and the key teaching of Jesus in the pericope is the freedom of the sons from the temple tax, which is not exactly grounded or supported by the predicted-but-never-narrated miracle.

[16] There is a slight problem here with the plural form in Matt 17:24, *ta didrachma*. The coin was the *didrachmon*, i.e., a coin worth two drachmas, which was roughly equivalent to the half-shekel needed for the annual temple tax. The plural may be generalizing (the tax paid by all adult males or the tax paid every year) or may be a set term for "the temple tax of the didrachmon." It is also possible, though, that *ta didrachma* represents an Aramaized form of *didrachmon*; see Bauckham ("The Coin," 245 n. 4) and the literature cited there. For other possible indications of an Aramaic substratum in the pericope (some highly speculative), see Horbury, "The Temple Tax," 282–83.

[17] The fact that Matthew has chosen the particular position of this story within the flow of his narrative to meet his own structural and theological concerns should make us careful about correlations with later Jewish texts like *m. Šeqalim* 1–2, which specify place of payment, time of payment (in the month before Passover, i.e., Adar), detailed modes of payment (including a surcharge), and exemption from the surcharge if a man pays for himself and another. Many questions need to be answered first: e.g., to what extent were these regulations in the Mishna ideals rather than strictly enforced provisions? To what extent and how were such laws, if real, enforced in Antipas' Galilee in the early part of the 1st century A.D.? These difficult questions, combined with the fact of Matthew's responsibility for the placement of the story within the structure of his Gospel, should make commentators wary of drawing detailed conclusions about a historical event in the life of Jesus.

[18] The basic rule of all Gospel exegesis holds true here: one must first interpret the text in its final form within the theological and literary context of the particular Gospel, and only then turn to questions of tradition and a possible connection with the histori-

cal Jesus. Davies-Allison, and more notably Derrett, Horbury, and Bauckham, jump too quickly to the question of the historical Jesus.

[19] Strangely, Bauckham ("The Coin," 226–27) acknowledges but then tries to play down the Matthean theme of the prominence of Peter; this seems to be a function of his desire to minimize Matthew's redactional hand in the story's formulation in favor of pre-Matthean tradition and ultimately a historical incident in the life of Jesus. Here as elsewhere in his exegesis this bias skews his interpretation.

[20] The similitude is a very general one ("the kings of the earth") and hardly refers to Roman practice in particular. More specifically, since Jesus in his question (v 25) mentions indirect taxes such as tolls (telē) as well as direct taxes such as the head tax (kēnsos), it is not true to say that his question applies in particular to Rome, which did not impose a poll tax on its own citizens. Even Roman citizens paid customs and other indirect taxes. On this point, see Bauckham, "The Coin," 221–22; the point is missed by Horbury, "The Temple Tax," 283.—Cassidy ("Matthew 17:24–27," 571–80) attempts to make the whole story refer to civil taxes paid to Rome rather than to the tax paid by Jews to support the Jerusalem temple. His arguments are well answered by Davies-Allison, *Matthew*, 2. 739–41; cf. Bauckham, "The Coin," 244–45 n. 1. One might add to their observations that throughout his argument Cassidy refers to taxation in *Judea*. But the Matthean story is set in Capernaum in Galilee, in the tetrarchy of Herod Antipas. It would seem that Antipas had his own system of civil taxation; he then in turn paid tribute to Rome.

[21] In Matthew's polemical theology (using language that would not be used by the ecumenically minded today), the kingdom of God is taken away from the people of Israel and given to another people, "my church" (Matt 21:43; 16:18). Hence it is those who follow Jesus who are the true "sons of the kingdom" in Matthew's eyes (13:38), while the former "sons of the kingdom," i.e., Israel, will be cast out from the eschatological banquet even as the Gentiles enter to enjoy it (8:11–12). Granted this highly negative tone of Matthew, who probably wrote his Gospel after his church had broken with the Jewish synagogue, it is extremely unlikely that Matthew understood the principle that "the sons are free" to apply to all Israelites and to mean that no Israelite should pay the temple tax because such a tax, by which God the Father would be taxing his own sons, was wrong from the start. According to this questionable interpretation, Jesus would be asserting that the temple should be supported by voluntary donations. In supporting this interpretation, Bauckham ("The Coin," 223–25) does not pay enough attention to the primary context of Matthean theology because he is so intent on reconstructing a supposed event in the life of Jesus. But even if we suppose that Matt 17:24–27 reflects some such event, it is difficult to believe that the historical Jesus would have held that the temple tax was in principle wrong and that the temple should be supported solely by voluntary offerings. (1) One may wonder whether Jesus would have been so out of touch with reality that he would have thought that the mammoth expenses entailed in running the Jerusalem temple could have been met solely by freewill offerings. In this connection Bauckham cites the Marcan story of the widow's mite; but whatever the original meaning of that story (which some interpret as a denunciation of the exploitation of widows by religious authorities), it is not *ad rem* to Bauckham's argument. (2) Bauckham (p. 246 n. 24) honestly admits that his theory seems to run counter to Jesus' apparent approval of paying tithes (Matt 23:23 ‖ Luke 11:42); the fine distinction he tries to make between the two types of levies does not solve the objection he himself raises. (3) Beyond all the individual questions there is the larger question of what exactly we mean when we say that the temple tax was "obligatory" for all Jews in Antipas' tetrarchy or in the Diaspora. In what sense obligatory? In the same sense that

Jews in the Roman province of Judea had to pay tribute to Caesar? Since there are indications from both Mishnaic and Qumranic sources (*m. Šeqal.* 1:3–4; 4Q *159* [Ordinances], a problematic text) that various groups claimed exemption from the tax, we are left wondering who collected the tax, who adjudicated claims of exemption, and who if anyone could use coercive police power to enforce collection of the tax from the recalcitrant in Antipas' Galilee or the Diaspora. In connection with this see Horbury, "The Temple Tax," 279, 282.

[22] In this pericope one could give *skandalizō* the milder meaning of "offend, anger, shock," but the clearly intended verbal connection with the first part of chap. 18 argues for the stronger theological meaning. Within Matthew's overall theological context, the collectors of the temple tax, not unlike "the scribes and the Pharisees" or "the Pharisees and the Sadducees," serve as generic, all-purpose representatives of official Judaism.

[23] On parallels in folklore and rabbinic literature, see Bauckham, "The Coin," 237–44; Davies-Allison, *Matthew*, 2. 741–42. Yet not all parallels are relevant, as Bauckham and Derrett ("Peter's Penny," 258–60, 262–65) point out. Our story, unlike some supposed parallels, does not speak of the lost item being recovered by the person who lost it; at any rate, it does not indicate who lost the coin; and the finding of the coin in the fish's *mouth* (as opposed to, e.g., its stomach) is unusual in ancient forms of the tradition. Still, the differences hardly justify the leap into historicity that Horbury ("The Temple Tax," 274–76) takes.—Bauckham (p. 243) observes that, strictly speaking, the chance finding of a coin in the mouth of a fish, while a rare and remarkable occurrence, is not in itself impossible and therefore is not a miracle by modern theological standards (which were not those of the ancient world anyway). This is true, but the Matthean story involves much more: a sudden request for a certain amount of tax money, which is answered by Jesus' immediate command to Peter to cast a hook into the Sea of Galilee and open the mouth of the first fish caught to get the exact amount needed to pay for the two of them. In such a case the improbability of the event is notably higher than that of a rare coincidence.

[24] Bauckham ("The Coin," 220) invokes the Mishnaic law about a surcharge on the tax (avoided if one man pays for another) in order to explain (explain away?) the pointed ending of v 27 ("for me and for you"). This is to import a point not present in Matthew's composition in order to avoid taking seriously a point that is present, namely, Peter's prominence in Matthew's Gospel and the neat connection Matthew makes between 17:27 and 18:1 (see also Bauckham, p. 227).—The exact correspondence between the amount of money needed and the amount the predicted miracle would supply is another reason why Matt 17:24–27 should not be put under Theissen's rubric of "gift miracle." (Theissen actually puts it under the rubric of "rule miracle," where it does not really fit either.) Typical of a gift miracle is the larger-than-life, superabundant, extravagant amount of food or other goods supplied by the miracle. The idea of *only* the exact amount needed is more Swiss or Scottish in spirit than Oriental. Bauckham ("The Coin," 233–34) is correct in saying that the coin-in-the-fish miracle comes closer to Theissen's "gift miracle" (or a miracle of divine provision, as Bauckham calls it) than to Theissen's "rule miracle"; but Bauckham fails to notice the absence of the element of the superabundant and extravagant. This absence makes the supposed miracle quite different in tone from the feeding of the multitude or the wine miracle of Cana.

[25] Since Bauckham ("The Coin," 227) is intent on playing down Matthew's redactional activity in 17:24–27, he is reduced to making the lame and unsubstantiated claim

that the connections created between 17:27 and chap. 18 by the use of *skandalizō* and "for me and you" were connections Matthew found in his source.

[26] Gundry, *Matthew*, 355. In my opinion, he places too much weight on phenomena that argue for Matthew's redactional hand but not necessarily for a total creation by Matthew. Gundry seems to be driven here by his desire to date the composition of Matthew's Gospel before A.D. 70.

[27] It will not do to claim that Matthew created the whole pericope to deal with the question of the obligation of paying the tax to the Roman temple of Jupiter Capitoline. Jesus' argument, which rests on the analogy between human kings and God the supreme King (who levies a tax to support his temple), would hardly fit the question of a tax paid to Jupiter Capitoline. On this, see Bauckham, "The Coin," 228. Indeed, such a contorted argument cannot even supply the reason why Matthew kept and redacted the Jewish-Christian tradition after its original problem had become anachronistic. Needless to say, Matthew has no problem retaining anachronistic Jewish material when he can find a suitable theological or parenetic purpose for it (e.g., Matt 5:23–24 on bringing a gift to the altar in the Jerusalem temple).

[28] See Strecker, *Der Weg der Gerechtigkeit*, 200; however, Strecker is not quite correct in listing the verb *teleō* among the *hapax legomena* of the pericope. This verb is used six other times by Matthew, though in these cases it means not "pay (tax)" but "finish." Gundry (*Matthew*, 355) rightly observes that Matthew could use a favorite word in more than one sense and that the shift in meaning would not strike him as much as it strikes us, who must use a totally different word for the sense of *teleō* in 17:24.

[29] An alternative suggestion would be that the tradition continued and concluded with Jesus' command that the tax be paid from the common purse, now that the theological principle of the freedom of himself and his followers had been established.

[30] For this view of the Matthean church, see Raymond E. Brown and John P. Meier, *Antioch and Rome* (New York/Ramsey, NJ: Paulist, 1983) 12–86 (by Meier); cf. Stephenson H. Brooks, *Matthew's Community. The Evidence of His Special Sayings Material* (JSNTSup 16; Sheffield: JSOT, 1987).

[31] Bultmann, *Geschichte*, 34–35.

[32] A recognition that Jesus' prophecy in 17:27 is placed there by Matthew simply to serve certain theological and literary concerns absolves us of the fruitless task of inventing reasons why the miracle is never narrated. I think the approach I have taken is preferable to that of Dodd (*Historical Tradition*, 227), who suggests that the tradition behind Matt 17:24–27 started out as a parabolic saying and that what we have in Matthew is a parabolic saying "almost in the act of making the transition" to a miracle story. This is possible; but as Derrett intimates in his respectful objection ("Peter's Penny," 262–65), it is difficult to imagine what the original parable said, how its argument by analogy worked if the original subject matter was not exemption from taxation, and how (or why) it came to be transformed into Matt 17:24–27.

[33] For detailed exegesis and lengthy bibliographies, see William R. Telford, *The Barren Temple and the Withered Tree* (JSNTSup 1; Sheffield: JSOT, 1980); and Sharyn Echols Dowd, *Prayer, Power, and the Problem of Suffering: Mark 11:22–25 in the Context of Markan Theology* (SBLDS 105; Atlanta: Scholars, 1988). Among the many articles on the pericope, a representative sampling would include Bruno Violet, "Die 'Verfluchung' des Feigenbaums," *Eucharistērion* (Hermann Gunkel Festschrift; FRLANT 19; 2 vols.; Göttingen: Vandenhoeck & Ruprecht, 1923) 2. 135–40; C. H. Bird, "Some *gar* Clauses in St. Mark's Gospel," *JTS* n.s. 4 (1953) 171–87; J. W. Doeve, "Purification

du temple et dessèchement du figuier," *NTS* 1 (1954–55) 297–308; Charles W. F. Smith, "No Time for Figs," *JBL* 79 (1960) 315–27; A. de Q. Robin, "The Cursing of the Fig Tree in Mark XI. A Hypothesis," *NTS* 8 (1961–62) 276–81; J. Neville Birdsall, "The Withering of the Fig-Tree," *ExpTim* 73 (1961–62) 191; Hans-Werner Bartsch, "Die 'Verfluchung' des Feigenbaums," *ZNW* 53 (1962) 256–60; Gerhard Münderlein, "Die Verfluchung des Feigenbaumes (Mk. XI.12–14)," *NTS* 10 (1963–64) 89–104; Richard H. Hiers, "Not the Season for Figs," *JBL* 87 (1968) 394–400; J. Duncan M. Derrett, "Figtrees in the New Testament," *HeyJ* 14 (1973) 249–65; Heinz Giesen, "Der verdorrte Feigenbaum—Eine symbolische Aussage? Zu Mk 11,12–14.20f.," *BZ* 20 (1976) 95–111; Wendy J. Cotter, " 'For It Was Not the Season for Figs,' " *CBQ* 48 (1986) 62–66.

[34] On the way in which Matthew thus changes the temporal schema Mark has created for "Holy Week," see Strecker, *Der Weg der Gerechtigkeit*, 93. For a defense of the basic historicity of Mark's chronology in chap. 11, see the excursus in Gundry, *Mark*, 671–91.

[35] See Telford, *The Barren Temple*, 74–75; also Violet, "Die 'Verfluchung' des Feigenbaums," 137; Gundry, *Matthew*, 415–17; Francis W. Beare, *The Gospel According to Matthew* (Peabody, MA: Hendrickson, 1981) 419.

[36] For general exegesis of Luke's parable of the fig tree, see Ernst, *Das Evangelium nach Lukas*, 418–20; Marshall, *Luke*, 552–56; Fitzmyer, *The Gospel According to Luke*, 2. 1003–1009.

[37] For a survey of various approaches to the pericope in the 19th and 20th centuries, see Telford, *The Barren Temple*, 1–25; or, more briefly, Giesen, "Der verdorrte Feigenbaum," 96–99; Robin, "The Cursing of the Fig Tree," 276–77; Münderlein, "Die Verfluchung des Feigenbaumes," 92–94. Giesen reduces the various solutions proposed to the problems of the cursing of the fig tree to the following types: (1) Jesus was looking for the "winter figs" that ripen in the following spring (then why say that "it was not the season for figs"?). (2) The story is an etiological legend that goes back to a particular fig tree along the road from Bethany to Jerusalem that suddenly withered (some add that Jesus had eaten from this tree). (3) The story developed from some saying or parable of Jesus, perhaps Luke 13:6–9. Others suggest that, while looking at the fig tree, Jesus quoted in a symbolic sense the words of Mic 7:1 ("My soul desires the first ripe-fig"), words misunderstood by his disciples; from this misunderstanding developed the miracle story. This is the approach of Robin, "The Cursing of the Fig Tree," 280; and Birdsall, "The Withering of the Fig-Tree," 191. (4) The story goes back to an "apocalyptic word" (not a curse) of Jesus that looked forward to the end-time events of his death and parousia, events that would occur so quickly that there would be no time for the fig tree to bear more fruit. When the end did not come, the church reinterpreted Jesus' word as a curse. This is the solution of Bartsch, "Die 'Verfluchung' des Feigenbaums," 256–60. Variations on this theme of imminent expectation of the end can be found in Violet, "Die 'Verfluchung' des Feigenbaums," 137–39 (with the escape hatch of a mistranslation of the original Aramaic); Hiers, " 'Not the Season for Figs,' " 394–400; and Derrett, "Figtrees in the New Testament," 249–65. (5) Mark's redaction uses the story as a symbol of how the Lord of all punishes everything that does not serve his divine rule. (6) The story originally referred to an action of Jesus during the feast of Tabernacles (so Smith, "No Time for Figs," 315–27), when there would be ripe summer figs. (7) Jesus' action is meant to demonstrate the power of faith and prayer (but those motifs are not in the story proper). (8) Giesen's own approach is to take the entire story as a symbol of the judgment passed on the fruitless

people of Israel and of their replacement with the new people of God. While Giesen tries to appreciate fully the redactional work and theology of Mark, his symbolism tends to become allegory; and he does not grasp sufficiently that the judgment symbolized in the story is aimed at the Jerusalem temple in particular, not Israel in general.

Many of the authors who attempt some explanation that posits an originating event in the life of the historical Jesus become involved in disputes over the precise type of fig or pod that Jesus was supposedly looking for—a highly speculative basis for exegesis. Telford (*The Barren Temple*, 28 n. 16) mentions the many conflicting claims among exegetes as to the nature and number of annual crops produced by the fig tree. According to Telford, "in reality, figs are usually gathered in one main harvest from the middle of August to well on in October. These are the 'summer figs' or *tĕʾēnîm* [sometimes called "late figs"], and have developed from buds sprouting on the new wood of the tree." From these figs in the full sense of the word must be distinguished various other growths on the fig tree: the little green knops (*paggîm*, unripe green figs), which develop from buds on the old wood in March-April and then mature in May-June as the "first-ripe" figs (*bikkûrōt*—however, many of the *paggîm* do not ripen and simply drop off); and the so-called "winter figs," which are neglected or immature summer figs that survived the winter and ripened with clement conditions in the springtime (they are thus "chance finds"). The leaves of the fig tree usually appear in April. This range of options has allowed exegetes to choose this or that type of growth and adjust the Marcan story accordingly. For example, if it is decided that (the historical) Jesus was actually looking for summer figs, the whole story is removed to around the time of the feast of Tabernacles in early autumn (so Smith, "No Time for Figs," 315–27), the setting at Passover being assigned to Mark's redactional hand. If, however, the story is kept at Passover, the *paggîm* may be invoked. Growths that are at best chance finds are declared to be what Jesus is seeking, and explanations are given why he—but apparently not his disciples—failed to eat at Bethany before setting out for Jerusalem and was in such a bad mood. The scenario becomes so complicated and imaginative that one thinks of the 19th-century "liberal lives" of Jesus. I suggest that it would be good to remind ourselves that the horticultural vocabulary that Mark uses in his story remains very general: *sykē* ("fig tree"), *sykon* ("fig"), *phylla* ("leaves"), *karpos* ("fruit"), and *riza* ("root"). If the whole sense of the story had hung upon a fine distinction among growths on the fig tree, one would think that Mark would have used language indicating the type of growth that was essential to grasping the story's meaning. Since that is not the case, various exegetes seize upon the hopelessly vague *ti* ("something") in 11:13, which can be conveniently identified with whatever growth is needed for a particular interpretation of the Marcan text. Often this procedure is invoked in service of a defense of the literal and detailed historicity of Mark's story as it stands. See, with varying emphases, Pesch, *Das Markusevangelium*, 2. 189–202; Gundry, *Mark*, 634–39, 647–55. I must confess that I find this whole approach contrived and questionable. In the main text I take an approach that seeks to avoid any and all horticultural speculation; theological speculation is bad enough.

[38] It must be remembered that we are dealing here with the theological interpretation of Mark and the other evangelists, and not necessarily with the intentions and actions of the historical Jesus. The question of the historicity of the triumphal entry and the cleansing of the temple will be treated in a later chapter.

[39] The Greek is *mēketi eis ton aiōna ek sou mēdeis karpon phagoi.* Two observations need to be made about the Greek text: (1) We have here an extremely rare case of the optative mood (*phagoi*) in Mark. It is all the more striking in that the optative was the proper mood for curses in classical Greek, while NT Greek tends to use the imperative

(see, e.g., Gal 1:8–9; cf. BDF, 194 §384; Herbert Weir Smyth, *Greek Grammar* [Cambridge, MA: Harvard University, 1920, 1956] 406 §1814b). C. F. D. Moule (*An Idiom-Book of New Testament Greek* [Cambridge: Cambridge University, 1960] 136) calls Mark 11:14 "the most vehemently prohibitive of all the examples" in the NT of the optative used to express a wish or a deprecation. Thus, Mark (or perhaps his source) seems at pains to make clear that this is a curse, a point which Peter then dutifully underlines in 11:21: ". . . the fig tree that you cursed (*hē sykē hēn katēraso*). . . ." Hence there is no reason to think that Peter is not correct in his evaluation of what Jesus said the previous day. (2) The phrase *eis ton aiōna* used with a negative (here both *mēketi* and *mēdeis*) regularly means "never," "never again"; cf. Bauer, *Wörterbuch* (6th ed.), col. 52, where Mark 11:14 (along with Mark 3:29, the only other time the phrase occurs in Mark) is cited as an example. Some commentators wish to interpret the negative + *eis ton aiōna* in 11:14 to mean "until the end of this age," "until the age to come." But such ideas have their own proper expressions in Greek: *ho mellōn aiōn, ho aiōn houtos, hē synteleia tou aiōnos*, used along with some preposition like *heōs* ("until"). "Until the end of the [or: this] age" would demand a construction such as is found in Matt 28:20: *heōs tēs synteleias tou aiōnos*. Critics like Violet ("Die 'Verfluchung' des Feigenbaums," 137–39) and Hiers (" 'Not the Season for Figs,' " 397–98) compare Mark 11:14 to Jesus' Last Supper logion in Mark 14:25: "Amen I say to you that I will no longer drink of the fruit of the vine until [*heōs*] that day when I drink it new in the kingdom of God." What is to be noted, however, is the *heōs* construction in 14:25, which is lacking in 11:14. Only by rewriting the logion, which is what Violet does, can one arrive at the imminent-eschatological sense these critics want.

[40] Since by my count there are five pericopes in chap. 11, since the cleansing of the temple stands in the center of the chapter, and since the cursing of the fig tree and the verification of the effect of the curse stand on either side of the cleansing, there is a natural temptation to see the whole of the chapter as a chiastic structure: A-B-C-B'-A'. As attractive as this would be, I do not think that the triumphal entry (11:1–11) and the challenge to Jesus (11:27–33) have enough in common to justify seeing them as corresponding (or even contrasting) pericopes in a chiastic structure.

[41] One notices here the hand of the editor (either Mark or a pre-Marcan collector of traditions), who prepares for the challenge to Jesus' authority (11:27–33) by saying that the high priests and the scribes *heard* Jesus' prophetic critique of the temple (11:18) on the previous day, just as the editor prepares for the verification of the effect of Jesus' curse (11:20–21) by saying that the disciples *heard* (*ēkouon*, literally, "were hearing") Jesus' curse on the previous day (11:14). On the redactional link between the two acts of hearing, see Giesen, "Der verdorrte Feigenbaum," 102. We see here a type of double intercalation, what one might call a "leapfrog" effect: the cursing of the fig tree jumps over the cleansing to link up with the verification of the curse, just as the cleansing leaps over the verification of the curse to link up with the challenge to Jesus' authority. Yet at the same time the curse and verification of the curse have been carefully separated and placed on either side of the cleansing so as to interpret it as a prophetic sign of judgment on the temple.

[42] See, e.g., Grundmann, *Das Evangelium nach Markus*, 232; Werner H. Kelber, *Mark's Story of Jesus* (Philadelphia: Fortress, 1979) 59–62; Elizabeth Struthers Malbon, *Narrative Space and Mythic Meaning in Mark* (San Francisco: Harper & Row, 1986) 122–23; Morna D. Hooker, *The Gospel According to Saint Mark* (Peabody, MA: Hendrickson, 1991) 265–66; John Paul Heil, *The Gospel of Mark As a Model for Action. A Reader-Response Commentary* (New York/Mahwah, NJ: Paulist, 1992) 225–28. It is remarkable how many commentators on Mark's Gospel spend time discussing the his-

torical date of the cleansing of the temple or the precise nature of the action and intention of the historical Jesus, without giving detailed consideration to the question of what Mark intends to convey by this scene as he places it within his overarching structure of chaps. 11–16. Too many commentaries on Mark are covert quests for the historical Jesus; the methodological confusion means that neither quest for Jesus nor commentary on Mark is done properly. Even those commentators who see the cleansing as a prophetic act announcing divine judgment are not always exact in their formulation. In the context of Mark 11, the judgment is on the temple and its authorities in particular, not on Israel in general.

[43] The reader will notice that nowhere in my discussion of Mark 11 do I mention v 26 ("But if you do not forgive, neither will your Father who is in heaven forgive your transgressions"). The reason for this is that almost all text critics and exegetes agree that v 26 is a later addition to the text by a Christian scribe who recognized that the substance of Mark 11:25 was also found in Matt 6:14 and who therefore completed the parallel by including the antithetical statement about not forgiving that is found in Matt 6:15. Besides not being in early witnesses that represent all text types, the addition in v 26 reveals its secondary nature by the use of the conditional form "*if* you do not forgive . . . ," which parallels the conditional form in Matt 6:14, instead of the temporal form ("*when* you stand to pray, forgive . . .") used in Mark 11:25. On the secondary nature of Mark 11:26, see Metzger, *Textual Commentary*, 110; Telford, *The Barren Temple*, 50, 64. Telford (pp. 50–56) goes on to maintain that Mark 11:25 and perhaps 11:24 are also later scribal additions to the Marcan text. The suggestion has not received wide acceptance, and rightly so; for the arguments against Telford's proposal, see Dowd, *Prayer*, 40–45.

[44] Again, it must be stressed that I speak here of *Mark's* redactional presentation and theology, not of the actual historical situation involved in Jesus' trial and death.

[45] Some scholars (e.g., Dowd, *Prayer*, 58) stress that it is Peter in 11:21 who calls Jesus' words in 11:14 a curse, while Jesus himself, in the sayings of 11:22–25, apparently interprets his words as a prayer. Actually, since Mark purposely presents us with two interpretations of the fig-tree miracle, one more "dogmatic" (the curse prophesying the destruction of the temple) and one more "parenetic" (the exhortation to Christians to have faith, to pray, and to forgive), one interpretation should not be played off against the other. In Mark's Gospel, when Peter says something that is theologically erroneous, Jesus tells him so in no uncertain terms (e.g., 8:32–33; 14:29–31). Nothing in 11:20–25 indicates that Jesus rejects Peter's designation of 11:14 as a curse. Moreover, I have already noted how the optative form of *phagoi*, most unusual in Mark, argues that 11:14 should be understood as a curse.

[46] For an extensive survey of the use of figs, fig trees, and other trees as theological images in the OT, Judaism, the NT, and the ancient Near East in general, see Telford, *The Barren Temple*, 128–250. Telford states (p. 135): "While the failure of the fig or the vine is given merely as a sign of distress in, for example, Jl. 1.7,12 and Hab. 3.17, the ravaged or withered fig-tree is a vivid emblem of God's active *punishment* of his people in Jer. 5.17; 8.13 Hos. 2.14; 9.10,16 and Am. 4.9 (cf. also Ps. 105.33 Is. 28.4; 34.4 Na. 3.12)." As Telford also points out, some of the prophetic passages are connected with the condemnation of temple worship and the sacrificial system (Jer 5:17–18; 8:12–23; Hos 2:11–13; 9:10–17; Amos 4:4–13). In Mic 7:1–4, God searches for an incorrupt and righteous people like a person engaged in a frustrated search for first-ripe figs. In some passages, God's punishment is actualized through the blasting, smiting, or ravaging of trees, especially the vine and the fig tree (e.g., Ps 105:33; Isa 24:6,7; Jer 6:6;

7:20; Hos 2:12; Amos 4:9). Telford shows how in later rabbinic literature the fig tree became a more direct image for individual concrete objects, e.g., the city of Jerusalem. However, in my opinion, the precise use of the fig tree as a symbol for the Jerusalem temple threatened with eschatological judgment is best attributed to the Christian author who decided to use the general image of the fig tree in the specific context of Jesus' last days in Jerusalem and of his cleansing of the temple in particular. The tireless search for "background" must not blind us to the creative use of the fig-tree image that the author of Mark 11:12–14, 20–21 demonstrates.

[47] Dowd (*Prayer*, 37–66) shows that the Marcan catechesis on faith, prayer, and forgiveness is not a foreign body in Mark's overall structure and theology; but even her holistic view of the text cannot hide some tensions and seams.

[48] There are also two sayings in the Coptic *Gospel of Thomas* from Nag Hammadi that include the motif of telling a mountain to remove itself to another place. In the translation of Bentley Layton (*The Gnostic Scriptures* [Garden City, NY: Doubleday, 1987] 389), saying 48 reads: "Jesus said: If two make peace with one another within a single house, they will say to a mountain, 'Go elsewhere,' and it will go elsewhere." Saying 106 (Layton, p. 398) reads: "Jesus said: When you [plural] make the two into one, you will become sons of man, and when you say, 'O mountain, go elsewhere!' it will go elsewhere." These two sayings are most likely dependent on and reworkings of the Synoptic tradition. Common to Mark 11:22–23 ‖ Matt 21:21, to Matt 17:19–20 ‖ Luke 17:5–6, and to 1 Cor 13:2 is the mention of faith as the necessary prerequisite for telling the mountain to move. Since Matt 17:20; 21:21; Luke 17:6; and 1 Cor 13:2 all agree on the conditional form "if you [Paul: I] have [Paul adds: all] faith," the criterion of multiple attestation indicates that this formulation represents the earliest form of the logion available to us. Significantly, while both saying 48 and saying 106 retain the structure of some sort of protasis ("if" or "when") as the condition for the ability to tell a mountain to move, the condition is no longer faith but rather the typically gnostic motif of overcoming duality by achieving oneness (making peace in one house, making the two one; cf. saying 22). In saying 106, the idea that all those addressed, when they achieve oneness, become "sons of man" (an echo of Jesus the Son of Man in the Synoptics?), i.e., true Gnostics, may reflect the pantheistic and/or polytheistic tone found in some of the sayings of the *Gospel of Thomas* (cf. saying 108). As Fieger (*Das Thomasevangelium*, 154) notes, saying 106 should therefore be judged to be more strongly gnostic than 48. Yet, as Fieger (p. 155) goes on to point out, even the symbolism of making peace in the one house refers to the gnostic idea of the return to ontological unity; rejection of the material world brings that inner peace, that recognition of the divine spark of light within, which makes possible for the Gnostic what is impossible for the hostile material world. Fitzmyer (*The Gospel According to Luke*, 2. 1143) thinks that "both forms [sayings 48 and 106] in the apocryphal Gospel [of Thomas] depend on Matt 17:20." In short, unlike Telford (*The Barren Temple*, 103), I would not leave open the possibility that sayings 48 and 106 in the *Gospel of Thomas* represent traditions lying behind the Synoptic Gospels.

A further insight that may be gained from comparing the versions of the saying on moving the mountain in Mark, Matthew, Luke, and 1 Corinthians is that all the versions except Mark place the mention of faith in a protasis: "If you have faith" (or, in 1 Cor 13:2: "If I have all sorts of faith"). Hence Mark himself may be responsible for the imperative construction at the end of Mark 11:22: "Have faith in God"; it is his way of joining the story of the verification of the efficacy of the curse (11:20–21) to his catena of sayings (11:22–25). Composition by Mark, who is certainly capable of some unusual locutions, may explain the rare use of *pistin theou* (literally, "faith of God") with the sense of an objective genitive: "faith *in* God."

[49] While, on the whole, the vocabulary in Mark and John is different at these points (Mark speaks in terms of asking with faith while John speaks—with his typical christological concentration—of asking "in my name"), both Mark 11:24 and all three sayings in John use some form of the verb *aiteō* in the 2d person plural. Moreover, both Mark 11:24 and John 15:7 conclude the promise with a clause worded in almost exactly the same way: Mark reads *kai estai hymin*, while John reads *kai genēsetai hymin*. Mark's form may be rendered "and it shall be yours." John's form could also be rendered that way, though more likely it means "and it shall be done for you." The assurance that Christian prayer will be answered by God appears with *aiteō* in other sources and contexts, including Q material (Matt 7:7–11 ‖ Luke 11:9–13), other passages in the Last Supper discourses of John (15:16; 16:24), James 1:5–6 (cf. 4:2–3), and notably 1 John 3:22; 5:14–15. Yet none of these comes as close in structure to the last words of Mark 11:24 as do the last words of John 15:7.

[50] While Koch (*Die Bedeutung*, 133) allows for this possibility, he prefers to think that the stray sayings became gradually attached to the story before Mark's redaction. In my view, Koch throughout his monograph resists unnecessarily the phenomena in the text that at times clearly argue for pre-Marcan complexes such as the basic material in Mark 11. Hence, he is forced to attribute the intercalation of the cursing of the fig tree and the cleansing of the temple to Mark alone; accordingly, the chain of stray sayings, which points in a different direction, has to be assigned to a vague and otherwise unexplained pre-Marcan process.

[51] So Taylor, *The Gospel According to St. Mark*, 408–10; Haenchen, *Der Weg Jesu*, 324–25; Lane, *Mark*, 338; Pesch, *Das Markusevangelium*, 2. 112–13 (who prefers the theory that Mark himself has collected the sayings, though he leaves open the possibility of a pre-Marcan collection); Hooker, *The Gospel According to Saint Mark*, 230–31. Curiously, Gundry (*Mark*, 507–8) resists the idea of a catechetical composition held together by catchwords, though he finally adopts a position of agnosticism (p. 508): "In the end, then, we should doubt our ability to decide with great certainty whether any, some, or all of these sayings and incidents originally belonged together." "Great certainty" is rarely if ever had in tracing the tradition history of Gospel material.

[52] For intercalation in Mark, especially in the Passion Narrative, see John R. Donahue, *Are You the Christ? The Trial Narrative in the Gospel of Mark* (SBLDS 10; Missoula, MT: SBL, 1973), esp. pp. 42, 58–63; cf. Donald Juel, *Messiah and Temple. The Trial of Jesus in the Gospel of Mark* (SBLDS 31; Missoula, MT: Scholars, 1977), esp. pp. 30–36 for his disagreements with the views of Donahue. Intercalation is certainly a characteristic of the Marcan tradition, by which I mean pre-Marcan collections of material as well as Mark's redactional work. In my view, it is possible that some of the intercalations usually attributed to Mark may have already existed in his sources. As we have already seen, the dovetailing of the raising of the daughter of Jairus with the healing of the woman with the hemorrhage (Mark 5:21–43) may be an example. I suggest here that the interweaving of the cursing of the fig tree with the cleansing of the temple may be another. To this extent I agree with Pesch (*Das Markusevangelium*, 2. 189–91), though I would not extend the pre-Marcan Passion Narrative as far as he does. For the view that the intercalation in Mark 11 is the work of the Evangelist himself, see Giesen, "Der verdorrte Feigenbaum," 102.

[53] On the phenomenon of the Marcan *gar* clauses, see Bird, "Some *gar* Clauses," 171–87. He points out that Matthew and Luke tend to eliminate Mark's troublesome

gar clauses in the narrative material, but less so in the sayings material. While Bird's general observations are helpful, I find his theory that the *gar* clauses point to cryptic allusions to specific OT texts highly imaginative. However, he does make an important point: these enigmatic *gar* clauses are found at various places throughout the Gospel; they are therefore most likely signs of Mark's hand rather than traditional elements. For further comments on Matthew's elimination of Mark's *gar* clauses and possible reasons for the elimination, see Cotter, " 'For It Was Not the Season for Figs,' " 63–64.

[54] On the question see Bultmann, *Geschichte*, 308–10; von Campenhausen, *Der Ablauf der Osterereignisse*, 35–42; Jean Delorme, "Résurrection et tombeau de Jésus," Paul de Surgy et al., *La résurrection du Christ et l'exégèse moderne* (LD 50; Paris: Cerf, 1969) 105–51; Edward Lynn Bode, *The First Easter Morning* (AnBib 45; Rome: Biblical Institute, 1970) 25 n. 1; Ludger Schenke, *Auferstehungsverkündigung und leeres Grab* (SBS 33; Stuttgart: KBW, 1971); Reginald H. Fuller, *The Formation of the Resurrection Narratives* (New York: Macmillan; London: Collier-Macmillan, 1971) 50–64; Xavier Léon Dufour, *Resurrection and the Message of Easter* (London: Chapman, 1974, originally 1971) 105–16; Pesch, *Das Markusevangelium*, 2. 519–41; Pheme Perkins, *Resurrection* (Garden City, NY: Doubleday, 1984) 114–24.

[55] Redaction, composition, and literary criticism have taught us to see Mark not just as an editor of previous traditions but as a creative author. That is true, but perhaps the enthusiasm of the contemporary literary criticism of the NT is in danger of making us forget that, even within the NT (to say nothing of the corpus of ancient Greek literature), Mark is not the greatest of Greek stylists. Although I do not agree with all his arguments or his conclusions, there is something to be learned from J. C. Meagher, *Clumsy Construction in Mark's Gospel* (Toronto Studies in Theology 3; New York/Toronto: Mellen, 1979).

[56] It may well be that the word *kairos* ("time" or "season") connotes the deeper theological sense of the appointed eschatological time of fulfillment or parousia (so Mark 1:15; 13:33; but cf. 10:30). However, in 11:13 as in 12:2, the meaning within the flow of the story must first of all be the time when the fruit (figs or grapes) ripens, the time of harvest. The deeper theological meaning is present only through and because of the natural, surface meaning in the story.

[57] For various opinions, see Hiers, "Not the Season for Figs," 394–400; Cotter, " 'For It Was Not the Season for Figs,' " 62–66. Cotter's remark is apposite (p. 62): "Mark's account of the cursing of the fig tree . . . is much like a chronic disorder: the patient is always on treatments and never really cured."

[58] See, e.g., the remarks by R. H. Lightfoot, *The Gospel Message of St. Mark* (London: Oxford University, 1950) 60–61; Bartsch, "Die 'Verfluchung' des Feigenbaums," 259–60. While I accept the idea of some sort of embryonic pre-Marcan Passion Narrative, I am doubtful of Pesch's claim that a detailed pre-Marcan Passion Narrative extended all the way from 8:27 to 16:8, with chaps. 14–16 revealing no significant addition by Mark (*Das Markusevangelium*, 2. 1–27). According to Pesch, all of chap. 11, with the exception of vv 24–25 (26), was part of this pre-Marcan Passion Narrative. The result of this sweeping theory is that phenomena that seem to most commentators to be signs of Mark's redactional hand must be attributed to the pre-Marcan redactor of the early Passion Narrative. Sometimes this becomes very forced (so, e.g., in 11:13e, 22–23). The driving engine of this whole approach seems to be a desire to declare as much material as possible historical.

[59] On this point see Raymond E. Brown, "John and the Synoptic Gospels: A Com-

parison," *New Testament Essays* (Garden City, NY: Doubleday [Image], 1968, originally 1965) 246–71.

[60] I say "roughly" because the anointing at Bethany precedes the triumphal entry in John but follows it in Mark.

[61] On this see Dodd, *Historical Tradition*, 160–62; Brown, *The Gospel According to John*, 1. 119.

[62] I presuppose here what appears to be the majority opinion among exegetes, namely, that the Fourth Evangelist transposed the cleansing of the temple to the beginning of the public ministry both to suffuse the whole of the Gospel with a Passover/Passion aura and to make way for the raising of Lazarus as the chief catalyst for the arrest of Jesus. On this point, see *A Marginal Jew*, 1. 381–82, and the discussion of the raising of Lazarus above. As I noted in *A Marginal Jew*, 1. 44, 52–53, I agree with the majority of 20th-century critical commentaries on John's Gospel that John draws upon a tradition similar to but independent of the Synoptics; in other words, John is not literarily dependent on Mark or any other Synoptic. This position has already been confirmed by my treatment of various pericopes (e.g., the healing of the centurion's servant or royal official's son) and will be confirmed again by my treatment of the walking on the water and the feeding of the multitude in this chapter. Hence the theory of David Seeley ("Jesus' Temple Act," *CBQ* 55 [1993] 263–83), viz., that Mark created the story of the cleansing of the temple, falls to the ground because of the independent attestation by John.

[63] I purposely say "no version of this miracle story," since it is often suggested that the origin of the story of the cursing of the fig tree may lie in the special Lucan parable of the barren fig tree (Luke 13:6–9). While this is possible in theory, three difficulties in particular must be pondered: (1) This theory of the tradition history of the Marcan curse miracle would demand that Mark (or, more likely, some pre-Marcan author) knew at least some of the special L tradition that lies behind Luke's Gospel. Especially if one accepts my position that the cursing of the fig tree is not a creation by Mark but belongs to a pre-Marcan complex that comprises most of chap. 11 of Mark's Gospel, one must push the individual story of the curse miracle back a good ways into the first Christian generation. Is it really likely that a Christian teacher or author, standing at an early stage of the development of the Marcan tradition, knew some of the special L tradition? To be sure, this is not impossible; but anyone who holds such a theory must be ready to explain what particular solution to the Synoptic problem he or she is adopting and how this solution makes such a scenario likely. (2) The thrust of the Lucan parable of the fig tree is noticeably different from, in some sense diametrically opposed to, the thrust of the Marcan curse miracle. In the Lucan parable, the barren fig tree, which has been visited by its owner for three years in a row, is nevertheless granted a reprieve of one more year, during which time great care will be taken with it, in the hope that it will produce fruit and so forestall its destruction. In effect, the parable announces the short time of grace still left for the audience of Jesus; the parable is an urgent call to repentance, in the hope that the audience may yet escape judgment and punishment. The cursing and withering of the fig tree say just the opposite. After one brief encounter (contrast the three years!), Jesus dooms the fig tree to destruction, which overtakes it by the next day. The message is that the fate of the Jerusalem temple is sealed; nothing can now prevent its imminent destruction. The difference in thrust is confirmed by the fact (pointed out by Fitzmyer, *The Gospel According to Luke*, 2. 1004) that only the most obvious words are common to both the curse miracle and the parable ("fig tree," "fruit," "he came," "found none"). (3) One may also ask how precisely we

are to conceive of the process by which, during the first Christian generation, a parable was transformed into a miracle story. While such a transformation is sometimes invoked by Gospel critics, concrete examples that command the assent of most scholars are hard to come by. It is interesting to note that, while Bultmann (*Geschichte*, 246) allows for the possibility of a miracle story developing out of a *saying* of Jesus, he does not think that, with the exception of the cursing of the fig tree, a miracle could have developed out of a *parable*.

In the light of all this, I agree with Telford (*The Barren Temple*, 233–37) that the Marcan story of the curse miracle probably did not develop out of the Lucan parable. However, if one wishes to maintain the view that the Marcan curse miracle arose out of the Lucan parable, that position would not alter the final judgment of my treatment of Mark 11:12–14,20–21, namely, that the story does not go back to some striking action of the historical Jesus that his disciples or audience took to be a miracle. On either reading, the story has its origin in Christian teaching.

[64] Whether this author was correct or not in his interpretation is not the point here. Exegetes differ on the question. E. P. Sanders (*Jesus and Judaism* [Philadelphia: Fortress, 1985] 61–76) strongly defends the view that, in "cleansing" the temple, the historical Jesus was actually symbolizing its destruction. Sanders's view is opposed by Craig A. Evans ("Jesus' Action in the Temple: Cleansing or Portent of Destruction?" *CBQ* 51 [1989] 237–70), who maintains that the historical Jesus was calling for a purification of temple practice.

[65] On the term *theologoumenon*, see *A Marginal Jew*, 1. 216–20 and 237 n. 41.

[66] I have restricted my list of OT punitive miracles to those in which a human agent (e.g., Moses, Elijah, or Elisha) is cursing, praying, commanding, or performing some miraculous gesture. Certain other punitive miracles have no human agent or mediator: e.g., the sudden death inflicted on Nadab and Abihu, two sons of Aaron the high priest, for offering an unauthorized incense-sacrifice to the Lord (Lev 10:1–2); the sudden death inflicted on Uzzah when he touched the ark of the covenant to steady it (2 Sam 6:6–7); the madness of Nebuchadnezzar in Dan 4:1–37, where Daniel interprets the king's dream but in no way causes or mediates the punishment.

[67] Interestingly, one of the divine child's punitive miracles (*Infancy Gospel of Thomas* 3:1–3) is to make a lad wither up completely "like a tree"; the lad is cursed by Jesus, who says that he will bear neither leaves nor root nor fruit. An echo of the story of the cursing of the fig tree may be present here; that the lad withers immediately may reflect Matthew's version rather than Mark's. (That the *Infancy Gospel of Thomas* knows at least some of the Synoptic Gospels seems clear from its last chapter [19:1–5], which is directly dependent on Luke 2:41–52; 1:42; 2:51–52.) The child Jesus also strikes dead a lad who accidentally knocks up against him (4:1), and those who then complain about Jesus to Joseph are struck blind (5:1). Later on (14:2) Jesus curses a teacher, who immediately faints and falls to the ground. One should note, however, that the *Infancy Gospel of Thomas* also portrays the child Jesus performing beneficent miracles, as well as undoing his curse miracles. For the text of the *Infancy Gospel of Thomas*, see Hennecke-Schneemelcher, *Neutestamentliche Apokryphen*, 1. 293–98.

[68] See Achtemeier, "Jesus and the Disciples as Miracle Workers in the Apocryphal New Testament," 149–86. Interestingly, with the exception of the infancy gospels, the tradition of Jesus as miracle-worker recedes from view, and practically no new miracles are attributed to him. The reverse happens to the apostles.

[69] As I have already noted, the Marcan story of the exorcism of the Gerasene demo-

niac does not really qualify as a curse miracle or a punitive miracle, although the possessed pigs panic, rush into the sea, and drown. (1) On the level of the story as presented by Mark, Jesus' own action is purely positive and liberating, namely, the freeing of a tormented man from a legion of demons. It is the demons who beg Jesus to let them enter the pigs, and it is the demoniac presence that then causes the pigs to rush into the sea and destroy themselves. (2) On the level of historical reconstruction, I have explained in my treatment of the exorcism why both text criticism and form criticism indicate that most likely the whole incident of the panicky pigs is a secondary addition to the basic story of Jesus' exorcism of the Gerasene demoniac.

[70] As the reader will notice, I have constructed this section to stress the argument from composition, source, and tradition criticism. However, if some reader should prefer another explanation of the rise and development of Mark 11 in general and 11:12–14, 20–21 in particular, I would maintain that the application of the two criteria of discontinuity and coherence are sufficient to show that the cursing of the fig tree most likely does not go back to an event in the life of the historical Jesus.

[71] The reader may wonder why I have spent so much time arguing for a position that would seem fairly obvious to most people. One reason that I have devoted so much space to this question is that, in theory, one could appeal to some of the criteria of historicity to mount an argument that the cursing of the fig tree does go back to the historical Jesus. (1) One could appeal to the criterion of embarrassment. After all, is it likely that early Christians, proclaiming Jesus as a gentle and loving Savior, would invent a story in which Jesus, in a fit of temper, destroys a harmless fig tree because it fails to provide him with fruit when it is not the season for fruit? Surely the story must come from the historical Jesus, for in due time the Marcan story is first abbreviated by Matthew and then omitted by an embarrassed Luke. *In reply*, I would remind the reader of a limitation of the criterion of embarrassment that I pointed out in Volume One of *A Marginal Jew* (pp. 170–71): what *we* judge embarrassing was not necessarily felt to be embarrassing by Christians of the 1st century A.D. Neither the pre-Marcan author, nor Mark, nor Matthew was embarrassed by this curse miracle; and the supposedly sensitive Luke was not embarrassed to attribute punitive miracles either to Gabriel, when the annoyed angel rebukes Zechariah in the Third Gospel (1:20), or to the heroes of Acts, Peter and Paul. In view of the lack of embarrassment about punitive miracles in the OT, in Mark, Matthew, and Luke in the NT, and in the apocryphal gospels and Acts, the argument from embarrassment loses most if not all of its force. (2) One may appeal to the criterion of discontinuity inasmuch as a punitive miracle aimed directly at a specific plant that is addressed and berated for its failings is rare if not unheard of in the Bible. *In reply*, I would note that this is true only to a certain degree. In the OT some of the ten plagues of Egypt (effected by a miracle-worker) were aimed at vegetative life, including trees (Exod 9:25: trees are splintered by the hail) and fruit (10:15: the fruit of the trees is consumed by the locusts). Obviously, the divine punishment is aimed through the trees and crops at a sinful people, the Egyptians. Not surprisingly, the equivalent plagues in the Revelation of John also damage or destroy crops and trees (Rev 6:6; 8:7) as both a symbol and a foretaste of the total destruction about to come upon Babylon. In a somewhat different vein, there is the peculiar case of the gourd plant in Jonah 4. The plant is not said to be cursed, but the story line makes it clear that God has caused it to sprout up and then die after only a day in existence. The plant provides a sort of parable in action, supporting God's debate with Jonah on the Deity's compassion for humanity, including sinful (but repentant) Gentiles. To be sure, Jesus' cursing of the fig tree does retain its special character insofar as the miracle-worker addresses a particular tree and punishes it for a particular fault, all with symbolic over-

tones. But this specific element is due to the desire of the pre-Marcan author to create a curse story that would serve as commentary on the cleansing of the temple.

[72] For extensive discussion and bibliography, see Rudolf Pesch, *Der reiche Fischfang. Lk 5,1–11/Jo 21,1–14* (Kommentare und Beiträge zum Alten und Neuen Testament; Düsseldorf: Patmos, 1969); a survey of literature and opinions can be found in the first two chapters (pp. 13–52). Further literature can be found in the articles of Günter Klein and Rudolf Pesch listed below. Out of the vast literature on the subject, the following works may be mentioned: Albert J. Matthews, " 'Depart from me; for I am a sinful man, O Lord' (Luke v. 8)," *ExpTim* 30 (1918–19) 425; M.-E. Boismard, "Le chapitre XXI de Saint Jean. Essai de critique littéraire," *RB* 54 (1947) 473–501; Robert Leaney, "Jesus and Peter: The Call and Post-resurrection Appearance (Lk v. 1–11 and xxiv. 34)," *ExpTim* 65 (1953–54) 381–82; Jindřich Mánek, "Fishers of Men," *NovT* 2 (1957) 138–41; Charles W. F. Smith, "Fishers of Men. Footnotes on a Gospel Figure," *HTR* 52 (1959) 187–203; Otto Betz, "Donnersöhne, Menschenfischer und der davidische Messias," *RevQ* 3 (1961–62) 41–70, esp. 53–61; Klaus Zillessen, "Das Schiff des Petrus und die Gefährten vom andern Schiff (Zur Exegese von Luc 5:1–11)," *ZNW* 57 (1966) 137–39; Günter Klein, "Die Berufung des Petrus," *ZNW* 58 (1967) 1–44; Stanley Marrow, "Jo 21: Indagatio in Ecclesiologiam Joanneam," *VD* 45 (1967) 47–51; Wilhelm H. Wuellner, *The Meaning of "Fishers of Men"* (New Testament Library; Philadelphia: Westminster, 1967); Francis Agnew, "Vocatio primorum discipulorum in traditione synoptica," *VD* 46 (1968) 129–47; Jean Delorme, "Luc v.1–11: Analyse structurale et histoire de la rédaction," *NTS* 18 (1971–72) 331–50; Wolfgang Dietrich, *Das Petrusbild der lukanischen Schriften* (BWANT 5/14; Stuttgart: Kohlhammer, 1972), esp. 23–81; Rudolf Pesch, "La rédaction lucanienne du logion des pêcheurs d'hommes (Lc., V, 10c)," *L'évangile de Luc—The Gospel of Luke* (BETL 32; revised and enlarged edition; ed. Frans Neirynck; Leuven: Leuven University/Peeters, 1989; originally 1973) 135–54.

[73] As I have already indicated, I think that chap. 21 of John's Gospel was added by a final redactor after the Evangelist completed the Fourth Gospel (and probably died). As Brown points out (*The Gospel According to John*, 2. 1077–85), this decision is not reached simply by a quick count of words that are not found elsewhere in John, but by a careful weighing of many different factors in chap. 21: vocabulary, grammar, style, and theological outlook—not to mention the awkward tacking on of a whole chapter to a work that has announced itself completed in chap. 20. For a detailed study of the literary aspects of chap. 21 that lead to the conclusion that the anonymous redactor is distinct from but a disciple of the Fourth Evangelist, see Boismard, "Le chapitre XXI," 473–501 (his emphasis on Lucan traits may be overdone); see also Marrow, "Jo 21," 47–51.

[74] As shall become evident, I do not in the end think that the miraculous catch of fish should be categorized as a gift miracle.

[75] The latter possibility cannot be dismissed out of hand. We probably have such a case in the washing of Jesus' feet by the repentant woman in Luke 7:36–50 vis-à-vis the anointing of Jesus' feet by Mary of Bethany in John 12:1–8. For this view see Brown, *The Gospel According to John*, 1. 449–52. For a different opinion see Fitzmyer, *The Gospel According to Luke*, 1. 684–88.

[76] For convenience' sake, in what follows I will often speak simply of "Luke" and "John." In reality, it is highly probable that the story of the catch of fish came to each author already ensconced in the respective setting witnessed in each Gospel. Hence "Luke" and "John" should be understood as code words for the special Lucan tradition

that Luke uses in 5:1–11 and the Johannine tradition that the final redactor of the Fourth Gospel uses in chap. 21.—Another problem of terminology arises: in what sense can a historian say that a particular event or tradition is pre-Easter or post-Easter, pre-resurrection or post-resurrection? Since, according to the definitions used in *A Marginal Jew* (1. 201 n. 2), the resurrection of Jesus, even theologically considered, must be termed "meta-historical," an event or a tradition is considered pre- or post-resurrection depending on whether it happened or arose prior to or after Jesus' death on the cross and the subsequent proclamation of his resurrection by his disciples (both of which are historical events). It is in this sense that "pre-resurrection" and "post-resurrection" are used here and elsewhere in this volume.

[77] Luke's rearrangement and redactional reformulation of the Marcan material concerning the beginnings of Jesus' public ministry lead to some tensions in the narrative. One is that Simon is referred to in passing in the story of the healing of his mother-in-law (Luke 4:38–39) without any identification of this "Simon" being given. Indeed, it is only by inference that the reader knows that the Simon referred to in 5:3 is the Simon of 4:38. This is a good reminder that Luke takes for granted that his readers know Simon Peter from Mark's Gospel, from various oral traditions, or from both; see Schürmann, *Das Lukasevangelium*, 1. 251.

[78] In my treatment of the Gospel narratives I regularly use "Sea of Galilee" as a useful generic label. Luke instead refers to this body of water by the more precise title of "the Lake of Gennesaret" (so in 5:1; elsewhere simply "the lake"). John's Gospel, besides using "the Sea of Galilee" (6:1), also uses "the Sea of Tiberias" (6:1; 21:1).

[79] Brown, *The Gospel According to John*, 2. 1077–1100; Fitzmyer, *The Gospel According to Luke*, 1. 559–64.

[80] I am dependent here, with a few additions and alterations, on the list given by Brown, *The Gospel According to John*, 2. 1090.

[81] At the end of his story Luke, almost as an afterthought, mentions James and John, the sons of Zebedee (5:10). At the very beginning of his story, before the action starts, the Johannine redactor lists Peter's companions, among whom are "the sons of Zebedee" (21:2); the sons of Zebedee are not mentioned again in the story. That they were referred to at all is strange; nowhere else in John's Gospel are the sons of Zebedee mentioned (to say nothing of their names being given). Even here the reader of John's Gospel never finds out what the names of the sons of Zebedee are. This "marginal" status of the sons of Zebedee in both the Lucan and Johannine narratives may indicate that originally only Peter was an actor alongside Jesus in the story. For the great emphasis on Peter in Luke's redaction of 5:1–11, see Zillessen, "Das Schiff," 137–39 (though he tends to allegorize); Dietrich, *Das Petrusbild*, 23–81.

[82] The imperfect tense of Luke's verb *dierrēsseto* ("were being torn apart") is probably a conative imperfect (so Max Zerwick-Mary Grosvenor, *A Grammatical Analysis of the Greek New Testament* [rev. ed.; Rome: Biblical Institute, 1981], 189): "were almost at the breaking point."

[83] See Bultmann, *Das Evangelium des Johannes*, 544; Brown, *The Gospel According to John*, 2. 1071; Lindars, *The Gospel of John*, 627; Schnackenburg, *Das Johannesevangelium*, 3. 423; Haenchen, *John 2*, 231; Heinrich Kasting, *Die Anfänge der urchristlichen Mission* (BEvT 55; Munich: Kaiser, 1969) 47. Schnackenburg points out that the recognition of Jesus by the beloved disciple in v 7 makes the hesitation of the other disciples to ask Jesus "Who are you?" in v 12 difficult to understand. John 21:7 shows the same tendency as the story of the empty tomb (John 20:1–10): a one-upmanship of Peter that

stresses the greater ability of the beloved disciple to sense the mystery with which both he and Peter are confronted. This should not be over-interpreted as a hostile polemic against Peter.

[84] With the typical one-upmanship of the Johannine tradition, it is the beloved disciple who moves Peter to action by declaring: "It is the Lord" (John 21:7). The indirect statements "that it is the Lord" (*hoti ho kyrios estin*) in 21:7,12 echo the words or thoughts of the beloved disciple or the group of disciples respectively. The title is not articulated by the narrator's own "voice" when he speaks on his own and from his own point of view.

[85] So, among many other scholars, Pesch, *Der reiche Fischfang*, 120–21. Van der Loos (*The Miracles of Jesus*, 670, 678) represents an older, uncritical type of exegesis that declares that the two stories accurately represent two different events, one at the beginning of the public ministry, the other after the resurrection. The obvious similarities are then explained on the grounds that Peter had proved unfaithful to his first call, which was occasioned by a startling catch of fish, and so after the resurrection Jesus reminded him of that first call by providing a second startling catch of fish. Needless to say, the fact that one story occurs only in Luke and the other only in the epilogue of John's Gospel is conveniently ignored at this point. Here we have a prime example of the harmonizing that infects van der Loos's whole book. It is regrettable to see Marshall (*Luke*, 200) following this tendency.

[86] When we ask about the original setting of the story, we are not necessarily presupposing that the story reflects some historical event. Rather, granted that the same basic story has been preserved in two different forms with two different settings, we are simply asking which setting was original to the story and which setting arose later as the story developed.—Contrary to most critics, Pesch in a sense waives the whole question of pre- or post-resurrection setting; see *Der reiche Fischfang*, 111–30. In his view, the miraculous catch of fish was originally a timeless miracle story without a specific context, a relatively late legend created by the church. While I disagree with Pesch's reconstruction of both the Lucan and Johannine traditions, I will not bother to engage him in point-by-point debate, since the final conclusion of his analysis is the same as mine: the story of the miraculous catch of fish does not go back to an event in the life of the historical Jesus.

[87] Earlier in his career Bultmann (*Geschichte*, 232) held that John 21:1–14 was a later composition, which in one way or another went back to Luke 5:1–11. However, in his commentary on John (*Das Evangelium des Johannes*, 546), Bultmann holds that the post-Easter setting is original. This second view is also the one he identifies as his own opinion in the fourth edition of the *Ergänzungsheft* (p. 83) to his *Geschichte*. Neither in his John commentary nor in the *Ergänzungsheft* does he signalize his change of opinion and explain the reasons that moved him to change his mind.

[88] Dibelius, *Formgeschichte*, 110; Agnew, "Vocatio," 135–37; Dietrich, *Das Petrusbild*, 23–81, esp. 76; Schürmann, *Das Lukasevangelium*, 1. 273–74; Grass, *Ostergeschehen*, 80; Smith, "Fishers of Men," 200; Klein, "Die Berufung des Petrus," 1–44, esp. 34–35; Marrow, "Jo 21," 48; Kasting, *Die Anfänge*, 47–52; Brown, *The Gospel According to John*, 2. 1089–94; Fitzmyer, *The Gospel According to Luke*, 1. 560–61. See the fourth edition of Bultmann's *Ergänzungsheft* (p. 83) to his *Geschichte* for a list of opinions on both sides. Ernst (*Das Evangelium nach Lukas*, 184–89) inclines to the view that Luke 5:1–11 derives from a post-resurrection appearance story, but he remains hesitant.

[89] This is emphasized especially by Klein, "Die Berufung des Petrus," 34–35.

Pesch's attempt to counter this argument by appealing vaguely to gnostic and docetic tendencies (never specified) is weak and unconvincing; see *Der reiche Fischfang*, 112–13.

[90] See, e.g., the ecumenical consensus in Raymond E. Brown, Karl P. Donfried, and John Reumann (eds.), *Peter in the New Testament* (Minneapolis: Augsburg; New York: Paulist, 1973) 85–89.

[91] See, e.g., Grundmann, *Das Evangelium nach Matthäus*, 420.

[92] For a detailed study of John 6:31–58 as a form of homiletic haggada, see Peder Borgen, *Bread from Heaven* (NovTSup 10; Leiden: Brill, 1965). One need not adopt all the views of Borgen to accept the basic insight about a homiletic development of the basic Jesus tradition by the Fourth Evangelist.

[93] On the theory that the transfiguration of Jesus is a retrojected resurrection appearance and on objections to such a theory, see Robert H. Stein, "Is the Transfiguration (Mark 9:2–8) a Misplaced Resurrection-Account?" *JBL* 95 (1976) 79–96.

[94] See Latourelle, *The Miracles of Jesus*, 162; Pesch, *Der reiche Fischfang*, 117–18; Dietrich, *Das Petrusbild*, 54. Dibelius (*Formgeschichte*, 110) seeks instead to explain the sudden confession of sinfulness by claiming that Peter sees himself a sinner by the stringent standards of Pharisaic piety. Coming "out of the blue" as it does, this explanation is grounded neither in the Lucan text nor in the historical reality of peasant life in early 1st-century Galilee. Against Dibelius's interpretation stands Kasting, *Die Anfänge*, 50 n. 17.—In any case, Dibelius thinks that the Lucan setting of the story is prior. Interestingly, while Dibelius allows that Luke 5:1–11 may simply be a development by the early church of the call story in Mark 1:16–20, he also allows for the possibility that the connection between the call of the first disciples and the abundant catch of fish goes back to some reminiscence of "historical reality," which was then developed into a legend.

[95] In favor of the view that "*his* house" in Mark 2:15 means Levi's house, in which Jesus has been invited to a meal, see Pesch, *Das Markusevangelium*, 1. 164–65; cf. Taylor, *The Gospel According to St. Mark*, 204; Gundry, *Mark*, 124. While various commentators suggest that the "his" might refer to either Jesus or Peter, Guelich (*Mark 1–8:26*, 101) is probably correct in stating that "the drift of the pericope seems to point to Levi as the host." Mark never says that Jesus had a house in Capernaum, and Peter does not appear in the immediate context.

[96] This is not sufficiently appreciated by Pesch, *Der reiche Fischfang*, 117–19.

[97] So Kasting, *Die Anfänge*, 47; Brown (*The Gospel According to John*, 2. 1111), who also mentions those commentators who deny that this is a scene of rehabilitation (e.g., Bultmann, *Das Evangelium des Johannes*, 551—though Bultmann admits that the "rehabilitation interpretation" is the usual one).

[98] On this point see Grass, *Ostergeschehen*, 79; Kasting, *Die Anfänge*, 49.

[99] On the way Luke connects the miraculous catch of fish to the Marcan tradition, see Fitzmyer, *The Gospel According to Luke*, 1. 560.

[100] On this see Latourelle, *The Miracles of Jesus*, 161; also the literary-critical approach of William S. Kurz, *Reading Luke-Acts. Dynamics of Biblical Narrative* (Louisville: Westminster/John Knox, 1993) 49.

[101] See Schürmann, *Das Lukasevangelium*, 1. 266–74.

[102] Schürmann, *Das Lukasevangelium*, 1. 270.

[103] Schürmann, *Das Lukasevangelium*, 1. 271.

[104] Theissen, *Urchristliche Wundergeschichten*, 112. The difficulty of classifying the miraculous catch of fish as any type of Gospel miracle story is noted by Pesch, *Der reiche Fischfang*, 125–27. As in the wine miracle of Cana, Jesus acts only indirectly in accomplishing the miracle. Moreover, unlike the other so-called nature miracles, the miraculous catch of fish lacks a clear prototype in the OT. Still, as I point out in the main text, the most astounding part of the miracle of the catch of fish is that what is miraculously supplied is then not used, since the supplying has only symbolic value. The context of resurrection appearance and the symbolism of call to ministry collaborate to make this miracle story sui generis.

[105] The singular nouns ("the loaf of bread" and "the fish") in 21:13 may intimate a multiplication of the food, thus recalling the feeding of the multitude in John 6:1–15. Since the Johannine story of the miraculous catch of fish regularly uses the plural form of *ichthys* for "fish" (and once the plural form of *opsarion* in v 10, perhaps under the influence of v 9), the singular *to opsarion* in 21:13 clearly harks back to the singular *opsarion* in v 9, all the more so because in both verses it is joined to *artos*, "loaf of bread."

[106] The precise form-critical category of the post-resurrection appearance in John 21:1–19 has been blurred by the combination of a number of different accounts and themes: the "protochristophany" to Peter, probably in the context of fishing; possibly another account of Jesus' appearance to a group of disciples in Galilee; the theme of table fellowship with the risen Lord, with eucharistic overtones; the triple affirmation of Peter's love for Jesus, reversing his triple denial; the theme of the commissioning of Peter and/or the disciples to become fishers of men and/or shepherds of the sheep; and the final call to "follow." On all this see Grass, *Ostergeschehen*, 74–85; Brown, *The Gospel According to John*, 2. 1082–1122; C. H. Dodd, "The Appearances of the Risen Christ: An Essay in Form-Criticism of the Gospels," *Studies in the Gospels* (R. H. Lightfoot Memorial; ed. D. E. Nineham; Oxford: Blackwell, 1967) 9–35, esp. 14–15. Dodd places John 21:1–14 in his second category of post-resurrection appearances, that of the "circumstantial" narratives, but notes the close contact with the fundamental motives underlying his first category, that of "concise" narratives. In consideration of the blend of different accounts and themes in John 21:1–14, I would prefer the vague label of "mixed narratives." Dodd remains skeptical about resolving the relationship between Luke 5:1–11 and John 21:1–14, since, in his view, the elements of a post-resurrection appearance are lacking in Luke 5, while what Luke 5 and John 21 have in common is not characteristic of post-resurrection appearances (p. 23). Perhaps Dodd's focus on the form-critical question is too narrow. As I have noted, the overall tone in Luke 5:1–11 of theophany and of Jesus as the Exalted One, the sudden and strange confession of sinfulness by Peter, and a thrust in the story that has more to do with commissioning Peter to apostolic ministry than with his initial call to discipleship must be taken into consideration. To be sure, Luke had to recast the tradition of the catch of fish in order to make it fit the beginnings of the ministry and to connect it with the tradition of Mark 1:16–20. But, even with all these changes, a good deal of Luke 5:1–11 still points to a post-resurrection context and to the tradition lying behind John 21:1–19.

[107] See, e.g., Bultmann, *Geschichte*, 232, 246. Such a position allows for all sorts of variations as to how the saying of Jesus first developed into a general story about a miraculous catch of fish and then bifurcated into specifically Lucan and Johannine forms. For example, Klein ("Die Berufung des Petrus," 1–44) stresses that the proper methodological approach to the problem of Luke 5:1–11 ‖ John 21:1–14 must be Jesus' saying about being fishers (or catchers) of men in the Marcan and Lucan traditions.

Klein judges the saying in Luke 5:10 ("From now on you shall be catching men") to be prior to the Marcan version and to be originally rooted in a post-resurrection setting. He even claims that a similar saying at some point fell out of the Johannine tradition lying behind John 21:1–14. Thus, the saying on fishing for or catching men stood at the origin of a tradition that then developed by two separate paths into a miracle-less narrative (Mark 1) and a miraculous narrative (Luke 5 ‖ John 21). It is sobering for the exegete to confront this confident reconstruction of the tradition with the equally confident but opposite view of Pesch in "La rédaction lucanienne," 135–54. Pesch claims that, far from being a piece of primitive tradition, the saying of Jesus in Luke 5:10 is Luke's redactional reformulation of the saying on fishers of men in Mark 1:17. (How Pesch's views fit into an overall explanation of the relationship of Luke 5:1–11 to John 21:1–14 can be seen in his monograph, *Der reiche Fischfang*.) Fortunately, it is not necessary for us to adjudicate these claims, since in the scenarios of both Klein and Pesch the miraculous catch of fish does not go back to some historical event in the public ministry of Jesus. Hence, despite the very different lines of argumentation, the upshot of the position of both authors is the same as far as the question we put to the texts is concerned.

[108] For a full treatment and extensive bibliography, see John Paul Heil, *Jesus Walking on the Sea* (AnBib 87; Rome: Biblical Institute, 1981). I am greatly indebted to the fine exposition given in this work of the versions of the story in Mark, Matthew, and John. It should be noted that Heil's major purposes are to discern the literary genre of the story, to present an exegesis of each version in turn, and to understand each version in the context of the respective Gospel. Heil does not intend to treat at length the question of the earliest hypothetical form of the story or the question of historicity. Besides Heil's work, other useful contributions include J. Kreyenbühl, "Der älteste Auferstehungsbericht und seine Varianten," *ZNW* 9 (1908) 257–96; Pietro Zarrella, "Gesù cammina sulle acque. Significato teologico di Giov. 6, 16–21," *La Scuola Cattolica* 95 (1967) 146–60; Albert-Marie Denis, "Le marche de Jésus sur les eaux. Contribution à l'histoire de la péricope dans la tradition évangélique," *De Jésus aux Evangiles. Tradition et rédaction dans les Evangiles synoptiques* (BETL 25; Joseph Coppens Festschrift, vol. 2; ed. I. de la Potterie; Gembloux: Duculot; Paris: Lethielleux, 1967) 233–47; Thierry Snoy, "La rédaction marcienne de la marche sur les eaux (Mc. VI, 45–52)," *ETL* 44 (1968) 205–41, 433–81; idem, "Marc 6,48: '. . . et il voulait les dépasser.' Proposition pour la solution d'une énigme," *L'évangile selon Marc. Tradition et rédaction* (BETL 34; ed. M. Sabbe; Leuven: Leuven University; Gembloux: Duculot, 1974) 347–63 (these articles reflect the work done in Snoy's Louvain doctoral dissertation of 1967, *Le marche sur les eaux. Etude de la rédaction marcienne*); Diego Losada, "Jesús camina sobre las aguas. Un relato apocalíptico," *RevistB* 38 (1976) 311–19; Hubert Ritt, "Der 'Seewandel Jesu' (Mk 6, 45–52 par). Literarische und theologische Aspekte," *BZ* 23 (1979) 71–84; Pinchas Lapide, "A Jewish Exegesis of the Walking on the Water," *Conflicting Ways of Interpreting the Bible* (Concilium 138; ed. Hans Küng and Jürgen Moltmann; Edinburgh: Clark; New York: Seabury, 1980) 35–40; J. Duncan M. Derrett, "Why and How Jesus Walked on the Sea," *NovT* 23 (1981) 330–48; Charles Homer Giblin, "The Miraculous Crossing of the Sea (John 6. 16–21)," *NTS* 29 (1983) 96–103; Harry Fleddermann, " 'And He Wanted to Pass by Them' (Mark 6:48c)," *CBQ* 45 (1983) 389–95; Charles Richard Carlisle, "Jesus' Walking on the Water: A Note on Matthew 14. 22–33," *NTS* 31 (1985) 151–55; David Finnemore Hill, "The Walking on the Water. A geographical or linguistic answer?" *ExpTim* 99 (1987–88) 267–69.

[109] Ritt, "Der 'Seewandel Jesu,' " 80.

[110] On the independence of John from Mark in the story of the walking on the water,

see Dodd, *Historical Tradition,* 196–222; the position of independence is defended by most authors of full-dress critical commentaries on John in recent decades, including Bultmann, Brown, Schnackenburg, and Haenchen. For the history of the controversy over John's independence of the Synoptics, see Smith, *John Among the Gospels.* Smith has taken an intriguing tack in bringing the apocryphal gospels within the ambit of the John-Synoptics question; see D. Moody Smith, "The Problem of John and the Synoptics in Light of the Relation between Apocryphal and Canonical Gospels," *John and the Synoptics* (BETL 101; ed. A. Denaux; Leuven: Leuven University, 1992) 147–62.

When we compare the versions of Mark and John below, we will see why John's version argues for independence from Mark. Two points are especially intriguing: (1) John's version, instead of looking like a later version of Mark's story as reworked by Johannine theology, appears more primitive and less markedly theological than Mark's. (2) Connected with this is the failure of John's version to fit snugly into the overarching theological purpose of chap. 6. One almost gets the impression that, if John had not found the walking on the water firmly imbedded in a traditional catena of early Christian stories, he would not have taken the trouble to include it in a succession of events in which it is more disruptive than helpful. Hence I find the attempt of J. Konings to derive John's version of the walking on the water in particular and John 6 in general from Mark's Gospel forced and unconvincing; see his article, "The Pre-Markan Sequence in *Jn.,* VI: A Critical Re-examination," *L'évangile selon Marc. Tradition et rédaction* (BETL 34; ed. M. Sabbe; Leuven: Leuven University; Gembloux: Duculot, 1974) 147–77. Note in particular his highly imaginative attempt on p. 170 to explain the structural and theological function of the walking on the water within the context of John 6.

[111] I postpone any consideration of the historicity of Peter's walking on the water in Matt 14:28–32a until the treatment of the historicity of Jesus' walking on the water is completed. Obviously, the historicity of the former depends totally on the historicity of the latter. As for Luke's omission of the Marcan account of Jesus' walking on the water, various theories are proposed: e.g., the story was not in the version of Mark that Luke possessed, or Luke found the story offensive or puzzling. In my opinion, the reasons for the omission are mostly literary: (1) the omission of the walking on the water is simply the beginning of Luke's "great omission" of material from Mark 6:45–8:26 (on which see Schürmann, *Das Lukasevangelium,* 1. 525–27; Fitzmyer, *The Gospel According to Luke,* 1. 770–71). One reason for omitting all this Marcan material is probably that, as a writer with a good eye and a sensitivity to Greco-Roman literary tastes, he realized that Mark's "bread section" contained two different versions of the same sort of material and themes. Hence he chose to jump from the first feeding of the multitude to Peter's confession of faith, bypassing the repetitions. As a good writer, he sees that the feeding miracle provides a more-than-adequate catalyst for Peter's confession; the story line is clarified and tightened. (2) Connected with the first consideration there may have been a very practical consideration about size and space. Luke's Gospel is a very long work, in fact (although Luke naturally could not have known this) the longest book in the NT (Acts, Luke's second volume, is second, with Matthew's Gospel a close third). The prolific Luke no doubt realized that, with all the non-Marcan material (Q and L) he wanted to include in his Gospel, some Marcan parts would have to be sacrificed. The "great omission," including the walking on the water, was the prime victim. (3) With his fierce focus on Jerusalem, the city of destiny, Luke may have wanted to omit material that would complicate the itinerary of Jesus and distract attention from the focus on Jerusalem. Hence Luke may have decided to avoid the meandering parts of Mark's story line, which has Jesus traveling north as far as Tyre and Sidon. On this point see Fitzmyer, *The Gospel According to Luke,* 1. 94. (4) A theological consid-

eration may have been mixed into these literary considerations: the omitted Marcan material contains pericopes that Luke may have found either irrelevant or offensive (e.g., the dispute on the tradition of the elders, washing hands, and food laws in Mark 7:1–23; the story of the Syro-Phoenician woman, with its comparison of Gentiles to dogs in 7:24–30, and the two strange miracle stories of the deaf and mute man in 7:31–37 and the blind man of Bethsaida in 8:22–26).

[112] See Oscar Cullmann, *Der johanneische Kreis. Zum Ursprung des Johannesevangeliums* (Tübingen: Mohr [Siebeck], 1975) 24, 84. For arguments in favor of such a traditional grid, see Dodd, *Historical Tradition*, 196–99, 212–22. It is interesting to note that, while Dodd's views and arguments are not exactly those of Cerfaux ("La section des pains," 471–85), they both arrive at the position that some traditional schema of stories lies behind both Mark 6–8 and John 6. Konings ("The Pre-Markan Sequence," 147–77) attempts to discredit the idea of a pre-Marcan/pre-Johannine cycle of stories behind Mark 6–8 and John 6; but, being based on the (in my view) erroneous theory of John's dependence on Mark, the attempt fails to convince. Indeed, if one holds to John's independence of Mark, it is almost impossible to avoid the conclusion that some sort of catena of early Gospel stories stands behind Mark 6–8 and John 6.

[113] See Denis, "Le marche de Jésus," 246. Here I disagree with Snoy ("La rédaction marcienne," 205–41), who argues at length that the feeding of the five thousand and the walking on the water were not joined in sequence before the Evangelist Mark. There are two basic weaknesses in Snoy's approach: (1) At the beginning of his argument (pp. 206–7), Snoy blithely brushes aside a pivotal problem: the same connection that occurs in Mark 6 occurs in John 6 as well. If, as most of the major 20th-century commentators on John's Gospel maintain with C. H. Dodd, John's tradition is independent of the Synoptics, the agreement between John and Mark on the connection between the feeding of the five thousand and the walking on the water is a decisive argument that the connection already existed in the pre-Marcan and pre-Johannine traditions. That both authors just happened by chance to invent the same connection, a connection whose rationale in John is by no means clear, is too much of a coincidence. (2) Snoy bases a great deal on the inconsistencies of time and place in the succession of the two stories. In my opinion, the geographical references are so unclear and muddled—as they are at times elsewhere in Mark—that it is perilous to construct any argument for or against a pre-Marcan connection between the two stories on the basis of geography. Moreover, if the apparent geographical and temporal contradictions were tolerable to Mark, how do we know that they were not tolerable to some pre-Marcan writer or composer of oral traditions?—It is perhaps telling that even Koch (*Die Bedeutung*, 36, 107), who is not given to positing large collections of pre-Marcan miracle stories, nevertheless supposes that the feeding of the multitude and the walking on the water were joined before Mark.

[114] See Dodd, *Historical Tradition*, 197.

[115] Speculation about references to the OT and Jewish motif of God helping the worshiper or the oppressed just person "at the break of day" or at dawn (see Pesch, *Das Markusevangelium*, 1. 360) seems out of place. In 6:48 Mark speaks vaguely of "about the fourth watch of the night," which could be a time around 3 a.m. just as easily as a time around 6 a.m.

[116] As Snoy ("La rédaction marcienne," 439) notes, the phrase *kai ekopasen ho anemos* ("and the wind died down," 6:51b) is identical to the phrase in Mark 4:39, in the story of the stilling of the storm. In the whole of the NT, this phrase—indeed, simply the verb *kopazō*—occurs only in these two Marcan passages, plus the Matthean parallel to

the walking on the water, Matt 14:32. Snoy sees this as a sign that in the story of the walking on the water the phrase is due to the redaction of Mark, who has taken it from its original setting in the stilling of the storm and placed it in a story where it is not as well integrated. If Snoy is correct, the pre-Marcan story was even less open to a "sea-rescue" interpretation than is its Marcan form.

[117] It is generally acknowledged by commentators on Mark that the end of v 51 and the whole of v 52 are redactional creations of Mark. This is argued at length by Snoy, "La rédaction marcienne," 433–81. On pp. 480–81, Snoy makes the interesting observation that by adding these verses Mark has modified to the point of inverting the traditional meaning of the miracle story. As an epiphany, the traditional story intended to illustrate the superhuman character of the person of Jesus and his quasi-divine power over the elements. In this there is nothing especially difficult to understand. It is Mark who introduces at the end of the story the idea of the hidden mystery of the true nature of Jesus, a mystery that in Marcan theology not even the epiphany of the walking on the water can dissolve for the obtuse disciples. On the redactional nature of 6:52 see also Quentin Quesnell, *The Mind of Mark. Interpretation and Method through the Exegesis of Mark 6,52* (AnBib 38; Rome: Biblical Institute, 1969) 61–67; Kertelge, *Die Wunder Jesu*, 145–46; Koch, *Die Bedeutung*, 107–8.

[118] Some authors use words like "epiphany" and "theophany" interchangeably, while others make various distinctions. Here I use "epiphany" as an umbrella-term, signifying a striking, extraordinary, and temporary appearance of a divine or heavenly figure in the earthly realm, often to a select individual or group of people for the purpose of communicating a message. When one is dealing with biblical stories, it is helpful to subdivide the term "epiphany" into a theophany (an appearance of God), an angelophany (an appearance of an angel), and a christophany (an appearance of Christ, especially the risen Christ). Since, in the biblical view of things, God cannot be directly and fully seen, his presence is usually signified by either a panoply of cosmic phenomena (e.g., earthquakes, lightning, thunder, clouds) or some sort of anthropomorphic figure that is understood to be not a perfect representation of God himself (e.g., Ezek 1:26–28, within the larger context of chap. 1). Obviously, then, there will always be a major difference when the trappings of an OT theophany are applied to an epiphany of Jesus in the NT: Jesus can be directly and fully seen, while God cannot. For further discussion of epiphany and theophany, see Heil, *Jesus Walking on the Sea*, 8–9; Jörg Jeremias, *Theophanie. Die Geschichte einer alttestamentlichen Gattung* (WMANT 10; 2d ed.; Neukirchen-Vluyn: Neukirchener Verlag, 1977); Theodore Hiebert, "Theophany in the OT," *Anchor Bible Dictionary*, 6. 505–11. Pesch (*Das Markusevangelium*, 1. 358) attempts to sketch the characteristic traits of an epiphany-story, but not all the traits he lists are verified in the walking on the water.

[119] Ritt ("Der 'Seewandel Jesu,'" 81) stresses the solemn formula *egō eimi* as the "absolute high point" of the miracle story: "not a miraculous *action* but a majestic miraculous *word*." Perhaps one can compromise here and see the action of Jesus' walking on the sea as the *central* event of the story, while the *egō eimi* stands further along in the text as the *climax* of the story. For Kertelge (*Die Wunder Jesu*, 147), the fact that both Mark and John have the key proclamation "It is I, fear not" shows that this is the real point of the tradition underlying both versions of the story and that the narrative is an epiphany-story; the central motif of the pre-Marcan story is the self-revelation of Jesus (p. 148).

[120] On this point see Gundry, *Mark*, 337, 342. I will be arguing this point as we move through the analysis of the story. A major influence in seeing the story as both an

epiphany and a sea rescue and in deciding which is primary or more original was Bult-mann, *Geschichte*, 231. While allowing for the possibility that the walking on the water was a variant that developed out of the miracle of the stilling of the storm (Mark 4:35–41 parr.), Bultmann preferred the view that the original motif was the walking on the water, to which the motif of the storm was added secondarily; so too Koch, *Die Bedeutung*, 104–5; Guelich, *Mark 1–8:26*, 346–47. As Ritt observes ("Der 'Seewandel Jesu,' " 77), both sides of the argument have been represented in the scholarly literature for some time: e.g., Ernst Lohmeyer held that the epiphany of Jesus was the primary material of the story, while Emil Wendling defended the position that the walking on the water developed out of the story of the stilling of the storm. Pesch (*Das Markus-evangelium*, 1. 358) prefers the formulation that the walking on the water is an epiph-any-story in which the motif of rescue, while present, has been massively reduced. Ritt himself argues against any sort of either-or approach; in his holistic view, an epiphany is by its very nature saving. One can agree with this valid insight and still not think that the proper designation of the genre of the walking on the water should include the label "sea rescue." Here I must part company with the otherwise helpful work of Heil (*Jesus Walking on the Sea*, 1–30), who argues for the correctness of the genre-designa-tion "sea-rescue epiphany."

I readily grant the observation of many critics that Mark 6:45–52 contains a number of phrases and motifs also found in the stilling of the storm in Mark 4:35–41: e.g., it was getting on toward evening, the disciples were going to the other shore, the crowd is left behind, the wind dies down, and the disciples are still without a clue about the identity of Jesus after they have witnessed his power over the forces of creation. Yet, despite many commentators' tendency to talk about a "storm" in 6:45–52, the word "storm," notably present in Mark 4:35–41 (v 37: *lailaps megalē anemou*, "a great storm of wind"), is notably absent in Mark 6:45–52. All Mark mentions is a strong contrary wind that makes the rowing difficult and slows down the boat's progress. There is no dire need or mortal danger from which the disciples must be rescued, and hence no desperate—and somewhat irreverent—cry from them to Jesus (4:38): "Teacher, do you not care that we are perishing?" (On the lack of danger in Mark's story of Jesus' walking on the water, see Denis, "Le marche de Jésus," 243–46; Haenchen, *John 1*, 282; cf. Pesch, *Das Markusevangelium*, 1. 360.) In contrast, when the disciples cry out in fear in Mark 6:49, it is not out of fear for their lives because of a storm, but out of fear at seeing Jesus, whom they take for a ghost. It is the epiphany itself that causes initial fear—as all good epiphanies should. Ritt's point about epiphanies being of their nature soteriological is well taken (see, e.g., his concluding comments in "Der 'Seewandel Jesu,' " 82–84), but the "saving element" in the story of the walking on the water has nothing to do with saving the disciples from mortal danger. It has much more to do with bestowing on them the saving, comforting, and fear-allaying presence of Jesus after the long night of separation. Quite literally, the primary saving element is inherent in the very event of epiphany, prior to and independent of any physical benefit that may or may not follow. As we shall see, I think that this point has some relevance for the question of the original *Sitz im Leben* of the walking on the water in the worship of the early church.

[121] In this Schnackenburg (*Das Johannesevangelium*, 2. 37) is in agreement with Bult-mann, *Das Evangelium des Johannes*, 155; and Brown, *The Gospel According to John*, 1. 253–54. The one notable exception to the primitive nature of John's version is the second miracle at the end of the story, i.e., the immediate arrival at the far side of the sea (v 21b).

[122] See Schnackenburg, *Das Johannesevangelium*, 2. 33–40.

[123] For example, Fortna (*The Fourth Gospel*, 80–93) thinks that "and it had already grown dark and Jesus had not yet come to them" in v 17 was added by the Evangelist; but he holds that the immediate arrival of the boat at the far shore was in the source, since in his view it is Jesus' role in bringing the disciples to shore that is the main point of the story in the Johannine tradition (p. 82). In contrast, von Wahlde (*The Earliest Version*, 100–101) maintains that the entire story in John 6:16–21 existed in the Evangelist's source; nothing has been added by the Evangelist. Uncertainty over such questions is one reason why I try to establish only the basic content of the primitive story, not its exact wording.

[124] For the debate on whether John's version of the walking on the water contains any great amount of Johannine theology or whether it has been retained basically because of its traditional connection with the feeding of the five thousand, see Zarrella, "Gesù cammina," 147–50. C. K. Barrett (*The Gospel According to St John* [London: SPCK, 1965] 232–33) rightly observes that, unlike the miracle of the feeding, the walking on the water is not directly expounded by John; in fact, it has little to do with the Johannine context. Barrett thinks that "John included the narrative (a) because it was firmly fixed in the tradition along with the miracle of the five thousand, and (b) in order to bring Jesus and the disciples back to Capernaum. . . ." See also Brown, *The Gospel According to John*, 1. 252; von Wahlde, *The Earliest Version*, 101. One can therefore see how questionable is the theory of Peter F. Ellis (*The Genius of John* [Collegeville, MN: Liturgical Press, 1984] 14–15), who maintains that the walking on the water is the structural and theological center of the whole of John's Gospel.

[125] Note that, unlike the feeding of the five thousand, the walking on the water is never called a "sign" by John. Hence it is illegitimate to include it in Jesus' reference to signs in John 6:26. The reference to signs in v 26 points back to John 6:2 in general ("they saw the signs that he worked on the sick") and to the feeding of the five thousand in particular. Hence Zarrella ("Gesù cammina," 150, 158–59) is incorrect in including the walking on the water under the rubric of "the sign" of John 6.

[126] See Jerome H. Neyrey, *An Ideology of Revolt* (Philadelphia: Fortress, 1988) 213–20.

[127] Ritt ("Der 'Seewandel Jesu,' " 81) makes the same point about Mark's account, where Ritt claims both meanings of *egō eimi* are present. According to Ritt, the proclamation of identity ("It is I, Jesus") is present in the "foreground," on the level of the action narrated in the story; the formula of self-revelation (the solemn "I am") is present in the "background," on the level of the deep meaning of the text.

[128] This is a commonplace among exegetes; see, e.g., Giblin, "The Miraculous Crossing," 97. While this observation is true in general, especially in comparison with Mark's version, there is still a certain oscillation of focus in John's version between the disciples and Jesus; see Zarrella, "Gesù cammina," 155.

[129] So rightly Bultmann, *Das Evangelium des Johannes*, 159. However, Bultmann goes too far when he favors omitting John 6:18 as a gloss (p. 159 n. 1). The reference to the wind whipping up the sea is not meant to prepare for Jesus' stilling of the storm, which in fact never takes place in John; rather, it explains why in v 19 the disciples have made relatively little progress in their rowing by the time Jesus comes to them.

[130] This is correctly seen by Giblin, "The Miraculous Crossing," 96. Giblin holds that John's story has a note of an epiphany, but John employs the epiphany to explain not a sea rescue but a sea crossing.

[131] The word *eutheōs* ("immediately") in John 6:21 should be taken in the strong

sense of "instantaneously," as is clear from the other two uses of the adverb in John: the cure of the paralytic (5:9) and the crowing of the cock after Peter's denial (18:27). We do not have here the Marcan phenomenon of the over-used and hence weakened *eythus*.

[132] On the immediacy of the arrival as miraculous, see Giblin, "The Miraculous Crossing," 97. Giblin makes the interesting suggestion that the immediate arrival at the far shore is the consequence of the coming of Jesus across the water, his self-identification, and the disciples' willingness to receive him. While this suggestion helps one appreciate the organic unity of the story, I think that it may go too far to claim, as Giblin does (p. 98), that the immediate miraculous arrival of the boat is the "main point of the narrative."

[133] Giblin ("The Miraculous Crossing," 98–99) suggests that the story of the walking on the water, including its miraculous conclusion, helps (1) to distinguish the believing disciples (as it turns out, the Twelve in particular) from the unbelieving crowd, (2) to prepare for Jesus' address to each group, and (3) to prepare for each group's reaction to Jesus, especially Peter's profession of faith (6:68–69). While this is an attractive idea, one must admit that nothing in the final part of chap. 6 indicates that the positive reaction of Peter and the Twelve is based on their experience of the walking on the water and the miraculous arrival of their boat at the far shore. How is the reader supposed to know that Peter's reaction is based on these miracles instead of or in addition to the great "sign" that dominates the chapter, the feeding of the five thousand? If the walking on the water and the miraculous arrival of the boat are so important, why are they not designated "signs" by the Evangelist?

[134] For an example of such harmonization, which shows more erudition than critical sense, see Heinz Kruse, "Jesu Seefahrten und die Stellung von Joh. 6," *NTS* 30 (1984) 508–30.

[135] As I have already indicated, I prefer to follow the Synoptic vocabulary in seeing the transfiguration of Jesus as a "vision" the disciples have of Jesus rather than a "miracle" that Jesus "performs."

[136] Indeed, in the highly metaphorical hymn in Job 9, "treading upon the back of the sea" may be meant to conjure up the image of God literally treading upon the back of the sea monster, just as in Ugaritic mythology the god Baal (= "Lord") battles and defeats the god Yamm (= "Sea"). On this see Heil, *Jesus Walking on the Sea*, 39–40.

[137] It is intriguing to note that just three verses later, in Job 9:11, Job says of God: "If he should pass by me, I would not see him. . . ." The language of "passing by" right after a mention of God walking on the sea is striking for anyone who knows the Marcan story of Jesus' walking on the water. However, the parallel in this case is merely verbal. God's "passing by" in Job 9:11 is the very opposite of a theophany; it is divine movement that, like most divine movement, is invisible to mere mortals like Job.

[138] We are fortunate to have this text attested in the fragments of the Targum of Job found in Cave 11 at Qumran (11QtgJob). For text and translation, see Fitzmyer and Harrington, *A Manual of Palestinian Aramaic Texts*, 36–39. Unlike some of the later "classical" targums, 11QtgJob is a fairly literal and sober translation of the Hebrew text of Job into Aramaic. Since this is true of the fragments we possess (including 38:8–11), it is reasonable to assume that the same would be true of the parts of the targum that have not come down to us. If one wishes to examine the corresponding material from the classical Targum of Job (ca. 4th–5th century A.D.), as well as other passages from rabbinic literature, these are conveniently collected by Heil, *Jesus Walking on the Sea*,

40–56. In my view, the later rabbinic material is of limited usefulness in our attempt to discern what would have been the primitive form of the story of the walking on the water, which presumably circulated among Christians sometime during the first half of the 1st century A.D.

[139] On this see Carroll Stuhlmueller, *Creative Redemption in Deutero-Isaiah* (AnBib 43; Rome: Biblical Institute, 1970); cf. Richard J. Clifford, *Fair Spoken and Persuading. An Interpretation of Second Isaiah* (New York/Ramsey, NJ/Toronto: Paulist, 1984) 59–67, esp. p. 66 n. 7.

[140] See Brown, *The Gospel According to John*, 1. CXXII–CXXV; John Painter, *The Quest for the Messiah* (Edinburgh: Clark, 1991) 107–28.

[141] So as not to encumber the main text, I mention there only the major theories suggested to solve the problem. For a detailed discussion of practically every suggestion ever made to explain the troublesome phrase "he wished to pass by them," see Snoy, "Marc 6,48," 347–63. Snoy (p. 348) is probably correct in maintaining the usual translation of the verb *thelō* as "wish" or "want." It is true that at times *thelō* means "to be about to" (= the verb *mellō*) in some classical authors, inscriptions, and papyri, but there is no indisputable case of such usage in the NT. As for the enigmatic verb *parerchomai* ("pass by"), Snoy gives a lengthy survey of opinions, refuting most of them on the way. In theory, *parerchomai* is open to any of the following interpretations: (1) the verb means arrive, rejoin; (2) the verb means transgress or traverse (this would make no sense here; the verb carries these meanings when applied to commandments or territories); (3) the verb means pass by or beyond someone, without stopping (this is Snoy's choice); (4) the verb means pass by, but it expresses the subjective impression the disciples had, not Jesus' intention (this is contrary to the express wording of the text, as well as the general point of view in the pericope); (5) Jesus wished to test the disciples' faith (this seems unlikely in Mark's Gospel, where the disciples are hopelessly obtuse); (6) Mark wished to indicate that for Jesus, walking on the sea was something quite natural, something he could continue to do without bothering about the disciples; (7) Jesus wished to get to the opposite shore ahead of the disciples and surprise them; (8) Jesus' walking on the water was not intended to be seen by the disciples, and only their distress led Jesus to rejoin them (yet Mark says that Jesus was walking *to* the disciples); (9) Jesus wishes to display to the disciples his power over the elements (yes, but then why did he want to pass by them?); (10) the verb fits in with other passages in Mark (the stilling of the storm, the epileptic boy, the Syrophoenician woman) where Jesus seems to refuse to occupy himself with others' needs or expresses his desire to withdraw and not be involved; (11) Jesus desires to keep his superhuman power secret; (12) the verb has the sense seen in OT theophanies at Sinai, when God "passes by" Moses or Elijah.

Snoy grants that Mark's scene is reminiscent of OT theophanies, but he prefers to take "he wished to pass by" as expressing the dialectic in Mark's "messianic secret." Jesus reveals himself yet he wishes to remain incognito. Hence, says Snoy, *parerchomai* should be taken in the literal sense of "passing by someone without stopping or letting oneself be recognized." In the end, because of the disciples' fear, Jesus decides to reveal his identity to them. For a critique of Snoy's theory of the "incognito," see Heil, *Jesus Walking on the Sea*, 72; Gundry, *Mark*, 340–41; and my remarks in the main text. While basically accepting Snoy's interpretation, Fleddermann (" 'And He Wanted to Pass by Them,' " 389–95) wants to add the idea from Amos 7:8; 8:2 that *parerchomai* refers to God's will to spare and so save his people. However, (1) the Marcan context, unlike the Amos context, does not contrast "passing through" (*dierchomai*) in the sense of punishing with "passing by" in the sense of sparing; (2) in the Amos texts "pass by" means sparing those who deserve punishment but who are forgiven and so saved by God; this does not fit the situation of the disciples witnessing the epiphany of Jesus. As I indicate in the main text, I think that *parerchomai* is best understood as a quasi-technical term from OT descriptions of theophanies; obviously, the sense changes somewhat when the epiphany no longer reveals Yahweh, who by definition cannot be directly and fully seen, but rather Jesus, who can. In technical terms, instead of a theophany in the strict OT sense (where God can be seen only indirectly, often through cosmic phenomena or anthropomorphic approximations), we have an epiphany of Jesus, in other words, a christophany (where the individual can be directly seen in his power and majesty).

[142] The Theodotion text is closer to the MT in using *anastēsetai* ("shall arise"), reflecting the MT's *ya'ămōd* ("shall stand").

[143] On the early nature and weighty message of the hymn in Phil 2:6–11, see Martin Hengel, *The Son of God* (Philadelphia: Fortress, 1976) 1–2, 76, 87; Ralph P. Martin, *Carmen Christi. Philippians ii. 5–11 in Recent Interpretation and in the Setting of Early Christian Worship* (rev. ed.; Grand Rapids: Eerdmans, 1983, originally 1967); Joseph A. Fitzmyer, "The Aramaic Background of Philippians 2:6–11," *CBQ* 50 (1988) 470–83.

[144] See the parallels highlighted by Ritt, "Der 'Seewandel Jesu,' " 80. An early and lengthy form of the post-resurrection-appearance theory was presented by Kreyenbühl in 1908 ("Der älteste Auferstehungsbericht," 257–96). Since he lacked any firm position on the Synoptic problem and preferred to judge priority from case to case, he wound up with the improbable solution that the earliest form of a narrative of a post-resurrection appearance in Galilee is preserved in the story of the walking on the water in Matthew 14, which reflects the Gospel of the primitive community. The stilling of the storm in Mark 4 and the present form of the walking on the water in Matthew 14 are later reworkings of the material by redactors who no longer understood the original post-resurrection appearance.

[145] Dodd, "The Appearances of the Risen Christ," 9–35, esp. 23–24. Dodd (p. 23) comments that the story of the walking on the water, "in its Johannine form, shows many of the features of post-resurrection narratives." He then applies to the Johannine story the five parts of his "concise" class of post-resurrection appearances: (1) the disciples were at sea and Jesus was not with them (theme of being bereft of the Lord); (2) they saw Jesus walking on the water (theme of the appearance of the risen Lord); (3) they were afraid, but Jesus hailed them with a word of reassurance (theme of greeting); (4) they were willing to receive him into the boat since they recognized him (theme of recognition); (5) however, the word of command is missing; instead, the voyage ends. While on the whole the story conforms to the concise type, some details, like the description of the violence of the wind and the distance from the shore remind one of the more detailed "circumstantial" narratives. Dodd (p. 24) goes on to observe that the Marcan form of the story "is farther away from the type of the post-resurrection narratives." The Marcan story is told from Jesus' point of view, and the disciples clearly take Jesus into the boat at the end of the story—both elements are contrary to post-resurrection narratives. Dodd, rightly in my opinion, ends by suggesting that the Johannine narrative is the more primitive form; the primitive form of the story was thus closer to a post-resurrection appearance than is its more developed Marcan form.

[146] *Contra* Ritt, "Der 'Seewandel Jesu,' " 74. The fact that the walking on the water is a well-composed, self-contained unit tells us something about the skill of the Christian(s) who created it, but tells us nothing about whether it was created from the beginning as a commentary on the feeding miracle. Ritt holds, however, that the two stories were already joined in the pre-Marcan tradition. He points out (p. 74) that otherwise it

is difficult to see why Mark's redactional comment about the disciples not understanding on the basis of the multiplication of the loaves (Mark 6:52) was not placed immediately after the feeding miracle, as opposed to its actual place after the walking on the water.

[147] Losada ("Jesús camina," 319) connects Mark's reference to the fourth watch of the night to the idea of the parousia, which, along with the theme of the cosmic triumph over nature, gives the passage an apocalyptic character. It is true that the early church saw the eucharist both as the continuation of table fellowship with the risen Lord and the anticipation of his final coming, but Losada may be asking too much of Marcan symbolism at this point. Since the reference to the fourth watch of the night is only in the Marcan form of the story, I would not want to use it to make any claims about the primitive story.

[148] One is reminded of Dibelius's comment (*Formgeschichte*, 232) that Mark's Gospel is a book of "secret epiphanies"; perhaps that is one reason why Mark would have been happy to keep the story of the walking on the water when he took over the pre-Marcan "bread cycle."

[149] If the walking on the water was created by the early church purely as a theological commentary on the feeding of the five thousand, one need not be surprised that no great care was taken to make all the geographical and temporal references in the two stories cohere. That these inconsistencies should not have bothered some early Christian author need not surprise us, since they did not bother Mark either. Hence I do not find the objections of Snoy ("La rédaction marcienne," 205–41) to a pre-Marcan link between the two stories, objections he bases largely on the supposed geographical and temporal contradictions, convincing.

[150] For a highly imaginative example of this approach, see Derrett, "Why and How Jesus Walked on the Sea," 330–48. Symptomatic of the whole article is the unsubstantiated declaration at its beginning: "The Walking on the Lake . . . is extremely difficult to imagine as having been fabricated *ex nihilo*." Actually, practically no one claims that it was fabricated *ex nihilo*. The vast OT substratum and the ongoing experience of the church provided the material for construction.—In theory, it is possible to take the phrase in John 6:19 usually translated as "walking on the sea" as meaning "walking by the sea," "walking on the seashore." Dodd (*Historical Tradition*, 198) readily admits this point, though he hastens to add: "Not that this is how John intended it [the story] to be read." He rightly points to the following narrative, which presupposes that Jesus has crossed the Sea of Galilee in some inexplicable way to Capernaum (see 6:25). Nevertheless, J. H. Bernard (*The Gospel According to St. John* [ICC; Edinburgh: Clark, 1928] 1. 186) held that "walking by the seashore" was the sense intended even in John's Gospel. In my view, that is obviously not the sense in the present form of the Gospel miracle stories—most blatantly so in Matthew's version, complete with Peter sinking beneath the waves. That it is not the sense in any of the Gospel versions of the story is evident to anyone who has explored the OT background of the story. As Brown (*The Gospel According to John*, 1. 252) points out against Bernard, to translate "by the seashore" in John 6:19 makes the story seem pointless. Since I think that the story came into existence precisely as a miracle story that was created by the church to comment on another miracle story, the whole question is moot.

[151] Ritt ("Der 'Seewandel Jesu,' " 81–82) speaks of Matthew's "redactional insert"; Held ("Matthäus als Interpret der Wundergeschichten," 194) explicitly states that the Peter incident, which displays typical Matthean vocabulary and style, comes from the

hand of Matthew. For Matthew's redaction of the Marcan story, see Held, pp. 193–95, 258–60; Carlisle, "Jesus' Walking on the Water," 151–55.

[152] Besides the standard Marcan commentaries, the following works on the pericope of the stilling of the storm may be consulted: Leopold Fonck, "Christus imperat ventis et mari," *VD* 3 (1923) 321–28; J. B. Bauer, "Procellam cur sedarit Salvator," *VD* 35 (1957) 89–96; Paul J. Achtemeier, "Person and Deed. Jesus and the Storm-Tossed Sea," *Int* 16 (1962) 169–76; idem, "Toward the Isolation of Pre-Markan Miracle Catenae," *JBL* 89 (1970) 265–91; idem, "The Origin and Function of the Pre-Marcan Miracle Catenae," *JBL* 91 (1972) 198–221; van der Loos, *The Miracles of Jesus*, 638–49; Xavier Léon-Dufour, "La tempête apaisée," *Etudes d'évangile* (Parole de Dieu; Paris: Editions du Seuil, 1965) 150–82; Gottfried Schille, "Die Seesturmerzählung Markus 4,35–51 als Beispiel neutestamentlicher Aktualisierung," *ZNW* 56 (1965) 30–40; Leander E. Keck, "Mark 3:7–12 and Mark's Christology," *JBL* 84 (1965) 341–58; Rudolf Pesch, "Zur konzentrischen Struktur von Jona 1," *Bib* 47 (1966) 577–81; Earle Hilgert, "Symbolismus und Heilsgeschichte in den Evangelien. Ein Beitrag zu den Seesturm- und Gerasenererzählungen," *Oikonomia. Heilsgeschichte als Thema der Theologie* (Oscar Cullmann Festschrift; ed. Felix Christ; Hamburg-Bergstedt: Herbert Reich Evang. Verlag, 1967) 51–56; Günther Bornkamm, "Die Sturmstillung im Matthäus-Evangelium," in Günther Bornkamm, Gerhard Barth, and Heinz Joachim Held, *Überlieferung und Auslegung im Matthäusevangelium* (WMANT 1; 5th ed.; Neukirchen-Vluyn: Neukirchener Verlag, 1968) 48–53; Kertelge, *Die Wunder Jesu*, 90–100; Luis F. Rivera, "La liberación en el éxodo. El éxodo de Marcos y la revelación del líder (4,35–8,30)," *RevistB* 32 (1971) 13–26; Koch, *Die Bedeutung*, 92–99; M. F. van Iersel and A. J. M. Linmans, "The Storm on the Lake," *Miscellanea Neotestamentica. Volumen Alterum* (NovTSup 48; ed. T. Baarda, A. F. J. Klijn, and W. C. van Unnik; Leiden: Brill, 1978) 17–48; Werner H. Kelber, *Mark's Story of Jesus* (Philadelphia: Fortress, 1979) 30–31; Jack Dean Kingsbury, "The 'Divine Man' as the Key to Mark's Christology—The End of an Era?" *Int* 35 (1981) 243–57; Kathleen M. Fisher and Urban C. von Wahlde, "The Miracles of Mark 4:35–5:43: Their Meaning and Function in the Gospel Framework," *BTB* 11 (1981) 13–16; Heil, *Jesus Walking on the Sea*, 118–27; Otto Betz, "The Concept of the So-Called 'Divine Man' in Mark's Christology," *Jesus der Messias Israels. Aufsätze zur biblischen Theologie* (WUNT 42; Tübingen: Mohr [Siebeck], 1987) 273–84; Latourelle, *The Miracles of Jesus*, 102–11; Albert Fuchs, "Die 'Seesturmperikope' Mk 4,35–41 parr im Wandel der urkirchlichen Verkündigung," *Studien zum Neuen Testament und seiner Umwelt* 15 (1990) 101–33.

[153] For a detailed consideration of the position of the stilling of the storm within the structure of the first part of Mark's Gospel, see Heil, *Jesus Walking on the Sea*, 118–27.

[154] This is a common view, held by, e.g., Schmidt, *Der Rahmen der Geschichte Jesu*, 150; Dibelius, *Formgeschichte*, 69 (less certain); Bultmann, *Geschichte*, 224 (more certain); Kertelge, *Die Wunder Jesu*, 90.

[155] A similar pattern is seen by Grundmann, *Das Evangelium nach Markus*, 102. A somewhat different progression of thought (revolving around the theme of death) is suggested by Gundry, *Mark*, 237. Because of his stringently conservative views, Gundry must claim that the thematic progression is simply a "happy coincidence" since "these stories occur together because the events narrated in them were historically interconnected by sea-crossings . . ." (p. 242). We are supposedly dealing with "historical chronology" as recollected by Peter. On the artificial and secondary nature of the Marcan context, see Léon-Dufour, "La tempête apaisée," 157–58, 180.

[156] On the special character of the miracle stories in Mark 4:35–5:43, see Taylor, *The*

Gospel According to St. Mark, 272; Kertelge, *Die Wunder Jesu*, 90; Fisher and von Wahlde, "The Miracles of Mark 4:35–5:43," 13–16 (though some of the common elements discerned by Fisher and von Wahlde seem forced, e.g., that all the miracles in this section of the Gospel are "primarily exorcisms" [p. 14]).

[157] For a healthy warning not to jump too quickly from lively, detailed stories to a judgment that they are eyewitness accounts, see Kertelge, *Die Wunder Jesu*, 90 n. 303, *contra* Taylor, *The Gospel According to St. Mark*, 272; cf. Lagrange, *Evangile selon saint Marc*, 125.

[158] Some commentators see a further unusual component in the story of the stilling of the storm. They claim that it is in effect some sort of confessional formula, hymn, or "ballad" with a set rhythmical form. Pesch, for example, divides the pericope into five strophes of three lines each. To achieve this pattern, though, he must begin the pericope at v 37 and eliminate v 40; even then, the individual lines (cola) vary greatly in length, and at times the last line of one strophe seems to belong more naturally to the next strophe. For other attempts of this sort see, e.g., Lohmeyer, *Das Evangelium des Markus*, 89; Schille, "Die Seesturmerzählung," 32–35; Grundmann, *Das Evangelium nach Markus*, 102–3. For a consideration and critique of various theories about the rhythmic structure of the text, especially in a hypothetical primitive version, see Kertelge, *Die Wunder Jesu*, 93–95; Guelich, *Mark 1–8:26*, 262; Gundry, *Mark*, 247. I will suggest below a much simpler primitive structure, built around the three mentions of "great" in the story.

[159] For various theories, see, e.g., Achtemeier, "Toward the Isolation," 265–91; idem, "The Origin and Function," 198–221; Keck, "Mark 3:7–12," 341–58; Pesch, *Das Markusevangelium*, 1. 198, 276; Koch, *Die Bedeutung*, 94 n. 14; Guelich, *Mark 1–8:26*, 261–63.

[160] For a more complex analysis of the form of the story, see Pesch, *Das Markusevangelium*, 1. 268–69. Some of his suggestions, though, are highly speculative: e.g., that the rebuke of cowardice and unbelief may be connected with the motif that the passenger who saves the others is often traveling incognito on the ship.

[161] That the stilling of the storm in its present wording demands a larger context is clear from the fact that neither Jesus nor "the disciples" are directly named in the story, which simply speaks of "he" and "they," often without the subject pronoun being expressed in the Greek. The present Marcan context makes the identities clear, and this may well have been true of a pre-Marcan collection. In the original isolated story, Jesus would have been named at least at the beginning. Whether the disciples were also named, or whether the other participants were originally just a vague "they," cannot be known. I think van Iersel and Linmans claim to know more than they can establish when they assert that the original miracle story did not tell about Jesus' disciples but about anonymous passengers who crossed the lake together with Jesus; see their "The Storm on the Lake," 19. How do we know that the original Christian audience listening to this story with its vague "they" resolved its vagueness in this direction rather than supposing that Jesus' companions in this story were his regular or constant companions, i.e., his disciples?—The double phrase in 4:35 ("on that day, as evening was coming on" [*en ekeinȩ tȩ hēmerȩ opsias genomenēs*]) looks like an example of Marcan duality and at least part if not all of it may reveal the hand of Mark (or possibly the pre-Marcan collector of miracle stories) stitching the beginning of the miracle cycle together with the parable discourse. Thus, the double temporal phrase may be just a narrative seam, and therefore to press it for symbolic value (the powers of darkness and chaos that threaten the disciples and that are defeated by Jesus) is unwarranted; so

rightly Gundry, *Mark*, 244, *contra* Pesch, *Das Markusevangelium*, 1. 269. At best the reference to the late hour may help explain why Jesus falls asleep in the boat (so Gundry and Kertelge), but no such connection is affirmed in the body of the story. In all this, we should remember that *opsias genomenēs* is a vague phrase, simply indicating that it was late in the day; in itself the phrase does not tell us whether sunset has occurred yet. Hence I do not see here a basis for deciding which part of the double temporal phrase comes from Mark and which part from the tradition. In contrast, Kertelge (*Die Wunder Jesu*, 91) favors the view that "as evening was coming on" belongs to the tradition, since it explains Jesus' falling asleep, while "on that day" comes from Mark.—As far as the historical verisimilitude of the time reference is concerned, van der Loos (*The Miracles of Jesus*, 638) observes: "the wind [on the Sea of Galilee] is nearly always stronger in the afternoon than in the morning or the evening, but when a storm gets up in the evening, it is all the more dangerous."

[162] Mark's usage argues for taking the phrase "in the boat" with "as he was"; see Gundry, *Mark*, 245; Koch, *Die Bedeutung*, 95.

[163] Theories about the function of the "other boats" in an earlier version of the story are listed by Pesch, *Das Markusevangelium*, 1. 270 n. 7. Pesch himself calls the mention of the other boats "a splinter of tradition" that eludes any sure interpretation; cf. Kertelge, *Die Wunder Jesu*, 91. Gundry (*Mark*, 238) tries to claim, not very convincingly, that Mark "introduces" the other boats; he suggests that this "only shows to what length Mark goes to introduce them here as a pointer to Jesus' magnetism." Gundry further hypothesizes that the Twelve are in the one boat with Jesus, "the rest of his disciples in the other boats." This simply reads into the text what is not there.

[164] Some of the commentators wax homiletic about how Jesus' sleep indicates his trust in God's providence; this is to read Matthew 6:25–34 into a Marcan miracle story concerned about other matters. To be blunt: God (or, the Father) is never mentioned in Mark 4:35–41; it is Jesus who by his own power and not by prayer to God stills the storm. Hence Taylor's reference (*The Gospel According to St. Mark*, 273, 276) to Jesus' trust in God is out of place in this context. On this question see Gundry, *Mark*, 239.— The historical and archaeological question of whether a boat on the Sea of Galilee would have had some sort of protected stern has received clarification from the discovery in 1986 of the remains of a hull of a wooden boat in the mud by the shore of the Sea about one mile north of Magdala on the western shore; for a short report, see Rainer Riesner, "Das Boot vom See Gennesaret. Entdeckung und Bergung," *BK* 41 (1986) 135–38; Jack Finegan, *The Archeology of the New Testament. The Life of Jesus and the Beginning of the Early Church* (rev. ed.; Princeton, NJ: Princeton University, 1992) 82. The boat, surprisingly well preserved and now housed in the Yigal Allon Museum at Kibbutz Ginnosar, dates from somewhere between the 1st century B.C. and the beginning of the 2d century A.D.; Finegan narrows this down to a period between 120 B.C. and A.D. 40. What remains of the boat measures 26.5 feet in length, 7.5 feet in beam, and 4.5 feet in depth. A stern is clearly visible in the structure, and it may be that the stern was covered by some sort of platform on which the steersman stood. If this be the case, one could imagine Jesus sleeping under the platform. Obviously, this valuable archaeological find does not prove the historicity of Mark 4:35–41; but it does ward off claims that the Gospel scene cannot be historical because the description of the arrangements in the boat does not correspond to what one would have found in a fishing boat on the Sea of Galilee in the 1st century A.D. On this see Gundry (*Mark*, 246), replying to Pesch's view (*Das Markusevangelium*, 1. 271) that Mark's depiction of the boat reflects the story in Jonah 1, i.e., a large ship plying the Mediterranean rather than a small boat on the Sea of Galilee.

[165] As we shall see, Guelich's interpretation (*Mark 1–8:26*, 267) is exaggerated: "Their cry [i.e., that of the disciples in 4:38] . . . does not come as a request but as an expression of *despair* and anger aimed at their 'Master' . . . who apparently cared little about them" (emphasis mine).

[166] On this see Gundry, *Mark*, 239.

[167] See Kertelge, *Die Wunder Jesu*, 92–93; Pesch, *Das Markusevangelium*, 1. 272; Guelich, *Mark 1–8:26*, 267. Gundry (*Mark*, 240) disputes the point, but he is too intent on the question of extra-Christian parallels. One should rather ask how Mark's language would strike a reader moving in order through Mark's Gospel, a reader who has so far met the combination of "rebuke" and "be muzzled" only in the exorcism story of Mark 1:21–28. Indeed, in Mark's Gospel the two words occur together—as a matter of fact, in the same sentence—only in Mark's first exorcism story and in the stilling of the storm. Gundry's approach to the question is too atomistic.

[168] So rightly Koch, *Die Bedeutung*, 97. Koch concludes correctly that the correspondence between the disciples' rough rebuke to Jesus and Jesus' rough rebuke to the disciples argues for the redactional nature of both.

[169] For "not yet" (*oupō*) as the original reading in the Greek text of 4:40, as opposed to "how . . . not" (*pōs ouk*), see Metzger, *Textual Commentary*, 84; Koch, *Die Bedeutung*, 97 n. 29.

[170] So rightly Guelich, *Mark 1–8:26*, 269; Gundry, *Mark*, 243–44. Kelber (*Mark's Story of Jesus*, 30–31) misses the point and the form-critical function of the fear motif when he claims that the disciples' fear is their reaction to Jesus' criticism. Fowler (*Loaves and Fishes*, 102) likewise fails to appreciate that the disciples' reverential fear before the divine is not in itself negative when he says that "the episode [of the stilling of the storm] concludes with the disciples *still afraid* . . ." (emphasis mine). There is no sense here of the background of the language of "fearing a great fear" in Jonah 1.

[171] See Heil, *Jesus Walking on the Sea*, 124–27; he suggests that the very use of exorcistic language in Mark 4:39 is meant to advance this idea of Jesus' "outdoing" his previous miracles of exorcism and healing.

[172] For the place of the disciples' question in 4:41 within Mark's development of the theme of the mystery of Jesus' person, known in the beginning of the Gospel story only to God and the demons, see Kingsbury, "The 'Divine Man,' " 253–54; cf. the structuralist analysis of the same point by van Iersel and Linmans, "The Storm on the Lake," 34–36. In claiming that the lack of a specific title reflects "a pre-paschal context," Latourelle (*The Miracles of Jesus*, 109) misses the whole point of Mark's theology here.

[173] Kertelge (*Die Wunder Jesu*, 93, 96) thinks that the main point of the story is the epiphany of Jesus; Koch (*Die Bedeutung*, 92–93) affirms that the story is both an epiphany and a sea rescue. Grundmann (*Das Evangelium nach Markus*, 105) speaks more cautiously when he says that the story receives a "theophanic trait." For a clearly articulated argument that the Marcan story of the stilling of the storm is a sea-rescue epiphany, see Heil, *Jesus Walking on the Sea*, 127–31.

[174] Van Iersel and Linmans ("The Storm on the Lake," 20) also deny that the primitive form of the story was an epiphany, but they do so on other grounds (the anonymity of the original spectators). Latourelle (*The Miracles of Jesus*, 102) calls it a "rescue" miracle, but also places in the same category what Theissen labels "gift miracles": the feeding of the multitude and the wine miracle of Cana.

[175] It seems to be in this sense that Dibelius (*Formgeschichte*, 90–93) speaks of his

Novellen ("tales," miracle stories) as "stories of epiphanies" and includes the stilling of the storm as one example.

[176] Heil (*Jesus Walking on the Sea*, 129) tries to get around this problem by equating Jesus' sleep with Jesus' absence; but it is the very physical presence of Jesus, as well as his presumed knowledge of what is going on, that makes the brusque approach and rebuke of his disciples possible. Jesus' sleep is no more his absence than his waking up is his appearance to people to whom he has previously been invisible or incognito. The importance of the element of absence or invisibility is one reason why I prefer to call the transfiguration of Jesus a vision (as does Matthew) rather than an epiphany. If one holds to the strict sense of epiphany, the transfiguration of Jesus is the epiphany of Moses and Elijah, not of Jesus. It is also a theophany of God the Father, revealed indirectly in the cloud and heavenly voice (Mark 9:7). In the story, Jesus is indeed trans-formed or trans-figured in his appearance, but he does not suddenly appear after having initially been invisible or absent from the scene; moreover, Mark reports no self-revelatory word of Jesus during the process of the transfiguration.

[177] Heil (*Jesus Walking on the Sea*, 130) tries to get around the lack of any self-revelatory formula spoken by Jesus at the end of the stilling of the storm. Heil interprets Jesus' rebuke to the disciples in Mark 4:40 thus: "Jesus thereby identifies himself with this manifestation of divine power and relates the epiphany directly to the situation of the disciples in order to evoke their response." It takes a great deal of imagination to turn Jesus' two-part rebuke in the form of rhetorical questions into a formula of self-revelation such as a heavenly being speaks at the climax of an epiphany. One senses in all this a stretching of definitions and form-critical categories to the breaking point.

[178] For a different evaluation of the absence of the disciples' question at the end of the walking on the water, see Heil, *Jesus Walking on the Sea*, 130–31: the disciples' questioning of Jesus' identity now becomes "complete non-understanding." Perhaps one might distinguish between the reason for the absence of the question in the primitive tradition and the function this absence assumes within the overarching redactional theology of Mark.

[179] On Matthew's dependence on Mark, see Held, "Matthäus als Interpret der Wundergeschichten," 189–92; and the full essay of Bornkamm, "Die Sturmstillung," 48–53. On Luke's dependence on Mark, see Fitzmyer, *The Gospel According to Luke*, 1. 726–29. For an attempt, fueled by apologetics, to deny the literary dependence of any one evangelist upon another, see Fonck, "Christus imperat," 321–28; for an example of what happens when one uncritically conflates all three accounts instead of weighing questions of sources and redactional theology, see Bauer, "Procellam cur sedarit Salvator," 89–96. Fuchs ("Die 'Seesturmperikope,'" 101–33, esp. 127–28) offers a modified version of the two-source theory in order to solve the problem of the minor agreements between Matthew and Luke in the stilling of the storm while preserving Marcan priority. Fuchs suggests that there was a second, revised edition of Mark, Deutero-Mark, which was the source that both Matthew and Luke used independently of each other. For our purposes, this modification of the two-source theory (into a "three-stage theory") would make no difference, since we are concerned with Mark's text and the primitive tradition lying behind it. However, it seems to me that, at least in this pericope, the minor agreements are explainable on the basis of developments and improvements of Mark's text undertaken independently by Matthew and Luke.

[180] On the use of "great" (Hebrew: *gādôl*) to structure Jonah 1, see Pesch, "Zur konzentrischen Struktur," 577–81.

[181] It may well be, though, that Mark's wording in v 38 replaced some earlier and

more typical form of a petition for a miracle. While possible, this is not absolutely necessary; it could be that the primitive story simply stated that the fearful disciples aroused Jesus from his sleep.

[182] Grundmann (*Das Evangelium nach Markus*, 105) observes that, with the exception of Jesus' commands, all the words spoken by the characters in the story are either the questions of the disciples to Jesus or the questions of Jesus to the disciples. We may have here Mark's contribution to the structure and rhetoric of the narrative.

[183] A convenient review of the various OT texts that depict Yahweh's triumph over the waters (or monster) of chaos and that are relevant to Mark 4:35–41 can be found in Achtemeier, "Person and Deed," 169–76. Since we have seen almost all of these texts when treating the story of Jesus' walking on the water, I do not repeat them here.

[184] The LXX translation of the Hebrew text is slightly different (Jonah 1:4): "And the Lord whipped up a wind (*pneuma*) upon the sea and there arose a great surge of rough waves (*klydōn megas*) on the sea, and the boat was in danger of shipwreck." Thus, the LXX of Jonah 1:4 does not have the exact Greek phrase for "great windstorm" found in Mark 4:37: *lailaps megalē*. However, the Hebrew words for "great windstorm" (*sa'ar-gādôl*) in Jonah 1:4 also occur in the Book of Jeremiah (MT 25:32), and in the LXX translation (Jer 32:32) they are rendered by *lailaps megalē*, the same phrase that we find in Mark.

Pesch in particular emphasizes the parallels in the Jonah story; see *Das Markus-evangelium*, 1. 270–73. As he points out on p. 271, we have in Jonah 1 and Mark 4 something more than just the common vocabulary usually found in a description of a sea storm. Both LXX Jonah 1:4 and Mark 4:37 proceed by way of a three-part sentence to describe the problem in the order of wind—water—boat. Each text begins with the mighty windstorm, notes how this in turn churns up the waters of the sea, and ends with observing how this endangers the boat. Such a parallel hardly seems accidental. Van Iersel and Linmans ("The Storm on the Lake," 21) are also strong on the influence of Jonah 1: "The partial parallelism [of the stilling of the storm] with Jonah I is hereby of essential importance. The fact that it was intended for this story [of the stilling of the storm] to be read in the light of the O.T. story is evident not only in a number of noteworthy corresponding details but also in the correspondence of the total situation." For a comparative list of parallels between Jonah 1 and the Synoptic stories of the stilling of the storm, see Léon-Dufour, "La tempête apaisée," 176.

[185] Mark 4:39 uses the verb *kopazō* ("grow weary") to depict the cessation of the wind; in Jonah 1:11–12 the same verb is used twice (once by the sailors, once by Jonah) to speak of the cessation of the sea's surging.

[186] Actually, in the LXX the closer grammatical parallel occurs earlier on in Jonah 1:10, *ephobēthēsan . . . phobon megan*, with the cognate or internal accusative; this corresponds exactly to Mark 4:41 (see BDR, 126 §153 1.a). In Jonah 1:16, the direct object "Lord" demands that "great fear" be put into the dative, *ephobēthēsan . . . phobǭ ton kyrion*. For the progressive expansion of the theme of fear in Jonah 1, see Pesch, "Zur konzentrischen Struktur," 578.

[187] So Pesch, *Das Markusevangelium*, 1. 269; Guelich, *Mark 1—8:26*, 269–70. See also the whole type-antitype use of Jonah in the Q sayings of Matt 12:39–41 || Luke 11:29–32. Since Matthew and Luke have taken the Jonah typology in different directions, we need not be surprised that the pre-Marcan miracle story goes its own way in developing its Jonah typology. Since we are concerned here with the various uses of Jonah in the early first-generation Christian tradition prior to Mark, it is not all that

relevant to object (as does Gundry, *Mark*, 246) that Mark himself does not develop (indeed, he does not even mention) the OT image of Jonah. Gundry's theological agenda leads him to try to neutralize the parallels to Jonah 1 as much as possible; he once again proceeds atomistically, i.e., taking each parallel in isolation and failing to appreciate what the convergence of all the parallels in a short compass indicates.

[188] It is interesting that van Iersel and Linmans ("The Storm on the Lake," 32) come to the same conclusion by a structuralist analysis of the text: "In Mk iv 35–41 the code of divine actions of Yahweh becomes the code of the actions of Jesus." Using the historical-critical approach, Latourelle (*The Miracles of Jesus*, 108) comes to basically the same conclusion: "The specific and unparalleled [?] aspect of the Gospel story is that Jesus acts with the power of Yahweh. His words make us think of the omnipotent words of Yahweh when he created the world. . . ."

[189] Other OT passages have also been suggested as parallels to the stilling of the storm, but some of the proposed parallels are farfetched. Gundry (*Mark*, 243) rightly rejects the claim of such authors as Otto Betz ("The Concept," 279–81) that Jesus' sea-crossing should be interpreted in light of Israel's crossing of the Reed Sea. The differences between the two stories are simply too great: e.g., crossing on foot versus crossing by boat, passage enabled by the wind versus passage impeded by the wind. Even more imaginative is the exodus typology of Rivera, "La liberación," 16.

[190] To all this material one could add many parallels from Greco-Roman myths and legends, some involving gods like Asclepius, Serapis, and the Dioscuri, others involving heroes like Aeneas or historical figures like Pompey, Julius Caesar, and Apollonius of Tyana; see Bultmann, *Geschichte*, 252–53; van der Loos, *The Miracles of Jesus*, 641–44; Pesch, *Das Markusevangelium*, 1. 273–74. However, in some of the stories we find instead the more general theme of divine protection at sea, as opposed to the specific idea that one of the imperiled figures in the boat works the miracle of calming sea and sky. Commentators also cite later rabbinic stories involving either a Jewish boy or Rabbi Gamaliel; see *y. Ber.* 9.13b and *b. B. Meṣ.* 59b. Both of these rabbinic narratives are probably influenced by the Jonah story, and both differ from the Gospel story in that the pious Jew invokes God in prayer for protection from the storm. A sea-rescue story can also be found in *T. Naphtali* 6:3–9 (see Heil, *Jesus Walking on the Sea*, 17–22), but its connections with the Gospel story of the stilling of the storm are sometimes exaggerated. In *T. Naphtali* 6:3–9, which is an allegory of Israel's exile and regathering narrated within a dream-vision, the boat carrying the patriarchs does break apart, Jacob is snatched away by the storm, Joseph escapes in a little boat, and the other patriarchs are scattered on planks. By the prayer of Levi, all are saved and reunited despite the shipwreck. Apart from (1) the general idea of a storm at sea and rescue from it and (2) the striking similarity of the phrase *lailaps anemou megalou* ("a storm of great wind"; cf. Mark 4:37: *lailaps megalē anemou*, "a great storm of wind"), there is little here in common with the Gospel story. One must also weigh the possibility that the text of the *Testaments of the Twelve Patriarchs* as we now have it is a product of Christian composition or at least Christian redaction. One may also add to the list of Jewish parallels a passage from the *Hôdāyôt* (Thanksgiving) psalms of Qumran. In 1QH 6:22–25, the person praying compares himself to a sailor caught in a fierce sea storm of wind and waves that brought him to the gates of death. But then (no doubt by God's aid) he became like a man who comes to a fortified city (the imagery suddenly changes at this point in the psalm). The imagery is very much that of the canonical Book of Psalms and the Book of Jonah, and the literary genre is obviously not that of a narrative or miracle story but of a psalm of lament and thanksgiving. Similar images can be found in 1QH 3:6,12–18; 7:4–5; on this see Heil, *Jesus Walking on the Sea*, 22–30.

While useful for establishing the widespread theme of sea rescue by a divinity throughout the ancient Mediterranean world, these parallels do not supply the immediate source for our Gospel story that the Book of Jonah and the Psalms do, for the latter are works—indeed, authoritative religious sources—presumably known to early Christian authors; the same cannot be said of Virgil's great epic poem the *Aeneid* or the Babylonian Talmud, both of which are often mentioned by scholars commenting on the Gospel story. After noting the parallels with the *Aeneid*, Taylor (*The Gospel According to St. Mark*, 273) adds with a smile: ". . . but had Mark read his Virgil?"

[191] Van Iersel and Linmans, "The Storm on the Lake," 18.

[192] That even in the primitive pre-Marcan tradition the Jesus who conquers the forces of chaos and saves the small ship of his church was seen to be the Risen One is held by Hilgert, "Symbolismus," 52.

[193] See, e.g., Lagrange, *Evangile selon saint Marc*, 123; Lane, *Mark*, 175.

[194] See Daniel Mark Epstein, *Sister Aimee. The Life of Aimee Semple McPherson* (New York: Harcourt, Brace, Jovanovich, 1993) 86. Commentators who have attempted a rationalistic explanation of the stilling of the storm, which would save the basic historical event while explaining away the specifically miraculous element, are discussed by Léon-Dufour, "La tempête apaisée," 154; van der Loos, *The Miracles of Jesus*, 639–40. A prime example of such an approach is given by Joseph Klausner, *Jesus of Nazareth* (New York: Macmillan, 1925) 269. He lists the stilling of the storm under those events that were "only apparently miraculous." "Under this head come events which happen in fact, but which have in them nothing of the miraculous and only appear so to the disciples."

[195] For example, van der Loos (*The Miracles of Jesus*, 640) summarizes the rationalistic approach of Heinrich E. G. Paulus thus: "Jesus certainly did not speak to the sea, but He doubtless cried out, as one usually does in such circumstances: what a dreadful storm! It must be over soon!" The disciples then misunderstood Jesus' remarks as the cause of the sudden calm.

[196] Klausner, *Jesus of Nazareth*, 269.

[197] So Pesch, *Das Markusevangelium*, 1. 276; Koch, *Die Bedeutung*, 94.

[198] Apart from the standard commentaries on John's Gospel, there is a vast array of books and articles on the first Cana miracle. A representative sampling includes: Hans Windisch, "Die johanneische Weinregel (Joh. 2,10.)," *ZNW* 14 (1913) 248–57; Karl Ludwig Schmidt, "Der johanneische Charakter der Erzählung vom Hochzeitswunder in Kana," *Harnack-Ehrung* (Adolf von Harnack Festschrift; Leipzig: Hinrichs, 1921) 32–43; Herbert Preisker, "Joh 2:4 und 19:26," *ZNW* 42 (1949) 209–14; Rudolf Schnackenburg, *Das erste Wunder Jesu (Joh. 2, 1–11)* (Freiburg: Herder, 1951); Johann Michl, "Bemerkungen zu Jo. 2, 4," *Bib* 36 (1955) 492–509; M.-E. Boismard, *Du baptême à Cana (Jean 1, 19—2, 11)* (LD 18; Paris: Cerf, 1956); Christian P. Ceroke, "The Problem of Ambiguity in John 2,4," *CBQ* 21 (1959) 316–40; Thomas Barrosse, "The Seven Days of the New Creation in St. John's Gospel," *CBQ* 21 (1959) 507–16; J.-P. Charlier, *Le signe de Cana. Essai de théologie johannique* (Etudes religieuses 740; Brussels: La pensée catholique; Paris: Office général du livre, 1959); Heinz Noetzel, *Christus und Dionysos* (Arbeiten zur Theologie 1; Stuttgart: Calwer, 1960); Carl Armerding, "The Marriage in Cana," *BSac* 118 (1961) 320–26; Richard J. Dillon, "Wisdom Tradition and Sacramental Retrospect in the Cana Account (Jn 2,1–11)," *CBQ* 24 (1962) 268–96; Jean-Paul Michaud, "Le signe de Cana dans son contexte johannique," *LTP* 18 (1962) 239–85 and 19 (1963) 257–83; J. Duncan M. Derrett, "Water into Wine," *BZ* 7 (1963)

80–97; André Feuillet, "The Hour of Jesus and the Sign of Cana," *Johannine Studies* (Staten Island, NY: Alba House, 1965) 17–37; A. Smitmans, *Das Weinwunder von Kana. Die Auslegung von Jo 2,1–11 bei den Vätern und heute* (BGBE 6; Tübingen: Mohr [Siebeck], 1966), containing a lengthy treatment (and bibliography) of the interpretation of the pericope in the patristic period as well as among modern exegetes; Paul W. Meyer, "John 2:10," *JBL* 86 (1967) 191–97; Francis E. Williams, "Fourth Gospel and Synoptic Tradition. Two Johannine Passages," *JBL* 86 (1967) 311–19; Matthias Rissi, "Die Hochzeit in Kana (Joh 2,1–11)," *Oikonomia. Heilsgeschichte als Thema der Theologie* (Oscar Cullmann Festschrift; ed. Felix Christ; Hamburg-Bergstedt: Herbert Reich Evang. Verlag, 1967) 76–92; Barnabas Lindars, "Two Parables in John," *NTS* 16 (1969–70) 318–29; A. Geyer, "The Semeion at Cana of the Galilee," *Studies in John* (NovTSup 24; Leiden: Brill, 1970) 12–21; Franz Zehrer, "Das Gespräch Jesu mit seiner Mutter auf der Hochzeit zu Kana (Joh 2,3f.) im Licht der traditions- und redaktionsgeschichtlichen Forschung," *Bibel und Liturgie* 43/3 (1970) 14–27; Joseph A. Grassi, "The Wedding at Cana (John II 1–11): A Pentecostal Meditation?" *NovT* 14 (1972) 131–36; Morton Smith, "On the Wine God in Palestine (Gen. 18, Jn. 2, and Achilles Tatius)," *Salo Wittmayer Baron Jubilee Volume* (3 vols.; Jerusalem: American Academy for Jewish Research, 1974) 2. 815–29; Albert Vanhoye, "Interrogation johannique et exégèse de Cana (Jn 2,4)," *Bib* 55 (1974) 157–67; Eta Linnemann, "Die Hochzeit zu Kana und Dionysos," *NTS* 20 (1974) 408–18; Stanley D. Toussaint, "The Significance of the First Sign in John's Gospel," *BSac* 134 (1977) 45–51; Raymond E. Brown, "The 'Mother of Jesus' in the Fourth Gospel," *L'évangile de Jean. Sources, rédaction, théologie* (BETL 44; ed. M. de Jonge; Gembloux: Duculot; Leuven: Leuven University, 1977) 307–10; Otto Bächli, " 'Was habe ich mit Dir zu schaffen?' Eine formelhafte Frage im A.T. und N.T.," *TZ* 33 (1977) 69–80; Ulrich Ruegg et al., "Zur Freude befreit. Jesus an der Hochzeit zu Kana (Johannes 2,1–12). Ein Geschenkwunder," *Wunder Jesu* (Bibelarbeit in der Gemeinde 2; ed. Anton Steiner and Volker Weymann; Basel: Friedrich Reinhardt; Zurich/Cologne: Benziger, 1978) 147–66; Richard M. Mackowski, " 'Scholar's Qanah.' A Re-examination of the Evidence in Favor of Khirbet-Qanah," *BZ* 23 (1979) 278–83; Raymond F. Collins, "Cana (Jn. 2:1–12)—The first of his signs or the key to his signs?" *ITQ* 47 (1980) 79–95; Rudolf Pesch, "Das Weinwunder bei der Hochzeit zu Kana (Joh 2, 1–12)," *Theologie der Gegenwart* 24 (1981) 219–25; Jeanne-Marie Léonard, "Notule sur l'évangile de Jean," *ETR* 57 (1982) 119–20; Johannes B. Bauer, " 'Literarische' Namen und 'literarische' Bräuche (zu Joh 2, 10 und 18, 39)," *BZ* 26 (1982) 258–64; Ingo Broer, "Noch einmal: Zur religionsgeschichtlichen 'Ableitung' von Jo 2,1–11," *Studien zum Neuen Testament und seiner Umwelt* 8 (1983) 103–23; Gerhard Lohfink, "Das Weinwunder zu Kana. Eine Auslegung von Joh 2,1–12," *Geist und Leben* 57 (1984) 169–82; Paul Trudinger, " 'On the Third Day There Was a Wedding at Cana.' Reflections on St John 2, 1–12," *DRev* 104 (1986) 41–43; J. N. Suggit, "John 2:1–11: The sign of greater things to come," *Neot* 21 (1987) 141–58; Rainer Riesner, "Fragen um 'Kana in Galiläa,' " *BK* 43 (1988) 69–71. See also the usual apologetic approaches of van der Loos, *The Miracles of Jesus*, 590–618; Latourelle, *The Miracles of Jesus*, 204–17.

[199] Although I designate the pericope as extending from v 1 to v 11 (along with Schnackenburg, *Das erste Wunder Jesu*, 1, and many others), some commentators end the pericope at v 12, with Jesus and his entourage descending to Capernaum. Bultmann (*Das Evangelium des Johannes*, 79 n. 4), for example, thinks that v 12 was already in the Evangelist's source, perhaps providing the transition to 4:46–54 (the healing of the royal official's son). I think that Bultmann is wrong on this point; but, be that as it may, I simply wish to affirm that, for our purposes in this volume, it is preferable to end the pericope with v 11: (1) From a form-critical point of view, the miracle story obviously

ends with the quasi-"acclamation" of the headwaiter in v 10 ("you have kept the good wine until now") plus the narrator's summarizing remark (both retrospective and prospective) in v 11 ("This was the first of the signs . . ."). From a form-critical perspective, v 12 is not part of the miracle story proper, but a transitional verse that moves Jesus from one venue to another. (2) Throughout this investigation of miracle stories, we have been asking about the earliest retrievable form of any given pericope (presumably, an individual story circulating in isolated form in the oral tradition) and any historical tradition that might lie behind it. Clearly v 12 could not have been the ending of a separate unit of oral tradition; its very purpose is to connect the Cana story with subsequent events. It is significant that Fortna (*The Fourth Gospel*, 59), while assigning at least part of v 12 to his "Signs Gospel," prefers to see it as the introduction to the healing of the royal official's son.—A number of commentators (e.g., Pesch, "Das Weinwunder," 222, 224; Latourelle, *The Miracles of Jesus*, 208–9) seem intent on keeping v 12 as part of the original tradition so that it can act as a support for a further theory: in the primitive tradition, it was the brothers and not the disciples of Jesus who were said to be present at the marriage feast along with Jesus and his mother. I find this substitution highly speculative; it misses the *inclusio* between the first mention of the disciples in v 2 and the second mention of them in v 11, and it presumes that later text-critical questions arising from the Greek manuscripts of John's Gospel give us entrée into early pre-Gospel forms of Johannine traditions—a very dubious supposition.

[200] For a detailed analysis of the structure of the story, see Pesch, "Das Weinwunder," 221.

[201] Here I draw from and adapt the observations of Dodd in his *Historical Tradition*, 223–24. As we have seen, the other candidates for "gift miracle" do not qualify: (1) in the story of the temple tax (Matt 17:24–27), Peter's finding of a coin in the fish's mouth is only predicted but never narrated, and the pericope as a whole is not a miracle story; (2) the miraculous catch of fish (John 21:1–14 || Luke 5:1–11) is in its origin a post-resurrection story, not a story of the public ministry; and the food provided is either mostly or entirely left behind uneaten by the people (the disciples called to follow Jesus) for whom it was provided.—Pesch ("Das Weinwunder," 220) observes that the category of gift miracle can be divided into two subcategories: a miracle of multiplication (so the feeding of the five thousand) and a miracle of transformation (so the first Cana miracle).

[202] Needless to say, the need is more pressing in the case of the feeding of the five thousand. In the first Cana miracle, the pressing need is rather the need of the host to avoid shame in an honor/shame culture, especially at such a public and pivotal event as a wedding feast. One can speak of need on the part of the guests insofar as guests regularly came and went during a wedding feast that spanned many days. Some guests might be arriving just as the wine has run out.

[203] This laconic announcement may be the reason why some manuscripts (notably the original hand of Sinaiticus) supplied a fuller explanation at the beginning of v 3: "They had no wine, for the wine of the wedding feast had been used up; then . . ."). Despite Bultmann's preference for this longer reading (*Das Evangelium des Johannes*, 80 n. 6), I think that the shorter reading adopted by *UBSGNT*[3] ("when the wine ran out") is original. As Metzger (*Textual Commentary*, 201) points out, the preponderance of early and good manuscripts argues for this shorter reading.

[204] A prime example of this highly fanciful approach, which takes for granted that we are dealing with a historical event that transpired almost exactly as John narrates it, can be found in Derrett, "Water into Wine," 80–97. To fill in what are perceived to be the

logical gaps in the story, Derrett calls upon the Babylonian Talmud, customs from India, a saying from modern Kurdistan, and unbridled imagination. The tenor of the whole can be surmised from one random sentence (p. 87): "Mary knew well that Jesus would not marry." The article reminds us that a scholar may be extremely erudite and completely uncritical.—Also highly imaginative, though not claiming to deal with the historical event, is Grassi, "The Wedding at Cana," 131–36; the parallels between John 2:1–11 and Acts 1–2 (not to mention the Book of Exodus, Joel, *Jubilees*, 1QS and CD, and various rabbinic works) remind one of the ingenuity of patristic exegesis. Unfortunately, even more sober exegetes are tempted to fill in what they perceive as gaps in the narrative; see, e.g., Lagrange, *Evangile selon Saint Jean*, 55.

[205] Besides functioning as a sort of admiring (though ignorant and therefore ironic) acclamation at the end of a miracle story (*contra* Meyer, "John 2:10," 193), the comment of the headwaiter also serves as a confirmation of the fact of the miracle, which has been narrated in an especially veiled and indirect manner.

[206] Here as elsewhere in this comparison I use the Johannine story of the multiplication of the loaves as the version most suited to an exercise in comparison-and-contrast with John 2:1–11.

[207] Perhaps one point indirectly made by the double reaction to the miracle is that the mere experiencing of the beneficial effects of a miracle does not equal or necessarily lead to belief in the miracle-worker. But this may be reading too much into the double ending.

[208] Note the specification: "of the public ministry." Quite different, of course, are the various miracles surrounding Jesus' conception and birth in the Infancy Narratives; but these are not worked by Jesus and do not belong to his public ministry (and correspondingly do not belong to the NT's core kerygma). For the sake of completeness, one should also mention the presence of the mother of Jesus at Luke's depiction of the gathering of the embryonic church in Jerusalem after Jesus' ascension and presumably therefore at the event of Pentecost (Acts 1:14; cf. 2:1).

[209] Another characteristic that sets the first Cana miracle apart from most of the other miracles in the Fourth Gospel is the lack of an interpretive discourse of Jesus following upon or interwoven within the miracle story. By a neat *inclusio*, only the second Cana miracle (the healing of the royal official's son in 4:46–54) evinces a similar lack of discourse material in or after the Johannine miracle story.

[210] For earlier attempts at detecting the Evangelist's hand, see, inter alia, Schmidt, "Der johanneische Charakter," 32–43; Meyer, "John 2:10," 191–97. I should alert the reader to a presupposition I am employing here: I do not think that an entire "Signs Gospel" existed before the present Fourth Gospel; hence, references in John 2:1–11 backward and forward to other parts of the Gospel must come from the hand of the Evangelist.

[211] See, e.g., Brown, *The Gospel According to John*, 1. 105; Suggit, "John 2:1–11," 146–47.

[212] So, among many others, Dodd, *The Interpretation of the Fourth Gospel*, 299–300; Boismard, *Du baptême à Cana*, 106–7; Suggit, "John 2:1–11," 147–48; with hesitance, Charlier, *Le signe de Cana*, 45. For "on the third day" referring to the resurrection, see Matt 16:21; 17:23; 20:19; 27:64; Luke 9:22; 18:33; 24:7,46; Acts 10:40; 1 Cor 15:4 (which shows that it was a set formula in a primitive Christian creed).

[213] Boismard, *Du baptême à Cana*, esp. 13–24. A similar schema, but with greater emphasis on ecclesiology, is presented by Barrosse, "The Seven Days," 507–16.

[214] The fanciful complications to which this can lead are seen in Trudinger, " 'On the Third Day,' " 41–43. The wedding feast at Cana is counted as the sixth day, which fittingly corresponds to the creation of man and woman on the sixth day in Genesis 1. Then Jesus goes down to remain (= rest) at Capernaum on the seventh day. At the same time, the sixth day is called the third day, alluding to the resurrection. The union of death and resurrection in John's Gospel explains how the sixth day (= Friday) can also be the third day in the sense of the resurrection (= Sunday). At this point we are engaging in the playful and highly imaginative exegesis of the Church Fathers.

[215] Brown (*The Gospel According to John*, 1. 105–6) gives a cautious evaluation of Boismard's theory and, even with some alterations, judges that the theory is "no more than . . . a *possible* interpretation." Brown also observes that a still more detailed exposition of Boismard's theory would interpret the seven days as running from Wednesday to Wednesday; this would seem to clash with the desire of some commentators to have "on the third day" refer to the resurrection, which involves Sunday. Still others see the Cana miracle taking place on a Tuesday; so, tentatively, Robinson, *The Priority of John*, 166–67. All this simply reminds us how speculative any calculation of the days is. Robinson gives a devastating critique of the seven-day schema on pp. 161–68. For the acceptance of the seven-day schema in a literary-critical instead of a historical-critical framework, see Staley, *The Print's First Kiss*, 74–94.

[216] Contrary to a common homiletic interpretation, a sober exegesis of the passage shows that, while a mutual relationship is established between mother and son, the mother of Jesus is entrusted to the care of the beloved disciple, and not vice versa. On the meaning of 19:26–27, see Schnackenburg, *Das Johannesevangelium*, 3. 323–28; Haenchen, *John 2*, 193; cf. Brown, *The Gospel According to John*, 2. 922–27. For various interpretations of the function of the mother of Jesus in the first Cana miracle, see Smitmans, *Das Weinwunder von Kana*, 54–63.

[217] On the OT background and meaning of the questions "What is that to me and you?" as well as its significance in the NT, see Bächli, " 'Was habe ich mit Dir zu schaffen?' " 69–80; also Brown, *The Gospel According to John*, 1. 99; Michl, "Bemerkungen," 492–509; Vanhoye, "Interrogation johannique," 162–65. Bächli points out that in the OT the phrase is not popular but rather elevated, formal language, with its *Sitz im Leben* in legal, political, and diplomatic activity. As a rhetorical question actually affirming a state of affairs, it creates a sense of distance between the two parties involved and affirms opposition between them. However, Vanhoye rightly emphasizes the openness of the rhetorical question to various meanings depending upon the context—and even the tone of voice.

Along with Brown, I think that the various nuances of the OT occurrences can be boiled down to two basic meanings: (1) When one party is unjustly bothering or threatening another, the injured party may object: "What have I done to you that you should do this to me?" (see Judg 11:12; 2 Chr 35:21; 1 Kgs 17:18). (2) When a person is asked to get involved in a matter that he feels to be no business of his, he may say: "That is your business. How am I involved?" (see 2 Kgs 3:13). While both meanings imply some type of refusal or disassociation because of a divergence of views or interests, the first meaning involves hostility while the second expresses simple disengagement. The hostile meaning appears in the demons' reply to Jesus (Mark 1:24; 5:7); a simple statement of disengagement seems to fit John 2:4. Brown goes on to note that some exegetes attempt to read into the Cana story a meaning of the phrase apparently present in 2 Sam 16:10, namely, "That is not *our* concern." In this case, Jesus would be associating Mary with himself, denying that either of them should be concerned with the problem of the lack of wine. But Jesus gives as the reason for his own disengagement the fact that "*my* hour has not yet come." Hence there seems to be a disengagement of Jesus from Mary's concern. Bächli (ibid., 79) observes that, while the usage in John 2:4 may have lost some of the original OT meaning of the formula, the distancing of the two parties can still be felt.—For the special case of 2 Sam 19:23, see Peggy L. Day, "Abishai the *śāṭān* in 2 Samuel 19:17–24," *CBQ* 49 (1987) 543–47.

[218] See Brown, *The Gospel According to John*, 1. 99. As a respectful address it is attested in pagan Greek literature, in Josephus, and in Jdt 11:1. Brown notes: "What is peculiar is the use of 'Woman' alone (without an accompanying title or a qualifying adjective) by a *son* addressing his *mother*—there is no precedent for this in Hebrew nor, to the best of our knowledge, in Greek"; similarly Michl, "Bemerkungen," 498–99.

[219] The exact nature of the symbolism is debated among scholars, but the question need not concern us here; see Brown, *The Gospel According to John*, 2. 922–27; Schnackenburg, *Das Johannesevangelium*, 3. 323–28.

[220] On the hour of Jesus as the hour of passion and glorification, see H. van den Bussche, "La structure de Jean I–XII," *L'évangile de Jean. Etudes et problèmes* (Recherches Bibliques; Bruges: Desclée de Brouwer, 1958) 61–107, esp. 79; Charlier, *Le signe de Cana*, 54; Feuillet, "The Hour of Jesus," 18–31; Smitmans, *Das Weinwunder von Kana*, 272–74; at greater length Wilhelm Thüsing, *Die Erhöhung und Verherrlichung Jesu im Johannesevangelium* (NTAbh 21; 2d ed.; Münster: Aschendorff, 1970) 88–100, esp. 92–96; Godfrey C. Nicholson, *Death As Departure. The Johannine Descent-Ascent Schema* (SBLDS 63; Chico, CA: Scholars, 1983) 147–48 (though he substitutes "departure from this world" and "return to the Father" for the concept of death). This point is missed by Michl ("Bemerkungen," 492–509); he makes Jesus' "hour" in 2:4 refer to the hour of the beginning of the ministry, including the ministry of miracles (p. 505). (One finds a similar position espoused in Lagrange, *Evangile selon Saint Jean*, 57; Boismard, *Du baptême à Cana*, 133–59; Dodd, *Historical Tradition*, 223; and Lohfink, "Das Weinwunder zu Kana," 174–75.) From this questionable judgment of Michl flow others made by him: (1) The decision to make v 4c a rhetorical question ("Has my hour not yet come?"), with the implied answer of "Yes, it has come." This then explains Mary's order to the servants. (2) The desire to soften the element of distancing and disassociation in the question in v 4b. Behind all the individual decisions is the basic error of not reading the pericope within the overarching theological and literary composition of the Evangelist; the pericope is treated more like a videotape replay of a historical event. The concern for historical verisimilitude and the psychological condition of the actors at Cana likewise weakens the approach of Ceroke, "The Problem of Ambiguity," 316–40.

Much more sensitive to the literary and theological context is Vanhoye, "Interrogation johannique," 159–62. With regard to whether 2:4c is a question, Vanhoye argues that the true parallel to John 2:4 is to be found in those NT passages where a question precedes a sentence with *oupō* ["not yet"] (Matt 16:9; Mark 4:40; 8:17). In such cases the sentence with *oupō* is also a question. But, along with Brown (*The Gospel According to John*, 1. 99), one must attend to the Johannine usage of *oupō*. The Fourth Evangelist uses *oupō* 11 times (12 times if one reads *oupō* twice in 7:8), and outside of 2:4 all the sentences are clearly declarative. Moreover, a number of the declarative sentences refer to the fact that Jesus' time or hour (*kairos* in 7:6,8; *hōra* in 7:30; 8:20) has not come or been fulfilled (on the cross). (The adverb *oupō* also occurs once in 1 John and twice in the Revelation of John, and in all three cases the sentences are declarative.)

Admittedly, the arguments of Vanhoye and Brown are finely balanced. I tend to agree with Brown for methodological reasons: it is better to judge John's usage by other passages in John (all of which use *oupō* in declarative sentences and some of which state that his hour has not yet come) than to appeal to the usage of Matthew and Mark, whose Gospels, in my opinion, John did not know and whose passages do not refer to the arrival of Jesus' hour. (As Vanhoye points out on p. 160 n. 1, the usage of the LXX cannot be invoked because in the OT *oupō* never occurs after a question.) Moreover, with all due regard to the ambiguity and double meaning employed in John's Gospel, I find it difficult to accept Vanhoye's claim (p. 166) that Cana is Jesus' hour in an initial sense and that the passion is his hour in the full sense (for a similar approach, see Schnackenburg, *Das erste Wunder Jesu*, 40–46). This does not seem to correspond to John's own usage of "hour" with a modifier: "his," "my," or "the" hour always means the hour of the cross, and nothing else. More extreme is the solution of Ceroke ("The Problem of Ambiguity," 327–30), who pushes the element of ambiguity in Jesus' words to the point that any coherent meaning seems to break down: somehow Jesus' words (in one way a question, in another way a declaration) mean both that the hour of miracles has come and that the hour of the passion has not come.

[221] Along with many other commentators, the theological cross-reference is emphasized by Preisker, "Joh 2:4 und 19:26," 209–14. Unfortunately, Preisker also mirrors many other commentators in being distracted by mariological concerns (pro or con) that go beyond the intention of the author and the thrust of the text.

[222] I purposely say "from the narrative"; there is a passing and slighting reference to her in the objection of the crowd to Jesus' claim to be the bread of life in 6:42: "Is this not Jesus the son of Joseph, whose father and mother we know?"

[223] So, e.g., Fortna, *The Fourth Gospel*, 49–58, esp. 55, 57–58; cf. Dillon, "Wisdom Tradition," 288–89; Zehrer, "Das Gespräch," 26; Collins, "Cana," 83.

[224] On this see Charles H. Giblin, "Suggestion, Negative Response, and Positive Action in St John's Portrayal of Jesus," *NTS* 26 (1979–80) 197–211; earlier forms of his insight can be found in Schmidt, "Der johanneische Charakter," 37–39; Feuillet, "The Hour of Jesus," 32–33. Giblin uses the wider category of "suggestion" instead of a precise petition for a particular miracle, and so he can include John 7:2–14 in his treatment. Since this pericope is most likely John's creation, it confirms the Evangelist's hand in the creation of the overall pattern. The thematic connection between the mother in chap. 2 and the brothers in chap. 7—in two pericopes that both use the pattern Giblin analyzes—also argues for the presence of the redacting hand of the Evangelist.

[225] A similar pattern can be found in the story of the Syrophoenician woman (Mark 7:24–30); some would also see it in the Q story of the centurion's servant/son, if Matt 8:7 par. is interpreted as an indignant question (a position I do not adopt). But at least the story of the Syrophoenician woman shows that the pattern we have isolated in John need not result from a redactor's disruptive insertion into a simpler miracle story, since the interchange between Jesus and the Syrophoenician woman seems to have been of the essence of the story from its inception. One should note, however, that there are some differences between the Johannine pattern and the one found in the story of the Syrophoenician woman; on this see Giblin, "Suggestion," 211.

[226] The wine provided by the host has run out (2:3), and the headwaiter speaks of keeping the "good wine until *now*," when all have already become drunk (2:10). Many translations soften the verb *methysthōsin* to phrases like "have drunk deeply" or "have drunk freely," but this sensitivity seems out of place at a peasant wedding feast in a hill-town of Galilee. Needless to say, the Evangelist, who is intent on the symbolic message of the pericope, does not pause to reflect upon the moral question involved in supplying

such a huge amount of wine to guests who may have already become drunk. In this connection, Collins ("Cana," 80) speaks of the "non-redemptive" character of this particular miracle. I take for granted here that one need not bother the educated reader with disputes about whether Jesus is supplying fine grape juice to people who have already drunk so much grape juice that they would not notice the difference between a fine and poor vintage of grape juice. Those who want to revisit the question may consult J. F. Ross, "Wine," *IDB*, 4. 849–52.

[227] For various OT texts illustrating the importance of wine in the material and spiritual culture of Israel, see Charlier, *Le signe de Cana*, 27–39. Léonard ("Notule," 119–20) tries to trace a detailed connection between John 2:1–11 and Isaiah 25, but much of the argumentation is forced.

[228] The translation is taken from A. F. J. Klijn, "2 (Syriac Apocalypse of) Baruch," *The Old Testament Pseudepigrapha*, 1. 630. The capacity of a "cor" probably varied during the biblical and postbiblical period. Brown (*The Gospel According to John*, 1. 105) gives an estimate of 120 gallons of wine; other estimates range from 35 to 60 gallons. Obviously, in this fanciful context the exact amount is beside the point, which is the incredible yield from one grape.

[229] For various OT texts depicting Yahweh and Israel in a marital relationship, see Charlier, *Le signe de Cana*, 17–26.

[230] I accept as a viable hypothesis that the Book of Revelation belonged in the broad sense to the Johannine stream of early Christianity; the very presence of the Book of Revelation within the Johannine stream reminds us that this stream was more diverse than what we might imagine from reading only the Johannine Gospel and Epistles. For an approach that instead places the Book of Revelation outside of the "Johannine school," see Elisabeth Schüssler Fiorenza, "The Quest for the Johannine School: The Apocalypse and the Fourth Gospel," *NTS* 23 (1976–77) 402–27.

[231] There is a more indirect reference in Paul's imagery about the Corinthian church in 2 Cor 11:2: "For I espoused you to one man [*andri* = male, husband] that I might present you as a chaste virgin to Christ."

[232] On this passage see, e.g., Brown, *The Gospel According to John*, 1. 152–56; Schnackenburg, *The Gospel According to St John*, 1. 416–17; Joachim Jeremias, "*nymphē, nymphios*," *TDNT* 4 (1967) 1099–1106, esp. 1101. Jeremias emphasizes that "nowhere in the OT is the Messiah presented as a bridegroom" (p. 1101); despite some disputed texts, he likewise claims that "in all later Jewish literature there is no instance of an application of the allegory of the bridegroom to the Messiah" (p. 1102).

[233] See, e.g., Charlier, *Le signe de Cana*, 64; for the treatment of the theme in both modern and ancient interpreters, see Smitmans, *Das Weinwunder von Kana*, 45, 207–17.

[234] There is an obvious opposition between "everyone" and "you" just as there is an opposition between the fine wine and the lesser wine and an opposition between the order of fine-wine-first-then-lesser-wine and the reverse order that this anonymous bridegroom has supposedly followed. With all this stress on oppositions in the context of eschatological fulfillment and replacement, the possibility arises that the Evangelist wishes the *pas anthrōpos* (usually translated "everyone") to be taken in its literal sense of "every human being" as opposed to the messianic bridegroom who has come into the world. On this see Suggit, "John 2:1–11," 153.

[235] The idea of Jesus providing the abundant wine of the end time at the eschatological marriage feast of the Messiah naturally conjures up for someone aware of both the

whole of the NT and later church tradition the idea of the wine of the eucharist. A number of commentators think that the Fourth Evangelist may have intended a eucharistic reference in John 2:1–11; so, e.g., Feuillet, "The Hour of Jesus," 33–34; Rissi, "Die Hochzeit," 87, 90–91; Geyer, "The Semeion," 18–19; Zehrer, "Das Gespräch," 25–26. Suggit ("John 2:1–11," 151) pushes the possibility to an extreme: e.g., the servants may represent deacons, and the headwaiter may represent the president of the eucharist. A much more sober argument for a eucharistic reference can be found in Dillon, "Wisdom Tradition," 280–96. However, I must admit that I remain skeptical about a eucharistic reference in the first Cana miracle. The influence of the great Oscar Cullmann has perhaps inclined us to see sacramental references in passages of the Fourth Gospel where the Evangelist might not have intended them. For Cullmann's tendency in this regard, see, e.g., his *Der johanneische Kreis*, 16–17; for a critique of this tendency, see Herbert Klos, *Die Sakramente im Johannesevangelium* (SBS 46; Stuttgart: KBW, 1970) 46. More to the point, the first Cana miracle uses the symbol of wine without ever mentioning blood, while the eucharistic part of the bread of life discourse (6:51–58) uses the graphic images of eating Jesus' flesh and drinking his blood without ever mentioning wine. In other words, since the Fourth Gospel lacks the Synoptic eucharistic words of Jesus at the Last Supper, which identify the wine with his blood, one looks in vain for a single passage in John that connects the two images of wine and blood. Without this connection somewhere in the Fourth Gospel, it is difficult to show that John intended a eucharistic reference in 2:1–11. On the various attempts by modern exegetes to see references to a sacrament (baptism, eucharist, or matrimony) in John 2:1–11, see Smitmans, *Das Weinwunder von Kana*, 50–54.

[236] Indeed, with the exception of Rev 18:23 (which alludes to Jer 7:34; 16:9; 25:10), every use of *nymphios* in the NT refers directly or indirectly to Jesus; interestingly, it is never used of God the Father. Once again, an attribute of Yahweh in the OT has been totally transferred by NT christology to Jesus.

[237] On this point see Schmidt, "Der johanneische Charakter," 41.

[238] The banquet with abundant wine may also conjure up the passages in the OT where the personified Wisdom of God is said to offer a banquet, symbolic of her teaching (e.g., Prov 9:5–6; Sir 24:19,21; 15:3). This idea is certainly present in the bread of life discourse in John 6, and some commentators would see it already present in John 2:1–11; so, in particular, Dillon, "Wisdom Tradition," 290–95; cf. Brown, *The Gospel According to John*, 1. 106–7. Personally, I am less certain about the reference to Wisdom's banquet in John 2:1–11.

[239] See, among many commentators who make this point, Schmidt, "Der johanneische Charakter," 40–41; Dodd, *The Interpretation of the Fourth Gospel*, 299; Neyrey, *An Ideology of Revolt*, 132; Painter, *The Quest for the Messiah*, 157. A number of exegetes wish to push the symbolism further by interpreting the number 6 as referring to the imperfection of the old religious order (7 being the number of perfection). This seems unlikely, since the wine that replaces the water is likewise contained in the six jars.— That the jars were made of stone fits well with their use for purification. In keeping with levitical purity laws (Lev 11:29–38), "if ritually contaminated, they [the stone jars] could be cleaned, whereas earthen jars would have to be broken" (Brown, *The Gospel According to John*, 1. 100).

My summary of the message of the pericope is meant to bring out the rich and complex nature of the theology of what looks at first like a simple and naive miracle story. I think it a mistake to decide which theological motif is the "main point" of the story and then relegate every other motif to the status of a redactional addition or relic of earlier tradition. The story carefully develops the multifaceted symbol of wine throughout the narrative: initial lack (v 3), the motif of Jewish purification (hence the theme of replacement in v 6), the massive quantity of the gift (two or three measures in each jar in v 6, filled up to the brim in v 7), the mysterious origin of the gift (v 9), the superior quality of the gift (v 10), and its eschatological nature (kept until now at the end of v 10).

[240] On this see Raymond E. Brown, *The Community of the Beloved Disciple* (New York/Ramsey, NJ/Toronto: Paulist, 1979).

[241] See Schnelle, *Antidocetic Christology*, 78: "Verse 11, which is crucial for understanding the miracle story, should be attributed entirely to the Johannine redaction."

[242] On "beginning" in 1 John, see Raymond E. Brown, *The Epistles of John* (AB 30; Garden City, NY: Doubleday, 1982) 97–100, 155–58. On the place of the OT and Jewish tradition within 1 John's concept of the "beginning," see Judith M. Lieu, "What Was from the Beginning: Scripture and Tradition in the Johannine Epistles," *NTS* 39 (1993) 458–77.

[243] On this see Meyer, "John 2:10," 192; Suggit, "John 2:1–11," 145. Both refer to Barrett, *The Gospel According to St John*, 161: "[in John 2:11] *archē* may mean more than the first of a series; not merely the first sign but 'a primary sign,' because representative of the creative and transforming work of Jesus as a whole." This point is missed by Schmidt ("Der johanneische Charakter," 35), who equates "beginning of the signs" with "first sign." Collins ("Cana," 80, 91) puts the matter well when he says: ". . . the account of the water-become-wine is the key to the Johannine signs just as much as it is the first of Jesus' miracles. . . . The account has not been written into the Johannine account so much to provide a description of a particular miracle as it has been written to say that all the signs of Jesus must be seen in the light of the hour of Jesus."

[244] For the various aspects of the key Johannine concept of "glory," especially as intimated in the first Cana miracle, see Lohfink, "Das Weinwunder zu Kana," 169–82.

[245] Although the sentence with the verb "believe" in 1:50 could be taken as a statement, most translations and commentators render it as a question. Brown makes the connection between 1:50 and 2:11 in *The Gospel According to John*, 1. 83.

[246] On this see Culpepper, *Anatomy of the Fourth Gospel*, 116; cf. Thompson, *The Humanity of Jesus*, 69–70; Schnelle, *Antidocetic Christology*, 74–75.

[247] Hence I think it is a mistake to see the miraculous catch of fish in John 21 as the third in a series of signs in a supposed signs source. The use of "third" in 21:14 refers to the third post-resurrection appearance of Jesus to his disciples; it represents an awkward attempt by the final redactor to tack on this story to an already completed Gospel. For the opposite view, that 21:1–14 was the third sign in a signs source (indeed, a Signs Gospel), see Fortna, *The Fourth Gospel*, 65–68; even Fortna warns (p. 66): ". . . from the outset it should be recognized that the assignment of this story [21:1–14] to the source is more hypothetical than for the other miracles."

[248] See the comment in Str-B, 2. 407–9.

[249] See the comment in Skehan and Di Lella, *The Wisdom of Ben Sira*, 391.

[250] Brown, *The Gospel According to John*, 1. 100.

[251] See, e.g., Martin Hengel, *Judaism and Hellenism. Studies in Their Encounter in Palestine during the Early Hellenistic Period* (Philadelphia: Fortress, 1974); idem, *The 'Hel-*

lenization' of Judaea in the First Century after Christ (London: SCM; Philadelphia: Trinity, 1989).

[252] This remains true, despite the attempt of Windisch ("Die johanneische Weinregel," 248–57) to show otherwise. The few supposed parallels he brings forward from classical literature do not really apply to the case in John 2:1–11. That the creation of fictitious customs for literary purposes was not unknown to ancient authors is shown by Bauer, " 'Literarische' Namen," 258–64.

[253] The earliest reference to a seven-day celebration of a wedding between a Jewish bride and a Jewish bridegroom is found in Tob 11:19 (in MSS B and A of the LXX; Tob 8:19 in the same MSS mentions 14 days). For rabbinical references, see, e.g., *m. Neg.* 3:2. An early reference to a seven-day wedding feast is found in Judg 14:12, but there (1) it is the wedding between Samson and a Philistine woman and (2) the narrator refers to the sort of wedding feast that young men used to celebrate (v 10).

[254] I realize that in assigning the whole of 2:1–11 to the creativity of the Evangelist I am going against the consensus of Johannine scholars, who see some coherent source behind the present story, whether or not this source was part of a written signs source (or Signs Gospel). But I think that a number of observations offered in the preceding treatment make that consensus less certain than some think: (1) As we have seen, a large part of the pericope can reasonably be assigned to John's hand. When all this Johannine material is subtracted, it is difficult to see what coherent story is left. (2) The story from start to finish fits into the literary structure and theological pattern of the Fourth Gospel; it has not been forced into that structure and pattern by some artificial additions. (3) There is no need to assign the explicit enumeration of the first and second signs of Cana (2:11; 4:54) to a signs source; the enumeration is perfectly understandable as a redactional *inclusio* that brackets the first part of Jesus' public ministry in John's Gospel. (4) There is no need to consider the dialogue between Jesus and his mother in 2:3–4 a disruptive addition. Granted John's pattern of initial request—apparent refusal—persistent faith—and final bestowal of the miracle in an unexpected way, the flow of the narrative in 2:1–11 makes perfect Johannine sense. The mistake is to try to understand it in realistic historical or psychological terms. From start to finish, it is a statement of John's theological program. (5) There is no need to consider the parenthetical comment of v 9 ("and he did not know whence it was, but the servants who had drawn the water knew") as the addition of a later hand (i.e., the Evangelist's). From chap. 21, added by the final redactor, we can see that the same person who is writing a narrative can also write the parenthetical comments that interrupt the narrative (see 21:7,19,20). Since ancient documents had neither footnotes nor parentheses signs, parenthetical comments had to be part of the main text. (6) The fact that John 2:1–11 contains a number of words that otherwise do not appear in John or in the NT as a whole (*hapax legomena*) does not necessarily prove that John is using a source. By everyone's admission, the first Cana miracle is a one-of-a-kind story in the NT; if the story is to be told at all, certain unusual words must be employed, no matter who is the first author. (7) It is often observed that, of all the miracle stories in the Fourth Gospel, only the first Cana miracle lacks a parallel or analogue in the Synoptic tradition (see, e.g., Fortna, *The Fourth Gospel*, 52). This may have a very simple explanation. While all of the other Johannine miracle stories do go back to some source (e.g., a written signs source) that contained parallels to the miracles in the Synoptic tradition, the first Cana miracle lacks such parallels to the Synoptics because it is purely the creation of the Evangelist.—To be sure, certain questions remain: e.g., why and whence the venue of "Cana of Galilee"? But the same question remains to be answered by any theory of a signs source or a Signs Gospel.

[255] Besides the OT motifs we have reviewed (abundance of wine in the end time, Yahweh as the bridegroom of Israel), these traditional themes might have included variant forms of Jesus' sayings that are represented in the Synoptic tradition by Mark 2:19–20 (the wedding guests cannot fast while the bridegroom is with them) and 2:22 (new wine must be put into new wineskins); the tradition of Jesus as one who associated with people noted for eating and drinking (Matt 11:19 par.); and the tradition that there was tension between Jesus and his family, including his mother (Mark 3:21,31–35; Luke 2:41–50). Thomas L. Brodie (*The Quest for the Origin of John's Gospel. A Source-Oriented Approach* [New York/Oxford: Oxford University, 1993] 74–75) goes so far as to see John 2:1–11 as the Evangelist's rewriting of Mark's presentation of the beginning of Jesus' ministry (Mark 1:21–39); this strange theory involves passing over more obvious Marcan parallels to John 2:1–11.

I have not bothered to treat in detail the suggestion made by Bultmann (*Das Evangelium des Johannes*, 83) and accepted by a number of British exegetes (e.g., Dodd, Lindars) that the first Cana miracle is connected with the Hellenistic cult of the wine god Dionysus. Simply as a matter of fact, many scholars have not been convinced by this position. It is telling that not some conservative apologist but rather the hardly credulous Haenchen points out the difficulties of such a theory; see his *John 1*, 177–78 and the literature cited there. Haenchen depends especially on Noetzel, *Christus und Dionysos*. Noetzel emphasizes the many differences between the myth and cult of Dionysus on the one hand and the Johannine vision of Christ in the Fourth Gospel on the other (see, e.g., *Christus und Dionysos*, 39–58). Specifically, he shows that nowhere in the Dionysus myth or cult is Dionysus said to turn water into wine. One point that Noetzel especially stresses is the late date of the association of the first Cana miracle with the feast of Epiphany; historically erroneous claims about the early connection between the two (supposedly involving the Dionysus cult) should have been put to rest long ago. It would seem that the connection was not made until the 4th century A.D. When the connection was made in Egypt, a desire to replace the myth and cult of Isis and Osiris may have played a part; Dionysus had nothing to do with it (pp. 29–38). On the extremely complicated history and intertwined themes of the feast of Epiphany, see Smitmans, *Das Weinwunder von Kana*, 165–86.

While admitting some of the weaknesses of Bultmann's position, Linnemann ("Die Hochzeit zu Kana," 408–18) criticizes Noetzel for his apologetic attempt to explain the story simply in terms of the OT and Jewish ideas (cf. Smitmans, *Das Weinwunder von Kana*, 34 n. 2). She allows for the possibility that an early Christian community purposely used the Dionysus legend because the Christians were engaging in dialogue and debate with pagans who sought in Dionysus the source of life. It was not a question of identifying Dionysus with Jesus or simply transferring the image of Dionysus to Jesus; rather, a counter-image was created by the Christians (pp. 416–17).

Linnemann helps clarify the point of the debate. Still, she never quite overcomes Noetzel's basic objection: there is no firm indication that the Dionysus legend or cult presented Dionysus as a god who turned water into wine. Nor does Linnemann ever explain adequately where she thinks a particular Christian community had contact with the mysteries of Dionysus. Other authors have tried to fill in these gaps. That the cult of Dionysus would have been known in the Syrian-Palestinian area around the time of the writing of John's Gospel is shown by Smith, "On the Wine God in Palestine," 815–29. However, contrary to Smith's claim, the text he produces from Achilles Tatius does not provide a "striking parallel" to John 2:1–11, since the key element of the miraculous transformation of a given amount of water into wine is absent. An attempt to remedy this basic weakness in the arguments of those championing the influence of the Dionysus cult on John 2:1–11 is offered by Broer in "Noch einmal," 103–23. While

Broer succeeds in pointing out some deficiencies in the position that emphasizes the OT and Judaism as the source of the Cana story's motifs, he does not really overcome the greatest difficulty of the position that champions an origin of the story in the Dionysus cult: there are no unambiguous texts from the pre-Christian period that depict the cult-god Dionysus changing water into wine. The texts Broer brings forward either do not bear the clear sense he wants to see in them or stem from the 2d century A.D. and later. In the end, Broer does more or less what the champions of the OT do: both sides stitch together various motifs from various texts to create the supposed source of the first Cana miracle.

Dodd (*Historical Tradition*, 224–28) combines Bultmann's theory of a folktale rooted in the Dionysus legend with a suggestion that behind v 10 lies a parable of Jesus. What exactly the content of this parable would be (a miracle?) is not clear. In his *The Interpretation of the Fourth Gospel*, 298–99, Dodd also highlights as general religious background for John 2:1–11 Philo's depiction of the Word as the "cupbearer" of God, who pours out the wine (instead of water) that symbolizes the gifts of God. Lindars ("Two Parables," 318–24), while differing with Dodd on some points, develops Dodd's suggestion about a parable by speculating that, besides the parable, the Cana story also derives in part from a miracle story in which the boy Jesus would have worked the wine wonder while still within his family circle, à la the *Infancy Gospel of Thomas*. Brown ("The 'Mother of Jesus,' " 308–9) finds himself "attracted" by this suggestion; a similar theory of derivation from a story about the child or boy Jesus is proposed by Pesch ("Das Weinwunder," 219–25), who appeals for support to the 2d-century apocryphal *Epistula Apostolorum* 4 (15)—5 (16). Personally, I doubt whether the *Epistula Apostolorum* gives us access to any independent tradition about the first Cana miracle; I think it more likely that the text in the *Epistula Apostolorum* is a very brief condensation of John 2:1–12. Taking a somewhat different tack, Williams ("Fourth Gospel," 311–16) suggests that John 2:1–11 is the Evangelist's dramatization of the parables and metaphors found in Luke 5:33–39, which are closer to the Cana story than the Marcan version of the sayings. One sees how the first Cana miracle invites ever more wide-ranging speculation.

The reader will forgive me if I do not pursue each of these theories in great detail. Even if the theory of, say, Bultmann, Linnemann, Broer, Dodd, or Lindars were correct (i.e., that the first Cana miracle derives from the Dionysus cult, from a parable of Jesus, or from a story about the child Jesus), the ultimate conclusion drawn would be the same as the one I present here on other grounds: the miracle story of John 2:1–11 does not go back to some event in the public ministry of the historical Jesus.

[256] For the usual position today, that John's Cana is Khirbet Qana, and not Kefr Kenna or Ain Qana, see Jack Finegan, *The Archeology of the New Testament. The Life of Jesus and the Beginning of the Early Church* (rev. ed.; Princeton: Princeton University, 1992) 62–65; James F. Strange, "Cana of Galilee," *Anchor Bible Dictionary*, 1. 827; Mackowski, "Scholar's Qanah," 278–84; Riesner, "Fragen," 69–71. Khirbet Qana is about nine miles north-by-northwest of Nazareth, while Kefr Kenna (the popular pilgrimage stop today) is about four miles northeast of Nazareth. John's Gospel may speak of "Cana of Galilee" (so in all occurrences: 2:1,11; 4:46; 21:2) to distinguish the town from Kanah in the territory of Asher "as far as great Sidon" (Josh 19:28), six miles southeast of Tyre. Also possible is an echo of the way John's Gospel plays off Galilee against Jerusalem and Judea. Only John mentions Cana in the NT; the Cana Josephus refers to (*Life* 16 §86) is probably likewise Khirbet Qana.

[257] For the sake of brevity, I often use the short phrase "the feeding of the multitude" or "the feeding story" to designate what is commonly called "the multiplication of the

loaves and fish." An advantage of the briefer label is that it restricts itself to words actually found in the story it is labeling. In contrast, "the *multiplication* of the loaves and fish" introduces an explanatory word that is pointedly not used in this miracle story, a story that (like the other gift miracle, the changing of water into wine at Cana) is notably "veiled" and indirect in its narration of the miracle proper.

Not surprisingly, with six different versions of the story of the feeding of the multitude in the Gospels, the literature on the subject is immense, even apart from the standard commentaries on Mark and John (our two primary sources). What follows is merely a representative sampling: G. H. Boobyer, "The Eucharistic Interpretation of the Miracles of the Loaves in St. Mark's Gospel," *JTS* 3 (1952) 161–71; idem, "The Miracles of the Loaves and the Gentiles in St. Mark's Gospel," *SJT* 6 (1953) 77–87; A. M. Farrer, "Loaves and Thousands," *JTS* 4 (1953) 1–14; Ethelbert Stauffer, "Antike Jesustradition und Jesuspolemik im mittelalterlichen Orient," *ZNW* 46 (1955) 1–30, esp. 20–29; idem, "Zum apokalyptischen Festmahl in Mc 6:34ff.," *ZNW* 46 (1955) 264–66; Alan Richardson, "The Feeding of the Five Thousand. Mark 6:34–44," *Int* 9 (1955) 144–49; Donald Fay Robinson, "The Parable of the Loaves," *ATR* 39 (1957) 107–15; H. Clavier, "La multiplication des pains dans le ministère de Jésus," *Studia Evangelica. Volume I* (TU 73; ed. Kurt Aland et al.; Berlin: Akademie, 1959) 441–57; P. Georg Ziener, "Die Brotwunder im Markusevangelium," *BZ* 4 (1960) 282–85; Alan Shaw, "The Marcan Feeding Narratives," *CQR* 162 (1961) 268–78; Hugh Montefiore, "Revolt in the Desert? (Mark vi. 30ff.)," *NTS* 8 (1961–62) 135–41; Frederick W. Danker, "Mark 8:3," *JBL* 82 (1963) 215–16; J. Knackstedt, "De duplici miraculo multiplicationis panum," *VD* 41 (1963) 39–51, 140–53; idem, "Die beiden Brotvermehrungen im Evangelium," *NTS* 10 (1963–64) 309–35; B. van Iersel, "Die wunderbare Speisung and das Abendmahl in der synoptischen Tradition," *NovT* 7 (1964) 167–94; Gerhard Friedrich, "Die beiden Erzählungen von der Speisung in Mark 6,31–44; 8,1–9," *TZ* 20 (1964) 10–22; A. G. Hebert, "History in the Feeding of the Five Thousand," *Studia Evangelica. Volume II* (TU 87; ed. F. L. Cross; Berlin: Akademie, 1964) 65–72; Alkuin Heising, "Exegese und Theologie der alt- und neutestamentlichen Speisewunder," *ZKT* 86 (1964) 80–96; idem, *Die Botschaft der Brotvermehrung* (SBS 15; 2d ed.; Stuttgart: KBW, 1967); Cyrille Vogel, "Le repas sacré au poisson chez les chrétiens," *RevScRel* 40 (1966) 1–26; A.-M. Denis, "La section des pains selon s. Marc (6,30—8,26), une théologie de l'Eucharistie," *Studia Evangelica. Volume IV* (TU 102; ed. F. L. Cross; Berlin: Akademie, 1968) 171–79; B. E. Thiering, " 'Breaking of Bread' and 'Harvest' in Mark's Gospel," *NovT* 12 (1970) 1–12; Roloff, *Das Kerygma*, 237–69; Kertelge, *Die Wunder Jesu*, 129–45; Hermann Patsch, "Abendmahlsterminologie ausserhalb der Einsetzungsberichte," *ZNW* 62 (1971) 210–31; Jean-Marie van Cangh, "Le thème des poissons dans les récits évangéliques de la multiplication des pains," *RB* 78 (1971) 71–83; idem, "La multiplication des pains dans l'évangile de Marc. Essai d'exégèse globale," *L'Evangile selon Marc. Tradition et rédaction* (BETL 34; ed. M. Sabbe; Leuven: Leuven University; Gembloux: Duculot, 1974) 309–46; Koch, *Die Bedeutung*, 99–104, 109–10; J. Duncan M. Derrett, "Leek-beds and Methodology," *BZ* 19 (1975) 101–3; Ignace de la Potterie, "Le sens primitif de la multiplication des pains," *Jésus aux origines de la christologie* (BETL 40; ed. Jacques Dupont; Leuven: Leuven University; Gembloux: Duculot, 1975) 303–29 (available in English translation as "The Multiplication of the Loaves in the Life of Jesus," *Communio* 16 [1989] 499–516); Karl Paul Donfried, "The Feeding Narratives and the Marcan Community," *Kirche* (Günther Bornkamm Festschrift; ed. Dieter Lührmann and Georg Strecker; Tübingen: Mohr [Siebeck], 1980) 95–103; Fowler, *Loaves and Fishes*, 43–148; Sanae Masuda, "The Good News of the Miracle of the Bread," *NTS* 28 (1982) 191–219; Ludger Schenke, *Die wunderbare Brotvermehrung. Die neutestamentlichen Erzählungen und ihre Bedeutung*

(Würzburg: Echter, 1983); Kruse, "Jesu Seefahrten," 508–30; P. W. Barnett, "The Feeding of the Multitude in Mark 6/John 6," *Gospel Perspectives. The Miracles of Jesus. Volume 6* (ed. David Wenham and Craig Blomberg; Sheffield: JSOT, 1986) 273–93; Jouette M. Bassler, "The Parable of the Loaves," *JR* 66 (1986) 157–72; Fritz Neuge-bauer, "Die wunderbare Speisung (Mk 6, 30–44 parr.) und Jesu Identität," *KD* 32 (1986) 254–77; Hugh M. Humphrey, "Jesus as Wisdom in Mark," *BTB* 19 (1989) 48–53; Angelika Seethaler, "Die Brotvermehrung—ein Kirchenspiegel?" *BZ* 34 (1990) 108–12; Giuseppe Segalla, "La complessa struttura letteraria di Giovanni 6," *Teologia* 15 (1990) 68–89; L. T. Witkamp, "Some Specific Johannine Features in John 6.1–21," *JSNT* 40 (1990) 43–59; Craig R. Koester, "John Six and the Lord's Supper," *LQ* 4 (1990) 419–37; Eduard Schweizer, "Joh 6,51c–58—vom Evangelisten übernommene Tradition?" *ZNW* 82 (1991) 274; Schnelle, *Antidocetic Christology,* 99–108, 194–208.

[258] For a survey of the similarities and differences between the first Cana miracle and the feeding of the multitude, see Dodd, *Historical Tradition,* 223–24, as well as my treatment of the first Cana miracle above.

[259] See Theissen, *Urchristliche Wundergeschichten,* 111. Theissen also maintains that "spontaneity" is a characteristic of gift miracles in the sense that the gift miracle is never called forth by a request. This is debatable; Theissen himself (p. 112) must allow for a possible exception in the approach of Jesus' mother to Jesus in John 2:3. Theissen (pp. 113–14) lists as a third characteristic the emphasis on the confirmation or "demon-stration" of the miracle.

[260] For detailed treatment of the Matthean and Lucan versions of the miracle, see Held, "Matthäus als Interpret der Wundergeschichten," 171–77; Fitzmyer, *The Gospel According to Luke,* 1. 761–69; Heising, *Die Botschaft,* 72–76; Schenke, *Die wunderbare Brotvermehrung,* 11–34, 157–73. Held points out how, in the first feeding of the multi-tude, Matthew states (14:19) that Jesus "breaking gave the loaves to the disciples, and the disciples [gave them] to the crowds." Nothing is said about Jesus doing likewise with the fish; Mark's statement (6:41) that "he [Jesus] divided the two fish among all [of them]" is simply dropped. Matthew thus makes clearer the allusion to the Last Supper. Fitzmyer (p. 764) supports seeing a reference to the eucharist in the Lucan version. That Matthew and Luke not only depend upon Mark's versions of the feeding story but also interpret them in a eucharistic sense is maintained by van Iersel, "Die wunderbare Speisung," 169–71, 190–94. More cautious about a eucharistic reference in Luke's version is Busse, *Die Wunder des Propheten Jesus,* 248.

[261] See Brown (*The Gospel According to John,* 1. 239, 244, with the accompanying charts on pp. 240–43) for a listing of the various agreements and disagreements. The charts in the present volume that illustrate my analysis of the stories of the multiplica-tion of loaves and fish reproduce Brown's charts with slight editorial modifications.

[262] I agree with most critics in judging that the "minor agreements" of Matthew and Luke against Mark in the feeding narratives are not sufficient to make probable a Q form of the story.

[263] Since this inquiry aims at (1) a likely sketch of what the most primitive form of the tradition would have looked like and (2) a decision about what if any event in the life of Jesus the tradition reflects, I do not pay much attention to the redactional changes and theological emphases of the various evangelists, especially Matthew and Luke, who for the most part simply modify Mark.

[264] Meier, *A Marginal Jew,* 1. 44, 52–53. On the independence of John from Mark in the feeding story, see (besides Brown and Dodd) Bultmann, *Das Evangelium des Jo-*

hannes, 155; Haenchen, *John 1*, 274; Schnackenburg, *Das Johannesevangelium*, 2. 28–31; also Heising, *Die Botschaft*, 77; Patsch, "Abendmahlsterminologie," 229; Witkamp, "Some Specific Johannine Features," 43–59. Some of the critics who hold for the literary independence of the Fourth Evangelist allow that the final redactor may have known at least some of the Synoptics.

[265] Brown, *The Gospel According to John*, 1. 236–44; Dodd, *Historical Tradition*, 196–211. A helpful review of the similarities and differences between the first Marcan and the Johannine versions is supplied by Barnett ("The Feeding of the Multitude," 273–93), who, like Brown and Dodd, comes to the conclusion that John is literarily independent of Mark (pp. 284–85).

[266] On this see Dodd, *Historical Tradition*, 208–9. John agrees with the second Matthean version in laying the scene on a hill or mountain *(to oros)* and in associating the feeding with miracles of healing that precede the feeding; John 6:1 is also strikingly similar to Matt 15:29 in mentioning the crossing of the Sea of Galilee.

[267] For example, all the Synoptics in the first feeding story use *ichthys* for "fish" (Mark 6:38 ‖ Matt 14:17 ‖ Luke 9:13), while John uses *opsarion* (John 6:9). In the second feeding story the diminutive form *ichthydion* is used in Mark 8:7 and Matt 15:34.

[268] On this point see J. Becker, "Das Johannesevangelium im Streit der Methoden (1980–84)," *TRu* 51 (1986) 1–78, esp. 22–23; Haenchen, *John 1*, 75.

[269] See Dodd, *Historical Tradition*, 206. The precise nature of the "desolate surroundings" or "wilderness" designated by *hē erēmos, ho erēmos topos*, or *hē erēmia* must be judged from the context, not from the words of the *erēm*-root taken in isolation. The general notion conveyed by these words is that of a region not regularly inhabited by sedentary humans engaging in agriculture. The words could refer to an absolute wasteland, but also to steppes or grassland used as pasturage. On this see Gerhard Kittel, "*erēmos*, etc.," *TDNT* 2 (1964) 657–60.

[270] I purposely use the image of a launching pad for 6:31a because one could well argue that it is 6:31b ("he gave them bread from heaven to eat") that is the true "text" of Jesus' "homily." For this view see Borgen, *Bread from Heaven*, 61.

[271] Among other things, Dodd (*Historical Tradition*, 196–222) ties his treatment of the feeding stories more closely to that of the story of the walking on the water; he also highlights the similarity between John 6:1 and Matt 15:29. He is perhaps a little more tentative than Brown on the question of John's independence of the Synoptics in the feeding story, but he still considers the view that John is independent to enjoy "substantial" probability (p. 211).

[272] See the succinct summary of the arguments for and against the "doublet theory" in van Cangh, "La multiplication des pains," 337–41.

[273] That the two Marcan versions go back ultimately to one tradition (and possibly to one historical event) is the view of the vast majority of critics today; see, e.g., Friedrich, "Die beiden Erzählungen," 10; Guelich, *Mark 1–8:26*, 401. Even an apologetic work like Latourelle's *The Miracles of Jesus* accepts the idea of one basic tradition and event (pp. 72–73). One of the few recent technical studies to maintain that the two Marcan versions go back to two distinct events in the life of Jesus is Kruse's article, "Jesu Seefahrten," 508–30, esp. 521–22; his psychologizing and harmonizing approach is reminiscent of the 19th-century "liberal lives" of Jesus. The same can be said of the openly apologetic study by Knackstedt, "Die beiden Brotvermehrungen," 309–35 (the substance of this article is also found in his two-part essay, "De duplici miraculo,"

39–51, 140–53); similarly, Neugebauer, "Die wunderbare Speisung," 273. Without making a definitive judgment, Gundry (*Mark*, 399) defends the possibility or even probability that the two Marcan narratives go back to two distinct events in the life of Jesus.

[274] Dodd, *Historical Tradition*, 196; Haenchen, *Der Weg Jesu*, 283–84; idem, *John 1*, 274; also Cerfaux, "La section des pains," 64–77; Taylor, *The Gospel According to St. Mark*, 628–32; Ziener, "Die Brotwunder," 283; Brown, *The Gospel According to John*, 1. 237–39; Denis, "La section des pains," 171–74; Lindars, *The Gospel of John*, 237–38; de la Potterie, "La multiplication des pains," 309; Humphrey, "Jesus as Wisdom in Mark," 49; Witkamp, "Some Specific Johannine Features," 43–45. For a detailed argument in favor of Mark 6–8 containing a traditional doublet, see Luke H. Jenkins, "A Marcan Doublet," *Studies in History and Religion* (H. Wheeler Robinson Festschrift; ed. Ernest A. Payne; London/Redhill: Lutterworth, 1942) 87–111. While I think the idea of two pre-Marcan cycles of tradition behind Mark 6–8 is a likely hypothesis, I am less confident about reconstructing the details of the two cycles.—On the whole question of the "bread section" in Mark, see my treatment of the healing of the blind man of Bethsaida above.

[275] A curious variant of this approach is proposed by Masuda, "The Good News," 191–219: a single bare-bones form of the feeding miracle existed in the tradition; Mark took it over and molded it into his two different accounts of the feeding miracle. There are many weak links in Masuda's chain of reasoning. To take but two examples: (1) Although he claims that details like the precise numbers in both Marcan accounts come from Mark's redaction (pp. 203–6), Masuda never explains the points of contact that each Marcan version has with the independent version in John 6:1–15 (e.g., the concrete numbers of five loaves, two fish, two hundred denarii, and five thousand men that John shares with the first Marcan version). (2) Masuda never adequately explains why the second Marcan version but not the first contains so many Marcan *hapax legomena*. Similar objections may be raised against the similar proposal of Donfried ("The Feeding Narratives," 95–103), who suggests that Mark adapted twice a single feeding story that he received from the oral tradition.

[276] Considered quite possible by Dibelius, *Formgeschichte*, 75 n. 1; rightly rejected by Koch, *Die Bedeutung*, 109.

[277] These Marcan *hapax legomena* include in vv 2–8 *prosmenō, nēstis, eklyō, hēkō, erēmia, ichthydion,* and *perisseuma*. In the transitional v 10, *meros* and *Dalmanoutha* are also Marcan *hapax legomena*. The words that occur only here and in Mark's redactional recollection of the feeding story in 8:20 are *spyris* and *tetrakischilioi*. Certain other words occur elsewhere in Mark, but only once or twice; and certain verbs occur only here in Mark in a particular form. Thus, on the whole, the vocabulary of the feeding of the four thousand is anything but strikingly Marcan. Kertelge (*Die Wunder Jesu*, 139) remarks: "In the feeding story proper [Mark 8:1–9] there is hardly a sentence or even a mere word that one could trace back to specifically Marcan interpretation." For an attempt to distinguish tradition from Marcan redaction in 8:1–10, see Fowler, *Loaves and Fishes*, 54–57.

[278] The coincidence hardly argues for literary dependence, since the two questions are quite different in wording: "Whence shall one be able to satisfy so many people with loaves of bread here in the wilderness?" in Mark 8:4; and "Whence shall we buy loaves of bread that these people may eat?" in John 6:5.

[279] For a defense of the position that Mark 6:32–44 is Mark's own creation, based on

the "second" feeding story, which is actually the one that existed in the tradition, see Fowler, *Loaves and Fishes*, 43–90. Against this view is Gundry, *Mark*, 397–98.

[280] In these common elements, two points should be noted: (1) While two hundred denarii are mentioned in both Mark 6 and John 6, the sense is slightly different in each case. In Mark 6:37, the disciples reply to Jesus' command that they give the people food to eat with the question: "Are we to go and buy two-hundred-denarii-worth of bread and give it to them to eat?" In contrast, in John 6:7 Philip denies that two-hundred-denarii-worth of bread would be enough to allow each person in the crowd to eat a little. In my view, the traditional motif of two-hundred-denarii-worth of bread has found expression in two different ways in Mark and John. Granted John's tendency to make miracles as mammoth as possible, I tend to think that he has turned a tradition that said the amount would be enough to feed the crowd into a negation of that estimate. (2) It is often claimed that the use of *kophinos* for "basket" in the first Marcan feeding story and the use of *spyris* for "basket" in the second reflects the difference between Jesus feeding a Jewish crowd in the first instance and his feeding a Gentile crowd in the second. Despite the association of *kophinos* with Jews in a passage from Juvenal, the idea that Greek-speaking people in general would associate one word with one ethnic group and the second with the other does not seem sufficiently proven. On this see Gundry, *Mark*, 398. The redactional intention of Mark to provide first a feeding of the Jews and then a feeding of the Gentiles is denied by Boobyer, "The Miracles of the Loaves and the Gentiles," 77–87 (Boobyer thinks that both crowds are made up of Gentiles); Friedrich, "Die beiden Erzählungen," 10–12; Koch, *Die Bedeutung*, 109–10. Thiering (" 'Breaking of Bread,' " 2–5) holds the unusual view that the first Marcan feeding symbolizes the preaching of the gospel to the "Judean Jews," while the second feeding symbolizes the preaching to the Hellenistic Jews from the whole world (the crowd of four thousand referring to the four corners of the world and the four winds). This kind of highly imaginative symbolic approach plagues all too many treatments of the feeding story: e.g., Farrer, "Loaves and Thousands," 1–14; Pesch, *Das Markusevangelium*, 1. 346–56, 400–405; Seethaler, "Die Brotvermehrung," 108–12; and much worse Robinson, "The Parable of the Loaves," 107–15 (the five loaves are the five books of the Law, the five thousand fed are the chosen of Israel, the twelve *kophinoi* are the twelve apostles, the two fish are the two Christian commandments that epitomize the Law and the prophets, the seven loaves are the seven Noachian laws, the seven *spyrides* are the seven Hellenist "deacons" [!], and the four thousand fed are the Gentiles). Friedrich ("Die beiden Erzählungen," 10–12) and Gundry (*Mark*, 396–97) stand firmly against such symbolic interpretations; Kertelge (*Die Wunder Jesu*, 141–42) considers them mere speculation.

[281] For the question of tradition and redaction in Mark, see van Iersel, "Die wunderbare Speisung," 173–77; Kertelge, *Die Wunder Jesu*, 129–31, 139–42; Koch, *Die Bedeutung*, 99–104, 109–10; Masuda, "The Good News," 191–219; Schenke, *Die wunderbare Brotvermehrung*, 135–51. To sample the variety of scholarly opinions concerning John 6:1–15, see Bultmann, *Das Evangelium des Johannes*, 155 (redaction seen in vv 4,6,14–15); Schnackenburg, *Das Johannesevangelium*, 2. 30–31 (redaction tightly interwoven with a traditional story that combined both Synoptic and non-Synoptic traits); Brown, *The Gospel According to John*, 1. 245–50 (with an evaluation similar to Schnackenburg's); Haenchen, *John 1*, 275 (with the possible exception of vv 14–15, the Evangelist has only lightly redacted the text of the source); Fortna, *The Fourth Gospel*, 79–93 (redaction in parts of vv 1,3,4,5,7,8,13,15; the whole of vv 2,4,6,12 seen as redactional); and von Wahlde, *The Earliest Version*, 97–100 (the whole story is traditional, except for vv 6 and 15).

[282] For example, von Wahlde sees it as part of the traditional story, while many other commentators (e.g., Bultmann, Schnackenburg, and Fortna) think that it is redactional; see von Wahlde's note on the variety of opinions in *The Earliest Version*, 99 n. 76.

[283] It should be stressed that, given the complexity of agreements and disagreements and the convoluted nature of the whole tradition history of the feeding story, one cannot presume that any version of the story—first Marcan version, second Marcan version, or the Johannine version—is always the earliest or always the latest form of the story. On this see Brown, *The Gospel According to John*, 1. 238.

[284] Used also by Guelich, *Mark 1–8:26*, 338.

[285] Both the first Marcan version (Mark 6:32–34, cf. v 45) and the Johannine version (John 6:1, cf. vv 16–17) place the feeding miracle by the Sea of Galilee. This is all the more striking in the Johannine version, since the larger narrative context of John's Gospel does not necessitate this setting. That is to say, John does not structure a good part of the ministry around various crossings of the Sea of Galilee, as Mark does. Hence the location of the miracle story by the Sea seems firmly rooted in the tradition. The extent to which the introductory verses in the first Marcan version (6:30–34) are redactional creations of Mark is debated by critics; see, e.g., Taylor, *The Gospel According to St. Mark*, 318; Pesch, *Das Markusevangelium*, 1. 347; Koch, *Die Bedeutung*, 99–102; Guelich, *Mark 1—8:26*, 337. A detailed consideration of the question can be found in Wilhelm Egger, *Frohbotschaft und Lehre. Die Sammelberichte des Wirkens Jesu im Markusevangelium* (Frankfurter Theologische Studien 19; Frankfurt: Knecht, 1976) 121–34; Egger sees 6:30–34 as the result of Mark consciously putting together various traditional motifs in order to highlight certain theological ideas in the following pericope (e.g., the relation of the disciples to Jesus, Jesus as Good Shepherd and teacher, the feeding of the multitude as a form of teaching). Fortunately, the question need not concern us here.

In contrast to the venue by the Sea of Galilee, it is difficult to make a decision about the presence or the absence of the "desolate place" or "wilderness" motif in the earliest form of the feeding story. Both Marcan versions have the motif; but apparently it was not present in the form of the story known to the Fourth Evangelist, for it is hardly conceivable that he would have eliminated a motif that fits so perfectly with his bread of life discourse. It is possible, though, that the motif was present at the earliest stage of the story in the Johannine tradition, but dropped out before the story reached the Evangelist.

[286] As Schnackenburg observes (*Das Johannesevangelium*, 2. 17), this is the only time that the Fourth Gospel mentions a large crowd "following" Jesus (in a way reminiscent of the Synoptic Gospels). "The Fourth Evangelist betrays here a knowledge of a wider (and longer) Galilean ministry of Jesus."

[287] Among the Marcan and Johannine versions, only the second Marcan version presents the crowd in dire need because the people have been with Jesus for three days and have nothing to eat, with the resulting danger that, if Jesus dismisses them, some of them will faint on the way home (8:2–3). Neither the first Marcan nor the Johannine version gives any indication of this dangerous situation.

[288] While the matter is not entirely clear, the Synoptic form seems to presuppose that the disciples check and report about their own supplies. For example, in Mark 6:38 (and likewise in Mark 8:5) Jesus asks his disciples: "How many loaves of bread do you have?" While both the Matthean and Lucan parallels to the first Marcan version cut down the dialogue at this point, both present the disciples speaking of what "we have"

(Matt 14:17 ‖ Luke 9:13). In contrast, in John's version, the disciple Andrew knows of a young lad *(paidarion)* who has five loaves and two fish. Possibly the lad "entered into" the Johannine version of the story when the Elisha story of 2 Kgs 4:42–44 began to exert an increasing influence on the tradition of Jesus feeding the multitude. In LXX 4 Kgdms 4:43 (= MT 2 Kgs 4:43) Elisha's servant, who objects that the twenty loaves available are too little for the hundred men, is called *ho leitourgos autou* (= *měšārětô* in the MT). But in 4:25 and 5:20 Elisha's servant (Gehazi) is called *to paidarion [autou]* (= *naʿărô* in the MT).

[289] It is remarkable that both the first Marcan version (6:19) and John's version (6:10) mention grass *(chortos)* in connection with Jesus' order that the crowd recline. (In Mark it is specified as "green grass," *chlōros chortos*). Some commentators see here an allusion in the tradition to LXX Ps 22:2 (= MT Ps 23:2) and Jesus as the Good Shepherd of Israel. However, the matter is not so clear. In LXX Ps 22:2, the word for grass is *chloē*, not *chortos*. Moreover, in John's version the mention of grass may be connected with the reference to Passover in 6:4; consequently, in the judgment of those critics who consider the reference to Passover an addition by the Evangelist, the mention of grass would also come from the Evangelist.

[290] While the participation of the disciples in the distribution of the loaves is mentioned in both Marcan versions (Mark 6:16; 8:6), the disciples disappear in the Johannine parallel: Jesus distributes the loaves to those reclining (John 6:11) with no mention of the disciples assisting. The absence of the disciples is probably due to the tendency of the Fourth Evangelist to push them into the background and place Jesus in the spotlight alone; on this "christocentric" thrust, see Heising, *Die Botschaft*, 79–80; Schnackenburg, *Das Johannesevangelium*, 2. 22–23; Lindars, *The Gospel of John*, 243; Haenchen, *John 1*, 272.

[291] In the primitive tradition the twelve baskets may have been meant to correspond to the twelve disciples; this is the one case where symbolism in numbers is a real possibility in the feeding story. While such an allusion would remain fairly clear in the Synoptic versions, it would be lost in the Fourth Gospel, which does not mention the group of the Twelve until the end of chap. 6 (6:70); on this see Schnackenburg, *Das Johannesevangelium*, 2. 23.—As for the mention of the number of persons who ate, both of the Marcan (and Matthean) versions place the number at the end of the story; along with the number of baskets filled with leftovers, this number emphasizes the spectacular nature of the miracle. Along with Lindars (*The Gospel of John*, 242), I think that John (and independently Luke) apparently felt that the mention of the number of people fed was awkwardly positioned at the end of the story and so moved this detail back to the point at which Jesus commands the crowd to recline. This also left John free to end the story with the reaction of the crowd (6:14–15).

[292] For a strong argument that John 6:14–15 is the creation of the Evangelist, see Schnackenburg, *Das Johannesevangelium*, 2. 23–27; likewise Schnelle, *Antidocetic Christology*, 103.

[293] So, e.g., Pesch, *Das Markusevangelium*, 1. 356: "The text [of the feeding of the multitude] is documentation for early Jewish-Christian . . . christology, not for the history of Jesus."

[294] Gift miracles in the Elijah-Elisha cycle include, besides 2 Kgs 4:42–44 (the twenty loaves that feed one hundred men), 1 Kgs 17:8–16 (during a drought, the jar of meal and the cruse of oil of the widow of Zarephath do not fail to supply food) and 2 Kgs 4:1–7 (a jar of oil fills all the other jars available to pay a debt of a widow of one of

the sons of the prophets). Further parallels in rabbinic stories and tales from many different cultures are supplied by van der Loos, *The Miracles of Jesus*, 624–27. Parallels from the Greco-Roman world in particular (including rabbinic literature) are discussed by van Cangh, "La multiplication des pains," 309–21. On p. 321 van Cangh comes to the conclusion that the best one can say about all the proposed parallels is that they demonstrate a widespread but vague pattern common to many popular cultures. But van Cangh claims that one cannot locate any precise parallel to the Gospel feeding stories in contemporary Greco-Roman and Jewish writings.

[295] The man in the story also brings something else, but the reading of the Hebrew text is disputed at this point; see John Gray, *I & II Kings* (OTL; Philadelphia: Westminster, 1963) 449 n. d.

[296] For a slightly different enumeration of parallels (focusing on Mark 6:32–44 alone), see Pesch, *Das Markusevangelium*, 1. 354; cf. Heising, *Die Botschaft*, 17–20, 31–38; van Cangh, "La multiplication des pains," 323–24. The strong similarities between the Gospel narratives of the feeding and 2 Kgs 4:42–44 argue well for the influence of the latter on the former; so rightly Haenchen (*John 1*, 271–72), *contra* Bultmann (*Das Evangelium des Johannes*, 157 n. 3), who does not consider the question in detail, but rather in customary fashion dismisses it with a rhetorical wave of the hand.

[297] So Guelich, *Mark 1–8:26*, 344; similarly, Roloff (*Das Kerygma*, 265), who claims however that Elisha-typology is to be found only in the Johannine version of the feeding story, and there only in individual motifs (the barley and the lad). The various parallels noted in the main text make this claim unlikely.

[298] It is typical of a number of treatments that, e.g., Heising (*Die Botschaft*, 19) emphasizes the similarities between the Elisha and Gospel narratives, while mentioning differences only in passing. Heising also places great weight on the supposed contacts between the Gospel narratives of Jesus feeding the multitude and the OT traditions of Moses feeding Israel with manna and quail in the wilderness (pp. 21–30). The central message of the Gospel story thus becomes the certification of Jesus as the new Moses of the end time, the eschatological prophet like Moses (pp. 51–60). While the Fourth Evangelist does develop the theme of Moses-and-the-manna, I do not think that it looms large in the primitive form of the Gospel feeding story.

[299] On this see Haenchen, *John 1*, 275–76.

[300] See Lindars, *The Gospel of John*, 242.

[301] Against the eucharistic interpretation in the Marcan versions are Boobyer, "The Eucharistic Interpretation," 161–71; Roloff, *Das Kerygma*, 241–51; Fowler, *Loaves and Fishes*, 139–47 (at least on the first reading of the Gospel); Neugebauer, "Die wunderbare Speisung," 269; Gundry, *Mark*, 331–32, 397. One should note that at least some of the critics who deny eucharistic allusions in the Marcan versions (e.g., Gundry) do so with a view to rejecting the larger claim that the story of Jesus feeding the multitude was simply created out of the eucharistic tradition of the early church. But denying the latter claim need not entail denying the former. Boobyer's treatment suffers from a different kind of difficulty. In his criticism of any eucharistic interpretation, Boobyer tends to push together two different questions: whether the feeding miracle itself was understood as a eucharist of sorts and whether the feeding miracle was secondarily given some eucharistic allusions or overtones by the later Christian tradition or by the evangelists. I would answer no to the former and yes to the latter. Another difficulty is that both Boobyer and Gundry take too literalistic an approach to the question of whether there are eucharistic allusions in the feeding miracle: e.g., they claim that the

presence of fish and the absence of wine in the feeding miracle preclude eucharistic allusions. But this is to confuse an allusion to a different event with a retelling of the same event in an alternate form.

In favor of sacramental overtones, in varying degrees, in the Marcan and/or the Johannine version are Richardson, "The Feeding," 146–49; Taylor, *The Gospel According to St. Mark*, 324, 359–60; Clavier, "La multiplication des pains," 440; Shaw, "The Marcan Feeding Narratives," 268–78 (with the suggestion that the first Marcan version refers more to the Last Supper, the second more to the eucharist of the church); Dodd, *Historical Tradition*, 200–205; van Iersel, "Die wunderbare Speisung," 167–94 (one of the fullest defenses of eucharistic allusions); Hebert, "History," 68, 69–70; Heising, *Die Botschaft*, 61–68; Brown, *The Gospel According to John*, 1. 246–47; Denis, "La section des pains," 174–79; Kertelge, *Die Wunder Jesu*, 140; van Cangh, "Le thème des poissons," 71, 80–81; idem, "La multiplication des pains," 330–34; Patsch, "Abendmahlsterminologie," 210–31; Lindars, *The Gospel of John*, 239; de la Potterie, "La multiplication des pains," 317–19 (claiming that the presence of a eucharistic reference is an almost unanimous opinion among commentators); Donfried, "The Feeding Narratives," 101–2; Masuda, "The Good News," 201–3 (only in Mark's redaction, not in his tradition); Bassler, "The Parable of the Loaves," 162 (only in the case of the "informed" or historical reader, not the "ideal" reader of modern reader-response criticism). Pesch's view is complex: on the one hand, the first Marcan version had no eucharistic overtones in the pre-Marcan tradition; that the Evangelist interpreted it eucharistically can be seen only from 8:14–21 (*Das Markusevangelium*, 1. 356). On the other hand, the second Marcan version already had eucharistic overtones in the tradition (pp. 402–4). Guelich (*Mark 1–8:26*, 343) prefers to speak of an "indirect influence" of the eucharistic tradition in the first Marcan version, which becomes more evident in the second Marcan version.

[302] For fuller comparisons between the various forms of the feeding miracle and the various forms of the Last Supper tradition, see van Iersel, "Die wunderbare Speisung," 167–94; Patsch, "Abendmahlsterminologie," 210–31 (with a better sense of the fluid nature of the oral eucharistic traditions that might have influenced the versions of the feeding miracle). All I am attempting here is a rough comparison between Mark 8:6–7 and what would have been the substance of the oral eucharistic tradition in the first Christian generation. As we can see from Mark and Paul, different versions of the eucharistic tradition circulated in the first generation; even the same church or group of Christians would probably have known and used different versions. At such an early stage Christians probably felt no need to proclaim the tradition in exactly the same words each time they used it. Consequently, we cannot be sure what form or forms of the eucharistic tradition would have been known to the person who formulated the tradition behind Mark 6:32–44. Granted this fluid situation, I view *eucharisteō* ("give thanks") and *eulogeō* ("bless") as functionally interchangeable, since both probably reflect the Aramaic pa''el *bārēk* (perfect) or *měbārēk* (participle) in the earliest Aramaic eucharistic traditions; cf. Brown, *The Gospel According to John*, 1. 234; Patsch, "Abendmahlsterminologie," 217–19.

[303] The point I am making here is that the primitive form of the feeding story seems to have been reordered in Mark 8:6–7 to create a second, separate act of Jesus pronouncing a blessing over some foodstuff and then having it distributed for others to eat. Such a reordering that creates two parallel actions of Jesus over food to be distributed is significant, despite the self-evident truth that fish is not wine. We are speaking here of allusions and structural parallels, not word-for-word identity. Gundry (*Mark*, 331–32, 397) seems too intent on demanding the latter; in his treatment of the relation of the

feeding stories in Mark to the eucharistic tradition he is, in my opinion, too literalistic and heavy-handed in weighing possible allusions.

[304] At times commentators see in the verb-plus-direct object in Mark 8:7 (*eulogēsas auta*, literally: "having blessed them") a different and more Greco-Roman concept of Jesus' words than the *eucharistēsas* ("having given thanks" [with no direct object]) of 8:6. The latter supposedly mirrors the Jewish form of "blessing," in which the blessing is addressed to God, who is blessed and thanked for the food over which the blessing is said. In contrast, *eulogēsas auta* is thought to express the pagan idea of directly blessing the food. While this is possible, the very fact that *eucharistēsas* stands in parallel position to *eulogēsas auta* leads me to think that the latter is to be understood in this particular context to mean "having pronounced a blessing [addressed to God] over them [i.e., the fish]." But I readily admit that the matter is far from clear, and the "Jewish-versus-pagan" interpretation may well be correct.

[305] "Giving thanks" (*eucharistēsas*) is also used for Jesus' action over the bread in the Pauline and Lucan versions of the supper (1 Cor 11:24; Luke 22:19). There is no mention of giving thanks or blessing over the cup in the Pauline and Lucan versions, since the cup word is introduced with the laconic "likewise the cup after they had eaten, saying. . . ."

[306] I say "some truth," because the observation, even before it is confronted with the factors I raise in the main text, must confront the objection of van Cangh, "La multiplication des pains," 330–31: It is true that Jesus' central action in the feeding of the multitude is based upon the ritual of a formal Jewish meal, but the same is true of Jesus' central action at the Last Supper. The problem consists precisely in determining the exact relationship, if any, between the eucharistic texts and the texts narrating the feeding miracle. As van Cangh observes (p. 331), "the parallel [between these two sets of texts] is too precise to be explained by mere coincidence. The four verbs that are characteristic of the accounts of the institution [of the eucharist] . . . are found associated together in the same way only in our narrative of the multiplication of the loaves."

[307] See *m. Ber.* 6:1 and especially 6:7: "This is the general rule; where there is a main food and aught that is but an accompaniment to it, the Benediction should be said over the main food and it need not be said over the accompaniment" (Danby translation). On all this see Roloff, *Das Kerygma*, 244; Guelich, *Mark 1–8:26*, 407. Referring in the main text to the eucharistic tradition, I use the phrase "the narrative" (in the singular) of Jesus' actions, even though in the original historical event (if we may presume historicity for the moment for the sake of argument) a meal would have separated the action over the bread from the action Jesus performed over the wine after he and his disciples had eaten. However, even in the two forms of the Last Supper narrative that preserve the memory that a meal separated the bread action from the wine action (i.e., 1 Cor 11:23–26 and Luke 22:19–20), the two separate actions have in fact been drawn together in parallel fashion in one very concise narrative. This tendency reaches its culmination in the Marcan-Matthean form of the narrative, where no mention is made of a meal intervening; the natural impression of a reader who knew only Mark or Matthew would be that the wine action followed immediately upon the bread action (though that is not explicitly said).

[308] As van Iersel observes ("Die wunderbare Speisung," 167–69), anyone who wishes to deny a eucharistic reference in the Gospel feeding stories must explain why all the evangelists bother to spell out in detail Jesus' actions over the bread—a point that is a fortiori a problem for those who stress that these were the common actions of a host at a formal Jewish meal. If they were so common, why are they spelled out in this story in

particular? Moreover, if we dispense with any eucharistic reference, we are hard-pressed to answer an obvious question: Why was this one miracle story so important to the early church that three different versions developed in the oral tradition and six versions appear in the Gospels?

[309] While there have been scholarly attempts to deny that John 6:51–58 refers to the eucharist (see, e.g., Koester, "John Six," 419–37), the vast majority of commentators read it as a statement on the eucharist, whether one attributes these verses to the Fourth Evangelist or to the final redactor of the Fourth Gospel. The abrupt change of vocabulary and ideas starting in 6:52–53 is simply too stark and the connections with eucharistic traditions both inside and outside the NT (e.g., Ignatius of Antioch's use of "flesh" rather than "body") are simply too strong to read 6:51–58 as just a metaphorical description of receiving Jesus' message in faith. On this see Schnelle, *Antidocetic Christology*, 194–208. To be sure, the question whether 6:51–58 comes from the Fourth Evangelist or the final redactor continues to be debated. For a stylistic argument in favor of 6:51–58 coming from the Evangelist, see Schweizer, "Joh 6,51c–58," 274; for a structural argument, see Segalla, "La complessa struttura letteraria," 68–89. Schnelle likewise favors the view that the eucharistic section of the bread of life discourse comes from the Evangelist, who is giving a eucharistic "twist" to traditional Johannine material.

[310] Schnelle (*Antidocetic Christology*, 101–2) insists that the use of the verb *eucharistein* without an object in John 6:11 shows "that the tradition of the Lord's Supper has affected 6:1–15," since the absolute use of *eucharistein* in the Four Gospels (and Paul) is restricted to the Last Supper narratives and the feeding stories. Dodd (*The Interpretation of the Fourth Gospel*, 333) thinks that the mention of Passover in John 6:4 indicates "that the evangelist intended at the outset to give a hint of the eucharistic significance of the narrative which follows."

[311] For example, in the first Marcan version of the feeding miracle, when the question of how the people are to be fed is raised between Jesus and his disciples, the disciples ask: "Shall we go and buy two-hundred-denarii-worth of bread and give it to them to eat?" Notice, only bread is mentioned in the suggestion. Jesus responds with a question that again mentions only bread: "How many loaves of bread do you have?" It is only after the disciples check that the first mention of fish is made: "Five [loaves] and two fish." Jesus' central action in v 41 begins with a mention of both loaves and fish, but the focus of the verse quickly narrows to the loaves. Only at the end of the verse, almost as an afterthought, are the two fish mentioned. Verse 43 likewise focuses on the bread and mentions the fish as an afterthought: "And they collected pieces of the broken bread, twelve baskets full, and [some] of the fish." If one reads v 44 according to Codex Vaticanus and Codex Alexandrinus, the story ends with a final emphasis on the loaves to the exclusion of the fish: "And those who ate the loaves of bread were five thousand men." (See Metzger [*Textual Commentary*, 92] on the text-critical problem in v 44.)

As I indicate in the main text, the second Marcan version restricts mention of the fish to a single verse (8:7); the rest of the story speaks only of loaves of bread and broken pieces of bread. In John's version, Jesus introduces the theme of bread (but not fish) by asking Philip (6:5): "Whence shall we buy loaves of bread that these people may eat?" Philip dutifully replies in terms of loaves of bread (v 7). It is Andrew in v 8 who mentions for the first time five loaves of bread and two fish. In v 11, Jesus' actions are first narrated totally in terms of the loaves of bread; only at the end of the verse do we hear what sounds like a vague afterthought: "And [some] of the fish, as much as they wanted." The subsequent collection of the leftovers is narrated entirely in terms of the pieces of broken bread (vv 12–13); no mention of fish is made. In short, then, in all three primary versions of the feeding story, there is a notable emphasis on the bread as opposed to the fish. One gets the impression that the fish are mentioned in the present versions of the story simply because they were part of the primitive story (and possibly the original historical event, if one occurred).

[312] With reference to the eucharistic traditions in particular, Kertelge (*Die Wunder Jesu*, 135–36) seeks to strike a careful balance. After an examination of the first Marcan version, he concludes that allusions to the Last Supper tradition are present in Mark and were present in the pre-Marcan tradition, but that they are secondary in nature and did not belong to the earliest form of the feeding story. In my view, the very fact that a number of capable critics deny any presence of eucharistic references in the Marcan versions indicates that, present or absent, the eucharistic allusions are not so massive and all-pervasive that they can explain the origin of the story of the feeding of the multitude. Van Iersel ("Die wunderbare Speisung," 182–83) suggests three reasons in particular why it is unlikely that the Gospel feeding story arose simply and solely as a cult legend connected with the Christian eucharist: (1) the presence of the fish motif in the miracle story, a motif absent in the eucharistic tradition; (2) the absence of the cup motif in the miracle story, a motif present in the eucharistic tradition; (3) the failure of the feeding miracle to reach the fully rounded form of a miracle story, a failure due to the fact that secondarily the miracle story developed into a type of cult legend (I find this third reason debatable).

Similarly, I do not think that the Gospel feeding miracle can be derived simply and solely from the Elisha-story of 2 Kgs 4:42–44. While I disagree with Roloff (*Das Kerygma*, 265), who claims that there are no allusions to the Elisha-story in the Synoptic versions of the feeding story, the very fact that he can maintain his position points out that the Elisha-story is not so all-pervasive in the Gospel narratives of Jesus feeding the multitude that the former can be taken to be the all-sufficient origin of the latter.

[313] Here I disagree with Heising (*Die Botschaft*, 56–60), who maintains that the literary genre of a "kerygmatic miracle story," showing in this case heavy influence from the stories of Moses providing manna to Israel in the wilderness and Elisha feeding one hundred men with twenty loaves, makes any judgment about the historicity of the Gospel feeding story impossible. For him, an a priori agnosticism is the only possible stance. It is his basic proposition that a form-critical category can somehow determine a judgment on historicity that I disagree with, as I have made clear from the beginning of my inventory of Gospel miracle stories. In this particular case, Heising allows for massive influence of the Moses-manna motif in the primitive Gospel story, something that I do not see or grant. Heising's agnostic approach seems to give way to a total rejection of historicity when he suggests (p. 59 n. 72) that the Gospel feeding story is best seen as a "Christ story" that belongs *entirely* (his emphasis) to the realm of the post-Easter proclamation of the risen and exalted Lord. Heising took a more cautious approach in his earlier work, "Exegese und Theologie," 80–96.

[314] Perhaps the best attempt to explain the presence of the fish in the feeding story on the basis of OT and pseudepigraphic traditions is that of van Cangh, "Le thème des poissons," 71–83; his position is also summarized in his "La multiplication des pains," 334–37. But even in these articles van Cangh must grasp at straws: e.g., he tries to associate the theme of fish with the theme of quail in the wilderness by pointing out that, in chap. 16 of the Book of Exodus, God sent both manna and quail to feed the Israelites in the wilderness (cf. Richardson, "The Feeding," 145) and that, in Gen 1:20–23, God created both birds and fish (including the sea monsters) on the fifth day. In the pseudepigraphic material that van Cangh reviews the most promising text is *2 Apoc. Bar.* 29:3–8: the Messiah is revealed, Behemoth (apparently a land monster)

comes forth from his place, Leviathan comes up from the sea, and both Behemoth and Leviathan serve as food for those who have survived the calamities of the last days (v 4). Great abundance of fruits, wine, and dew is also provided (vv 5–7). In v 8 the manna from heaven is given again. However, one must remember that the *Syriac Apocalypse of Baruch* was written somewhere around the beginning of the 2d century A.D., and feeding off of Behemoth and Leviathan (along with fruit, wine, dew, and manna) at the end of time is a far cry from eating bread and fish in a "wilderness" or deserted spot by the Sea of Galilee. Much more fanciful is the attempt by Vogel ("Le repas sacré," 1–26) to explain the fish in the Gospel meal stories as reflecting a sacred meal of fish celebrated by 1st-century Christians.

[315] Cf. the application of the criteria of historicity to the feeding story by de la Potterie, "La multiplication des pains," 322–27. While I basically agree with de la Potterie's use of the criteria of multiple attestation and coherence, I would not invoke as he does the supposed criterion of necessary explanation (pp. 323–24), which he takes over from René Latourelle (see, e.g., Latourelle's "Critères d'authenticité historique des Evangiles," *Greg* 55 [1974] 609–37, esp. 628). As I explained in Volume One of *A Marginal Jew* (p. 194 n. 66), I do not think that "necessary explanation" is properly speaking a criterion of historicity alongside the other particular criteria (e.g., embarrassment, discontinuity, multiple attestation, and coherence) used in the quest for the historical Jesus. Rather, all logical argumentation works with the postulate of a necessary explanation to be sought. "Necessary explanation" is just another form of the principle of the sufficient reason, an overarching philosophical principle presupposed in all forms of argumentation, be they strictly historical or not. As a matter of fact, every serious scholar who has ever written on the historical Jesus would claim that he or she has presented the truly necessary explanation of the data concerning Jesus. The principle of necessary explanation does not in itself adjudicate such opposing claims. Moreover, de la Potterie invokes in his argument from necessary explanation material that may come from the early Christian tradition or the redaction of the evangelists rather than from some original historical event. For example, the enthusiasm of the crowd that hails Jesus as prophet and king (John 6:14–15) may be a contribution of the Johannine tradition or John's redaction. Similarly, we cannot be sure from a historical point of view that the feeding of the multitude was closely connected with Peter's confession of faith (at Caesarea Philippi à la Mark or at Capernaum à la John?). Such a connection certainly existed in an early cycle of stories about Jesus' Galilean ministry that was known both to the Marcan and to the Johannine tradition. But this cycle of stories is already a product of an early Christian crafting of the tradition; one cannot automatically move from it to an original chain of historical events with a clear line of cause and effect. Like almost all the other miracle stories in the Gospels, the feeding of the multitude cannot be assigned to one set time in the ministry of Jesus with any certainty or even high probability.

[316] Lindars (*The Gospel of John*, 238) considers this argument especially weighty: ". . . the account is so well attested that there is no need to doubt that a real incident lies behind it."

[317] This is a widely accepted aspect of the historical Jesus, supported by critics as various as Joachim Jeremias (*New Testament Theology*, 115–16), Günther Bornkamm (*Jesus of Nazareth*, 80–81), Norman Perrin (*Rediscovering the Teaching of Jesus*, 102–8), E. P. Sanders (*Jesus and Judaism*, 208–9, though more restrained on the issue than many others), and John Dominic Crossan (*The Historical Jesus*, 332–33, 341–44).

Sanders does well to issue a word of caution about sweeping statements concerning Jesus' table fellowship and its meaning. As most questers for the historical Jesus admit in their more sober moments, the Gospel material on table fellowship that has a good claim to historicity is not plentiful. Some of the narrative material in particular may be redactional (e.g., Luke 15:1–2). Nevertheless, among the available Gospel texts are some sayings that we have already examined at length and judged historical: (1) Matt 11:18–19 presents Jesus as mocked as a glutton and wine-drinker, a friend (in this context, especially through eating and drinking) of the socially despised toll collectors and "sinners" (non-observant Jews who had broken with the covenant community of Israel and were considered equivalent to Gentiles). Seen in conjunction with v 18, this portrait of Jesus in v 19 contains implicitly an unfavorable contrast with John the Baptist, who was an abstemious ascetic, but so much so that some judged him crazy ("he has a demon"). The criterion of embarrassment argues for the historicity of this two-part saying; the early church was hardly interested in creating mocking caricatures of its Risen Lord as a bon vivant who suffered by comparison with John the Baptist. What is important in this saying is that it attests not only to Jesus' frequent appearance at festive meals but more importantly to his use of such a joyous context to reach out to the social and religious "lowlifes" of Jewish Palestine. (2) Jesus' reason for using precisely the context of a festive meal for such outreach becomes clear in a second authentic saying (Matt 8:11–12 || Luke 13:28–29), in which Jesus prophesies that many will come from east and west to recline at the heavenly banquet with the Israelite patriarchs, while those who have rejected his ministry will find themselves in turn rejected and so excluded from the final banquet. Jesus' use of banquets as a vehicle of his ministry among his fellow Jews is thus to be seen as a preparation for and an anticipation of the final banquet in the kingdom. (3) This link between present and future banquet is confirmed by Jesus' affirmation at the Last Supper (Mark 14:25) that he would not drink wine (the sign of a festive meal) again until he did so in the kingdom of God (fully come). Thus, the "Last Supper" was meant by Jesus to be literally the last of a whole series of meals celebrating in anticipation the joy of the heavenly banquet even as they opened up participation in the banquet to one and all, even those who were morally or socially suspect.

These various sayings are supported by narrative material found in both Mark (2:13–17, the meal with toll collectors and sinners after the call of Levi) and L (Luke 19:1–10, Jesus' request for and acceptance of hospitality and table fellowship from Zacchaeus, the chief toll collector of Jericho; on Zacchaeus see John P. Meier, "The Bible as a Source for Theology," *The Catholic Theological Society of America Proceedings 43* [1988] 4 n. 11). It is intriguing to note that, while we have very few names of male disciples of Jesus in the Synoptic Gospels outside the circle of the Twelve, two that we do have (Levi and Zacchaeus) both belong to toll collectors, associated in the Gospels with the theme of table fellowship and hospitality. The claim that Jesus celebrated table fellowship (most notably with toll collectors and sinners) as a sign and anticipation of the final banquet in the kingdom is thus supported by the criterion of multiple attestation of both sources (Mark, Q, and L) and forms (sayings and narratives).

Jesus' table fellowship with sinners is also supported by the criteria of embarrassment and discontinuity. As Sanders (*Jesus and Judaism*, 176) observes, "a high tolerance for sinners was not a characteristic of the early church, as far as we can know it." The early Christians, as we read in Paul's letters, saw themselves as "the holy ones" of the end time, and Paul proclaims loudly that certain morally or religiously offensive actions (incest, partaking in pagan cult and cultic meals, lack of concern for the poor at the eucharist) exclude the offender from church fellowship in general (1 Cor 5:1–5; 2 Cor 2:5–11) and from the eucharist in particular (1 Cor 10:14–22; 11:17–34). Paul's churches were not the only ones to separate offending members from fellowship (which no doubt included table fellowship); denial of fellowship was a known mechanism in the Matthean and Johannine churches as well (Matt 18:15–20; 1 John 2:19; 5:16–17; 3 John 9–10). The early church, as a missionary group anxious to recommend itself to the society it wished to win over, realized the importance of "looking good"—a concern apparently not high on the list of Jesus' priorities. This in itself may explain why material about Jesus' "open commensality" (to use Crossan's phrase), which included sinners, is not widely attested in the Gospels; it did not jibe with the church's own practice.

[318] In the Synoptic Gospels (the only place in the NT in which their relationship with Jesus is noted), the "toll collectors" (*hoi telōnai*) are most likely minor functionaries who collected the payment of tolls or customs (indirect taxes) on goods being transported across borders; hence we hear of them in connection with commercial centers at border crossings (Capernaum and Jericho). In older translations of the Bible and in older biblical commentaries they were often referred to as "publicans" or "tax collectors." On this see John R. Donahue, "Tax Collector," *Anchor Bible Dictionary*, 6. 337–38. "Sinners" is a very broad term that includes anyone who was viewed by Jewish society in general to be living a life antithetical to God's will as expressed in the Law. In particular, it may refer to those Jews who had abandoned practice of the Law and lived like Gentiles. On the problem of identifying "sinners" in the Gospels, see E. P. Sanders, "Sin, Sinners (New Testament)," *Anchor Bible Dictionary*, 6. 43–44. Sanders observes (p. 43): "It is probable that Luke has expanded the theme of Jesus' appeal to toll collectors and sinners, but the theme itself reflects the ministry of Jesus."

[319] For a survey of theories, see van der Loos, *The Miracles of Jesus*, 627–31; Heising, *Die Botschaft*, 56 n. 71 (continuing on pp. 57–59); Roloff, *Das Kerygma*, 245 n. 152; de la Potterie, "La multiplication des pains," 304–8. Heinrich Eberhard Gottlob Paulus, a 19th-century rationalist, championed the "purely natural" explanation of Jesus setting an example by sharing his bread, with the edified audience, especially the rich among them, then following suit. Karl Friedrich Bahrdt favored the view that "Jesus was standing at the secret entrance to a cave, from which intimates kept on handing Him bread which had been stacked in the cave beforehand" (van der Loos, p. 628). Pierre Nahor suggested that devout rich ladies provided the loaves and fish to prevent the crowd from going hungry. It is against any and all such rational explanations (explanations that try to keep most of the story but find a way to omit the miraculous element) that David Friedrich Strauss championed his "mythological" approach to the Gospel miracle of the feeding of the multitude: the miracle is a clothing of early Christian ideas in garb that looks like history. Rejecting the mythological approach, Christian Hermann Weisse suggested that the Gospel feeding story derives from a parable of the historical Jesus. With his suggestion that Jesus distributed morsels of bread, Albert Schweitzer combined a naturalistic explanation with his own theological emphasis on Jesus' ideas of messiahship and imminent eschatology. Ethelbert Stauffer, basing himself on parallels from Qumran, maintained that the Gospel story reflects a Passover feast that Jesus celebrated in Galilee in A.D. 31 (one year before his death), a feast Jesus pointedly observed not in the Jerusalem temple but in a celebration without sacrifice in Galilee. Hugh Montefiore believed that the Gospel feeding miracle reflected an attempted revolt in the wilderness. Faced with all these different reconstructions, some highly imaginative, I think it best to keep one's claims modest.

[320] An alternate version of this suggestion (noted in passing by Lindars, *The Gospel of John*, 238–39) is that the lad mentioned in John 6:9 set an example by sharing what he had, and everyone else followed suit. Lindars adds his judgment: "This is the 'lunch basket' theory; it can scarcely be regarded as a serious possibility." See also the criticism of Hebert, "History," 68–69.

[321] Albert Schweitzer, *Geschichte der Leben-Jesu-Forschung* (Siebenstern-Taschenbuch

77/78 and 79/80; 2 vols.; Munich/Hamburg: Siebenstern Taschenbuch, 1966, originally 1906) 2. 430. Hebert ("History," 69) is more sympathetic to Schweitzer's approach than to Paulus's, but he feels that it is still inadequate.

[322] Cf. Haenchen, *John 1*, 276: ". . . the primitive community combined a memory
of a meal of Jesus and his disciples beside the Sea of Galilee with the OT story of Elijah
[*sic*, for Elisha]. . . ." See also Hebert, "History," 68: "A real incident must surely be
behind the narrative, but it has been so transformed that it is impossible for us to say
exactly 'what happened.' " Schenke (*Die wunderbare Brotvermehrung*, 116–17) feels that
all one can say is that behind the story of Jesus feeding the multitude lies Jesus' well-
attested habit of holding meals with all levels of society.

[323] The point is well put by de la Potterie, "La multiplication des pains," 308: "Indeed, it is not the task of a historian to declare an event miraculous."—For an attempt
to place the feeding of the multitude within the context of Jesus' Galilean ministry,
leading up to Peter's confession of faith at Caesarea Philippi, see Clavier, "La multiplication des pains," 445–49. In my opinion, Clavier is too confident about our ability to
reconstruct the order of events in the Galilean ministry. When we arrive at the most
primitive form of the feeding story available to us, it is an isolated pericope with no
indication of its place within the larger flow of Jesus' ministry in Galilee.

[324] Besides acting as a summary, this section seeks to give a final reply to the questions raised in Chapter 17, section II. C., "Keeping Our Questions Modest."

CONCLUSION TO VOLUME TWO

I. SETTING THE STAGE[1]

Volume One of *A Marginal Jew* simply set the stage on which the adult Jesus of Volume Two would step. Even after the prolonged investigation of Volume One, the stage setting remained spartan: somewhere around 7 or 6 B.C., a few years before the death of Herod the Great (4 B.C.), a Jew named Yēshûaʿ (= Jesus) was born, most likely in Nazareth of Galilee, though possibly in Bethlehem of Judea. At any rate, Jesus certainly grew up in Nazareth, a small hilltown in Lower Galilee, as can be seen from the fact that "Nazorean," "Nazarene," or "of Nazareth" became almost his second name. His mother was named Miryam (= Mary) and his putative father Yôsēf (= Joseph). The Synoptic Gospels name four brothers of Jesus: Jacob (= James), Joseph, Judah (= Jude), and Simon; sisters are mentioned but go unnamed.

The presence in the immediate family circle of so many personal names that hark back to the glorious days of the patriarchs, the exodus, and the conquest of the Promised Land ("Jesus" being a shortened form of the Hebrew name of "Joshua") is noteworthy. It may point to a family milieu that shared in the reawakening of Jewish national and religious identity in Galilee, a milieu that longed for the restoration of Israel in all its glory. Such expectations may have been especially prominent in Jesus' family if—as seems likely—Joseph (Jesus' putative father) was thought to be a descendant of King David.

Jesus' family would have been imbued with an "uncomplicated" type of Jewish piety probably widespread among the peasants of Lower Galilee. Ordinary Galilean Jews from the lower strata of society, particularly in the countryside, would have had no time for or interest in the theological niceties, the special observances, and the fierce disputes of the Essenes, the Pharisees, or the Sadducees. For these Galilean Jews of the countryside, fidelity to the Jewish religion meant fidelity to the basics spelled out in the Mosaic Law: circumcision, observance of the Sabbath, observance of kosher food laws, and pilgrimage to the Jerusalem temple, whose sacrificial ritual during the great feasts was the high point of the annual cycle of their religious life. Surrounded as they were by a fair number of Gentiles and a fair amount of Hellenistic culture (as close as Herod Antipas' capital at Sepphoris), these Galilean Jews of the countryside would cling tenaciously to the basics of their religion as "boundary symbols" reinforcing their identity.

As the firstborn of his family, Jesus would naturally have received special attention from his parents. He was trained as a woodworker, presumably following in the footsteps of Joseph, who apparently died before Jesus began his public ministry. Jesus' mother Mary, his brothers, and his sisters were alive during his ministry, and at least some of them survived into the early days of the church. Signs of tension between Jesus and his family surface in the Gospels once the ministry begins. John's Gospel goes so far as to make the blunt claim that "not even his brothers believed in him" (John 7:5). This statement is all the more startling because one of the brothers, Jacob (= James), later became the leader of the Christian Jews in Jerusalem and died a martyr's death.

Jesus spoke Aramaic as his ordinary language, with perhaps a smattering of Greek picked up for commercial and social purposes. Knowledge of the sacred language of Hebrew was probably gained by listening to and perhaps being taught to read the Scriptures in the synagogue in Nazareth. If more formal instruction in the sacred writings and traditions of his people was arranged for by Joseph, it would have remained on a fairly elementary level; there is no indication that Jesus received "higher" education. Whether he could read at all is debatable, though I incline to the view that he was literate. For the most part, the Jesus of the public ministry would have delivered his teaching orally in Aramaic to ordinary Jews; in disputes with learned scribes or pious Pharisees he might have quoted the Scriptures in Hebrew.

Jesus' position as the woodworker of Nazareth would have assured him a modest but average standard of living, as compared to that of most other Jews in the Galilean countryside. He would seem poor in our eyes, but he was no poorer than the vast majority of Galilean Jews. His socioeconomic status as well as his status as a pious Jewish layman from a pious Jewish family also assured him that modicum of honor in an honor/shame society without which ordinary people would have found existence very difficult.

One characteristic, though, made him stand out in his town. As far as we can tell, Jesus never married, a point that automatically made him atypical, ab-normal (in the root sense of the word), and to that extent "marginal" to mainstream Jewish society. Nevertheless, while this choice was highly unusual among the Jews of his time, figures like the Baptist and some of the Essenes show that it was not unheard of. Jesus' early adulthood was otherwise unremarkable. With almost all of his life spent under the notably long and relatively peaceful reign of Herod Antipas, the tetrarch of Galilee (reigned 4 B.C.–A.D. 39), Jesus could probably have chosen to live out his days in the small-town tranquillity and obscurity of Nazareth.

But Jesus chose otherwise. Somewhere around A.D. 28, Jesus broke with his honorable though modest socioeconomic status, his settled life in Nazareth, and his close family ties to undertake the unusual role of an itinerant celibate layman proclaiming the imminent arrival of the kingdom of God. Being about thirty-four years old at the time he began his ministry, Jesus would have already seemed unusual or socially marginal in the eyes of his fellow Jews by his conscious choice of a celibate state. He now made himself even more unusual or marginal by his consciously chosen ministry of an itinerant prophet of the end time. He had obviously lost the honor accruing to his former state of life. Whether he gained a new kind of honor in the eyes of at least some Jews depended on whether or not his audience believed him.

It is at this point, after the stage has been set, that Volume Two begins. Actually, as Volume Two gets under way, we must first back up slightly to consider someone who for Jesus was much more than a stage prop: John the Baptist.

II. COMING ON STAGE AND BEGINNING THE DRAMA

The public ministry of the marginal Jew named Jesus takes its beginning from the public ministry of another marginal Jew, John the Baptist. Without John as his mentor and matrix, the Jesus of the public ministry is hardly intelligible. Somewhere around A.D. 28, while Antipas was tetrarch of Galilee and Perea, Pontius Pilate prefect of the Roman province of Judea (A.D. 26–36), and Joseph Caiaphas high priest in Jerusalem (A.D. 18–36), an ascetic Jewish prophet named John appeared in the lower Jordan valley, proclaiming an imminent, fiery judgment that was about to engulf all Israel. Protection from the wrath to come could be gained only by repentance, reform of one's life, and a special water baptism received at the hands of John (hence his surname "the Baptist"). According to John, the final judgment was to be administered by an eschatological figure whom John vaguely referred to as "the stronger one" or "the one who comes." This mysterious figure would show his superiority to John by baptizing with the holy spirit instead of with mere water.

Many Jews flocked to the Jordan for the protective water baptism of John, who at the very least looked like *a* if not *the* prophet sent by God to prepare his sinful people for the last days. Among the Jews who accepted John's call to national repentance was Jesus, who submitted to John's baptism in the Jordan River ca. A.D. 28. Jesus therefore knew John, accepted his eschatological message and baptism, and in that sense at least became his disciple. Whether John personally knew Jesus any more than he knew all the other Jews he baptized is unclear. If Jesus stayed on for a while in the inner circle of John's disciples, John would obviously have come to know Jesus personally and have had a still greater impact on him. Such an "apprenticeship" among John's disciples is often taken for granted by critics. It seems likely, although strictly speaking it cannot be proven.

Whether immediately after his baptism or after a stay in John's entourage, Jesus emerged from the Baptist's movement to inaugurate his own "public" ministry—a ministry, indeed, more "public" than John's in that it knew no geographical limitation within Israel. Moving from the Jordan valley to Galilee, Jesus reached out to Jews of all stripes, the respectable and (especially) the sinful, the rich and (especially) the poor,[2] as he journeyed through Galilee, the Decapolis, Perea, Judea, and particularly to Israel's spiritual capital, Jerusalem. Even Samaritans and pagans were not denied passing contact.

With this change in and expansion of venue came also a more expansive message. To be sure, Jesus never totally broke with or "apostatized" from the Baptist and his program. One could still hear from Jesus John's message of imminent judgment. The supposedly meek and gentle Jesus was quite capable of thundering woes against the Galilean towns that failed to heed his call to repentance. Moreover, Jesus continued to use baptism as a symbol of the purification needed to escape the fire to come. He was not about to scrap the ritual that had been so pivotal so recently in his own life. In other words, a Jesus totally disconnected from John's baptism and his preaching of eschatological judgment is a creation of modern exegetes. In a real sense, John always remained Jesus' mentor.

Nevertheless, like the venue of Jesus' ministry so the emphasis of Jesus' message shifted from John's. Jesus' proclamation was marked much less by threats of doom and much more by the good news that God was about to come in power to save and restore his sinful and scattered people. Here too Jesus made a conscious choice. He seized upon the relatively rare phrase "the kingdom of God" and used it to evoke the triumphant coming of God as king to rule Israel in the last days, a coming promised in the Book of Isaiah and celebrated in the Psalms.

In using the multifaceted, multilayered symbol of "the kingdom of God," Jesus conjured up in his audience's imagination the whole biblical drama of God's kingly rule over his creation and over his people Israel. It was God the King who in the beginning had called order out of chaos, who had saved a ragtag group of refugees from the slavery of Egypt and chosen them as his people Israel, who had exiled and scattered his people for their sins, and who now in this last hour was gathering, healing, and forgiving his people in preparation for final judgment and final salvation. It was this dynamic, multivalent, "salvation-history-in-a-nutshell" quality of "kingdom of God" that allowed Jesus to use it both of his pivotal ministry in the present moment and of the denouement of his ministry, soon to come.

On the one hand, the kingdom of God meant for Jesus the full appearance of God's victorious rule over the world in the near future. It was with a sober awareness that all was not yet perfect in Israel that Jesus taught his disciples to pray to the Father: "Your kingdom come." It was with anguish and yet trust that Jesus told his disciples at his last fellowship meal that he would not drink wine again until he drank it in the kingdom of God. One is tempted to stretch a point here by saying that Jesus went to his death promising himself the kingdom of God he had promised others. To be sure, though, the banquet in the kingdom was not meant for Jesus alone. He had promised that many others would come from the east and the west to recline with the patriarchs of Israel at the final banquet in the kingdom. Then and then alone would the hungry be fully fed, the mourners be finally comforted, the inequities of this world be reversed, and all the promises listed in Jesus' beatitudes be kept—kept for him as well as for those who heard him.

On the other hand, the kingdom was not just a future reality. If Jesus had simply prophesied an imminent coming of God to rule Israel with a full and definitive display of power, the Nazarene would not have differed all that much from some of the OT prophets, the writers of Jewish apocalypses, or John the Baptist. Jesus proved to be a more complicated and puzzling figure because the kingdom he proclaimed as coming was the kingdom he also proclaimed as present in his ministry (Luke 17:21): "The kingdom of God is in your midst." In some sense this was true of Jesus' powerful preaching and teaching, especially of his riddle-like parables, which confronted listeners with a kingdom of God that challenged and threatened their present ways of thinking and living. To hear these parables of the kingdom properly was to experience the coming of the kingdom into one's own existence. But the experience of the kingdom Jesus gave was not simply a modern, existentialistic "word event." Jesus wanted his fellow Jews to experience the kingdom present in action in their everyday lives. Hence he made the final banquet of the kingdom present and palpable in his table fellowship, which he shared most strikingly with social and religious outcasts.

While all this is true, Jesus himself emphasized that the presence of God's rule was especially experienced in the exorcisms and healings he performed. With an allusion to the absence of miracles in the Baptist's ministry, Jesus pointed out to John's inquiring envoys the stunning difference in his own ministry. Now at last Isaiah's prophecies of Israel's healing in the end time were being fulfilled (Matt 11:5 par.): "The blind see, the lame walk, lepers are cleansed, the deaf hear, the dead are raised"—all as part of Jesus' larger program of proclaiming the good news of salvation to Israel's poor. In particular, Jesus saw his exorcisms as a striking sign that even now, in the lives of individual Israelites, Satan's hold over God's people was being broken. Even now, on the limited turf of concrete Israelite lives, God's rule was triumphant (Luke 11:20): "If by the finger of God I cast out demons, then the kingdom of God has come upon you." Thus, in both word and deed, Jesus made God's future kingdom a present experience, at least in some partial or proleptic sense. Jesus was not just another prophet uttering more prophecies about the future. He was the prophet who was accomplishing what the prophets had foretold (Matt 13:16–17 ‖ Luke 10:23–24): "Happy the eyes that see what you see, and the ears that hear what you hear. For I say to you that many prophets and kings longed to see what you see and did not see it, and to hear what you hear and did not hear it."

For the crowds that followed Jesus, his supposed miracles were no doubt the most striking and attractive element of his ministry, the one that gave his mysterious talk about the kingdom of God palpable impact and meaning for ordinary Jews. For all his rejection of crass faith based on "miracles-on-demand," Jesus obviously appreciated the value of miracles as pedagogy, as propaganda, and especially as the present enactment of the powerful rule of God that he promised for the future. Miracles loom large in the Four Gospels because they first loomed large in the ministry of the historical Jesus. A good deal of the popular excitement over Jesus was fed by reports of his exorcisms, his healings of the infirm (especially people suffering from paralyzed limbs or from blindness), and even of his raising the dead.[3]

This belief in Jesus as a prophet who was at the same time a miracle-worker—a belief that goes back to his ministry—furnishes an important key to understanding who people thought Jesus was and perhaps even who *he* thought he was. In the OT, very few of Israel's prophets are reported to have worked a whole series of miracles as a regular part of their ministry. Early on in the Hebrew Scriptures, Moses as the "proto-prophet" stands alone in this regard, and later on only the prophets Elijah and Elisha were known especially as miracle-workers. Around the time of Jesus, some pious Jews were celebrated for the efficacy of their prayers, some others performed exorcisms, and no doubt others dabbled in practices we would label magic. In relating the turbulent years preceding the First Jewish Revolt, Josephus mentions popular leaders whom scholars call "sign prophets." These prophets *promised* their followers great miracles of deliverance, but apparently they did not go around performing miracles as a regular way of gaining adherents.

Thus, Jesus' customary activity of miracle-working, so characteristic that it is mentioned by Josephus as well as the Gospels and Acts, did make him stand out from most of the other religious leaders in the Palestinian Judaism of his day, including John the Baptist. Regular miracle-working by an itinerant prophet active in northern Israel would naturally conjure up thoughts of Elijah and Elisha. In particular, the belief that, in addition to a whole range of miracles, Jesus raised the dead—a miracle attributed in the Hebrew Scriptures to Elijah and Elisha but not to Moses—would have cast him in the mold of the former two prophets.

III. A PRELIMINARY SKETCH OF A SYNTHESIS[4]

The pieces of the puzzle thus begin to fit together: (1) At the very least, in some vague sense Jesus was seen by others and himself as an eschatological prophet. He proclaimed the imminent coming of God's kingly rule and reign. (2) Yet, unlike the Baptist, Jesus proclaimed and celebrated the kingdom of God already present in his ministry. It was present in his powerful preaching and teaching, present in his table fellowship offered to all, including toll collectors and sinners; but most strikingly it was present, palpable, and effective for his Jewish audience in his miracles. (3) These miracles, especially the supposed miracles of raising the dead, would almost inevitably cast Jesus in the role of Elijah or Elisha. Being an itinerant prophet as well as a miracle-worker, a prophet who operated particularly in northern Israel, a prophet who spoke rather than wrote—all this would make the fit still closer.

Would his Jewish audience think of him more in terms of Elijah or Elisha? From Malachi through Ben Sira to the NT and beyond into the rabbinic literature, Elijah was *the* eschatological prophet par excellence, the prophet whose return from heaven (whither he had been taken up in a fiery chariot) would signal the last days, the regathering and cleansing of Israel, the resolving of all legal questions, and the coming of God to rule in full power.[5] Hence the eschatological prophet and miracle-worker from Nazareth would naturally be connected with Elijah rather than Elisha.[6] Whether people thought that Jesus was literally the returned Elijah or rather another prophet clothed with Elijah's mantle and fulfilling Elijah's role is the kind of abstruse question and fine distinction that probably did not exercise the minds of many of Jesus' Jewish followers at the time. Whatever his precise relation to the Elijah of old, Jesus the eschatological prophet was acting out the role of the eschatological Elijah as he both proclaimed the imminent coming of God's rule and made that rule a reality even now by his miracles. It was this convergence and configuration of different traits in the one man named Jesus—traits that made him the Elijah-like eschatological prophet of a kingdom both future and yet made present by his miracles—that gave Jesus his distinctiveness or "uniqueness" within Palestinian Judaism in the early 1st century A.D.[7]

All this stands in stark contrast to one popular portrait of the historical Jesus often found in literature today: Jesus was a kindhearted rabbi who preached gentleness and love in the spirit of Rabbi Hillel. This domestication of a strange 1st-century marginal Jew bears a curious resemblance to the domestication of Jesus undertaken by Thomas Jefferson some two centuries ago. The advantage and appeal of the domesticated Jesus is obvious: he is instantly relevant to and usable by contemporary ethics, homilies, political programs, and ideologies of various stripes. In contrast, a 1st-century Jew who presents himself as the eschatological prophet of the imminent arrival of God's kingdom, a kingdom that the prophet makes present and effective by miracles reminiscent of Elijah and Elisha, is not so instantly relevant and usable. Yet, for better or for worse, this strange marginal Jew, this eschatological prophet and miracle-worker, *is* the historical Jesus retrievable by modern historical methods applied soberly to the data.

Still, this is not the whole story, the entire configuration. Besides being the eschatological prophet and miracle-worker clothed in the aura of Elijah, Jesus not only taught his Jewish followers general ethical imperatives (e.g., love and forgiveness) but also presumed to give concrete directions on how to observe the Mosaic Law (*hălākôt*). Some of his pronouncements on the Mosaic Law led to disputes with other Jewish groups, not least of all because at times Jesus, while certainly affirming the Law as God's word to Israel, took it upon himself to rescind or change some individual institutions in the Law: e.g., divorce, oaths and vows, and, in the opinion of some exegetes, even the kosher food laws of the Torah. This element of concrete-and-controversial directives as well as general teaching on the Law added further spicy ingredients to an already heady brew. Jesus not only presented himself as the eschatological prophet of the coming kingdom of God, not only presented himself as the Elijah-like miracle-worker who made the future kingdom already effective and palpable to his followers, but at the same time presented himself as a teacher who could tell Israelites how to observe the Law of Moses—indeed, who could even tell Israelites what they should or should not observe in the Law.

Thus, the so-called "charismatic" nature of Jesus, which one can discern in his prophetic ministry and miracle-working, also surfaces in his teaching on the Law. As a true charismatic, Jesus located his authority to interpret and even change the Law not in recognized traditional channels of authority (the Law with its accepted modes of interpretation, the rulings of priests or authoritative courts, or the sayings of famous teachers) but rather in his own ability to know directly and intuitively what was God's will for his people Israel in the last days. This is just another aspect of his claim to be the charismatic prophet of the end time, a claim now extended from strictly prophetic and miraculous activity into the more "scribal" activity of interpreting the Law and guiding concrete behavior. At this point, the convergence and configuration of multiple roles in the one man called Jesus become extremely dense and complicated.

In bringing the teaching of Jesus on the Law into this preliminary synthesis, I realize that I have gone beyond the limits set for Volume Two of *A Marginal Jew* and have anticipated what awaits us in Volume Three. For methodological reasons, the portrait and synthesis possible at the end of Volume Two are necessarily restricted in scope. With slight exaggeration, one might say that Volume Two has focused mainly on "Jesus seen in himself." With the one exception of John the Baptist, I have not highlighted Jesus' relations and interactions with other individual Jews and groups of Jews. The focus has rather been on Jesus' core message (the kingdom of God) and his salient actions (miracles) seen "in themselves" and in their relation to each other—and not primarily in their relation to their audience or recipients.[8]

Now that we have this preliminary focus on Jesus, we can begin to widen the spotlight, as it were, to bring into the circle of light the various individuals and groups affected by and responding to his words and deeds. The widening circle will include his immediate entourage of disciples (especially the Twelve), the larger and looser group of those Jews favorably disposed to him (disciples in a wider sense), and the various socioeconomic or religious groups with whom he interacted (e.g., toll collectors and sinners, Pharisees and Sadducees).

This widening of the circle will naturally involve us in the key question of Jesus' relation to the Mosaic Law, both in his interpretation and in his praxis of it. The stance of this eschatological prophet, herald of the future-yet-present kingdom, and Elijah-like miracle-worker to the Mosaic Law, especially when he enters into debate over it with other Jewish groups, will make all the more pressing the central question: Who does this man think he is? We have found something of a partial answer to this question in Volume Two, though without involving ourselves directly in the complicated questions of (1) what eschato-logical or messianic designations and titles existed in Judaism at the time of Jesus and (2) which, if any, of these designations might have been used of Jesus or by Jesus during his public ministry. For a fuller answer to these questions, we must move on to Volume Three. But at least some basic patterns and guide-posts have emerged to direct our steps down the long and dusty road.

NOTES TO CONCLUSION

[1] Since this conclusion of Volume Two aims at being a brief summary and a tight synthesis of results achieved so far, I do not repeat here all the arguments, text references, and bibliography mentioned in the course of the first two volumes of *A Marginal Jew*; end notes are kept to a bare minimum. For details the reader is referred to the relevant sections of the two volumes.

[2] As we have seen already and will see again, Jesus gave special attention to social and religious outcasts, to the downtrodden and the poor. Nevertheless, this special concern should not be read in an exclusivistic sense. People like the synagogue leader Jairus, the rich toll collector of Jericho Zacchaeus, the centurion or royal official whose "boy" Jesus healed, the Pharisees who hosted Jesus at their tables—all these varied actors in the story remind us that Jesus did not let his concern for the outcast and the poor turn into narrow and mean-spirited partisanship. Moreover, to say that Jesus was concerned about the poor does not in the end say very much. About 90 percent of Galilean Jews would probably have qualified as "poor" in some sense of the word. On "poverty" in Jesus' Galilee, see *A Marginal Jew*, 1. 281–83.

[3] Throughout this sketch and especially in the description of Jesus' miracles the reader may feel disappointed, for to some the presentation may seem "flat" and without development. Surely, some will object, there must have been change and development in Jesus' preaching and miracle-working during the two years or more of his public ministry. For instance, Jesus may have at first continued the Baptist's fiery message of judgment and then switched to a more compassionate message of forgiveness and healing when he discovered that he had the power to heal illnesses. Or perhaps, in his miracle-working ministry, Jesus at first relied heavily on physical means (spittle, laying on of hands) but then discovered that his mere word was sufficient to work miracles. The answer to these and all other "developmental" theories of Jesus' ministry is simple: yes, of course, these and countless other scenarios of Jesus' development, both in inner consciousness and outward activity, are possible. But do the data in the Gospels make these scenarios anything more than possible? The answer must be: no. As we saw in Volume One (pp. 406–9), one of the major contributions of form criticism was to dissolve the chronological frameworks of the public ministry as found in the Four Gospels; they were seen to be the creations of the four evangelists. The early oral tradition of the church contained individual stories and sayings of Jesus, as well as collections of stories and sayings. But, before the work of the evangelists, apparently there was no overarching chronological framework that ordered all the material of the public ministry. Here, then, is the root of the problem. Once we acknowledge the artificial nature of the order of events in each of the Gospels, we necessarily admit that, for most of the material of the public ministry, there is no before or after, as far as the modern critic attempting historical reconstruction is concerned. To be sure, there was a real before and after in the actual historical events as they unfolded in Palestine ca. A.D. 28–30. But that historical order is unknown and unknowable to us today. Needless to say, we are free to supply our own "probable" order of external events or of Jesus' psychological development, but such an order is just as artificial as the chronological framework created by the evangelists. An important distinction that I made during the discussion of Jesus' youth (Volume One, p. 254) is applicable here as well. *That* Jesus changed and developed his ideas and practice during the public ministry is highly probable; *what* exactly that change

was and how it took place is unknowable to us today. Imaginative theories of the development of Jesus' consciousness or ministerial praxis serve no purpose beyond helping to sell books.

[4] As I acknowledge in the main text of this section, for the purpose of rounding out this preliminary sketch of a synthesis I anticipate a consideration of Jesus as teacher of the Mosaic Law that is still to come in Volume Three. This is done simply to avoid leaving the reader hanging in midair. The substantiation of my brief remarks about Jesus' relation to the Law must await a full treatment in the next volume.

[5] See, e.g., Mal 3:23–24 in the MT (4:5–6 in English translations); Sir 48:1–11; Luke 1:17; John 1:19–21; Mark 9:11–13; Rev 11:3–6; *m. 'Ed.* 8:7; *m. Soṭa* 9:15. Later Jewish and Christian versions of an *Apocalypse of Elijah*, which may go back to a Jewish source written ca. A.D. 100, expanded and varied Elijah's connection to and role in the end-time events. On this see Orval S. Wintermute, "Elijah, Apocalypse of," *Anchor Bible Dictionary*, 2. 466–69.

[6] However, one must allow for the fact that the stories about Elijah and Elisha so resembled one another that the two figures may well have blended in the popular mind. But, since it was Elijah who made such a spectacular exit from this world and was expected—even within the OT period—to return in the last days, the composite figure would most likely have been thought of under the label of Elijah.

[7] Here in particular one might be tempted to construct a grand "developmental" theory embracing both John the Baptist and Jesus. John prophesied the imminent arrival of the eschatological figure whom he called "the one who comes." In keeping with some strains of Jewish eschatology at the time, John may have used this mysterious phrase "the one who comes" as a cryptic description of Elijah, the last human precursor of God himself. During his time in John's circle of disciples, Jesus would have grown used to such an expectation. When he began his own eschatological ministry, and especially when he discovered his power to perform Elijah-like miracles, Jesus would have come to see himself as the Elijah whose coming John had promised. Like so many developmental theories, this one is both engaging and unprovable. Throughout the volumes of *A Marginal Jew*, I purposely eschew any highly speculative theory that "explains it all" in favor of a judicious weighing of evidence in order to arrive at modest but fairly secure conclusions about what the historical Jesus did and said.

[8] On the importance of Jesus' relationships with other people and groups of people for understanding Jesus himself, see Witherington, *The Christology of Jesus*, esp. 33–143. I agree with his basic point, but have decided to keep such a consideration until Volume Three.

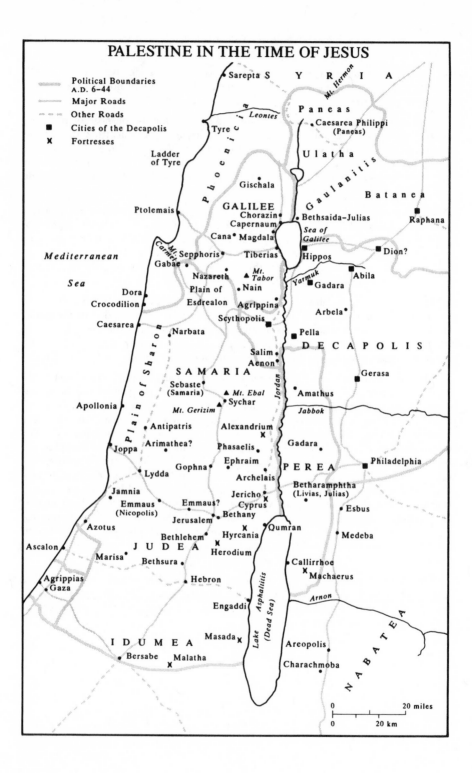

PALESTINE IN THE TIME OF JESUS

Political Boundaries
A.D. 6-44
Major Roads
Other Roads
■ Cities of the Decapolis
✗ Fortresses

Sarepta S Y R I A

Mt. Hermon

Leontes

Paneas

Tyre

Caesarea Philippi
(Paneas)

Ladder
of Tyre

U l a t h a

Phoenicia

Gischala

G a u l a n i t i s

B a t a n e a

Ptolemais

GALILEE
Chorazin
Capernaum
Cana Magdala

Bethsaida-Julias

Raphana

Sea of
Galilee

Sepphoris
Gabae

Tiberias

Hippos

Dion?

Mediterranean

Mt. Carmel

Nazareth

Mt.
Tabor

Abila

Sea

Plain of
Esdrealon

Nain

Yarmuk

Gadara

Dora
Crocodilion

Agrippina

Arbela

Caesarea

Scythopolis

Narbata

Pella

D E C A P O L I S

Plain of Sharon

Salim
Aenon

Gerasa

S A M A R I A

Jordan

Sebaste
(Samaria)

Mt. Ebal
Sychar

Amathus

Apollonia

Mt. Gerizim

Jabbok

Antipatris

Alexandrium ✗

Gadara

Arimathea?

Phasaelis

P E R E A

Philadelphia

Joppa

Gophna

Ephraim

Lydda

Archelais

Jamnia

Emmaus?

Jericho
Cyprus

Betharamphtha
(Livias, Julias)

Emmaus
(Nicopolis)

Bethany

Esbus

Azotus

Jerusalem ✗

Hyrcania

Qumran

Medeba

Bethlehem

Hezron ✗
Herodium

Ascalon

Marisa

Bethsura

J U D E A

✗

Callirrhoe

Agrippias
Gaza

Hebron

Machaerus ✗

Engaddi

Lake Asphaltitis
(Dead Sea)

Arnon

I D U M E A

Masada ✗

Areopolis

Bersabe

Malatha ✗

Charachmoba

N A B A T E A

0   20 miles

0   20 km

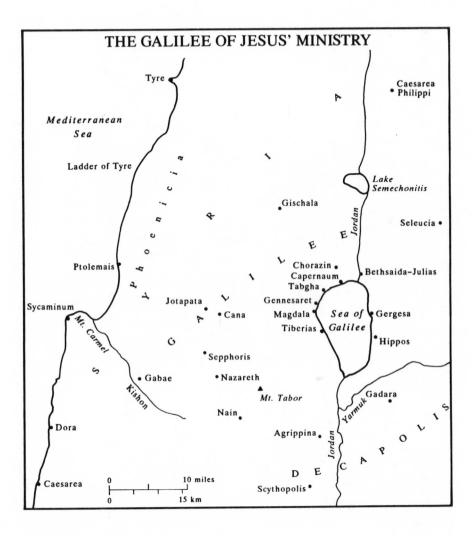

THE GALILEE OF JESUS' MINISTRY

Tyre

Mediterranean
Sea

Ladder of Tyre

Phoenicia

Caesarea
Philippi

Lake
Semechonitis

Gischala

Jordan

Seleucia

Chorazin
Capernaum
Tabgha

Bethsaida–Julias

Ptolemais

GALILEE

Jotapata

Cana

Gennesaret

Magdala

Sea of
Galilee

Gergesa

Sycaminum

Mt. Carmel

Tiberias

Hippos

Sepphoris

Gabae

Nazareth

Kishon

Mt. Tabor

Gadara

Nain

Yarmuk

Jordan

Dora

Agrippina

DECAPOLIS

Caesarea

0   10 miles

0   15 km

Scythopolis

THE FAMILY OF HEROD THE GREAT

Herod the Great had ten wives. Only the wives and descendants of direct interest to students of the NT are listed here.

b. = born
d. = died
r. = reigned
m. = married
K. = King
E. = Ethnarch
T. = Tetrarch

King Herod the Great
b. ca. 73 B.C.
d. 4 B.C.

m. MARIAMME I (Hasmonean) d. 29 B.C.

Aristobulus IV d. 7 B.C.; m. Bernice I

Herod (of Chalcis)
m. Bernice II
r. Chalcis A.D. 41–48 (K.)
d. A.D. 48

Herod Agrippa I
r. tetrarchies of Philip and Lysanias as K. from A.D. 37—tetrarchy of Antipas added A.D. 40—Judea and Samaria added A.D. 41–44
d. A.D. 44

Herodias
m. (1) Herod (misnamed Philip)*
(2) Herod Antipas

MARIAMME II

Herod (misnamed Philip)
m. Herodias

Salome III
m. Philip

MALTHACE (Samaritan)

Archelaus
r. 4 B.C.–A.D. 6 (E.)

Herod Antipas
m. (1) Daughter of Aretas IV (Nabatean K.)
(2) Herodias
r. 4 B.C.–A.D. 39 (T.)

CLEOPATRA (of Jerusalem)

Philip
m. Salome III
r. 4 B.C.–A.D. 34 (T.)
d. A.D. 34

*Mark's Gospel confuses Herod, the son of Mariamme II, with Philip; this has led some NT scholars to speak (wrongly) of "Herod Philip" as Herodias' first husband.

1052

THE REGNAL YEARS OF THE
ROMAN *PRINCIPES* (EMPERORS)

Compared with the dates of the Prefects/Procurators of Judea, Samaria, and Idumea

OCTAVIAN (AUGUSTUS)   [Prefects]

    31 B.C. (battle of Actium)   Coponius   A.D. 6–9

    27 B.C. (assumes title of Augustus)   M. Ambivius   9–12 (?)

    A.D. 14 (dies)   Annius Rufus   12–15 (?)

TIBERIUS

    14–37   Valerius Gratus   15–26

        Pontius Pilate   26–36

        Marcellus   36–37

GAIUS (CALIGULA)

    37–41   Marullus   37–41 (?)

CLAUDIUS   [Reign of Agrippa I over the restored

    41–54   kingdom of the Jews, 41–44]

        [Procurators]

        C. Cuspius Fadus   44–46

        Tiberius Julius Alexander   46–48

        Ventidius Cumanus   48–52

NERO

    54–68   M. Antonius Felix   52–60 (?)

        Porcius Festus   60–62 (?)

        Lucceius Albinus   62–64

        Gessius Florus   64–66

GALBA, OTHO, VITELLIUS

    (all in 69)

        Jewish Revolt   66–70

VESPASIAN

    69–79

List of Abbreviations

1. Abbreviations of the Names of Biblical Books (with the Apocrypha)

Gen	Nah	1-2-3-4 Kgdms	John
Exod	Hab	Add Esth	Acts
Lev	Zeph	Bar	Rom
Num	Hag	Bel	1-2 Cor
Deut	Zech	1-2 Esdr	Gal
Josh	Mal	4 Ezra	Eph
Judg	Ps (*pl.*: Pss)	Jdt	Phil
1-2 Sam	Job	Ep Jer	Col
1-2 Kgs	Prov	1-2-3-4 Macc	1-2 Thess
Isa	Ruth	Pr Azar	1-2 Tim
Jer	Cant	Pr Man	Titus
Ezek	Eccl (*or* Qoh)	Sir	Phlm
Hos	Lam	Sus	Heb
Joel	Esth	Tob	Jas
Amos	Dan	Wis	1-2 Pet
Obad	Ezra	Matt	1-2-3 John
Jonah	Neh	Mark	Jude
Mic	1-2 Chr	Luke	Rev

2. Abbreviations of the Names of Pseudepigraphical and Early Patristic Books

Adam and Eve	Books of Adam and Eve	*Gos. Eg.*	Gospel of the Egyptians
2-3 Apoc. Bar.	Syriac, Greek Apocalypse of Baruch	*Gos. Heb.*	Gospel of the Hebrews
Apoc. Mos.	Apocalypse of Moses	*Gos. Naass.*	Gospel of the Naassenes
As. Mos.	Assumption of Moses	*Gos. Pet.*	Gospel of Peter
1-2-3 Enoch	Ethiopic, Slavonic, Hebrew Enoch	*Gos. Thom.*	Gospel of Thomas
		Prot. Jas.	Protevangelium of James
Ep. Arist.	Epistle of Aristeas	*Barn.*	Barnabas
Jub.	Jubilees	*1-2 Clem.*	1-2 Clement
Mart. Isa.	Martyrdom of Isaiah	*Did.*	Didache
Odes. Sol.	Odes of Solomon	*Diogn.*	Diognetus
Pss. Sol.	Psalms of Solomon	*Herm.*	Hermas,
Sib. Or.	Sibylline Oracles		
T. 12 Patr.	Testaments of the Twelve Patriarchs	*Man.*	Mandate
		Sim.	Similitude
T. Levi	Testament of Levi	*Vis.*	Vision
T. Benj.	Testament of Benjamin, etc.	*Ign. Eph.*	Ignatius, Letter to the Ephesians
Acts Pil.	Acts of Pilate	*Magn.*	Ignatius, Letter to the Magnesians
Apoc. Pet.	Apocalypse of Peter		
Gos. Eb.	Gospel of the Ebionites	*Phld.*	Ignatius, Letter to the Philadelphians

Pol.	Ignatius, Letter to Polycarp	*Mart. Pol.*	Martyrdom of Polycarp
Rom.	Ignatius, Letter to the Romans	Pol. *Phil.*	Polycarp to the Philippians
Smyrn.	Ignatius, Letter to the Smyrnaeans	*Bib. Ant.*	Ps.-Philo, Biblical Antiquities
Trall.	Ignatius, Letter to the Trallians		

3. Abbrebiations of Names of Dead Sea Scrolls and Related Texts

CD	Cairo (Genizah text of the) Damascus (Document)	1QS	*Serek hayyahad* (*Rule of the Community, Manual of Discipline*)
Hev	Nahal Hever texts		
Mas	Masada texts	1QSa	Appendix A (*Rule of the Congregation*) to 1QS
Mird	Khirbet Mird texts		
Mur	Wadi Murabba'at texts	1QSb	Appendix B (*Blessings*) to 1QS
P	Pesher (commentary)	3Q15	Copper Scroll from Qumran Cave 3
Q	Qumran		
1Q, 2Q, 3Q, etc.	Numbered caves of Qumran, yielding written material; followed by abbreviation of biblical or apocryphal book	4QFlor	*Florilegium* (or *Eschatological Midrashim*) from Qumran Cave 4
		4QMess ar	Aramaic "Messianic" text from Qumran Cave 4
QL	Qumran literature	4QPrNab	Prayer of Nabonidus from Qumran Cave 4
1QapGen	*Genesis Apocryphon* of Qumran Cave 1	4QTestim	*Testimonia* text from Qumran Cave 4
1QH	*Hôdāyôt* (*Thanksgiving Hymns*) from Qumran Cave 1	4QT Levi	*Testament of Levi* from Qumran Cave 4
1QIsa^{a, b}	First or second copy of Isaiah from Qumran Cave 1	4QPhyl	Phylacteries from Qumran Cave 4
1QpHab	*Pesher on Habakkuk* from Qumran Cave 1	11QMelch	*Melchizedek* text from Qumran Cave 11
1QM	*Milhāmāh* (*War Scroll*)	11QtgJob	*Targum of Job* from Qumran Cave 11

4. Targums

Tg. Onq.	Targum Onqelos	Tg. Ps.-J.	Targum Pseudo-
Tg. Neb.	Targum of the Prophets		Jonathan
Tg. Ket.	Targum of the Writings	Tg. Yer. I	Targum Yerušalmi I*
Frg. Tg.	Fragmentary Targum	Tg. Yer. II	Targum Yerušalmi II*
Sam. Tg.	Samaritan Targum	Yem. Tg.	Yemenite Targum
Tg. Isa.	Targum of Isaiah	Tg. Esth I, II	First or Second Targum
Pal. Tgs.	Palestinian Targums		of Esther
Tg. Neof.	Targum Neofiti 1		*optional title

5. Abbreviations of Orders and Tractates in Mishnaic and Related Literature.

To distinguish the same-named tractates in the Mishna, Tosepta, Babylonian Talmud, and Jerusalem Talmud, we use italicized *m.*, *t.*, *b.*, or *y.* before the title of the tractate. Thus *m. Peʾa* 8:2; *b. Šabb.* 31a; *y. Mak.* 2.31d; *t. Peʾa* 1.4 (Zuck. 18 [=page number of Zuckermandel's edition of the Tosepta]).

ʾAbot	ʾAbot	Moʿed Qat.	Moʿed Qatan
ʿArak.	ʿArakin	Maʿas. Š.	Maʿaśer Šeni
ʿAbod. Zar.	ʿAboda Zara	Našim	Našim
B. Bat.	Baba Batra	Nazir	Nazir
Bek.	Bekorot	Ned.	Nedarim
Ber.	Berakot	Neg.	Negaʿim
Beṣa	Beṣa (= Yom Ṭob)	Nez.	Neziqin
Bik.	Bikkurim	Nid.	Niddah
B. Meṣ.	Baba Meṣiʿa	Ohol.	Oholot
B. Qam.	Baba Qamma	ʿOr.	ʿOrla
Dem.	Demai	Para	Para
ʿErub.	ʿErubin	Peʾa	Peʾa
ʿEd.	ʿEduyyot	Pesaḥ.	Pesaḥim
Giṭ.	Giṭṭin	Qinnim	Qinnim
Ḥag.	Ḥagiga	Qidd.	Qiddušin
Ḥal.	Ḥalla	Qod.	Qodašin
Hor.	Horayot	Roš. Haš.	Roš Haššana
Ḥul.	Ḥullin	Sanh.	Sanhedrin
Kelim	Kelim	Šabb.	Šabbat
Ker.	Keritot	Šeb.	Šebiʿit
Ketub.	Ketubot	Šebu.	Šebuʿot
Kil.	Kilʾayim	Šeqal.	Šeqalim
Maʿaś.	Maʿaśerot	Soṭa	Soṭa
Mak.	Makkot	Sukk.	Sukka
Makš.	Makširin (= Mašqin)	Taʿan.	Taʿanit
Meg.	Megilla	Tamid	Tamid
Meʿil.	Meʿila	Tem.	Temura
Menaḥ.	Menaḥot	Ter.	Terumot
Mid.	Middot	Ṭohar.	Ṭoharot
Miqw.	Miqwaʾot	Ṭ. Yom	Ṭebul Yom
Moʿed	Moʿed	ʿUq.	ʿUqṣin

Yad.	Yadayim	Zabim	Zabim
Yebam.	Yebamot	Zebaḥ	Zebaḥim
Yoma	Yoma (= Kippurim)	Zer.	Zeraʿim

6. Abbreviations of Other Rabbinic Works

ʾAbot R. Nat.	ʾAbot de Rabbi Nathan	Pesiq. R.	Pesiqta Rabbati
ʾAg. Ber.	ʾAggadat Berešit	Pesiq. Rab Kah.	Pesiqta de Rab Kahana
Bab.	Babylonian	Pirqe R. El.	Pirqe Rabbi Eliezer
Bar.	Baraita	Rab.	Rabbah (following
Der. Er. Rab.	Derek Ereṣ Rabba		abbreviation for
Der. Er. Zuṭ.	Derek Ereṣ Zuṭa		biblical book: Gen.
Gem.	Gemara		Rab. [with periods]
Kalla	Kalla		= Genesis Rabbah)
Mek.	Mekilta	Ṣem.	Ṣemaḥot
Midr.	Midraš; cited with	Sipra	Sipra
	usual abbreviation	Sipre	Sipre
	for biblical book; but	Sop.	Soperim
	Midr. Qoh. =	S. ʿOlam Rab.	Seder ʿOlam Rabbah
	Midraš Qohelet	Talm.	Talmud
Pal.	Palestinian	Yal.	Yalquṭ

7. Abbreviations of Nag Hammadi Tractates

Acts Pet. 12 Apost.	Acts of Peter and the Twelve Apostles	Gos. Phil.	Gospel of Philip
Allogenes	Allogenes	Gos. Thom.	Gospel of Thomas
Ap. Jas.	Apocryphon of James	Gos. Truth	Gospel of Truth
Ap. John	Apocryphon of John	Great Pow.	Concept of our Great Power
Apoc. Adam	Apocalypse of Adam		
1 Apoc. Jas.	First Apocalypse of James	Hyp. Arch.	Hypostasis of the Archons
2 Apoc. Jas.	Second Apocalypse of James	Hypsiph.	Hypsiphrone
		Interp. Know.	Interpretation of Knowledge
Apoc. Paul	Apocalypse of Paul		
Apoc. Pet.	Apocalypse of Peter	Marsanes	Marsanes
Asclepius	Asclepius 21–29	Melch.	Melchizedek
Auth. Teach.	Authoritative Teaching	Norea	Thought of Norea
		On Bap. A.	On Baptism A
Dial. Sav.	Dialogue of the Savior	On Bap. B	On Baptism B
Disc. 8–9	Discourse on the Eighth and Ninth	On Bap. C	On Baptism C
		On Euch. A	On the Eucharist A
Ep. Pet. Phil.	Letter of Peter to Philip	On Euch. B	On the Eucharist B
		Orig. World	On the Origin of the World
Eugnostos	Eugnostos the Blessed		
Exeg. Soul	Exegesis on the Soul	Paraph. Shem	Paraphrase of Shem
Gos. Eg.	Gospel of the Egyptians	Pr. Paul	Prayer of the Apostle Paul

Pr. Thanks.	Prayer of Thanksgiving	Treat. Res.	Treatise on Resurrection
Sent. Sextus	Sentences of Sextus	Treat. Seth	Second Treatise of the Great Seth
Soph. Jes. Chr.	Sophia of Jesus Christ		
Steles Seth	Three Steles of Seth	Tri. Trac.	Tripartite Tractate
Teach. Silv.	Teachings of Silvanus	Trim. Prot.	Trimorphic Protennoia
Testim. Truth	Testimony of Truth		
Thom. Cont.	Book of Thomas the Contender	Val. Exp.	A Valentinian Exposition
Thund.	Thunder, Perfect Mind	Zost.	Zostrianos

8. Abbreviations of Commonly Used Periodicals, Reference Works, and Serials

(Titles not found in this list are written out in full. Titles of periodicals and books are italicized, but titles of series are set in roman characters, as are acronyms of authors' names when they are used as sigla.) Short, one-word titles not on this list are not abbreviated.

AAS	*Acta apostolicae sedis*	ALBO	Analecta lovaniensia biblica et orientalia
AASOR	Annual of the American Schools of Oriental Research	ALGHJ	Arbeiten zur Literatur und Geschichte des hellenistischen Judentums
AB	Anchor Bible		
AcOr	*Acta orientalia*	AnBib	Analecta biblica
ACW	Ancient Christian Writers	ANEP	J. B. Pritchard (ed.), *Ancient Near East in Pictures*
AfO	*Archiv für Orientforschung*	ANESTP	J. B. Pritchard (ed.), *Ancient Near East Supplementary Texts and Pictures*
AGJU	Arbeiten zur Geschichte des antiken Judentums und des Urchristentums	ANET	J. B. Pritchard (ed.), *Ancient Near Eastern Texts*
AH	F. Rosenthal, *An Aramaic Handbook*	Ang	*Angelicum*
AJA	*American Journal of Archaeology*	AnOr	Analecta orientalia
		ANQ	*Andover Newton Quarterly*
AJBA	*Australian Journal of Biblical Archaeology*	ANTF	Arbeiten zur neutestamentlichen Textforschung
AJP	*American Journal of Philology*		
AJSL	*American Journal of Semitic Languages and Literature*	ANRW	*Aufstieg und Niedergang der römischen Welt*
AJT	*American Journal of Theology*	AOAT	Alter Orient und Altes Testament

AOS	American Oriental Series	BAR	*Biblical Archaeologist Reader*
AP	J. Marouzeau (ed.), *L'Année philologique*	*BARev*	*Biblical Archaeology Review*
APOT	R. H. Charles (ed.), *Apocrypha and Pseudepigrapha of the Old Testament*	*BASOR*	*Bulletin of the American Schools of Oriental Research*
Arch	*Archaeology*	BBB	Bonner biblische Beiträge
ARW	*Archiv für Religionswissenschaft*	BBET	Beiträge zur biblischen Exegese und Theologie
ASNU	Acta seminarii neotestamentici upsaliensis	*BCSR*	*Bulletin of the Council on the Study of Religion*
ASOR	American Schools of Oriental Research	BDB	F. Brown, S. R. Driver, and C. A. Briggs, *Hebrew and English Lexicon of the Old Testament*
ASS	*Acta sanctae sedis*		
AsSeign	*Assemblées du Seigneur*		
ASSR	*Archives des sciences sociales des religions*	BDF	F. Blass, A. Debrunner, and R. W. Funk, *A Greek Grammar of the NT*
ASTI	*Annual of the Swedish Theological Institute*		
ATAbh	Alttestamentliche Abhandlungen	BDR	F. Blass, A. Debrunner, and F. Rehkopf, *Grammatik des neutestamentlichen Griechisch*
ATANT	Abhandlungen zur Theologie des Alten und Neuen Testaments		
		BeO	*Bibbia e oriente*
AtBib	H. Grollenberg, *Atlas of the Bible*	BETL	Bibliotheca ephemeridum theologicarum lovaniensium
ATD	Das Alte Testament Deutsch		
ATR	*Anglican Theological Review*	BEvT	Beiträge zur evangelischen Theologie
Aug	*Augustinianum*		
AusBR	*Australian Biblical Review*	BFCT	Beiträge zur Förderung christlicher Theologie
AUSS	*Andrews University Seminary Studies*	BGBE	Beiträge zur Geschichte der biblischen Exegese
BA	*Biblical Archaeologist*		
BAC	Biblioteca de autores cristianos	BHEAT	Bulletin d'histoire et d'exégèse de l'Ancien Testament
BAGD	W. Bauer, W. F. Arndt, F. W. Gingrich, and F. W. Danker, *Greek-English Lexicon of the NT*	BHH	B. Reicke and L. Rost (eds.), *Biblisch-Historisches Handwörterbuch*

BHK	R. Kittel, *Biblia Hebraica*	*BTB*	*Biblical Theology Bulletin*
BHS	*Biblia hebraica stuttgartensia*	*BTS*	*Bible et terre sainte*
		BurH	*Buried History*
BHT	Beiträge zur historischen Theologie	*BVC*	*Bible et vie chrétienne*
		BWANT	Beiträge zur Wissenschaft vom Alten und Neuen Testament
Bib	*Biblica*		
BibB	Biblische Beiträge		
BibBh	*Bible Bhashyam*	*ByF*	*Biblia y fe*
BibLeb	*Bibel und Leben*	BZ	*Biblische Zeitschrift*
BibOr	Biblica et orientalia	BZAW	Beihefte zur *ZAW*
BibS(F)	Biblische Studien (Freiburg, 1895–)	BZNW	Beihefte zur *ZNW*
		BZRGG	Beihefte zur *ZRGG*
BibS(N)	Biblische Studien (Neukirchen, 1951–)	*CAH*	*Cambridge Ancient History*
BIES	*Bulletin of the Israel Exploration Society (= Yediot)*	*CahEv*	*Cahiers évangile*
		CahRB	Cahiers de la Revue biblique
BIFAO	*Bulletin de l'institut français d'archéologie orientale*	Cah Théol	Cahiers théologiques
		CAT	Commentaire de l'Ancien Testament
Bijdr	*Bijdragen*	*CB*	*Cultura bíblica*
BIOSCS	*Bulletin of the International Organization for Septuagint and Cognate Studies*	*CBQ*	*Catholic Biblical Quarterly*
		CBQMS	Catholic Biblical Quarterly—Monograph Series
BJPES	*Bulletin of the Jewish Palestine Exploration Society*	CC	Corpus christianorum
		CCath	Corpus catholicorum
		CH	*Church History*
BJRL	*Bulletin of the John Rylands University Library of Manchester*	*CHR*	*Catholic Historical Review*
		CIG	*Corpus inscriptionum graecarum*
BK	*Bibel und Kirche*		
BKAT	Biblischer Kommentar: Altes Testament	*CII*	*Corpus inscriptionum iudaicarum*
BLit	*Bibel und Liturgie*	*CIL*	*Corpus inscriptionum latinarum*
BN	*Biblische Notizen*		
BO	*Bibliotheca orientalis*	*CIS*	*Corpus inscriptionum Semiticarum*
BR	*Biblical Research*	*CJ*	*Classical Journal*
BSac	*Bibliotheca Sacra*	*CJT*	*Canadian Journal of Theology*
BSOAS	*Bulletin of the School of Oriental (and African) Studies*		
		CNT	Commentaire du Nouveau Testament
BT	*The Bible Translator*	ConB	Coniectanea biblica

ConBNT	Coniectanea biblica, New Testament	EHAT	Exegetisches Handbuch zum Alten Testament
ConBOT	Coniectanea biblica, Old Testament	EKKNT	Evangelisch-katholischer Kommentar zum Neuen Testament
ConNT	*Coniectanea neotestamentica*		
CP	*Classical Philology*	*EKL*	*Evangelisches Kirchenlexikon*
CQ	*Church Quarterly*		
CQR	*Church Quarterly Review*	*EncJud*	*Encyclopedia Judaica* (1971)
CRAIBL	*Comptes rendus de l'académie des inscriptions et belles-lettres*	*EnchBib*	*Enchiridion biblicum*
		ErIsr	Eretz Israel
		ErJb	*Eranos Jahrbuch*
CRINT	Compendia rerum iudaicarum ad Novum Testamentum	*EstBib*	*Estudios bíblicos*
		EstEcl	*Estudios eclesiásticos*
		EstTeol	*Estudios teológicos*
CSCO	Corpus scriptorum christianorum orientalium	*ETL*	*Ephemerides theologicae lovanienses*
CSEL	Corpus scriptorum ecclesiasticorum latinorum	*ETR*	*Études théologiques et religieuses*
		EvK	*Evangelische Kommentare*
CTJ	*Calvin Theological Journal*	*EvQ*	*Evangelical Quarterly*
CTM	*Concordia Theological Monthly (or CTM)*	*EvT*	*Evangelische Theologie*
CTQ	*Concordia Theological Quarterly*	*EWNT*	H. Balz and G. Schneider (eds.), *Exegetisches Wörterbuch zum Neuen Testament*
CurTM	*Currents in Theology and Mission*		
DACL	*Dictionnaire d'archéologie chrétienne et de liturgie*	*ExpTim*	*Expository Times*
		FB	Forschung zur Bibel
		FBBS	Facet Books, Biblical Series
DBSup	*Dictionnaire de la Bible, Supplément*	FC	Fathers of the Church
DJD	Discoveries in the Judaean Desert	FRLANT	Forschungen zur Religion und Literatur des Alten und Neuen Testaments
DRev	*Downside Review*		
DS	Denzinger-Schönmetzer, *Enchiridion symbolorum*	GAT	Grundrisse zum Alten Testament
DTC	*Dictionnaire de théologie catholique*	GCS	Griechische christliche Schriftsteller
EBib	Études bibliques		
EDB	L. F. Hartman (ed.), *Encyclopedic Dictionary of the Bible*	GKB	Gesenius-Kautzsch-Bergsträsser, *Hebräische Grammatik*

GKC	*Gesenius' Hebrew Grammar*, ed. E. Kautzsch, tr. A. E. Cowley	IB	*Interpreter's Bible*
		IBS	*Irish Biblical Studies*
		ICC	International Critical Commentary
GNT	Grundrisse zum Neuen Testament	IDB	G. A. Buttrick (ed.), *Interpreter's Dictionary of the Bible*
GRBS	*Greek, Roman, and Byzantine Studies*	IDBSup	Supplementary volume to *IDB*
Greg	*Gregorianum*		
GTA	Göttinger theologische Arbeiten	IEJ	*Israel Exploration Journal*
GTJ	*Grace Theological Journal*	Int	*Interpretation*
		IOS	*Israel Oriental Society*
HALAT	W. Baumgartner et al., *Hebräisches und aramäisches Lexikon zum Alten Testament*	ITQ	*Irish Theological Quarterly*
		JA	*Journal asiatique*
		JAAR	*Journal of the American Academy of Religion*
HAT	Handbuch zum Alten Testament		
HDR	Harvard Dissertations in Religion	JAC	Jahrbuch für Antike und Christentum
HeyJ	*Heythrop Journal*	JAL	Jewish Apocryphal Literature
HibJ	*Hibbert Journal*		
HKAT	Handkommentar zum Alten Testament	JANESCU	*Journal of the Ancient Near Eastern Society of Columbia University*
HKNT	Handkommentar zum Neuen Testament	JAOS	*Journal of the American Oriental Society*
HNT	Handbuch zum Neuen Testament	JAS	*Journal of Asian Studies*
HNTC	Harper's NT Commentaries	JB	A. Jones (ed.), *Jerusalem Bible*
HR	*History of Religions*	JBC	R. E. Brown et al. (eds.), *The Jerome Biblical Commentary*
HSM	Harvard Semitic Monographs		
HSS	Harvard Semitic Studies	JBL	*Journal of Biblical Literature*
HTKNT	Herders theologischer Kommentar zum Neuen Testament	JBR	*Journal of Bible and Religion*
		JDS	Judean Desert Studies
HTR	*Harvard Theological Review*	JEH	*Journal of Ecclesiastical History*
HTS	Harvard Theological Studies	JEOL	*Jaarbericht . . . ex oriente lux*
HUCA	*Hebrew Union College Annual*	JES	*Journal of Ecumenical Studies*
HUT	Hermeneutische Untersuchungen zur Theologie	JETS	*Journal of the Evangelical Theological Society*

JHNES	Johns Hopkins Near Eastern Studies	JSSR	*Journal for the Scientific Study of Religion*
JHS	*Journal of Hellenic Studies*	*JTC*	*Journal for Theology and the Church*
JJS	*Journal of Jewish Studies*	*JTS*	*Journal of Theological Studies*
JMES	*Journal of Middle Eastern Studies*	*Judaica*	*Judaica: Beiträge zum Verständnis . . .*
JNES	*Journal of Near Eastern Studies*	KAT	E. Sellin (ed.), Kommentar zum A. T.
JPOS	*Journal of the Palestine Oriental Society*	KB	L. Koehler and W. Baumgartner, *Lexicon in Veteris Testamenti libros*
JPSV	*Jewish Publication Society Version*		
JQR	*Jewish Quarterly Review*	*KD*	*Kerygma und Dogma*
JQRMS	Jewish Quarterly Review Monograph Series	*KJV*	*King James Version*
		KIT	Kleine Texte
JR	*Journal of Religion*	*LB*	*Linguistica biblica*
JRelS	*Journal of Religious Studies*	LCC	Library of Christian Classics
JRH	*Journal of Religious History*	LCL	Loeb Classical Library
JRS	*Journal of Roman Studies*	*LCQ*	*Lutheran Church Quarterly*
JRT	*Journal of Religious Thought*	LD	Lectio divina
JSHRZ	Jüdische Schriften aus hellenistisch-römischer Zeit	*LLAVT*	E. Vogt, *Lexicon linguae aramaicae Veteris Testamenti*
JSJ	*Journal for the Study of Judaism in the Persian, Hellenistic and Roman Periods*	*LPGL*	G. W. H. Lampe, *Patristic Greek Lexicon*
		LQ	*Lutheran Quarterly*
JSNT	*Journal for the Study of the New Testament*	*LR*	*Lutherische Rundschau*
		LS	*Louvain Studies*
JSNTSup	Journal for the Study of the New Testament—Supplement Series	LSJ	Liddell-Scott-Jones, *Greek-English Lexicon*
		LTK	*Lexikon für Theologie und Kirche*
JSOT	*Journal for the Study of the Old Testament*	*LTP*	*Laval théologique et philosophique*
JSOTSup	Journal for the Study of the Old Testament-Supplement Series	*LumVie*	*Lumière et vie*
		LW	*Lutheran World*
JSS	*Journal of Semitic Studies*	*McCQ*	*McCormick Quarterly*
		MDB	*Le monde de la Bible*
		MDOG	Mitteilungen der deutschen Orient-Gesellschaft

MeyerK	H. A. W. Meyer, Kritisch-exegetischer Kommentar über das Neue Testament
MGWJ	Monatsschrift für Geschichte und Wissenschaft des Judentums
MM	J. H. Moulton and G. Milligan, The Vocabulary of the Greek Testament
MNTC	Moffatt NT Commentary
MPAIBL	Mémoires présentés à l'académie des inscriptions et belles-lettres
MScRel	Mélanges de science religieuse
MTZ	Münchener theologische Zeitschrift
Mus	Muséon
MUSJ	Mélanges de l'université Saint-Joseph
NAB	New American Bible
NCB	New Century Bible
NCCHS	R. D. Fuller et al. (eds.), New Catholic Commentary on Holy Scripture
NCE	M. R. P. McGuire et al. (eds.), New Catholic Encyclopedia
NEB	New English Bible
Neot	Neotestamentica
NFT	New Frontiers in Theology
NHS	Nag Hammadi Studies
NICNT	New International Commentary on the New Testament
NICOT	New International Commentary on the Old Testament
NIV	New International Version

NJBC	New Jerome Biblical Commentary
NJV	New Jewish Version
NKZ	Neue kirchliche Zeitschrift
NovT	Novum Testamentum
NovTSup	Novum Testamentum, Supplements
NRT	La nouvelle revue théologique
NTA	New Testament Abstracts
NTAbh	Neutestamentliche Abhandlungen
NTD	Das Neue Testament Deutsch
NTF	Neutestamentliche Forschungen
NTS	New Testament Studies
NTTS	New Testament Tools and Studies
Numen	Numen: International Review for the History of Religions
OBO	Orbis biblicus et orientalis
OIP	Oriental Institute Publications
OLP	Orientalia lovaniensia periodica
OLZ	Orientalische Literaturzeitung
Or	Orientalia (Rome)
OrAnt	Oriens antiquus
OrChr	Oriens christianus
OrSyr	L'Orient syrien
OTA	Old Testament Abstracts
OTL	Old Testament Library
PAAJR	Proceedings of the American Academy of Jewish Research
PCB	M. Black and H. H. Rowley (eds.), Peake's Commentary on the Bible

PEFQS	Palestine Exploration Fund, Quarterly Statement	REJ	Revue des études juives
		RelS	Religious Studies
		RelSoc	Religion and Society
PEQ	Palestine Exploration Quarterly	RelSRev	Religious Studies Review
PG	J. Migne, Patrologia graeca	RES	Répertoire d'épigraphie sémitique
PGM	K. Preisedanz (ed.), Papyri graecae magicae	ResQ	Restoration Quarterly
		RevExp	Review and Expositor
Phil	Philologus	RevistB	Revista bíblica
PJ	Palästina-Jahrbuch	RevQ	Revue de Qumran
PL	J. Migne, Patrologia latina	RevScRel	Revue des sciences religieuses
PO	Patrologia orientalis	RevSem	Revue sémitique
PSB	Princeton Seminary Bulletin	RGG	Religion in Geschichte und Gegenwart
PSTJ	Perkins School of Theology Journal	RHE	Revue d'histoire ecclésiastique
PTMS	Pittsburgh Theological Monograph Series	RHPR	Revue d'histoire et de philosophie religieuses
PVTG	Pseudepigrapha Veteris Testamenti graece	RHR	Revue de l'histoire des religions
		RIDA	Revue internationale des droits de l'antiquité
PW	Pauly-Wissowa, Real-Encyclopädie der klassischen Altertumswissenschaft	RivB	Rivista biblica
		RNT	Regensburger Neues Testament
PWSup	Supplements to PW	RQ	Römische Quartalschrift für christliche Altertumskunde und Kirchengeschichte
QD	Quaestiones disputatae		
QDAP	Quarterly of the Department of Antiquities in Palestine	RR	Review of Religion
		RRef	La revue reformée
		RSO	Rivista degli studi orientali
RAC	Reallexikon für Antike und Christentum	RSPT	Revue des sciences philosophiques et théologiques
RANE	Records of the Ancient Near East		
RArch	Revue archéologique	RSR	Recherches de science religieuse
RB	Revue biblique		
RCB	Revista de cultura bíblica	RSV	Revised Standard Version
RE	Realencyclopädie für protestantische Theologie und Kirche	RTL	Revue théologique de Louvain
		RTP	Revue de théologie et de philosophie
REA	Revue des études anciennes	RUO	Revue de l'université d'Ottawa
RechBib	Recherches bibliques		

RV	*Revised Version*
SacEr	*Sacris erudiri*
SANT	Studien zum Alten und Neuen Testament
SB	Sources bibliques
SBA	Studies in Biblical Archaeology
SBAW	*Sitzungsberichte der bayerischen Akademie der Wissenschaften*
SBB	Stuttgarter biblische Beiträge
SBFLA	*Studii biblici franciscani liber annuus*
SBJ	*La sainte bible de Jérusalem*
SBLASP	Society of Biblical Literature Abstracts and Seminar Papers
SBLDS	SBL Dissertation Series
SBLMasS	SBL Masoretic Studies
SBLMS	SBL Monograph Series
SBLSBS	SBL Sources for Biblical Study
SBLSCS	SBL Septuagint and Cognate Studies
SBLTT	SBL Texts and Translations
SBM	Stuttgarter biblische Monographien
SBS	Stuttgarter Bibelstudien
SBT	Studies in Biblical Theology
SC	Sources chrétiennes
ScEccl	*Sciences ecclésiastiques*
ScEs	*Science et esprit*
SCHNT	Studia ad corpus hellenisticum Novi Testamenti
SCR	*Studies in Comparative Religion*
Scr	*Scripture*
ScrB	*Scripture Bulletin*

ScrHier	Scripta hierosolymitana
SD	Studies and Documents
SE	Studia Evangelica I, II, III, etc. (= TU 73 [1959], 87 [1964], 88 [1964], 102 [1968], 103 [1968], 112 [1973])
Sem	*Semitica*
SHT	Studies in Historical Theology
SJ	Studia judaica
SJLA	Studies in Judaism in Late Antiquity
SJT	*Scottish Journal of Theology*
SMSR	*Studi e materiali di storia delle religioni*
SNT	Studien zum Neuen Testament
SNTSMS	Society for New Testament Studies Monograph Series
SO	Symbolae osloenses
SOTSMS	Society for Old Testament Study Monograph Series
SP	J. Coppens et al. (eds.), *Sacra pagina*
SPap	*Studia papyrologica*
SPAW	*Sitzungsberichte der preussischen Akademie der Wissenschaften*
SPB	Studia postbiblica
SPC	*Studiorum paulinorum congressus internationalis catholicus 1961* (2 vols.)
SR	*Studies in Religion/ Sciences religieuses*
SSS	Semitic Study Series
ST	*Studia theologica*
STANT	Studien zum Alten und Neuen Testament
STDJ	Studies on the Texts of the Desert of Judah

Str-B	[H. Strack and] P. Billerbeck, *Kommentar zum Neuen Testament*
StudNeot	Studia neotestamentica
StudOr	Studia orientalia
SUNT	Studien zur Umwelt des Neuen Testaments
SVTP	Studia in Veteris Testamenti pseudepigrapha
SymBU	Symbolae biblicae upsalienses
TAPA	*Transactions of the American Philological Association*
TBei	*Theologische Beiträge*
TBl	*Theologische Blätter*
TBü	Theologische Bücherei
TBT	*The Bible Today*
TCGNT	B. M. Metzger, *A Textual Commentary on the Greek New Testament*
TD	*Theology Digest*
TDNT	G. Kittel and G. Friedrich (eds.), *Theological Dictionary of the New Testament*
TDOT	G. J. Botterweck and H. Ringgren (eds.), *Theological Dictionary of the Old Testament*
TextsS	Texts and Studies
TF	*Theologische Forschung*
TGl	*Theologie und Glaube*
THKNT	Theologischer Handkommentar zum Neuen Testament
ThStud	*Theologische Studiën*
TLZ	*Theologische Literaturzeitung*
TP	*Theologie und Philosophie*
TPQ	*Theologisch-Praktische Quartalschrift*
TQ	*Theologische Quartalschrift*
TRE	*Theologische Real-enzyklopädie*
TRev	*Theologische Revue*
TRu	*Theologische Rundschau*
TS	*Theological Studies*
TSK	*Theologische Studien und Kritiken*
TToday	*Theology Today*
TTZ	*Trierer theologische Zeitschrift*
TU	Texte und Untersuchungen
TWAT	G. J. Botterweck and H. Ringgren (eds.), *Theologisches Wörterbuch zum Alten Testament*
TWNT	G. Kittel and G. Friedrich (eds.), *Theologisches Wörterbuch zum Neuen Testament*
TynBul	*Tyndale Bulletin*
TZ	*Theologische Zeitschrift*
UBSGNT	United Bible Societies *Greek New Testament*
UNT	Untersuchungen zum Neuen Testament
USQR	*Union Seminary Quarterly Review*
VC	*Vigiliae christianae*
VCaro	*Verbum caro*
VD	*Verbum domini*
VE	*Vox evangelica*
VF	*Verkündigung und Forschung*
VKGNT	K. Aland (ed.), *Vollständige Konkordanz zum griechischen Neuen Testament*
VP	*Vivre et penser* (= *RB* 1941–44)
VS	Verbum salutis
VSpir	*Vie spirituelle*
VT	*Vetus Testamentum*

VTSup	Vetus Testamentum, Supplements	*ZAW*	*Zeitschrift für die alttestamentliche Wissenschaft*
WDB	*Westminster Dictionary of the Bible*	*ZDMG*	*Zeitschrift der deutschen morgenländischen Gesellschaft*
WHAB	*Westminster Historical Atlas of the Bible*		
WHJP	World History of the Jewish People	*ZDPV*	*Zeitschrift des deutschen Palästina-Vereins*
WMANT	Wissenschaftliche Monographien zum Alten und Neuen Testament	*ZHT*	*Zeitschrift für historische Theologie*
		ZKG	*Zeitschrift für Kirchengeschichte*
WO	*Die Welt des Orients*	*ZKT*	*Zeitschrift für katholische Theologie*
WTJ	*Westminster Theological Journal*		
WUNT	Wissenschaftliche Untersuchungen zum Neuen Testament	*ZMR*	*Zeitschrift für Missionskunde und Religionswissenschaft*
WVDOG	Wissenschaftliche Veröffentlichungen der deutschen Orientgesellschaft	*ZNW*	*Zeitschrift für die neutestamentliche Wissenschaft*
		ZRGG	*Zeitschrift für Religions-und Geistesgeschichte*
WZKM	*Wiener Zeitschrift für die Kunde des Morgenlandes*	*ZTK*	*Zeitschrift für Theologie und Kirche*
WZKSO	*Wiener Zeitschrift für die Kunde Süd-und Ostasiens*	*ZWT*	*Zeitschrift für wissenschaftliche Theologie*

9. *Miscellaneous Abbreviations*

LXX	The Septuagint
MT	Masoretic Text
NT	New Testament
OT	Old Testament
par(r).	parallel(s) in the Gospels
Vg	The Vulgate
VL	Vetus Latina (Old Latin)
‖	two pericopes (often in the Q document) that are basically parallel, though possibly with some differences in wording

SCRIPTURE INDEX

Author Index

SUBJECT INDEX